THE OXFORD HANDBOOK OF

DIALECTICAL
BEHAVIOUR
THERAPY®

THE OXFORD HANDBOOK OF

DIALECTICAL BEHAVIOUR THERAPY®

Edited by

MICHAELA A. SWALES

OXFORD
UNIVERSITY PRESS

OXFORD

UNIVERSITY PRESS

Great Clarendon Street, Oxford, OX2 6DP,
United Kingdom

Oxford University Press is a department of the University of Oxford.
It furthers the University's objective of excellence in research, scholarship,
and education by publishing worldwide. Oxford is a registered trade mark of
Oxford University Press in the UK and in certain other countries

© DBT is a registered trademark of Marsha M. Linehan

© Oxford University Press 2019

The moral rights of the authors have been asserted

Impression: 3

Published in the United States of America by Oxford University Press
198 Madison Avenue, New York, NY 10016, United States of America

British Library Cataloguing in Publication Data

Data available

Library of Congress Control Number: 2018943676

ISBN 978–0–19–875872–3

Printed and bound by
CPI Group (UK) Ltd, Croydon, CR0 4YY

To Marsha Marie Linehan for her creativity, dedication, and scientific acumen

FOREWORD

WHEN I teach clinicians how to understand what it is like for individuals who are suicidal, I have for many years told them the following story. It gives a glimpse into the world of the suicidal person and into the hell that they experience.

The suicidal person is like someone trapped in a small room with high walls that are stark white. The room has no lights or windows. The room is hot, humid, and the red-hot coals on the floor of hell are excruciatingly painful; there is no water to cool down even one piece of coal or soothe the person's thirst for just one moment. The person searches for a door out to a life worth living but cannot find it. Scratching and clawing on the walls does no good. Screaming and banging brings no help. Falling against the wall and trying to shut down and feel nothing gives no relief. Praying to God and all the saints brings no salvation. The room is so painful that enduring it for even a moment longer appears impossible; any exit will do. The only door out the person can find is the door of suicide. The urge to open it is great indeed.

I developed Dialectical Behaviour Therapy (DBT) to address the pain and suffering of suicidal people with a borderline personality disorder diagnosis and to aid them in finding a life worth living. Since the early days of testing the treatment, researchers and clinicians from across the US, Europe, and further afield have taken the treatment and considered how its benefits could be brought to other client groups. This book is a testament to that work. It synthesizes developments over the last twenty-five years in both the theoretical underpinnings of the treatment, its application to an ever-widening set of clinical problems, and its implementation in routine clinical practice. Everything a clinician, academic, therapist-in-training, or student needs to know about DBT is here in these pages. Reviewing the contents pages, I am delighted to see all the major aspects of the treatment addressed by experts in the field, many of whom are my former students or colleagues.

I first met Michaela twenty years ago when she came to Seattle to learn DBT. She was half of the first team to train in my treatment from the UK. From small beginnings in her own clinical service, she has gone on to systematically disseminate DBT throughout the UK, more recently in Ireland and further afield. Michaela is a skilled clinician and trainer who knows DBT from the inside out. Her passion and commitment to train therapists in effectively relieving their clients' suffering has borne fruit in her work with the British Isles DBT Team that under her leadership delivers high-quality DBT training to hundreds of therapists every year. Her earlier books written jointly with Heidi Heard provide a succinct introduction to the treatment (*DBT: Distinctive Features*, Swales &

Heard, 2017) and a comprehensive trouble-shooting guide to problem solving in DBT (*Changing Behaviour in DBT: Problem-solving in action*, Heard & Swales, 2016). This book complements Michaela's earlier work by bringing together, as only a few people can, the breadth of DBT expertise from across the globe to produce the first desk reference for DBT. As you read, I hope that you, as I have, enjoy exploring the ways in which DBT has been applied and developed and that you are inspired either to begin or to continue your own journey using DBT.

Marsha M. Linehan, 2018

PREFACE

My first encounter with DBT was entirely serendipitous. On qualifying as a clinical psychologist in 1992, I moved to North Wales to commence a joint academic and clinical post. My main motivation in accepting the post was it afforded me the opportunity to study for my PhD with Mark Williams, future co-developer of Mindfulness-based Cognitive Therapy (Segal, Williams, & Teasdale, 2012). The clinical component of the post was based in an inpatient adolescent unit run along modified therapeutic community lines treating young people with mental health problems, many of whom were suicidal and self-harming. In the early 1990s self-harm behaviour was less commonly discussed and, as a newly trained clinician, I knew next to nothing about how to help my mainly female clients. During my training, I had received just one morning session on the subject of self-harm and the session had been more theoretical than practical. Thankfully, Mark had spent some time with Marsha Linehan at the Applied Psychology Unit in Cambridge, where she had spent a sabbatical. She had sent him a draft of her manuals and he passed them on to me to read. I still remember receiving them—a heavy box full of densely printed pages. I had no idea that reading those pages would change the course of my career. In those draft versions of the manuals I found an approach I could relate to and that I could use with my young clients. I began conducting skills training on an individual basis, discovering the benefits of holding ice-cubes and noticing—rather than acting on—thoughts.

Some months later Mark received information about a training opportunity in DBT. Marsha was offering a two-week Intensive Training™ course in Seattle that involved one week of didactic instruction and a further week some five months later where we had to present our DBT programmes and a clinical case. Mark, with his customary foresight, found a means by which he could send me and Barry Kiehn, the Consultant Psychiatrist in my service, to Seattle for this training. And so it was that I found myself at a training half way around the world, becoming part of the first team trained in DBT in the UK.

The Intensive Training™ was a fascinating experience in a number of ways. First, I had never visited the US before, nor travelled on a long-haul flight (which, as I had then a flight phobia, was quite a challenge!). Second, the training truly was "intensive." We began at 8:30am, finished at 5pm for dinner, and returned to the classroom at 7pm for two hours of skills training. Also, Marsha's teaching style was to lecture you relentlessly for almost the entire time—with the occasional video of therapy that was typically shown at lunchtime. She had an incredible presence and could hold the attention for that length of time—but it was *intensive*! Finally, with hindsight, that training was instrumental in the dissemination of DBT into Europe. I, Martin Bohus, from Germany,

Weis Van Den Bosch, from the Netherlands, and a team from the Karolinska Institute in Stockholm attended the training; we all went on to deliver DBT training in our respective countries.

One moment from that training remains evocative for me of the style of the treatment. During a lunchtime, we viewed part of a therapy session throughout which the client held a doll. One participant interrupted the viewing to ask why Marsha had "allowed" the client to "regress to her childhood" in this way? Marsha beautifully demonstrated the strategy of mindful describing, stripping away the assumptions made by the questioner: how did he know that the client had been attached to dolls as a child? What did he mean by "regressing," precisely? What behaviours indicated the client had "regressed"? In the ensuing discussion, the questioner, and the audience, began to see the behavioural, non-judgmental style of the treatment in action, stripping back the assumptions and simply sticking with what was observed. The client was holding a doll: that was all. When it was evident that she had made her point, Marsha paused and then said "You know ... I couldn't stand the doll either, so I asked her to keep it in her bag for subsequent sessions." At this, the entire room erupted into laughter, diffusing the tension, and revealing to us the direct, yet non-pathologizing style of the treatment in action.

The European contingent trained along with teams from Seattle and other parts of the US, which proved useful in my later experience as a trainer. In the early days of training, often the treatment would be accused of being "West Coast" or "too American." Following on from Marsha's demonstration in the "doll" incident, I would ask myself what it was in the treatment that was leading to such interpretations or assumptions. Often delegates would adduce the taking of phone calls and practising mindfulness as "American" or "West Coast." My experience alongside US therapists on my Intensive Training™ meant I could convincingly argue that those aspects of DBT were no more typical of US therapy than the UK. Such assumptions, therefore, were not necessarily reasons to modify the treatment for implementation in the UK. This was an important and useful lesson on many occasions. When applying DBT, new practitioners often find it difficult to change their behaviour. Frequently, there is a temptation to change the treatment to what feels more comfortable and familiar when, instead, learning the new strategy or technique is what is required. Over the years, I have trained practitioners who work in a variety of settings with a wide range of client groups, as well as therapists in Norway, Ireland, and more recently in Poland. Holding to the principles of the treatment and discovering how to apply them flexibly, without making assumptions about what can or cannot be done in a particular context, is vital in introducing evidence-based practices into new settings.

Bringing DBT to the wider NHS community in the UK began with a small grant awarded to Mark Williams, me, and Heidi Heard, Marsha's graduate student whom I had met at my Intensive Training™ in Seattle. This grant supported Heidi to come to Bangor University and commence establishing DBT teams in North Wales and further afield. Heidi's arrival also allowed me to focus more thoroughly on developing competency as a DBT therapist through weekly videotaped supervision of my individual therapy and skills classes.

Independent training in DBT in the UK began in 1997, first with the formation of a small team, supported by trainers from the US and in association with the Psychological Therapies Research Centre at the University of Leeds, and then from 2001 with a commercial partner. One of the first actions the company took was to recognize the unique position of the training team as the only group licensed to deliver in the UK and Ireland Marsha's US-developed and standardized training materials. The company sought and received permission from the then-Department of Trade and Industry within the UK government to trade as *British Isles DBT Training* (biDBT), a special designation in a trading name that is restricted to companies pre-eminent in their field.

Partnering with a limited company changed the way training was delivered. Instead of only offering training when and if there seemed to be sufficient interest, which in the early years was an annual Intensive Training™, the company began working to a schedule and to focus on disseminating the product! This created a number of interesting dialectical tensions. All trainers typically at that time had other full-time positions in the NHS and so had limited availability to provide training and were motivated to limit the amount of training they provided. The company, on the other hand, was motivated to provide as much training as possible to maximize the rate of diffusion and putative client benefits. Finding syntheses to the economic realities of running a technology transfer company with the values of high-quality training and sustainable teams remains a constant feature of the relationship between clinicians who deliver the training and the company who produce the business plan. In utilizing a partnership with a private company, we found that we delivered more training, reached more clients, and that the rate of diffusion compared favourably with other international training organizations in the US and Germany (Swales, Taylor, & Hibbs, 2010), who used slightly different training models. Whether this was a consequence of the training model or attributable to other factors at the time (e.g., an increased focus on evidence-based treatment, publication of national guidelines for treating borderline personality disorder, concerns over costs of inpatient treatment) remains unknown.

Training others in DBT transformed my understanding of what is required to deliver evidence-based treatments in practice. It became increasingly apparent to my co-trainers and I that ensuring evidence-based treatments reached clients in a form that would ensure similar clinical outcomes was not just a matter of training mental health professionals. Moving away from basic research into psychological processes in suicidal behaviour towards studying these problems of implementation and dissemination was precipitated by a Knowledge Transfer Programme (KTP) that focused on improving the dissemination and sustainability of DBT. Two people were instrumental in helping me see the relevance and possibility of such a programme grant. Richard Hastings, then at Bangor University, suggested the idea of a collaboration between the academic department and a commercial partner. My husband Richard Hibbs, Managing Director of biDBT, brought his expertise as a statistician and operational research analyst to modelling the challenge of disseminating and implementing a psychotherapy with mathematical precision. The programme of research resulted in a book in the Distinctive Features of CBT series (Swales & Heard, 2009) and two papers on implementation;

the first, a conceptual piece on the recursive nature of DBT and how the principles of pre-treatment can be applied to preparing organizations for embedding the treatment (Swales, 2010a), and then a more practical piece on selecting and training a team of professionals to deliver DBT (Swales, 2010b). As planned, over the course of the grant, the number and capacity of training places increased speeding up the dissemination of the treatment in the UK. Subsequent outputs from the KTP focused on modelling this dissemination of the treatment through the UK health system and on factors impacting the sustainability of the treatment (Hibbs, Swales, & Taylor, 2010; Swales, Taylor, & Hibbs, 2012). These topics have become front and centre in my thinking and in research to improve access to DBT. Without the vison of the 'Two Richards' none of this would have been possible.

Teaching others how to implement DBT has been informed constantly by my experience of delivering and sustaining others to deliver the treatment in my own NHS organization. Being an expert in DBT does not inoculate you from the challenges of implementing innovations in a public healthcare organization—my own programme and those in the network of teams I support have experienced temporary closures resulting from insufficient personnel and lack of organizational commitment. Perhaps this is just as well—it has kept my teaching alive and relevant to new teams arriving for training.

In the years since my first trip to Seattle in 1994, I have had the privilege of hearing and seeing the work of other exponents of the treatment in widely varying contexts, settings, and with many different client groups. Those experiences have consolidated my faith in the flexibility of DBT to address the concerns of those clients whose difficulties are multiple, complex, and risky, and that often lead to marginalization by treatment services. In editing this book, I wanted to bring to others in one volume those experiences from which I have learned and benefitted. The great pleasure of editing this volume has been liaising with all my colleagues in the DBT community and making new relationships. The chapters here encompass the current knowledge base of DBT and the understandings we have garnered of its theoretical bases, clinical applications, and implementation over the last twenty-five years. Oxford Handbooks are associated with academic excellence and rigour; typically, chapters have a scholarly focus. Many of the chapters in this volume present and evaluate the treatment from such a perspective. Deliberately, I complemented that focus with chapters showcasing the clinical rigour of DBT and one chapter presenting the view of a recipient of DBT. While Louise Brinton Clarke's chapter is a single voice, its presence provides a powerful reminder of the reasons for all the work presented in this book. Poignantly she discusses her experience of completing DBT in a system that did not provide treatment for her PTSD, a topic discussed by Harned & Schmidt and Bohus & Priebe in their chapters. I hope and trust that readers of this volume will benefit in reading the work of the experts who have contributed to this volume as I have in listening and discussing with them during its production.

And for those of you still wondering about my flight phobia, DBT was instrumental in curing me. Travelling regularly to Seattle provided ample opportunities for exposure

ACKNOWLEDGEMENTS

MARSHA Linehan has dedicated her life to developing and testing a treatment that provides an alternative to the unbearable and enduring suffering of people who are suicidal. This book is dedicated to that work.

I am grateful to all of the contributors of chapters to this book for their willingness to take time to produce the work contained in its pages. We all owe a huge debt of thanks to Marsha Linehan for developing the treatment that many of us have spent most of our clinical and academic lives implementing, delivering, teaching, studying, and understanding. None of us could have learned what we have about the treatment and its possibilities without the courage and commitment of all the clients we have worked with over the years who have been willing to trust us to help them find a "route out of hell." While we may offer a map and resources to aid them in their journey, it is they who have to walk the frequently long and difficult route out. We honour them.

My greatest debt of gratitude is to Heidi Heard, my former supervisor, mentor, colleague, co-author, and friend. Early in my career she taught me the therapeutic skills of DBT and went on to model and shape my competency as a trainer and consultant in DBT. In the early days of DBT we travelled the length and breadth of the UK for many weeks a year living in dodgy hotel rooms and wrestling with the challenging fit of DBT to NHS systems. During the writing of our two books, Heidi has grappled with my wordy prose and my absence of grammatical education to shape me into a more conceptually clear author. She is an unstinting support and purveyor of wise counsel to me in the running of the biDBT training team that she founded and graciously handed over to my directorship in 2002. Heidi, I give you my profound thanks.

In my early days as a rookie trainer I was fortunate to learn not only from Heidi, but also from Charlie Swenson, Kelly Koerner, and Kate Comtois, all of whom trained on the first DBT Intensive Trainings™ delivered in the UK. All four of these individuals are inspirational trainers of the treatment, capable of conveying both its precision and compassion in their teaching. From them I learned skills in the judicious use of time in training and the delicate balance of didactic with clinical examples and experiential learning.

On the biDBT training team we remind ourselves that *DBTers do everything in teams*. I have benefitted over the years from many teams who have trained, supported, and encouraged me in my DBT journey. I have been part of creative and energizing clinical teams, strong and flexible DBT teams, academic teams, and the British Isles DBT Training (biDBT) Team. Without them all, this book would not have been possible.

Three teams deserve a special mention. The team of international researchers, clinicians, and trainers that forms the Strategic Planning Meeting (SPM) that gathers each year in Seattle, has provided a welcome home for exploring my own research into the sustainable implementation of DBT and almost every participant in SPM was badgered into providing a chapter for this book. Thank you to members of the steering committee of SPM, Martin Bohus, Alan Fruzzetti, Melanie Harned, Katie Korslund, Marsha Linehan, Andre Ivanoff, and Shelley McMain, for drawing together each year a stimulating programme that evaluates and challenges us to think about the treatment and ways forward in research. I have also had much fun, as well as critical reflection, at SPM meetings discussing with Kate Comtois and Sara Landes the implementation of "the thing" that is DBT.

Especial thanks to the biDBT Training Team who travel extensively throughout the UK and Ireland disseminating and training the treatment. Without Christine Dunkley, Janet Feigenbaum, Amy Gaglia, Stephanie Hastings, Heidi Heard, Carolyn Hinds, Jim Lyng, and Maggie Stanton, my DBT journey would not be possible and certainly would be much less fun! Special mention to Christine, Heidi, and Jim, who, at different times and in different ways fulfilled the role of the editor's editor! As always, any errors of judgment or accuracy are all my own.

Particular thanks to my Radically-Open DBT (RO-DBT) clinical team, and to Tom Lynch, the treatment developer. For the first time in twenty years I had the opportunity to treat adults rather than adolescents, which proved smoother than I had imagined. Modifying my therapeutic style, after many flying hours in the therapy chair, to treat people whose main problem was "over-" rather than "under-control," was more difficult, presenting numerous challenges that were often hard to greet with openness and enthusiasm! Without my dedicated team of Stephanie Hastings, Carolyn Hinds, James Lea, and Pip Thomas, it would have been impossible. Together we learned new ways of doing things and had a lot of fun in the process. Working on a randomized clinical trial was also a long-held ambition made all the more rewarding by the contributions from the other researchers in the team who selflessly and non-judgmentally shared their own challenges, expertise, and advice.

The dissemination and implementation of training in DBT in the UK and Ireland would not be possible without the dedicated administration team who, behind the scenes, coordinate training schedules, organize venues, book training teams, register delegates, and make sure all the logistics of trainers, delegates, and materials all end up in the right place at the right time. Thanks to Dan Owen, Barbara Nicholls, Ceri Davies, and Brandon Humphreys for your contribution.

I have benefitted personally, as has the British Isles Training Team, from its association with the Linehan Institute and BTech LLC, and its previous incarnations. Initially with Shari Manning and Helen Best, and more recently, with Andre Ivanoff and Tony duBose, I have shared the joys and trials of disseminating a treatment at a national level and have learned much from their experiences from the other side of the pond! I am delighted that all of them contributed to this volume.

Through close affiliation with BTech LLC I have been fortunate to train with many colleagues from the US and to welcome them to the UK. Training alongside colleagues from the US brought me many benefits both in learning and disseminating the treatment and in keeping alive the dialogue about applying the principles of the treatment in different types of healthcare systems. Thanks to Jennifer Sayrs, Alec Miller, Alex Chapman, and Melanie Harned for sharing in this way.

Over the years my dedication to training and disseminating DBT has taken me away from my "home" DBT team. I have always benefitted and been grateful for those dedicated clinicians who took up the slack and covered for me in my many absences. My thanks to Angela Brennan, Robin Glaze, Barry Kiehn, Bronwen Platt, and Pip Thomas.

I am grateful to my colleagues at the North Wales Clinical Programme for their forbearance as DBT frequently takes me away from the office. I am especially thankful to have had two very supportive managers during the course of this project who have valued it and supported my involvement in it. Finding such flexibility and unstinting support is rare in hard-pressed public services, which makes me especially grateful to Dr. Sara Hammond-Rowley and Professor Robert Jones.

Thanks to my long-standing personal assistant and friend, Dr. Barbara Baragwanath, who has worked with me on all of my book projects and for whom no task is too small or too big to be completed without energy and commitment. This, for reasons beyond our control, will be our last book project together, so a particularly bittersweet thank you to you, Barbara.

Thanks to Martin Baum, Senior Commissioning Editor at Oxford University Press, for approaching me about this book. Without his desire for a Handbook in DBT, I would never have thought of editing one! A particular thanks to Charlotte Holloway, Senior Assistant Commissioning Editor, who has been calm, patient, unflappable, and a fount of sage advice about the process of a project of this magnitude. Haripriya Ravichandran, Anitha Alagusundaram and the copyediting team at Newgen have patiently copyedited the work of all of the authors in this book. Thank you for saving us from the worst of our grammatical inelegancies – we take full responsibility for the rest!

Projects like this can never be completed without the support of family who more often see your back as you spend more time interacting with the computer than with them! To my parents, Pat and Eric, who instilled in me the values of hard work and dedication to others. Those values have driven the course of my career. Profound thanks to Richard, Tom, and Caitlin for sharing me with my work, with DBT, and most recently with this book.

Michaela A. Swales, 2018

TABLE OF CONTENTS

SECTION I INTRODUCTION

> **KEY MESSAGES FOR CLINICIANS**
> - DBT is an integrative treatment, synthesizing behavioural theory, principles of Zen practice, and dialectics.
> - DBT was developed in an endeavour to solve the problem of chronic suicidality presenting in clients with a borderline personality disorder diagnosis.
> - DBT was the first treatment to demonstrate clinical efficacy with this client group.
> - Since the publication of the treatment manuals, DBT has been adopted and adapted for clients in a range of settings and with different clinical presentations and diagnoses.

SECTION II THEORETICAL UNDERPINNINGS OF DBT

> **KEY MESSAGES FOR CLINICIANS**
> - Since the publication of Linehan's original treatment manual (Linehan, 1993) there has been considerable progress in understanding the biological underpinnings of BPD.
> - There is strong evidence of hyperactivity in the limbic system and decreased activation of the prefrontal cortex, which may contribute to affective instability in BPD, although it is unclear how *specific* these findings are to BPD.
> - Extensive studies of brain activation during pain processing in BPD patients demonstrate changes that complement patient reports of the physical and psychological impact of NSSI.
> - The hyperactivity in the limbic system may also impede functional behaviour in social interactions.

KEY POINTS FOR CLINICIANS
- Borderline personality disorder (BPD) emerges as a result of high-risk transactions between inherited vulnerabilities, such as trait impulsivity, and invalidating developmental contexts.
- These transactions, which are characterized by invalidation and coercive processes, socialize emotion dysregulation over time and across development.
- Emerging research has identified certain child and caregiver characteristics that increase risk for an invalidating developmental context. However, mismatch between the needs of the child and that of his or her caregiver's abilities may also contribute to invalidation.
- Dialectical Behavior Therapy (DBT) for at-risk adolescents and families offers an opportunity to intervene on the invalidating environment and reduce contextual risk for adult BPD.

KEY MESSAGES
- Behavioural theory guides many aspects of DBT.
- Behavioural theory and practices help DBT therapists assess and understand their clients' behaviour.
- Functional or chain analyses can help the DBT therapist assemble a case formulation that paves the way to potentially helpful interventions.
- Behavioural theory encourages DBT clinicians to be specific about behaviour, to take an active role in therapy, and to present opportunities for clients to learn new behaviours.

KEY MESSAGES FOR CLINICIANS
- Zen as a practice has a 2,500-year history.
- Zen forms the basis of acceptance technology found in DBT.
- Zen practice principles are compatible with behaviour therapy.
- Zen provides a set of new targets for both client and therapist.
- DBT core mindfulness and reality acceptance skills are an outgrowth of Zen practice

KEY POINTS FOR CLINICIANS
- A dialectical strategy is any strategy that looks for what is left out of one's position, then facilitates movement toward a synthesis of the two opposing positions.
- Dialectical strategies include magnifying tension between two poles, entering the paradox, and the use of metaphors.
- While the dialectical strategies were developed within DBT, several evidence-based treatments utilize a dialectical approach.

SECTION III THE STRUCTURE OF TREATMENT

HENRY SCHMIDT III AND JOAN C. RUSSO

> **KEY POINTS FOR CLINICIANS**
> - Successful programmes pay close attention to the structural elements of DBT.
> - It is critical to understand Linehan's description of the functions of treatment when making decisions about the structure of treatment.
> - Structural elements of a programme include the physical infrastructure, as well as the customs and practices of the treatment (such as agreements, therapist strategies, careful attention to language, and requests for review of one's work).
> - A sound and well-followed programme structure will enable clinicians and clients to more easily focus on the critical interactions of treatment.
> - Each programme needs to create a "programme manual" which defines the treatment provided, particularly when it has been adapted from the original model described by Linehan.

JENNIFER H. R. SAYRS

> **KEY POINTS FOR CLINICIANS**
> - DBT team is an essential element of comprehensive DBT.
> - DBT team supports therapists' capability and motivation, and overall adherence to the DBT manual.
> - Agreements, structure, and roles are important in running an effective DBT team.
> - The same principles and strategies used with clients in DBT are implemented in DBT team.

COLLEEN M. COWPERTHWAIT, KRISTIN P. WYATT, CAITLIN M. FANG, AND ANDRADA D. NEACSIU

> **KEY POINTS FOR CLINICIANS**
> - Rely on research to inform decision-making and clinical practice when adapting DBT skills training.
> - The principles and strategies that guide DBT skills training are the *same* as the principles and strategies underlying DBT as a whole.
> - Consider case conceptualization, treatment targets, and contingencies when making decisions about how to best engage a client and teach skills.
> - Discuss clinical decisions and skills training adaptations with the DBT consultation team.

SHIREEN L. RIZVI AND KRISTEN M. ROMAN

> **KEY POINTS FOR CLINICANS**
> - Focus on generalization is a critical part of effective treatment but is often overlooked.
> - Changes in technology mean a greater focus on generalization can occur via the mediums of phone, texts, and emails.
> - This chapter provides guidelines for effectively consulting to the client in order to increase generalization of skills.

KEY MESSAGES FOR CLINICANS
- Team leads take responsibility for two functions of a DBT programme: Structuring the environment, and enhancing therapists' capabilities and motivation to treat.
- DBT team leads take responsibility for organizational pre-treatment: establishing which organizational goals are relevant to the DBT programme, orientating the or-ganization to the resources needed, and gaining commitment from the organiza¬tion to support the programme.
- DBT team leads assess the assets of their staff and programme and address any identified deficits.
- DBT team leads ensure that the consultation team fulfils its function of enhancing therapists' skills, capacities, and motivation to deliver the treatment, and that they take a lead in helping the team address any problems that arise in the functioning of the team.

SECTION IV   CLINICAL APPLICATIONS OF DBT

KEY MESSAGES FOR CLINICIANS
- Case conceptualization is iterative and organic, and changes as the treatment progresses.
- Case conceptualizations should be clear and concise so that they can be communicated easily to the client and to team members.
- Case conceptualization uses the tenets of DBT to assess causal and consequential factors of behaviours.
- Case conceptualization assists the therapist and the client in determining specific interventions to use in treatment, as well as the means to determine the effectiveness of the interventions.

KEY POINTS FOR CLINICIANS
- Assessment in general, and behavioural chain analysis (BCA) specifically, is a critical strategy in DBT. Lack of assessment or errors in assessment can lead to difficulties in treatment.
- BCA can function to challenge clients' common experience and belief that events "come out of the blue" and aids clients in learning that emotions, actions, or thoughts result from certain interactions or transactions with the environment.
- BCA can be a validating experience for a client, especially when a client may think they that they are engaging in a problem behaviour simply because "something is wrong" with them. BCA provides understanding of their experience, which can lead to decreased judgments and increased use of skills.
- When doing BCA, the therapist should describe things behaviourally and non-judgmentally, as well as focus on a single instance of a behaviour.
- All components of BCA (e.g., thoughts, emotions, vulnerability factors, or consequences) provide opportunities for intervention.
- When assigning homework generated from solution analysis, the DBT therapist should also use commitment and troubleshooting strategies to increase the likelihood the client will complete the task.
- BCA can be a difficult task for both the client, who may feel shame at discussing problem behaviours, and for the therapist. Practice, non-judgmental language, and validation can ease the difficulty.

KEY POINTS FOR CLINICIANS

- Each emotion is designed to elicit a different action.
- Each emotion has a unique signature in a number of domains; temperature, fa¬cial expression, breathing, muscle tone, posture, gesture, voice tone, actions in the environment.
- Emotion regulation involves a number of steps that can be coached through behav¬ioural rehearsal:
  - Identify the emotion.
  - Ascertain what level, if any, would fit the facts.
  - Up or down-regulate the emotion by paying attention to the domains of that emotion, until it reaches an appropriate level.
  - Remember to do what is appropriate for the amount of the emotion that does actually fit the facts.
- Coaching distress tolerance or de- arousal strategies will not strengthen the client's emotion regulations skills.
- An over-reliance on distress tolerance at the expense of emotion regulation may result in clients failing to make anticipated progress in therapy.

KEY POINTS FOR CLINICIANS

- Although challenging, clinicians working with people who self-harm should make comprehensive psychosocial assessments of the patient's psychiatric disorder (including assessment of comorbidity with personality disorders and/or substance misuse), risks, resources, and needs in order to provide adequate treatment and protection.
- Many clinicians fear reinforcing suicidal behaviours should they systematically address the topic of suicidality in therapy sessions—hence, they avoid it. This is not advisable; the risk must be repeatedly re-evaluated and actively addressed since the risk scenario may rapidly change in these patients due to their increased affective reactivity and impulsivity.
- Important aims in the treatment are to prevent relapse or escalation of self-harm and other high-risk behaviours, and to develop a crisis plan or safety plan is regarded essential. To treat psychiatric conditions, improve social and occupational functioning, and improve quality of life are also highly prioritized treatment aims for the longer term.
- DBT has a well-documented efficacy in reducing suicidal behaviours and NSSI, emergency room visits, psychiatric hospital days, and a wide range of symptoms and behaviours related to suicidality.
- DBT adopts a behavioural approach to suicide and self-harm in order to identify antecedents and consequences either causing or maintaining the behaviours.
- In DBT, suicidal behaviours are treated directly and specifically and given top priority. DBT offers multiple and specific strategies to prevent and manage suicidal crises, such as teaching patients skills in emotion regulation, distress tolerance, and interpersonal problem solving.
- Keeping patients alive while they are making progress in treatment builds in DBT on a strong therapeutic relationship that balances the therapeutic strategies of validation and change.

KEY MESSAGES FOR CLINICIANS

- Definition of validation: requires attention, *genuine* understanding, and communicates that understanding which is applied to specific behavioural targets (e.g., emotions, skillful actions, thoughts, etc.).
- Validation is a key social behaviour in part because it soothes negative emotional arousal, and thus is essential in any relationship, is part of every modern psychotherapy, and is a key strategy in DBT.
- In DBT we only validate *valid* behaviours; invalidating *invalid* behaviours are part of DBT change strategies.
- Validation communicates acceptance and understanding, builds the therapeutic relationship, and facilitates and balances change.
- At times, validation may be considered a reinforcer, and facilitates change and learning.
- Validation also may be considered an eliciting stimulus, signaling that a different repertoire of responses is likely to be effective, and inviting different, more regulated responses.
- There are multiple levels, or types of validation; type of validation must fit the situation and goals, as well as be appropriate to the way(s) in which a behaviour is valid.

KEY POINTS FOR CLINICIANS

- Few models of cognitive-behaviour therapy emphasize attending to and treating clients' in-session clinical behaviours as much as Dialectical Behaviour Therapy (DBT).
- The term "in-session clinical behaviour" (ICB) encompasses any client behaviour, including a therapy-interfering behaviour (TIB) or secondary target, that occurs during a treatment session and adversely impacts either the treatment session or other aspects of the client's life.
- A key principle of behaviour therapy asserts that interventions are most effective when they stop an episode of a clinical behaviour as quickly as possible and immediately elicit a more adaptive behaviour instead.
- To enhance clients' understanding of and collaboration in treating ICBs, DBT clinicians describe the form of an ICB with behavioural specificity and without assumptions about the function or intent.
- DBT clinicians enhance motivation to address ICBs partly by relating in-session behaviours to out-of-session behaviours and to the clients' goals.
- DBT clinicians use behavioural theory and Linehan's biosocial theory to develop a behavioural conceptualization of the proximal factors causing and maintaining ICBs.
- Solution implementation ranges from applying a single intervention to conducting a comprehensive solution analysis, depending on the context and number of key controlling factors for the ICB.

KEY POINTS FOR CLINICIANS

- Therapists:
  have their own mindfulness practice.
  model a mindful and dialectical philosophy.
- Use a variety of practices.
- Keep the practice simple and give clear instructions.
- Take feedback after a practice to shape mindful awareness.
- Behaviourally rehearse mindfulness skills in session.
- Coach a non-judgmental stance in the tone of voice, facial expression, body posture, thoughts, and language.
- Assess the level of skill for each client and provide coaching to strengthen this.
- Identify and problem-solve obstacles to being mindful.
- Combine mindfulness with other skills.
- Highlight opportunities for generalizing the skill.
- Make clear the relevance of using the skill in the client's everyday life.

KEY POINTS FOR CLINICIANS

- DBT with parents or families utilizes the same theory and overlapping strategies as DBT with individuals; some targets may vary, there are additional skills and strategies, and we use "double chains" to assess and understand the ways family members affect each other.
- Intervening with parents, partners, or other family members is essential when they are "on the chain" toward self-harm or suicidal behaviour—that is, when what they do is either a precipitating event or reinforcer for these life-threatening behaviours. The targets then include reducing aversive and invalidating responses overall, and eliminating positive and negative reinforcement of suicidal and self-harming behaviours.
- Parent and family skills include emotion self-management, relationship mindfulness, accurate expression, validation, and radical acceptance.
- The key transactional focus is to decrease the cycle of inaccurate expression and invalidating responses, and instead build up accurate expression and validating responses.
- Family interventions may occur in family therapy, or in multi-family groups, with or without the patient.
- Family sessions can sometimes be chaotic, so there are specific strategies employed with families to manage them and keep them productive.
- It is essential to empower parents and other family members with skills and to help them be effective within their roles.

SECTION V EVIDENCE FOR DBT

ERIN M. MIGA, ANDRADA D. NEACSIU, ANITA LUNGU, HEIDI L. HEARD,
AND LINDA A. DIMEFF

KEY MESSAGES FOR CLINICIANS

- Efficacy of Comprehensive DBT is substantiated for suicidal and self-injurious treatment populations, and comorbid BPD and substance use, and DBT generally evidenced superior treatment retention to control treatments.
- DBT-Skills only has well-established empirical evidence for efficacy with treatment resistant depression, anxiety, binge eating, and bulimia disorders.
- Quality assurance method strengths included standardized assessments, blind raters, and adequate randomization. Limitations included lack of power analyses, in-study reliability, and only 13% of trials conducted follow up assessment at least one year later.
- 35% of all DBT trials utilized formal adherence ratings, when reported scores ranged from 3.8–4.2, indicating generally adequate treatment adherence.
- 58% of studies reported some or all clinicians received intensive or intensive-equivalent DBT training, most prior to study start.
- More attention is needed towards increasing accessibility and prevalence of ongoing adherence monitoring, supervision, and baseline DBT training.

CARLA J. WALTON AND KATHERINE ANNE COMTOIS

KEY MESSAGES FOR CLINICIANS

- Overall, in routine clinical settings, treatment with DBT leads to improvement in terms of decreasing suicidal and non-suicidal self-injury (NSSI), days admitted to psychiatric hospitals, depression, and general psychiatric symptoms.
- In the settings reported in this chapter, most of the clinicians had attended ten-day intensive DBT training, either before or during the study.
- There is large variability in routine clinical settings regarding the amount of follow-up consultation received after initial training.
- Drop-out rates for treatment are higher when DBT is delivered in routine clinical settings, as compared to research settings. More research is needed to explore reasons for drop-out and ways to decrease drop-out.
- Many routine clinical settings include phone coaching only during office hours. It is unclear what impact, if any, this modification from the standard protocol has on outcomes.

KEY MESSAGES FOR CLINICIANS

- DBT is the treatment for BPD that offers Level 1 (highest level) evidence of efficacy and effectiveness and is the only treatment with sufficient data for meta-analyses.
- Cost-effectiveness studies in treating people with BPD are few in number and highly varied in their design and variables measured, so conclusions need to be considered with caution; more prospective methodologically robust studies are needed.
- Data on cost-savings from reduced hospital days remains largely descriptive although DBT has the most objective data, to date.
- Despite these current limitations, funders and administrators must make decisions on the best current information available.
- Current information of means of reduced mental hospital days suggest that providing DBT is in most situations likely to be financially cost-effective by virtue of hospital cost savings alone.
- In addition, it is reasonable to expect cost savings to increase over the years following treatment as positive client outcomes translate into both increased health cost savings and decreased costs of providing treatment.
- More systematic assessment of health costs, costs of other services (police, justice, ambulance, social services, housing), and lost income productivity would further enhance future cost-effectiveness analyses.
- DBT offers an evidence-based option for treating people with BPD that is likely to meet the financial objectives of funders, economists, accountants, administrators, providers, and consumers.

KEY POINTS FOR CLINICIANS

- When reviewing literature on mediators and mechanisms of change, determine whether the researchers have established "statistically significant mediators" or met additional criteria necessary to be considered a mechanism of change.
- The effectiveness of DBT treatment strategies depends upon a strong therapeutic relationship. When DBT therapists adopt a dialectical stance that balances acceptance and change, clients are more open to emotional experiencing and expression, and new learning experiences.
- Increased emotional awareness and acceptance, attentional control, emotional modulation, and use of adaptive coping skills are change processes associated with positive outcomes in DBT. Therapist interventions focused on enhancing each of these processes are likely to yield beneficial effects.

KEY MESSAGES FOR CLINICIANS

- The label of borderline personality disorder can be more damaging than helpful.
- Non-DBT services that continue to label clients as having BPD when they no longer meet the criteria for the disorder are unhelpful—once a broken leg is healed, it is no longer a broken leg. Clinicians need to emphasize this point to their clients, as well as to the systems in which they work.
- DBT should be delivered by confident, competent, and courageous practitioners who are not afraid to both challenge and set limits for their clients.
- The rationale behind some of the skills (e.g., exposure via mindfulness) require repeated explanation; clients may have difficulty in understanding the purpose of learning the skills.
- Consistency is key; DBT needs practitioners who are prepared to engage for at least two cycles of the skills programme. They must also be willing to work consistently as an individual therapist with their clients.
- DBT works, if the correct elements are in place—motivation from the client, a certain level of understanding from the client, and the appropriate, skilled practitioner are all needed for success in DBT.

SECTION VI ADAPTING THE TREATMENT FOR NEW CLINICAL POPULATIONS

KEY MESSAGES FOR CLINICIANS

- Dialectical Behavior Therapy has been adapted and has been shown to be effective for multi-problem, complex adolescents with and without risk for suicide and/or non-suicidal self-injury.
- DBT-A includes all of the same modes of standard, adult DBT—individual therapy, group skills training (offered in the teen adaptation in a multi-family skills training group format), telephone consultation, and therapist consultation team.
- Parental support and involvement is a critical component of DBT-A, which is facilitated through additional modes of family sessions, parenting sessions, and parent phone coaching.
- There are particular challenges to working with multi-problem youth and their families, such as managing confidentiality, suicidal risk, rapport, and establishing/maintaining commitment to the treatment.
- Research, including the completion of two randomized controlled trials, now supports the adaptation of DBT for adolescents. Future directions include applying DBT with younger children and in school settings.

KEY POINTS FOR CLINICIANS

- Because eating pathology can function as a strategy to cope with emotion sensitivity and vulnerability, dialectical behaviour therapy (DBT) can fill a needed gap for individuals who have not responded to standard treatment approaches.
- The following characteristics in individuals with eating disorders (ED) may indicate the utility of a DBT approach:
  a. Failed treatment attempts with evidence-based treatment approaches.

KEY MESSAGES FOR CLINICIANS

• Co-occurring Borderline Personality Disorder (BPD) and Substance Use Disorders (SUD) are associated with higher risk behaviours and with greater treatment engagement challenges than either independently.

• DBT adapted for SUDs includes all aspects of the standard model of DBT for BPD with added formulations, strategies, and skills for addressing problems of addiction.

• DBT-SUD includes attachment strategies to help prevent individuals with BPD and SUDs from "falling out of treatment."

• DBT-SUD addresses the challenges involved with structuring clients' living environments and the treatment environment with a re-balancing of the Consultation to the Client and Intervening in the Environment DBT case management strategies.

• A modified primary target treatment hierarchy helps provide an integrated treatment of BPD and SUD related problem behaviours.

• The Active Passivity vs. Apparent Competency dialectical dilemma formulation and related secondary targets of passive coping and inaccurate communication are particularly useful for maintaining phenomenological empathy and responding strategically to lying, a common challenge in SUD presentations.

• Implementation challenges of DBT-SUD involve synthesizing standard DBT principles and strategies with SUD treatment best practices such as opioid replacement medications, and addressing common complications of individuals struggling with SUDs such as severe life chaos and the potential for SUD contagion among clients.

• Several RCTs provide at least modest to moderate support of DBT with and without SUD modifications for co-occurring BPD and SUD. Preliminary evidence extends DBT-SUD effectiveness to new populations including co-occurring SUD and eating disorders and primary substance use disorders, and to diverse ethnic, linguistic, and geographic settings.

KEY MESSAGES FOR CLINICIANS
- DBT is adopted in forensic settings as a treatment model for characteristics of Borderline Personality Disorder and other emotion regulation disorders.
- DBT is also adopted in forensic settings as general behavioural programming to address risk factors of criminal recidivism.
- Examples and language used throughout DBT standard manuals need to be modified to match a forensic population and setting conditions: this does not constitute treatment "adaptation."
- Modifications to standard DBT (Linehan, 1993a, b) in forensic settings most commonly include skills-only interventions, shortening group session length, incorporating targets related to dynamic criminogenic risk factors, and adding coping skills related to stressors in the institution.
- Variation across studies and lack of methodological rigor call for more research to reach conclusions regarding the effectiveness of implementing DBT in forensic settings.

KEY MESSAGES FOR CLINICIANS
- Decide on whether what is being offered is a crisis resolution programme, where there is a need for a brief admission focused on quick discharge, or a specialist treatment unit. This might depend more on the actual length of stay versus the desired one. The length of stay for patients will inform treatment targets in individual therapy and also the breadth of DBT skills taught in the Skills Training Groups.
- In terms of treatment targets, focus on those behaviours that got the patient into inpatient treatment and keep them there—watch for "mission creep" and having to treat every last problem that actually could be managed in the community once the risk has abated.
- The evidence for short-term DBT programmes indicates teaching a concentrated version of DBT skills (fewer skills taught more frequently) with a focus on crisis resolution.
- The evidence for longer-term DBT programmes emphasizes the importance of structuring the environment with a strong emphasis on behavioural principles and discharge.
- Maximize the opportunities to strengthen and generalize the use of skillful behaviour.
- Pay attention to Rathus and Miller's (2000) dialectical dilemmas for treating suicidal adolescents and their families, and how they manifest themselves in inpatient settings.

KEY MESSAGES FOR CLINICIANS
- The complexity and severity of mental illness are increasing across college campuses; this includes increasing rates of anxiety, depression, and suicidality.
- Of the surveyed CCC directors, 94% report a steady increase in the number of students arriving on campus with severe psychological problems (Gallagher, 2014).
- Research on DBT in the CCC shows promising results regarding reductions in suicidality, life problems, and psychopathology and increases of adaptive coping skills. More research is needed examining implementation, standard DBT protocol, and utilizing more controlled designs.
- Designing a DBT programme within your CCC operating under different policies and parameters than the CCC as a whole may be a way to implement standard DBT without violating policies regarding session limits and contact outside of business hours.

- Implementing brief DBT skills group is an evidence-based, time-limited treatment for a wide range of students that requires a lesser degree of training than standard DBT.
- The biosocial theory in its current form as a theory of emotion dysregulation is relevant and appropriate for explaining many common symptoms found in college students.
- Before implementing DBT, a thorough assessment of the needs and goals of the CCC and student body is necessary.
- After implementing a new DBT programme, the CCC should conduct a thorough outcome evaluation to assess progress toward goals.
- Challenges to implementation include (1) misfit between CCC structure or scope of practice and DBT treatment practices, (2) low support from university administration, (3) misfit between DBT theory and clinician's beliefs about treatment or pre-existing theoretical orientations, (4) difficulties obtaining commitment from students to participate in new treatment modalities, and (5) challenges arising from students in treatment together who know one another from classes or elsewhere on campus.

KEY MESSAGES FOR PRACTITIONERS
- DBT-C retains the theoretical model, principles, and therapeutic strategies of standard DBT.
- DBT-C incorporates almost all of the adult DBT skills and didactics into the curriculum, but modified to the developmental and cognitive level of pre-adolescent children.
- DBT-C includes a parent-training component.
- A major departure from standard DBT is the treatment target hierarchy, which emphasizes increasing adaptive patterns of parental responding as central to improving the child's emotional and behavioural regulation.

KEY POINTS FOR CLINICIANS
- DBT Skills in schools offers a unique upstream approach to provide adolescent emotion regulation skills.
- DBT STEPS-A is designed at the universal level and to be delivered by general education teachers.
- DBT STEPS-A is part of a continuum of DBT services that can be provided in school-based settings, is developed for school-based adolescents, and is adapted from Marsha Linehan's DBT.

KEY POINTS FOR CLINICIANS
- Vocational activity is an important goal for recovery from mental ill health.
- Adaptations of DBT focusing on employment have shown positive results.
- DBT for employment can be delivered as a group-based treatment, thus improving cost-effectiveness.
- All three adaptations of DBT for employment provide all five functions of standard DBT.
- The adaptations of DBT for employment have been developed as stage 2 treatments, provided to those individuals who are no longer engaging in high-risk behaviours.

KEY POINTS FOR CLINICIANS

- Accommodations to DBT for individuals with ID need to remain adherent to the model; the delivery mechanisms are altered, rather than core processes.
- It is essential for the DBT therapist to have heightened self-awareness regarding perceptions and communication patterns to foster positive transactional patterns in the client.
- The DBT therapist treating individuals with ID must understand how to manage factors associated with cognitive load in order to design and adjust treatment interventions.
- The therapist needs to understand, be empathetic about, and manage the complex environmental factors that impact the lives of individuals with ID.
- The complex and detailed skills curricula that form part of standard DBT require some adaptation for clients with ID. The Skills System is one such adaptation that provides the client with an accessible emotion regulation skills framework that promotes self-regulation and co-regulation processes to enhance the generalization of skills into the individual's natural environment.

KEY POINTS FOR CLINICIANS

- DBT+DBT PE is delivered in three stages, with Stage 1 using DBT to achieve behavioural control, Stage 2 targeting PTSD via the DBT PE protocol, and Stage 3 using DBT to address any problems that remain after PTSD is treated.
- During the pre-treatment phase of DBT, therapists begin orienting clients to the DBT PE protocol and establishing effective contingencies regarding achieving behavioural control in order to receive PTSD treatment.
- Stage 1 DBT is delivered without adaptation with the goal of helping clients to achieve the stability and skills necessary to safely and effectively engage in subsequent PTSD treatment.
- Clients must meet specified, principle-driven readiness criteria to begin the DBT PE protocol in Stage 2, including a requirement of abstinence from all forms of suicidal self-injury and NSSI for at least two months.
- The DBT PE protocol is an adapted version of Prolonged Exposure (PE) therapy that uses the core procedures of in vivo exposure to feared but objectively safe situations and imaginal exposure and processing of trauma memories.
- The DBT PE protocol includes three treatment phases: pre-exposure (2–3 sessions), exposure (flexible number of sessions), and termination/consolidation (1 session).
- On average, the DBT PE protocol is started after 20 weeks of DBT and lasts 13 sessions.
- Research supports the feasibility, acceptability, safety, and effectiveness of integrating the DBT PE protocol into DBT for suicidal and self-injuring clients with BPD, PTSD, and multiple additional diagnoses.
- Successful implementation of the DBT PE protocol in routine practice settings requires attention to several common client-, therapist-, and programme-level barriers.

KEY POINTS FOR CLINICIANS
- DBT-PTSD is a safe and highly effective multicomponent treatment programme for complex PTSD.
- Thus far, there is no evidence that ongoing self-harm is a safety risk or negative predictor for treatment outcome.
- Borderline patients with co-occurring PTSD should search for a trauma-focused treatment.
- In most cases, there is no need for patients with complex PTSD or PTSD and BPD to complete standard DBT ahead of a specifically designed treatment programme for treating trauma.

SECTION VII IMPLEMENTATION OF DBT

KEY MESSAGES FOR CLINICIANS
- When considering DBT trainings to enhance implementation, trainings that facilitate discussion or answering of questions or consultation are important as stake-holders work through determining how DBT will fit in their setting.
- Trainers must have experience with a range of solutions to typical appropriateness concerns so clinicians, agencies, or systems do not implement DBT in a rigid way that fits the manual, but not their clinical structure.
- A DBT pilot programme is an implementation strategy that can be evaluated to determine whether it should be implemented more widely.
- Once a pilot project is determined to be successful, expanding the programme to improve reach to appropriate clients is a vital next step.
- Those considering implementing DBT could use the data presented within this chapter about barriers to inform an implementation plan (e.g., knowing that staff turnover is an issue, plan for how to address it using the suggestions provided).
- DBT fidelity appears to be associated with more training.

KEY MESSAGES FOR CLINICIANS
- Successful implementation of DBT involves multi-level change within organizations.
- As a complex activity, tensions are inevitable among stakeholders when implementing DBT. Dialectics offer a means of promoting flexibility and resolving the challenges of implementation.
- Three common dialectical dilemmas occur during implementation of DBT:
    1. Tension between adopting and adapting DBT.
    2. Tension between risk management and delivering the treatment as intended.
    3. Tension between meeting both the needs of the system and the needs of providers.

SARAH K. REYNOLDS AND COLLEEN M. LANG

KEY MESSAGES FOR CLINICIANS

- The challenge for clinicians implementing comprehensive DBT in private practice is to determine how to implement modes of treatment that meet all of functions of DBT. The modes may differ from standard DBT, but the practitioner must be able to articulate how each function is served by the modes provided.
- Solo practitioners can best deliver standard comprehensive DBT by utilizing a shared location that enables cross-referrals between therapists' skills groups while maintaining separate business entities.
- The dual roles of business manager and individual therapist can be difficult to balance. Many DBT clinicians may have negative judgments of earning money from clients "in-need" and must seek dialectical solutions that honour business, service to clients, and personal limits.
- For private practice DBT, an essential topic in the pre-treatment phase is orientation to all business and payment-related policies. Potential problems such as non-payment, late cancellations/no-shows, etc., are conceptualized and targeted as TIBs.
- The consultation team is an essential component for any practitioner wishing to use DBT in their solo practice.

DANIEL M. FLYNN, MARY KELLS, AND MARY JOYCE

KEY MESSAGES FOR CLINICIANS

- Existing knowledge about DBT implementation for teams can be applied to implementation at a system-level.
- System change requires innovation champions who understand both the evidence-based treatment model as well as the political and societal climate within which it exists.
- Innovation champions cannot achieve change alone; change requires DBT champions and health service management working together to facilitate successful implementation.
- Research evaluation of all aspects of implementation is essential so as to understand, refine, and address potential implementation barriers.

ANTHONY P. DUBOSE, YEVGENY BOTANOV, AND ANDRÉ IVANOFF

KEY POINTS FOR CLINICIANS

- The global demand for DBT stems from high levels of mortality and morbidity due to suicide, the need for effective treatments for disorders of emotion regulation, and an increased demand for evidence-based mental health treatments.
- Due to the resource-intensive framework of DBT, careful examination of past implementation efforts is necessary for continued success in the international implementation of DBT.
- DBT implementation includes the required programmatic elements of the treatment and the provider behaviours that need to align with the strategies of the treatment.
- For successful international DBT implementation, factors including technology, language/translation, variability in healthcare systems, and challenges of working in a foreign country must be considered.

KEY POINTS FOR CLINICIANS
- The demand for DBT is outpacing the supply of clinicians trained in delivering it effectively.
- DBT is compatible with the implementation of technology, including persuasive technology, modularity, and logical flow.
- There is growing research support for the use of technology to both augment and supplant DBT, including videos, mobile apps, and computerized interventions.
- There are several mobile apps on the market that can be downloaded and used in therapy, although there appears to be no research on these applications.

SECTION VIII TRAINING IN DBT

KEY MESSAGES FOR CLINICIANS
- Along with evidence-based psychological treatments, there is also a need for evidence-based training.
- An intensive model of training in DBT was developed to meet the growing demand that could not be met through traditional training methods.
- The model of DBT intensive training typically is provided as a bipartite training consisting of two five-day workshops separated by a period for self-study and implementation.
- Strategies and principles of the treatment are also incorporated within the training, such as mindfulness at the start of each training day and chain analyses targeting behaviours that interfere with training.
- Early evaluations of DBT intensive training has demonstrated successful initial implementation and adoption of DBT modes. However, further research is needed to examine long-term sustainability and treatment penetration.

KEY MESSAGES FOR CLINICIANS

- Translating evidence-based therapies from research settings to routine community settings requires that interventions provided, in both form and content, match those delivered as part of the research protocol in order to maintain outcomes.
- Treatment adherence and treatment fidelity: DBT uses "treatment adherence" to describe therapists' behaviours used when conducting the therapy, and "treatment fidelity" when discussing therapy modes offered in DBT programmes.
- DBT is a complex therapy to master given the abundance of treatment strategies, all of which are context specific. DBT is a principle-driven, not protocol-driven, therapy, although protocols do also exist within DBT.
- The DBT Adherence Coding Scale (DBT ACS), created for research purposes, establishes whether a therapist's therapy provision matches the behaviours set out in the treatment manual.
- The DBT ACS scale reflects the complexity of the treatment and requires the review of an entire therapy session and the subsequent coding of therapist strategies on 66 items, some of which embody complex "if-then" rules of therapy.
- Currently DBT does not have a scale that is briefer, easier to administer, or easier to deploy in community settings to measure therapist competence.
- Research on the acquisition of and the increase of competence in DBT suggests that more training and supervision leads to increased use of DBT strategies.
- Consultation team habits can shape the DBT practice of its team members.

SECTION IX IN CONCLUSION

KEY POINTS FOR CLINICIANS

- Since the publication of the first treatment trial in 1991 evidential support for using DBT for clients with suicidal behaviour in the context of BPD has been complemented by promising adaptations and outcomes in other populations.
- DBT's flexible modular structure has aided the process of adopting and adapting the treatment for new client groups and new populations.
- Building on DBT's flexible transdiagnostic basis to realize its potential to reach a greater number of clients suffering from difficulties in the experience and management of emotion should be a focus for the next two decades.
- Understanding more about effective mechanisms, both in treatment and for training staff, to deliver consistently improved outcomes for clients will aid the dissemination endeavour.
- Synthesizing the desire to disseminate the treatment and improving reach with ensuring fidelity to maintain clinical outcomes is a central issue for DBT now and into the future
- Despite DBT's success in delivering good clinical outcomes many clients remain functionally impaired in the medium to longer term. Dedicated research to understanding and scoping this problem would be a useful focus for the next decade.

- Funding research to examine which modes of treatment and which treatment lengths and intensities are most effective remains a priority. "Big data" collected in routine practice settings may assist with this task.
- DBT is well placed to adapt to forthcoming changes in diagnostic classification that utilize a dimensional trait based approach to describing difficulties.
- DBT as a principle-based treatment fits well with ideas of interventions that focus on evidence-based principles of change.

LIST OF CONTRIBUTORS

Seth R. Axelrod, Ph.D., School of Medicine, Yale University, USA

Helen Best, Treatment Implementation Collaborative, LLC, USA

Kelly A. C. Bhatnagar, The Emily Program, Department of Psychological Sciences, Case Western Reserve University, USA

Martin Bohus, Central Institute of Mental Health, Medical Faculty Mannheim, Heidelberg University, Germany

Lauren Bonavitacola, Cognitive & Behavioral Consultants of Westchester & Manhattan, USA

Tali Boritz, Psychologist, Department of Psychiatry, University of Toronto, Canada

Yevgeny Botanov, Department of Psychology, Millersville University, USA

Louise Brinton Clarke, Primary Care Community Health Team, Betsi Cadwaladr University Health Board, Bangor, UK

Julie F. Brown, School of Social Work, Simmons College, USA

Alexander L. Chapman, Clinical Science Department of Psychology, Simon Fraser University, USA

Carla D. Chugani, School of Medicine, University of Pittsburgh, USA

Katherine Anne Comtois, Department of Psychiatry and Behavioral Sciences, University of Washington, USA

Colleen M. Cowperthwait, Department of Psychiatry and Behavioral Sciences, Duke University Medical Center, USA

Sheila E. Crowell, Department of Psychology, University of Utah, USA

Elizabeth T. Dexter-Mazza, Mazza Consulting and Psychological Services, USA

Linda A. Dimeff, Portland DBT Institute, Inc., USA; Evidence-Based Practice Institute, LLC, USA

Anthony P. DuBose, Linehan Institute/Behavioral Tech, LLC, USA

Christine Dunkley, Department of Psychology, Bangor University, UK and British Isles DBT Training, UK

Caitlin M. Fang, Department of Psychiatry and Behavioral Sciences, Duke University Medical Center, USA

Janet D. Feigenbaum, Research Department, Clinical, Educational and Health Psychology, University College London, UK

Daniel M. Flynn, Cork Kerry Community Healthcare, Health Service Executive, Ireland

Emily Fox, St Andrew's Healthcare, Northampton, UK

Alan E. Fruzzetti, McLean Hospital and Department of Psychiatry, Harvard Medical School, USA

Amy Gaglia, British Isles DBT Training Team, Wrexham, UK

Jeremy L. Grove, Department of Psychology, University of Utah, USA

Melanie S. Harned, Department of Psychology, University of Washington, USA

Heidi L. Heard, Department of Psychology, University of Washington, US, and British Isles DBT Training, UK

André Ivanoff, Columbia University, USA & Linehan Institute/Behavioral Tech, LLC

Mary Joyce, National Suicide Research Foundation, Ireland

Mary Kells, Health Service Executive, Cork Kerry Community Healthcare, Ireland, UK.

Roy Krawitz, Department of Psychological Medicine, Auckland University, New Zealand

Sara J. Landes, Department of Psychiatry, University of Arkansas for Medical Sciences, USA; Central Arkansas Veterans Healthcare System, USA

Colleen M. Lang, Behavioral Wellness of NYC, USA, and St. John's University, USA

Marsha M. Linehan, Department of Psychology, University of Washington, USA

Anita Lungu, Lyra Health, USA

Jim Lyng, School of Psychology, Trinity College Dublin, Ireland

Shari Manning, PhD, Treatment Implementation Collaborative, LLC, USA

Phillip L. Marotta, School of Social Work, Columbia University, USA

Caitlin Martin-Wagar, The Emily Program, Department of Psychology, University of Akron, USA

James J. Mazza, College of Education, University of Washington, USA

Shelley F. McMain, Centre for Addiction and Mental Health/University of Toronto, Canada

Lars Mehlum, Institute of Clinical Medicine, University of Oslo, Oslo

Erin M. Miga, Department of Psychology, University of Washington, USA

Alec L. Miller, Cognitive & Behavioral Consultants of Westchester & Manhattan, USA

Maria V. Navarro-Haro, Hospital General de Cataluyna, Spain

Andrada D. Neacsiu, Department of Psychiatry and Behavioral Sciences, Duke University Medical Center, USA

Inga Niedtfeld, Department of Psychosomatic Medicine, Mannheim/Heidelberg University, Germany

Francheska Perepletchikova, Department of Psychiatry, Weill Cornell Medicine, NY, USA

Kathlen Priebe, Institute of Psychiatric and Psychosomatic Psychotherapy; Central Institute of Mental Health, Mannheim, Heidelberg University, Germany

Jill H. Rathus, Department of Psychology, Long Island University, USA

Sarah K. Reynolds, Private Practice, New York, NY, USA

Shireen L. Rizvi, Rutgers University, USA

Kristen M. Roman, CBT/DBT Associates, New York, NY, USA

Allison K. Ruork, M.A., Department of Psychology, University of Nevada, USA

Joan C. Russo, DBT-Linehan Board of Certification, USA

Jennifer H. R. Sayrs, Evidence-Based Treatment Centers of Seattle, USA

Henry Schmidt III, President, Behavioral Affiliates, Inc., USA

Sara C. Schmidt, Department of Psychology, University of Washington, USA

Maggie Stanton, Department of Psychology, Bangor University, UK, and British Isles DBT Training, UK

Michaela A. Swales, School of Psychology, Bangor University, UK

Amanda A. Uliaszek, Departments of Psychology and Psychological Clinical Science, University of Toronto Scarborough, Canada

Carla J. Walton, Hunter New England Mental Health Service, Australia

Chelsey R. Wilks, Department of Psychology, University of Washington, USA

Gregory E. Williams, Department of Psychological Clinical Science, University of Toronto Scarborough, Canada

Lucene Wisniewski, LLC, Department of Psychological Sciences, Case Western Reserve University, USA

Randy Wolbert, Behavioral Tech LLC, USA

Kristin P. Wyatt, Department of Psychiatry and Behavioral Sciences, Duke University Medical Center, USA

Richard J. Zeifman, Ryerson University, Canada

SECTION I

INTRODUCTION

CHAPTER 1

··

DIALECTICAL BEHAVIOUR THERAPY

Development and Distinctive Features

··

MICHAELA A. SWALES

INTRODUCTION

···

DIALECTICAL behaviour therapy (DBT) began in the early 1980s out of efforts to address the problems of repetitive suicidal behaviour using behaviour therapy. Testing the new therapy with individuals with a diagnosis of borderline personality disorder (BPD), a group with high rates of suicidal behaviour, drove the development of a treatment that not only successfully treated suicidal and self-harm behaviour, but was also the first treatment to demonstrate effectiveness with clients with a BPD diagnosis for whom no previous treatment had been effective (Linehan, Armstrong, Suarez, Allmon, & Heard, 1991). Thus, DBT radically changed the treatment landscape for clients with a personality disorder diagnosis and heralded in an era of increased therapeutic optimism. While other BPD treatments have since been developed and tested (e.g., Schema-focused therapy, Young, Klosko, & Weishaar, 2003; Mentalization-based therapy, Bateman & Fonagy, 2006; Transference-focused psychotherapy, Yeomans, Clarkin, & Kernberg, 2015), DBT remains the most well researched and evaluated of all treatments for BPD (Stoffers-Winterling et al., 2012). This chapter, in part, draws on presentations given by Linehan in recent years, most notably her address to the British Psychological Society Division of Clinical Psychology as part of its 50th Anniversary celebrations, entitled "DBT: Where we were, where we are and where we are going" (September, 2015)[1]. The chapter begins by describing the development of DBT in the early 1980s, before moving on to orient the reader to the structure of the handbook. *The Oxford Handbook of Dialectical Behaviour*

---

[1] Marsha Linehan kindly gave her permission for me to draw on these talks in preparing this chapter.

Therapy charts the progress of DBT in the twenty-five years since the manuals were published and brings together experts in the field to review the theory, research, clinical practice, and implementation of DBT.

DEVELOPMENT OF DBT

Linehan was converted from an interest in Freudian psychology to the beginnings of her life-long passion for behaviourism (Linehan, 2016) by reading the work of Walter Mischel (1968) in social learning theory and later by the work of Staats (1975) and Bandura (1969). Linehan describes how behavioural descriptions of mental disorders and their causes that illuminate how you might intervene to alter these causes and maintaining factors was central to her interest in behaviour therapy. The centrality of data and evidence-gathering underpinning behaviourism was exciting and energizing (Linehan, 2016). At the time of Linehan's work in the early 1980s, suicide was, as it still is, a major public health problem. Her early career interest was in the application of behavioural theories to suicidal behaviour (Linehan, 1981), which led her to seek grant funding for treatment development. In developing the new treatment there were many challenges to address and problems to solve. First, ensuring that clients who really needed the treatment both attended and engaged effectively with the treatment; second, that interventions were based on a coherent theory that could guide intervention; and finally, that therapists could stay the course of treatment.

Solving the Challenge of Change

DBT was born in the crucible of applying behavioural theory and practice to the problem of suicide and self-harm, in what Linehan and Wilks (2015) describe as a "trial-and-error clinical effort." In rigorously applying problem solving to highly suicidal individuals, therapists working in Linehan's lab noticed that clients were struggling to tolerate the extreme focus on change that the behavioural treatment demanded. Clients experienced the demands for change as fundamentally invalidating and often abandoned the treatment endeavour. In response, therapists were tempted to shift to a more acceptance-based approach. Indeed, many therapists in the face of client distress are tempted to limit requests for change and move to a palliative care approach for clients with severe difficulties in the hope that this will relieve their distress. Paradoxically, such a move rarely has the desired effect. For clients in extreme distress with multiple problems, not helping them change their circumstances—whether those are external or internal to the person—is also experienced as invalidating, and as a *therapeutic* option, it is untenable.

This central dilemma led to two core aspects of what became DBT. First, change-based and acceptance-based approaches were required at the heart of the treatment; and second, a structural or philosophical context was required to "house" the two contrasting approaches. In terms of a change-based technology, DBT draws on behavioural theory and practice to address the problems of the client, deploying *a radical behaviourist approach* to both overt and covert human behaviours. While the initial treatment manual is entitled *Cognitive-behavioral treatment of borderline personality disorder* (Linehan, 1993a), the treatment focuses more on behaviourism than cognition in comparison to many other treatments in the CBT stable. The central role of behavioural or functional analysis as the approach to conceptualizing change reveals Linehan's roots in behaviourism.

Selecting which particular acceptance-based perspective to contrast with the emphasis on change was not so self-evident. All psychological therapies incorporate acceptance to a degree, and some, for example, Rogerian Client-Centred therapy (Rogers, 1946), consider acceptance the heart of the treatment. Yet, even in Rogerian therapy, the central drive of acceptance is change (Linehan & Wilks, 2015). Linehan sought a more fundamental approach to acceptance—one that was not aimed at change at all. Linehan had a long-standing interest and connection with both Eastern and Western acceptance traditions, first with contemplative prayer (West) and later with Zen (East) (Linehan & Sargent, 2017). Even in Linehan's pursuit of what is considered an Eastern practice (Zen), dialectically, she studied with two Zen masters who were both Catholic priests.

Alongside a small number of other Western practitioners, she was curious about the relevance and application of the principles of Zen and the associated practice of mindfulness within healthcare. While Kabat-Zinn had brought mindfulness into intervention in psychological medicine (Kabat-Zinn, 1991), Linehan was the first to incorporate mindfulness into a psychological treatment. Others have subsequently followed, for example, Mindfulness-Based Cognitive Therapy (Segal, Williams, & Teasdale, 2002), Acceptance and Commitment Therapy (Hayes, Strosahl, & Wilson, 1999). Uniquely, she translated the principles and practice of mindfulness into a set of skills that could be taught to clients who were experiencing high levels of distress and dysregulation (Linehan, 1993b; 2015).

The role of acceptance in DBT incorporates some of the functions of acceptance in other treatments, for example, emphasizing acceptance of the difficulty of a task can motivate a client to change. Commonly in treatment, clients trying to change their behaviour may experience shame and anger, and experience high levels of self-criticism and judgment, describing themselves as "stupid" or "idiotic." Such emotions and thoughts demotivate clients from persisting with strategies that may—with time, coaching, and finesse—yield significant benefits. Therapists moving in to accept and validate firstly that changing is difficult, and secondly, that experiencing frustration and self-criticism is normal when trying to change behaviour, helps clients to regulate their affect, leading to increased persistence in the process of change. Acceptance in DBT, however, has a more radical place. There are moments that require complete and total acceptance, with no agenda for change at all: acceptance for its own sake. For example, many clients have experienced multiple and repeated traumas in the past. Therapists need to help clients develop complete and total, i.e., *radical*, acceptance that they did not have a safe and secure childhood. In coming to fully accept the past, current circumstances, or both, clients may experience profound change—this may be the consequence of acceptance, but it is not its goal.

The extreme contrast between the determined focus on change demanded by behavioural theory and the equally firm embodiment of acceptance required, both conceptually and practically, a philosophical perspective to house the two approaches. Dialectics fulfils this role in the treatment. Dialectics permeates the treatment both as a world view and as a method of persuasion. A dialectical world view argues for no single perspective on reality as owning the whole truth; multiple perspectives are not only possible, but desirable. Reality is complex and oppositional, and the tension between opposing views of reality pulls for resolution and synthesis, which then evolves into new tensions (see Figure 1.1). A dialectical world view embraces change as the only constant and points to finding the validity in multiple perspectives on reality.

These early developments of the treatment in terms of its philosophical foundations drove a new set of therapist strategies. First, therapists needed competence in behaviourism, the technology of change, and mindfulness, the technology of acceptance. Both of these technologies can be considered as contrasting perspectives on reality, and both have an essential validity. Secondly, application of strategies stemming from dialectics that emphasize the capacity to see both poles of a dialectic assists therapists in moving between positions of acceptance and change to find new solutions to client problems. The constant motion between positions of acceptance and change drives the speed, movement, and flow of therapy (Swenson, 2016, Ch. 13). Finally, stemming from Zen, therapists also require skills in radical acceptance of the client as he or she is in the moment, including the slow and episodic rate of progress in treatment and the high risk of suicide.

Conceptualizing the Central Problem of Borderline Personality Disorder

The federal grant funding Linehan received to test her developing treatment required that outcome research focused on a mental disorder diagnosis. Given the risk of suicide and frequency of self-harming behaviour (then described as parasuicide) in individuals with a BPD diagnosis, Linehan chose this client group for the first treatment trial. Choosing to address suicidal behaviour within BPD led to two additional problems requiring resolution. Firstly, the treatment was originally conceptualized and developed for suicidal behaviours, not for a *disorder*. DBT required a way to focus on the mechanisms underpinning both suicidal behaviour and BPD as a way of reconciling this dialectic. Secondly, and related to the first, DBT required a model for understanding BPD that related to treatment. The treatment model needed to be capable of guiding effective therapy (behavioural roots), non-pejorative and engendering compassion (acceptance roots), and compatible with current research data. Reviewing what was known about BPD and incorporating what was known already about suicidal and self-harm behaviour from earlier research and treatment development in her laboratory, Linehan

FIGURE 1.1 M. C. Escher, *Liberation*. For me, this image personally represents the transactional nature of change experienced in the treatment.

developed a theory focusing on the centrality of emotion dysregulation as the core problem for clients. DBT highlights the pervasive nature of the emotion regulation difficulties clients experience and how the criterion behaviours of a BPD diagnosis (e.g., interpersonal difficulties, identity disturbance, behavioural control problems such as self-harm and impulsive behaviours) are all either natural consequences of being emotionally dysregulated, or serve as attempts to re-regulate. DBT articulates a dialectical model of pathogenesis—the *biosocial theory*—in which biological vulnerabilities transact with pervasively invalidating environments such that, over time, environmental responses increase biological sensibilities, and these in their turn prompt further invalidation from the environment, resulting in the behavioural patterns associated with emotional dysregulation in BPD. The biosocial theory not only drives a compassionate approach to the problems with which clients present, but also orients therapists towards solving the affective difficulties that clients experience (Linehan, 1993a).

Supporting Therapists to Treat

During the early stages of treatment development, the impact of treating individuals at chronic high risk for suicide became all too evident; therapists experienced fear, often accompanied by urges to discharge the clients or no longer treat the client group. For any treatment to be successful, therapists need to be able to stay the course alongside their clients. DBT, therefore, needed both to assist therapists to effectively treat the high levels of risk presented by the client group, and to address the intense emotional reactions engendered both by the level of risk and by the intense emotional pain of the clients.

Responding to therapists' anxiety about client risk of suicide, and based on her earlier work in the field of suicidal behaviour (Linehan, 1981), Linehan developed a structured approach both to treating recent suicidal behaviours, using comprehensive problem solving, as well as describing how to respond to a current suicidal crisis (Linehan, 1993a, Ch. 15). As a behavioural treatment, DBT focuses on analysing the function of suicidal and self-harm behaviour and, in line with the biosocial theory of BPD, particularly addresses affective variables that prompt or maintain the behaviour. DBT conceptualizes suicidal and self-harm behaviours as attempts at problem solving where the problem is both unbearable from the client's perspective, and where alternative solutions have either failed or resources are unavailable. In a suicidal crisis, therapists conceptualizing suicidal behaviour as a problem, rather than a solution, may fail to see clients' desperation to escape a current situation. DBT encourages therapists, dialectically, to redirect their efforts to finding alternative, more effective solutions for whatever problem that the client is endeavouring to solve, i.e., to find the validity in the client's desire to escape a situation and to formulate and implement a non-suicidal plan to reach the client's objective.

In addition to managing therapist anxiety by developing expertise in suicidal behaviour management, Linehan also structured the therapy to address therapists' intense emotional reactions to their clients' behaviours. Difficulties in their own emotional regulation frequently led, in addition to fear, to problems with anger and hostility, all of which often resulted in endeavours to control, reject, or attack the client. Alternatively, either in direct response to client behaviours or in an endeavour to re-regulate their own anger and distress, therapists also were equally prone to excessive empathy, leading them to leap into the pool of despair with their clients, effectively abandoning therapy. Remaining fixed at one pole or oscillating between extremes of emotional response constituted dialectical failures. DBT introduced the Consultation Team, where all therapists treating clients meet to seek assistance from their team members on how to most effectively implement treatment and, crucially, how to avoid such dialectical failures. While the use of such treating teams was, and still is, standard in the conduct of psychotherapy randomized controlled trials (RCTs) to control adherence in the delivery of a treatment under test, DBT uniquely exported this idea into the treatment itself, making the DBT Consultation Team an integral component of the treatment.

BRIEF ORIENTATION TO THIS HANDBOOK

This volume comprises nine sections. The second section discusses recent developments in our understanding and knowledge of the biosocial theory, as well as the three theoretical foundations underpinning the treatment; behaviourism, Zen, and dialectics. The comprehensive multi-modal nature of DBT is described in chapters in Section III, while Section IV tackles the clinical application of DBT. Section V reviews the evidence base for DBT, and considers questions of efficacy, effectiveness, financial cost-effectiveness, and mechanisms of action. Adaptations of DBT in different settings and with different populations are reviewed in Section VI, with Sections VII and VIII considering issues in implementation and training, respectively. Each chapter has a set of key messages for clinicians, which can be found both in the chapter and with the contents pages to assist in navigating the varied, diverse, and stimulating contributions made to this volume by experts in their field. Section IX concludes the volume, summarizing DBT's progress to date and looking to the future.

SECTION II: THEORETICAL UNDERPINNINGS OF DBT

At the time of writing of the original treatment manual (Linehan, 1993a), there was promising evidential support for the biosocial theory. In the 25 years since, knowledge of the biological vulnerabilities of BPD, and their neural substrates, has increased apace. Bohus Niedtfeld and Bohus in their chapter review these recent data and indicate what the most recent research might indicate about future directions in therapy. Grove and Crowell in their chapter discuss invalidating family contexts as a risk factor for BPD and consider factors that contribute to the development of these contexts and how they might be ameliorated. Knowledge of these processes assists therapists in understanding and validating the substantial challenges faced by their clients in overcoming their difficulties.

The subsequent chapters in the section consider the three philosophies that form the bedrock of the therapeutic interventions within the treatment; behaviourism, Zen, and dialectics. DBT's emphasis on *behavioural*, rather than cognitive, theory drives a distinctive approach to treatment. As a radical behaviourist treatment, DBT conceptualizes everything an individual does—thinking, emoting, acting, sensing—as a behaviour that can be understood as cued and maintained using behavioural theory. DBT's perspective sees clients' problems as disordered behaviour, leading DBT therapists to target specific behaviours, rather than particular diagnoses. Distinctively, thinking in this way means that, once the disordered behaviour (which may include thinking, emoting, or other internal experiences) is no longer observed by others or experienced by the client, then the disorder is gone. This perspective, both at the time of its original inception, but also currently, provides hope that stigmatizing diagnoses such as BPD can be removed by the systematic application of behavioural interventions. DBT also takes a behavioural, rather than a volitional, approach to motivation. Thus, DBT therapists focus on emotions, thoughts, and environmental contingencies that interfere with both learning and executing more skillful behaviours. Addressing motivation in this way helps therapists focus effectively on factors blocking clinical progress, rather than blaming the client for failing to progress. In his chapter, Chapman describes the behavioural theory component of the treatment in more detail, specifically its application to suicidal behaviours and non-suicidal self-injury.

As briefly elucidated earlier, the behavioural change emphasis of the treatment required an acceptance counter-point to enable clients with high levels of emotional sensitivity to tolerate and engage with the treatment. Zen as a practice centres on complete and total acceptance of the present moment. Aitken (1982) expresses this principle as follows: "the essential world of perfection is this very world" (p. 63). From this perspective, the world, including ourselves, is perfect; the best that can be. Neither the world nor ourselves can be different because we are created or caused by all that has preceded this very moment. Wolbert, in his chapter, discusses in greater detail the philosophical basis of Zen and how this impacts the treatment conceptually and in terms of therapeutic strategies and skills. He describes Linehan's early experiences with contemplative practices and Zen, and how she came to unite them with behavioural theory. The chapter illustrates both the contrasts and similarities between Zen and behavioural theory.

Dialectics provides a structural philosophical context to "house" behavioural theory and Zen practice. In essence, dialectics posits that truth emerges through the posing of an argument or thesis, which then elicits a counter-argument or antithesis demonstrating the inaccuracy in some or all of the original argument. This process leads to a new proposition or synthesis, which, in its turn, forms a thesis eliciting a new antithesis. In the course of therapy, DBT therapists and their clients encounter many such debates. The client wants to die; the therapist disputes that dying is a good idea. In so doing, the client argues for why they wish to die; perhaps they are overwhelmed with anxiety about current debt. The therapist validates the difficulty of solving the debt problem and how anxiety in these circumstances makes sense, yet holds the view that dying is not a solution to debt. The client experiences the therapist's comments as indicating that the problems are understood and valid, which reduces slightly their emotional distress and enables the therapist to work with them on both decreasing anxiety and solving the debt problem. Resolving such dialectical tensions is a common part of the treatment.

Dialectical philosophy emphasizes relatedness and that there are multiple perspectives on reality, all of which hold some aspect of the truth. This perspective encourages therapists to remain flexible in searching for solutions, remaining perpetually aware of what they may have missed out in their understanding of a problem or a situation. Because of its respect for multiple perspectives, dialectics helps teams work with clients with complex problems where frequent opportunities for disagreements about care emerge. Commonly, teams working with clients who have been given a BPD diagnosis experience strong disagreements that threaten to "split" the team. Typically, this process is driven in part by strong emotion, but also by beliefs that one course of action or one interpretation of a client's behaviour is "right", which then leads team members to argue more strongly to assert their own position. For a team following a dialectical philosophy, all team members embrace the idea that there are multiple perspectives on reality, all of which may hold some perspective on the truth. The task of the team is to explore the multiple perspectives to find a new truth or synthesis that will assist the therapist and client to move forward.

On an inpatient unit, a client frequently ties ligatures. Half the staff team think that the client, overwhelmed with her trauma symptoms, finds the noise and the signs of emotional distress in other patients hard to tolerate. The other half of the staff team think that staff attention during the observation period subsequent to an incident reinforces the behaviour. Initially at a ward round, the team disagree about which is the correct perspective—half of the team asserting that the client needs more support, and the other that the client should be discharged. One of the team members highlights to the team that they have lost a dialectical perspective that allows the team to explore the validity in both perspectives. Following this dialectical discussion, the team are more open to noticing what is happening for the client at these times. Further assessment reveals that the client *is* overwhelmed by the noise on the inpatient unit *and* that the location of the observation post-incident, in non-communal areas that are quieter, are *both* controlling variables. This allows the team to rally around solutions that increase access to quieter spaces at particular times of day and to increase the therapy focus on regulating emotions in the face of distress in others. Using dialectics as an overarching framework to draw on both the change and acceptance perspectives permeates the treatment. Sayrs and Linehan describe the principles of dialectics more comprehensively and highlight how these are used within the treatment.

Section III: The Structure of Treatment

The original DBT programme was structured to address the capability and motivational deficits that are the consequence of growing up in invalidating environments when emotionally sensitive (Linehan, 1993a). Commonly, such environments respond to private communication in erratic, extreme, or inappropriate ways, intermittently reinforce more intense forms of emotional communication, and over simplify the challenge of solving problems, resulting in difficulties in labelling, experiencing, and managing emotions, tolerating distress, and forming realistic goals and expectations. Addressing the extent of the resultant problems meant that delivering therapy solely via a once-a-week individual therapy appointment was impractical. Rather, Linehan designed DBT as a programmatic treatment comprising 1) weekly skills training groups, during which a six-month curriculum of skills was taught twice; 2) weekly individual therapy, during which the therapist targeted specific problematic behaviours and treated any motivational issues (emotions, thoughts, and contingencies interfering with effective behaviour); 3) out-of-hours telephone consultation, in which the client could access their therapist for skills coaching to avoid crises and increase skills generalization; and 4) consultation team for therapists, where therapists discussed how to provide the best quality of treatment to their clients and received support to manage the emotional demands of the work.

The comprehensive nature of the treatment presented a challenge for implementation into routine settings as therapists wishing to provide DBT needed to work in teams and provide multiple modalities of therapy to groups of clients (of which more in Section VII). In training others to deliver the treatment, Linehan recognized that these modalities mapped onto particular functions delivered by DBT programmes. These are: *enhancing client capabilities* (skills training groups); *enhancing client motivation* (individual therapy); *generalization* of treatment gains outside of therapy (telephone consultation); and *enhancing therapist capabilities and motivation* (consultation team). Focusing on *function* rather than *form* or *modality* provides a degree of flexibility for using the treatment in other settings. So, for example, in inpatient settings, skills groups may occur multiple times in the week and generalization may occur via milieu skills coaches rather than via contact with the individual therapist. Analysing DBT treatment in this way also highlights an additional function that, in the treatment development work, had been provided, in part, by the structure of the RCT. This final function, *structuring the treatment environment*, focuses on ensuring that the wider treatment environment facilitates the delivery of the programme. This function may encompass modalities of treatment that relate either to the wider healthcare system—for example, meetings between the DBT team lead and senior managers within the healthcare organization to discuss resources, or to other groups within the clients' life whose support of the treatment will likely improve clinical outcomes—for example, a support group for partners and parents of adult clients in the DBT programme or training in the basic tenets of the DBT model for milieu staff in an inpatient unit. Section III begins with a description by Schmidt and Russo of the structure and practical challenges of running a DBT programme. Chapters that follow discuss the modalities of treatment: Sayrs discusses the principles and challenges in setting up and running an effective consultation team; Cowperthwait, Wyatt, Fang, and Neacsiu address the principles and practicalities of skills training in the treatment; and Rizvi and Roman discuss how to take the therapy out of the consulting room using various strategies to enhance generalization. The section concludes with a chapter by Swales and Dunkley on the skills that team leaders require to set up and run a comprehensive DBT programme.

SECTION IV: CLINICAL APPLICATIONS OF DBT

Central aspects of formulating and treating clients are tackled in Section IV. Clients presenting with suicidal behaviour who also have problems consistent with a diagnosis of BPD almost always have multiple additional diagnoses and problems. DBT addresses this clinical complexity by taking a staged and targeted approach to treatment, establishing first what are the current treatment priorities and then hierarchically targeting the behaviours required to achieve those priorities. So, for example, typically clients who are suicidal with a BPD diagnosis enter treatment at Stage 1, where the priority is to achieve behavioural stability. Within Stage 1, DBT therapists hierarchically organize treatment targets prioritizing first *life-threatening behaviours*, then *therapy-interfering behaviours*, and finally *quality of life-interfering behaviours*, which, in DBT terms, are those behaviours that seriously destabilize the client and often lead to intervention by others (Swales & Heard, 2017). As a problem-solving treatment, during Stage 1, DBT therapists systematically conduct behavioural and solution analyses to actively reduce the targeted behaviours. Over time, therapists begin to see patterns of responding within client behaviours allowing for a more systematic approach to solution implementation and generation (Koerner, 2012). Once the client has achieved behavioural stability, they may enter Stage 2, where the focus is on emotionally processing the past and therapists will derive, in collaboration with their clients, appropriate targets for this stage. Manning describes DBT's approach to case conceptualization in her chapter, providing a detailed clinical case example; Landes describes how to effectively conduct behavioural and solution analyses; and Dunkley addresses conceptual and practical issues in the application of emotion regulation within behavioural and solution analyses. Mehlum, from the perspective of a suicidologist, discusses how these approaches and strategies in DBT actively address suicidal behaviours.

DBT focuses on the therapeutic relationship to provide both a validating and supportive context in which clients can learn and in which to resolve issues arising within the therapeutic relationship that appear elsewhere in the clients' lives and cause difficulty. In their chapter, Fruzzetti and Ruork discuss the conceptual and practical aspects of applying validation in DBT and how DBT therapists might maximize the validating nature of the therapeutic relationship. Heard addresses treating in-session clinical behaviours, both those behaviours that are "therapy-interfering" and those that may not interfere with the therapy, but importantly link to other targets of therapy, illustrating the movement in the treatment between in-session and out-of-session behaviour.

As described earlier, DBT was the first psychotherapy to utilize mindfulness as a set of skills to assist clients to remain mindfully awake to the present moment. While mindfulness and its teaching are now commonly offered in mental health services and further afield, the teaching of mindfulness is a skilled endeavour, particularly where clients may be suicidal and highly emotionally labile. The way in which Linehan organizes mindfulness skills assists in this challenging task. Stanton and Dunkley elucidate the ways in which DBT therapists teach and train mindfulness in their clients.

Given the hypothesized role of family environments in the development and maintenance of problematic behavioural patterns, the involvement of families in treatment presents many challenges. Just as behaviours of family members may prompt certain problematic behaviours from clients, clients' difficulties also present problems for family members. Intervening effectively in these transactional patterns may prove important in improving clinical outcomes. Fruzzetti addresses the circumstances in which involving families in treatment may be useful and the practicalities of conducting family sessions.

Section V: Evidence for DBT

As the first treatment for BPD to establish evidence of efficacy, it is perhaps unsurprising that DBT is the most intensively researched treatment in its field (Stoffers-Winterling et al., 2012). Evidence for DBT is the focus of Section V. Miga, Neacsiu, Lungu et al. comprehensively review the RCT evidence for DBT and, in particular, focus on the quality of those trials and what may safely be deduced from them. Walton and Comtois review evidence from effectiveness studies to establish whether the gold standard results reviewed by Miga and colleagues can be expected in routine clinical settings. They also review qualitative studies that discuss the client experience of DBT. This is followed by Clarke's chapter in which she provides a personal client perspective on the experience of DBT. In many healthcare settings, there are concerns about the financial implications of intensive treatments such as DBT. The chapter by Krawitz and Miga analyses data addressing these concerns.

What is Working in DBT?

Since the first published trial of DBT, researchers and clinicians have questioned which aspects of the treatment drive its efficacy. Potential contenders to explain DBT's outcomes initially circled around the issue of whether anyone other than the treatment developer could deliver the outcomes seen in the early trials, and whether the outcomes were entirely attributable to expert psychotherapy. DBT has been examined in multiple RCTs, across multiple sites and countries, and tested by researchers other than the treatment developer. All of these studies reported similar outcomes to studies by Linehan, indicating that the treatment can be learned and delivered by others to deliver similar outcomes for clients (see Miga et al., this volume).

More recent research has examined mediators and moderators of treatment both from data in existing studies, for example, Neacsiu, Rizvi, and Linehan (2010), and in a recent dismantling study (Linehan et al., 2015). Both lines of research demonstrate that clients' learning and application of skills (see Cowperthwait, Wyatt, Fang, & Neacsiu, this volume), in a context of robust management of suicidal behaviours (Mehlum, this volume), is central to effective outcomes. The chapter by Boritz, Zeifman, and McMain reviews what is known about moderators and mediators of outcome in DBT.

SECTION VI: ADAPTING THE TREATMENT FOR NEW CLINICAL POPULATIONS

DBT's success in treating a previously hard-to-help group led to interest in using the treatment with other client groups with similar behavioural patterns. Maintaining fidelity plays a central role in the effective implementation of evidence-based treatments (McHugh, Murray, & Barlow, 2009). Only after implementation with fidelity has failed should modifications to an evidence-based treatment be considered (Fixsen, Naoom, Blasé, Friedman, & Wallace, 2005). As modifying a complex treatment like DBT, with many potentially effective components, risks losing those parts of the intervention that make it effective, all such modifications need to be evaluated. DBT researchers setting out to treat a new population hold to the principles and practices of DBT and modify only where absolutely necessary, while keeping track of evidence of effectiveness. This approach maintains an evidence-based approach to DBT. The application and adaptation of DBT to client populations who differ by diagnosis, types of behavioural problems, differential contexts, environments, and cultures has occupied clinicians and therapists for more than two decades since training began in DBT. The fruits of this labour can be found in Section VI.

In some circumstances, adaptations may be minimal. For example, they may be confined to the functions and modes of the treatment and modifications to behavioural targets but with no or limited changes to the underpinning theory. Examples of such adaptations are described in more detail by Rathus, Miller, and Bonavitacola in the chapter on adolescent DBT, by Bhatnager, Martin-Wagar, and Wisniewski in the chapter on eating disorders, and by Axelrod in the chapter on substance use disorder adaptations. Other adaptations have also required modifications to the biosocial theory of the disorder being treated, for example, DBT programmes for offenders with diagnoses of Anti-Social Personality Disorder, discussed by Ivanoff and Marotta. Delivering DBT in some contexts may require a degree of structural adaptation, for example, in inpatient settings as described in the chapter by Fox and by Uliasek, Chugani, and Williams in the chapter on DBT in College Counselling Centres. Delivery of DBT to some client groups may require substantial adaptation to both the structure and content of the programme, for example, the work of Perepletchikova in delivering DBT to pre-adolescent children and their parents, and of Brown working with individuals with an intellectual disability. Yet other adaptations have focused exclusively on delivering the skills component of the treatment to clients in particular settings, for example, the work by Mazza and Dexter-Mazza in adapting DBT for delivery in school settings (STEPS-A) as part of routine lesson plans, and the work of Feigenbaum in targeting DBT skills for clients with a personality disorder diagnosis aiming to return to work. While the focus on skills is prominent in these adaptations, other functions of the treatment may also be addressed, e.g., motivation, as part of the skills group in these settings.

Some of these adaptations have substantial empirical evidence, including RCTs supporting them, for example, DBT for adolescents, others have more modest evidence, for example, DBT for eating disorders, whereas yet others are only just beginning their evidential journey, for example, STEPS-A and DBT for employment-related difficulties.

Improving Outcomes in DBT

Researchers have begun to address for whom DBT works best and how to enhance outcomes. Analysis of client outcomes from amalgamated data from several DBT studies indicated that in addition to delivering good outcomes for suicidal behaviour, DBT also improved outcomes for major depression, substance misuse, and eating disorders, yet outcomes for anxiety disorders were not as good as behavioural treatments for anxiety disorders in non-suicidal individuals (Harned et al., 2008). One possible explanation for this difference is that high-risk individuals often struggle to tolerate the distress of exposure-based treatments without their suicidal behaviours escalating, and therapists, anxious about the escalation of risk, avoid conducting exposure-based treatments as a result. This difficulty was creatively solved by Harned, Korslund, Foa, & Linehan (2012), who combined an exposure-based protocol with judicious use of contingency management procedures to effectively treat suicidal individuals with BPD and PTSD. Bohus has also developed a different synthesis to solve this problem also within the framework of DBT. Harned and Schmidt, and Bohus and Priebe describe these adaptations in their respective chapters and provide interesting examples of DBT researchers and treatment developers working to solve complex clinical problems within the framework created by DBT.

SECTION VII: IMPLEMENTATION OF DBT

The dissemination and implementation of DBT has revealed significant challenges, many of them akin to the challenges of any innovation in practice and specifically to other interventions in the healthcare field. Comtois and Landes review what has been learned from these endeavours from an implementation science perspective on DBT. Subsequent chapters by Best and Lyng, Reynolds and Lang, and Flynn, Kells, and

Joyce illustrate the challenges and how they might be addressed in public and private healthcare systems and at a national level respectively. DuBose, Botanov, and Ivanoff review the global dissemination and implementation efforts to date, in particular highlighting the significant challenges in ensuring that the treatment reaches all those whom it might reasonably be expected to help. Given that the need for DBT exceeds the availability of trained therapists to deliver it, the following chapter, by Lungu, Wilks, and Linehan, considers the role of novel technology in dissemination efforts.

SECTION VIII: TRAINING IN DBT

While DBT has an impressive reach, DBT demand is higher than the resources available to provide adequate treatment. Successful training methods have been developed, as described by DuBose, Botanov, Navaro-Harro, and Linehan in their chapter on the Intensive Training Method^{TM}, and much has been learned about the process of training therapists to adherence, discussed in the chapter by Gaglia, yet there are insufficient trained therapists to deliver treatment and trainers to train the therapists. Successfully resolving these challenges may require empirically-based modifications to the treatment that may be less intensive to deliver for less severe presentations and increased access to training and supervision via online methods.

CONCLUSION

DBT is an integrative treatment resting on the foundations of behaviourism, Zen, and dialectics focusing on the challenge of affect regulation for clients presenting with multiple, and frequently complex, problems. This volume elucidates the theoretical foundations before describing in greater detail the ways in which DBT addresses the challenges of treating clients with these problems, both structurally and strategically. The focus on affect regulation difficulties was rapidly recognized as a problem for many groups of clients, not just those for whom the treatment was first developed. The various groups and settings for which DBT has been adapted and modified are also represented in what follows. From the very first, Linehan was concerned to address issues of implementation of the treatment, from how to train therapists effectively to how to embed the treatment in clinical settings. What we know from the work in this area and, perhaps more importantly, the problems we need to solve are also represented here. Each chapter has a set of key messages for clinicians, which can be found both in the chapter itself and within the contents pages to assist in navigating the varied, diverse, and stimulating contributions made to this volume by experts in their field.

KEY MESSAGES FOR CLINICIANS

- DBT is an integrative treatment, synthesizing behavioural theory, principles of Zen practice, and dialectics.
- DBT was developed in an endeavour to solve the problem of chronic suicidality presenting in clients with a borderline personality disorder diagnosis.
- DBT was the first treatment to demonstrate clinical efficacy with this client group.
- Since the publication of the treatment manuals, DBT has been adopted and adapted for clients in a range of settings and with different clinical presentations and diagnoses.

REFERENCES

Aitken, R. (1982). *Taking the path of Zen*. San Francisco: North Point Press.

Bandura, A. (1969). *Principles of behaviour modification*. New York: Holt, Rinehart & Winston.

Bateman, A., & Fonagy, P. (2006). *Mentalization-based treatment for Borderline Personality Disorder: A practical guide*. New York: Oxford University Press.

Fixsen, D. L., Naoom, S. F., Blasé, K. A., Friedman, R. M., & Wallace, F. (2005). *Implementation research: A synthesis of the literature*. Tampa, FL: University of South Florida, Louis de la Parte Florida Mental Health Institute, The National Implementation Research Network.

Harned, M. S., Chapman, A. L., Dexter-Mazza, E. T., Murray, A., Comtois, K. A., & Linehan, M. M. (2008). Treating co-occurring Axis I disorders in recurrently suicidal women with borderline personality disorder: A 2-year randomized trial of dialectical behavior therapy versus community treatment by experts. *Journal of Consulting and Clinical Psychology, 76*(6), 1068–1075.

Harned, M. S., Korslund, K. E., Foa, E. B., & Linehan, M. M. (2012). Treating PTSD in suicidal and self-injuring women with borderline personality disorder: Development and preliminary evaluation of a Dialectical Behavior Therapy Prolonged Exposure Protocol. *Behaviour Research and Therapy, 50*(6), 381–386.

Hayes, S. C., Strosahl, K. D., & Wilson, J. G. (1999). *Acceptance and commitment therapy: An experiential approach to behaviour change*. New York: Guilford Press.

Kabat-Zinn, J. (1991). *Full catastrophe living: Using the wisdom of your body and mind to face stress, pain, and illness*. New York: Delta.

Koerner, K. (2012). *Doing dialectic behavior therapy: A practical guide*. New York: Guilford Press.

Linehan, M. M. (1981). A social-behavioral analysis of suicide and parasuicide: Implications for clinical assessment and treatment. In H. Glazer & J. F. Clarkin (Eds.), *Depression, behavioural and directive intervention strategies* (pp. 229–294). New York: Garland Press.

Linehan, M. M. (1993a). *Cognitive-behavioral treatment of borderline personality disorder*. New York: Guilford Press.

Linehan, M. M. (1993b). *Skills training manual for treating borderline personality disorder*. New York: Guilford Press.

Linehan, M.M. (2015). *DBT® Skills Training Manual*, 2nd Edition. New York: Guilford Press.

Linehan, M. M. (2016). Behavior therapy: Where we were, where we are and where we need to be going. *Cognitive and Behavioral Practice*, *23*(4), 451–453. https://doi.org/10.1016/j.cbpra.2015.12.002

Linehan, M. M., Armstrong, H. E., Suarez, A., Allmon, D., & Heard, H. L. (1991). Cognitive behavioural treatment of chronically parasuicidal borderline patients. *Archives of General Psychiatry*, *48*, 1060–1064.

Linehan, M. M., Korslund, K. E., Harned, M. S., Gallop, R. I., Lungu, A., Neacsiu A. D., McDavid, J., … Murray-Gregory, A. M. (2015). Dialectical behavior therapy for high suicide risk in individuals with borderline personality disorder: a randomized clinical trial and component analysis. *JAMA Psychiatry*, *72*(5), 475–482.

Linehan, M. M., & Sargent, K. (2017). Brief thoughts on Zen and behaviour therapy. In A. Masuda & W. T. O'Donohue (Eds.), *Handbook of Zen, mindfulness and behavioral health* (pp. 251–254). New York: Springer.

Linehan, M. M., & Wilks, C. R. (2015). The course and evolution of Dialectical Behavior Therapy. *American Journal of Psychotherapy*, *69*(2), 97–110.

McHugh, R. K., Murray, H. W., & Barlow, D. H. (2009). Balancing fidelity and adaptation in the dissemination of empirically-supported treatments: The promise of transdiagnostic treatments. *Behavior Research & Therapy*, *47*, 946–953.

Mischel, W. (1968). *Personality and assessment*. New York: John Wiley and Sons.

Neasciu, A. D., Rizvi, S. L., & Linehan, M. M. (2010). Dialectical behaviour therapy skills use as a mediator and outcome of treatment for borderline personality disorder. *Behaviour Research and Therapy*, *48*(9), 832–839.

Rogers, C. R. (1946). Significant aspects of client centered therapy. *American Psycholgist*, *1*, 415–422.

Segal, Z. V., Williams, J. M. G., & Teasdale, J. D. (2002). *Mindfulness-based cognitive therapy for depression: A new approach to preventing relapse*. New York: Guilford Press.

Staats, A. (1975). *Social behaviourism*. Homewood, IL: Dorsey Press.

Stoffers-Winterling , J. M., Völlm, B. A., Rücker, G., Timmer, A., Huband, N, & Lieb, K. (2012). Psychological therapies for people with borderline personality disorder. *Cochrane Database of Systematic Reviews*. DOI: 10.1002/14651858.CD005652.pub2

Swales, M. A., & Heard, H. L. (2017). *Dialectical behaviour therapy: Distinctive features*, 2nd Edition. London: Routledge.

Swenson, C. R. (2016). *DBT® Principles in action: Acceptance, change and dialectics*. New York: Guilford.

Yeomans, F. E., Clarkin, J. F., & Kernberg, O. F. (2015). *Transference-focused psychotherapy for Borderline Personality Disorder: A clinical guide*. Arlington, VA: American Psychiatric Publishing.

Young, J., Klosko, J., & Weishaar, M. (2003). *Schema therapy: A practitioner's guide*. New York: Guilford Press.

SECTION II

THEORETICAL UNDERPINNINGS OF DBT

CHAPTER 2

UNDERSTANDING THE BIO IN THE BIOSOCIAL THEORY OF BPD

Recent Developments and Implications for Treatment

INGA NIEDTFELD AND MARTIN BOHUS

INTRODUCTION

CURRENTLY, most researchers disentangle three core domains of psychopathology in borderline personality disorder (BPD): affective dysregulation, interpersonal disturbances, and problems in identity. There is an ongoing debate about the hierarchy of these domains and their potential interactions (e.g., Schmahl et al., 2014). From a sociobiological point of view, most of the interpersonal and individual problems of BPD patients (such as rejection sensitivity, difficulties in belonging, cooperation, chronic loneliness, and negative self-esteem) can be seen as being driven by dysfunctional emotion processing (e.g., Lis & Bohus, 2013). From a developmental point of view, dysfunctional interpersonal experiences (such as traumatic invalidation, insecure attachment, early loss, or sexual abuse) can be seen as leading to dysfunctional social cognitions that transact with problems in emotion regulation.

Dialectical behaviour therapy (DBT) conceptualizes disturbed affective regulation as a core feature of BPD and as a driving force behind several serious dysfunctional behavioural patterns including suicidal ideation and suicide attempts, maladaptive interpersonal behaviours, and impulsive coping behaviours such as alcohol abuse (Conklin, Bradley, & Westen, 2006; Jahng et al., 2011; Linehan, 1993; Links, 2007; Yen et al., 2004). Initially, this theory was mainly based on Marsha Linehan`s clinical experience. However, within the last 20 years, several studies have confirmed alterations of the emotion processing system in BPD on behavioural, structural, and neurofunctional levels under both everyday life conditions and experimental conditions.

This chapter sums up the recent findings in BPD with regard to brain function and neurotransmission and relates them to the core symptoms of BPD psychopathology: disturbed emotion processing (underlying affective instability), behavioural dysregulation (including altered pain processing, dissociation, and impulsivity), and interpersonal disturbances.

EMOTION DYSREGULATION IN BPD

Principles

This section gives a short overview of the current taxonomy of emotion processing in general before discussing the distinct mechanisms of dysfunctional emotion processing in BPD.

From a psychosocial perspective, emotions essentially are complex and evolved patterns of response to both external and internal stimuli, providing a fast, situational interpretation along with a corresponding action tendency. Emotion processing involves automatic and intentional processes that influence the occurrence, intensity, duration, and expression of emotions. There is a wide spectrum of theories on how emotions can influence self-theory, identity, decision-making, social interaction, and even policy (for overview, see Lewis, Haviland-Jones, & Barrett, 2008).

Among others, Ochsner and Gross (2014) have proposed a model of emotion regulation that emphasizes the explicit or implicit appraisal of external or internal emotional cues that trigger a set of experiential, physiological, and behavioural response tendencies. This model has already influenced treatment development for BPD (Neacsiu, Linehan, & Bohus, 2014) and might serve as a current basis for research. According to this model, emotions can be modulated automatically or by either manipulating the input to the system (*antecedent-focused emotion regulation strategies*) or by manipulating the output of the regulation process (*response-focused emotion regulation strategies*). Antecedent-focused strategies include both implicit and explicit strategies, such as situation selection or modification and cognitive techniques (e.g., reappraisal, attention deployment, or reframing of the situation), while response-focused strategies include both implicit and explicit strategies that can be subdivided into physiological, cognitive, and behavioural processes.

Ochsner and Gross's model does not consider the potential role of emotional awareness or experiential avoidance (EA) in emotion regulation. One could argue that emotion regulation is mostly an automatic process, independent from cognitive meta-awareness. On the other hand, recent research has clearly demonstrated the potential role of EA in the pathogenesis of psychological disorders. EA not only includes any behaviour that seeks to avoid, or escape from, unwanted internal experiences or those external conditions that elicit them, but also the pure awareness of activated emotions. Consequently, increasing emotional awareness and emotion acceptance is currently seen as an important mode of action in psychotherapy in general and in BPD. Schramm and colleagues (2013) showed that borderline personality features were associated with significantly higher levels of EA and difficulties in emotion regulation. Hierarchical regression analyses showed that EA made a small but significant incremental and independent contribution to borderline features when added to a model that already included difficulties in emotion regulation.

On a neuroanatomical level, the central areas involved in the "emotion regulation circuitry" are thought to be the dorsolateral and ventral areas of the prefrontal cortex (including the anterior cingulate cortex, ACC), as well as the amygdala, the hippocampus, and the insula (Ochsner & Gross, 2014). It should, however, be stressed that these regions fulfil several functions besides emotion regulation. Ochsner and Gross suggested a psychobiological circular model of emotion processing whereby emotions are generated and modulated by interplaying macro- and micro-circuits of "bottom-up" and "top-down" processes. According to this model, central areas such as the amygdala and the insula are involved in the evaluation of external and internal stimuli regarding their emotional valence. These stimuli are further processed in the hypothalamus and in brain stem regions in order to activate autonomic and behavioural responses. In parallel, prefrontal and parietal cortical areas serve to allocate attention and to activate potential behavioural responses. Regulatory processes associated with areas of the lateral and medial prefrontal cortex (MPFC) act to control and modulate emotional activation, thereby covering typical response-focused regulation strategies. Recent studies suggest a regulatory hierarchy, whereby the dorsolateral prefrontal cortex (DLPFC) and areas of the anterior medio-prefrontal cortex modulate the cingulate, which in turn modulates the amygdala and further subcortical areas (Meyer-Lindenberg & Weinberger, 2006).

Importantly, these regulatory interactions are sensitive to genetic variation in candidate genes that have been reported to have an impact on personality as well as on the risk for affective disorders and for which gene-environment interactions with early childhood trauma have been found (Meyer-Lindenberg & Tost, 2006; Ochsner & Gross, 2004; Pezawas et al., 2005). Recent work has extended these results to genome-wide significant risk variants for severe psychiatric disorder and has suggested a common circuitry for emotion regulation and extinction of emotional responses on which genetic and environmental risk factors converge (Meyer-Lindenberg & Tost 2012). Regulatory processes can also be activated by cognitive reappraisal, by changing attention, or by activating memories. These cognitive strategies result in an activation of lateral and medial prefrontal areas which, in turn, involve the ACC and ultimately dampen emotional arousal by attenuating the activity of the amygdala, the mid-cingulate, and areas of the insula (for review, see Ochsner & Gross, 2005). These mechanisms of emotion regulation are subject to genetic variation, to maturing processes, and to inter-individual variation, as well as to environmental risk factors such as early adversity or poverty. Notably, during adolescence, there appears to be a marked imbalance between increased sensitivity and susceptibility of subcortical limbic areas to emotional stimuli and not yet fully mature prefrontal areas. This imbalance may account for the tendency towards high emotional activation and impulsivity during adolescence in general (reviewed in e.g., Spear, 2000).

Altered Emotion Activation in BPD

A large body of studies has used functional Magnetic Resonance Imaging (fMRI) during emotional challenge. In these studies, negative pictures or auditory scripts are presented to investigate brain correlates of emotional responding in those with BPD, as compared to healthy individuals. Most of the studies point to an increased activity of limbic brain regions, such as the amygdala, in BPD (Donegan et al., 2003; Herpertz et al., 2001; Koenigsberg et al., 2009; Krause-Utz et al., 2012; Minzenberg, Fan, New, Tang, & Siever, 2007; Niedtfeld et al., 2010; Schulze et al., 2011). Since the amygdala is important during the generation of emotional responses (Ochsner & Gross, 2014), it was concluded that BPD patients show exaggerated emotional responding. Several studies in BPD patients show that this was not only true for negative emotional stimuli, but also for neutral pictures in BPD patients (Donegan et al., 2003; Koenigsberg et al., 2009; Krause-Utz et al., 2012; Niedtfeld et al., 2010). Moreover, when presented repeatedly with the same negative picture stimuli, patients showed diminished habituation of the amygdala (Dudas et al., 2016; Koenigsberg et al., 2014). Similarly, patients showed prolonged amygdala response in experimental tasks that directly induced fear (Kamphausen et al., 2012; Krause-Utz, Keibel-Mauchnik, Ebner-Priemer, Bohus, & Schmahl, 2016). Similar to amygdala hyper-reactivity, an enhanced reactivity of the insula was also shown in patients with BPD as compared to healthy participants during the presentation of negative stimuli (Beblo et al., 2006; Krause-Utz et al., 2012; Niedtfeld et al., 2010; Schulze et al., 2011). The insula is implicated in the processing of interoceptive signals from the body, negative emotions, and pain perception (Damasio et al., 2000; Menon and Uddin, 2010).

The outlined results of increased limbic (i.e., amygdala and insula) reactivity correspond to clinical observations of heightened emotional responsivity in patients with BPD (Crowell, Beauchaine, & Linehan, 2009; Gilbert et al., 2009; Kamphausen et al., 2012). However, the first meta-analysis on emotion processing in BPD reported contradictory findings of decreased amygdala activity during processing of negative emotions relative to neutral conditions in patients with BPD compared to healthy controls (HC) (Ruocco, Amirthavasagam, Choi-Kain, & McMain, 2013). Of course, meta-analyses always include the possibility of selection biases (e.g., concerning the studies selected and the inclusion of different numbers of contrasts into the analysis). The most recent meta-analysis on emotion processing in BPD (Schulze, Schmahl, & Niedtfeld, 2016) confirmed increased amygdala activation during negative emotion processing in BPD. Interestingly, this effect was most pronounced in medication-free samples.

Additional to alterations in limbic brain regions, a large body of neuroimaging studies in BPD point to lower activation of prefrontal brain regions in patients with BPD, as compared to healthy volunteers (Leichsenring, Leibing, Kruse, New, & Leweke, 2011; Lis, Greenfield, Henry, Guile, & Dougherty, 2007; O'Neill & Frodl, 2012; Schmahl,

Elzinga, et al., 2004). Additionally, studying baseline regional glucose metabolism with positron emission tomography (PET), BPD patients show lower baseline metabolism in prefrontal brain regions (de la Fuente et al., 1997; Juengling et al., 2003; Lange, Kracht, Herholz, Sachsse, & Irle, 2005; Salavert et al., 2011). In the most recent meta-analysis on emotional processing in BPD, reduced activity of the bilateral DLPFC was reported (Schulze et al., 2016). Apart from the DLPFC, implicated in the voluntary regulation of emotional responses (Ochsner & Gross, 2014), some studies also point to altered brain responses in the ACC (Minzenberg et al., 2007). The ACC is supposed to mediate top-down regulation of the amygdala (Hariri, Mattay, Tessitore, Fere, & Weinberger, 2003). Based on these studies, it can be concluded that reduced brain activation during emotional challenge corresponds to a deficient modulation of negative emotions in BPD.

Studies using working memory tasks also showed increased susceptibility to emotional stimuli, leading to lower task performance. When emotional picture stimuli served as distractors within an emotional working memory task, patients with BPD as compared to HC showed higher amygdala activity, and fewer correct reactions (Krause-Utz et al., 2012). The amygdala was also more strongly activated when emotional pictures were presented within an n-back task, (a well-established short-term memory paradigm), together with slower reaction times (Prehn et al., 2013). Distraction by fearful facial expressions also resulted in higher ACC and amygdala activation in a modified flanker task (a response inhibition test used to assess the ability to suppress responses that are inappropriate in a particular context; Holtmann et al., 2013).

In order to investigate interaction between limbic and frontal brain regions in BPD, some studies examined brain connectivity. The first study found reduced connectivity between prefrontal and limbic structures during baseline activity using positron emission tomography (New et al., 2007). Two studies experimentally inducing fear found stronger connectivity of the amygdala and ACC (Cullen et al., 2011) as well as ventromedial prefrontal cortex (vmPFC) (Kamphausen et al., 2012). In response to pictures of facial expressions, BPD patients exhibited increased amygdala coupling with the hippocampus and dorsomedial PFC (Krause-Utz et al., 2014). When viewing repeatedly presented negative pictures, those with BPD showed higher coupling between amygdala and insula (Koenigsberg et al., 2014). The authors conclude that BPD patients fail to habituate to emotional stimuli, possibly resulting in increased affective instability (Koenigsberg et al., 2014).

Altered Emotion Regulation in BPD

The studies cited above suggest that emotion dysregulation in BPD might be caused by hyper-responsive "bottom-up" processing in limbic structures, while "top-down" prefrontal control mechanisms might be less effective. However, it is important to note that this pattern of fronto-limbic dysregulation during emotion processing is not specific for BPD, but also is present in affective disorders (Etkin & Wager, 2007; Groenewold, Opmeer, de Jonge, Aleman, & Costafreda, 2013).

Subsequently, voluntary emotion regulation was investigated using a well-established reappraisal paradigm (Ochsner, Bunge, Gross, & Gabrieli, 2002). Within this paradigm, pictures are presented to elicit emotional responses and participants are instructed to change their emotional response via cognitive reappraisal. Investigating explicit emotion regulation in BPD, three studies found reduced recruitment of prefrontal brain regions (Koenigsberg et al., 2009; Lang et al., 2012; Schulze et al., 2011). The first study instructed participants to distance themselves from emotional stimuli and found lower activity in DLPFC and ventrolateral PFC (VLPFC) in BPD patients (Koenigsberg et al., 2009). In line with these results, cognitive reappraisal resulted in lower activity of the orbitofrontal cortex and higher activity of the insula in BPD patients as compared to HC (Schulze et al., 2011). The third study showed similar effects of reduced recruitment of regulatory brain regions but compared a group of patients with BPD and trauma history to healthy individuals with trauma history and a group of non-traumatized healthy individuals (Lang et al., 2012). Notably, traumatized BPD patients and trauma-exposed healthy individuals both showed the aforementioned alterations, thereby questioning the specificity of the discussed findings for subjects with BPD.

Although these studies on explicit emotion regulation point to alterations in the recruitment of prefrontal brain areas, no differences to HC were found with regard to subjective arousal ratings as an indication of reappraisal success (Koenigsberg et al., 2009; Lang et al., 2012; Schulze et al., 2011). This could be explained by a lower ability to reflect on their own emotions for patients with BPD (New et al., 2013), but might also point to compensatory strategies that were not directly investigated within these studies. Notably, some other studies in BPD also observed differences between subjective and biological responses in BPD (Gilbert et al., 2009; Hazlett et al., 2007; Herpertz et al., 2001).

Since emotion dysregulation is the main target of DBT, some neuroimaging studies investigating alterations after treatment found normalization of limbic hyper-reactivity (Goodman et al., 2014; Niedtfeld et al., 2017; Schmitt, Winter, Niedtfeld, Schmahl, & Herpertz, 2016; Schnell & Herpertz, 2007; Winter et al., 2016). After successful therapy, patients exhibited changes in brain activity, pointing to reduced hypersensitivity of limbic brain regions and increased prefrontal brain activity during emotional challenge. An early study investigated six BPD patients before and after a 12-week residential DBT treatment. In response to negative pictures, patients showed reduced activity of insula and ACC after successful psychotherapy (Schnell & Herpertz, 2007). Investigating habituation processes, negative pictures were presented repeatedly to patients before and after standard DBT. The amygdala was activated to a lesser extent after 12 months of DBT, pointing to improved habituation (Goodman et al., 2014). Notably, these studies did not include a control group of patients without DBT, and so they cannot differentiate between DBT-specific effects and unspecific therapy, or time, effects. Three recent studies were done in a large project investigating different emotion regulation strategies (reappraisal, distraction, and pain) before and after a 12-week residential DBT treatment (Niedtfeld et al., 2017; Schmitt et al., 2016; Winter et al., 2016), as compared to treatment as usual and HC subjects. When engaging in reappraisal of negative pictures, those with BPD showed decreased anterior insula and dorsal ACC activity during and after DBT. Therapy responders also showed reduced activation in amygdala, ACC, orbitofrontal, and DLPFC, together with increased limbic-prefrontal coupling (Schmitt et al., 2016). In the second study, DBT treatment responders also showed reduced ACC activity when viewing negative (as compared to neutral) pictures. During cognitive distraction from negative pictures, decreased activity in the right inferior parietal lobe was found in BPD patients after DBT (Winter et al., 2016). The third study examined the effect of pain on emotional reactions and found that pain-mediated affect regulation (i.e., amygdala deactivation in response to painful stimulation) was reduced after DBT treatment (Niedtfeld et al., 2017). Most recently, it was shown that BPD patients can learn to regulate amygdala activity more directly using neurofeedback (Paret et al., 2016). Over four training sessions, an increase in amygdala-ventromedial prefrontal cortex connectivity was observed, pointing to improved emotion regulation.

Taken together, there is strong evidence for limbic hyper-reactivity in BPD, leading to intense and long-lasting emotional reactions. Additionally, down-regulation of emotional arousal seems to be deficient in BPD, as shown by decreased recruitment of prefrontal regulation networks. These two aspects might result in affective instability in BPD. However, it is important to note that most of these effects might be not specific to BPD patients. A study in healthy subjects with childhood maltreatment demonstrated functional alterations that were strikingly similar to the findings described here for BPD (Dannlowski et al., 2012). It is possible that adverse childhood experiences lead to alterations in limbic brain regions, which in turn increase the risk for the development of psychiatric disorders in general (Gilbert et al., 2009). With regard to BPD, it has been argued that the co-occurrence of adverse childhood experiences and dysfunctional emotion regulation, together with increased impulsivity and interpersonal problems, might be more specific for the development of BPD (Crowell et al., 2009).

BEHAVIOURAL DYSREGULATION

Non-Suicidal Self-Injury and Altered Pain Processing

Closely linked to emotion dysregulation in BPD is dysfunctional behaviour, the most prevalent being non-suicidal self-injury (NSSI; also referred to as self-injurious behaviour, deliberate self-harm, or self-injury; Welch, Linehan, Sylvers, Chittams, & Rizvi, 2008). Patients report injuring themselves to reduce aversive tension and negative emotions (Kleindienst et al., 2008). During NSSI, many patients report analgesic phenomena (Shearer, 1994). Based on patient reports with regard to the emotion-regulation effect of pain (Klonsky, 2007), the effects of painful stimuli in BPD have been extensively studied leading to several robust findings. First, studies repeatedly observed that pain sensitivity is reduced in BPD (Bohus et al., 2000; Cardenas-Morales et al., 2011; Ludäscher, Bohus, Lieb, Philipsen, & Schmahl, 2007; McCown, Galina, Johnson, de Simone, & Posa, 1993; Russ et al., 1992; Schmahl et al., 2006; Schmahl, Greffrath et al., 2004; Schmahl et al., 2010). Second, pain perception and pain thresholds, studied with a spatial discrimination task, using electroencephalography (EEG) as well as subjective ratings (Schmahl, Greffrath et al., 2004), confirmed an alteration of the affective-emotional processing of pain in BPD, but found no impairment in the sensory-discriminative component of pain (Schmahl, Greffrath et al., 2004). Third, neural pain processing investigated in neuroimaging studies found that painful heat stimuli resulted in increased DLPFC activation in participants with BPD, as compared to HC, together with deactivation in the amygdala and the perigenual ACC (Schmahl et al., 2006). These results were interpreted as an increased top-down regulation, possibly due to an altered appraisal of pain (Schmahl et al., 2006). Using a similar study design, BPD patients (with and without comorbid PTSD) were compared to patients with PTSD (Kraus et al., 2009). In response to pain, BPD patients with comorbid PTSD showed stronger amygdala activation than the other patient groups, but no differences were found with regard to subjective pain sensitivity (Kraus et al., 2009). Painful stimuli in BPD also resulted in lower connectivity between posterior cingulate cortex and DLPFC (Kluetsch et al., 2012), which might be interpreted as less self-relevance during the appraisal of pain. When patients were asked to imagine an act of NSSI, BPD patients showed activation in the DLPFC (Kraus et al., 2010). Fourth, the role of pain in emotion regulation was investigated more directly using picture stimuli to elicit negative affect, combined with thermal stimuli to induce heat pain (Niedtfeld et al., 2010). Although amygdala and insula brain activity decreased over time, this was not specific for painful stimulation. When looking at brain connectivity, painful temperature stimuli resulted in enhanced coupling between prefrontal and limbic regions in BPD, pointing to increased inhibition of limbic arousal (Niedtfeld et al., 2012). Findings of increased connectivity between amygdala and medial frontal gyrus (BA8 and BA9) suggest attentional distraction processes (McRae et al., 2010). Moreover, connectivity between insula and DLPFC could also implicate altered appraisal of pain (Treede, Apkarian, Bromm, Greenspan, & Lenz, 2000). In addition to temperature stimuli, the effect of pain on emotion regulation was tested with an incision into the forearm (tissue damage), or a sham condition (Reitz et al., 2012; Reitz et al., 2015). Tissue damage in BPD, as compared to HC, resulted in reduced amygdala activation, together with increased connectivity of amygdala and superior frontal gyrus (BA8) (Reitz et al., 2015).

Apart from neuroimaging studies, there is evidence that engaging in NSSI can be partly explained by a dysregulation of the endogenous opioid system (EOS; see Bandelow, Schmahl, Falkai, & Wedekind, 2010). This neuropeptide system includes three classes of opioids: β-endorphin, enkephalin, and dynorphin (μ-, δ-, and κ-opioid receptors; Dhawan et al., 1996). Disturbance in β-endorphin (and probably enkephalin) is closely related to NSSI. The EOS becomes activated when the organism faces physical, social, or emotional pain, or stress (Bresin & Gordon, 2013; Stanley et al., 2010). It is known that the activation of the EOS mediates the sensation of pain, as well as analgesic effects. Furthermore, activation of the EOS can induce euphoria and diminish inner tension and other emotional states (Bandelow et al., 2010; Stanley & Siever, 2010). One study stated that patients engaging in NSSI tend to have lower baseline levels of β-endorphin (and probably enkephalin) in cerebrospinal fluid (CSF) and plasma compared to HC and other patient groups (Stanley et al., 2010). Additionally, Prossin and colleagues (2010) found greater μ-receptor availability for patients with BPD compared to HC, possibly due to a lower β-endorphin tone. Chronically low basal levels of β-endorphin are associated with an increase in negative affect, feeling of chronic emptiness, dysphoria, and lack of a sense of well-being, all symptoms often described by patients engaging in NSSI (Stanley & Siever, 2010; Zubieta et al., 2003). Importantly, tissue damage during NSSI leads to a release of β-endorphin (and probably enkephalin). Direct results of the temporary heightened β-endorphin level might be the described decrease in negative affect, aversive tension, and other related symptoms reported by patients with NSSI. However, further research is needed to support this assumption.

Bresin and Gordon (2013) summarized that disturbed EOS activity can be related to NSSI in two ways. First, low levels of β-endorphin and relatively normal levels of dynorphins can lead to a disturbed function of the EOS, resulting in dysphoric and/or dissociative feelings and increased urges for NSSI. Second, low levels of β-endorphin lead to increased sensitivity or availability of μ- opioid receptors also resulting in increased urges for NSSI (Bresin & Gordon, 2013). Taken together, interpreted in terms of an EOS dysregulation theory, NSSI could be understood as a dysfunctional attempt to trigger a higher opioid level. The EOS may also be involved in other core symptoms of BPD such as disrupted interpersonal relationships, risky sexual contacts, attention-seeking behaviour, and dissociation (see Bandelow et al., 2010), but the empirical data is sparse.

The conclusion is that tissue damage as a proxy for NSSI results in reduction of subjective stress levels, psychophysiological stress reactions, and brain correlates of emotional dysregulation. These studies underline the assumption that NSSI can be interpreted as a dysfunctional attempt to regulate emotions.

Dissociation

During periods of negative affect and heightened arousal, those with BPD frequently experience dissociative states (Korzekwa, Dell, Links, Thabane, & Fougere, 2009; Stiglmayr et al., 2005; Stiglmayr et al., 2008). These aversive states can trigger dysfunctional behaviour like NSSI (Kemperman, Russ, & Shearin, 1997; Kleindienst et al., 2008). During dissociative states, psychological functions like memory, attention, and the perception of the body and the environment are disrupted, leading to symptoms of analgesia, amnesia, depersonalization, and derealization (American Psychiatric Association, 2000).

Research into brain function during dissociative states in PTSD, indicates increased prefrontal activity and reduced activity in the amygdala and insula suggesting emotional over-modulation (Lanius et al., 2010; Sierra and Berrios, 1998; Wolf et al., 2012). Transferring these findings to BPD, dissociative states were induced in BPD using script-driven imagery (Ludäscher et al., 2010; Winter et al., 2015). Findings on increased activation in inferior frontal gyrus and lower limbic activation are in line with research on dissociative states in PTSD. Other studies analysed the effects of self-reported state dissociation on task performance, but without direct induction of dissociation. They report a negative correlation of dissociation and limbic activity (Krause-Utz et al., 2012), as well as correlations of dissociation with brain connectivity of the insula and default mode network (Wolf et al., 2011). (This network is most commonly shown to be active when a person is not focused on the outside world and the brain is at wakeful rest. But it is also active when the individual is thinking about others, thinking about themselves, remembering the past, and planning for the future.) From these studies, the conclusion is that dissociative states resemble a dysfunctional strategy to regulate negative emotional states, because it is marked by increased activation of prefrontal brain regions and reduced limbic activity.

Impulsivity

A further core symptom of BPD is impulsive behaviour, such as reckless spending, unprotected sex, substance abuse, and binge eating. Based on the heritability of serotonergic neurotransmitter function, which is related to impulsive and aggressive behaviour and deficient inhibitory control, the proposal is that serotonergic dysfunction might serve as an endophenotype of BPD (Goodman, New, Triebwasser, Collins, & Siever, 2010; Mak & Lam, 2013; McCloskey et al., 2009).

At the neurobiological level, alterations in several neurotransmitter systems (dopamine, serotonin, glutamate, GABA) have been found (Hoerst et al., 2010; Soloff, 2003), possibly contributing to heightened impulsivity (Yanowitch & Coccaro, 2011). With regard to brain metabolism, serotonergic responses were investigated using serotonin receptor agonists. After fenfluramine challenge (a marker for serotonin activity in the brain), HC subjects showed an increased prefrontal (OFC, DLPFC) activity measured with PET, as compared to the placebo condition, which was not observed in BPD (New et al., 2002; Siever et al., 1999; Soloff, Meltzer, Greer, Constantine, & Kelly, 2000). In the posterior cingulate cortex, serotonin receptor agonist meta-chlorophenylpiperazine (M-CPP) led to reduced activity in HC, but increased activation in BPD (New et al., 2002). With a similar study design, the working group found that amygdala activity was not altered in BPD patients under M-CPP (New et al., 2007). Another study showed increased hippocampal 5HT receptor binding, suggesting alterations in the serotonin system in BPD (Soloff et al., 2007). These alterations seem to be genetically determined, because aggression was linked to a haplotype of the serotonergic gene tryptophan-hydroxylase 2 in BPD (Perez-Rodriguez et al., 2010).

When aggression was experimentally induced in patients with intermittent explosive disorder, they showed an increased metabolism in amygdala and OFC, and a decreased metabolism in DLPFC, as compared to HC (New et al., 2009). With the same paradigm, lower metabolic rate in the striatum was found only for male patients with BPD (Perez-Rodriguez et al., 2012). This is in line with another study pointing to an important role of frontal-striatal circuits for aggression in BPD (Leyton et al., 2001). With regard to possible psychopharmacological treatments, the cortical glucose metabolism in BPD tended to normalize in response to a selective serotonin reuptake inhibitor (New et al., 2004).

In sum, previous research points to alterations in the serotonergic system in BPD. However, many studies found gender differences in serotonergic responses, leading to heterogeneity of findings (i.e., stronger effects in male patient populations; New et al., 2003; Soloff, 2003; Soloff et al., 2005). It is also important to note that the serotonin system tightly interacts with other neurotransmitter systems, which have also been shown to be altered in BPD. The concentrations of glutamate and GABA differ from HC subjects, and correlate with self-reported impulsivity in BPD (Ende et al., 2016; Hoerst et al., 2010).

Aside from transmitter levels, recent neuroimaging studies applied behavioural tasks to assess different aspects of impulsivity (Sebastian et al., 2014). In response to a Go/No-Go task (a task to measure a participant's capacity for sustained attention and response control), patients with BPD or antisocial personality disorder showed less prefrontal brain activity, but activation of more distributed networks (superior, medial, and inferior frontal gyri) during response inhibition (Vollm et al., 2004). Other researchers stated that the empirical basis of behavioural measures of impulsivity is weaker than investigations with self-report questionnaires and pointed out that negative affect might be an important mediator of behavioural impulsivity in BPD (Sebastian, Jacob, Lieb, & Tuscher, 2013). After induction of negative affect, BPD patients had a higher error rate in an emotional variant of the Go/No-Go task, along with decreased brain activation in perigenual ACC and orbitofrontal cortex, as well as increased activation of the insula and dorsal ACC (Silbersweig et al., 2007). After the induction of negative mood states with auditory scripts, another study reported more amygdala activation as well as lower activity in subgenual ACC (Jacob et al., 2013). Other studies point in the same direction, namely that deficits in impulse control in BPD are most pronounced in the presence of negative emotional stimuli (Baer, Peters, Eisenlohr-Moul, Geiger, & Sauer, 2012; Fertuck, Lenzenweger, Clarkin, Hoermann, & Stanley, 2006) and during experimentally induced stress (Cackowski et al., 2014). Summing up the findings described here, heightened impulsivity in BPD seems to be (at least partly) genetically determined, is marked by serotonergic dysfunction, and leads to impaired response inhibition, especially during states of high arousal.

INTERPERSONAL DISTURBANCES

Instability in relationships seems to be one of the most stable symptoms in BPD (Gunderson, 2007; Gunderson et al., 2011). Dysfunctional behaviours like NSSI or suicide attempts are more likely to occur in the context of interpersonal problems (Brodsky, Groves, Oquendo, Mann, & Stanley, 2006; Welch & Linehan, 2002). This has led some authors to propose that interpersonal sensitivity could be one causal factor for emotional instability (Gunderson, 2007; Stanley & Siever, 2010). Alternatively, one could argue that interpersonal problems in BPD are driven by dysfunctional emotion processing (Domes, Schulze, & Herpertz, 2009) due to limbic hyper-reactivity (Niedtfeld et al., 2010).

Given the enduring nature of interpersonal problems for patients with BPD, treatments need to focus on improving social functioning (McMain et al., 2009). In line with this need, recent research in BPD has focused increasingly on social cognition (Lis & Bohus, 2013). At the neurobiological level, processing of facial expressions was studied first. Those with BPD showed heightened activity in limbic regions in response to negative, but also neutral, facial expressions, mirroring the results from emotional challenge studies (Donegan et al., 2003; Frick et al., 2012; Holtmann et al., 2013; Mier et al., 2012; Minzenberg et al., 2007; Prehn et al., 2013). Additionally to amygdala hyper-reactivity, lower activity in the subgenual ACC was observed in response to fearful faces, whereas subgenual ACC activation was heightened in response to angry facial expressions (Minzenberg et al., 2007). Apart from limbic alterations, pictures of facial expressions also led to lower activation in the DLPFC and inferior frontal gyrus, as compared to healthy subjects (Guitart-Masip et al., 2009; Holtmann et al., 2013; Mier et al., 2012; Radaelli et al., 2012). Other studies investigated higher social-cognitive processes, such as theory of mind and empathy. During those tasks, lower activation of right superior temporal sulcus and DLPFC was observed in patients with BPD (Dziobek et al., 2011; Frick et al., 2012; Mier et al., 2012). More specifically, lower cognitive empathy in BPD was found to correspond to heightened activity in the middle and posterior insula in BPD (Dziobek et al., 2011). The authors conclude that social-cognitive processing might be impeded by emotional interference.

Some studies investigated behavioural aspects of social interaction and their neural correlates (Jeung, Schwieren, & Herpertz, 2016). Using an economic exchange game, BPD patients were found to have difficulties maintaining cooperation with an interaction partner over the course of the experiment (King-Casas et al., 2008). These behavioural effects were correlated with insula activation, which was differentially activated in HC depending on the fairness of the transaction but was heightened in BPD irrespective of the actual fairness of the interaction partner (King-Casas et al., 2008). The conclusion is that heightened insula activity in BPD results in a diminished ability to differentiate between fair and unfair interactions and therefore in difficulties establishing trust in social interactions (King-Casas et al., 2008; Meyer-Lindenberg, 2008).

Apart from interpersonal trust, the processing of social exclusion was examined, since self-report of patients with BPD often point to high rejection sensitivity in BPD (Staebler, Helbing, Rosenbach, & Renneberg, 2010), indicating that those with BPD are prone to expect and perceive rejection by others. The first study induced social exclusion with a card game and examined neural correlates using functional near-infrared spectroscopy (Ruocco et al., 2010). The authors report higher activity in medial prefrontal cortex in BPD, as compared to HC. This activation was correlated to fear of abandonment and rejection sensitivity (Ruocco et al., 2010). Another study used the cyberball paradigm (Williams & Jarvis, 2006) to induce social inclusion and exclusion with a ball-tossing game during neuroimaging (Domsalla et al., 2014), and found that BPD patients, as well as HC, felt excluded during social exclusion, but crucially BPD patients also felt more excluded during the inclusion condition. Irrespective of experimental conditions, those with BPD showed more activity in dorsal ACC and medial prefrontal cortex, pointing to increased processing of potential social threat. Investigating pain processing after social inclusion, a recent study used the cyberball paradigm in combination with painful heat stimuli (Bungert et al., 2015). Those with BPD exhibited higher insula activity in response to pain after social exclusion, and a less differentiated amygdala and insula response to inclusion as compared to exclusion in patients with high rejection sensitivity. From this body of research, the conclusion is that high limbic activity in BPD impedes functional social interaction behaviour because it hinders discrimination between prosocial and potentially threatening social behaviour of interaction partners. Again, limbic hyper-reactivity seems to contribute to problems at the interpersonal level.

IMPLICATIONS FOR PSYCHOTHERAPY

Across all paradigms investigating patients with BPD using neuroimaging methods, limbic hyper-reactivity (e.g., in the amygdala and insula) and diminished recruitment of frontal brain regions (e.g., the ACC, OFC, and DLPFC) were found. This imbalance between frontal and limbic brain regions can be linked to emotion dysregulation, impulsivity, and interpersonal disturbances. These clinical features of BPD appear to be closely linked to each other, underpinned by similar neural mechanisms.

Recent studies have revealed the importance of skills acquisition as a moderator variable of successful DBT (Linehan et al., 2015). One might argue that most of the DBT skills serve as quickly working self-administered mental instructions that enable clients to explicitly regulate their emotional system. There has been relevant progress in elucidating the neural underpinnings of emotion dysregulation in BPD. As a next step, research should focus on the distinct mechanisms of neural function of skills and tailor the treatment according to the needs of individual patients.

KEY MESSAGES FOR CLINICIANS

- Since the publication of Linehan's original treatment manual (Linehan, 1993) there has been considerable progress in understanding the biological underpinnings of BPD.
- There is strong evidence of hyperactivity in the limbic system and decreased activation of the prefrontal cortex, which may contribute to affective instability in BPD, although it is unclear how *specific* these findings are to BPD.
- Extensive studies of brain activation during pain processing in BPD patients demonstrate changes that complement patient reports of the physical and psychological impact of NSSI.
- The hyperactivity in the limbic system may also impede functional behaviour in social interactions.

References

American Psychiatric Association. (2000). *Diagnostic and Statistical Manual of Mental Disorders, 4th Edition, Text Revision (DSM-IV-TR)*. Washington, DC: American Psychiatric Association.

Baer, R. A., Peters, J. R., Eisenlohr-Moul, T. A., Geiger, P. J., & Sauer, S. E. (2012). Emotion-related cognitive processes in borderline personality disorder: a review of the empirical literature. *Clinical Psychology Review, 32*, 359–369.

Bandelow, B., Schmahl, C., Falkai, P., & Wedekind, D. (2010). Borderline personality disorder: a dysregulation of the endogenous opioid system? *Psychological Review, 117*, 623–636.

Beblo, T., Driessen, M., Mertens, M., Wingenfeld, K., Piefke, M., Rullkoetter, N., . . . Woermann, F. G. (2006). Functional MRI correlates of the recall of unresolved life events in borderline personality disorder. *Psychological Medicine, 36*, 845–856.

Bohus, M., Limberger, M., Ebner, U., Glocker, F. X., Schwarz, B., Wernz, M., & Lieb, K. (2000). Pain perception during self-reported distress and calmness in patients with borderline personality disorder and self-mutilating behavior. *Psychiatry Research, 95*, 251–260.

Bresin, K., & Gordon, K. H. (2013). Endogenous opioids and nonsuicidal self-injury: a mechanism of affect regulation. *Neuroscience and Biobehavioral Reviews, 37*, 374–383.

Brodsky, B. S., Groves, S. A., Oquendo, M. A., Mann, J. J., & Stanley, B. (2006). Interpersonal precipitants and suicide attempts in borderline personality disorder. *Suicide & Life-Threatening Behavior, 36*, 313–322.

Bungert, M., Koppe, G., Niedtfeld, I., Vollstadt-Klein, S., Schmahl, C., Lis, S., & Bohus, M. (2015). Pain processing after social exclusion and its relation to rejection sensitivity in borderline personality disorder. *PLoS ONE, 10*, e0133693.

Cackowski, S., Reitz, A. C., Ende, G., Kleindienst, N., Bohus, M., Schmahl, C., & Krause-Utz, A. (2014). Impact of stress on different components of impulsivity in borderline personality disorder. *Psychological Medicine, 44*, 3329–3340.

Cardenas-Morales, L., Fladung, A. K., Kammer, T., Schmahl, C., Plener, P. L., Connemann, B. J., & Schonfeldt-Lecuona, C. (2011). Exploring the affective component of pain perception during aversive stimulation in borderline personality disorder. *Psychiatry Research, 186*, 458–460.

Conklin, C. Z., Bradley, R., & Westen, D. (2006). Affect regulation in borderline personality disorder. *The Journal of Nervous and Mental Disease, 194*, 69–77.

Crowell, S. E., Beauchaine, T. P., & Linehan, M. M. (2009). A biosocial developmental model of borderline personality: Elaborating and extending Linehan's theory. *Psychological Bulletin, 135*, 495–510.

Cullen, K. R., Vizueta, N., Thomas, K. M., Han, G. J., Lim, K. O., Camchong, J., . . . Schulz, S. C. (2011). Amygdala functional connectivity in young women with borderline personality disorder. *Brain Connectivity, 1*, 61–71.

Damasio, A. R., Grabowski, T. J., Bechara, A., Damasio, H., Ponto, L. L. B., Parvizi, J., & Hichwa, R. D. (2000). Subcortical and cortical brain activity during the feeling of self-generated emotions. *Nature Neuroscience, 3*, 1049–1056.

Dannlowski, U., Stuhrmann, A., Beutelmann, V., Zwanzger, P., Lenzen, T., Grotegerd, D., . . . Kugel, H. (2012). Limbic scars: Long-term consequences of childhood maltreatment revealed by functional and structural magnetic resonance imaging. *Biological Psychiatry, 71*, 286–93.

de la Fuente, J. M., Goldman, S., Stanus, E., Vizuete, C., Morlán, I., Bobes, J., & Mendlewicz, J. (1997). Brain glucose metabolism in borderline personality disorder. *Journal of Psychiatric Research*, *31*, 531–541.

Dhawan, B. N., Cesselin, F., Raghubir, R., Reisine, T., Bradley, M. M., Portoghese, P. S., & Hamon, M. (1996). International Union of Pharmacology. XII. Classification of opioid receptors. *Pharmacological Reviews*, *48*, 567–592.

Domes, G., Schulze, L., & Herpertz, S. C. (2009). Emotion recognition in borderline personality disorder - a review of the literature. *Journal of Personality Disorder*, *23*, 6–19.

Domsalla, M., Koppe, G., Niedtfeld, I., Vollstadt-Klein, S., Schmahl, C., Bohus, M., & Lis, S. (2014). Cerebral processing of social rejection in patients with borderline personality disorder. *Social Cognitive and Affective Neuroscience*, *9*, 1789–97.

Donegan, N. H., Sanislow, C. A., Blumberg, H. P., Fulbright, R. K., Lacadie, C., Skudlarski, P., ... Wexler, B. E. (2003). Amygdala hyperreactivity in borderline personality disorder: implications for emotional dysregulation. *Biological Psychiatry*, *54*, 1284–93.

Dudas, R. B., Mole, T. B., Morris, L. S., Denman, C., Hill, E., Szalma, B., ... Voon, V. (2016). Amygdala and dlPFC abnormalities, with aberrant connectivity and habituation in response to emotional stimuli in females with BPD. *Journal of Affective Disorders*, *208*, 460–466.

Dziobek, I., Preissler, S., Grozdanovic, Z., Heuser, I., Heekeren, H. R., & Roepke, S. (2011). Neuronal correlates of altered empathy and social cognition in borderline personality disorder. *Neuroimage*, *57*, 539–48.

Ende, G., Cackowski, S., Van Eijk, J., Sack, M., Demirakca, T., Kleindienst, N., ... Schmahl, C. (2016). Impulsivity and aggression in female BPD and ADHD patients: Association with ACC glutamate and GABA concentrations. *Neuropsychopharmacology*, *41*, 410–8.

Etkin, A., & Wager, T. D. (2007). Functional neuroimaging of anxiety: a meta-analysis of emotional processing in PTSD, social anxiety disorder, and specific phobia. *American Journal of Psychiatry*, *164*, 1476–88.

Fertuck, E. A., Lenzenweger, M. F., Clarkin, J. F., Hoermann, S., & Stanley, B. (2006). Executive neurocognition, memory systems, and borderline personality disorder. *Clinical Psychology Review*, *26*, 346–75.

Frick, C., Lang, S., Kotchoubey, B., Sieswerda, S., Dinu-Biringer, R., Berger, M., ... Barnow, S. (2012). Hypersensitivity in borderline personality disorder during mindreading. *PLoS ONE*, *7*, e41650.

Gilbert, R., Widom, C. S., Browne, K., Fergusson, D., Webb, E., & Janson, S. (2009). Burden and consequences of child maltreatment in high-income countries. *Lancet*, *373*, 68–81.

Goodman, M., Carpenter, D., Tang, C. Y., Goldstein, K. E., Avedon, J., Fernandez, N., ... Hazlett, E. A. (2014). Dialectical behavior therapy alters emotion regulation and amygdala activity in patients with borderline personality disorder. *Journal of Psychiatric Research*, *57*, 108–116.

Goodman, M., New, A. S., Triebwasser, J., Collins, K. A., & Siever, L. (2010). Phenotype, endophenotype, and genotype comparisons between borderline personality disorder and major depressive disorder. *Journal of Personality Disorder*, *24*, 38–59.

Groenewold, N. A., Opmeer, E. M., de Jonge, P., Aleman, A., & Costafreda, S. G. (2013). Emotional valence modulates brain functional abnormalities in depression: evidence from a meta-analysis of fMRI studies. *Neuroscience & Biobehavioral Reviews*, *37*(2), 152–63.

Guitart-Masip, M., Pascual, J. C., Carmona, S., Hoekzema, E., Berge, D., Perez, V., ... Vilarroya, O. (2009). Neural correlates of impaired emotional discrimination in borderline personality disorder: an fMRI study. *Progress in Neuro-Psychopharmacology & Biological Psychiatry*, *33*(8), 1537–45.

Gunderson, J. G. (2007). Disturbed relationships as a phenotype for borderline personality disorder. *American Journal of Psychiatry*, *164*, 1637–40.

Gunderson, J. G., Stout, R. L., McGlashan, T. H., Shea, M. T., Morey, L. C., Grilo, C. M., … Skodol, A. E. (2011). Ten-year course of borderline personality disorder: Psychopathology and function from the Collaborative Longitudinal Personality Disorders Study. *Archives of General Psychiatry*, *68*(8), 827–837.

Hariri, A. R., Mattay, V. S., Tessitore, A., Fera, F., & Weinberger, D. R. (2003). Neocortical modulation of the amygdala response to fearful stimuli. *Biological Psychiatry*, *53*, 494–501.

Hazlett, E. A., Speiser, L. J., Goodman, M., Roy, M., Carrizal, M., Wynn, J. K., … New, A. S. (2007). Exaggerated affect-modulated startle during unpleasant stimuli in borderline personality disorder. *Biological Psychiatry*, *62*, 250–255.

Herpertz, S. C., Dietrich, T. M., Wenning, B., Krings, T., Erberich, S. G., Willmes, K., … Sass, H. (2001). Evidence of abnormal amygdala functioning in borderline personality disorder: a functional MRI study. *Biological Psychiatry*, *50*, 292–298.

Hoerst, M., Weber-Fahr, W., Tunc-Skarka, N., Ruf, M., Bohus, M., Schmahl, C., & Ende, G. (2010). Correlation of glutamate levels in the anterior cingulate cortex with self-reported impulsivity in patients with borderline personality disorder and healthy controls. *Archives of General Psychiatry*, *67*, 946–954.

Holtmann, J., Herbort, M. C., Wustenberg, T., Soch, J., Richter, S., Walter, H., Roepke, S., & Schott, B. H. (2013). Trait anxiety modulates fronto-limbic processing of emotional interference in borderline personality disorder. *Frontiers in Human Neuroscience*, *7*, 54. https://doi.org/10.3389/fnhum.2013.00054

Jacob, G. A., Zvonik, K., Kamphausen, S., Sebastian, A., Maier, S., Philipsen, A., … Tuscher, O. (2013). Emotional modulation of motor response inhibition in women with borderline personality disorder: an fMRI study. *Journal of Psychiatry & Neuroscience*, *38*, 164–72.

Jahng, S., Solhan, M. B., Tomko, R. L., Wood, P. K., Piasecki, T. M., & Trull, T. J. (2011). Affect and alcohol use: An ecological momentary assessment study of outpatients with borderline personality disorder. *Journal of Abnormal Psychology*, *120*, 572–584.

Jeung, H., Schwieren, C., & Herpertz, S. C. (2016). Rationality and self-interest as economic-exchange strategy in borderline personality disorder: Game theory, social preferences, and interpersonal behavior. *Neuroscience & Biobehavioral Reviews*, *71*, 849–864.

Juengling, F. D., Schmahl, C., Hesslinger, B., Ebert, D., Bremner, J. D., Gostomzyk, J., … Lieb, K. (2003). Positron emission tomography in female patients with borderline personality disorder. *Journal of Psychiatric Research*, *37*, 109–15.

Kamphausen, S., Schroder, P., Maier, S., Bader, K., Feige, B., Kaller, C. P., … Tuscher, O. (2012). Medial prefrontal dysfunction and prolonged amygdala response during instructed fear processing in borderline personality disorder. *The World Journal of Biological Psychiatry*, *14*(4), 307–318.

Kemperman, I., Russ, M. J., & Shearin, E. N. (1997). Self-injurious behavior and mood regulation in borderline patients. *Journal of Personality Disorders*, *11*, 146–157.

King-Casas, B., Sharp, C., Lomax-Bream, L., Lohrenz, T., Fonagy, P., & Montague, P. R. (2008). The rupture and repair of cooperation in borderline personality disorder. *Science*, |*321*, 806–10.

Kleindienst, N., Bohus, M., Ludascher, P., Limberger, M. F., Kuenkele, K., Ebner-Priemer, U. W., … Schmahl, C. (2008). Motives for nonsuicidal self-injury among women with borderline personality disorder. *The Journal of Nervous and Mental Disease*, *196*, 230–6.

Klonsky, E. D. (2007). The functions of deliberate self-injury: A review of the evidence. *Clinical Psychology Review*, *27*, 226–39.

Kluetsch, R. C., Schmahl, C., Niedtfeld, I., Densmore, M., Calhoun, V. D., Daniels, J., ... Lanius, R. A. (2012). Alterations in default mode network connectivity during pain processing in borderline personality disorder. *Archives of General Psychiatry*, 69(10), 1–11.

Koenigsberg, H. W., Denny, B. T., Fan, J., Liu, X., Guerreri, S., Mayson, S. J., ... Siever, L. J. (2014). The neural correlates of anomalous habituation to negative emotional pictures in borderline and avoidant personality disorder patients. *American Journal of Psychiatry*, 171, 82–90.

Koenigsberg, H. W., Fan, J., Ochsner, K. N., Liu, X., Guise, K. G., Pizzarello, S., ... Siever, L. J. (2009). Neural correlates of the use of psychological distancing to regulate responses to negative social cues: A study of patients with borderline personality disorder. *Biological Psychiatry*, 66, 854–863.

Korzekwa, M. I., Dell, P. F., Links, P. S., Thabane, L., & Fougere, P. (2009). Dissociation in borderline personality disorder: A detailed look. *Journal of Trauma & Dissociation*, 10(3), 346–367.

Kraus, A., Esposito, F., Seifritz, E., Di Salle, F., Ruf, M., Valerius, G., ... Schmahl, C. (2009). Amygdala deactivation as a neural correlate of pain processing in patients with borderline personality disorder and co-occurrent posttraumatic stress disorder. *Biological Psychiatry*, 65, 819–822.

Kraus, A., Valerius, G., Seifritz, E., Ruf, M., Bremner, D., Bohus, M., & Schmahl, C. (2010). Script-driven imagery of self-injurious behaviour in patients with borderline personality disorder: A pilot fMRI study. *Acta Psychiatrica Scandinavica*, 121(1), 41–51.

Krause-Utz, A., Elzinga, B. M., Oei, N. Y., Paret, C., Niedtfeld, I., Spinhoven, P., ... Schmahl, C. (2014). Amygdala and dorsal anterior cingulate connectivity during an emotional working memory task in borderline personality disorder patients with interpersonal trauma history. *Frontiers in Human Neuroscience*, 8, 848.

Krause-Utz, A., Keibel-Mauchnik, J., Ebner-Priemer, U., Bohus, M., & Schmahl, C. (2016). Classical conditioning in borderline personality disorder: An fMRI study. *European Archives of Psychiatry and Clinical Neuroscience*, 266, 291–305.

Krause-Utz, A., Oei, N. Y., Niedtfeld, I., Bohus, M., Spinhoven, P., Schmahl, C., & Elzinga, B. M. (2012). Influence of emotional distraction on working memory performance in borderline personality disorder. *Psychological Medicine*, 42(10), 2181–2192.

Lang, S., Kotchoubey, B., Frick, C., Spitzer, C., Grabe, H. J., & Barnow, S. (2012). Cognitive reappraisal in trauma-exposed women with borderline personality disorder. *Neuroimage*, 59, 1727–1734.

Lange, C., Kracht, L., Herholz, K., Sachsse, U., & Irle, E. (2005). Reduced glucose metabolism in temporo-parietal cortices of women with borderline personality disorder. *Psychiatry Research*, 139, 115–126.

Linehan, M. M., Korslund, K. E., Harned, M. S., Gallop, R. J., Lungu, A., Neacsiu, A. D., ... Murray-Greggory, A. M. (2015). Dialectical behaviour therapy for high suicide risk individuals with borderline personality disorder: a randomized clinical trial and component analysis. *JAMA Psychiatry*, 72(5), 475–482.

Lanius, R. A., Vermetten, E., Loewenstein, R. J., Brand, B., Schmahl, C., Bremner, J. D., & Spiegel, D. (2010). Emotion modulation in PTSD: Clinical and neurobiological evidence for a dissociative subtype. *American Journal of Psychiatry*, 167, 640–647.

Leichsenring, F., Leibing, E., Kruse, J., New, A. S., & Leweke, F. (2011). Borderline personality disorder. *Lancet*, 377, 74–84.

Lewis, M., Haviland-Jones, J. M., & Barrett, L. (2008). *Handbook of emotions*. New York, NY: Guilford Press.

Leyton, M., Okazawa, H., Diksic, M., Paris, J., Rosa, P., Mzengeza, S., ... Benkelfat, C. (2001). Brain regional alpha-[11C]methyl-L-tryptophan trapping in impulsive subjects with borderline personality disorder. *American Journal of Psychiatry, 158,* 775–782.

Linehan, M. M. (1993). *Cognitive-behavioral treatment of borderline personality disorder.* New York: The Guildford Press.

Links, P. S., Eynan, R., Heisel, M. J., Barr, A., Korzekwa, M., McMain, S., & Ball, J. S. (2007). Affective instability and suicidal ideation and behavior in patients with borderline personality disorder. *Journal of Personality Disorder, 21,* 72–86.

Lis, E., Greenfield, B., Henry, M., Guile, J. M., & Dougherty, G. (2007). Neuroimaging and genetics of borderline personality disorder: A review. *Journal of Psychiatry & Neuroscience, 32,* 162–173.

Lis, S. & Bohus, M. (2013). Social interaction in borderline personality disorder. *Current Psychiatry Reports, 15,* 338.

Ludäscher, P., Bohus, M., Lieb, K., Philipsen, A., & Schmahl, C. (2007). Elevated pain thresholds correlate with dissociation and aversive arousal in patients with borderline personality disorder. *Psychiatry Research, 149,* 291–296.

Ludäscher, P., Valerius, G., Stiglmayr, C., Mauchnik, J., Lanius, R. A., Bohus, M., & Schmahl, C. (2010). Pain sensitivity and neural processing during dissociative states in patients with borderline personality disorder with and without comorbid posttraumatic stress disorder: A pilot study. *Journal of Psychiatry & Neuroscience, 35,* 177–184.

Mak, A. D., & Lam, L. C. (2013). Neurocognitive profiles of people with borderline personality disorder. *Current Opinion in Psychiatry, 26,* 90–96.

McCloskey, M. S., New, A. S., Siever, L. J., Goodman, M., Koenigsberg, H. W., Flory, J. D., & Coccaro, E. F. (2009). Evaluation of behavioral impulsivity and aggression tasks as endophenotypes for borderline personality disorder. *Journal of Psychiatric Research, 43,* 1036–1048.

McCown, W., Galina, H., Johnson, J., de Simone, P. A., & Posa, J. (1993). Borderline personality disorder and laboratory-induced cold pressor pain: Evidence of stress-induced analgesia. *Journal of Psychopathology and Behavioral Assessment, 15,* 87–95.

McMain, S. F., Links, P. S., Gnam, W. H., Guimond, T., Cardish, R. J., Korman, L., & Streiner, D. L. (2009). A randomized trial of dialectical behavior therapy versus general psychiatric management for borderline personality disorder. *American Journal of Psychiatry, 166,* 1365–1374.

McRae, K., Hughes, B., Chopra, S., Gabrieli, J. D., Gross, J. J., & Ochsner, K. N. (2010). The neural bases of distraction and reappraisal. *Journal of Cognitive Neuroscience, 22,* 248–262.

Menon, V., & Uddin, L. Q. (2010). Saliency, switching, attention and control: A network model of insula function. *Brain Structure & Function, 214,* 655–667.

Meyer-Lindenberg, A. (2008). Psychology. Trust me on this. *Science, 321,* 778–780.

Meyer-Lindenberg, A., & Weinberger, D. R. (2006). Intermediate phenotypes and genetic mechanisms of psychiatric disorders. *Nature Reviews Neuroscience, 7*(10), 818–827. doi:10.1038/nrn1993

Meyer-Lindenberg, A., Buckholtz, J. W., Kolachana, B., Hariri, A. R., Pezawas, L., Blasi, G., ... Weinberger, D. R. (2006). Neural mechanisms of genetic risk for impulsivity and violence in humans. *Proceedings of the National Academy of Sciences of the United States of America, 103,* 6269–6274.

Meyer-Lindenberg, A., & Tost, H. (2012). Neural mechanisms of social risk for psychiatric disorders. *Nature Neuroscience, 15,* 663–668.

Mier, D., Lis, S., Esslinger, C., Sauer, C., Hagenhoff, M., Ulferts, J., ... Kirsch, P. (2012). Neuronal correlates of social cognition in borderline personality disorder. *Social Cognitive and Affective Neuroscience, 8*(5), 531–537.

Minzenberg, M. J., Fan, J., New, A. S., Tang, C. Y., & Siever, L. J. (2007). Fronto-limbic dysfunction in response to facial emotion in borderline personality disorder: An event-related fMRI study. *Psychiatry Research, 155*, 231–243.

Neacsiu, A., Linehan, M., & Bohus, M. (2014). Dialectical behavior therapy: An intervention for emotion dysregulation. In J. J. Gross (Ed.), *Handbook of emotion regulation.* New York, NY: Guilford Press.

New, A. S., Buchsbaum, M. S., Hazlett, E. A., Goodman, M., Koenigsberg, H. W., Lo, J., ... Siever, L. J. (2004). Fluoxetine increases relative metabolic rate in prefrontal cortex in impulsive aggression. *Psychopharmacology (Berlin), 176*, 451–458.

New, A. S., Carpenter DM, Perez-Rodriguez MM, Ripoll LH, Avedon J, Patil U, Hazlett EA, Goodman M. (2013). Developmental differences in diffusion tensor imaging parameters in borderline personality disorder. *J Psychiatr Res., 47*(8),1101–1109. doi: 10.1016/j.jpsychires.2013.03.021. Epub 2013 Apr 28.

New, A. S., Hazlett, E. A., Buchsbaum, M. S., Goodman, M., Koenigsberg, H. W., Iskander, L., ... Berman, K. F. (2005). Midbrain dopamine and prefrontal function in humans: interaction and modulation by COMT genotype. *Nature Neuroscience, 8*, 594–596.

New, A. S., Hazlett, E. A., Buchsbaum, M. S., Goodman, M., Mitelman, S. A., Newmark, R., ... Siever, L. J. (2007). Amygdala-prefrontal disconnection in borderline personality disorder. *Neuropsychopharmacology, 32*, 1629–1640.

New, A. S., Hazlett, E. A., Buchsbaum, M. S., Goodman, M., Reynolds, D. A., Mitropoulou, V., ... Siever, L. J. (2002). Blunted prefrontal cortical 18fluorodeoxyglucose positron emission tomography response to meta-chlorophenylpiperazine in impulsive aggression. *Archives of General Psychiatry, 59*(7), 621–629.

New, A. S., Hazlett, E. A., Newmark, R. E., Zhang, J., Triebwasser, J., Meyerson, D., ... Buchsbaum, M. S. (2009). Laboratory induced aggression: A positron emission tomography study of aggressive individuals with borderline personality disorder. *Biological Psychiatry, 66*, 1107–1114.

Niedtfeld, I., Kirsch, P., Schulze, L., Herpertz, S. C., Bohus, M., & Schmahl, C. (2012). Functional connectivity of pain-mediated affect regulation in borderline personality disorder. *PloS ONE, 7*, e33293.

Niedtfeld, I., Schmitt, R., Winter, D., Bohus, M., Schmahl, C., & Herpertz, S. C. (2017). Pain-mediated affect regulation is reduced after dialectical behavior therapy in borderline personality disorder: A longitudinal fMRI study. *Social Cognition and Affective Neuroscience, 12*(5), 739–747.

Niedtfeld, I., Schulze, L., Kirsch, P., Herpertz, S. C., Bohus, M., & Schmahl, C. (2010). Affect regulation and pain in borderline personality disorder: a possible link to the understanding of self-injury. *Biological Psychiatry, 68*, 383–391.

O'Neill, A., & Frodl, T. (2012). Brain structure and function in borderline personality disorder. *Brain Structure & Function 217*, 767–782.

Ochsner, K. N., Bunge, S. A., Gross, J. J., & Gabrieli, J. D. (2002). Rethinking feelings: an FMRI study of the cognitive regulation of emotion. *Journal of Cognitive Neuroscience 14*, 1215–1229.

Ochsner, K. N., & Gross, J. J. (2004). Thinking makes it so: A social-cognitive neuroscience approach to emotion regulation. In R. F. Baumeister & K. D. Vohs (Eds.), *Handbook of self-regulation: Research, theory, and applications* (pp. 229–255). New York: Guilford Press.

Ochsner, K. N., & Gross, J. J. (2005). The cognitive control of emotion. *Trends in Cognitive Sciences, 9,* 242–249.

Ochsner, K. N., & Gross, J. J. (2014). The neural bases of emotion and emotion regulation: A valuation perspective. In J. J. Gross (Ed.), *Handbook of emotion regulation* (pp.23–42). New York, NY: Guilford Press.

Paret, C., Kluetsch, R., Zaehringer, J., Ruf, M., Demirakca, T., Bohus, M., ... Schmahl, C. (2016). Alterations of amygdala-prefrontal connectivity with real-time fMRI neurofeedback in BPD patients. *Social Cognition and Affective Neuroscience, 11,* 952–960.

Perez-Rodriguez, M. M., Hazlett, E. A., Rich, E. L., Ripoll, L. H., Weiner, D. M., Spence, N., ... New, A. S. (2012). Striatal activity in borderline personality disorder with comorbid intermittent explosive disorder: Sex differences. *Journal of Psychiatric Research, 46,* 797–804.

Perez-Rodriguez, M. M., Weinstein, S., New, A. S., Bevilacqua, L., Yuan, Q., Zhou, Z., ... Siever, L. J. (2010). Tryptophan-hydroxylase 2 haplotype association with borderline personality disorder and aggression in a sample of patients with personality disorders and healthy controls. *Journal of Psychiatric Research, 44,* 1075–1081.

Pezawas, L., Meyer-Lindenberg, A., Drabant, E. M., Verchinski, B. A., Munoz, K. E., Kolachana, B.S., ... Weinberger, D. R. (2005). 5-HTTLPR polymorphism impacts human cingulate-amygdala interactions: a genetic susceptibility mechanism for depression. *Nature Neuroscience, 8,* 828–834.

Prehn, K., Schulze, L., Rossmann, S., Berger, C., Vohs, K., Fleischer, M., ... Herpertz, S. C. (2013). Effects of emotional stimuli on working memory processes in male criminal offenders with borderline and antisocial personality disorder. *The World Journal of Biological Psychiatry, 14,* 71–78.

Prossin, A. R., Love, T. M., Koeppe, R. A., Zubieta, J. K., & Silk, K. R. (2010). Dysregulation of regional endogenous opioid function in borderline personality disorder. *American Journal of Psychiatry, 167,* 925–933.

Radaelli, D., Poletti, S., Dallaspezia, S., Colombo, C., Smeraldi, E., & Benedetti, F. (2012). Neural responses to emotional stimuli in comorbid borderline personality disorder and bipolar depression. *Psychiatry Research, 203,* 61–66.

Reitz, S., Kluetsch, R., Niedtfeld, I., Knorz, T., Lis, S., Paret, C., ... Schmahl, C. (2015). Incision and stress regulation in borderline personality disorder: neurobiological mechanisms of self-injurious behaviour. *British Journal of Psychiatry, 207,* 165–172.

Reitz, S., Krause-Utz, A., Pogatzki-Zahn, E. M., Ebner-Priemer, U., Bohus, M., & Schmahl, C. (2012). Stress regulation and incision in borderline personality disorder: a pilot study modeling cutting behavior. *Journal of Personality Disorders, 26,* 605–615.

Ruocco, A. C., Amirthavasagam, S., Choi-Kain, L. W., & McMain, S. F. (2013). Neural correlates of negative emotionality in borderline personality disorder: An activation-likelihood-estimation meta-analysis. *Biological Psychiatry, 73,* 153–160.

Ruocco, A. C., Medaglia, J. D., Tinker, J. R., Ayaz, H., Forman, E. M., Newman, C. F., ... Chute, D. L. (2010). Medial prefrontal cortex hyperactivation during social exclusion in borderline personality disorder. *Psychiatry Research, 181,* 233–236.

Russ, M. J., Roth, S. D., Lerman, A., Kakuma, T., Harrison, K., Shindledecker, R. D., ... Mattis, S. (1992). Pain perception in self-injurious patients with borderline personality disorder. *Biological Psychiatry, 32,* 501–511.

Salavert, J., Gasol, M., Vieta, E., Cervantes, A., Trampal, C., & Gispert, J. D. (2011). Fronto-limbic dysfunction in borderline personality disorder: a 18F-FDG positron emission tomography study. *Journal of Affective Disorders, 131,* 260–267.

Schmahl, C., Bohus, M., Esposito, F., Treede, R. D., Di Salle, F., Greffrath, W., ... Seifritz, E. (2006). Neural correlates of antinociception in borderline personality disorder. *Archives of General Psychiatry, 63*, 659–667.

Schmahl, C., Greffrath, W., Baumgartner, U., Schlereth, T., Magerl, W., Philipsen, A., ... Treede, R. D. (2004). Differential nociceptive deficits in patients with borderline personality disorder and self-injurious behavior: laser-evoked potentials, spatial discrimination of noxious stimuli, and pain ratings. *Pain, 110*, 470–479.

Schmahl, C., Herpertz, S. C., Bertsch, K., Ende, G., Flor, H., Kirsch, P., ... Bohus, M. (2014). Mechanisms of disturbed emotion processing and social interaction in borderline personality disorder: state of knowledge and research agenda of the German Clinical Research Unit. *Borderline Personality Disorder and Emotion Dysregulation, 1*, 12. doi:10.1186/2051-6673-1-12

Schmahl, C., Meinzer, M., Zeuch, A., Fichter, M., Cebulla, M., Kleindienst, N., ... Bohus, M. (2010). Pain sensitivity is reduced in borderline personality disorder, but not in posttraumatic stress disorder and bulimia nervosa. *The World Journal of Biological Psychiatry, 11*, 364–371.

Schmahl, C. G., Elzinga, B. M., Ebner, U. W., Simms, T., Sanislow, C., Vermetten, E., ... Bremner, J. D. (2004). Psychophysiological reactivity to traumatic and abandonment scripts in borderline personality and posttraumatic stress disorders: A preliminary report. *Psychiatry Research, 126*, 33–42.

Schmitt, R., Winter, D., Niedtfeld, I., Schmahl, C., & Herpertz, S. C. (2016). Effects of psychotherapy on neuronal correlates of reappraisal in female patients with borderline personality disorder. *Biological Psychiatry: Cognitive Neuroscience and Neuroimaging, 1*(6), 548–557.

Schnell, K., & Herpertz, S. C. (2007). Effects of dialectic-behavioral-therapy on the neural correlates of affective hyperarousal in borderline personality disorder. *Journal of Psychiatric Research, 41*, 837–847.

Schulze, L., Domes, G., Kruger, A., Berger, C., Fleischer, M., Prehn, K., ... Herpertz, S. C. (2011). Neuronal correlates of cognitive reappraisal in borderline patients with affective instability. *Biological Psychiatry, 69*, 564–573.

Schulze, L., Schmahl, C., & Niedtfeld, I. (2016). Neural correlates of disturbed emotion processing in borderline personality disorder: A multimodal meta-analysis. *Biological Psychiatry, 79*, 97–106.

Schramm, A. T., Venta, A, & Sharp, C. (2013). The role of experiential avoidance in the association between borderline features and emotion regulation in adolescents. *Personality Disorders, 4*, 138–144.

Sebastian, A., Jacob, G., Lieb, K., & Tuscher, O. (2013). Impulsivity in borderline personality disorder: a matter of disturbed impulse control or a facet of emotional dysregulation? *Current Psychiatry Reports, 15*, 339.

Sebastian, A., Jung, P., Krause-Utz, A., Lieb, K., Schmahl, C., & Tuscher, O. (2014). Frontal dysfunctions of impulse control—a systematic review in borderline personality disorder and attention-deficit hyperactivity disorder. *Frontiers of Human Neuroscience, 8*, 698.

Shearer, S. L. (1994). Phenomenology of self-injury among inpatient women with borderline personality disorder. *Journal of Nervous and Mental Disease, 182*, 524–526.

Sierra, M., & Berrios, G. E. (1998). Depersonalization: Neurobiological perspectives. *Biological Psychiatry, 44*, 898–908.

Siever, L. J., Buchsbaum, M. S., New, A. S., Spiegel-Cohen, J., Wei, T., Hazlett, E. A., ... Mitropoulou, V. (1999). d,l-fenfluramine response in impulsive personality disorder assessed with [18F]fluorodeoxyglucose positron emission tomography. *Neuropsychopharmacology, 20*, 413–423.

Silbersweig, D., Clarkin, J. F., Goldstein, M., Kernberg, O. F., Tuescher, O., Levy, K. N., . . . Stern, E. (2007). Failure of frontolimbic inhibitory function in the context of negative emotion in borderline personality disorder. *American Journal of Psychiatry, 164*, 1832–1841.

Soloff, P. (2003). Impulsivity, gender, and response to fenfluramine challenge in borderline personality disorder. *Psychiatry Research, 119*, 11–24.

Soloff, P. H., Meltzer, C. C., Becker, C., Greer, P. J., & Constantine, D. (2005). Gender differences in a fenfluramine-activated FDG PET study of borderline personality disorder. *Psychiatry Research, 138*, 183–195.

Soloff, P. H., Meltzer, C. C., Greer, P. J., Constantine, D., & Kelly, T. M. (2000). A fenfluramine-activated FDG-PET study of borderline personality disorder. *Biological Psychiatry, 47*, 540–547.

Soloff, P. H., Price, J. C., Meltzer, C. C., Fabio, A., Frank, G. K., & Kaye, W. H. (2007). 5HT2A receptor binding is increased in borderline personality disorder. *Biological Psychiatry, 62*, 580–587.

Spear, L. P. (2000). The adolescent brain and age-related behavioral manifestations. *Neuroscience & Biobehavioral Reviews, 24*, 417–463.

Staebler, K., Helbing, E., Rosenbach, C., & Renneberg, B. (2010). Rejection sensitivity and borderline personality disorder. *Clinical Psychology & Psychotherapy, 18*(4), 275–283.

Stanley, B., Sher, L., Wilson, S., Ekman, R., Huang, Y. Y., & Mann, J. J. (2010). Non-suicidal self-injurious behavior, endogenous opioids and monoamine neurotransmitters. *Journal of Affective Disorders, 124*, 134–140.

Stanley, B., & Siever, L. J. (2010). The interpersonal dimension of borderline personality disorder: Toward a neuropeptide model. *American Journal of Psychiatry, 167*, 24–39.

Stiglmayr, C. E., Ebner-Priemer, U. W., Bretz, J., Behm, R., Mohse, M., Lammers, C. H., . . . Bohus, M. (2008). Dissociative symptoms are positively related to stress in borderline personality disorder. *Acta Psychiatrica Scandinavica, 117*, 139–147.

Stiglmayr, C. E., Grathwol, T., Linehan, M. M., Ihorst, G., Fahrenberg, J., & Bohus, M. (2005). Aversive tension in patients with borderline personality disorder: a computer-based controlled field study. *Acta Psychiatrica Scandinavica, 111*, 372–379.

Treede, R.-D., Apkarian, A. V., Bromm, B., Greenspan, J. D., & Lenz, F. A. (2000). Cortical representation of pain: functional characterization of nociceptive areas near the lateral sulcus. *Pain, 87*, 113–119.

Vollm, B., Richardson, P., Stirling, J., Elliott, R., Dolan, M., Chaudhry, I., . . . Deakin, B. (2004). Neurobiological substrates of antisocial and borderline personality disorder: Preliminary results of a functional fMRI study. *Criminal Behavior and Mental Health, 14*, 39–54.

Welch, S. S., & Linehan, M. M. (2002). High-risk situations associated with parasuicide and drug use in borderline personality disorder. *Journal of Personality Disorders, 16*, 561–569.

Welch, S. S., Linehan, M. M., Sylvers, P., Chittams, J., & Rizvi, S. L. (2008). Emotional responses to self-injury imagery among adults with borderline personality disorder. *Journal of Consulting and Clinical Psychology, 76*, 45–51.

Williams, K. D., & Jarvis, B. (2006). Cyberball: A program for use in research on interpersonal ostracism and acceptance. *Behavior Research Methods, 38*, 174–180.

Winter, D., Krause-Utz, A., Lis, S., Chiu, C. D., Lanius, R. A., Schriner, F., . . . Schmahl, C. (2015). Dissociation in borderline personality disorder: Disturbed cognitive and emotional inhibition and its neural correlates. *Psychiatry Research, 233*, 339–351.

Winter, D., Niedtfeld, I., Schmitt, R., Bohus, M., Schmahl, C., & Herpertz, S. C. (2016). Neural correlates of distraction in borderline personality disorder before and after dialectical behavior therapy. *European Archives of Psychiatry and Clinical Neuroscience, 267*(1), 51–62.

Wolf, E. J., Lunney, C. A., Miller, M. W., Resick, P. A., Friedman, M. J., & Schnurr, P. P. (2012). The dissociative subtype of PTSD: A replication and extension. *Depression and Anxiety*, *29*, 679–688.

Wolf, R. C., Sambataro, F., Vasic, N., Schmid, M., Thomann, P. A., Bienentreu, S. D., & Wolf, N. D. (2011). Aberrant connectivity of resting-state networks in borderline personality disorder. *Journal of Psychiatry and Neuroscience*, *36*, 402–411.

Yanowitch, R., & Coccaro, E. F. (2011). The neurochemistry of human aggression. *Advances in Genetics*, *75*, 151–169.

Yen, S., Shea, M. T., Sanislow, C. A., Grilo, C. M., Skodol, A. E., Gunderson, J. G., … Morey, L. C. (2004). Borderline personality disorder criteria associated with prospectively observed suicidal behavior. *American Journal of Psychiatry*, *161*, 1296–1298.

Zubieta, J. K., Ketter, T. A., Bueller, J. A., Xu, Y., Kilbourn, M. R., Young, E. A., & Koeppe, R. A. (2003). Regulation of human affective responses by anterior cingulate and limbic mu-opioid neurotransmission. *Archives of General Psychiatry*, *60*, 1145–1153.

CHAPTER 3

INVALIDATING ENVIRONMENTS AND THE DEVELOPMENT OF BORDERLINE PERSONALITY DISORDER

JEREMY L. GROVE AND SHEILA E. CROWELL

INTRODUCTION

DIALECTICAL behaviour therapy (DBT) is an effective intervention for the treatment of borderline personality disorder (BPD), self-inflicted injury (SII), and many other conditions characterized by pervasive emotion dysregulation. This effectiveness can be credited, in part, to the strategies, assumptions, and aetiological theories that guide implementation of adherent DBT. For example, a central tenet of DBT is that clients are doing the best that they can *and* that they need to do better in every context and relationship. Thus, the DBT therapist simultaneously absolves the client of blame while challenging her to make dramatic and unprecedented changes in her daily life. This dialectic is one of the more revolutionary aspects of DBT and, to this day, challenges the status quo within the mental health field. To remove blame from the client is to suggest that there are complex yet treatable causes for her distress—understandable reasons for skills deficits, which can be targeted effectively in treatment. At the same time, new skills must generalize well beyond the therapy room. Therefore, the DBT client carries the therapy into her daily life through skills group, environmental interventions, daily diary tracking, and regular out-of-session contact with her therapist. These aspects of DBT differ dramatically from standard conceptualizations of clients, which often presume that psychopathology emerges due primarily to significant biological deficits. This traditional doctor-patient ("us-them") mentality often precludes out-of-session contact and reinforces rigid boundaries.

To understand these revolutionary aspects of DBT, one must trace the treatment back to its core a etiological premise: the biosocial theory (Crowell, Beauchaine, & Linehan, 2009; Linehan, 1993). In essence, the biosocial theory emphasizes trans-actions between biological sensitivities and environmental risk factors in the devel-opment of BPD, rather than either of these processes alone. More specifically, a core assumption of this model is that BPD emerges as a result of complex transactions be-tween individual-level biological vulnerabilities (e.g., trait impulsivity, trait anxiety) and contextual risk factors. These transactions potentiate the development of emotion dysregulation and later BPD via complex socialization processes (e.g., reinforcement of negative affect). Thus, the biosocial theory is a model based upon learning experi-ences and how these experiences shape behaviour over the course of development. In many cases, strategies that were once intermittently effective and adaptive at an earlier stage become gradually less effective in new learning environments. In this regard, the biosocial theory is very consistent with the developmental psychopathology perspec-tive, whose adherents view psychological risk and resilience as products of biology × environment interactions across development (Cicchetti & Rogosch, 1996).

This chapter briefly reviews the biosocial theory, with a particular focus on invalidating developmental contexts as a contributing factor to BPD development (Linehan, 1993). Importantly, invalidation is a dimensional construct, which can range from mild misunderstandings or criticism to severe maltreatment. It focuses primarily on milder forms of invalidation within the family context, given that the effects of abuse are well-documented (Ball & Links, 2009). It also reviews emerging empirical work on factors that may contribute to the development of invalidating contexts. Next, it dis-cusses the biosocial theory in the context of specific DBT intervention strategies that may be effective at reducing risk for invalidation and, by extension, borderline person-ality development among vulnerable youth. Finally, it concludes with recommendations for future research on contextual risk for BPD.

THEORETICAL PERSPECTIVE: THE BIOSOCIAL THEORY

A thorough review of the biosocial theory would include a detailed overview of re-cent biological research (e.g., genetic and epigenetic processes, neurotransmitter func-tion, etc.), which is reviewed in Chapter 2 of this volume (see also Crowell & Kaufman, 2016 a,b). Briefly, the biosocial theory is a model of BPD development that describes complex longitudinal transactions between a biologically vulnerable child and his environment—with an emphasis on the caregiver-child relationship. A key tenet of the biosocial theory is that invalidation is more likely to occur when there is a *mismatch* between child and environment. Hence, psychopathology can emerge within any household, even if no other member of the family shows distress. That said, there is clear evidence that certain inherited vulnerabilities confer risk for invalidation, and ultimately, BPD. In particular, trait impulsivity and trait anxiety are highly heritable, and contribute to the (correlated) externalizing and internalizing trajectories to BPD, respectively. Emotional sensitivity is another biological vulnerability that appears to be important for later development of emotion regulation difficulties. These vulnerabilities have been explored in a number of different ways, including neurotransmitter, HPA-axis (e.g., cortisol), and psychophysiological functioning (e.g., Beauchaine, 2015; Beauchaine & McNulty, 2013; Doom & Gunnar, 2013; Gross & Hen, 2004). Below, we briefly review their neurobiological underpinnings.

Trait impulsivity, or the tendency to engage in reward-seeking behaviours with minimal forethought, is highly heritable (~.8) and emerges early in development (Beauchaine & Gatzke-Kopp, 2012; Beauchaine, Hinshaw, & Pang, 2010; Beauchaine & McNulty, 2013; Caspi & Silva, 1995). Trait impulsivity has been linked with specific neural substrates (see Beauchaine, Zisner, & Sauder, 2017 for a review). For instance, the mesolimbic dopaminergic (DA) system, which includes neural projections from the nucleus accumbens and ventral striatum, is one subcortical region that contributes to behavioural manifestations of impulsivity (Swartz, 1999). Dysfunction of this system, particularly hypofunctioning of the mesolimbic DA system, is an a etiological contributor to childhood externalizing disorders and anhedonia (Beauchaine et al., 2013; Gatzke-Kopp, 2011). Hypodopaminergic expression is believed to produce an aversive, irritable state, from which individuals are motivated to escape by engaging in reward-seeking and novelty-seeking behaviours. However, because the positive effects of such behaviours are temporary, individuals tend to continue seeking rewards (see Zisner & Beauchaine, 2016). Behaviourally, these biological vulnerabilities manifest as irritability, boredom, hyperactivity, and impulsivity. The *mesolimbic* DA system functions as an emotion generation system and is a predominant neural influence on impulsivity among children. The *mesocortical* DA system, which typically develops into and beyond adolescence, becomes increasingly important for regulating impulsivity (Zisner & Beauchaine, 2016). The interplay of these neural systems across development is complex. For example, early manifestations of behavioural impulsivity can have evocative effects on the environment, which can delay the maturation and development of top-down inhibitory control systems and exacerbate behavioural and emotional problems. Impulsive youth, especially females, are highly susceptible to invalidation and criticism in both home and school environments. In one longitudinal study, young girls with ADHD were at elevated risk for engaging in self-inflicted injury by adolescence—an early-emerging feature of BPD (Hinshaw et al., 2012).

Trait anxiety is also highly heritable, and rooted in behavioural inhibition, a temperamental construct characterized by shyness, passive avoidance of real and perceived threat, and fearfulness in novel contexts (Gray & McNaughton, 2000). Trait anxiety is associated with activity and reactivity of a number of neural structures innervated by serotonin (5HT), including the amygdala, posterior cingulate cortex, and the septo-hippocampal system (Corr & McNaughton, 2016). Inhibitory control and cognitive flexibility are two important processes that regulate these sub-cortical mechanisms of trait anxiety (Otto, Misra, Prasad, & McRae, 2014; White, McDermot, Degnan, Henderson, & Fox, 2011), and dysfunction of these top-down regulatory systems is associated with BPD traits (Baer, Peters, Eisenlohr-Moul, Geiger, & Sauer, 2012). Inhibitory control is associated with the right inferior frontal cortex, and activation in the dorsolateral prefrontal cortex (PFC), anterior cingulate cortex (ACC), and the ventral PFC (see Bridgett, Burt, Edwards, & Deater-Deckard, 2015 for review). Excessive inhibitory control can result in over-controlled and avoidant behaviours, especially in the absence of approach-related motivational tendencies (Kagan, 2013). Cognitive flexibility is a key aspect of emotion regulation, including attentional shifting/control and reappraisal, and has been linked with dorsolateral and medial PFC, and anterior cingulate cortex (Bissonette, Powell, & Roesch, 2013). In general, trait anxiety is highly predictive of a range of internalizing disorders across the lifespan, and may be associated with an internalizing trajectory towards BPD development (e.g., Kagan, 2013). For example, ADHD, which is a common diagnostic precursor for BPD features, is associated with harsh and overly critical parenting styles (Danforth, Connor, & Doerfler, 2016; Hinshaw et al., 2012). Children with comorbid trait impulsivity *and* trait anxiety may be more likely to internalize these criticisms, ultimately developing an angry or hostile interpersonal style over time (e.g., Crowell & Kaufman, 2016a).

Emotional sensitivity, or a propensity toward negative affect in infancy, is another temperamental vulnerability to BPD with a biological basis. It has been suggested elsewhere that this vulnerability, particularly when met with environmental risk, contributes to the emergence of emotion regulation problems in childhood/adolescence. Vulnerability to negative affectivity is mediated by central DA functioning, with low levels associated with irritability (Forbes & Dahl, 2005). Recent fMRI studies suggest that emotional sensitivity may be linked with heightened activation in the dorsolateral PFC, ventrolateral PFC, and dorsomedial PFC, and the ACC in response to negatively valenced stimuli (see van Zutphen, Siep, Jacob, Goebel, & Arntz, 2015 for review). Emotional sensitivity may be an important moderator for the association between trait impulsivity/anxiety and later development of BPD. That is, children who are highly attuned to emotional stimuli, sensitive to context, and easily dysregulated may be especially vulnerable to invalidating contexts.

Of course, child vulnerabilities alone are rarely sufficient to cause BPD. Invalidating environments also contribute to emergence of emotion dysregulation—a tendency to experience intense, prolonged, and highly aversive emotions (Cicchetti, Ackerman, & Izard, 1995). Linehan (1993) defines invalidating contexts as those that regularly reject or ignore a child's displays of emotional behaviour, while occasionally responding to extreme and highly aversive emotional outbursts with warmth, support, or solicitousness. In essence, these environments simultaneously punish normative expressions of emotion and reinforce more extreme emotional displays. Consequently, the child fails to learn how to label and communicate emotional needs, except via highly aversive and intense emotional expressions. Such negative social exchanges shape the behaviour of both parent and child, which over time results in increased frequency and intensity of negative interactions. Across development, evocative effects of early borderline features can increase risk for future invalidation across contexts (e.g., peers). As a result, pervasive deficits in emotional, behavioural, cognitive, interpersonal, and identity functioning become increasingly stable, thereby perpetuating risk for future invalidation across contexts (see Crowell, Puzia, & Yaptangco, 2015). Thus, for treatment providers, targeting the developmental context could offer a significant window of opportunity to reduce long-term contextual risk and prevent development of BPD.

TYPES OF INVALIDATING ENVIRONMENTS

Invalidation occurs when a person receives explicit or implicit communication from others that his or her internal experiences (e.g., emotions, thoughts, perceptions of theirs or others' behaviour, etc.) are insignificant, incorrect, inappropriate, or not an appropriate reaction to a given situation (Fruzzetti, Shenk, & Hoffman, 2005). An invalidating developmental context is one in which invalidation occurs regularly. In other words, a child's emotional experiences are frequently met with punishment, such that the caregiver responds with inappropriate, extreme, and/or negative responses, or simply does not respond at all. Consequently, over time, the child fails to learn how to appropriately label or express emotions in a way that communicates their needs effectively.

Child maltreatment is a known contextual risk factor for BPD (Bornovalova et al., 2013; Fossati, Madeddu, & Maffei, 1999; Gratz, Latzman, Tull, Reynolds, & Lejuez, 2011; Soloff, Lynch, & Kelly, 2002; Zanarini, Gunderson, Marino, Schwartz, & Frankenburg, 1989). This represents an extreme form of invalidation because it evokes intense emotional responses in the child along with communication from perpetrators and/or family members that such emotions are unjustified, wrong, or should remain private. As a result, the child's emotional processing abilities are disrupted, which affects her ability to identify and modulate painful emotions (Dannlowski et al., 2012; Pollak, Cicchetti, Hornung, & Reed, 2000). Furthermore, children who are abused may become hypervigilant to threat and may learn avoidant behaviours to minimize risk of further abuse (Ford, Fraleigh, Albert, & Connor, 2010). Such behaviours can generalize beyond the original abusive context, thereby placing the child at risk for further invalidation and/or decreasing the likelihood of corrective emotional experiences (Carlson, Furby, Armstrong, & Shlaes, 1997; Malinosky-Rummell & Hansen, 1993).

Sociocultural invalidation is another important construct, though it is seldom discussed as an a etiological factor for BPD. In general, we define sociocultural invalidation as the experience of chronic social stress related to discrimination, prejudice, isolation, or stigma on the basis of biologically determined, unchangeable character-istics (e.g., race/ethnicity, sexual orientation, etc.), cultural background, or disability (Meyer, 2003). Sociocultural invalidation can occur in a macro- or micro-level context (Ridgeway, 2006). Macro-level sociocultural invalidation involves societal values and/or norms that communicate that emotions, actions, needs, and beliefs of an individual are wrong, inappropriate, or inconsistent with the majority view (e.g., the very public and longstanding debate of gay marriage rights). In contrast, micro-level sociocultural invalidation is experienced on a personal level, often overtly (e.g., racial slurs), but also via covert gestures (e.g., micro-aggressions). Importantly, children who are minorities report these types of invalidating experiences early in life (Bigler & Liben, 2006). To date, there is limited research on sociocultural invalidation as a contextual risk factor for BPD. However, at least one study found an association between sexual minority status and BPD (Reich & Zanarini, 2008). Importantly, many individuals who meet criteria for BPD do not report abuse, neglect, or sociocultural invalidation. This suggests that subtle interaction patterns within families can also confer risk for BPD. These more elusive family dynamics are critical to understand because they are amenable to intervention and have the potential to reduce distress within the entire family system.

Evidence for the Invalidating Environment Theory

The invalidating environments theory outlines specific mechanisms by which subtle, yet chronic, patterns of problematic communication between caregivers and at-risk youth confer contextual risk for BPD among vulnerable and/or sensitive youth. Three compo-nents are at the crux of this theory. First, children at risk for BPD experience chronic in-validation within the family context, such that these environments routinely dismiss or reject children's displays of emotion, which, by virtue of inherited vulnerabilities, may be intense and overwhelming. Second, invalidating and coercive environments inter-mittently reinforce extreme and contextually inappropriate emotional responses, while punishing relatively normative emotional displays by the child. Consequently, children learn that extreme displays of negative emotions are sufficient in gaining emotional support from parents or avoiding of parental demands/conflict. Third, over time, these parent-child dynamics shape chronic emotion dysregulation, such that emotions are ex-perienced more frequently, intensely, and for longer periods of time relative to individ-uals without emotion regulation difficulties.

The first component of the invalidating environment theory describes invalidation as repeated communication by the caregiver to the child, in one form or another, that his or her emotions and related needs, thoughts, and behaviours are invalid, unjustified, or inappropriate. Communication may be overt and/or coercive (e.g., "Stop crying or I'll give you something to cry about!"), or covert and/or unintentional, such as the caregiver failing to understand, recognize, or consider the child's emotional responses. Prior research demonstrates convergent findings across cross-sectional and longitudinal studies that parental invalidation characterized by conventional definitions of invalidation is associated with development of BPD symptoms in at-risk youth (Dixon-Gordon, Whalen, Scott, Cummins, & Stepp, 2016; Johnson, Cohen, Chen, Kasen, & Brook, 2006; Sauer & Baer, 2010; Selby, Braithwaite, Joiner, & Fincham, 2008; Stepp, Whalen, Pilkonis, Hipwell, & Levine, 2012). Importantly, the biosocial theory recognizes that invalidating environments are not solely due to either the caregiver or the sensitive child. Instead, it argues that both child and contextual variables interact to produce an invalidating context, which can be further compounded by external forces (e.g., poverty, environmental stressors).

The second component of the invalidating environment theory posits that caregivers intermittently reinforce extreme and intense emotional expression via a number of problematic interaction patterns. For instance, Linehan (1993) first observed that invalidating contexts often consist of caregivers who ignore, do not tolerate, or inadvertently punish mild to moderate displays of emotional expressions, yet extreme emotional displays tend to elicit particular attention. In other words, the child learns that extreme displays of emotions garner attention from caregivers, regardless of whether the attention is positive or negative. Over time, this intermittent reinforcement of extreme emotions results in chronic emotion dysregulation, such that the child is more likely to experience intense negative emotions that are slow to return to baseline.

Coercive processes within the family context are also associated with intermittent reinforcement of problematic emotions and behaviours, particularly aggression and delinquency (Patterson, DeBaryshe, & Ramsey, 1989; Snyder, Schrepferman, & St. Peter, 1997). Similar to Linehan's (1993) theory, coercion theory (Patterson et al., 1989) hypothesizes that aversive and aggressive tactics between parents and child escalate over time due to their effectiveness at reducing similarly aversive behaviours in the interacting partners (i.e., escape conditioning). Children raised in these types of contexts learn that the most successful method for ending disagreement is to escalate conflict, from which the interaction partner on the receiving end is motivated to escape. Over time, these negative operant reinforcement processes result in more extreme escalating behaviours in both children and parents, and consequently reinforce anger, aggression, and emotion dysregulation in the child (Patterson et al., 1989). Furthermore, such behaviours generalize across other contexts (e.g., peers, school, etc.), often resulting in conduct problems (e.g., aggression towards peers; Ostrov, Crick, & Stauffacher, 2006), which further perpetuate hostile parenting practices (Scaramella & Conger, 2003). Coercion theory has historically been applied to conduct and/or antisocial personality disorder development in impulsive and temperamentally difficult adolescent and young adult males. However, a similar pattern of coercive interactions between caregiver and child has been observed in youth who exhibit BPD traits (e.g., Crowell et al., 2013). This is not surprising, given that antisocial and borderline personality disorder share biological vulnerabilities and contextual risk factors (Beauchaine et al., 2009; Crowell, Yaptangco, & Turner, 2016).

Empirical evidence supports both Linehan's and Patterson's theories as they are applied to the aetiology of BPD. For instance, one recent study demonstrated that family contexts characterized by a lack of support in regulating emotions and higher levels of conflict are associated with adolescent development of emotion dysregulation and SII (Adrian, Zeman, Erdley, Lisa, & Sim, 2011). Similarly, Stepp et al. (2014) assessed children aged 5–8 and their parents annually over a nine-year period and found moderate associations between child BPD symptoms and increases in harsh parenting behaviours. Specifically, as BPD symptom severity waxed and waned over a span of nine years, so too did the practice of harsh parenting behaviours. Further, the authors demonstrated a reciprocal association between adolescent-reported harsh punishment and low caregiver warmth and adolescent BPD symptoms.

These processes have also been observed in laboratory settings. In a recent study, we examined mother-daughter dyads in self-injuring adolescents and healthy controls. Participants were instructed to engage in a mother-daughter conflict discussion. Dyadic interactions were coded using both global and microanalytic systems, which allowed for a highly detailed characterization of mother-daughter interactions. We found that, compared to control dyads, self-injuring dyads were more likely to escalate conflict and more importantly, de-escalation of conflict occurred only once one member of the dyad became highly dysregulated (Crowell et al., 2013). More recently, we examined similar mother-daughter interaction patterns in a different sample using nonlinear dynamic systems approaches designed to detect causal processes in timeseries data (Crowell et al., 2017). Interestingly, we found that mothers' behaviour had a driving effect on both behaviour and psychophysiological responses of self-injuring adolescents, whereas the converse was not true (i.e., daughters' behaviour did not drive behavioural or physiological changes in mothers). In depressed dyads, mother behaviour drove teen behaviour but not physiological responses and typical controls demonstrated no driving effects. Taken together, these results suggest that self-injuring and depressed teens are more sensitive than controls and that self-injuring youth may be especially sensitive to parental inputs (Crowell et al., 2017).

In yet another study, Whalen et al. (2014) demonstrated parent-child interaction patterns that might confer risk for *or* protection against long-term risk for BPD. The authors examined parent-child dyads in the laboratory using a similar conflict discussion task in a sample of at-risk youth and then examined associations between coded interactions and BPD symptom development prospectively over a two-year period (ages 15 through 17). Findings indicated that positive maternal affective behaviour (e.g., supportive/validating behaviour, effective communication skills, etc.) and positive dyadic affective behaviours (e.g., positive escalation, general satisfaction with interaction, etc.) predicted decreases in BPD severity scores over time. Furthermore, they found that dyadic negative escalation (e.g., negative escalation, dissatisfaction with interaction, etc.) was associated with overall higher levels of adolescent BPD symptom severity scores, though this effect was not found for negative maternal affective behaviours. Thus, subtle transactions characterized by invalidation and coercion can be captured in laboratory contexts and are predictive of BPD development over time.

The final component of the invalidating environment theory is that emotion dysregulation among adolescents becomes increasingly stable over time and across contexts, leading to BPD and other severe forms of psychopathology. Although there are many methods for assessing emotion dysregulation, psychophysiological response patterns are especially interesting because they occur rapidly in response to environmental inputs and they fall largely outside of conscious awareness. One of the most widely used psychophysiological measures is respiratory sinus arrhythmia (RSA), which is thought to be a biomarker for emotion regulation abilities (see Beauchaine, 2012). Across numerous studies, low resting RSA is associated with psychopathology, social impairments, emotional inflexibility, and poor capabilities to modulate emotional responses (see Price & Crowell, 2016 for a review). Although further research is needed to determine how emotion dysregulation and low RSA are shaped across development, there is now consistent evidence of low RSA in self-injuring adolescents (Crowell et al., 2006) and adults with BPD (Koenig, Kemp, Feeling, Thayer, & Kaess, 2016). Although we have found that child RSA is associated with parent behaviours, such as aversiveness during conflict (Crowell et al., 2013; 2014), prospective research examining parent-child interactions, emotion dysregulation, RSA, and BPD traits is sorely needed.

Risk Factors for Invalidating Developmental Contexts

Invalidating environments are a product of transactions between an at-risk child and environmental risks, especially the caregiver-child dynamic. Nonetheless, there are known individual-level (i.e., child and caregiver) and environmental characteristics that may increase the probability of an invalidating developmental context, including child characteristics such as early temperament, inherited vulnerabilities, and externalizing behaviours. On the caregiver side, parental psychopathology and parenting strategies also increase risk for invalidation. Furthermore, poor caregiver-child fit may also confer risk for invalidation.

Child Characteristics

Temperament and Vulnerability Traits. Childhood temperament refers to individual differences across broad domains, such as extraversion/surgency (i.e., outgoing and sociable), negative affectivity, and effortful control (Shiner et al., 2012). Children at risk for BPD may be more likely to exhibit negative affectivity (i.e., tendency to experience shyness, discomfort, sadness, frustration) and low effortful control (i.e., poor self-regulation). Indeed, a recent longitudinal study found that among young girls between the ages of five and eight, high emotionality (i.e., negative affectivity), high activity level (i.e., high energy, disinhibition), low sociability (i.e., hesitant to engage with others), and shyness significantly predicted BPD symptoms between the ages of 14 and 19 (Stepp, Keenan, Hipwell, & Krueger, 2014). As mentioned above, trait impulsivity, trait anxiety, and emotional sensitivity may also confer risk for invalidation. For example, impulsivity could elicit caregiver invalidation by virtue of associated emotional and behavioural problems (i.e., evocative effects). Similarly, children who exhibit negative affectivity and emotional sensitivity may be more likely to perceive, and react intensely to, caregiver behaviours (e.g., Crowell et al., 2017). Thus, vulnerable children may have emotional needs that exceed caregiver capacity, increasing risk for invalidation (Crowell et al., 2009).

Externalizing Symptoms. Children diagnosed with externalizing disorders (e.g., Attention Deficit Hyperactivity Disorder (ADHD), Conduct Disorder (CD), and Oppositional Defiant Disorder (ODD)) are at significant risk for developing BPD (Beauchaine, Klein, Crowell, Derbridge, & Gatzke-Kopp, 2009; Fossati et al., 2015; Hinshaw et al., 2012; Stepp, Burke, Hipwell, & Loeber, 2012). Importantly, these disorders share features that might contribute to contextual risk, including neurocognitive impairment, behavioural and emotional problems, anger and hostility, and academic problems (Anckarsäter et al., 2006; Harty, Miller, Newcorn, & Halperin, 2009; Minde et al., 2003). Several longitudinal studies underscore the association between child and adolescent externalizing disorders and BPD. For instance, Stepp and colleagues (2012) used data from the Pittsburgh Girls Study, which oversampled children raised in low SES families, and examined prospective associations between childhood externalizing disorders (i.e., ADHD and ODD) and BPD symptoms between 8 and 14 years of age. Here, they demonstrated that ADHD and ODD symptoms at age eight predicted BPD symptoms at age 14. Furthermore, the rate of growth change in ADHD symptoms between eight and ten and ODD symptoms between 10 and 14 predicted BPD symptoms. Therefore, even though only a fraction of children diagnosed with ADHD and/or ODD later develop BPD, externalizing symptoms are a clear risk factor for later personality disorder traits (see also Crowell & Kaufman, 2016a).

Caregiver Characteristics

Parental Psychopathology. Parental psychopathology is a common correlate of youth with borderline traits and may increase risk for the disorder. Longitudinal research examining parental psychopathology as a predictor of child BPD is limited. However, there is a large and growing literature examining child outcomes for *mothers* with BPD, with less attention on fathers. For example, Eyden, Winsper, Wolke, Broome, and MacCallum (2016) recently conducted a systematic review of 33 studies investigating parenting behaviours of mothers with BPD and found that, relative to mothers without BPD, mothers with the disorder tended to engage in maladaptive parenting behaviours (e.g., more insensitive, intrusive, overprotective, hostile, less engaged, etc.). The authors hypothesize that maternal emotion dysregulation may be a mechanism underlying problematic parenting behaviours. Antisocial and mood disorder features in caregivers have also been linked with externalizing and internalizing disorders in offspring

(Kaufman et al., 2017; Repetti, Taylor, & Seeman, 2002), and parental substance abuse has been specifically linked with BPD symptoms in offspring (Stepp, Olino, Klein, Seeley, & Lewinsohn, 2013). Several factors might explain transmission of internalizing and externalizing problems between caregiver and offspring. Specifically, parental psychopathology could confer risk via propensity to invalidate, misunderstand, or neglect emotional responses of the child. In addition, parents with emotion regulation difficulties, BPD, or Anti-Social Personality Disorder (ASPD), may be more likely to negatively reinforce emotional reactivity via conflict escalation and coercive parenting tactics (Stepp et al., 2013).

Parenting Practices. Evidence suggests that parenting practices, family emotional climate, and modelling may interact with parent and child vulnerabilities to confer risk for emotion dysregulation and psychopathology (e.g., Morris, Silk, Steinberg, Myers, & Robinson, 2007). Furthermore, inconsistent discipline and parental involvement is associated with increased severity of childhood ADHD symptoms over time (Ellis & Nigg, 2009; Lindahl, 1998; Ullsperger, Nigg, & Nikolas, 2016), independent of associated conduct problems (Hawes, Dadds, Frost, & Russell, 2013). Similarly, in a study examining a parenting intervention, children had better outcomes when their mothers decreased inconsistent and inattentive parenting (Muratori et al., 2015). The Children in the Community Study (CIC; Cohen, Crawford, Johnson, & Kasen, 2005), which prospectively examined personality disorder development in community adolescents followed into adulthood, found that maternal inconsistency predicted the development and maintenance of BPD 2.5 years later (Bezirganian, Cohen, & Brook, 1993).

Overprotective and over-controlling parenting styles may also contribute to invalidation. Recent research has focused on the concept of parental psychological control, or parenting behaviours characterized by problematic contingencies that function to shape child behaviour. These contingencies are problematic because while they can serve to control behaviour early in development, they inhibit later emotional development and strain the caregiver-child relationship in the long-term (Barber, Olsen, & Shagle, 1994). Further, the contingencies may not be entirely clear to the child, in part because they often contrast with normative development of agency and autonomy in the child. These parenting behaviours may include withholding warmth and affection and/or eliciting guilt and shame at times when the child expresses normative autonomous behaviour. Often, these contingencies are enforced with overprotective, overly critical, and intrusive parenting behaviours. Parental psychological control has been consistently linked with internalizing and externalizing disorders in childhood and adolescence (Barber et al., 1994; Kuppens, Laurent, Heyvaert, & Onghena, 2013; Nanda, Kotchick, & Grover, 2012). One longitudinal study investigated whether temperamental traits (i.e., harm avoidance and novelty seeking), child psychopathology, and perceived parenting style in 15-year-old children contributed to BPD symptoms five years later (Arens, Grabe, Spitzer, and Barnow, 2011). The authors found that internalizing disorders and Harm Avoidance × Overprotective Parenting predicted BPD. Thus, parental psychological control may be relevant to BPD development.

Parenting behaviours characterized by excessive and harsh punishment have long been associated with the subsequent development of externalizing psychopathology in offspring. For instance, one meta-analysis found that higher levels of physical punishment were associated with significant increases in child conduct problems (Gershoff, 2002). Although prior work has examined antisocial and conduct problems in males at risk for ASPD, recent research has also uncovered a similar pattern for BPD. For example, a recent prospective investigation by Hallquist, Hipwell, & Stepp (2015) demonstrated that parenting behaviours associated with harsh parenting, poor self-control, and negative emotionality prospectively predicted BPD symptoms in adolescent girls. These findings are corroborated by another longitudinal study indicating that parenting behaviours characterized by low warmth and harsh punishment prospectively predicted a BPD diagnosis in adulthood (Winsper, Zanarini, and Wolke, 2012).

Caregiver-Child Fit

Poor fit between the caregiver and child may also contribute to invalidating contexts. Indeed, Linehan (1993) theorized that many different types of families can become invalidating. For example, a child with low individual-level vulnerability may still experience invalidation within a family context that is extremely taxed and unable to meet the child's emotional needs (e.g., financial difficulties, serious chronic illness within the family, etc.). Alternatively, caregivers who are relatively untaxed and skillful, but nonetheless lack the parenting resources to meet the needs of an extremely sensitive and highly demanding child may also inadvertently foster an invalidating developmental context. Although research on caregiver-child fit is limited, one prospective study demonstrated that, among other variables, family life stress prospectively predicted BPD symptoms at age 28 (Carlson, Egeland, & Sroufe, 2009). Hence, risk for invalidating developmental contexts and BPD varies widely as a function of unique combinations of external factors and individual-level characteristics of both parent and child.

REDUCING CONTEXTUAL RISK FOR
BPD: DIALECTICAL BEHAVIOUR THERAPY

DBT has been adapted to treat self-injurious and suicidal behavior in adolescents (Miller, Rathus, & Linehan, 2006). A thorough review of adolescent DBT (DBT-A) is provided in Rathus, Miller, and Bonavitacola in Chapter 25 of this volume (see also MacPherson, Cheavens, & Fristad, 2013 for thorough review). At its core, adolescent DBT-A incorporates the same principles and tenets as traditional DBT (e.g., behavioural science, Zen practice, etc.). Furthermore, the modes and functions of DBT-A are virtually the same as the adult version, such that the treatment incorporates individual therapy, skills group, telephone coaching, and a therapist consultation team. However, because DBT-A was adapted to be developmentally appropriate, there are noteworthy differences. For instance, just as all other DBT-informed treatments emphasize the biosocial theory in case formulation and treatment, the same is true for DBT-A. Accordingly, a significant aspect of the treatment targets the adolescent's family environment, which typically involves the invalidating and coercive processes reviewed in the previous section, in addition to the adolescent's own vulnerabilities (e.g., emotion dysregulation, maladaptive coping). The central task of this intervention is to shape the adolescent to use his or her own skills to cope with challenges within a supportive environment that reinforces adaptive, skillful behaviour and extinguishes maladaptive behaviours. In other words, DBT-A seeks to address the problematic biology × environment interactions that confer risk for adult BPD.

One of the most important adaptations for DBT-A is the inclusion of the multi-family skills group component. Multi-family skills group is structured to address both sides of the biology × environment transactions that confer risk for adult BPD. Skills modules that address individual vulnerabilities include mindfulness, emotion regulation, distress tolerance, and interpersonal effectiveness. These modules are also taught in the adult version of DBT. Importantly, the skills covered in the multi-family skills group are useful for both parents and adolescents, both with respect to their relationships with one another as well as for addressing their own private issues that might affect the environment in various ways. For instance, one important element of DBT-A is teaching parents and adolescents to replace invalidating and coercive strategies with those more conducive to positive parent-child interactions (e.g., validation, dialectics, behavioural principles, etc.). These skills are applied and reinforced in family sessions involving the individual therapist, adolescent, and parents, which typically occur on a regular basis (e.g., once every four individual sessions for part of a session).

Parent Coaching

In some cases, the parent-child dynamic is so problematic that family sessions devolve rapidly into conflict. In other cases, one member of the parent-child dyad is highly critical while the other is highly sensitive, which can lead to one-sided attempts at problem solving that fail to generalize outside of the therapy room. Sometimes two parents disagree about their parenting approach, are struggling with their own psychological distress, or have never experienced the benefits of parenting support. These are just some of the circumstances in which parent coaching would be preferred over intermittent contact with the adolescent's primary therapist. The goal of parent coaching is to support caregivers in their efforts to generalize skills outside of the therapy room and into the relationship with their child. To our knowledge, there have been no empirical tests of parent coaching as an adjunctive DBT treatment, in spite of calls to include loved ones in treatment (see e.g., Crowell, 2016). Therefore, the principles of parent coaching are largely derived from clinical expertise and the theoretical framework of DBT-A (e.g., adolescent-family dialectical dilemmas; Miller, Rathus, & Linehan, 2006). Broadly speaking, key components of parent coaching include: strengthening the parent-child relationship through val-idation and conflict de-escalation, maintaining consistent expectations and rules and enforcing the rules through predictable contingencies, reducing individual parent vulnerabilities through self-care and regular skills use, and strengthening the couple relationship (where applicable). Parent coaching allows caregivers to stay in-volved in treatment while allowing the adolescent to maintain a special and confi-dential relationship with their therapist. Thus, coaching is especially useful in cases where a parent is reaching out to the primary therapist more often than the adoles-cent or when occasional sessions are otherwise insufficient to meet parent needs. For other key components of DBT-A and how it targets invalidating environments, see Chapter 25 by Rathus et al., this volume.

IMPLICATIONS AND FUTURE RESEARCH

Taken together, the findings reviewed here indicate that: (1) BPD emerges as a result of high-risk transactions between individual vulnerabilities (e.g., trait impulsivity and trait anxiety) and invalidating developmental contexts; (2) these transactions, such as invali-dation and coercive processes, socialize emotion dysregulation over time; (3) there are child and caregiver characteristics that may increase the probability of an invalidating environment; and (4) DBT for adolescents and families offers an opportunity to directly intervene in the invalidating environment, minimize blame, and reduce contextual risk for adult BPD. Nonetheless, there are important limitations in our understanding of how invalidating environments confer risk for BPD. First, while there has been an increase in longitudinal evidence on the development of BPD, to our knowledge, no prospective research has directly examined the full biosocial model of BPD develop-ment. Instead, most studies have only addressed one or several hypotheses rather than the model in its entirety. Further, prior longitudinal studies have relied on methods that limit our capacity to draw conclusions about the complex biology × environment trans-actions inherent in the biosocial model.

Second, our review of the literature was almost exclusive to the invalidating *family* context. However, as briefly mentioned, there are other forms of invalidation that likely predict the development of BPD. For instance, although there has been a substantial amount of research conducted on childhood sexual abuse, we know very little about in-validation on the societal level and its impact on the development of BPD. In particular, recent epidemiological studies indicate that sexual minority status in adolescence is predictive of SII and suicide completion, above and beyond other factors (Stone et al., 2014). In fact, suicide is the leading cause of death among sexual minorities between the ages of 10 and 24. Further, sexual minority youth are six times more likely to com-plete suicide relative to non-sexual minority youth (Stone et al., 2014). Future research should investigate the extent to which societal invalidation contributes to unfortu-nate and life-threatening outcomes among this population, as well as other minority groups who may be likely to experience this type of invalidation (e.g., racial/ethnic minorities, etc.).

Third, additional research should examine the influence that early adolescent peer relationships have on the development of maladaptive emotion regulation/avoidance strategies that typically emerge in late adolescence. Biology × environment transactions occur within *and* outside of the family environment. For instance, we know from prior research that at-risk adolescents tend to socialize with other at-risk peers (i.e., delinquent peer group formation; Beaver, Wright, & DeLisi, 2008). Further, such peer groups influence the likelihood that at-risk adolescents will initiate maladaptive behaviours (e.g., SII; You, Zheng, Lin, & Leung, 2016). However, mechanisms by which these relationships confer additive risk for maladaptive behaviours are less clear. In particular, studies that investigate susceptibility and contagion of peer behaviours (e.g., SII) could improve our efforts to reduce contextual risk for BPD.

In conclusion, there has been significant progress in research investigating contextual risk for BPD over the past decade. Although the biosocial theory is just one of several theoretical frameworks that outlines the development and course of BPD, the findings reviewed in this chapter lend support to the assumption that invalidating environments, in combination with individual vulnerabilities, confer risk for adult psychopathology. BPD has historically been labelled as a pervasive, treatment-resistant condition that emerges in adulthood. However, empirical data contradict these long-held assumptions. In fact, BPD may not only be treatable but also perhaps preventable, particularly if evidence-based interventions are implemented earlier in the course of the BPD trajectory. In other words, early identification of risk factors and precursors to BPD is absolutely critical and these indicators often appear much earlier than adulthood. Given the findings reviewed herein, interventions that target contextual risk (e.g., invalidating family environments), in addition to individual-level risk factors, may be particularly effective.

KEY POINTS FOR CLINICIANS

- Borderline personality disorder (BPD) emerges as a result of high-risk transactions between inherited vulnerabilities, such as trait impulsivity, and invalidating developmental contexts.

- These transactions, which are characterized by invalidation and coercive processes, socialize emotion dysregulation over time and across development.

- Emerging research has identified certain child and caregiver characteristics that increase risk for an invalidating developmental context. However, mismatch between the needs of the child and that of his or her caregiver's abilities may also contribute to invalidation.

- Dialectical Behavior Therapy (DBT) for at-risk adolescents and families offers an opportunity to intervene on the invalidating environment and reduce contextual risk for adult BPD.

REFERENCES

Adrian, M., Zeman, J., Erdley, C., Lisa, L., & Sim, L. (2011). Emotional dysregulation and interpersonal difficulties as risk factors for nonsuicidal self-injury in adolescent girls. *Journal of Abnormal Child Psychology, 39,* 389–400.

Anckarsäter, H., Stahlberg, O., Larson, T., Hakansson, C., Jutblad, S. B., Niklasson, L., . . . Gillberg, C. (2006). The impact of ADHD and autism spectrum disorders on temperament, character, and personality development. *American Journal of Psychiatry, 163,* 1239–1244.

Arens, E. A., Grabe, H. J., Spitzer, C., & Barnow, S. (2011). Testing the biosocial model of borderline personality disorder: Results of a prospective 5-year longitudinal study. *Personality and Mental Health, 5,* 29–42.

Baer, R. A., Peters, J. R., Eisenlohr-Moul, T. A., Geiger, P. J., & Sauer, S. E. (2012). Emotion-related cognitive processes in borderline personality disorder: a review of the empirical literature. *Clinical Psychology Review, 32,* 359–369.

Ball, J. S., & Links, P. S. (2009). Borderline personality disorder and childhood trauma: evidence for a causal relationship. *Current Psychiatry Reports, 11*(1), 63–68.

Barber, B. K., Olsen, J. E., & Shagle, S. C. (1994). Associations between parental psychological and behavioral control and youth internalized and externalized behaviors. *Child Development, 65,* 1120–1136.

Beauchaine, T. P. (2012). Physiological markers of emotion and behavior dysregulation in externalizing psychopathology. *Monographs of the Society for Research in Child Development, 77,* 79–86.

Beauchaine, T. P. (2015). Respiratory sinus arrhythmia: A transdiagnostic biomarker of emotion dysregulation and psychopathology. *Current Opinion in Psychology, 3,* 43–47.

Beauchaine, T. P., & Gatzke-Kopp, L. M. (2012). Instantiating the multiple levels of analysis perspective in a program of study on externalizing behavior. *Development and Psychopathology, 24,* 1003–1018.

Beauchaine, T. P., Hinshaw, S. P., & Pang, K. L. (2010). Comorbidity of attention-deficit/hyperactivity disorder and early-onset conduct disorder: Biological, environmental, and developmental mechanisms. *Clinical Psychology: Science and Practice, 17,* 327–336.

Beauchaine, T. P., Klein, D. N., Crowell, S. E., Derbridge, C., & Gatzke-Kopp, L. (2009). Multifinality in the development of personality disorders: A biology × sex × environment interaction model of antisocial and borderline traits. *Development and Psychopathology, 21,* 735–770.

Beauchaine, T. P., & McNulty, T. (2013). Comorbidities and continuities as ontogenic processes: Toward a developmental spectrum model of externalizing psychopathology. *Development and Psychopathology, 25,* 1505–1528.

Beauchaine, T. P., Zisner, A. R., & Sauder, C. L. (2017). Trait impulsivity and the externalizing spectrum. *Annual Review of Clinical Psychology, 13,* 343–368.

Beaver, K. M., Wright, J. P., & DeLisi, M. (2008). Delinquent peer group formation: Evidence of a gene × environment correlation. *The Journal of Genetic Psychology, 169,* 227–244.

Bezirganian, S., Cohen, P., & Brook, J. S. (1993). The impact of mother-child interaction on the development of borderline personality disorder. *The American Journal of Psychiatry, 150,* 1836–1842.

Bigler, R. S., & Liben, L. S. (2006). A developmental intergroup theory of social stereotypes and prejudice. *Advances in Child Development and Behavior, 34,* 39–89.

Bissonette, G. B., Powell, E. M., & Roesch, M. R. (2013). Neural structures underlying set-shifting: roles of medial prefrontal cortex and anterior cingulate cortex. *Behavioural Brain Research, 250,* 91–101.

Bornovalova, M. A., Huibregtse, B. M., Hicks, B. M., Keyes, M., McGue, M., & Iacono, W. (2013). Tests of a direct effect of childhood abuse on adult borderline personality disorder traits: a longitudinal discordant twin design. *Journal of Abnormal Psychology*, *122*, 180.

Bridgett, D. J., Burt, N. M., Edwards, E. S., & Deater-Deckard, K. (2015). Intergenerational transmission of self-regulation: A multidisciplinary review and integrative conceptual framework. *Psychological Bulletin*, *141*, 602–654.

Carlson, E. A., Egeland, B., & Sroufe, L. A. (2009). A prospective investigation of the development of borderline personality symptoms. *Development and Psychopathology*, *21*, 1311–1334.

Carlson, E. B., Furby, L., Armstrong, J., & Shlaes, J. (1997). A conceptual framework for the long-term psychological effects of traumatic childhood abuse. *Child Maltreatment*, *2*, 272–295.

Caspi, A., & Silva, P. A. (1995). Temperamental qualities at age three predict personality traits in young adulthood: Longitudinal evidence from a birth cohort. *Child Development*, *66*, 486–498.

Cicchetti, D., Ackerman, B. P., & Izard, C. E. (1995). Emotions and emotion regulation in developmental psychopathology. *Development and Psychopathology*, *7*, 1–10.

Cicchetti, D., & Rogosch, F. A. (1996). Equifinality and multifinality in developmental psychopathology. *Development and Psychopathology*, *8*, 597–600.

Cohen, P., Crawford, T. N., Johnson, J. G., & Kasen, S. (2005). The children in the community study of developmental course of personality disorder. *Journal of Personality Disorders*, *19*, 466.

Corr, P. J., & McNaughton N. (2016). Neural mechanisms of low trait anxiety and risk for externalizing behavior. In T. P. Beauchaine & S. P. Hinshaw (Eds.), *The Oxford Handbook of externalizing spectrum disorders* (pp. 220–238). New York, NY: Oxford University Press.

Crowell, S. E. (2016). Biting the hand that feeds: Current opinion on the interpersonal causes, correlates, and consequences of borderline personality disorder. *F1000Research*, *5*.

Crowell, S. E., Baucom, B. R., McCauley, E., Potapova, N. V., Fitelson, M., Barth, H., . . . Beauchaine, T. P. (2013). Mechanisms of contextual risk for adolescent self-injury: Invalidation and conflict escalation in mother–child interactions. *Journal of Clinical Child & Adolescent Psychology*, *42*, 467–480.

Crowell, S. E., Baucom, B. R., Yaptangco, M., Bride, D., Hsiao, R., McCauley, E., & Beauchaine, T. P. (2014). Emotion dysregulation and dyadic conflict in depressed and typical adolescents: Evaluating concordance across psychophysiological and observational measures. *Biological Psychology*, *98*, 50–58.

Crowell, S. E., Beauchaine, T. P., Gatzke-Kopp, L., Sylvers, P. D., Mead, H., & Chipman-Chacon, J. (2006). Autonomic correlates of attention- deficit/hyperactivity disorder and oppositional defiant disorder in pre-school children. *Journal of Abnormal Psychology*, *115*, 174–178.

Crowell, S. E., Beauchaine, T. P., & Linehan, M. M. (2009). A biosocial developmental model of borderline personality: Elaborating and extending Linehan's theory. *Psychological Bulletin*, *135*, 495–510.

Crowell, S. E., Butner, J., Wiltshire, T. J., Munion, A. K., Yaptangco, M., & Beauchaine, T. P. (2017). Evaluating emotional and biological sensitivity to maternal behavior among depressed and self-injuring adolescent girls using nonlinear dynamics. *Clinical Psychological Science*, *5*(2), 272–285.

Crowell, S. E., & Kaufman, E. A. (2016a). Borderline personality disorder and the emerging field of developmental neuroscience. *Personality Disorders: Theory, Research, and Treatment*, *7*, 324–333.

Crowell, S. E., & Kaufman, E. A. (2016b). Development of self-inflicted injury: comorbidities and continuities with borderline and antisocial personality traits. *Development and Psychopathology, 28*, 1071–1088.

Crowell, S. E., Puzia, M. E., & Yaptangco, M. (2015). The ontogeny of chronic distress: Emotion dysregulation across the life span and its implications for psychological and physical health. *Current Opinion in Psychology, 3*, 91–99.

Crowell S. E., Yaptangco M., & Turner, S. L. (2016). Coercion, invalidation, and risk for self-injury and borderline personality traits. In T. J. Dishion and J. J. Snyder (Eds.), *The Oxford Handbook of coercive relationship dynamics* (pp. 182–193). New York, NY: Oxford University Press.

Danforth, J. S., Connor, D. F., & Doerfler, L. A. (2016). The development of comorbid conduct problems in children with ADHD: An example of an integrative developmental psychopathology perspective. *Journal of Attention Disorders, 20*, 214–229.

Dannlowski, U., Stuhrmann, A., Beutelmann, V., Zwanzger, P., Lenzen, T., Grotegerd, D., . . . Lindner, C. (2012). Limbic scars: long-term consequences of childhood maltreatment revealed by functional and structural magnetic resonance imaging. *Biological Psychiatry, 71*, 286–293.

Dixon-Gordon, K. L., Whalen, D. J., Scott, L. N., Cummins, N. D., & Stepp, S. D. (2016). The main and interactive effects of maternal interpersonal emotion regulation and negative affect on adolescent girls' borderline personality disorder symptoms. *Cognitive Therapy and Research, 40*, 381–393.

Doom, J. R., & Gunnar, M. R. (2013). Stress physiology and developmental psychopathology: Past, present, and future. *Development and Psychopathology, 25*, 1359–1373.

Ellis, B., & Nigg, J. (2009). Parenting practices and attention-deficit/hyperactivity disorder: New findings suggest partial specificity of effects. *Journal of the American Academy of Child and Adolescent Psychiatry, 48*, 146–154.

Eyden, J., Winsper, C., Wolke, D., Broome, M. R., & MacCallum, F. (2016). A systematic review of the parenting and outcomes experienced by offspring of mothers with borderline personality pathology: Potential mechanisms and clinical implications. *Clinical Psychology Review, 45*, 85–105.

Forbes, E. E., & Dahl, R. E. (2005). Neural systems of positive affect: Relevance to understanding child and adolescent depression? *Development and Psychopathology, 17*, 827–850.

Ford, J. D., Fraleigh, L. A., Albert, D. B., & Connor, D. F. (2010). Child abuse and autonomic nervous system hyporesponsivity among psychiatrically impaired children. *Child Abuse & Neglect, 34*, 507–515.

Fossati, A., Gratz, K. L., Borroni, S., Maffei, C., Somma, A., & Carlotta, D. (2015). The relationship between childhood history of ADHD symptoms and DSM-IV borderline personality disorder features among personality disordered outpatients: The moderating role of gender and the mediating roles of emotion dysregulation and impulsivity. *Comprehensive Psychiatry, 56*, 121–127.

Fossati, A., Madeddu, F., & Maffei, C. (1999). Borderline personality disorder and childhood sexual abuse: A meta-analytic study. *Journal of Personality Disorders, 13*, 268–280.

Fruzzetti, A. E., Shenk, C., & Hoffman, P. D. (2005). Family interaction and the development of borderline personality disorder: A transactional model. *Development and Psychopathology, 17*, 1007–1030.

Gatzke-Kopp, L. M. (2011). The canary in the coalmine: The sensitivity of mesolimbic dopamine to environmental adversity during development. *Neuroscience & Biobehavioral Reviews, 35*, 794–803.

Gershoff, E. T. (2002). Corporal punishment by parents and associated child behaviors and experiences: A meta-analytic and theoretical review. *Psychological Bulletin, 128*, 539–579.

Gratz, K. L., Latzman, R. D., Tull, M. T., Reynolds, E. K., & Lejuez, C. W. (2011). Exploring the association between emotional abuse and childhood borderline personality features: The moderating role of personality traits. *Behavior Therapy, 42*, 493–508.

Gray, J. A., & McNaughton, N. (2000). *The neuropsychology of anxiety: An enquiry into the functions of the septo-hippocampal system*, 2nd Edition. New York: Oxford University Press.

Gross, C., & Hen, R. (2004). The developmental origins of anxiety. *Nature Reviews Neuroscience, 5*, 545–552.

Hallquist, M. N., Hipwell, A. E., & Stepp, S. D. (2015). Poor self-control and harsh punishment in childhood prospectively predict borderline personality symptoms in adolescent girls. *Journal of Abnormal Psychology, 124*, 549–564.

Harty, S. C., Miller, C. J., Newcorn, J. H., & Halperin, J. M. (2009). Adolescents with childhood ADHD and comorbid disruptive behavior disorders: Aggression, anger, and hostility. *Child Psychiatry & Human Development, 40*, 85–97.

Hawes, D. J., Dadds, M. R., Frost, A. D., & Russell, A. (2013). Parenting practices and prospective levels of hyperactivity/inattention across early-and middle-childhood. *Journal of Psychopathology and Behavioral Assessment, 35*, 273–282.

Hinshaw, S. P., Owens, E. B., Zalecki, C., Huggins, S. P., Montenegro-Nevado, A. J., Schrodek, E., & Swanson, E. N. (2012). Prospective follow-up of girls with attention-deficit/hyperactivity disorder into early adulthood: Continuing impairment includes elevated risk for suicide attempts and self-injury. *Journal of Consulting and Clinical Psychology, 80*, 1041–1051.

Johnson, J. G., Cohen, P., Chen, H., Kasen, S., & Brook, J. S. (2006). Parenting behaviors associated with risk for offspring personality disorder during adulthood. *Archives of General Psychiatry, 63*, 579–587.

Kagan, J. (2013). Behavioral inhibition as a temperamental vulnerability to psychopathology. In T. B. Beauchaine & S. H. Hinshaw (Eds.), *Child and adolescent psychopathology* (pp. 227–250). Hoboken, NJ: Wiley.

Kaufman, E. A., Puzia, M. E., Mead, H. K., Crowell, S. E., McEachern, A., & Beauchaine, T. P. (2017). Children's emotion regulation difficulties mediate the association between maternal borderline and antisocial symptoms and youth behavior problems over 1 year. *Journal of Personality Disorders, 31*, 170–192.

Koenig, J., Kemp, A. H., Feeling, N. R., Thayer, J. F., & Kaess, M. (2016). Resting state vagal tone in borderline personality disorder: A meta-analysis. *Progress in Neuro-Psychopharmacology and Biological Psychiatry, 64*, 18–26.

Kuppens, S., Laurent, L., Heyvaert, M., & Onghena, P. (2013). Associations between parental psychological control and relational aggression in children and adolescents: A multilevel and sequential meta-analysis. *Developmental Psychology, 49*, 1697–1712.

Lindahl, K. M. (1998). Family process variables and children's disruptive behavior problems. *Journal of Family Psychology, 12*, 420–436.

Linehan, M. M. (1993). *Cognitive behavioral treatment of borderline personality disorder*. New York: Guilford.

MacPherson, H. A., Cheavens, J. S., & Fristad, M. A. (2013). Dialectical behavior therapy for adolescents: Theory, treatment adaptations, and empirical outcomes. *Clinical Child and Family Psychology Review, 16*, 59–80.

Malinosky-Rummell, R., & Hansen, D. J. (1993). Long-term consequences of childhood physical abuse. *Psychological Bulletin, 114*, 68–79.

Meyer, I. H. (2003). Prejudice, social stress, and mental health in lesbian, gay, and bisexual populations: Conceptual issues and research evidence. *Psychological Bulletin, 129*, 674–697.

Miller, A. L., Rathus, J. H., & Linehan, M. M. (2006). *Dialectical behavior therapy with suicidal adolescents.* New York: Guilford Press.

Minde, K., Eakin, L., Hechtman, L., Ochs, E., Bouffard, R., Greenfield, B., & Looper, K. (2003). The psychosocial functioning of children and spouses of adults with ADHD. *Journal of Child Psychology and Psychiatry, 44*, 637–646.

Morris, A. S., Silk, J. S., Steinberg, L., Myers, S. S., & Robinson, L. R. (2007). The role of the family context in the development of emotion regulation. *Social Development, 16*, 361–388.

Muratori, P., Bertacchi, I., Giuli, C., Lombardi, L., Bonetti, S., Nocentini, A., . . . Lochman, J. E. (2015). First adaptation of Coping Power Program as a classroom-based prevention intervention on aggressive behaviors among elementary school children. *Prevention Science, 16*, 432–439.

Nanda, M. M., Kotchick, B. A., & Grover, R. L. (2012). Parental psychological control and childhood anxiety: The mediating role of perceived lack of control. *Journal of Child and Family Studies, 21*, 637–645.

Ostrov, J. M., Crick, N. R., & Stauffacher, K. (2006). Relational aggression in sibling and peer relationships during early childhood. *Journal of Applied Developmental Psychology, 27*, 241–253.

Otto, B., Misra, S., Prasad, A., & McRae, K. (2014). Functional overlap of top-down emotion regulation and generation: An fMRI study identifying common neural substrates between cognitive reappraisal and cognitively generated emotions. *Cognitive, Affective, & Behavioral Neuroscience, 14*, 923–938.

Patterson, G. R., DeBaryshe, B. D., & Ramsey, E. (1989). *A developmental perspective on antisocial behavior* (Vol. *44*, No. 2, p. *329*). Washington, DC: American Psychological Association.

Pollak, S. D., Cicchetti, D., Hornung, K., & Reed, A. (2000). Recognizing emotion in faces: Developmental effects of child abuse and neglect. *Developmental Psychology, 36*, 679–688.

Price, C. J., and Crowell, S. E. (2016) Respiratory sinus arrhythmia as a potential measure in substance use treatment–outcome studies. *Addiction, 11*, 615–625.

Reich, D. B., & Zanarini, M. C. (2008). Sexual orientation and relationship choice in borderline personality disorder over ten years of prospective follow-up. *Journal of Personality Disorders, 22*, 564.

Repetti, R. L., Taylor, S. E., & Seeman, T. E. (2002). Risky families: Family social environments and the mental and physical health of offspring. *Psychological Bulletin, 128*, 330–366.

Ridgeway, C. L. (2006). Linking social structure and interpersonal behavior: A theoretical perspective on cultural schemas and social relations. *Social Psychology Quarterly, 69*, 5–16.

Sauer, S. E., & Baer, R. A. (2010). Validation of measures of biosocial precursors to borderline personality disorder: Childhood emotional vulnerability and environmental invalidation. *Assessment, 17*, 454–466.

Scaramella, L. V., & Conger, R. D. (2003). Intergenerational continuity of hostile parenting and its consequences: The moderating influence of children's negative emotional reactivity. *Social Development, 12*, 420–439.

Selby, E. A., Braithwaite, S. R., Joiner, T. E. Jr, & Fincham, F. D. (2008). Features of borderline personality disorder, perceived childhood emotional invalidation, and dysfunction within current romantic relationships. *Journal of Family Psychology, 22*, 885–893.

Snyder, J., Schrepferman, L., & St. Peter, C. S. (1997). Origins of antisocial behavior negative reinforcement and affect dysregulation of behavior as socialization mechanisms in family interaction. *Behavior Modification, 21*, 187–215.

Soloff, P. H., Lynch, K. G., & Kelly, T. M. (2002). Childhood abuse as a risk factor for suicidal behavior in borderline personality disorder. *Journal of Personality Disorders, 16*, 201–214.

Shiner, R. L., Buss, K. A., McClowry, S. G., Putnam, S. P., Saudino, K. J., & Zentner, M. (2012). What is temperament now? Assessing progress in temperament research on the twenty-fifth anniversary of Goldsmith et al. *Child Development Perspectives, 6*, 436–444.

Stepp, S. D., Burke, J. D., Hipwell, A. E., & Loeber, R. (2012). Trajectories of attention deficit hyperactivity disorder and oppositional defiant disorder symptoms as precursors of borderline personality disorder symptoms in adolescent girls. *Journal of Abnormal Child Psychology, 40*, 7–20.

Stepp, S. D., Keenan, K., Hipwell, A. E., & Krueger, R. F. (2014). The impact of childhood temperament on the development of borderline personality disorder symptoms over the course of adolescence. *Borderline Personality Disorder and Emotion Dysregulation, 1*(1), 18.

Stepp, S. D., Olino, T. M., Klein, D. N., Seeley, J. R., & Lewinsohn, P. M. (2013). Unique influences of adolescent antecedents on adult borderline personality disorder features. *Personality Disorders: Theory, Research, and Treatment, 4*, 223–229.

Stepp, S. D., Whalen, D. J., Pilkonis, P. A., Hipwell, A. E., & Levine, M. D. (2012). Children of mothers with borderline personality disorder: Identifying parenting behaviors as potential targets for intervention. *Personality Disorders: Theory, Research, and Treatment, 3*, 76–91.

Stepp, S. D., Whalen, D. J., Scott, L. N., Zalewski, M., Loeber, R., & Hipwell, A. E. (2014). Reciprocal effects of parenting and borderline personality disorder symptoms in adolescent girls. *Development and Psychopathology, 26*, 361–378.

Stone, D. M., Luo, F., Ouyang, L., Lippy, C., Hertz, M. F., & Crosby, A. E. (2014). Sexual orientation and suicide ideation, plans, attempts, and medically serious attempts: Evidence from local youth risk behavior surveys, 2001–2009. *American Journal of Public Health, 104*, 262–271.

Swartz, J. R. (1999). Dopamine projections and frontal systems function. In B. L. Miller & J. L. Cummings (Eds.), *The human frontal lobes: Functions and disorders* (pp. 159–173). New York, NY: Guilford Press.

Ullsperger, J. M., Nigg, J. T., & Nikolas, M. A. (2016). Does child temperament play a role in the association between parenting practices and child Attention Deficit/Hyperactivity Disorder? *Journal of Abnormal Child Psychology, 44*, 167–178.

van Zutphen, L., Siep, N., Jacob, G. A., Goebel, R., & Arntz, A. (2015). Emotional sensitivity, emotion regulation and impulsivity in borderline personality disorder: A critical review of fMRI studies. *Neuroscience & Biobehavioral Reviews, 51*, 64–76.

Whalen, D. J., Scott, L. N., Jakubowski, K. P., McMakin, D. L., Hipwell, A. E., Silk, J. S., & Stepp, S. D. (2014). Affective behavior during mother–daughter conflict and borderline personality disorder severity across adolescence. *Personality Disorders: Theory, Research, and Treatment, 5*, 88–96.

White, L. K., McDermott, J. M., Degnan, K. A., Henderson, H. A., & Fox, N. A. (2011). Behavioral inhibition and anxiety: The moderating roles of inhibitory control and attention shifting. *Journal of Abnormal Child Psychology, 39*, 735–747.

Winsper, C., Zanarini, M., & Wolke, D. (2012). Prospective study of family adversity and maladaptive parenting in childhood and borderline personality disorder symptoms in a nonclinical population at 11 years. *Psychological Medicine, 42*, 2405–2420.

You, J., Zheng, C., Lin, M. P., & Leung, F. (2016). Peer group impulsivity moderated the individual-level relationship between depressive symptoms and adolescent nonsuicidal self-injury. *Journal of Adolescence, 47*, 90–99.

Zanarini, M. C., Gunderson, J. G., Marino, M. F., Schwartz, E. O., & Frankenburg, F. R. (1989). Childhood experiences of borderline patients. *Comprehensive Psychiatry, 30*, 18–25.

Zisner, A., & Beauchaine, T. P. (2016). Midbrain neural mechanisms of trait impulsivity. In T. P. Beauchaine & S. P. Hinshaw (Eds.), *The Oxford Handbook of externalizing spectrum disorders* (pp. 184–200). New York, NY: Oxford University Press.

CHAPTER 4

BEHAVIOURAL FOUNDATIONS OF DBT

Applying Behavioural Principles to the Challenge of Suicidal Behaviour and Non-suicidal Self-injury

ALEXANDER L. CHAPMAN

THE DEVELOPMENT AND THEORETICAL FOUNDATIONS OF DBT

A transaction of theory, science, and clinical experience influenced the development of DBT. When Dr. Marsha Linehan originally set out to develop a treatment to help complex, highly suicidal individuals, she began with the existing state of the art. At the time, the state of the art was cognitive-behavioural therapy (CBT), informed by the "cognitive revolution" and behavioural principles established and refined over a century of theoretical and treatment development. Although CBT might be considered an uneasy marriage of theoretical perspectives (Farmer & Chapman, 2008), evidence has amassed that CBT is efficacious for a variety of clinical problems (Hofmann, Asnaani, Vonk, Sawyer, & Fang, 2012).

In applying CBT with highly suicidal, complex clients, Linehan discovered some of the pitfalls of a largely change-oriented treatment paradigm. Although treatment led to behaviour change, complex, multi-problem clients often had difficulty accepting the message that they simply need to change their thinking and behaviour in order to develop less painful lives. Clients sometimes experienced this approach as invalidating and overly simplistic (i.e., a simple solution for what they experienced as unbearable, complex suffering). While CBT appeared potentially effective, it was not acceptable enough to implement on a broad scale with complex, highly suicidal individuals with borderline personality disorder (BPD).

To address these limitations of existing approaches, Linehan (1993a) sought ways to incorporate perspectives (dialectical theory, see Chapter 6) and practices (mindfulness, zen practice, acceptance, see Chapter 5) to convey acceptance and help clients accept themselves. A growing emphasis on the balance and synthesis of acceptance and change emerged and was found to be effective. DBT evolved into something akin to an expert martial artist skillfully adapting to different self-defence situations. The martial artist must continually remain focused and adapt to the behaviour of her or his opponent or sparring partner. At times, the most effective approach might be to engage in a preemptive strike or counter the opponent's attack in a forceful manner. At other times, it can be effective to go with the flow, allowing the partner to attack while deflecting, evading, and redirecting, or to simply step back and observe. The expert martial artist also moves back and forth between a loose, relaxed muscle state, and quick, explosive movements. Indeed, relaxed muscles move more quickly than tense muscles when speed is of the essence. Similarly, the DBT therapist toggles back and forth between acceptance and change-oriented skills and strategies, at times stepping back, observing, assessing, and conveying acceptance, and at other times, moving in to help the client change behaviour. Zen practice and dialectical principles guide the use of acceptance, helping the therapist flexibly navigate the sometimes complex and challenging behaviour of multi-problem clients. The core principles of body mechanics and physics help the martial artist effectively navigate a variety of practical situations, and to execute the most effective moves when needed. Similarly, the structure and practice of DBT remains rooted in behavioural theory and science.

Just as the knowledge of when and why to use a "hard" versus "soft" approach helps the martial artist adapt to different situations, zen practice and dialectics work together with behavioural theory in DBT. As with behavioural theory, zen practice emphasizes the present, concrete experience, observable behaviour, and the transient nature of self and identity. Dialectical theory is a transactional world view suggesting that identity and truth are both absolute and relative, similar to the contextual view of "truth" and the inseparability of behaviour and context in behavioural theory (see Hayes & Brownstein, 1986; Skinner, 1953). Given that many of the challenges faced by complex clients involve difficulties understanding and regulating emotions, emotion theory and science also inform DBT. Consistent with behavioural theory, contemporary emotion theory and science frames emotional states as multi-component responses with important, practical social-behavioural functions (Gross, 1998, 2013). This view is consistent with a behavioural perspective, in which emotions can be considered responses, antecedents, or consequences of behaviour (Farmer & Chapman, 2016). While the aim of this chapter is not to explicate commonalities across the perspectives underlying DBT, behaviourism, zen practice, dialectics, and emotion science meld effectively within a treatment that is practical, acceptable, and effective.

Behavioural Theory and DBT

Although there are several schools of behavioural theory, the behavioural framework of DBT most closely resembles that of *social behaviourism*, first described by Arthur

Staats and further elaborated in his 1996 book *Behavior and personality: Psychological behaviorism*. As with other behavioural approaches, this framework emphasizes the role of reinforcement contingencies, learning history, and observable environmental events in current behaviour. In comparison with some schools of behaviourism (radical behaviourism, for example), however, psychological behaviourism attempts to integrate a behavioural approach with various areas of psychology (e.g., cognitive, developmental, biological, personality) and more strongly emphasizes the role of classical conditioning, temperament, and biological variables (Chapman & Linehan, 2005; Staats, 1996). Because of this, psychological behaviourism easily accommodates theory and research on emotions and emotion regulation, temperament, and personality.

Psychological behaviourism proposes that "person × environment" transactions occurring throughout an individual's learning history shape basic behavioural repertoires (another way to describe "personality" within this approach; Staats, 1996). These basic behavioural repertoires are a person's characteristic behaviours, emotions, thoughts, and actions in particular contexts, and these repertoires evolve as new learning and experiences accrue. An emotionally vulnerable person raised in an invalidating environment, for example, may have developed a basic behavioural repertoire for situations involving perceived rejection or abandonment. This repertoire might involve emotions of shame and anger and behaviours of contact seeking, intense emotional expression, or withdrawal. Any of these behaviours may have been reinforced during the individual's learning history. Withdrawing from those who are critical or rejecting can be self-protective and result in negative reinforcement (through avoidance of mistreatment or punishment), whereas contact-seeking and escalating emotional expression may be intermittently reinforced through increased support and attention (Linehan, 1993a). Throughout treatment, the individual may learn alternative responses to perceived rejection, such as cognitive reappraisal of the cue for perceived rejection, "checking the facts" (Linehan, 2015), strategies to accept or regulate emotions, relationship-enhancing assertiveness skills, and so on. The behavioural repertoire in situations previously associated with rejection can change in response to new learning.

Consistent with this example, the *biosocial theory* proposes that BPD develops as a result of transactions between a temperament characterized by heightened emotional vulnerability and an environment that invalidates the individual's emotions, thoughts, and actions (Crowell, Beauchaine, & Linehan, 2009; Linehan, 1993a; Chapters 2 and 3, this volume). This transaction results in deficits in the behavioural repertoires or skills required to effectively regulate emotions and navigate interpersonal relationships. The suicidal client with BPD often has developed repertoires characterized by self-damaging escape or avoidance behaviours in the context of strong emotions, perceived rejection, and interpersonal conflict. Close relationships are often both desired and frightening, as the expression of emotions and thoughts were only inconsistently reinforced and periodically punished. Within a DBT framework, due to this transaction of temperament and environment, the individual has not learned the skills needed to understand and regulate emotions and navigate relationships effectively. Thus, the suicidal client with BPD may need to learn and practice new skills regularly in relevant situations. Over time, the basic behavioural repertoires that mark the legacy of her or his learning history and biology can change.

DBT as a Learning-oriented Treatment

Based largely on a behavioural, skills-deficit model to understand complex, multi problem clients, DBT is a learning-oriented treatment. This point can be easily lost. The nature of the clients often treated in DBT might suggest that the treatment focuses primarily on the reduction of imminent and harmful problem behaviours, such as self-injury and suicide attempts. The primary purpose of the treatment, however, is not to reduce harmful behaviours, but rather, to increase behaviours that will facilitate and maintain a life worth living. At the same time, it would be impossible to develop a life worth living without eliminating suicidal behaviour and learning new, life-enhancing behaviours. When it comes to multi-problem clients with BPD, the skill-deficit model of DBT suggests that clients often need to learn how to attend to and live in the present moment (mindfulness skills), understand and regulate emotions (emotion regulation skills), tolerate distress and avoid acting on impulse (distress tolerance skills), and manage interpersonal relationships more effectively (interpersonal effectiveness skills).

These skills typically are taught formally in a structured skills training group (Linehan, 1993a, 2015), but each unique client may need to learn specific behaviours that do not always fall neatly within the skills training curriculum. Some of these might include organization, self-management, navigating specific interpersonal situations (for example, job interviews), and so on. There is, therefore, a balance in DBT of a standardized skills-instruction approach with an idiographic approach targeting challenges and areas of growth for each individual client. This balance is perhaps most challenging to strike in the context of skills training, where there is a structured curriculum and several clients to help at once. The behaviourally oriented DBT therapist, therefore, must be adept at assessing and understanding where clients are on the shaping curve for various skills, what they need to focus on, and how to effectively adapt teaching methods.

AN INTEGRATIVE BEHAVIOURAL FRAMEWORK FOR UNDERSTANDING SUICIDAL AND SELF-INJURIOUS BEHAVIOUR

Behavioural formulations of problem behaviours often emphasize a few key variables. It can be useful to organize these variables within the following categories: antecedents, person variables, behaviours, and consequences (following Farmer & Chapman, 2008,

2016; see also the Stimulus Organism Response Consequences (S-O-R-C) model first described by Goldfried & Davison, 1976). *Antecedents* include conditions that set the occasion for a particular behaviour. *Person variables* include factors such as learning history and individual differences (e.g., temperament, personality). *Behaviours* comprise relevant actions, emotions, and thoughts, often focusing on the target behaviour (e.g., suicidal or self-injury related actions, emotions, and thoughts). Finally, *consequences* involve events following the target behaviour that might increase (reinforcement) or decrease (punishment, extinction) the likelihood that the behaviour will occur again under similar circumstances. This section discusses several factors that fit within each domain in view of contemporary theories and research on self-injury and suicidal behaviour. Figure 4.1 shows how these variables fit together.

Antecedents

Within a behavioral model, antecedents come in a couple of key varieties. *Discriminative stimuli* signal the likelihood of reinforcing or punishing consequences if the individual were to engage in particular actions (Farmer & Chapman, 2016). *Establishing operations*, including conditions that alter the reinforcing effects of particular consequences (Laraway, Snycerski, Michael, & Poling, 2003; Michael, 2000). As an example, discriminative stimuli for a woman who self-injures following a conflict with her partner could include the presence of the partner, the time of day, and so forth. These stimuli may signal that, if she self-injures, the conflict will end, the partner will stop demanding that she search for a job, and support and attention will be forthcoming. Establishing operations, including social isolation or deprivation, might make reinforcers involving attention and support particularly potent.

Antecedents occasioning suicidal or self-injurious behaviours often include those related to stress, psychological, or physical pain (including illness). Research consistently has shown that recent stressors, such as loss of employment or relationships, or diagnoses of chronic illnesses, among other adverse life events, are associated with elevated suicide risk. Similarly, NSSI often is preceded by negative emotional states or events (Chapman, Gratz, & Brown, 2006; Kleindienst et al., 2008; Klonsky, 2007). Joiner's *Interpersonal-Psychological Theory of Suicide* (IPTS; 2005) proposes that two key antecedents include perceived burdensomeness (the perception that one is a burden on others) and thwarted belongingness (e.g., social rejection, exclusion, ostracism, alienation). According to the IPTS model, these factors increase suicide risk by increasing the individual's desire to commit suicide. Similarly, the three-step model of suicide emphasizes these factors as well as the individual's sense of connectedness to others (Klonsky & May, 2015). Within this framework, when connectedness is weaker than pain (physical or psychological), suicidal ideation intensifies. Perceived burdensomeness, lack of connectedness, thwarted belongingness, and psychological or physical pain may function as establishing operations, increasing the value of the reinforcement (e.g., emotional escape or relief; social consequences, such as increased support or attention).

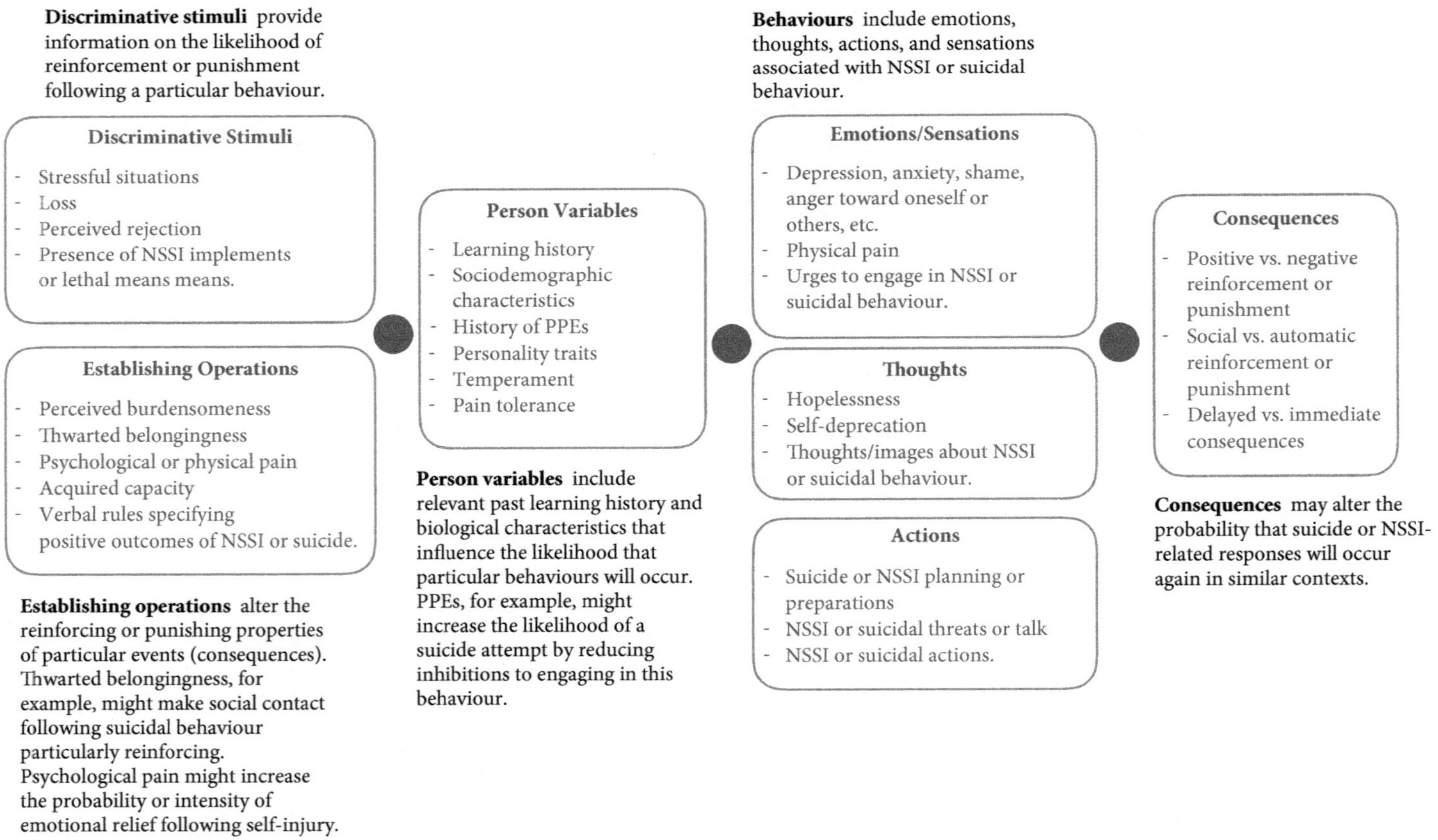

Discriminative stimuli provide information on the likelihood of reinforcement or punishment following a particular behaviour.

Discriminative Stimuli

- Stressful situations
- Loss
- Perceived rejection
- Presence of NSSI implements or lethal means means.

Establishing operations alter the reinforcing or punishing properties of particular events (consequences). Thwarted belongingness, for example, might make social contact following suicidal behaviour particularly reinforcing. Psychological pain might increase the probability or intensity of emotional relief following self-injury.

Establishing Operations

- Perceived burdensomeness
- Thwarted belongingness
- Psychological or physical pain
- Acquired capacity
- Verbal rules specifying positive outcomes of NSSI or suicide.

Person Variables

- Learning history
- Sociodemographic characteristics
- History of PPEs
- Personality traits
- Temperament
- Pain tolerance

Person variables include relevant past learning history and biological characteristics that influence the likelihood that particular behaviours will occur. PPEs, for example, might increase the likelihood of a suicide attempt by reducing inhibitions to engaging in this behaviour.

Behaviours include emotions, thoughts, actions, and sensations associated with NSSI or suicidal behaviour.

Emotions/Sensations

- Depression, anxiety, shame, anger toward oneself or others, etc.
- Physical pain
- Urges to engage in NSSI or suicidal behaviour.

Thoughts

- Hopelessness
- Self-deprecation
- Thoughts/images about NSSI or suicidal behaviour.

Actions

- Suicide or NSSI planning or preparations
- NSSI or suicidal threats or talk
- NSSI or suicidal actions.

Consequences

- Positive vs. negative reinforcement or punishment
- Social vs. automatic reinforcement or punishment
- Delayed vs. immediate consequences

Consequences may alter the probability that suicide or NSSI-related responses will occur again in similar contexts.

FIGURE 4.1 Integrative behavioural model of NSSI and suicidal behaviour.

Person Variables

Person variables include aspects of the individual's learning history, temperament, biological, or other individual characteristics that influence the likelihood of NSSI or suicidal behaviour. When it comes to suicidal behaviour, some of these variables include sociodemographic factors, such as age, sex, socioeconomic status, historical or familial factors, among others (Chapman, Ferreira, & Law, in press). Other person variables might include personality traits, such as impulsivity or neuroticism.

Within Joiner's model, one important person factor includes a history of exposure to painful and provocative events (PPEs) and the resulting development of the *acquired capacity* to enact suicide behaviours. Indeed, not all people who want to commit suicide are capable of enacting a suicide plan. Attempting suicide requires actions that are painful, distressing, and generally opposed to human survival instincts. According to this model, people acquire the capacity to enact suicidal behaviours through learning experiences involving repeated exposure to PPEs. PPEs can include NSSI, extreme sports, serious injuries, exposure to the injury or death of other people (e.g., in combat or through traumatic events), or other events involving bodily damage. Exposure to PPEs reduces the psychological and physical aversiveness of self-inflicted bodily damage; the individual becomes increasingly courageous and willing to carry out the behaviours required to enact a suicide attempt. In behavioural terms, acquired capacity may build in part through processes often associated with exposure therapy for phobias and other anxiety disorders (e.g., inhibitory learning; Craske et al., 2008). Other related person variables in this framework include factors that reduce aversion to suicidal behaviours, such as high pain tolerance.

The DBT approach to suicide, NSSI, and other target behaviours also emphasizes skill deficits as important person variables. People vary in their capacity to engage in behaviours that reduce or prevent risk of NSSI and suicide. Skill deficits may develop through a transaction of individual vulnerabilities (e.g., emotion vulnerability) and developmental environments that do not equip the individual to effectively manage emotions or navigate interpersonal relationships (Crowell et al., 2009; Linehan, 1993a; Chapters 2 and 3, this volume). Some of the skills needed to reduce or prevent NSSI or suicidal behaviour might include recognizing, labelling, and regulating emotions, tolerating distress, solving stressful interpersonal problems, and so forth. The solution often is to first understand the individual client's skill deficits and then to teach and train the client in relevant skills.

Behaviours

Behaviours include actions, thoughts, emotions, and sensations related to suicidal or self-injurious behaviours. Suicide and NSSI-related actions include a broad range of behaviours. Some examples include planning or preparing for suicide or NSSI, researching methods of NSSI or suicide, talking about or threatening to engage in these behaviours, acquiring or increasing access to harmful or lethal means, writing suicide notes, and so on. Some clinicians may prefer to keep NSSI or suicide ideation or urges in the category of antecedents, but for the purposes of this chapter, these are included as behaviours. As discussed later in the chapter, a behavioural orientation requires specificity regarding behaviours. In developing a case formulation of a client's suicidal or NSSI-related behaviours, it is helpful to clearly specify the topography of these actions, in terms of frequency, duration, and intensity.

Consequences

Consequences include events that might reinforce, punish, or extinguish suicide and NSSI-related behaviours. Within the DBT framework, suicidal and self-injurious behaviours function both as solutions to problems and as problems in their own right. Suicide attempts and NSSI often result in negative reinforcement via escape, reduction, or avoidance of emotional pain or other overwhelming or intolerable experiences, such as thoughts or sensations (Baumeister, 1990; Chapman et al., 2006; Gratz, 2003; Gratz, Chapman, Dixon-Gordon, & Tull, 2016; Klonsky, 2007; Reitz et al., 2015). In this way, these behaviours are short-term solutions to the problem of emotional misery and suffering. Self-injurious and suicidal thoughts and behaviours repeatedly occur and periodically are reinforced in distressing situations. In the longer term, suicidal and self-injurious behaviours impede the development of a life that is worth living.

Due to powerfully reinforcing consequences, suicide attempts and NSSI can become over learned and easily prompted in particular contexts. Suicidal, and in particular, self-injurious behaviours, are likely to result in more immediate, reliable reinforcement and require less effort than the skills that the client needs to overcome these behaviours and build a life worth living in the long run. Consistent with the matching principle (Hernstein, 1961), behaviours that reliably result in immediate reinforcement and require minimal effort are more likely to be maintained compared with more effortful behaviours with less consistent immediate consequences. For a client struggling with depression (see Hopko, Lejuez, Ruggiero, & Eifert, 2003; Lejuez, Hopko, & Hopko, 2001, 2002), remaining in bed, for example, is reliably associated with avoidance of discomfort (physical effort, anxiety, etc.) and requires minimal effort. NSSI also can become a low-effort, highly reliable way to achieve immediate negative reinforcement (typically, emotional relief or escape; Brown, Comtois, & Linehan, 2002; Kleindienst et al., 2008). Anecdotally, however, clients periodically report self-injuring without any resulting alleviation of emotional distress or identifiable positively or negatively reinforcing environmental consequences. It is likely, therefore, that these behaviours are subject to intermittent reinforcement schedules, which makes them particularly resistant to extinction.

Other models of NSSI and suicidal behaviour similarly emphasize the functional aspects of these behaviours. Within the Four-Function Model (Nock & Prinstein, 2004), for example, automatic and social forms of positive and negative reinforcement maintain NSSI. The term *automatic* refers to reinforcement occurring internally, such as changes in emotions, thoughts, or sensations. *Social* refers to reinforcement occurring externally, in the social environment. For any self-injuring individual, NSSI might be maintained by a combination of social or automatic reinforcement involving the removal (negative reinforcement) or addition (positive reinforcement) of conditions that increase the likelihood that these behaviours will occur again in similar contexts. Given the preponderance of evidence suggesting that NSSI results in relief from internal states (thoughts, emotions, sensations), the experiential avoidance model of NSSI emphasizes the role of automatic negative reinforcement (Chapman et al., 2006) in the maintenance of this behaviour.

Assessing and Understanding Problem Behaviour

Within DBT, therapists use a behavioral approach to the understanding and treatment of specific behavioural problems. Behavioural approaches to assessment and treatment generally have a few key principles in common. First, the aim of assessment is to generate hypotheses about the factors maintaining the client's behaviour. Each client is unique; thus, the behavioural therapist takes an idiographic approach to understand factors related to the individual client's behaviour. Second, treatment is a hypothesis-testing endeavour. DBT therapists assume that assessment will highlight possible hypotheses and related directions for therapy, but that the effects of therapy ultimately confirm or disconfirm what we think we know about our clients. Third, behavioural approaches involve an iterative interplay of assessment and treatment. The expert martial artist in the earlier example must continually assess and re-assess the situation, respond appropriately, adjust, and adapt. Similarly, the behaviourally oriented DBT therapist continually monitors the effects of treatment and adjusts her or his formulation, generates new hypotheses, and further adjusts treatment in an iterative process. With these principles in mind, this section discusses how DBT therapists can use behavioural assessment to build and refine their conceptualization of NSSI and suicidal behaviour.

Principles for the Use of Chain Analyses in Dialectical Behaviour Therapy

One key way to understand and plan for the treatment of NSSI and suicidal behaviour is to conduct functional or "chain" analyses when these behaviours occur. Fairly specific to DBT, the term "chain analysis" emphasizes the observation that behaviour often occurs within a chain of events. Chain analysis, however, is essentially synonymous with the more widely used behavioural term *functional analysis*. A chain analysis is a detailed assessment of the antecedents, behaviours, and consequences associated with a discrete episode of a problem behaviour. When a client, for example, has self-injured, the therapist and client discuss the events, thoughts, actions, and emotions that preceded NSSI, the topography of the NSSI, and the events or consequences following this behaviour. The purpose and practice of chain analysis in DBT has been described extensively elsewhere (Chapter 13, this volume; Rizvi & Ritschel, 2013); thus, this chapter makes a few key points about chain analysis and focuses on key principles as well as how this assessment strategy can be used to build a behavioural formulation of NSSI or suicidal behaviour.

The aim of a chain analysis is to assess and understand the variables that control and maintain problem behaviours. In this way, chain analyses form the building blocks of an evolving case formulation, help the client and therapist to understand patterns of behavior, and highlight potentially fruitful directions for intervention. Sometimes, however, the key function of chain analysis as an assessment strategy gets lost in clinical practice. Because chain analyses often involve detailed discussions of behaviours that may elicit shame, clinicians sometimes misconstrue or even use chain analyses as aversive consequences for problem behaviour. In institutional settings, following the occurrence of self-injurious or suicidal behaviour, patients sometimes are required to complete chain analysis paperwork immediately, or prior to their next therapy session. Even when the intention is not to use chain analysis as an aversive strategy, this arrangement still has the trappings of a punishment procedure. It is important to remember that the aim of a chain analysis is to collaboratively determine the factors that need to change in order to help the client overcome problem behaviours and move closer to a life worth living.

Based on these considerations, a chain analysis should ideally be conducted in a collaborative manner with awareness of behaviours to increase or reinforce. As a collaborative exploration of behaviour, chain analyses can teach clients important skills needed to reflect on and understand their own behaviour. Ultimately, clients may benefit if they learn to step back and reflect with curiosity on factors that sometimes lead them astray. When clients are engaged in chain analyses, they are actively thinking through and discussing events leading up to or following NSSI or suicide attempts, and observing and describing associated thoughts, emotions, and actions, and so forth. These are important behaviours to reinforce and build throughout therapy. As a result, it is useful to consider how to reinforce the client's engagement in chain analyses. While reinforcement is by definition idiographic, some reinforcing behaviours on the part of the therapist could include collaborative, responsive behaviour, nonjudgmental discussion of problem behaviours and related events, validation of valid aspects of the client's behaviour, encouragement, praise, and so forth (for discussions on the use of therapeutic reinforcement, see Farmer & Chapman, 2016; Kohlenberg & Tsai, 1991).

At the same time, therapists might also consider whether the reinforcers for engaging in the chain analysis may actually reinforce the problem behaviour. It is possible that, for some clients, the opportunity to discuss their experiences and receive attention and support from the therapist might reinforce NSSI or suicidal behaviour.

These consequences are not likely, however, to be the paramount reinforcers for harmful behaviours. Reinforcers occurring close in time to the target behaviour(s) are likely to be most influential. In standard outpatient therapy, however, the client may not see the therapist for several days following an episode of NSSI or suicidal behaviour. The most powerful reinforcers for these behaviours (commonly involving negative reinforcement in the form of escape from aversive emotions, thoughts, or sensations; Chapman et al., 2006; Klonsky, 2007) are likely to occur much more proximally, such as within seconds or minutes. Notwithstanding, it is still possible that therapist behaviours during the next meeting might reinforce suicidal behaviour or NSSI. Indeed, this is the primary rationale for the 24-hour rule, whereby therapists are not available for between-session communication (e.g., phone, email, text messaging) within 24 hours of NSSI or suicidal behaviour (Linehan, 1993a). Therefore, if chain analyses could potentially reinforce these behaviours, the therapist might systematically withdraw reinforcement, for example, by taking on a more matter-of-fact demeanour, subtly withdrawing warmth, being less soothing or validating, and so forth (Linehan, 1993a).

Another important consideration is that chain analyses work best when clients have received adequate orientation to this assessment strategy. It is easy to imagine how challenging and offputting it would be to be interrogated about the minute details of a potentially embarrassing behaviour (e.g., NSSI, suicide attempts) without knowing why. Chain analyses, therefore, are often most effective when the therapist has provided a clear rationale for this assessment strategy, as well as orientation regarding what to expect.

For example, "William" was struggling with severe anxiety, depression, and NSSI. His primary goals were to improve his relationship with his wife and children, and to maintain meaningful employment. He came to his therapy session after having self-injured for the first time in a few weeks. Although his therapist had previously orientated him to the value and procedures of chain analyses, it was still very helpful for the therapist to reorientate William and make the link between the current chain analysis and his therapy goals salient:

> Remember how, when this has happened before, we have done what's called a chain analysis? This involves putting our heads together like detectives to examine in a lot of detail how you ended up going down the path to self-injury this time around. I know that one of your most important goals is to improve your relationship with your wife and your children, and that anxiety and other emotions often have played an important role in your self-injury. While I don't know exactly what happened at this time, if we figure out ways to better manage your emotions, we could make a big difference in your relationship as well. I know that one of the reasons you have wanted to stop cutting yourself is that it really stresses out and worries your wife. You've also mentioned how it's hard for your wife when you get kind of stuck in anxiety and worry, or when you end up withdrawing to the bedroom when you're feeling sad and down. If emotions were involved at all in your self-injury this time around, we might be able to start chipping away at those patterns.

Understanding Behavioural Patterns: Moving from Chain Analysis to Case Formulation

Chain or functional analyses can be used, over time, to refine case formulation and identify key behavioural patterns to target in treatment. A clinician, for example, may have conducted several chain analyses focusing on the same behaviour. Over time, the patterns underlying this behaviour start to emerge, and it becomes clear that a few basic patterns are involved. Once enough chain analyses have been conducted that no new substantial patterns are emerging, it can be useful for the therapist to spend less time assessing and more time engaging in targeting these patterns with problem-solving strategies. This idea of key patterns of behaviour to target is similar to the notion of "basic behavioural repertoires" mentioned earlier and include situations, thoughts, emotions, sensations, actions, and consequences associated with a problem behaviour. Repeated chain or functional analyses can coalesce into a story or description of the client's typical patterns with respect to problem behaviours. Box 4.1, for example, includes a simplified narrative description of one pattern related to William's NSSI, labelled "Self-Injury at Work." See Figure 4.2 for how this pattern might fit into the functional analysis framework described previously. Figure 4.2 also includes suggested interventions for each domain.

THE BEHAVIOURAL FLAVOUR AND STYLE OF DIALECTICAL BEHAVIOUR THERAPY

In addition to guiding ongoing assessment, case formulation, and interventions for self-injurious, suicidal and other problem behaviours, behavioural theory also influences the style and manner in which DBT sessions are conducted. The way the therapist speaks with the client, the activities occurring in a session, and so forth, often reflect DBT's behavioural underpinnings in several ways. Some key aspects of the flavour and style of DBT that are rooted in behavioural principles include (a) non-judgmental behavioural specificity, (b) an engaged, attentive, and mindful therapeutic style, and (c) an emphasis on action.

Non-Judgmental Behavioural Specificity

Behavioural theory emphasizes the importance of specific, observable behavioural targets, often formulated in terms of behavioural excesses or deficits (Farmer & Chapman, 2016; Linehan, 1993a). Accordingly, in DBT, clinicians are expected to formulate and discuss behaviour in a behaviourally specific manner. As mentioned earlier, this often involves clearly specifying the topography of the behaviour in terms of frequency, intensity, and duration. Clearly specifying those behaviours that the client is aiming to increase

Box 4.1   Narrative description of "William's" pattern: Self-injury at work

This pattern typically occurs when William is anticipating an upcoming, regularly scheduled group staff meeting at work. He thinks he is a social misfit, as he doesn't seem to have established close relationships with co-workers in the same way that others have, and he is generally quite shy and reticent around others. He judges himself as socially inept as well. In anticipation of the meeting, he feels anxious about the prospect of talking in front of others, fearful that he will be chastised for inadequate performance, and thinks he will be judged negatively by co-workers (and his boss) during the meeting. He experiences self-deprecating thoughts and related shame. In the few hours leading up to the meeting, William experiences sensations of heat, tension, and tightness in the jaw. He has the thought that he "can't take this" and will "mess up" or embarrass himself if he remains this anxious. He also believes, "If I cut myself, I'll be calmer and more able to get through the meeting." He then experiences urges to self-injure. Sometimes, he considers or engages in alternative coping strategies (breathing, taking a walk, mindfulness), but on occasions when he self-injures, he normally quickly abandons these other strategies and begins to seek implements with which to self-injure. He then usually surreptitiously cuts or scratches himself on his arm or wrist at his cubicle or in the restroom. During cutting, William feels alert and focused on cutting and does not experience anxiety, shame, or anticipatory thoughts about the upcoming meeting. Afterward, he usually feels calm and relaxed. Sometimes, he experiences delayed feelings of guilt or shame, in addition to worry that someone might notice or discover his wounds at work, or that his wife will notice his self-injury when he gets home. He typically feels calm and "mellow" up until the meeting, during which he feels slightly tense but comforted and distracted by the sensations and appearance (sometimes, he quickly takes a look at his wound) of his injury. Later that evening, William's wife sometimes notices a new cut or scar (although he generally conceals his wounds in these situations), expressing frustration and concern. At times, arguments ensue. Relevant aspects of William's learning history include the experience of inconsistent and unpredictable punishment. He described times when he would be sitting and reading a book, and his father would storm in and start yelling at him about tasks he had not done around the house (often, tasks he did not even realize he should be doing). This history appears to have resulted in hypervigilance about possible negative evaluation or behavioural sanctions and fear of others' judgments, increasing his vulnerability to anxious apprehension about meetings. William also has reported that he has generally always been shy and socially awkward (not knowing what to say to other peers or how to strike up conversations) and was often left out of activities in school and occasionally bullied. In terms of temperament or personality, William generally tends to be anxious, inhibited, and risk averse. He also has yet to learn and reliably use effective strategies to manage anxiety, and he also appears to have deficits in skills needed to connect socially with acquaintances. William began self-injuring periodically in his late teens.

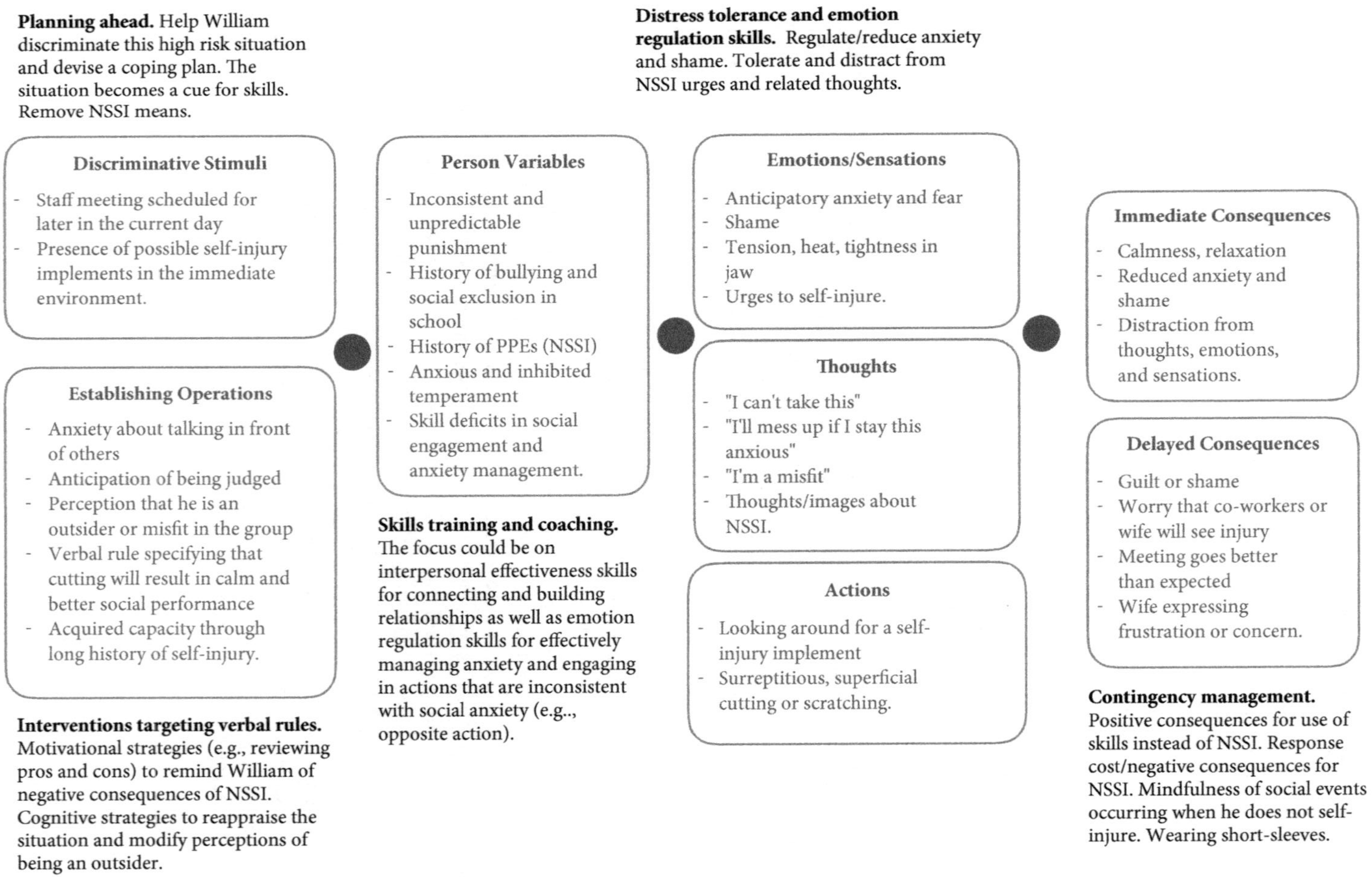

Planning ahead. Help William discriminate this high risk situation and devise a coping plan. The situation becomes a cue for skills. Remove NSSI means.

Distress tolerance and emotion regulation skills. Regulate/reduce anxiety and shame. Tolerate and distract from NSSI urges and related thoughts.

Discriminative Stimuli

- Staff meeting scheduled for later in the current day.
- Presence of possible self-injury implements in the immediate environment.

Person Variables

- Inconsistent and unpredictable punishment
- History of bullying and social exclusion in school
- History of PPEs (NSSI)
- Anxious and inhibited temperament
- Skill deficits in social engagement and anxiety management.

Emotions/Sensations

- Anticipatory anxiety and fear
- Shame
- Tension, heat, tightness in jaw
- Urges to self-injure.

Immediate Consequences

- Calmness, relaxation
- Reduced anxiety and shame
- Distraction from thoughts, emotions, and sensations.

Establishing Operations

- Anxiety about talking in front of others
- Anticipation of being judged
- Perception that he is an outsider or misfit in the group
- Verbal rule specifying that cutting will result in calm and better social performance
- Acquired capacity through long history of self-injury.

Thoughts

- "I can't take this"
- "I'll mess up if I stay this anxious"
- "I'm a misfit"
- Thoughts/images about NSSI.

Delayed Consequences

- Guilt or shame
- Worry that co-workers or wife will see injury
- Meeting goes better than expected
- Wife expressing frustration or concern.

Actions

- Looking around for a self-injury implement
- Surreptitious, superficial cutting or scratching.

Interventions targeting verbal rules. Motivational strategies (e.g., reviewing pros and cons) to remind William of negative consequences of NSSI. Cognitive strategies to reappraise the situation and modify perceptions of being an outsider.

Skills training and coaching. The focus could be on interpersonal effectiveness skills for connecting and building relationships as well as emotion regulation skills for effectively managing anxiety and engaging in actions that are inconsistent with social anxiety (e.g., opposite action).

Contingency management. Positive consequences for use of skills instead of NSSI. Response cost/negative consequences for NSSI. Mindfulness of social events occurring when he does not self-injure. Wearing short-sleeves.

FIGURE 4.2 Case formulation of "William's" pattern: Self-injury at work.

or decrease helps both the therapist and the client to collaboratively determine whether progress is being made and if therapeutic interventions are affecting important targets.

Therapists encouraging behavioural specificity also can help clients learn to effectively observe and understand their patterns of behaviour, thoughts, and emotions. A client seeking help for problems with anger management, for example, would benefit from clearly and specifically delineating problem behaviours associated with anger (i.e., behaviours that will likely be targeted to decrease in therapy). It is helpful to know that the adolescent client yells and curses at her parents two or three times a week and threatens suicide a couple of times per month. These episodes usually occur when the client's parents have refused her request to borrow money, stay out late with friends, or when they ask her to work on her homework. Suicide threats usually occur if the client's yelling has not resulted in the parents acquiescing to her demands. This information is more useful than the information that the client simply has anger management problems or has "blow-ups" at home. When the client is aware of her specific target behaviours (and the contexts in which they occur), she can begin to observe, describe, and keep track of them. When she understands the specific contexts in which these behaviours occur, she and her therapist will be able to devise skills and strategies to use in those specific contexts. Simply focusing on anger management or suicide threats generically can result in cookbook-style interventions that neither specifically map onto the client's unique challenges nor provide the client with the understanding needed to ultimately become her own therapist.

Clients, however, normally do not begin treatment well-practised at specifically observing and describing their own behaviours, thoughts, and emotions (indeed, neither do some therapists), or the contexts in which these occur. As a result, in DBT, therapists often coach clients on how to be behaviourally specific. When a client, for example, states that she "really blew up" on Friday, the therapist is not under any delusion that the client has just conveyed useful information. Instead, the DBT therapist would help the client specifically describe what actually happened on Friday. When hearing the phrase "blew up," remembering the behavioural framework discussed earlier can help generate several useful questions about the antecedents, behaviours, and consequences involved in this episode.

- When and where did the episode occur?
- What was happening prior to the episode?
- What was the client thinking, feeling, and doing?
- Were other people present, and if so, what were they doing?
- What does she mean by "blew up"?
- What behaviours did she engage in?
- How long did this episode continue?
- What thoughts, emotions, sensations, or urges occurred during the episode?
- What thoughts, emotions, sensations, or urges occurred following the episode?
- What events occurred in the immediate environment during or after the episode?
- Were there any delayed or lasting consequences?

It also is helpful for the therapist to model behavioural specificity. Therapists can do this by talking in a behaviourally specific manner about their own behaviours, thoughts, and emotions. They may also demonstrate behavioural specificity by rephrasing what the client has said in more specific terms. Speaking in clear, objective, non-judgmental terms also helps to model the behavioural specificity. Often, clients also describe emotions in fairly vague terms, such as upset, unhappy, depressed, stressed out, and so on. When this occurs, the therapist can simply ask the client to clarify what she or he means by upset, etc. DBT therapists also are often explicit with their clients regarding the importance of non-judgmental specificity. Along these lines, it can be useful to orient the client to the importance of being specific, as shown in the following example:

> I think our treatment is going to work best for you if we get specific about the problems occurring in your everyday life. When you feel "bad," knowing what kind of bad it is, whether it's sadness, anger, shame, and so on, will help us figure out what skills will help you deal with your emotions. If you're having a hard time with problem behaviours, like blowing up at others, it's important for me to know exactly what happened. So, I'm going to ask you to describe it to me from the perspective of a fly on the wall, or a video camera that can talk. If I have a really clear picture of the problems and challenges you're facing, I'll have a better idea of how to help you overcome them. So, whenever you say something that's not quite specific enough, I might ask you some questions to narrow down exactly what happened, how you're feeling, what you did, and so on. Does that sound reasonable?

Active and Attentive Therapeutic Style

The therapist's style in DBT often can be described as engaged, attentive, and mindful. Of course, this therapeutic style is not unique to DBT. Many cognitive-behavioural therapists are active, directive, engaged, and attentive. Indeed, the active and sometimes directive style of cognitive and behavioural therapists likely distinguishes them from many humanistic or psychodynamic counterparts. Arguably, behavioural principles contribute to this common flavour of both DBT and CBT.

As described earlier, DBT is a learning-oriented treatment. An overarching goal is for clients to learn behaviours that help them move toward important goals and establish a desired quality of life. To help clients learn new behaviours, the therapist often must teach and model these behaviours, observe the client's changes in behaviour, and provide instruction and coaching on effective responses (Chapman et al., in press; Farmer & Chapman, 2016; Linehan, 1993b, 2015). Accordingly, behavioural approaches historically have emphasized an active role for the therapist. Traditionally, in behavioural parent training, for example, the therapist takes on an active role as a teacher and a coach. Behavioural parent training often involves instructing and modelling new parenting skills, observing parent-child interactions, coaching parents in effective strategies, and so forth. This work often has occurred in families' natural environments, which facilitates the generalization and transfer of skills to everyday life (Forehand, Jones, & Parent, 2013).

In DBT, the therapist also often functions as a teacher and a coach. In the example of William's self-injury pattern discussed earlier, the DBT therapist might focus on ways to help William communicate his needs effectively to his wife before the chain of events leading to NSSI are well underway. As described below, the therapist might, for example, (a) teach William about potentially helpful skills, (b) model the use of these skills, (c) prompt William to try out the skills, (d) observe his use of skills, (e) provide coaching and feedback, and (f) repeat these steps as needed.

Teaching. The therapist could teach William about a few key interpersonal effectiveness and emotion regulation skills. As William seems primarily to have trouble connecting with co-workers and feels like an outsider, some of the newer supplementary DBT skills could be useful. These include skills for building new relationships (Linehan, 2015). Emotion regulation skills involving opposite action to shame or anxiety (regarding upcoming gatherings or meetings) and relaxation skills, such as paced breathing, could also be very useful. The therapist could teach William key points about these skills, describe their rationale, and clarify when and why to use them.

Modelling. The therapist would often then model the use of the skills. The therapist might demonstrate how to use skills to build or enhance relationships, such as how to begin or continue discussions with people, when and how to approach a small group of people, and so on. The therapist could also model the use of paced breathing or other skills by showing how and where to focus the breathing (abdomen/diaphragm), as well as appropriate posture and rate. In terms of opposite action, the therapist might model confidently approaching social situations, using direct and confident body language and eye contact, and so forth. The therapist also can model skill use by describing how she or he has used such skills in the past as well as the associated positive consequences of doing so (Farmer & Chapman, 2016; Linehan, 1993a).

Prompting skills practice and dragging out behaviour. It also would be essential to prompt William to practise the skills. As a learning-oriented treatment, DBT sessions are not just "talk therapy". Instead, the therapist is active, often directive, and seeks to facilitate active learning opportunities in each individual or group session. Instruction, discussion, and exploration are valuable, indeed integral components of therapy, but therapy focused primarily on talking would be expected to have limited effects. Imagine trying to learn the violin or martial arts by simply discussing music or martial arts theory with an instructor on a weekly basis. How confident would a martial arts student feel stepping into a competition when she or he has never had the chance to try out new moves, manoeuvres, or self-defence strategies with the instructor present to provide feedback, coaching, and reinforcement of effective performance? (As a martial arts practitioner, I would not feel very confident in this situation!) DBT therapists, therefore, look for opportunities to "drag out" (activate) new behaviours in session. When clients engage in new behaviours, the therapist observes carefully and provides appropriate coaching and feedback.

Observing. As mentioned, behavioural theory encourages DBT therapists to take an attentive and mindful approach to therapy. Accordingly, the therapist's role is often mindfully to observe the client's behaviour while she or he is trying out new skills. The therapist in the William example would, therefore, attend closely to the ways in which William is using the interpersonal effectiveness or emotion regulation skills. Attention should be given to what William is doing well or correctly as well as areas for improvement.

Coaching. Coaching involves providing feedback about a client's behaviour, and emphasizing effective behaviours and areas for improvement. If the skills were new to William, the therapist might focus more on what William is doing correctly, rather than what he needs to do differently. Over time, however, coaching would aim to help William further strengthen, refine, and generalize his use of the skills. Just as a coach during a hockey game is an active participant in the game (albeit from the bench), the DBT therapist is an active participant observer in session with her or his client.

Attention to Content, Context, and Process

Behaviourally oriented DBT therapists also must actively attend to behaviour at both the level of content and process. *Content* has to do with the particular form or topography of the behaviour and includes what the client is specifically doing or saying. An angry client struggling with road rage, for example, might be scowling and glaring, waving her or his hands, saying, "This fool can't drive!", sitting in an overly rigid or tense manner, and so on. When it comes to *process*, the therapist must be attentive to the *type* of behaviour the client is engaging in, and determine whether this is a behaviour targeted to increase or decrease. The road rage client, from this perspective, may be engaging in complaining or ruminating about other drivers. The DBT therapist who is attentive to the type of behaviour occurring might consider whether this behaviour is likely to improve or exacerbate the client's difficulties with road rage. Another example might be the client who says that therapy is not working, that she is feeling very depressed, and that she wishes to quit therapy. Content-based observations would specifically focus on what the client is saying as well as the client's observable behaviour. At the level of process, the therapist would attend to the type of behaviour the client is engaging in, the likely utility of this behaviour, and how it functions in the current therapeutic context. For some clients, talking about quitting therapy may function to divert discussions from difficult problem areas. For others, this behaviour may be an adaptive way of expressing the desire to quit or pursue other options. Helpful observations at the level of process, therefore, require the therapist to remain aware of her or his case formulation of the individual client at all times. This, of course, is a hallmark of behavioural therapy.

A behavioural framework encourages attention to the context in which client behaviour occurs, both within and outside of therapy sessions. As described earlier, context is a critical ingredient to attend to in both functional/chain analyses and case formulation. Within any given session, it is also useful for DBT therapists to attend to ways in which the therapeutic context may occasion, reinforce, or otherwise influence client behaviour. When a client repeatedly talks about suicidal ideation, for example, therapeutic discussions might focus on that topic to the exclusion of important quality of life issues. If these quality of life issues were solved, it is possible that the client's suicidal urges or desires would also reduce. Yet, some quality of life issues are painful to address, such as challenges in relationships, traumatic events, losses, events that occasion feelings of shame, and so forth. The therapist must strike a delicate balance in this situation. While it is always important to attend to and take suicidal behaviours seriously, the therapist also must avoid negatively (by allowing the avoidance of painful discussions) or positively (e.g., by differentially providing attention when suicide talk arises) reinforcing these behaviours. The therapist attending to principles of contingency management will have a greater chance of striking an effective balance in this situation (for further, detailed discussion of the role of context and content in therapy, see Hayes, Jacobson, Follette, & Dougher, 1994; Kohlenberg & Tsai, 1991; Heard, Chapter 17, this volume).

SUMMARY

Behavioural theory forms an essential part of the theoretical foundation of DBT. Behavioural theory informs the DBT therapist's approach to assessing, understanding, and formulating problem behaviours, including suicidal behaviour and NSSI, as well as any other behaviours targeted in treatment. Regular chain or functional analyses can help illuminate consistent behavioural patterns and coalesce into a useful case formulation. The general behavioural framework specifying antecedents, person variables, behaviours, and consequences can help guide the therapist's organization and understanding of the client's behavioural patterns. The case formulation should highlight hypotheses and potentially effective intervention strategies. Behaviourally oriented therapists, however, should always remember that their formulations and hypotheses are simply works in progress to be refined further throughout therapy. Behavioural theory also influences the style of DBT. DBT therapists tend to be active, sometimes directive, and attentive, and to look for opportunities to help clients learn new behaviours by prompting or dragging out behaviour, observing, coaching, and providing feedback. DBT therapists also remain aware of client behaviour in terms of content, context, and process. Together with a dialectical emphasis on the synthesis of acceptance and change, zen principles, and basic emotion science, behavioural theory helps the DBT therapist respond flexibly to new, complex, and challenging situations, ultimately guiding their clients toward lives that are worth living.

KEY MESSAGES FROM THIS CHAPTER

- Behavioural theory guides many aspects of DBT.
- Behavioural theory and practices help DBT therapists assess and understand their clients' behaviour.
- Functional or chain analyses can help the DBT therapist assemble a case formulation that paves the way to potentially helpful interventions.
- Behavioural theory encourages DBT clinicians to be specific about behaviour, to take an active role in therapy, and to present opportunities for clients to learn new behaviours.

REFERENCES

Baumeister, R. F. (1990). Suicide as escape from self. *Psychological Review, 97*, 90–113.

Brown, M. Z., Comtois, K. A., & Linehan, M. M. (2002). Reasons for suicide attempts and nonsuicidal self-injury in women with borderline personality disorder. *Journal of Abnormal Psychology, 111*, 198–202.

Craske, M. G., Kircanski, K., Zelikowsky, M., Mystkowski, J., Chowdhury, N., & Baker, A. (2008). Optimizing inhibitory learning during exposure therapy, *Behaviour Research and Therapy, 46*, 5–27. http://dx.doi.org/10.1016/j.brat.2007.10.003

Chapman, A. L., Ferreira, J. S., & Law, K. C. (In press). Suicide. In O. J. Sahler, J. Carr, J. B. Frank, J. Nunes (Eds.), *The behavioral sciences and health care*, 4th Edition. Oxford: Hogrefe Publishing.

Chapman, A. L., Gratz, K. L., & Brown, M. Z. (2006). 'Solving the puzzle of deliberate self-harm: The experiential avoidance model', *Behaviour Research and Therapy, 44*, 371–394.

Chapman, A. L., & Linehan, M. M. (2005). Dialectical behavior therapy for borderline personality disorder. In M. Zanarini (Ed.), *Borderline personality disorder* (pp. 211–242). Boca Raton, FL: Taylor & Francis.

Crowell, S. E., Beauchaine, T. P., & Linehan, M. M. (2009). A biosocial developmental model of borderline personality: Elaborating and extending Linehan's theory. *Psychological Bulletin, 135*, 495–510.

Farmer, R. F., & Chapman, A. L. (2008). *Behavioral interventions in cognitive-behavior therapy: Practical guidance for putting theory into action*. Washington, DC: APA Publications.

Farmer, R. F., & Chapman, A. L. (2016). *Behavioral interventions in cognitive-behavior therapy: Practical guidance for putting theory into action*, 2nd Edition. Washington, DC: APA Publications.

Forehand, R., Jones, D. J., & Parent, J. (2013). Behavioral parenting interventions for child disruptive behaviors and anxiety: What's different and what's the same. *Clinical Psychology Review, 33*, 133–145.

Goldfried, M. R., & Davison, G. C. (1976). *Clinical behavior therapy*. New York: Hold, Rinehard, and Winston.

Gratz, K. L. (2003). Risk factors for and functions of deliberate self-harm: An empirical and conceptual review. *Clinical Psychology: Science and Practice, 10*, 192–205.

Gratz, K. L., Chapman, A. L., Dixon-Gordon, K. L., & Tull, M. T. (2016). Exploring the association of deliberate self-harm with emotional relief using a novel implicit association test. *Personality Disorders: Theory, Research, and Treatment, 7*, 91–102.

Gross, J. J. (1998). The emerging field of emotion regulation: An integrative review. *Review of General Psychology, 2*, 271–299.

Gross, J. J., (Ed.) (2013). *Handbook of emotion regulation*, 2nd Edition. New York: The Guilford Press.

Hayes, S. C., & Brownstein, A. J. (1986). Mentalism, behavior-behavior relations, and a bezhavior-analytic view of the purposes of science. *The Behavior Analyst, 9*, 175–190.

Hayes, S. C., Jacobson, N. S., Follette, V. M, & Dougher, M. (Eds.) (1994). *Acceptance and change: Content and context in psychotherapy*. Reno, NV: Context Press.

Hernstein, R. J. (1961). Relative and absolute strength of response as a function of frequency of reinforcement. *Journal of the Experimental Analysis of Behavior, 4*, 267–272.

Hofmann, S. G., Asnaani, A., Vonk, I. J. J., Sawyer, A. T., & Fang, A. (2012). The efficacy of cognitive behavioral therapy: A review of meta-analyses. *Cognitive Therapy and Research, 36,* 427–440.

Hopko, D. R., Lejuez, C. W., Ruggiero, K. J., & Eifert, G. H. (2003). Contemporary behavioral activation treatments for depression: Procedures, principles, and progress. *Clinical Psychology Review, 23,* 699–717.

Joiner, T. E. (2005). *Why people die by suicide.* Cambridge, MA: Harvard University Press.

Klonsky, E. D. (2007). The functions of deliberate self-injury: A review of the evidence. *Clinical Psychology Review, 27,* 226–239.

Klonsky, E. D., & May, A. M. (2015). The three-step theory (3ST): A new theory of suicide rooted in the "idea-to-action" framework. *International Journal of Cognitive Therapy, 8,* 114–129.

Kleindienst, N., Bohus, M., Ludäscher, P., Limberger, M. F., Kuenkele, K., Ebner-Priemer, U. W., ... Schmahl, C. (2008). Motives for nonsuicidal self-injury among women with borderline personality disorder. *Journal of Nervous and Mental Disease, 196,* 230–236.

Kohlenberg, R. J., & Tsai, M. (1991). *Functional analytic psychotherapy: Creating intense and curative therapeutic relationships.* New York: Plenum Press.

Laraway, S., Snycerski, S., Michael, J., & Poling, A. (2003). Motivating operations and terms to describe them: Some further refinements. *Journal of Applied Behavior Analysis, 36,* 407–414.

Linehan, M. M. (1993a). *Cognitive behavioral treatment of borderline personality disorder.* New York: The Guilford Press.

Linehan, M. M. (1993b). *Skills training manual for treating borderline personality disorder.* New York: The Guilford Press.

Linehan, M. M. (2015). *Dialectical behavior therapy skills training manual,* 2nd Edition. New York: The Guilford Press.

Lejuez, C. W., Hopko, D. R., & Hopko, S. D. (2001). A brief behavioral activation treatment for depression. Treatment manual. *Behavior Modification, 25,* 255–286.

Michael, J. (2000). Implications and refinements of the establishing operation concept. *Journal of Applied Behavior Analysis, 33,* 401–410.

Nock, M. K., & Prinstein, M. J. (2004). A functional approach to the assessment of self-mutilative behavior. *Journal of Consulting and Clinical Psychology, 72,* 885–890.

Reitz, S., Kleutsch, R., Niedtfeld, I., Knorz, T., Lis, S., Paret, C., ... Schmahl, C. (2015). Incision and stress regulation in borderline personality disorder: Neurological mechanisms of self-injurious behaviour. *The British Journal of Psychiatry, 207,* 165–172.

Rizvi, S. L., & Ritschel, L. A. (2013). Mastering the art of chain analysis in dialectical behavior therapy. *Cognitive and Behavioral Practice, 21,* 335–349.

Skinner, B. F. (1953). *The Possibility of a Science of Human Behavior.* New York: The Free House.

Staats, W. W. (1996). *Behavior and personality: Psychological behaviorism.* New York: Springer Publishing Company.

CHAPTER 5

MODIFYING BEHAVIOUR THERAPY TO MEET THE CHALLENGE OF TREATING BORDERLINE PERSONALITY DISORDER

Incorporating Zen and Mindfulness

RANDY WOLBERT

INTRODUCTION

DIALECTICAL Behaviour Therapy can be conceptualized as the transaction between behavior therapy and Zen contemplative practice, held together with a dialectical philosophy. When first developed, mindfulness practices had not yet been incorporated into psychotherapy. Marsha Linehan chose to augment behaviour therapy with Zen practice. This chapter begins with a brief history of Zen and discusses the need for an acceptance-based practice to balance behaviour therapy within the treatment. It describes the Zen beliefs contained in the four noble truths and precepts, and how these translate into the principles and practice of Zen. It then considers both the differences between and compatibility of Zen and behaviour therapy. Finally, it discusses how Zen practice modifies behaviour therapy in DBT. Most of the stories and anecdotes are from Linehan's Zen Dharma talks given during her Zen Sessions held over the past ten years.

WHAT IS ZEN?

Zen is the Japanese form of the Sanskrit word *Dhyana*, or meditation. Zen originated from Buddhism, known as Chan "quietude", which was brought to China in the sixth century by the Indian monk Bodhidharma. From China, Chan spread to Japan in the twelfth century, where it became known as Zen "Meditation" (Jurgensmeyer, 2006). Zen does not emphasize the study of sacred texts, or worship deities. According to Bodidharma, the practice is "Not dependent on the written word, Transmission apart from the scriptures; directly pointing at one's heart, seeing one's nature, becoming Buddha". Zen more concerns itself with the regular practice of meditation to break through the restraints of concepts and dualistic thinking, in particular, letting go of concepts of good and bad, right and wrong, or separation between the mental and physical, and to "see reality as it is". Zen teaches that all beings have the capacity to attain enlightenment because we already have Buddha nature. As noted by Zenji in his *Song of Zazen*, "All beings by nature are Buddha, as ice by nature is water; apart from water there is no ice, apart from beings no Buddha" (Hakuin, c. 1750), Buddha being a person who has awakened from ignorance into wisdom. Our inability "to see reality as it is" is clouded by greed, hatred, and ignorance.

While words and concepts can be useful tools, we live in a dualistic world, and mistaking them for reality can prevent us from seeing the true nature of reality. "Seeing reality as it is" is also known as Satori, or Kenshō: an experience of oneness with the universe. The Zen practitioner has to have the desire for Kenshō to the same degree as someone having gulped down a red-hot iron ball wishes to vomit it up (Koun, 2005) but cannot; however, the moment the thought of Kenshō passes through your mind, it is gone. Zen practice is being fully present in this one moment. Being present, as described by Linehan, allows you to crack open the moment and find joy.

There are several schools of Zen including Rinzai, Soto, and Sanbo Kyodan. The Japanese lineage of the Chinese Linji school, founded during the Tang Dynasty (600–900 CE), became the Rinzai School that emphasizes Kenshō, which is insight into one's true nature. This insight is followed by continued practice, including zazen (formal sitting mediation) and Kōan study, which leads to a gradual deepening of understanding. Koun Yamada (2005) presents a collection of Kōan, or teaching stories, in *The Gateless Gate*. Kōans are stories, dialogues, questions, or statements designed to provoke doubt and in the resolution of the doubt, to further the practice of Zen. An example of an introductory Kōan is "what is the sound of one hand clapping?" Following a set of introductory Kōans, students progress through a series of Kōan manuals written as 'cases'. Students present the Kōan case to their teacher, recite the verse connected with the Kōan, and then are asked by their teacher to demonstrate Buddha Nature by solving the Kōan (see Box 5.1). Kōans have been passed down to Zen teachers by their own teachers for many generations. Buddha Nature, the true nature of reality and being, is characterized by both form and emptiness, defies conceptual explanation, and instead must

> **Box 5.1 Joshu's Dog**
>
> The Case
> A monk asked Joshu in all earnestness, "Does a dog have Buddha nature or not?"
> Joshu said, "Mu!"
> The Verse
> Dog-Buddha nature!
> The Perfect manifestation, the absolute command.
> A little "has" or "has not",
> And Body is lost! Life is lost!

be experienced. The Soto school, the Japanese lineage of the Chinese Caodong School founded during the Tang dynasty, deemphasized Kōans and emphasized zazen. The essence of practice is gradual cultivation of existing Buddha Nature. The Sanbo Kyodan line, also a Japanese school of Zen, is based on three treasures; the Sangha (community of Zen practitioners), the Dharma (the teachings of the Buddha and Buddha Nature), and the Buddha (the perfection of enlightenment). Founded by Hakuun Yasutuni in 1954, it promotes Zen for lay practitioners and people of other faith (non-Buddhist) communities and cultures. Sanbo Kyodan considers zazen and Kōan study essential for realizing Zen in everyday life.

THE NEED FOR ACCEPTANCE IN ORDER TO BALANCE CHANGE

During the late 1970s and early 1980s, Linehan's attempts to treat suicidal behaviours through the use of standard cognitive behavioural techniques were not effective, or as Linehan once described it: "They blew-up". Clients experienced the emphasis on the behavioural change strategies as disregarding their obvious suffering, and perhaps blaming them for their problems. This experience led to high levels of emotion dysregulation, rendering any implementation of learned skillful behaviour nearly impossible; it often resulted in high degrees of anger, verbal attacks on the therapist, non-collaboration in treatment, or dropping out of therapy (Linehan, 1993). Linehan realized that she needed to include elements of acceptance to her treatment in order to both decrease the extreme suffering of her clients and to facilitate the changes necessary for them to build a life worth living.

In 1985, mindfulness had not yet migrated from Eastern practice traditions to western psychology practice. Linehan had a background in Christian contemplative prayer and so sought recommendations for good teachers of acceptance. The two sources she found were Shasta Abbey, run by a Soto woman Zen Rōshi (Zen Master), and Willigis Jäger, a Benedictine Priest in Germany who also happened to be a Zen Rōshi. First, Linehan spent three months at Shasta Abbey learning the practice of Radical Acceptance conveyed through the practice of monastery life; observing noble silence, conducting assigned work tasks (not all of which were done willingly!), and acquiring the capacity to accept what is, instead of holding preferences for things to be different from what they are. In one of her Zen dharma talks Linehan describes that she knew that she had found what she was looking for at Shasta Abbey.

Linehan returned to clinical practice and attempted to persuade her clients to practice mindful meditation, known in Zen as zazen. She tried to bring the traditions of Soto Zen that she had learned at Shasta Abbey into the practice. Clients did not see the point of removing their shoes, sitting on the floor in meditation, or counting breaths. Linehan thought perhaps that the more active mindfulness practice of walking meditation, known as Kinhin, might be better suited for her clients. After giving instructions to follow her she started down the hallway. After a period of time she turned around and discovered that only one client had followed her. This experience powerfully emphasized the need to find other ways for her clients to benefit from the practice of zazen without doing a formal meditation practice.

Subsequently, Linehan spent three months at a monastery in Germany and ultimately became a Zen student of Willigis Jäger Rōshi. She regularly returned to Germany to study with Willigis, translating what she learned from him on the practice of zazen and the principles and practices of Zen into behavioural terms and strategies. All she learned during her study of Zen in these early years of treatment development was distilled into the seven mindfulness skills in DBT (Wise Mind; Observe, Describe and Participate—the 'what' skills; Non-judgmentally, One-Mindfully and Effectively—the "how" skills; Linehan, 2015). She presented all of the materials contained in DBT related to mindfulness first to Jäger and later to her second teacher, Pat Hawk Rōshi, to verify the congruence of the mindfulness-based skills in DBT with Zen practice.

Linehan continued to study Zen and is part of two different Zen "lines", Willigis Jäger Rōshi and Pat Hawk Rōshi. A Zen lineage is a line of transmission of the teachings of Buddha (Dharma) from one generation to the next. All Zen lineages trace their line of succession back to Shakyamuni Buddha (discussed later). Zen masters (Rōshi) can only be recognized as such and confirmed by another Zen master (this process is known as receiving transmission). Linehan's first and primary teacher is Willigis Jäger, who later sent her for instruction with Pat Hawk, a Zen Master in the Diamond Sangha school of Zen founded by Robert and Anne Aitken. Linehan received transmission (given Rōshi status) from Pat Hawk prior to his death in 2012. Her transmission as a Rōshi in the Diamond Sangha was confirmed by Willigis Jäger in the Leere Wolke Lineage.

Why Zen?

There are several reasons why Linehan chose Zen as a balance to behavioural theory and practice in the treatment. Zen is a practice, and not a religion. If religious concepts had been included in the many meditation/mindfulness practices in DBT, it is likely that a whole segment of individuals who could benefit from the therapy would be alienated. Jäger (http://www.benediktushof-holzkirchen.de/zen/63-zen.html) teaches Zen from a trans-confessional viewpoint; a practice that is suitable for everyone from the orthodox, to fundamentalists, to atheists. According to Jäger, "Zen is Zen and will always be Zen, irrespective of whether it is taught and practiced in the East or the West. The core of Zen is always the same, aimed at experiencing reality".

Maller (2016) explains further by saying, "The relationship of religion to truth is like that of a menu to a meal. The menu describes the meal as best it can. It points to something beyond itself. As long as we use the menu as a guide we do it honor. When we mistake the menu for the meal, we do it and ourselves a grave injustice".

So why Zen, and not mindfulness-based psychotherapies or other mindfulness-based treatments? At the time that Linehan was developing DBT the only mindfulness-based treatment widely available in western circles was Mindfulness-Based Stress Reduction developed by Jon Kabat-Zinn in the late 1970s. Jon Kabat-Zinn took Vipassana meditation principles and removed the Buddhist framework and de-emphasized the connection between mindfulness and its various spiritual traditions. He combined meditation with hatha yoga and studied the effect on psoriasis, pain, anxiety, and stress (Kabat-Zinn, 1990). Linehan was the first researcher to incorporate principles of mindful meditation adopted from Zen into a psychological treatment. Unlike other researchers, Linehan did not seek to downplay the connection between spiritual experience and the psychological benefits of mindfulness practice. While not ignoring the spiritual aspects of practice, she kept with the trans-confessional spirit of Zen espoused by Jäger.

ZEN AND THE FOUR NOBLE TRUTHS

Siddhārtha Gautama, Shakyamuni Buddha, or simply the Buddha, is believed to have lived and taught in Eastern India sometime between the sixth and fourth centuries BCE. His teachings were passed on by oral tradition and not written down till 400 years or so after his death. He was born a prince and was the heir to the throne in the province. At the age of 29, he left the palace, his wife, and his son to be among his subjects. Discovering the existence of suffering in the world, he began an ascetic life style begging for alms. His belief, along with his companions at that time, was that enlightenment could only be found through deprivation of worldly goods and self-mortification. After almost dying from starvation he was rescued by a village girl and regained his strength and abandoned the ascetic lifestyle in favour of a more middle path of moderation. He began to believe that meditation was the path to enlightenment. He sat beneath a Bodhi tree vowing to stay there until he achieved enlightenment. After sitting for 49 days he achieved awakening (enlightenment), which, for Siddhārtha (now the Buddha), was an end to the endless cycle of rebirth, suffering, and dying again. Following his experience, the Buddha began to teach others how to become awakened, which he continued to do for the next 45 years until his death.

The Buddha's first sermon was to his previous companions from his ascetic lifestyle days in a place known as Deer Park. The Buddha was interested in everyone discovering the fundamental nature of all things (Buddha Nature) and delivered his first sermon on the Four Noble Truths, from which the principles and practices of Zen are derived. The following briefly describes the Four Noble Truths and how these lead to the practices of Zen (O'Brien, 2014).

1. The Truth of Suffering. Suffering exists in the world: being born, ageing, experiencing physical or emotional pain, becoming sick, and eventually dying all involve suffering. Associating with people that you do not want to be around or being absent from those you care about also involves suffering. Finally, not getting what we want involves suffering. The path towards the end of suffering begins with acceptance that suffering exists. Using the metaphor of a physician, the diagnosis is that we have suffering.

2. The Truth of the Cause of Suffering. Craving or clinging causes suffering. Searching for someone or something outside of ourselves to make us happy causes suffering. The cause of this clinging or craving arises out of greed, hatred, and ignorance. We grow frustrated that the world does not conduct itself in tune with our expectations or desires. We cling to the notion of a permanent and independent self. This cause of suffering is seen as karma, or the law of cause and effect. Every behaviour produces more behaviours. Behaviours arising out of greed, hatred, or ignorance produce more behaviours arising out of greed, hatred, or ignorance. Continuing with the metaphor of the physician, this is the cause of the diagnosis of suffering.

3. The Truth of the End of Suffering. Extinguishing craving leads the way out of this suffering. Willpower alone will not end the craving. The conditions that gave rise to the cravings in the first place are still within. This requires contemplation and observation in our everyday lives: the willingness to learn through experience, and not intellect. As we are able to stop clinging to the belief that things should be different than they are, suffering begins to decrease and is replaced by greater level of joy. This is the physician indicating that there is hope for the end of suffering.

4. The Truth of the Path that Frees us from Suffering. The way out of suffering is by walking the eight-fold path. This is not a belief, but rather living and walking the path through the experience of our senses.

The Eightfold Path, or the Middle Way, can be seen as engaging in skillful living and includes "right understanding" into the nature of reality; "right intention" to realize enlightenment; "right speech" using compassion towards others; "right actions" of being ethical and compassionate; "right livelihood" being helpful and not harmful to the rest of the earth; "right effort" cultivating the wholesome, letting go of the unwholesome; "right mindfulness" and awareness of the whole mind and body; and "right concentration" for a regular formal mindfulness practice. This path can be seen as the prescription to treat suffering.

Right understanding and right attitude are considered wisdom. Right understanding develops the capacity to see karma, or the law of cause and effect. In the context of DBT, understanding causal relationships is essential for both the behaviour therapist and the client, and is the way of ultimately letting go of judgments. Right attitude does not harbour thoughts and feelings of greed and anger, as these prevent the experience of joy: "Right understanding (and right functioning) of the mind does not come from thinking, but from actively and attentively observing the complex constellation of energies and activities of mind" (Smithers, 1991). Right speech, right action, and right livelihood are seen as good conduct. As the Buddha says, "Teach this triple truth to all.... A generous heart, kind speech, and a life of service and compassion are the things which renew humanity". This is the golden rule magnified, the "acting as if". Zen teaches that boundaries are, in fact, a delusion; being compassionate to others is being compassionate to yourself, and harming others is harming yourself. James Gordon noted that "Altruism ... the doing for others has tremendous physical benefits ... we should probably prescribe that for people" (Gordon, 2015). Right effort, right mindfulness, and right concentration constitute mental development. This requires practising willingness over willfulness. The Buddha says that "the secret of health for both mind and body is not to mourn the past nor worry about the future, but to live the present moment wisely and earnestly".

Zen Practice Principles

Zen practice leads to the ability to see reality as it is, revealing the experience of the true self and the true nature of the universe. This experience leads to an understanding that all individuals, and reality as a whole, are one; boundaries are artificial delusions that prevent us from seeing reality as it is. Knowing that attachment to wanting things to be different is the root of suffering. True freedom can only come by letting go of attachments, radically accepting that the world is perfect as it is, and that everything is as it should be. Reality as a whole, including our own actions and reactions, are impermanent: the only reality is now.

Zen further teaches that all individuals have the inherent capacity for enlightenment, which is the capability of acting intuitively from Wise Mind. Wise Mind has the capacity to enter into the paradox experiencing form and self as both empty and full. Wise Mind simultaneously experiences "being" mind and "doing" mind, and, as with many aspects of Zen, must be experienced as it defies definition with words: "In order to avoid suffering expanding one's awareness wide enough to contain opposites without resolving them" (Hawk, 2009).

Linehan translated the principles of Zen practice into a set of "how" and "what" skills (Linehan, 2015). These skills require staying mindful of the current moment, seeing reality as it is without attachment, and accepting reality without judgment. If a thought or emotion is observed as only a thought or emotion, then the individual can be free from the *attachment* to that thought or emotion. Furthermore, as the ability develops to observe our own experiences as a means of understanding the world, it then allows "disattachment" from experiences and the ability to describe them without judgment. Zen practice is finding the Middle Way, as outlined by the Buddha, and to use skillful means along the path.

COMPATIBILITY OF BEHAVIOUR THERAPY AND ZEN PRACTICE

Behaviour therapy commits to changing behaviours utilizing the techniques of problem-solving, determining behaviours to increase and decrease and removing barriers to achieving desired goals. In contrast, Zen accepts what is. Zen practice consists of bringing our bare attention to the present moment. It is being yourself, with nothing extra, in harmony with the way things are. Zen is the practice of looking directly at life as it is.

While behavioural science and Zen practice appear to be polar opposites, the conclusions of both practices as to the nature of reality are surprisingly convergent. In discussing the practice of Buddhism in conjunction with science, the Dalai Lama said that "My confidence in venturing into science lies in my basic belief that, as in science so in Buddhism, understanding the nature of reality is pursued by means of critical investigation: if scientific analysis were conclusively to demonstrate certain claims in Buddhism to be false, then we must accept the findings of science and abandon those claims" (Dalai Lama, 2005).

So, what is the convergence between behaviour therapy and Zen Practice? Linehan addressed this question in a talk given to honour Willigis Jäger's ninetieth birthday in 2015. She identified seven similarities between Zen and behaviourism. First, both Behaviour Therapy and Zen recognize no self or no independent self. Behaviour therapists, rather than focusing on the concept of an independent or permanent self, focus on learning experiences and their transactions with environmental events. Patterns of behaviour exist but they are always changing. For example, we could say that a person is walking but once they stop, where is walking? In Zen, the concept of an independent self is simply a delusion invented by the brain. Zen practice removes this delusion recognizing the non-dualistic nature of the universe: To actually see our true nature. Secondly, both behaviour therapy and Zen recognize unity; Zen as the oneness of the universe and behaviour therapy as the connection between behaviours and the context in which they occur. Any analysis of cause and effect requires the recognition of unity.

> If you are a poet, you will see clearly that there is a cloud floating in this sheet of paper. Without a cloud, there will be no rain; without rain, the trees cannot grow; and without trees, we cannot make paper. The cloud is essential for the paper to exist. If the cloud is not here, the sheet of paper cannot be here, either. We can say that the

cloud and the paper inter-are. 'Interbeing' is a word that is not in the dictionary yet, but if we combine the prefix 'inter-' with the verb 'to be', we have a new verb, 'inter-be'" (Hanh, 2012).

Thirdly, while it may seem to contradict unity, both approaches also recognize individuality. Just as a rug is a whole complete object, it comprises many threads. Behaviour therapists recognize that behaviours are ideographic and treatment is adjusted to fit the individual. Similarly, there is no notion of "one size fits all"; Zen and the Zen teacher will assist the student by fitting the practice to meet the student's needs.

Fourthly, both Zen and behaviour therapy adopt a non-judgmental worldview reflected in the way that they interact with each other, students, and clients. As noted, Zen possesses a set of precepts encouraging moral behaviour but nowhere in Zen are found the concepts of good and bad. Willigis Jäger illustrated this point by saying that a pound of gold and a pound of shit are the same: they are one. From a behavioural perspective all behaviour is caused and therefore given the causes, how could a different result be expected? To change behaviour one must change the causes. In both Zen and behaviour therapy, corrective feedback is given in the spirit of kindness and compassion without the application of moral judgements.

Focus on the present is the fifth commonality central to both Zen and behaviourism. Behaviour therapy focuses on the attainment of current goals by addressing barriers that prevent clients from reaching their goals. A behaviour chain analysis yields the controlling behaviours that mainting the problematic behaviours, which in turn prevent the attainment of goals. While the analysis concerns behaviours occurring in the recent past, the focus of the session revolves around the barriers preventing more skillful behaviour in the current moment. In Zen the only thing that exists is this present moment; for example, a Zen timepiece would just say "now". The past is already gone and the present has not yet occurred. The practice of Zen is to be wide-awake and fully present in this one moment.

Zen and behaviour therapy emphasize practice—the sixth convergence. Being a Zen student requires rigorous daily practice as directed by the teacher. The behaviour therapist teaches clients new skills, conducts behavioural rehearsal in session, and assigns homework outside of session.

Finally, both approaches utilize exposure and opposite action. In behaviour therapy the technique known as exposure presents the client with painful cues and blocks avoidance so that the client actually experiences the associated emotion and learns that the pain will subside, i.e. facing the suffering rather than avoiding it. Robert Aitken Rōshi, the founder of the Diamond Sangha, said, "The first truth is that life is suffering. Avoidance of suffering leads to worse suffering". In behaviour therapy, acting opposite to the emotion can reduce an unwanted emotion. Hawk said, "Practice these things (wisdom, compassion, and freedom from desires) as if you already have them." Aitken also described this same practice: "Act as if you have compassion and you will find that you always did" (Aitken, 1982). Both the practice of Zen and behaviour therapy encourage the acquisition of and use of skillful means. In DBT, practising skillful means is the path towards a life worth living. In Zen, practising skillful means is the path towards enlightenment.

How Zen Practice Modifies the Delivery of Behaviour Therapy in DBT

The principles and practices of Zen are woven into the fabric of DBT. This section expands on the presence of Zen within the ultimate goals of therapy, the targets of treatment, therapeutic strategies and relationships, and the skills taught to clients.

Goals of Treatment

The goal of behaviour therapy is change. The goal of Zen or mindful practice is simply mindful practice. The side effects of mindful practice appear to be decreased suffering, increased happiness, increased control of your mind, and the capability of experiencing reality as it is without delusion. According to Linehan, this involves moving beyond knowing and experiencing connection to the universe, towards essential goodness and essential validity. The change behaviour therapy seeks first requires acceptance. Acceptance is an essential element across all spiritual and humanistic traditions. Ultimately, radical acceptance is the willingness to experience life as it is, not how we want it to be, i.e. letting go of clinging and attachments. Radical acceptance is freedom from desiring that things should be different from what they are, and it is a necessary skill or practice to acquire in the pursuit of joy. According to Linehan, the experience of joy is actually the experience of freedom, of being content with life as it unfolds, and of being free from having to have everything that you want. But this is not simply letting go of desires or preferences. Freedom needs to be internalized as an inner release from 'demand' itself: the kind of freedom that comes when the compulsions to have, to own, and to be someone, disappear (Hillman, 2015). Freedom means letting go of any expectations of life experiences, radical acceptance of the way things are, and a continual turning of the mind towards acceptance; ultimately, this freedom leads to joy.

New Therapist Strategies

Zen principles within DBT require that therapists embrace and teach acceptance alongside principles of change from behaviour therapy. To balance these, therapists require spaciousness of mind; they must dance with movement, speed, and flow—doing adeptly what is needed, when it is needed. The therapist must also practice radical acceptance, i.e., always staying in touch with the unity of all things, and secure in the experience of the real relationship between equals. The process of treatment is transactional in nature and approached with humility. DBT therapists must radically accept that individuals with BPD tend to make slow episodic progress and that working with suicidal individuals portends the possibility of suicide by these clients.

New Client Targets

The practice of Zen adds several new client targets to DBT, in particular, targets around acceptance. Clients have to accept one set of problems in order to work on another. They have to accept the mistakes of the past, the reality of the present, and limitations on the future. Accepting the past is the way out of suffering; refusing to accept maintains the status quo of a miserable existence. Acceptance of the reality of the present as the only moment that matters, the only moment that we control. The pain of the present exists as it is. Suffering occurs when dwelling in the past. Thinking "things have always been this way" intensifies and perpetuates the misery. Speculating on the future prompts further suffering, and thoughts that the future will not differ from the present can lead to anxiety. Beck (1993) says sagely that "there is nothing other than this present moment; there is no past, there is no future; there is nothing but this. So, when we don't pay attention to each little *this*, we miss the whole thing". Residing in this one moment allows problem solving to occur, and the residing in a different moment inevitably results in suffering.

Zen practice teaches clients reality acceptance skills that focus on tolerating distress without avoiding the present, or by creating additional suffering by acting impulsively or destructively (e.g., engaging in non-suicidal self-injury, using drugs and/or alcohol). Radical acceptance requires relinquishing efforts to control everything, which, almost always, makes things worse. The skill of observing without trying to attach meaning to what is observed requires letting go of the propensity to listen to our brains, or in Hawk's words, "our pattern-making machines" (Hawk, 2010). The emotion of fear leads to thinking, rather than observing; fear will vanish if the moment is spent in observation, but it will remain if it is analysed. According to the Boddidharma, "If you use your mind to study reality, you won't understand either your mind or reality. If you study reality without using your mind, you'll understand both". Finally, as noted, Zen practice helps clients to experience completely connection to others, essential goodness, and essential validity. As Tarrant (2008) sums, "Suffering is what happens when we are lonely and forget that we participate in the world".

New Client Skills: Wise Mind and Mindfulness Skills

In Zen, all sentient beings have the inherent capacity for Wise Mind. Wise Mind is so much more than the synthesis of emotion mind and reasonable mind (Linehan, 1993;

Linehan, 2015): it is seeing and responding to what is. Hawk describes Wise Mind as coming home when homesick. In spiritual practices, Wise Mind can also be called enlightenment, wisdom, compassion, and freedom—our essential being or true self. From a religious perspective, it could be the deity from which wisdom flows. Since all things are in unity, Wise Mind means accessing the wisdom of the universe, where we are no longer alone and are able to share in the wisdom of the ages. Finding Wise Mind is necessary for a life worth living. As described in the serenity prayer, Wise Mind is knowing the difference between what can, and what cannot, be changed.

A DBT therapist believes that every client has a Wise Mind; he or she teaches clients how to access it by going deep within and how to act from it. All of the DBT mindfulness skills assist clients and therapists alike to inhabit Wise Mind in a more sustained way. For a therapist to skillfully help a client find, and act from, Wise Mind, he or she must also practise mindfulness. Being mindful not only requires some type of formal meditation practice, but also requires that therapists bring the essence of mindfulness to all that they do. Mindfulness is required when conducting therapy, and in all other aspects of daily living.

The practice of mindful meditation starts with *observing*, rather than analysing reality. Psychotherapists are taught to analyse, but Zen practice lets go of analysis as intellectual knowledge is worthless in Zen, and experiential knowledge is of greater value. For example, intellectualizing that you are worthwhile is less useful than experiencing yourself as worthwhile. Oxenhandler (1996) suggests that "There is something sacred about the moment when we fall out of the habit-realm. So often it is precisely such a gap, a sense of wonder or questioning at what we take for granted, that brings us to the path in the first place".

The act of *describing* follows the skill of observation, as that which is not first observed through your senses cannot be described. Describing puts words around what is observed; it is a way of labeling thoughts as thoughts, emotions as emotions, and actions as actions. The describing skill provides a means of communicating observations to others. But while describing is not part of traditional Zen practice, a student must describe their observations when speaking with their teacher. Linehan added describing to the canon of mindfulness skills in order to assist clients with high levels of dysregulation, as these clients can experience intensified distress using observation alone.

Participating is the experience of oneness. It is letting go of the delusion of boundaries, and rather than just observing and describing reality, the client becomes one with it. The experience of oneness eliminates the concepts of good and bad.

The skill of *effectiveness* arose from Linehan's experience at Shasta Abbey. The Abbot gave each of the students a dime (which used to be the cost of a phone call from a pay phone). She told the students that they may experience an awakening so profound that they may find themselves incapacitated by joy: The dime was to call for assistance! Individuals who have had such experiences have a strong desire to stay with the experience or repeat it—to stay "on top of the flagpole", so to speak. Sooner or later, however, the house requires cleaning, money must be earned, and groceries bought. The skill of effectiveness is doing what is needed. According to an old Zen saying: "Before enlightenment, chop wood, carry water. After enlightenment, chop wood, carry water". Within Zen, morality is not rooted in abstract notions of good and bad; instead, behaviours, including mental ones, are described and evaluated in terms of their effectiveness in relation to goals.

Zen and the Therapeutic Relationships in DBT

DBT Consultation Team as a Zen Sangha

The study of Zen occurs within the context of a community, or Sangha. The Sangha fosters the teachings of Zen, trains students in the disciplines, practices, and devotions of Zen, and provides suitable surroundings, instruction, and support for the practice of Zen. A Zen teacher guides the Zen Sangha along the path of awakening. Experiences of the student are presented to the teacher for verification. In DBT, the consultation team serves the function of enhancing clinicians' motivation and capabilities to provide DBT, which could be considered to share some characteristics with a Zen Sangha. Ultimately, the team acts as the vehicle that provides guidance to the community of therapists providing treatment to a community of clients. Although the consultation team can be viewed as non-hierarchical in nature, each consultation team has a team leader. Typically, the leader has greater experience and knowledge than other team members in the treatment, with the added responsibility of maintaining DBT programme fidelity. The team leader assures that all team members adhere to the principles that guide DBT and continually deepen their knowledge, skills, and abilities in the practice of DBT. Other team members and the team leader verify the conduct of DBT.

DBT Therapist as Teacher

The therapeutic relationship between a therapist and client in DBT mirrors the relationship between a student and teacher in Zen. A Zen teacher guides the inexperienced student along a spiritual journey fraught with difficulties and doubt. In Zen it is necessary to have a teacher who understands Zen, has been recognized as a teacher by the Zen community, and who has been granted authority by a Zen master (Rōshi) to teach and lead others. DBT therapists act as guides to building a life worth living, must possess the requisite knowledge and skills in the treatment, and be recognized as such by the DBT community. Both DBT and Zen consider the relationship between client and therapist, student and teacher, to be a real relationship between equals.

CONCLUSION

There is an old Zen story (author unknown) about a king whose people had grown soft and entitled. Dissatisfied with this state of affairs, he hoped to teach them a lesson. His plan was simple. He would place a large boulder in the middle of the main road, completely blocking entry into the city. He would then hide nearby and observe their reactions. How would they respond? Would they band together to remove it? Or would they get discouraged, quit, and return home? With growing disappointment, the king watched as subject after subject came to this impediment and turned away. Or, at best, tried halfheartedly before giving up. Many openly complained or cursed the king, fortune, or bemoaned the inconvenience; none managed to do anything about it. After several days, a lone peasant came along on his way into town. He did not turn away. Instead he strained and strained, trying to push it out of the way. Then an idea came to him, and he scrambled into the nearby woods to find something he could use for leverage. Finally, he returned with a large branch he had crafted into a lever and deployed it to dislodge the massive rock from the road. Beneath the rock were a purse of gold coins and a note from the king, which said:

> "The obstacle in the path becomes the path. Never forget, within every obstacle is an opportunity to improve our condition."

One of the first scientists to introduce acceptance in the form of mindfulness into psychotherapy was Marsha Linehan. Mindfulness is now considered a mainstream or complementary treatment for multiple physical and psychological maladies. Within the obstacle of non-acceptance, Linehan was able to see opportunity. The new path includes acceptance in the form of mindfulness, which can lead to relief in the lives of many suffering individuals.

Key Messages for Clinicians

- Zen as a practice has a 2,500-year history.
- Zen forms the basis of acceptance technology found in DBT.
- Zen practice principles are compatible with behaviour therapy.
- Zen provides a set of new targets for both client and therapist.
- DBT core mindfulness and reality acceptance skills are an outgrowth of Zen practice.

REFERENCES

Aitken, R. (1982). *Taking the path of Zen*. London: Macmillan.

Beck, C. J. (1993). *Nothing special: Living Zen*. San Francisco: Harper.

Dalai Lama, (2005). *The universe in a single atom: The convergence of science and spirituality*. New York: Random House.

Gordon, J. (2015). The evolution of medicine. *On Being*, Interviewed by Krista Tippett. Retrieved from http://www.onbeing.org/program/mark-hyman-james-gordon-and-penny-george-the-evolution-of-medicine/8183.

Hakuin E. (c.1750). *Zazen Wasan—Song of Zazen*, trans. Robert Aitken. Retrieved from https://villagezendo.org/practice/suggested-readings/zazen-wasan/.

Hanh, T. N. (2009). *Answers from the heart: Practical responses to life's burning questions.* Berkeley, CA: Parallax Press.

Hanh, T. N. (2012). *Awakening of the heart: Essential buddhist sutras and commentaries.* Berkeley, CA: Parallax Press.

Hawk, P. (2009). *Zen dharma talk tucson.*

Hawk, P. (2010). *Zen dharma talk tucson.*

Hillman, J. (2015). American zeitgeist and a shift in ages. In Pythia Peay (Ed.), *America on the couch: Psychological perspectives on American politics and culture* (pp. 425–436). Brooklyn: Lantern Books.

Jäger, W. *Zen home page benediktushof.* Retrieved from https://www.benediktushof-holzkirchen.de/zen/63-zen.html.

Jurgensmeyer, M. (Ed.) (2006). *Oxford handbook of global religions.* Oxford: Oxford University Press.

Kabat-Zinn, J. (1990). *Full catastrophe living: Using the wisdom of your body and mind to face stress, pain, and illness.* New York: Delacorte Press.

Kabat-Zinn, J. (2012). Opening to our lives. *On Being.* Interview by Krista Tippet. Retrieved from http://www.onbeing.org/program/opening-our-lives/138.

Koun, Y. (2005). *The gateless gate: The classic book of Zen koans.* Somerville, MA: Wisdom Publications.

Linehan, M. M. (1993). *Cognitive behavioral treatment for borderline personality disorder.* New York: Guilford Press.

Linehan M. M. (1996). Dialectical behavior therapy for borderline personality disorder. In B. Schmitz (Ed.), *Treatment of personality disorders.* Munich: Psychologie Verlags Union.

Linehan, M. M. (2015). *DBT skills training manual, second edition.* New York: Guilford Press.

Maller, A. S. (2016). Buddhism meets Hasidism. *Tricycle 25*(4). Retrieved from https://tricycle.org/magazine/buddhism-meets-hasidism/.

O'Brien, B. (2014). *Rethinking religion: Finding a place for religion in a modern, tolerant, progressive, peaceful and science affirming world,* ten directions.

Oxenhandler, N. (1996). Twirling a flower. *Tricycle 5*(3). Retrieved from https://tricycle.org/magazine/twirling-a-flower-the-question-form/.

Smithers, S. (1991). Minding the storehouse. *Tricycle 1*(1). Retrieved from https://tricycle.org/magazine/minding-storehouse/.

Tarrant, J. (2008). *Bring Me the rhinoceros: And other Zen koans that will save your life.* Boulder, CO: Shambhala Publications.

CHAPTER 6

MODIFYING CBT TO MEET THE CHALLENGE OF TREATING EMOTION DYSREGULATION

Utilizing Dialectics

JENNIFER H. R. SAYRS AND MARSHA M. LINEHAN

INTRODUCTION

DIALECTICS has many meanings. It can refer to a world view, a set of assumptions about fundamental processes of change, a form of dialogue or discourse, or a way of thinking. Dialectics as a world view can be contrasted with an absolute or universalistic world view and with a relativistic world view. In a universalistic world view, fixed universal truths are sought and one seeks to understand and adhere to the universal or correct order of things. In a relativistic world view, truth is relative, there is no a priori order to be found, and appreciation and description of diverse ordering is sought. Dialectics takes the middle path: fixed truths exist but only for the briefest moment before they evolve into new truths, and truths are relativistic in that they only exist in relation to their context. In a dialectical world view, truth both evolves over time and is found through "efforts to discover what is left out of existing ways of ordering the universe, and then to create new orderings which embrace and include what was previously excluded" (Basseches, 1984, p. 11).

With respect to dialogue, dialectics refers to the Socratic techniques of logical analysis of contradictory facts or ideas (thesis and antithesis) with a view to the resolution of their real or apparent contradictions (synthesis). This same process carried out internally by the individual is dialectical thinking. The goal is to come to a synthesis. Dialectical discourse develops by a continuous unification of opposites. This coming together is not the result of compromise, or a sacrifice of positions on either end, but a complex interplay where both extremes coexist. The result is an entirely new context, greater than the sum of the two. Because reaching a synthesis moves the interaction to a new context, with a new thesis and antithesis, a benefit of a dialectical discourse is that one can come to see the limits of one's present context, and see beyond those limits to additional possibilities.

Many psychotherapy approaches have strategies involving movement between thesis and antithesis. Any time a therapist examines a client's current ineffective strategies, explores what is being left out, and suggests new solutions to the client, and creates a move from thesis to antithesis. For example, in cognitive therapy, the therapist assesses the client's thoughts (theses) and facilitates movement to more rational, effective thoughts (antitheses). While this movement from thesis to antithesis is part of a dialectical strategy, it is not, in and of itself, dialectical. There is a second necessary component, which is movement from the antithesis to a synthesis of thesis and antithesis. Kegan (1982) highlights this difference: dichotomous strategies are those in which the old is abandoned for the new, as in the cognitive therapy example here, and dialectical strategies *incorporate* the old with the new, creating new and as yet unforeseen opportunities to solve the problem. Dialectical treatment strategies are those springing from a dialectical world view, intentionally designed to both foster the reconciliation of opposites within the therapeutic context and to model and strengthen dialectical response patterns of the client.

Dialectics were first described in a therapy context within dialectical behaviour therapy (DBT; Linehan, 1993). DBT is a form of cognitive behavioural therapy (CBT) that has both a dialectical world view to guide interventions as well as a number of specific dialectical strategies. The addition of dialectics was made primarily in response to the often extreme and polarized behavioural patterns and treatment dilemmas that arose in treatment with clients who experience emotion dysregulation and multiple, chronic problems. The dialectical stance can help improve clients' flexibility and tolerance of ambiguity, allowing new solutions to emerge from very difficult problems. Swenson (2016) describes the utility of dialectics within DBT, to help the therapist navigate impasses with a client, move both the client and therapist from rigidity to flexibility, find the wisdom in both poles of a situation and move toward synthesis, and throughout all of this, maintain collaboration between the therapist and client even when the therapy is stuck.

EVIDENCE-BASED TREATMENTS AND DIALECTICS

Dialectical treatment strategies have never been tested in isolation. However, there are data supporting treatment packages that incorporate dialectics. For example, a number of randomized clinical trials have shown efficacy for DBT with clients meeting criteria for borderline personality disorder in reducing suicide attempts, treatment drop-out, drug abuse, and emotion dysregulation (e.g., depression and high anger), and improving social and global adjustment (for a review, see Rizvi, Steffel, & Carson-Wong, 2013; see also Chapters 20 and 21, this volume).

Acceptance and Commitment Therapy (ACT; Hayes, Strosahl, & Wilson, 1999), another treatment package that emphasizes dialectical strategies (e.g., extensive use of metaphor and a strong emphasis on acceptance as an actual change strategy) has also been shown to be efficacious. In randomized controlled trials, ACT or ACT-based protocols have demonstrated efficacy in areas such as depression, pain, substance use, psychosis, and others (see https://contextualscience.org/state_of_the_act_evidence for a list of randomized controlled trials).

Several other evidence-based CBT approaches utilize strategies which have much in common with dialectics, including motivational interviewing (Miller & Rollnick, 2002 and Rosengren, 2009), mindfulness-based cognitive therapy (Segal, Williams, & Teasdale, 2002), relapse prevention (Marlatt & Donovan, 2005), and acceptance-based behaviour therapy (Roemer & Orsillo, 2002; Roemer, Orsillo, & Salters-Pedneault, 2008). A discussion of the use of dialectics in CBT along with additional examples can be found in Fruzzetti and Fruzzetti (2009).

When Are Dialectical Strategies Beneficial?

Dialectical strategies are useful when polarization occurs. The emphasis on movement and the larger context facilitates depolarization of interactions. For example, if a client insists that he or she needs to continue to use drugs, and the therapist insists the use must stop in order to have a productive life, therapeutic progress may halt. In such a case, the client has the thesis, the therapist the antithesis, and no synthesis is occurring (i.e., no movement). A useful synthesis that can function as the catalyst to further movement may be to agree with the client that drugs are helping to avoid a problem the client does not know how to solve, and therefore are useful (thesis), and at the same time they are creating other problems that are interfering with the client's life (antithesis). Therefore, a new solution to the client's problem (needing to feel better) must be generated. By synthesizing, or holding both poles as true, the therapist maximizes client collaboration while shifting away from self-destructive solutions for problems.

Other examples of getting stuck are when the client and therapist both end up on one pole and movement stops. For example, both may agree that a client's husband is not treating her well. Without seeing the antithesis (the husband's behaviour is caused by and makes sense given his learning history and the continuous interplay between him and his wife) and the synthesis (the husband's behaviour must change in order to keep the client happy, *and* the husband's behaviour makes sense given his context), the therapist and client can get stuck where the husband becomes "bad;" understanding does not evolve and solutions are not generated.

These strategies can also be used to get the client's attention when therapy is stagnating. A client will probably not expect a therapist to agree that drugs are useful in a certain sense, and doing so may confuse the client enough to make him or her sit up and listen. To remain dialectical, the therapist must of course also discuss why drugs are not an effective long-term solution to the problem, but this balanced approach can keep the client off-kilter enough to move the treatment forward.

DIALECTICAL STRATEGIES: STEP-BY-STEP

Steps in developing a dialectically informed treatment are as follows.

Step 1: Adopt and model a dialectical world view. It is extremely difficult to implement a set of dialectical treatment strategies within a guiding world view that is non-dialectical. Thus, the first task for the therapist who wants to integrate dialectics into treatment is to adopt such a view. This may be more difficult than it first appears, as it requires the therapist to wholeheartedly give up being right all of the time or having an absolute grasp on truth. It also demands that the therapist avoid falling back into imprecise thinking of "anything goes," or easing up on the effort to discover what is being excluded from the current perspective when differences and divisiveness are encountered.

There are three characteristics of a dialectical world view (Basseches, 1984). First, this world view is holistic and contextual. Most simply put, everything is related to everything else and events or phenomena cannot be understood independent of the context in which they occur, nor can the context be understood independent of the events that comprise it. The coherence of the overall phenomenon is primary, not the separate elements. From this perspective, *disorder is systemic.* Thus, rather than looking for a primary element that caused a client's problematic responses, be it cognition, biochemistry, action patterns, or the environment, the therapist searches for the pattern of relationships among elements that influences the system of client and environmental responses. Therapy is aimed at modifying these relationships.

Second, instead of conceptualizing static elements as entering into relations with other, external elements and the relations among elements are viewed within the context of the greater whole. From this perspective, *identity itself is relational.* One cannot be a therapist or a client, for example, outside of a therapeutic relationship. Disorder occurs when one's identity is generated from a part without reference to the whole. For example, while the sense of being isolated and an outsider may indeed be quite valid (as an element of the whole), such an experience arises from a lack of appreciation for one's connections to both others and to the universe (the whole). A dialectical therapist might suggest to a client who is feeling unloved that she views herself as one ingredient in a greater whole, rather than an independent element. Thus, the client may feel alone *and* learn to acknowledge the connections that exist within a dialectical world view. This client might focus on connections to loved ones who are not near, or strangers who may have had similar experiences, in an effort to feel more connected with other components of the whole.

Third, a dialectical world-view suggests that reality itself is a fundamental process of ongoing change. As relations change, a change in the whole occurs, and in turn, as the whole is altered, the relationship between these parts is changed. Dialectics refers to the logic of process, not to that of structure. Instead of searching for static elements from which the existence of an event or phenomena is formed, the *process* by which these elements evolve is sought. From this perspective, *change is both continual and transactional.* In contrast to an interactional diathesis-stress model of mental disorder, where the focus is on the unidirectional impact of one variable on another, a dialectical model focuses on the reciprocal impact of environment on person and person on environment, as well as the ongoing evolution of both in transaction. Dialectical therapists attend not only to their own impact on the client, but also the client's impact on them, and their joint influence on clinical outcome. For example, dialectics would suggest that attending to the reinforcement contingencies operating on the therapist within a clinical dyad is just as important as the reinforcement contingencies applied to the client by the therapist.

This perspective can be extremely beneficial in that it removes judgment and blame from the conceptualization of a problem. Instead of concluding that the client is "the problem," the therapist and client will look at the many transactions between the client and the multiple variables in the environment. Therapist and client will look for the validity in the client's responses to the environment, and the environment's understandable responses to the client, repeatedly over time, and how to alter these processes to create a more effective pattern. This moves the perspective off the "identified patient" and onto where interventions in the larger system may be useful.

Focusing on the continual process of change lends itself to teaching the client to become more dialectical. Arbitrarily keeping a treatment frame the same across time might be artificial, and as a result, detrimental to the client. The dialectical therapist instead allows for change within the therapeutic relationship and coaches the client how to tolerate such natural change. This is not to say that change should be *created* to help the client; on the contrary, it is learning about the natural course of change that can be therapeutic. This approach synthesizes the desire for the client to maintain consistency with the fact that change is always occurring, which facilitates learning to tolerate and even embrace such change. For example, a therapist's limits about the extent of out-of-session contact with the client may evolve over time, and there is no reason to artificially keep the rules in therapy the same simply to avoid exposing the client to such variability. By being awake to the evolving nature of the therapeutic relationship, a dialectical therapist can improve the quality of the relationship, minimize frustration and burnout, and more closely mimic relationships occurring outside of therapy. Similarly, two providers working with the same client may have vastly different limits in their interactions with the client, and allowing the client to become accustomed to such inconsistency, while providing support for the difficulties it creates, may enhance the client's flexibility.

Step 2: Balance treatment strategies and therapeutic positions. The primary dialectical strategy is balance: the balanced use of strategies and therapeutic positions by the therapist, and constant attention to the reality that for any point an opposite or complementary position can be held. From a dialectical stance, the therapist combines acceptance with an emphasis on change, flexibility with stability, nurturing with challenging, a focus on capabilities with a focus on limitations and deficits, and offering problem solutions oriented to change with solutions oriented to tolerating what is. It is important to note that "balance" does not refer to a 50–50 division. To be dialectical, a therapist would fully embody both poles and strategically implement strategies from either pole as needed. For example, the therapist can fully accept and understand the client exactly as she is, while at the same time deeply understand the need for change. The strategies implemented in any interaction will be based on what is needed in the moment, from a stance of full acceptance and full change. This could result in an entire session focused solely on validation, or solely on change. By holding both acceptance and change as strongly important in each interaction, the therapist will do exactly what is needed in the moment.

There are three essential characteristics of a dialectical stance in therapy. First, speed is of the essence. This keeps the client off balance and facilitates change so the balance between acceptance and change can be maintained. Second, alertness to each movement and response of the client is required. The therapists must respond just enough to each move of the client to maintain the therapeutic flow. As noted by Linehan, "the therapist has to be as alert as if he or she and the patient really were balanced at opposite ends of a teeter-totter perched on a high wire over the Grand Canyon" (1993, p. 202). Third, the therapist must move with certainty, strength, and total commitment. Dialectics is not "wishy-washy." The therapist gives him or herself over to being just as he or she is in one moment, while being open to quickly moving to another position in the next.

Step 3. When polarization occurs, work for a synthesis. The most essential and unique theme of a dialectical process is the pattern of thesis, antithesis, and synthesis. The dialectical therapist notices when a dialectical impasse has been reached, searches for what is left out of both the therapist's and client's current behaviours and ways of ordering reality, and then works with the client to create new orderings that embrace and include what was previously excluded. Consider a woman who enters therapy saying she cannot change (thesis). Her family says she can change if she wants to (antithesis). The synthesis may more fully develop the thesis and antithesis (she can learn to change) or replace the contradiction by transforming one of the opposites into the other (wanting to change might itself require change). Another useful strategy in this situation, behavioural shaping (reinforcing small increments of improved behaviour), is also a dialectical treatment strategy in that it incorporates simultaneous acceptance of a client's limitations and realization of the capacity for change.

A clinical example of synthesis and movement is provided in a situation where a therapist disagrees with a client's decision regarding a particular problem. For example, contrary to the therapist's advice, a client goes to the local emergency room whenever suicidal, says that he or she is going to attempt suicide if left alone, and is admitted to an inpatient unit. The therapist views this series of events as reinforcing the client's repeated suicidal behaviours. Going onto an inpatient unit is an escape from difficult life situations; over time the need to escalate suicidality to get the ER staff to continue to hospitalize the client is leading to more serious risk and, in time, the pattern will lead to the client's suicide. The thesis, as proposed by the therapist, could be stated as, "Hospitalization in response to suicidal behaviours increases the likelihood of further suicidal behaviours and eventual suicide."

The antithesis to this approach is that suicidal thoughts and plans are a result of the client being overwhelmed by life's adversities and overcome with unendurable anguish. An inpatient setting reduces the client's sense of alienation and provides an opportunity to work on problems leading to thoughts and plans of suicide. Denying admission to the inpatient unit to a recurrently suicidal person is cruel, invalidates the client's need for help, and makes the situation worse. The client therefore becomes more suicidal. Being kept in such a painful environment means the client will eventually commit suicide. The antithesis proposed by the client is, "Keeping me out of the hospital when I am suicidal will increase the likelihood of further suicidal behaviours and eventual suicide." This is an alternative point of view, but one that is equally polarized and static.

A synthesis to these poles is to consider both sides of the issue at once, see the validity in each pole, and look for what is being left out of both positions. What options other than hospitalization (and reinforcement of suicidal behaviours) and refusal to hospitalize (leaving the client alone to deal with intolerable anguish) are being ignored? How could the therapist's need to "do no harm" be reconciled with the client's need for help? In this situation, the client is not considering the harmful consequences of hospitalization. The therapist is not considering that the client's pain is sometimes so intense that immediate outside help is essential. The therapist must first fully grasp and embrace both poles, then consider other forms of intervention that will provide the client with assistance in staying alive that does not simultaneously constitute reinforcement for the suicidal behaviour. For example, the therapist might agree to admit the suicidal client to a medical (not psychiatric) unit, or to admit the client to his or her most hated inpatient unit with plans in place to provide protection but none of the activities that constitute reinforcement. Or the client and therapist might find an alternative, non-reinforcing, placement with relatives or friends.

Step 4. When one dialectical strategy doesn't work, try another. Any strategy that involves looking for what is left out (finding the antithesis), synthesizing thesis and antithesis, and allowing the synthesis to move the interaction forward into a new tension between thesis and antithesis, is a dialectical strategy. There are many ways to accomplish this. Thus, in one session the therapist may need to move from strategy to strategy until one of them allows the therapist and client to find the synthesis. Dialectical strategies from DBT are as follows.

Magnify the tension between opposites. It is the tension between opposites or between parts and wholes that propels change. At times it can be useful for the therapist to magnify the tension to unbalance the client's position and push change. The *devil's advocate* technique, developed by Goldfried (1978), is a good example. The therapist presents an extreme prepositional statement (thesis), then asks if the client believes it. Once the client agrees, the therapist begins arguing the antithesis in an extreme way, playing devil's advocate. Through the process of back and forth argument, synthesis can be brought about. For example, the therapist asks for a commitment to treatment and to no self harm for the duration of the treatment (thesis), and the client agrees. The therapist moves to the antithesis in an extreme fashion, asking, "Now, why on earth would you want to agree to this? Wouldn't you rather be in a therapy where you're allowed to self harm? I'm not going to let you out of this agreement. Why would you agree to this?" Assuming the therapist has been extreme enough, the client will come to synthesize two poles: acknowledging the difficulty and seriousness of the commitment while simultaneously strengthening the arguments against self harming. A typical response to this strategy is, "No, I can't keep living this way. It's affecting my relationships and my self-respect. I want to stop harming myself. I fully understand how difficult this is, and it is worth it to me." (Of course, if a client responds with, "You're right! I shouldn't do this treatment!" the therapist can quickly switch to other strategies.)

Extending is another strategy that can magnify and highlight the tension between opposites. The technique was adapted from Aikido and is similar to strategic family therapy's psychological judo: joining with the person's movement in a particular direction, moving with him or her, then extending the person's movement beyond where he or she was intending to go, leaving him or her slightly off balance (Linehan, 1993). Extending is useful when clients are polarized and make very dramatic or extreme statements as a means to solve a problem. It is also useful when the therapist is frustrated and can't think of another response. For example, when a client states, "If I can't see you today, it's all over. That's it!" instead of responding to the overt content of the statement by discussing why the therapist cannot see the client on such short notice, why this is not an effective way to request a session, and so on, the therapist can join with the client ("Oh, no!"), move with the client ("It sounds like things are really bad right now."), and then move beyond the client's statement, or extend the statement, leaving the client off balance ("Are you suicidal? It sounds like you are really not doing well! And I can't see you until tomorrow. If you are going to kill yourself you are probably too upset to have a session anyway. Let me get off the phone and call 911. Or can you get yourself to the hospital immediately?"). When extending, a therapist responds to the part of the statement the client is least expecting. Instead of talking about whether to have a session, the therapist responds to the implicit threat and its consequences. Such a response can cause the client to back off from the extreme nature of the statement. Again, the introduction of an antithesis when the client is very polarized provides conditions ripe for synthesis, where more options are available to the client.

In another example, the client may say that he or she wants to use drugs "just to see what it's like." The therapist, instead of arguing, "Don't do it," agrees, then takes it to the extreme. The therapist may say, "Right, you want to try *everything* once, even including AIDS and poking yourself in the eye with a pencil." The client is then forced to move toward the middle, or synthesis, of the argument, by stating, "Well, I suppose some things are dangerous even if done only once" as the therapist moves to an alternate synthesis that "some risk is an inherent part of life." Even if the client still isn't completely convinced that he or she doesn't want to experiment, this provides the therapist the room needed to discuss the problem more freely without continuous argument. This strategy has, as a result, expanded the realm of available outcomes.

Enter the paradox. Entering the paradox involves moving into a paradox, or tension between poles, by highlighting seeming contradictions in two positions and leaving the contradiction hanging, letting the client tolerate the tension between the two. The therapist might ask, "It seems like you want to work on this target and you don't," without saying more. This approach is often very foreign to clients' approach to their lives, which may be more "black and white" or rigid than flexible. A therapist might strongly and genuinely validate a client's position ("I understand completely how it is reasonable for you to believe I don't care about you"), while simultaneously disagreeing with it ("and it is reasonable for me to disagree"). This models for the client how two positions can both be true at once, letting the client tolerate that tension and find that the solution lies in neither pole but in the synthesis. Again, this approach can throw the client off balance, providing conditions necessary for depolarization and the generation of creative new solutions.

One relatively straightforward strategy aimed at finding a synthesis by highlighting a paradox is changing the word "but" to "and." This strategy is used in DBT, and is described as the *and versus but* technique by Hayes and his colleagues (Hayes et al., 1999). The therapist has the client substitute the word "but" with "and." The word "but" indicates the words placed after the word "but" contradict the statement preceding the word "but." For example, "I love my boyfriend, but I am always so angry at him," communicates the anger contradicts the woman's love for her boyfriend. The statement implies that one or the other statements must change, because they are at odds with each other, which can create polarization. This approach is dichotomous, involving abandoning the thesis for the antithesis. To move the client toward a synthesis, she can remove the word "but" and substitute the word "and": "I love my boyfriend, *and* I am always so angry at him." Here, there is no contradiction; both statements are true. By allowing both statements to stand as they are, the client has synthesized the two poles, which moves the client forward, depolarizes the statement, and provides a new context from which solutions can be generated.

Another example of entering the paradox is that of *making lemonade out of lemons*, where the therapist takes a situation that appears problematic and re-conceptualizes it as an opportunity or benefit. For example, when a client informs his or her therapist that he or she could not complete the assigned therapy homework or task during the week, the client generally expects the therapist to be disappointed. But with this strategy, the therapist can respond with, "How wonderful! Now we have an opportunity to figure out what the obstacle was." The therapist constantly looks for what can be gained from a difficult or problematic situation (what was left out of the client's perspective), so the treatment can continue to progress. There is a danger with this strategy, however. If, by using this strategy, the therapist inadvertently invalidates the difficulty or pain of the situation (i.e., implies that the lemon was really lemonade all along), progress will halt. The therapist must be careful not to simply move from thesis to antithesis ("You should stop complaining and appreciate the good in the situation"), and instead synthesize the two points ("Things are really painful right now, *and* there are some aspects of this problem from which you might benefit"). Another example of lemonade arose with a client in withdrawal from heroin. Instead of going with the thesis ("This is too hard to tolerate!") or antithesis ("It will be worth it,"), the therapist can find the synthesis, "I know you're miserable, and this is the most worthwhile misery you will probably ever experience." This response can help the client to tolerate a safe withdrawal with medical help while validating its difficulty.

Develop metaphors. Metaphors, or the use of stories, parables, myths, or other alternate forms of describing a situation, are used in many treatments, primarily because they provide an indirect, less threatening form of communication. Metaphors have many benefits, including increasing client understanding of complicated points and enhancing client memory. Metaphors are also dialectical strategies, in that they can provide fertile ground for antithesis and synthesis when polarization has occurred. Metaphors are the path to the dialectic, in other words. When the story is less emotional and somewhat removed from the actual situation, the client may suddenly be able to see what is being left out and synthesize the two poles. When the story is then related back to the original problem, the client may see the problem within a new context.

The therapist, in creating the metaphor, must be very careful to capture the essence of the thesis and antithesis. A misaimed metaphor can confuse the client and divert the discussion. But a metaphor that accurately reflects the problem and its ramifications can be extremely powerful. For example, clients often become frustrated with therapists for pushing for change when the client is experiencing a great deal of pain and wants soothing from the therapist. The client is a person standing on white hot coals begging for water to be poured on his or her feet. The therapist might ask, "Who cares for you more, the person who pours water over your feet or the person who runs onto the coals to push you off?" Or, in a behavioural skills training session, a client says, "I don't do skills." The therapist responds, "You remind me of a house builder who says I don't do walls." To the client who consistently avoids behaviours necessary for change, "You are a person sitting in a corner of the back room of a burning building with only one door out. Running through the smoke and flames around the door is the only escape. Let's run." In this example, the thesis, "This hurts too much for me to do anything," and the antithesis, "You must change," are synthesized ("The temporary increase in pain will in the long run help you to feel better,") and the client suddenly has more options available to solve the problem.

Having many metaphors at one's fingertips is important in order to select one that accurately captures the situation. In addition to the metaphors provided in the Linehan and Hayes et al. texts, many useful stories are provided in DeMello (1982).

CONCLUSION

Dialectical strategies can take many forms. The underlying principle of such strategies is a focus on the process of change within a context. This context is made up of constantly changing components, which, in turn, are part of yet another, greater context.

A dialectical strategy is one where the therapist and client can search for what is being left out in the current thesis and synthesize the thesis and antithesis, continuing the evolution toward a new thesis. The examples provided demonstrate how these emphases can be translated to the therapy room. By providing clients with conditions for synthesis when treatment progress has halted, clients and therapists may be better able to view the "bigger picture," from which new solutions are available and therapeutic movement can resume.

KEY POINTS FOR CLINICIANS

- A dialectical strategy is any strategy that looks for what is left out of one's position, then facilitates movement toward a synthesis of the two opposing positions.
- Dialectical strategies include magnifying tension between two poles, entering the paradox, and the use of metaphors.
- While the dialectical strategies were developed within DBT, several evidence-based treatments utilize a dialectical approach.

REFERENCES

Basseches, M. (1984). *Dialectical thinking and adult development*. New Jersey: Ablex Publishing Corporation.

De Mello, A. (1982). *The song of the bird*. New York: Doubleday.

Fruzzetti, A. R., & Fruzzetti, A. E. (2009). Dialectics in cognitive and behavior therapy. In W. T. O'Donohue & J. E. Fisher (Eds.), *General principles and empirically supported techniques of cognitive behavior therapy* (pp. 230–239). Hoboken, NJ: John Wiley & Sons, Inc.

Goldfried, M. R., Linehan, M. M., & Smith, J. L. (1978). The reduction of test anxiety through cognitive restructuring. *Journal of Consulting and Clinical Psychology, 46*, 32–39.

Hayes, S. C., Strosahl, K. D., & Wilson, K. G. (1999). *Acceptance and Commitment Therapy: An experiential approach to behavior change*. New York: Guilford Press.

Kegan, R. (1982). *The evolving self: Problem and process in human development*. Cambridge, MA: Harvard University Press.

Linehan, M. M. (1993). *Cognitive-behavioral treatment of borderline personality disorder*. New York: Guilford Press.

Marlatt, G. A., & Donovan, D. M. (2005). *Relapse prevention: Maintenance strategies in the treatment of addictive behaviors*, 2nd Edition. New York: Guilford Press.

Miller, W. R., & Rollnick, S. (2002). *Motivational interviewing*, 2nd Edition. New York: Guilford Press.

Rizvi, S. L., Steffel, L. M., & Carson-Wong, A. (2013). An overview of dialectical behavior therapy for professional psychologists. *Professional Psychology: Research and Practice, 44*(2), 73–80.

Roemer, L., & Orsillo, S. M. (2002). Expanding our conceptualization of and treatment for generalized anxiety disorder: Integrating mindfulness/acceptance-based approaches with existing cognitive-behavioral models. *Clinical Psychology: Science and Practice, 9*(1), 54–68.

Roemer, L., Orsillo, S. M., & Salters-Pedneault, K. (2008). Efficacy of an acceptance-based be-
    havior therapy for generalized anxiety disorder: Evaluation in a randomized controlled trial.
    Journal of Consulting and Clinical Psychology, 76(6), 1083–1089.

Rosengren, D. B. (2009). *Building motivational interviewing skills: A practitioner workbook.*
    New York: Guilford Press.

Segal, Z. V., Williams, J. M. G., & Teasdale, J. D. (2002). *Mindfulness-based cognitive therapy for
    depression: A new approach to preventing relapse.* New York: Guilford Press.

Swenson, C. R. (2016). *DBT principles in action.* New York: Guilford Press.

THE STRUCTURE OF TREATMENT

CHAPTER 7

THE STRUCTURE OF DBT PROGRAMMES

HENRY SCHMIDT III AND JOAN C. RUSSO

IMPLEMENTING DIALECTICAL BEHAVIOUR THERAPY: AN INTRODUCTION

WHATEVER one's trade or avocation, there is generally a collection of tools, rules, and materials to become familiar with. Mastery is an indication that one has a deep understanding of how to best operate within the bounds defining the activity. Musicians know their instruments, and generally play within set tunings and time sequences. Chess masters adopt the pieces, their moves, and play on a set board. By practising our play within the rules and on the board we are given, we develop mastery. Failing to attend to either aspect will result in less satisfactory outcomes (or will birth a new activity). Each new activity we learn starts with a goal, a set of instructions, and the tools and materials to work with.

This chapter is intended to assist those preparing to begin a treatment programme offering Dialectical Behaviour Therapy (DBT), and to provide tips to programmes already established. The person responsible for leading the team is identified as the "team leader" or "programme manager", although these duties may be shared with others across programmes. We presume reader familiarity with the theory and practices of the model as described originally by Linehan (1993a, 1993b), and expanded upon by Linehan and her colleagues in subsequent publications, presentations, and trainings. There have been DBT programmes established around the world in the past 25 years, most comprising a single team. Smaller programmes may only have a few team members, while large programmes may include multiple teams working across a system of care or within a facility, sharing clients across time and settings. A single chapter is too brief to describe in full all aspects of every possible programme configuration. The discussion herein offers suggestions for how to organize and streamline treatment tasks and processes.

Although the number of details presented may seem daunting at first, keep in mind that DBT originated in a few standardly equipped therapy offices, with several binders of freshly printed handouts and an organized approach to conducting and documenting treatment. At some point, maybe from the beginning, Marsha added a mindfulness bell. In some settings it may not need to get much more complicated than that.

Much larger programmes face both challenges and opportunities in setting up shop. In some settings (e.g., residential), programme structure necessarily becomes more complex as the number of staff increases and roles and responsibilities are shared. The discussion of how to implement a principle-driven treatment in the real world involves balancing a need to adapt to one's clients and surroundings against a desire to replicate a treatment model with as much fidelity as possible (Koerner, Dimeff, & Swenson, 2007; Best & Lyng, this volume). Although this chapter speaks to anybody running a DBT programme, it is up to the practitioner or programme manager to identify the demands of their practice, and select from the following recommendations accordingly.

This chapter briefly describes the functions of comprehensive treatment as identified by Linehan, Cochran, & Kehrer (2001), and then addresses the structure of the DBT programme. It starts by discussing the space in which treatment is housed. Following that, it reviews the structural elements of each of the modes of treatment identified by Linehan originally (1993a), materials and supplies that support the programme, and finally the elements of administration. Where Linehan has remained silent in administrative matters, we have occasionally referenced best clinical practice recommendations from other sources.

Whenever possible, the information here has been derived from programme descriptions made available by the developer of DBT and her associates, favouring those descriptions that have been tested in outcome research. Most of these are published, and are referenced here and in other chapters of this volume. Additional information has been gleaned from working with Linehan and her colleagues specifically on the topic of programme certification, and from the creative approaches shared with us by many professionals implementing DBT in settings around the world.

DEFINING "PROGRAMME STRUCTURE"

We define programme structure as those tangible and intangible elements that operate in a fixed way, generally to support treatment objectives or processes. This chapter is important because, as Robinson notes, "we can easily ignore [structure] and take it for granted—it's just an underlying platform, often invisible, though it shapes everything that is built on top of it" (2015, p. 11). In DBT, structure is present across all modes of treatment. Taking the example of chess, the game includes the board, the pieces, and the rules. The players and the succession of plays are free to vary, but the structure is maintained across every game played. Otherwise, one is not playing chess. In DBT, structure would encompass the setting and administration of treatment, the materials used, and the practices spelled out in the treatment manuals.

The structural elements of DBT have various sources. In some instances, Linehan adopted or created structure based on the best science supporting her goals, such as specific skills taught for emotion regulation, or the use of the diary card for more accurate reporting and tracking of client data between sessions. Other structural elements of treatment are driven by principles of treatment or theoretical assumptions of the client population, such as the specific selection of skills taught and the sequencing of treatment. There are some elements that are somewhat arbitrary or derived from common practice, such as length of session. And, as in the most straightforward of designs, the structure or form of some aspects of treatment is derived directly from its intended function (Sullivan, 1896).

FUNCTION MATTERS

Decisions about treatment implementation and adaptations should be made with consideration of the principles and functions of treatment. The functions of comprehensive DBT were introduced in 2001 (Linehan, Cochran, & Kehrer, 2001) and have been referenced in many publications since. To review briefly, Linehan identified and described five functions of comprehensive treatment: 1) engaging and motivating clients and 2) providers, 3) client skill acquisition and 4) generalization, and 5) structuring the environment.

Beginning with the first function, it is expected that clients may require early and ongoing assistance in motivation for treatment. Formal treatment does not begin until the client makes a commitment to work on agreed-upon targets in therapy with her individual therapist (and attend skills group). Linehan attends to this in a variety of ways across treatment. In her manual and subsequent training materials, she presented specific therapist strategies to develop client motivation and strengthen commitment. Client engagement is tracked from the beginning; Linehan included a daily client self-report of "urge to quit therapy" on the diary card as a variable to actively monitor and address in session as needed. In addition, clients are expected to call and take calls from their therapist between sessions, to support motivated action in crisis, and repair the relationship between therapist and client, if needed. Skills trainers develop relationships with each client and track attendance at skills group closely, and the group work is designed to be sufficiently challenging, interesting, and fun. Skills trainers may also take or initiate phone calls to clients between sessions. Clients are oriented to a "4-miss" rule in treatment, and the consultation team swings into action if it appears that a client will miss a third consecutive treatment session. Finally, Linehan identified "treatment-interfering-behaviour (TIB)" as a high-level target for treatment across all modes of treatment, stressing the need to directly address barriers to a productive therapeutic relationship. From a logical perspective, if a client is not engaged in (and practising within) treatment, outcomes are likely to suffer greatly. Thus, this function is a high priority across all modes of treatment identified in Linehan's original treatment manual.

Working with high-risk and challenging client behaviours without support is a predictor of therapist burnout (Deutsch, 1984) and treatment drift. Thus, Linehan noted the need to attend to therapist motivation to provide treatment. She developed the Consultation Team specifically to address this function. Team meetings focus on enhancing therapist capabilities, maintaining treatment adherence and outcomes, and providing ongoing support to team members. The meetings also include ongoing training, which allows therapists to remain current with new developments in basic science and treatment, and encourages participation in professional networks. Role plays, video review, and clinical discussions held during the meeting can control for therapist drift from the treatment, improving outcomes and client responses. Further, the team may provide support to a therapist during challenging periods of treatment. Agreements on how to interact with fellow team members further guide conversation (and cognitions) to reduce negative or destructive emotions, as do recommendations for a routine mindfulness practice. The commitment to therapist motivation is one made by the team to each individual therapist, and by each individual therapist who agrees to follow a sound practice to maintain his or her engagement.

Theorizing that client dysfunctional behaviour is a means of solving problems in the client's life, Linehan (1993a) highlighted the need to supply clients with alternate and more productive means of solving the same problems. "Supporting client skill acquisition and generalization" (Functions 3 and 4) requires that we help clients learn new skills, and apply those skills to all relevant settings. At times, this is done within the session, as when a therapist teaches a client to regulate her emotions and then encourages her to use that skill in-session when arousal interferes with treatment. In other instances, a skill may be taught formally in group or as needed in session, with the intent that the client will apply the skill to some situation outside of treatment. Skills taught in group (Linehan, 1993b) were developed to address the deficits generally identified in the client population as a whole; skills focused on in session are often selected specifically for the individual client in a given context. Practising skills is the guiding principle underlying most DBT structure.

Finally, Linehan noted the centrality of environment in supporting behaviour, and as a critical factor in behaviour change. The fifth function is "structuring the environment so that effective behaviours, rather than dysfunctional behaviours, are reinforced" (Linehan et al., 2001, p. 486). More broadly construed, the function can be understood as utilizing structure to support the many principles and goals of treatment, within the treatment setting and beyond. When considering generalization of behaviour and maintenance of treatment gains, the function of "structuring the environment" may extend to assisting the client to structure her own environment, including relationships, employment, spirituality, and general health. All of these changes are in pursuit of a client-identified "life worth living." The balance of this chapter will be devoted to the ways in which the treatment environment itself is structured to support the modes and other aspects of treatment.

It is critical to understand the principles and functions of treatment when considering the elements that support it. Linehan has provided extensive material for our consideration on both function and form of DBT, and has been explicit in discussing these over the evolution of the treatment. She noted in a recent retrospective that "[m]odularity can be used to separate the functions of a treatment/intervention into independent modules such that each module contains everything necessary to carry out one specific aspect of the desired treatment" (Linehan & Wilks, 2015, p. 101). To take one example, Linehan identified that skills groups directly support the function of client skills acquisition. As noted, groups are also offered in a way that is intended to enhance client engagement in treatment. In the development of DBT, skills groups were ultimately created as a mode of treatment apart from individual sessions to enable skills development across the course of treatment. For clients commonly in crisis, a skills group was offered in a well-defined classroom-style format. Here a core set of skills were taught that the client and therapist could draw on and strengthen in individual sessions. Further, the nature of the ground rules of skills sessions (e.g., no discussion of self-harm, no intimate relationships with members of the group) along with the didactic approach created a clear and pragmatic approach which lowered the likelihood of eliciting strong emotional responses, thus reducing impediments to learning and unintended reinforcement of dysfunctional behaviour. Thus, the functions of skills groups are directly supported by setting, style of delivery, and rules.

Although Linehan proposed that a modular treatment could focus on one function of treatment per module, it may be a matter of emphasis rather than exclusivity. In practice, each mode of DBT requires attention to more than one function. Anybody who has seen Linehan conduct skills training knows that she pays close attention to engaging and motivating her clients throughout the session, and diary cards and homework review both heavily emphasize skill generalization. Whether adopting or adapting the model, following the principles and understanding the reasoning beneath Linehan's recommended practices will help to ensure that the functions of treatment continue to be supported in your programme environment.

THE STRUCTURE OF TREATMENT IN THE ORIGINAL MANUALS

Linehan devoted a chapter in her original text (1993a, pp. 165–196) to the structure of treatment specific to target behaviours. That chapter introduces target hierarchies for each mode of treatment, and clarified therapist responsibilities. It also largely discusses what should occur within sessions, and it is here that Linehan introduces the individual diary card. This chapter also clearly identifies that it is the client's individual therapist who bears ultimate responsibility for addressing the client's target behaviour(s) in standard outpatient DBT. Linehan also briefly describes the Consultation Team meeting, and presents a set of agreements that therapists committed to uphold in her clinic.

The skills manual released concurrently (Linehan, 1993b) introduced the skills diary card, dozens of client handouts, scripted lecture content and discussion points for each skills group session, and agreed-upon rules of conduct. A leader and co-leader were recommended for group, and their roles described, along with a predictable sequence of group activities, starting with a mindfulness exercise.

Each mode of treatment has its own structural demands, based upon the setting, its functions and the tasks to be performed. Linehan (1993a) noted that the hierarchies and division of responsibilities can be altered to suit other settings or client populations, but that the resulting changes must be defined and explained to programme participants and in the adapted programme manual. She singles out milieu-based programmes as an example, noting that the target hierarchy may change and that careful description of the milieu (as a separate mode of treatment) would be desirable, with its primary function being skill generalization. Such an arrangement was later described by Swenson and colleagues (2001). Thus, across all forms of DBT, Linehan envisioned that the functions of treatment would apply, although the modes may be altered to respond to local demands and opportunities. There are additional chapters in the original text (Linehan, 1993a) similarly focused on structure of treatment, including instructions for case management, conducting sessions, and a focus on crisis management and suicide assessment and response. As an introduction to the structure of treatment, each of these chapters is important to revisit in its original form.

As Linehan and her colleagues have further described and researched treatment in the ensuing 25 years since her initial research was published (Linehan, Armstrong, Suarez, Allmon, & Heard, 1991), more detail has been provided concerning the structure of treatment (see Chapters 8–11 and 25–36, this volume). Many of those elements are catalogued below. This review may seem overly complex to some, or too simplistic to others. For many, a discussion of programme structure will not hold near the excitement of therapy descriptions and session transcripts, and understandably so. The proposition here is that, by clarifying and organizing the predictable elements of a programme in order to best support clinicians and clients, a therapist's attention may focus more consistently and completely to the challenging and, for some, more rewarding aspects of treatment.

HOUSING THE TREATMENT

The space where treatment occurs is perhaps one of the more obvious elements of structure, often considered initially when looking for a practice site and again when considering how to grow or streamline operations. A comfortable waiting area and bathroom, a locked file room (with locked cabinets), rooms for individual sessions, a larger room for skills groups and Consultation Team meetings, and some means of communication between client and therapist in between sessions are the essentials needed for a comprehensive programme. Small programmes may need to solve *only* these problems in terms of space. Larger programmes may need more space to house administrative staff and infrastructure, increasingly including secure areas for computer servers and client files. A "break room" and storage space for supplies can almost always be put to good use.

Adaptations of the model will have different space requirements. Treatment targeting youth or vulnerable adults with a caregiver will demand larger rooms for therapy sessions (parts of which the caregivers may attend), and for skills groups (clients plus caregivers). A milieu-based approach (e.g., day treatment, inpatient, forensic) will require an infrastructure to support other activities provided to clients (e.g., education, recreation, vocational training, spiritual practice, meals, etc.). DBT adaptations may have separate treatments offered specifically for caregivers (e.g., parent training), or for common client targets (e.g., food preparation and nutrition), which may call for additional rooms and configurations, or even separate space for non-DBT providers to work and deliver their services. Some populations may benefit from on-site daycare for children of clients or for very young siblings in adolescent multi-family groups. Thus, an understanding of the modes of treatment to be offered and the needs of the clients to be treated within the programme will dictate space requirements.

Additional "Housing" Consideration: Wiring the Programme

Technology is constantly evolving and improving the ways in which we can work with each other and clients. Telecommunications, electronic records, and storage and retrieval of files locally and online must be addressed in today's programmes. Linehan (1993a) introduced in her manual that real-time communication between client and therapist must be available between sessions. Phone calls (and, increasingly, texts or other means of contact) support client skill generalization, crisis management, and the client-therapist relationship. Thus, programmes must decide how clinicians will field and respond to communications in the office and beyond, and clarify to clients how to reach their therapists. Therapists must be able to consult one another as well, and have ready access to contact information for others in the client's network included in a given client's crisis plan. All of these tasks are able to be completed more conveniently than in the past via current technology; ensuring reliable and secure means of communication and access to file information is a decision worth researching, and making early.

The software and information technology supporting treatment documentation and information retrieval is an important and (often) expensive decision, and mapping out the programme demands can help in shopping or negotiating with vendors. These decisions are not DBT-specific, but it is important to balance the need to maintain confidentiality and have complete records against therapist convenience. Managers may be tempted to purchase a standard client management and file documentation programme, although many come with limitations the DBT clinician needs to work around. A second option is to work with a knowledgeable software developer to create a records system tailored to the needs of a DBT team. The ability to upload and store texts, emails, and photos as part of a client's record is important, and many clinicians find it convenient to be able to access and update client charts remotely. Whatever the solution, it is important to also have a plan (technological assistance, work-arounds, etc.) if the system goes down.

Further, as technology becomes more readily available and less expensive, its application to the treatment setting is on the rise. Linehan (1993a) recommended that sessions be recorded for clients to listen to at a later point in order to strengthen session interventions, revisit important elements of the session that were missed due to lack of attention or dissociation, and remind themselves of the connection to the therapist in moments of doubt during the week. Clients can now record sessions on their phones; digital recorders can be purchased inexpensively. Some programmes videorecord skills group sessions for clients to review if they have missed a session. In this case, video files must be stored, able to be viewed by clients, and a schedule for deleting the files needs to be maintained. Review of therapist performance in sessions and skills groups is also recommended (e.g., Heard & Swales, 2016). Clinicians will need a means of recording and storing their work with clients, and they should be oriented before hire to the expectation that their sessions will be videotaped for supervision and/or peer review in Consultation Team. Obtaining informed consent from clients for recording will also be needed. A system for storing, reviewing, and deleting the files should be clearly documented and followed. Technology solutions will require some budget for maintenance of the system, trouble-shooting when fails, and updates.

Finally, the rapid development of technology has also led to an explosion of available content that can be used to support treatment. The Internet provides lectures, discussions, and slideshows on DBT topics and material relevant to clinical work. Whereas it was once common to share articles and books with one another (and with clients), clinicians now can develop and share examples of content found on the web. The active teaching and experiential emphasis in DBT leads us to be on the lookout for new and engaging ways of explaining and presenting material to clients. Video and audio content can engage and inform clients with high production values, augmenting the lecture materials and handouts that have traditionally been used in DBT. For this reason, many therapists will want to have ready access to a computer (or tablet) and the Internet in their sessions, now relatively standard for all office environments.

Folowing this discussion of some of the more concrete programme demands for a given location, the next section covers the structure that supports modes of treatment.

STRUCTURE AND MODES OF TREATMENT

As the modes are predominant in discussions of DBT, we have maintained that form here. For each mode, we identify elements stipulated by Linehan in her writing, such as the agreements, forms, or rules she introduced, as well as more practical considerations. Some elements touch more than one mode, as with the example of updating client files above, or providing updates on client behaviour in skills group to individual therapists. As each function is impacted by the other four, no mode is entirely independent from the others. We will highlight those instances as well.

Consultation Team

The core of the weekly DBT programme schedule is the Consultation Team meeting. It is the mode most closely aligned with the functions of "engaging and motivating therapists," as well as a core aspect of "structuring the environment to support (adherent) treatment." Some programmes may only include clinicians who offer either individual or group sessions, excluding treatment providers considered "adjunct" (e.g., nutritionists, psychiatrists, vocational therapists, etc.) and office staff. Other programmes may insist that these individuals also provide services using DBT principles and practices, and thus these individuals must attend Consultation Team. All DBT team hires must commit to attending the meetings, abiding by the assumptions and commitments, and participating fully. Thus, in some instances, given the challenges in changing schedules for busy clinicians already on the team, lack of availability to attend the DBT Consultation Team meeting may in fact preclude employment at a given programme.

Linehan has defined roles to be assigned in the meeting: team leader, observer, time-keeper, and note-taker. Given the expectation that all team members will need consultation, meetings must have few enough members that there is time on the agenda to speak regularly, although not necessarily every week. The Consultation Team Agreements (Linehan, 1993a, pp. 117–119) support clinicians in their work with each other, providing specific tools (e.g. behaviourally specific speech, non-judgmental language, and a non-defensive posture) to address therapists' communication and emotional well-being, and to support effective treatment when the going gets tough. Common practice is to read one agreement at the beginning of each team meeting (after mindfulness). Typically, a card is provided to the observer as well, to remind them what to highlight if observed. These can be stored with the agenda and other documents used for the meeting, or with the mindfulness bell.

Consultation Team Meeting Structure

The Consultation Team meetings in Linehan's training clinic were comprised of two separate elements: weekly training for therapists, and a second hour of consultation to the therapist. Although she ran these meetings consecutively, they may be broken out to different days of the week, and not all team members need attend the same training topic. Training should routinely review aspects of the treatment to maintain clinician skills, and also introduce topics relevant to the programme, including research in DBT and the related sciences as it is published.

The Consultation Team portion of the meeting provides the opportunity for clinicians to receive support in several ways from fellow team members (Sayrs, Chapter 8, this volume). Because there is so much to do in a short time each week, members of well-established Teams prepare ahead of time, remain focused in their presentations and when giving advice, and are clear in their request. The number of team members in a given Consultation Team should be related to the amount of support needed by its individuals; those still learning treatment will need more time on a more regular basis. Larger programmes, comprising more than eight to ten DBT providers, should consider dividing the teams. The programme's clinical lead or local manager overseeing all treatment delivery may choose to attend all Consultation Team meetings to ensure fidelity and to monitor treatment for all clients. When clinicians are meeting in different team meetings, skills groups trainers will need to consider how to relay client behaviour in skills group to therapists weekly in the meetings they do not attend. (One solution is to have the skills group leader and co-leader attend different Team meetings. Another is to provide updates to all clinicians via email and notes on client behaviour in each client's file.)

Determining whether regular review of session videos will be done in this forum or separately is another factor in determining the size of the group. It is possible for video review to occur outside of the team meeting, to be discussed during the meeting. This requires clinicians to find additional time in their schedules for video review.

Consultation Team Notes

Consultation Team meetings generate information that needs to be tracked in client files or for programme purposes. Most teams develop a standard set of forms allowing them to accomplish these goals. Regarding client files, brief notes on discussions and the clinical justification for decisions made can be important to retain; the discussion does not need to be documented in detail. Notes are helpful reminders to clinicians of the rationale for clinical decision-making. Further, seeking input from peers is also best practice or "due diligence" when responding to high-risk or novel situations with clients. (Seek guidance from a local attorney and professional organizations on what to include in notes in your location.) The individual keeping notes can write up an entry during the meeting, which can be reviewed by the clinician prior to placement in the client's file. Instances where a therapist is asking for "validation" or other forms of support in their work do not need to be documented, and clearly would not be attached to client files.

Discussions during the meeting also may generate follow-up items, such as when a therapist commits to complete overdue notes, or agrees to bring a chain analysis to team. These items are noted along with the date due, then brought forward on the agenda for the appropriate team meeting to be reviewed. A standard agenda form can be helpful in tracking agenda items occurring weekly, those being reviewed from past meetings, and items unique to a given week. These forms should be stored in a binder or electronic file for reference.

Meetings may also serve as a source of data for programme self-evaluation. For instance, managers may wish to ensure that all therapists are routinely asking for consultation, or track whether therapists participating in the meeting offer support or guidance on a regular basis. There may be interest in tracking the requests and topics of therapists, to prioritize trainings or address programmatic issues. Many of these tasks may fall to the designated "note-taker," a role that typically rotates by meeting. This level of notes does not need extensive content if the categories are clear. For instance, the note-taker may simply use hash marks to indicate when a speaker is using "behaviourally specific language," or tally up at the end of each meeting the category of request from therapists, and whether members spoke during the meeting. These variables tracked may shift over time, as attention to a variable may improve its occurrence, opening space for other targets to be tracked. Some teams have members conduct a self-evaluation after each meeting, or periodically throughout the year as a means of gathering information directly from each provider on their participation and experience. This information can be used to intervene early before problems become extensive, to plan additional training, and to re-affirm accountability that targets are being addressed effectively and met. Data collection is balanced against other demands, to ensure that meeting time is primarily reserved for therapist support and direction. If doing regular review of session videos, then a schedule for that should be maintained, as well.

Individual Therapy for DBT Clients

The individual therapist oversees the course of treatment for each of his or her DBT clients in the programme. Linehan (1993a) assigned many responsibilities to the clinician in this primary role. In programmes in which an interdisciplinary team is providing treatment, the individual therapist may share some of these responsibilities (e.g., case management, orientation to the overall programme, skill generalization) with others. It is the programme manager's responsibility to ensure that the essential functions of treatment occur, and to ensure that treatment providers understand their roles and responsibilities. This information should be spelled out in new employee materials, job descriptions, and the programme manual.

The programme manual should clearly define the programme's client population, and address a client's ability to participate effectively in the programme itself as well as with the other clients. Most, but not all, research trials on DBT have excluded clients with active psychotic disorders and severe cognitive limitations, for example. Similarly, programmes should plan carefully when placing highly aggressive or exploitative individuals alongside more vulnerable clients in skills group or other shared activities. (Individual skills training is always an option, although more costly.) Clients are generally only accepted to a programme when there is an individual therapist and a group slot available, so client managers in larger programmes will need to track multiple individual therapists and group membership, and schedule clients weeks before an opening occurs. While some clinicians may keep their own calendars, scheduling software has become common in supporting the many functions (contact information, communications, scheduling) of client management.

The programme manager and individual therapists will need to consider the issues that may arise in working with specific client populations, and plan accordingly. Programmes treating drug-using clients may need means of storing and/or disposing of legal or illicit drugs or drug paraphernalia brought in by clients. Weapons, chemicals, and other items may be surrendered when treating suicidal or aggressive clients, and a policy and plan for managing them will be needed. In some settings, such as residential programmes working with highly suicidal clients, it may be important to remove access to means to self-harm from areas accessible to clients. Being thoughtful about the situations that may arise can lead to early planning and development of practice guidelines for staff and providers to follow. Ask for guidance from experts (medical or governmental for disposal of chemicals and medication; law enforcement for handling weapons, etc.) in crafting your policy.

While there are no formal assessments other than Behaviour Chains required in DBT, sufficient initial assessment may be required to ensure that clients meet criteria to enter the programme, support diagnoses or other baseline measures, provide information for reimbursement of treatment, and to permit adequate treatment planning. Insurance, healthcare networks or government agencies may require additional data collection at intake and throughout treatment. It is poor practice to ask clients or staff to spend time on assessment material that will not be used, and a liability to have data that is not reviewed or addressed, so be thoughtful when crafting assessment batteries. To support DBT, assessment activity should be guided by a biopsychosocial and transactional understanding of behaviour, attempting to understand client target behaviours across time and in their environmental contexts.

When considering the functions and tasks of individual sessions, it is important that therapists have ready access to materials used to orient clients to treatment (pre-treatment), review skills, and document important information discussed in session (e.g., chain analyses). For those therapists just learning the treatment, a "checklist" kept on their desk of topics to cover in orientation, and a reminder of the hierarchy and sequence for a typical DBT session can be very helpful. Therapists need blank or individualized diary cards for each client at each session. A whiteboard is considered essential in some programmes to assist with teaching points or to record chain information as a client provides it. Some whiteboards come with printers to preserve the information, or it can be copied by hand (or photographed) so that the client can take it home and review it afterward, and so that session work can be maintained in the client's treatment file. Although it may seem unnecessary to note, ensuring sufficient sound-proofing or "white noise" (when sound-proofing is not an option) to provide confidentiality to clients and to reduce sound intrusion from outside the room is a best practice in almost all settings. (In forensic and some other settings, it may be inadvisable to conduct therapy out of view of other staff, yet the content of sessions need not be routinely directly monitored and should be kept confidential from other clients.)

The following suggestions for the variety of documentation to consider is organized in the order it would most likely happen as a new client enters treatment.

Intake: Informed Consent for Treatment

As you develop your manual (see Developing the Programme Manual) you will want to clarify, along with local statute and practice, what is included in the consent forms that clients (and/or guardians) will review and sign. Programme managers should obtain legal guidance to ensure they understand what is required, and that their consent forms follow local guidelines. You will need signed forms consenting to treatment (with a corresponding description of treatment that the client has read and understands), and applicable consents to request or share information with significant others or other providers. It is important to inform clients that DBT is provided as a team approach, and that clinical information will be shared with others on the team. Programmes that review individual sessions and/or skills group through video or audio recordings should include language requesting consent to be recorded in session, with clear information about what will be done with the recordings, how they will be protected, and when they will be destroyed. For programmes planning evaluation or to be certified by external agencies, consent to have clinical materials reviewed during that process should be sought.

Starting Treatment: Pre-Treatment

"Pre-treatment" refers to the time period prior to and overlapping with the first several sessions with a DBT therapist (Linehan, 1993a). There is a fair amount of information exchanged during the pre-treatment phase to ensure that clients are making an informed choice, that the treatment is appropriate for the client, and that clinicians are comfortable committing to working with the client. Linehan (1993a) noted that it might take up to four sessions to cover all of these tasks sufficiently. Some clinicians may wish to supplement these discussions with handouts, and access to a whiteboard can be helpful in diagramming and punctuating the discussion. As it is a discussion that will be had with each new client, and sometimes repeated with clients and significant others, it can be helpful to streamline one's approach and ensure that the desired handouts, forms, and tools are readily available. Some programmes ask clients to sign a "contract" noting that they have been oriented to treatment and agree to actively participate. The pre-treatment phase is important, and the amount of information to be provided to clients is somewhat extensive, so a checklist reminding clinicians of what to cover can also help avoid errors of omission in this process (see Hales, Terblanche, Fowler, & Sibbald, 2008).

Given the high-risk behaviours exhibited in this population, a Crisis Response Plan should be developed at the commencement of treatment with each client exhibiting Stage 1 behaviour. This would include information about the client's address, all means of contact (phone, messaging, email), and addresses and contact information for significant others who may be able to contact the client or be asked to intervene in a crisis. Contacts may include family, friends, or non-related caregivers; in some instances, a social network map is created (McMain, Sayrs, Dimeff, & Linehan, 2007). For clients who are at high risk of dropping out, a list of a client's favoured locations to feel safe, self-soothe, or "hide out" when avoiding responsibilities of life may be identified. The goal is to enable quick and efficient mobilization of resources in a crisis event. Thus, this information needs to be tailored to each client and readily available to clinicians at all hours and from just about any location.

Assessment

Beyond screening assessments to ensure clients meet critieria for the programme, the only assessment specifically described and required by Linehan (1993a) in DBT is the "behavioural chain analysis" (BCA; also see Rizvi & Ritschel, 2014). The BCA focuses on a specific instance of a target behaviour, with the goal of identifying the variables that exert influence on that particular presentation of the behaviour. Target behaviours are determined using the DBT Target Hierarchy (Linehan, 1993a), as agreed upon with clients. Some programmes have developed worksheets or forms for clients and therapists to use when completing chain analyses. Many clinicians rely strictly on chains done verbally in session. Some utilize a whiteboard to provide a visual representation of the chain elements. As chain analysis directly informs the treatment (via solution analysis), it is important to document the important elements. Include the notes or a photo of the whiteboard in the client's working files, to be referred back to later in treatment. A copy of the BCA can also be offered to the client, who may wish to study it later or share it with a significant other.

Treatment Plans

The treatment plan combines elements of CBT and case management, specific to each client. It should derive directly from the case conceptualization (Rizvi & Sayrs, in print; Manning, Chapter 12, this volume), based on target behaviours identified during pre-treatment and subsequent behaviour chain analyses done. The common strategies for behaviour change are based on the problem-solving paradigm (Heard & Swales, 2016), and include exposure, skill acquisition and generalization, contingency management, and cognitive restructuring. These strategies are applied to the controlling variables and behavioral patterns identified in the case formulation, and it is to these that the treatment plan should refer when mapping out treatment for the coming period. As the individual therapist is directing all relevant treatment, the roles and functions of additional care providers should be clarified in the treatment plan. Involvement of parents, partners or other significant supports for the client may also be important elements in structuring the client's environment. The treatment plan may also identify variables to be tracked over the subsequent period of treatment on diary cards or during session, to assess client compliance with the treatment plan (e.g., skills use or completion of exposure sessions), and symptom or behaviour change. The therapist should complete initial treatment plans soon after a client has committed to treatment, and keep them current with updates at least every 90 days and a treatment summary at the end of treatment. Some programmes may wish to create a standardized treatment plan, to structure the therapists' activities and to ensure that relevant aspects of treatment are documented and not overlooked. Employ peer reviews of charts to ensure that paperwork is complete and that assessment data is consistently collected, and driving treatment and transition.

A well-organized treatment plan will assist clinicians to focus on what is essential, and does not waste clinician time on irrelevant tasks. Well-written plans are clear to clients when reviewed with them, and allow the team lead or other members to quickly assess for quality assurance. All written documents should prioritize behavioural descriptions and plain speech over diagnostic labels, highly technical language, or excessive jargon. In many jurisdictions clients can access their own records, and some programmes freely share treatment plans and notes with clients (or co-create them with the client). Following Linehan's "consultation to the client" prescription and evolving practice recommendations, clinical documents should be written "for the benefit of the client" (Davis, 2014, p. 51). Given that practitioners are expected to be able to explain every aspect of the programme to clients and their supporters, maintaining plain speech in treatment documents provides an opportunity to be brief and straightforward, search for appropriate language, and describe and interpret client behaviour non-judgmentally. Other professionals receiving your documents will appreciate the clarity as well.

Treatment Documentation: Case Notes

Linehan has not recommended a particular format for DBT case notes. Conceptually, the case notes document the progress in the implementation of the treatment plan. Important elements to track in case notes include:

- current client engagement and goals identified for the session;
- session interventions;
- new information regarding client behaviour or circumstances, including chain and solution analyses;
- a rationale for target change (when indicated);
- environmental interventions, including contact with significant others and preparation for end of treatment; and
- homework assigned.

In some ways, a solution analysis for a recent behaviour may provide an update and amendment to the treatment plan on record. In this way, the treatment plan remains current and subsequent session and homework interventions remain clearly rooted in the most recent assessment data.

The Diary Card

Linehan introduced the Diary Card to be used in all DBT individual sessions following the pre-treatment phase (Linehan, 1993a). Diary Cards typically track client variables identified on the treatment plan or more recent solution analyses. Completed Diary Cards are typically retained and stored in client files. They provide data on progress of treatment, and the content should drive the session agenda for a given week. Diary Cards may also provide significant data at a programme level for managers to periodically review. Blank diary cards need to be available to hand to each client at the end of a session. Tailoring the cards for each client and printing them from an office printer at the end of each session is common; electronic diary cards (or an app) may take the place of printed cards in coming years.

Treatment Summary

Standard treatment summaries are used with DBT clients and most programmes require them as an aspect of closing a client's file. Case notes preceding the end of treatment should document the efforts made to structure the client's environment, generalize skills and other behaviours across relevant domains of functioning, and connection to needed services to support client gains following DBT (or efforts to re-engage clients who drop out of treatment).

Skills Group Training

As noted earlier, the rules, format, and style of delivery of group serve to engage clients and to help them adopt new behaviour. Typically, Skills Group leaders provide the handouts and homework sheets for the skills being taught in each class. Recent revisions of the skills training manuals (Linehan, 2015a, b) have enabled purchasers to download skills handouts and worksheets from the website; many programmes copy the skills directly from the manual (permitted by copyright agreement with the publisher). Some programmes provide the Skills Training Manual to clients; others encourage the clients to purchase them.

Skills trainers need time before group to gather the relevant materials (mindfulness supplies, handouts, cue up video if being used, etc.), and this time should be protected on a clinician's schedule. For skills leaders just learning the skills, more time is needed each week to thoroughly review the materials and prepare for the training (teaching story, metaphors, scientific support for the skill, modelling example, experiential exercise to practise the skill, etc.). If a token economy is being implemented in skills group, co-leaders need to ensure that the tokens or tracking sheet and any reinforcers handed out in group are available.

There is a separate diary card form allowing clients to track skills that they learn and practice throughout treatment. These are typically reviewed by individual therapists during sessions, and are brought to Skills Group, to monitor whether clients are making efforts to try new skills, and increasing their overall use of skills (generalization). Unlike the individual diary cards, skills group cards reflect the set of skills that all clients are learning and practising. Thus, an identical card can be used for all clients, modified from the original (Linehan, 1993b, 2015) to reflect the specific skills taught in the programme. Although Linehan's (1993a) original treatment studies used the same card for individual therapy and Skills Group (front and back), it is possible to have a separate card for each mode, and the client should bring both cards to individual sessions.

Attendance is tracked at each Skills Group, and a progress note is kept on each client's participation during the session. These chart notes allow the individual therapist to stay informed of the skills being taught currently and client participation in group. Clients who are at risk of missing four consecutive Skills Groups must be brought to the attention of the individual therapist and/or the team, so tracking the consecutive number of missed groups for each client is important. Skills group leaders and individual therapists should strategize together how to ensure that these clients do not drop out of treatment by missing more groups. Individual therapists also may address motivation, skills de-velopment and contingency management for group behaviour, so it is also important to track and communicate Skills Group-interfering behaviour and improvement.

Some programmes offer a "graduation ceremony" for clients who are ending treat-ment or their period of skills training, in which case a calendar should be maintained to track departures after each module, and who is switching to a new group, such as a "graduate group," (Comtois, Kerbrat, Atkins, Harned, & Elwood, 2010). If there are adaptations to skills materials, or selection of materials from non-researched sources, they should be carefully considered and a rationale for the substitutions should be in-cluded in the programme manual and other relevant documentation.

Telephone Coaching

The last DBT mode of treatment is telephone coaching, which allows clients to access consultation from their clinician between sessions. The phone coaching target hier-archy and guidelines were also published in the original manual (Linehan, 1993a). As noted earlier, therapists or clients may initiate phone calls, and a plan for communi-cation outside of session is agreed upon at the start of treatment, and may be revised as treatment progresses (further details, including the use of other means of out-of-session contact such as text and email, can be found in Rizvi & Roman, Chapter 10, this volume). Clear information on how clients are to communicate with therapists should be included in client orientation, the consent forms, and in the programme manual. Some programmes make use of a rotating "on-call" schedule for coverage, or an inde-pendent crisis response service; such arrangements do not allow for repair of the client-therapist relationship or updates between sessions, and independent services may not be able to support skill generalization without sufficient knowledge of DBT Skills.

Therapists "observe limits" (Linehan, 1993a) regarding out-of-session contact, and discuss them directly with clients in the pre-treatment phase and as needed in in-dividual sessions. Therapists also discuss other resources available to the client when the therapist cannot immediately respond. Clients are expected to follow their Crisis Response Plan in high-risk situations while awaiting the therapist's response. Keeping a record of these calls in the client's chart documents interventions, patterns of contact, and increasing client effectiveness as treatment progresses. Calls typically last about ten minutes or less, may be rehearsed with clients in session, and may be discussed or tar-geted during the client individual sessions.

Ancillary Treatments used in DBT

Linehan recognized that DBT may be helpful for clients and in settings which require the involvement of ancillary professionals, such as psychiatrists for medication manage-ment, chemical dependency specialists, dietitians, specialists in exposure or other ther-apies, youth advocates, case managers, etc. These professionals may attend Consultation

Team meetings if they agree to follow the principles and practices of DBT in their work with clients. It is important to note, again, that Linehan viewed the individual therapist as primarily responsible for the course of a client's treatment, so decision-making should reflect this, without straying beyond the clinician's areas of competence. Appropriate confidentiality agreements will be needed if information is shared with professionals from agencies outside the DBT programme. At the administrative level, agreements with outside agencies or contracted professionals should be signed and placed in programme files, and roles and responsibilities defined in the programme manual.

Supplies

Organizing and streamlining the programme space allows providers to focus on clinical work. Planning how to streamline routine tasks can reduce last-minute stress as clinicians prepare for the next meeting, or group, or session. Developing routines and checklists to ensure replenishment of commonly used materials in a timely manner can free up clinician energy and time on any given day to consider the content being delivered, in a more focused and mindful way.

DEVELOPING THE PROGRAMME MANUAL

Each programme should develop its own working "programme manual" that spells out the relevant policies and procedures of the clinic and defines the clients and providers, as well as the principles, practices, and materials used in the DBT treatment offered in your facility. The programme description serves as a statement of intent for the programme. It should answer most questions about treatment delivery, noting the practice and referring to published treatment manual(s) for more in-depth discussion of programme elements, when possible. (It may go without saying that each therapist should have a well-thumbed copy of the source materials.) Many programme characteristics may be identical with Linehan's (1993a) published manual. Even with source materials clearly identified, there may be locally defined characteristics of treatment (which clients, length of treatment, skill training calendar, etc.). Where there are deviations from the published manuals, the programme should document the local practices in more detail, including a rationale for the changes. Variations from Linehan's original work may be small (e.g., clients may not need to have a recent history of self-harm) or large (e.g., length of treatment may be weeks, not months).

The programme manual is the operations guide for clinicians and other staff serving on the team, and it should specify roles and proficiencies for each position. The programme manual is the document to which the programme holds itself accountable. Programme guidelines regarding the core elements of treatment will be strengthened by careful consideration; decisions made in response to a critical event may be overly influenced by the emotions of the moment. It is not uncommon to find that problems in treatment delivery were exacerbated when a programme deviated from its intended focus or area of expertise, deliberately or through inattention. Programme manuals also provide information and language that can be incorporated into a brochure, a website, and descriptions for referral sources or other providers in the community. As the science changes, it is expected that DBT programmes will also. Programme manuals will need periodic updating.

ADMINISTRATION AND HUMAN RESOURCES

In small programmes functioning as a collection of independent practitioners, the administrative tasks may fall to the individual clinicians themselves who, with the exception of Skills Group and team meetings (which are collectively set), manage their own appointment calendars. In these programmes, clinicians may create and select their own treatment brochures, website information, consent forms, etc.

In larger programmes or programmes-within-programmes, team resources, policy and even practice decisions may be made at a level above the team. In these cases, it is important to be very clear at what level DBT Principles and Practices are informing decision-making. DBT team members hold themselves, and each other, to a high level of accountability and transparency regarding the delivery of treatment. Goals and desired outcomes are clearly defined and monitored. When administrative decisions appear to undercut (or outright contradict) the principles of DBT, it can be a blow to team morale and an ongoing source of frustration. Programmes within larger systems will likely want to be assertive in clarifying the approach to the other professionals with whom they (and/or their clients) will have regular interaction. With administrators, it is important that the structure of the programme and the support needed be clearly identified prior to the programme commencing. Especially in matters of staffing, if DBT programme staff is assigned the same "job classification" as staff working elsewhere in the organization, administrators may see the positions as "interchangeable," and thus place an equal-level staff with no interest in DBT in the "vacant position" on the team. This can be disastrous, clearly, and is but one of many examples of how a team must define and protect its programme.

Hiring, Training, and Retention

The effectiveness of the team is directly and consistently influenced by the knowledge, skills, and abilities of team members. While it is ideal to hire new team members who are already well trained and proficient in DBT, in reality, additional training will likely be needed following hire. In larger systems, extensive training for cohorts of hires will need to be addressed. A meta-analysis of published studies on training of therapists noted that research was able to document that " ... therapists did reach proficiency levels in adherence, competence, and skill, particularly in CBT" (Beidas & Kendall, 2010, p. 25). Importantly, therapists did not become proficient without organization-level support (ongoing supervision and feedback). Thus, considerable resources need to be devoted to creating a competent team.

While, in theory, any behaviour can be trained, some aptitudes may be critical factors in new hires. Previous history of adherence to evidence-based practices and a positive response to supervision instruction are good behaviours to assess for. In DBT language, "willingness" is a critical attribute, highlighting flexibility in the provider's ability to take multiple perspectives of a given situation, to eschew rigid or avoidance-based responses, and to try new ways of behaving (thinking, acting). Therapists must demonstrate an ability to learn new content related to treatment, and allow their behaviour to be shaped via feedback from clients and supervisors. A non-judgmental approach to treatment-related behaviour of clients and fellow clinicians is also essential. Most skilled practitioners recognize that clinical excellence is not an outcome that one achieves at a given point, but rather an ongoing practice, and so they see themselves as constantly needing to learn and improve skills. Linehan is both adaptive (changing emphasis and practice based on new research) and disciplined (emphasizing sound principles, maintaining a mindfulness practice) in her approach to treatment, and the best DBT therapists are likely to possess these traits.

Given the significant investment in training and supervision that each new employee requires, it is important to be selective when hiring, and to create hiring practices that will enable you to best predict the applicant's current skills and future behaviour. Many programme managers conduct a specific commitment session (with problem solving of potential barriers and perhaps some "devil's advocate") with candidates prior to making an offer of employment.

The best training typically involves a combination of reading, formal lecture, demonstration and practice with feedback, and ongoing supervision (Hawkins & Sinha, 1998). Larger programmes may be able to designate a portion of an employee's schedule to reading and attendance of formal training. For smaller programmes, these activities may take place on an employee's own (unpaid) time. Licensed (and licence-eligible) individuals can seek and maintain DBT certification in modes of treatment as an aspect of professional development.

Programmes offering supervision will need to factor the time of the supervisor and supervisee into the weekly schedule, and additional time for the supervisor if session materials (video, chart notes) are reviewed ahead of meeting. It is important to set clear, behaviourally defined benchmarks for the employee to achieve as employment progresses, and identify the resources available to the employee to learn and master the skills. Managers should include direct observation in addition to other measures (e.g., client reports and data) in employee evaluations. Employees who successfully learn and demonstrate treatment competencies and contribute positively to the team should be retained and promoted, while those who fail to master competencies may be better suited to an alternative therapy modality which fits their training and clinical practice.

Schedule

Beyond scheduling therapists into training and consultation, client scheduling needs to incorporate a means of tracking appointments kept, rescheduled, and missed, to support the 4-miss (or programme-identified miss) rule for both individual sessions and Skills Group attendance. This informs a standard element in the agenda for consultation team (clients at risk of missing four appointments). Programmes may have an interest in monitoring and improving outcomes of client retention, a hallmark outcome of clinical research and strong argument for providing DBT in the first place. If clients are dropping out at numbers significantly greater than found in the research, it may be important to re-visit client inclusion criteria, therapist adherence, or other factors that may be impacting retention. As the individual therapist is primarily responsible for the treatment provided, therapists should retain a large degree of control over session scheduling and communication with clients concerning changes of schedule to ensure that engagement is addressed and to avoid reinforcing client avoidance or other dysfunctional behaviour.

DATA COLLECTION

Outcomes

There are several principles to consider when thinking about data collection in a DBT programme (Rizvi, Monroe-DeVita, & Dimeff, 2007). The first is to note that, broadly, there are two classes of information a programme can assess and monitor: behaviour changes in clients (outcomes), and whether the programme is being implemented as intended (adherence). Given limited resources, including therapist time, it is often most effective to pick just a few things to measure at any given time. There is much data to be found in just the day-to-day operation of a programme, so it can be most efficient to see whether that data (e.g., attendance, diary card data, case notes) can be effectively organized so it can be used to answer programme questions. Diary cards already track the client's self-report on frequency of target behaviours, intensity of urges, and use of skills. Such data can be entered into a database for periodic analysis, and also graphed in real time to provide ongoing feedback to the client and therapist concerning treatment effectiveness. More recent developments of digital diary cards and DBT-related apps for smartphones may improve ability to access, store, and analyse client data. (Be certain that these digital aids can be uploaded to programme servers, and that such programmes securely maintain client confidentiality.)

In addition to target behaviours (self-harm acts, medical seriousness), Linehan et al.'s (1991) early research reported on psychiatric hospital admissions and days in hospital, among other variables. Although few programmes will have the resources to collect data as extensively as is done in formal research settings, each programme can identify and track the client behaviours targeted by its clinicians. Standard DBT may track client self-harm. An eating disorder programme or substance use intervention may focus on outcomes relevant to those client populations (in addition to self-harm, if present). Programmes that treat a diverse set of clients can evaluate effectiveness across all cases by ensuring that the targets are behaviourally specific and reliably tracked. Analysis of data is only possible with as complete and accurate a record as possible, so periodic checks on data collection and thorough training for those gathering and storing the data is essential. Consent forms should notify clients that clinical data will be tracked and analysed for programme performance (and any other purposes), and, of course, client privacy must be protected.

Linehan et al. (1991) also tracked client psychological variables (e.g., depression, anxiety, anger, etc.) using questionnaires and interviews. Some programmes may decide to periodically request that clients complete such measures to track change across the treatment period. In order to compare scores, it is important to utilize the same measure at each period. Programmes planning to do this will need to select the instruments and identify who is responsible for having the client complete the forms when due. (Thus, the assessments will need to be scheduled for regular intervals.) Data input and eventual analysis should be factored into a programme budget (either employee hours or a separate line item).

When considering what data to track, one set of benchmarks is the list of outcome data published in research studies for a given client population or target behaviour. Programmes should strive to meet the levels of client improvement found there. If these levels are not met, it can be helpful to seek consultation. Note that behavioural outcomes (e.g., incidence of self-harm) may not correspond with changes in psychological variables (anxiety, anger), so it may be wise to track both. For those adapting the classic treatment for behaviours already researched using DBT, it is important to determine whether the alterations in programme have decreased effectiveness (e.g., client retention, reduction in target behaviour). Other programme adaptations may apply DBT to new client populations or behaviours. In these instances, programme outcomes can be compared to published studies treating the same behaviour (e.g., recidivism rates, client retention), with the goal of improving outcomes or reducing costs.

Programmes may also use data collection as part of a larger strategy to inform clients and others about treatment effectiveness, to lobby for additional resources, or to provide assurance that adaptations made are improving outcomes and quality of care for new client populations. Documenting cost savings (e.g., reduction in psychiatric hospitalization days or use of psychiatric medications without an increase in adverse events), improved outcomes across domains that matter to clients, or provider satisfaction can all be persuasive in proposals to expand the programme, attract new clients, and encourage talented providers to join the team.

Programme Fidelity

In addition to clinical treatment outcomes with clients, programmes can also evaluate whether they are operating the way they should. This is referred to as fidelity or adherence to the treatment model. The benchmark here for comprehensive DBT programmes is Linehan's (1993a) treatment manual and associated descriptions of treatment, and any specific alterations defined in the local programme manual. Many teams monitor their adherence to the model informally, through discussion in the Consultation Team or review and discussion of therapist sessions. More formal methods can be used to augment these informal checks and balances. For instance, programmes may track client diary card completion for each client, or whether a plan has been discussed by the Consultation Team for a client who has missed two or three sessions in a row. Programmes can add a simple check box to case notes to track whether a Chain is done for a given target behaviour, that a role play/experiential exercise was done in session, or to track that clients exhibiting PTSD symptoms are offered and provided exposure treatment (Harned, Korslund, & Linehan, 2014). Consultation Team notes can track the frequency of each therapist placing him/herself on the agenda, or contributing to the discussion (as expected). Such variables can be identified as cornerstones of the treatment and tracked for the duration of the programme, or be a temporary focus to shape up clinician behaviour when key elements of treatment are perceived to be underutilized. Even though such measures may seem trivial to an experienced team, knowing that specific variables are being reviewed periodically can have the effect of increasing performance of each clinician, and adherence has been demonstrated to improve client outcomes in DBT (Linehan et al., 1999) as in other treatments. Demands placed on providers must be balanced, of course, against a tendency to collect more data than is reviewed, which is clearly a waste of time.

Adaptations and treatment in different settings (e.g., forensic, psychiatric inpatient) may have specific challenges in providing treatment that will encourage a focus on particular aspects of the programme. For instance, in prison settings there can be a variety of reasons that a daily schedule is thrown off (unit disruption, campus-wide lockdown, staff do not turn up for work). In lax programmes, it can be easy to skip groups and not re-schedule. Thus, a manager may request a monthly account of the groups held, compared against the expected number of groups, and address programmes that consistently struggle to meet the expectation. For other sources of inspiration, it can also be helpful to consider the five functions of comprehensive treatment discussed earlier. Balancing data collection to look at how the programme supports (and measures) client engagement, skill acquisition and generalization, and therapist motivation can ensure that all core aspects of the programme are balanced and functioning well.

SUMMARY

DBT truly is a team sport; you can't do it alone. Programme managers provide important leadership in creating an effective structure for DBT to flourish. Programme structure supports treatment delivery, reminds us what to do when, and ideally rewards us for doing what we should (while blocking or discouraging dysfunctional behaviour). Linehan and her colleagues have done an exemplary job over the years of describing and defining the treatment from a principle-driven perspective, as well as providing us with a description of the fixed rules and other structural elements needed. The treatment experience can be vastly rewarding and, much like the games of chess or Go, one's skills within it have an almost limitless ability to develop over the course of a career. Committing to implement this model to the utmost of one's ability requires familiarity with the tools and structure of DBT. Deciding not to use the elements of treatment or to select only portions of the model to implement is to decide to master a different activity, and we should expect different outcomes. A well-organized programme helps clinicians and clients alike. This chapter introduced and reviewed the structural elements of DBT for Team Leaders and managers, and provided examples of ways to address them. Each programme will be unique, tailored to its providers, clients and resources. We urge the reader to continue to use your own creativity in your particular environment, and to share your solutions to the common problems of treatment delivery, not just in style and content, but also in the many ways of structuring the treatment environment for success.

KEY POINTS FOR CLINICIANS

- Successful programmes pay close attention to the structural elements of DBT.
- It is critical to understand Linehan's description of the functions of treatment when making decisions about the structure of treatment.
- Structural elements of a programme include the physical infrastructure, as well as the customs and practices of the treatment (such as agreements, therapist strategies, careful attention to language, and requests for review of one's work).
- A sound and well-followed programme structure will enable clinicians and clients to more easily focus on the critical interactions of treatment.
- Each programme needs to create a "programme manual" which defines the treatment provided, particularly when it has been adapted from the original model described by Linehan.

REFERENCES

Beidas, R. S., & Kendall, P. C. (2010). Training therapists in evidence-based practice: A critical review of studies from a systems-contextual perspective. *Clinical Psychology: Science and Practice*, *17*, 1–30.

Comtois, K. A., Kerbrat, A. H., Atkins, D. C., Harned, M. S., & Elwood, L. (2010). Recovery from disability for individuals with borderline personality disorder: A feasibility trial of DBT-ACES. *Psychiatric Services*, *61*, 1106–1111.

Davis, C. (2014). Creative treatment planning at a home for troubled adolescents. *CYC-Online*, 49–57. Retrieved on May 29, 2016 from: http://www.cyc-net.org/cyc-online/cycol-0208-davis.html

Deutsch, C. J. (1984). Self-reported sources of stress among psychotherapists. *Professional Psychology: Research and Practice*, 15(6), 833–845.

Hales, B., Terblanche, M., Fowler, R., & Sibbald, W. (2008). Development of medical checklists to improve quality of patient care. *International Journal for Quality in Health Care*, 20, 22–30.

Harned, M. S., Korslund, K. E., & Linehan, M. M. (2014). A pilot randomized controlled trial of Dialectical Behavior Therapy with and without the Dialectical Behavior Therapy Prolonged Exposure Protocol for suicidal and self-injuring women with borderline personality disorder and PTSD. *Behaviour Research and Therapy*, 55, 7–17.

Hawkins, K. A., & Sinha, R. (1998). Can line clinicians master the conceptual complexities of dialectical behavior therapy? An evaluation of a State Department of Mental Health training program. *Journal of Psychiatric Research*, 32(6), 379–384.

Heard, H., & Swales, M.A. (2016). *Changing behavior in DBT: Problem solving in action.* New York, NY: Guilford Press.

Koerner, K., Dimeff, L. A., & Swenson, C. R. (2007). Adopt or adapt?: Fidelity matters. In L. A. Dimeff & K. Koerner (Eds.), *Dialectical behaviour therapy in clinical practice* (pp. 19–36). New York, NY: Guilford Press.

Linehan, M. M. (1993a). *Cognitive behavioural therapy of borderline personality disorder.* New York, NY: Guilford Press.

Linehan, M. M. (1993b). *Skills training manual for treating borderline personality disorder.* New York, NY: Guilford Press.

Linehan, M. M. (2015a). *DBT Skills Training Manual*, 2nd Edition. New York, NY: Guilford Press.

Linehan, M. M. (2015b). *DBT skills training: Handouts and worksheets,* 2nd Edition. New York, NY: Guilford Press.

Linehan, M. M., Armstrong, H. E., Suarez, A., Allmon, D., & Heard, H. L. (1991). Cognitive-behavioural treatment of chronically parasuicidal borderline patients. *Archives of General Psychiatry*, 48, 1060–1064.

Linehan, M. M., Cochran, B. N., & Kehrer, C. A. (2001). Dialectical behaviour therapy for borderline personality disorder. In D. H. Barlow (Ed.), *Clinical handbook of psychological disorders: A step-by-step treatment manual*, 3rd Edition. (pp. 470–522). New York, NY: Guilford Press.

Linehan, M. M., Schmidt, H., III, Dimeff, L. A., Craft, J. C., Kanter, & J., Comtois, K. A. (1999). Dialectical behavior therapy for patients with borderline personality disorder and drug-dependence. *American Journal of Addiction*, 8, 279–292.

Linehan, M. M., & Wilks, C. R. (2015). The course and evolution of dialectical behavior therapy. *American Journal of Psychotherapy*, 69(2), 97–110.

McMain, S., Sayrs, J. H. R., Dimeff, L. A., & Linehan, M. M. (2007). Dialectical behaviour therapy for individuals with borderline personality disorder and substance dependence. In L. A. Dimeff & K. Koerner (Eds.), *Dialectical behavior therapy in clinical practice* (pp. 145–173). New York, NY: Guilford Press.

Rizvi, S. L., Monroe-DeVita, M., & Dimeff, L. A. (2007). Evaluating your Dialectical Behavior Therapy program. In L. A. Dimeff & K. Koerner (Eds.), *Dialectical behavior therapy in clinical practice* (pp. 326–350). New York, NY: Guilford Press.

Rizvi, S. L., & Ritschel, L. A. (2014). Mastering the art of chain analysis in dialectical behavior therapy. *Cognitive and Behavioral Practice*, 21, 335–349.

Rizvi, S. L., & Sayrs, J. H. R. (in print). Assessment-driven case formulation and treatment planning in dialectical behavior therapy: Using principles to guide effective treatment. *Cognitive and Behavioral Practice.*

Robinson, B. J. (2015). *Holacracy: The new management system for a rapidly changing world.* New York, NY: Henry Holt.

Sullivan, L. H. (1896). The tall office building artistically considered. *Lippincott's Magazine* (March 1896), 403–409.

Swenson, C. R., Sanderson, C., Dulit, R. A., & Linehan, M. M. (2001). The application of dialectical behavior therapy for patients with borderline personality disorder on inpatient units. *Psychiatric Quarterly*, *72*(4), 307–324.

CHAPTER 8

RUNNING AN EFFECTIVE DBT CONSULTATION TEAM

Principles and Challenges

JENNIFER H. R. SAYRS

INTRODUCTION

As a comprehensive treatment, dialectical behaviour therapy (DBT) has several functions or jobs it must serve in order to be effective. All of these functions are considered important when treating high-risk, challenging clients with multiple, chronic problems; in order to be considered "full" or "comprehensive" DBT, these functions must be addressed in some way. Being a principle-driven treatment, however, means DBT offers a great deal of flexibility in how these functions are met. Linehan (1993) first discussed these functions in her DBT treatment manual (see also Schmidt & Russo, this volume); they include:

- Increasing capability (i.e., teaching skills; typically accomplished via skills training group).
- Increasing motivation (i.e., arranging variables such that the client is more likely to engage in effective behaviour, less likely to engage in ineffective behaviour; most often addressed in individual therapy).
- Generalizing skills to the client's environment (i.e., strategies to get the new behaviour to occur in the client's own environment; this includes strategies such as phone calls and texts with the therapist outside of session, homework assignments, and listening to recordings of the previous session at home).
- Structuring the environment (i.e., a variety of ways to arrange the environment such that it supports DBT; this may be done with the individual therapist, a family therapist, case manager, and/or other providers or strategies).
- Building therapist motivation, capability, and adherence to the treatment manual, i.e., "hold the therapist inside the treatment," (Linehan, 1993, p. 101); NB: therapists typically address this within a DBT team.

Individual therapy and skills have received significant attention in books, workshops, and webinars focused on training DBT therapists. Relatively speaking, DBT team has received much less focus. This is notable, as the team is considered an essential element of DBT, the fulcrum, so to speak, where therapists can recalibrate and centre themselves to provide the best treatment possible.

This chapter—as well as a forthcoming book (Sayrs & Linehan, in press)—aims to provide more guidance regarding running an effective DBT team. This is important both because of the essential nature of team to the effectiveness of DBT, and because DBT teams are quite different from traditional treatment teams. The principles of DBT team and treating the therapist are becoming more widely used in other treatments as well; non-DBT providers can also use these guidelines, translating them to fit their own treatment principles. For the sake of brevity, this chapter focuses only on DBT teams.

Linehan (1993) first described the concept of DBT team, and it has since been summarized by others, including Swenson (2016) and Koerner (2012). Even so, it seems many of the guidelines for DBT team have been widely used but not fully documented, which motivated Marsha Linehan and me to write a manual for DBT teams. After being on the same teams for many years, directing our own teams, and teaching and consulting to a large number of DBT teams and therapists, we wanted not only to delineate the basic guidelines for teams, but also to share the successes and challenges we have seen in our tenure as DBT therapists and teachers. We have spent many hours discussing DBT team and the many lessons we have learned over the years—some of them painful! This chapter represents a brief summary of those experiences and discussions, but in no way should it be interpreted as a set of rules. Teams can learn from our own and others' experiences, follow these principles, and adapt the specific structure to their own needs.

The Function of DBT Team

DBT team has two purposes. These purposes are closely intertwined, and actually have the same purpose: adherence to the DBT manual. Providing the most effective, adherent care possible (i.e., care that most closely follows the DBT manual), means attending to two factors:

1. Therapist motivation. Team helps maximize providers' motivation to deliver effective treatment to their clients. Motivation can refer to several aspects: teams can provide a "safe haven," where therapists are comfortable being vulnerable, and where they share and receive support. Teams can help a therapist feel cared about, an "insider" in a group of like-minded individuals. Teams can even be a source of fun! Just as in DBT treatment, motivation also means lining up the controlling variables such that effective therapist behaviours are reinforced, and ineffective

behaviours are minimized. Motivation refers to what makes a person act in a certain way; team can enhance motivation by helping to set up the environment such that the therapist is steered toward the most effective action possible.

2. Capability. Teams also aim to increase each therapist's capability. This refers to the skill with which the treatment is delivered, and the ability to implement each strategy along with any additional treatment protocols.

This chapter describes how the structure and culture of DBT team can help enhance the therapist's motivation and capability. Any discussion of therapists in this chapter refers to anyone who is a member of the DBT team, follows the DBT team agreements, and has client responsibility in some manner; this includes not only the individual DBT therapist, but also all other DBT providers, including skills trainers, pharmacotherapists, and others. The degree, level of education, or profession are not as important as the training in, experience with, and dedication to DBT and the team agreements, as well as current clinical work with DBT clients.

What is Different About DBT Team?

A Community of Therapists

There are a few components of DBT team that make it very different from traditional treatment teams in other, non-DBT settings. First, DBT team is a *community of therapists treating a community of clients*. This means that all therapists on the team treat all the clients, as a team. This is different from traditional teams, where therapists have their own clients and others on the team do not know much about those clients, and are perhaps less invested in their treatment as a result. This notion is taken so seriously in DBT that, if one therapist has a client who dies by suicide, all members of the team say they had a client die by suicide. It is not someone else's client, it is "our" client. This also means that if members of the team notice a therapist has fallen out of adherence from the manual, such as reinforcing ineffective client behaviour or failing to intervene with a client when needed, they have an obligation to say something, because *it is also their client*.

Therapy for the Therapist

The second component that sets DBT apart from traditional teams is the practice of providing *therapy for the therapist*. In DBT teams, the team provides therapy for each therapist, *not* for the clients. The therapists put themselves on the agenda, not the clients. And the team addresses obstacles to the therapist staying motivated and providing adherent DBT, rather than addressing client behaviours or problems. For example, in a traditional team, a therapist might bring up a client who is refusing to do homework; in

DBT team the therapist brings up their own difficulty with getting a client to do homework, along with their difficulty in regulating their own frustration. The team focuses on the *therapist's* behaviour, and how to remove obstacles to the therapist's skill and motivation.

Vulnerability

Relatedly, the membership of a DBT team may be different than a traditional team. All members of the DBT team are required to have some sort of responsibility for a client. This does not mean everyone provides DBT individual therapy or even skills training, but administrators and supervisors would not be on the team unless they provide some type of direct clinical care. Students and trainees must also have some type of clinical contact. This means that therapists taking a break from seeing clients would also take a break from DBT team. Providing therapy for the therapist requires a level of vulnerability that is not needed in traditional teams. Therapists may end up sharing personal problems that are interfering with clinical care, or admit to their team that they made a mistake about which they feel significant shame. It is extremely difficult to be this vulnerable, if other members of the team are not "down in the trenches" with you, experiencing as much risk and vulnerability as you. I have consulted with multiple teams where an administrator offers advice to the front-line/milieu staff, and even if that administrator has clinical training, the front-line staff roll their eyes! It is so easy to oversimplify clinical challenges when you are not working with clients, and conversely, easy to experience such advice as invalidating when given by someone who does not see clients. In order to both maximize vulnerability in the team and to avoid oversimplification of addressing therapist challenges, all members of the team have some sort of clinical responsibility.

Emphasis on Dialectics

The final distinction of DBT team is the emphasis on dialectics. The core dialectic in DBT is that of acceptance and change; this is no different in DBT team. DBT teams do not focus solely on supporting the therapist, nor solely on changing the therapist, nor is this a 50–50 balance. DBT teams focus intensely on support, and intensely on change. Both are fully present in every team meeting. Whether the team spends the entire time validating, or the entire time working to change a therapist's intervention, or some combination, the meeting is based on what is effective in the moment. For example, a therapist may say, "I already have a solution, but jeez, am I feeling overwhelmed. Can you please help me with that?" The team may want to confirm that the solution is effective, but most of the time in the team meeting will then be spent on validating the therapist and reinforcing the effective strategies they have implemented already. Another therapist may say, "Let's not spend any time on validating me, I just need a solution and fast!" In these circumstances, the team may spend virtually no time validating—rather, they will assess and generate solutions to help the therapist. Many other dialectics will arise in team as well, where members of the team represent two seemingly opposite positions, such as ending treatment with a client versus continuing treatment, or validating a therapist versus reducing the therapist's judgments. In DBT team, the therapists will try to uphold both poles and work toward a synthesis for dialectics that arise in team.

NEW DBT TEAM MEMBERS

With these elements in mind, this section addresses bringing new therapists into the team. As in DBT therapy, setting a precedent for team culture, and getting early, solid commitments can make team functioning and problem solving much easier when later difficulties arise. The way in which new members join the team can have a significant impact on the team's functioning, and is considered the foundation of the team's culture.

When a new therapist joins the team, they are asked to make a commitment to the team and to all of the team agreements. The commitment strategies (Linehan, 1993) are used with the potential teammates just as they are used with a potential client. It is essential that every team member join the team voluntarily. This typically is not a problem, although there may be two obstacles to voluntary team membership. First, certain work settings require participation on the DBT team, which works against the commitment process and a voluntary agreement to join the team. In this type of situation, the commitment strategies and discussion of team agreements should occur in the job interview, since once the job starts the new employee will have no choice but to attend team. Second, involuntary participation in team can occur if a therapist is not fully oriented to what is involved in DBT team. They may agree to joining the team, not realizing the level of vulnerability involved, and that the focus is on the therapist rather than on the clients. I learned this lesson many years ago, when I failed to orient a new therapist sufficiently, and accepted her quick agreement to join the team. Once on the team, she insisted that judging clients was the only way to work through frustration, and that she needed to "vent" in team in order to provide DBT. Had I oriented her better to phenomenological empathy and non-judgmental stance, we could have had an honest conversation about the requirements of team before she joined. Instead, there were awkward moments in team and difficult discussions outside of team, before she finally decided to leave. Much distress could have been avoided, had I only followed this guideline!

There are a number of agreements the therapist will "sign on" to before joining the team. These agreements will be shaped by the nature of your team, your agency, and the clients you see. The agreements below are widely used and fairly standard in DBT teams. I have found them to be extremely helpful in my own team as well as to the many teams I have trained and consulted. Once again, these are not rules, but rather guidelines to consider as you create agreements that fit your team the best. Most teams will use the standard DBT Consultation Team Agreements (Linehan, 1993, pp. 116–117). Briefly these are:

1. Accept a dialectical philosophy; search for what is left out of any discussion; strive to identify the other pole and help the team move to a synthesis (*dialectical agreement*).
2. Avoid serving as intermediaries for clients with other team members (*consultation to the patient agreement*); instead, team members will use the "consultation to the client" strategy and coach clients to navigate those interactions themselves, as often as possible. Team members may strategically and mindfully engage in environmental intervention with each other on behalf of a client on rare occasions when the cost of not intervening outweighs the cost of intervening (Linehan, 1993). Such environmental intervention is done infrequently to provide the client with opportunities for new learning whenever possible.
3. Observe your own limits (*observing-limits agreement*); stretch limits when needed; approach others' limits non-judgmentally, even when they are different from your own.
4. Agree that consistency between team members is not required (*consistency agreement*); inconsistency, when it occurs naturally, is an opportunity for clients to practise their skills.
5. Be non-judgmental, compassionate, and phenomenologically empathic to teammates, clients, clients' family members, yourself, and others (*phenomenological empathy agreement*).
6. Have humility to admit mistakes and difficulties, be fallible, have willingness to allow other team members to help solve/address these, and remain open to feedback as opposed to taking a defensive stance (*fallibility agreement*). Be willing to address one's own team-interfering behaviour.

Additional agreements to consider in orienting new team members are as follows; more detailed discussion can be found in Sayrs and Linehan (in press).

7. Provide DBT; do not combine, alternate between, or add in other treatment modalities unless doing so effectively and mindfully (e.g., in DBT, adding another CBT manual may be appropriate while treating clients with quality-of-life-interfering targets, such as OCD or binge eating).
8. Conceptualize clients and each other's behaviour from a behavioural perspective; do not combine or add in other theoretical models (if the team is not providing DBT, the team will identify a consistent theoretical model for the team to operate within).
9. Treat team meetings in the same way you treat any other therapy sessions, i.e., attend weekly as often as possible, do not double-schedule, arrive on time, stay until the end, come to meetings adequately prepared, and speak in every team (although you do not need to be on the agenda in every team); participate in team by sharing the roles of meeting leader, observer, note-taker, and/or any other roles essential to the team.

10. Consider yourself part of a community of therapists treating a community of clients.

11. Provide "therapy for the therapists" on the team; address your own and others' obstacles to providing DBT with fidelity to the manual. This means speaking up when a therapist has veered from the manual, even when that person has more experience than you, or might get upset, or is your boss, or if you are not sure if you are "right."

12. Be available to fulfil the role for which you joined the team (e.g., individual therapist, skills trainer, pharmacotherapist); all members of the DBT team have client contact and clinical responsibility.

13. Call out the "elephant in the room" even if others do not. In other words, when there is a tension in the room, it is important to label and discuss it. Each member will work to address unspoken "elephants," including speaking up if team is frustrating or not useful, broaching topics even when afraid of another team member's response, and not treating each other or yourself as too fragile to handle the discussion.

14. Remain one-mindful and focused in team, rather than doing two things at once; e.g., do not attend to phone calls, texts, notes, or other distractions during team, and do not engage in side conversations in team.

15. Assess sufficiently before offering solutions.

16. Strive to follow the assumptions about clients and therapy (Linehan, 1993; Sayrs & Linehan, in press).

17. Follow team policy regarding providing coverage for each other, missing team, and missing appointments with clients.

18. Continue focusing on all these agreements, even when feeling burned out, frustrated, tired, overworked, underappreciated, hopeless, ineffective, etc.

Not only is it important to establish and strengthen commitment to all of these agreements ahead of time, but therapists will also need to troubleshoot, as well. This involves anticipating problems with following these agreements, and solving those problems in advance whenever possible. Identifying that certain agreements will be difficult to follow, and addressing those difficulties earlier rather than later, is important. For example, an incoming therapist may commit to the team and all of the agreements, but identify that being vulnerable in a group is very challenging. The new therapist, along with their teammates, can then begin to discuss solutions, such as a shaping strategy for gradually sharing more in team.

THE STRUCTURE OF YOUR TEAM

Once you have your team members established, and all are voluntarily participating in your team, your next focus can be the team structure. There is a great deal of flexibility in how you run your team, but teams will need certain systems to maintain their culture and effectiveness. I want to emphasize that there is no "right" way to do this; I will provide suggestions and principles, then you can choose how to implement these to best support your team. Each team will look different, and no team needs to follow these in a rote way.

Managing Time

Teams need a way of managing their time. This is most often done by implementing an agenda, and assigning a "*meeting leader*," who monitors how time is spent in the team meeting. The meeting leader starts the meeting by making sure an agenda is set, conducting a mindfulness exercise, and then moving the team through the agenda items. The meeting leader will inform the team when it is time to move on to another topic, and will highlight for the team when one agenda item is taking time away from other essential agenda items. This role is different from that of team leader, who is overseeing the programme as a whole; the meeting leader role can rotate regularly and everyone in the team can take a turn as meeting leader over time.

As part of managing time, teams need an agenda. Typical agenda items include:

- A mindfulness practice. This should be brief, with a brief discussion after. It may be five minutes of silence where each member practises independently, or one member may lead everyone through an exercise.
- The meeting leader reads one Therapist Consultation Agreement, in an effort to remind the team of the culture of the team. The leader can choose any agreement they wish; the purpose is to keep the agreements salient during team time. The Therapist Consultation Agreements are written out in full in Linehan (1993, pp. 117–119), are discussed in Sayrs and Linehan (in press), and are a subset of the team agreements listed previously. They include the dialectical agreement, consultation-to-the-patient agreement, observing-limits agreement, consistency agreement, phenomenological empathy agreement, and fallibility agreement.
- Briefly review the last team meeting's notes, which may result in additional items being placed on the agenda.
- Therapists provide therapy for the therapist. This takes up the bulk of team time (more will be said about this phase of team later in the chapter).
- Teams often close with reports of therapists' and clients' effective behaviour.

Additional, optional items for the agenda include:

- Therapist of the week, a rotating role where a therapist has several minutes to present a case formulation, show a video, or role-play a particular situation. This is done on a rotating basis (as opposed to therapists requesting this time when distress is high), to allow topics that may typically fly under the radar to be addressed by the team.

- Assigning out-of-town coverage.
- Informing team members which skills were taught and homework assigned in recent groups.
- Psychiatrists or other team members may need to give brief updates to the team. It is important this portion remain brief, because it veers away from therapy for the therapist. If psychiatrists, teachers, or others have an issue to discuss, they put themselves on the agenda and receive therapy for the therapist just as the rest of the team does.
- Some teams benefit from briefly sharing how they are doing personally. If the team has time, each member can provide a short update on anything going on for them (level of burnout or distress, their mother-in-law is visiting, their child is ill, etc.). Teammates will then have a better idea of the context for any clinical issues, as well as feel closer to each other and more connected. These updates should again be very brief, and any issue that is interfering with clinical care can go on the therapy for the therapist portion of the agenda.

The agenda can be set at the start of team; some teams do this verbally, with the meeting leader asking each member if they'd like to be on the agenda, and writing out an informal agenda. Other teams use a form that is completed at the start of team, with each member quickly placing themselves on the agenda, and still others use a whiteboard to create the agenda, which has the benefit of being visible to all team members. Teams that need to be more efficient with their time may benefit from a written agenda, so they do not spend extra time discussing what will be on the agenda.

What goes on the agenda? The key principle here is to provide therapy for the therapist. This means therapists put *themselves* on the agenda, not clients. Therapists bring up any obstacles to their own skill and motivation. This could include a wide variety of issues, including lack of knowledge, lack of skill in a certain area, emotion, problems with the functioning of the team, and any other situation or issue that interferes with adherence or motivation.

Certain topics do not belong on the agenda. Therapists do not address every problem they have, only those professional or personal issues that interfere with excellent client care. Team does not provide a licence to say absolutely anything to a teammate, either. DBT team places value on a direct discussion of problems in team, within the context of using skills and maintaining your own and your teammates' motivation to attend team and provide DBT. Using non-judgmental stance, the describe skill, DEAR MAN, and any other relevant skills will be essential when discussing problems in team. There are also some topics that do not belong in team; some may need one-on-one attention from the team leader (e.g., certain legal or ethical issues, highly personal issues, or if a member is not responsive to team's repeated interventions). Some problems may also be beyond the capacity of the team, due to time constraints or role constraints. For example, if a therapist's personal relationship is impacting the therapy provided to clients, and is taking up significant team time and not improving, the team may recommend marital or individual therapy. The team can still monitor the therapist's capability and motivation, and know the therapist is seeking solutions outside of team.

Prioritizing agenda items can be extremely helpful in managing team time. Many DBT teams use a rating system to indicate how urgent the agenda item is. Our team uses a 1–5 rating system that matches the diary card rating, with 5 being most urgent and 1 being least. If we rate an item at 5, the team will be sure to discuss that item in this team; if we rate an item at 1, our item may get postponed until the following week. Priority can be based on the DBT hierarchy, with life-threatening behaviour that the therapist is struggling to manage warranting highest priority, and clinical difficulties relating to quality-of life-interfering behaviour may get rated lowest. Time-sensitive questions, such as a session occurring immediately after team, may also get high priority, as will high therapist distress that may impact multiple clients if not addressed immediately. Because this is therapy for the therapist, the therapist is only placed on the agenda once, and the therapist only takes one turn in team, rather than taking multiple turns for multiple client issues.

How do we move through the agenda? Once the agenda is set, the meeting leader helps the team work its way through the agenda, providing therapy for the therapist. We recommend that therapists state exactly what they need from the team prior to starting the agenda item. Instead of starting the agenda item with a long description of the client, you can tell team exactly what you need. This will help the team stay on track and use time most efficiently. Many DBT teams offer therapists the following options to tell the team exactly what is needed:

- I need help with assessment.
- I need help with problem solving.
- I need help building empathy for my client.
- I need validation.

Our team added additional choices, based on our own team's needs:

- I need help with my own burnout.
- I need help figuring out what I need.

When a therapist on our team starts an agenda item, they will say, "I'm putting myself on the agenda, and I need help with …" This reminds everyone to focus on therapy for therapist, and helps the team address the issue that needs the most attention.

The team can then respond with assessment questions, solutions, validation, irreverence, acceptance skills and change skills, and any other component of DBT that will help the therapist. The observer and all members of the team can watch for the team placing more emphasis on the client, remembering the focus will need to remain on the therapist, and whatever is getting in the way of the therapist's motivation and capability.

For example, in our team, a therapist placed herself on the agenda for failing to follow through with a suggestion provided by the team in our last meeting. The therapist said she needed help with assessment, to understand what was interfering with her following through. The team did a missing links analysis (Linehan, 2015), and identified the therapist experienced fear in session, just before implementing the strategy. The team then assessed whether the fear was justified or not; they agreed the fear was justified (the client was likely to walk out of the session, as evidenced by previous behaviour), then engaged in problem solving to find a way to increase the client's tolerance of the intervention. The team also validated the fear extensively, while keeping the pressure on the therapist to go back into the session and implement the strategies discussed in team.

Maintaining the Culture of the Team

Teams need a system for alerting the team when a therapist has deviated from the manual or the team agreements listed earlier. Many teams use the *observer role* to meet this need. The observer role often rotates; the team member in the observer role monitors the team for moments when other teammates veer from the team culture, including when someone is judgmental or non-dialectical. The observer can highlight the moment for the team (teams often ring a bell or otherwise alert everyone), and the team can correct course.

Teams can have the observer monitor for any behaviours that the team is trying to shape or maintain. Here is a brief list of items from the team agreements that observers typically monitor during team time. You can add additional reminders as they are relevant to your own team.

OBSERVER REMINDERS: The observer will ring the bell if any of the following occur:

- A therapist did not speak during team.
- Non-mindfulness; a therapist did two things at once.
- A therapist was late or unprepared.
- A therapist was defensive.
- A therapist made judgmental or non-compassionate comments about other therapists, clients, him/herself, and/or others.
- Solutions were offered before sufficient problem definition/assessment occurred.
- A team member was treated as "fragile"—there was an elephant in the room that was not discussed.
- A dialectic went unresolved.

Once the observer (or anyone else, for that matter) has highlighted a problem, the team will then decide how to deal with the situation. Responses can vary widely, including a quick restatement, a gentle reminder, an irreverent comment, direct confrontation, validation, chain analysis, and/or solution analysis. Typically, teams want to reserve their time for agenda items, and pause only briefly to address these issues. If a problem in team continues, the team can place that therapist or problem on the agenda for a more extended exploration.

Documentation

Teams need a system for documenting decisions and suggestions generated in the team. Teams can use the *note-taker role* to fulfil this function. Without such a system, teams can lose track of suggestions or skills discussed. For example, a therapist may tell the team they are working on building empathy for a client who is engaging in therapy-interfering behaviour. The team may challenge the therapist to try a particular skill in the next session. Without the reminder to discuss this again in the following team, the therapist could easily avoid or forget to practise, and the team may not remember to follow up.

The note-taker may use a form that works for the team, or just take notes in a blank document. It helps for the note-taker to focus the notes on the therapist, not the client, to again maintain the emphasis on therapy for the therapist. The solutions generated in team should be documented as suggestions and not mandates from the team; the therapist, hopefully alongside the client, can get into Wise Mind and choose which solutions are most effective.

Assigning Roles

The team will need a system for assigning and rotating roles. The team leader or an administrative person can set up a schedule and distribute it to team members. This will include at a minimum the meeting leader, observer, and note-taker, with other roles the team deems helpful, such as room preparation or therapist of the week. Some teams rotate roles weekly, others monthly.

Coordinating Clinical Coverage

One of the many wonderful benefits of being on a DBT team is the ability to arrange coverage with clinicians who are familiar with your clients. Team members agree, as part of joining the team, to arrange coverage for their own absences, as well as to provide coverage for teammates as needed. In our team, therapists jump to volunteer to cover for teammates, knowing that doing so will mean they can themselves take time off now and then. The culture of easily obtaining coverage—whether for an extended vacation, maternity leave, or just a weekend off from phone coverage—further enhances the sense of a community of therapists treating a community of clients.

Different agencies will have different rules about how coverage works. In our clinic, if a therapist is out of town, they must arrange for someone to be "in town" to back them up, even if they have taken their cell phones with them. This is to be sure that someone is physically available should a client need to be seen in person. While this is rarely the case, it is one of our requirements. If a therapist would like to be off phone coverage for a period of time, they must have a specific therapist(s) assigned who will take calls from clients. They have to write up a document with emergency contact information as well as the skills plans and any other relevant information. This coverage can be arranged in team, or if it cannot be done quickly, will be arranged outside of team.

In our team, arranging coverage is easy enough, and therapists can make their travel arrangements as long as they confirm they have someone available to cover. In other teams, where they have fewer licensed therapists or other obstacles to ready coverage, the therapist may need to get permission from the team before purchasing tickets or otherwise locking in their travel plans. This is in addition to any agency requirements regarding vacation; it is important the team is involved in travel plans to be sure the clients are offered continuous care.

Absence from Team

A topic closely related to organizing clinical coverage is missing team. Your team will need some type of system to deal with therapists' absence from team. As noted in the team agreements, therapists treat their commitment to attend team as seriously as they treat their session time with clients. When you are absent from team, even if it is for reasons that everyone agrees are important, the team misses out on your contribution. Your absence causes harm. That does not mean you cannot miss team, but correction/overcorrection is a useful strategy for acknowledging and rectifying the team's loss. For example, I miss team several times each year to teach workshops. The team has no problem with me balancing teaching and providing therapy . However, I am aware that each time I am away, I am not there to help provide therapy for the therapist, to add my ideas and experience to the discussion, and to support my team.

To follow the principles of correction/over-correction (Linehan, 1993), the correction acknowledges and fixes the damage caused, and the over-correction goes beyond the correction, such that the team can actually experience benefit from the absence. For example, if I am away for vacation, I might buy my team treats from the city I am visiting, to acknowledge the damage and let them know I was thinking of them while I was away. For over-correction, I might offer to cover for someone else, or email an interesting article to them, or offer another such gesture that hopefully makes them feel my absence had some "up side." When I am absent for a training, my over-correction can be to bring back something I learned while I was away, so my team benefits, too.

Other strategies from DBT can be implemented for team absences, as well. When someone is late or misses team without planning it, the team can assess what happened (e.g., chain analysis or missing links analysis; Linehan, 2015) and which strategies can be used to prevent it again. For example, if someone is chronically late to team because they run over time in the session just before team, they might use DEAR MAN (Linehan, 2015) to request the client move their session time, or set an alarm in session to make sure they end on time. Such discussions can cause some tension in team; often team members will ask the team not to discuss the tardiness because they are too stressed out already and do not want pressure from the team. The team can respond by reminding the teammate about the agreements and the importance of maintaining the culture; if the therapist has already committed to the agreements, there will likely be more willingness to engage in this discussion.

In our team, we try not to take up agenda time discussing tardiness, because that takes away more time from the team. Instead, we email the team a chain analysis and at least one solution, as well as a commitment to implement the solution before next team meeting. If that turns out to be insufficient, we then move the discussion into team, and address how it is that the solutions were not sufficient to solve the problem.

Team Leader

The team leader is essential in DBT team. This role is distinct from that of the meeting leader; the team leader oversees the health of the team, shaping and maintaining the well-being of the team and overall programme. As such, this role does not rotate, as other roles in DBT team can. The team leader does not need to be the most experienced or have a particular training or education background; the only requirements are that they know DBT very well, and, most importantly, are willing and enthusiastic to guide the team.

The team leader's guidance can be invaluable, particularly in larger teams, or teams set within an agency. The tasks of the team leader can vary widely depending upon the setting, but most often the team leader's tasks include overseeing the team's health, managing team logistics (e.g., meeting time, length of team, and so on), interacting with and gaining support from administration, recruiting team members, on rare occasions facilitating the departure of a team member, as well as any other tasks that help the team.

Most important, however, is the role the team leader plays in supporting and maintaining team culture. The team leader creates the structure for the commitment process for new members, makes sure the structure of team supports the team agreements, models effective team behaviour (modelling vulnerability and therapy for the therapist, as opposed to acting as an instructor or trying to control team members' behaviour), and intervenes as necessary when the team is struggling. The team leader's job can be difficult at times; Swales and Dunkley (this volume) provide further discussion of the role of team leader.

PROBLEMS IN TEAM

As in DBT treatment, having agreements, systems, and structure in place can help prevent many problems. That does not mean there are not problems, however! Having a group of people talk about very personal topics, while treating clients with extremely emotional situations and behaviours, provides fertile ground for intense emotion in team, and relatedly, interpersonal conflict.

While each team and problem will be unique, we have found a few key principles and strategies to be helpful across most problems. If these seem familiar to you, they should! In brief, these problems are dealt with using DBT. Each team member is a DBT therapist to every team member, with all of the skills and strategies at play. To begin with, focus on remaining non-judgmental, dialectical, and willing. Look for what is being left out in your own and others' positions, and try to validate the valid in both poles. Do not get stuck on rules; instead, look for how DBT principles and strategies (see Linehan, 1993, 2015) can define your path forward. Review the agreements regularly, and remember your teammates have committed to following them, and it is perfectly reasonable to ask them to follow them. Speak up; identify problems early, and use the describe skill to label and define them. Check the facts. Assess carefully, using chain analysis and missing links analysis as needed. In assessing the problem, make sure to ask about therapists' emotion, as that seems to be a thread through many team issues: therapists can become fearful, frustrated, sad, or ashamed with their own behaviour, their clients, or teammates. Just as in DBT, maintaining the focus on emotion will help tremendously in problem solving. Brainstorm solutions together, using all the change strategies at your disposal (contingency management, cognitive strategies, exposure, and skills). Get a commitment and troubleshoot. Use validation and reciprocal strategies throughout this process. And importantly, remember not all problems need to be solved, or solved perfectly. All team members will need to use distress tolerance in order to let some problems slide, or there will be no time to provide therapy for the therapist! All of these DBT strategies, intertwined with humour, caring, compassion, irreverence, and an easy manner, will allow the team to solve the problems that need solving, and get back to the best client care possible.

A range of problems will arise during the life of a team. Those that appear frequently, along with suggestions for how a team might begin to wrestle with them using the strategies described here, are provided in Box 8.1 (see Sayrs and Linehan (in press) for additional examples and further discussion).

All teams have struggles and tense moments. Problems such as difficult interactions in team, wondering if teammates have judged you, or not agreeing with anything that is said, are all going to happen quite frequently. If the team spends all of its time solving these, pausing the agenda to discuss interpersonal tension or non-verbal communications each time, there will be no time to talk about clinical issues. The team can work toward a dialectical balance of addressing those problems that interfere with therapist motivation and capability, and ignoring those that are not severe enough to interfere with adherent treatment.

Box 8.1 Examples of DBT team problems and suggested solutions

1. You believe another team member was judgmental toward you when you brought up a challenging clinical situation. If your emotions are high, you might respond in a variety of ways, such as becoming quiet, judging in return, or looking irritated such as rolling your eyes. Strategies for managing this might include:

   • Be direct, describe non-judgmentally what happened. The observer or other teammates will hopefully also notice you have become quiet and highlight the change in your demeanour.

   • Check the facts, and ask if the therapist was indeed judging. Judgments are shortcuts, they skip over the facts and summarize the situation as "good" or "bad." Asking your teammate to unpack the judgment and use the describe skill instead may help move the conversation to a more matter-of-fact exploration of what they are trying to express.

   • A DEAR MAN may be needed to ask that they restate what they said.

   • Radical acceptance and distress tolerance may be needed, to tolerate that your teammate has high distress for other reasons, and is simply not being very friendly today.

   • Self soothe, to tolerate the distress and stay in the conversation even though it is upsetting.

   • Remember dialectics: There is validity in your pole, but there is likely validity in your teammate's pole, as well. Somewhere in the judgment is likely a nugget of gold, and trying to find that may help you and your client.

2. You feel like the team is being cold and invalidating, when all you really want is validation. Some strategies might include:

   • Make sure you told the team what you wanted (validation). Highlight again that you were asking for validation.

   • The observer, your teammates, and you can all highlight that the team is focusing on solutions when in fact that is not what you asked for.

   • Check the facts. Are you understanding your team accurately?

   • Use describe, and tell the team what you are experiencing. You can add in a DEAR MAN to request more validation. For example, "When you say that, I feel like you're not understanding my experience at all. Then I get all anxious and frustrated and can't think straight. Can I try telling you again, and this time you focus on validating me? It'll really help me hear your feedback better if you can do that."

   • Irreverent humour can also break up a stuck conversation, such as, "You all have degrees in this! Validate me already!"

3. Your teammate responds to every suggestion by saying, "That won't work."

   • Describe the pattern out loud, so there are no elephants in the room.

   • Assess first, to be sure the problem is clearly understood. For example, the therapist may say they already did a chain analysis, but upon assessment discover they forgot to assess events after the target behaviour, including which consequences may be maintaining the behaviour.

Box 8.1 Continued

- Find out what has already been tried, and what has not worked. It can be very frustrating when the team launches into suggestions before assessing this!

- Assess the therapist's emotion. It may be that the solutions could work but frustration or fear is so high, the therapist cannot process what the team is saying. The team may also discover the therapist implemented strategies effectively, but is too frustrated to communicate clearly to the team.

- The team can then help suggest emotion regulation or distress tolerance skills. Validation will likely also help regulate the emotion, so the team can get back to addressing the problem.

4. You are burned-out.

- It is essential to deal with burnout, ideally long before it becomes burnout. When a therapist experiences an ongoing state of frustration, exhaustion, or other challenges related to clinical work, it can impact all of their clients and the entire team.

- The term "burnout" is very vague, and means a variety of things to different people. Carefully defining what you meant by "burnout" will be an important step.

- Then assess the situation. The team will need to understand the relevant variables in order to help. It may help to monitor your mood throughout the day, to see when frustration, fear, or certain thoughts arise. When do you notice distress? What happens just before? What thoughts, what emotions, what urges occur? How do you manage the distress? Search for ineffective strategies that provide relief in the short term but maintain the problem in the long term (e.g., escape fantasies such as, "I'll just quit and become an accountant!"). These questions will help pinpoint the problem and maximize the effectiveness of the interventions.

- The team can then provide support and problem solving. All of the DBT strategies and skills can come into play in this discussion.

- While the team can support and offer suggestions, it remains your own responsibility to implement the solutions, keep the team informed, and get additional help if needed. Burnout can be very serious, particularly when treating high-risk clients. Keeping quiet, getting frustrated with team, not trying their solutions, or expecting the team to solve the problem without your participation are all problematic for a number of reasons. Team can help keep your focus on solving the problem, but it will be essential that you engage in this process fully.

5. A person on team talks for too long.

- Teams will need to highlight this problem directly, calling out the elephant in the room.

- Assess if the length of this person's turn is longer because it serves a function for them, such as obtaining more validation or they believe the detail is essential to get adequate assistance from the team.

- Teams can discuss strategies for managing time in team, both in general and for this specific person. The team will need to both define the problem and facilitate solution generation.

- Having each therapist state what they need (e.g., assessment, problem solving, empathy, validation; see discussion earlier in this chapter) before they start their turn helps everyone focus on the problem and avoid unnecessary details.

(continued)

> **Box 8.1 Continued**
>
> - When our team was very large, we started having every therapist write down the number of minutes they would need on the agenda. The meeting leader watched the time and kept them to that number, until/unless the team agreed the topic warranted additional time. This dramatically reduced the time spent on details that were not relevant to the problem.
> - Remain dialectical! Spending extra time on certain issues may be valid, *and* the rest of the team needs time, too. Attending to the validity of both will help the team navigate these situations skillfully.

Conclusion

DBT team is considered one of the required components of comprehensive DBT and is aimed at addressing therapist capability and motivation, with the overarching goal of enhancing adherence to the DBT manual. While important, DBT team has received relatively less attention in DBT manuals, workshops, and other training materials. With this chapter, and a forthcoming book (Sayrs & Linehan, in press), I hope to bring more attention to principles and strategies useful in running an effective DBT team.

DBT team is quite different from traditional consultation teams. Providing DBT as a community of therapists, focusing on therapy for therapists rather than clients, requiring therapists to have clinical responsibility and therefore vulnerability in team, and emphasizing dialectics all make DBT team unique. The agreements, structure, and roles discussed here facilitate effective team meetings, and the DBT strategies help teams assess and deal with problems as they arise. Because every DBT team will have its own strengths and difficulties, these are described here as principles and not rules; each team can adapt the strategies to fit their needs.

Treating clients with multiple, chronic problems associated with emotion dysregulation can be very challenging. More than just a set of strategies, DBT team is a place that can help therapists feel motivated, rejuvenated, supported, and more capable as they meet the challenges of providing this treatment. It is my hope that this chapter provides at least a starting point for developing and maintaining a successful DBT team, where every DBT therapist can get the support needed to provide the best treatment possible.

Key Points for Clinicians

- DBT team is an essential element of comprehensive DBT.
- DBT team supports therapists' capability and motivation, and overall adherence to the DBT manual.
- Agreements, structure, and roles are important in running an effective DBT team.
- The same principles and strategies used with clients in DBT are implemented in DBT team.

REFERENCES

Koerner, K. (2012). *Doing dialectical behavior therapy: A practical guide.* New York: Guilford Press.

Linehan, M. M. (1993). *Cognitive-behavioral treatment of borderline personality disorder.* New York: Guilford Press.

Linehan, M. M. (2015). *DBT skills training handouts and worksheets*, 2nd Edition. New York: Guilford Press.

Sayrs, J. H. R., & Linehan, M. M. (in press). *A community of therapists: A manual for DBT team.* New York: Guilford Press.

Swenson, C. R. (2016). *DBT Principles in action.* New York: Guilford Press.

CHAPTER 9

SKILLS TRAINING IN DBT

Principles and Practicalities

COLLEEN M. COWPERTHWAIT,
KRISTIN P. WYATT, CAITLIN M. FANG, AND
ANDRADA D. NEACSIU

OUTPATIENT comprehensive (or "full-model") Dialectical Behaviour Therapy (DBT; Linehan, 1993) has been successfully disseminated outside of formal research settings (Comtois, Elwood, Holdcraft, & Simpson, 2007; Comtois, Kerbrat, Atkins, Harned, & Elwood, 2010). DBT is a time-intensive, complex treatment for multidiagnostic, high-severity clients, requiring a one-year commitment to at least three hours of treatment per week (i.e., one hour of individual therapy and two hours of group skills training). Comprehensive DBT includes individual psychotherapy, group skills training, phone coaching, and a consultation team for therapists. Community practices must have several resources to offer DBT (e.g., multiple therapists, time for consultation team, an avenue for 24-hour coaching) and must engage in intensive training to implement the treatment with fidelity (Harley, Sprich, Safren, Jacobo, & Fava 2008). Therefore, in community-based practice, DBT is frequently shortened or modified to fit existing resources or client presentations (e.g., age, comorbidity, severity of high-risk behaviours; Linehan, 2015b; Linehan et al., 2015; Nixon, McLagan, Landell, Carter, & Deshaw, 2004).

Modifications specifically to the skills-training mode of treatment include shortening the treatment from one year to six months or less, providing skills training as a standalone treatment, reducing the number of skills taught, providing individual rather than group skills training, and including family members into skills training groups. The implementation of these adaptations of the treatment in the "real world" is often inconsistent with the evidence base for DBT (Koerner & Dimeff, 2000; Scheel, 2000), despite there being a burgeoning literature of evidence-based DBT adaptations (Harley, Baity, Blais, & Jacobo, 2007; Linehan et al., 2015). Thus, community therapists are encouraged to find evidence-based adaptations, rather than making their own modifications to standard DBT.

This chapter provides evidence and clinical guidelines for implementing evidence-based adaptations to DBT skills training. To justify these recommendations, the chapter first reviews the theoretical underpinnings of skills training, the function and content of each skill module, and empirical support for DBT skills training. Then specific recommendations are provided regarding skills training group structure and practical considerations, including research-informed clinical decisions, regarding various models of DBT skills training.

Theoretical Underpinnings
of Skills Training

Historically, Linehan added skills training to DBT because she identified pervasive skills deficits as a core problem of adults who met criteria for Borderline Personality Disorder (BPD) and who engaged in suicidal behaviour (Linehan, 1993a, 1993b, 2015a, 2015b). According to the biosocial theory, behavioural dysfunction that is typical for BPD arises when there is a poor fit between a temperamentally emotionally sensitive and reactive individual and the environment. The emotionally vulnerable individual and the environment shape and reinforce extreme behaviours in each other. The environment provides insufficient modelling, coaching, and cheerleading of expressive behaviours, followed by either excessive punishment or intermittent reinforcement of extreme expressive behaviours. Over time, this transaction leads to deficits in the skills necessary to regulate emotions and tolerate emotional distress, which in turn leads to maladaptive behaviours employed in an attempt to regulate negative affect and/or inhibit emotional responses (Courtney-Seidler, Klein, & Miller, 2013; Crowell, Beauchaine, & Linehan, 2009; Linehan, 1993a; Linehan & Dexter-Mazza, 2008). In DBT, therefore, we see those who meet criteria for BPD as having pervasive emotion dysregulation stemming from skills deficits.

This conceptualization can be extended beyond BPD to affective disorders (see e.g., Neacsiu, Bohus, & Linehan, 2013), to substance use that serves an emotion regulation function (see e.g., Axelrod, Perepletchikova, Holtzman, & Sinha, 2011), as well as to other maladaptive behaviours (e.g., hair pulling, skin picking, explosive anger) that can be construed as consequences of emotional dysregulation (see e.g., Keuthen et al., 2012). In practice, emotionally dysregulated clients are taught to trust their experiences, label emotions accurately, engage in experience and expression of emotions, modulate arousal, tolerate distress, and replace problematic regulation behaviours with effective behaviours (Harned, Banawan, & Lynch, 2006; Linehan, 1993a, 2015b; Lynch, Chapman, Rosenthal, Kuo, & Linehan, 2006). If the *invalidating environment* is still present, parents and caretakers are taught to adapt contingencies to promote effective behaviours as well as to learn essential skills needed to interact with the primary patient (Miller, Rathus, & Linehan, 2007; Miller, Rathus, Linehan, Wetzler, & Leigh, 1997; Rathus & Miller, 2014).

DIALECTICAL BEHAVIOUR THERAPY SKILLS TRAINING CONTENT AND STRUCTURE

In DBT skills training, the focus is on teaching skills and increasing skills use in everyday situations. Four overarching skill sets are taught in a skills training group: core mindfulness, interpersonal effectiveness, emotion regulation, and distress tolerance. These skills were developed to target emotional, behavioural, interpersonal, cognitive, and social dysregulation and skill deficits that are characteristic of those who meet criteria for BPD, as well as for those who have difficulties with emotion regulation.

Core mindfulness skills are psychological and behavioural versions of meditation skills usually taught in Eastern spiritual practices, including Zen. These skills emphasize observing, describing, and participating in the present moment effectively, one-mindfully and non-judgmentally; they are central to all DBT skills and techniques and taught at the beginning of each of the other modules (Linehan, 1993a, 1993b, 2015a, 2015b; Linehan & Dexter-Mazza, 2008). DBT mindfulness skills were initially designed to target self-dysregulation, including identity disturbance or unstable self-image or sense of self, as well as to reduce vulnerability to dissociation, paranoid thinking, and over-personalization (Lynch, Morse, Mendelson, & Robins, 2003). In our clinical experience, in populations where identity disturbance is less common, mindfulness skills can also be helpful in the context of high intensity emotion, allowing a patient to identify information beyond emotion-based perceptions and cognitions.

Interpersonal effectiveness skills include assertively asking for something or refusing requests, building relationships with others, maintaining self-respect in interpersonal situations, modulating intensity of asking or refusing, and using behavioural principles, mindfulness, and dialectics to shape relationships. These skills were originally designed to target interpersonal dysregulation that often resulted in intense and chaotic interpersonal relationships and fear of being abandoned. In the recent revision of the DBT skills training manual (Linehan, 2015a), the interpersonal effectiveness skills were significantly enhanced, adding relationship skills that go beyond the basics. For clients with a BPD diagnosis, all interpersonal effectiveness skills are critical. Others with emotion dysregulation may have some, but not all, of these skills and a more in-depth assessment of skills deficits is needed to offer the most appropriate set of skills for the client at hand.

Emotion regulation skills are behavioural strategies that can be used to downregulate acute and chronic emotional arousal, including understanding emotions and their functions, mindfully experiencing and labelling emotions, reducing vulnerability to negative emotions, increasing positive emotional experiences, checking facts, problem solving, or acting opposite to the emotional urges. These skills are applicable and necessary for clients with emotional dysregulation who meet criteria for a variety of disorders. In different formats, many contemporary treatments for affective disorders, substance use, eating disorders, or impulsive/compulsive disorders teach these skills to clients, e.g., Unified Protocol for Transdiagnostic Treatment of Emotional Disorders (Barlow et al., 2010); Skills Training in Affect and Interpersonal Regulation (Cloitre, Koenen, Cohen, & Han, 2002); Emotion Regulation Group Therapy (Gratz & Gunderson, 2006); Emotion Regulation Therapy for Chronic Anxiety and Recurring Depression (Mennin & Fresco, 2013).

Distress tolerance skills include crisis survival and reality-acceptance strategies. Crisis survival skills are short-term strategies to tolerate painful life events without engaging in impulsive actions, such as self-harm and suicidal behaviours. Acceptance skills focus on radically accepting painful situations that are unlikely to change, the goal of radical acceptance being to reduce suffering (Linehan, 1993a, 1993b, 2015b; Linehan & Dexter-Mazza, 2008). Most people who endorse emotion dysregulation report knowing some of the crisis survival skills (see e.g., Neacsiu, Smith, & Fang, under review). Nevertheless, learning several options for tolerating distress, as well as the concept of intense emotion as distress, that can be tolerated with skills is novel for most clients. Reality acceptance skills are also relevant for a variety of clinical presentations, as evidenced by the inclusion of these skills in many contemporary treatments for a variety of disorders (e.g., Unified Protocol for Transdiagnostic Treatment of Emotional Disorders, Barlow et al., 2010; Acceptance and Commitment Therapy, Hayes, Strosahl, & Wilson, 2012; Emotion Regulation Therapy for Chronic Anxiety and Recurring Depression, Mennin & Fresco, 2013).

Group skills training is highly structured and lasts 2 to 2.5 hours. The skills training group is taught by one "leader" who is responsible for content and learning, and one "co-leader" who is responsible for process and management of group dynamics. The first half of group consists of mindfulness practice and a review of written homework from the previous week. The second half of group consists of direct instruction of new DBT skills and a homework assignment. It takes approximately six months to teach all four skills training modules, although length of time depends on the number of skills selected for teaching (Neacsiu et al., 2013). Depending on the severity of the clients in group and of the evidence-based adaptation selected, clients can be learning skills in a group format, anywhere from a few weeks to a full year, where they go through skills several times (Linehan & Dexter-Mazza, 2008). The *core mindfulness* module is repeated between each of the other three modules, and new clients may enter skills training while the group is learning the *core mindfulness* module (Linehan, 1993a, 1993b, 2015a, 2015b; Linehan & Dexter-Mazza, 2008). Thus, the skills training group may be made up of clients at different points in treatment and working on different stages of target behaviours.

EMPIRICAL DATA EVALUATING DIALECTICAL BEHAVIOUR THERAPY SKILLS GROUPS

There is a growing body of research evaluating the efficacy of DBT skills group as a standalone treatment. In her most recent DBT skills training manual, Linehan (2015b) presented a review of 15 randomized controlled trials (RCTs) investigating DBT skills training groups. Her review highlights the efficacy of standalone skills training in reducing emotion-related dysfunction, including: depression, anger, emotion dysregulation, emotional intensity, and affective instability (Feldman, Harley, Kerrigan, Jacobo, & Fava, 2009; Harley et al., 2008; Lynch et al., 2003; Safer, Telch, & Agras, 2001; Soler et al., 2009; Telch, Agras, & Linehan, 2001; Van Dijk & Katz, 2013; Waltz et al., 2009; Whiteside, 2011). DBT skills-only interventions have been successfully adapted to address a variety of presenting concerns and diagnoses, including eating disorders (Safer, Robinson, & Jo, 2010; Safer et al., 2001; Telch et al., 2001), problematic alcohol use (Whiteside, 2011), attention-deficit/hyperactivity disorder (ADHD, Fleming, McMahon, Moran, Peterson, & Dreessen, 2015; Hirvikoski et al., 2011), and with individuals who have perpetrated intimate partner violence (Cavanaugh, Solomon, & Gelles, 2011). Skills groups have also been modified for use in diverse treatment settings, including correctional facilities (Bradley & Follingstad, 2003; Shelton, Kesten, Zhang, & Trestman, 2011; Shelton, Sampl, Kesten, Zhang, & Trestman, 2009) and in vocational rehabilitation for individuals with severe mental disorders (Koons et al., 2006). Across these diverse clinical presentations and specialized treatment settings, DBT skills groups without concurrent individual therapy have been effective in reducing dysfunction specific to these populations (Linehan, 2015b; Valentine, Bankoff, Poulin, Reidler, & Pantalone, 2015).

Since the literature review published in the Linehan (2015b) skills training manual, a number of RCTs have emerged that evaluate the efficacy of standalone DBT groups. Neacsiu and colleagues (2014) found that DBT skills group alone was superior to an activities-based support group in improving emotion dysregulation and anxiety among a transdiagnostic sample of adults with anxiety, depression, and high emotion dysregulation. Furthermore, skills use mediated longitudinal changes in emotion dysregulation and anxiety, highlighting skills use as one active mechanism of change in DBT. This study highlights that DBT skills training is effective not only for specific psychiatric diagnoses, but also in transdiagnostic adult samples (Neacsiu, Eberle, Kramer, Wiesmann, & Linehan, 2014). Of importance, this study did not use any individual therapy (e.g., DBT or TAU) in conjunction with skills training. While the intervention was successful, it yielded high drop-out rates, and one of the primary reasons cited for drop-out was wanting individual therapy in addition to the skills training class (Neacsiu et al., 2014).

There have also been two investigations applying standalone DBT groups to address dysfunction among undergraduate students. Uliaszek and colleagues (2016) conducted an RCT comparing the efficacy of DBT group skills training to group positive psycho-therapy in improving "severe emotion dysregulation" among a sample of treatment-seeking undergraduate students. While both groups demonstrated improvements in psychiatric presentation, adaptive skill use, and well-being, students in the DBT group showed lower attrition, higher attendance, and higher ratings of therapeutic alliance than students in the control group (Uliaszek, Rashid, Williams, & Gulamani, 2016). Fleming et al. (2015) found that college students with ADHD showed greater treatment response rates and clinical recovery after receiving DBT skills training, compared to receiving DBT skills handouts alone.

There have also been two RCTs exploring the differential impact of DBT-informed skills training groups. The first study compared the efficacy of the Living Through Distress (LTD) programme, which is a DBT-informed skills group for inpatients, to treatment as usual (TAU) for psychiatric inpatients with BPD or deliberate self-harm (DSH). This study found that participants who went through the LTD program showed improvements in emotion regulation, compared to controls (Gibson, Booth, Davenport, Keogh, & Owens, 2014). Another study investigating the relative efficacy of a DBT-informed skills group to treatment as usual (TAU) found that, compared to TAU, DBT skills were effective in increasing primary "assertive" anger, which mediated symptom reduction, particularly within clients' social roles (Kramer et al., 2016).

In addition to these RCTs, there are a number of open trials and pilot investigations also pointing to the efficacy of DBT skills training as a standalone treatment. These studies suggest that DBT skills training may be useful in addressing dysfunction among individuals with BPD and other serious mental illnesses, as well as in reducing long-term use of mental health services. For example, one study found that a six-month standalone DBT group for clients with BPD and other severe mental illnesses produced significant improvements in functioning and severity of anxiety and depression (Vickers, 2016). An open trial investigating the impact of a DBT-informed emotional coping skills group for individuals with parasuicidal behaviours found completing the DBT skills training programme was associated with a 30% reduction in inpatient admissions and a reduction in mean number of inpatient days at one-year and two-year follow-up, with more than half of participants having no admissions in the year after completing the skills group (Sambrook, Abba, & Chadwick, 2007; Booth, Keogh, Doyle, & Owens, 2014). This work suggests that DBT skills training might be one effective way to reduce long-term cost of care for this population. Collectively, research on standalone DBT skills groups highlights the potential for the use of DBT skills to address a range of psychiatric disorders and transdiagnostic indices of clinical dysfunction.

There has also been work investigating the role of skills training in DBT for BPD. Recent mediation analyses (Neacsiu, Rizvi, & Linehan, 2010), dismantling studies (Linehan et al., 2015), and RCTs (Neacsiu et al., 2014) provide preliminary support for the theory that maladaptive behaviours (i.e., self-harm, substance use) are evidence of skills deficits, highlighting the importance of skills training to introduce new behavioural skills to reduce maladaptive behaviours in BPD. Skills training may be a driving mechanism underlying symptom improvement in DBT. For example, a randomized trial comparing the efficacy of standard DBT (individual and DBT skills group), DBT skills group with case management, and individual DBT with an activities-based support group for patients with BPD and recent parasuicidality found that all three groups showed comparable decreases in suicidality. However, the standard DBT and DBT skills with individual case management conditions significantly outperformed individual DBT without skills training on NSSI frequency and depression and anxiety severity (Linehan et al., 2015). Additionally, post-hoc analyses of previous positive outcomes in RCTs (Linehan et al., 1999a, 2002, 2006) of DBT for BPD indicated that the use of DBT skills fully mediated reductions in suicide attempts and improvements in depression severity and control over anger, and partially mediated decreases in NSSI (Neacsiu et al., 2010). Although more work is needed to replicate these findings, this research highlights the importance of skills training in treating several core symptoms of BPD (Linehan et al., 2015).

PRINCIPLES OF SKILLS TRAINING IN DIALECTICAL BEHAVIOUR THERAPY

This section discusses the broad principles of DBT skills training in a group format, with subsequent elaborations on how to successfully apply these principles in practice. Principles that guide DBT skills training groups are the same principles that guide DBT as a treatment package, including Zen, behaviour therapy, and dialectical philosophy, with dialectics serving to synthesize acceptance-based Zen and change-based behaviour therapy. As in DBT as a whole, DBT skills training group is organized around a treatment hierarchy and relies on assumptions of both therapists and clients.

Zen

Mindfulness and acceptance-based strategies in DBT are primarily informed by Zen philosophy, which emphasizes attentional control and compassion. Attentional control means both mindfully and non-judgmentally participating in the present moment, even a painful moment, while, at the same time, remaining alert and open to any experience that might arise. Mindfulness and acceptance permeate all aspects of skills training: the mindfulness module is repeated six times during one year, a short mindfulness practice begins and ends each group session, and group leaders model and shape use of mindfulness throughout. For example, group leaders often encourage clients to think non-judgmentally and be effective (both mindfulness skills) when teaching interpersonal effectiveness, emotion regulation, or distress tolerance skills.

The Zen philosophy concept of compassion and loving kindness influences DBT therapist assumptions. At times, working with complex and emotionally dysregulated clients can lead group leaders to feel frustration towards their clients and towards the group as a whole. In these moments, it is critical that DBT therapists, group leaders, and clients all maintain a genuine belief that clients are doing the best they can, given the circumstances that led to current behaviours. This assumption may help group leaders feel less judgmental towards clients who are having difficulty learning or applying new DBT skills and instead shift the focus towards solution analysis.

Behaviour Therapy

Principles and practices from change-oriented behaviour therapy are dialectically balanced with acceptance-based Zen. In skills training, behavioural principles include setting clear behavioural targets, using contingency management and shaping, teaching and employing stimulus control as needed, and conducting behavioural analyses. Behavioural targets are hierarchically organized: 1) extinguishing therapy-destroying behaviours (e.g., extreme behaviours that emerge in group that seriously threaten the continuation of treatment for one or more group members), 2) increasing skills acquisition, strengthening, and generalization, and 3) decreasing therapy-interfering behaviours (TIBs: Linehan, 1993a, 1993b, 2015b).

Increasing skills acquisition. Behavioural skills training procedures of modelling, instruction, rehearsal, and feedback are critical for the goal of increasing skills acquisition. In essence, DBT directly tells and shows clients what to do. If the target behaviour is difficult or complex, shaping and prompting are also employed to help with skills acquisition. The new skills training manual (Linehan, 2015a) includes clear and detailed verbal instructions for each skill, with step-by-step directions, visual illustrations (i.e., handouts) and thoughtful homework assignments (i.e., worksheets). The detail in the manual has led some to falsely assume that repeating these instructions *is* DBT skills training (but if that were the case, there wouldn't be a chapter for us to write!). Verbal instruction is one of a complex set of strategies and principles at play in DBT skills training. Examples and metaphors add vibrancy to verbal instruction and promote reader engagement. For example, when teaching mindful observation, telling clients an Adam Payne favorite (Payne & Reynolds, 2014): "Minds are like puppies: they run around and sniff butts!", tends to be an irreverent attention-grabbing teaching tool in demonstrating that minds wander and the goal is to notice them doing so.

Modelling as a strategy has immense flexibility in application. Sharing examples or stories of DBT skill use; showing effective communication with group co-leader, directly with clients, or with oneself (via thinking out loud); and role-playing with a co-leader or client are all forms of modelling. In our groups, clients have consistently provided feedback that they find therapist self-involving self-disclosure stories using skills to be among the most helpful and validating teaching strategies. For example, one of the authors shares a story in the context of interpersonal effectiveness skills in which, while moving house, movers changed their quoted price mid-way through the already-stressful move. The author disclosed urges to yell, cry, and engage in many ineffective interpersonal behaviours with the movers. She then describes that she engaged in momentary radical acceptance, allowing her to identify that her priority was to get the proposed higher price reduced (as opposed to making the movers "feel bad" which is what her emotional mind would have had her do). Therefore, she describes crafting a "DEAR MAN GIVE FAST" (for explanations of these acronyms, see Linehan, 2015a, 2015b) that led her to attaining her objective. The leader can choose to stop the story at the point where the skills to use were identified, and then can use verbal prompting, shaping, and verbal instruction to get the group to craft a "DEAR MAN ... " together.

Strengthening skills use. Behavioural rehearsal, reinforcement of skillful behaviour, and feedback and coaching are behavioural procedures used to improve likelihood and accuracy of skill application (Linehan, 1993a). Behavioural rehearsal may be used via role-plays, in real situations in group, or imaginally. Clients are taught the benefit of behavioural rehearsal via the skill of "Cope Ahead", where clients are instructed to engage in behavioural rehearsal by describing the problem to be coped with, generating coping strategies, and imaginally envisioning themselves practicing the plan they have just developed. Outside of teaching this directly, participants may be asked to role-play interpersonal effectiveness skills with each other, lead a mindfulness practice that emphasizes one of the six mindfulness skills in each group, and encourage group members to identify judgments or emotions that may interfere with their homework or learning. All these examples are additional illustrations of behavioural rehearsal used in group skills training.

Opportunities for reinforcement of skillful behaviours are endless in group skills training. Depending on the group, reinforcement may consist of verbal and non-verbal praise, or more concrete reinforcers such as stickers or candy. All of the authors have had success getting written homework from clients by offering stickers (an experience that surprised us all!). In group, we carefully attend to all possible skillful behaviours that could be reinforced, from bringing of a skills binder to class to masterfully executing a skill during a role play. In the case of behaviour where some aspects are skillful and others are not, the leader has a choice to use shaping with differential reinforcement of skillful behaviours and ignoring the ineffective behaviour (i.e., extinction procedures), or to pair the reinforcement with feedback and coaching. For example, in the case of a client who used opposite action (e.g., by sharing that the homework was not completed and shame arose), shaping could be used to reinforce the behaviours used to correctly implement the skill (e.g., "You said it to all of us in a clear way which is so hard and at the same time can help shame go away"), whereas feedback and coaching may include that the client's behaviour did not clearly demonstrate "all the way," (e.g., "looking down when you say it is shame consistent and will keep the emotion going") with provision of example behaviours demonstrating "all the way" (e.g., "look up, say it out loud like it's your Oscar speech").

Increasing skills generalization. Following Linehan's (1993b) recommendations, skill trainers aim to promote flexible responses in each context (response generalization)

and skillful behaviours across contexts (stimulus generalization). For response generalization, the therapist may acknowledge the multiple possible skills to use in any given
situation. For example, when a client feels sad and hopeless about engaging in an ineffective behaviour, he/she may have the option to use crisis survival (use cheerleading
statements), emotion regulation (problem solve how to avoid ineffective behaviour in
the future), or mindfulness (experience and label sadness as the bodily sensations that it
is comprised of). For stimulus generalization, skills homework practices and in session
role-plays are intended as behavioural rehearsal exercises to promote generalization of
skills use to other environments. For example, after learning how to turn the mind in
group towards acceptance that everyone is expected to speak, clients may be encouraged to identify a difficult problem that they are not accepting, and to practice turning
the mind when prompts for non-acceptance arise.

Targeting problematic behaviour in skills training. We also rely heavily on behaviour therapy techniques when targeting therapy-destroying and -interfering behaviours. Client TIBs frequently observed in our skills groups include lack of homework
completion, arriving to group late, missing group, attending to skills-irrelevant stimuli,
and refusing to speak in group. Skills trainers' TIBs that we have observed in our groups
include reinforcing ineffective behaviour, over- or under-preparing for group, or presenting material ineffectively (e.g., too quickly, providing unclear explanations, absence
of relatable examples). Client therapy-destroying behaviours are less frequent in our experience, and might include engaging in self-injurious behaviour in group, selling drugs
to other group members, making violent threats to others, or frequently interrupting
others when they speak. Targeting TIBs in group can involve creative applications of
learning principles (e.g., extinction, reinforcement, punishment, behavioural analytic assessment), though Linehan (2015b) notes two primary strategies: 1) ignoring behaviours
that are short in duration, and 2) firmly asking the client to stop the behaviour and subsequently focusing on continued skills training. Additional behavioural strategies may
include prompting a client to use a skill to promote consequent effective engagement,
removing distracting stimuli (i.e., stimulus control), and, of course, referring targeting
of the problematic behaviour to the individual therapist. For example, a co-leader might
suggest that a group member who appears to be emotionally dysregulated practise paced
breathing, ask members who are using their cell phones in group to put their phones out
of sight, or remove the clock from the skills training room to manage clock-watching.

Therapy-destroying behaviours must be addressed right away. For these behaviours,
behavioural assessment and functional analysis as well as a clear skills and contingency
management plan are recommended steps. For example, we recently encountered an instance of one group member attempting to sell drugs to other group members on break,
which clearly violates our rule against participants tempting others to engage in problem
behaviours inside or outside of group. In this case, group leaders alerted the offending
group member's individual therapist, who conducted a chain analysis to clarify contributing variables and the function of this behaviour, generate a skills plan to target the
function of the behaviour and other contributing variables, and clearly describe consequences of future instances of attempting to sell drugs to group members. In this case,

the behaviour functioned to increase positive emotions and feelings of social connect-edness and competence, and the skills plan entailed spending time with a friend and building mastery prior to skills group, paired with stimulus control plans of where to keep excess drugs, opposite action to urges to bring drugs to group, and crisis survival skills to tolerate these urges as needed. A contingency plan was developed based on the stimuli that served as reinforcers for that client, and entailed being told to leave the group session at the moment an additional group drug deal proposition is discovered, followed by that client bringing a repair and making an appropriate apology to group the following week, and receiving their favorite candy bar from the group leaders on break for absence of this behaviour for four groups in a row.

Furthermore, contingency clarification can be a helpful tool in managing TIBs. For example, in the case of lack of homework completion, we orient group members as to what are possible consequences of not completing their homework: dragging out of be-haviour in having them complete the exercise during homework review, with the leader prompting for responses to each important part of the worksheet as other group mem-bers observe, or, alternatively, engaging in a brief behavioural chain to identify barriers to homework completion and possibilities for intervention. For many group members, they report motivation to avoid these two possible outcomes, and thus complete their homework prior to attending group.

Exposure procedures may also be helpful in targeting TIBs. For example, in the case that a group member is missing groups due to shame or anxiety, individual therapists may coordinate with group skills trainers to implement graduated exposure exercises, such as first simply attending group, then speaking once during group, then asking one question during group, etc.

Dialectics

"Dialectics" refers to the philosophy that there is no absolute truth, nor is truth relative; rather, seemingly opposite ideas, viewpoints, or emotions can be true at the same time. Within DBT, a dialectical philosophy highlights that there may be function in dysfunc-tional or maladaptive behaviours, and there may be accuracy in distorted cognitions. By learning to reduce "either-or" thinking and view the world through a lens in which there is no absolute truth, clients become open to novel problem-solving strategies (Harned et al., 2006; Linehan, 1993a; Lynch et al., 2006).

The core dialectic in DBT, and in skills training group, is the balance between ac-ceptance and change. Both therapists and clients work on accepting behaviours (i.e., thoughts, emotions, actions) as the very best the client can do, while simultaneously pushing clients to do better, try harder, and be more motivated to change. This is ac-complished by teaching both acceptance- and change-based skills. Acceptance-based skills include skills taught in the mindfulness and distress tolerance modules, particu-larly radical acceptance. Change-based skills include those skills taught in the emotion regulation and interpersonal effectiveness modules.

Having both a leader and a co-leader in skills training group is particularly effective for highlighting dialectical thinking and balancing acceptance—and change-oriented strategies. Leaders and co-leaders can use the dialectical strategy of offering balanced solutions by deliberately disagreeing with each other or offering different skills that a client could use in a particular situation. For example, during the interpersonal effectiveness module, one group member asked for help navigating a situation at work where he felt a friendly co-worker was unjustly taking credit for the group member's work. The group leader suggested a change-oriented skill and recommended clarifying priorities and figuring out if the friendship with the co-worker or getting the credit he deserved was more important. The group co-leader offered an acceptance-oriented distress tolerance skill, and suggested that the client practise radically accepting that sometimes things aren't fair.

A critical dialectical approach to group is to balance heavily change-oriented content with validation. Validation is discussed extensively in DBT training materials (see Linehan, 2015b). All levels need to show up in every group, with an emphasis on higher levels, including normalizing client reactions and radical genuineness (Validation Levels 5 and 6; see Fruzzetti & Ruork, this volume). For example, when a client shared a homework example of having a particularly strong emotional reaction to finding out his partner had cheated on him, the group leader asked the group members to raise their hands if they would have felt similarly. All group members, and both group leaders, raised their hands, which the client found hugely validating.

In addition to modelling dialectical thinking and balanced solutions, skills trainers also rely heavily on dialectical and stylistic strategies in skills training group, including balancing consulting-to-the-patient with environmental intervention, magnifying tension, and using metaphors and stories as teaching skills. Our consultation team recently used the dialectical strategy of balancing consulting-to-the-patient with environmental intervention to help one client navigate group-interfering behaviour by another client in her group. One group member, "Jane," repeatedly asked another group member "Rebecca" to go out on dates with her after group. Jane's behaviour made Rebecca feel uncomfortable, and contributed to Rebecca's missing a number of groups in order to avoid awkward interactions with Jane. Our consultation team recommended that Rebecca's individual therapist coach her on using "DEAR MAN" and "FAST" to ask Jane to stop asking her out on dates. Our team also recommended that the group leaders review group rules and expectations in the next group session, with a particular emphasis on the rule prohibiting romantic or confidential relationships between other group members.

Group leaders can use the dialectical strategy of devil's advocate when teaching pros and cons by highlighting cons of resisting crisis urges: "Gosh, using skills in that moment sounds like it would take a lot of work!"; "It doesn't seem fair that everybody else around you gets to be ineffective and you have to use skills!", etc. This strategy often encourages clients to "argue back" to the group leaders and give reasons to use distress tolerance skills, even in the presence of high-intensity emotion and ineffective behavioural urges. Group leaders can also use balanced strategies on the opposite end of the dialectic by engaging in behaviours consistent with validating nurturance, as well as firm requests for additional change behaviours. For example, we provide validation that attending and fully participating in a skills training group can be frightening for a so-cially anxious client. At the same time, we advise socially anxious clients to "make lem-onade out of lemons," and use skills training group as an opportunity to practice distress tolerance while engaging in goal- and value-consistent behaviour.

Skilled group leaders also make heavy use of metaphors and analogies as teaching tools when teaching skills. Metaphors and stories help clients associate new concepts with concepts from everyday life that they understand well. For example, one group leader in our clinic teaches "ABC PLEASE" skills as the equivalent of getting a flu shot. Getting a flu shot doesn't reduce your exposure to the flu virus, but it decreases the prob-ability that you'll get the flu once exposed. In the same way, engaging in pleasure and mastery events daily and taking care of your physical body may not eliminate your ex-posure to stressful life events, but does reduce vulnerability to emotion mind.

Skills Training Group Structure

Traditional DBT skills training groups have the following components: announcements, mindfulness practice, homework review, break, new skill, homework assignment, and (optional) closing ritual. Although each of these components is elaborated upon in the Linehan (2015b) manual, additional clinical strategies are discussed below.

Announcements

This section of group includes opportunities for leaders to announce changes to group scheduling, the anticipated joining of new members or graduation of existing group mem-bers, communications from absent group members, and anticipated substitute co-leaders. These can be helpful in highlighting opportunities for skill use as relevant to group, as some group members can find some of these events to be emotionally evocative. Announcements also allow an opportunity for group members to alert group leaders to anticipated absences and lateness. This section of group is especially relevant when new members join for intro-ductions of group members to one another and can be used for an ice-breaker activity (e.g., dyads discussing favourite movies and sharing with group, each client sharing a fun fact about themselves) to begin increasing group cohesion immediately.

Mindfulness Practice

Mindfulness practices are short (2–5 minutes) experiential exercises that are aimed to focus the clients' attention on the new skills to be taught, as well as to strengthen use and clarify concepts related to mindfulness skills use. Several factors warrant attention in choosing and conducting a mindfulness practice. A variety of practices across groups are necessary for generalization, as well as strengthening of various mindfulness skills (e.g., observe, describe, non-judgmentally) and to foster member engagement. While mindfulness skills can be applied to anything, many resources provide suggestions of practices appropriate for group skills training (e.g., Hall, 2013; Linehan, 2015a; Miller et al., 2007; Rathus & Miller, 2014). The recommendation is that practice instructions begin with a story to add meaning and promote recall of the practice, with clear concise instructions, including which mindfulness skills will be used in the practice (for practical considerations related to leading mindfulness, see http://behavioraltech.org/resources/leadMindfulness.cfm). It can also be helpful to anticipate reactions to the practice and give clear instructions for these reactions (e.g., mind wandering, if wilfulness shows up). After the practice, each member and leader is encouraged to contribute to allow for skills trainers to provide feedback, relevant instruction, and modelling. At times, conducting a mindfulness practice relevant to the skills module or specific skill can be particularly helpful, especially with increasing response generalization of mindfulness skills.

For example, one of our team's favourite participate mindfulness practices is throwing dance moves. To lead this practice in skills group, a leader might say:

> "With some of the recent world events, my dog being sick, preparing for the holidays, and managing my day-to-day life, I've noticed my mind wandering away from whatever I'm doing a lot. With that in mind, I'd like to start group off today with a practice that helps us all get into this moment, doing one thing, all the way. This practice is a participate practice called throwing dance moves. I want us all to use our mindfulness skill of participate; that is, fully throwing ourselves into this activity. The way this practice works is very much like we are playing catch. One person will perform a dance move, any dance move, and "throw" it to another group member. That member receiving the dance move will repeat the dance move thrown, and will then initiate a different dance move of their choosing, and throw that dance move to another member. [Leader can demonstrate by initiating a dance move and throwing it to the co-leader, to mimic leader's dance move and initiate their own co-leader dance move.] You can be as creative as you wish. When I ring the bell, I invite you to fully throw yourself into this activity, fully attending to the present moment. You may notice your mind wandering to worries or judgments about the practice, or doing other things that pull you away from participating. When you notice yourself being pulled out of participate, notice what pulled you away from fully participating, and throw yourself back into the practice. Any questions? [pause] I'll ring the bell three times to begin and once to end. To start, let's have everyone stand up, and I'll initiate the first dance move."

Further guidance on teaching Mindfulness in DBT can be found in Stanton and Dunkley, this volume.

Homework Review

During homework review, each group member is prompted to share his or her efforts at applying the skill taught the previous week. Prompts for specific verbal behaviour (e.g., tell me which distress tolerance skill you used and how you used it) can be helpful in this process to promote targeted, relevant responses. Homework review, even in the most shaped of groups, presents many opportunities for TIBs, quite frequently including not completing homework exercises, not wanting to share, or being tangential when asked about the situation and the skills used. We have found three strategies to be effective in managing these TIBs: behavioural chain analysis, missing links analysis, and dragging out behaviour. For example, when a client told his group that he did not do any homework, the group leader encouraged him to recall if there were any situations over the past week where he was skillful or could have been skillful but wasn't. If the client insists that no such situations occurred, giving an example, such as "well, you're here now which means you engaged in effective behaviour to show up! That's skillful!" can model how to identify and label skillful behaviour. The group leader may follow with "is there anything else like this that you did this week?" to continue to work on dragging out behaviours.

New Skill

New skill material is chosen based on the curriculum chosen for any given population (e.g., Linehan, 2015a, schedule 1), skills strengths and deficits observed in the group, and members' level of experience with skills training (i.e., all members have participated in multiple modules vs. five new members joined last week). For example, for skills deficits, if teaching a skills group for which anger problems is highly prevalent among members, the group leader may choose to quickly orient the group to the Ways to Describe Emotions handout and breadth of emotions covered, while having each member of the group take turns reading sections from the anger handout, or when teaching opposite action, emphasize opposite action applications to anger. For an experienced group, in which most members have learned states of mind and the what and how skills of mindfulness several times, a leader may choose to teach "being" mind and "doing" mind and/ or loving kindness meditation instead. While Linehan (2015b) provides many teaching points for each skill, highlighting all of these is not possible. It does, however, highlight which points she consistently uses with high frequency with check marks and stars, which can help the leaders focus their teaching. The factors identified here for selection of new skills can also be useful in selection of teaching points. For example, in a group with several anxious achievers who tend to overdo unpleasant task completion and inhibit engagement in enjoyable behaviours, a group leader may choose to highlight a greater number of teaching points for short-term accumulate positives, engage the group in discussion points, and target barriers to engaging in these behaviours. In contrast, in a group where engaging in pleasant activities is a strength among group members, less time would be spent on material to increase behavioural frequency, and the leader would likely emphasize mindfulness of the enjoyed activity and unmindfulness of worries, with fewer teaching points.

Skills acquisition, strengthening, and generalization strategies are the primary methods used for teaching new skills. Skills acquisition strategies are teaching behaviours that promote development of new behaviour and include verbal instruction and modelling, while skills strengthening strategies increase use of or facility in using a new behaviour and include role-plays, coaching, in vivo practice, and reinforcing skillful behaviour. Generalization strategies help the client use skills behaviours flexibly in contexts relevant to their life and include demonstrating skills as applicable to variety of contexts and providing several variations of skill application for one context. In teaching a new skill with acquisition, strengthening, and generalization strategies, it is important to use strategies from each category to promote all three of these skills training goals. For example, in teaching "DEAR MAN", the leader might sequentially describe the function of the skill (acquisition: verbal instruction), model using "DEAR MAN" with a co-leader or group member (acquisition), provide verbal instructions for each skill of the acronym (acquisition), engage the group in drafting a "DEAR MAN" together (strengthening: rehearsal and coaching from leaders), followed by role plays in pairs (strengthening), with leader and co-leader walking around to give feedback (strengthening: coaching, reinforcement of skillful behaviour, feedback), asking group members how they could use this skill in their lives (generalization), and assigning homework practice (generalization). Encouraging group members to share examples, ask questions, and to use the "participate" skill paired with contingent reinforcement can be particularly valuable for in vivo practice and role-plays. In the authors' experiences, leader self-disclosure, relevant examples provided by leaders and other members, and exercises requiring skill application with feedback in group are perceived by group members as most beneficial.

Homework Assignment

Following teaching of a new skill(s), relevant homework worksheets and/or activities are assigned. Leaders can select the particular worksheet or ask the group to choose one of the options. Concisely reviewing the task instructions may be helpful. Homework exercises beyond worksheets can be effective forms of generalization. Having group members build distress tolerance kits (i.e., an individualized collection of items that are particularly effective in helping the person calm down, such as a favourite candle, a photograph of a loved one, a Sudoku book, or an index card with written reminders of skills to use, which clients keep in one place in order to make sure these items are easily accessible during a crisis) with subsequent show and tell in group is a frequently used example of this strategy.

Closing Ritual

A closing ritual, such as sharing one observation about group, or setting an intention for the week, is optional, although it can provide additional opportunities for practising DBT skills. Closing observations allow for additional practice of observe and describe mindfulness skills, for which clients may share any observation they made during the skills training session, while setting an intention provides an opportunity for clients to commit to using a skill (beyond assigned homework) before the next session, and allows trainers and group members to cheerlead and provide accountability and reinforcement for skill use. Closing rituals are also helpful to highlight contingencies. Group leaders frequently share observations at this point about our emotional experiences when something skillful or unskillful happened in group, or about planned or unplanned absences of group members.

Deviation from Curriculum

In some cases, effectively leading a skills group includes dialectically flexing from the structured plan. Deviating from the set curriculum involves both addressing a client response in the moment and then returning to what was taught, as well as deliberately altering the curriculum. Actively applying fundamental DBT strategies, such as speed, movement, and flow, can be especially helpful in managing client responses in skills group. At times, shared mindfulness observations, homework review examples, and client contributions during teaching of new skills can become circumstantial, tangential and/or emotionally dysregulating for some participants. Speed, movement, and flow is integral in helping the group progress in these circumstances. Skillful leaders will quickly read and respond to a client with an appropriate behavioural management strategy and immediately shift back to skills training.

Altering curricula usually takes two forms: either more time is allotted for the planned curriculum or additional materials are added (e.g., optional skills). Slowed pace may occur particularly when therapy-destroying behaviour (including when TIBs becomes group-destroying) takes up significant group time, which then allows insufficient time for material. In addition, certain skills can contribute to dysregulation or lack of understanding in different groups, at which time functional validation in slowing down can be appropriate. For example, many clients find radical acceptance to be emotionally evocative, and thus, if using schedule 1 or 2 (Linehan, 2015b), the leader may choose to spend additional time with radical acceptance instruction and practice, and finish turning the mind the following week. Similarly, many clients find understanding emotions skills, particularly what emotions do for you and a model for describing emotions, to be cognitively challenging to understand and therefore, subsequently emotionally dysregulating. Given that, per schedule 1, six emotion regulation handouts are to be covered on week one, it can be an effective alternative when these circumstances occur to break these two high cognitive load skills into two separate days of skills training.

Adding additional skills can be effective in the service of responsiveness to the group, or at times, when it becomes clear that additional skills are needed to promote learning of skills in the chosen curriculum. For example, when teaching "GIVE", some groups have sufficient difficulty with "V" for validation, such that additional time has been made to incorporate other material (i.e., interpersonal effectiveness handouts

17: *Validation*, 18: *A How to Guide to Validation*, 18a: *Identifying Validation*, Linehan, 2015a, 2015b; additional modelling, behavioural rehearsal opportunities) to promote understanding and extra practice of validation.

PRACTICAL CONSIDERATIONS

Starting a New Skills Training Group

As with any clinical service, beginning a skills group requires many considerations, including population, setting, treatment manual, curriculum, leaders, consultation team, measuring outcomes, and reimbursement. Clinical considerations are addressed in the subsequent paragraphs, while administrative concerns are beyond the scope of this chapter.

First, it is important to consider the population to participate in the group. As previously noted (see "Empirical Data Evaluating DBT Skills Groups" section), DBT skills training has successfully been applied with positive outcomes to numerous populations and age ranges (Linehan, 2015b). Defining clear inclusion and exclusion criteria is key to informing subsequent decisions and appropriate referrals (e.g., Linehan et al., 1999; Mehlum et al., 2014; Neacsiu et al., 2014). Common inclusion and exclusion criteria considered are diagnoses, age, sex/gender, suicidal and homicidal behaviour, psychosis, and behaviours with possible contagion effects (e.g., substance use, disordered eating; Caudill & Marlatt, 1975; Dishion & Tipsord, 2011). Although the bulk of the RCTs of outpatient DBT have been conducted with adults with BPD, BPD is characterized by comorbidity; over 90% of adults with BPD also meet criteria for a mood disorder, 64% meet criteria for a substance use disorder, 88% meet criteria for an anxiety disorder, and 53% meet criteria for an eating disorder (Zanarini et al., 1998). As a result, DBT skills training groups, even those for adults who meet diagnostic criteria for BPD, are functionally multidiagnostic. In community-based settings, opening DBT skills training groups to those without a diagnosis of BPD by providing multidiagnostic skills training groups may also maximize the number of clients who could benefit from learning skills (Blackford & Love, 2011; Booth et al., 2014; Harley et al., 2007).

Upon clarification of population, the most relevant skills manual (e.g., Linehan, 2015b; Mazza, Dexter-Mazza, Miller, Murphy, & Rathus, 2016; Rathus & Miller, 2014) and, if relevant, curriculum must be chosen (e.g., 24 weeks Linehan, 20 weeks McMain, 16 weeks Neacsiu; see Linehan, 2015b). Curricula may be chosen based on presenting concerns of potential group members, group member experience with and mastery of core DBT skills, or time constraints imposed by treatment setting or payers. There are some benefits to specialized skills training groups and curricula for specific diagnostic and target behaviours. The newest skills training manual (Linehan, 2015b) includes skills training adaptations for specific populations, including BPD plus comorbid substance use disorder, transdiagnostic emotion dysregulation, or "advanced" skills groups. Benefits of specific diagnostic and behaviour-specific groups include pointed emphasis on relevant skills. For example, non-suicidal depressed or anxious clients may not need to spend six weeks learning crisis survival skills, and may be best suited to a curriculum emphasizing emotion regulation, whereas clients with substance use disorders often miss out on the opportunity to learn DBT skills for addictive behaviours, including "Addict Mind/Clean Mind/Clear Mind", "Dialectical Abstinence", "Burning Bridges", and "Alternative Rebellion".

Furthermore, the open or closed nature and relevant contingencies are worthy of consideration. In outpatient settings, groups are typically closed for the majority of the cycle, with entry of new members at specific time points. In treatment settings that utilize curricula offering repeating mindfulness modules between other skills modules, new members can often enter skills group during mindfulness review or in the first few weeks of the following module. However, in other settings (e.g, substance abuse treatment facilities), the DBT team and co-leaders may prioritize capitalizing on clients' current commitment to behavioural change and allow new group members to join mid-module rather than waiting until the next review of mindfulness.

Outside of the actual skills training group, adherence to the treatment as a whole is critical. Clients who are enrolled in full-model DBT in our clinic must have individual DBT therapists who sit on our consultation team. Unless a skills training group is using a supported curriculum for a specific targeted population (e.g., Neacsiu et al., 2014), it is recommended that clients who are referred to DBT skills group must be enrolled in weekly individual therapy with an individual therapist who agrees to manage crises and TIBs. Adherence to the treatment also includes consultation team and group leaders/skills trainers. A group that teaches DBT skills but doesn't have the leaders on a DBT consultation team is *not* a DBT group! A therapist consultation team helps ensure the goals set forth for the group are being achieved in a manner consistent with DBT skills training principles and assumptions and provides the necessary support for skills trainers working with a challenging population. Additionally, skills group leaders should be intensively trained, or receiving adequate DBT training or supervision, and participate in consultation team. Although many DBT programmes "rotate" skills training roles, in which one leader will review homework and the other will teach one week and then roles will swap the following week, in order to implement DBT skills training with fidelity there should be one clear leader and one clear co-leader for at least an entire module, and ideally, for the entire six months of skills training.

Finally, it is important to consider targets and measurement of progress towards targets for any group. Skills acquisition, strengthening, and generalization are broad targets of DBT skills training, and additional targets may vary substantially based on the skills training group population. Linehan (2015b) lists many reliable and valid measures for various relevant targets. For example, in our clinic our standard intake packet for referrals to our DBT program includes the *Beck Depression Inventory,*

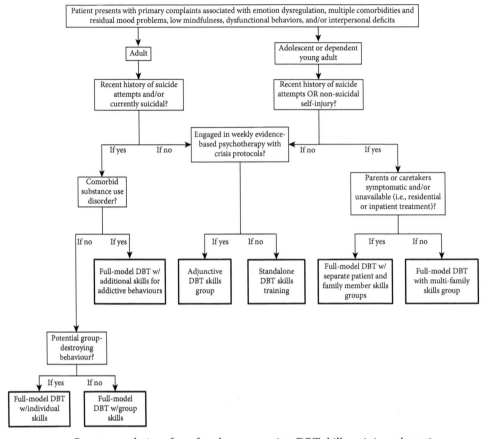

FIGURE 9.1 Recommendations for referral to appropriate DBT skills training adaptation.

second edition (BDI-II; Beck, Steer, & Brown, 1996), the Beck Anxiety Inventory (BAI; Beck, Epstein, Brown, & Steer, 1988), the Borderline Symptom List-23 (BSL-23; Bohus et al., 2009) and the Difficulties in Emotion Regulation Scale (DERS; Gratz & Roemer, 2004).

Research-Informed Clinical Decisions

DBT is often shortened or modified on the basis of resources or characteristics of the clinic where the treatment is provided (Linehan et al., 2015; Nixon, McLagan, Landell, Carte, & Deshaw, 2004), and, in our clinical experience, many of these adaptations have not been evaluated in large randomized controlled efficacy or effectiveness trials. Common adaptations include offering skills training only, as opposed to offering "full-model" DBT, offering some clients individual skills training, as opposed to group skills training, and including family members in skills training, as opposed to treating only the identified patient. For each adaptation, there are case examples that are representative of clinical referrals received in our clinic which briefly review what empirical support there is for each adaptation, and insight is provided into decisions made when we decide to modify skills training. Figure 9.1 offers a quick guide to clinical decision making in the form of a decision tree containing recommendations for which DBT skills training adaptation to consider with particular clinical presentations.

Full-model DBT versus skills training-only

Case Example: "Charles"

Charles is a 32-year-old Caucasian man with a history of generalized anxiety disorder, ADHD, and dysthymia. He has no history of suicide attempts, suicidal ideation, or NSSI. He has been engaged in weekly individual psychotherapy for the past two years at a private clinic in the community, which he has found helpful for improving insight and decreasing self-judgmental thoughts. His individual therapist referred him to our clinic for DBT skills group in order to improve mindfulness and gain emotion regulation and coping skills.

Case Example: "Devon"

Devon is a 56-year-old African-American man with a history of alcohol and prescription painkiller abuse, major depression, one suicide attempt lifetime, attempted carbon monoxide poisoning in his garage one month ago when his wife filed for divorce, and current hopelessness and passive suicidal ideation. He has been intermittently attending individual therapy at a community-based behavioural health clinic for the past five months and has not made significant gains. His individual therapist referred him to our clinic for DBT skills group in order to reduce suicidality and substance use.

Group skills training-only DBT may be more cost-effective than comprehensive DBT or individual DBT in community settings (Harley et al., 2007). Group skills training-only DBT may maximize resources by allowing clinicians to treat multiple people at one time and minimize training and supervision requirements because it follows a well-specified protocol (Blackford & Love, 2011). DBT skills-only groups alone can result in significant reductions in maladaptive behaviours (Neacsiu et al., 2014) and improvements in emotional regulation, mood, and general psychiatric symptoms (Booth et al., 2014; Fleming et al., 2015; Koons et al., 2006; Koons et al., 2001).

Based on these data we know that skills-only can work for people who have affective or attentional disorders. Further, there is some evidence from the recent component analysis study that DBT skills training, without individual DBT therapy, is effective for reducing NSSI frequency and depression and anxiety severity (Linehan et al., 2015). However, the "DBT skills only" condition in this trial was not truly only skills training group; it included concurrent non-DBT individual therapy and crisis management. It is important to note that there is currently no data to suggest that an outpatient skills-only intervention without concurrent weekly individual therapy is effective for highly suicidal adults or adults with a BPD diagnosis. Therefore, it is recommended that adults who are determined to be "high risk," as in clients who present with suicidality or homicidality with plan, intent, and means, those who have any history of suicide attempts or homicidal acts, or those who engage in severe treatment interfering- or treatment-destroying behaviours, should be referred to full-model DBT. Those who are lower risk, as in those with a history of self-harm but not suicidal ideation, those with primary diagnoses of mood or anxiety disorders, or those who are currently engaged in weekly, evidence-based individual therapy, may be good candidates for group skills training as an adjunctive treatment.

Clinical Decision: "Charles"

After consultation with the DBT team, we determined Charles to be low risk for life-threatening and severe therapy-interfering behaviours and agreed to admit Charles to an adult DBT skills group without requiring him to participate in full-model DBT. As part of skills-only DBT in our clinic, we required Charles to sign a release of information for our programme to consult with his individual therapist, and required his individual therapist to provide crisis support and management of TIBs for Charles; we did not provide phone coaching to Charles. If we were concerned about life-threatening or therapy-interfering behaviour, we followed the written crisis plan that the individual therapist provided prior to us admitting Charles into the group and we called the individual therapist to alert him of the behaviours happening and to transfer responsibility to him.

Clinical Decision: "Devon"

Given Devon's recent suicide attempt, current suicidal ideation, and availability of lethal means, substance use, social isolation and recent loss of significant relationship, depression and hopelessness, and ambivalence about individual therapy, we determined Devon to be a high-risk patient who we were uncomfortable admitting to the programme for only DBT skills. After consultation with the DBT team, we recommended full-model DBT, including individual DBT, telephone coaching, and DBT skills training group, all provided by clinicians on our DBT consultation team in our programme.

Individual versus group skills training

Case Example: "Candace"

Candace is a 39-year old African-American woman with a history of PTSD, with multiple sexual traumas beginning in childhood and notable life-threatening and therapy-interfering behaviours of suicidal and homicidal ideation, non-suicidal cutting, and anger problems. She presented to our clinic with high willingness upon referral by her psychiatrist and committed to DBT to increase behavioural control of crisis behaviours prior to engaging in PTSD treatment. While Candace had engaged in low-lethality behaviour with intent to kill on one occasion several years ago and had engaged in other instances of homicidal planning behaviour, assessment indicated that these behaviours were reliably directed toward perpetrators of her abuse. In addition, she experienced passive homicidal ideation in response to anger and/or hurt arising from interactions with many others beyond perpetrators. Based on chain analyses, these behaviours appeared to serve a communication function for Candace (i.e., she engaged in these behaviours to solicit support from her social environment and to communicate anger and hurt).

Case Example: "James"

James is a 20-year-old Caucasian man with a history of psychotic depression, social anxiety disorder, polysubstance abuse, and three hospitalizations for serious suicide attempts. He arrived at our clinic after being suspended from his job for making homicidal threats during an argument with a co-worker. James' substance use and suicide attempts served to regulate high-intensity painful emotion, and his homicidal threats served a communication function when he didn't know how to effectively communicate his needs in anxiety-provoking interactions. It was clear that James could benefit from skills training, and we began orientation and commitment to full-model DBT. James was unwilling to commit to group skills training because he was anxious about being in a group setting. At the same time, James had a goal of being able to get back to work, which would require tolerance of interpersonal situations.

The majority of clients seeking DBT are multi-diagnostic clients with severe emotion regulation difficulties, and these clients may experience acute distress and crisis more regularly than other populations. As such, it is important that these clients have a space to both acquire new skills and apply them to crises that emerge in their daily lives. This is one important reason that DBT includes both *group skills training* to acquire, strengthen, and generalize skills, and *individual therapy* to apply these skills to difficult life events. Based on the hierarchy guiding individual DBT, it is difficult to successfully conduct skills training in the context of individual therapy. Skills training follows a different hierarchy, and there is a distinct set of expectations from group leaders and other group members that increases the likelihood of skills acquisition in this mode of treatment.

Group skills training provides opportunities for vicarious learning, support from other group members with similar problems, and informal exposure to interpersonal situations. However, there are some situations in which individual skills training may be warranted. Some individuals may be aggressive or engage in group-interfering behaviours that are difficult to manage, which may have a negative impact on the group, or have significant anxiety and be unable to fully habituate to the group, which may inhibit their ability to process information during sessions. Given the significant clinic resources required to conduct individual skills training and important social and interpersonal benefits of participating in a group, we rarely recommended individual skills training and there is very little research as of yet to guide this decision. For example, some studies have demonstrated the superiority of group therapy over individual therapy for PTSD (e.g., Sripada et al., 2016), while meta-analyses have demonstrated that both individual and group interventions for PTSD are effective (Powers, Sigmarsson, &

Emmelkamp, 2008). Some studies of treatment of social anxiety have demonstrated the superiority of individual therapy over group therapy (e.g., Stangier, Heidenreich, Peitz, Lauterbach, & Clark, 2003), while others demonstrate that individual and group interventions for social anxiety may operate via distinct mechanisms of change (Hedman et al., 2013).

Therefore, the decision whether to pursue individual versus group skills training should be evaluated on a client-by-client basis with careful consideration of contingencies and attention to what is being reinforced. For example, individuals may need temporary individual skills training if there are long waitlists for group entry and their maladaptive behaviours are too severe to be placed on a waitlist. We may consider individual skills training if we believe that the client may engage in group-destroying behaviour or may not be a good temperamental fit for the group (e.g., placing an aggressive or homicidal male in a group made up of predominantly traumatized women). We may also recommend individual skills training if the client is unwilling or unable to commit to a full six months of skills training, so as to not disrupt group dynamics by attending infrequently or leaving group prematurely. Adults who cannot attend group skills training due to logistical reasons (e.g., timing of groups, not having space in group, not having enough clients in need to form a group) may need to begin skills training with an individual trainer, while working to problem solve logistical issues with the individual therapist.

Should a client need individual skills training, it is ideal to have skills training led by a second therapist who is not the client's primary individual therapist. This allows for more clear delineation of responsibilities, with the second therapist focusing on skills training and the primary therapist focusing on crisis management and skills application. If a second skills trainer is not available, the primary individual therapist can also provide skills training; however, it is important that both the client and therapist are disciplined in allowing sufficient time for skills training. This can be difficult to achieve, as there are often pressing problems in the client's life that feel more urgent than formal skills training. In order to increase the probability of success within this model, the individual therapist should consider: 1) having separate sessions for individual therapy and individual skills training, preferably in different rooms, or 2) focusing on skills directly relevant to the client's presenting concern and integrate skills didactics into the session.

Clinical Decision: "Candace"

In considering individual or group skills training for Candace, social support and the likelihood of homicidal communications occurring as group-destroying behaviour was considered. Given relevant history, we judged the likelihood that homicidal urges would be directed at other group members to be low. Although our team considered that Candace would likely experience feelings of hurt and anger in skills training group, we believed that her experiencing these emotions in the context of group would offer opportunities for skills strengthening and generalization. We decided the strengths of skills group in providing validation, social support, and corrective learning experiences outweighed the risks of Candace engaging in group-destroying homicidal communications directed toward group members.

Clinical Decision: "James"

After consultation with the DBT team, we decided to pursue short-term individual skills training plan with James, with the intention of his transitioning into group skills training. Individual skills training focused on distress tolerance in order to give James the skills he needed to tolerate group without engaging in serious group-destroying behaviours, such as making inflammatory statements or homicidal threats.

Multi-family versus identified patient- or family member-only group

Case Example: "Bethany"

Bethany is a 25-year-old Caucasian woman with a history of BPD, panic disorder, and bulimia. She arrived at our clinic after completing a six-month residential programme in an out-of-state treatment facility specializing in eating disorders. She is currently living at home with her parents and three younger siblings and she just got her first job working at a clothing store at the local mall. By her parents' reports, Bethany has few relationships outside of her family and has few independent living skills. By Bethany's report, her parents' relationship is characterized by conflict, and her mother has a history of BPD and anorexia, neither of which is currently well treated.

Case Example: "Ariana"

Ariana is a 19-year-old Latina woman with a history of BPD, multiple drug overdoses with ambivalent intent to die, NSSI (cutting), panic attacks, and PTSD after being raped by an acquaintance at 16. She arrived at our clinic after completing a four-month residential DBT programme in a treatment facility out of state. Although she is financially dependent on her father, since returning from the residential treatment facility, she was welcomed back to her position at her old job, moved out of her father's home and into an apartment with room-mates, and passed her driver's licence test. Ariana's father attended the intake appointment, and both Ariana and her father reported goals of fostering Ariana's independence, avoiding future hospitalizations, and targeting symptoms of PTSD. Ariana's father was also observed to be behaviourally, cognitively, and emotionally dysregulated himself, to engage in pervasively invalidating behaviours, to intermittently reinforce ineffective behaviours of Ariana's, and to fully exhibit secondary targets observed in families of BPD teens.

Significant others and family members of adults and adolescents with BPD show higher levels of psychological distress than the general population (Ekdahl, Idvall, & Perseius, 2014; Hoffman, Buteau, Hooley, Fruzzetti, & Bruce, 2003; Scheirs & Bok, 2007). These findings, as well as our understanding of the biosocial theory and how emotion dysregulation develops, emphasize the particular importance of decreasing family member criticism, and increasing validation and emotion management within families of men and women with emotion dysregulation and/or BPD (Miller, Glinski, Woodberry, Mitchell, & Indik, 2002).

There are several models of DBT skills training that include family members. For example, in standard outpatient DBT for adolescents, parents are included in multi-family skills training groups. In this model family members partake in skills training along with the identified patient, in order to intervene simultaneously on individual and environmental factors that contribute to adolescent emotional and behavioural dysfunction (Woodberry, Miller, Glinski, Indik, & Mitchell, 2002). The addition of family members into multi-family skills training groups also provides a common vocabulary for therapeutic techniques within families, enhances generalization of skills, models appropriate management of disruptive behaviours, and provides in vivo opportunities for family members to enhance validation, support, and effectiveness (MacPherson, Cheavens, & Fristad, 2012; Miller et al., 2007). Including multiple families also allows for feedback and skills practice across families (Ekdahl et al., 2014; Rathus & Miller, 2014).

In settings where family members are not available to attend groups with the identified patient, such as residential, inpatient, or correctional facilities, it may be necessary to implement separate groups, one for patients and another for family members. There are several models of family member-only groups that meet with different frequencies and use different curricula (Ekdahl et al., 2014; Hoffman, Fruzzetti, & Buteau, 2007; Hoffman et al., 2005; Nixon et al., 2004; Rajalin, Wickholm-Pethrus, Hursti, & Jokinen, 2009; Wilks et al., 2016). DBT-informed skills training programmes for family members of adults who have emotion dysregulation and/or BPD provide psychoeducation, teach validation and dialectical thinking, and offer a built-in support network (Hoffman, Fruzzetti, & Swenson, 1999; MacPherson et al., 2012). Family members who complete DBT-informed skills training programmes self-report improvements in overall psychiatric distress, depression severity, and perceived burden (Hoffman et al., 2007; Hoffman et al., 2005; Rajalin et al., 2009; Wilks et al., 2016). Those family members experiencing clinically significant anxiety and depression at the start of treatment appear to particularly benefit from DBT skills training (Ekdahl et al., 2014).

The addition of family members into treatment should be evaluated on a client-by-client basis, with careful consideration of treatment targets and contingencies. Among adolescents, family members should be included in skills training as much as is feasible. However, in young adults and adults, in cases where family members may be perpetrating traumatic invalidation or abuse, or if the treatment targets of the identified patient are more explicitly focused on developing independence than on changing family-level dynamics, it may be more beneficial to see the client independent of his or her family members.

Clinical Decision: "Bethany"

After consultation with the DBT team, we decided to place Bethany in a young adult multi-family skills training group, which includes both of her parents in skills training group weekly. The DBT team believed that multi-family group was best for Bethany and her parents in order to intervene directly on family-level factors that may be maintaining maladaptive behaviour, including targeting Bethany's parents' excessive caretaking that has blocked her developing independent functioning and Bethany's mother's own emotion dysregulation and ineffective coping.

Clinical Decision: "Ariana"

In consultation with DBT team, we considered multi-family young adult group for her and her father, given her father's aforementioned significant contribution to target behaviours, as well as adult skills training group. Given Ariana's desire to foster independence in treatment, her father's unwillingness to participate, and her recent residential independence (and thus decreased contact with the pervasively invalidating home environment created by her father and step-mother), our team decided to place Ariana in an adult skills training group, rather than the young adult multi-family skills training group which would include her father, in order to enhance her sense of self-efficacy and competence to solve her own problems.

CONCLUSION

Linehan has included over 100 skills in her newest skills training manual (Linehan, 2015a, 2015b) that covers problems relevant across psychopathology. This exciting set of clinical tools has immense appeal to both therapists and clients, and the DBT literature offers a rich and complex set of options for how to best teach these skills to clients. There are some important take home points to consider when thinking of teaching DBT skills to adults and adolescents with psychopathology. First, it continues to be of utmost importance to follow the newest evidence and as much as possible rely on research to inform clinical practice and decision-making. This is the only way to effectively serve patients and to not engage them in extensive work that has unknown or iatrogenic effects. Second, principles and strategies taught in individual DBT must also be applied in skills training DBT. A skills trainer cannot be effective without having a solid theoretical foundation in dialectics, behavioural principles, and Zen. Third, clinical decision making with regards to the specific type of skills training experience to offer to a client needs to be discussed and agreed upon with the DBT team. A skills trainer not on team does not offer DBT skills training. Fourth, when dependent adults or adolescents are concerned, context must also be targeted by the intervention to enhance likelihood of success. Fifth, the case conceptualization for a client is critical in the decision-making process regarding how to best teach skills to the client.

KEY POINTS FOR CLINICIANS

- Rely on research to inform decision-making and clinical practice when adapting DBT skills training.
- The principles and strategies that guide DBT skills training are the *same* as the principles and strategies underlying DBT as a whole.
- Consider case conceptualization, treatment targets, and contingencies when making decisions about how to best engage a client and teach skills.
- Discuss clinical decisions and skills training adaptations with the DBT consultation team.

REFERENCES

Axelrod, S. R., Perepletchikova, F., Holtzman, K., & Sinha, R. (2011). Emotion regulation and substance use frequency in women with substance dependence and borderline personality disorder receiving dialectical behavior therapy. *The American Journal of Drug and Alcohol Abuse*, *37*(1), 37–42. doi:10.3109/00952990.2010.535582

Barlow, D. H., Farchione, T. J., Fairholme, C. P., Ellard, K. K., Boisseau, C. L., Allen, L. B., & Ehrenreich-May, J. (2010). *Unified protocol for transdiagnostic treatment of emotional disorders*. New York: Oxford University Press.

Beck, A. T., Epstein, N., Brown, G., & Steer, R. A. (1988). An inventory for measuring clinical anxiety: psychometric properties. *Journal of Consulting and Clinical Psychology*, *56*(6), 893–897. doi: 10.1037/0022-006X.56.6.893

Beck, A. T., Steer, R. A., & Brown, G. K. (1996). *Manual for the Beck Depression Inventory—II*. San Antonio, TX: Psychological Corporation.

Blackford, J. U., & Love, R. (2011). Dialectical Behavior Therapy group skills training in a community mental health setting: a pilot study. *International Journal of Group Psychotherapy*, *61*(4), 645–657. doi:10.1521/ijgp.2011.61.4.645

Bohus, M., Kleindienst, N., Limberger, M. F., Stieglitze, R.-D., Domsalla, M., Chapman, A. L., ... Wolf, M. (2009). The short version of the Borderline Symptom List (BSL-23): development and initial data on psychometric properties. *Psychopathology*, *42*, 32–39. doi:10.1159/000173701

Booth, R., Keogh, K., Doyle, J., & Owens, T. (2014). Living Through Distress: A skills training group for reducing deliberate self-harm. *Behavioural and Cognitive Psychotherapy*, *42*, 156–165. doi:10.1017/S1352465812001002

Bradley, R. G., & Follingstad, D. R. (2003). Group therapy for incarcerated women who experienced interpersonal violence: A pilot study. *Journal of Traumatic Stress*, *16*(4), 337–340. doi:10.1023/A:1024409817437

Caudill, B. D., & Marlatt, G. A. (1975). Modeling influences in social drinking: an experimental analogue. *Journal of Consulting and Clinical Psychology*, *43*, 405–415.

Cavanaugh, M. M., Solomon, P., & Gelles, R. J. (2011). The Dialectical Psychoeducational Workshop (DPEW): the conceptual framework and curriculum for a preventative intervention for males at risk for IPV. *Violence Against Women*, *17*(8), 970–989. doi:10.1177/1077801211414266

Cloitre, M., Koenen, K. C., Cohen, L. R., & Han, H. (2002). Skills training in affective and interpersonal regulation followed by exposure: A phase-based treatment for PTSD related to childhood abuse. *Journal of Consulting and Clinical Psychology*, *70*(5), 1067–1074. doi:10.1037/0022-006X.70.5.1067

Comtois, K. A., Elwood, L., Holdcraft, L. C., & Simpson, T. L. (2007). Effectiveness of dialectical behavior therapy in a community mental health center. *Cognitive and Behavioral Practice*, *14*(4), 406–414. doi:10.1016/j.cbpra.2006.04.023

Comtois, K. A., Kerbrat, A. H., Atkins, D. C., Harned, M. S., & Elwood, L. (2010). Recovery from disability for individuals with borderline personality disorder: a feasibility trial of DBT-ACES. *Psychiatric Services*, *61*(11), 1106–1111. doi:10.1176/appi.ps.61.11.1106

Courtney-Seidler, E. A., Klein, D., & Miller, A. L. (2013). Borderline personality disorder in adolescents. *Clinical Psychology: Science and Practice*, *20*, 425–444. doi:10.1111/cpsp.12051

Crowell, S. E., Beauchaine, T. P., & Linehan, M. M. (2009). A biosocial developmental model of borderline personality: elaborating and extending Linehan's theory. *Psychological Bulletin*, *135*(3), 495–510. doi:10.1037/a0015616

Dishion, T. J., & Tipsord, J. M. (2011). Peer contagion in child and adolescent social and emotional development. *Annual Review of Psychology, 62*, 189–214.

Ekdahl, S., Idvall, E., & Perseius, K. I. (2014). Family skills training in Dialectical Behaviour Therapy: The experience of the significant others. *Archives of Psychiatric Nursing, 28*, 235–241. doi:10.1016/j.apnu.2014.03.002

Feldman, G., Harley, R., Kerrigan, M., Jacobo, M., & Fava, M. (2009). Change in emotional processing during a dialectical behavior therapy-based skills group for major depressive disorder. *Behaviour Research and Therapy, 47*(4), 316–321. doi:10.1016/j.brat.2009.01.005

Fleming, A. P., McMahon, R. J., Moran, L. R., Peterson, A. P., & Dreessen, A. (2015). Pilot randomized controlled trial of dialectical behavior therapy group skills training for ADHD among college students. *Journal of Attention Disorders, 19*(3), 260–271. doi:10.1177/1087054714535951

Gibson, J., Booth, R., Davenport, J., Keogh, K., & Owens, T. (2014). Dialectical behaviour therapy-informed skills training for deliberate self-harm: A controlled trial with 3-month follow-up data. *Behaviour Research and Therapy, 60*, 8–14. doi:10.1016/j.brat.2014.06.007

Gratz, K. L., & Gunderson, J. G. (2006). Preliminary data on an acceptance-based emotion regulation group intervention for deliberate self-harm among women with borderline personality disorder. *Behavior Therapy, 37*(1), 25–35. doi:10.1016/j.beth.2005.03.002

Gratz, K. L., & Roemer, L. (2004). Multidimensional assessment of emotion regulation and dysregulation: development, factor structure, and initial validation of the Difficulties in Emotion Regulation Scale. *Journal of Psychopathology and Behavioral Assessment, 26*(1), 41–54. doi: 10.1023/B:JOBA.0000007455.08539.94

Hall, K. (Ed.). (2013). *Mindfulness exercises for DBT therapists*. Scotts Valley, CA: CreateSpace Independent Publishing Platform.

Harley, R. M., Baity, M. R., Blais, M. A., & Jacobo, M. C. (2007). Use of dialectical behavior therapy skills training for borderline personality disorder in a naturalistic setting. *Psychotherapy Research, 17*(3), 362–370. doi:10.1080/10503300600830710

Harley, R. M., Sprich, S., Safren, S., Jacobo, M., & Fava, M. (2008). Adaptation of dialectical behavior therapy skills training group for treatment-resistant depression. *The Journal of Nervous and Mental Disease, 196*(2), 136–143. doi:10.1097/NMD.0b013e318162aa3f

Harned, M. S., Banawan, S. F., & Lynch, T. R. (2006). Dialectical behavior therapy: an emotion-focused treatment for borderline personality disorder. *Journal of Contemporary Psychotherapy, 36*, 67–75. doi:10.1007/s10879-006-9009-x

Hayes, S. C., Strosahl, K. D., & Wilson, K. G. (2012). *Acceptance and commitment therapy: The process and practice of mindful change*, 2nd Edition. New York: Guilford Press.

Hedman, E., Mörtberg, E., Hesser, H., Clark, D. M., Lekander, M., Andersson, E., & Ljótsson, B. (2013). Mediators in psychological treatment of social anxiety disorder: Individual cognitive therapy compared to cognitive behavioral group therapy. *Behaviour Research and Therapy, 51*, 696–705. doi:10.1016/j.brat.2013.07.006

Hirvikoski, T., Waaler, E., Alfredsson, J., Pihlgren, C., Holmström, A., Johnson, A., Nordström, A. L. (2011). Reduced ADHD symptoms in adults with ADHD after structured skills training group: results from a randomized controlled trial. *Behaviour Research and Therapy, 49*(3), 175–185. doi:10.1016/j.brat.2011.01.001

Hoffman, P. D., Buteau, E., Hooley, J. M., Fruzetti, A. E., & Bruce, M. L. (2003). Family members' knowledge about borderline personality disorder: Correspondence with their levels of depression, burden, distress, and expressed emotion. *Family Process, 42*, 469–478.

Hoffman, P. D., Fruzzetti, A. E., & Buteau, E. (2007). Understanding and engaging families: an education, skills and support program for relatives impacted by borderline personality disorder. *Journal of Mental Health, 16*(1), 69–82. doi:10.1080/09638230601182052

Hoffman, P. D., Fruzzetti, A. E., Buteau, E., Neiditch, E. R., Penney, D., Bruce, M. L., ... Struening, E. (2005). Family Connections: a program for relatives of persons with borderline personality disorder. *Family Process, 44*(2), 217–225. doi:10.1111/j.1545-5300.2005.00055.x

Hoffman, P. D., Fruzzetti, A. E., & Swenson, C. (1999). Dialectical behavior therapy—family skills training. *Family Process, 38*(4), 399–414. doi:10.1111/j.1545-5300.1999.00399.x

Keuthen, N. J., Rothbaum, B. O., Fama, J., Altenburger, E., Falkenstein, M. J., Sprich, S. E., ... Welch, S. S. (2012). DBT-enhanced cognitive-behavioral treatment for trichotillomania: A randomized controlled trial. *Journal of Behavioral Addictions, 1*(3), 106–114. doi:10.1556/JBA.1.2012.003

Koerner, K., & Dimeff, L. A. (2000). Further data on Dialectical Behavior Therapy. *Clinical Psychology: Science and Practice, 7*(1), 104–112. doi:10.1093/clipsy/7.1.104

Koons, C. R., Chapman, A. L., Betts, B. B., O'Rourke, B., Morse, N., & Robins, C. J. (2006). Dialectical behavior therapy adapted for the vocational rehabilitation of significantly disabled mentally ill adults. *Cognitive and Behavioral Practice, 13*(2), 146–156. doi:10.1016/j.cbpra.2005.04.003

Koons, C. R., Robins, C. J., Tweed, J. L., Lynch, T. R., Gonzalez, A. M., Morse, J. Q., ... Bastian, L. A. (2001). Efficacy of dialectical behavior therapy in women veterans with borderline personality disorder. *Behavior Therapy, 32*(2), 371–390. doi:10.1016/S0005-7894(01)80009-5

Kramer, U., Pascual-Leone, A., Berthoud, L., de Roten, Y., Marquet, P., Kolly, S., ... Page, D. (2016). Assertive anger mediates effects of Dialectical Behaviour-informed skills training for Borderline Personality Disorder: A randomized controlled trial. *Clinical Psychology & Psychotherapy, 23*(3), 189–202. doi:10.1002/cpp.1956

Linehan, M. M. (1993a). *Cognitive-behavioral treatment of borderline personality disorder.* New York: Guilford Press.

Linehan, M. M. (1993b). *Skills training manual for treating borderline personality disorder.* New York: Guilford Press.

Linehan, M. M. (2015a). *DBT skills training handouts and worksheets,* 2nd Edition. New York: Guilford Press.

Linehan, M. M. (2015b). *DBT Skills Training Manual,* 2nd Edition. New York: Guilford Press.

Linehan, M. M., Comtois, K. A., Murray, A. M., Brown, M. Z., Gallop, R. J., Heard, H. L., ... Lindenboim, N. (2006). Two-year randomized controlled trail and follow-up of Dialectical Behavior Therapy vs. therapy by experts for suicidal behaviors and Borderline Personality Disorder. *Archives of General Psychiatry, 63,* 757–766. doi:10.1001/archpsyc.63.7.757

Linehan, M. M., & Dexter-Mazza, E. T. (2008). Dialectical Behavior Therapy for Borderline Personality Disorder. In D. H. Barlow (Ed.), *Clinical handbook of psychological disorders: A step-by-step treatment manual,* 4th Edition (pp. 365–420). New York: Guilford Press.

Linehan, M. M., Dimeff, L. A., Reynolds, S. K., Comtois, K. A., Welch, S. S., Heagerty, P., ... Kivlahan, D. R. (2002). Dialectical behavior therapy versus comprehensive validation therapy plus 12-step for the treatment of opioid dependent women meeting criteria for borderline personality disorder. *Drug and Alcohol Dependence, 67*(1), 13–26. doi:10.1016/S0376-8716(02)00011-X

Linehan, M. M., Korslund, K. E., Harned, M. S., Gallop, R. J., Lungu, A., Neacsiu, A. D., ... Murray-Gregory, A. M. (2015). Dialectical Behavior Therapy for high suicide risk in individuals with borderline personality disorder: A randomized clinical trial and component analysis. *JAMA Psychiatry, 72*(5), 475–482. doi:10.1001/jamapsychiatry.2014.3039

Linehan, M. M., Schmidt, H., Dimeff, L. A., Craft, J. C., Kanter, J., & Comtois, K. A. (1999). Dialectical behavior therapy for patients with borderline personality disorder and drug-dependence. *The American Journal on Addictions, 8,* 279–292.

Lynch, T. R., Chapman, A. L., Rosenthal, M. Z., Kuo, J. R., & Linehan, M. M. (2006). Mechanisms of change in dialectical behavior therapy: theoretical and empirical observations. *Journal of Clinical Psychology, 62*(4), 459–480. doi:10.1002/jclp.20243

Lynch, T. R., Morse, J. Q., Mendelson, T., & Robins, C. J. (2003). Dialectical behavior therapy for depressed older adults: a randomized pilot study. *The American Journal of Geriatric Psychiatry, 11*(1), 33–45. doi:10.1176/appi.ajgp.11.1.33

MacPherson, H. A., Cheavens, J. S., & Fristad, M. A. (2012). Dialectical behavior therapy for adolescents: theory, treatment adaptations, and empirical outcomes. *Clinical Child and Family Psychology Review*, doi:10.1007/s10567-012-0126-7

Mazza, J. J., Dexter-Mazza, E. T., Miller, A. L., Murphy, H. E., & Rathus, J. H. (2016). *DBT skills in schools: Skills training for emotional problem solving for adolescents DBT STEPS-A.* New York: Guilford Press.

Mehlum, L., Tørmoen, A. J., Ramberg, M., Haga, E., Diep, L. M., Laberg, S., . . . Grøholt, B. (2014). Dialectical behavior therapy for adolescents with repeated suicidal and self-harming behavior: a randomized trial. *Journal of the American Academy of Child and Adolescent Psychiatry, 53*, 1082–1091.

Mennin, D. S., & Fresco, D. M. (2013). Emotion regulation as an integrative framework for understanding and treating psychopathology. In A. M. Kring & D. S. Sloan (Eds.), *Emotion regulation and psychopathology* (pp. 356–379). New York: Guilford Press.

Miller, A. L., Glinski, J., Woodberry, K. A., Mitchell, A. G., & Indik, J. (2002). Family therapy and dialectical behavior therapy with adolescents: Part I: Proposing a clinical synthesis. *American Journal of Psychotherapy, 56*(4), 568–584.

Miller, A. L., Rathus, J. H., & Linehan, M. M. (2007). *Dialectical behavior therapy with suicidal adolescents.* New York: Guilford Press.

Miller, A. L., Rathus, J. H., Linehan, M. M., Wetzler, S., & Leigh, E. (1997). Dialectical behavior therapy adapted for suicidal adolescents. *Journal of Practical Psychiatry & Behavioral Health, 3*(2), 78–86. doi:10.1097/00131746-199703000-00002

Neacsiu, A. D., Bohus, M., & Linehan, M. M., (Eds.) (2013). *Dialectical behavior therapy skills: an intervention for emotion dysregulation, Vol. 2.* New York: Guilford Press.

Neacsiu, A. D., Eberle, J. W., Kramer, R., Wiesmann, T., & Linehan, M. M. (2014). Dialectical behavior therapy skills for transdiagnostic emotion dysregulation: A pilot randomized controlled trial. *Behaviour Research and Therapy, 59*, 40–51. doi:10.1016/j.brat.2014.05.005

Neacsiu, A. D., Rizvi, S. L., & Linehan, M. M. (2010). Dialectical behavior therapy skills use as a mediator and outcome of treatment for borderline personality disorder. *Behaviour Research and Therapy, 48*. doi:10.1016/j.brat.2010.05.017

Neacsiu, A. D., Smith, M., & Fang, C. M. (under review). Challenging assumptions from emotion dysregulation psychological treatments. *Depression and Anxiety.*

Nixon, M. K., McLagan, L., Landell, S., Carter, A., & Deshaw, M. (2004). Developing and piloting community-based self-injury treatment groups for adolescents and their parents. *The Canadian Child and Adolescent Psychiatry Review, 13*(3), 62–67.

Payne, A., & Reynolds, S. (2014). *Behavioral tech DBT foundational training.* Queens Village, NY: Linehan Institute.

Powers, M. B., Sigmarsson, S. R., & Emmelkamp, P. M. G. (2008). A meta-analytic review of psychological treatments for social anxiety disorder. *International Journal of Cognitive Therapy, 1*(2), 94–113. doi:10.1521/ijct.2008.1.2.94

Rajalin, M., Wickholm-Pethrus, L., Hursti, T., & Jokinen, J. (2009). Dialectical behavior therapy-based skills training for family members of suicide attempters. *Archives of Suicide Research, 13*, 257–263. doi:10.1080/13811110903044401

Rathus, J. H., & Miller, A. L. (2014). *DBT skills manual for adolescents*. New York: Guilford Press.

Safer, D. L., Robinson, A. H., & Jo, B. (2010). Outcome from a randomized controlled trial of group therapy for binge eating disorder: comparing dialectical behavior therapy adapted for binge eating to an active comparison group therapy. *Behavior Therapy*, *41*(1), 106–120. doi:10.1016/j.beth.2009.01.006

Safer, D. L., Telch, C. F., & Agras, W. S. (2001). Dialectical Behavior Therapy for bulimia nervosa. *American Journal of Psychiatry*, *158*(4), 632–634. doi:10.1176/appi.ajp.158.4.632

Sambrook, S., Abba, N., & Chadwick, P. (2007). Evaluation of DBT emotional coping skills groups for people with parasuicidal behaviours. *Behavioural and Cognitive Psychotherapy*, *35*(2), 241–244.

Scheel, K. R. (2000). The empirical basis of dialectical behavioral therapy: Summary, critique, and implications. *Clinical Psychology: Science and Practice*, *7*, 68–86. doi:10.1093/clipsy/7.1.68

Scheirs, J. G. M., & Bok, S. (2007). Psychological distress in caretakers or relatives of patients with borderline personality disorder. *International Journal of Social Psychiatry*, *53*, 195–203.

Shelton, D., Kesten, K., Zhang, W., & Trestman, R. (2011). Impact of dialectic behavior therapy–corrections modified (DBT-CM) upon behaviorally challenged incarcerated male adolescents. *Journal of Child and Adolescent Pediatric Nursing*, *24*, 105–113. doi:10.1111/j.1744-6171.2011.00275.x

Shelton, D., Sampl, S., Kesten, K. L., Zhang, W., & Trestman, R. L. (2009). Treatment of impulsive aggression in correctional settings. *Behavioral Sciences & the Law*, *27*(5), 787–800. doi:10.1002/bsl.889

Soler, J., Pascual, J. C., Tiana, T., Cebrià, A., Barrachina, J., Campins, M. J., ... Pérez, V. (2009). Dialectical behaviour therapy skills training compared to standard group therapy in borderline personality disorder: A 3-month randomised controlled clinical trial. *Behaviour Research and Therapy*, *47*, 353–358. doi:10.1016/j.brat.2009.01.013

Sripada, R. K., Bohnert, K. M., Ganoczy, D., Blow, F. C., Valenstein, M., & Pfeiffer, P. N. (2016). Initial group versus individual therapy for posttraumatic stress disorder and subsequent follow-up treatment adequacy. *Psychological Services*, *13*(4), 349–355. doi:10.1037/ser0000077

Stangier, U., Heidenreich, T., Peitz, M., Lauterbach, W., & Clark, D. M. (2003). Cognitive therapy for social phobia: Individual versus group treatment. *Behaviour Research and Therapy*, *41*(9), 991–1007. doi:10.1016/S0005-7967(02)00176-6

Telch, C. F., Agras, W. S., & Linehan, M. M. (2001). Dialectical Behavior Therapy for binge eating disorder. *Journal of Consulting and Clinical Psychology*, *69*(6), 1061–1065. doi:10.1037/0022-006X.69.6.1061

Uliaszek, A. A., Rashid, T., Williams, G. E., & Gulamani, T. (2016). Group therapy for university students: A randomized control trial of dialectical behavior therapy and positive psychotherapy. *Behaviour Research and Therapy*, *77*, 78–85. doi:10.1016/j.brat.2015.12.003

Valentine, S. E., Bankoff, S. M., Poulin, R. M., Reidler, E. B., & Pantalone, D. W. (2015). The use of Dialectical Behavior Therapy skills training as stand-alone treatment: A systematic review of the treatment outcome literature. *Journal of Clinical Psychology*, *71*(1), 1–20. doi:10.1002/jclp.22114

Van Dijk, S., & Katz, J. J. (2013). A randomized, controlled, pilot study of dialectical behavior therapy skills in a psychoeducational group for individuals with bipolar disorder. *Journal of Affective Disorders*, *145*(3), 386–393. doi:10.1016/j.jad.2012.05.054

Vickers, J. (2016). Assessing a six-month dialectical behaviour therapy skills-only group. *Mental Health Practice*, *19*(8), 26–30. doi:10.7748/mhp.19.8.26.s19

Waltz, J., Dimeff, L. A., Koerner, K., Linehan, M. M., Taylor, L., & Miller, C. (2009). Feasibility of using video to teach Dialectical Behavior Therapy skill to clients with borderline personality disorder. *Cognitive and Behavioral Practice, 16*, 214–222. doi:10.1016/j.cbpra.2008.08.004

Whiteside, U. (2011). *A brief personalized feedback intervention integrating a motivational interviewing therapeutic style and dialectical behavioral therapy skills for depressed or anxious heavy drinking young adults* (Unpublished doctoral dissertation). University of Washington.

Wilks, C. R., Valenstein-Mah, H., Tran, H., King, A. M. M., Lungu, A., & Linehan, M. M. (2016). Dialectical behavior therapy skills for families of individuals with behavioral disorders: Initial feasibility and outcomes. *Cognitive and Behavioral Practice*, doi:10.1016/j.cbpra.2016.06.004

Woodberry, K. A., Miller, A. L., Glinski, J., Indik, J., & Mitchell, A. G. (2002). Family therapy and dialectical behavior therapy with adolescents: Part II: A theoretical review. *American Journal of Psychotherapy, 56*, 585–602.

Zanarini, M. C., Frankenburg, F. R., Dubo, E. D., Sickel, A. E., Trikha, A., Levin, A., & Reynolds, V. (1998). Axis I comorbidity of borderline personality disorder. *American Journal of Psychiatry, 155*, 1733–1739.

CHAPTER 10

GENERALIZATION MODALITIES

Taking the Treatment out of the Consulting Room—Using Telephone, Text, and Email

SHIREEN L. RIZVI AND KRISTEN M. ROMAN

DIALECTICAL Behaviour Therapy (DBT) has received broad empirical support and has been disseminated to a multitude of settings and populations (Rizvi, Steffel, & Carson-Wong, 2013). When originally developed by Marsha Linehan in the 1970s and 1980s, there were many novel components of the treatment that have since become a staple of more "mainstream" psychotherapy. For example, DBT was one of the first mental health interventions to incorporate mindfulness; today, mindfulness is ubiquitous in the mental health field. However, there are other components of DBT that remain somewhat unique to the model and which have not been so broadly adopted. One of these components is phone consultation, or consultation to the client outside the therapy sessions. As one of the four modes of DBT treatment, phone consultation is explicitly designed to assist a client in generalizing what is learned in treatment to their "real world." This chapter discusses the importance of the function of generalization, the mode of phone consultation, and the myriad other ways in which generalization can be addressed within the DBT model, including ways in which technology can help facilitate the process. It also addresses some of the common obstacles to incorporating generalization modalities into DBT treatment.

Role of Generalization within the Broader Dialectical Behavioural Therapy Model

DBT is a comprehensive psychosocial treatment. As such, it is designed to achieve five functions: enhancing capabilities (i.e., skillful behaviour), generalizing capabilities, improving motivation, structuring the environment, and enhancing and maintaining therapist capabilities and motivation. These functions are addressed, in standard out-patient DBT, by four treatment *modes*: skills training, individual therapy, phone coaching, and the therapist consultation team (Linehan, 1993). Skills training is designed to help clients acquire new skills in order to increase effective behaviours and decrease ineffective or maladaptive behaviours. Increasing motivation is frequently addressed in individual therapy, as is the topic of how to structure the client's own environment so that skillful behaviour is more likely to be reinforced/strengthened. The therapist consultation team provides support to the therapists and aims to reduce burnout while simultaneously increasing therapist adherence to the model (see Sayrs, Chapter 8, this volume).

The function of generalizing capabilities is extremely important and often over-looked. An assumption of the DBT model is that learning and practising skills and new behaviours in one therapy session and one skills group per week (roughly 2.5–3 hours out of the 168-hour week) is not enough for these new behaviours to become an inte-grated part of a client's behavioural repertoire. Rather, there needs to be an explicit focus on helping a client not just become an ideal therapy client (e.g., well-regulated in ses-sion, effective problem-solver in session) but also a person who can transfer these skills from within the therapy session into daily life. Therefore, this skills generalization func-tion of DBT is vitally important to clients' improvement in skills use during treatment and sustained improvement after DBT ends.

In the DBT manual, Linehan (1993) describes generalization of capabilities as being accomplished by: 1) teaching skills in a particular way that promotes acquisition and generalization; 2) phone coaching between sessions; 3) recording of sessions for clients to re-listen to between sessions; 4) in-vivo behavioural rehearsal of skills; and 5) struc-turing the environment to promote skills use. This chapter focuses on phone coaching, the form of skills generalization most often associated with generalization. However, it is important for a DBT clinician to not overlook these other critical aspects of skills gen-eralization in their treatment approaches.

"Traditional" Phone Coaching

Traditional phone coaching was conceptualized as allowing and encouraging DBT cli-ents to call their primary therapists for help using skills in day-to-day situations and crises that arise between sessions. A fundamental idea is that a week is a long time to go between sessions, especially when clients have a number of crises in the interim. It is more effective for both the client and the therapist to speak about skillful behaviour in times when it is needed than to have a posthoc conversation about what the client "should have" done several days later. As such, phone coaching is typically presented as an option on an as-needed basis. However, it sometimes includes scheduled client-initiated phone calls if a client is in need of greater assistance for a period of time and the therapist wants to reduce the possibility that certain behaviours and emotional expressions of being in a crisis are being reinforced by extra time with therapist. Practically speaking, availability of phone coaching means that therapists share a contact number at which they can be reached outside the session (different strategies for addressing practical considerations will be detailed below).

The targets of phone coaching, in hierarchical order, are: 1) decrease suicide crisis behaviours; 2) increase application of skills to everyday life; and 3) resolve interpersonal crises, alienation, or sense of distance between client and therapist. Linehan emphasizes that the focus is not necessarily on problem resolution, but rather helping clients use skills to cope with or tolerate their current situation. That is, the emphasis for phone coaching is to keep the calls brief and focused on the present moment, not to turn the phone coaching session into another individual therapy hour. For example, clients will often call after receiving bad news, such as finding out they have to move out of their apartment in a month or finding out they failed a test. Tempting as it may be to help clients resolve their crises over the phone by engaging in problem solving to find a new apartment or getting back on track academically, effective phone coaching sessions instead focus on helping the client tolerate the distress of the news, check the client's interpretations of the news, or regulate emotions prompted by the news. Calls tend to proceed more smoothly when therapists validate their clients' concerns as significant stressors that will require session time to resolve, and that the call will focus on helping them cope until that can happen.

As part of the focus on skills generalization, traditional phone coaching also uses a "24-hour-rule." After engaging in suicidal or self-harm behaviours, clients are not allowed to contact their therapists for phone coaching for a period of 24 hours. This rule adds an aversive consequence to the act of self-injury (to counteract the number of reinforcers that likely help to maintain the behaviour) and is intended to promote asking for help and using skills *before* the situation turns into a crisis, making it more likely that skillful behaviour rather than crisis-generating behaviour persists. Therapists in DBT tell clients that once they self-harmed, they have already solved the problem (albeit ineffectively) and therefore no longer need the therapist's help with skills. It is important to remember to orient the client to the 24-hour rule in advance and to keep in mind that a therapist would still conduct a brief risk assessment if a client states that they are currently at risk of engaging in suicidal behaviour before terminating the call (see Ben-Porath & Koons, 2005 for more information). Also, the 24-hour rule might be modified for adolescents (Miller & Rathus, 2006).

The act of calling the therapist on the phone is in itself practising a new behavioural skill for clients who struggle to ask for help effectively. By calling, clients may be practising interpersonal effectiveness (asking for a help in a way that elicits help from others) and self-validation of being deserving of help. Because phone coaching breaks the mould of the traditional client/therapist relationship and allows for a more naturalistic form of contact between client and therapist, the idea is that this skill set will be more likely to generalize to interactions with others in the client's life when practised regularly and shaped by the therapist.

ALTERNATIVES TO TRADITIONAL PHONE COACHING

Since the development of DBT, there have been monumental changes in how people communicate with one another. As such, the traditional phone coaching of DBT has had to evolve. Using the United States as an example, 92% of Americans own cell phones (Anderson, 2015) and therapists are far more likely to give out their personal cell phone number than their home telephone number for coaching. These changes have also meant that therapists are much more likely to be "available" 24 hours a day. (In the past, if therapists weren't near their office phone or their home phone, then a client couldn't immediately get in touch with them.) The options now available for communication between a therapist and client include phone, email, text messaging, mobile apps, and social media. While issues related to technology privacy and HIPAA are outside the scope of this chapter, it is important for clinicians to be aware that each medium carries its own advantages and risks.

With this range of options available for outside-of-session communication, it is essential that DBT therapists remember the *function* of coaching which is to promote skills generalization. Thus, is it important to think about how to flexibly achieve this function via different mediums. Although clients and therapists alike may prefer texting, because of ease of use, if texting does not help with skills generalization with a particular client, then the therapist should encourage calling instead. If a client likes to email the therapist long descriptions of their problems but then closes up and is unresponsive during session, then the therapist can identify excessive emailing as therapy-interfering behaviour, rather than facilitating change, and target it as such.

PRACTICAL ISSUES TO CONSIDER WITH COACHING

As with any task in DBT, the first step involved in introducing a new procedure is to orient the client to it by explaining what it is and its rationale. Many clients have never before been *encouraged* to call their therapist. Thus, this policy represents a dramatic shift from prior messages they may have received and it often involves a period of adjustment. The general recommendation is to introduce outside-of-session coaching options during one of the first few individual therapy sessions. Providing a thorough orientation to the reasons for and limits around phone coaching in advance helps address the fact that many clients in DBT are quite sensitive and could easily interpret this orientation after-the-fact as punitive (Ben-Porath, 2015). A handout explaining the procedures is also a useful tool to accompany the discussion. During this orientation, it is important for the therapist to remind the client about any privacy considerations. For example, the therapist should state and include in any handouts that she cannot guarantee confidentiality via email as appropriate. It is also helpful to remind the client at this point that it is impossible to guarantee with 100% certainty that all phone, email, and text communications will be received.

In the following scenario, a therapist (T) introduces phone coaching to a client (C) in their second session:

T: *This week I want to introduce phone coaching so that you can start making use of it as soon as possible. Let's first talk about why phone coaching is a part of DBT. There are a few reasons that we have phone coaching, the first of which is to help you apply the skills that you'll be learning to situations in your daily life, including when you have urges to engage in suicidal behaviours. We say that it's kind of like taking a timeout in the middle of a sports game. Did you play any sports growing up?*

C: *Yeah—basketball.*

T: *Awesome. It was probably much more helpful for your coach to give you in-the-moment feedback during a timeout on what you and your teammates were doing and what you could try rather than waiting until the next week in practice when the opportunity has passed and you might not remember all of the specifics of the moment. Phone coaching is kind of like that. For example, you can call me when you're having urges to yell at your wife or cut yourself, and I can coach you on what skills might work in that moment. It's really important that you call before you act on the urge to cut yourself rather than after, so we get a chance to try and come up with some skills you can use instead of acting on the urge [Note: the therapist would later explain the 24-hour rule]. Make sense?*

C: *Yeah. But I should probably only really call if it's a real emergency, right? I don't want to bother you.*

T: *That's considerate of you. But actually, we use phone coaching for a range of situations, not just emergencies. And as a DBT therapist, I take this on as part of my job, so I'm actually really glad when my clients reach out for help. That brings me to the second reason we have phone coaching, which is to give people an opportunity to practise asking for help effectively. Asking for help tends to be challenging for a lot of people. Do you have any trouble asking for help?*

C: *(laughs) Yep.*

T: *You're definitely not the only one! Many people find it hard to ask for help at all, or they end up waiting until it reaches a crisis level and the person they ask may be so overwhelmed that they don't know how to help. Phone coaching encourages you to ask for help before things escalate and before you engage in any kind of suicidal behaviour, which will likely help you do so in other relationships, too. Got it?*

C: *Yeah, that makes sense.*

T: *Okay, so the last reason we have phone coaching is to help repair the relationship between you and me as needed. For example, let's say I were to inadvertently offend you and after leaving the session you found yourself stewing about how angry with me you were. It's much better to have a brief check-in between our sessions to talk through what upset you, rather than have you sit with it until the following week, when it might get so bad that you don't even want to show up.*

C: *Hopefully that won't happen!*

T: *Hopefully—but if it does, we will be sure to address it. There are a few more things I want to mention . . . keep in mind that I will not always be able to respond to your calls or texts immediately. (Said with easy manner): Like you, I do things other than work. So sometimes I'm sleeping or in the middle of something and won't be able to respond right away. For example, if a client was calling me right now I wouldn't know it because I'm meeting with you and my phone is on silent.*

C: *Right.*

T: *So, if you don't catch me, I'll ask that you leave me a voicemail with a brief summary of what's been going on and what skills you've tried so far.*

C: *Okay.*

T: *Finally, I just want to mention a couple things about the use of technology for phone coaching. One is that privacy cannot be 100% ensured with phone calls, texts, and emails. Another is that sometimes technology fails, so there could be a time that I don't receive a contact from you because of an issue with my phone or your phone.*

Another critical component of orienting clients to phone coaching is helping them understand what to expect when they reach out to their therapists. Setting realistic expectations about how long the calls will be and what will happen in the call begins the process of shaping clients into calling for coaching effectively. It may be helpful to explain explicitly to some clients that what happens in phone coaching calls is quite different than what happens in individual therapy sessions. For example, calls are not likely to have extensive problem solving, nor is the therapist likely to spend a lot of time validating the client when the focus is on getting immediate skills generation and practice.

To illustrate even more clearly what a coaching call will look like, a therapist might do a brief role play of a call during the session. This can be particularly helpful if a client is shy, has social anxiety, or tells the therapist that she would be hesitant to call. Another way to help clients more quickly get accustomed to phone coaching is to schedule a time during the week after orienting (e.g., during the most emotionally vulnerable time in the client's week, such as Saturday afternoon) that the client will call the therapist for coaching. This helps clients get a sense of what situations it would be helpful to call in, see how it might be useful to them, and takes the pressure off determining when is a "good" time to call. Below is an example of a therapist (T) setting clear expectations with a client (C) and initiating a role play to practise a coaching call.

T: *Phone coaching calls are pretty quick—no more than about 10–15 minutes. What will happen is, you'll call me . . . I'll ask you to quickly summarize what's been going on and what skills you've tried so far . . . we'll generate some ideas of what skills*

would be helpful and develop a plan... you will let me know if you think anything
will get in the way of the plan... and then we'll get off the phone and you'll try it
out. You're always welcome to call me back after to let me know how it went. Any
questions?

C: *No, that sounds good.*

T: *Okay, great. Since we have some extra time, why don't we try this out in session so*
you can get a sense of what it would be like and get some practice actually asking
me for help. Let's pretend like you are calling for coaching because you're feeling
really anxious at work and having difficulty getting work done.

In this scenario, the therapist could actually step out of the office and have the client practice calling them in that moment. This behavioural rehearsal increases the likelihood that a similar phone call would occur outside of session.

Despite a therapist's well-executed orientation to phone coaching, it is to be expected that some clients may initially struggle with the guidelines outlined and call in ways that can frustrate their therapists. It helps to recall the DBT assumption that clients are "doing the best that they can *and* need to also do better." Clients cannot be expected to call for phone coaching "perfectly" without getting a chance to try it out and get feedback, as well as learn the skills in DBT that will help them elicit phone coaching in more effective ways. If clients are exhibiting dysfunctional interpersonal behaviours, they will also exhibit dysfunctional behaviours with outside-of-session communication. Therapists might also remind themselves to validate their clients (e.g., "How could it be otherwise?"), practise distress tolerance skills themselves with initial phone coaching behaviour, and seek consultation on how to best shape their clients.

The "How To's" of Coaching

Linehan (1993) described three primary targets for phone calls between sessions: 1) reducing suicide crisis behaviours; 2) increasing skills generalization; and 3) facilitating relationship repairs between the therapist and client. As this chapter focuses specifically on skills generalization, discussion is limited to that aspect of phone coaching. Ideally, skills generalization is the focus of the majority of phone calls elicited by clients. For more information on addressing the other two targets of phone coaching, see Linehan (1993).

An effective skills generalization call generally consists of a client reaching out to the therapist during a situation in which she is having difficulty thinking of or applying appropriate skills. She may be experiencing urges to engage in a harmful behaviour and/or feel stuck in not knowing how to proceed. The client then is looking for help in how to take the "lessons" from therapy and apply them to the real-life situation that she is facing. How a therapist responds to this contact is affected by several factors, including how long the client has been in treatment and what skills she has already learned, how the client is asking for help, history of previous coaching contacts, and where the client is on the shaping curve of skills generalization, etc. As discussed earlier, the therapist wants to keep phone coaching contact brief (a rule of thumb is fewer than 15 minutes), focused on what skills to use *now*, and an immediate plan of action. Phone coaching contacts are not the time to explore the problem in depth, nor to turn it into another therapy session. In that way, they may often feel unsatisfying to both the client and the therapist. However, with continued focus on the purpose of the phone coaching, both parties can adjust to the nature of it with some practice.

While skills generalization is most often thought of as resulting from a client calling for help in the moment using skills, there are other types of calls that can serve a similar function of reinforcing skills use. Therapists can instruct clients to call with good news and to report on effective use of skills, which should be met with lots of reinforcement from the therapist (Ben-Porath & Koons, 2005). It may be tempting to put more energy and time into crisis-related calls, as they are more likely to prompt anxiety in the therapist. However, in doing so, the therapist runs the risk of reinforcing crisis-generating behaviours more so than skills use. Therapists can also call clients to offer praise for skillful behaviour that they have become aware of, such as a behaviour that a client has been coached to try in skills group or a client meeting their goal of a 90-day period of sobriety (Ben-Porath & Koons, 2005).

ALTERNATIVES TO PHONE COACHING

Over the past few years, it has appeared notable that many clients prefer to communicate with their therapists via text messaging. This tends to be the case even more so with younger clients and adolescents. Recent reports indicate that people under 50 are more likely to communicate via text than phone calls (Newport, 2014), and thus, it is important not to necessarily pathologize the client's desire to communicate via text. There are some situations in which it would be very difficult for a person to call but is appropriate to text (during a work meeting, for example). If a therapist is comfortable with communicating via text messages (and concerns about privacy have been adequately addressed), skills generalization via text can at times be used very effectively.

That said, there are some principles to use when considering using texting as a medium for skills generalization. The first is to make sure that the client is using it to seek help effectively and with an eye toward become more effective in her life. Often, clients use text as a medium by which they can express dissatisfaction or complaints without specifically asking a question or for help. For example, sending a text that reads "I can't take it anymore" is not an effective way to communicate distress and a therapist would need to work with the client to shape this behaviour over time to be more effective. The second is to make sure to not reinforce passive problem solving by responding to texts without encouraging phone calls when calls would be much more likely to be effective and efficient. Finally, if a client is not using texting effectively and is not responsive when needed via text, the therapist needs to address it as therapy-interfering behaviour in a comprehensive way.

For example, in the following scenario, a client (C) reaches out via text to her therapist (T):

C: *I'm having some difficulty regulating right now and could use some help, if you have time.*

T: *Sure. Can you call?*

C: *Not really. I'm in a staff meeting and don't want to step out.*

T: *Ok. Let's see if we can do this. What problem are you experiencing and what have you tried so far?*

C: *I can't stop thinking about a fight I had last night with my boyfriend. I'm afraid I'm going to cry and call attention to myself. My boss has already given me feedback about my emotions.*

T: *That sounds really painful. What skills have you tried?*

C: *Distract over and over. Keep telling myself not to think about it. But it just keeps getting worse.*

T: *Ok, try to not tell yourself to just stop—that might be having the opposite effect! Can you practice Participate? What would it look like to throw yourself into your work meeting right now?*

C: *Probably stop texting you! And take notes or something?*

T: *Good idea. Why don't you try to be the best staff member in the world right now? Be attentive to your boss. Write down everything he says. Keep redirecting your attention back. How much longer is the meeting?*

C: *20-30 minutes.*

T: *Good, just keep doing it and doing it. Call me when it's over, ok?*

C: *Ok. Thanks.*

In this scenario, the whole text exchange lasted less than five minutes. It was focused on skills and did not try to solve larger problems than the current moment. In addition, it involved a situation in which texting, as opposed to talking, made sense and was used effectively. Far too often, therapists stay in texting mode when it would be far more effective and efficient to talk one-on-one. Therapists are encouraged to prompt the client to call when these situations arise (e.g., "This sounds like something that might be better discussed over the phone. Can you give me a call?").

There are other alternatives to "traditional" phone coaching that have been influenced by technological advances. Mobile phone applications ("apps") have been developed to help clients track behaviours and urges and to assist in skills use and there are a number that exist in the marketplace. It is important to note that there is virtually no data on the effectiveness of such apps in terms of their value in skills generalization. The only DBT app to be empirically investigated is the DBT Coach (Rizvi, Dimeff, Skutch, Carroll, & Linehan, 2011; Rizvi, Hughes, & Thomas, 2016) which is not available on the marketplace. The data from a recent pilot study of the DBT Coach, which includes interactive coaching in the majority of the DBT skills, indicated that use of the app was related to immediate reductions in subjective distress and urges to self-harm (Rizvi et al., 2016).

However, these results are tempered by the fact that clients used the app rarely despite having constant access to it. These data are similar to the data reviewed below on phone coaching and highlight the obstacles to engaging in skills generalization tasks.

Another pilot trial has investigated the use of web-based platforms to provide in vivo coaching in skills (Chu, Riziv, Zendegui, & Bonavitacola, 2015). In this study, two adolescents with school-refusal behaviour were provided with a standard course of DBT for adolescents (Miller & Rathus, 2006) augmented by the provision of early morning web-based coaching (via a secure platform). The rationale for this coaching was that youth with school-refusal behaviour most need help at times when therapists are typically not available (early mornings when urges to avoid school are typically highest) and therapists could have a larger impact on behaviour by intervening in those vulnerable moments. Although the sample was quite small, it was notable that the web-based coaching was deemed feasible and desirable by the clients. This type of coaching should be explored further and may indicate a possible future direction of skills coaching.

Common Barriers to Phone Coaching

While DBT's strategies for generalization of new skills and effective behaviour opens up the possibility for immense change in a client's life, it also brings with it new challenges that are not typically encountered in the standard one-hour therapy model. This section outlines several common barriers to effective skills coaching and presents some possible solutions.

Unfortunately, the environment being too powerful can influence DBT therapists' ability to implement phone coaching "by the book." Therapists may be limited by organizational demands, such as not being allowed to give out personal phone numbers to clients or take phone calls outside of "work hours." Although not providing phone coaching now places a programme outside the requirements of adherent comprehensive DBT, there are some solutions for helping remain focused on the area of skills generalization. For example, in the situation of therapists not being allowed to give out personal numbers, answering services or new technology such as free mobile phone applications that allow individuals to provide a phone number other than their personal line, may be effective alternatives. For those who are prohibited from being in contact with clients after hours, encouraging clients to make use of crisis lines while also developing clear coping plans in individual sessions may be an acceptable substitute, depending on the nature of the client's problems. When possible, if a setting makes use of an on-call clinician for calls after hours, ensuring that these clinicians are trained in DBT skills and principles is encouraged.

Some therapists may decide that they are not willing to be constantly available for phone coaching because of how it might impact their lifestyle. In this case, a therapist may set a limit and tell clients that they take calls only between certain hours, and that after those hours a client will be asked to a call a crisis line. A team might also decide to have phone coaching provided by a rotating clinician, so, for example, one therapist would provide phone coaching for all clients seen by the team for a week at a time, after which the responsibility rotates to another clinician. While these models have worked for some therapists and teams, how this impacts clients' willingness to call for coaching and the quality of the coaching should be considered. For example, it can be challenging to provide coaching for someone else's client when you are not aware of their specific target behaviours and skills being focused on in sessions.

For certain types of clients, therapists should be aware that being unable to utilize the phone coaching component of DBT might drastically limit a client's progress in treatment, as well as amplify risk. Linehan emphasizes the importance of contact via phone in her original text: "I believe strongly, as do a number of experts … in the treatment of suicidal patients (including those who meet criteria for BPD), [that patients] must be told that they can call their therapists at any time—night or day, work days or holidays if necessary" (1993, p. 503). Therefore, a therapist being asked to do DBT in a setting that does not allow for phone coaching may consider advocating for this limit to be adjusted for DBT clients, and present the relevant evidence on why this is an essential component.

Another common barrier related to skills generalization occurs when clients consistently fail to call for help when it would likely be effective to do so. When clients are not calling for phone coaching before engaging in suicidal behaviour or self-harm (or any other top-priority target such as binge eating, impulsive sex, or shoplifting), this should be identified as a therapy-interfering behaviour and addressed in individual sessions as such. Typically, DBT therapists deploy behavioural and solution analysis, to accurately identify and treat barriers to calling for help.

Some common reasons for clients not calling are self-invalidating beliefs about their problems (e.g., "I shouldn't need help", "This isn't a big deal") or themselves ("I do not deserve help") or beliefs about how it would impact the therapist (e.g., not wanting to "bother" or "burden" them). In these cases, questioning around beliefs about needing and asking for help is often appropriate. Drawing out the advantages and disadvantages of holding onto certain myths about asking for help (see Interpersonal Effectiveness Handout 2A in new version of skills manual, Linehan, 2015) can sometimes facilitate clients' greater understanding of what they may be missing by not using this mode of DBT. In some situations, it can be helpful to have the client check the facts with the therapist about how they feel about being called for phone coaching (e.g., on a weekend). We often tell clients in a genuine way that we would be thrilled to see their name pop up on our cell phones for the first time because we know how big of a step that would be for them and how helpful it could be. Use of irreverent comments such as, "Give me a try. I'm really good at this," can also be helpful to encourage calling. As any well-trained behaviourist knows, the first time a client calls for coaching should be met with an abundance of reinforcement.

Some other clients might not call for coaching due to ambivalence about wanting to use skills or DBT treatment in general, forgetting it is an option (especially early in treatment), or confusion about what it is. In response to ambivalence, therapists can revisit commitment strategies such as pros/cons. For clients having trouble remembering that it is an option, highlighting possible opportunities for calling while doing solution analysis for problem behaviours and creating physical cues to call (e.g., post-it notes, iPhone reminders, a particular background photo on the client's cell phone that she associates with the therapist, having the skills binder in a noticeable place) have worked well for us in the past. Scheduling a planned time for the client to practise calling for coaching is also a very effective strategy. Expecting the client, rather than the therapist to initiate the call provides practise in calling and an opportunity to test out beliefs about bothering the therapist, what happens during a call, how helpful it will be, etc. Another common reason for not calling is misunderstandings related to the parameters and purpose of phone coaching. We once had a client who when asked why she did not call for coaching in a particular situation said, "Oh, I thought I could only call you for coaching once per week," even though this was not outlined anywhere in the orientation. Other clients have wrongly assumed they had to know exactly what they were asking for (even early in treatment) before calling. Clearly, reviewing the function and guidelines around phone coaching from time to time can be helpful in instances like this.

When clients lack the interpersonal skills to initiate the phone call or social anxiety impacts their ability to do so, it can often be helpful to role-play a coaching call in session to drag out the new behaviour and provide an opportunity for exposure to the feared situation in order to practise tolerating their anxiety and testing out their beliefs about what will happen.

Given that phone coaching involves factors of both the client and the therapist, it is also important to consider barriers to effective phone coaching related to the therapist. One of the most common is the potential conflict between therapists' personal limits and clients' need for skills coaching. DBT therapists are committing to accepting phone calls outside of sessions as a part of the job. There is an assumption that certain clients, especially early in treatment, may need to call regularly during periods of time (although the data, as reviewed briefly further on, indicate that this is less likely to be a problem).

Some solutions to help keep phone coaching within therapists' limits include keeping the nature of the calls skills-focused and brief to limit therapist burnout and frustration, and therapists giving themselves permission to let calls go to voicemail until they feel more willing to stop what they are doing for coaching. Therapists may find it helpful to remind themselves that not being immediately available could also benefit clients in the long term by decreasing dependency and giving them an opportunity to try skills out on their own first, without help. DBT therapists are alert to phone calls exceeding their personal limits and addressing it in therapy as soon as possible, before resentment and burnout builds up. This feedback is best delivered in person during individual therapy sessions couched with a lot of validation. Some therapists are hesitant to deliver this kind of feedback because of fears of the client's reaction or unrealistic beliefs about what they "should" be able to tolerate as a DBT therapist. Feedback about infringing therapist limits is important for clients to hear, however, as they are likely engaging in the same burnout-increasing behaviours with other people in their lives. Therapists and clients may also develop a coping card with a list of five skills to try before calling the therapist for coaching. This strategy not only reduces the likelihood of therapist burnout, but also promotes skills generalization in itself because the client is practising developing a solution on her own. It can also help shape calls into being skills-focused (Ben-Porath, 2004). Another strategy for keeping calls goal oriented and skills focused is to have clients fill out a worksheet to organize their thoughts prior to calling for phone coaching. This worksheet might include items on defining the problem, identifying what skills have been tried already, and listing other individuals from whom they sought help before contacting the therapist.

Research on Phone Coaching

Unfortunately, there has been very little research on phone coaching in DBT, both in terms of frequency and content as well as relationship to treatment outcome. Such research is necessary to determine the effects of coaching on both clients and therapists and to provide informative data to those therapists considering phone coaching. Despite phone coaching being widely accepted as necessary for suicidal clients, dismantling studies have yet to be conducted to confirm that phone coaching is an essential component of DBT.

Interestingly, some data about phone coaching from the very first randomized controlled trial of DBT (Linehan, Armstrong, Suarez, Allmon, & Heard, 1991) was provided in a published letter to the editor by Linehan and Heard (1993). They described a monthly mean of 2.4 (SD = 2.5) coaching calls in a sample of 22 participants diagnosed with BPD who received 12 months of standard DBT. This frequency of calls was not significantly different from the treatment as usual (TAU) condition which had a mean of 1.6 (SD = 2.0). However, the method for recording call frequency in this study was a therapist interview at the end of treatment and therefore these data likely reflect an estimate. Using the same methodology, Chalker and colleagues (2015) reported a median of one call per month per client over a 12-month DBT treatment trial in a sample of 63 participants diagnosed with BPD. In this study, more frequent contacts were associated with a reduction in drop-out and psychological symptoms, and an increase in client and therapist satisfaction.

Recently, we have examined the data on phone coaching in the Rutgers University research and training clinic (Oliveira & Rizvi, 2016). Instead of therapist interviews, weekly session notes in which therapists were directly asked to report on intersession contact (phone, email, or text) were coded and analysed. The sample consisted of 51 clients with BPD in a six-month DBT treatment programme, of whom 35 were treatment completers. Results indicated that the average number of contacts for coaching per month was 2.55 (SD = 4.49) and a median of 11 calls over the course of the six months of treatment (i.e., fewer than two calls per month). Interestingly, four of the 35 treatment completers accounted for 56% of the contacts in this study. Together, these data suggest that, except for a few notable outliers, the average number of phone calls per client per month is 1–2. This suggests that the problem is not necessarily clients using coaching too much (except for a few), but instead using it too little to be meaningfully helpful. Future research is needed in this area. Specifically, research that focuses on *what* contributes to clients learning to generalize skills to their own environment would greatly impact our thinking on the value of phone coaching and ways in which to increase its use if necessary.

Conclusions

Skills generalization is an essential and often-overlooked function in DBT treatment. This chapter has outlined how it fits into the comprehensive treatment model and has elaborated on ways to maximize skills generalization and troubleshoot common roadblocks in the modern era. Phone coaching is the most common way that skills generalization is promoted, and modern technology has expanded the breadth of phone coaching modalities to include text messaging, emails, and mobile apps. A skilled DBT therapist works to manage behavioural principles (e.g., shaping), personal limits, and the skills deficits and goals of each individual client to maximize the potential benefits within this modality. To date, research in the area of phone coaching is limited, and further study of clients' use of and the benefits of phone coaching is encouraged.

KEY POINTS FOR CLINICANS

- Focus on generalization is a critical part of effective treatment but is often overlooked.
- Changes in technology mean a greater focus on generalization can occur via the mediums of phone, texts, and emails.
- This chapter provides guidelines for effectively consulting to the client in order to increase generalization of skills.

REFERENCES

Anderson, M. (2015). Technology device ownership: 2015. *Pew Research Center*. Retrieved from http://www.pewinternet.org/2015/10/29/technology-device-ownership-2015.
Ben-Porath, D. D. (2004). Intersession telephone contact with individuals diagnosed with borderline personality disorder: Lessons from dialectical behavior therapy. *Cognitive and Behavioral Practice*, 11, 222–230.

Ben-Porath, D. D. (2015). Orienting clients to telephone coaching in dialectical behavior therapy. *Cognitive and Behavioral Practice, 22*(4), 407–414.

Ben-Porath, D. D., & Koons, C. R. (2005). Telephone coaching in dialectical behavior therapy: A decision-tree model for managing inter-session contact with clients. *Cognitive and Behavioral Practice, 12*(4), 448–460.

Chalker, S. A., Carmel, A., Atkins, D. C., Landes, S. J., Kerbrat, A. H., & Comtois, K. A. (2015). Examining challenging behaviors of clients with borderline personality disorder. *Behaviour Research and Therapy, 75*, 11–19.

Chu, B. C., Riziv, S. L., Zendegui, E. A., & Bonavitacola, L. (2015). Dialectical behavior therapy for school refusal: Treatment development and incorporation of web-based coaching. *Cognitive and Behavioral Practice, 22*(3), 317–330.

Linehan, M. M. (1993). *Cognitive behavioral treatment of borderline personality disorder*. New York: Guilford Press.

Linehan, M. M. (2015). *DBT skills training handouts and worksheets*, 2nd Edition. New York: Guilford Press.

Linehan, M. M., Armstrong, H. E., Suarez, A., Allmon, D., & Heard, H. L. (1991). Cognitive-behavioral treatment of chronically parasuicidal borderline patients. *Archives of General Psychiatry, 48*(12), 1060–1064.

Linehan, M. M., & Heard, H. L. (1993). Impact of treatment accessibility on clinical course of parasuicidal clients: in reply to R.E. Hoffman [letter to the editor]. *Archives of General Psychiatry, 50*, 157–158.

Miller, A. L., & Rathus, J. H. (2006). *Dialectical behavior therapy with suicidal adolescents*. New York: Guilford Press.

Newport, F. The new era of communication among Americans (published online 10th November 2014). Retrieved from http://www.gallup.com/poll/179288/new-era-communication-americans.aspx. accessed 10th January 2017.

Oliveira Viera, P., & Rizvi, S. L. (2016). *Patterns of phone coaching in DBT: Frequency and relationship to therapeutic alliance, suicidal behaviors, and baseline severity*. Research presentation at the annual conference of the International Society on the Improvement and Teaching of Dialectical Behavior Therapy (ISITDBT), New York, NY.

Rizvi, S. L., Dimeff, L. A., Skutch, J., Carroll, D., & Linehan, M. M. (2011). A pilot study of the DBT coach: An interactive mobile phone application for individuals with borderline personality disorder and substance use disorder. *Behavior Therapy, 42*(4), 589–600.

Rizvi, S. L., Hughes, C. D., & Thomas, M. C. (2016). The DBT Coach mobile application as an adjunct to treatment for suicidal and self-injuring individuals with borderline personality disorder: A preliminary evaluation and challenges to client utilization. *Psychological Services, 13*(4), 380–388.

Rizvi, S. L., Steffel, L. M., & Carson-Wong, A. (2013). An overview of dialectical behavior therapy for professional psychologists. *Professional Psychology: Research and Practice, 44*(2), 73.

CHAPTER 11

STRUCTURING THE WIDER ENVIRONMENT AND THE DBT TEAM

Skills for DBT Team Leads

MICHAELA A. SWALES AND CHRISTINE DUNKLEY

INTRODUCTION

Two distinctive features of dialectical behaviour therapy (DBT; Swales & Heard, 2017) are its programmatic nature (Schmidt & Russo, this volume) and the centrality of the consultation team (Sayrs, this volume). Both of these aspects of the treatment featured in the early research trials of DBT and both, unusually in the case of the Consultation Team, were "exported" into the routine practice of the therapy. To deliver a programmatic treatment requires a degree of structuring of the organizational environment that is not typically required for the delivery of single modality treatments (Swales, 2010). A DBT programme must deliver weekly skills groups, weekly individual therapy, weekly consultation team, and support therapists in offering telephone consultation (Linehan, 1993a; Swenson, 2016). All of this requires structuring of the treatment environment to allow the programme to develop and sustain itself (Comtois & Landes, this volume; Best & Lyng, this volume). DBT consultation team functions to drive and maintain the team delivering adherent therapy with a client group who frequently engage in behaviours that therapists find stressful and that may lead to therapist burnout (e.g., suicidal behaviours, and hostility; Linehan, Cochran, Mar, Levensky, & Comtois, 2000). The team lead is the person to whom much of the work of structuring the environment and leading the consultation team falls. However, little has been written about this role, its tasks, and the skills required to perform it effectively. This chapter aims to fill that gap.

STRUCTURING THE ENVIRONMENT

As a function of DBT, *structuring the environment* has two components. One requires therapists to deliver treatment modalities that structure the clients' environments to support skillful living, for example, offering groups for family members of clients' receiving DBT that teach skills and strategies of the treatment (e.g., Fruzetti, this volume) or, in inpatient settings, awareness sessions for new staff teaching the biosocial theory (e.g., Fox, this volume). The second focuses on structuring the treatment environment more broadly to enable comprehensive DBT to be delivered. This function is primarily the responsibility of the team lead and, if not executed well, a DBT programme is unlikely to be comprehensively implemented or sustained.

The Team Lead and the Organizational Interface

Installing and maintaining a DBT programme requires commitment from both the organization hosting the treatment and from the staff delivering the programme. The team lead has a central place in resolving problems and dilemmas that arise both with the wider organization and with staff on the team. The first task of the team lead for installing a DBT programme is to conduct *organizational pre-treatment* (Swales, 2010); here, the initial stage involves identifying the goals of the organization proposing to host that programme. Typically, healthcare organizations publish their mission statements or key goals and standards on their webpages or in their annual report. Reviewing these documents represents a good place for a team lead to begin identifying what his or her organization hopes to achieve. Most organizations have goals relating to improving the standard of patient care, decreasing patient mortality, improving client experience, or delivering evidence-based interventions. DBT often fairly easily matches these higher, executive-/board-level goals. Challenges arise with middle-level organizational management, which is where these broad goals become translated into day-to-day reality. DBT as a comprehensive programme of care requires changes in the way systems work and how staff spend their time. Initially, it requires staff training and time devoted to programme development. Not all of these tasks will fit with middle-management needs to solve immediate service problems, e.g., waiting lists where cost pressures may be more evident. DBT team leads require skills in identifying goals of the organization at different levels in order to clearly link the outputs of the DBT programme to those goals, and must take a lead in resolving incompatible goals in preparation for installation of the DBT programme (Swales, 2010).

> *Case study*: Sadie worked in a large public healthcare organization that delivered both general healthcare as well as mental healthcare to a large population spread over a large semi-rural area. The executive board had goals for delivering evidence-based healthcare in a wider cultural climate of concern about suicide rates and self-harm, both of which

the national government had targeted for reduction. A presentation to the Executive Board was made by Sadie and a service user from a neighbouring healthcare organization who had been successfully treated with DBT. This swayed senior management to endorse investing in a pilot programme in one local area. Sadie anticipated, however, that persuading Simon, the local mental health team manager, would require a different type of presentation. Sadie knew Simon was under pressure from senior management to reduce waiting times, and that he was also concerned about staff sickness resulting from large caseloads of service users with high-risk behaviours. Persuading Simon to release some of his staff for training would require helping him see that the waiting time problems were in part caused by a small sub-set of service users repeatedly presenting in crisis (the group for whom Sadie planned to offer DBT), and helping him make a case to senior management that the waiting time problems may not be solved until the DBT team was up and running and effectively dealing with the high-risk service users. This would also take some time. Sadie conducted an audit identifying which service users repeatedly presented in crisis and was able to link these cases with episodes of staff sickness and cancellations of the routine work of the team. Sadie arranged for both her and Simon to make a second presentation to the Board, during which they outlined potential implementation problems. They highlighted that, while implementing DBT would help with reducing self-harm and re-presentations, it may take some time before the team were sufficiently skilled to impact on these outcomes. They discussed how addressing the waiting time problem might be delayed during the early stages of implementation of DBT, and requested the senior team reduce demands for shorter wait times just until the programme was established. While Board members worried about potential fines for missing the waiting-time target, they agreed to pilot DBT in one locality, so that waiting-time initiatives in other parts of the mental health service could mitigate the risk of financial penalties.

Sadie demonstrated two further features of *organizational pre-treatment* in preparation for starting her programme; orientating the system to the programme and what it might realistically achieve, including linking DBT programme goals to organizational goals of reducing suicidal and self-harming behaviours, and gaining commitment from the system for the investment of time and money required (Swales, 2010). This careful set up by Sadie of the pilot project helped the new initiative make a promising start. Sadie continued to meet regularly with Simon throughout the implementation to assess the impact on issues important to his role and to clearly communicate the stage of development of the DBT project. Together they provided written briefings to the Board on the progress of the implementation.

DBT team leads ensure that they know and understand the different goals of their organization at the various levels within the organization, and that they actively consider how the DBT programme may deliver on these goals. Typically, this requires that DBT teams have in place methods to monitor clinical outcomes or other material changes, as well as reporting systems by which these can be communicated to their stakeholders. If a DBT team has a record of delivering outcomes relevant to the organization, e.g., a decrease in serious suicidal events or hospital bed days, then the team lead has a platform from which to negotiate for additional DBT resources when needed. Without demonstrable outcomes, financially pressed organizations may find committing re-source to a high-intensity programme difficult.

DBT team leads are responsible for addressing programme-destroying behaviour that arises either from inside (discussed later) or outside the DBT team. The most common programme-destroying behaviour of organizations is withdrawing already-allocated re-source from the DBT team (Swales, Taylor, & Hibbs, 2012). Teams commencing training in DBT must commit to allowing ten to 12 hours a week per person to learn, and then deliver, the treatment programme. Frequently, organizations do not make appropriate adjustments in staff job plans to free up this time, or they reduce the number of hours available. Combine this with the typical staff turnover in mental health services and a DBT programme may be on the edge of viability within a few years of training. The team lead in these circumstances approaches and negotiates additional resource from the system, emphasizing the connection between DBT and the organization's goals. If following attempts at problem-solving the issues, none is forthcoming, the team lead devises and applies necessary contingencies. Once a DBT team has fewer than 20 hours a week of staff time devoted to it, running a programme becomes either impossible or cost ineffective. If the DBT team lead cannot secure sufficient staff time, they must signal that they will close the programme and then follow through with this contingency if no resource is forthcoming.

Leading the DBT Team: Tasks and Skills

For DBT team leads to operate effectively they need to be recognized both by the DBT team and the wider organization, and must possess authority to make decisions about the team and the implementation of the DBT programme. With newly installed teams, identifying the team lead can be a challenge. When teams are first trained, the person acting as team lead may be the person who has coordinated the training initiative, but that may not always be the case. Also, despite orientation, individuals may not yet have embraced that the aim of coming to training is to deliver a service. So, for any of these reasons, the person nominated as the team lead at the time of training may not actually possess any authority over the implementation process. Teams are advised to resolve this issue as soon as possible. In some more established teams, there may be an identi-fied role or position as team lead and an individual may have been specifically recruited into this role. In other cases, team leads may have been selected because of their long-standing commitment within their service, and therefore they already command re-spect from colleagues. Authority may be earned by having or developing more expertise in DBT than the rest of the team, or simply by showing a high level of enthusiasm and willingness to accomplish team tasks.

Assessing Team Assets

Once in a position of authority, DBT team leads assess the assets of their programme, the most important of which is the staff. Skilled team leads build strong relationships based on an understanding of each person's skills, and an awareness of what reinforces or punishes their membership of the team. As in any modality of DBT, team leads must assess rather than assume what skills and capacities a team member possesses, as well as what motivates them to deliver DBT. An initial assessment of a new team member's training and self-identified strengths and weaknesses in the treatment can be a useful starting point. New team members can be encouraged to share their own assessment with the team on arrival and obtain feedback as their work unfolds, in order to hone the accuracy of their own assessment. Skills groups and consultation team provide therapists with opportunities to identify, describe, and reinforce team member capacities, as well as to give corrective feedback. Teams that regularly observe each other's work via video or audio tape also provide opportunities for reflection and learning.

What motivates team members to learn and deliver DBT varies considerably. Some team members may be reinforced by the treatment's emphasis on adherence and continuous skill development, some may love the chaos and intensity of the clients being treated, others are motivated by the access to multiple and different sources of consultation, and yet others by the experience of being "all in it together." Astute team leads, aware of these contingencies, work to maximize the reinforcement for each team member and encourage team members to do the same. Radical acceptance that each person is not motivated in the same way will benefit the capacity of the team to work effectively together. In addition to initial assessment of capacities and motivating factors, annual meetings between the team lead and individual members provide a useful opportunity to reflect on skills, strengths, and areas for development. These meetings also provide a valuable opportunity to review whether the team and programme continues to reinforce and motivate that person and to address any other more personal issues that could reduce effectiveness. The frequency of these meetings can be increased to assist therapists that, from time to time, may need additional support.

As part of the routine work of the team an awareness of the strengths of each member should be cultivated. Team leads are instrumental in promoting this attitude by observing out loud particular skills and expressing appreciation for them. Utilizing particular skills of team members to improve the effectiveness of the team spreads the workload, and conveys a sense of the value of different contributions. Thus, the team lead may delegate tasks such as drawing up the skills group rota and coverage for annual leave to a team member with high levels of organizational skills whom she knows, from their individual meetings, is reinforced by the mastery he experiences from organizing the team. She may also encourage a new team member to consult with a creative and experienced skills trainer who has a talent for enthusing anxious beginners in the treatment. Experienced and skilled team leads, in knowing their team, develop a sense of the dialectical styles, and can identify the natural validators, the team members who can hold hope when all hope seems gone, those who can notice the smallest green shoot of change in a morass of tangled weeds, and who can insist that, even in appalling circumstances, the most apparently unskilled client IS capable of making a move in a different direction. When the team becomes unbalanced, calling on the specific strengths in the team can aid finding new syntheses; team leads may also encourage individuals to develop their capacities in the opposite direction to which they naturally lean. Inviting a team member who typically pushes for change to operate from an acceptance position and another who more easily holds a validating stance to only generate change solutions can help the team develop its flexibility.

Addressing Team Deficits

Alongside assessing and reinforcing team skills and capacities, team leads also accept responsibility for addressing deficits in the team. The first, and most important, is ensuring that there are sufficient staff to deliver the programme. Sustainability of the DBT team typically requires a recruitment strategy to address staff turnover. Capacity and willingness to learn and deliver DBT will need to be included in job descriptions and person specifications, particularly in services where any given appointment may have multiple roles in the service. Negotiating a training budget for new therapists joining the team and for existing staff to remain in touch with treatment development will also buffer the programme against changes in personnel over time. Secondly, team leads take responsibility for promoting retention of staff on the team. Based on knowledge of each person, effective team leads ensure that reinforcers for team membership are in place and that they take an active stance to problem-solve punishers of engagement in DBT.

> **Case Study:** *Sadie found that, despite regular meetings with Simon the mental health manager, some members of the DBT team were being rostered to conduct generic "duty" assessments on the days of consultation team meetings. These therapists missed team frequently and, as the team used a "repairs" policy for non-attendance (Linehan, 1993a), were having to repair frequently which demotivated them from attending when they were free to do so. Sadie first met with Simon to comprehend the challenge from his perspective. He was struggling with an absence of administrative support and found covering the rota for routine assessments difficult, in particular, ensuring leave requests were honoured. Sadie discussed this with the DBT team and one of the team members with a flair for spreadsheets offered to meet with Simon and set up a more manageable system. This intervention improved the situation markedly, but did not totally solve the problems. A couple of team members who also had input into the "duty" system reported that they were often asked to cover staff who had other meetings and responsibilities; reasonable requests by colleagues who were perfectly entitled to ask. In consultation team Sadie and the team rehearsed the DEAR MAN GIVE FAST skills to improve their ability to refuse such requests, and also conducted some cognitive restructuring to recognize that, simply because the person asking had a legitimate request, it did not naturally follow that the DBT team member must acquiesce. Role-plays on team of how to decline skillfully proved most useful in helping team members solve the problem and improve consultation team attendance.*

Finally, in addressing deficits, team leads require a staff development strategy. This will be based on assessments of skills on entry to the team which is updated with information from observed skills in groups, consultation team, and from video review. Team leads may reserve part of the weekly consultation team for teaching and revision of key topics in DBT, support attendance at training events in DBT and in approaches that DBT draws upon (e.g., applied behavioural analysis, CBT, mindfulness-based approaches), and may develop and encourage participation in local or national DBT networks to ensure the programme and its members remain up to date with new knowledge in the treatment.

In addition to a strong focus on skill development, team leads require the authority to "fire" ineffective team members. These may be team members who fail to acquire sufficient knowledge and skill to execute competent DBT despite repeated help and support, who refuse to embrace delivering DBT and continually introduce other models to their understanding and delivery of treatment, who do not adhere to the consultation team agreements, and, in particular, those who do not embrace fallibility and refuse to discuss their work or are repeatedly defensive in the face of feedback. All of these problems may be responsive to structured feedback from the team lead outside of the consultation team meeting. Therapists may be provided with strategies and support to resolve these issues. If, however, there is insufficient improvement in a timely manner, the DBT team lead must be able to ask and insist that the team member leave the DBT team.

Team Lead Skills

The role of the DBT team lead is *not* for the faint hearted! To effectively lead a DBT team, the lead requires skills in conflict resolution and decision making combined with a willingness to seek outside assistance as and when necessary. They also need the skills and motivation to utilize their authority strategically in resolving difficulties on the team. Fortunately, almost all of the DBT skills and strategies are useful in the service of leading and directing the team, bearing in mind that leads must also apply the skills to themselves.

Individuals who join DBT teams possess wide ranges of strengths, skills, and orientations to life and its vicissitudes. Clients treated by DBT teams engender strong emotions and complex thinking patterns in those who seek to help them (Linehan et al., 2000). The diversity of these emotions, thoughts, and beliefs is the very essence of what can make an effective, functioning dialectical team if handled well. However, wide variations in perspectives and approaches can lead to conflict and tension. The skill to accurately and non-judgmentally identify and label conflicts in goals and between people is essential. Teams will then have more opportunities to use those tensions in the service of creative and effective solutions for patients and therapists. The team lead must also apply validation and problem-solving strategies to positively connote all sides of the dialectical debate and be willing and capable of doing so in the face of high emotional arousal in both themselves and others.

Typically, these aforementioned skills of a mindful, validating, problem-solving stance will inspire willingness and loyalty to resolve conflicts from the rest of the team. Other strategies may also help here, e.g., working hard to acquire resources for the team, being willing to step in and protect team members from outside demands, or simply making sure a good quality cup of coffee or tea is on offer at the start of consultation team.

Inevitably, in the life of a busy team there are multiple decisions that need to be made in response to changes in the wider system in which the programme sits, to changes in the DBT evidence base and within the team itself, e.g., sickness, maternity leave, or other absences. DBT team leads require skills in leading thorough pros and cons analyses of alternative courses of action for the team maintaining a dialectical focus. Often through such discussions a natural "favourite" or optimal course of action will emerge. When this does not occur, skillful team leads have the capacity to take a decision based on the analysis and bring those who disagreed with the chosen course of action along with them, which likely will include the willingness to problem solve unwanted and/or unexpected impacts of their decision.

Case Study: 18 months into the DBT implementation Sadie reviewed her programme with a team lead in a neighbouring healthcare organization. The colleague encouraged Sadie to consider implementing out-of-hours phone consultation with clients, as in their programme this had both reduced the numbers of self-harm incidents and sped up the rate at which the behaviour came under control. Sadie returned to her team and conducted a pros and cons analysis of expanding their phone offering to clients. Team members could see the potential benefits and at the same time some had significant concerns about the impact on their personal lives and about potential liability issues. No obvious solution presented itself. Sadie validated each team member's perspective and doubts, as well as providing evidence to counteract concerns (cognitive restructuring). She conducted some work with the wider environment (policy development and reimbursement arrangements) to mitigate liability worries. Nevertheless, the impasse remained. Sadie, as team lead, took the decision that from a date six months in the future the programme would be offering out-of-hours phone calls and that by that date all members of the team must either be in a position to offer the phone contact or arrangements must have been made for them to leave the team. Sadie in announcing her decision validated that offering out-of-hours phone contact could legitimately be outside someone's personal limits and that she would support anyone in this position to leave the team. Over the next three months, team members increasingly started extending their limits with the phone such that only one team member remained who was not willing to participate in the new arrangements. Helping that person to leave was then discussed further on the team. After some discussion with the wider system it was agreed that the team member who was leaving would cover some of the non-DBT workload for one of his team colleagues so that she could take up the DBT hours he was vacating.

At times, team leads need to utilize their consultation team to help resolve potential programme-destroying or -interfering behaviours by the host organization. This requires a particular skill set from team leads. First, they need to orientate the team to providing them with effective consultation—having a clear definition of the problem needing a solution can help here, combined with reminders to team members to always assess, never assume, and remaining dialectical. While receiving consultation, the team lead must remain vigilant to ineffective interventions, e.g., excessive validation in the absence of problem solving, or reinforcement of hopeless or judgmental thinking. If the

---

Box 11.1   Team leads utilize authority strategically

- Ignore
- Model
- Highlight
- Assess
- Problem solve
- Advise
- Instruct
- Insist
- Add contingencies

---

issue for which consultation has been requested elicits strong emotions in the team lead, she may nominate the observer to monitor these behaviours.

Team leads need to consider utilizing their authority strategically. In Box 11.1 a range of strategies are listed in order of intensity, from lowest to highest. Frequently, problems arise in the organization that impact on the team or its members and the most effective long-term strategy is to simply ignore the issue. For example, comments that imply a negative attitude to DBT often fall into this category. At other times, the systems behaviour cannot be ignored without some cost to the DBT programme and in these circumstances some assessment of the problem is warranted, as in Sadie's programme where consultation team attendance was adversely affected by another team rota. If necessary, the team lead must apply contingencies to a problematic behaviour. For example, if the wider system constantly removes staff from the DBT team and does not agree to replace them or to train replacement staff, the team lead may need to decide at what staffing level the programme is no longer viable, orientate the system, and, if that level is reached, follow through with closing the programme. As with patients, team leads are advised to base the use of such non-conservative strategies on the failure of strategies lower in the hierarchy.

A particular challenge arises for the team lead when there is a complaint by a client against the DBT team or an individual therapist within it. The DBT principle that all clients of the team are treated by the team as a whole means the team lead shares equal responsibility for any deficiencies in delivering the treatment. Team leads may experience the urge to close ranks in these circumstances, and defend against a complaint or rush to highlight mitigating factors. The balancing act required is to both hold and support the team, and model fallibility—that there may be a nugget of truth in the complaint being made, which, if addressed, can lead to improved outcomes for future patients. The team lead must be sensitive to the "blame culture" in many organizations, and be careful not to assert rank that puts herself out of the firing line. Equally there is a responsibility to ensure that spurious or malicious allegations are not upheld. Constantly asking the dialectical question, "are we missing anything here?" can be helpful in negotiating this particular minefield.

Box 11.2   Common dialectical dilemmas for team leads

- Utilizing authority versus enhancing collaboration.
- Focus on other versus focus on self.
- Obligation to management versus obligation to the team.
- Holding standards versus allowing mistakes.
- Rigid adherence to form versus lack of attention to form.
- Taking on tasks versus delegating tasks.
- Influencing priorities versus being influenced by other's priorities.
- Carrying morale versus being demoralized.

During tenure as a DBT team lead, a number of dialectical dilemmas are likely to arise. Knowing the typical issues that present themselves (see Box 11.2) helps in both spotting the problem and identifying both ends of the dialectic, which is needed to move towards a synthesis. Sadie, in working to resolve the out-of-hours phone consultation issue, was particularly attentive to the dialectic of "*utilizing authority*" over "*enhancing collaboration*", whereas in her negotiations about attendance at consultation team she moved closer to an "*obligation to the team*" versus her "*obligation to the wider service*" in her search for synthesis. Team leads struggling to work creatively to synthesize the dilemmas of their team and system may benefit from outside consultation, either from another team leader, or from an external expert.

ENHANCING THERAPISTS' CONSULTATION AND MOTIVATION TO TREAT

The weekly consultation team is a mandatory component of DBT therapy. Regular consultation allows the patient to benefit from multiple perspectives on her case, and ensures therapists do not drift from the treatment. It also provides peer support to therapists in dealing with high-risk cases and challenging behaviour. This is the feature of the consultation team that Linehan (1993a) refers to as "therapy for the therapist." So, it is in pursuit of these functions that the team lead must give her energy and dedication.

Probably the best metaphor for the team lead role is as the skipper on a yacht in the America's Cup. The destination of an adherent programme has already been set by Linehan, so there should be no dispute about the direction of travel. Every person must make a contribution to making the boat go faster—no dead weight is allowed. In calm seas with an effective team, the skipper can undertake routine tasks and enjoy the ride with everyone else, and a hierarchical structure is not necessary. The skipper does not need to have exactly the same specialist knowledge as every other team member, and will take advice. But if the craft is blown off track, the skipper takes responsibility to solve the problem, in consultation with the other experts on the boat. This ability to move back and forth between leader and team member is an art of dialectical balance—too much authority and the boat will list, not enough, and it will stall. Over a prolonged period, the skipper cannot always be at the helm—others will take turns at the tiller, and any team member must be able to navigate the boat if called upon to do so.

The strategies at the team lead's disposal (see Box 11.1) are listed in a hierarchy of the least to the most active intervention. When looking at issues that arise during consultation team meeting, the team lead may keep this list to hand, and reflect on which level of intervention is needed. The DBT principle of using more active procedures only after conservative ones have failed might be a useful guide.

Structuring the Consultation Team

The team lead will check that people attend consultation team meetings. Simply keeping a register can help, but certainly any unscheduled misses require investigation by whatever method (some consults require that a written chain is circulated to everyone after a miss, so as not to spend precious time of regular attenders problem-solving for those who were late or absent). A common issue for a team lead here is that if she challenges a poor attender, the other team members suddenly becoming absorbed in examining the rim of their coffee cups, leaving the team lead to be the "bad guy." Confronting team-interfering behaviour is a whole-team issue, and at the same time the lead will see to it that everyone participates, taking the helm if necessary, but highlighting when others have withdrawn from the discomfort of the task. She might say, "Paulo, why don't you help Mandy put her side of the situation, while Amal supports what I am saying, and the others can help us find a synthesis." Mindfully describing what is required is much more helpful than seething internally at the lack of support.

Seeing that the team follows some kind of agenda will help ensure the functions are met. The chapter on consultation team outlines the options (see Sayrs, this volume), but a problem may occur for the team lead when members fail to follow the agenda, or do so superficially. Therapists are reinforced for going off track, particularly in supportive DBT teams that have high stress from the organization. Getting together with others under similar strain and "having a moan" can be hugely validating and soothing. Sometimes the cue that permits or encourages moaning might be as simple as *being seated in a circle with other staff members, holding coffee cups*. This socially relaxed format (particularly if cake is added!) can induce a bonding session over shared organizational woes. Unfortunately, clients do not necessarily improve in direct proportion to soothing given to their therapist in this context. There is an amount of sharing that offers relief, beyond which it becomes simply distracting. Team leads may be loath to inhibit this behaviour because the emotional support looks very like "therapy for the therapist."

One solution might be to highlight the pattern of behaviour and offer bonding time as a reward for work done on the official agenda. Surprisingly, when this opportunity is made formal rather than implied, it often loses its appeal. In this case, the team lead must ensure that the consult itself is rewarding. Making sure members get help with difficult cases, and share ideas that they would not have come up with individually, is the natural reinforcer of increased attention to the agenda.

Team leads need additional skill to spot when agenda-following has become a superficial tick-box exercise. For example, the reading of one of the consult agreements becomes a formality, read then forgotten, or the mindfulness exercise ends and the chair immediately says, "right, so what have we got on our list?" as though nothing has happened. Worse is when the agenda fills up with business items, e.g., numbers of people waiting for assessment, holiday cover, requests for training from other teams, etc. Such issues may indicate that the agenda is serving as *something to get through*, rather than an effective guide for the work of the team. DBT consultation team requires mindful participation by all team members where their emotions and behaviours, as well as their intellect, are engaged. Time pressures cause many organizational meetings to be conducted as "grab and go" sessions, and the consultation meeting is as vulnerable as any other. The team lead can use the strategy of "modelling" to convey the message "I am here to both get something valuable and contribute fully, and there is nowhere else I need to be right now." Business items can be deferred to email or a once-monthly business hour, so that the consultation team meeting can focus on giving members valuable insights, strategies, and support to provide better DBT.

One of the team lead's responsibilities is to ensure that the team members adhere to the roles assigned to them, whether as the observer, note-taker, time-keeper, or leader of the mindfulness practice. Slippage is everyone's responsibility, but the team lead acts as the "back-stop," blocking the type of collusion that permits a lapse of structure. We have seen on many occasions that the leader's attitude makes all the difference. A laissez-faire position will lead to an unspoken assumption that structure and roles are for the initial period of DBT training only, and not a part of ongoing work.

Team leads who model coming to consultation meeting having prepared a question in advance set a positive tone for their team. Professionals tend towards providing narrative descriptions of events, rather than defining the problem that they require help with, for example, "My chains with this patient have been so similar on the last three occasions, but nothing is changing and I fear I am missing something. Here is the chain and my solutions, can you help?" Therapists can be forgiven for making this mistake as other meetings may value and expect verbal reports from them. Shifting focus to the function of *receiving* consultation takes time. In our experience therapists often fail to recognize that they have slipped into recounting mode, so the behaviour of requesting help must be modelled and highlighted frequently by the team lead until it is established. One myth for the team lead to challenge is that a huge amount of background information is required before anyone could possibly make a helpful suggestion. In fact, the opposite may be true; the more others know of wider circumstances the more potential biases are introduced, and the less behavioural analysis will be done on the current scenario.

Because the team lead may also be a manager, another tripping point may be when issues are raised that have service implications. For example, a therapist wants to extend therapy with a client, and yet the team lead/manager is called to account for people waiting for DBT who have not yet received treatment. In this case, it is helpful to mirror the therapy in not jumping in too quickly to solve the problem. Better to ask, "What are our options?" and then evaluate the pros and cons. One con is the fate of people currently waiting, and a second con is the team leader's feelings about having to justify the extension. These will be evaluated against the benefits of extending therapy. The position of simply outranking the team member would be anti-DBT, and at the same time the implications for both the DBT service and the potential backlash to the team lead of any decision must be taken into account.

Leaders may use more active strategies when dealing with off-model behaviour from team members. Particular problems occur when members deliver non-behavioural formulations, e.g., referring to attachment theory or psychodynamic constructs. Therapists may have a strong background in other models, and it helps to point out that these have their place and value—they just do not belong in DBT. Trying to integrate other models is akin to bringing a motorcycle on board the DBT boat: in another setting it would be an excellent mode of transport, but on a high-speed yacht there is nowhere for it to go and it will only slow proceedings down. It is in confronting alternative formulations that the team lead may resort to highlighting, then advising, then instructing, before finally insisting on a DBT approach.

Handling Issues and Problems in Consultation Team

The "naming of elephants" (Koerner, 2012) is sometimes a thankless task, particularly if there are behaviours indicating judgments of other team members—eye-rolling, sighing, tutting while others are talking (behaviours that incidentally therapists dislike if clients do them in skills training group). Worse however, can be the situation where people have a grievance but say nothing during consult, preferring to gather in cliques outside of the meeting to express an opinion. Again, it is not the team lead's sole responsibility to "name elephants," but she can guide the team to a dialectical approach in resolving them.

Case Study: In Sadie's team Kara was upset because Emma had failed to inform her about an important meeting that was nothing to do with DBT. The noticeable behaviour in consult was Kara frowning and staring at Emma, who steadfastly refused to look her way, but showed obvious discomfort that was potentially reinforcing the staring behaviour. Everyone was aware of it, but Sadie was left, by default, to step in. After naming the behaviour and conducting an assessment Sadie encouraged Kara to notice, "When I am in consult and see Emma my mind returns to her omission to tell me about the meeting, and I interpret her looking away from me as not caring". Emma was able to acknowledge "I notice a sensation of guilt when Kara looks at me and if I look away it feels marginally more bearable." In this situation, the acknowledgement of guilt

made enough of a difference to enable both parties to be more mindful that during con-
sultation team they needed to focus on DBT matters. This assessment was more func-
tional than simply instructing Kara and Emma to keep non-DBT issues for outside the
meeting. Not one of the other team members thought it was up to them to raise this
non-DBT incident, although all of them knew it had happened. This is an example of
the principle that the team lead may not have caused the problems but may have to
solve them anyway. However, being routinely left to do so becomes another elephant to
be named.

Sometimes simply being the team lead draws fire from team members, particularly in times of upheaval. Elephant-naming here probably takes the form of "describing"— "I notice that people are responding slowly when I ask a question, or disagreeing frequently when I make a point, or not smiling when I say hello. Is there something I am doing that is making this more likely to happen?" The team lead may add, "And can I draw on help from the observer just to make sure we describe things behaviourally?" The greatest skill of the team lead here is to communicate genuine curiosity without defensiveness, truly modelling the fallibility agreement. This is a whole-body skill—the leader has to check for tension in her stomach, her jaw, or the pursing of her lips, and welcome feedback with a lightness of touch. This is applying the treatment to both herself and the team—the facts are always friendly, and finding them out is one step closer to solving them. Another skill being called for is one of mindfulness, as even the very best team lead can exhibit problematic behaviours. The team lead may find it helpful to have a list of common but toxic thoughts that are likely to derail her attempts at remaining dialectical, for example:

> *After all I do for the team. They have no idea how hard I work. This is typical coming*
> *from X. They are so ungrateful. X is not pulling his/her weight. Why am I the one being*
> *called to account? Why do I bother? What's the point? If X hadn't done (this or that) we*
> *would not be having this conversation ... etc.*

If these thoughts arise the leader can notice, "*I am being unmindful*" or "*that is an unhelpful thought.*" Just as when responding to client accusations a therapist needs to check for what is valid before moving onto what is not justified, the team leader can use this opportunity to model that skill.

> ***Case Study:*** *While Sadie was trying to sort out the issues with the host organization,*
> *her team accused her of being distracted in consultation team and focusing more on*
> *programme issues than her client work. Sadie's initial response was that she was being*
> *judged harshly, especially as she was trying to save the programme. She noticed the*
> *thought, "they have no idea what pressure I am under". Taking a moment to ask her-*
> *self, "what's valid in what is being said", she was able to respond, "I guess it is true that*
> *the programme issues have come to the fore of my mind, and I recognize I have not told*
> *everyone the pressures I face. On the other hand, the client work cannot progress with*
> *no programme, and I don't want to lower the mood of consult with too much detail of*
> *those pressures. Can we see a way forward so I can divide my time better, and also get*

some support?" Immediately, two team members offered to brainstorm contingencies for the organization and come to meetings with Sadie if needed. The team also agreed that Sadie should discuss at least one client issue before a business item. It was agreed to trial this and see if it made any difference, either in a positive or negative way, and review in one month.

Sometimes the grievance with the team lead is unjustified, e.g., blaming the team leader for decisions that have been made democratically. One team agreed to deny late-comers any coffee as a contingency measure. Those affected began making jibes at the team lead, who ignored that behaviour in order not to reinforce it.

A consultation team member may have strong feelings about an issue that did not go his or her way, but actually still throw their efforts behind the team. For example, a skills group had to change location which caused problems for the skills leader. In the consultation team meeting she was clearly unhappy, but she did everything to make the new location a success. It was not necessary for her to inhibit all her disappointment and frustration, as that would not constitute "therapy for the therapist." Rather, the group as a whole were willing to absorb some of her misery, and offer solace. The leader highlighted that distress about a change that caused such inconvenience is warranted. The real skill for team leads is being able to work that dialectical line—knowing when to ignore and when to address an issue, and to accept that sometimes an error will be made, but as long as consultation team continues, there is always another chance to problem solve.

A consultation team may be new or have run for many years and still not know DBT well enough to deliver adherent therapy. In the case of new teams, there may have been insufficient time to acquire the skill, whereas for established teams, skills may never have been acquired or have become stale. Mistakes made early on may have become accepted as standard practice. Constantly keeping an eye on the level of adherence within the team and working on solutions may fall to the team lead. Solutions may involve going back to the manuals, training materials, or research literature to look up answers to tricky questions. External supervision or consultation may be sought, and the team will be encouraged to do role-playing, bring in tapes of sessions, and provide written chain and solution analyses to give feedback to each other. Without someone accepting this as a role, the likelihood of these things happening in a busy clinical environment is virtually zero. This begs the question of how can the team lead motivate *themselves* to do such things that are time-consuming, labour intensive, and potentially exposing. We would suggest that networking with other team leads can provide an opportunity to both compare notes and encourage each other. Attendance at DBT events and conferences can help rejuvenate the flagging team, or act as a source of pride for those currently feeling on top of their game.

Getting help when demoralized is harder for a team lead than other team members, because she is expected to carry the team through difficulties, and her attitude has a profound effect on morale. It is often when the rest of the team is low that the team lead feels like giving up, as it is lonely to feel like the only one pulling the load. Taking a systematic approach can start to unite the team, even if only in their collective unhappiness—providing this moves on to problem solving. The team lead might start by saying, "a number of people, myself included, are feeling demoralized at the moment, and there are many controlling variables. If we draw up a list we can sort them into the most demoralizing at the top, to those ongoing niggles at the bottom, and then work out solutions, options and any potential quick wins."

> *Case study:* Here is a list drawn up by Sadie's team when members became disheartened:
>
> 1. Staffing levels have dropped and other demands on time are creeping up. This makes it harder to get away for skills group and consultation team.
> 2. Non-DBT staff are making comments such as "it's ok for you guys while we have to take on more cases."
> 3. There are two members in skills group who complain loudly each week that the skills are not working, and the whole group sits with their shoulders hunched looking at the floor when they say those things.
> 4. Two of us are having thoughts such as "why am I doing this? I'm not very good at it."
> 5. People have started giving apologies for consultation team, so it is harder to get ourselves to attend.
>
> Once the list was drawn into a hierarchy, the team united in trying to problem solve. Sadie arranged role-play practice of how to respond to the skills group clients, for example, smiling and saying, "You are in exactly the right place! We can help you with this—can you describe what you did and we will all see if we can work out what got in the way." Also, the team brainstormed some active mindfulness exercises to get clients up and out of their hunched posture at the start of skills group.
>
> The consultation team mindfulness exercise for three weeks was for therapists to identify and call to mind some "shining moments" in DBT, to notice unmindful judgments of oneself, and to rephrase that mindfully—"I am having the thought I am not good at this." Sadie also organized some external supervision and sent two members to a workshop which revitalized their interest. The team put on a half-day training for non-DBT staff to show some behavioural principles in action, and the result was a little more support from colleagues.
>
> Only by taking a systematic approach was Sadie able to get help for herself and the rest of the team.

Encouraging Adherence in Other Modalities of Treatment

Team leads ensure that adherence to DBT does not slip down the agenda in any of the other modalities, and so keeping up to date with DBT practice is essential. Receiving supervision where video or audio tapes are rated on the University of Washington Adherence Rating Scale is a good way to ensure personal fidelity to the model. Learning points from supervision can be shared with other team members, either through summarizing in written format or playing examples from supervised tapes in consultation team. A number of countries now have DBT accrediting bodies, and attaining accredited status can reassure the team that at least one member is delivering the therapy in an adherent manner. Fear of having their therapy scrutinized or judged can make encouraging therapists towards accreditation a challenge. Fortunately, most people who have successfully navigated the process are so delighted with the learning it brings that the initial fear of exposure quickly dissipates. If only one team member is able to go for accreditation, we recommend that the team lead is the first to take the plunge. Leading by example is both an opportunity to inspire others, and to learn the skills needed for adherence so they may be disseminated to the rest of the team.

CONCLUSION

DBT team leads play a pivotal role in the sustainability of DBT. Like Janus, they have two faces—one facing the team and one facing the outer organization. Effective team leads embed the DBT team within the wider organization and lead the team to deliver on organizational goals related to DBT's key outcomes. Team leads work to establish and maintain a cohesive, flexible, and adherent team of clinicians who together feel supported to continue treating their clients. They may even have some fun along the way.

KEY MESSAGES FOR CLINICIANS

- Team leads take responsibility for two functions of a DBT programme: Structuring the environment, and enhancing therapists' capabilities and motivation to treat.
- DBT team leads take responsibility for organizational pre-treatment: establishing which organizational goals are relevant to the DBT programme, orientating the organization to the resources needed, and gaining commitment from the organization to support the programme.
- DBT team leads assess the assets of their staff and programme and address any identified deficits.
- DBT team leads ensure that the consultation team fulfils its function of enhancing therapists' skills, capacities, and motivation to deliver the treatment, and take a lead in helping the team address any problems that arise in the functioning of the team.

REFERENCES

Koerner, K. (2012). *Doing Dialectical Beahviour Therapy: A practical guide*. New York, NY: Guilford Press.

Linehan, M. M. (1993a). *Cognitive-behavioral treatment for borderline personality disorder*. New York, NY: Guilford Press.

Linehan, M. M., Cochran, B. N., Mar, C. M., Levensky, E. R., & Comtois, K. A. (2000). Therapeutic burnout among borderline personality disordered clients and their therapists: Development and evaluation of two adaptations of the Maslach Burnout Inventory. *Cognitive and Behavioral Practice*, *7*(3), 329–337.

Swales, M. A. (2010). Implementing DBT: Organisational pre-Treatment. *Cognitive Behaviour Therapist*, *3*, 145–157.

Swales, M. A., & Heard, H. L. (2017). *Dialectical behaviour therapy: Distinctive features*, 2nd Edition. London: Routledge.

Swales, M., Taylor, B., & Hibbs, R. A. B. (2012). Implementing dialectical behaviour therapy: Programme survival in routine healthcare settings. *Journal of Mental Health*, *21*(6), 548–555.

Swenson, C. R. (2016). *DBT® principles in action: Acceptance, change & dialectics*. New York, NY: Guilford Press.

CLINICAL APPLICATIONS OF DBT

CHAPTER 12

CASE FORMULATION IN DBT

Developing a Behavioural Formulation

SHARI MANNING

I N its broadest sense, case conceptualization is the use of the tenants of a psychological theory to gather knowledge about human behaviour and to develop a treatment plan that is consistent with the theory (Nelson et al., 2007). The foci and language of case conceptualizations have developed from the different schools of psychotherapy and use the model's theory of aetiology and maintenance of the disorder to develop a formulation to guide treatment. According to Ingram (2006), case conceptualization is a means of condensing and summarizing information to understand and treat the client.

Behavioural case conceptualizations should be clear and concise in order to communicate them easily to members of treatment teams and to the client. They should be precise and use operationally specific language. Case conceptualizations should be comprehensive and should generalize across the client's behavioural patterns. Case conceptualization should match empirically validated principles and, importantly, case conceptualizations should be useful and meaningful to facilitate treatment planning and decision making by the client and the therapist (Dawson & Moghaddam, 2016). Formulations can vary in temporal scope from case-based to episode-based or moment-based, and formulations may evolve during the course of treatment. Therefore, ongoing monitoring, testing, and assessment during treatment are necessary: monitoring can take the form of session-by-session progress reviews using quantitative measures, and formulations can be modified if an intervention is not as effective as hoped.

Persons (1989) describes a cognitive behavioural approach to providing evidence-based hypothesis testing to psychotherapy and clinical work. The three elements of her approach include assessment, formulation, and intervention. The Dialectical Behaviour Therapy (DBT) case conceptualization brings together all three elements into one cohesive plan that begins with assessments, creates a formulation, implements interventions, and then begins again until the client meets her goals and terminates treatment.

Table 12.1   Dialectical Behaviour Therapy case conceptualization template

1. Demographics including diagnosis, treatment history, and reason for referral
2. Initial assessment:
    a. Five areas of dysregulation
    b. Client's strengths
    c. Client's deficits
3. Biosocial theory
4. Stage of treatment
5. Life Worth Living Goal(s)
6. Behaviourally defined problems to be addressed
7. Primary target hierarchy (for all Stages)
8. Secondary targets
9. Hypotheses of controlling variables for problem behaviour
10. Solution analysis plan for controlling variables
11. Predicted outcomes and their measurement

In DBT (Linehan, 1993), case conceptualization is described as collaborative and transparent, and changes as the treatment progresses, and as in all aspects of DBT, the client is involved. There is no single case conceptualization for DBT. However, DBT clinicians most often use variations on standard cognitive behavioural case conceptualizations in that they identify behavioural patterns and, as described by Persons and Tompkins (2007), move from symptom to disorder to problem to case. The DBT case conceptualization presented in this chapter begins with disorder and symptoms, then moves to problems and, ultimately, to a case much like Persons describes. Table 12.1 lists the components of DBT case conceptualization discussed in this chapter.

Some DBT therapists formally write out all the sections of their case conceptualizations. Others might include the various sections in different parts of their medical record, e.g., the demographics in the psychosocial history, the targets, and controlling variables are included in the treatment plan. Some DBT clinicians write out parts of the case conceptualization, but not others. Whether written formally in the case record or not, skilled DBT therapists can describe their conceptualization of their clients and commonly share these with their clients continuously orientating them to their case formulation and involving them in changes to the conceptualization. The conceptualization of the treatment is created prior to treatment and changes through the therapy as goals, targets, and stages change. Within the conceptualization of the entire case, specific behaviours are analysed, hypotheses are generated, and interventions are implemented. Because client behaviours change during the course of treatment, the case conceptualization constantly evolves (Persons & Tompkins, 2007), and should be flexible and sufficiently concise so that it can be easily understood by other clinicians and by the client if it is shared with him/her. The case conceptualization should also use behaviour-specific language, e.g., "Client tells his partner that he will 'hit him so hard his teeth will rattle'" instead of "client is verbally aggressive." The case should be non-judgmental and non-pejorative, e.g., "the client engages in self-harm behaviour that is environmentally reinforced when his spouse apologizes for upsetting him," instead of "the client manipulates his spouse."

This chapter describes many of the topics that are addressed in DBT case conceptualizations. Although it is not imperative that all sections are included in a case formulation, there must be enough to create what Persons (1989) describes as the conceptual rationale and justification for the treatment/behavioural plan.

With the advent of DBT individual certification (www.dbt-lbc.org), case conceptualization has become a prominent piece of testing clinicians' abilities to formulate a case through a DBT or behavioural lens. The sections of case conceptualization presented in this chapter represent all of the sections required in the case conceptualization demonstration for DBT individual clinician certification. Since DBT is now used to treat all genders, I will use feminine and masculine pronouns interchangeably in this chapter.

ASSESSMENT

Most frequently, therapists begin the treatment with an extensive assessment of the client's behaviours. These assessments may include diagnostic testing, completion of programmatic and individual outcome measures, and DBT-specific interviews. The diagnostic assessments are conducted to ensure that the client meets any diagnostic criteria for the treatment, for a programme that bases inclusion on diagnosis, or that she has specific behavioural problems and meets inclusion criteria, for a programme that treats clients with specific behavioural patterns.

The pre-treatment assessment is the beginning of the case conceptualization in DBT. During the assessment, the therapist and the client are creating the therapeutic alliance and the therapist asks many questions to further understand the client's experience from a DBT framework, specifically the five areas of dysregulation (emotional, interpersonal, behavioural, cognitive, and self) treated in DBT and the biosocial theory of aetiology of emotion regulation disorders.

In assessing the five areas of dysregulation, the therapist examines the problem areas treated in DBT. At its core, DBT conceptualizes the problems that the client experiences as related to pervasive emotion dysregulation. During pre-treatment, the therapist assesses clients' over or under control of emotions and related behaviours. The therapist asks about specific emotions, beginning to examine, for example, the role of shame, guilt, sadness, and anger in the client's life. Behavioural dysregulation is often a consequence of emotion dysregulation and/or functions to regulate emotions. For example, the client may have urges to cut when shame is high, e.g., a Subjective Units of Distress (SUDs) number of 80 out of 100. She may also cut because it brings down anger from SUDs of 90 to 20 or 30. Interpersonal dysregulation is a consequence of emotion dysregulation. Because of fluctuating emotions and liability of emotions, client's behaviours related to establishing and maintaining balanced relationships with others often result in chaotic, and unpredictable relationships. Self-dysregulation is also consequential to emotion dysregulation. Because high emotional arousal impedes cognitive processing, clients with high emotional dysregulation cannot subjectively examine their own experiencing and determine likes and dislikes, goals, values, sexual orientation, gender orientation, etc. Finally, high emotions cause problems with attentional control and focus. Assessing cognitive dysregulation involves assessing dissociation, paranoia, brief psychosis, and problems with concentration that evolve from the emotion dysregulation.

An integral piece of the initial assessment is an evaluation of the client's strengths and obstacles to change. The therapist aims to identify capabilities and resources that can be built upon in the treatment as well as identifying barriers that will require problem solving and troubleshooting. For example, the client's strengths may be having a stable place to live, a church community, and the ability to study and learn as evidenced by completion of an undergraduate college degree. The deficits may include an ex-spouse who periodically does not pay support, thus increasing the client's emotions, having never worked a full-time job, and having a chronic health disorder that causes extreme fatigue.

Assessment of strengths and deficits involves asking specific questions about current capabilities, resources, and knowledge that can affect the treatment delivery (Saleebey, 1996). Some of the areas assessed are: social support, family, finances, housing, intellectual strengths or deficits, vocational and educational capabilities, social/leisure activities, religious beliefs and community, reasons for living, behaviours in the repertoire that are DBT skills, and co-occurring mental health and/or medical issues.

As the therapist assesses the areas treated in DBT, the beginnings of a formulation evolve. The therapist and the client begin to draw a picture of the patterns in the client's life as related to emotions, then, the therapist and the client examine the aetiological features of the development of the problems that are interfering with her life.

BIOSOCIAL THEORY OF AETIOLOGY AND MAINTENANCE OF DISORDER

DBT requires some explanation of the development and maintenance of the behaviours that bring the patient to DBT. Often, the initial assessment at intake for DBT begins to identify, by self-report, the client's experience of her innate experience of emotional stimuli and how her environment responded to her in childhood. DBT uses a biosocial theory (Linehan, 1993) to explain the evolution of the pervasive emotion dysregulation of its clients. The biosocial theory is composed of innate emotional vulnerability transacting over time with an invalidating environment.

When conceptualizing emotional vulnerability, the therapist and the client examine the client's experience of emotional stimuli over time beginning as early in the child's life as possible. The client describes her emotion sensitivity (how easily she responds to emotional stimuli), her emotional reactivity (the intensity of her response), and how long it takes her to return to baseline emotion. People with emotion regulation disorders usually have a combination of high sensitivity, high reactivity, and slow return to baseline. As this is described to the therapist, a picture of the client's emotional experiencing evolves.

In addition to being an emotionally vulnerable child, the client's environment responded in ways that were not helpful. This invalidating environment could be anywhere on the continuum from a family in which there was sexual trauma, to chaotic divorce, to extreme overcontrol, to an environment in which parents or caregivers were not as emotionally vulnerable as the child and therefore did not model or teach how to regulate extreme, lengthy emotions.

The environment may have responded in a combination of three ways that increase invalidation (Linehan, 1993). The environment may have criticized, pathologized, or negated in some way the child's communication of her private experiences. For example, a client whose parents had lavish dinner parties and frequently told her that she ruined the evening when she said she was tired and wanted to go to bed. Another way in which the environment may invalidate the child is by intermittently reinforcing or by punishing emotional displays. In another example, Sue was a child in a large family. When she communicated being sad, no one heard or responded unless she got loud and threw herself on the ground, sobbing. Over time, softly crying and asking for help was extinguished and she was "trained" to have loud emotional expressions. A client who is taught "quit that crying or I'll give you something to cry about" is having emotional displays punished. Finally, children can be invalidated in an environment that communicates that solving life's problems is simple.

The purpose of the assessment of emotion vulnerability and its transaction with the invalidating environment is to ascertain the current patterns of functioning that are evident in the client's life. Over time, the emotionally vulnerable child and the invalidating environment transact or influence each other. The child responds to the environment and the environment responds to the child. The child's learning results in the behaviours that are present in the therapy.

Early on in developing the case conceptualization, the therapist and the client are working together to look at the client's behavioural (emotions, cognitions, and actions) patterns that have resulted from the biosocial theory. For example, in the case of the client who was always extremely emotionally sensitive and whose parents did not respond to her emotional communications until she was on the floor sobbing, the therapist worked with the client to describe her behaviour as a set of transactions between herself and her parents. The therapist and the client worked together to define current behaviours, e.g., becoming extremely distressed at work, having thoughts of not being listened to by others, and an increase in shame and frustration in the context of her learning from her childhood environment

STAGE OF TREATMENT

In DBT, the modes of treatment delivered are dependent upon the stage of treatment. In turn, the stage of treatment is dictated by the behaviours of the patient. It is important to accurately identify the stage of treatment in order to move people through the correct stages and formulate a treatment plan. The initial pre-treatment assessment determines the stage of treatment in which the client enters DBT. If there are multiple severe problems in multiple areas of functioning, the client is considered to be in Stage 1 DBT. Stage 1 involves moving the client towards her life goals by stabilizing behaviour. During Stage 1, the client is in weekly DBT individual psychotherapy, weekly skills training group and receives coaching via telephone, text, or email within the therapist's limits. In Stage 1, the primary therapist and the client work together to determine goals, identify problems that interfere with the acquisition of goals, and treat problem behaviours. During Stage 1, the DBT primary therapist works with the client to formulate hypotheses of drivers (respondent and/or operant) of problem behaviours that are agreed upon targets. During Stage 2, emotional avoidance and its related behaviours are assessed and treated, primarily through exposure protocols. In Stage 3, clients are moving out of DBT by targeting single problems that may or may not be diagnostically oriented. Stage 3 targets may include vocational issues, medical issues, or single problem mental health issues, e.g. depression, relationship issues. The problem is assessed, and the variables associated with the problem are determined and treated. If there is an evidence-based treatment available for the problem, the evidence-based treatment is used.

LIFE WORTH LIVING GOAL(S)

Every client in DBT's treatment plan, and thus the conceptualization of his behaviour, is based on the client's stated life worth living goals (LWLGs). In DBT, the overarching goal is achieving a life worth living. These goals include the activities, people, jobs, and events that would make the client's life full and complete. They are incompatible with life-threatening behaviours, e.g., suicide, self-harm, homicide, assault. The LWLGs are not therapy or mental health goals, such as "I want to get out of the hospital and live in the community." Getting out of the hospital is a problem that the DBT individual client must solve on the way to meeting a LWLG. The LWLGs are the foundation of the therapy in DBT. All problem behaviours are evaluated in terms of their interference with the specific goals. New behaviours are assessed in terms of whether they bring the client closer to or push them farther from their LWLGs. As patterns of behaviour become more evident and their functions are conceptualized, the therapist links problems and solutions back to the goals.

When determining LWLGs at the beginning of therapy, therapists resist determining whether those goals are realistic. The therapist does not yet know what is possible and impossible for the client. Later in the therapy, the therapist, knowing better what the client's strengths and capabilities are, may voice reluctance or concern about the goals. However, the process of DBT, learning to access wise mind, will help the client learn to determine his own goals and what is realistic or not.

A DBT therapist worked with a client who stated, in pre-treatment, that his LWLG was to go to Harvard Medical School. The therapist was very concerned because he did not consider the goal "realistic." The client had never graduated from secondary school and was in his thirties. With the help of the DBT Consultation Team, the therapist let go of being attached to whether or not the client could get to Harvard and began with conceptualizing a list of problems to be solved to get him there. The first was to stay out of the hospital and the second was to finish high school. As the client and the therapist worked together, the client finished secondary school and became a phlebotomist. He reframed his own LWLGs into goals that made sense as he became more regulated.

The LWLGs are not only a starting place for conceptualizing treatment in DBT, but they also establish a link between what the client wants in his life and the therapy. DBT therapists help the client to visualize the LWLG in as much detail as possible to make them concrete and to more easily identify the problems that interfere with achieving the goals. Throughout the treatment, the client and the therapist revisit the LWLGs to assess progress and to redefine the goals as needed. Table 12.2 lists the steps in moving from establishment of LWLGs through treatment in DBT, the process through which the case conceptualization is formulated.

Table 12.2 Road map for DBT

Step 1:	Determine Life Worth Living Goal(s).
Step 2:	Translate LWLG into specifically defined problems (increase or decrease).
Step 3:	Translate the problems into the Primary target hierarchy.
Step 4:	Get commitment to target the problems.
Step 5:	Pick several of the targets from Step 2 for monitoring on diary card.
Step 6:	Conduct thorough behavioural assessment of the target behaviours.
Step 7:	When the behaviour occurs, conduct chains, looking for controlling variables. Begin generating and implementing solutions.
Step 8:	After several chains, generate a hypothesis about a controlling variable and test it. Repeat for possible controlling variables.
Step 9:	Begin treatment based on the assessments/chains that address the controlling variables. Usually, they will involve contingency management, cognitive modification, exposure and/or behavioural skills.
Step 10:	Update the diary card to reflect refinement in goals and problem behaviours.
Step 11:	Repeat steps again for all target behaviours until client achieves LWLGs.

BEHAVIOURALLY DEFINED PROBLEMS

After determining the LWLGs, the patient and the therapist create a list of behaviourally defined problems that must be solved in order to reach the LWLGs. Many find it helpful to think of these as the barriers to achieving the LWLGs. These will not all be mental health problems, but may include some. They will not all be problems that will be addressed in the treatment. Some will be homework for therapy, e.g., in the example of the client who wants to go to Harvard, the therapist may spend a few minutes of a session problem solving whom to contact about enrolling for Adult Education and getting commitment to do so for homework one week. Unless a desired behaviour does not occur, in which case missing links analysis or behavioural chain analysis are conducted, the therapist moves on to the next related problem, e.g., securing secondary school transcripts. The problems are classified as behaviours to increase, behaviours to decrease, and problems to be solved. Below is a list of some of the problems that had to be solved to help the client get to Harvard:

1. Decrease suicide behaviour by overdose (they kept him in the hospital and he could not go to school).
2. Decrease cutting behaviours (they increased his shame and maintained avoidance of activities outside of the home).
3. Decrease behaviours that result in hospitalization (suicide communications, suicide planning, suicide letter writing).
4. Increase compliance with psychiatrist's orders (to get out of hospital).
5. Determine the requirements for finishing secondary school.
6. Contact Adult Education to enrol in preparation for finishing school.
7. Decrease staying in bed 20 hours per day.
8. Increase timely completing of assignments, even when they seem "stupid".
9. Decrease depression (increase medication compliance and increase behavioural activation).
10. Decrease anxiety (decrease ruminating about the future, decrease physiological arousal of increased heart rate, muscle tension, racing thoughts, and sensations of breathlessness).
11. Decrease avoidance of cues related to post-traumatic stress disorder (PTSD).
12. Decrease premature drop out from therapy (he had a history of doing so).

These problem lists are often extensive and change as the treatment continues to resolve problems, complete tasks, and when new problems emerge.

PRIMARY TARGETS

In DBT the therapist categorizes and creates agendas by using a target hierarchy. The primary targets in Stage 1 DBT are sorted into the following categories: life-threatening behaviours, therapy-interfering behaviours, quality-of-life-interfering behaviours, and behavioural skills. The first three targets are behaviours to be decreased, and the fourth target is behaviours to be increased.

Life-threatening behaviours (LTBs) are those that pose physical danger to self or others. They consist of suicide, self-harm, homicide, and assaultive behaviours. Within each category, the behaviours are classified as urges, actions, and ideation. Therapy-interfering behaviours (TIBs) are behaviours by the client or the therapist that interrupt the treatment. TIBs can affect behavioural change as well as the motivation of the therapist, the client, or, in the case of TIBs in skills training group, other clients. TIBs are often sub-classified as non-compliant behaviours, non-collaborative behaviours, or non-attending behaviours (Linehan, 1993). Quality-of-life-(QOL) interfering-behaviours are all other behaviours that must be decreased for the client to achieve his LWLGs. They include behaviours associated with other psychiatric diagnoses and those that seriously destabilize the client's life, such as drinking, depression, medical disorders, behaviours related to Bipolar Disorder, using drugs, gambling, binging, purging, running away, quitting jobs/schools/relationships prematurely, staying in bed for days, or other avoidance behaviours. In order to decrease the primary target behaviours, clients must engage in new behaviours. In DBT, these behavioural skills are taught in skills training group and include core mindfulness skills, interpersonal effectiveness skills, emotion regulation skills, and skills for tolerating distress.

As clients progress through Stage 1, part of the conceptualization includes deciding on if/when Stage 2 treatment for post-traumatic stress disorder (PTSD) or other disorders or behaviours related to experiential and/or emotional avoidance should begin. Clinicians often manage some of the behavioural consequences of PTSD (nightmares, flashbacks, dissociation, extreme avoidance) in Stage 1 but only directly target trauma in Stage 2 when behavioural dyscontrol has stabilized. Stage 2 targets usually include decreasing experiential avoidance, increasing emotional experiencing, increasing down-regulation following emotional experiencing, decreasing emptiness, and decreasing feelings of non-belonging (Chapters 35 and 36, this volume, discuss the treatment of PTSD in DBT in more detail).

Stage 3 targets are determined based on single problems being targeted during the treatment contract. Examples of Stage 3 targets include increasing job-related skills, decreasing interpersonal conflict in a specific relationship, decreasing depressive symptoms, or increasing behavioural activation. If the client has progressed through the stages in DBT in a fashion where they have attended skills training group, increasing generalization of the DBT behavioural skills is also targeted in Stage 3. Whenever there is a previously established evidence-based treatment for a behaviour, e.g., post-partum depression or anxiety, its targeted behaviours will be included in the Stage 3 targets. If Stage 3 includes moving toward discharge from psychotherapy, requisite behaviours and any tapering of services will be included in the conceptualization of Stage 3 targets.

Secondary Targets

Secondary targets are most frequently identified throughout the course of treatment as opposed to being determined in the initial sessions. Secondary targets are defined as those behaviours that maintain primary target problem behaviours (Linehan, 1993). They are behaviours that are observed in the client's responses in individual psychotherapy, e.g., "I don't deserve to feel better" (the secondary target of self-invalidation), or that arise when she becomes dysregulated in session. Secondary targets are also identified as controlling variables on a chain of a dysfunctional behaviour, e.g., when the cognitive link "I don't deserve to feel better" (also the secondary target of self-invalidation) occurs on the path to suicidal, self-harm and other problem behaviours.

The secondary targets are made up of six poles along three behavioural continuums. Not every client has all three polarities but usually when one pole can be identified, its polar opposite can also be identified (see Linehan, 1993, p. 67).

The first set of secondary targets is the most prevalent in clients with emotion regulation disorders. Emotional vulnerability and self-invalidation are the consequences of the biosocial theory. Emotion vulnerability describes the current manifestation of the exquisite sensitivity and reactivity to emotional stimuli that contributed to and was further developed during the course of the client's development. Clients often describe the experience of their vulnerability as being emotionally out of control, reporting that, "I can't take any more of this" or "I can't stand it." They may structure their lives in such a way as to not allow any emotional experiencing in order to keep emotions at bay. In self-invalidation, clients adopt the characteristics of their invalidating environment. They will negate their experiences, punish their emotional expression, or display perfectionistic or set unrealistic expectations for themselves. While in self-invalidation, clients may say, "I'm a bad person" or "I don't deserve ...."

Active passivity and apparent competence occur in an interpersonal context. Typically, clients with active passivity present with a passive problem-solving style. Perhaps because they may not know how to solve their life problems or they believe that only others can solve their problems for them, they actively engage in behaviours that elicit help from others. Often, other people describe clients as being "aggressive," or "demanding" that others solve their problems. Other times, clients may remain passive and do nothing to solve their own problems until the problem becomes so significant that someone else intervenes for them, e.g., not paying a bill for months until someone else pays it for the client, thus reinforcing a sense of incompetence in solving her own problems and beliefs that others are more skilled in solving their life problems. Many times, people in the client's environment become frustrated at the client's lack of problem-solving abilities and motivation.

Apparent competence occurs when the environment treats the client as if she is more competent than she sees herself. Apparent competence may be present when the client masks emotional expression and uses phrases such as "I am fine" when she is in emotional distress or when she appears to tolerate a stressful situation with less emotion than previously. When the client exhibits apparently competent behaviour, the environment responds to her as if she is more competent than she experiences herself, thus further invalidating her experience.

The dialectical dilemmas of "unrelenting crisis" and "inhibited grieving" are related to loss and negative emotions. Clients often experience significant loss and sadness when young and become increasingly sensitized to it over time. The secondary target of unrelenting crisis describes problematic decision making that may also occur in the face of legitimate crisis and loss. Many DBT clients experience extreme tragedy in their lives. In response to a crisis, clients engage in problematic escape behaviours that often further compound the original crisis. As the problems mount, clients engage in more problematic escape behaviours, often further prolonging the pain and distress. Inhibited grieving occurs when clients shut down to avoid or escape painful emotions: it may occur volitionally or reflexively. Clients often articulate the fear that they will be overcome by emotion (emotion vulnerability) and in response they disconnect from experiencing emotion.

DETERMINING CONTROLLING VARIABLES AND PATTERNS OF PROBLEM BEHAVIOURS: FORMULATION

After LWLGs, problems, and targets are determined, the client and the DBT therapist begin to systematically address all the targets. These sections of the case conceptualization are the most organic in that they change with each new behaviour until specific, repeated behavioural patterns are identified. The client and therapist collaboratively choose targets, and then begin with a behavioural assessment of the target. The therapist assesses the frequency of the behaviour (how often it occurs), the intensity of the behaviour (strength of urges, ideations, emotions), the topography (what the behaviour looks like, free of global or evaluative words), and the duration (how long it lasts). The behavioural assessment represents not only the first step of targeting a behaviour, but also the first step of conceptualizing the specific behaviour and ultimately changing it through treatment interventions. After collaboratively labelling the behaviour to add to the diary card, the client and the therapist analyse the behaviour when it occurs in order to generate hypotheses about the controlling variables and the coordination of treatments or solutions.

HYPOTHESES ABOUT CONTROLLING VARIABLES

As targeted behavioural events occur, the client and the therapist work together to conduct behavioural chain analyses of the behaviour. Persons (1989) identifies the hypothesis as the heart of the case conceptualization and it is the main feature of the "treatment plan" in DBT. The purpose of the chain analysis is to obtain a detailed assessment of the antecedents and consequences of the behaviour, including functional and dysfunctional variables. After creating the linear examination of the behavioural events, the therapist and the client generate hypotheses about the controlling variables including the function of the behaviour. Controlling variables are those pieces of the chain that are believed to affect the problem behaviour. The contextual controlling variables are found in the vulnerability factors, prompting event, and/or links (cognitive, emotion, action, sensation, events). The consequential controlling variables are determined from the internal (proximal and distal) and environmental (proximal and distal) consequences.

Included in the hypothesis is the function of the behaviour. Does the behaviour occur in response to contextual variables (respondent), to access consequential variables (operant), or both? For example, three chain analyses were done on a client's behaviour of cutting her wrist four to six times with a razor blade in order to form an overarching hypothesis about the causes and consequences of the behaviour. The resulting hypothesis suggested that when the client was not sleeping because she was studying for tests (vulnerability factor), combined with the belief that she had been criticized by a professor (cognitive link), she would experience an increase in shame (emotion link); hence, cutting resulted in a decrease in muscle tension, heart rate, and racing thoughts (proximal internal consequence) and her roommates would gather around her and offer encouragement (distal environmental consequence). The behaviour is conceptualized as functioning both respondently and operantly.

THE SOLUTION ANALYSIS OR TREATMENT PLAN FOR SPECIFIC BEHAVIOURS

Once a therapist and client have determined a hypothesis or sequence of hypotheses about the problem behaviour, the therapist then implements treatment for each of the controlling variables. In DBT, there are five basic interventions, or treatments: problem solving, skills training, cognitive modification, exposure (predominantly solutions for the respondent variables of the behaviour), and contingency management (predominantly for the operant variables of the behaviour). The DBT behavioural skills can be solutions for most variables either respondent or operant. The solution is matched to its corresponding controlling variable. Table 12.3 lists possible controlling variables and their positions on chains, as well as examples of possible solutions. Because not every solution will be used to eliminate a problem behaviour, Table 12.3 is comprised of generic solutions from multiple client behaviours.

Once a solution is identified, it is implemented and practised. The therapist and the client discuss other places in the client's life that similar solutions can be utilized. This step is the transition of the formulation of a specific behaviour to the client's overall conceptualization. Finally, the therapist secures a commitment from the client to engage in

Table 12.3 Solutions by position on the chain

Position on Chain	Possible Solutions	Examples of Possible Interventions
Vulnerability Factors	Problem solving	Removing lethal means. Skills for seeking medication change.
	Behavioural skills	PLEASE for sleep, Crisis survival skills. Mindfulness to current emotion.
	Exposure	Loneliness, boredom.
	Cognitive modification	Changing *"My life stinks"*.
Prompting Events (PE)	Problem solving	Decreasing conflict with spouse.
	Behavioural skills	DEAR MAN GIVE
Link *These should be in the order that they occur in the chain		
Cognition	Cognitive modification	Changing *"I am a burden"*. Dialectical thinking. Decreasing rumination.
Emotion	Exposure to classically conditioned emotion	Shame, sadness before PE.
Actions/Events	Problem solving	Stimulus control. Dealing with others' behaviours. What to do when unexpected things happen.
Any Link	Behavioural skills	Mindfulness skills. Distress tolerance. Interpersonal effectiveness. Emotion regulation.
Consequences (Positive, Negative, Neutral)		
Proximal/Distal	Behavioural skills	Replacement behaviours for ways to get "relief," asking for help instead of cutting.
	Cognitive modification	Contingency clarification *"If you don't want your parents to X, don't Y"*.
	Contingency management	Shape new behaviours. Reinforce new behaviours. Punish old behaviours. Extinguish old behaviours.
Environmental	Contingency management	Change environments (don't respond in X way). Reinforce environment.
	Behavioural skills	Interpersonal skills.
After Effects	Behavioural skills	Repairing for guilt. Decreasing vulnerability to negative emotions using ABC PLEASE.
	Exposure	Shame in session.
	Problem solving	Review/remove means. Repair any damage resulting from the problem behaviour.

the new behaviours derived from the solution analysis, and analyses that solution to determine any places that the solution could be derailed.

After the problem behaviour is treated and decreases/stops, therapists and clients determine a new behaviour and the process is repeated. After treating several behaviours, a conceptualization of repeated controlling variables will emerge. These patterns, or the insight analysis (Linehan, 1993), are then treated with the same interventions described earlier. After treating these patterns, the therapist and the client will determine when to move to different stages, e.g., moving to treat PTSD in Stage 2 after life-threatening and severe QoL-interfering behaviours are resolved.

Outcomes

Determining when to start treating a new problem behaviour or to move to a new Stage of treatment requires specific outcomes. When agreeing to target a behaviour, the therapist and the client collaborate to decide the desired outcome, e.g., decreasing hours in bed each day, decreasing depression, stopping cutting, and how it will be measured. The outcome measure may come from a standardized instrument, e.g., the Borderline Symptom List 23 (Bohus et al., 2009) or the Difficulties in Emotion Regulation Scale (Gratz & Roemer, 2004) or it may be derived from behaviours tracked on the diary card. For instance, the diary card monitors suicide action (yes/no), suicide urges (0–5), and suicide ideation (0–5) daily, and diary cards are completed each week. Over the first few months of treatment, the therapist and client can expect suicide actions to end and for urges and ideation to decrease. Dates from the diary card can determine when the behavioural expectations are met. When the measures change to an agreed-upon score, the treatment moves to different problem behaviours or new stages of treatment. Outcomes can be evaluated monthly, quarterly, by skills module or by treatment contract. To assure quick determination of progress, it is important to choose outcomes that are meaningful to both the client and the therapist, are tracked easily by the client, and not overly complicated.

Appendix 1 provides a completed example of the case conceptualization of a current DBT client. The client "Mary" has been in a comprehensive DBT programme for 21 weeks, including pre-treatment.

There is no single "approved" version of a DBT case conceptualization. This chapter includes frequently utilized sections of a DBT case conceptualization. The case conceptualization examines past and present, causal, and consequential aspects of client behaviour to inform a meaningful treatment plan. The DBT case conceptualization begins formulation on the day that the potential DBT client arrives for his assessment and intake, changes as the client proceeds through the treatment, and dictates the final skills plan that is written with the client as part of termination and consolidation. Whether every section is written in a formal document or woven throughout the client's health

KEY MESSAGES FOR CLINICIANS

- Case conceptualization is iterative and organic, and changes as the treatment progresses.
- Case conceptualizations should be clear and concise so that they can be communicated easily to the client and to team members.
- Case conceptualization uses the tenets of DBT to assess causal and consequential factors of behaviours.
- Case conceptualization assists the therapist and the client in determining specific interventions to use in treatment, as well as the means to determine the effectiveness of the interventions.

record and case notes, the conceptualization is the DBT thinking that informs the entirety of the client's treatment with DBT.

APPENDIX 1

DBT Case Conceptualization for "Mary"

Demographics

Mary is a 26-year-old female referred to the DBT programme following a near-lethal suicide attempt. She was brought into the emergency department of the local hospital unconscious and had ingested 120 tablets of her anti-psychotic medication, 20 tablets of benzodiazepine, and had consumed an unknown amount of wine. Mary was in the Intensive Care Unit for three days and was on dialysis for eight days before being admitted to the psychiatric hospital where she was a patient for two weeks. Mary has had six previous inpatient psychiatric admissions as an adult and one six-month admission to a psychiatric residential treatment facility when she was sixteen and seventeen. In addition to multiple, near-lethal suicide attempts, she cuts herself multiple times per month, drinks to the point of blackout, and binges and purges. When she was referred to the DBT programme as part of her discharge plan from the psychiatric inpatient facility, she was administered the Structured Clinical Interview for DSM Disorder – Personality Disorder (SCID-PD) and was given diagnoses of borderline personality disorder and post-traumatic stress disorder. She also was diagnosed with fibromyalgia and chronic migraines.

Mary is the third of five children. Both of her parents are college educated. Her father worked while her mother remained at home to rear the children. Mary reports that an uncle who lived one block from her family sexually molested her between the ages of five and seven by. At age seven, she told her parents of the abuse. They ended their relationship with the uncle and refused to talk about the abuse again. When Mary suffered with symptoms of PTSD (flashbacks, nightmares, dissociation, and experiential avoidance), Mary was told that her abuse was in the past and she should "move on and let it go."

Initial Assessment: Areas of Dysregulation, Strengths, and Weaknesses

1. **Emotional dysregulation**

   Mary reports extreme, intense and undercontrolled emotions. Fear and shame are predominant emotions. Mary states that she has realized that all emotions are "bad" and that she would be "better off" if she just did not have emotions.

2. **Interpersonal dysregulation**

   Mary was married for under two years. She states that her husband left her because he could not tolerate the "chaos." She describes intermittent relationships with friends who often prematurely terminate their relationships with her, often in response to actions that she takes when drunk. Her relationship with her family is intact, although she believes that her siblings "put up with" her because her parents require them to do so.

3. **Behavioural dysregulation**

   Mary has suicide and self-harm (cutting) behaviour. She drinks eight to ten glasses of wine five nights a week and states that, when drunk, she often texts friends and acquaintances which results in people terminating their relationships with her. She binges on food two to three times per week, eating half gallons of ice cream and bags of potato chips. Mary purges almost daily, sometimes in response to binging, sometimes after drinking and sometimes because "it helps me feel better."

4. **Self-dysregulation**

   Mary states that she "does not know" herself. She is unclear of her likes and dislikes, her values, or her goals.

5. **Cognitive dysregulation**

   Mary is unclear of the exact frequency of her dissociative behaviours but believes that she dissociates multiple times daily. She has short-term and long-term memory deficits and problems controlling her attention.

6. **Strengths**

   Mary has strong family support. Although they continue to invalidate her by simplifying and criticizing her problems, they also are active in her treatment when invited. Mary describes that her parents are willing to do "anything her therapist tells them to do." They frequently provide financial support during times when she is unemployed and about to lose housing, and give her spending money when she has none. She eats at her parents' home several days a week and spends holidays with them, even though Mary reports that most visits end up in verbal disagreements.

   Mary is intelligent and educated. She has a bachelor's degree in accounting, experience as a bookkeeper, and is proficient at securing employment. She has her own home. Mary states that she is "tenacious" and works hard when she has goals.

7. **Deficits**

   Mary's physical illnesses make it difficult to activate her in the service of goals. She reports two to three migraines per month. When she has the migraines, she "must" get in bed and stay there until the migraine stops, usually at least one day, sometimes two. The chronic pain from her fibromyalgia impacts her mobility and her behavioural activation. Mary lacks support outside of her family. She has had intermittent, very brief romantic relationships that have resulted in her belief that she does not deserve love. When she is angry at her family, Mary has no other support in the way of friends.

Biosocial Theory

During the initial interview with her therapist, Mary reported that she has always had extreme emotions. Mary remembers crying for hours (slow return to baseline) as a child and her family tells her that she was "inconsolable." She describes herself as "losing control" and "raging" at others. Mary states that she has always had emotions when others did not (sensitivity). For example, she has always become very distressed by movies and television shows. Even as a child, she remembers crying because of something she had seen or a story she was told. She has always "gone from 0 to 100" (reactivity) when other people do not seem to be experiencing any emotion. Mary states that she has high joy and happiness as well as other emotions. Mary reports that others in her family are not as emotional as she is. Mary states that she looks physically different to the other four children in her family. According to Mary, the rest of her family are petite, slender, and graceful. Mary is tall and states that she has never been coordinated. Mary reports that she often felt out of place in her family and that her parents said things to her like, "Don't embarrass the family." During family dinners, when she dropped food or did not use "appropriate table manners," her father would excuse her from the table and send her to her room. Later, her mother would come to her room and tell her how she had ruined dinner. Mary says that she was often told that she could not join family outings unless she agreed to "behave." Her experience is that, as hard as she tried, she has never met expectations. When she was told that her behaviour was "sub-par," Mary would "melt down," and would then be told that she could not join the next event.

As an adult, Mary identifies shame and anger as her two most prevalent emotions. She describes herself as a volcano that bubbles beneath the surface most of the time and then explodes. Often the "explosions" result in her threating or cursing at others. Afterward, she is overcome with shame, guilt, and sadness at her own behaviour, which then precipitates suicidal urges, self-harm actions, drinking, and excess spending.

Stage of Treatment

Mary is in Stage 1 DBT. She has problems across multiple domains (work, family, friends). She has suicidal and self-harm behaviours, as well as alcohol abuse, binging and purging, and overspending. She has lost six jobs in the last 3.5 years, all because she has missed too many days of work. Many of those days were because she was in bed with chronic pain associated with fibromyalgia and migraines. She has chaotic relationships with both friends and family. Stage 2 will be indicated to address Mary's problems with the causal factors related to experiential avoidance.

Life Worth Living Goals (in Mary's words):

1. Begin to date again with the goal of finding a man to share my life with. He would be kind, enjoy the beach, and going to the movies.
2. Have four or five girlfriends who talk several times a week, and plan outings and weekend trips together.
3. Strengthen the relationship with my parents so that I don't "need" them. Then, I can have them to my home for dinner and have adult conversation with them.

Problems Needing Solving (in Mary's words):

1. Decrease suicidal ideation, urges, and actions.
2. Decrease inpatient hospitalizations.

3. Decrease self-harm behaviour.

4. Increase money to spend on activities with family, friends, and romantic partners.

5. Increase job attendance/decrease number of days of work missed because of pain.

6. Decrease days at home in bed.

7. Decrease number of drinks per night.

8. Decrease number of nights spent drinking.

9. Increase participation in reputable online dating sites.

10. Increase leisure activities (movies, theatre, dining).

11. Decrease physical pain.

12. Increase hours out of bed, even during times of increased pain.

13. Decrease isolating in order to binge.

14. Decrease purging behaviours.

15. Decrease nightmares.

16. Decrease flashbacks.

17. Decrease dissociation.

18. Increase staying present when "pleasant" events occur.

19. Decrease avoidance of cue for sadness, shame, and fear.

Primary Targets:

Life-threatening behaviours:

- Decrease suicidal actions (overdose, planning, communications).
- Decrease suicidal urges.

Decrease suicide ideation:

- Decrease non-suicidal self-injurious behaviour (cutting with razor blades, burning with cigarettes/lighters).

Therapy-interfering behaviours:

- Decrease missed appointments due to physical illness.
- Decrease non-compliance (no/incomplete diary card).

Quality-of-life-interfering behaviours:

- Decrease alcohol consumption to one to two drinks, four nights per week.
- Decrease bingeing on food.
- Decrease purging, both post-binge and without bingeing.
- Decrease days of staying in bed.
- Decrease avoidance of places or events where there are people Mary doesn't know.
- Decrease frequency and intensity of flashbacks.

- Decrease frequency and intensity of nightmares.
- Decrease dissociation.

Behavioural skills to increase:

- Increase attentional control by practising being one-mindful.
- Increase non-judgmental stance with self and others.
- Increase distracting and self-soothing for chronic pain.
- Increase radical acceptance of pain.
- Increase use of GIVE skills to attend to relationships.

Increase PLEASE skills to increase sleep and address medical issues:

- Increase mindfulness to current emotion.
- Increase Check the Facts.
- Increase Opposite Action for fear, shame, and sadness.

Secondary Targets

During the course of treatment, in-session behaviour and links on the chains of Mary's primary target behaviours have demonstrated all of the six secondary targets. The first set of behaviours, and the most pervasive, are emotion vulnerability and self-invalidation. Mary's experience of emotions is that they are overwhelming and should be avoided. She attempts to create an environment that does not prompt emotion. When emotions are cued, they are extremely uncomfortable and Mary's cognitions are that she cannot tolerate the emotion. Mary frequently judges herself, her emotions, and her responses to her emotional cues. She sets unrealistic goals for herself and believes that if she "just quit letting things get to me," she would no longer struggle in life. Mary vacillates from unrelenting crises to inhibited grieving. Her drinking functions to avoid emotions, especially the fear and shame that are related to her childhood sexual trauma. In the presence of emotional situations, Mary will drink, binge, and purge. After a period of behavioural dysregulation, Mary will stay in bed to "recover" and because she "can't face" reality. The consequences of the time in bed are losses of jobs, inability to pay bills, and friends terminating relationships because she has taken too many "rain checks." Mary dissociates, withdraws, and avoids cues for emotional experiencing.

Mary often minimizes the pain in her life. In her family of origin, doing so has been reinforced. Often, when Mary is experiencing physical pain or difficulty regulating emotions and/or behaviours, her family tells her that she should "just grin and bear it." The consequence of the history with her family is that she does not express emotion in a way to which others respond. In therapy, she frequently under-reports her own difficulties.

Mary has been punished for asking for help and at the same time, others (her family and her ex-husband) have intervened, especially when finances were involved. For example, when Mary has stopped going to work and has lost her job, her family has provided support to keep her in her home and with necessities.

Controlling Variables for Targeted Behaviours

Thus far in treatment, suicidal actions, self-harm actions, and purging have been targeted for treatment. There are some overlapping controlling variables in the behavioural patterns. All three behaviours function operantly and respondently. The suicidal behaviours targeted included one suicide attempt by overdose on a week's supply of her medical and psychiatric medications (she has them dispensed weekly at the pharmacy) and one action of pulling out all of her medications and lining them up in front of her. When she spilled her wine on the medications, they dissolved and the attempt was not made.

Hypothesis for Suicide Action

Problem behaviours in this hypothesis include suicide action of overdosing by taking seven days' worth of medication, suicide action of lining up medications to be swallowed with alcohol, and calling her mother and saying that she was going to commit suicide by overdose (a total of four events since the beginning of treatment). This behaviour is respondent to sleep disturbance, disappointment and sadness, and thoughts of being alone. This behaviour is operant for physical relaxation, sleep, emergency room visit, and mother's intervention. A possible reinforcer that is already being blocked is admission to the psychiatric unit.

> Vulnerability Factors: Ongoing conflict with mother (disagreements about money, what to do about grandfather who is in a nursing home) that result in disturbed sleep.
> Prompting Events: Friend/acquaintance says no to an invitation to go to a movie or dinner.
> Emotion Links: Disappointment and shame.
> Cognitive Link: "I am always going to be alone."
> Proximal Internal Consequences: Muscle tension decreases, body relaxes.
> Distal Internal Consequences: Body relaxes to the point of falling asleep (approximately one to one-and-a-half hours post event).
> Distal Environmental Consequences: Taken via ambulance to emergency room; mother summoned by emergency room staff and comes to hospital. Historically, the overdoses result in inpatient hospitalization (reinforcing).

Hypothesis for Self-harm Behaviours

Problem behaviours in this hypothesis include cutting 10–15 times on arms and/or legs with a straight-edged razor blade; burning herself 5–10 times on arms and/or legs with a lighter or cigarette; running blades' blunt edges over arms and visualizing cutting.

> Vulnerability Factors: Two to three days' worth of nightmares that interrupt sleep, night terrors, any potential change in financial status, e.g., parents say that they are going to withdraw financial support.
> Prompting Event: Receiving bills in the mail.
> Emotion Links: Fear and shame.
> Cognitive Link: Rapid thoughts related to "I am going to die alone and homeless."
> Sensation Link: "Heart feels like it is going to beat out of my chest."

Distal Internal Consequences: Heart rate slows down close to normal, thoughts slow down, "I can begin to figure out how to get the money."

Distal Environmental Consequences: Parents take the bills from her "to keep me from freaking out."

Hypothesis for Purging

Problem behaviours in this hypothesis include 5–15 minutes after eating meal as previously prescribed by dietician, takes one box of laxatives (12 tablets) and vomits until there is nothing but stomach acids. This behaviour occurs twice to three times per week. Note: there is currently a preliminary hypothesis that this behavioural pattern is different from purging after a binge. Although there may be some overlap in controlling variables, there are also differences.

Vulnerability Factors: Nightmares that interrupt sleep, three to four days of eating "healthy" as prescribed by dietician. Increasing worry thoughts about gaining weight.

Prompting Event: Clothes, usually pants, require more effort to button/zip.

Emotion Links: Fear and shame.

Cognitive Links: "Nobody is ever going to want me if I am fat." "I am always going to be alone."

Sensation Link: Heart racing, muscles tighten, stomach feels bloated, difficulty breathing.

Proximal Internal Consequences: Heart rate slows, muscles loosen, breathing evens, thoughts calm down.

Distal Internal Consequences: As laxatives begin to take effect, sensation of being bloated ends, weight is lower the next day.

Controlling Variables Consistent Across Behaviours

Patterns have emerged across suicide, self-harm, and purging. These are:

Vulnerability Factor: Disturbed sleep for several days.

Cognitive Links: "No one is ever going to want me," thoughts related to being alone forever.

Emotion Link: Shame, fear, and sadness.

Consequences: Slowed heart rate, muscle tension easing.

Solution analysis for the variables controlling suicide, self-harm, and purging:

Exposure: Shame, fear, and sadness.

Cognitive Modification: Change extreme language, decrease self-judgments, dialectical thinking.

DBT Behavioural Skills: Mindfulness to Current Emotion, PLEASE skill, Nightmare Protocol for Sleep, Temperature, Intense Experience, Paced Breathing (TIP) skill to decrease emotional arousal, sensations, and as replacement skill for bringing down physiological arousal, Take a Non-judgmental Stance Skill, Check the Facts.

Problem Solving: Removing means to self-harm of razor blades and laxatives, stimulus control for medications; study how to get to sleep (decrease vulnerability factors); discuss referral to nutritionist/dietician.

Contingency Management: Block emergency room visits unless medical risk is very high, advanced directive to emergency room that requests minimal interaction and no "special favours," e.g., food. No "warm fuzzies" from mom. Parents do not buy things after attempt. To reinforce use of skills: Contact therapist when used skills and she will send a cat meme. Mom will come to visit when there is no self-harm.

Outcomes

The therapist administered the Borderline Symptom List 23 (Bohus et al., 2009) at pre-treatment and at the end of each skills training module. The BSL total summary score at pre-treatment was 91 and at the end of the first module was 78. At the end of the second module, Mary's BSL-23 total score was 70. She is currently in her third module. The DBT diary card is being used to measure suicide action (yes/no) and suicide urge and ideation (0 to 5). At pre-treatment, Mary had suicide action, including suicide communications, at least once a week. At pre-treatment, Mary's weekly mean suicide urge and suicide ideation scores were 5.0 each. Currently, Mary's suicide actions have decreased to <2 per month and her daily suicide urge and ideation scores are an average 3.1 and 4.0, respectively. At pre-treatment, Mary had two or more self-harm actions per week. Currently, she has <1 per week. Mary's self-harm urges and ideations have decreased from an average 5.0 each to 4.0 each. Purging behaviours are now the focus of intervention. Currently, Mary's urges to purge range from 3.0 to 5.0 (0 to 5 scale) at some point each day. She engages in purging behaviour two to three times per week.

References

Bohus, M., Kleindienst, N., Limberger, M., Stieglitz, R. D., Domsalla, M., Chapman, A., ... Wolf M. (2009). The short version of the Borderline Symptom List (BSL-23): development and initial data on psychometric properties. *Psychopathology, 42,* 32–39.

Dawson, D. L., & Moghaddam, N. G. (2016). *Formulation in action: Applying psychological theory to clinical practice.* New York: Walter de Gruyter.

Gratz, K. L., & Roemer, L. (2004). Multidimensional assessment of emotion regulation and dysregulation: Development, factor structure, and initial validation of the difficulties in emotion regulation scale. *Journal of Psychopathology and Behavioral Assessment, 26*(1), 41–54.

Harned, M. S. (2014). The combined treatment of PTSD with borderline personality disorder. *Current Treatment Options in Psychiatry, 1,* 335–344.

Ingram, B. L. (2006). *Clinical case formulations: Matching the integrative treatment plan to the client.* Hoboken, NJ: John Wiley & Sons, Inc.

Linehan, M. M. (1993). *Cognitive behavioral treatment of borderline personality disorder.* New York: Guilford Press.

Nelson, T. S., Chenail, R. J., Alexander, J. F., Crane, D. R., Johnson, S. M., & Schwallie, L. (2007). The development of core competencies for the practice of marriage and family therapy. *Journal of Marital and Family Therapy, 33,* 417–438.

Persons, J. B. (1989). *Cognitive therapy in practice: A case formulation approach.* New York: Norton.

Persons, J. B., & Tompkins, M. A. (2007). Cognitive-Behavioral Case Formulation. In: T. D. Eells (Ed.), *Handbook of psychotherapy case formulation* (pp. 290–316). New York: Guilford.

Saleebey, D. (1996). The strengths perspective in social work practice: extension and cautions. *Social Work, 41*(3), 296–305.

CHAPTER 13

CONDUCTING EFFECTIVE BEHAVIOURAL AND SOLUTION ANALYSES

SARA J. LANDES

INTRODUCTION TO CHAIN ANALYSIS

BEHAVIOURAL chain analysis (BCA), often referred to simply as chain analysis, is a functional assessment tool that DBT therapists and their clients use in identifying the controlling variables for problematic behaviours and seeking the most effective solutions to treat those behaviours. These analyses, which occur almost every session, increase therapists' and clients' understanding of what prompts problem behaviours and what links these prompting events to target behaviours. By investigating what follows problem behaviours, behavioural analyses identify how consequences might affect the reoccurrence of the problem behaviour (Miller, Koerner, & Kanter, 1998).

Dominos provide a useful metaphor for comprehending behavioural analyses. Knocking the first domino in a closely stacked set causes the rest of the dominos to fall. This trick only works if the dominos are set close enough together. If the gap is too large, the next domino will not fall. Chain analyses work in the same way. If the "links" in the chain (information about what happened) are not close enough together in time, the chain of events will not make sense. A successful chain has links sufficiently close together that the series of events makes sense and clarifies how the problem behaviour occurred, much like how dominos fall when set close together. This chapter reviews the processes of conducting BCAs that elucidate the controlling variables of target behaviours, thus providing a solid grounding for identifying and implementing effective solutions to assist clients in resolving the difficulties that led them into therapy. The chapter begins by reviewing the rationale for behavioural analyses, before describing the pragmatics of conducting them. A clinical example follows ahead of a discussion and review of the principles and practices of effective solution analyses. The chapter concludes with some of the common challenges in completing behavioural and solution analyses.

WHY DO A CHAIN ANALYSIS?

There are a number of reasons a therapist may choose to use a chain analysis. First, behavioural analysis helps the therapist (who was likely not present when the behaviour occurred) understand what occurs when a client (who may not be aware of exactly what happened) engages in a problem behaviour. The detailed review of the sequence of events ahead of and following a target behaviour challenges clients' common experience and belief that events "come out of the blue"; rather, conducting a BCA aids clients in learning that emotions, actions, or thoughts do not "just happen," but result from certain interactions or transactions with the environment.

Second, completing a BCA provides the therapist with an empirical method to test out theories about the controlling variables of a client's behaviour. For example, a therapist may hypothesize that drinking alcohol makes a client more vulnerable to arguments with his wife. Completing an analysis on an instance of an argument with his wife would allow the therapist and client to see if alcohol use was a vulnerability factor in that situation. Doing numerous analyses over time for the same type of behaviour allows the therapist and client to assess for a behavioural pattern (e.g., most, but not all, arguments occur after the client has been drinking).

Third, the process of completing a chain, highlighting what led up to a problem behaviour and identifying what consequences might be maintaining a behaviour (despite a client's desire to stop the behaviour), can be a validating experience for a client. This is especially true when a client may think or hear from others that they are "just crazy" or decide that they are engaging in a problem behaviour because "something is wrong" with them. Clients are less likely to believe these derogatory explanations when they can observe the causes of their behaviour, and that it "makes sense." Understanding their own behaviour and having their experience validated can impact on other behaviours. For example, if a client understands the reasons for her self-harm when she experiences high emotion (because it provides relief), she may have fewer judgmental thoughts about herself after cutting. Decreased judgments may allow the client to utilize skills more effectively or report the behaviour on a diary card and ask for help in coping with her strong emotions.

Finally, and perhaps most importantly, BCA provides the therapist with ideas for selecting solutions to prevent future occurrences of the target behaviour. In identifying what prompts and maintains target behaviours, despite a client's efforts to change, BCA aids the therapist in generating, evaluating, and implementing solutions with the client. With a better understanding of the controlling variables of a target behaviour, the therapist can generate more ideas about where and how to intervene.

BEING BEHAVIOURAL

DBT therapists conduct BCAs on single specific instances of a target behaviour (e.g., cutting the arm on Tuesday evening, rather than all cutting behaviour last week). This allows the therapist and client to evaluate what led up to and what followed the problem behaviour in a specific instance. When describing behaviour, the focus should be on describing the form or "topography" of the behaviour. For example, when a client says he had "road rage" while driving, that does not describe exactly what happened. "Road rage" could include a number of behaviours, such as yelling, using swear words, driving faster, driving too closely to another car, feeling angry, having tense muscles, etc. When a client uses a term that may have different meanings to different people or is vague, DBT therapists prompt him or her to be more specific about what happened, even when a therapist may assume they and the client share a similar definition of a term, such as "having a fight" or "being depressed." A therapist can ask the following questions to obtain a more behavioural description:

- What does "road rage" look like?
- What do other people see when you have "road rage"?
- Can you be more specific about what you did?
- What were you saying to yourself while it was happening?
- What were you feeling in your body?
- What exactly did you and she say?
- What happened first? Then what happened? And what happened after that?

For those who are less inclined to think behaviourally, defining behaviour in terms of its frequency (how many times it occurred), duration (how long it lasted), and intensity (strength of experience) will prove useful. Example questions using these defining characteristics of behaviour include:

- Frequency: good for thoughts and actions
  - How many times did you have that thought?
  - How many times did you honk the horn at the other car?
- Duration: good for emotions and actions
  - How long were you angry?
  - How long did the flashback last?
  - How long did you yell?
- Intensity: good for emotions, thoughts, urges, and physical sensations
  - How angry were you, on a scale from 0–100?
  - How much did you believe that thought, on a scale from 1–10?
  - How intense was your stomach pain, on a scale from 1–10?
  - How strong was the urge to swerve at the other car, on a scale from 0–100?

Readers wanting more information or a refresher on behavioural thinking and addressing consequences are encouraged to read "Don't Shoot the Dog!: The New Art of Teaching and Training" (Pryor, 1999).

CONDUCTING THE FIRST BEHAVIOURAL CHAIN ANALYSIS WITH THE CLIENT

A therapist beginning a BCA simply requires something to write with and something to write on. Many therapists use paper and pen, while some use white boards on an office wall. Using something simple like paper and pen teaches the client that no special tools or handouts are needed. Switching from a handout to paper and pen often results in less therapy-interfering behaviour, such as, "I lost the handout and didn't do the homework" and a change to more therapy-enhancing behaviour (e.g., a client of the author wrote out a chain on an empty pizza box for homework). Therapists who wish to use handouts, or see one for reference, are encouraged to use the one in the DBT Skills Training Manual (Linehan, 2015).

When teaching clients about BCA for the first time, DBT therapists often focus on beginning with the problem behaviour before reviewing the prompting event, the consequences of the behaviour, and finally the links in the sequence between the prompting event and the behaviour. This sequence, reviewed in more detail later, is not in chronological order. Once clients are familiar with the structure and method of a BCA, therapists can revert to conducting them in chronological order. Nevertheless, therapists may wisely ask for details of the behaviour, prompting event, and consequences ahead of further details in circumstances where the client is particularly loquacious or where time is of the essence, for example, where the session agenda is full. See Figure 13.1 for a visual of all components of a chain analysis.

Problem Behaviour

A BCA starts with identifying the problem behaviour. A problem behaviour is something the client does, not something someone else does, that causes them difficulty. For example, a client's mother yelling at her would not be a problem behaviour picked for analysis (even though it causes a problem for the client). The mother yelling may, however, be the prompting event that leads to a problem behaviour. In such circumstances, the problem behaviour of the client might be cutting her arms after being yelled at by her mother. The ultimate goal of a chain analysis is to help the client to do something more effective the next time they are in a similar situation. Therefore, the therapist should pick behaviours over which they have some control. Questions a therapist can ask a client to help identify the problem behaviour are:

FIGURE 13.1 All components of a chain analysis.

- What did you do that caused problems for you or others around you?
- What did that look like? What would it have looked like to others?

Prompting Event

Next, DBT therapists identify the prompting event for the problem behaviour. The term prompting event refers to whatever set the problem behaviour in motion. The prompting event can also be called the trigger, cue, or antecedent stimulus. Prompting events are external (e.g., something in the environment, outside the person, like the actions of another person or the nature of the location or terrain). There is nothing that inherently makes something a prompting event; it simply happens to be the stimulus that triggers a behaviour in a person. For example, walking past a lilac bush may be a prompting event for someone who was assaulted near a lilac bush and may result in the problem behaviour of drinking. However, for others, walking past a lilac bush may prompt nothing other than recollections of summer evenings.

The client may not always know or be able to identify the prompting event (which is also true of other components of the chain). Sometimes things happen quickly and the prompting event passes unnoticed. Some behaviours are so well learned that they happen more or less automatically, with little awareness of the client, so that he or she may be unable to recall later what prompted the behaviour. In the absence of certainty, the therapist and the client can hypothesize about what might have precipitated a problem behaviour. A key part of treatment often involves helping the client pay closer attention to the next similar situation to clarify hypotheses generated in session. Questions a therapist can ask a client to help identify the prompting event include:

- What set this off?
- What was going on just before you (insert problem behaviour)?
- What was the situation you were in when it happened?
- When did you first know you were heading toward the problem behaviour?
- When did the problem start?

Consequences

Next, DBT therapists identify the short-term and long-term consequences of the problem behaviour. Identification of the immediate or short-term consequences of the behaviour will help the therapist and client understand what is maintaining the behaviour. Reinforcing consequences strengthen the problem behaviours and result in maintenance of these behaviours over time. Therapists also highlight long-term consequences of the behaviour. Knowing that their current behaviour may result in unwanted or unpleasant long-term consequences may increase clients' motivation to work on their behaviour. Sometimes the long-term consequences are not yet apparent and the client and therapist may have to hypothesize what these consequences may be. Questions a therapist can use to help identify the consequences of problem behaviours are:

- What happened after (insert problem behaviour)? How does that work for you?
- What was the consequence of you doing that? Were there other consequences?
- What was the result of you doing that? What else?
- Did you get something you wanted in the short-term?
- Does this cause you any problems in the long run?
- Are there possible problems that could happen in the long run?

At this point, three components of the chain have been presented: the prompting event, problem behaviour, and consequences. Returning to the domino metaphor, if one had just these three dominos set up to represent the pieces of information in chronological order, the dominos would not successfully fall, as they would be spaced too far apart. More information is needed to fill in the gaps to understand what happened between the prompting event and the problem behaviour.

Links in the Chain: Actions, Events, Thoughts, Emotions, Physical Sensations, and Urges

To fill in the gaps, the therapist and client need to identify the links in the chain, or what happened between the prompting event and the problem behaviour. Links include the following categories: actions (of the client), events (e.g., actions of others, events outside of the client), thoughts, emotions, physical sensations, and urges. For many situations, the client may have experienced the prompting event and the problem behaviour as happening immediately one after the other. The therapist may need to prompt the client to play back the situation "in slow motion" to establish more clearly what happened. With a client who reports that she cut herself after her mother yelled at her, the therapist can validate that it likely felt that she cut herself immediately after her mother yelled and, at the same time, it is unlikely that she was sitting with a razor next to her wrist as her mother yelled. The client probably had thoughts about the yelling, may have responded with her own yelling, left the room, felt angry, had an urge to do something to get rid of the negative emotion, experienced physical sensations that go along with anger, and had to get something to cut with … all before cutting. These would all be considered links in the chain.

The more links in the chain, the more useful the behavioural analysis. When finished, each link in the chain is a potential place for intervention (e.g., using a skill, saying something different, changing the environment in some way to prevent it supporting the behaviour) for the next time something similar happens. When going through a chain, the therapist should notice what kind of links the client reports and ask about the remaining categories of links. Some therapists like to write the categories on the paper being used to write out the chain as a prompt for the clients and themselves. While asking about all types of links is important, therapists must ensure that they retain the chronological order of links in order to accurately analyse the behavioural chain of events. For example, for effectively implemented exposure, therapists must know the cue for the problematic emotion, how the emotion is expressed, and the relevant escape behaviours. Therefore, remembering which came first in the sequence is vital. Therapists assist clients who tend to "clump" emotions together, e.g., "I felt sad, ashamed, and guilty when my mother yelled at me" to pause and consider which emotion came first and what other thoughts, sensations, and urges accompanied it before the next emotion came along. In this way, DBT therapists expand and increase the awareness of their clients and the opportunities to successfully intervene. Clients may not notice or remember all categories of links; for example, some clients find it more difficult to notice urges than other types of link. Instead, they may only notice actions they actually engage in. When a therapist asks about each type of link during the analysis clients will learn to notice these in the future, as they become more aware of what transpires before, during, and after problem behaviour.

There is no set rule about how many links are "enough." After the therapist has queried each type of link and established a temporal order, reviewing the chain with the client to assess whether anything significant is missing may prove helpful. If nothing is missing and the therapist and client feel they have a good understanding of what happened, they likely have enough information to proceed.

In terms of how much detail is needed for each link, a DBT therapist only needs a description that allows them to understand what happened in that specific moment. For example, when asking about thoughts, a therapist would want to know the content of the thought. Therapists practising from other models might ask about the intensity of the thought or how much the client believed the thought, but that information is not necessary for a behavioural analysis. If the therapist and client decide to intervene with thoughts, the therapist may ask for more detail when working on an intervention. During a chain, the therapist and client are assessing what happened in a specific instance of behaviour; asking about the history of a link, such as when the client started having this type of thought, or about what the thought means to them is unnecessary for an effective behavioural analysis. Information about the history of problems can easily derail a therapist from moving ahead with assessment of a specific behaviour and choosing interventions. Questions a therapist can use to help identify links are:

- What happened next?
- What were you thinking?
- What were you feeling? Did you have any emotions?
- What emotions showed up?
- What physical sensations did you have?
- If you had an emotion, did you have physical sensations that go along with that emotion (e.g., flushed face, clenched fists when angry)?
- Did you notice an urge or need to do something?
- What happened around you? Did others do anything? Did things change around you?
- What did you do next?

Vulnerability factors

Finally, DBT therapists identify the vulnerability factors that increased the likelihood that the client would engage in the problem behaviour on that day and at that time. Vulnerability factors can be either acute (e.g., feeling sick, hungry, tired, recent fight with a friend) or chronic vulnerability factors (e.g., strained relationship with mother, chronic pain, chronic sleep deficit, not taking medications as prescribed). For example, a client may report that she would not have yelled at her partner if she had not been tired and had a difficult day at work (vulnerability factors). Sometimes, treatment targets vulnerability factors directly, so that a problem will be less likely to occur. Targeting vulnerability factors specifically typically occurs later in treatment; early in treatment attempting to resolve vulnerability factors offers a poor return on the investment of time.

How are vulnerability factors different from prompting events? Vulnerability factors make a person more likely to react to a prompting event. For example, having poor sleep and feeling tired is a vulnerability factor increasing the likelihood that the client will react to a partner's criticism (the prompting event). Vulnerability factors set the tone for what happens. Questions a therapist can use to help identify vulnerability factors are:

- What made you vulnerable?
- Why this day/time and not before or another time?
- Was there anything going on earlier that day or the day before that made you more vulnerable or more likely to have the problem?
- Did you have anything else going on that day that made dealing with this more difficult?

When conducting a behavioural analysis the first goal is assessment. A therapist may be tempted to intervene on obvious targets (e.g., challenging a thought), but it is best to wait. Otherwise, the therapist may become distracted and fail to complete the chain resulting in insufficient information to select interventions most effectively. At the same time, DBT therapists often briefly reinforce behaviours while completing the chain. For example, a therapist can point out that a client's awareness of a situation is increasing (e.g., "that's great that you noticed your physical sensations, when we started you had difficulty doing that"). In reinforcing the client for engaging in the chain, DBT therapists aim to promote the experience of analysing behaviour as helpful and useful, as opposed to aversive or provoking shame. Not all clients are reinforced by the same therapist behaviours, so DBT therapists pay attention to the effect their statements have on a client (e.g., does he talk more or less after the intended reinforcement?).

EXAMPLE OF A CHAIN ANALYSIS

Below is a fictional transcript of a BCA completed with a hypothetical client who has already been oriented to the task. This client, Lucy, is a 22-year-old woman who lives with her parents and has a part-time job. She is working on decreasing cutting behaviours and other behaviours (e.g., drinking) that function to avoid painful emotions and on increasing skills, with a focus on emotion regulation. Lucy's main diary card targets are non-suicidal self-injury (NSSI), drinking alcohol, and productive activity.

Case Example

Therapist: In reviewing your diary card, it looks like you cut yourself on Friday and drank until you got drunk on Wednesday. Let's do a chain on the cutting, as that's in the life-threatening category.

Client: Yeah, okay. I figured we would do that if I put it on the diary card.

Therapist: Oh really? When did that thought cross your mind?

Client: Yeah, that night when I filled out my diary card, I thought, "shoot, now we have to talk about this."

Therapist: Did you have an urge to not put it on the diary card?

Client: Just a little bit, but I remembered that you told me in the beginning that the information is only meant to help me and I think talking about it is helping.

Therapist: That's great. I'm so glad you put it on the diary card so we can keep working on this. So, let's describe the problem behaviour first. What did "cutting" look like?

Client: Well, I cut my arm twice with a razor blade. It wasn't deep and didn't bleed.

Therapist: Okay. Do you have an idea of what the prompting event was?

Client: Well, I was just having one of those days, feeling really bad. Cutting makes me feel better.

Therapist: Was there something specific that happened during the day that made you feel bad or out of control?

Client: Hmmm ... let me think. [pause] Well, my mom yelled at me when she got home because I hadn't done the chores she asked me to do.

Therapist: Ah, okay. That seems related to the zero for the day for productive activity on your diary card. Not being productive could be a vulnerability factor. What happened next?

Client: I don't know. I just cut myself and felt better.

Therapist: We know from previous chains there are usually some steps in between. Walk me through what happened between your mom yelling and cutting. What were you thinking?

Client: Well, my first thought was "She's always so mean to me" and I yelled back at her. But then I thought about not doing my chores and of course she's mad, so I was thinking "I can't do anything right."

Therapist: What happened next?

Client: I just kept thinking about how I can't do things right and how I'm such a loser.

Therapist: What emotions were you having?

Client: Well, first I was angry that she was yelling at me. That's when I wanted to yell back at her.

Therapist: Did you notice the urge to yell before yelling?

Client: Maybe a little bit.

Therapist: Okay, what other emotions?

Client: When I realized it made sense she was yelling because I don't do things, I felt like a loser and was really sad. I just wanted to get away, so I locked myself in the bathroom because our other doors don't have locks. My dad was yelling when I locked myself in there and then my parents were arguing.

Therapist: Okay, you had an emotion of sadness, thoughts about being a loser, and urge to get away.

Client: Yeah, I just wanted it to stop. I wanted to stop feeling so bad.

Therapist: So, you had that thought and urge. What physical sensations did you notice with these emotions?

Client: My stomach hurt and I was tense. When I was in the bathroom, I felt ashamed that I'm 22 and locking myself in a bathroom and that my parents are arguing because of it. That's when my face felt so hot.

Therapist: So, in the bathroom you started to feel shame?

Client: Yeah. That's when I thought I just want to die. I wanted this to just stop. I hate feeling that way.

Therapist: That does sound like a horrible way to feel. What happened after you had those thoughts and urges?

Client: I got out the razor blade I have hidden in the bottom cabinet. I knew I would feel better, so I cut my arm twice.

Therapist: What were the short-term consequences? Did it make you feel better?

Client: Yeah, it's like immediate relief. I don't feel so tense and it kind of lets my negative emotions out.

Therapist: As we've talked about before, we can see why this behaviour is hard to stop doing—it's very reinforcing in the moment. That's why the long-term consequences are so important; we have to figure out good reasons to stop.

Client: Yeah, I know. The main one I thought of later was having to do one of these chains.

Therapist: What are other long-term consequences or reasons to change?

Client: Well, my mom tells me that me cutting makes my parents trust me less and it makes them angry that I'm not using skills. And I might have more scars.

Therapist: Those sound like they could be helpful motivators. I know the possible long-term consequence I really worry about is that we know that self-harm increases the likelihood of you dying by suicide by accident. We need you alive so you can create this life worth living and so you can reach your goal of travelling to different countries.

Client: Yeah, I know.

Therapist: So, let's take a look at our chain to see if we are missing anything important so we can move on to coming up with solutions for you to try. We don't seem to have much in the way of vulnerability factors. What made you more likely on that day at that time to cut?

Client: Well, I was really tired and I keep having some problems with one of my friends. I was already upset.

Therapist: Okay, I'm adding that. Is anything else important missing?

Client: No, I don't think so.

TARGETING THE COMPONENTS OF A BEHAVIOURAL CHAIN ANALYSIS

The more "links in the chain" that can be identified, the better, as each of those links is now a possible point of intervention. This section reviews what types of treatment interventions can be used on different links. The section that follows reviews some of the principles of solution generation, evaluation, and implementation that guide therapists in deciding which interventions to implement based on the behavioural analysis.

Vulnerability Factors

Preventing or reducing the occurrence of vulnerability factors can make a problem behaviour less likely to occur. The PLEASE skill targets many common vulnerability factors, including treating physical illness, healthy eating, taking medications as prescribed, avoiding non-prescribed drugs, sleep, and exercise. For a client who has identified feeling overly tired and stopping their psychiatric medications, PLEASE is a great skill for reducing these vulnerability factors. Added benefits of the PLEASE skill include its common-sense flavour and familiarity to clients and also that it tends to be within their repertoire (e.g., many people have the skills and ability to increase physical activity by walking). Other vulnerability factors may be more complicated and require a number of skills to address, such as having a strained relationship with a friend that makes a client vulnerable to arguing with them, such as Lucy in the above example. For Lucy, interpersonal skills such as DEAR MAN and GIVE and emotion regulation skills might be a great fit for addressing something that can be both a problem behaviour and a vulnerability factor for self-harm.

Prompting Events

Reducing or eliminating contact with prompting events can prevent or reduce a problem behaviour (stimulus control). For example, a client can use opposite action to avoid entering a bar that is a prompting event for substance use. Deploying stimulus control for problematic prompting events needs to be used with care, as therapists do not want to inadvertently teach clients that avoidance is always effective. Avoidance of some prompting events can actually perpetuate problems by preventing the client from learning that certain situations are not inherently dangerous or from learning to cope more effectively. Additionally, some prompting events, like attending family gatherings or going to work, are part of daily life. Therefore, rather than encouraging avoidance, therapists will sometimes need to work with the client to change their reaction to prompting events. Changing the reaction to the prompting event can include changing the problematic response (problem behaviour) by using exposure principles and procedures, or it can include changing any of the links in the chain that occur between the prompting event and the problem behaviour. Another way of addressing prompting events is to create new prompting events for positive alternative behaviours. For example, being in the presence of sober people will likely promote recovery. So, a client can be encouraged to deliberately associate with abstinent people (e.g., through joining Alcoholics Anonymous).

Links in the Chain

Intervening with the links in the chain (actions, events, thoughts, feelings, physical sensations, or urges) will include use of all of the DBT change procedures; skills training, exposure, contingency management, and cognitive modification. For example, when addressing problematic thoughts in a chain, a therapist might choose to use thought records to challenge thoughts or teach the skill of non-judgmental stance. A therapist might want to help the hypothetical client Lucy with addressing her thoughts of being a loser, as it comes up in different contexts. Emotions and physical sensations are related, but separate, links in the chain. Many clients find identifying emotions easiest by focusing on the physical sensations they are having at the same time (others may use thoughts or urges to help them identify what emotion they are experiencing). Some examples of interventions for emotions and physical sensations might include mindfulness of emotion, opposite action, or TIP.

Therapists may also choose to target urges as they appear in the chain. Many clients have difficulty noticing when they have urges and often report that they do not have an urge before engaging in a behaviour (e.g., they "just do it"). Discussing the concept of experiencing an urge (often by noticing thoughts or physical sensations, sometimes both) before engaging in a behaviour (even if the experience is brief) can often be an intervention in and of itself. Highlighting that there may be a choice point before engaging in a behaviour can be a new idea for clients. For those clients who have difficulty noticing or do not notice urges, having the therapist continuing to inquire about urges in each chain can also function as an intervention, as it prompts them to consider whether or not they experienced an urge. Over time, this prompting can generalize to their daily life and they may start to notice urges.

If simply noticing proves insufficient to manage urges, therapists may teach and encourage "urge surfing," a skill that was developed as part of an adaptation of DBT for Substance Use Disorder (Linehan & Dimeff, 1997). For this skill, urges are compared to waves that dissipate over time. The goal is to surf the urge as one would surf the wave, riding it until it goes away (knowing that it may take some time for this to happen and that it will eventually happen). Essentially, the therapist teaches the client to wait out an urge until it subsides, providing imagery as an aid.

Finally, a therapist may also intervene with the consequences of the behaviour. There are three general ways to change consequences: have the client change his or her own consequences, include someone from the client's life to change consequences, or the therapist, as a source of consequences, modifies his or her response to the behaviour. Clients can deliberately provide different consequences for themselves, as a way of shaping their own behaviour. One way to do this is to reinforce oneself for doing something more effective. For example, a client could reward herself for completing a therapy homework assignment by spending time relaxing with a "schlocky" magazine. Rewards are just one way a client can provide their own reinforcement. Other methods of reinforcement include the client allowing herself to feel pride at moving closer to a goal, or writing down accomplishments to see improvement. These types of reinforcement are more likely to be natural reinforcers and are easier to maintain over time.

Significant others in the client's life may modify consequences for a client by responding differently to the client's behaviour. Family members can be taught how to reinforce or praise changes that they observe or to stop reinforcing problematic behaviour. For example, a husband can be taught to reinforce gradual change in interpersonal interactions by noticing and commenting on behaviour he likes or appreciates in his wife to highlight the impact of the new behaviour, things his wife may not have noticed in the moment. Thus, the wife gains both a positive experience of hearing her behaviour change is appreciated by her husband and she becomes aware of a reinforcer she may not have come in contact with in the moment. Her husband might say, "I noticed that you didn't raise your voice when we disagreed earlier. I appreciated that and it made it easier for me to have the conversation with you." Some individuals find outright praise (e.g., "It's so great you did that") uncomfortable, so highlighting the impact and stating appreciation can be more natural and less aversive. Others in the client's life can also be taught that change is gradual and may take some time. Orienting them to the process may make it easier for them to reinforce gradual approximations of changes the client is trying to make. This can help avoid having someone waiting until the client gets it "just right" before reinforcing him or her.

As orienting is an important DBT strategy, the therapist can also teach the client how to orient others around him or her to the new effective behaviour they are working on (e.g., interpersonal skills), what it looks like, and how they are hoping to be reinforced by others. Bringing the client's significant other into the treatment session and discussing and agreeing ways that the significant other can respond to desirable and undesirable behaviours by the client can be especially valuable. This can aid the change process, and set things up so the client will experience the new reactions of the other person as acts of support. In session, asking the client, in the presence of the significant other, how they would like the other person to respond may be especially helpful. When choosing this intervention strategy, therapists should select someone in the client's life amenable to helping the client change his or her behaviour and who seems likely to have the capacity to reinforce approximations of new, more effective behaviour.

The therapist is a critical source of consequences for the behaviours of the client, whether the therapist intends to be or not. Therefore, the therapist needs to be mindful of their impact on the client. In the relationship with the therapist, the client may try out new behaviours and take risks, such as trusting more, or becoming emotionally closer to the therapist. The therapist needs to recognize positive changes of all kinds by the client and provide reinforcement for doing something more effective.

As mentioned, different people find different consequences to be reinforcing. For example, some people may find praise reinforcing, while others experience it as aversive. When attempting to reinforce a client, the therapist needs to notice the effect their behaviour has on the client. A therapist can ask about the impact (e.g., "What was it like for you when I said good job? Would you like it better if I responded differently?"). The therapist can also provide modestly aversive consequence for doing something ineffective (e.g., having the client do chains in session, being disappointed when the client fails to follow through on a therapeutic commitment or task assignment).

Intervening with consequences is frequently not the best intervention to choose either with a new client or when a client is new to behavioural analysis. Contingency management, while often vital to effective behaviour change, may prove a more difficult intervention to implement successfully, especially when relying on others to provide different consequences. Gradually shaping behaviour change by modifying therapist responses to client behaviours occurs from the beginning in DBT, however. For example, DBT therapists often remain matter-of-fact and do not increase warmth in the face of suicidal communications by their clients. In circumstances where clients have typically received more input and higher levels of warmth in response to such communications, this subtle change in response to these behaviours by DBT therapists aims to weaken suicidal communications from the commencement of therapy.

Solution Analysis

The previous section reviewed different types of interventions a therapist can use with different links in a chain analysis. The aim was not to list all of the possible interventions, but to show how targeting different links in a chain could suggest different possible interventions. Once a therapist and client have completed the chain analysis, the next step is to complete a solution analysis to decide how the client can be more effective the next time a similar situation arises. The first step in solution analysis requires the therapist to identify the client's goals, needs, or desires. The therapist and the client both need to be aware of what the client wants to achieve (e.g., to stop cutting, to not yell at his wife, to reduce road rage). Identification of these goals should occur early in therapy and therefore is not needed before every chain. Tying the interventions selected together to the client's personal goals in this way usually increases his or her motivation to follow through.

A solution analysis begins with the therapist and the client reviewing the chain as a whole and discussing possible places for intervention. When the therapist points out every place for intervention, illustrating that there are many opportunities for change, it can generate hope. The therapist may say, "Let's look at our completed chain. I see a lot of options for us in picking a place to intervene or make a change. We could work on thoughts, emotions, your actions, urges, physical sensations, vulnerability factors, the prompting event, or consequences." Next, the therapist asks the client where they would like to target (e.g., a specific thought or a particular emotion).

Once a link to work on is agreed, the therapist and the client brainstorm possible solutions. When brainstorming, possible solutions are not initially evaluated; the focus is on generating as many solutions as possible. When a therapist first introduces solution analysis to a client, they can assist with brainstorming if it appears the client needs help generating solutions and then fade this assistance over time. To increase the number of solutions generated, a therapist can tell the client that at least ten possible solutions need to be generated. When generating solutions, the therapist can give solutions that may seem a little outrageous or silly to prompt the client to think "outside the box" or be more creative. For example, a therapist might suggest that the client sing nursery rhymes in the car if he has difficulty with road rage. Solutions can also include things that the client has tried before, even if they were not successful, and would like to try again with new skills, or try differently.

Once a number of solutions have been generated, the therapist can have the client look at each of them and pick the two that seem like the best options. The therapist should go along with the client's preferences where possible, but also use clinical judgment to make sure that the selections are likely to be effective. Considerations to bear in mind when selecting solutions are those that will be easy to implement (e.g., the client has the needed skills, has access to items needed to do the solution), are most likely to be effective, and are ones the client is willing to do. For each solution, the therapist and the client should evaluate them further and identify obstacles that might get in the way of implementing each one.

After the client chooses a solution, the therapist and the client will troubleshoot the solution to identify obstacles and ways of overcoming them, to increase the likelihood that they will implement the solution and that it will go well. Issues to consider or questions a therapist can ask the client when troubleshooting a solution include:

- Do you know how to do this?
- Do you have the skills you need to do this?
- Do you have access to items you need for this solution? If not, do you have means to get them?
- How likely is it that you would try this solution?
- What might get in the way of you doing this?
- Is there anyone who could help you with this or who could reinforce you for doing this?
- When are you going to try this? What day? What time?

The solution the client has chosen will be the assigned homework for the week. The therapist must follow up on the homework in the next session. Forgetting to do so decreases the likelihood that the client will complete the homework next time. More details on solution analysis and common problems in its execution can be found in Heard and Swales (2016).

Intervening on Common Links

Intervening with common links in a chain is one of the most effective ways of choosing where to intervene. Common links are those that tend to show up across many instances of the same problem behaviour or across instances of different problem behaviours. For example, a client may tend to have similar thoughts or emotions in different situations where the problem behaviour occurs. Targeting or intervening on these common links can give the therapist and client "more bang for the buck" because it will address something that occurs often and across situations.

Some providers like to keep copies of chains and lay them out to review with clients. Through review, they identify common links such as similar thought patterns, urges, or behaviours in different situations. Another way to assess for common links across chains is to use the table presented here. By entering brief information into a table such

Table 13.1   Blank Assessing Common Links handout

Chain 1	Chain 2	Chain 3
Problem Behaviour	Problem Behaviour	Problem Behaviour
Vulnerability factors	Vulnerability factors	Vulnerability factors
Prompting Event	Prompting Event	Prompting Event
Thoughts	Thoughts	Thoughts
Actions	Actions	Actions
Emotions	Emotions	Emotions
Physical sensations	Physical sensations	Physical sensations
Urges	Urges	Urges
Events	Events	Events
Short-term consequences	Short-term consequences	Short-term consequences
Long-term consequences	Long-term consequences	Long-term consequences

as Table 13.1, a therapist and client can easily identify common links. These common links will help the therapist identify key treatment strategies to use. For example, if a client often has distorted thoughts about a situation, cognitive restructuring or cognitive therapy will likely be one of the treatment strategies.

To use Table 13.1, simply enter links into the appropriate categories. Using this method will make it easier to look at categories of behaviour (e.g., thoughts), but will not allow for examining the sequence of events. To focus on sequence, reviewing completed chains as described earlier is most effective. A completed example from the fictional client, Lucy, earlier is presented in Table 13.2 to demonstrate how different behaviours can serve the same function (in this case, avoiding the experience of emotion). In this example, there are a number of common links, such as thoughts (e.g., I'm such a loser) and short-term consequences (e.g., relief). Table 13.2 also shows how consequences from one chain (e.g., harder to sleep at night) also show up in other chains as vulnerability factors (e.g., little sleep the night before).

PRACTICALITIES

When to Do a Chain?

Chain analysis should be used throughout therapy. With a new client, chains should be completed on the most recent and most severe instances of non-suicidal self-injury and suicide attempts. In ongoing therapy, chains are conducted in each session. A helpful format for structuring a session comprises review of the diary card, conducting a chain

Table 13.2 Example of completed Assessing Common Links handout

Chain 1	Chain 2	Chain 3
Problem Behaviour	**Problem Behaviour**	**Problem Behaviour**
Cutting arm with razor blade 2 times on Friday	Sleeping most of the day on Sunday	Drinking until drunk (7 beers) on Wednesday
Vulnerability factors	**Vulnerability factors**	**Vulnerability factors**
Upset from argument with friend Tired	Hungover Hungry	Little sleep the night before Still upset with friends
Prompting Event	**Prompting Event**	**Prompting Event**
Mom yelled at me for not doing chores	Saw pictures on social media of friends at a party I wasn't invited to	Coming home from work and not having any social plans
Thoughts	**Thoughts**	**Thoughts**
"She's always so mean to me." "I can't do anything right." "I'm such a loser." "I just want this to stop."	"My friends hate me." "I'm such a loser." "They wouldn't care if I disappeared."	"I'm such a loser." "Everyone else has things to do." "Why do I suck at everything?"
Actions	**Actions**	**Actions**
Yelled at mom Locked self in bathroom	Cried Posted hurtful comments on picture on social media Threw phone	Looked at social media Cried Watched TV
Emotions	**Emotions**	**Emotions**
Anger Sadness Shame	Sadness Embarrassment Anger	Sadness Anger Shame
Physical sensations	**Physical sensations**	**Physical sensations**
Face was hot Stomach hurt Tense	Face was hot Clenched fists Stomach hurt	Tightness in chest Face was hot Tense all over
Urges	**Urges**	**Urges**
Yell at mom Stop feeling so bad To just die	Yell at friends Say mean things on social media Block friends on social media Stop feeling so bad Stop feeling like a loser Pull the covers over my head and sleep	Not have emotion Escape
Events	**Events**	**Events**
Dad yelled at me while in bathroom Parents arguing	Friend texted to ask me to take down mean comment	None noted in chain

Table 13.2 Continued

Chain 1	Chain 2	Chain 3
Short-term consequences	**Short-term consequences**	**Short-term consequences**
Relief from emotions and physical sensations Decreased negative emotion Less physical tension	Avoid interaction with friends Avoid seeing more comments Keeps me from saying more rude things Relief Less physical tension	Less physical tension Enjoyed TV shows more Felt good physically from being drunk Not as aware of negative emotions
Long-term consequences	**Long-term consequences**	**Long-term consequences**
Parents are more angry Parents trust me less I might have more scars Have to do a chain in therapy Increase likelihood of dying by suicide by accident	Harder to apologize to friends after more time has passed Felt bad about not being productive Parents irritated with me Harder to sleep at night, which makes me vulnerable the next day	Hangover Guilt about drinking Impaired sleep

on the highest target behaviour, completing a solution analysis, rehearsing the chosen solutions, assigning homework of the chosen solution, obtaining commitment, and troubleshooting barriers to implementation.

Tips for Getting Started

When introducing a new task, the therapist needs to properly orient the client to the task. With chain analysis, orienting can include introducing it and discussing the rationale, rehearsing what to do (e.g., going through the chain and what each component is), pointing out how the therapist and client will be doing this together, and stressing how practice will make it easier. Especially with new tasks, it is helpful to offer support while learning. A therapist can do this in a number of ways. As described previously, a therapist can emphasize that chain analysis is a collaborative task that they and the client will work on together. This can be highlighted by sitting side by side with the client while working on the chain. In the beginning, the therapist can ask more questions to elicit information in the chain; they will want to fade out this assistance over time and encourage the client to be asking these questions themselves to figure out the components of the chain (as the eventual goal is for them to be able to complete a chain independently and have a tool to use once therapy is over). Sometimes the hardest part of doing a chain is starting and picking the problem behaviour. When doing a chain on a target behaviour for the first time, it is best to pick either the most recent or most severe instance of the behaviour. These are usually the instances that are most easily remembered. The therapist can also ask the client if there is an instance that sticks out most in their memory.

This is Hard—How Do I Stick With It?

Conducting a behavioural analysis can be difficult for both the client and the therapist. So, how can a therapist keep going when they (as the provider) are having difficulty? Some therapists report that practising doing chains, either with someone else or on their own behaviour, is helpful both before trying it in session or when they have been struggling with them in session. How can a therapist keep going when the client is having difficulty? First and foremost, validate! Chain analysis is a difficult task (as the therapist may know themselves) that requires a lot of effort. Highlighting these facts can be validating for the client and knowing that the therapist understands may help them keep going with the task. In addition, doing chains can be shame-provoking for some clients (imagine discussing a very personal problem that is causing intense difficulty in life and examining it in great, specific detail with another person!). The therapist should check in with the client about their experience during the analysis (e.g., what emotions are they experiencing, what thoughts are they having, etc.) to assess for the occurrence of shame or guilt, if conducting the analysis causes the client to make judgments about him or herself, or if they are experiencing the urge to avoid doing chains.

Clients may find behavioural analysis aversive or punishing (i.e., thinking "I engage in a behaviour that's a problem for me and every time I report it to my therapist, we have to do a chain"). At the same time, an aversive contingency may not be a bad thing; clients sometimes report not engaging in problem behaviours because they did not want to do a chain in session. Provided the therapist ensures that they treat the controlling variables for the behaviour, a temporary cessation in the behaviour as a result of an aversive contingency may provide a valuable therapeutic window that therapists can capitalize on. Conducting analyses of successful behaviours may minimize clients' experiences of shame or a sense of punishment. Analysing success experiences can also help identify what was different and suggest ways of increasing clients' effective behaviours.

To further address the problem of experiencing shame when doing a chain, therapists should ensure that they and their clients describe behaviour in a chain that is factual and non-judgmental. For example, a client may say, "like an idiot, I yelled at her." The client is adding a judgment of himself (an idiot) to his description of his behaviour (yelling). The therapist can highlight this by saying something like, "our goal is to just describe what happened and not judge you for your behaviour. Remember, doing a chain helps us see why this happened and is a way of figuring out something different to do next time." If the client thought of himself as an idiot in the situation that is being chained, the therapist can add that to the chain as a thought, "I thought I was an idiot." Highlighting this as a thought also distinguishes it from fact.

Clients Who Don't Remember or Say "I Don't Know" Often

Chain analysis can be done with clients who have difficulty remembering or often reply to questions with the response "I don't know." Clients who dissociate frequently can

also learn to complete behavioural analyses successfully. While chains are more difficult with those with memory problems, below are some tips on how to proceed more
successfully.

The therapist should first educate the client about memory. The therapist can discuss
with the client the negative impact of stress and high emotional arousal on memory;
therefore, difficulty remembering details about a stressful event or interaction make
sense when the client frequently experiences stress and intense emotions. At the same
time, memory does work in situations where it is not expected to work well. For example, with practice, individuals can remember information from times when they may
have engaged in dissociation. The therapist can also talk about memory as similar to any
other skill; it improves with repeated practice over time. Basically, the therapist's goal is
to highlight that "yes, your experience of having difficulty remembering makes sense
and at the same time, you are able (with practice and effort) to remember more over
time." Being dialectical, the therapist validates the client's experience and shows how
doing chains despite this experience can be effective.

Therapists may need to offer more support and additional prompts for those with
memory difficulties in order to set the stage for a chain (e.g., getting an overall feel of
what happened that day). For example, a therapist can ask questions like:

- When did you wake up that morning?
- What did you do during the day?
- Did you have breakfast?
- Where were you when it happened?
- Who was with you?

Therapists can also offer hypotheses for gaps in memory. For example, a therapist might
say "I wonder if you might have been angry when your friend didn't call you back?"

However, there may be some gaps that the therapist and client will not be able to fill in.
The therapist and client can hypothesize what might have happened, given that the client
might know how he or she would normally think, feel, or act in a similar situation like that,
and the therapist may also have some ideas based on their interactions and knowledge
of the client. These hypotheses can function as good starting points for self-monitoring
homework; the therapist may assign the client to notice if the hypotheses were correct in
the next similar situation or they may want to ask others in their life if this is true.

As clients continue to practice chain analysis, they are training themselves to improve
their skills in remembering. Over time, they will likely find that the gaps are smaller. The
therapist can highlight that remembering is a skill and skills improve with consistent
practice, just like learning a new language or how to play basketball.

In gathering information needed to fill out a chain analysis, therapists may find it
helpful to remember that people are often not very good observers of their own behaviour.
Sometimes things happen too quickly to be noticed. Sometimes clients are emotionally
upset or otherwise too distracted to pay close attention to what is happening. To help clients
report more accurately on their behaviour and its prompting events and consequences,
therapists might consider discussing the diary card as a way to practise self-monitoring.

Different Variations on Doing a Chain—Doing Briefer Chains

Once a client has learned how to analyse behaviour, the therapist can vary the length of chains according to the needs in that session (Koerner, 2010). For example, a therapist can do a brief chain lasting five minutes or so to get a quick assessment of a behaviour. When does it make sense to do a briefer chain? Examples may include:

- When the therapist and client are past the beginning of therapy and the client already knows how to do a chain and understands the main components (and therefore may need less prompting and discussion of what each type of link includes).
- When the therapist has already chained this behaviour a number of times before and has a good idea of the common links in the chain. In this instance, the therapist may want a brief chain to see if the specific instance of behaviour is similar to previous instances of behaviour before moving on to the solution analysis.
- When the behaviour is not a primary target. If a behaviour is important to understand in the moment, but may not be a focus of treatment, the therapist may not wish to devote as much time to a chain.

Using Chain Analysis Outside of Session

When doing chain analysis with a client, in addition to talking with the client in session to better identify different parts of the chain (e.g., prompting events), the therapist can ask the client to complete a chain analysis each time the problem behaviour occurs during the week. If the client completes a chain analysis soon after the problem behaviour occurs, that information is likely to be more accurate than if done much later. When a chain is completed closer in time to the actual behaviour, errors in terms of memory or recall are minimized.

Teaching chain analysis as a tool to use outside of session teaches clients that they can "be their own therapists" once sessions have ended. Using a chain, they can identify a problem behaviour, what prompts it, the links in the chain that highlight what happens after the trigger and before the behaviour, what maintains it, and what makes them more vulnerable to engaging in the behaviour. Armed with this information, they can apply the tools learned in therapy to address different links in the chain.

CONCLUSION

As described, behavioural chain analysis (BCA), or chain analysis, is a critical assessment tool used in DBT. Functional assessment of a problem behaviour allows for identification of all the steps that led to a problem behaviour (i.e., thoughts, emotions, physical sensations, urges, actions, and events) and the consequences that occurred after that maintain the behaviour (i.e., the short-term consequences that reinforce the behaviour) and provide reasons for change (i.e., the long-term consequences one might wish to avoid). Using BCA in conjunction with problem solving strategies, DBT therapists and clients can collaboratively generate solutions in solution analysis. Each link in the chain offers an opportunity for intervention and multiple opportunities for intervention can generate hope. Therapists can teach clients how to use BCA and solution analysis in their own lives. It can be used at a session level to determine next steps for changes (e.g., client trying a new skill) and also at a broader level to identify common links for targeting therapy in general (e.g., using cognitive techniques for judgmental thoughts that are common links across problem behaviours).

KEY POINTS FOR CLINICIANS

- Assessment in general, and behavioural chain analysis (BCA) specifically, is a critical strategy in DBT. Lack of assessment or errors in assessment can lead to difficulties in treatment.

- BCA can function to challenge clients' common experience and belief that events "come out of the blue" and aids clients in learning that emotions, actions, or thoughts result from certain interactions or transactions with the environment.

- BCA can be a validating experience for a client, especially when a client may think they that they are engaging in a problem behaviour simply because "something is wrong" with them. BCA provides understanding of their experience, which can lead to decreased judgments and increased use of skills.

- When doing BCA, the therapist should describe things behaviourally and non-judgmentally, as well as focus on a single instance of a behaviour.

- All components of BCA (e.g., thoughts, emotions, vulnerability factors, or consequences) provide opportunities for intervention.

- When assigning homework generated from solution analysis, the DBT therapist should also use commitment and troubleshooting strategies to increase the likelihood the client will complete the task.

- BCA can be a difficult task for both the client, who may feel shame at discussing problem behaviours, and for the therapist. Practice, non-judgmental language, and validation can ease the difficulty.

REFERENCES

Linehan, M. M., & Dimeff, L. A. (1997). *Dialectical behavior therapy manual of treatment interventions for drug abusers with borderline personality disorder*. Seattle, WA: University of Washington.

Heard, H. L., & Swales, M. A. (2016). *Changing behaviour in DBT: Problem solving in action*. New York: Guilford.

Koerner, K. (2010, November). *Strengthening behavioural analysis and commitment strategies*. Presented at the annual conference of the International Society for the Improvement and Teaching of Dialectical Behaviour Therapy. San Francisco, CA.

Linehan, M. M. (2015). *DBT skills training handouts and worksheets*, 2nd Edition. New York: Guilford Press.

Miller, A. L., Koerner, K., & Kanter, J. (1998). Dialectical behaviour therapy: Part II. Clinical application of DBT for patients with multiple problems. *Journal of Practical Psychiatry and Behavioural Health, 4*, 84–101.

Pryor, K. (1999). *Don't shoot the dog!: The new art of teaching and training*. New York, NY: Bantam.

CHAPTER 14

CONCEPTUAL AND PRACTICAL ISSUES IN THE APPLICATION OF EMOTION REGULATION IN DIALECTICAL BEHAVIOUR THERAPY

CHRISTINE DUNKLEY

HELPING clients to regulate their emotions is a central component of conducting DBT. Linehan (1993) conceptualized problem behaviours, such as self-harm and suicide attempts, were either a result of clients' dysregulated emotions, or direct attempts to avoid or reduce aversive emotional sensations. Linehan's biosocial theory suggests that clients with Borderline Personality Disorder (BPD) experience their emotions much more intensely than the average person, have emotions that are triggered more quickly, and take longer to return to a baseline emotional state. An entire module of skills training is devoted to emotion regulation, supported by updated handouts and worksheets in the 2015 version of the skills manuals (Linehan, 2015a, b). These materials effectively assist the clinician to teach emotion regulation during the first stage of skills enhancement, called the acquisition phase.

The second and third stages of learning the skill are those of strengthening and generalization, which should be carried out via the individual therapy and phone coaching modalities. Given the importance of emotion regulation skills it is vital that therapists continue to reinforce them outside of skills training class. If this goes well, the end result is usually a reduction in actions that clients previously employed to reduce emotional pain. Where emotion-driven problem behaviours persist, it is often because emotion regulations skills are not being properly strengthened and generalized. This chapter focuses on how to enhance the skill of the primary therapist in understanding the concepts of emotion regulation, and to improve his or her confidence in rehearsing and coaching this skill in all the modalities of therapy.

DANGERS OF OVER-COACHING DISTRESS TOLERANCE

Anecdotal evidence from supervisors suggests that during behavioural chain and solution analysis therapists often over-rely on coaching distress tolerance skills. The same may be true within telephone coaching, although these conversations are less likely to be recorded and played in supervision. It is possible that while the Distress Tolerance module is appropriately named, both therapists and clients wishfully misread the title as either Distress Elimination or Distress Reduction.

Why else do therapists prefer to coach distress tolerance skills? Let's say a patient, Emma, calls her therapist to say that she is thinking of harming herself. She recounts how at work that day she was viciously bad-mouthing a colleague without knowing that the victim of her rant was close enough to hear her words. Later she heard that the girl had gone home feeling ill, and that her unkind words had been reported to others in the office. Emma noticed that no one sat with her during break and the person who usually gives her a lift home left early without waiting. Her mind is thinking over these events and her distress is high.

This scenario provides an excellent opportunity for the client to practice emotion regulation. From a mounting emotional storm (e.g., shame, guilt, fear, sadness) she can learn to discern *which* emotion is dominant (e.g., guilt). With help, Emma can work out whether this emotion fits the facts (e.g., she *did* do a hurtful thing, so some guilt is justified). The therapist can coach her to weigh up how much guilt is appropriate (100%? 50%? 30%?) and what she needs to do to problem-solve that warranted part of it (e.g., make a repair to the victim). For excess guilt, Emma can practise "opposite action" and use her wise mind to judge at what point she must stop down-regulating, i.e., her emotion is at the appropriate level. Throughout this exercise she will be strengthening her ability to remember all the different components to opposite action, some of which are biological and some behavioural. She can marvel at the effect that even simple steps such as changing her body posture and facial expression have on the sensations in her body. Her therapist can guide her to notice if her mind leaves the current scenario to revisit all the other times she has felt guilty, and to be mindful of any judgments of herself and others. She can begin to see first-hand how those associations amplify and prolong the intensity of her emotion. Through this painstaking process of investigation, behavioural rehearsal, and evaluation Emma can learn how to approach a guilt-inducing incident without harming herself.

All these coaching actions depend on the busy mental health professional being willing to pick apart a complex emotional experience, remembering the unique signature of each emotion, its function, action urge, and regulatory systems. However, if the clinician shifts attention *away* from the emotion itself and focuses on the *level of distress* it engenders, he or she can bypass all those layers of complexity and prioritize tolerating the distress, usually by urging the client to distract herself. In this scenario Emma might be advised to turn her mind to another activity such as watching a comedy DVD or having a bath with aromatherapy oils. If she engages mindfully enough in the new activity, the distress will be more bearable.

Is it any wonder that the therapist feels drawn to promote this second option? Faced with a patient who is threatening self-harm and who wants relief from emotional pain, taking the simplest route seems logical and appealing. Unfortunately, this is like trying to fix a broken leg by taking an analgesic. The client learns new ways, albeit less harmful ones, to avoid emotion, but in doing so, fails to gain mastery over experiencing emotions. Furthermore, she is not developing the sense of self that comes from being emotionally literate, nor is she understanding what each emotion has to tell her about her values, dislikes, hopes, and disappointments. Not only does the client fail to progress, but the therapist also loses a chance to assist her, through the process. The in-depth walk-through with the client is vital in increasing the *clinician's* confidence in the skill, and in his or her ability to problem-solve obstacles to implementation. These missed opportunities mean that both parties are less likely to turn to emotion regulation in the future.

KNOWING THE EMOTIONS

A truly effective emotion-regulation trainer needs to develop an almost obsessive interest in each emotion, its function, and its action urge. He or she needs to embrace a dialectical approach, which means there is no "one size fits all" strategy. The therapist has to help the client "read" the situation, decipher the emotion, and discern the valence required, then up- or down-regulate as appropriate. The following section describes the main principles of emotion theory.

"E-motions" are designed to Elicit **Motion**, i.e., they are bodily prompts to a particular action. Each emotion evolved to occur in a specific situation, and to prompt the action which more often than not was helpful in those circumstances. Table 14.1 provides a list of the main "families" of emotions, and it is advisable for therapists to get into the habit of using the term "emotion" instead of "feeling" as the latter word has wider connotations. For example, "I *feel* betrayed" might denote an *emotion* of anger, sadness or disgust, plus the *thought* "someone has betrayed me".

Table 14.1 summarizes what Linehan means when she refers to an emotion "fitting the facts" (Linehan, 2015a, b). She points out that sometimes emotions can be

Table 14.1   Emotion functions and action urges

Name	Situation (when the emotion fits the facts)	Function	Action urge
Anger	When blocked in pursuit of a goal or threatened.	To give energy to burst through the obstacle or fight off the threat	To attack.
Sadness	When there is a loss.	(2 stages) 1. Conserve resources to prevent further loss. 2. Mobilize help to retrieve what is lost.	1. To withdraw. 2. To seek or pine for the lost item, situation, or person.
Fear	When life or health is in danger.	To preserve life by avoiding danger.	(2 stages) 1. To avoid or run away. 2. If danger gets too close to avoid, then to freeze until it passes.
Joy	When an activity has potential benefits to health or quality of life.	To maximize gains.	To do more of whatever set off the joy.
Shame	When an action committed carries a risk of expulsion by the group.	To minimize the likelihood of expulsion.	To hide either one's person or one's misdemeanour.
Guilt	When an action committed transgresses group norms, which may have been internalized as a personal moral code or set of values (but is not so great to warrant expulsion).	To maximize the chances of remaining in the group.	To make reparation.
Envy	When another person has a desired advantage in possessions, relationship, situation, or status	To reduce the discrepancy.	To either acquire or destroy the thing that is coveted.
Jealousy	When there is a perceived risk that another person might wish to take or destroy a possession, relationship, situation, or status.	To keep what is precious away from potential rivals.	To jealously guard the precious item, person, status, or situation.
Disgust	When there is a danger of toxic contamination (including social contamination).	To prevent harm from association with toxic substances or morally repugnant behaviours.	To recoil from or repel the potential contaminant.
Interest	When encountering a stimulus with potential to yield further knowledge or benefits.	To expand the potential range of knowledge or benefits.	To attend to, explore, or pursue the interesting stimulus.
Surprise	When encountering a stimulus that is contrary to expectations.	To allow adjustments to accommodate a change in circumstances.	(2 stages) 1. Stop. 2. Reappraise and assimilate the contradictory information.

understandable, but inappropriate to the circumstances. Thus, if a client previously has had few social contacts, then fear of walking into an evening class for the first time is understandable; in reality, however, there is no actual danger.

THE UNIQUE SIGNATURE OF EACH EMOTION

Each emotion is recognized by its distinct combination of features that affect the body (interested readers are referred to handout 5, p. 213 in Linehan, 2015b model for explaining emotions). These features might be grouped into "domains" as follows:

- Temperature
- Facial expression
- Breathing
- Posture
- Gesture
- Muscle tone
- Voice tone
- Actions (or urges to act) within the environment

The signature of each emotion is unique. For example, shame is a "hot" emotion, whereas pure fear is "cold". Anger is associated with tension in the muscle tone, whereas in sadness the body loses rigidity and muscles become floppy. Disgust has a twisted recoiling body posture, but in anger the body posture is square and forward. There is a two-way maintenance cycle between these domains and the intensity of the emotion. Thus, if the patient is coached to physically act opposite to the emotion-specific signature in each domain, the intensity of that emotion will reduce, e.g., within the domain of temperature, an angry patient cooling down will feel marginally less angry, whereas a sad patient warming up will feel marginally less sad. Each domain addressed in this way will down-regulate the intensity by a couple of degrees. Table 14.2 summarizes the unique signatures of the most common emotions therapists help clients learn to regulate during therapy.

There are three essential points for the individual therapist to remember:

1. **Only one emotion can be regulated at a time.** This is why the identification of the emotion is such an important part of DBT (Linehan, 1993, p. 45). Some therapists encourage clients to clump emotions together, by asking "What else were you feeling? What other emotions did you have?" This is likely to overwhelm the client and delay or prevent down-regulation. Where a client describes two or more emotions together, the therapist may ask what the facial expression was like, which is likely to give clues to the most dominant emotion.

Table 14.2 Signature features of emotions

Name	Temp	Facial expression	Breathing	Posture	Gesture	Muscles	Voice	Actions
Anger	Hot	Scrunched brow, jaw clenched, eyes narrowed, lips pursed, intense staring.	Quick, shallow, "huffing and puffing" (at some extreme levels of rage the breathing may become unnaturally slow in preparation for a pre-emptive strike).	Rigid, squaring up to someone or taking a "shrugging off" posture; pointedly turning away.	Chin jutting, fist raising, finger jabbing, stomping, or finger/foot tapping (if the person is struggling to contain rage, the head may be lowered, and eyes narrowed in preparation for a pre-emptive strike).	Tense, clenched.	Raised, accusatory, curt, snappy.	E.g., banging doors, making threats, following the person around.
Sadness	Cold	Downcast eyes, mouth turned down, crying or eyes misting over, eyebrows slant from raised in the centre to low outer edge.	Long sighs or intermittent sobs.	Loose, sagging, lying down or curling up, but without tension in muscles.	Slow movements, dragging body rather than purposeful movement.	Floppy, lack of muscle tension.	Low, slow, breathy, or whiny.	Withdrawing, or seeking out reminders of the lost thing/person.
Fear*	Cold*	Eyes wide, eyebrows pulled towards centre mouth open but pulled down at the corners.	Holding breath or rapid shallow breaths.	Defensive; rigid, making self smaller – pulling limbs inwards, shoulders up. Arms and legs folded over body.	Flinching or shrinking, nail-biting or fingers covering mouth.	Tense, rigid, trembling.	Silent or hushed.	Freezing, becoming inactive, staying indoors, avoiding contacts.
Anxiety* stage 1 of fear	Hot*	Darting eyes under furrowed brow. Novel situations produce wider eyes.	Rapid and shallow.	Escape-ready; shoulders raised limbs tensed but forward. Perching on the end of the seat.	Pacing, fidgeting, hand-wringing, jumpy movements.	Tense.	Intense staccato speech.	Avoiding, checking, reassurance-seeking.

Emotion	Temperature	Face	Breathing	Posture	Movement	Muscle tone	Voice	Behaviour
Joy	Pleasantly warm	Open, smiling, upward-looking, eyebrows raised, cheek muscles raised.	Regular.	Expansive, elongated.	Upward movements, speediness and lightness of step, open hands, clapping, embracing.	Fluid with some tone, but not tense.	Light, musical, varied in tone.	Approaching, seeking out and remaining by the source of joy, or reminders of it.
Guilt	Uncomfortably warm	Lips together but teeth open behind closed lips, head slightly tilted down but eyes up, brows centre-raised.	Slower and into upper chest cavity.	Very slightly shrugged shoulders.	Shrugging, open-handed supplication or hands laid at sides palms up.	Moderate tension.	Restricted, lower in volume, but urgent in tone.	Apologizing, appeasing.
Shame	Hot	Gaze angled diagonally downwards, no eye contact.	Slower and into upper chest.	Head lowered, hiding behind hair or hands.	Curling up, shrinking, turning away.	Droopy, but tensing up on approach by others.	Absent.	Self-denigration or self-accusing, withdrawing or hiding.
Disgust	Cool	Upper lip curled on one side, scrunched nose, turning face to the side.	Breath holding or exaggerated exhaling (heart rate falls in disgust).	Twisted body postures, lack of symmetry in the body.	Recoiling with head or body, tilting head, pointedly looking away.	Tensed stomach muscles, gag reflex in throat.	Scathing or sneering tone.	Recoiling from or repelling something noxious. Being hostile or critical towards the source of the disgust.

(continued)

Table 14.2 Continued

Envy	Hot	Lowered brow, eyes narrow. Lips in a fixed line or "fake smiling".	Even,	Posture is rigid with inhibition of movement	Few gestures as signs of this emotion are often deliberately inhibited.	Muscles are stiff, no fluidity.	Speech may sound forced.	Fantasizing about damaging what the envied person has, or taking actions to acquire or destroy it.
Jealousy	Hot	Scrunched brow, jaw clenched, eyes narrowed, lips pursed.	Shallow, rapid.	Postures enabling scanning of the environment or perceived threat, or standing with hands on hips as if to block others.	"Back off" gestures— hand waving, finger pointing, pushing movements.	Tense.	Slightly raised pitch, sense of urgency in tone.	Standing guard over what is precious, warning others off. Checking for signs or proof of threat.

* Fear may actually be a 2 phase emotion, while the organism can still flee, the emotion is hot with an urge to run, when danger gets too close the blood runs cold and movement is frozen.

2. **One size does not fit all.** It stands to reason that differentiating between emotions is pointless if the same action is taken to reduce each. For example, in the domain of "posture", dropping the shoulders and lowering the chin will de-intensify anger, but where the problem emotion is shame the emotion will intensify via the same actions. Some domains are more important to certain emotions, and less important to others. For example, temperature is less important in disgust, but facial expression (the curl of the upper lip) and posture (the recoiling motion of the body) are vital. In guilt, changing voice tone and inhibiting apologetic gestures is more powerful than changing facial expression. It is important not to confuse de-arousal strategies for emotion regulation.

3. **Emotions should be regulated only to the level of intensity that is appropriate to the circumstances.** A common therapist error is to imply that an emotion should be eradicated, when instead it needs only to be de-intensified. Sometimes this discrepancy in valence is referred to as the emotion being "unwarranted by degree". Here, too much down-regulation may lead the client to assume that the therapist lacks understanding because the warranted part of the emotion has been invalidated. Just as an emotion can be too strong, it can also be too weak for the situation, e.g., finding out a friend has defrauded you out of your life savings, and experiencing "slight disappointment".

DISCERNING THE APPROPRIATE LEVEL
FOR AN EMOTION

The emotion regulation skills are aptly named—"regulation" being the ability to move the emotion up and down on a scale, much as one might alter the temperature on a central-heating thermostat. To do this the client must be able to work out how much of the emotion is appropriate in each situation. For example, here are some scenarios that may involve varying degrees of guilt:

> Forgetting to send a card for a friend's birthday.
> Forgetting her birthday having previously agreed to arrange a party for her.
> *Deliberately* "forgetting" to arrange the party in order to save work.
> Having sex with her partner.

Regulating the emotion relies on being able to discern two levels of the emotion. Firstly, how much guilt is currently being experienced? Secondly, how much of that guilt is valid? When helping clients with personality disorder, it is more helpful to validate at Level 5—normative validation. So, while it is *understandable* (Level 4 validation; Linehan, 2015) that arranging a party is quite an ordeal for someone with mental health issues, it is *normal* (V5) to feel guilty if the promise to do it is forgotten, and to

feel even more guilty if the "forgetting" was intentional. However, a person who deliberately "forgets" to organize a friend's birthday may be experiencing too little guilt, and
to reach culturally acceptable norms the therapist may need to help to up-regulate the
emotion. Meanwhile, other slights pale into insignificance if the person is sleeping with
her friend's partner.

In the following example, anger has cropped up as a link in the chain of a self-harming
behaviour. Miriam's ex-partner Kevin promised to repay a loan so that she can put a
deposit on her new rental apartment. When Kevin turned up protesting that he does
not have the cash, Miriam noted that he was wearing brand new boots. The therapist
is going to help Miriam work out what level of anger might be appropriate, and in the
second extract will show how to regulate to that level.

Therapist: So, is that when your urge to cut yourself was highest?

Miriam: It was after he had gone and I was just thinking about it. He just makes me
so mad, he has money for boots—MY money, but now I might lose the apartment
because he hasn't paid me back.

Therapist: So, did you correctly identify at the time that the emotion was anger?

Miriam: Yes, I knew it was anger, and that I just wanted to get rid of that horrible
feeling somehow.

Therapist: So, if you had been able to regulate your anger on that day, do you think
your urge to cut would have gone up or down?

Miriam: Definitely down

Therapist: Ok, let's see if we can get it down by rehearsing now. First, we have to
decide whether the anger fits the facts. Were you blocked in pursuit of a goal or
threatened?

Miriam: Yes, the threat is losing the flat, and I am blocked from paying the deposit.

Therapist: Excellent. Next, we have to decide how much anger on a 0 to 100 scale
you think is appropriate for this incident.

Miriam: 100%, because my problem was ALL his fault.

Therapist: Ok, so are you saying this is the most anger-provoking thing Kevin has
ever done, and is likely to ever do?

Miriam: No way! He is always doing stuff like this.

Therapist.   Then where does it sit in the list of things he has done or might do? Top?
Bottom? Middle? Higher? Lower?

Miriam: Hmm ... he's pretty infuriating. Maybe half way?

Therapist: So, would you want to be about half as angry as you are capable of
being? Check in with your wise mind, how angry would a *wise* person have been
about this?

Miriam: I'm not sure, maybe not at all?

Therapist: Well, that wouldn't be very wise—if you never have any anger when
people let you down, they might end up taking advantage of you, but it sounds like
you think a wise person might be less angry than 50%.

Miriam: Well yes, I suppose so. He winds me up all the time, so I don't want to
waste my time on thinking about him.

Therapist: But we want to keep some anger, right? Because this is how we allow our
emotion to guide us.

Miriam: Yes... I dunno ... About 30% then?

Therapist: OK, but remember I'm not here to tell you the level. You have to keep working it out until it *feels* wise to you. Consult your wise mind, say to yourself, "what's the most appropriate level of anger to have here, that would not be over the top, but not just giving in?" Your anger is trying to help you, we don't want to ignore it—after all he *has* let you down. But too much anger means when something even worse happens we don't have an increased level of anger to show. It's like if you always shout at your kids no matter what they do, then they might as well be naughty—they will get the same level of anger from you regardless.

Miriam: (Pondering) Er... Well I think 40% is actually about right—it is a big deal if I lose the apartment.

Therapist: Great—and how much anger did you have on the day?

Miriam: 90%!

Therapist: So now I am going to help you to practise getting it down, but when we get to the "40% angry" level we have to stop and work out how to represent that level to Kevin in a firm, but wise, way.

Miriam: Ok, that sounds good, because I don't see why he should just get off the hook.

Therapist: Neither do I. So, let's practise some down-regulating or YOU will be the one taking all the blame for angry behaviour, when some of your crossness with Kevin was perfectly legitimate.

Identifying Justified Emotional Intensity: Strategies to Shape Clients' Skills

In teaching clients strategies to shape their skills in how to identify justified emotional intensity, it is important for the therapist to interact with the client in an open and understanding way. The following list shows three ways in which a therapist can provide support to a client who is learning to shape his or her emotion regulation skills.

1. The therapist acknowledges a degree of the client's emotion is justified, which is validating for the client. This type of validation fosters willingness as the client can see that the therapist is not simply dismissing the emotional response.

2. The therapist encourages the client to work out the appropriate level of the emotion without telling the client what it should be. Evoking "wise mind" is important for the treatment of "identity disturbance" in BPD. It also allows for personal differences in emotional expression while still attempting to put some parameters around what is considered acceptable.

3. Coaching the skill of discernment is time-consuming, and the therapist must appreciate that this is time well spent. When the client begins to self-regulate emotional responses to situations, it makes a huge difference to her behaviour when the client physically experiences an emotional surge.

ACTING OPPOSITE IN EACH DOMAIN

Again, using the example of Miriam, the therapist demonstrates the art of regulation—moving the emotion down to the appropriate level using Opposite Action, and problem-solving the valid part of the emotion.

> **Therapist:** So, after Kevin left you had the urge to cut yourself, and you correctly identified that you were angry at 90%, where 40% would have been more the level that your wise mind tells you is appropriate. So, we want to get the unwarranted anger down. Do you remember the domains we talked about—the ways in which the anger plays out in your body?
>
> **Miriam:** (Unsure) Er … maybe …
>
> **Therapist:** Here is a prompt card with them all written on. (*Gives card with this list on it: Temperature, Facial expression, Breathing, Posture, Gesture, Muscle tone, Voice tone, Actions within the environment.*) Now, the first one is temperature. So, what was your temperature that day?
>
> **Miriam:** I was really hot.
>
> **Therapist:** And so … ?
>
> **Miriam:** Er… I should cool myself down. I could have opened the window and let in some fresh air. Or had a cold drink from the fridge.
>
> **Therapist:** Or both. You can also keep a cold flannel in the fridge and put it on your neck or wrists.
>
> **Miriam:** I suppose so.
>
> **Therapist:** Write yourself a note to do that when you get home… (hands her pen and paper). What's the next domain?
>
> **Miriam:** Facial expression (laughs). Yes, if you'd seen my face you'd have known immediately how I was feeling.
>
> **Therapist:** Well it turns out there is a two-way message going from your body to your face and your face back to your body. If you change your face to relax the muscles and let your jaw hang loose a bit, you will actually feel less angry. So, scrunch up your face like you did that day, and try to get a bit angry here with me now—think about those boots! Then we will practise smoothing out the lines on your forehead with your fingertips, wiggling your eyebrows, allowing your jaw to relax. While we're at it, let's work on your body posture too, as that is another domain—lean back in your chair a bit more, and let your shoulders drop, yes, that's right, now do those face things that we just talked about.
>
> **Miriam:** (Follows the instructions.)
>
> **Therapist:** What do you notice?
>
> **Miriam:** Well, I'm definitely not as angry—but isn't that just the passage of time that makes it go down?
>
> **Therapist:** Ok, let's see—sit up and tense all your muscles, frown really hard and clamp your teeth and lips together. Clench your fists while you remember what Kevin did, and let's notice what happens to the anger.
>
> **Miriam** (Follows instructions) Yes. I can feel it go up when I purse my lips, and hold myself tensely. And again when I frown. I can just picture those new boots in my mind's eye.

Therapist: This is so important, Miriam, I want you to have absolute confidence that if you need to get anger down you can do it. Now here's a big domain for anger—your breathing. How was it on the day? Show me.

Miriam: (Starts to breathe heavily and rapidly.)

Therapist: Ok, now you are building up your breath inside like an explosion is on its way, I want you to lengthen your outbreath as though you are blowing up a balloon, long, deep breaths. And lay back in your seat again, shoulders down. Face smoothed out, just like before.

Miriam: (Follows instructions) That does feel better.

Therapist: Are we down to 40% angry yet? Remember we are not going to take this all the way to zero. You have to listen to your emotions or they come back stronger. We just want to get to a level of crossness, rather than complete fury.

Miriam: Yes, it is definitely lower (Miriam looks at the "domains" card that the therapist has given to her). What does it mean when it says "actions in the environment" on the card?

Therapist: That's things you do that might make it worse, like if you chased him down the street, shouting, or if you were stomping around your kitchen banging cupboard doors.

Miriam: I did do a bit of that.

Therapist: Then the anger would stay around longer or get bigger. So, what would Opposite Action look like?

Miriam: Walking more slowly, I guess, and moving things gently. But it would be so hard!

Therapist: I agree. So, tell me what you are thinking because whatever it is it will make perfect sense, and I might be able to help you with it.

Miriam: That he is getting away with it while I am here without the cash.

Therapist: Are you thinking that if you cut yourself or remain furious then he will suffer in some way, maybe by feeling guilty? Or that you would keep it up till you see him again?

Miriam: When you say it like that … no, he won't suffer at all.

Therapist: OK, let's carry on getting it down then. What about "voice tone", which is another domain and includes the "tone" you use in your head.

Miriam: What … ? Do you mean saying to myself, "he is SUCH a LOSER".

Therapist: (Laughs) Yes that would do it. That would pump the anger up a notch.

Miriam: (Wails) But I CAN'T just be nice about him!

Therapist: Of course not! We have to keep our 40% anger. So, try making a mindful statement to yourself that sums up the situation as accurately as possible. I call this "touching your truth". Keep the judgments out of it and just state the facts. The best statements are dialectical, so they say, "on the one hand this, and on the other hand that". Speaking it either in your head or out loud can really help reduce emotion.

Miriam: This is hard. OK. "On the one hand I am so mad at him for buying new boots when he owes me money. On the other hand, at least he came around and I could see he felt bad about it".

Therapist: Does that work for you?

Miriam: Not really, it feels like I'm just making allowances. I don't think it was that big of him to come around. He might have just felt bad because he knew I wouldn't be lending him any more money.

Therapist: Then change the statement. Try using the word angry instead of "mad". It might have a better down-regulating effect.

Miriam: "On one hand I am angry with him for buying boots when he owes me money. On the other hand, I'd rather it was boots than drugs, and he is not as aggressive these days."

Therapist: Well? How was that?

Miriam: I guess I was less angry. But am I just letting him off the hook?

Therapist: If we don't work out a way for you to tell him how cross you are about this, then yes. But when you were alone that evening, after he'd gone, did it affect him at all whether you were FURIOUS or a bit cross?

Miriam: No, he wouldn't even know either way.

Therapist: Exactly, so we need to put you back in control of your emotion levels, so that you can decide on an appropriate course of action, and not end up harming yourself. Have another go at the statement, and this time you can include your intention to take this up with him again.

Miriam: "On one hand I am angry with him for buying boots and not paying what he owes, and I will phone him again on Tuesday when he gets paid. On the other hand, at least it was boots not drugs, and he is less aggressive these days."

Therapist: How was that?

Miriam: That felt so much better. I can't believe that just talking it out loud like that has such an effect.

Therapist: It's because you are acting opposite in the other domains, too. One of the action urges in anger is to attack people, so when you add in your dialectical statement you are also acting a little bit kind—the opposite of attack. Remember that you need to keep checking whether your emotion regulation efforts are working or not by trying them out, and if it isn't working you have to change something and try again. If you do this you will get more confident in your ability to reduce emotion without resorting to hurting yourself.

PROBLEM-SOLVING IN EMOTION REGULATION

For the justified part of the emotion the client must devise a plan of action and follow it through. In the example above, Miriam must work out how to get her money for the deposit on the apartment. She may need help to come up with creative solutions. The following list shows some examples that Miriam can use to devise a plan of action:

- Use her DEAR MAN and FAST skills (Linehan, 2015, Chapter 8) to negotiate a repayment plan with Kevin.
- Plan to reissue her request to Kevin on payday, before he has spent the money.
- Sell some of Kevin's motorcycle accessories that he left with her.
- Accept that Kevin is unlikely to come up with the money and attempt to borrow or earn the money elsewhere.

- Find a cheaper alternative to the new apartment.

The emotion is there to alert Miriam to being blocked in pursuit of her goal. However, both clients and therapists can sometimes mistakenly assume that getting rid of the emotional sensation is the primary goal, and that once it becomes bearable the job is done. If the *justified* part of the emotion is ignored, the client never learns to appreciate its message about something important about themselves or their situation. A strong desire to down-regulate painful emotional states is what subtly pushes clients and therapists towards the distress tolerance skills. However, over-relying on these techniques—and, in particular, distraction—will result in the client presenting in a characteristic way, which may include:

1. Reporting frequently that "skills don't work".
2. Showing no change in their circumstances, no movement towards a "life worth living".
3. Complaining that his or her level of distress is actually increasing, rather than reducing.
4. Seeking more "solutions" that numb the body—e.g., an increase in prescription drugs, alcohol, food-restriction, over-the-counter medication, street drugs, or excessive sleeping.

If these signs persist well into treatment, the therapist should strongly suspect that the client is failing to solve problems that should legitimately be addressed, e.g. accommodation, employment, relationships (particularly loneliness), finance, legal issues, or unresolved physical health problems, and that the client is not recognizing that the emotions accompanying these problems are justified. Landes (this volume) and Heard and Swales (2015) outline the principles behind finding and rehearsing appropriate solutions.

Solutions that Require Simultaneous Tracking

One reason that therapists sometimes neglect solutions to ongoing or longer-term problems is because it appears to conflict with the moment-by-moment nature of a chain and solution analysis. Thus, solutions that the client can implement at the time of the target behaviour take priority. For example, if a patient has self-harmed because she is lonely on a Friday evening, the primary solutions will revolve around how to manage the sadness of not being with anyone that day, how to gainfully occupy the evening, perhaps seeking company, how to be mindful of harmful thoughts ("nobody cares about me"), and how to avoid contact with any harmful implements. Opposite action will help diminish the intensity of the sadness.

The therapist must then create a "simultaneous track" for the client to follow over a period of days or weeks to solve the bigger problem of ongoing loneliness. This will involve "friend-recruiting" activities, e.g., checking for social groups or classes in the local area, finding out how to join, getting herself to go along, introducing herself by name to other participants. The tasks are broken down into what needs to be done each day or couple of days, over perhaps two or three weeks. Therapists can do the tracking on the current diary card or create a new diary card to keep a record of progress towards the desired level of friendship. This "solution tracking" goes on alongside the tracking of dysfunctional behaviour on the regular diary card.

This is an inherently dialectical approach; the client needs better interpersonal skills in order to recruit and retain friends, and yet needs friends to practise her fledgling interpersonal skills. Progress will not be linear, but rather takes a corkscrew trajectory, where the client circles towards and away from the goal, encountering and solving fresh obstacles with the help of the therapist. At the end of the individual session each week the client and therapist should monitor the simultaneous track, and if the client has any intense problems on this journey, they are likely to surface in the target hierarchy. The main point is that the question "should we focus on solving the micro problems or the bigger problems?", should be answered with "both, simultaneously."

Summary of Strategies for Regulating Unjustified Emotions or Emotions Unwarranted by Intensity

1. The therapist teaches the client to retain the level of emotion that fits the facts.
2. The therapist assumes that, despite learning the skill in skills class, the client will not know how to put the skill into practice. It is only when the client can demonstrate the skill in front of the therapist that it will be evident that the skill can be used in daily life.
3. A prompt card is used to remind the client of the domains they have to alter to down-regulate the unjustified part of the emotion.
4. The therapist helps brainstorm practical solutions for the part of the emotion that is warranted.
5. The client is encouraged to follow a shaping protocol (utilized across all the skills, not just emotional regulation) when regulating the emotion:
   - Employ the skill
   - Evaluate
   - Adjust
   - Re-employ (re-evaluate, re-adjust)
   - Start again.
   - Continue until you get as close as you can to the desired result.
6. The client may need to create a simultaneous track to address problems that will take time and effort to solve.

REGULATING APPROPRIATE SADNESS

Many therapists struggle to help with regulating sadness because it is often highly appropriate. Problems arise when the clinician tries to reduce the emotion without attending to its valid content. In the following scenario, Alison is an adolescent who has been prevented by her foster-mother from accepting a party invitation from her new friend Holly; the argument is that Holly is a stranger who might lead Alison astray. Alison had urges to harm herself, and her therapist is conducting a chain and solution analysis.

Therapist: Well done that you did not actually cut yourself, but it sounds as though when you had that urge, it was because you wanted to change something—what was cutting yourself going to improve for you?

Alison: It would have made me feel better—I just felt awful.

Therapist: Can we work out what that emotion was?

Alison: Well, I was so mad at them for not letting me go out, just because they've never met Holly—they have no idea what it's like to be at a new school. She might never ask me again, just because of them.

Therapist: So, we're trying to work out the emotion. Were you clenching your jaw and frowning, with your muscles all tense?

Alison: No, I was curled up on the bed, sobbing.

Therapist: Ah, OK. Well, I could be wrong, but it sounds like you were maybe feeling sad?

Alison: Yes, because I really, really wanted to go to the party.

Therapist: That makes complete sense to me—you had just met Holly and were really pleased to get the invitation, and then you were not able to go. So, do you remember how we down-regulate sadness?

Alison: Is it to try and cheer yourself up, like play a comedy DVD or something?

Therapist: No, not to start off with, because emotions are messages to us, and we have to read the message and work out what it is telling us. So, what do we know about sadness? When does it fit the facts? When there is a . . .?

Alison: Loss.

Therapist: Yes! So, what had you lost in that moment?

Alison: I wasn't able to go to the party.

Therapist: Absolutely right. So, at that level the sadness did "fit the facts". You did have a loss in that very moment—you were not at the party. So, what's the first thing that sadness programmes us to do when we have lost something?

Alison: (Shrugs.)

Therapist: It helps us to not make any further losses, so it gets us to hole up and make sure we conserve our resources. So, question one in sadness is how can I be sure my losses don't get any bigger? Was there anything you could have done to prevent more losses, and I'm thinking particularly with Holly.

Alison: I did text and say, "sorry I can't come".

Therapist: Did that help you to feel connected to Holly? Your sadness is telling you she's an important person in that moment. You need to satisfy the emotion that all is not lost with Holly. What else could you have said?

Alison: (Grumpily) That I would sneak out and come anyway.

Therapist: (Laughs) Well, you're in the right ball-park! Maybe something like, "I'm grounded, and I even thought of sneaking out, but I'd get caught". How would you react to that if you were in Holly's shoes?

Alison: I'd be disappointed, but at least it doesn't sound like a brush-off.

Therapist: The thing is, if you weren't sad about it, then after you had texted "can't come" to Holly, you would just have got on with your evening, but the sadness is saying, "Hey, this matters", so it is actually trying to help you. If you listen to it, then it is prompting you to minimize that loss if you can. The trick is to say something that keeps the relationship friendly, using your GIVE skills. Perhaps add in that you would see her on Monday. If you had sent that kind of text would your sadness have gone up, or down?

Alison: If I had said I would see her on Monday, then yeah, it would go down. But then I think, but she might never give me another invitation ...

Therapist: Here's where you need to watch out, because this is an "unmindful thought". If you are not mindful, then your brain starts to predict all the possible losses you might have to face in your entire relationship with Holly, or even with other people. If we get on that track then before we know where we are, our sadness is huge and unmanageable. So, remember to keep it to the loss of that moment. You can say to yourself, "I am sad that I am not at the party tonight", and if your mind wanders to other sad things, gently guide it back to this moment. Learning to be sad mindfully is a great skill. Try saying that mindfully.

Alison: "I'm sad because I am not at the party tonight."

Therapist: Now the next phase of sadness is about getting support for yourself. As a species, humans are designed to rally round when something is lost, to pool our resources, and help recover whatever we can. There are a number of ways to draw in this help. One way is to "send out a distress flare" by crying big ploppy tears! Tears catch the light and tell people—*I need help.* You were crying on your bed, but we need to forge some kind of alliance when we're sad. Who could you speak to or call?

Alison: Nobody, they were all at the party! And I would just look like a loser if I rang then, while they were there.

Therapist: It could be true that at 8:00pm on a Friday, there weren't many people you could call. So, either you can work down a list of people and find someone NOT at the party—like your aunt Meg, for instance (Alison makes a scornful face). Ok, here's the thing. If there really isn't anyone you can connect with when you are sad, you can do something I sometimes do if I am working away from home and something upsets me. I think of one of my friends or family members, and imagine how I am going to tell them about this incident the next time I see them. I imagine what I will say to them, and what they will say to me. It's kind of getting some comfort from them, but in my imagination—and it works really well if you can predict what that person is most likely to say. Do you have a friend who you think would have been sympathetic?

Alison: Amy. She had already texted to say "I can't believe you're not coming".

Therapist: So, you're in your room lying on your bed and you think, "*next time I see Amy I am just gonna tell her what a horrid time I had while they were all at the party*". You can really ham it up if you like, tell her the worst bits—like, '*and it was really freezing in my room, so I was just sitting there in my duvet drinking cocoa like an old lady and thinking of you all having a great time ... .*" Can you picture her face?

Alison: Yes, she'd laugh if I said that, but in a good way, I guess. She'd say, "Ali, you saddo, the party was lame". Even if it was really good she'd say that 'cos she calls everything lame.

Therapist: If you can picture any response then you are doing a good job of conjuring her up in your mind. This is the skill of staying connected to people even if they're not there. But it also means you have to follow up—you have to seek out Amy when you go back to school and tell her that thing. So, if you had made plans to tell Amy your woes while you were on your bed, do you think you would have felt more sad or less sad?

Alison: A bit less.

Therapist: Now we have to make sure that in the presence of some comfort, even if it is the imaginary kind, you don't go overboard in being sad. We want the right amount of sadness for missing *this* party, *this* evening; we don't want to trip into TRAGIC sadness. How much sadness would be appropriate? Is it the saddest thing that could possibly happen?

Alison: No. I never said it was.

Therapist: So, we want to get just the right amount of crying. Do you think on that day your sadness was too big or not big enough for missing the party that evening?

Alison: Probably too big. I was thinking about a lot of other sad things too.

Therapist: That's normal, but really unhelpful, so remember to be mindful. So, I'd advise on any sadness to try and acknowledge the loss and cry some willing tears, and not block them or hold your breath or distract yourself, for at least seven minutes. Really accept that you are sad about this one loss in this moment. Proper wet tears if you can get them, and comfort yourself while you cry, because it *is* a sad thing. If you really let yourself relax into those tears, and don't add in any other sadness you will probably be done long before the seven minutes are up.

Alison: I can cry for hours.

Therapist: But probably you block and fight the tears, and then escalate to include all the other things you might be sad about.

Alison: Yes. I did that.

Therapist: Now, when you want to stop crying, and this only works when you have allowed yourself to be appropriately sad, then you can act opposite to sadness. Sadness is cold, so warm yourself up. It's a still emotion, so get yourself moving, and it prompts withdrawing so seek out other people. You lose your appetite, so get some food to eat, and your breathing is in big sighs, so shorten them. Your muscles go floppy so tense them up, and your posture is all curled up so get yourself upright and take up as much space as you can. It's hard to be sad if you are punching the air! Now only do this when you have done all the other stuff, or your sadness will come back stronger. So, let's have a practice at those things and I will coach you in what to do, and then you can see how well they work.

Summary: Strategies for Therapists for Treating Appropriate Sadness

1. Before trying to down-regulate sadness, the therapist explores the ways in which it is valid.

2. The therapist explains the function of sadness before attempting to regulate it.

3. The therapist helps the client to conceptualize the sadness mindfully—what is lost in THIS moment.

4. At no point does the therapist suggest distraction or suggest that the main aim is to reduce distress. Instead, the client is encouraged to problem-solve the loss of the moment.

5. The client is only taught how to down-regulate an inappropriate level of sadness when she has understood how to acknowledge and problem-solve the warranted part of it.

6. The client is encouraged to check out how the strategies might have affected her level of sadness during the critical period.

UP-REGULATING EMOTIONS

Most of the problems that clients experience with emotion regulation can be attributed to an excess of emotion. Occasionally there is a need for the therapist to coach the client how to up-regulate an emotion when it does not appear at an appropriate time. Some clients have become so detached from their emotional experiencing that they do not register any characteristics of what would be a perfectly normal response. The following dialogue shows an example of the therapist coaching the up-regulation of justified anger.

Therapist: So you went in to your neighbour Carrie's flat, and walking past the bedroom door you saw your jacket on the bed, the one you thought you must have left somewhere?

Elsa: Yes, it's quite an unusual design and my eye was drawn to it.

Therapist: And you confronted her?

Elsa: I just said, "is that my jacket, the one you knew I've been looking for"? She just shrugged.

Therapist: And at that moment what was the emotion?

Elsa: I don't remember feeling anything really. These things happen, I guess.

Therapist: I could imagine feeling pretty angry if it turned out one of my friends had been taking my things without permission, or very sad at the thought they would do that.

Elsa: (Jokily) Perhaps you should see a therapist and they could help you with that!

Therapist: (Seriously) I know you are taking a light-hearted approach to this, but I'm worried that the urges you had to self-harm later might be as a result of not really having any emotion about this event. If you HAD experienced some emotion right then, which do you think would have been most justified—it's a very personal thing—Anger? Sadness? Disgust?

Elsa: What's the point? It doesn't get you anywhere.

Therapist: Too much emotion can be a problem, it's true, but none at all is just as problematic. It makes it look as though what Carrie did is ok with you. Emotions communicate to others about us, and actually help in the relationship. So, which emotion do you think you might have felt more strongly?

Elsa: I think what she did was really out of order, so if I'd felt anything, it would probably have been anger.

Therapist: Just think right now of the moment you made that discovery—picture yourself back there. Say to yourself, "She is SO out of order". Now is there any sensation in your body?

Elsa: (Looks uncomfortable) Not really, look—I absolutely don't want to lose my rag. My dad used to get really violent when he was angry. I hate violence. It made us all nervous wrecks.

Therapist: It makes perfect sense that you would be reluctant to feel that anger, given your history, and nobody likes feeling angry with a friend. But some anger was appropriate here, and blocking or ignoring it could result in that tense feeling later, that you sought to relieve by cutting your arm. So, let's look at your fear of being angry and apply the same emotion regulation protocol: does it fit the facts? Is your dad here now? Or is there a real likelihood that you might physically attack Carrie?

Elsa: No. Dad's long gone, and I have never been violent.

Therapist: So, your fear doesn't fit the facts, and we should act opposite to that fear and allow a little anger about this situation. If there is a danger of the anger going too high then we will down-regulate it—do you remember how to do that?

Elsa: I remember learning this in group—relaxing all your muscles and smoothing out your forehead, and leaning back in the chair? There are some breathing things, too, right? This doesn't apply to me though. I'm good at not getting angry. I don't do anger.

Therapist: It's possible that when you say to yourself "these things happen" and distract yourself, as you did by going home and playing your computer game, you kind of disconnect the angry feeling from what set it off. Then, later on, you have this tension that you don't recognize as being related to Carrie taking the jacket. When you allow yourself to feel angry, you might start thinking, "this is out of control". We want to allow some sensations of anger without them going too high, so those physical strategies you mentioned will help. Now here with me replay that moment that you challenged her about the jacket and she shrugged it off.

Elsa: "That was so out of order ... "

Therapist: Say it like you really mean it and furrow your brow a little so you feel more cross. Sit up, get a bit more tension in your body. Think about what you would want to say to her, right there and then.

Elsa: (Raises her voice a little) "This is SO out of order, I can't believe you have got my jacket and have absolutely nothing to say for yourself" (Starts to cry).

Therapist: Well done. Now, when you made the statement did you feel some anger in your body?

Elsa: Yes, I think it was justified to say that to Carrie.

Therapist: And then when you started to cry, did you feel sad? Or were they angry tears?

Elsa: I was really sad, because she betrayed my trust.

Therapist: And when you felt sad, did the anger go down?

Elsa: Yes, the tension went.

Therapist: It's OK if that happens. It's quite common, and we don't need to worry about that, providing you express that crossness first. If you had gone straight to being sad without letting Carrie know there was anger in there, too, then that would have been an issue, but getting angry and then crying is a much more healthy way to dissipate tension than cutting yourself. Even those few moments of accurate expression of the emotion is helpful. Over time, we will look to stretch out the amount of anger you can tolerate without dissolving into tears. But for a first attempt, well done! You got angry, you expressed it appropriately, then you got sad and cried, and nobody got harmed. We will look out for other practice opportunities until anger is no longer something to fear.

Summary: Strategies for Up-regulating Emotional Responses

1. The therapist identifies a situation in which an appropriate emotional response failed to appear.
2. The therapist instructs the client to display some of the features of the emotion.
3. Any fears the client has are addressed using the same protocol—does it fit the facts?
4. The client is asked to replay the scenario, including the emotional response that was previously missed out.
5. The therapist validates any legitimate responses.
6. The learning points (e.g., that the emotion was experienced and no bad things happened) are highlighted at the end of the behavioural rehearsal.

CONCLUSION

People who regularly experience very painful emotions will naturally seek solutions that reduce the unpleasant bodily sensations, and may even resort to harming or destroying the body, wherein lies the seat of their pain. Once a person has gone down the route of suicidality and self-harming behaviour (or other body-numbing strategies), both the ability to decipher the function of the emotion as well as how to address the issue it is bringing to their attention is lost.

As if this loss of problem-solving ability were not enough, the emotion itself will not— as the client wishes—simply disappear, but it will instead return with greater urgency in an attempt to get the message through. The repeated blocking of incoming emotional signals eventually renders the client a victim of relentless overwhelming sensations. At this point it appears to the client as though the emotions meld into each other, and the entire experience simply becomes distressing.

In some cases, the therapist is tempted to respond not to the discrete emotion the client is having, but to the distress it produces, and seeks to adopt the quickest method to reduce it: distraction. This merely perpetuates the cycle. Instead, the therapist should help the client to meticulously unpick each emotion, work out its function, and alter the intensity of it (up or down) until it is within the appropriate range. With practice, the client becomes truly mindful of each emotion as it occurs, harnesses the problem-solving features of it, and naturally dissipates the remainder. They are then able to describe themselves as having the skill of emotion regulation.

KEY POINTS FOR CLINICIANS

- Each emotion is designed to elicit a different action.
- Each emotion has a unique signature in a number of domains; temperature, facial expression, breathing, muscle tone, posture, gesture, voice tone, actions in the environment.
- Emotion regulation involves a number of steps that can be coached through behavioural rehearsal:
  - Identify the emotion.
  - Ascertain what level, if any, would fit the facts.
  - Up- or down-regulate the emotion by paying attention to the domains of that emotion, until it reaches an appropriate level.
  - Remember to do what is appropriate for the amount of the emotion that does actually fit the facts.
- Coaching distress tolerance or de-arousal strategies will not strengthen the client's emotion regulations skills.
- An over-reliance on distress tolerance at the expense of emotion regulation may result in clients failing to make anticipated progress in therapy.

REFERENCES

Heard, H. L., & Swales, M. A. (2016). *Changing behavior in DBT: Problem solving in action.* New York: Guilford Press.

Linehan, M. M. (1993). *Cognitive-behavioral treatment of borderline personality disorder.* New York: Guilford Press.

Linehan, M. M. (2015a). *DBT skills training manual*, 2nd Edition. New York: Guilford Press.

Linehan, M. M. (2015b). *DBT skills training: Handouts & worksheets*, 2nd Edition. New York: Guilford Press.

CHAPTER 15

DBT AS A SUICIDE AND SELF-HARM TREATMENT

Assessing and Treating Suicidal Behaviours

LARS MEHLUM

CHRONIC SUICIDALITY AND SELF-HARM— CHALLENGING, BUT POSSIBLE TO TREAT

DIALECTICAL behaviour therapy (DBT) was designed specifically for the treatment of "chronically parasuicidal individuals with Borderline Personality Disorder" (BPD) (Linehan, 1993). "Chronically parasuicidal" meant repetitive "intentional, acute self-injurious behaviour with or without suicidal intent, including both suicide attempts and self-mutilating behaviours." The terminology of suicidal and self-harming behaviours has changed over the years; currently we would label this type of behaviour as repetitive or chronic self-harm—again embracing both suicidal and non-suicidal self-injurious (NSSI) behaviour (Mehlum, 2009). While terminology has changed, the clinical population in question remains the same. These patients present themselves in equally high numbers at emergency departments at general hospitals after having self-harmed (NICE, 2009). They are often experiencing suicidal crises for which they are frequently admitted to acute psychiatric care, and they may engage in countless episodes of self-cutting or other NSSI as attempts to regulate painful and overwhelming emotions. Although our knowledge on self-harming behaviour has increased over the last three decades, healthcare providers still perceive these behaviours in their patients as extremely stressful, and this will sometimes lead to anger, anxiety, and even burnout. Ill-advised therapeutic interventions and hospitalizations, ineffective practice, and treatment failure may easily be the result. Many patients with BPD and chronic self-harming behaviour are only offered short-term generic or crisis-oriented treatments, but such approaches to the treatment have the potential of creating self-confirming vicious circles that reinforce dysfunctional behaviours at the cost of patients' prognosis with regard to further suicidal behaviours. The risks are indeed high; 60–70% of people with BPD attempt suicide at some point in their life (Oldham, 2006) and the risk of completed suicide is raised more than tenfold compared to healthy controls (Black, Blum, Pfohl, & Hale, 2004).

There is still no firm evidence of curable effects of pharmacotherapy for BPD or for suicidal or NSSI behaviour linked to BPD (Stoffers et al., 2012; Miga et al., this volume). There is some evidence that pharmacological treatments can be helpful when used to reduce specific symptoms, including anger, anxiety, depression symptoms, hostility, and impulsivity, which are frequently seen in patients with BPD (NICE, 2009). It is, however, unclear whether these effects are the consequence of treating comorbid disorders. Thus, effective treatment of BPD and associated suicidal and NSSI behaviour will rely on psychotherapeutic interventions in the foreseeable future.

DBT is not the only psychotherapeutic intervention having demonstrated efficacy in reducing suicidal and NSSI behaviour in patients with borderline personality disorder (NICE, 2009), but it certainly is the treatment that has provided the most robust evidence for such efficacy (Stoffers et al., 2012). This chapter discusses some of the challenges of treating suicidal and NSSI behaviour in patients with BPD and gives an overview of how these challenges are dealt with in DBT. Finally, it provides a brief review of the empirical literature on the clinical outcomes of interest.

CHALLENGES IN TREATING SUICIDAL AND NON-SUICIDAL SELF-HARMING PATIENTS WITH BORDERLINE PERSONALITY DISORDER

Suicidal and Non-suicidal Self-harming Behaviour

Although people with BPD constitute a heterogeneous group with regard to symptoms and behaviours, self-destructive behaviours—a diagnostic criterion of this syndrome—are present in the majority of patients and they range from self-mutilation via suicide attempts to completed suicide. Although the boundaries between non-suicidal and suicidal self-harm are not very sharp, clinical experience suggests that NSSI behaviours tend to be more strongly linked to difficulties of regulating emotions and cognitions, while suicidal self-harm will have stronger associations with depressive states and hopelessness. While suicidal ideation seems to be chronically present (Mehlum, Friis, Vaglum, & Karterud, 1994), borderline patients are not at equally high risk of suicidal behaviour most of the time. When in suicidal crises, however, BPD patients seem more inclined than any other patient group to actively seek assistance from emergency services (Mellesdal et al., 2015). Many clinicians are inclined to believe that suicidal behaviour in patients with BPD mainly is a question of communicative gestures with no strong intention to die. This is not supported by empirical evidence. Suominen, Isometsa, Henriksson, Ostamo, and Lonnqvist (2000) compared patients with (mainly DSM-IV cluster B disorders) and without personality disorders in consecutive cases of attempted suicide referred to general hospitals, and found no difference between the groups in terms of suicide intent, hopelessness, or lethality. When having made suicide attempts, individuals with cluster B personality disorder and a pattern of repetitive NSSI, seem, however, to rate the lethality of their attempts as lower and the likelihood of rescue as higher compared to people without such non-suicidal self-harm (Stanley, Gameroff, Michalsen, & Mann, 2001).

What Increases the Risk of Suicide in Borderline Patients?

Emotion dysregulation and instability and a pronounced sensitivity to environmental stress are characteristics of the borderline syndrome closely linked to suicidal and NSSI behaviour (Sher et al., 2016). But what seems to facilitate suicidal behaviour more than anything else is impulsivity, which is a personality trait found to be a predictor for suicidal behaviour across a wide range of psychiatric disorders (Mann, Waternaux, Haas, & Malone, 1999; Soloff, Lynch, Kelly, Malone, & Mann, 2000). There is strong research evidence for a biological substrate for impulsivity related to lower levels of CNS 5-HT documented in numerous studies (Oquendo & Mann, 2000). Individuals with pronounced impulsivity are more vulnerable for suicidal crises to be provoked by negative life events and stress. Linehan's biosocial theory highlights the interplay between a biological vulnerability and negative environmental factors in the formation early in life of a reduced capacity to regulate emotion, increasing the risk of several types of dysfunctional behaviours, among them self-harming behaviour (Linehan, 1993). Self-destructive impulsivity probably represents the clinically most challenging part of the borderline syndrome and why several current treatment models for BPD target the ability to control self-destructive impulses and tolerate unpleasant affect.

BPD has extensive comorbidity with other psychiatric disorders, and comorbidity is the rule, rather than the exception (Skodol et al., 2002). Psychiatric comorbidity seems in general to strongly increase the severity of suicidal behaviour (Beautrais et al., 1996) and this seems to be even more pronounced in cases of comorbidity (Corbitt, Malone, Haas, & Mann, 1996). This is not unexpected since comorbidity often implies more complex and hard-to-treat disorders and more severe symptomatic strain on the patient. Comorbidity with personality disorders is particularly common in suicide-attempting patients (Corbitt et al., 1996). This has been confirmed by studies in representative patient samples where the suicide risk in the presence of at least one personality disorder was found to be ten to 15 times greater than in the absence of such disorders (Haw, Hawton, Houston, & Townsend, 2001). Such comorbidity in suicidal patients often complicates clinical evaluations and treatments.

Problems with Staying in Treatment

An important aspect of BPD individuals' problems is their difficulty with regulating their relationships with other people and maintaining nurturing close interpersonal relationships over time (Linehan, 1993). This extends to the clinical setting, where BPD patients all too often very soon feel disappointed, rejected, or invalidated by their therapists. Many patients bring with them from their past experiences of abuse, trauma, neglect, and rejection from families, friends, and previous healthcare providers. Building a trusting relationship with the patient can therefore prove quite a difficult challenge, but it is nevertheless indispensable, since most clinicians would agree that a strong therapeutic alliance is among the most important suicide preventative aspects of treatment. Ending of treatments or transitions from one service to another notoriously evoke substantial distress and emotional reactions in patients with BPD. Fonagy and Bateman (2006) highlight that the frequent therapist changes commonly experienced by BPD patients often result in poorer clinical outcomes. It is important to note that in patients with BPD, completed suicide is often seen relatively late in the course of the illness, frequently after several failed treatment attempts (Paris, 2007).

Treating Suicidal and Non-suicidal Self-injury Behaviours in BPD Patients: Current Best Practice

Most clinical guidelines, among them the UK NICE guidelines (NICE, 2011), recommend that clinicians working with people who self-harm should make comprehensive psychosocial assessments of the patient's psychiatric disorder (including assessment of comorbidity with personality disorders and/or substance misuse), risks, resources, and needs. Risk assessments should include assessments of risk of repetition of self-harm and risk of completed suicide, and should consider suicide intent, medical lethality, and circumstances of both current and past suicidal behaviour. Assessment of the patient's risks and needs should also include assessment of current life difficulties, such as possible interpersonal conflicts or loss, exposure to traumatic stress, lack of social support, financial problems, work place/school problems, physical ill-health, and problems linked to sexual orientation. To conduct such assessments is, however, often challenging for many clinicians, since crisis-related short-term treatment interventions do not often go easily hand in hand with the need for a systematic evaluation of the patient. An adequate clinical evaluation with assessment of the severity and seriousness of suicidal behaviour in the individual patient is, however, essential in order to provide adequate treatment and protection. The risk must be repeatedly re-evaluated as the risk scenario may rapidly change in these patients due to their increased affective reactivity and impulsivity. Many clinicians fear reinforcing suicidal behaviours in their BPD patients should they systematically address the topic of suicidality in therapy sessions—hence, they avoid it.

People who have self-harmed frequently need therapeutic support for more than the first few days or weeks after the episode; this is particularly important for patients with repetitive self-harm behaviour. Longer-term treatment requires that clinicians develop a trusting, supportive, and engaging relationship with their patients and maintain continuity of this relationship. Clinicians should be aware of the stigma often still associated with self-harm and adopt a non-judgmental approach. It is important that clinicians ensure that people are fully involved in decision-making about, planning, and setting goals for their own care. Important aims in the treatment are to prevent relapse or escalation of self-harm, and to stop or reduce other high-risk behaviours. To develop a crisis plan or safety plan is regarded as essential. Treating psychiatric conditions, improving social and occupational functioning, and increasing quality of life are high priority treatment aims for the longer term. There is limited evidence on the efficacy of pharmacological treatment in the acute phase of self-harming behaviour, and as such, medication should therefore not be initiated to manage self-harm unless it is otherwise indicated (for example to treat depression or bipolar disorder). Patients should rather be offered psychosocial treatments in the form of a structured care based on an explicit theoretical approach. A limiting factor in practice is that many therapists have not been trained to deliver treatment programmes to an adherent standard (Fairburn & Cooper, 2011). This is currently a severe challenge to patients, care providers, and care systems planners in most countries.

Patients who have repetitive or chronic self-harm associated with BPD are often high users of inpatient treatment (Mellesdal et al., 2015). There is, however, no evidence that long-term hospitalization is effective in the treatment of BPD. Most experts suggest that if hospital admission is needed, it should be brief and the focus should be on crisis management (NICE, 2009). Clinicians often find the question of hospitalization one of the most problematic decisions to make in the management of suicidal crises in BPD patients. This decision carries risks in several ways. There is the real risk that the patient—if not protected by the hospital environment—may actually take her own life. If hospitalized, on the other hand, the problems may actually become worse through a negative interplay with staff or fellow patients, which could then lead to escalating suicide threats, self-mutilation, or suicidal behaviour. In sum, there are reasons to avoid hospital admission. If the need for protection makes hospitalization unavoidable, this intervention should be brief and it is recommended to set a fixed date of discharge ("next morning" or "over the weekend") and clearly inform the patient and her family about this.

TREATMENT OF SUICIDAL AND NON-SUICIDAL SELF-HARMING BEHAVIOURS: THE DBT STANCE

Treatment Targeting

DBT adopts a clear hierarchy of targets, with life-threatening behaviours treated as top priority. In many treatment approaches, it is assumed that a reduction of suicide risk will be achieved primarily through improvement of the psychiatric disorder causing the symptoms and suffering leading to suicidal behaviours. Thus, the main strategy is to treat the disorder and not the suicidality. However, clinical studies have shown that in patients with BPD and repetitive self-harm behaviour, high levels of suicidality may persist over extended periods of time, even when other symptoms subside (Mehlum et al., 1994). In contrast, DBT aims to treat suicidal behaviours directly since these behaviours can be treated independently of any other psychiatric disorder and such treatment should be given without delay to increase patient safety. From a DBT standpoint, suicidal behaviours represent disordered *behaviour* and are not simply a consequence of a psychiatric diagnosis that will remit when the disorder is treated.

DBT regards suicidal and NSSI behaviour as maladaptive problem solving and aims at replacing it with more functional and healthy coping behaviours. The patient and the therapist will agree to work collaboratively towards this goal and the patient is then asked to self-monitor her suicidal ideation, urges to self-harm, and any acts of non-suicidal or suicidal self-harm on a daily basis. This approach substantially differs from that taken in most other treatments. Most patients and therapists find suicidal behaviour so aversive to discuss that they prefer to avoid addressing it. In DBT, however, the therapist clarifies from the outset of treatment that she will check for self-harming behaviour *on a routine basis, not only in crises,* and that explicitly addressing and reducing such behaviours will be regarded as a highly prioritized focus of the treatment. When adopting this approach and addressing self-harm in a calm, matter-of-fact, and non-judgmental manner, therapists usually will greatly reduce the risk of inadvertently reinforcing self-harming behaviours.

A Behavioural Approach

DBT was developed for the treatment of chronically suicidal and NSSI patients with BPD at a time when most clinicians regarded these patients as difficult, if not impossible, to treat, and when most clinicians resorted to hospitalizing their borderline patients to prevent suicide, even though there was no evidence that this would lead to improvement or reduced suicide risk. In the careful construction of her new treatment approach for this patient group, Linehan was fully aware of the genuine risk of suicide and dedicated much attention to finding new ways to help therapists manage the risk at the same time as they helped their patients towards a life worth living.

Even though DBT never has claimed to be a treatment for suicide prevention, it certainly has a number of innovative features proactively targeting self-harming and suicidal behaviours. Among the most important was perhaps the simplest, and yet so easily forgotten: to regard suicidal ideation, suicide attempts, and NSSI as *behaviours*, and to adopt a phenomenological and non-pejorative way of thinking and talking about these behaviours. Linehan realized that simply avoiding discussing self-harming behaviour with patients in the hope that it would eventually disappear was ineffective. Whereas therapists typically regard suicidal and NSSI behaviours as problems, patients very often view them as solutions (Linehan, 1993). The truth is that both therapists and patients are right; self-harming behaviours work *and* they constitute a severe and often life-threatening problem. Non-suicidal self-harm is a strongly negatively reinforced behaviour through its often rapid and striking effect in reducing arousal and intolerable emotions (see Chapman, this volume). The patient is unlikely to stop this behaviour unless she finds alternative ways of regulating or tolerating negative emotions. Similarly, repetitive suicidal behaviours are often highly conditioned responses to stress factors, situations, or cues that set off a chain of emotions, thoughts, and behaviours leading to overt suicidal behaviour. The behavioural approach adopted in DBT actively and explicitly explores these chains of events and the contingencies involved without reinforcing the behaviour.

In recent years, DBT's strategy of conducting an "ideation-to-action" analysis in order to acquire a more detailed understanding of how suicide risk progresses from ideation to potentially lethal suicide attempts has been much more widely acknowledged (Klonsky, Qiu, & Saffer, 2017). In DBT, the standard approach of obtaining this information is for the therapist and patient to collaboratively conduct a moment-to-moment chain analysis of environmental and behavioural events linked to suicidal behaviour (see Landes, this volume). Predisposing psychological, physiological, and environmental factors and prompting events and what were links in the chain, such as emotions or thoughts, leading to the self-harming behaviour are described in detail. How other people responded and what the consequences were of the self-harm are also noted. Determining if suicidal behaviour is primarily respondent (linked to prompting cues or events) or operant (linked to consequences of the behaviours) is of primary importance. Therapists conduct chain analyses when needed at every stage in the treatment and these analyses guide the treatment towards clients' short- and long-term goals. Patients often perceive chain analyses as, at least, moderately aversive. While to instigate such aversive stimuli is certainly not the therapist's primary intention in using the method, it may undoubtedly serve to counteract any reinforcing effects that may arise from discussing self-harming behaviour.

Changing Behaviours Through the Use of Skills Training

For patients with a pattern of repetitive self-harming behaviour, it is essential not only to clarify salient factors involved in the current episode, but also to connect these factors to overall behavioural patterns. This information should then be used as a basis for conducting an analysis of possible solutions. If the suicidal behaviour is primarily respondent, solutions should involve stopping eliciting events and teaching skills for preventing, coping with, or increasing tolerance for such events. Solutions could also include treating associated disorders such as substance abuse or depression (see Axelrod, this volume). For operant suicidal behaviour it is, of course, important to not reinforce this behaviour, but rather reinforce non-suicidal, adaptive responses while validating the suicidal feelings, but *not* the suicidal behaviour. A central part of DBT is the teaching of behavioural skills with the aim of replacing maladaptive behaviours with skillful behaviour. Studies have shown that increasing skills use is an important mechanism of change for suicidal behaviour (Neacsiu, Rizvi, & Linehan, 2010). It is beyond the scope of this chapter to describe the wide range of skills used in DBT to help patients change emotions, cognitions, or overt behaviours that are links in the chain of events leading to suicidal or NSSI behaviour (see Cowperthwait et al., this volume).

Crisis Strategies

For highly suicidal patients, suicidal crises are expected to occur during the treatment, particularly during the first weeks and months. Hence, DBT includes protocols for managing crises and crisis telephone calls (see Rizvi & Roman, this volume). These protocols are designed to reduce the risks of suicide and severe injury in the short term, while not increasing the risk of suicidal behaviours in the long run. Central to this endeavour is distinguishing between suicide attempts on the one hand and NSSI on the other, even though the line between these two cannot be sharply drawn. Patients can learn how to self-monitor urges to NSSI and suicidal behaviour, and also learn how to distinguish between these behaviours. When crises emerge, this distinction is important with respect to what intervention approach to adopt. During therapy sessions therapists will assist clients in recognizing the differing controlling variables for each type of behaviour and which skills and solutions to use in each case. A second strategy that facilitates crisis management is for the patient and therapist early in treatment to develop a safety plan describing which high-risk situations or emotional states the patient needs to be aware of (that trigger the use of the safety plan), what the patient can do herself to manage the situation (e.g. problem-solving skills), from whom in the environment the patient can seek help, and what professional helpers (with telephone numbers) are available.

Although many clinicians often reject the notion that patients can call them for help between sessions, the field of suicide prevention generally recognizes that suicidal people frequently need crisis support at different hours of the day and even night (Mann et al., 2005). In DBT, therapists are encouraged to take calls from patients between sessions, while at the same time observing their personal limits to prevent therapist burnout. When developing a treatment for suicidal patients, Linehan (2011) had to solve the dilemma of providing effective crisis intervention when needed without reinforcing crisis behaviours. The solution was to provide patients with ample opportunities to call, not only when in crisis, but also when in need of coaching to use skills to solve problems in regulating emotions, cope with interpersonal relationships, ask for help appropriately, and tolerate distress. In this way, any contingency between suicidal behaviours and therapist assistance via telephone calls could be mitigated. In her clinical trials, Linehan found no correlation between number of telephone crisis calls and number of self-inflicted injuries in patients who received DBT, while there was indeed such positive correlation in patients who received treatment as usual (Linehan & Heard, 1993). It is important to note that in DBT, patients are encouraged to call *before* suicidal crises, or at least before they have harmed themselves, for their therapist to be able to coach them in the use of crisis strategies or skills. If the patient has already self-harmed, the so-called "24-hour rule" applies, which means that the patient cannot call her therapist for support or coaching in the 24 hours following self-harm, with the exception of telephone contact necessary for basic medical management.

Strong Therapeutic Alliance

DBT puts a strong emphasis on the therapeutic alliance. This is of particular relevance to suicide prevention, since, at times, it will probably only be the strong therapeutic alliance that will keep the patient alive. Overcoming many of the core problems chronically suicidal patients with BPD struggle with involves exposure to intense emotional pain. There is no other way for the patient to build a life worth living than for her to go through this pain. A strong therapeutic alliance is, however, needed in order for the patient to be able to work her way through these painful emotions. Given BPD patients' constellation of personality traits, it is no surprise that forming and keeping a strong therapeutic alliance may be difficult, both from the perspective of the therapist and of the patient. There are many ways in which DBT therapists aim to strengthen the therapeutic alliance and a full review of these strategies falls outside the scope of this chapter (interested readers are referred to chapters by Heard, and by Fruzzetti & Ruork, this volume). Therapists create a collaborative relationship with a validating, nurturing environment where therapeutic techniques can be delivered and new learning can take place (Swales & Heard, 2007). Among factors that seem to strengthen a therapeutic alliance is for the patient to notice progress early in treatment, however small this improvement may be. Setting overly ambitious targets early in the treatment may be counter-productive. Therapists actively motivate and engage patients in the treatment through using both validation and commitment strategies to counteract early drop-out.

Family Approach in the Treatment of Teenagers

Many studies have shown that both suicidal and NSSI behaviour in adolescents may be strongly linked to family problems (Brent, 2010). In some cases, these problems are causal factors, while in other instances, families who may not have caused the problems may nevertheless inadvertently augment them. In all cases, however, families play an important role in finding solutions and helping adolescents make progress in their treatment. The current research literature seems to indicate that interventions hoping to effectively reduce suicidal behaviour in adolescents will all need to include some sort of family support and must also address family dysfunction (Brent et al., 2013). In DBT a range of family strategies have been included in an adaptation of the treatment for adolescents and their families developed by Miller, Rathus, and Linehan, 2007. This form of DBT includes all of the modalities of standard DBT, but has made modifications to be able to address typical dilemmas experienced by families who have a child with emotion dysregulation and suicidal behaviour. These dilemmas are addressed by including parents in family therapy sessions and by including them in the skills training. DBT skills training in this adaptation is organized in multi-family groups where parents participate on equal terms with adolescents, which means that they need to learn the skills being taught just as much as everyone else. This is of particular value to parents, since assisting their adolescents to generalize skills use to their daily life outside of therapy sessions will be easier when they have intimate knowledge themselves of what skills are required and the challenges of deploying them effectively in a crisis (see Rathus et al., this volume).

Efficacy of DBT on Suicidal and Non-suicidal Self-harming Behaviour: the Research

The empirical support for DBT has been reviewed in detail in other chapters of this book (interested readers are referred to Miga et al., and Walton & Comtois, this volume). This section considers outcomes of interest to our topic, namely suicidal and NSSI behaviour, as well as to symptoms and dysfunctions closely associated with such behaviour, and finally, the use of emergency health services due to suicidal crises. Though the majority of DBT trials have employed a sound research methodology, they have had to struggle with many of the same challenges as other psychotherapy studies, including limited sample sizes, problems of defining and measuring core outcomes, non-normal distribution of data, and strong heterogeneity of samples, just to mention some of the most salient problems complicating data analysis and interpretation. Suicidal and NSSI behaviour have mostly been clearly defined in DBT trials (contrary to many other psychotherapy studies). However, even in high-risk patient populations, such as people with BPD and a history of repeated suicide attempts, the natural rate of new suicide attempts during the course of a trial is low, thus making it difficult to measure change over time and between-group differences. Some studies have, therefore, reported both suicidal and NSSI behaviours as a collective category.

Suicidal Behaviour

Follow-up studies have consistently shown that people who make a suicide attempt run a high risk of repeated suicide attempts and suicide during the first year after the incident (Haw, Bergen, Casey, & Hawton, 2007; Suominen et al., 2004). Improved care following a suicide attempt has thus been highlighted as a high priority area for its considerable suicide preventive potential (Mann et al., 2005). To this day, however, there are only a limited number of treatments that have demonstrated their capacity to effectively reduce suicidal behaviour in clinical populations of suicide attempters. It is fair to say that DBT stands out as the treatment with the strongest empirical support for such efficacy across diagnostic groups and treatment contexts (Stoffers et al., 2012).

Linehan's first randomized clinical trial (Linehan, Armstrong, Suarez, Allmon, & Heard, 1991) did not distinguish between suicide attempts and NSSI, but reported on "parasuicide" as a collective category, as mentioned previously. Patients with BPD receiving one year of standard DBT reported significantly fewer parasuicide episodes than patients receiving one year of treatment as usual (TAU). The major treatment gains with respect to this primary outcome seem to have occurred during the first four months of treatment, and they were maintained during the first six months post-treatment (Linehan, Heard, & Armstrong, 1993). In the years following Linehan's initial study, several additional trials at independent sites replicated the finding of DBT's superiority over other treatments in reducing suicidal behaviours in patients with BPD (Turner, 2000; Koons et al., 2001), while others have found the same favourable treatment response in DBT with respect to suicidal behaviour, but no significant outcome differences between treatment conditions (Carter, Willcox, Lewin, Conrad, & Bendit, 2010; Clarkin, Levy, Lenzenweger, & Kernberg, 2007; Verheul et al., 2003), either because their sample sizes were too small, or because the base rate of suicide attempts was too low. In a later randomized trial comparing one year of standard DBT with therapy by experts for patients with BPD, Linehan reported on suicide attempts separately (Linehan et al., 2006). Here, patients receiving DBT had half the rate of suicide attempts of patients in the comparison group. Since both treatments had been delivered by experts, treatment gains could not be explained simply by therapists' general level of expertise and experience or their allegiance to treatment. The many strategies in DBT focusing on treating suicidal behaviours (mentioned previously in this chapter) that are usually not found in other treatment models, even when they are delivered at a high level of expertise, may account for these differences in outcome. An obvious example is the central place of skills training in DBT. In a secondary analysis of data from three RCTs, Neacsiu et al. (2010) demonstrated that DBT skills use mediated the decrease in suicide attempts over time, suggesting that to increase skills use is a mechanism of change for suicidal behaviour. In a more recent study, Linehan further evaluated the relative importance of the skills training component of DBT in treating suicidal patients with BPD by comparing one year of DBT skills training as a stand-alone treatment with DBT without skills training and with standard DBT in which both skills training and individual therapy are included (Linehan et al., 2015). Over the one-year treatment period and one-year follow-up, similar improvements in the frequency and severity of suicide attempts and in the level of suicidal ideation were observed in all three treatment conditions. This finding, seemingly in contrast to Linehan's previous findings of a mediating role of skills training in decreasing suicide attempts over time, suggests that reductions in suicidal behaviours in DBT rely on more than skills training, as we have discussed.

In the largest RCT on psychotherapeutic interventions for suicidal patients with BPD to date, McMain and colleagues compared one year of standard DBT with general psychiatric management and found that patients in both conditions improved significantly and similarly in the frequency and severity of episodes of both suicidal and NSSI behaviours (McMain et al., 2009) and these treatment gains were sustained two years after treatment (McMain, Guimond, Streiner, Cardish, & Links, 2012). It is important to note that in McMain's study "general psychiatric management" was in reality a high-standard coherent treatment developed and manualized for the trial to comply with the APA Practice Guideline for the Treatment of Patients with Borderline Personality Disorder (American Psychiatric Association Practice, 2001). The treatment consisted of psychodynamic psychotherapy, case management, and pharmacotherapy. These findings suggest that significant differences between high-standard treatments in reductions of suicidal behaviour in patients with BPD should probably not be expected.

An increasing number of adaptations of DBT for various patient populations have emerged during recent years. Perhaps the most salient of these has been the DBT-adaptation for adolescents, mentioned previously. Both suicidal and NSSI behaviour is highly prevalent in adolescents (Madge et al., 2008), making DBT a potentially relevant treatment to offer in this age group. A brief (four months) version of DBT for adolescents developed by Miller and colleagues (Miller, Rathus, & Linehan, 2007) was found to significantly reduce self-harm (suicidal behaviours and NSSI were not reported separately) and suicidal ideation in adolescents with borderline features, compared with enhanced usual care in a randomized trial by Mehlum et al. (2014). These treatment gains were achieved early in the treatment and were sustained one year (Mehlum et al., 2016) and two years (Mehlum et al., unpublished manuscript) post-treatment.

Non-suicidal Self-Harm

Several studies have, wisely, reported separately on suicide attempts and non-suicidal self-harm (or NSSI). This is important since, as mentioned, treatments should address these behaviours differently and therefore the outcomes should also be assessed both separately and differently. Due to a number of reasons, NSSI behaviours are, however, far from easily assessed. There are a multitude of different types of self-harm and unless each of them is explicitly addressed in the assessment interviews, they will often remain undetected and unmeasured. Episodes of NSSI may occur extremely frequently, up to dozens of episodes per day, and the question is how to count them and how to estimate changes over time and between treatment groups with such highly non-normally distributed data.

Among studies having reported separately on suicide attempts and NSSI is the Dutch study of standard DBT by Verheul and colleagues in which no difference in suicide attempts between patients who had received one year of standard DBT or TAU was found (Verheul et al., 2003). The decrease in NSSI was, however, significantly greater for the DBT-group, and this effect was sustained even six months post-treatment (Van Den Bosch, Koeter, Stijnen, Verheul, & Van Den Brink, 2005). Pistorello treated suicidal college students with BPD features through seven to 12 months of either DBT or optimized TAU, and found that subjects who received DBT had a significantly lower number of episodes of NSSI, lower level of suicidal ideation, and stronger reductions in BPD criteria (Pistorello, Fruzzetti, MacLane, Gallop, & Iversson, 2012). In Linehan's important component analysis, DBT with skills training performed significantly better than DBT without skills training in reducing the frequency of NSSI episodes (Linehan et al., 2015), suggesting that skills training is a necessary component to achieve treatment response in NSSI, but possibly not in suicidal behaviour.

Use of Emergency Services and Psychiatric Admission

In Linehan's original study, patients who received DBT had significantly fewer psychiatric inpatient days both during the treatment year and during the follow-up (Linehan & Heard, 1993). In her 2006 study comparing DBT with therapy by experts, emergency room visits for suicidality were reduced by more than 50% in DBT patients, and in-patient admissions for suicidality were reduced by more than 70% (Linehan et al., 2006). These outcomes were sustained during the one-year post-treatment follow-up. These findings have been replicated in studies at independent sites (Koons et al., 2001; Turner, 2000). The capacity of DBT to reduce psychiatric hospitalization is important for several reasons. First, there is no clear rationale for admitting suicidal patients with BPD, as hospitalization has not been shown to reduce suicide rates in patients with BPD (NICE, 2009). The obvious high cost of psychiatric inpatient care should therefore favour any treatment that is able to provide treatment response without making costly inpatient care necessary. Second, hospitalization is very disruptive for most patients' daily lives and for any outpatient treatment they may receive. Finally, several treatment procedures—particularly the ones aimed at reducing suicidal behaviour—risk reinforcing in patients with BPD the very behaviour they intend to reduce; each new incident of suicidal behaviour is "rewarded" with more care and concern from therapists and nursing staff.

Other Outcomes Associated with Risk of Suicidal and Non-suicidal Self-harming Behaviour

A wide range of symptoms, dysfunctions, emotions, and behaviours have been found to be associated with risk of suicidal and NSSI behaviour in individuals with BPD, and within the limited space available here, only a few will be mentioned. A large proportion of patients with BPD have comorbid depression, and suicidal behaviour in these patients seems often to be strongly associated with depressive states. It is therefore of particular interest that a range of clinical trials have found that DBT leads to stronger reductions in the severity of depressive symptoms than comparison treatments (Koons et al., 2001, Mehlum et al., 2014; Pistorello et al., 2012; Turner, 2000). Similarly, stronger reductions in the level of hopelessness have been reported in several trials (Koons et al., 2001; Mehlum et al., 2014). A number of trials have demonstrated that criteria for BPD or borderline symptoms have been significantly more reduced in patients receiving DBT than in those who received comparison treatments (Mehlum et al., 2014; Pistorello et al., 2012), and these effects have, interestingly, been found in studies of young patient groups. Trait-like behaviours or dysfunctions such as anger (Koons et al., 2001; Linehan et al., 1991; Turner, 2000), impulsiveness (Turner, 2000), and emotion dysregulation (Turner, 2000) have also been found to be significantly more reduced in patients with BPD receiving DBT.

CONCLUSIONS

DBT is a comprehensive treatment delivered through several modalities and with a range of strategies relevant to preventing suicidal and NSSI behaviour. The efficacy of DBT in reducing suicidal behaviour and NSSI, emergency room visits, psychiatric hospital days, and a range of symptoms and behaviours related to suicidality is well documented through numerous randomized trials. We lack firm evidence, however, as to which strategies in DBT are the exact mechanisms of change with respect to self-harming behaviours. Currently, it seems likely that strategies such as adopting a behavioural approach to suicide and self-harm in order to identify antecedents and consequences either causing or maintaining the behaviours are central. Treating suicidal behaviours directly and specifically and making such treatment the top priority may also be important. Multiple and specific strategies to manage suicidal crises and to prevent suicidal crises from occurring may also promote good outcomes. In particular, teaching patients a range of skills in emotion regulation, distress tolerance, and interpersonal problem solving combined with a focus on generalization of skills use to crises and other challenging situations in their daily lives may drive clinical outcomes. Keeping patients alive while they are making progress in treatment builds in DBT on a strong therapeutic relationship that balances the therapeutic strategies of validation and change.

KEY POINTS FOR CLINICIANS

- Although challenging, clinicians working with people who self-harm should make comprehensive psychosocial assessments of the patient's psychiatric disorder (including assessment of comorbidity with personality disorders and/or substance misuse), risks, resources, and needs in order to provide adequate treatment and protection.

- Many clinicians fear reinforcing suicidal behaviours should they systematically address the topic of suicidality in therapy sessions—hence, they avoid it. This is not advisable; the risk must be repeatedly re-evaluated and actively addressed since the risk scenario may rapidly change in these patients due to their increased affective reactivity and impulsivity.

- Important aims in the treatment are to prevent relapse or escalation of self-harm and other high-risk behaviours, and to develop a crisis plan or safety plan is regarded essential. To treat psychiatric conditions, improve social and occupational functioning, and improve quality of life are also highly prioritized treatment aims for the longer term.

- DBT has a well-documented efficacy in reducing suicidal behaviours and NSSI, emergency room visits, psychiatric hospital days, and a wide range of symptoms and behaviours related to suicidality.

- DBT adopts a behavioural approach to suicide and self-harm in order to identify antecedents and consequences either causing or maintaining the behaviours.

- In DBT, suicidal behaviours are treated directly and specifically and given top priority. DBT offers multiple and specific strategies to prevent and manage suicidal crises, such as teaching patients skills in emotion regulation, distress tolerance, and interpersonal problem solving.

- Keeping patients alive while they are making progress in treatment builds in DBT on a strong therapeutic relationship that balances the therapeutic strategies of validation and change.

REFERENCES

American Psychiatric Association Practice (2001). Practice guideline for the treatment of patients with borderline personality disorder. American Psychiatric Association. *American Journal of Psychiatry*, *158*(10 Suppl), 1–52.

Beautrais, A. L., Joyce, P. R., Mulder, R. T., Fergusson, D. M., Deavoll, B. J., & Nightingale, S. K. (1996). Prevalence and comorbidity of mental disorders in persons making serious suicide attempts: A case-control study. *American Journal of Psychiatry*, *153*(8), 1009–1014.

Black, D. W., Blum, N., Pfohl, B., & Hale, N. (2004). Suicidal behavior in borderline personality disorder: Prevalence, risk factors, prediction, and prevention. *Journal of Personality Disorders*, *18*(3), 226–239.

Brent, D. (2010). What family studies teach us about suicidal behavior: Implications for research, treatment, and prevention. *European Psychiatry*, *25*(5), 260–263.

Brent, D. A., McMakin, D. L., Kennard, B. D., Goldstein, T. R., Mayes, T. L., & Douaihy, A. B. (2013). Protecting adolescents from self-harm: A critical review of intervention studies. *Journal of the American Academy of Child & Adolescent Psychiatry*, *52*(12), 1260–1271.

Carter, G. L., Willcox, C. H., Lewin, T. J., Conrad, A. M., & Bendit, N. (2010). Hunter DBT project: Randomized controlled trial of dialectical behaviour therapy in women with borderline personality disorder. *Australian & New Zealand Journal of Psychiatry*, *44*(2), 162–173.

Clarkin, J. F., Levy, K. N., Lenzenweger, M. F., & Kernberg, O. F. (2007). Evaluating three treatments for borderline personality disorder: A multiwave study. *American Journal of Psychiatry*, *164*(6), 922–928.

Corbitt, E. M., Malone, K. M., Haas, G. L., & Mann, J. J. (1996). Suicidal behavior in patients with major depression and comorbid personality disorders. *Journal of Affective Disorders*, *39*(1), 61–72.

Fairburn, C. G., & Cooper, Z. (2011). Therapist competence, therapy quality, and therapist training. *Behaviour Research and Therapy*, *49*(6–7), 373–378.

Fonagy, P., & Bateman, A. (2006). Progress in the treatment of borderline personality disorder. *British Journal of Psychiatry, 188*, 1–3.

Haw, C., Bergen, H., Casey, D., & Hawton, K. (2007). Repetition of deliberate self-harm: A study of the characteristics and subsequent deaths in patients presenting to a general hospital according to extent of repetition. *Suicide and Life-Threatening Behavior, 37*(4), 379–396.

Haw, C., Hawton, K., Houston, K., & Townsend, E. (2001). Psychiatric and personality disorders in deliberate self-harm patients. *British Journal of Psychiatry, 178*(1), 48–54.

Klonsky, E. D., Qiu, T., & Saffer, B. Y. (2017). Recent advances in differentiating suicide attempters from suicide ideators. *Current Opinion in Psychiatry, 30*(1), 15–20.

Koons, C. R., Robins, C. J., Tweed, J. L., Lynch, T. R., Gonzalez, A. M., Morse, J. Q., ... Bastian, L. A. (2001). Efficacy of dialectical behavior therapy in women veterans with borderline personality disorder. *Behavior Therapy, 32*(2), 371–390.

Linehan, M. M. (1993). *Cognitive-behavioral treatment of borderline personality disorder.* New York, Guilford Press.

Linehan, M. M. (2011). Dialectical behavior therapy and telephone coaching. *Cognitive and Behavioral Practice, 18*, 2.

Linehan, M. M., Armstrong, H. E., Suarez, A., Allmon, D., & Heard, H. L. (1991). Cognitive-behavioral treatment of chronically parasuicidal borderline patients. *Archives of General Psychiatry, 48*(12), 1060–1064.

Linehan, M. M., Comtois, K. A., Murray, A. M., Brown, M. Z., Gallop, R. J., Heard, H. L., ... Lindenboim, N. (2006). Two-year randomized controlled trial and follow-up of dialectical behavior therapy vs therapy by experts for suicidal behaviors and borderline personality disorder. *Archives of General Psychiatry, 63*(7), 757–766.

Linehan, M. M., & Heard, H. L. (1993). Impact of treatment accessibility on clinical course of parasuicidal patients: In reply to R.E. Hoffman. *Archives of General Psychiatry, 50*, 157–158.

Linehan, M. M., Heard, H. L., & Armstrong, H. E. (1993). Naturalistic follow-up of a behavioral treatment for chronically parasuicidal borderline patients. *Archives of General Psychiatry, 50*(12), 971–974.

Linehan, M. M., Korslund, K. E., Harned, M. S., Gallop, R. J., Lungu, A., Neacsiu, A. D., ... Murray-Gregory, A. M. (2015). Dialectical behavior therapy for high suicide risk in individuals with borderline personality disorder: A randomized clinical trial and component analysis. *JAMA Psychiatry, 72*(5), 475–482.

Madge, N., Hewitt, A., Hawton, K., de Wilde, E. J., Corcoran, P., Fekete, S., ... Ystgaard, M. (2008). Deliberate self-harm within an international community sample of young people: Comparative findings from the Child and Adolescent Self-harm in Europe (CASE) Study. *Journal of Child Psychology and Psychiatry, 49*(6), 667–677.

Mann, J. J., Apter, A., Bertolote, J., Beautrais, A., Currier, D., Haas, A., ... Hendin, H. (2005). Suicide prevention strategies: A systematic review. *JAMA: The Journal of the American Medical Association, 294*, 2064–2074.

Mann, J. J., Waternaux, C., Haas, G. L., & Malone, K. M. (1999). Toward a clinical model of suicidal behavior in psychiatric patients. *American Journal of Psychiatry, 156*(2), 181–189.

McMain, S. F., Guimond, T., Streiner, D. L., Cardish, R. J., & Links, P. S. (2012). Dialectical behavior therapy compared with general psychiatric management for borderline personality disorder: Clinical outcomes and functioning over a 2-year follow-up. *American Journal of Psychiatry, 169*, 11.

McMain, S. F., Links, P. S., Gnam, W. H., Guimond, T., Cardish, R. J., Korman, L., & Streiner, D. L. (2009). A randomized trial of dialectical behavior therapy versus general psychiatric management for borderline personality disorder. *American Journal of Psychiatry*, 166(12), 1365–1374.

Mehlum, L. (2009). Clinical challenges in the assessment and management of suicidal behaviour in patients with bordeline personality disorder. *Epidemiologia E Psichiatria Sociale*, 18(3), 184–190.

Mehlum, L., Friis, S., Vaglum, P., & Karterud, S. (1994). The longitudinal pattern of suicidal behaviour in borderline personality disorder: A prospective follow-up study. *Acta Psychiatrica Scandinavica*, 90(2), 130.

Mehlum, L., Ramberg, M., Tormoen, A. J., Haga, E., Diep, L. M., Stanley, B. H., … Grøholt, B. (2016). Dialectical behavior therapy compared with enhanced usual care for adolescents with repeated suicidal and self-harming behavior: Outcomes over a one-year follow-up. *Journal of the American Academy of Child and Adolescent Psychiatry*, 55(4), 295–300.

Mehlum, L., Tormoen, A. J., Ramberg, M., Haga, E., Diep, L. M., Laberg, S., … Grøholt, B. (2014). Dialectical behavior therapy for adolescents with repeated suicidal and self-harming behavior: A randomized trial. *Journal of the American Academy of Child and Adolescent Psychiatry*, 53(10), 1082–1091.

Mellesdal, L., Gjestad, R., Johnsen, E., Jorgensen, H. A., Oedegaard, K. J., Kroken, R. A., & Mehlum, L. (2015). Borderline personality disorder and posttraumatic stress disorder at psychiatric discharge predict general hospital admission for self-harm. *Journal of Traumatic Stress*, 28(6), 556–562.

Miller, A. L., Rathus, J. H., & Linehan, M. M. (2007). *Dialectical behavior therapy with suicidal adolescents*. New York: Guilford Press.

Neacsiu, A. D., Rizvi, S. L., & Linehan, M. M. (2010). Dialectical behavior therapy skills use as a mediator and outcome of treatment for borderline personality disorder. *Behaviour Research and Therapy*, 48(9), 832–839.

NICE (2009). *Borderline Personality Disorder: Recognition and Management. Clinical Guideline.* Retrieved from http://nice.org.uk/guidance/cg78

NICE (2011). *Self-harm in over 8s: Long-term management. NICE Guidance.* London: National Institute for Health and Care Excellence.

Oldham, J. M. (2006). Borderline personality disorder and suicidality. *American Journal of Psychiatry*, 163(1), 20–26.

Oquendo, M. A., & Mann, J. J. (2000). The biology of impulsivity and suicidality. *Psychiatric Clinics of North America*, 23(1), 11–25.

Paris, J. (2007). *Half in love with death. Managing the chronically suicidal patient.* New York: Routledge.

Pistorello, J., Fruzzetti, A. E., MacLane, C., Gallop, R. J., & Iversson, K. M. (2012). Dialectical behavior therapy (DBT) applied to college students: A randomized clinical trial. *Journal of Consulting and Clinical Psychology*, 80(6), 8.

Sher, L., Fisher, A. M., Kelliher, C. H., Penner, J. D., Goodman, M., Koenigsberg, H. W., … Hazlitt, E. A. (2016). Clinical features and psychiatric comorbidities of borderline personality disorder patients with versus without a history of suicide attempt. *Psychiatry Research*, 246, 261–266.

Skodol, A. E., Gunderson, J. G., Pfohl, B., Widiger, T. A., Livesley, W. J., & Siever, L. J. (2002). The borderline diagnosis I: Psychopathology, comorbidity, and personality structure. *Biological Psychiatry*, 51(12), 936–950.

Soloff, P. H., Lynch, K. G., Kelly, T. M., Malone, K. M., & Mann, J. J. (2000). Characteristics of suicide attempts of patients with major depressive episode and borderline personality disorder: A comparative study. *American Journal of Psychiatry*, 157(4), 601–608.

Stanley, B., Gameroff, M. J., Michalsen, V., & Mann, J. J. (2001). Are suicide attempters who self-mutilate a unique population? *American Journal of Psychiatry, 158*(3), 427–432.

Stoffers, J. M., Völlm, B. A., Rücker, G., Timmer, A., Huband, N., & Lieb, K. (2010). Pharmacological interventions for borderline personality disorder (Review). *Cochrane Database of Systematic Reviews, 6*, CD005653. doi: 10.1002/14651858.CD005653.pub2

Stoffers, J. M., Völlm, B. A., Rucker, G., Timmer, A., Huband, N., & Lieb, K. (2012). Psychological therapies for people with borderline personality disorder. *Cochrane Database of Systematic Reviews, 8*, CD005652.

Suominen, K., Isometsa, E., Suokas, J., Haukka, J., Achte, K., & Lonnqvist, J. (2004). Completed suicide after a suicide attempt: A 37-year follow-up study. *American Journal of Psychiatry, 161*(3), 562–563.

Suominen, K. H., Isometsa, E. T., Henriksson, M. M., Ostamo, A. I., & Lonnqvist, J. K. (2000). Suicide attempts and personality disorder. *Acta Psychiatrica Scandinavica, 102*(2), 118–125.

Swales, M. A., and Heard, H. L. (2007). The therapy relationship in dialectical behaviour therapy. In P. Gilbert and R. Leahy (Eds.), *The therapeutic relationship in the cognitive behavioral psychotherapies* (pp. 185–204). New York: Routledge.

Turner, R. M. (2000). Naturalistic evaluation of dialectical behavior therapy—oriented treatment for borderline personality disorder. *Cognitive and Behavioral Practice, 7, 7.*

Van Den Bosch, L. M., Koeter, M. W., Stijnen, T., Verheul, R., & Van Den Brink, W. (2005). Sustained efficacy of dialectical behaviour therapy for borderline personality disorder. *Behavior Research and Therapy, 43, 10.*

Verheul, R., Van Den Bosch, L. M., Koeter, M. W., De Ridder, M. A., Stijnen, T., & Van Den Brink, W. (2003). Dialectical behaviour therapy for women with borderline personality disorder: 12-month, randomised clinical trial in The Netherlands. *British Journal of Psychiatry, 182*, 135–140.

....

CHAPTER 16

VALIDATION PRINCIPLES AND PRACTICES IN DIALECTICAL BEHAVIOUR THERAPY

....

ALAN E. FRUZZETTI AND ALLISON K. RUORK

Introduction

....

THE links between validation and healthy social relationships, and the importance of validation in soothing negative emotions, have been understood for generations. Thich Nhat Hanh notes that in the ancient Buddhist writings of the *Lotus Sutra*, "compassionate listening brings about healing" (1998, p. 79). Similarly, validation of one type or another has had an essential role in almost every psychotherapy since Freud's dominance waned, including Rogerian or client-centred psychotherapy (cf. Rogers, 1961), existentially orientated psychotherapy (cf. Binswanger, 1956), cognitive therapy (cf. Safran & Segal, 1996), behaviour therapy (cf. Kohlenberg & Tsai, 1991), mentalization-based therapy (cf. Bateman & Fonagy, 2004), and, of course, dialectical behaviour therapy (DBT, Linehan, 1993). Indeed, Linehan's incorporation of aspects of Rogers' approach to validation (e.g., Rogers & Truax, 1967) was intentional. Nevertheless, the role, implementation details, and theoretical understanding of validation vary widely across psychotherapies. This chapter highlights the role of validation in DBT, and how those principles are put into practice.

First, in DBT the term "validation" (a noun) actually reflects a *process*. This includes several steps: 1) the client engages in some behaviour, which could be doing something overtly (including verbally), experiencing an emotion or desire, thinking, behaving in a pattern, etc.; 2) the client may, or may not, express the behaviour accurately (words, tone, body posture, facial expression, etc.); 3) the therapist pays attention and attempts to understand the client's experience and behaviour(s) from the client's perspective; and, finally, 4) expresses that understanding, usually verbally. This last bit is often what is called "validation," but it is essential to put that activity into context, recognizing that when the therapist validates, he or she is responding to a client behaviour, and highlighting what is truly understandable, or legitimate (valid) about that behaviour (for our purposes, both public/overt behaviours and private ones like experiencing emotion or thinking, will be considered "behaviours"). Thus, validation is really a process that includes the therapist taking the client's experience seriously and communicating in an honest way that some client behaviour (experience, action, etc.) is understandable and legitimate in one or more ways. Thus, validation is the expression of genuine understanding of a person's experience or behaviour (emotion, want, thought, sensation, action, etc.), and how that behaviour or experience "makes sense" (Fruzzetti & Iverson, 2004; Linehan, 1993).

We will now describe the theory or principles underlying validation in DBT. Following that we will describe client behaviours and experiences to validate and when to do so, various ways to validate (levels, or types of validation), and finally, discuss what it means (and what to do) when therapist validation apparently fails, or results in increased client distress and dysregulation.

THEORY AND PRINCIPLES OF VALIDATING IN DBT

Validation is a social behaviour with both social and emotional consequences for the person whose behaviour is being validated. Precision requires that we describe specifically how validating and invalidating responses work in DBT, within a behavioural framework. For example, although validation is often considered to be a reinforcer, we will explain how this can be true, but also how much more sophisticated validating responses can be.

Validation can function in a number of ways, including: (1) to increase therapist/client rapport and strengthen the therapeutic alliance, (2) dialectically, as a means of balancing change-oriented strategies by communicating acceptance and understanding, (3) as the key therapist change behaviour in discrimination training, primarily as a reinforcer of nascent skillful behaviour and clinical progress; (4) as an eliciting stimulus (including as an establishing operation); and (5) to model and strengthen self-validation. In addition, we will highlight the important role of *invalidation* (of invalid behaviours) in DBT. However, we will begin by noting the various client behaviours (or targets) that the therapist might validate.

Targets for Validating Responses

Most important in DBT, therapists validate only *valid* behaviours, and *only* in the way(s) that the behaviour is valid. Put another way, it must be clinically effective to validate whatever behaviour is targeted. The therapeutic relationship is a real relationship between two people, who also have distinct roles. Validating something invalid risks significant disruption to the relationship (and possibly reinforcing dysfunction). In addition, validating something invalid could strengthen that invalid behaviour, and risk iatrogenic consequences: "Without a clear understanding of what behaviours are necessary to get from the client's current state of functioning, to that which the client aspires to, validation is in danger of strengthening iatrogenic outcomes, at worst, or stagnation, at best" (Linehan, 1997, p. 374).

For example, imagine that a person is extremely anxious getting into his or her friend's car. The facts are, the friend has an excellent driving record, and has a new car with up to date safety features. It is a sunny day, the roads are clear and dry, and there is little traffic. Is the anxiety valid based on the present moment situation? Clearly, it is not. So, what is valid about the anxiety? First, it has "existential" validity: the person actually feels it. So, just acknowledging his or her anxiety is one way to validate ("you seem really anxious right now"). Maybe the anxiety has nothing to do with getting into the car. Perhaps the person is going to get some extensive medical or dental procedures and has had painful experiences with similar procedures in the past. Then, the anxiety makes sense in another way (anticipatory anxiety). However, imagine the person had a serious car accident a few weeks ago. Then, the anxiety might be based on that recent experience (classically conditioned anxiety). Either way, any validating response beyond an acknowledgement of the reality of the anxiety would require some understanding of the causes and conditions that gave rise to it. The most validating thing to do might be to ask questions, and help the person understand his or her own experience better, which would lead to opportunities to validate more fully (and might lead to opportunities to help alleviate his or her suffering, too). So, validation targets must be valid, not imagined, not patronizing, and must be connected to the person's history and experiences, as well as understood in the present moment situation.

Colloquially, people often speak about validating a person (e.g., "she validated me"). Although that kind of language speaks to the rather large impact that validation can have, in DBT the therapist is typically validating a specific behaviour or experience of the person. Of course, in DBT, behaviour is anything a person does (or does not do), and includes experiencing emotion, thinking, wanting, talking, other forms of expression, other overt behaviours, sensing, awareness, and so on. In principle, any of these behaviours, or the absence of any of these behaviours, could be validated. The key piece is that the therapist accurately perceives the behaviour (or its absence), and is trying to understand its legitimacy in context.

For example, the client might simply look sad. The therapist might simply notice this and validate it as part of the client's experience (e.g., "you look really sad"). This can have a variety of salutary effects (as explained below), including helping to soothe the client's painful emotion and perhaps to invite or elicit more fully accurate expression. The client might further explain that his or her plans with a friend fell through, and the client is really disappointed. Knowing how lonely the client is, the therapist might further validate the client's sadness: "It makes a lot of sense that you'd be disappointed. Anybody would in this situation."

Yet, targets for validation can be much broader than this. Thinking, especially non-judgmental thinking and accurate appraisals, are all easily validated because they are not likely provocative and are easy to understand. Of course, judgments, misappraisals, and problematic thinking *can* be validated, but it is trickier, and these must be validated in quite different ways. If a client says, "I know I'm just a terrible, awful person," the therapist *can* validate what is actually valid about this kind of self-invalidating thinking and statement: "I know you often *think* very judgmentally about yourself." The therapist might add additional, more change-oriented interventions immediately, of course (e.g., "What actually happened? What did you do? Can you be more descriptive?" or, simply, "Can you say that again, without the judgments?"). But, leading with the validating statement may be essential to let the client know that the therapist *does understand* his or her experience, and its importance to the client, prior to targeting it for change.

In addition to emotional experiences (especially painful ones) and thinking, the therapist can also validate what the client wants (even if it's not likely, or even impossible, to get it), how difficult certain tasks might be, his or her point of view (even if ineffective, or logically inconsistent), sense of being out of control, and other private experiences. It is also very important to validate new, more skillful behaviours of all kinds (e.g., mindfulness/awareness, interpersonal skills, managing distress effectively, managing emotions, self-validation, accurate expression, and "wise mind" of any kind). Validating these targets is, of course, the key way that DBT therapists instantiate "acceptance" in DBT, and provide balance to change strategies. Again, as a process, mindful, non-judgmental awareness of the client and his or her experience and patterns, along with curiosity and awareness of treatment targets, all inform what behaviours or targets (and how) the therapist validates.

Validation and the Therapeutic Alliance

Validation communicates acceptance, understanding and legitimacy of an individual's thoughts, feelings, behaviour and experiences. By doing so, validation strengthens the therapeutic alliance. This can make validation a powerful tool even in the early stages of the therapeutic relationship. This communication of understanding, acceptance and legitimacy increases positive affect and decreases negative affect. In experimental social situations, subjects were randomly assigned (without them knowing) to receive either validating or invalidating responses when experiencing distress, and subjected to ongoing stressors. Validation reduced negative emotional arousal according to both self-report and psychophysiological indices of negative emotion even while the stressors continued, whereas invalidation resulted in no reduction in negative arousal (Shenk & Fruzzetti, 2011). Thus, validation can have a very soothing effect on negative emotional arousal. Fruzzetti and colleagues have demonstrated the soothing effects of validation in a variety of clinical situations, including with families (Payne & Fruzzetti, 2017; Shenk & Fruzzetti, 2014) and in chronic pain patients (Edlund, Carlsson, Linton, Fruzzetti, & Tillfors, 2015; Linton, Boersma, Vangronsveld, & Fruzzetti, 2012).

This is particularly important for dysregulated clients who may have intense and/or dysregulated emotion in the therapy session. By finding the valid part and validating the client's experiences, even if extreme, the therapist can help the client reduce negative affect and dysregulation, improving both the relationship and the client's ability to benefit from treatment. However, further research is needed to determine how much of the alliance is a direct result of validation per se, as opposed to the whole "package" of acceptance and change strategies delivered dialectically.

There are other likely effects of therapist validation, even of dysregulated emotion. By soothing with validation, the client's negative emotion is reduced, which likely not only improves the alliance, but also may help reduce drop-out. For example, Wnuk et al. (2013) found that stronger client-reported alliance predicted treatment completion (vs. drop-out).

Of course, as noted earlier, dysregulated emotion is not the only target of therapist validation. Validating client desires and goals, increasing use of skills, and in-the-moment wise-mind, as well as validating the reality of dysfunctional behaviours (urges to suicide, relapse, drop out of treatment, etc.) all help to build a strong and therapeutic relationship with the client and set the foundation for effective change.

Validation to Balance Change

Change is difficult, and pressure to change can quickly create friction and become counterproductive. Validation, because it soothes negative emotion and strengthens the relationship, while communicating understanding of the difficulties present, is the "grease" that reduces this interpersonal friction and allows the therapist to keep pushing for needed (and desired) change, even when it is very difficult. It can make sense *both* that the client "feels" like giving up, *and* also wants to climb out of painful situations and emotions. In DBT, the therapist validates the former in the service of the latter.

Thus, the ratio of acceptance and validation to change strategies will be based on the individual client, both in terms of the client's interpersonal style and his or her progress in the course of therapy. Focusing exclusively on change can communicate to clients that they are unacceptable and are making insufficient progress and/or are not working hard enough (regardless of effort), and can be perceived as overwhelming This often results in increased fear, anxiety, shame, and hopelessness which can impede change and growth and increase negative reactions toward the therapist. When the therapist-client relationship is newer and more uncertain for the client (and the therapist is less aware of the client's experiences and patterns), more validation strategies can be more frequent. In later stages of therapy when the client is more comfortable, the therapist knows the client better, and the relationship between client and therapist more stable, the balance can be adjusted to include an increase in change oriented strategies (Linehan, 1997).

New environmental stressors or events, increased demands, and discussion of new, potentially difficult, topics should also be accompanied by increased validation (Linehan, 1997). This increase likely helps clients feel understood and comfortable discussing sensitive topics or when faced with challenges. It is important for the therapist to approach each client and situation individually when determining how to balance change strategies with acceptance and validation, and to determine how much validation, and in what ways, are needed to continue to work effectively on important change targets.

Validation as a Reinforcer

Clearly, validation has enormous acceptance appeal, and acceptance properties: Validation communicates acceptance and understanding of the client's experience. Thus, validation is a potent and positive "stimulus" or event for anyone, including clients. Thus, validation has the potential to function as a reinforcer, a necessary piece of any operant change strategy.

When validation is employed as a reinforcer, it should be contingent on the client showing improved, or at least desirable, behaviour that represents clinical progress. One simple application of this is in discrimination training. In behaviour therapy, discrimination training is a process in which, in a given situation, one behaviour is reinforced and others are not. For example, language learning is almost entirely a process of discrimination training: in the presence of a cup full of water, a small child might say "luf" and be ignored (intentionally, or because the parent or caregiver has no idea what the child wants). However, when the child says "dink" the adult smiles and gives the child the cup, and says, "drink?" Later, the child says, "dink" and the adult says, "drink ... say D R ink" and the child says "drink" (or something closer to that), at which point the adult gives the cup of water to the child. Many, many behaviours are learned through discrimination training.

In DBT for example, the client might appear really angry. The therapist might validate: "you look really angry," and the client might nod, indicating that is correct. When queried about what happened (perhaps formally, by doing a chain analysis), it might turn out that a couple of the teen client's friends ate lunch together earlier that day, while the client was busy making up work that was missed the previous week when the client was home with the flu. After figuring this out, the therapist might query further, "Hmm. I know that you're feeling angry, that you would have preferred to have had lunch with your friends rather than making up missing school work (validating the reality of the client's emotion). If you notice that part ... that you really wanted to have lunch with them and missed out on it, do you notice any other emotion?" The client might notice, and express, "yeah, I suppose ... I really missed out ... they had fun, I am really disappointed, too." The therapist, having directed the client's attention to perhaps the primary emotion in the situation, would likely validate the primary emotion (disappointment) differently than the previous, likely secondary emotion (anger): "Of course ... that WOULD be disappointing ... anybody would be disappointed then." Over time, discrimination training would help this client learn to identify, label, and express primary emotions more accurately. And, validating the emerging, more skillful behaviour is simultaneously likely to reinforce and thus increase that behaviour, while extinguishing older, less skillful alternatives.

This kind of discrimination training around emotion, in particular, is dialectical: yes, you feel that emotion (secondary) AND there is another emotion (primary) that may be important to notice and manage. Anger is not wrong in that situation, but rather is perhaps less justified, less primary, than disappointment, and other people will more immediately be able to understand, and hence validate, the primary emotion, by definition. It is more effective to spend more time with primary emotions, which are much more readily regulated (Fruzzetti, Crook, Erikson, Lee, & Worrall, 2008). In order for this kind of discrimination training to be effective, there must be differential validation for the different behaviours. Thus, secondary emotions would typically be validated in one way (noticed, reflected, acknowledged), whereas primary emotions would be validated differently (with more enthusiasm, normalized, and tied to being effective). These distinctions about different ways to validate will be described in detail in a later section.

Even in situations not warranting discrimination training per se, validation can still be a reinforcer (intentionally or not). For example, a therapist might validate a client who reports having tried using skills but was not particularly successful in its application, yet continued to try, by saying: "It sounds like you tried really hard, and felt really frustrated when it didn't work the way you expected, but you didn't give up!" Note that the therapist also could have responded with praise instead: "That's so wonderful that you tried to be skillful in that situation!" Either way, it is very likely that the therapist wants the client to continue to practice skills in that situation (wants to reinforce that behaviour). Clearly, there is at least a bit of overlap between praise (the expression of approval) and validation (communicating understanding about the client's experience). Praise can, at times, have validating components, and validating responses can concurrently communicate approval (praise). However, in DBT, validation is a far more important therapist activity.

Similarly, validation functions to provide clients with feedback more globally, about themselves as acceptable human beings, and their behaviours as not "crazy" (Fruzzetti & Iverson, 2004; Linehan, 1997). It models thinking about oneself, as well as behaviour and the origins of that behaviour, using a non-judgmental and non-pejorative attitude. This can be particularly important for clients who construct a sense of meaning from understanding the development of their behaviour. Clients may also be in need of confirmation that their behaviour is appropriate, reasonable or normal, particularly if they are isolated, or have been raised in, or are currently in, environments which never or rarely provided this information, and may have even punished such behaviour, leading to a preponderance of self-judgments and self-invalidation (Fruzzetti, Shenk, & Hoffman, 2005; Linehan, 1997).

Validation as an Eliciting Stimulus to Change Behaviour

It may seem like a strange idea that a therapeutic *response* to a client could also act as an eliciting stimulus. However, behavioural theory tells us that, in a stream of behaviours, various behaviours can have different functions, depending on the analysis (cf. Skinner, 1953).

In the transactional or biopsychosocial model for emotion dysregulation and bor-derline personality disorder, chronic and pervasive invalidation (of valid behaviours and experiences) is understood to be a key developmental feature of the client's family and/or social environment (Crowell et al., 2009; Fruzzetti et al., 2005; Linehan, 1993). Invalidation, then, is a very common experience for DBT clients, and likely elicits a pat-terned response that includes: escalating negative emotional arousal (including fear and perhaps anger associated with the person doing the invalidating, and also shame), corresponding reductions in cognitive complexity and flexibility, increased anger and shame, and escape urges associated with social disconnection and rejection, and a variety of other problematic and unskillful reactions. In a sense, being invalidated is a "signal" that the other person is not understanding, and possibly not valuing, your ex-perience, and consequently is likely to proceed in ways that block goals and feel hurtful and disappointing (Fruzzetti & Worrall, 2010). This signal cues up a whole variety of possibly appropriate (but potentially maladaptive) learned responses.

In contrast, it is likely that a validating response, in particular in situations in which invalidating ones have been common, will elicit an entirely different pattern, or reper-toire: de-escalating negative emotional arousal, increased awareness, increased capac-ity for thinking and problem solving, and cognitive flexibility, more connection to the person doing the validating, and increased generally skillful behaviour associated with arousal reduction and social connection. Thus, not only does validation soothe arousal, it may elicit an entirely more skillful set of behaviours because it "signals" that this very different set of responses is warranted and likely will be effective.

Validation to Model and Strengthen Self-Validation

When therapists validate their clients, they provide the initial step in teaching and increasing the clients' abilities to identify and describe their own emotion in a non-judg-mental or non-pejorative way (Linehan, 1997). This may be particularly important for clients who have been in especially invalidating environments, as these environments tend to teach the client not to trust their own emotional experiences (Fruzzetti et al., 2005). Validation of their valid experiences helps them learn to trust their own experi-ence, and helps to reduce client passivity, in two ways: first, by modelling appropriate validation the client can learn various ways to self-validate, and the different ways that both public and private behaviours can be valid. Second, by reinforcing clients' mindful awareness (noticing their own internal experiences, without prejudice or judgment), they build trust in themselves as "wise" observers, increase self-awareness, and reduce passivity (Fruzzetti et al., 2005; Linehan, 1997).

One risk is that a clinician will validate client self-mistrust. This is most likely to occur when the therapist validates, and therefore reinforces, client self-denigration or self-mistrust, or even very basic self-awareness. For example, a client might seek reassurance from the therapist about what he or she is feeling or wanting, not trusting his or her own self-awareness. If the therapist supplies the "answer" (e.g., by telling the client what it looks like the client is feeling or wanting), not only is the opportunity for new learning lost, but the therapist may inadvertently reinforce the client for looking externally for internal answers. In order to prevent this the therapist must generally avoid the use of strong validation strategies immediately following dysfunctional behaviours, in particular those which are maintained by eliciting validation from the social environment. Therefore, it is especially important that clinicians validate differentially, primarily using stronger validation following valid behaviour that is to be strengthened, including acts of self-awareness and self-trust and client expression of confidence in their own abilities to know what they feel, want, like, and so on (Linehan, 1997).

Early in treatment, the client may have a very poor skill repertoire vis-à-vis private behaviours (what the client thinks, wants, feels, etc.), and the therapist may be willing to provide a lot of help and suggestions based on external cues, normative emotions, and so on. Over the course of DBT, the therapist's role, or help, in the same situation would generally be expected to fade out. Subsequently, the therapist should more and more frequently answer questions about the client's emotions, and even questions about what skills to use, with "what do you think?" and use validation in a dialectical manner more regularly.

The Role of Therapist Invalidating Invalid Behaviours

No discussion of therapist validation would be complete without acknowledging that sometimes it is important for therapists actually to *invalidate* clients' invalid behaviour. For example, a client in her very first session might say, "I can tell that you already regret taking me on as a client, that you don't like me." Assuming, of course, that this is not at all the therapist's experience, there are a number of ways to respond to this, including trying to figure out what the cue for that thought (or fear, or whatever else is being expressed) was, typically by doing a chain analysis, even if brief. This will help the therapist find something valid to validate. A valid "kernel" that might be found through such a chain could be, "given that you've had a lot of experiences with relationships blowing up, I can understand how you might worry a bit about me, and our relationship" (or something similar). However, at some point in the conversation, after finding something(s) valid to validate, it is important that the therapist actually invalidate the client's invalid statement (and thought or emotion), and say clearly, "Actually, you've read me wrong. I realize you don't know me well, so I don't expect you to believe me much (likely acknowledging or validating the client's experience of mistrust), but, truth be told, I am actually quite glad to meet you today, and have not had any regrets about us working together."

However, even this "invalidation of the invalid" runs the risk of reinforcing self-judgments and passivity (see above), so if the client were to continue to express these kinds of thoughts and fears, the therapist would offer less and less direct reassurance because doing so would begin to validate the invalid behaviours of the client being passive and unskillful (reacting to the therapist based on historical reactions from others, rather than the growing history they have together), and instead increasingly ask the client to rely on his or her own experiences with the therapist (relationship mindfulness, present moment) to answer his or her own question. Subsequently, the therapist could then validate the client's valid experiences and statements. For example, the client, after being queried what his or her experience was right now, might then say, "well, you have not done anything yet to support my fears about this" or "I guess right now it seems like you are just listening to me." The therapist can then validate the valid, "right, you are reading me right." Note that the behaviour being validated is the client's skillful noticing of what is real in the moment (relationship mindfulness), which is relatively unlikely to reinforce dysfunctional requests for reassurance, mistrust of his or her own experience, or general passivity.

LEVELS OR TYPES OF VALIDATION

Linehan (1997) described six levels of verbal validation that together account for most of the acceptance strategies in DBT: (1) paying attention to the client, active listening, and openness to what the client is experiencing; (2) accurate reflection, acknowledgement of the client's experience; (3) articulating client unverbalized behaviour; (4) validating client behaviour based on previous learning or other client limitations; (5) validating the client's behaviour as normative; and (6) radical genuineness. We will add an additional level: (7) selective self-disclosure of the therapist as validation of the client's experience. In addition, doing what is needed in the moment, or being responsive to the client's needs, may be considered "functional" validation (responses that are not verbal per se). Although this framework of levels or types of validation was developed specifically for use in DBT, it could be used across many treatment approaches, all of which utilize one or more types of validation.

Of course, validation is important across all relationships, not just in psychotherapy, and a similar schematic can be employed to understand validation in close relationships (e.g., Fruzzetti, 2006), and validation has similar effects across different relationships. The "higher" levels of validation depend on the therapist already having utilized one or more of the previous levels of validation, and the higher levels are hierarchically both more complex and more complete (Linehan, 1997). However, the most effective type of validation is the level or type that fits the situation, and the therapeutic goals, in the moment.

Level 1: Openness, Paying Attention, and Active Listening

Level 1 validation requires the therapist to listen and observe what the client is saying, as well as the client's emotional expression, with curiosity and openness. The focus of this level is to be interested in what the client says and does, to not make assumptions, and to pay close attention to nuances of response (e.g., expression, posture, vocal tone) during the interaction as well as more clearly demonstrated behaviour. This process of active, interested listening communicates to clients that they are taken seriously and heard. However, it is not without challenges, as it requires the clinician to find a balance between paying close attention to the client and filtering and applying this information based on therapeutic targets, case conceptualization, and the client's history (Linehan, 1997).

Level 1 validation is particularly important during the beginning of treatment as it facilitates the building of rapport and getting to know the client, but is essential throughout treatment for the client, and is similarly essential in other modes of DBT (skills training, generalization opportunities, consultation team, family interventions). Open and active listening requires the clinician to remain largely focused and engaged in the present moment. However, this does not mean that the therapist remains silent. Instead, reciprocal communication strategies should be used to *communicate* this level of attention and openness. Ordinary conversation cues, such as "Mmhmm" or "uh-huh" and nodding, "What happened next?" "What were you thinking while this happened?" further communicates that the therapist is tracking and understanding both the client's story and perspective (Fruzzetti, 2006; Linehan, 1997).

It is important that the therapist participate in the world of the client. The therapist does so by taking the client's perspective. This is frequently achieved by finding an experience or quality within the therapist, or his or her own experience to convey understanding. This might be done through the use of metaphor, analogy, or an imaginal story, which matches and highlights the client's experience in some essential way so that the client knows that the therapist understands. This may require frequent checking in with the client to ensure that the therapist's understanding matches the client's perspective as well as the facts of the situation (Linehan, 1997). However, in order to be effective, the clinician cannot become lost in the client's experience. In order to achieve a balance, it is important to be mindful of the client's goals and compare the content of the client's responses with these goals, never deviating from therapeutic activities that work toward those goals. For example, a therapist can be empathic and take the perspective of a client who reports having engaged in some dysfunctional behaviour which previously had been effective in some way (e.g., self-harm). In addition to finding the validity in the dysfunctional behaviour, the therapist must also determine the ways in which the behaviour is invalid, including how it thwarts the client's long-term goals. Thus, it is important to pay attention both to what is valid (acceptance), and also to what is dysfunctional (invalid in achieving long-term goals). Effective therapeutic decision-making can then follow, accordingly.

Level 2:   Accurate Reflection and Acknowledging the Experience of the Client

Level 2 validation requires the therapist to acknowledge or reflect clients' thoughts, experiences, feelings, behaviours, and assumptions back to them accurately. In a sense, this is simply acknowledging the client's phenomenology. This conveys (to a greater degree than Level 1 validation) that the therapist understands the context of their experiences and their responses to such experiences. Level 2 validation corresponds to what the client has actually said, or what can be directly observed by the clinician, with no additions or interpretations, regardless of other knowledge or awareness on the part of the therapist. In order to reflect accurately the therapist must understand the events, and context, of the client's perspective and experience. Through an iterative process of accurately reflecting and acknowledging the client's experience, the client can correct and clarify any misunderstandings, and thus facilitate the therapist and client to work collaboratively from there.

It is important for clinicians to reflect and acknowledge the client's feelings and experiences, without necessarily treating these responses as facts. For a client who is currently suicidal, and says despondently "It's never going to get better!" Rather than reflecting as a fact the idea that the client's situation will not improve, the therapist might instead reflect, "It sounds like you're feeling really hopeless right now, and you're thinking it will never get better." The former is inaccurate, the latter accurate. The therapist must identify both the client's perspective and the facts. However, at this level of validation the therapist does not discuss how the client's experiences and responses correspond to the facts (if they are at all different), but rather simply acknowledges them as the client's experience.

Level 3: Articulating Unverbalized Experiences or Behaviours

In Level 3 validation the therapist is able to articulate the client's unverbalized (unspoken) feelings, wishes, needs, or thoughts by "reading" the client's behaviour in context and combining it with their understanding of the client's history and perspective. The client may not have verbalized something for a variety of reasons, and no assumptions are necessarily made about the motivation for not verbalizing them. For example, the client: 1) may simply be unaware of his or her behaviour (e.g., an emotion); 2) may not have the words (or other skills) to verbalize it; 3) may be having a negative and/or judgmental reaction to the behaviour; 4) may be afraid to verbalize it to the therapist, and/or have an aversive history around similar verbalizations; 5) may be overwhelmed; or there may be many other possible reasons.

This form of validation further communicates to clients that they are understood, and does so at a deeper level than the previous two forms of validation. "Reading" a client accurately requires sensitivity and empathy for the client's perspective, history, patterns, and responses. Articulating unverbalized emotion can also communicate to clients that their responses are predictable and justified in the context of their experiences and environment. However, this is only implied, because at this level of validation the therapist does not explicitly state this. Clients often invalidate their own experiences, even if they are initially able to accurately label them, which makes this a particularly powerful form of validation. When clients are unable to label their thoughts or emotions, particularly in the case of painful emotions, articulating the unverbalized may help them gain a better understanding of themselves.

In situations in which clients miss their own primary emotions, the therapist can offer a Level 3 validation, something like, "in that situation, I wonder if you might have also felt ___." Notice how this is offered as a hypothesis, not something the therapist is 100% certain about. This affords the client the opportunity to "try it on" and see if it is accurate, and provide further accurate expression of his or her own.

It is important that clinicians articulate unverbalized responses that represent both client strengths and weaknesses, as this helps to communicate that the client is accepted as is, and understood, by the therapist. In contrast, ignoring, or only validating clients' strengths, can communicate that client struggles or dysfunctional behaviours (or lack of skills) are unacceptable, and that the therapist is not capable of or interested in completely understanding them.

Therapists should be cautious when using Level 3 validation. The risk is that therapists will become overly attached to a particular theory or may interpret the observed functions of a behaviour as corresponding to a particular intent. For example, a client who threatens suicide at the prospect of being left by a loved one may be viewed as "manipulative," instead of being perceived as desperate and hopeless. Worse, any protest on the part of the client may be viewed as further proof of the validity of the therapist's theory. Empathy for the client's perspective and experience (good Level 1 validation) is important to help prevent this. In addition, developing multiple hypotheses may help the clinician avoid becoming overly attached to a single one, and respond flexibly to disconfirming or contradictory evidence (Linehan, 1997).

Level 4: Validating in Terms of Previous Learning or Other Limitations

This type of validation acknowledges that certain thoughts, feelings, and overt behaviour are understandable in the context of the client's learning history or current limitations (e.g., medical illness or other limiting client factors), even if the behaviour is otherwise problematic or invalid. Almost all behaviour serves a function, and is adaptive in the context within which it is learned, and can therefore be validated. This level of validation is based on the therapist acknowledging the likely previously adaptive function of behaviour.

For example, Jasmine was previously repeatedly assaulted by her former partner, Bob, but she was able to leave him. Now, several years later, she has found a new partner, Bryan, who has never been aggressive or violent with her (nor with anyone else), and they have a generally good relationship. However, when they do have a disagreement, and Bryan gets upset, he does sometimes take a deep breath and appears upset. When he does that, Jasmine becomes overwhelmed with fear. However, because of that fear, she does not tell Bryan about her experience. She does tell her therapist, however, that she is afraid of Bryan and wants to leave him. This occurs many months into treatment, following many examples of Jasmine telling her therapist how loving and kind Bryan is, and having had several sessions that included him because he wanted to know how best to support Jasmine and her treatment. After getting a detailed description of the event, it was apparent that Bryan was never verbally, or non-verbally, threatening. However, his deep breath bore a similarity to what Bob had done many times just prior to exploding in a violent rage. They agreed to have a session with Bryan, and he explained that he was just confused and didn't know what to say, because Jasmine had seemed to withdraw from their discussion and seemed distant and aloof. He described being sad, not angry. The therapist offered a Level 4 validation: "It makes sense that you would be very afraid in that moment, given the awful experiences you had with Bob." Of course, in this situation, they had also successfully identified a change target for Jasmine (with help from Bryan): how to respond to Bryan in the moment, and not to respond to him as if he were Bob. This example highlights the importance of accepting and validating the reality of the client's prior learning without judgment.

Another example might be a client who lacks skills for managing overwhelming emotion, and has been cutting to manage these emotions since her late teens. Despite learning several new skills, and being committed to not self-harming, she is frustrated that she still has such strong urges to cut and says, "What is wrong with me?!" A Level 4 validation might be, "It makes sense that you still have high urges to cut; it's the only thing you had that worked for you to get any relief from your emotional pain for a long time." Depending on the type of behaviour it may also be important for the therapist to add that while the client's behaviour makes sense in the context of his or her history, it may no longer be serving the client's long-term interests and goals. Building on the previous example, the therapist might say "... and now we've got to work on practising skills and giving you more options that are effective in reducing your dysregulated emotions, so that your brain will learn to rely on those skills instead." Thus, Level 4 validation can often be an acceptance step on the way toward a change goal.

Level 5: Validation as Normalizing the Client's Behaviour or Experience

Level 5 validation occurs when the therapist acknowledges that the client's behaviour is legitimate, justifiable, and *normative*. The therapist understands, and communicates, that the client's behaviour or experience is essentially how anybody would respond to such a situation. At this level of validation, the therapist must find the "kernel of truth" in the client's behaviour, highlighting aspects of their responses which make sense in the current context (Linehan, 1993, 1997). While the client's response to a situation may also make sense in terms of previous learning, the behaviour is justified based on its own merit and acknowledging previous learning history is not necessary, and in fact may be invalidating.

Level 5 validation can be used when the client's behaviour is based on empirical fact and is normative within the client's culture. For example, imagine a person walking into his or her flat and discovering two burly people inside who are stealing her belongings and ransacking the flat. Fear is completely normal, and running back out the door would

LEVELS OR TYPES OF VALIDATION   339

make sense ... anybody would be scared in that situation. Even if this client has a severe anxiety disorder, it is important to validate that the fear in this situation is completely normative, and not present because of her generalized conditioning to fear cues, nor is her fear because she has an anxiety disorder, PTSD, and so on. In fact, validating at Level 4 ("it makes sense that you were afraid, given your anxiety disorder") would be quite invalidating in this situation, because the situation was truly dangerous.

Some behaviours require a Level 5 validating response, as the example above illustrates. The experience of primary emotions, and the accurate expression of primary emotions, because by definition they are universal and adaptive, typically would be validated in a Level 5 way. For example, feeling sadness and grief at the death of a close relative or friend is normative, as would be shame at being ridiculed in public, or joy upon receiving love and attention from a person you care about. Primary emotions almost always provide at least one "kernel of truth" that can be validated in a Level 5 way.

In fact, most behaviours that are simply normative and do not lead directly to dysfunction are validated this way. However, determining when Level 5 validation is appropriate can be a complex process in some situations. The therapist infrequently has direct access to all relevant empirical facts and must rely on reporting from the client, and as a result may need to conduct a fair amount of sleuthing in order to get a more complete picture in specific situations. In these cases, it is important for the therapist to balance effectiveness with what is right, or correct. The complex nature of validation at this level requires careful examination on the part of the therapist, and constant focus on the client's long-term goals.

One way for the therapist to proceed also overlaps a little bit into Level 6 (below), requiring the therapist to imagine how he or she might feel, what she or he might think, want, or do in a given situation (like the one a client is in, or describing). This activity equalizes the relationship in some ways, instantiating half of the relationship dialectic in DBT: that the therapist and client are equal human beings with equal value, *and* also have very separate roles in the therapy. If the therapist would think, feel, or act in a similar manner to the client, that is some evidence that the behaviour is normative. Communicating this shared responding ("I would feel that way/do that/want that too!") provides both a Level 5 validating response and also carries over into Level 6.

Level Six: Treating the Person as Valid—Radical Genuineness

Validation Levels 1 through 5 may be viewed as specific ways to validate specific behaviours. Level 6 differs in both level and kind: the individual as a person is validated rather than specific behaviours or even patterns of responses. Level 6 validation treats the client as a legitimate, capable person of equal status, worthy of respect, while maintaining strong empathy for his or her individual difficulties and challenges, similar to the person-oriented approach pioneered by Carl Rogers (1961). This is in stark contrast to what Stage 1 clients may be accustomed to in their natural environment: being treated as fragile, incompetent, broken, or disgusting, and often in a condescending manner. In Level 6, the client is neither to be feared as overly powerful nor as overly fragile. In a real relationship, we treat the other person as an equal human being, of course simultaneously recognizing his or her pain and limitations on the one hand, and skills, strengths, and competencies on the other. The same is true in DBT.

Level 6 validation requires the clinician to be completely, or radically, genuine within the therapeutic relationship (while still dialectically within the therapist role). Radical genuineness requires that the clinician be mindful of the present moment while reacting to the client spontaneously. In order to achieve this genuineness, the therapist must be willing to abandon certain narrow conceptions about the professional role and respond to the client empathically. In this context, both confrontational (irreverent) and cheerleading techniques can be examples of Level 6 validation, as can expressions of genuine warmth and caring, and helping the client to tolerate painful emotions. By not treating the client as fragile or incompetent, irreverence and confrontation communicate that the client is a complete individual, capable of change and who does not need to be handled gently or with fear. Cheerleading also communicates to the client that he or she is capable of change and able to overcome challenges and difficulties in life. By having confidence and believing in the client the therapist validates these capabilities and the client's individual wisdom. However, it is important that the clinician balance hope and confidence in the client's abilities with realistic expectations and validation of how hard these difficulties and challenges are for the client. Without this balance, cheerleading can be perceived as invalidating by the client.

In addition, radical genuineness also allows, and may even require, the therapist to push, or simply allow, the client to experience his or her primary emotion, even when it is painful. In this case, it would reflect recognition of the validity of the emotion (Level 5) plus an appreciation for the strength of the client to tolerate even intense emotions *within a validating therapeutic environment* (assuming the client does have sufficient skills to do this productively). Of course, this also requires the clinician to be able to tolerate the client's intense emotions, and the therapist's own intense emotions as a genuinely open, caring, and compassionate human being who is empathically present with the client and his or her experience.

For example, sometimes clients tell us about events in their lives that are difficult to hear, and were painful, or even traumatic, for the client. Level 6 validation might include the therapist allowing herself or himself to tear up, be present with the sadness, genuinely feeling a lot of empathy for the client and hold a belief in the client's ultimate ability to move to sadness, with sufficient skills, support, and validation. The therapist might simply say, "I feel so sad hearing this story" (or, "I am impressed how you got through that"). Of course, other responses might be needed if the client does not yet have the capacity to tolerate that much negative emotion. In those situations, validating using Level 2 (noticing, reflecting) and Level 5 (normalizing), followed by coaching to tolerate and reduce the client's arousal using distress tolerance or emotion regulation skills might be required.

Thus, Level 6 is less about specific verbal responses to specific client disclosures and more about the therapist's comportment: respecting the client and his or her strengths at all times and validating the person, even while recognizing even significant skill deficits and dysfunctional repertoires, and acting with awareness of both.

Level 7:   Validating through Self-Disclosure

Level 7 validation occurs when the client discloses vulnerabilities that the therapist has also experienced, and shares with the client. Through self-disclosure of his or her own vulnerabilities (reciprocal communication) the therapist validates the client's experiences. This level of validation may be viewed as an extension of Levels 5 and 6, since it both normalizes the client's experience and treats them as a legitimate person of equal status, albeit in a very specific way. As a result, it has many of the benefits of both levels, and is a powerful tool for strengthening the therapeutic alliance. In some cases, it may also provide opportunities for modelling effective behaviour and patterns of response for the client. An example of Level 7 validation for a client who describes consistently evaluating his performance on tasks as poor, and then proceeds to ruminate or withdraw from engaging in other tasks (regardless of the facts of his or her performance), could be "I often have had the thought that I've performed poorly too. It's easy for me to get caught up in that thought and judge myself really harshly and then I end up feeling awful." Of course, this must quickly be followed by honest indications that the *therapist can manage this effectively*, or else the client could begin to worry about the therapist. In this example, the therapist could then facilitate a discussion of observing thoughts as thoughts and other mindfulness strategies the therapist has used successfully (and sometimes even unsuccessfully).

As with all self-disclosure, it is crucial that therapists be genuine and aware of the function of their self-disclosure. If the function serves to communicate to the client that he or she is understood, and not isolated in this experience, then this is likely to be experienced as validating. Of course, validation must primarily serve the client and the client's goals.

WHEN VALIDATION APPARENTLY "FAILS"

Sometimes the therapist offers what he or she thinks will be a validating response, but instead of soothed emotions and more collaboration, the client responds with escalated negative emotions. The therapist might think, "validation didn't work!" However, assuming that the client heard our actual words and tone (and that we said what we think we said), we might instead consider the possibility that we *did not understand* the client's experience, and so our communication of understanding was really a communication of misunderstanding. In other words, we were *invalidating*.

The most important step at this point is what *not* to do: Do not insist that your statement was validating. Instead, notice what happened, and use Level 6 validation: "I thought I understood what you were telling me, but you have reacted really negatively, so I have to assume that I missed the boat, that I misunderstood something important. Can you help me understand? I really want to." Of course, if really dysregulated, it may be important to coach the client to help him or her re-regulate first, then engage in the reparative behaviour.

The point here is that validation, by definition, communicates an understanding of the client's experiences and other behaviours. If the client does not "feel" understood, either the therapist's understanding, or communication, is lacking. Consequently, for clients who have a difficult time expressing themselves accurately, validation can be very difficult (Fruzzetti et al., 2005; Fruzzetti, 2006). Thus, it is important to use the consultation team to practice, stay non-defensive, and keep trying.

SUMMARY AND CONCLUSION

Validation is a complex behaviour. Some client behaviours are valid in one way (e.g., historically), but not others (e.g., in the present situation). Other client behaviours (e.g., primary emotions) are always valid, in every way. Being able to invalidate invalid behaviours (occasionally) gives us credibility and direction to validate valid ones. Validation can be understood with great precision behaviourally, but also includes the humanity and softness of client-centred therapy. Validation in DBT includes validation of the person as a stance and overarching behaviour (Level 6), begins with enormous openness and attention and maintains that activity at all times (Level 1), while still striving to find very specific behaviours in the moment (e.g., emotions, wants, actions, thoughts, sensations) that are valid in a particular way, and to validate them in that particular way (Levels 2–5). Because validating another human being soothes his or her negative emotions, validation is a powerful tool for therapists. And, because therapists and clients are people, validation is also simply the right thing to do, as it is in any relationship.

KEY MESSAGES FOR CLINICIANS

- Definition of validation: requires attention, *genuine* understanding, and communicates that understanding which is applied to specific behavioural targets (e.g., emotions, skillful actions, thoughts, etc.).

- Validation is a key social behaviour in part because it soothes negative emotional arousal, and thus is essential in any relationship, is part of every modern psychotherapy, and is a key strategy in DBT.

- In DBT we only validate *valid* behaviours; invalidating *invalid* behaviours are part of DBT change strategies.

- Validation communicates acceptance and understanding, builds the therapeutic relationship, and facilitates and balances change.

- At times, validation may be considered a reinforcer, and facilitates change and learning.

- Validation also may be considered an eliciting stimulus, signalling that a different repertoire of responses is likely to be effective, and inviting different, more regulated responses.

- There are multiple levels, or types of validation; type of validation must fit the situation and goals, as well as be appropriate to the way(s) in which a behaviour is valid.

REFERENCES

Bateman, A., & Fonagy, P. (2004). *Psychotherapy for borderline personality disorder: Mentalization Based Treatment.* London: Oxford University Press.

Binswanger, L. (1956). Existential analysis and psychotherapy. In E. Fromm-Reichmann & J. L. Moreno (Eds.), *Progress in psychotherapy* (pp. 144–168). New York: Grune & Stratton.

Crowell, S. E., Beauchaine, T. P., & Linehan, M. M. (2009). A biosocial developmental model of borderline personality: Elaborating and extending Linehan's theory. *Psychological Bulletin, 135*(3), 495–510. doi:10.1037/a0015616

Edlund, S. M., Carlsson, M. L., Linton, S. J., Fruzzetti, A. E., & Tillfors, M. (2015). I see you're in pain: The effects of partner validation on emotions in people with chronic pain. *Scandinavian Journal of Pain, 6*, 16–21.

Fruzzetti, A. E. (2006). *The high conflict couple: A dialectical behavior therapy guide to finding peace, intimacy, and validation.* Oakland, CA: New Harbinger Publications.

Fruzzetti, A.E., Crook, W., Erikson, K., Lee, J., & Worrall, J. M. (2008). Emotion regulation. In W. T. O'Donohue & J. E. Fisher (Eds.), *Cognitive behavior therapy: Applying empirically supported techniques in your practice*, 2nd Edition (pp. 174–186). New York: Wiley.

Fruzzetti, A. E., & Iverson, K. M. (2004). Mindfulness, acceptance, validation and "individual" psychopathology in couples. In S. C. Hayes, V. M. Follette, & M. M. Linehan (Eds.), *Mindfulness and acceptance: Expanding the cognitive-behavioral tradition* (pp. 168–191). New York: Guilford Press.

Fruzzetti, A. E., Shenk, C., & Hoffman, P. D. (2005). Family interaction and the development of borderline personality disorder: A transactional model. *Development and Psychopathology, 17*, 1007–1030.

Fruzzetti, A. E., & Worrall, J. M. (2010). Accurate expression and validation: A transactional model for understanding individual and relationship distress. In K. Sullivan & J. Davila (Eds.), *Support processes in intimate relationships* (pp. 121–150). New York: Oxford University Press.

Kohlenberg, R. J., & Tsai, M. (1991). *Functional Analytic Psychotherapy: A guide for creating intense and curative therapeutic relationships.* New York: Plenum.

Linehan, M. M. (1993). *Cognitive-behavioral treatment of borderline personality disorder.* New York: Guilford Press.

Linehan, M. M. (1997). Validation and psychotherapy. In A. Bohart & L. S. Greenberg (Eds.), *Empathy and psychotherapy: New directions to theory, research, and practice* (pp. 343–392). Washington, DC: American Psychological Association.

Linton, S. J., Boersma, K., Vangronsveld, K., & Fruzzetti, A. (2012). Painfully reassuring? The effects of validation on emotions and adherence in a pain test. *European Journal of Pain, 16*(4), 592–599.

Nhat Hanh, T. (1998). *The heart of the Buddha's teaching: Transforming suffering into peace, joy, and liberation.* Berkeley, CA: Parallax Press.

Payne, L., & Fruzzetti, A. E. (2017). *Effects of brief, intensive DBT parent interventions on suicidal adolescents: A randomized trial.* In review.

Rogers, C. R. (1961). *On becoming a person: A therapist's view of psychotherapy.* Boston: Houghton Mifflin.

Rogers, C. R., & Truax, C. B. (1967). The therapeutic conditions antecedent to change: A theoretical view. In C. R. Rogers (Ed.), *The therapeutic relationship and its impact* (pp. 97–108). Madison, WI: University of Wisconsin Press.

Safran, J. D., & Segal, Z. V. (1996). *Interpersonal process in cognitive therapy*. New York: Jason Aronson.

Shenk, C., & Fruzzetti, A. E. (2011). The impact of validating and invalidating responses on emotional reactivity. *Journal of Social and Clinical Psychology, 30*, 163–183.

Shenk, C., & Fruzzetti, A. E. (2014). Parental validating and invalidating responses and adolescent psychological functioning: An observational study. *The Family Journal, 22*, 43–48. doi: 10.1177/1066480713490900

Skinner, B. F. (1953). *Science and human behavior*. New York: The Free Press.

Wnuk, S., McMain, S., Links, P. S., Habinski, L., Murray, J., & Guimond, T. (2013). Factors related to dropout from treatment in two outpatient treatments for borderline personality disorder. *Journal of Personality Disorders, 27*(6), 716–726.

CHAPTER 17

RESPONDING TO CLIENTS' IN-SESSION CLINICAL BEHAVIOURS

HEIDI L. HEARD

INTRODUCTION

SINCE Freud's development of psychoanalysis, many models of psychotherapy have attended to how clients' behaviours during sessions relate to their behaviours elsewhere and to how the treatment of clinical behaviours in sessions changes behaviour outside of therapy. Few models of cognitive-behaviour therapy, however, emphasize attending to and treating clients' in-session clinical behaviours as much as Dialectical Behaviour Therapy (DBT; Linehan, 1993a) does. The DBT adherence rating scale (Linehan & Korslund, 2003) partly captures this focus when it rates whether a therapist "is awake to in-session" behaviour and "relates in-session to out-of-session behaviour." Furthermore, the original DBT target hierarchy (Linehan, 1993a; see chapter 12 in this volume) includes "therapy-interfering" behaviours (TIBs) just after "life-threatening" behaviours, because suicidal clients with borderline personality disorder (BPD), for whom Linehan (1993a) originally developed DBT, have a reputation for being difficult to treat due to, at least partially, such TIBs. Though some TIBs occur outside of treatment sessions, many occur during sessions, with some being so severe or chronic that they destroy the session or the therapeutic relationship.

Besides TIBs, clients engage in a range of behaviours during treatment sessions that have clinical relevance. Any intense emotion or maladaptive cognition that controls an out-of-session target behaviour may also occur during sessions. All of the "secondary targets" identified by Linehan (1993a) can occur during sessions. Even if such behaviours do not impede a treatment session, clinicians still attend to them, consistent with a key principle of behaviour therapy which asserts that interventions are most effective when they stop an episode of a clinical behaviour as quickly as possible and immediately elicit a more adaptive behaviour instead. Though adaptive behaviours learned in treatment sessions may not generalize automatically to clients' daily lives, treating a clinically relevant behaviour during a session increases the likelihood that the client will become mindful of the behaviour in daily life and will have the motivation and capability to change the behaviour.

For the purposes of this chapter, the term "in-session clinical behaviour" (ICB) encompasses any client behaviour, including a TIB or secondary target, that occurs during a treatment session and adversely impacts either the treatment session or the rest of the client's life. ICBs range from obvious actions such as a client throwing a cup across the room, running out of the room in tears, or refusing to try a new skill, to more subtle behaviours such as a client staring into a cup, saying something self-invalidating and inaccurate about learning a skill, or expressing a few tears in response to any challenge from the therapist. ICBs may prove quite disruptive to the session, such as several clients asking fellow skills class members "to go on strike," or not at all, such as a client repeatedly making judgmental statements about his or her spouse.

This chapter reviews key principles and strategies involved in responding to the full range of ICBs. It provides examples of how to respond in an array of treatment contexts (e.g, individual psychotherapy, skills training class, and telephone coaching). It also highlights prevalent therapist errors in responding to ICBs, describes common causes for the errors, and suggests ways to correct them. As responding to an ICB begins with observing the behaviour, the chapter begins with this topic. Next, it reviews principles to apply when behaviourally describing an ICB, identifies factors to consider when deciding whether or not to treat the behaviour, and discusses how to enhance the client's motivation to address it. The chapter then discusses developing behavioural conceptualizations of the proximal factors leading to and maintaining ICBs, while attending to time and other contextual constraints that may preclude a detailed behavioural chain analysis. The chapter next describes cognitive-behavioural procedures (e.g, skills training, contingency management, exposure, stimulus control, and cognitive restructuring) and other related strategies used to change ICBs. An effective intervention may require no more than for a clinician to provide a cue for a client to use a particular skill or to ignore a behaviour to extinguish it. Alternatively, the intervention may require a comprehensive solution analysis and the implementation of multiple cognitive-behavioural procedures. Finally, the chapter summarizes other key sets of strategies involved in treating ICBs.

OBSERVING AND DESCRIBING ICBS

Observing

Responding strategically to an ICB begins with observing the behaviour. Clinicians rarely miss severe TIBs, and many DBT therapists effortlessly notice the full range of

ICBs. Novice DBT therapists, however, sometimes struggle to observe subtle ICBs. Initially, learning how to apply the core strategies of their treatment modality (e.g., conducting behavioural chain and solution analyses in individual therapy, teaching a skill in skills training class) may consume their entire attention. Fortunately for novice group skills trainers, they can reduce the number of strategies to learn at one time by dividing the skills training tasks and the observing and responding to ICB tasks between the two skills trainers.

After developing basic competency in the core strategies, some DBT novices naturally begin to notice more subtle ICBs, while others continue to miss important behaviours. Therapists without a background in treatments that focus on in-session behaviours, the elements of primary emotions, or cognitive processes may have more difficulty noticing certain types of ICBs. For example, many therapists without training in the cognitive component of cognitive-behaviour therapies quickly begin to observe judgmental thinking because of the emphasis in DBT on this cognitive style, but they fail to notice other types of problematic cognitive patterns, such as over-generalizing and catastrophizing. If therapists recognize their vulnerability to missing certain types of ICBs, they may remedy the weakness through additional study. For example, therapists who lack a familiarity with problematic cognitive patterns should review the patterns mentioned by Linehan (1993a, 2015), and which are described in more detail in cognitive research or traditional cognitive-behaviour therapy. They can then generate a list of examples from their own clients to monitor during sessions. Similarly, therapists who have had little training in the basic elements of primary emotions should review the description of these elements in the DBT skills training manual (Linehan, 1993b, 2015).

Unfortunately, therapists often cannot know what they have missed and thus must rely on DBT supervisors or consultation teams reviewing treatment sessions to identify patterns of failing to observe important ICBs. Sometimes supervisors and teams can identify these patterns without listening to a clinician's session. For example, if a review of a written chain analysis of an out-of-session target reveals a therapist's tendency to miss certain types of links, the review may indirectly identify a tendency not to observe the same types of behaviours when they occur during sessions. In one case, when a DBT team reviewed the chain analysis of a novice DBT therapist with extensive experience in cognitive therapy, they noticed that she excelled at identifying cognitive links but tended to include emotional links in the analysis only when clients mentioned an emotion by name. When the therapist reflected on how well she observed clients' emotions in session she realized that she probably had missed lower levels of emotional expressions, particularly shame. After reviewing the basic elements of emotions, the therapist watched portions of old therapy sessions from several clients to increase her ability to notice emotional expressions during sessions. Because of the subtlety of many ICBs, DBT supervisors and teams often cannot rely upon clinicians' verbal reports or even written chain analyses, and instead need to watch therapy sessions to notice important ICBs. In one case, a therapist became concerned that she had missed something in her case formulation because her client, Leala, worked collaboratively during sessions, completed homework between sessions, and used phone coaching as suggested, yet Leala had demonstrated less progress than reasonably expected. When the DBT team listened to a portion of a session, they noticed that Leala exhibited several behaviours which resembled traits of dependent personality disorder. For example, she repeatedly asked her therapist which skills to use rather than generating her own, and when she generated her own skills the solutions usually involved someone else supporting her. Consequently, her progress had stalled because the treatment had not attended to behaviours which interfered with generalizing solutions to the natural environment. The therapist had not noticed these behaviours, partly because of a lack of experience in treatments focusing on interactions between clients and therapist, and partly because Leala always used an array of effective interpersonal skills when asking the therapist for advice and support. After the team's consultation, the therapist reflected on telephone coaching sessions with Leala and realized that a similar pattern of behaviours occurred in that context.

Finally, clinicians may know which ICBs they should observe but still fail to observe the behaviours if they become unmindful during sessions. Therapists who have not strengthened their own mindfulness abilities may demonstrate a general lack of mindfulness throughout the session. More often, therapists have specific cognitions, emotions, or impulses that distract them away from or otherwise interfere with the task of observing clients' ICBs. For example, some therapists become "attached" to completing "perfect" behavioural chain analyses and therefore ignore anything unrelated to the content of the analysis. Other therapists worry about clients' reactions to highlighting ICBs. After therapists have identified an absence of mindfulness and the reasons for it, they implement the same solutions for the problem(s) that they teach clients.

Describing

Responding to ICBs requires DBT clinicians to describe clients' actual behaviours, at least to themselves, and usually to the clients as well. Although the steps of deciding whether or not to respond to an ICB do not necessarily require a clear behavioural definition, the process of defining an ICB can help clinicians to decide. This chapter addresses the topic of describing before deciding. The chapters by Chapman and Landes (this volume) discuss behavioural definition in the context of treating target behaviours. The topic has particular importance in responding to TIBs as a poorly defined TIB notably increases the likelihood of the client disagreeing with the clinician about the behaviour. The principles used to effectively define TIBs have relevance to other ICBs as well.

A key principle of defining ICBs is to describe the form of the behaviour with sufficient specificity for the client to know exactly which behaviours the clinician has noticed. In Leala's case, her therapist might have labelled all of the behaviours highlighted by the DBT team as "dependent" because the behaviours all appear as criteria of dependent personality disorder, but "dependent" does not describe the form of any behaviour. Instead, her therapist described specifically what she had noticed Leala say or do, such as "I've noticed that you usually ask me for solutions before generating any yourself" or "I've noticed that all of the solutions you generated involve someone else helping you".

Behavioural specificity helps clients to recognize which behaviours need to change, and clinicians to develop effective treatment plans to promote the change. In the case of Barney, a patient in a forensic hospital, when his therapist told him that he needed "to act less passively" during sessions, his behaviour did not shift. After consultation from the team, the therapist instead described the specific ICBs as "automatically responding by saying, 'I don't know'" during behavioural chain analyses and solution generation, "automatically rejecting solutions before trying them" and repeatedly "asking [the therapist] to solve environmental problems" for him. With a few specific behaviours to change, rather than a general personality style, Barney's motivation to change the behaviours improved. Furthermore, as soon as the therapist had a description of specific behaviours, she immediately realized that she had not yet developed a sufficient formulation of or treatment plan for the behaviours. Similarly, when a skills trainer asked the DBT team for consultation on a client who "doesn't participate" in skills training, the client's therapist suggested that the skills trainer first needed to specify the behaviours that constituted participating or the client may not know what to change. The skills trainer identified two TIBs: "not practising the mindfulness exercise" and "refusing to practise new skills". The team noticed, however, that the therapist mentioned two other behaviours that were neither required in skills training nor relevant to the client's daily life, namely "voluntarily contributing to group discussions about new skills" and "giving other members feedback on their homework". If the therapist had not specified the behaviours, the team could not have corrected this error.

Behavioural specificity also reduces the likelihood of clinicians and clients disagreeing about whether the behaviour has occurred. In the case of Kelly, a client in a forensic programme, when her therapist highlighted Kelly's "aggressive" behaviour during the session, Kelly responded by saying, "I am NOT being aggressive". Fearing that this disagreement about the ICBs could escalate tension in the session and stall the treatment, the therapist began to review dialectical strategies to find a synthesis. After realizing that she had not assessed Kelly's understanding of "aggressive", she also realized that she had not defined what she meant by the term. She then described the two most problematic ICBs that she had noticed, namely "using a loud voice to say critical things about the treatment" and "clenching fists while leaning forward in the chair". Although Kelly, who defined aggressive as hitting someone, throwing furniture, or at least yelling, could reasonably argue whether she had acted aggressively, she could not reasonably deny the more specific behaviours.

As another key principle, behavioural descriptions should exclude value judgments about the behaviour and assumptions or interpretations about its intent or function. For example, a therapist would say, "You just threatened to harm yourself if I don't extend the session", rather than "You're trying to manipulate me", or "I've noticed that you seldom complete your homework", rather than "I think that you're sabotaging the therapy". One therapist described a set of his client's ICBs as frequently "using extreme language" and "giggling", "always rating emotions as extremely high without attending to variability", and "telling unnecessary dramatic stories in the middle of treatment tasks." He did not define the behaviours as "attention-seeking" as such a description not only fails to specify the forms of the behaviours that the therapist observed, it would also have indicated that the therapist had made assumptions about the client's intent or the behaviours' function. Indeed, when the therapist analysed these behaviours separately, he learned that they had three different functions. Assuming rather than assessing intent and function notably increases the likelihood of therapists developing inaccurate behavioural formulations and insufficient treatment plans. Furthermore, historically, clinicians referring to "attention-seeking" have often had unspoken negative judgments about the function as well as the behaviour, despite the fact that attention is "probably [one of] the most powerful and versatile of all secondary reinforcers" (Wilson & O'Leary, 1980). As with having a lack of specificity, judging a behaviour or confusing a behaviour with its intent or function notably increases the likelihood of conflict between the therapist and client. Based on fact, behavioural descriptions offer little opportunity for error or disagreement, but statements about motive based on assumptions or interpretations can easily elicit disagreement or prove erroneous.

Closely related to the previous principle, clinicians may use an ICB's consequences (including its function) to refine the behavioural description, but not as a substitute for the description. For example, if a client asked the therapist personal questions that pushed the therapist's limits, the therapist would not define the ICB as "pushing my limits". Instead, the therapist might identify "asking questions about my private life that have no relationship to treatment" or "asking questions about my private life so often that it pushes my limits". Both descriptions contain the critical component of identifying the client's behaviour. Clinicians sometimes erroneously combine a description of the consequences with assumptions about the function of the behaviour. In one case, a new DBT inpatient therapist asked the DBT team for consultation on how to respond to a client who "pitted me against other members of the staff". When the team began to analyse the client's behaviour, they soon discovered that the therapist had identified his assumption about the intent of the behaviour and how he "felt" as a consequence of it, not the client's actual behaviour. The client only had told him, albeit unskillfully, how other members of the staff had helped her more than the therapist. When the therapist analysed this behaviour, he learned that the client had a very different intent than he had assumed. The client simply had wanted to increase her therapist's use of other "helpful" interventions by describing them; she had not intended to set him in competition or conflict with the staff.

After describing and analysing specific ICBs, clinicians and clients may then use a shorthand for patterns of behaviours. For example, after clients learn what constitutes judgmental and self-invalidating statements, simply labelling the form (e.g., judgmental, self-invalidating) rather than describing the content usually proves sufficient to elicit clients' recognition of the ICB. Similarly, a therapist and client may agree to use "willful" as a shorthand for certain ICBs if analyses of those ICBs have confirmed that the links leading to them match the definition of "willful," particularly that the client intentionally engaged in the ICBs. Kelly and her therapist agreed to use "aggressive" as a shorthand to refer to the pattern of behaviour, but the therapist still described the specific behaviours when she noticed them.

DECIDING WHETHER TO TREAT AN ICB

When DBT clinicians notice ICBs they can decide not to attend to the behaviour, and instead simply highlight it or implement cognitive-behavioural procedures to treat it. Besides the DBT target hierarchies, several factors influence the decision whether or not to treat an ICB. Consistent with targeting in general, therapists focus first on behaviours with the most severe, immediate consequences. Thus, TIB's generally receive attention before other ICBs.

Therapy-interfering Behaviours

As TIBs consist of behaviours that directly impede treatment progress, the consequences of a behaviour, not just its form, determine whether a clinician identifies a behaviour as a TIB. For example, phoning for skills coaching late at night only becomes a TIB if it pushes the limits of that client's therapist. Focusing on an assumption, interpretation, or personal judgment about an in-session behaviour, instead of its actual consequences, sometimes causes clinicians to mistakenly label a behaviour as a TIB. In one case, a new skills trainer labeled "knitting in group" as a TIB based on the assumption that the client "must not be paying attention". The client's individual therapist, however, knew that the knitting, though not entirely mindful, helped the client to regulate her emotions and decreased the likelihood of dissociation during skills class. As the knitting did not adversely impact anyone else in the class either, it did not meet the criteria for a TIB. During sessions clients often engage in unusual or clinically relevant behaviours that may cause problems in another setting, but that don't interfere with treatment. In one case, a client repeatedly sat with her back to the class during skills training, but participated in the mindfulness exercise, reviewed her homework, practised the new skills, and spoke loudly enough that everyone could hear her. Over the years clients have successfully completed the required in-session tasks while sitting on the floor, lying prone on the floor, sitting as close to the skills trainers as possible, and as far from the trainers as possible.

To manage multiple TIBs, clinicians often develop a sub-hierarchy of target priorities. After prioritizing TIBs based on the severity of their consequences, clinicians may consider their respective frequencies, the relative ease or speed of treating them, and their relationships to other targets in the hierarchy. Prioritizing the first two factors can increase the treatment's efficiency by decreasing the number of TIB episodes more quickly, while prioritizing the third factor can enhance the effectiveness of treating other targets.

Therapists may consider the same factors when deciding whether to implement solutions that remedy a TIB momentarily, or whether to take the time and more fully treat the behaviour to stop it permanently. For example, if a client sometimes impulsively says, "I don't remember" during behavioural chain analyses, the therapist may respond by simply generating a hypothesis or asking a few additional questions designed to help the client to remember. If the client repeatedly says, "I don't remember" during analyses, the therapist may decide to take the time to conduct a behavioural chain analysis and comprehensive solution analysis for the behaviour. In one case, when a pair of adolescent clients, Lisa and Susanna, interfered with a skills class by passing off-task notes to each other, the co-trainer blocked the behaviour by simply moving to sit between them. If, however, the same or a similar behaviour had caused significant problems for one of the clients at school, the skills trainer also may have taken some time during the break or at the end of skills class to briefly discuss the behaviour with the client and generate skills that the client could use at school as well.

Other In-session Clinical Behaviours

When deciding whether to respond to an ICB that doesn't interfere with treatment, therapists consider similar variables, although in slightly different ways. Whereas therapists respond to TIBs to improve the effectiveness of treatment sessions, they respond to other ICBs to improve the client's effectiveness in daily life. Thus, the most critical factor is how the behaviour relates to a primary target, a secondary target, another behavioural pattern, or the client's treatment goals. In Angie's case, the client repeatedly made judgmental comments about her husband and co-workers during therapy sessions. The comments never interfered with treatment, but they did appear as links in the chain leading to a set of behaviours which resulted in her husband threatening to divorce her, and another set of behaviours which resulted in her losing a previous job and receiving poor reviews on her current job. Thus, the therapist decided to respond to these judgmental statements whenever they occurred during a session. In contrast to treating a TIB, the frequency of the ICB in the client's daily life matters even more than the frequency during sessions. If a client engages in several of these ICBs frequently during a session, it often proves more effective to respond repeatedly to one or two behaviours rather than to multiple behaviours; in using the former tactic, the therapist can help the client to strengthen new skills and other solutions sufficiently without the client becoming overwhelmed by too many new solutions. Selecting behaviours that are easier to change (i.e., require less intervention from the therapist or less effort from the client) may increase the likelihood of reinforcing clients for working on ICBs more generally. Among ICBs that don't interfere with treatment, therapists may also prioritize responding to those that the client already has motivation to change over those that elicit more ambivalence from the client. The next section discusses how to enhance client's motivation to treat ICBs in general. Finally, because an ICB that does not interfere with treatment seldom becomes the main agenda item for a session, the therapist considers the time required to respond effectively to the ICB so that sufficient time remains to address the main agenda.

One case illustrates several of these principles. A newer client made judgmental, hopeless, and non-judgmental self-invalidating statements with equal impact and frequency during sessions and in daily life. The therapist initially tried to treat each behaviour whenever it occurred, both during sessions and as a link in behavioural chain analyses, but quickly discovered that the client needed a more complex set of solutions for the hopeless thoughts. The therapist and client agreed to treat judgmental and self-invalidating thinking when they occurred during sessions, but only to notice hopeless thinking during sessions until the client could better manage the other two types of thinking. After successfully learning to use mindfulness for the judgmental thoughts, and mindfulness and cognitive restructuring for the self-invalidating thoughts, the client had more motivation to address the more complex hopeless thoughts.

MOTIVATING CLIENTS TO TREAT AN ICB

As the treatment of most ICBs involves clients' collaboration, clinicians try to maximize clients' motivation to treat the behaviours. As discussed in the 'Describing' section, the way that a therapist describes an ICB to a client can determine whether the client understands the problem and agrees to treat it, or disagrees that a problem even exists. Therapists further enhance motivation to address ICBs by relating in-session behaviours to out-of-session behaviours (Linehan & Korslund, 2003) and the clients' goals. Leala's motivation to work on generating solutions that did not require help from others improved when her therapist highlighted how similar behaviours in her daily life caused significant conflict in valued personal relationships and had even caused some relationships to end. Kelly agreed to attend to her aggressive behaviour during sessions only after her therapist related it to Kelly's violent behaviours elsewhere that had resulted in arrests, jail, and court-ordered treatment. When Barney's therapist linked his automatic rejection of solutions to other behaviours that extended his detention on the forensic in-patient unit, Barney's motivation to work on the TIB increased. When trying to motivate a client to work on stopping a TIB in particular, a therapist may also clarify a contingent relationship between the client's behaviours and the DBT programme. For example, many clients diagnosed with BPD want to continue DBT after they have completed their initial DBT contract, and many programmes allow clients to continue if they have demonstrated significant progress in reducing treatment targets, including TIBs. Clarifying this contingency motivates many clients to work on reducing TIBs, especially as the initial contract nears its end.

Similarly, a therapist may use self-involving self-disclosure to clarify the impact of a client's TIB on the therapist's ability and motivation to conduct the treatment. In one case, a client, who valued her relationship with the therapist, had a pattern of becoming mute during telephone coaching sessions and demonstrated little motivation to work on changing this pattern until the therapist used self-disclosure, saying, "When you become mute, my motivation to continue coaching plummets and I have an urge to end the call". Therapists often combine clarifying the aversive consequences of the TIB on the treatment and linking a change in the TIB to the client's goals. This occurred in the case of Cathy, a divorced woman whose youngest child left home part way through her first year of DBT. When Cathy began to phone repeatedly for "a chat" rather than skills coaching a couple of months after the child left, her therapist responded by saying, "When you phone me without wanting skills coaching it makes me want to stop being available after office hours. You've also said that many of your friends have withdrawn from you because you've pushed their limits. Maybe if we solve the problem in therapy, you can use the same solutions to recover those friendships".

Clarifying contingencies and otherwise reviewing reasons to address an ICB suffices to engage many clients, but when clients remain insufficiently motivated, therapists sometimes erroneously continue to rely on this set of strategies alone. In such instances, a therapist usually has forgotten to assess for other factors (i.e., other than a lack of attention to consequences) that control the client's motivation. For example, one therapist sought consultation regarding a client, Martin, who engaged in behaviours similar to Kelly, but in a manner that interfered more with treatment. The therapist described the specific behaviours, and Martin agreed with the description, but then added, "So what?" After the therapist described how the behaviours distracted her from focusing on the main target for the session, Martin said, "That's your problem". When the therapist linked the in-session behaviours to out-of-session targets, Martin said, "I wouldn't get in trouble for this [aggressive behaviour] anywhere else". As the therapist began to challenge this, Martin appeared increasingly aggressive. The therapist then asked her DBT team how she could convince Martin about the importance of treating these TIBs. The team hypothesized that emotion, more than a lack of understanding about the behaviours' consequences, controlled Martin's apparent unwillingness to treat the aggressive TIBs. They suggested that the therapist conduct a brief analysis of Martin's new TIB: essentially refusing to target another TIB. When Martin next refused to work on reducing aggressive in-session behaviours, the therapist applied the team's consultation and learned that fear primarily inhibited his motivation to reduce in-session aggressive behaviour. Contributing to the fear, he believed that he would appear "weak" and "be out of control" and the therapist would "just push [him] around". He also believed that if he appeared less aggressive elsewhere, other people also would think him "weak" and "push me around" and would "take advantage of me". With this critical information, the therapist successfully developed a set of solutions to decrease Martin's fear while also increasing his motivation to treat in-session aggressive behaviours. Key solutions included cognitive restructuring (for his belief about "being out of control" and his therapist "pushing him around") and opposite-to-emotion action for unwarranted fear, as well as the therapist committing to teaching him how to assert himself without appearing aggressive.

When Edie, a patient on a secure unit said, "I want to quit DBT" because "it's pointless", her therapist initially relied upon reviewing the pros of continuing and the cons of quitting treatment. As she did so, however, Edie became more adamant about quitting. The therapist's DBT team suggested that, instead of responding only to the content of "it's pointless", the therapist should assess all of the key controlling variables for saying "I want to quit" and then implement solutions for those variables as well. In the next session when Edie said "I want to quit", her therapist completed a brief behavioural chain analysis and discovered several variables controlling the behaviour, particularly fear, shame, and self-invalidating thoughts. After Edie and her therapist implemented solutions for these variables, especially the shame and fear, Edie's urges to quit decreased notably and the overt behaviour stopped.

Conceptualizing Causal Factors for an ICB

When DBT clinicians decide to treat an ICB, they use behavioural theory and Linehan's biosocial theory (1993a; Grove & Crowell, this volume) to develop a behavioural conceptualization of the proximal factors causing and maintaining the ICB. As with other primary and secondary targets, ICBs may be under the control of antecedents, consequences, or both. The conceptualization may be limited to a single hypothesis about a knowledge or skill deficit or a motivational issue, or it may be based on a comprehensive assessment using a behavioural chain analysis to identify a variety of links (interested readers are referred to chapter 13 in this volume for a detailed discussion of behavioural chain analyses).

The actual comprehensiveness of a conceptualization varies with the therapeutic context and the time available for analysis. For example, a detailed behavioural chain analysis could prove unintentionally embarrassing for a client in the context of a skills training class. Furthermore, skills trainers or skills coaches usually have less time to analyse ICBs than do individual therapists. Indeed, in some situations a clinician may need to generate hypotheses about causal factors without involving the client in the formulation. In the case of Susanna and Lisa, who disrupted their skills class by passing notes, the co-trainer did not want to disrupt the class further by involving them in the analysis of their behaviour. Instead, she quickly hypothesized that each note prompted the next and that a "positive" emotion reinforced the passing. This hypothesis sufficed to generate a solution which stopped that episode of the behaviour.

Fortunately, in comparison to analysing out-of-session targets, clinicians in any treatment modality have the advantage of being present when ICB occurs and thus have more information about the behaviours and possible causal factors. Furthermore, they can enhance the efficiency of their conceptualizations by using pattern recognition strategies (Linehan, 1993a). For example, in one instance when a client began making extreme judgmental statements about skills training during the class, the skills trainer reasonably hypothesized, without needing to stop skills training for an analysis, that her own challenging of the client's behaviour a moment before had prompted the client's TIB. Based on the content and vocal tone of the client's statements and the client's facial expression and body posture, the trainer also reasonably hypothesized that anger contributed to the TIB. She knew that the client had acquired the skill of "opposite to emotion action" but had not yet had time to strengthen it. Furthermore, she learned from the client's individual therapist during DBT consultations that the client often experienced anger as a secondary emotion to shame and that the anger functioned to decrease the shame. Although the skills trainer knew that she had missed some contributing factors, her set of hypotheses and pattern recognition provided her with a sufficient formulation to generate an effective set of solutions to stop this episode of the TIB.

If therapists have insufficient information for pattern recognition of a TIB as well as little time for assessment, they usually can maximize the efficiency of their assessment by focusing on identifying the emotional links, as highlighted in the biosocial theory, and the function of the behaviour, as emphasized in behavioural theory. For example, during a suicide crisis call with her individual therapist, Josephine began to reject all of the skills that the therapist generated, repeatedly saying, "That won't work". The therapist initially accepted Josephine's statements and generated alternative skills, but then he noticed Josephine rejecting skills that had a history of working for her. The therapist realized that he needed to assess the TIB of automatically rejecting solutions but had minimal time to do so. He decided to focus on assessing the function of the TIB and soon realized that the behaviour functioned to prevent Josephine from experiencing loneliness, a contributing factor to her suicidal urges, by prolonging the phone call. This formulation of the function of the TIB allowed the therapist to generate a solution, contingency management, to stop the TIB quickly and return to treating the suicidal urges, now with a particular focus on generating solutions for the loneliness.

The optimal comprehensiveness of a conceptualization is the degree required to generate a solution analysis that, when fully implemented, changes the behaviour permanently. For example, if a client at the beginning of treatment frequently deviates from the behavioural chain analysis and instead begins to provide a narrative of his or her day, an analysis of this behaviour may first reveal that the client did not understand the therapist's orientation to behavioural chain analyses. If treating the knowledge deficit permanently stops the deviations, therapists then do not need to assess for other controlling variables, such as a wish to please or to interest therapists. Often, however, teaching clients more about behavioural chain analyses does not stop them from deviating away from the analyses. Therapists then need a more comprehensive conceptualization of the function and other factors controlling the deviating in order to generate all necessary solutions. For many clients, analysing out-of-session targets elicits aversive emotions, such as shame, guilt, and disgust; deviating away from those analyses functions to reduce the emotions. Other clients seek sympathy from their therapists and expect the narrative of their day to elicit more. An experience of excitement while telling a particular story reinforces the behaviour for some clients.

The optimal degree of formulation depends partly upon the number and complexity of critical factors controlling the behaviour. TIBs usually involve more extensive analysis than other ICBs. For example, a pattern of in-session self-invalidation simply may be a classically conditioned response to certain in-session cues (e.g., any request to implement a new solution), whereas a refusal to practise a new skill may be controlled by the same type of in-session cues and self-invalidation, plus notable fear and a history of the therapist reinforcing such refusals. A relatively simple ICB, however, still may have multiple critical controlling factors. For example, both classical and operant conditioning may have shaped in-session self-invalidation. The client may persist with self-invalidating statements during sessions because of a combination of in-session cues and the therapist unintentionally reinforcing the statements, perhaps by responding with more validation or the removal of the relevant cue (e.g. withdrawing the request to practise the new skill). Similarly, antecedents may primarily control judgmental thoughts about others, and early in treatment the client may lack only sufficient mindfulness skills to notice and let go of these thoughts. In many cases, however, judging also has reinforcing consequences, such as self-validation. No matter how skillful these clients become at mindfulness, the probability that they will use the skill diminishes notably if the reinforcement for judging remains. In the case of Angie, the client who repeatedly made judgmental comments about her husband, an initial, limited analysis of the behaviour indicated that Angie lacked the mindfulness skills to decrease this type of thinking, so the therapist focused on skills training. The ICB persisted, however, after Angie clearly had acquired and strengthened the mindfulness skills. A comprehensive analysis of the behaviour revealed that Angie persisted in judging her husband because the behaviour provided her with self-validation. Her therapist then focused on helping Angie to develop a repertoire of other self-validating statements that would not damage her marriage.

IMPLEMENTING SOLUTIONS

Using the conceptualization of factors controlling an ICB, the therapist then generates, evaluates, and implements interventions for those factors. Depending on the context and number of key controlling factors, therapists may implement a single intervention or may conduct a comprehensive solution analysis (Heard & Swales, 2016; Linehan, 1993a) with the client. Similar to developing the behavioural conceptualization, for example, skills trainers often have limited opportunity to generate solutions and may only implement cueing for a single skill or change a single contingency. The time available for implementation also influences, of course, which solutions a therapist generates. For example, providing a prompt for an existing skill requires less time than teaching a new skill. Formal exposure to treat a re-occurring in-session emotion might require a significant portion of the session; in contrast prompting or even teaching a client to change body posture and facial expression requires relatively little time. Whether the ICB occurs only during treatment sessions also influences the selection of solutions, as behaviours that occur in the client's non-treatment environments as well will eventually require solutions that generalize to those environments.

Just as a behavioural chain analysis is the servant to a solution analysis, so, too, does solution generation serve solution implementation when responding to ICBs. Clinicians sometimes generate appropriate interventions but then either fail to implement them at all or implement them insufficiently. For example, while conducting exposure for a client's unwarranted emotion during a session, a therapist might inadvertently miss a critical way in which the client avoids the relevant stimuli. Besides not knowing how to implement a particular solution, motivational factors often contribute to clinicians fully implementing a solution. For example, a therapist may not follow through with exposing a client to an in-session cue because of the therapist's own discomfort with the client's increasing emotion during the exposure procedure. Some therapists have hesitated to implement potentially effective aversive consequences generated by the consultation team because such consequences "make [them] feel mean". Even if they have sufficiently implemented a solution in a given moment, clinicians sometimes fail to persist with or repeat that solution as needed throughout the session. For example, if a therapist has decided to implement extinction for an ICB, he or she must continue to respond to the behaviour with a non-reinforcing response throughout the session and beyond. Therapists sometimes underestimate the extent to which clients need prompts throughout a session to elicit new behaviours before those behaviours become permanent. One therapist prematurely stopped prompting a client to use mindfulness skills during a session as she feared "nagging" the client. Another therapist stopped prompting a client to return to the behavioural chain analysis despite the effectiveness of the prompts because she became "tired" of "constantly pulling [the client] back". Of course, therapists can also persist with a single solution for too long. Prolonged persistence often results from a problem with the conceptualization or solution generation rather than solution implementation. For example, a therapist might ineffectively continue with cognitive restructuring as a solution because he or she only identified cognitive distortions in the conceptualization and failed to identify emotions as essential factors. A therapist might become overly attached to establishing more relationships as a solution for loneliness because he or she does not know any other solutions for loneliness. Though clinicians may identify such implementation issues themselves, the identification often depends upon the consultation team role-playing or listening to recordings of therapy sessions.

Brief Interventions

In some situations, clinicians may have the opportunity to implement only a single solution. Such situations include skills training classes, phone consultations, the end of individual sessions, and individual sessions in which other targets have priority. In some of these situations, clinicians may not even have the opportunity to discuss solutions with the client and implement the solution "silently" instead. This type of solution often involves blocking behaviour. In the incident with Susanna and Lisa, their skills trainer decided to block their note passing by simply moving her chair to sit between them. One skills trainer simply held up her hand like a stop sign toward any client who interrupted another client during skills training.

Clinicians may also implement contingency management without discussing the solution with clients. For some clients, a clinician's frown or clipped voice tone suffices to stop the client's TIB. Therapists may extinguish impulsive responses of "I don't remember" by simply persisting with a behavioural chain analysis. In skills class, if a trainer believes that a client reported not completing the homework partly to avoid participating in the homework review, the trainer may still focus on the client for the same time, using the time either to prompt the client to complete the homework in the moment or to analyse what interfered with the homework completion. The following week, if the client collaborates with the homework review the therapist may reinforce this behaviour by reducing the time focusing on the client. Alternatively, if a clinician's conceptualization suggests that attention reinforces a TIB, the clinician may withdraw attention to extinguish behaviour and then reinforce alternative behaviours with more attention. Though therapists generally discuss contingency management options with clients, both to enhance collaboration and to ensure that clients link their behaviour to the consequences, sometimes consequences have more impact if they occur immediately and without discussion. For example, if a therapist explains to a client that leaning forward and making eye contact was intended to express interest and thus reinforce the client's collaboration, the expression of interest may lose in impact what it has gained in clarity.

Usually a clinician has at least the opportunity to say something brief, and sometimes this may be enough to change an ICB. Indeed, simply increasing a client's awareness of the behaviour or its consequences (i.e., contingency clarification) occasionally suffices to stop an ICB without the therapist needing to generate any solutions. Clients may stop ICBs as soon as they become aware of them through clinicians highlighting or describing the behaviours. For example, asking, "Did you notice that statement was an overgeneralization?" might lead directly to the client using cognitive restructuring to change his or her thinking. A clinician may need only to ask a client to stop a behaviour or briefly clarify the consequences of the behaviour to sufficiently shift the client's motivation to immediately inhibit the behaviour. For example, a therapist might highlight each instance of the client taking time to divert away from the behavioural chain analysis means less time for the client's agenda items at the end of the session. In one case, during a suicide crisis call, the client began clicking the trigger of a gun. The sound interfered with the therapist concentrating on treating the client's suicidal urges. Based on past crisis calls and her general relationship with the client, the therapist hypothesized that the client's TIB did not function to elicit any particular response from the therapist, but was more likely a mindless behaviour resulting from the client having the gun near him (similar to playing with a pen while holding it). The therapist thus initially responded by saying, "Clicking the gun is distracting me from helping you. If you want me to continue helping you, you need to stop playing with it". The client immediately stopped the TIB, and the phone consultation returned to addressing the client's suicide crisis (including permanently removing the gun).

Briefly presenting a client with a cue—a stimulus control procedure—related to a specific solution often suffices to prompt the client to implement the solution. Clinicians, especially skills trainers, use this intervention most often to remind clients to use skills that clients already have in their repertoires. For example, a therapist might say, "Be mindful of your judgmental thoughts" or "I think that opposite action will reduce your shame". Similarly, a therapist might prompt a client to generate his or her own solutions. If a client's ICB causes problems in non-treatment environments as well, then the therapy also will need to attend to how the client can structure cues in those environments (see Heard & Swales, 2016, for a discussion of stimulus control in DBT).

In some situations, implementing contingency management may only require that the therapist first briefly introduce the client to the new consequence(s). In the case of Josephine, the client who repeatedly rejected her therapist's solutions during a coaching call, the therapist had little time to treat the TIB and thus simply introduced an aversive consequence for the behaviour. He said, "My solutions seem to be of no help to you. If that continues, there won't be any reason for us to continue and I'll end the call". With this new contingency in place, Josephine immediately stopped automatically rejecting the therapist's solutions. When Josephine accepted and rehearsed solutions instead, her therapist reinforced the behaviour by offering to schedule a follow-up coaching session.

Lengthier Solutions

Other interventions require more and variable amounts of time. If the formulation of the ICB suggests that a lack of basic information primarily controls the behaviour, clinicians would, of course, provide the client with the relevant didactic information. As previously mentioned, therapists might need to provide a client with more orientation to the process of a behavioural chain analysis to prevent the client from telling a story instead. A client who has not rated daily skills use on the diary card only because he or she did not understand the scale would require only more information about the scale. In skills classes clients sometimes provide prolonged feedback on their homework. Although this behaviour could have a problematic interpersonal function, it can also result if clients want to please or impress the skills trainers, but do not understand exactly what type of feedback the trainers need. In the latter instances, the skills trainers would provide more instructions about homework feedback to correct the problem.

In many instances, a formulation of the factors controlling an ICB indicates that the client requires skills training (interested readers are referred to Chapter 9 by Cowperthwait and colleagues, this volume), not just a prompt to use a skill. When newer clients have not covered the needed skill in skills training class, the individual therapist must provide instruction, modelling, or both, although only in those aspects of the skill needed to change the current ICB. For example, a therapist would instruct and model for a client how to "act opposite" only to the elements of the emotion that the client experienced in that moment of the session. Therapists also use skills acquisition procedures if the formulation suggests that the client has either misunderstood or not learned a critical component of the skill. For example, if a therapist hypothesizes that a client has refused to practise "radical acceptance" because the client mistakenly believes that radical acceptance implies agreement, then the therapist would clarify the parameters of the skill and model how to apply it in that situation. The amount of skills acquisition work in such situations varies. For example, it requires only a few moments to teach a client that "deserve" can also indicate a judgmental thought. Alternatively, if a therapist has prompted a client to be more mindful during a session and the client instead distracts with a mindfulness exercise, it might require longer for the therapist to teach the client the difference between mindfully participating in session tasks and practising a mindfulness exercise that distracts from those tasks. In some instances, clients need additional skills strengthening or assistance in generalizing a skill to the session, rather than training in the basics of the skill. For example, in response to a prompt to use "opposite action" for an unwarranted emotion in a session, a client may act opposite to major overt behaviours but need more shaping on identifying and acting opposite to facial expressions and cognitive behaviours. In response to a prompt to implement "radical acceptance" a client readily might accept that an event has occurred, but forget or struggle to extend that acceptance to the consequences of the event. Another client might have learned to skillfully use "check the facts" for cognitive distortions leading to suicide attempts, but have difficulty generalizing the skill to other types of cognitive distortions that occur during a treatment session.

Although exposure procedures may require longer than a single skill to implement, the initial investment can prove a better long-term investment. In Cindy's case, the behavioural chain analysis of her refusal to complete a diary card in the session indicated that the diary card prompted thoughts about her recent behaviours and that those memories elicited shame of unwarranted intensity. The shame seemed the most dysfunctional link in the chain. When the same behaviour occurred in the previous session, her therapist had coached her to act opposite to the shame and complete the diary card. Though this had succeeded in that session, it had not stopped the TIB permanently. As Cindy did not have any recent suicidal targets and such shame had interfered with behavioural chain analyses as well, her therapist decided to focus on treating the TIB more thoroughly with exposure and more permanently break the link between the cue and the emotion. Thus, when Cindy began to complete the diary card by rushing through it as quickly as possible, her therapist blocked this behaviour, reminded Cindy to complete the task mindfully, and re-presented the diary card. Although repeated exposure trials during the session required more time, they provided Cindy with a significantly lower shame response to her behaviours on the diary card, as well as a completed diary card.

In many instances, contingency management requires notably more time to implement than in the examples described in the previous section. For example, using correction-overcorrection requires not only that the client stop (i.e., correct) a TIB, but also that he or she then overcorrect for it, which usually requires more time. For example, when one client repeatedly made a variety of impulsive, unmindful statements (e.g., assumptions, judgments, overgeneralizations) that interfered with the therapy session, the formulation of this set of TIBs suggested that the statements resulted from a motivational deficit rather than a skills deficit. The therapist shifted the client's motivation to use the relevant skills in the session by stating that each instance of such statements would lead to a homework assignment relevant to the statement (over-correction), in addition to the usual in-session rehearsal of more mindful, factual statements (correction). Although orientating the client to the new contingency required little time, the therapist also had to check later that the client had completed the homework. Fortunately, as the client's homework assignments increased during the session, the relevant TIBs decreased, such that the client only had three additional pieces of homework to review.

Comprehensive Solution Analysis

Though some ICBs alter sufficiently after implementing a single solution, many require a combination of CBT procedures. For a simple cognitive or emotion ICB, a pair of solutions may effectively change the behaviour. For example, a client who had completed the distress tolerance module, but not the emotion regulation module, sometimes had surges of intense, unwarranted shame during sessions. The therapist first successfully treated these episodes of shame through a combination of cueing the client to use a "TIPP" skill and teaching "opposite action", eventually replacing the teaching with strengthening, and then just cueing. In the case of a client who repeatedly made catastrophizing statements during sessions, the analysis of the ICB suggested that the client lacked both an awareness of the behaviour and the skill to think another way. A combination of mindfulness and "check the facts" skills stopped the statements. In another case, the client not only lacked awareness of her "dramatic" statements (e.g., catastrophizing, overgeneralizing), but also gained reinforcing consequences from them in the form of interest, sympathy, or reassurance from others, including, initially, her therapist. Reducing these statements required a combination of mindfulness strengthening and contingency management.

In many instances, particularly when treating TIBs, the client will require multiple solutions to change the multiple factors contributing to the ICB. As described in an earlier section, Edie's therapist had identified fear, shame, and self-invalidating thoughts as critical factors in Edie's statement that she wanted to quit therapy, with the TIB functioning primarily to reduce the two emotions. More specifically, while conducting a behavioural chain analysis on an out-of-session target, Edie had begun to think, "I'm so stupid for still doing this. I should have stopped by now", and to feel moderate, but unwarranted, levels of shame. She then began to think, "This is pointless; I'll never change", and to feel moderate, unwarranted fear. The fear escalated and then she thought, "They'll keep me here forever. I've got to leave now". When she declared her intention to quit DBT, her fear and shame decreased a little. The therapist began the solution generation and implementation for the TIB by focusing on reducing Edie's fear, as its intensity would interfere with other solutions. To reduce Edie's arousal, the therapist cued her to use breathing skills. Next, the therapist coached Edie on how to "act opposite" to the components of fear and then to the components of shame. At this point, Edie's worry about an involuntary admission abated. Edie and her therapist then examined the evidence for the self-invalidating assumption about Edie's capacity for change. For the judgmental self-invalidation, the therapist cued Edie to implement mindfulness. The therapist reinforced Edie's work on self-invalidation with cheerleading.

Responding to ICBs with Other Strategies

Though problem-solving strategies usually have the most prominent role in responding to ICBs, other sets of DBT strategies certainly have strong supporting roles, especially dialectical, validation, and stylistic strategies. For example, remaining awake to in-session behaviours is a prerequisite to responding to ICBs. Self-involving self-disclosure about the consequences of a TIB often motivates a client to collaborate in the treatment of that TIB and sometimes suffices to stop the need for other solutions. Clinicians balance such reciprocal strategies with irreverent strategies. Generally remaining matter-of-fact can help prevent clinicians from becoming overly polite and ironically prolonging a TIB. For example, a clinician would state, "I want you to stop X behaviour" rather than asking, "Do you want to stop X behaviour?", to which the client could honestly respond, "No". One inpatient had a pattern of judgmentally referring to staff members and other patients as "bitch" or "bastard". When he did this during an individual DBT session, his therapist responded by using the terms in their literal sense. Such a response surprised and confused the client, causing him to stop his litany of judgmental statements and attend to the therapist, who then had a chance to treat the ICB.

In addition to their normal role in the treatment, validation strategies often play a special role in the treatment of TIBs. TIBs, particularly those that cross clinicians' "limits", can prompt varying degrees of therapist anger. Searching for the validity of a client's behaviour provides an extremely efficient way for therapists to act opposite to their anger, as it can effectively reduce the clinician's anger, identify key factors controlling the client's behaviour, and, if shared with the client, improve the client's motivation to change the behaviour. In Josephine's case, her therapist experienced notable frustration when Josephine repeatedly rejected solutions during a phone consultation and had a strong urge to end the phone call. Although ending the call would have removed the opportunity for Josephine to reject solutions, it would not have removed her suicidal urges. When the therapist identified the function of the behaviour as loneliness, his frustration with Josephine decreased. He then provided functional validation, by focusing on solutions for the loneliness, which increased Josephine's willingness to collaborate.

Dialectics influences the response to ICBs in multiple ways. Besides balancing acceptance and change strategies, clinicians use specific dialectical techniques. In the case of Martin, the client who initially refused to address his in-session TIB because he feared appearing "weak" and "out of control", his therapist "entered the paradox", stating that "only when you let go of your attachment to being in control will you have the control you want". Therapists also try to balance acceptance and change solutions when generating multiple solutions. In the case of Cathy, who phoned for a chat rather than skills coaching when she felt lonely, her therapist generated a dialectical set of skills for the loneliness which equally included skills to decrease loneliness and to tolerate it; the therapist also made the continuation of any call contingent upon Cathy participating in skills coaching. The therapist coached, or at least prompted, Cathy to use interpersonal skills to decrease the likelihood of being alone (e.g., expressing interest during conversations with friends), "check-the-facts" to decrease catastrophizing and overgeneralizing thoughts that exacerbated the loneliness, "radical acceptance" of and "turning the mind" toward coping with being on her own for a period of time, mindfulness to develop a sense of connection, and "accumulating positive emotions" when alone.

Adhering to dialectical principles, DBT clinicians attend to the system of the therapy relationship. Dialectical principles specifically direct clinicians' attention toward transactions between therapists and clients and the way in which they reciprocally influence each other. In most relationships, individuals interact in ways that, intentionally or not, influence the behaviour of the other individual. Clinicians thus consider how their own behaviours may have prompted or reinforced clients' ICBs. For example, when one therapist complained to her team about her client repeatedly "going off-track" during behavioural chain analyses, the team listened to a portion of the last session and discovered that the therapist had probably reinforced the behaviour by continuing to listen to the client and had then prompted the behaviour by asking a few questions related to the "off-track" topic. As this example also illustrates, client's ICBs often have validity within the context of the current therapy relationship. Martin's fear of his therapist trying to "control" him when she initially tried to motivate him to work on his aggressive behaviour had validity to the extent that she persisted with only trying to convince him that he needed to stop the behaviour. As exemplified in the previous section, clinicians' own natural, personal responses (e.g., frowning, expressing disapproval, withdrawing attention) to ICBs often extinguish or punish those behaviours, while clinicians' personal responses (e.g., smiling, providing verbal validation, expressing interest) to clients' skillful, healthier behaviours can reinforce those behaviours in therapy sessions.

CONCLUSION

DBT clinicians remain mindful of and ready to respond to clients' ICBs. DBT individual therapists keenly attend to their clients' in-session behaviours even while focusing on treating an out-of-session target. When a therapist notices an in-session behaviour that has clinical relevance, he or she uses standard DBT principles and strategies to respond to the behaviour with the ultimate aim of not only changing the behaviour in the session, but also in the client's daily life as well. Thus, DBT individual therapists do not consider most TIBs simply as obstacles to avoid or overcome so that therapy can proceed. Instead, therapists treat them as examples of the behaviours that occur in clients' lives outside of therapy and as the most immediate opportunities to change those behaviours. When developing a formulation for the causal factors of an ICB, clinicians consider how their own behaviour may have prompted or reinforced the ICB. They also use or alter their personal responses to ICBs to decrease the likelihood of the behaviour re-occurring and to reinforce clients' skillful behaviours. Considering the consistent attention to clients' in-session behaviours and therapists' roles in that behaviour, one may imagine that Freud would very much have enjoyed working as a DBT therapist.

KEY POINTS FOR CLINICIANS

- Few models of cognitive-behaviour therapy emphasize attending to and treating clients' in-session clinical behaviours as much as Dialectical Behaviour Therapy (DBT).
- The term "in-session clinical behaviour" (ICB) encompasses any client behaviour, including a therapy-interfering behaviour (TIB) or secondary target, that occurs during a treatment session and adversely impacts either the treatment session or other aspects of the client's life.
- A key principle of behaviour therapy asserts that interventions are most effective when they stop an episode of a clinical behaviour as quickly as possible and immediately elicit a more adaptive behaviour instead.
- To enhance clients' understanding of and collaboration in treating ICBs, DBT clinicians describe the form of an ICB with behavioural specificity and without assumptions about the function or intent.
- DBT clinicians enhance motivation to address ICBs partly by relating in-session behaviours to out-of-session behaviours and to the clients' goals.
- DBT clinicians use behavioural theory and Linehan's biosocial theory to develop a behavioural conceptualization of the proximal factors causing and maintaining ICBs.
- Solution implementation ranges from applying a single intervention to conducting a comprehensive solution analysis, depending on the context and number of key controlling factors for the ICB.

REFERENCES

Heard, H. L., & Swales, M. A. (2016). *Changing behaviour in DBT*. New York: Guilford Press.

Linehan, M. M. (1993a). *Cognitive-behavioral treatment of borderline personality disorder*. New York: Guilford Press.

Linehan, M. M. (1993b). *Skills training manual for treating borderline personality disorder*. New York: Guilford Press.

Linehan, M. M. (2015). *DBT skills training manual*, 2nd Edition. New York: Guilford Press.

Linehan, M. M., & Korslund, K. E. (2003). *Dialectical behaviour therapy adherence manual*. Seattle: University of Washington, Unpublished manual.

Wilson, G. T., & O'Leary, K. D. (1980). *Principles of behaviour therapy*. Englewood Cliffs, NJ: Prentice-Hall.

CHAPTER 18

TEACHING MINDFULNESS SKILLS IN DBT

MAGGIE STANTON AND CHRISTINE DUNKLEY

INTRODUCTION

MINDFULNESS is a central skill in Dialectical Behaviour Therapy (DBT), and as such, runs throughout the teaching that takes place (see Wolbert, this volume). It is unique in being taught at the start of every skills module and practised at the beginning of every DBT skills class. DBT differs from other mindfulness-based therapies in explicitly teaching mindfulness as a skill. Marsha Linehan (1993, 2015b) identified the skills clients need to acquire in developing mindfulness. She divided out what clients need to do to be mindful (i.e. the three "What Skills" of observe, describe, and participate) and how they need to practise them (i.e. the three "How Skills" of non-judgmentally, one-mindfully, and effectively). In the "What Skills", Linehan makes a distinction between observing, i.e., noticing experiences in the present moment, and describing, i.e., the activity of putting words on the experience. This is unusual when teaching mindfulness, as most mindfulness approaches emphasize observing *without* putting words onto the experience. However, by introducing observing and describing as two distinct skills, she identifies the need for clients to both be more skillful at paying attention to information coming in through their senses in the moment, and also to be able to describe this to themselves and others in a non-judgmental and accurate way that is as close to the observed experience as possible. In this way, clients are dealing with the reality of the situation, rather than a mind-version of events.

Unlike other mindfulness approaches, such as Mindfulness-Based Stress Reduction (Kabat-Zinn, 2013), and Mindfulness-Based Cognitive Therapy (Segal, Williams, & Teasdale, 2013), DBT not only makes a distinction between observing and describing but also between observing and participating, and teaches these as separate skills.

Participation requires being fully aware and present in the current moment, without the running commentary our minds can often give on the experiences we are having. Through practising participation clients learn to move from observing and describing to develop a way of *being* in the experience. The aim is for clients to participate more mindfully in their lives, do one thing at a time, lose the rules, comparisons, assumptions, and judgments their minds give them, and focus on effective behaviours that are in line with their goals and values. When clients are behaving in this way, it helps them to access the mindfulness skill of "Wise Mind".

The concept of wisdom guiding one's actions (including both knowledge and an intuitive sense) is evident throughout the mindfulness literature, but DBT is unique in teaching it explicitly. Linehan recognized that acting wisely was a key skill for clients whose impulsivity often leads to high-risk or unhelpful behaviours. When faced with the challenge of teaching this concept, Linehan defined the mindfulness skill of "Wise Mind" as the synthesis of emotion and reason states of mind, thus emphasizing the dialectical nature of taking a wise mind approach or decision. We give an example of a client using the wise mind skill in the "Modelling a Mindful and Dialectical Philosophy" section of this chapter.

Linehan recognized that for clients to become mindful they required not only skills in *what* to do, but also in *how* to be mindful. Thus, she identified the "How Skills" to define the way in which mindfulness is carried out, i.e., non-judgmentally, one-mindfully, and effectively. Judgments are shorthand ways of communicating. The difficulty for clients is when they forget this and react to judgments as if they are reality. Also, judgments can increase the intensity of emotions. Clients learn to take a non-judgmental stance by labelling judgments or describing the observed experience more factually. In this way, clients are responding to the actual situation and the emotion frequently reduces. The "How Skills" also emphasize the importance of doing one thing at a time, thus focusing on the present, rather than what *has* happened or what *may* happen, and being effective rather than participating in value judgments of how things *should* be.

As we have described, DBT differs from other mindfulness-based approaches in having an explicit focus on teaching mindfulness as a set of skills. Initially, it teaches clients *what* and *how* to be mindful, i.e., to acquire the skill. Over time the client hones the skill and generalizes it so that he or she incorporates mindfulness into daily life as a different way of being. Thus, the DBT therapist needs to pay attention to the behavioural step they are focusing on when teaching this skill to clients, i.e., acquiring the skill, strengthening the skill, or generalizing its use to the natural environment. Many clients will have their first encounter with mindfulness when they attend skills group, so the chapter begins by discussing teaching mindfulness in this modality, with its main focus on skill acquisition, with some skills strengthening via in-session rehearsal and homework practice. Individual therapy is where clients learn to strengthen the skill by applying mindfulness to the specific problems and difficulties they have encountered; thus, the chapter covers this aspect next. Finally, the DBT therapist is always aware of the need for the client to generalize the skill into their lives, so the chapter concludes with coaching mindfulness in the phone contact modality.

The chapter provides examples from different settings and with various client groups. While ages and challenges may vary, the principles are the same, so that, within the chapter, therapists can find suggestions to enrich their practice of teaching mindfulness in DBT.

Teaching Mindfulness in Skills Group

The function of the skills training modality is to enhance the capability of the client by acquiring and strengthening the skill of mindfulness. Tips to teach mindfulness include:

1. Explaining what mindfulness is, and how and when the skill is relevant;
2. Brief mindfulness practices, usually with a specific focus;
3. Taking feedback after a practice to shape mindful behaviour; and
4. Homework setting and review, to strengthen and begin to generalize the skill.

Throughout the group sessions, the therapist aids skill acquisition by modelling a mindful approach to their own and others experiences.

What is Mindfulness?

Often clients will come to skills group unsure what mindfulness is, and unless therapists are clear in their teaching, clients may leave skills group even more confused. It is essential to begin with a simple definition of mindfulness, and how it can be helpful. At its essence, mindfulness:

> "... means paying attention in a particular way: on purpose, in the present moment, and non-judgmentally."
>
> (Kabat-Zinn, 1994, p. 4)

If clients are to acquire a skill, they need to understand how it will be personally relevant. Therefore, it is useful to give examples of using mindfulness to which clients can relate. Here we provide an example of engaging clients and demonstrating how acquiring the skill of mindfulness may help them:

> Have you ever been to a party and been sure everyone's having a good time except you, so you left? Or made a doctor's appointment but assumed the doctor would say you were making an unnecessary fuss about your symptoms so you cancelled it? Or been in a new situation, like maybe starting skills group today, and worried all morning about what you would say or do? So, would it have been helpful to have the skill of noticing when your mind went to these thoughts and be able to bring it

onto what you wanted to think about? So that you could stay at the party, or go to the doctor's appointment, or even come to group without having all that worry attached? If so, then mindfulness is the skill for you.

In this way, the therapist is able to link client goals to mindfulness and define mindfulness as the ability to put the client's attention on the focus of his or her choice.

In-group Practice

Acquiring the skill of mindfulness is achieved via in-group practices and feedback. In mindfulness, there are essentially two types of practice, i.e., opening the mind or being aware of experiences, and bringing attention to a particular focus. In DBT the practices tend to be more of the latter type, as these are generally easier for clients who experience high emotions and engage in impulsive behaviours. In these practices, the therapist presents a stimuli, e.g,. sounds, for the clients to focus on. The instruction is to notice if the mind wanders and gently guide it back to the focus. It is important that the therapist does not over-complicate the practices and remembers to only ask clients to do one thing at a time. The art of teaching mindfulness is in keeping the practice simple. Be clear if the focus of the practice is on observing, describing, or participating. Let the clients know whether the practice is guided or not, how it will start and stop, as well as what to do if their attention wanders (i.e., remind clients that this is normal, and gently to bring their mind back to the focus, and be willing to do this many times). Throughout the teaching, the message to convey is that the purpose of practising is to acquire the skill in order to be able to apply it when needed (i.e. generalized to the environment). Mindfulness is not about sitting quietly staring at an object, but rather a skill for everyday life (Dunkley & Stanton, 2017). Thus, when the children are shouting over a game, the dog is yapping, and the client can feel their irritation rising, they can mindfully turn their attention back to the present (e.g., cooking the evening meal, stirring the sauce in the pan, the smell of the tomatoes, the feel of the spoon in their hand). It is possible to do this because the skill of turning one's attention to a focus has been practised many times. Mindfulness is on the acceptance, rather than change, end of the dialectic. Mindfulness doesn't stop the dog yapping or the kids shouting. Rather, by accepting this *is* the reality of the situation, the client can choose to focus on what *they* want to turn their mind to, and in doing this, they are in the driver's seat of their mind (Linehan, 1993).

Skills group leaders need to convey to clients the importance of practising mindfulness with their eyes open. Daily life occurs with our eyes open, and the aim is to lead a more mindful life. If a client wants to close their eyes, then therapists encourage them to practise keeping their eyes open over time, or for part of the practice. The therapist may suggest the client tries noticing the urge to close their eyes without acting on it and take an interest in what happens to the urge. DBT differs from some other therapies by keeping the practices short. This is because clients often have painful and difficult thoughts, emotions, and sensations. It can be counter-productive to sit with these experiences, even for a short time. In keeping the practices short, and having therapists engage in the practice too, clients are more apt to try mindfulness and apply it in their lives.

When planning mindfulness practice, the DBT therapist needs to consider how it will relate to the skill being taught in that session, or to themes that are particularly relevant to the clients in the group at that time. The following examples show how the therapist has thought through a mindfulness practice that would be useful, and planned it accordingly.

Dan's Mindfulness Plan

Dan worked in a forensic DBT team with male clients who had extreme difficulty noticing sensations in their bodies. The topic for group was the mindfulness "What Skills". For the "observe" aspect of mindfulness, Dan prepared a guided exercise around the men drinking water. This included directing their attention to the feel of the cup in their hand, its weight and temperature, as well as noticing the sensation of the water in their mouth, the taste as it passed over their tongue, and their muscles as they contracted and relaxed with each swallowing action. In this way Dan focused the mindfulness practice to direct the client's attention to their sensations and increase their awareness of information coming in through their senses.

Suzy's Mindfulness Plan

Suzy was planning mindfulness for the beginning of skills group. The topic that week was the interpersonal effectiveness DEAR MAN skill (Linehan, 2015a). Suzy knew that assumptions were likely to crop up when clients tried to listen mindfully to another person. She planned a mindfulness exercise that was likely to generate some assumptions about what others were going to say. She asked the group to tell a story, each member only adding one word to the tale before it passed to the person next to them. In the feedback after the practice and when role-playing the DEAR MAN skill, Suzy was able to highlight assumptions the clients made and help them to refocus on just listening to the other person.

Feedback after a Practice

Practising is very important, but clients acquiring a skill requires more than them just practising it, in the same way as an athlete does not learn the long jump simply by jumping many times. Both clients and athletes learn from their trainer's instruction and feedback about how to develop and hone their skills. Immediately following a mindfulness practice in skills class, there is an opportunity to take feedback from a couple of group members in order to shape their awareness of the actions of their mind by highlighting both their mindful and unmindful behaviour (Dunkley & Stanton, 2014). Questions such as "What did you notice during that practice?" can be very helpful in guiding clients to give feedback on their experience, rather than giving an overview or general account. The following dialogue continues with the example of the therapist "Suzy" and provides an illustration of taking feedback after the story telling:

Joe: *When the story started 'Once upon a ...' I thought Mary next to me would say 'time'. When she said 'Wednesday' I couldn't think of anything to say.*

Therapist: *So you made an assumption Mary would say "time?"* (Curious and interested, labelling the assumption.)

Joe: *(Nods).*

Therapist: *Did you notice you had made an assumption?* (Drawing attention to the actions of his mind.)

Joe: *No, my mind went blank and I thought "why hasn't she said time?" Everyone always says "time".*

Therapist: *Isn't it interesting that the assumption got in the way of being able to think of something to say, and led to another assumption about "everyone always saying time"?* (Curious and interested. Highlighting the consequence of the assumption.)

Joe: *Yes, I hadn't thought of it like that.*

Therapist: *Next time that happens, you could try labelling the thought as an assumption and bring yourself back to what is actually happening.* (Setting practice to strengthen and begin to generalize the skill.)

Later when the clients were practicing the DEAR MAN skill, the therapist was able to re-mind the class to notice assumptions and mindfully bring their attention onto what the other person was actually saying.

In this example, the therapist planned the practice around assumptions while losing attachment to any particular outcome. In this situation, if no assumptions come up, then the therapist's task is to recognize any attachment they had to highlighting assumptions without judging themselves, and deal with the feedback in the moment. In being mindful, the therapist unhooks from attachments. If the therapist becomes aware of thoughts about how they "*want it to be*" or "*think it should be*" in class, they notice the attachment and re-focus on the feedback they *are* getting. In order to do this, therapists need to practise mindfulness themselves. In fact, modelling their own use of mindfulness by taking a curious, interested approach to their own and others' experiences is perhaps one of the most important acquisition strategies a DBT therapist will use (Kuyken et al., 2010; Linehan, 2015b). Regular mindfulness practice helps the therapist notice and let go of judgments, stay in the moment of the class, and focus on being effective. In addition, sharing examples of their own use of mindfulness enables clients to see how to generalize the skill. In the following example, the therapist was teaching the mindfulness "How Skill" of doing one thing in the moment and using a personal story to demonstrate the point.

"I was sitting on the bench, watching my daughter playing, texting my friend about meeting up in the week and eating an apple I had found in my bag. I realized I was doing three things at a time and all of them were suffering. I wasn't enjoying being

with my daughter at the park, or even watching her closely; I wasn't paying attention to my friend telling me about the film she wanted us to see; and I wasn't even
noticing the apple I was eating. When I became aware, I put my phone and the apple
in my bag and went over to my daughter. I watched as she climbed the slide and
queued for her turn. Her face was excited as she talked to the other children. She
saw me looking and pulled a face at me. Being mindful is doing one thing at a time
and when we do that, we are in that moment of our lives, whatever that may be. It
may not be the most exciting or even pleasant moment, but it is the moment we are
living and we only get it once. Are there times when you do more than one thing at
once? What have you noticed when that happens?" (Here the therapist uses self-
involving self-disclosure, makes the teaching point that mindfulness is about doing
one thing in the moment, whether that is pleasant or not, and looks for examples
from the group.)

In our experience, one of the most difficult mindfulness skills to acquire, for clients
as well as therapists, can be the "How Skill" of taking a non-judgmental stance, i.e.,
identifying judgments and knowing what to do when they are recognized. An important teaching point is that judgments are both the content and delivery of what is
said. A judgmental stance can be in the tone of voice, facial expression, body posture,
thoughts, and/or language. By changing these, it is possible to adopt a more mindful
approach. Therapists need to be clear and specific in their instructions as clients will
often be confused if simply told to "let go of judgments". The group leader needs to
give feedback on what they see and coach the client in what to do, as in the following
scenario.

Matt was learning mindfulness in the adolescent skills group. He was reporting what
he had noticed in a participation practice of making a paper plane and flying it.

Matt: *I'm just crap at this! My plane was pathetic!*
Therapist: *Judging yourself and judging the plane! Were you having those thoughts
   during the practice?* (Labelling judgments and locating when they occurred in time.)
Matt: *Yes, I'm rubbish at this.*
Therapist: *And still judging yourself. Do those thoughts about being "rubbish"
   and "crap" ever happen outside of this room?* (Highlighting patterns, identifying
   opportunities for generalization.)
Matt: *Yes, all the time!*
Therapist: *I'd like to help you with that because from what you've told me it can make
   it really hard to do things. Would you be interested?* (Noticing consequences and
   gaining commitment.)
Matt: *I guess so.*
Therapist: *Mindfulness is taking the judgments out of what you are saying by
   describing factually what you mean. Have a go.* (Coaching skill acquisition.)
Matt: *Well, I squashed the plane nose and one of the wings tore so it didn't fly as far as
   I wanted it to.*

Therapist: *Great job! It looked like you were still judging yourself a bit though because you were frowning and your tone of voice was quite harsh as you said that. Could you say it again relaxing your forehead and lightening your tone of voice to see if you can let go of the judgments from your expression and voice too?* (Strengthening the skill.)

Matt: (Repeats his words with relaxed forehead and lighter tone.) *That felt different. I'm still disappointed but not so much.*

Therapist: *Would you be willing to try doing that next time those judgments crop up?* (Looking for opportunities and commitment to generalize the skill.)

If Matt had said "*I loved that practice*" or "*I hated that practice*" he would have been giving his opinion of the practice. This is a key teaching point: an opinion is not a judgment. When asked: "Did it look or sound judgmental?" clients and therapists are usually accurate at identifying whether there was a judgment or not. If Matt simply had not done the practice (as will happen from time to time in skills class) then the therapist would take feedback in the usual way. By asking questions and being curious about what happened, the therapist would unpick the events with Matt to notice the actions of his mind, how it influenced his not taking part in the practice, and the consequence of this for him.

When teaching mindfulness, therapists need to identify the teaching points and decide the strategies to communicate these most effectively to the group. Using the full range of stories (from books, magazines, TV, the internet, etc.), metaphors, personal experience, and practices brings the teaching alive. While skills can be taught individually, learning mindfulness in a group enables clients to benefit from other members' experiences. It can be easier for a client to pick out patterns of unmindful behaviour when they see it in someone else, or hear the feedback from another group member. In a rolling programme where clients can join the group at the start of each module, comments and feedback from more experienced group members can be really beneficial to newcomers. Group discussions can be a very powerful teaching technique, particularly when conveying the concept of participating more mindfully in one's life. In the following example, the therapist keeps the introduction to the participation practice short (so as not to give a lot of time to think about it), takes feedback in the usual way, then uses group discussion to relate the learning to everyday life.

The therapist began the participation practice by explaining it was a group mirroring exercise. He invited the clients to throw themselves in and follow his movements as if they were his reflection in a mirror. The therapist made different shapes with his body, crouching, twisting, and hopping, which group members copied. After the practice, the therapist took feedback. Josh said he'd had lots of thoughts of looking stupid and this made it hard to do. Kim reflected she'd been completely in the experience, not aware of anything except watching and the feel of her body. Baako commented he kept thinking "I don't want to be doing this".

In the discussion afterwards, the therapist encouraged the group to think how these experiences relate to participating mindfully in their lives, and asked "How often do we have a running commentary on what we are doing (often with a very negative analyst!)? How frequently do we try to reject our experiences because they are not as we want them to be? How much of the time are we in the moment of our lives fully experiencing it? Does this change the nature of the experience?"

Through discussion, clients were able to identify how little of the time they were participating in the moment of their lives and, when they were, the experience had a different quality. They each committed to a time during the week when they would practise participation, e.g., washing their face mindfully, walking to the shop mindfully, eating mindfully, and report back next week.

Setting Homework and Taking Feedback

Having clearly set the homework practice to strengthen the new skill from the previous week, the aim of homework feedback is to assess the level of the skill for each client and strengthen the skill by:

- Highlighting and reinforcing when the client has been (or has attempted to be) mindful;
- Providing behaviourally specific feedback to enhance awareness of the actions of their mind;
- Noticing with the client any consequences of being mindful; and
- Problem solving around any obstacles they may have encountered when using the mindfulness skill in their everyday lives.

A common obstacle can be forgetting to practise mindfulness. The usual memory aids work well for this e.g., putting a reminder on your phone, using an available app (which many clients find useful). The reminder alerts the client to notice and to carry out mindfully whatever they are doing in that moment. If the client has not done the mindfulness homework, it is important to "drag" the skill in session. For example, if the task was to eat mindfully and the client has not done it, the therapist will ask them to eat (or drink some water if no food is available) mindfully in the group. The therapist can ask "What did you notice when drinking the water?" In this way, the therapist can ensure the client has at least some practice and feedback to strengthen their acquisition of the new skill. The client may say they did not do the practice because they could not see the point. In this case, skills trainers both validate the difficulty of doing the task in the presence of this thought, while also making it explicit how, for *this* client, having *this* skill will enable them to move closer to *their* specific goals.

We have reviewed strategies and techniques for teaching mindfulness in the skills training modality (acquiring the skills). The primary modality for clients to learn to strengthen the skills and weave them into their lives is in individual therapy, which we now cover in the next section.

Mindfulness Skills in Individual Therapy

Once clients have learned the skill of mindfulness in the skills training modality, the individual therapist's goal is to strengthen this skill in both the one-to-one sessions and the telephone coaching modalities. Mindfulness is strengthened in four ways:

1. Highlighting opportunities for mindfulness;
2. Behavioural rehearsal and corrective feedback;
3. Modelling a mindful and dialectical philosophy; and
4. Combining mindfulness with other skills.

Highlighting Opportunities for Mindfulness

During individual sessions, there is an opportunity to watch carefully for the specific problems associated with a deficit of mindfulness. The therapist can also catch these tendencies in his or her own behaviour, thereby modelling how everyone is influenced by the same phenomena. The list below is not exhaustive, but covers some of the main unmindful behaviours that the therapist needs to observe and highlight.

a. Feeling overwhelmed or distracted in a situation by memories or associations with a previous event or earlier circumstances.
b. Becoming emotionally dysregulated by predictions of the future without recognizing that these events are not happening currently, and are perhaps not inevitable.
c. Making assumptions about the current situation and responding to these as though they are factual, without proper evaluation.
d. Fighting against the reality of a current situation, and dwelling instead on how the circumstances could, or should, be different.
e. Allowing attention to narrow to one set of factors in a given context, and missing or ignoring other significant variables.
f. Being a passive recipient of the contents of the mind, rather than actively adjusting awareness and attentional control when needed.
g. Failing to recognize that internal phenomena such as thoughts, sensations, or emotions are transient and will pass.
h. Using judgmental or interpretive descriptions that introduce an unnecessary bias which distracts from what is actually being observed or experienced.

In order to effectively model mindfulness, the therapist will both highlight behaviours from the list above, and have phenomenological empathy for the misery they cause when they occur. Too often clients are advised to "use your skills" when they are suffering intensely, which is akin to asking an orthopaedic patient to perform his own surgery.

In the following example, the client, Kim, is working on solving the problem of not having transport to appointments.

Kim: *There's no point in asking my daughter to help me out with transport, she's not interested.*

Therapist: *Is that a thought you are having, or have you asked her?* (Enhances curiosity about internal phenomena; labels a "thought".)

Kim: *I don't need to ask, I just know she won't help.*

Therapist: *I'm just noticing a lot of unmindful statements here and I am worried that they might influence what you eventually decide to do. I wonder if we can describe this more mindfully. For example, you could say, "I am having the thought, my daughter won't help with the transport".* (Models mindful describing and requests an active rehearsal from the client.)

Kim: *I am having the thought, "my daughter won't help with the transport".*

Therapist: *Great. Now when you say, "she's not interested", it sounds like you know what she's thinking right now, but maybe it is more of an assumption or even a fear about how she might react if you were to ask?* (Seeks clarification on the nature of the internal phenomenon.)

Kim: *I guess it's a fear.*

Therapist: *Then just say that.* (Encourages keeping to simple factual statements.)

Kim: *I'm having the thought that my daughter won't help with the transport. I'm afraid that if I ask her she will not be interested in helping me.*

Therapist: *Let's just stop for a moment and see if those two statements feel any different. Try saying the original statement you made about your daughter, and say it with all the expression you used at the time, sort of scrunching your face and using the same judgmental tone.* (Encourages the client to evaluate her new skilled behaviour.)

Kim: *Why? I thought you wanted me NOT to do that?*

Therapist: *I want you to have confidence in the skill, so that you can really notice the difference yourself – if there is any. I'm not here to make your life worse; it is painful enough. I'd like you to just evaluate for yourself if the mindful statement is any less intense than the other.* (Gives a genuine rationale for what is being asked of the client.)

Kim: *Ok.* (Screws up her face and uses a harsh tone.) *There's no point asking my daughter to help me out with the transport, she's NOT interested.*

Therapist: *Now say it the mindful way; and remember to take those judgments out of your tone and relax your face.* (Advises the client to try out different ways of responding and to evaluate which feels better in an attempt to encourage use of this skill outside of the therapy room.)

Kim: *I'm having the thought, "my daughter won't help with the transport" and I'm afraid that if I ask her she will not be interested.*

Therapist: *What did you notice? And don't be afraid to tell the truth, if it doesn't make any difference that's OK. The facts are always useful to know, so if this mindful statement is genuinely not helping we can weave in some other skills.* (Models a mindful and dialectical approach, remaining factual and focusing on what works without attaching to one particular outcome.)

Kim: *It did seem less upsetting. It's funny but when I said it mindfully for some reason I didn't feel quite so scared at the prospect of asking. I think I was probably worried that she will say "no", but even if she did I won't be any worse off.*

Therapist: *And yet it might not have gone that way, even when you restated it mindfully. You could have been just as afraid or just as convinced that it was pointless. I'm not really trying to get you to be happier or more positive. Some things will be painful no matter what. My goal here is so that you can just see and describe things as they are, without adding in extra things to be afraid of or worried about. Then we can decide more wisely what we are going to do about them.* (Models how to approach a situation mindfully, without judging it as good or bad.)

The example here shows how the therapist drags new behaviour from the client, and then gets her to check out whether this is more, or less, helpful. This is a set of strategies designed to focus the client's attention on the natural reinforcers of being more mindful. The therapist also remains mindful, and doesn't assume that improvements will happen, but instead checks the facts with the client.

Behavioural Rehearsal in Individual Sessions

When conducting a behavioural chain and solution analysis the therapist will want to ensure that the client can perform the required skill exactly when needed. This "re-run" of specific links in the chain, i.e., substituting new behaviour for the unskilled action, makes it more likely that the client will behave differently. This brief snippet of a session demonstrates how NOT to strengthen a mindfulness skill:

Nadia: *My favourite nurse, Katherine, was doing admission forms with the new patient, leaning towards her and looking all concerned about her. I was just hanging around in the corridor thinking, "So it's fine for me to be left out here, no one cares, I just don't matter".*

Therapist: *What skill could you have used?*

Nadia: *Hmmph. Mindfulness I guess.*

Therapist: *Right, you need to notice your thoughts and let them go.*

Nadia: *OK.*

Here the therapist has merely highlighted a skill to use, but has not assessed or rehearsed the client's ability to perform it on the day. The client has given a verbal agreement with no real understanding of any obstacles that could get in the way.

Below is the same scenario, showing how to strengthen the skill:

Nadia: *My favourite nurse, Katherine, was doing admission forms with the new patient, leaning towards her and looking all concerned about her. I was just hanging around in the corridor thinking, "So it's fine for me to be left out here, no one cares, I just don't matter".*

Therapist: *It sounds like those thoughts were making an unpleasant situation even worse?* (Highlights the role of an internal phenomenon, a thought, in altering the client's experience.)

Nadia: *Yes, I hate waiting around, I really wanted to see Katherine because she hadn't been on duty at all over the weekend.*

Therapist: *So if you had been more skillful, what would you have liked to be able to do? I'm guessing you didn't really want to be hanging around in the corridor?* (Enquires about what would be a skillful or normal behaviour in the situation where a person you wish to speak to is unavailable.)

Nadia: *I'd like to have just gone back to the day-room, maybe chat with Joe until Katherine was free. I just couldn't, I was just working myself up.*

Therapist: *It is really hard. Did you think of any skill to use that could have helped?* (Checking whether the client can generate the appropriate skill.)

Nadia: *Well, maybe mindfulness, but I couldn't do it.*

Therapist: *Did you have a go?* (Checking if the client actually tried the skill or only thought about it.)

Nadia: *Not really. Anyway, why should I? Katherine could see I was waiting, she could've hurried up.*

Therapist: *It might be one solution to think of ways that you could alert Katherine that you were waiting, but are there ever other situations where you just have to wait, like it or not?* (Validates at Level 5 that it is fine to wish to alert someone to the fact you are waiting, and then refocuses on the higher-value learning opportunity, in this case, how to wait effectively.)

Nadia: *All the time.*

Therapist: *So if we could work out how to use mindfulness even in those horrible circumstances, maybe it would help at other times, too?* (Gives a rationale for the use of a mindfulness skill.)

Nadia: *Huh. Yes. OK.*

Therapist: *So let's say you decide to walk down the corridor to the dayroom, but want to do it mindfully—what could you pay attention to? Remember that we want to use as many of our senses as possible as these are giving us moment-by-moment information from the real world. It helps us to unhook from all that "mind-traffic".* (Guides the client in what to do to walk mindfully and turn her attention to what is in her actual surroundings.)

Nadia: *Well, there are pictures on the walls – stuff we did in art. There's a big collage of a tree where we all made leaves to stick on the branches. So, should I distract myself by looking at the collage?*

Therapist: *That's a good question. In that moment, you were walking down the corridor, so you might as well walk mindfully, noticing with enhanced awareness what is around you. Your actual experience was walking past the collage and so it was your thoughts that pulled you away from that. We don't use mindfulness to distract us from our thoughts, we notice that sometimes our thoughts distract us from being present in our life.* (Uses the opportunity to correct the client's misapprehension that mindfulness is distraction.) *So imagine walking down the corridor paying attention to that collage. Describe passing it, describe it mindfully.* (Encourages behavioural rehearsal.)

Nadia: *I'm walking past the collage and I can smell a mixture of paint and glue from the leaves. I see the brown trunk of the tree, going up towards the ceiling, and the green leaves with silver veins.*

Therapist: *Great. Can you feel anything, or hear anything?* (Gives praise as a reinforcer and asks for more detail to shape mindful behaviour.)

Nadia: *I can hear Katherine talking to the new patient, not what they are saying but just kind of muttering.*

Therapist: *Maybe that's not the best thing to attend to, although you can if you want – as long as you describe it mindfully to yourself. But remember there is always a variety of things to choose, how about the sound your feet are making on the floor, and the feel of each step? You choose.* (Gives corrective feedback, encourages the client to be more discerning in where to put her attention.)

Nadia: *I don't want to focus on Katherine, so I'll do the feet thing.*

Therapist: *OK, off you go. And I am going to test you, because I am going to say some of the unwanted thoughts that you were having, and your job is to turn your mind back to the collage.* (Demands more rehearsal and orientates the client to an additional challenge.)

Nadia: *I'm walking down the corridor and I can hear my shoe hit the floor with a kind of tapping sound, I'm looking at the collage and can see green leaves with silver writing ... I can smell the dried paint and ...*

Therapist: (Whispers in Nadia's ear) *I just don't matter, no one cares about me.* (Testing whether the client can turn her attention in the presence of the problematic thought.)

Nadia: *That's true, I was just left waiting around in the corridor.*

Therapist: *Remember we are just trying to walk mindfully, we're not concerning ourselves with whether the thoughts are true or not. They make you miserable, so let's not focus on them.* (Gives corrective feedback.)

Nadia: *So I have to be a push-over?*

Therapist: *Hmm ... well let's see ... when you spent quite a lot of time thinking those thoughts on that day—did they help you to not be a push-over? If they did actually improve the situation for you then we don't need to move our attention away from them. Remember we are just trying to do what's effective. That's one of our mindfulness "How Skills" that you learned in skills class.* (Highlights the component of mindfulness being practised.)

Nadia: *No, the thoughts didn't help me, they just wound me up.*

Therapist: *So have another go and this time when you notice the thought, turn your mind to the collage again.* (Gives clear instructions.)

Nadia: *I'm walking down the corridor and I can hear my footstep on the floor, I can feel my toes inside my shoes. I'm looking at the collage and I can see the green leaves ...*

Therapist: (Whispers in Nadia's ear) *They think it's fine to leave me out here.* (Produces the problematic cue so that the client can more realistically rehearse the skill.)

Nadia: *Er.. uh ... and I can ... er... I can smell the paint and the glue ...*

Therapist: *Much better.*

Nadia: *It was hard!*

Therapist: *Yes, so well done for turning your mind back to the collage. Remember you might have to do that quite a few times in the space of two or three minutes.* (Adds additional instructions for the practice of the skill.)

In this version of the scenario, the therapist goes into detail of *how* the skill is done. Getting the client to rehearse in session flushes out some problems, for example, how

Nadia gets distracted when she has the thoughts "why should I do it?" and "so I have to be a push-over?" These inhibiting factors are only revealed during the rehearsal. Then solutions are found and tested out to see if Nadia can become more proficient, even in the presence of those uninvited thoughts.

Modelling a Mindful and Dialectical Philosophy

The example above also highlights another principle of mindfulness, that as the session unfolds second by second, an internal state can change. Nadia's motivation goes up and down; a sudden unhelpful thought causes it to fall, where trying out a new behaviour raises it again. The therapist must remain mindful to these fluctuations, cheerleading during effective behaviour and problem solving when obstacles arise. The clinician does not conceptualize the client as either "willing" or "unwilling", but notices which controlling variables move her closer and further away from effectiveness. There is no assumption that if motivation is high it will stay that way, or if it has waned that it has gone for good. The only question is: *what is happening in THIS moment, and what is needed in order to move forward in a valued direction?*

Modelling non-attachment is a difficult skill to master, because it is human nature to have preferences in how things turn out. The therapist constantly models the relentless pursuit of problem-solving with non-attachment to outcome. This does not mean a lack of interest in the result of any solutions, but being open to seeing each turn of events, for example, as another move in an ongoing game of chess. At the end of the session with Nadia, the therapist points out that although on this occasion she felt differently as a result of the mindfulness (the chess move went favourably for her) it could just as easily have gone the other way. This is an advanced form of being non-judgmental and realizing that whatever happens does not have to be deemed good or bad—it just is as it is.

During therapy, dialectical tensions arise, and the therapist helps the client to resolve them mindfully. In the following scenario, Ben had urges to harm himself the previous week when he got into an argument with the manager of a local day centre about his poor attendance.

> **Ben:**   *The thing is, I don't want to keep going to the day centre. I've been going for years now, but I just think it's not for me anymore. I don't need the support I used to. I don't like the new person who has taken charge. It's time I moved on. It's only once a week, so I'm not going to miss it that much.*
>
> **Therapist:**   *It sounds as though you've made a decision to leave?* (Level 3 validation, verbalizing the unspoken.)
>
> **Ben:**   *Yes definitely.*
>
> **Therapist:**   *I'm just wondering which mind is most active in this right now, you know – when we use the skill of "Wise Mind"?* (Highlights the opportunity to use the skill of "Wise Mind".)
>
> **Ben:**   *Maybe my reason mind – I've weighed up the value of going to the day centre, and it's just not that high these days.*

Therapist: *Yes, everything you say makes sense to me. And let's be clear, I'm not trying to change your mind, I can see that you have moved on a lot since you started at day centre, and this might be an opportunity to do new things. I just want us to check in with your Wise Mind. So, what would the other mind say? Emotion mind?* (Gives a rationale and describes the first step that is required.)

Ben: *I don't have much emotion about it—it's fine.*

Therapist: *Just sit with it for a minute, say to yourself, "I have decided to leave the day centre". Picture yourself leaving, relax your muscles and just see if any emotion comes up.* (Gives clear instructions on how to do the skill.)

Ben: (Slowly exhales and inhales as he has been taught in skills class) *"I have decided to leave the day centre". OK. Well, I feel a bit sad about leaving some of the people I have known for a long time. Particularly JayCee. I think she will be gutted when I go. And maybe I'm a bit scared too, if I'm honest.*

Therapist: *That's what we were looking for, which doesn't mean you should stay. We want to acknowledge that when you think of leaving, all your reasons to stay don't disappear, and if you were to think of staying, all your reasons to leave wouldn't disappear either. Both positions are valid. So now we want to get a "Wise Mind" statement that just acknowledges the truth in both sides. Something that when you say it to yourself it seems to capture where you are with it right now.* (Gives clear instructions on what the client needs to actually do.)

Ben: *I want to leave the day centre after six years, because it doesn't do the same for me anymore, and it is time to move on . . .*

Therapist: (Prompts) *– and at the same time . . .* (Encourages an active response for the client.)

Ben: *. . . And at the same time, I will be sad to leave my friends behind, and I'm scared I might regret leaving.*

Therapist: *Now allow yourself, body and mind, to fully occupy that position and see if it sums up both sides, if it is wise you will sense it inside of yourself.* (Clear instructions on what to do.)

Ben: *No it doesn't feel quite right.*

Therapist: *Excellent noticing. So just keep going till it fits your sense of what's true for you, in this moment, right now.* (Offers praise as a reinforcer, as the client is working well.)

Ben: *Er . . . "I want to leave the daycentre after six years, because it doesn't benefit me anymore, and at the same time I will miss my friends, and I'm scared of not having it there as back up". That feels more accurate. I don't think I will regret leaving over all, but it will still be a loss.*

Therapist: *So did that feel like a "Wise Mind" statement? This is a whole-body skill, so I always put my hand on my tummy when I do it.* (Gives a personal disclosure.)

Ben: *Yes, it wasn't exactly comfortable, but it felt true.*

Therapist: *So why do you think I got you to do that? I mean, we ended up in the same place with you still deciding to leave, didn't we? So why did we go through all that "Reason Mind, Emotion Mind, Wise Mind" stuff?* (Checks that the client is aware of the value of this practice.)

Ben: *I suppose that even though my decision is the same, I feel a bit different about it. I'm more prepared for the emotions that will come with leaving. And saying out loud, "I'll miss the back-up" was better than "I'll regret it".*

Therapist: *That's it! If we don't make Wise Mind decisions then as each wave of emotion or logic floods in we get buffeted – pulled this way and that. "Wise Mind" helps us to step back and contemplate all sides. Let's say tomorrow you break an ankle—your Wise Mind statement might be "I want to leave the day centre as it is not helping me any more, and at the same time I need additional support till my ankle heals". "Wise Mind" is adaptable.* (Highlights the dialectical nature of the skill.)

The excerpt above demonstrates how mindfulness and dialectics sit hand-in-glove. When we are being dialectical, we take more than one perspective. Yet it is impossible to be truly dialectical without being in the moment. Each new moment could bring an alternative perspective, as the therapist points out at the end of the dialogue.

Therapists are constantly looking at how to bring home the message that "this moment may feel like any other, but you have never actually been here before, in this time and space, with these unique circumstances". Being able to fully inhabit the present involves the client unhooking from their memories, associations, assumptions, and predictions. The client becoming more aware of the influences on his or her own mind helps to counter the disturbed sense of identity that is a common feature of BPD (American Psychiatric Association, 1994).

Combining Mindfulness with Other Skills

Therapists strengthen clients' abilities to combine mindfulness (often referred to as a "core" skill for this reason) with other skills in individual therapy. Almost all the other skills require a degree of mindfulness to do them, and this is often included in the handout, for example, as the M in the DEAR MAN skill, or in the "Mindfulness of Emotion" handout from the emotion regulation module (see Linehan, 2015a).

In the next dialogue, the client, an adolescent, has had urges to overdose after an argument with her foster mother.

Jodie: *I couldn't settle to watch TV in my room. I kept thinking, why did I say those things? Then I thought, nobody cares about me, and I felt really sad. That's when I wanted to overdose.*

Therapist: *I'm wondering how we got from "Why did I say those things" to "Nobody cares about me"? Was there anything in between?* (Assessing for any missing links.)

Jodie: *Just that I am horrid. She didn't want me to stay out too late in case I got attacked or something, and I just flew at her. No wonder I keep getting moved on, but she just annoys me. It's not all my fault! She doesn't bother explaining properly.*

Therapist: *Now I need you to be mindful here because it is important—did you have the thoughts about her being annoying at that time when you couldn't settle, or only now, when we're discussing it?* (Encouraging the client to notice how events unfold moment-by-moment.)

Jodie: *Not at the time. I just felt cross with myself.*

Therapist: *Was it cross with yourself first of all, or did some guilt come first?* (Paying attention to sequencing.)

Jodie: *She DOES annoy me, though. It's not all me!*

Therapist: *It seems like even if I just mention feeling guilty you fly off into another emotion. Can I ask you—might you have felt guilty that night before you got sad? I wasn't there, so you have to check in with yourself to find this out, and I could be wrong. So if there was no guilt, it's fine to say so, as it might just have been anger, or you might have gone straight to feeling sad.* (Encouraging mindful reflection.)

Jodie: (Quietly) *I did feel some … but …*

Therapist: *I get it that this feels painful. Remember from skills class that the first thing we do in emotion regulation is to name the emotion and see if it fits the facts. The problem we have got here is that your mind keeps pulling away from naming a feeling of guilt, like your hand would if you touched a hot surface. If we are going to down-regulate that painful guilt, we need to be mindful that it is there, even when our mind tries to go down the fire escape! Try just describing mindfully, "I felt guilty because I regret some things I said to Freya in our argument".* (Using mindful describing to help name the emotion).

Jodie: *"I regret all those horrible things I said. No wonder people don't like me".*

Therapist: *Now that time the pendulum swung the other way—almost like instead of shying away from the hot surface you are throwing yourself onto it. Let's have another go.* (Giving corrective feedback in the moment.)

Jodie: *I felt guilty … because … but it wasn't all my fault.*

Therapist: *I'm wondering if when you acknowledge guilt you start to judge yourself. Does your mind say, "If I'm guilty then I'm bad"?* (Level 3 validation: mind reading.)

Jodie: *Well that's what it means, isn't it?*

Therapist: *So if we had people who never felt any guilt about anything, what kinds of things might they do?* (Moves from mindfulness to highlighting dysfunctional cognitions.)

Jodie: *Maybe they would … steal things … or be nasty to people.*

Therapist: *And if they felt guilty? More or less likely to steal?* (Gentle thought challenging.)

Jodie: *Er … yeah, OK … probably less likely …*

Therapist: *So we don't have to say that guilt is either good or bad, only whether it fits the facts. But if we are going to down-regulate it we need to be mindful of any judgments we are making. So, let's try that first step of emotion regulation again, naming the emotion, and if you notice you are judging yourself or the emotion, gently turn your mind back to describing mindfully. Then once we have decided how much guilt is justified, we can work out how to make a repair. For any excess guilt, we can use the skill of Opposite Action, and I can help you with that, too.* (Returns to the skill of emotion regulation.)

Here Jodie's therapist is trying to coach some emotion regulation skills, such as naming the emotion and working out whether it fits the facts, but the client is hindered by her inability to remain mindful. At each stage, the clinician assesses the problem and moves skillfully back and forth between working on the emotion and coaching mindfulness, even weaving in a little cognitive restructuring along the way. Questions such as, "Did you have that thought at the time?" help orient Jodie to notice when her mind confuses one time period with another. This painstaking attention to each moment in which the session itself unfolds also calls for a high degree of mindfulness on the part of the therapist.

GENERALIZING MINDFULNESS SKILLS

Having examined teaching in skills group to aquire mindfulness skills and how these skills are then strengthened in individual therapy, the chapter concludes by reviewing how therapists help clients to generalize the skill of mindfulness into their lives. The main modality to address this function is coaching on the phone, where the aim is to strengthen the skill of mindfulness and generalize it into all relevant settings. Coaching by phone modality is brief and focused. In the following example, the client, Becky, has phoned her individual therapist at 11pm for coaching as she has a test in the morning, can't sleep, and has high urges to self-harm. Becky is three months into treatment and hasn't self-harmed for some weeks.

> **Therapist:** *It's great you phoned for coaching Becky. Can I just check I've understood the problem? It sounds like you're trying to get to sleep and your mind keeps going into the future to thoughts about the test and how you're going to fail. You've tried distracting yourself by reading, but the thoughts keep intruding and the urges to cut yourself are getting stronger. So, the function of cutting yourself is to get away from the thoughts?* (Reinforces with praise. Summarizes the mini chain of events and function of the urge to engage in the problem behaviour.)
>
> **Becky:** *Yes, that's it. I just can't bear it!*
>
> **Therapist:** *I get that it's really hard, and I want us to look at what skills you can use. I'm just wondering if telling yourself you can't bear it is making it easier or harder for you?* (Highlights the unmindful description. Draws the client's attention to the consequence.)
>
> **Becky:** *Harder I guess.*
>
> **Therapist:** *Try saying it more mindfully. Maybe try: "This is hard for me".* (Highlights opportunities for mindfulness. Strengthens the skill by coaching behavioural rehearsal of mindful describing.)
>
> **Becky:** *"This is hard for me". It is!*
>
> **Therapist:** *That sounds a bit different.* (Highlights the consequence of a more mindful description.)
>
> **Becky:** *Yes. I don't think it's quite so hopeless when I say it that way.*
>
> **Therapist:** *Yes, what we say to ourselves matters because we are listening. So, let's see if using the mindfulness "describe" skill is helpful in describing the problem. Have a go.* (Engages the client in skill strengthening by coaching behavioural rehearsal of mindful describing.)
>
> **Becky:** *Well, I'm trying to get to sleep and I keep getting thoughts that I will fail the test tomorrow and I don't want to think that, so I have the urge to cut myself to get rid of the thoughts.*

Therapist: *Well done. So, if we could come up with a skill to help you notice when your mind goes into the future and down a path with lots of worry thoughts about the test, would that be useful?* (Moves to solution generation.)

Becky: *Yes, I guess I need to try mindfulness but that's really hard to do.* (Client identifies potential solution.)

Therapist: *I was thinking mindfulness could be helpful, too. We could look at the sleep protocol if you think that would be more effective. Remember the mindful effectiveness skill: "focus on what works". What do you think would be more effective in this situation tonight?* (Models a mindful and dialectical philosophy in solution analysis.)

Becky: *I think mindfulness.*

Therapist: *OK. Sometimes when it's hard to be mindful it can help to use a metaphor. I remember you liked the puppy metaphor we spoke about in group. Do you remember we said our mind is like an untrained puppy, running off digging up the flowerbeds and mindfulness is training our mind to come to the focus of our choosing, like training the puppy to come when we call? It sounds like your mind is off digging up the test worry thoughts.* (Uses metaphor to coach the mindfulness skill of noticing where the client's attention has gone and to return it to the focus of their choosing.)

Becky: (Laughing) *Yes, it is. I remember that!*

Therapist: *OK, so if you were going to use this skill when you notice the worry thoughts, what would you turn your attention to?* (Coaches using the skill. Highlights focusing attention in the moment.)

Becky: *Well I'll be lying in bed, so my breath, I guess.*

Therapist: *Brilliant. We rehearsed similar examples in individual therapy before, so let's try it. Can you get into bed and keep the phone on? Lie down and close your eyes. You'll need to speak out loud what you are doing so I know, and I will play the role of the thoughts hitting you and we'll see how it goes.* (Uses behavioural rehearsal to strengthen the mindfulness skill).

Becky: *I'm noticing my breath as I breathe in.*

Therapist: (Therapist takes the role of the worry thoughts to assess solution implementation, for skill strengthening and generalization) *"I'm going to fail the test".*

Becky: *That's the puppy digging up worry thoughts. I'm noticing the rise and fall of my chest.*

Therapist: (Therapist takes the role of the worry thoughts to assess solution implementation, for skill strengthening and generalization) *"I'll never pass".*

Becky: *That's a worry thought. I'm noticing the air coming in my nose is cool.*

Therapist: *Well done! If you do that, do you think the urge to cut yourself will go up, down, or stay the same?"* (Assesses whether the skill will be effective in reducing urges.)

Becky: *Go down. I'm going to give it a try.* (Client gives commitment to try the skill.)

Therapist: *Great. Do you think anything will get in the way of you doing it?* (Looks for potential obstacles to problem solve.)

Becky: *No, I'm going to give it a try.* (Client strengthens commitment to try the skill.)

Therapist: *Brilliant Becky. Call me if you need coaching in using the skills, and if I don't hear from you tonight, text me in the morning to let me know how you get on.*

Becky: *I will. Thanks.*

So we can see how, in this scenario, the therapist coaches Becky to describe the problem more mindfully, choose a solution, and then implement it using behavioural rehearsal to identify whether the use of mindfulness will be effective in reducing the urges to self-harm.

It is arguably in the coaching by phone modality that therapists derive most personal benefit from mindfulness. Therapists are often concerned that a call such as the one in this example will disturb them, and they will be unable to sleep themselves. By practising mindfulness, the therapist can be mindful in the moment of the call and also notice when their mind goes to thoughts of the client after the call has finished. Then the therapist can bring their attention back to what they are doing in the moment. Mindfulness can also help them take a non-judgmental stance towards the client and their difficulties, as well as towards themselves as therapists and coaches (Heard & Swales, 2016). In practising in this way, therapists enhance their own mindfulness skills.

Conclusion

Throughout the chapter, we have described how the DBT therapist can teach the skill of mindfulness so that it is acquired in skills training, strengthened in individual therapy, and generalized in the coaching by phone mode. Thus, the client is provided with a range of opportunities to become competent and confident in weaving mindfulness skills into their everyday lives.

Key Points for Clinicians

- Therapists:

  have their own mindfulness practice.

  model a mindful and dialectical philosophy.
- Use a variety of practices.
- Keep the practice simple and give clear instructions.
- Take feedback after a practice to shape mindful awareness.
- Behaviourally rehearse mindfulness skills in session.
- Coach a non-judgmental stance in the tone of voice, facial expression, body posture, thoughts, and language.
- Assess the level of skill for each client and provide coaching to strengthen this.
- Identify and problem-solve obstacles to being mindful.
- Combine mindfulness with other skills.
- Highlight opportunities for generalizing the skill.
- Make clear the relevance of using the skill in the client's everyday life.

REFERENCES

American Psychiatric Association. (1994). *Diagnostic and statistical manual of mental disorders, (DSM-IV)*, 4th Edition. Arlington: American Psychiatric Association.

Dunkley, C., & Stanton, M. (2014). *Teaching clients to use mindfulness skills: A practical guide.* New York: Routledge.

Dunkley, C., & Stanton, M. (2017). *Using mindfulness skills in everyday life: A practical guide.* New York: Routledge.

Heard, H. L., & Swales, M. A. (2016). *Changing behaviour in DBT: Problem solving in action.* New York: Guilford Press.

Kabat-Zinn, J. (1994). *Wherever you go, there you are: mindfulness meditation for everyday life.* London: Piatkus Books.

Kabat-Zinn, J. (2013). *Full catastrophe living: Using the wisdom of your body and mind to face stress, pain, and illness.* New York: Bantam Dell.

Kuyken, W., Watkins, E. R., Holden, E. R., White, K., Taylor, R. S., Byford, S., . . . Dalgleish, T. (2010). How does mindfulness-based cognitive therapy work? *Behaviour Research and Therapy, 48*, 1105–1112.

Linehan, M. M. (1993). *Cognitive-behavioral treatment of borderline personality disorder.* New York: Guilford Press.

Linehan, M. M. (2015a). *DBT skills training handouts and worksheets*, 2nd Edition. New York: Guilford Press.

Linehan, M. M. (2015b). *DBT skills training manual*, 2nd Edition. New York: Guilford Press.

Segal, Z. V., Williams, M. G., & Teasdale, J. D. (2013). *Mindfulness based cognitive therapy for depression*, 2nd Edition. New York: Guilford Press.

CHAPTER 19

DIALECTICAL BEHAVIOUR THERAPY WITH PARENTS, COUPLES, AND FAMILIES TO AUGMENT STAGE 1 OUTCOMES

ALAN E. FRUZZETTI

INTRODUCTION

FAMILY interventions can be an efficient and effective way to augment outcomes for individuals in Dialectical Behaviour Therapy (DBT). Comprehensive DBT always includes five functions: 1) skill acquisition; 2) skill generalization; 3) improving the motivation of the client to employ skills rather than old, dysfunctional responses (this typically includes chain and solution analyses, troubleshooting, commitment, rehearsal, etc., punctuated with validating responses); 4) intervening in the environment (social, family, work, administrative, etc.) to reduce impediments to skillful improvements and to help those environments instead promote improvements, and become more validating; and 5) enhancing the motivation and skills of DBT treatment providers. Interestingly, family interventions are relevant to the first four of these five functions: 1) family interventions typically include learning skills needed to reduce harmful conflict, solve relationship problems, and build better relationships; 2) bringing the family into a family group or family therapy affords the client the opportunity to practise his or her skills in the actual environment in which they are needed (family interactions); 3) when a parent, partner, or other close person provides the prompting event for a client's chain, or reinforces (positively or negatively) the client's dysfunctional behaviours, or punishes (or ignores) incremental improvements and skillful behaviour, family interventions can have a direct impact on patient motivation to use skills; and 4) the family environment is often a key place in which newer, skillful behaviours are ignored or punished, and/or dysfunctional client behaviours are inadvertently reinforced. Thus, intervening directly with families can be extremely efficient.

Family interventions may take many forms: 1) psychoeducational multi-family groups that include the patient (Hoffman, Fruzzetti, & Swenson, 1999); 2) psychoeducational multi-family groups that do not include the patient (that is, for parents, partners, siblings, grandparents, and other caregivers separately; Ekdahl, Idvall, & Perseius, 2014; Flynn et al., 2017; Hoffmann, Fruzzetti, & Buteau, 2005; Hoffman et al., 2007); 3) skill groups that include family members (Rathus & Miller, 2014); more standard couple or family therapy (Fruzzetti & Payne, 2015); or, some combination of these.

Of course, in DBT, the treatment target hierarchy places Stage 1 targets above others, and within Stage 1 focuses first on those behaviours that are life threatening. A transactional understanding of problem behaviours recognizes that parents, partners, and other loved ones can often be very relevant to the chain of a client's self-harm, suicidal behaviour, or aggression. Because in these circumstances the role of the family member is so important, and often neglected in individual DBT, this chapter focuses primarily on DBT family interventions in Stage 1, and emphasizes interventions related to life-threatening behaviours. However, the interventions described can readily be adapted for intervention around other targets later in treatment. Overall, this chapter outlines the circumstances under which DBT family interventions might be particularly useful, the specific targets to be addressed and treatment target hierarchy to be followed, a general protocol for how to conduct a family session, and various helpful strategies to use in-session when DBT family interventions are utilized.

INDIVIDUALS AND FAMILIES IN CHAOS

The transactional or biosocial model of borderline personality disorder (BPD) and related disorders maintains a dialectical position: severe psychopathology such as BPD and related problems can be understood as the result of an emotionally vulnerable person transacting with others in an invalidating environment (Fruzzetti, Shenk, & Hoffman, 2005; Fruzzetti & Worrall, 2010). Of course, this is not to blame the emotionally vulnerable individual or the members of her or his family for psychological difficulties. Rather, this model is descriptive, with clear intervention targets, and it is essential that every DBT family therapist utilize his or her consultation team to stay non-judgmental toward all relevant parties, and empathic toward family members as well as the client.

Indeed, families of clients with BPD are a heterogeneous group. Family members range from being physically and/or sexually abusive to highly verbally critical, to burned out and hopeless, to gentle, over-burdened, and caring. Additionally, all of them have their own learning histories. Family interventions may help patients and their family members achieve stability regardless of where on this continuum family members may fall, and thus are likely to benefit both patients and family members. Clearly, for example, it is vital to eliminate physically or sexually aggressive or abusive behaviour in order to allow an individual to move toward stability, and reducing pervasive criticisms and other forms of verbal invalidation help to diminish the toxicity in any family environment. However, there are many other, perhaps subtler, family behaviours (by their presence or absence) that may contribute to both individual and relationship dysfunction. The *treatment target hierarchy* for family interventions in Stage 1 is: 1) eliminate physical and sexual aggression and abuse; 2) remove reinforcers for suicidality or self-harm; 3) reduce invalidating family behaviours that are antecedents (or the removal of which are negative reinforcers) to life-threatening individual behaviours; 4) reduce invalidating behaviours in general; and 5) increase family behaviours that might promote skillful alternative behaviours of the identified patient (e.g., appropriate warmth and attention, validating responses, good problem solving).

Because we employ a transactional model, modifying the identified patients' behaviour to support the changes that their family members make is also essential. For example, a client might typically escalate quickly (i.e., extinction burst) when a family member stops performing a particular kind of "caretaking" behaviour that seems to reinforce dysfunction despite good intentions (e.g., providing a lot of soothing or withdrawing reasonable demands following self-harm). In order for the family member to change this pattern, the patient must a) understand and be committed to the new pattern, and b) have a plan in place to manage her or his likely escalating distress when actually faced with the situation. Effective interventions will address both sides of this transaction in order to improve the situation for both the patient and her or his family.

ASSESSMENT

Because remediating the identified patient's primary targets is the raison d'être for employing family interventions in Stage 1, further assessment is needed only to identify the secondary targets or specific transactional behaviours on the identified patient's dysfunctional chain(s) that will be the focus of intervention. That is, key family behaviours will already have been identified in individual DBT as relevant or controlling variables (targets) on the chain to crisis or other problematic target behaviours. Subsequent assessments will simply need to assess further the details of the interaction in order to know which behaviour(s) members of the family will try to alter, and which skills the therapist must teach in order to help them to do so. Of course, bringing the family in for treatment also affords the therapist, and therefore the whole treatment team, a welcome opportunity for direct assessment of family interactions in the service of the individual patient's case conceptualization, and affords opportunities for higher levels of validation of the individual patient and her or his family members (see Fruzzetti & Payne, in press, for more details about family assessment in DBT). The next section explores both antecedents and consequences of individual dysfunctional behaviour that may become targets for intervention.

Antecedents on the Chain to Dysfunctional Behaviours

> Maria often had difficulty waking up in the morning and frequently was late for work at her part-time job. After getting out of bed late one morning, Maria's mother began scolding her and telling Maria that she was "worthless and lazy" and would "never amount to anything." Maria's shame escalated as she went into the bathroom to take a shower. When she saw a razor in the bathroom, she impulsively cut herself with it on the inside of her thigh, bandaged it up, took her shower, dressed, and went to work a little bit late.

Maria's example highlights how certain kinds of criticisms and other forms of invalidating responses can create, or exacerbate, negative emotional arousal on the way to dysfunctional behaviours. If Maria's mother acted this way often, and if Maria's cutting was significantly more likely following similar instances of invalidation, reducing her mother's criticisms and judgments could be important targets for intervention. Of course, her DBT therapist would also target teaching Maria how to manage her shame differently when responding to invalidation, and could also encourage Maria to use her interpersonal effectiveness skills (Linehan, 2015) to help her mother to use a different approach. But direct intervention with Maria's mother would also be a reasonable, potentially effective, and efficient strategy that could benefit Maria, her relationship with her mother, and thus, her mother as well.

Any time family members do things that are an important part of dysfunctional chains, it is reasonable to consider family intervention. However, in order to be efficient, assessment should determine that problematic family behaviours are a *necessary* or causal part of the chain. That is, if Maria likely would have cut herself that morning even if her mother had not been critical and judgmental, targeting other links on the chain would be more effective.

Many kinds of invalidation show up as relevant antecedents of severely dysfunctional client behaviour: criticisms, judgments, minimizing pain, blaming the client for all of his or her problems, and being physically or emotionally unavailable are common examples. But a partner having sexual affairs (or related demonstrations of attraction to others), lying about whereabouts or activities, partners or other family members ignoring patient requests not to be touched or not to engage in sexual activities (or any forced sexual behaviours), or anyone's attempts to *dishonestly* and intentionally mislead the client despite her initially "knowing" the truth of the situation (sometimes referred to as "gaslighting," after the eponymous films) may also be invalidating antecedents to dysfunction and should be addressed.

Of course, at other times, family members may do things that are helpful in averting dysfunctional outcomes, or they may help to create a more validating environment in general. Most family members have, at least at times, worked very hard to be helpful to their loved one. It is important also to assess for these validating and helpful behaviours, both to provide balance in the session (opportunities to support and validate family members, or as examples to prevent judgments by the therapist, identified patient, or themselves) and to catalogue successes to build upon in the future.

The individual DBT therapist, in collaboration with the identified patient, conducts the initial behavioural or chain analysis with the client, and passes this information on to the family DBT therapist (if the family therapist is not also the individual therapist). It is up to the family DBT therapist, in collaboration with all relevant members of the family (identified patient plus anyone else whose behaviours are on the chain), to look more specifically at what each person can do differently. Typically, this is in the form of a *double chain*, in which the behaviours of the relevant family member (thoughts, emotions, actions) are woven around, or in parallel with, the patient's chain (see Figure 19.1). Just as with chain analysis with an individual, it is essential to assess a *specific* interaction chain from a *specific* episode, rather than asking about interactions that occur frequently or behaviours that are perceived to be problematic in general. As shown in Figure 19.1, the therapist should start by asking the patient to describe, and perhaps write on a white board or large sheet of paper, the chain already completed (the "upper" chain in Figure 19.1), and then ask the family member to describe his or her chain, leading up to and overlapping the time frame of the patient's chain (the "lower" chain in Figure 19.1). It is important for the therapist to elicit judgments, appraisals, attributions, emotional arousal, and other private reactions in each person (the "open" links in Figure 19.1), as well as ascertaining specific things said or done (e.g., public links, behaviours relevant to both people, shown as shaded links in Figure 19.1). As the therapist identifies any of these behaviours, or any other forms of invalidation, he or she can make a note to address them later, or they can be targeted right away. Just as with individual chain and solution analysis, it is not always necessary to complete the entire chain; often, understanding (and finding solutions to) one or more segments of the chain is sufficient for a successful intervention.

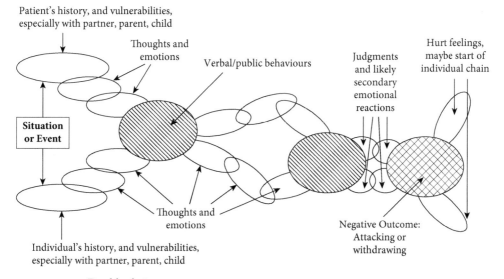

FIGURE 19.1 Double chain.

Identifying Relevant Family Responses to Dysfunctional Individual Behaviours

Paul spent long hours at work, at the gym, or with his friends. His wife, Sophie, had few friends, a long history of high suicide urges and several suicide attempts, and spent much of her time waiting for Paul to be home with her. Early one evening Sophie became increasingly suicidal as she imagined Paul with another woman. She thought about calling him on his cell phone, but she felt humiliated that she was "so needy and clingy and untrusting." Sophie went back and forth between rage at Paul for leaving her alone so often and shame and humiliation for "needing him so much" and for "not trusting him, despite the fact that he has been so good to me." Around 8:30pm she cut herself in the bathroom, and was still sitting there on the floor when Paul came home around 9:00pm. Sophie was medically stable (not requiring sutures), and Paul lay down with her on the bathroom floor, stroked her hair, and reassured her about how much he loved her. Paul then urged Sophie to call him on his cell phone so he could "come home to help her" any time she felt unsafe by herself.

It is important to identify all of the relevant consequences of the individual's problematic behaviour. For example, cutting might only be negatively reinforced by brief relief from high negative arousal (as was the case in Maria's example), and thus the family member's behaviour is relevant primarily as an antecedent (prompting event). Or, problematic behaviours such as suicidality or cutting might also be socially positively reinforced with warmth and attention, in addition to the relief (negative reinforcement) experienced by loneliness being replaced with being cared for (both of these seem relevant in the example of Sophie and Paul). Thus, it is essential to identify what actually *changes* immediately following the primary target behaviour and explore this as a possible reinforcer.

Of course, not all social consequences that reinforce dysfunctional behaviours are necessarily positive reinforcers. For example, increasing suicidality or even increasing depressive responses may be negatively reinforced by a family member becoming less invalidating, less demanding, or less aversive (Biglan et al., 1985). Similarly, family members may simply not notice or fail to reinforce self-management or skillful behaviours, or may even actively punish them. For example:

Rita worked hard in DBT skills training to learn mindfulness, emotion regulation, distress tolerance, and interpersonal effectiveness skills. As time went on, she became somewhat less blameful of herself and less accepting of the blame that her partner, Ralph, placed on her. She skillfully asked Ralph to try to state his complaints about her in a less judgmental, more constructive way. Ralph became enraged and hit Rita with the back of his hand, giving her a bruise and a laceration on her cheek. Clearly, this kind of response to enhanced skills would make Rita's (or anyone's) attempts at self-management more difficult.

Thus, in addition to assessing for problematic (invalidating, aversive) antecedents, it is important to assess for all four possible problematic family consequences: 1) positively reinforcing dysfunctional behaviours; 2) negatively reinforcing dysfunctional behaviours; 3) failing to reinforce self-management or skillful behaviours; and 4) punishing skillful behaviours. Once identified, the therapist can target these dysfunctional and problematic consequences for change.

It is also important to try to find examples of family consequences that have been helpful, or might be helpful, if provided in a more predictable, sustained, or uncontaminated way. These examples provide both an opportunity to validate and appreciate family members and examples of behaviours they already have in their repertoires upon which even more effective responses can be built.

For example, a family member might on occasion (or even regularly) notice small improvements in self-management in their loved one and respond warmly (e.g., "I can see that you really struggled with being angry a little while ago, and it's great that you were able to let it go; now it will be easier to just enjoy our time together tonight"). No assessment would be complete without identifying reinforcers for client self-managing, crisis reducing, or otherwise skillful behaviours, thereby enabling the therapist later to use these examples in supporting family members to replace their problematic consequences with responses like these.

INTERVENTION TARGETS AND STRATEGIES

The first target in DBT with couples and families is to facilitate individuals getting their own seriously dysfunctional behaviours under control. Safety (for everyone involved) is the paramount goal, and before other targets are considered, the family environment must be immediately safe, or made safe (i.e., no imminent harm—neither self-harm nor aggression against another). After establishing safety, the next steps in family interventions augment individual treatment, and include more thorough orientating and committing family members to treatment, and psychoeducation regarding emotion dysregulation and the biosocial or transactional (non-blaming) model. Psychoeducation can be offered "as needed" (i.e., when a topic is relevant to the family) or in a more curricular fashion (i.e., as part of a structured group programme).

Regardless, as previously discussed, after ensuring there is no ongoing physical or sexual aggression, in Stage 1, the therapist first targets stopping any family reinforcement of patient life-threatening dysfunctional behaviours, then focuses on reducing judgments and invalidation directed toward the identified patient (and reducing her or his judgments and invalidation of others in the family), and finally, targets enhancing validation in support of the identified patient's skillful self-management. First, however, it is important to consider issues and processes that do not occur in individual DBT, and instead that are unique to working with families.

Important DBT Therapist Strategies with Families

Family work with dysregulated people can be difficult, and even chaotic, and progress can be slow. This section describes several strategies that DBT therapists can utilize with families in order to maximize therapy effectiveness.

Helping family members and clients not look bad. Therapists have a lot of training in active and empathic listening and validation, and do not live in the same household as their clients and clients' family members. These, and other factors, make it much easier for therapists to be less reactive, less critical, and less invalidating, and warmer and more validating than many family members can. However, if the therapist makes these responses look easy, or is the primary provider of validating responses, it can make parents or partners look very unskillful at best, and ignorant and incompetent at worst. Thus, it is important *not* to validate the patient (or family members) in big ways or to validate too quickly. Rather, it is important to help family members validate each other through coaching and practice. In the family context, all family members, and their relationships, are the clients.

Liking the client and family members. Although this may seem obvious, sometimes therapists hear only one perspective on a chain or about an event, and it can be difficult to remember that at least one other perspective (that of the other family member) is missing. Moreover, sometimes family members (as well as patients) become reactive, angry, invalidating, demanding, and difficult to work with. Even in these situations, it is essential to remember that all behaviour has a cause, even if the chain(s) that created the problem behaviour are not known or understood. Of course, this does not excuse or condone problematic behaviour, but rather it helps with finding a non-judgmental stance, and to bring curiosity and acceptance to these situations, allowing the therapist to maintain collaboration with everyone in the room.

Blocking dysfunction and redirecting toward skillful alternatives. Blocking dysfunctional behaviour early, and often, in family sessions is essential: the family already does these things at home and does not need to practise dysfunction in the session; no one needs to be exposed to invalidation more than already occurs in daily life. Although there may be merit in seeing a dysfunctional pattern play out *once*, letting it continue simply does damage to family relationships and wastes precious family therapy time. Playfulness, for example, can make it easier to block. It is important to block dysfunctional behaviours as soon as they emerge. A simple "stop" might suffice, but collaborating on the signal to stop can be helpful, as can helping family members learn skills to inhibit their ineffective behaviours.

DBT communication strategies. The dialectic of reciprocal (warm, genuine) and irreverent (unorthodox, playful, even humorous) in DBT is most important when working with families. Family members need to know that the therapist understands and takes them seriously, and also, as mentioned, they need to feel liked and appreciated. Playful irreverence, the use of self-deprecating (but not self-invalidating or judgmental) examples can be helpful, as can a simple, matter-of-fact tone when problems emerge.

Revolving door strategy. On occasion, even the most skillful therapist cannot successfully block and redirect certain family members or patients. When this happens, the therapist may send one or more family members out into the waiting room for a while. During this time, the therapist can assess to understand the problem behaviour, coach and rehearse needed skills with the remaining family member, and then bring the other(s) back to give the conversation/transaction another chance to succeed. For example, with a suicidal teen in the waiting area, it may be possible both to validate the parent more, without the teen feeling increased shame and burden, and/or push the parent harder without embarrassing him or her in front of the child.

Establishing Safety

In order for family therapy to be effective, the treatment context itself must promote safety and well-being, and the DBT family therapist must quickly recognize, block, and redirect (with skills) emerging crisis behaviours. Thus, prior to addressing any other target, the therapist must assess that no one is currently in the middle of a life-threatening crisis (high risk for imminent suicidal behaviour, self-harm, or aggressive/violent behaviour). This assessment should be done quickly at the beginning of every family session (it should be an item on the diary card, if at all relevant), and near the end of any session in which de-escalation of one or more family members is not achieved. If someone is at high risk, immediate intervention is warranted. However, the role of the DBT family therapist can be quite complex in Stage 1 when dealing with such a crisis. For example, while the explicit target is to help deliver changes in the family to augment individual treatment, the identified patient also has individual DBT therapy, either with this same therapist (in overlapping roles), or with another therapist. It is important to be clear how to proceed in either of these circumstances when life-threatening crises emerge.

Family DBT Therapist is also the Individual DBT Therapist. When one therapist provides both treatment modalities, he or she has the advantage of knowing a lot about the identified patient's behavioural patterns and her or his emerging skills. Also, if the family therapist has good training as an individual DBT therapist, she or he will be familiar with DBT crisis strategies (Linehan, 1993), and be able to intervene seamlessly in the crisis. In this situation, the therapist can coach the client to use effective skills whenever either of them notices the client starting to become dysregulated and moving toward self-harm or aggressive behaviours. The disadvantage, of course, is that the individual attention could, in some situations, reinforce escalation and crisis behaviours, and possibly interfere with the therapist balancing relationships with all family members. Regardless, imminent life-threatening crises must be addressed right away in a manner consistent with the client's treatment plan for crisis situations.

Client has a Different Individual DBT Therapist. The identified patient instead may have a different individual DBT therapist. The advantage of this arrangement is that the family DBT therapist can simply refer the client back to the individual therapist for crisis intervention and stabilization. However, one disadvantage is that the family DBT therapist may not identify the crisis "chain" early on and may be less able to avert a crisis. Another possible disadvantage, especially if the therapist does not have a lot of training and experience in individual DBT, is that she or he may not have the repertoire to intervene in the crisis effectively if it emerges in the family session. Good communication between the individual DBT therapist and the family DBT therapist can mitigate these potential problems, as would good crisis intervention training for everyone on the team. In all situations in Stage 1, the family DBT therapist must be familiar with the crisis treatment plan and be able to implement it. Ideally, the DBT family therapist is on the same team as the individual therapist (if not the same person), in order to maximize efficiency and communication.

Of course, someone in the family other than the identified patient could become high risk for self-harm or aggressive/violent behaviour. If this occurs, the therapist would of course employ DBT crisis strategies and do whatever might be necessary to ensure her or his safety if still at risk toward the end of the session (e.g., facilitate the person utilizing crisis strategies, facilitate the person going to a psychiatric emergency service or hospital). In cases of high risk for family violence, a safety plan should also be developed right away and follow-up arranged.

Orientating and Committing to Treatment

DBT with couples and families requires a clear orientation to the nature of the treatment and any available alternatives. Family members must be informed how the treatment is conducted and evaluated, how their presenting problems and concerns will be organized in a treatment target hierarchy, the assessment procedures that will be conducted, how long treatment will last (at least initially), and what factors might result in a change in the treatment "contract." Although evaluating the "pros and cons" of DBT family interventions (versus other available treatments, or no treatment) is an important step, with briefer family interventions this must be done quickly and efficiently, typically requiring only a small part of the first session. In fact, even prior to committing explicitly to family DBT, family members may complete pre-treatment assessments and, if appropriate, begin to complete daily self-monitoring charts or diary cards.

Typically, the identified patient will have explained the rationale for family DBT (i.e., to augment individual treatment) to her or his family members, and the initial meeting should begin by ensuring that this rationale is clear and acceptable to all present. In order to foster collaboration, the therapist should go to great lengths to explain, and to demonstrate by her or his comportment, that these will be "blame-free" sessions, and that the therapist will try to provide benefits to family members as well as to the patient (a good example of dialectics in action).

It is not uncommon for families of people with BPD to be blamed by others, including professionals, and often to blame themselves for the identified patient's dysfunctional behaviours. Many family members may be reluctant even to engage in family therapy because of prior invalidation and blame from professionals. Recognizing this and addressing

it quickly and forthrightly with families is important to establish an effective working relationship with the family. On the other hand, many family members blame the identified
patient, not only for her or his own dysfunction, but for the entirety of their family's distress as well. It is similarly important to block this tendency, should it emerge, and attempt
to allay fears that the treatment sessions might degenerate into "blame" sessions.

Family members also need to be orientated to treatment targets. Specifically, they need to
be informed that: 1) both individual DBT and family DBT have specific targets that are organized into an explicit hierarchy which requires more severe or out-of-control behaviours
be resolved (i.e., to become "in-control") before less-severe behaviours are addressed; 2) the
overarching goal of all applications of DBT is to help clients create and maintain a life worth
living according to their own core values; and 3) goals include helping the family become a
"validating social environment" which supports individual well-being and satisfying relationships for all its members. Consequently, treatment targets are arranged hierarchically
according to how severely they interfere with the client or family's quality of life. The main
targets for family sessions (Stage 1) are helping to reduce the identified patient's behaviours that are out of control by reducing the behaviours of family members that contribute
to these problematic behaviours (or, increasing family behaviours that might support significant client behavioural improvements). In particular, behavioural safety and stability
across three domains are paramount: 1) life-threatening behaviours, including suicidal and
self-injurious behaviours, aggression and violence (as a perpetrator or victim), and child
abuse and neglect; 2) therapy-interfering behaviours (e.g., the individual client does not
come to session, is not collaborative, or does not adhere to agreed-upon between-session
practice targets); and 3) severe quality-of-life-interfering behaviours, such as maintaining
an ongoing affair, severe drug abuse or debilitating depression, criminal activity that might
lead to incarceration, or other out-of-control behaviours that severely limit quality of life
or family stability. Thus, improving the family environment, per se, is not a target for intervention in Stage 1 (but may be in Stage 2). However, it is important to point out that having a
more stable family member (i.e., the patient) would likely improve the quality of the overall
family environment, and that family interventions address problems relevant to the whole
family and often lead to higher levels of family satisfaction generally.

Having orientated family members to all of these issues, the therapist should then engage in a brief discussion of the pros and cons of committing to family DBT (cf. Linehan,
1993). This discussion is designed in part so that the therapist or another family member
may ease any concerns family members might have, thus facilitating commitment. Or,
hearing a new concern, the therapist may want to alter one or more targets or intervention
strategies, either to facilitate commitment to the treatment and/or to enhance the outcome.
A simple verbal agreement to treatment is all that is required to move on to the next step.

Orienting to the Biosocial/Transactional Model

Explaining the biosocial or transactional model (Fruzzetti et al., 2005; Fruzzetti, 2006,
2018; Fruzzetti & Worrall, 2010; Niedtfeld & Bohus, this volume) so that family members

understand both sides of the transaction (i.e., the vulnerable and often dysregulated individual in an invalidating social or family environment) is an important step in establishing collaboration. This dialectical position is to create the understanding that each person influences the other, in reciprocal fashion, and behaves within the limits of their biological functioning and their lifetime of learning. Specifically, the biosocial model can be explained with a few examples: 1) if a person is particularly sensitive, even ordinary interpersonal "bumps" can be very painful, and that person could start doing things to avoid interpersonal interactions or desperately try to get other people to be more gentle, soothing, etc.; 2) even a resilient person will experience a lot of pain if repeatedly rejected, criticized, devalued, misunderstood, or blamed; 3) a sensitive person who is regularly criticized, blamed, etc., might feel excruciating pain; and 4) a resilient person who experiences enough pain will become increasingly sensitive. BPD involves a great deal of emotional sensitivity, whether the person was born that way (biologically based from the beginning) or learned to be that way over time (learned, but now biologically vulnerable). Thus, both individuals and family members may be doing the best they can, but still be hurting each other. Ameliorating the pain of the identified patient *and* of other family members is the goal of family interventions.

As noted, it is important to maintain that blame and other judgments are not a part of the transactional/biosocial model and, moreover, are corrosive to the individuals involved and their relationships. Discussing these issues also presents an opportunity to suggest that the first step toward breaking the cycle of blame, shame, anger, and dysfunction is letting go of judgments and blame, and instead looking for opportunities to use the transactions in the family for improvements. The therapist may be able to engender a little bit of realistic hope for both the identified patient and for overall family well-being this way.

Teaching Family Skills

Depending on the specific chain, a variety of psychoeducation and skills may be needed, both in the session and out (see Fruzzetti, Gunderson, & Hoffman, 2014, for details about family psychoeducation and skill groups). Table 19.1 summarizes relevant DBT family and relationship skills shown to be very helpful in stabilizing families, reducing distress, and increasing family member well-being. Multiple studies have demonstrated reduced caregiver burden, depression, and grief, and increased mastery and sense of empowerment among family members following DBT family skills training in one format or another (e.g., Ekdahl et al., 2014; Flynn et al., 2017; Hoffman et al., 2005, 2007; Rajalin, Wickholm-Pethrus, Hursti, & Jokinen, 2009). A recent study also found that teens of parents who received DBT family skills training reported greater improvements in validating responses and parent availability, and more reductions in invalidating responses, than did teens whose parents did not receive DBT family skills training, resulting in greater improvements in emotion regulation (Payne & Fruzzetti, 2018). Further details about these skills may be found in Fruzzetti (2006, 2018), Fruzzetti and Payne (2015), or Rathus and Miller (2014).

DBT family skills may be taught separately in a DBT family skills group that is completed prior to DBT family therapy, or concurrently. Or, DBT family skills may be taught

Table 19.1 Family and relationship skills

Emotion Self-Management	Utilizes distress tolerance, mindfulness, and emotion regulation skills to modulate negative emotional arousal, thereby allowing effective engagement in family interaction.
Relationship Reactivation	Spend more non-negative time together (a version of exposure, to reduce avoidance of each other when one has become an "aversive stimulus"), and engage in enjoyable activities together with awareness and connection.
Mindfulness	Particular attention is paid to learning to identify and describe wise-mind goals and desires, awareness of primary emotions.
Accurate Expression	Descriptive, accurate expression of primary emotions, wise-mind goals, and desires.
Relationship Mindfulness	Non-judgmental awareness of, and open-minded attention to, the other person, while maintaining awareness of wise-mind relationship goals, including ongoing awareness of love for and commitment to the other person.
Validation	Accurate expression of understanding, acceptance, and the legitimacy of the other person's experience and behaviour.
Radical Acceptance	Letting go of ineffective attempts to change the other person, including grieving the loss of desired changes, and subsequent awareness of what was missed due to the intensive or singular focus on trying to get the other person to change.
Dialectical Problem Solving	Utilizing all of the listed skills, collaborative engagement in solving problems of one or both people in the relationship, or problems that create destructive conflict, pain, and distance, with awareness of the legitimacy of both perspectives.

more organically, right on the double chain, as the need for specific skills becomes apparent. Either way, it is essential to target replacement of problematic or dysfunctional "links" on the chain with more skillful alternatives, and not to assume that family members already have these skills in their repertoires. Although these skills do not necessarily need to be taught in any particular order, some skills do build on other skills. For example, validation is not possible without first mastering emotion self-management (to modulate attention and emotion) and good relationship mindfulness (to be able to pay attention, in a genuine way, to the other person, with the goal of understanding him or her). Thus, it is important to observe family members directly, and not necessarily begin by teaching complex skills like validation.

Stabilizing Current Family Crises

There are many forms of non-life-threatening family crises that have the potential to create or exacerbate individual distress and dysfunction, and/or to interfere with family interventions. Problems such as eviction from housing, loss of a job, legal problems that could lead to imprisonment, extramarital affairs, etc., can become the focus of family interventions, despite these not being the original rationale for family interventions.

With family interventions in Stage 1 it is usually important not to try to solve these problems in their entirety per se, but rather to help stabilize the situation sufficiently so that the main targets of this treatment modality can again be the focus of attention (if not already accomplished). This typically might involve structured problem solving with a lot of coaching in emotional self-management for many or all family members. However, the number of opportunities or sessions available for family intervention can be limited, so it is important to remember that managing external crises not related to client Stage 1 behaviours is not the focus of this mode, at least until patient safety and stability are achieved. Rather, when crises arise, the goal is to help the family to stabilize quickly and then immediately move back to the original agenda: augmenting individual treatment by reducing judgments and invalidation, altering family contingencies to support individual skills and progress, eliminating reinforcement of dysfunctional behaviours, and increasing accurate expression and validation. Having noted this hierarchy, of course it is possible that family crises are directly related to patient instability, and must be addressed more fully in order to help patients become safe and stable.

Case Example

Cheryl was in individual DBT and she and her husband, Bill, agreed to spend several sessions with a DBT couple therapist to help Bill understand Cheryl's treatment and find ways to facilitate her progress. Careful chain analyses of Cheryl's recent suicide attempts led to the hypothesis that Bill's criticism, contempt, and devaluing Cheryl were important antecedent links. Moreover, Bill felt very guilty and became very nurturing in the hours and days following Cheryl's suicide attempts, possibly negatively reinforcing (and maybe even also positively reinforcing) her suicidality and suicide attempts. Modifying these behaviours were the targets for family intervention.

However, in the second session, Bill reported that he was in danger of losing his job and both Cheryl and Bill were understandably very distressed about the impact this would have. Both were on edge, highly emotionally aroused, and focused on all of the potentially negative things that might occur in the coming months. The DBT couple therapist helped them sort out the facts of the situation from their fears about what might happen, helped them problem solve how to get more information, and provided Bill with some resources for job hunting and unemployment assistance. Then she reoriented the couple back to their targets, helped them use mindfulness skills (one of the targets for the session anyway) to observe their fearful thoughts and redirect their attention to the goals for the present session, and proceeded to spend the rest of the session working on how they could modify their arguments to be less toxic for their relationship and less likely to elicit dangerous levels of negative emotional arousal in Cheryl. After some progress on these targets, it became realistic to consider how each of them could actually support each other in this employment crisis, rather than have it be an additional stressor leading to further criticisms, blame, and distance.

Eliminating Reinforcers for Dysfunctional Behaviour

Moving reinforcers for dysfunction (e.g., in the example with Bill, who was more intensely involved, solicitous, loving, and soothing toward his partner Cheryl when she was suicidal or following her suicide attempts) may be crucial in getting problem behaviours under control. However, it is important not to simply remove those behaviours from the family member's repertoire. Rather, the target is for him or her to be soothing and solicitous contingently when the identified patient is doing well or asking for closeness or support in non-dysfunctional ways (or have loving and caring behaviour not be contingent at all, but provided on regular basis—a "fixed schedule"). It is also important to target the family member increasing positive responses overall, with validation, warmth, and attention no longer contingent on dysfunctional behaviours of the identified patient. Notice that love and care are *moved*, not *re*moved. That is, we would never ask Bill to be less loving, caring, and soothing, but we might ask him to do so either non-contingently (i.e., on a regular or fixed schedule) or contingent on Cheryl expressing that she wants companionship or to be close. This way, she does not need to escalate into dysfunction to get what she wants, and is not in danger of an extinction burst around suicidal behaviours.

Orient Family Members to How Behaviours Might Function. The process of doing a thorough chain analysis sets the stage for the therapist to explain the concept of *function* to family members unfamiliar with this concept. Once reinforcers for problem behaviours (or the absence of reinforcers for skillful behaviours) have been identified, the therapist can use these specific examples to explicate how each family member influences the other. In addition, it can be useful to provide some common examples of transactions both to highlight the concept of the function of behaviours as well as to show how understandable problematic behaviours are on both sides of the transaction. This also may help reduce blame and judgment. For example, demonstrating how a child's tantrum in the candy aisle of a grocery store may be positively reinforced by giving the child candy, and how, in return, when the child ceases the tantrum, that may negatively reinforce (remove the aversive stimulus) the parent for giving in, nicely illustrates family transactions. These kinds of examples are often familiar to families and validate how difficult it is to change dysfunctional patterns of interaction.

Anticipate Extinction Bursts. Family members need to understand, anticipate, and have a plan for getting through an extinction burst if the target is stopping something that seems to have reinforced dysfunction in the past (but as previously mentioned, not around suicidal behaviours). Again, continuing with the tantrum example (or other examples, such as the likelihood that urges for nicotine or other drugs increase for a while after a person quits using, and eventually decrease), family members must be orientated to how problems might become more intense for a while until stability is restored, or a new equilibrium is achieved.

Direct questions to the identified patient can help elucidate what to expect and, in turn, facilitate the development of a detailed management plan for everyone involved. For example, Rose imagined that if her parents stopped soothing her after she cut herself that she might become more suicidal or have even stronger urges to cut herself again. Having agreed that, indeed, their soothing was likely reinforcing Rose's dysfunctional behaviour, the therapist was able to have them role-play the scenario to see what might happen. Rose said that she likely would become afraid that her parents don't love her any more, would feel increasingly angry, and probably would say very nasty things to them, after which they would withdraw (and/or criticize her). Rose needed a lot of coaching and practice in distress tolerance. The parents' new target behaviour involved saying to Rose, "I do love you, but you need to go get yourself calmed down, back in control. After you do, we can take a walk together, but we won't talk about your cuts or being suicidal. Can I help you with any skills?" Both of Rose's parents needed a lot of coaching to be able to maintain this position. The therapist pointed out that Rose really wanted them to love her and pay attention to her, and that they had committed to doing this any time *except* when she was verbalizing suicidality or following self-harm. The therapist and both parents agreed that it would be most effective, and likely the easiest path, for Rose to give up discussing her suicidality and self-harm urges and behaviours with them entirely, and instead save those discussions for her DBT therapist. However, they committed to being responsive to Rose's requests for attention and help. In fact, this plan alleviated Rose's father's fears: he realized that he had gotten into a pattern of distancing himself from Rose, at least in part out of fear of her dysfunctional behaviours, as well as his self-blame that he wasn't able to help her more. Not surprisingly, his distance seemed often to be a trigger or antecedent to Rose's dysfunctional behaviours, and it was useful to highlight this reciprocal pattern, or transaction. By focusing his loving concern on Rose when she was less distressed (or simply asked effectively), they both got more of what they wanted from each other, which made it easier for both of them to implement the plan after two sessions of practice and troubleshooting. It also took some of the burden off Rose's mother. Initially, Rose had reported high daily thoughts about suicide and urges to self-harm for more than a year, and had cut herself an average of six times per month over this period. Within a month of implementing this plan, Rose's thoughts about and urges to engage in self-harm or suicidal behaviour fell to zero, and she ceased cutting herself completely. Of course, this could only be possible if getting her parents' love and attention were the primary reinforcers of her suicidality and self-harm, and it may often be the case that there are other, additional reinforcers.

Balance Change Targets, and Perceived Benefits, Across Family Members. If one or more family members perceive that changes they make will come at great cost to them, this may interfere with a successful outcome, despite possible benefits to another family member (including the identified patient). For example, asking (or allowing) a spouse or partner to take a time out to curtail aversive conflict escalation might be experienced as both invalidating of her/his desire for closeness or resolution (reassurance, under-standing, etc.) and as threatening to the relationship (e.g., "I want more from you, but you are leaving. I don't trust that you'll come back."). This may be true even if the time out might be essential to reduce the aversive and destructive transaction, facilitate regulating emotions, and thereby reduce or eliminate judgmental verbal statements or even more aggressive behaviours. In the case of time outs, it is important for the person leaving not to blame the other, and instead state explicitly why he or she is leaving briefly (e.g., "I am taking time out to keep *myself* from saying something nasty" or "to regulate myself"), and then to state clearly what he or she is going to do and explicitly when he or she will return, in order to alleviate abandonment or other fears (e.g., "So, I'm going to go for a walk to the park. I'll be back in about half an hour.").

Another problem can occur if one family member thinks that she or he is bearing more than her or his share of the burden of change, which can lead to resentment and reduce the likelihood of attaining improvements. If one person perceives that he or she is burdened unfairly with the responsibility for change and improvement, the therapist must address and validate this concern without validating its veracity per se. That is, the family member can make an appraisal that something is unfair, but fairness or unfair-ness should not be reified; others may make very different appraisals. For example, the therapist might say, "You are right, I am asking you to do a lot here, and it makes sense how you might think it's unfair." Because perceptions of unfairness can decrease mo-tivation, the therapist and family should then address the issue in a dialectical manner, either changing the balance of burden or the appraisals of unfairness attached to the present balance.

The therapist can avoid many pitfalls by tasking all family members with skill prac-tices, and assign to each one practices relevant to his or her deficits. It may be especially useful for the therapist (often in consultation with the treatment team) to find dialec-tical solutions, as well as quid pro quo solutions, to problematic interactions.

Enhancing Commitment. Of course, translating dialectical targets into good out-comes requires successful implementation. Most behaviour changes are difficult and are likely to lapse if not reinforced quickly. Therefore, the DBT family therapist must help the family members rehearse new solutions many times, walk through the steps of the new solution carefully, and look for emotional reactions, judgments, negative appraisals, etc., that might interfere with skill implementation outside the session. Hammering out this detailed commitment to the solution (Fruzzetti & Payne, 2015; Linehan, 1993) al-lows everyone to anticipate problems that may occur when starting new behaviours and work them out ahead of time.

Reducing Judgments and Invalidating Interactions

There is a large literature linking critical, negative, or invalidating family behaviours to individual psychopathology, and conversely, a significant literature demonstrating that living with someone with serious individual psychopathology can be stressful and burdensome (cf. Fruzzetti & Worrall, 2010; Hoskins, 2014; Shenk & Fruzzetti, 2014; Whisman & Uebelacker, 2009). Clearly, judgmental, critical, and invalidating family behaviours can increase individual distress and vulnerability, increase risk for further emotional escalation and dysregulation, and be triggers for self-harm and other crisis behaviours. They are particularly toxic when they lead to rapid negative escalation of emotion and conflict, which, of course, is the hallmark of both BPD (in individuals) and distressed relationships. When chain analyses do not indicate *specific* reinforcers for dysfunctional (Stage 1) individual behaviours, reducing invalidating family behaviours overall is the main target.

Because this is a whole *class* of behaviours, careful chain analysis typically is not needed. Simply eliciting examples from family members from their diary cards affords the opportunity to teach the needed steps to rework these interactions: 1) identify escalating emotions and judgments about others; 2) tolerate whatever distress the other person's behaviour has triggered; 3) manage negative emotional arousal; 4) let go of judgments and restate the situation descriptively to oneself; 5) use relationship mindfulness to remember, and experience, love and commitment for the other person; and then 6) either not respond at all or respond non-judgmentally and descriptively (or even in a validating manner).

The first step toward a successful and skillful solution is generally to teach family members both individual mindfulness skills (Linehan, 2015) and relationship mindfulness skills (Fruzzetti, 2006, 2018) by using real examples from family interactions. Most family members readily agree that it is easier to avoid invalidating responses *when aware* that their goal is to be effective in the relationship (as opposed to being "right" or wanting retribution). But they also realize that, when emotions escalate and they feel fear, shame, disappointment, anger, or related strong emotions, it is difficult to slow down and respond effectively. By practising "observing" skills, clients can interrupt their escalating emotional arousal before it gets very high. Then, "describing" skills allow clients to self-validate their emotions and slow down a bit, making it easier not to "buy into" judgmental attributions about their family member. If family interactions have been soured for years, this can be very difficult and take a lot of commitment and practice. The most important transactional goal of this first step is simply to slow down long over-learned negative, critical, and invalidating responses, to drive a kind of wedge between the person's private initial reactions (emotion, judgmental thought) toward their family member and their verbal and non-verbal responses, including not only words but also facial expressions, changes in breathing patterns, and other public displays.

Recognizing one's own rising emotional arousal and associated judgments is just the first step, of course. Then the person must be well practised in inhibiting invalidating responses by practising tolerating having judgmental thoughts and strong emotional reactions without immediately acting on them. Practising remembering that the other person is someone he or she loves can lead to a believable synthesis. For example, "I love my teen AND he is driving me crazy at the moment" captures both sides. In addition, distress tolerance skills (Linehan, 2015) can be employed to help family members distract away from the stimulus (judgmental thought or negative emotional escalation in reaction to what the other person just did or said) so as to keep arousal in check, or to let go of ineffective responses and become willing to work on improving the situation, typically by letting go of judgments and recalling larger goals and genuine relationship connections. Non-judgmental self-validation can be helpful (e.g., "I really don't like this" or "I prefer that he/she would do this differently!").

The next step is to return to describe the context or situation, the trigger (the other person's behaviour), and the individual's reaction mindfully. Often, this is enough to provide balance to the situation and truncate escalation. Then the person can either simply not respond to the triggering behaviour, or can respond to it more effectively.

For example, one couple frequently got into rapidly escalating fights in which both said very critical and judgmental things to the other that they later regretted. These fights were often on the chain of behaviours that led both of them to use drugs, both of them to become physically aggressive, or led one partner to a suicidal crisis. No specific statements or reactions were identified as regular triggers. Rather, small misunderstandings or negatively perceived statements became incendiary, eliciting a downpour of nasty responses from each. They both described their reaction time as virtually instantaneous. Their DBT family therapist helped them to practise the steps illustrated here. They began by trying to "observe" their own escalating arousal, rather than "participating" in it early on. It turned out that, as they became more aware of their own reactions, in fact, the typical pattern was longer and more slowly escalating than they had thought—but they had previously ignored the lower levels of arousal because of fear or hopelessness that it would escalate, because their history confirmed this fear, and they had no skills to do it differently. However, by noticing dislikes and annoyances earlier on, they were smaller and easier to tolerate, and they found that they had more choices (ways of accepting the situation or trying to change the situation). By interrupting their own emotional reactions, it was easier to describe the situations or the other's behaviour, and to remember their commitment to the relationship, which in turn made it easier either to let go of the annoyance or try to get the other person to do something differently via skillful means. Seeing the transaction, rather than blaming each other, helped them slow down. They were also able to employ some humour in the task, which also alleviated tension and made the task more successful (e.g., in a sing-song voice one would say "now I am noticing that you just said that in a different tone of voice, one that I thought just for a moment might have been a little critical—but before I pound my chest and say something nasty, I thought I'd just ask you for a little clarification," after which both would laugh and any needed repair could be made).

Reducing critical, blaming, and other invalidating behaviours can be very difficult, both because so much negative emotion is involved and because these destructive responses have been conditioned over time. Regardless, every invalidating response not spoken, or that is transformed into something more effective, can make an important difference in that moment.

Increasing Validation as Antecedents and Consequences of Skillful Self-Management

Often, therapists find that family members reward skillful behaviours of the identified patient, do not reinforce dysfunction, are not judgmental, and are not high in destructive conflict. However, even in these families, there may be deficits in warmth and validation, creating a kind of "dead" or "dormant" family environment that is low on closeness and high on disengagement (Fruzzetti, 1996). Or, after interventions are successful, families may reduce their invalidating responses and have few remaining positive interactions. For these families, the target would be to *reactivate their relationship* (doing enjoyable things in parallel, or together, which is another family or relationship skill—see Table 19.1). In this case, the skill is to create or enhance the family environment or relationship to make it both more enjoyable and more validating in general, and to reinforce real engagement, time together, and increasingly skillful behaviour, specifically.

Increasing Validation as a Stimulus Control Strategy. Certain kinds of cues can be conditioned to elicit or "pull for" more functional behaviour, just as certain other cues have been conditioned to elicit dysfunctional responses. Promoting validation as a way to pull for skillful behaviour from the identified patient is one way to employ validation as a stimulus control strategy. Simply put, when family members validate each other's (valid and effective) behaviour, in particular, their emotions and wants, it helps to maintain stability of the interactions and of each individual's own emotions, and signals closeness, acceptance, and understanding. This helps reduce painful negative emotional arousal and allows a more regulated repertoire to be available to the client.

Thus, the targets here are for family members to: 1) increase the overall rate of validating behaviours; and/or 2) specifically try to validate the identified patient's emotions and value as a human being and family member. Teaching validation explicitly (Fruzzetti, 2006, 2018) can be a useful way of highlighting both targets for validating the identified patient in support of her or his individual treatment targets, and finding appropriate ways to validate. If the identified patient is working on being less judgmental, devaluing, and blaming of herself, family members can validate her primary emotions and validate her behaviour descriptively, even if she can't at that moment. For example, Jennifer had planned to go out with a friend but the friend cancelled at the last minute. Jennifer seemed quite upset and it was her usual pattern to blame herself for relationship problems and become quite judgmental of herself (e.g., "I must have done something to upset her. I'm such an idiot. She probably hates me now. I've managed to alienate somebody else."), which would contribute to heightened emotional arousal (shame and fear). Prior to getting training in validation, her mother would have told her, "Don't worry about it, it's no big deal. You'll do something with her next week." Instead, with validation training, she simply said, "I know you wanted to spend some time with her tonight. I'm guessing you are disappointed", thus validating both Jennifer's desires and her primary emotion. When her mother validated disappointment (rather than being invalidating), it helped Jennifer focus on this emotion (disappointment), instead of her secondary emotion (shame), which helped her recognize her disappointment as valid. This self-validation interrupted her escalation and she was able to problem-solve, and then engage in alternate, albeit second choice, enjoyable and safe activities.

Notice and Reinforce Skillful Behaviour. It is also important to coach families to communicate about their targets so that they can reinforce each other. Often, in clients with severe problems, improvements go unnoticed and are therefore not reinforced. This may be because family members have become conditioned to be watchful for problematic behaviours or signs of impending crisis, because family members are burned out, or because the initial exhibitions of new skills do not much resemble what they will look like after substantial practice. Regardless, the chances of reinforcing new behaviours can be enhanced by simply being aware of what the identified patient is trying to accomplish. The therapist can help the patient practise communicating her or his targets and progress, and family members can practise supporting and reinforcing both this communication and any incremental progress.

However, family members sometimes notice new behaviours, but can be judgmental of them, and therefore fail to reinforce them. For example, they might think (judgmentally) that their family member "should be able to do it better" or "isn't trying hard enough." Even though they may not express these judgments to the person out loud, at the very least they are not reinforcing progress. When identified, it is important to go back to the steps described here to deal with judgments and invalidating responses, even if they are only thoughts (and not overtly communicated). It can be helpful to remind family members just how powerful validation can be in shaping new behaviours, and simple role-playing can be used to illustrate this point.

Finally, the therapist will have identified positive behaviours and responses during the assessment. Using family members' own previous successes and existing strengths as examples not only validates those behaviours, but also makes it easier for family members to understand what they can do to be helpful. They don't need to become "saints," but rather can use their genuine love and concern for their loved one to help her or him toward greater stability, self-control, and a higher quality of life. And being skillful will have reciprocal benefits for them, as well.

CONCLUSION

Because humans live in a transactional family and/or social environment, it may be helpful to utilize both sides of the transaction in treatment, and not rely only on helping the client navigate an invalidating environment more successfully, or give all the responsibility for increasing validation to the client. DBT family interventions include: 1) helping family members change antecedents of their loved one's behaviour that support dysfunction, including reducing invalidation that results in a lot of negative emotional escalation; 2) providing brief family psychoeducation about emotions, emotion dysregulation, and the transactional model; 3) directly teaching family members a wide range of skills; 4) helping them weave these skills into their daily lives and transactions with their loved ones; 5) helping family members reduce or eliminate those behaviours that reinforce suicidality and other dysfunctional responses; 6) reducing invalidating responses in general; and 6) increasing validating responses. These interventions can be effective and beneficial for both patients and their families.

KEY POINTS FOR CLINICIANS

- DBT with parents or families utilizes the same theory and overlapping strategies as DBT with individuals; some targets may vary, there are additional skills and strategies, and we use "double chains" to assess and understand the ways family members affect each other.

- Intervening with parents, partners, or other family members is essential when they are "on the chain" toward self-harm or suicidal behaviour—that is, when what they do is either a precipitating event or reinforcer for these life-threatening behaviours. The targets then include reducing aversive and invalidating responses overall, and eliminating positive and negative reinforcement of suicidal and self-harming behaviours.

- Parent and family skills include emotion self-management, relationship mindfulness, accurate expression, validation, and radical acceptance.

- The key transactional focus is to decrease the cycle of inaccurate expression and invalidating responses, and instead build up accurate expression and validating responses.

- Family interventions may occur in family therapy, or in multi-family groups, with or without the patient.

- Family sessions can sometimes be chaotic, so there are specific strategies employed with families to manage them and keep them productive.

- It is essential to empower parents and other family members with skills and to help them be effective within their roles.

REFERENCES

Biglan, A., Hops, H., Sherman, L., Friedman, L. S., Arthur, J., & Osteen, V. (1985). Problem-solving interactions of depressed women and their husbands. *Behavior Therapy*, 16, 431–451.

Ekdahl, S., Idvall, E., & Perseius, K. I. (2014). Family skills training in DBT: The experience of the significant others. *Archives of Psychiatric Nursing*, 28(4), 235–241.

Flynn, D., Kells, M., Joyce, M., Corcoran, P., Herley, S., Suarez, C., . . . Groeger, J. (2017). Family Connections versus optimised treatment-as-usual for family members of individuals with borderline personality disorder: Non-randomised controlled study. *Borderline Personality Disorder and Emotion Dysregulation*, 4. DOI: 10.1186/s40479-017-0069-1

Fruzzetti, A. E. (1996). Causes and consequences: Individual distress in the context of couple interactions. *Journal of Consulting and Clinical Psychology*, 64, 1192–1201.

Fruzzetti, A. E. (2006). *The high conflict couple: A dialectical behavior therapy guide to finding peace, intimacy, and validation*. Oakland, CA: New Harbinger.

Fruzzetti, A. E. (2018). *Families and borderline personality disorder: A dialectical behavior therapy guide to finding peace in your family*. Oakland, CA: New Harbinger.

Fruzzetti, A. E., Gunderson, J. G., & Hoffman, P. D. (2014). Psychoeducation. In J. M. Oldham, A. Skodal, & D. Bender (Eds.), *Textbook of personality disorders*, 2nd Edition (pp. 303–320). Washington, DC: American Psychiatric Publishing.

Fruzzetti, A. E., & Payne, L. G. (2015). Couple therapy and the treatment of borderline personality and related disorders. In A. Gurman, D. Snyder, & J. Lebow (Eds.), *Clinical handbook of couple therapy*, 5th Edition (pp. 606–634). New York: Guilford Press.

Fruzzetti, A. E., & Payne, L. G. (in press). Assessment of parents, couples, and families in Dialectical Behavior Therapy. *Cognitive and Behavioral Practice.*

Fruzzetti, A. E., Shenk, C., & Hoffman, P. D. (2005). Family interaction and the development of borderline personality disorder: A transactional model. *Development and Psychopathology*, *17*, 1007–1030.

Fruzzetti, A. E., & Worrall, J. M. (2010). Accurate expression and validation: A transactional model for understanding individual and relationship distress. In K. Sullivan & J. Davila (Eds.), *Support processes in intimate relationships* (pp. 121–150). New York: Oxford University Press.

Hoffman, P. D., Fruzzetti, A. E., & Buteau, E. (2007). Understanding and engaging families: An education, skills and support program for relatives impacted by Borderline Personality Disorder. *Journal of Mental Health*, *16*, 69–82.

Hoffman, P. D., Fruzzetti, A. E., Buteau, E., Penney, D., Neiditch, E., Penney, D., . . . Struening, E. (2005). Family Connections: Effectiveness of a program for relatives of persons with borderline personality disorder. *Family Process*, *44*, 217–225.

Hoffman, P. D., Fruzzetti, A. E., & Swenson, C. R. (1999). Dialectical Behavior Therapy—Family skills training. *Family Process*, *38*, 399–414.

Hoskins, D. H. (2014). Consequences of parenting on adolescent outcomes. *Societies*, *14*, 506–531. DOI:10.3390/soc4030506

Linehan, M. M. (1993). *Cognitive-behavioral treatment of borderline personality disorder.* New York: Guilford Press.

Linehan, M. M. (2015). *DBT skills training manual*, 2nd Edition. New York: Guilford Press.

Payne, L. & Fruzzetti, A. E. (8, Submitted for review). Effects of brief, intensive DBT parent skills training on suicidal adolescents: A randomized trial.

Rajalin, M., Wickholm-Pethrus, L., Hursti, T., & Jokinen, J. (2009). Dialectical behavior therapy-based skills training for family members of suicide attempters. *Archives of Suicide Research*, *13*(3), 257–263.

Rathus, J. H., & Miller, A. L. (2014). *DBT skills manual for adolescents.* New York: Guilford Press.

Shenk, C., & Fruzzetti, A. E. (2014). Parental validating and invalidating responses and adolescent psychological functioning: An observational study. *The Family Journal*, *22*, 43–48. DOI: 10.1177/1066480713490900

Whisman, M. A., & Uebelacker, L. A. (2009). Prospective associations between marital discord and depressive symptoms in middle-aged and older adults. *Psychology and Aging*, *24*, 184–189. DOI: 10.1037/a0014759

SECTION V

EVIDENCE FOR DBT

CHAPTER 20

DIALECTICAL BEHAVIOUR THERAPY FROM 1991–2015

What Do We Know About Clinical Efficacy and Research Quality?

ERIN M. MIGA, ANDRADA D. NEACSIU,
ANITA LUNGU, HEIDI L. HEARD,
AND LINDA A. DIMEFF

QUALITY ASSURANCE IN DIALECTICAL BEHAVIOUR THERAPY RANDOMIZED CONTROLLED TRIALS: A CRITICAL REVIEW

DIALECTICAL Behaviour Therapy (DBT) is an internationally recognized evidence-based treatment (EBT) for clients who meet criteria for multiple diagnoses including Borderline Personality Disorder (BPD; Kliem, Kröger, & Kosfelder, 2010; SAMHSA, 2006; Stoffers et al., 2012). Originally developed to address suicidal behaviour (Linehan, 1993a, b; Linehan, Armstrong, Suarez, Allmon, & Heard, 1991), DBT has been expanded and evaluated as a psychosocial treatment for a wide variety of dysfunctional behaviours (e.g., non-suicidal self-injury (NSSI), drug use) across multiple disorders. Its success with different psychological problems and attractiveness to clinicians has led to an exponential increase in DBT research conducted. A PsycInfo search shows an average of ten peer reviewed DBT publications per year from 1993 until 2000, 64 publications per year from 2001 to 2010, and 94 per year since 2011. Since the last major review of the DBT RCTs (Lynch, Trost, Salsman, & Linehan, 2007), there have been over 600 additional publications analysing the theory, effectiveness, and complexity of this treatment internationally, 24 of these publications include RCT data (e.g., Linehan et al., 2006; McMain et al., 2009; van den Bosch, Verheul, Schippers, & van den Brink,

2002). To date, 31 distinct RCTs have been conducted on DBT and DBT skills only, with a total of approximately 38 publications culminating from these RCTs. The rapid proliferation of research mirrors the clinical enthusiasm about this treatment: over 180 sites nationwide have providers trained in DBT (SAMHSA, 2012). Nevertheless, DBT trials have been criticized for lacking scientific rigour. For example, one meta-analysis found that trials testing treatments labelled as "third wave", such as DBT and Acceptance and Commitment Therapy (ACT), were less methodologically rigorous than CBT trials published in the same years and journals (Öst, 2008).

The goal of this review is to provide a review and scientific analysis of the DBT literature with an emphasis on the clinical and research quality of each trial in order to inform researchers and clinicians about the relative strengths and limitations of research trials that purport to be testing DBT vs. a comparison treatment. More specifically, it examines in detail for each RCT whether sufficient evidence supports that DBT was indeed the intervention delivered and what conclusions can be drawn given the research methodology employed. This level of analysis informs a critical discussion about which outcomes on DBT are the result of adherently conducted and rigorously tested research, and which outcomes are less conclusive due to the relative lack of research quality assurance. Finally, it provides preliminary recommendations for future clinical trials and highlights where future DBT research is needed.

BIRD'S-EYE VIEW OF DIALECTICAL BEHAVIOUR THERAPY

DBT was developed in the late 1980s, when Marsha Linehan's attempts to apply standard behavioural therapy to chronically suicidal, multi-diagnostic clients with severe behavioural dyscontrol failed (Linehan, 1993a, b). Through iterative attempts, Linehan found that achieving a dialectical balance and synthesis between a focus on change and a focus on acceptance was most effective at keeping clients in treatment and helping them reach their own treatment goals. DBT therefore extends CBT by including acceptance-based strategies such as validation, mindfulness, radical genuineness, and reciprocal communication. (See Linehan & Schmidt, 1995 for a thorough review.) Case conceptualization in DBT is based on the biosocial theory, which posits that clients who meet criteria for BPD have pervasive emotion dysregulation, which is the result of a transaction between environmental invalidation and a biological vulnerability to emotional reactivity (Linehan, 1993a). Within this framework, dysfunctional behaviours (e.g., suicide attempts, NSSI, substance use, self-injury, disordered eating) are seen as maladaptive emotion regulation strategies likely to have been reinforced by one's environment and/or the intrinsic relief of an aversive emotional state. The goal in DBT is to replace these dysfunctional (though sometimes quite effective) short-term coping strategies with skillful, functional behaviours that help clients progress toward their long-term goals and build a "life worth living". (For a thorough review of the biosocial conceptualization, see Crowell, Beauchaine, & Linehan, 2009; Grove & Crowell, and Niedtfeld & Bohus, this volume.)

Comprehensive DBT includes five treatment functions: 1) enhance clients' skillful behaviour; 2) increase clients' motivation to use effective skills; 3) help clients generalize skillful behaviour; 4) enhance therapists' capabilities and motivation to treat difficult clients; and 5) structure the clients' environment in a way that facilitates clinical progress. The structure of DBT follows the recommendations set forth by the 2009 National Institute for Health and Clinical Excellence (NICE) guidelines for BPD treatments. These guidelines suggest that BPD treatments should: 1) be structured; 2) be explicit and take an integrated approach used by both provider and treatment team; and 3) contain a built-in mechanism for therapist supervision and support. In line with these recommendations, the DBT functions are met through the four modes of treatment: weekly individual psychotherapy (including family sessions as needed), group skills training, between-session coaching contact (by telephone or milieu-based), and clinician consultation team. The recommended DBT model for adults with BPD and/or suicidal behaviour is 12 months of weekly individual therapy, skills training, and team with phone coaching as needed. The DBT skills class includes four modules (Mindfulness, Emotion Regulation, Interpersonal Effectiveness, and Distress Tolerance) that are covered in six months. Standard DBT recommends that patients go through these modules twice to enhance skills acquisition, strengthening, and generalization.

Whether all functions and modes of treatment are necessary, and whether the intensity, duration, and frequency the treatment manual recommends are optimal, remain empirical questions. More recently, research has begun to examine the efficacy and effectiveness of sub-components of the standard DBT model, such as skills training, for a variety of populations with a multitude of clinical presentations. Yet a systematic review and critique of the evidence base for the DBT skills training component alone is lacking. Therefore, in order to critically and thoroughly examine the DBT research literature, this chapter includes randomized controlled trials that test comprehensive DBT (defined here as individual DBT, phone coaching, group skills training, and therapist consultation team), DBT skills only (defined here as DBT skills training) as well as DBT components (defined here as comprehensive DBT without one or more components in a configuration distinct from DBT skills only).

QUALITY ASSURANCE IN PSYCHOTHERAPY RANDOMIZED CLINICAL TRIALS

Randomized controlled trials (RCTs) are considered the "gold standard" for psychotherapy research due to design characteristics that allow a systematic test of the efficiency and effectiveness of psychological interventions. More specifically, RCTs use a control condition for comparison and randomization to balance known and unknown prognostic factors in the assignment of treatment conditions. Nevertheless, designing and conducting clinical research trials involves many decisions in addition to the use of a control group and randomization procedures. As a consequence, studies following an RCT design can vary greatly in terms of quality of the research design and implementation, which in turn directly influences the strength of the conclusions that can be inferred from the results. For psychotherapy research, two key dimensions to be used in evaluating quality of a study are: 1) the quality of the research procedures employed; and 2) the extent of adherence to the treatment model. Evaluating the quality of research procedures helps to derive accurate conclusions on treatment effect, while the adherence to treatment certifies the precise treatment provided. One of the challenges of critically summarizing research findings is the insufficient reporting in research papers of precise information that allows quality assurance evaluation. This section details the pieces of information that enable quality assurance evaluation for both categories mentioned: quality of research procedures, and adherence to the treatment model.

Quality Assurance Through Research Procedures

Quality of research procedures can be systematically assessed with developed measures that include evaluations along several dimensions, such as definition and delivery of treatment, outcome measures and data analysis methods, determination of assessor reliability and use of blind assessment, characteristics of the comparison treatment, and clinician training and supervision. Unfortunately, many systematic reviews and meta-analyses fail to systematically account for study quality by not factoring in information on the dimensions above in their results/outcome presentation. One evaluation of 11 meta-analyses and 127 RCTs revealed that the overall trial quality was not systematically addressed and was weak when considering characteristics such as blind assessment and randomization procedures. This resulted in an overestimation of intervention impact among the low-quality studies (Juni, Altman, & Egger, 2001; Moher et al., 1998).

Quality Assurance Through Adherence to the Treatment Model

Quality assurance in the area of adherence to the treatment model helps address the question as to whether the client actually received the treatment under consideration. Adherence to the treatment model has two facets: clinician adherence to treatment and programme fidelity. Clinician treatment adherence is defined as the "degree to which a therapist uses *prescribed* procedures and avoids *proscribed* procedures" within treatment delivery (see Schoenwald et al., 2011, p. 33). Prescribed procedures are those that are required for adherent delivery of the treatment, while proscribed procedures include those explicitly prohibited or implicitly prohibited (i.e., omitted) in the manual. Programme fidelity in turn refers to a particular study "staying true to the original program design" (see O'Connor, Small, & Cooney, 2007, p. 1).

Clinician adherence to treatment has crucial implications for patient care, as high adherence has been linked to more successful patient outcomes in a number of treatments, including Multisystemic Therapy (Henggeler, Schoenwald, Borduin, Rowland, & Cunningham, 1998), Assertive Community Treatment (Test, 1992; Test & Stein, 1976), and Trauma-Focused Cognitive Behavioural Therapy (TF-CBT; Cohen, Mannarino, & Deblinger, 2006, as cited in McHugh & Barlow, 2012). In addition, relative to high-fidelity programmes, programmes with low fidelity have been linked to poorer programme performance (McHugo, Drake, Teague, & Xie, 1999) and attenuated treatment effects (Henggeler, Melton, Brondino, Scherer, & Hanley, 1997).

Adherence and fidelity assessments are thus two quality assurance methods that address the question: "Are individual clinicians and treatment programmes delivering the treatment they say they are delivering?". Adherence and fidelity are typically achieved through training (which can be didactic and/or competency based), supervision, consultation, and adherence monitoring. Ensuring that the treatment delivered is adherent to the treatment model does *not* solely involve didactic training of the therapists. Based on findings from implementation science, traditional didactic training alone does little to effect clinician behaviour change (see Beidas & Kendall, 2010 for a review). In contrast, competency-based training, which includes direct feedback and coaching/supervision, leads to more sustainable change in clinician behaviour (Miller, Yahne, Moyers, Martinez, & Pirritano, 2004).

Training, Adherence, and Fidelity for DBT Providers

DBT training options range from didactic (e.g., 1–2 day workshops) to didactic and competency based (e.g., 10–day intensive or core clinical training, which includes formal teaching on DBT plus consultation on programme and clinical cases; full day training held once weekly for eight weeks, which includes didactic and competency-based methods). Informed by research supporting that ongoing monitoring, consultation, and assessment of clinician acquisition of skill is also needed for successful treatment implementation and to prevent treatment drift (Bellg et al., 2004; McHugh & Barlow, 2012; Sholomskas et al., 2005), some DBT training models have evolved to provide ongoing monitoring, consultation and real-time, expert coaching to facilitate DBT programme implementation and shape clinician behaviour (for examples, see Behavioral Tech's Dialectical Behaviour Therapy Team-Building Intensive, available at: behavioraltech.org/training/IndependentPractitioners.cfm, or Practice Ground, an online learning community founded by Koerner and colleagues, available at: http://www.practiceground.org/willow-wellbeing-which-path-is-right/).

DBT adherence is assessed by trained adherence coders using an empirically validated instrument that has 66 items, 12 sub-scales, and a global adherence scale. Each item is a behaviourally defined and operationalized DBT strategy linked to the adherence manual (Linehan & Korslund, 2003) and follows an "if–then" algorithm, which takes into account whether a particular strategy is necessary, and sufficient given the context of the treatment session and the necessary strategies outlined in the DBT treatment manual. Scores range from 0 to 5.0, with an adherence threshold score of 4.0 and above indicating an adherent session. The process of adherence coding and adherence training is currently overseen by the University of Washington, where coders can receive training as well as resources to achieve inter-rater reliability with a gold standard. The DBT adherence measure has undergone several iterations (see Linehan et al., 1991; Linehan, Lockard, Wagner, & Tutek, 1996) and continues to be under development.

Despite the recent training advancements and extant research findings regarding fidelity and ongoing monitoring, treatment studies often fail to report specific details regarding adherence and training, or forego it altogether. To address this aspect, additional steps were taken (e.g., contacting the authors asking for specific quality assurance details pertaining to their studies) to systematically present what aspects of DBT training (didactic and competency based), adherence, programmatic, and clinical consultation, occured across controlled trials and treatment sites, and what quality assurance elements are underutilized or overlooked. To this end, the list shows: 1) a training rating based on whether training was structured, scheduled, and included didactic and competency-based training methods; 2) supervision methods; 3) adherence reporting; and 4) the "overall study quality" rating, based on the empirically validated psychotherapy quality rating scale RCT-PQRS (Kocsis et al., 2010; see Appendix). This information is presented in Table 20.1.

QUALITY ASSURANCE IN DIALECTICAL BEHAVIOUR THERAPY RANDOMIZED CONTROLLED TRIALS

Search Method and Selection Criteria

In conducting this review, the search terms "Dialectical Behavior Therapy" and "DBT" were entered into the PsycInfo EBSCO host search engine. Studies were included if they met the following criteria: 1) RCTs that compared DBT to an active control condition or waitlist; 2) applied standard DBT, an adaptation of DBT, and/or purported to apply DBT; and 3) had been published in a peer-reviewed journal. Studies were excluded that were: non-randomized controlled trials, quasi-experimental studies,

Table 20.1 Summary of clinician training, quality assurance methods, and primary outcomes in DBT RCTs

Authors	Treatment Length and DBT Modes[a]	Population and Problem Behaviours Investigated	DBT Training of Therapists[b]	Frequency and Type of Supervision/ Consultation Received	Primary Outcomes	Formal DBT Adherence Ratings	Overall Study Quality[c] (0–7)
DBT for Borderline Personality Disorder (BPD): Studies with Adherence Ratings[d]							
Linehan et al. 1999	12-month Comprehensive DBT	Females, comorbid BPD and drug dependence	NA	Weekly supervision. Supervisor: Marsha Linehan	DBT > TAU in reducing substance abuse.	Yes/Mean score: 3.91	5
Koons et al. 2001	6-month Comprehensive DBT	Females, BPD	2	Bimonthly (one clinician) Individual peer-based supervision	DBT > TAU in reducing suicidal ideation (SI), hopelessness, anger, and Beck depression; DBT only: reductions in NSSI, anger, and dissociation; DBT = TAU in reducing HAM-D depression and BPD symptoms.	Yes/Mean score: 3.8	5
Linehan et al. 2002	12-month Comprehensive DBT	Females, comorbid BPD and opiate dependence	NA	Weekly Clinicians met weekly to review tapes and discuss clinical material with supervisor	DBT = CVT-12S initially reducing opiate use, CVT-S: increased opiate use in last four months of treatment; DBT = TAU in decreasing SI.	Yes/Mean score: 3.94	5

(continued)

Table 20.1 Continued

Authors	Treatment Length and DBT Modes[a]	Population and Problem Behaviours Investigated	DBT Training of Therapists[b]	Frequency and Type of Supervision/ Consultation Received	Primary Outcomes	Formal DBT Adherence Ratings	Overall Study Quality[c] (0-7)
Van den Bosch et al. 2002; Verheul et al. 2003 (original study)	12-month Comprehensive DBT	Females, BPD (53% with comorbid substance use disorder (SUD))	2	Weekly individual and group supervision. Tape-based monitoring. Supervisor: van den Bosch	NSSI reduced in DBT & increased in TAU; effects moderated by NSSI severity. DBT > TAU in fewer drop-outs; DBT > TAU in reducing BPD symptoms; DBT = TAU in reducing substance use (no change in either condition).	Yes/ Median score: 3.8	4
Linehan et al. 2006; Harned et al. 2008; Bedics et al. 2012	12-month Comprehensive DBT	Females, highly suicidal,& BPD	2	Weekly Supervisor: Marsha Linehan	DBT > Community Treatment by Experts (CTBE) in reducing suicide attempts; DBT > CTBE in reducing use of crisis services; CTBE > DBT in fewer drop-outs; DBT > CTBE in reducing substance use disorders; DBT = CTBE in reducing SI and Major Depressive Disorder (MDD) remission, anxiety & eating disorders.	Yes/ Mean Score: 4.0	7

Study	Treatment	Population	N	Supervision	Outcome	Adherence	Quality
McMain et al. 2009	12-month Comprehensive DBT	Males and females, BPD	2	Weekly individual supervision plus approximate monthly expert consultation; Consultants: Koerner & Dimeff, DBT trainers	DBT = GPM in reducing suicidal behaviour, use of crisis services (significant decrease in both conditions).	Yes/ Median score: 4.06	6
Linehan et al. 2015	12-month Comprehensive DBT & 12-month Standard Skills-Only DBT (DBT-S) & 12-Month Individual Therapy–Only DBT (DBT-I)	Females, highly suicidal & BPD	3	Weekly group supervision across conditions. Individual supervision as needed if a research therapist fell out of adherence	DBT = DBT-S = DBT-I in reducing suicidal attempts and ideation, as well as use of crisis services. DBT & DBT-S > DBT-I in reducing NSSI.	Yes/Mean score of DBT and DBT-S: 4.20, Mean score of DBT-I: 4.16	6

DBT for BPD: Studies without Adherence Ratings

Study	Treatment	Population	N	Supervision	Outcome	Adherence	Quality
Linehan et al. 1991, 1993, 1994	12-month Comprehensive DBT	Females, highly suicidal & BPD	NA– treatment under development	Weekly Individual, tape-review based supervision Supervisor: Linehan	DBT > TAU in reducing suicidal behavior and NSSI & inpatient days; DBT > TAU in fewer drop outs; DBT = TAU in decreasing suicidal ideation (SI).	No	4
Turner 2000	12-month Individual DBT with use of psychodynamic conceptualization—DBT skills in individual therapy format	Males & females, BPD and suicidal behaviour	1	Weekly Group supervision centered around tape review Supervisor: Turner	DBT > TAU in reducing in self-harm/suicide behaviour (both conditions reduced behaviour, DBT: greater gains); DBT > TAU in reducing inpatient days & improving mental health functioning.	No	4

(continued)

Table 20.1 Continued

Authors	Treatment Length and DBT Modes[a]	Population and Problem Behaviours Investigated	DBT Training of Therapists[b]	Frequency and Type of Supervision/ Consultation Received	Primary Outcomes	Formal DBT Adherence Ratings	Overall Study Quality[c] (0–7)
Clarkin et al. 2007	12-month Comprehensive DBT	Males and females, BPD and suicidal behaviour	3	Weekly supervision Supervisor: Stanley	DBT = Transference Focused Psychotherapy (TFP) = Schema-Focused Treatment (ST) in reducing depression & anxiety; TFP = ST (not DBT) in reducing anger and impulsivity; only TFP significantly reduced irritability & assaultive behaviour.	No	6
Carter al., 2010	6-month DBT Modifications to phone consultation	Females, BPD	2	Weekly	DBT = TAU + Waitlist (WL) in reducing NSSI, hospital admissions, and length of stay in hospital.	No	4
DBT for personality disorder traits and self-injurious behaviour: Studies with Adherence Ratings							
Pistorello et al. 2012	7–12 month Comprehensive DBT	Males and females, BPD	2	As needed individual supervision and phone consultation	DBT > Optimized Treatment as Usual (O-TAU) in reducing NSSI, SI, & depression. DBT > 0-TAU greater gains for more severe baseline suicidality.	Yes/Mean score: 3.92	6

Priebe et al. 2012	12-month Comprehensive DBT	Males and females, BPD criteria, self injurious behaviour (NSSI), a Personality Disorder (PD) not limited to BPD	2	Frequency not specified Five therapists had 40 hours of supervision during study. Individual supervision included tape review. Supervisors: Amy Gaglia & Tim Mold, team manager. Expert supervision from Heidi Heard, DBT trainer	DBT> TAU in reducing NSSI.	Yes/Mean score: 4.1	5
Mehlum et al. 2014	19-week Comprehensive DBT	Adolescent males and females, BPD traits, and NSSI	3	Monthly one-hour group consultation. Consultants: Alec Miller & Sarah Reynolds	DBT > Enhanced usual care (EUC) in reducing self-harm, depressive symptoms, and suicidal ideation.	Yes/ Mean score: 4.11 individual sessions, 4.18 group skills class	6

DBT for personality disorder traits: Studies without Adherence Ratings

Feigenbaum et al. 2012	12-month Comprehensive DBT	Males and females, PD (93% BPD)	3	Frequency and type not specified 1–2 days of expert consultation/year. Consultant: Heidi Heard	DBT = TAU in reducing self-harm, suicide attempts, rate and length of hospitalizations.	No	5

(continued)

Table 20.1 Continued

Authors	Treatment Length and DBT Modes[a]	Population and Problem Behaviours Investigated	DBT Training of Therapists[b]	Frequency and Type of Supervision/ Consultation Received	Primary Outcomes	Formal DBT Adherence Ratings	Overall Study Quality[c] (0-7)
DBT for mood and other behavioural disorders: Studies with Adherence Ratings							
Goldstein et al. 2015	36 sessions, alternating between one hr individual and family skills training sessions As needed phone coaching Consultation team	Adolescent females and males, BPD	1	Weekly tape review and supervision	DBT > TAU in reducing depressive symptoms DBT: reductions in mania and emotion dysregulation over time, but not TAU DBT = TAU in reducing suicidal ideation and attempts.	Yes/no scores reported	5
DBT for mood and other behavioural disorders: Studies without Adherence Ratings							
Lynch et al. 2007 (Study 2: Distinct sample from Lynch et al. 2003)	24 weekly individual and group sessions As needed phone coaching Consultation team	Older adult males and females, MDD + 1 PD	3	See Lynch et al. 2003	DBT + medication management (DBT+ MED) > MED in reaching faster MDD remission.	No	6
Courbasson et al. 2012	12-month Comprehensive DBT	Females, concurrent ED (Anorexia Nervosa (AN), Binge Eating Disorder (BED) and/or Bulimia Nervosa (BN)) and SUD	NA	Frequency and type not specified	DBT > TAU in fewer drop-outs; all analyses done in DBT pre-post b/c low retention in TAU; DBT reduced dysfunctional eating behaviours; attitudes, severity, and substance use.	No	3

Bohus et al. 2013	Inpatient 23 individual sessions (DBT + formal exposure) over 12 weeks 11 90-minute DBT skills training groups (16.5 hrs total) Approx. 54 group sessions re: PTSD psychoeducation, art and music therapy, mindfulness, self-esteem Use of consultation team not reported	Females, Post-Traumatic Stress Disorder (PTSD) and 50% PTSD & BPD	3	Weekly Live, online supervision centred around video review Supervisors: Bohus, treatment developer & Steil	DBT > TAU in reducing PTSD.	No	6

DBT skills plus coaching for depression: Studies without Adherence Ratings

Lynch et al. 2003	28 weekly 2-hour skills groups 30-minute scheduled phone contact + diary card review As needed phone coaching Consultation team	Older adult males and females, MDD	3	Frequency not specified. All group and planned phone sessions audiotaped and reviewed Supervisor: Lynch	Remission from depression (DBT > MED) gap even wider at follow up.	No	6

DBT skills only for emotion dysregulation: Studies with Adherence Ratings

Neacsiu et al. 2014	16 weekly 2-hr DBT group sessions Consultation team	Males and females, high emotion dysregulation and anxiety and/or depressive disorder	2	Weekly Tape-based supervision	DBT-ST > ASG (Activities Skills Group) in reducing emotion dysregulation and anxiety, increasing skills use. DBT-ST = ASG in treatment acceptability and reducing depression severity.	Yes/Mean score: 4.0	6

(continued)

Table 20.1 Continued

Authors	Treatment Length and DBT Modes[a]	Population and Problem Behaviours Investigated	DBT Training of Therapists[b]	Frequency and Type of Supervision/Consultation Received	Primary Outcomes	Formal DBT Adherence Ratings	Overall Study Quality[c] (0-7)
DBT skills only for BPD: Studies without Adherence Ratings							
Soler et al. 2009	13 weekly 2-hr skills groups Included all original skills, no repetition of skills content Use of consultation team not reported	Males and females, BPD	NA	Not described	DBT > supportive group therapy (SGT) in reducing depression, anxiety, irritability, anger, and affect instability.	No	4
DBT skills only for mood and behavioural disorders: Studies without Adherence Ratings							
Bradley & Follingstad 2003	18 weekly 2.5-hr skills groups (nine DBT skills, nine narrative writing assignments) Use of consultation team not reported	Incarcerated females with childhood abuse histories.	1	Not described	DBT-ST > no contact in reducing depression symptoms, anxious arousal, dissociation	No	2
Harley et al. 2008; Feldman et al. 2009	16 weekly 1.5-hr skills groups Consultation team	Females, treatment resistant MDD	2	No	TAU + DBT-ST > TAU + WL in reducing depression symptoms from week 0–week 16.	No	4
Hirvikoski et al. 2011	14 weekly 2-hr skills groups on Mindfulness and Emotion Regulation Use of consultation team not reported	Males and females, Attention Deficit Hyperactivity Disorder (ADHD)	2	Bimonthly individual supervision during study period (2–3 hours); Group supervision, including all research therapists	DBT-ST > TAU in reducing ADHD symptoms.	No	5

Study	Intervention	Population			Outcome		Rating
Van Dijk et al. 2012	12 weekly 90-min DBT group sessions Use of consultation team not reported	Males and females, Bipolar I or Bipolar II Disorder.	1	None	DBT-ST = WL in reducing depressive symptoms, improving mindfulness-based self-efficacy and emotional self-control.	No	3
Fleming et al. 2015	8 weekly 90-min DBT group sessions & weekly 10–15 min coaching calls Consultation team	Adolescent males and females, ADHD	3	Not described	DBT-ST > Skills handouts (SH) in reducing executive functioning (EF) problems, and EF recovery at post treatment and follow up. DBT-ST = SH in ADHD inattentive problems. DBT-ST rated as acceptable and satisfactory to participants.	No	4

DBT skills only for eating disorders: Studies without Adherence Ratings

Study	Intervention	Population			Outcome		Rating
Telch et al. 2001	20 weekly 2-hour DBT skills training sessions Diary cards used and individualized treatment plans developed in group Use of consultation team not reported	Females, BED	NA	Not described	DBT > WL in reducing binge eating and weight related concerns.	No	4
Safer et al. 2001	20 weekly 50-min DBT skills in individual session format No consultation team reported	Females, BN	NA	Not described	DBT > WL in reducing rates of binge/purging.	No	4

(continued)

Table 20.1 Continued

Authors	Treatment Length and DBT Modes[a]	Population and Problem Behaviours Investigated	DBT Training of Therapists[b]	Frequency and Type of Supervision/Consultation Received	Primary Outcomes	Formal DBT Adherence Ratings	Overall Study Quality[c] (0–7)
Safer et al. 2010; Safer et al. 2011	20 weekly 2-hour DBT skills group. Replicated format of Telch et al. 2001. Use of consultation team not reported	Males and females, BED	NA	Frequency not specified; Conducted by a DBT expert independent from the study, identity unknown	DBT > Active comparison group therapy (ACGT) in more rapid reductions in binge frequency and achieving binge abstinence; DBT > ACGT in fewer drop-outs.	Yes/ Scores not reported; used instrument derived from BRTC adherence measure adapted for DBT-BED	5
Hill, Craighead, & Safer, 2011	12 weekly DBT skills plus diary card in individual session format (15 hrs total) Consultation team	Females, BN	1	Weekly Supervisor: Hill	Appetite Focused DBT (DBT-AF) rated highly acceptable by participants and therapists; DBT-AF > control in reducing objective binge episodes at week six.	No	5

[a] Comprehensive DBT is defined as weekly individual therapy, weekly skills training, inter-session phone coaching, and therapist consultation team. If a study did not deliver Comprehensive DBT, specific modes were outlined.

[b] The training criteria is intended to provide a more systematic, parsimonious, and objective illustration of the range of DBT training methods offered. "Formal training" is defined in this review as having the following elements: scheduled, structured training, which includes both didactic and competency-based training methods.

NA– Insufficient information available or no information available to determine a rating

0- No formal training reported (e.g., self-taught)

1- Minimal formal training (e.g., at least some team members completed at least one formal workshop before the study began, but no team members completed equivalent of ten-day formal training)

2- Moderate formal training (e.g., some but not all members had completed equivalent of ten-day training before study began, some or whole team completed equivalent of ten-day formal training after study began)

3- Maximal formal training (e.g., all members completed the equivalent of ten-day formal training before study began)

^c Item 25 from Psychotherapy Quality Assurance Rating Scale (see Appendix for full scale). Omnibus rating: please provide an overall rating of the quality of the study, taking into account the adequacy of description, the quality of study design, data analysis, and justification of conclusions. 1 = exceptionally poor; 2 = very poor; 3 = moderately poor; 4 = average; 5 = moderately good; 6 = very good; 7 = exceptionally good. Raters utilized the following factors when factoring in score: Use of 1 year + follow-up, adequate analyses and design (use of Bonferroni + ITT analyses), adequate measurements (blind and reliable raters + standardized instruments), appropriately stating claims based on results, active control group.

^d Studies were organized in the table first by population, and secondarily by whether the study conducted adherence ratings

pre-post designs, case studies, and unpublished DBT studies (e.g., dissertations). Studies were not excluded on the basis of specific client outcomes tested, diagnostic criteria at baseline, treatment frequency/duration, and mention of fidelity/ adherence assessment. Because quality assurance methods such as programme fidelity and therapist adherence are typically consistent for studies conducted within the same research group, the information was organized by clustering the DBT trials conducted at the same site.

The aim was to systematically review the quality of research procedures followed across DBT RCT studies using the RCT of Psychotherapy Quality Rating Scale (RCT-PQRS) to quantify the evaluation. The RCT-PQRS (Kocsis et al., 2010) is a validated measure that can be used to evaluate the quality of the research conducted following an RCT model. The scale contains 25 items that encompass six domains: description of subjects, definition and delivery of treatment, outcome measures, data analysis, treatment assignment, and overall quality of study. The measure has high internal consistency ($\alpha = .87$, with a correlation between first 24 items and overall quality item 25: $\alpha = .88$) (See RCT-PQRS in Appendix).

To assess quality of research, each study was rated using a revised version of the RCT-PQRS scale. The first and second author reviewed and discussed the scale criteria together to establish clear guidelines for rating DBT studies, in particular on the RCT-PQRS scale. The first and second author then rated 11% of the studies independently, compared ratings, and resolved any discrepancies in applying this scale. The first author then reviewed and rated the remaining studies, consulting with the second author as needed. Ratings focused on trials rather than on publications. If multiple papers were published from the same RCT, only the main RCT publication was rated; secondary publications utilizing the original sample were summarized in the review, but not rated. Overall study quality ratings of each trial are presented in Table 20.1. A specific rating of training methods was devised based on a scale developed by the first and fourth authors. Each trial was then rated by first and fourth author, with 89% concordance rates. Discrepant ratings were then discussed and resolved. More detailed ratings of each study are available upon request to the first author. Qualitative information about each study's research methodology derived from the scale will be included for each study. Studies are presented according to treatment population, and then secondarily organized according to whether standard DBT was delivered (as assessed by intensity and duration of treatment as well as DBT modes) *and* adherence ratings conducted. These studies are presented first within the population category and reviewed more fully, and primary results are included. Studies that were determined to deviate from standard DBT *and* did not conduct adherence ratings are subsequently and briefly reviewed. Further, the first author followed up individually with each RCT's first or second author to ascertain more specific information on training methods beyond what was included in the publication. Of those contacted, 71% replied and provided more detailed information on training methods, adherence, and supervision.

Summary and Critique of Studies Conducted by Treatment Developer

DBT for BPD. Linehan and colleagues conducted four RCTs assessing the effectiveness of 12–month comprehensive DBT: two in treating 44 and 101 chronically suicidal women with BPD (Linehan et al., 1991; Linehan et al., 2006), and two in treating 28 and 33 females with comorbid BPD and substance dependence (Linehan et al., 1999; Linehan et al., 2002).

In treating suicidal women with BPD, DBT was initially compared to treatment-as-usual (TAU) and later to community treatment by non-behavioural experts (CTBE), a control condition designed to rigorously account for many potential confounds such as clinician expertise, allegiance to treatment provided, adequate clinical supervision, and institutional prestige. DBT was superior to TAU and CTBE in reducing episodes of non-suicidal self-injury (NSSI), medical risk, hospitalizations, treatment drop-outs (Linehan et al., 1991, 1994, 2006; Linehan, Heard, & Armstrong, 1993), remission from substance dependence, and comorbid disorders (Harned et al., 2008), in improvements in positive introject (Bedics, Atkins, Comtois, & Linehan, 2012), and in reducing experiential avoidance and anger expression (Neacsiu, Lungu, Harned, Rivsi, & Linehan, 2014). There were no significant differences between DBT and TAU or CTBE in reducing suicidal ideation, depression, hopelessness (Linehan et al., 1991, 1993, 1994, 2006), shame, guilt, anger suppression, and anxiety (Neacsiu et al., 2014) or in improving outcomes for Axis I disorders outside of substance abuse (Harned et al., 2008). CTBE study findings in particular suggest that clinical improvements in the DBT condition did not result from therapeutic attention, support, and expertise alone, but rather from specific, active DBT treatment ingredients.

Strengths of the first published trial (Linehan et al., 1991) include close attention to clinician supervision, consideration of an active control group as an ethical, optimal alternative to wait-list, and blind, reliable outcome raters. Limitations include insufficient description of clinician background training, lack of follow-up assessment, intent-to-treat and power analyses, unclear methodology regarding inclusion/exclusion criteria, and the use of non-standardized instruments (Linehan et al., 1991). Furthermore, a DBT adherence instrument had not been created at the time that this RCT was conducted, so lack of full adherence reporting is another limitation. Strengths of the second trial (Linehan et al., 2006) include follow-up assessment, rigorous statistical analyses, the use of an active, expert treatment comparison group, and full adherence reporting, while limitations include insufficient power analyses, and use of several non-standardized outcome measures.

In treating substance-dependent BPD women, 12-month DBT was augmented with opiate replacement medication and was compared initially to TAU and then with Comprehensive Validation Therapy with 12-step (CVT+12S). DBT was superior to control conditions in leading to significantly greater reductions in substance abuse at the end of treatment and after one year and in greater improvements in social and global adjustment (Linehan et al., 1999; Linehan et al., 2002). DBT was superior to TAU regarding participant retention (Linehan et al., 1999), although CVT+12S was superior to DBT in retaining 100% of subjects, as compared to 64% in the DBT condition (Linehan et al., 2002). There were no significant differences between conditions in NSSI, suicide attempts, anger (Linehan et al., 1999), and psychopathology (Linehan et al., 2002). Post hoc analyses from the 1999 study revealed a notable finding relevant to our review. Participants treated by consistently adherent clinicians had significantly higher proportion of clean urinalyses at 12 months as compared to those treated by clinicians with inconsistent adherence ratings. While the small sample size of adherent DBT clinicians (N = 4) precludes any definitive conclusions, this data combined with clinical observation led the treatment developer to hypothesize a relationship between DBT adherence and treatment outcomes (Linehan et al., 1999).

Strengths of the above trials treating substance-dependent BPD women include follow-up assessment, intent-to-treat analyses (which help eliminate analytic bias caused by drop outs), clinician training by experts, and use of blind, independent raters to minimize assessment bias (Linehan et al., 1999; Linehan et al., 2002). An additional strength of the 2002 study was the use of an active condition, which holds intervention factors (e.g., manualized therapy approach, academic treatment setting, common treatment factors for opiate addicts, and therapist experience and commitment) stable across conditions. Chief limitations of both studies were a lack of within-study reliability of diagnostic and outcome measures, and lack of full reporting on adherence ratings, which weakens the ability to draw conclusions about the quality of assessment and treatment delivered.

Most recently, Linehan et al. (2015) conducted a component analysis comparing 99 females with BPD and suicidal behaviour randomized across Comprehensive DBT, DBT-Skills training only (DBT-S), and DBT individual therapy only (DBT-I). Regardless of condition, providers utilized a standardized suicide assessment and management protocol. All three conditions resulted in similar reductions in suicide attempts and ideation, as well as use of crisis services, and the two DBT conditions incorporating skills training outperformed DBT-I in reductions in NSSI. Comprehensive DBT had fewer drop-outs and greater reductions in hospitalizations post-treatment as compared to the other two conditions. Strengths include the of use of blind, reliable raters, rigorous statistical analyses and comparison conditions, full adherence reporting, and adequate attention to the importance of rigorous clinician training in assessing and managing suicide risk. Limitations include significant differences in treatment dose across conditions due to treatment drop out, and some inclusion of non-standardized outcome measures.

Studies Conducted Outside Site of Treatment Development

Many researchers have begun examining DBT's efficacy beyond the site of treatment development. As for any other evidence-based treatment, it is important for the evidence base testing DBT vs. comparison treatments to expand beyond the treatment developer in order to assess DBT's efficacy across sites, researchers, clinicians, and treatment populations. At the same time, attempts to replicate findings can be compromised without adequate quality assurance methods in place, such as attention to model fidelity and adherence. For this reason, we present subsequent studies with attention to whether adherence ratings were conducted and the standard DBT model was followed.

DBT for BPD: Studies with DBT adherence ratings. Koons and colleagues (2001) published one of the first RCTs testing comprehensive DBT outside of the DBT development site, in which a sample of female veterans diagnosed with BPD were randomized to either a six–month comprehensive DBT condition (N = 10) or to TAU (N = 10). Participants in the DBT condition demonstrated statistically greater reductions in suicidal ideation, depression, hopelessness, and anger at post-treatment as compared to participants in TAU. There were no between condition differences in changes in self-harm behaviours, dissociation, or utilization of crisis services.

Chief strengths of the study include full adherence reporting, adequate clinician adherence, and training. Limitations include lack of blind raters, no follow-up assessment, a small sample size, and low baseline levels of NSSI, which may have contributed to floor effects and a failure to detect between–condition differences on NSSI.

Van den Bosch and colleagues (2002) conducted the first DBT RCT outside of the US in a Netherlands outpatient programme. Females diagnosed with BPD (53% with comorbid substance use disorders, SUD) were randomized to 12-month comprehensive DBT (N = 27) or TAU (N = 31). Participants in the DBT condition had significantly higher reductions in NSSI and impulsive acts (van den Bosch, Verheul, Schippers, & van den Brink, 2002) and lower drop-out rates (37% vs. 77%; Verheul, van den Bosch, Koeter, De Ridder, Stijnen, & Van Den Brink, 2003) compared to TAU participants. No significant between-condition differences were observed in reduction of substance use problems (van den Bosch et al., 2002), or in frequency and course of suicidal behaviour. DBT was superior to TAU for clients who were more severe in their self-harming behaviour, but not for those whose self-harm severity was low (Verheul et al., 2003). Strengths of the original 2003 RCT (Verheul et al., 2003) include the use of intent-to-treat (ITT) analyses, full adherence reporting, and clear description of DBT clinician training. Limitations include lack of blind raters, lack of interrater reliability to ensure unbiased and sound assessment, and failure to conduct follow-up assessment to assess whether clinical improvements hold over time.

McMain et al. (2009) conducted a large-scale RCT in which men and women diagnosed with BPD and recent suicidal behaviour were randomized to receive either 12 months of comprehensive outpatient DBT (N = 90) or general psychiatric management (N = 90). Psychiatric management consisted of weekly psychodynamically informed individual treatment, case management, and symptom-specific medication management. There were no differences between conditions in decreases in BPD criteria, suicidal behaviour, depression, anger, and utilization of healthcare services. Strengths of the study include the use of blind, reliable diagnostic assessors, rigorous statistical analyses, full adherence reporting, and the use of an expert treatment comparison group to control for allegiance and non-specific therapy effects. Limitations include the lack of follow-up assessment as to whether clinical improvements were sustained in either condition.

DBT for BPD: Studies without DBT adherence ratings. A sample of 24 men and women with BPD and suicidal behaviour were randomized to 12-month outpatient DBT-informed treatment (N = 12) or to client-centred therapy (CCT; N = 12; Turner, 2000). The DBT condition did not follow the comprehensive treatment model, but rather consisted of weekly individual therapy sessions (including DBT treatment strategies and psychodynamic case conceptualization and strategies) with DBT skills training incorporated within the individual sessions. Both conditions were offered a total of six groups that focused on clients' close outside relationships; DBT skills training was not provided in the DBT condition. The author did not specify whether DBT consultation team or phone coaching was incorporated. Compared to the CTT condition, participants in the DBT-informed condition showed significantly higher decreases in suicidal and self-harming behaviour, anger, depression, impulsivity, and hospitalizations, and also higher increases in overall mental health functioning at the end of treatment and at one year follow-up.

Strengths of this study include use of adequate diagnostic methodology, blind independent outcome assessors, weekly supervision, and ITT analyses. However, this study tested a treatment that departed from comprehensive DBT in significant ways without providing a solid rationale for why the changes in treatment were needed, in particular, the inclusion of psychodynamic techniques in conceptualizing the clients is a significant departure from the cognitive behavioural theoretical foundation of DBT. Other limitations include a lack of adherence ratings, insufficient DBT clinician training, and lack of inter-rater reliability for interview assessment and unclear durability of treatment gains (i.e., no follow-up assessment). Therefore, in our perspective this study implemented a treatment that departed from standard DBT to such an extent that its outcomes cannot be included as evidence for the efficacy of comprehensive DBT for suicidal and self-injurious populations.

Clarkin, Levy, Lenzenweger, & Kernberg (2007) conducted a multi-site treatment study where 90 men and women diagnosed with BPD were randomized to 12 months of either DBT, Transference Focused Psychotherapy (TFP; Clarkin, Yeomans, & Kernberg, 1999), or Dynamic Supportive Treatment (ST; Rockland, 1992). DBT and TFP were superior to ST in reduction in suicidality; TFP and ST were superior to DBT in reductions in anger; and TFP was superior to both DBT and ST in improvement in irritability, aggressive behaviour, and impulsivity (Clarkin et al., 2007). There were no differences between conditions in improvements of depression, anxiety, global functioning, and interpersonal adjustment. Study strengths include the use of active comparison treatments that controlled for allegiance and non-specific therapy effects, outcome measures assessed by blind raters with established reliability, and the provision of regular therapist supervision. Limitations include the lack of follow-up assessment, insufficient detail regarding therapist training, and lack of adherence score reporting.

Carter, Willcox, Lewin, Conrad, & Bendit (2010) conducted an RCT in which 73 females diagnosed with BPD were randomized to a six-month Australian outpatient DBT programme (N = 38) or TAU + waitlist control condition (N = 35). Phone consultation deviated from the standard model in that coaching was provided by an on-call member of the consultation team during daytime hours and the local psychiatric hospital between 10:30 pm and 8:30 am. Findings revealed no significant between-condition differences in hospital admissions or reductions in NSSI behaviours. Findings from secondary analyses revealed that those in the DBT condition demonstrated significant improvements in physical and psychological quality of life, the quality of their environment (e.g., physical safety, access to healthcare), and disability (days spent in bed).

Study strengths include the use of blind raters, intent to treat analyses, and the use of multiple sources for outcome measures beyond self-report. In terms of weaknesses, the authors note that they may have received insufficient training, supervision was not mentioned, and adherence was not conducted. The comparison condition was a TAU+ waitlist to DBT, and it is possible that for some participants, the expectation of receiving DBT in the future may have an effect on clinical outcomes. Lastly, the phone-coaching mode included deviations from the standard DBT model. Therefore, in our perspective, due to the extent to which the study deviated from standard DBT, this study cannot be included in the body of literature examining the effectiveness of comprehensive DBT for those diagnosed with BPD.

DBT for personality disorder traits and self-injurious behaviour: Studies with DBT adherence ratings. DBT has also been researched among college students (Pistorello, Fruzzetti, MacLane, Gallop, & Iverson, 2012). Sixty-three college students (81% female) with histories of suicidal behaviour or self-injury, and three or more BPD diagnostic criteria, were randomized to a seven- to 12-month comprehensive DBT condition (N = 31) or an optimized (well-trained and supervised) TAU (O-TAU) condition of psychodynamic orientation (N = 32). All practicing clinicians across both conditions were trainees, and therefore a "supervision by expert" paradigm was adopted, consistent with a typical counselling centre model. Results indicated that DBT participants showed significantly greater decreases in suicidality, depressive behaviours, self-injurious behaviour, and BPD behaviours, as compared to the control participants. No between-group differences were found on treatment retention. Study strengths include the use of blind, reliable diagnostic and outcome assessors, in-study power analyses, full adherence reporting, sufficient attention to clinician training and supervision, and an active control condition. One limitation is overgeneralizing trial-specific results to conclude that DBT is effective with suicidal, multi-problem college students more generally.

Priebe et al. (2012) randomized 40 males and females with histories of self-injury and BPD or a different personality disorder to 12-month comprehensive DBT (N = 20) or TAU (N = 20) within the UK National Health Service. Results indicated that the 48% of participants who remained in DBT had greater reductions in self-harm as compared to study drop-outs. Further, those participants in DBT had greater reductions in total days of self-injury over the treatment course, as compared to those in TAU, although no significant between-group differences were found on secondary outcomes, including BPD symptoms, general psychiatric symptom severity, or general life satisfaction (Priebe et al., 2012). The authors conjecture that the high drop-out rate in the DBT condition may be due to the wide inclusion criteria (e.g., BPD plus a substance use disorder), which have historically been associated with higher drop-out rates, although, the study used a more strinent test of drop-out (two misses in a row) than other DBT studies reviewed here. Further, the authors note that public clinical services in the UK are free, which may have been a disincentive for individuals to stay in an intensive treatment such as DBT when they have access to other free healthcare alternatives. Study strengths include full adherence reporting, and the testing of DBT in a naturalistic, public service context with an emphasis on DBT cost-effectiveness. Limitations include lack of description of clinician training and supervision methods, and lack of reliable blind raters and follow-up assessment.

Most recently, a shortened form of DBT has been researched among adolescents (Mehlum et al., 2014). Seventy-seven adolescents (88% female) with histories of suicidal behaviour and self-injury and one or more BPD diagnostic criteria were randomized to a 19-week comprehensive DBT condition (N = 39) or an enhanced usual care (EUC) condition of therapists with a psychodynamic or cognitive-behavioural orientation (N = 38). Results indicated that DBT participants showed significantly greater decreases in suicidal thoughts, depressive behaviours, and self-injurious behaviour, as compared to the EUC participants. No between-group differences were found on treatment retention, and both conditions had high retention rates. Study strengths include the use of blind, reliable diagnostic and outcome assessors, in-study power analyses, full adherence reporting of DBT, and an active control condition. Limitations include insufficient explanation of and rationale for the shortened (i.e., 19-week) adaptation of DBT, unequal treatment doses between conditions, and lack of follow-up assessment.

DBT for personality disorder traits with or without self-injurious behaviour: Studies without DBT adherence ratings. Feigenbaum et al. (2012) randomized 42 males and females with BPD symptoms and/or a different personality disorder to 12-month comprehensive DBT (N = 26) or TAU (N = 16) within a publicly funded, specialist PD clinic. Results indicated that both conditions resulted in significantly reduced deliberate self-harm (DSH) rates, although no between-group differences were found. No significant reductions were found on suicide attempts or rate or length of inpatient hospitalizations in either condition. Study strengths include the use of an active control group and validated, reliable outcome measures, and the authors' attention to the importance of clinician training. Despite attention to clinician background training, clinicians did not receive ongoing expert supervision, and adherence and follow-up assessment were not conducted.

DBT for mood disorders: Studies with DBT adherence ratings. Most recently, Goldstein et al. (2015) conducted a pilot RCT comparing a DBT adaptation (N = 14) to psychosocial TAU (N = 6) for adolescents with bipolar disorder. The DBT adaptation consisted of 36 sessions, alternating weekly between individual therapy and a family skills sessions (tapering in frequency across the treatment year), plus phone-based skills coaching and consultation team. Results indicated that this DBT adaptation was feasible and rated as satisfactory to participants, and DBT outperformed TAU in reductions in symptoms of depression and mania. Strengths include the use of blind, reliable raters and standardized instruments, while limitations include insufficient sample size, significant baseline differences across conditions in clinical acuity (greater baseline suicide attempts in DBT condition), failure to report adherence ratings, as well as between-condition differences in treatment dose. Such condition differences make it difficult to disentangle whether DBT-specific ingredients are contributing to clinical change among this sample of adolescents with BPD and suicidality.

DBT for mood disorders: Studies without DBT adherence ratings. Lynch et al. (2007) randomized 35 older adults with comorbid depression and personality disorder diagnosis who were deemed medication non-responders in an earlier treatment phase. Individuals were randomized to a 24-week Comprehensive DBT+MED (N = 21) or MED only (N = 14) condition. No between-group differences were found in HAM-D depressive symptoms post-group (end of 24-week DBT skills group training), post-treatment (end of DBT treatment or medication management at week 30), or follow-up (15 months after randomization). Finally, at post-treatment and follow-up, participants in DBT+MED had lower self-reported sensitivity and aggression in interpersonal relationships than those in MED alone. Study strengths include clinician training by the treatment developer, follow-up assessment, and detailing a strong rationale and systematic process regarding adapting DBT for older adults with depression and personality disorders. Limitations include lack of adherence monitoring, failure to ensure that outcome assessors were blind to condition, and greater clinical contact in DBT+MED condition than in the MED alone condition, which prevents determining whether DBT-specific ingredients contributed to clinical improvement.

Courbasson, Nishikawa, & Dixon (2012) randomized 21 females with eating disorders (ED) and SUD to 12-month comprehensive DBT (N = 13) or TAU (N = 8). Because the TAU condition was associated with unexpected elevated drop-out rates and worsening of ED-SUD symptoms over time, recruitment of participants to TAU was stopped prematurely due to the ethical concerns of delivering a treatment that may be iatrogenic. Failure to maintain a control condition prevented the authors from making direct comparisons between treatment conditions and maintaining the research design integrity of an RCT, and therefore conclusions about DBT's relative effectiveness for this ED-SUD population cannot be made.

Bohus and colleagues (2013) randomized 82 females with Post-Traumatic Stress Disorder (PTSD) related to childhood sexual abuse and BPD to a 12-week inpatient DBT+PSTD (N = 43) or treatment as usual condition (TAU-WL; N = 39). Individuals in the DBT+PTSD condition received twice-weekly DBT+ exposure treatment in individual session format, DBT skills training, and other treatment groups unrelated to DBT. Adults treated with TAU were encouraged to see a therapist of their choice (except DBT+PTSD) and were offered the opportunity to enter into DBT+PTSD at the end of the study period. DBT=PTSD outperformed TAU in significantly greater reductions in PTSD, depression, and global functioning. No between-group differences were found on BPD criteria or dissociation.

Study strengths include use of blind, reliable raters for diagnostic measures, power analyses, follow-up assessment, provision of weekly supervision, and clear rationale for and explication of DBT adaptation. Limitations include lack of formal DBT adherence ratings, which makes it difficult to draw conclusions about DBT's effectiveness for this population, and insufficient description of clinician training.

Summary and Critique of Studies Conducting DBT Skills+Phone Coaching

Several more recent RCTs have begun investigating the effectiveness of DBT skills only or skills only *plus phone coaching* for the treatment of various problem behaviours and diagnoses, including BPD with and without co-occurring substance dependence, ED, Major Depressive Disorder (MDD), emotion regulation difficulties and problem drinking, Attention Deficit Hyperactivity Disorder (ADHD), and BPD.

DBT skills plus coaching for depression: Studies without DBT adherence ratings. Lynch and colleagues (2003) conducted a pilot investigation of 34 older adults with MDD randomized to a 28-week medication management condition (MED; N = 17) or DBT skills training plus medication management (DBT-ST+MED) and phone coaching (N = 17). The DBT condition consisted of 28 two-hour weekly skills groups based on Linehan's manual in a modified format, including psychoeducation for depression. Weekly scheduled 30-minute phone contact with individuals focused on diary card review and problem solving, and additional phone-based skills coaching included as needed. Individuals in the DBT+MED condition were superior to MED-only in that those in DBT+MED showed decreases in depression scores and hopelessness, and significant increases in adaptive coping. Individuals in both the DBT+MED and MED-only conditions demonstrated significant reductions in clinician-administered depression scores at post-treatment, which were maintained at six-month follow up. A significantly greater proportion of DBT+MED individuals were in remission from depression with the gap between remission rates widened further at follow-up. Strengths include follow-up assessment, and reliable, independent outcome assessors, while limitations include lack of adherence monitoring and failure to control for contact hours across conditions, which make it difficult to draw strong conclusions about DBT's favourable results for this population.

Summary and Critique of Studies Conducting DBT Skills Only

DBT skills only for emotion dysregulation: Studies with DBT adherence ratings. Most recently, Neacsiu, Eberle, Kramer, Wiesmann, & Linehan (2014) conducted a pilot RCT to examine DBT skills training among a sample of non-BPD patients who met criteria for high emotion dysregulation. Forty-four adults with high emotion dysregulation and an anxiety and/or depressive disorder were randomized to a 16-week DBT skills condition (DBT-ST; N = 22) or activities-based support group (ASG; N = 22). DBT-ST utilized skills, treatment strategies, and targets drawn directly from the Linehan (1993b) manual, pared down to accommodate an adapted 16-week course, including shortening the interpersonal effectiveness and mindfulness modules. Group participants tracked their skills use with daily diary cards. Participants in both conditions reported significant decreases in emotion dysregulation across time, although those in DBT-ST had significantly greater and faster improvements. Those in the DBT condition reported significant increases in skills use and maintained these gains during follow-up, while those in the control condition did not. Contrary to what was predicted, those in DBT-ST lost some of their gains in anxiety, depression, and emotion dysregulation, while those in ASG continued to show improvements. Participants found both treatment conditions acceptable, although treatment drop-out was relatively high (32% and 59% in DBT-ST and ASG, respectively).

Strengths of this pilot study include a detailed explication of the DBT skills curriculum, attention to feasibility and acceptability as a pilot intervention, adherence monitoring on both conditions, and the use of an active control condition to control for common treatment factors. One limitation included a lack of adequate training for all clinicians delivering DBT skills.

DBT skills only for BPD: Studies without DBT adherence ratings. Soler et al. (2009) conducted an RCT in which males and females diagnosed with BPD were randomized to a 13-week outpatient short-term DBT skills training (DBT-ST; N = 29) or a non-behavioural standard group therapy conducted by psychodynamically trained therapists (SGT; N = 30). Authors state that DBT skills training included all skills from the Linehan (1993b) manual in an abbreviated format, with no repetition of modules. DBT participants demonstrated significant reductions in depression, anxiety, irritability, anger, and greater treatment retention, as compared to the SGT participants. No between-condition differences were found in frequency of suicide attempts, NSSI, or emergency-room visits. Study strengths include the use of a rigorous control group with expert therapists and ITT analyses. Limitations include insufficient information on clinician training and supervision, insufficient rationale for abbreviated skills format (and explanation as to how they taught all skills in 13-week format), lack of adherence monitoring, and lack of follow-up assessment to determine whether results from this treatment were sustained.

DBT skills only for mood disorders: Studies without DBT adherence ratings. Bradley and Follingstad (2003) randomized 49 incarcerated women with childhood physical and/or sexual abuse histories to either DBT skills+writing condition (N = 24) or a no-contact comparison condition (N = 25). The DBT skills condition was comprised of nine 2.5-hour skills training sessions supplemented by nine sessions of structured writing assignments to promote meaningful narrative description of life experiences. DBT+writing was superior to the no-contact condition in leading to clinically significant decreases in depression, dissociation, and other PTSD behaviours (such as anxious arousal and intrusive experiences). One of the chief study strengths was the testing of DBT skills in a novel prison environment. Limitations include a lack of blind, reliable raters, lack of adherence ratings or clinician supervision, and inadequate detail on treatment content. More definitive conclusions about the efficacy of DBT skills with this population cannot be drawn without the inclusion of an active comparison group, due to the significant deviations from the standard DBT skills group content and structure.

Harley and colleagues (2008) conducted an RCT examining the effectiveness of DBT skills for individuals with depression (treatment-resistant type). Female participants were randomized to a 16-week DBT-based skills group (N = 13) or waitlist control group (N = 11). Both DBT skills and participants were free to receive outside treatment as usual during study, and the majority of the participants across conditions were in non-CBT individual treatment. DBT was superior to waitlist in that those in DBT skills demonstrated significantly greater improvements in depression over the course of treatment, although both conditions showed reductions in depressive symptoms. A follow-up study utilizing this sample indicated that individuals in both DBT skills and waitlist conditions demonstrated increases in emotional processing over time. However, greater emotional processing was associated with decreases in depressive symptoms in the DBT group, and *increases* in depression in the waitlist condition (Feldman et al. 2009).

Strengths of this pilot study include use of blind and reliable HAM-D assessors, adequate explication of background clinician training, six-month follow up assessment, and a detailed overview of the 16-week DBT skills curriculum. Limitations include the lack of an active control group, no adherence monitoring, and limited sample size (Final N = 19) to detect between group differences. Additionally, authors did not control for the potential effects of concurrent individual therapy, which makes it difficult to attribute improvements to DBT-specific factors.

Van Dijk, Jeffrey, & Katz (2012) conducted a pilot RCT to examine DBT skills training among a sample of patients with Bipolar Disorder. Twenty-six adults with Bipolar I or Bipolar II disorder were randomized to a 12-week DBT skills condition (N = 13) or waitlist control condition (N = 13). The DBT skills condition utilized skills drawn directly from the Linehan (1993b) manual, pared down to accommodate an adapted 12-week course, and with an additional emphasis on mindfulness practice. No between-group differences were found; both conditions demonstrated significant improvements in depressive symptoms, mindfulness-based self-efficacy, and emotional self-control. Those in the DBT condition demonstrated a trend towards a more significant improvement in depressive symptoms and mindfulness-based self-efficacy relative to the control condition. Individuals in the DBT group were also highly satisfied with the leaders, format, and skills content. Strengths of this pilot study include a clear, detailed explication of the DBT skills curriculum, and attention to treatment feasibility and acceptability as a pilot intervention. Limitations include a lack of adherence monitoring, lack of active control group, and inadequate description of clinician training and supervision provided.

DBT skills only for eating disorders: Studies without DBT adherence ratings. Telch, Agras, and Linehan (2001) randomized females diagnosed with Binge Eating Disorder (BED) to 20 weekly two-hour DBT skills training sessions adapted for BED (N = 22) or a waitlist control condition (N = 22). The skills programme was an adaptation of the Linehan (1993b) manual with the treatment rationale and strategies consistent with the model of binge eating as a difficulty in emotion regulation (Telch, Agras, & Linehan 2000). Interpersonal Effectiveness, one of the standard four modules taught in DBT skills group, was not taught as part of this DBT adaptation. Diary cards and chain analyses were utilized in the skills group to aid in targeting, assessing, and intervening on ineffective behaviour during skills group. Individualized treatment plans were developed in the last two skills group sessions to facilitate ongoing skills practice and reductions in binge eating. DBT skills training outperformed the waitlist control group in reducing binge eating behaviours. At post-treatment, a significantly greater proportion of those in DBT had stopped binge eating for the previous four weeks (89% vs. 12.5% of waitlist individuals). DBT individuals reported significantly fewer weight, shape, and eating concerns, and fewer urges to eat when experiencing anger, as compared to controls. No between-group differences were found on dietary restraint and other mood problems, such as depression or anxiety.

In a study conducted by Safer, Telch, and Agras (2001), females with Bulimia Nervosa (BN) and sub-threshold BN were randomized to a preliminary evaluation of a 20-week two-hour DBT skills programme (N = 14) or waitlist control condition (N = 15). As in the above study, authors adapted the Linehan (1993b) treatment manual to more closely target behaviours associated with BN (see Wiser & Telch, 1999 for more details). DBT skills training was superior to the control condition in decreasing frequency of both binge eating and purging behaviours, as well as in decreasing emotional eating and negative effect. Of the DBT clients, 29% (N = 4) were abstinent at post-treatment, as compared to 0% of the waitlist control individuals. Of the DBT individuals, 36% (N = 5) reduced binge-eating episodes and purging by 88% and 89% respectively at post-treatment, while 0% of the control condition participants reported reduction in binge-purge episodes.

Strengths shared by both studies include a clear rationale for deviations from standard protocol, while shared limitations include insufficient attention to clinician training, lack of adherence monitoring, and a lack of active control condition, which precludes drawing more definitive conclusions that DBT-specific elements were related to the improvement in ED symptoms (Safer et al., 2001; Telch et al., 2001).

Almost ten years following Safer and Telch's original RCTs, Safer and colleagues (2010) conducted an RCT in which 101 males and females with BED were randomized to a 20-week DBT skills training (N = 50) or an active comparison group therapy utilizing a supportive, Rogerian orientation (ACGT; N = 51). The treatment manual was adapted for BED based on the original DBT skills manual (Safer et al., 2001; Safer, Telch, & Chen, 2009; Telch et al., 2000). Individuals in DBT had significantly lower drop-out rates, greater reductions in eating disorder restraint at post-treatment and follow-up, and greater reductions in self-reported eating concerns at post-treatment. Further, participants in the DBT group achieved binge-eating abstinence and reductions in binge frequency more rapidly than those in ACGT, although between-group differences at follow-up were non-significant. This study advanced beyond the previous studies examining DBT skills training for eating disorders in its use of an active, rigorous control condition (which controlled for therapeutic contact, support, and total contact hours), use of DBT-BED adherence monitoring, and multiple time point follow-up assessment, which enabled the researchers to test whether DBT treatment effects held over time. Study limitations include inadequate description of training and supervision, and inclusion of blind raters to ensure unbiased assessment.

Most recently, Hill, Craighead, and Safer (2011) compared a 12-week skills training in individual session format (N = 18) modified to include Appetite Awareness Training (AAT) to a six-week delayed treatment control (N = 14) for BN. The DBT skills training followed Safer's DBT for Binge Eating and Bulimia manual (Safer et al., 2001; Telch et al., 2000) while the AAT incorporated followed Craighead's Appetite Awareness Workbook (Craighead, 2006). DBT diary card and chain analysis tools were utilized and modified to include appetite monitoring. At treatment mid-point, participants in the appetite-focused DBT (DBT-AF) reported lower frequency of purges and objective binge episodes over the previous month, lower overall eating pathology, and improved appetite awareness, but not improved emotional awareness, as compared to controls. Intent-to-treat analyses revealed that 62% of DBT-AF participants no longer met full or sub-threshold criteria for BN, and 72% of post-treatment reduction in binge episodes occurred by week six; improvement similar among treatment completers. No significant between-group differences were found for subjective binge episodes, negative affect, emotional eating, or self-efficacy. Strengths include a thorough explanation and rationale for the treatment adaptation provided, high client and therapist ratings of treatment acceptability, and blind, reliable raters for both diagnostic and outcome assessments. Limitations include lack of an active control group and follow-up assessments; future research is needed to determine if this adaptation outperforms other treatments over time. Lastly, the waitlist controls were invited into DBT-AF at six weeks, preventing a comparison of the full 12-week DBT-AF treatment to a control condition.

DBT skills only for ADHD: Studies without DBT adherence ratings. One of the most recent randomized controlled trials was conducted in a Swedish outpatient clinic for adults diagnosed with ADHD (Hirvikoski et al., 2011). Participants were randomized to a two-hour 14-week DBT-informed skills training for ADHD (N = 26) or a loosely structured discussion based control group centred on ADHD topics (N = 25). The DBT followed the German adaptation of the DBT skills workbook (Hesslinger et al., 2004) with adaptations for a Swedish population. A review of the content of the DBT skills training sessions reveals significant deviations from the standard DBT skills model, including the addition of ADHD psychoeducation, medication management, teachings on stress management and organization, behavioural analysis, and the omission of standard Distress Tolerance and Interpersonal Effectiveness content. DBT was superior to control in leading to a significant reduction in ADHD symptoms for those in DBT skills group only. While participant-rated satisfaction and treatment feasibility was high in both groups, the DBT skills group was rated as more credible at pre- and post-treatment. No significant reductions in comorbid psychiatric difficulties (mood disorders, learning disabilities, sleep problems) were found in either group.

Strengths include a clear, detailed explication of the DBT skills curriculum, follow-up assessment, and attention paid to treatment feasibility and acceptability as a pilot intervention. Limitations include a lack of adherence monitoring, and inadequate description of clinician training and supervision provided. Lack of adherence monitoring and significant deviations from the standard skills format weaken our ability to draw conclusions about the extent to which DBT skills are effective for an ADHD population.

Most recently, Fleming et al. (2015) conducted a pilot RCT testing the feasibility and efficacy of an adapted eight-week DBT skills only condition (N = 17) to skills handouts (SH; N = 16) for college students with ADHD. Results indicated that participants found the DBT skills only both acceptable and feasible, and the DBT skills condition outperformed skills handouts in reducing problems in executive functioning (EF) and leading to higher rates of recovery into the normal range on ADHD and EF. Interestingly, participants rated mindfulness and structuring environment as most useful, and ADHD psychoeducation as least useful. Study strengths include a detailed explication of the skills intervention, follow-up assessment, and adequate clinician training. Limitations include lack of an active, rigorous control condition, small sample size, and lack of adherence monitoring.

Summary of DBT Quality Assurance Methods

The first aim of the review was to provide a comprehensive summary of the research findings from DBT RCTs to date, informed by the quality assurance methods utilized by each trial. The second aim was to provide a summary on quality assurance methods utilized across the DBT RCTs, including the use of adherence ratings, supervision, and other training methods. Only 52% (N = 16) of the 31 distinct research trials reviewed described the use of adherence monitoring in their study. Of these 16 RCTs, three trials reported conducting self-assessed adherence or adherence informally assessed by an on-site DBT supervisor, and eleven trials utilized formal, systematic adherence ratings derived from standardized research instruments. When reported, global adherence scores ranged from 3.8–4.2, indicating generally adequate adherence. One trial requested standardized adherence assessment through the University of Washington, but it was not available to them (Carter et al., 2010). As a follow-up examination of the data, we compared outcomes of the ten comprehensive DBT studies that obtained adherence ratings to the nine studies that neither utilized a standard adherence measure nor obtained ratings. A review of the data reveals no major differences; regardless of whether the trial conducted adherence assessment, roughly 50% of the 19 studies favoured DBT across all primary outcomes, and approximately a quarter of studies resulted in zero primary outcomes favouring DBT. Additional empirical investigations are needed to explore the extent to which DBT adherence is (or is not) linked to favourable clinical outcomes.

In terms of training available to clinicians, a wide range of training methods was used: 58% (N = 18) of studies reported that some or all of their clinicians received intensive or intensive-equivalent training (didactic and competency-based training), with the majority of clinicians receiving intensive training prior to study start. The modal number of trials received a rating of "2" on our training scale, indicating that some clinicians (but not all) had received formal DBT training before or during study. Of the studies, 52% explicitly mentioned participating in an on-site training consisting of seminars and other didactic methods before and/or during the study, and

77% reported that their clinicians received ongoing supervision or consultation, although the nature, frequency, and duration of supervision were often unspecified. When supervision or consultation was delivered, 61% of the supervision/consultation was performed by at least one individual with recognized expertise in DBT (defined in this review as a nationally or internationally recognized DBT trainer and/or treatment developer). While follow-up assessment with first authors yielded much richer and more promising information about the use of consultation, supervision, and training methods in each RCT, it is notable that less than 10% of studies *published* sufficient detail/level of training and supervision to fully inform consumers, despite what we know about the importance of ongoing supervision to maintain model fidelity (McHugh & Barlow, 2012).

Results from the quality assurance rating of study methodology reveal that across DBT trials, strengths included the use of standardized diagnostic and outcome instruments, blind raters, and adequate randomization methods (including ensuring that samples were comparable at baseline). Limitations included lack of rigorous data analytic methods—only 10% of original RCTs reviewed utilized corrections for multiple comparisons, such as the Bonferroni method, few to none of the studies reviewed conducted adequate in-study power analyses, and the majority of studies failed to present in-study reliability on diagnostic and outcome assessments. Of the trials, 48% conducted some post-treatment follow-up assessment, and only 13% conducted follow-up assessment a year or more later. Additional attention is needed to increase the rigour of data analytic methods, and to increase the use of follow-up assessment to test sustainability of clinical improvements over time.

DISCUSSION

The primary aim of this review was to provide a comprehensive summary and critique of the standard DBT and DBT skills only RCTs to date. The secondary aim of our review was to provide an evaluative overview of quality assurance methods used in DBT studies to date, with particular attention to clinician training, adherence monitoring, and quality of research procedures followed. To this aim, we rated DBT RCTs on a revised version of the Psychotherapy Quality Rating Scale (RCT-PQRS; Kocsis et al., 2010) to inform our conclusions regarding DBT's effectiveness for particular clinical populations and problem behaviours from the perspective of quality assurance.

Division 12 Task Force designates a treatment as having "well-established empirical evidence" once two or more RCTs reveal superior results to an active or placebo condition criterion (Chambless & Hollon, 1998). Based on this criterion, Comprehensive DBT has well-established evidence for efficacy with suicidal and self-injurious behaviours, comorbid BPD, and substance use problems, as well as for high treatment retention. Following the same criteria, the DBT skills only treatment model has well-established empirical evidence for efficacy with treatment-resistant depression, binge eating, and bulimia disorders. Below we provide more detailed conclusions on DBT's efficacy organized by the primary categories of DBT targets: life-threatening behaviours, treatment-interfering behaviours (such as therapy drop-out), and quality of life (QoL)-interfering behaviours (such as mood and substance disorders). Secondarily, we provide recommendations for future research on DBT and quality assurance.

Comprehensive DBT and Life-threatening Behaviours

Comprehensive DBT has solid research support for its treatment of suicidal behaviours (Koons et al., 2001; Linehan et al., 1991; Pistorello et al., 2012); and NSSI behaviours (Linehan et al., 1991; Linehan et al., 2006; Pistorello et al., 2012; Priebe et al., 2012; van den Bosch et al., 2002). The use of DBT adherence ratings and rigorous control groups in several of these RCT trials (Linehan et al., 2006; Pistorello et al., 2012) lend further confidence to DBT's favourable outcomes on suicidal and NSSI behaviours. While still other studies found that DBT outperformed control groups on both suicidal and self-injurious behaviours, consumers of research should take caution before drawing conclusions from studies that lack fidelity to the standard DBT treatment model (Turner, 2000). At the same time, further research is needed to parse apart what elements of a DBT-informed treatment (as used in Turner's study) are leading to significant improvements in suicidal behaviour. Several DBT RCT trials that met a high quality-assurance standard (provided rigorous control groups and adherence to treatment) failed to find significant differences in reduction of all suicidal behaviours across treatment conditions (Linehan et al., 2002; Linehan et al., 2006; Linehan et al., 2015; McMain et al., 2009). One possible explanation for this finding is that clinician expertise and experience in treating suicidal and multi-problem clients (factors common to rigorous comparison groups used in these particular studies) are key factors in the effective treatment of suicidal behaviour. Some DBT RCT studies *without* a high quality-assurance standard failed to detect between group differences in NSSI and other significant areas of dysregulation (Carter et al., 2010; Goldstein et al., 2015). In such cases, the findings may also be attributable to small sample size and a floor effect resultant from low NSSI base rates, as suggested in Koons et al. (2001).

Comprehensive DBT and Treatment-Interfering Behaviour

Treatment-interfering behaviour (TIB) in DBT includes, but is not limited to, client behaviours such as dropping out of treatment, lateness, aggressive behaviour towards therapist or group members, and refusal to collaborate in treatment. This review focuses exclusively on one type of TIB—treatment drop-out. A large number of studies

found that DBT was superior to the comparison group in terms of treatment retention (Courbasson et al., 2012; Linehan et al., 1991; Linehan et al., 1999; Linehan et al.,
2006; Verheul et al., 2003). In contrast, one study found the comparison treatment
(Comprehensive Validation+12-step) had significantly lower drop-out rates than
DBT, which may be partially attributable to the condition's strong emphasis on validation and warmth (Linehan et al., 2006). Taken together, these findings indicate
that DBT's multi-pronged emphasis on commitment strategies, genuine validation
of the patient's experience, and delivery of practical coping skills and structure to
enhance the quality of patients' lives likely play a synergistic role in promoting treatment retention. In other studies, DBT treatment drop-out was high (i.e., 52–56%). In
studies by both Feigenbaum et al. and Priebe et al., wide inclusion criteria may have
led to higher drop-out for several reasons: not only could broader inclusionary criteria lead to especially complex cases prone to drop-out, but such broad criteria (e.g.,
other PDs besides BPD) may extend beyond the existing evidence base of clients that
DBT can effectively treat and retain. Feigenbaum et al. (2012) also posits that lower
quality treatment delivered by one DBT therapist may have contributed to the high
drop-out rate, whilst Priebe et al. used a more conservative drop-out rule in comparison to other studies.

Comprehensive DBT and Quality of Life-Interfering Behaviour

Several trials provide evidence that comprehensive DBT with a systematic focus on
substance use may be an efficacious treatment for comorbid BPD and substance abuse,
compared to control groups (Harned et al., 2008; Linehan et al., 1999; Linehan et al.,
2002). The failure to detect significant between-group differences in substance use
within van den Bosch's 2002 study may be due to the absence of substance-specific treatment strategies, such as dialectical abstinence and adaptive denial, which were included
in the Linehan et al. 1999 and 2002 studies. Still other studies found that DBT outperformed controls in reducing other behaviours that may interfere with QoL, such as
anger (Koons et al., 2001; Linehan et al., 1993), depressive behaviours (Koons et al., 2001;
Pistorello et al., 2012), and hospitalizations (Linehan et al., 1991; Linehan et al., 2006).
While these results are promising, more studies assessing adherent, standard DBT for
life quality behaviours are needed before one can confidently state that DBT is efficacious in these domains. In a comparison between DBT and two other BPD treatments
(transference-focused psychotherapy and supportive therapy), transference-focused
therapy led to the widest range of improvements in impulsivity, anger, and assaults,
compared to DBT and supportive therapy (Clarkin et al., 2007). Without the use of
formal adherence ratings to more precisely assess treatment delivered in each condition, it is difficult to make definitive conclusions or interpretations of the data. Follow-
up research that uses formal adherence ratings and provides a closer focus on each

treatment's mechanisms of action could clarify further whether TFP outperforms DBT in these domains, and if so, why. Overall, comprehensive DBT holds promise for reducing behaviours that interfere with QoL, such as substance use, anger, and depressive behaviours, particularly if such behaviours are systematically targeted in the context of a DBT treatment hierarchy framework. The research evidence on DBT skills only in the following section may also inform what particular QoL behaviours may be effectively targeted within Comprehensive DBT, once life-threatening behaviours have been effectively treated and reduced.

DBT Skills Only and Quality of Life-Interfering Behaviour

DBT skills only and mood disorders. The evidence base for DBT skills only has expanded rapidly more recently, with the majority of the skills-only studies published in the past five years. Results from the skills-only studies reveal the efficacy of DBT skills for depression (two independent RCTs and one RCT for skills only plus coaching) and anxiety symptoms (two independent RCTs). Mixed research support and fewer research trials have been conducted for DBT skills only in treating BPD, ADHD, BPD-related mood problems, and high emotion dysregulation, and several implications and limitations are worth mentioning. First, 92% of the skills-only studies failed to assess DBT adherence, which prevents stronger conclusions being drawn about what exact treatment is being delivered in the majority of DBT skills studies. Secondly, while a few RCTs on DBT skills to date favour DBT for select mood-related outcomes (Goldstein et al., 2015; Soler et al., 2009), DBT skills conditions has not been shown as superior to comparison conditions in reducing suicide attempts, self-injury, or hospitalizations. Additional research is needed on DBT skills only before more definitive conclusions can be drawn about the appropriateness of DBT skills only as a standalone treatment for those with severe emotion dysregulation, notably suicidal and NSSI behaviour.

Such research questions about the efficacy of skills only are beginning to be explored via component-analyses studies designed to isolate what mode of treatment (or particular skills) lead to clinical change. DBT emotion regulation skills led to reductions in BPD criteria, including NSSI, relative to other skills conditions (Dixon-Gordon, Chapman, & Turner, 2013), and a more recent component analysis at the site of treatment development indicates that those conditions with skills training components out-performed DBT-individual therapy alone in reducing NSSI (Linehan et al., 2015). Furthermore, in their 2014 study, Neacsiu et al. revealed that adherently delivered DBT skills outperformed an active control condition in reducing high emotion dysregulation and anxiety symptoms.

DBT skills only and eating disorders. The majority of the DBT skills-only studies for ED utilize a small sample size, lack adherence monitoring, incorporate additional treatment strategies beyond "skills only", and utilize non-active waitlist control conditions (see Hill et al., 2011; Safer et al., 2001; Telch et al., 2001) which, taken together, limit claims that DBT skill-specific factors are leading to treatment effects for an eating disordered population. On the other hand, Safer et al.'s (2010) enhanced sample size, use of adherence monitoring, and rigorous control group matched to contact hours and treatment modality enhance our confidence in DBT skills conditions' faster binge remission and lower treatment drop-out. Research is needed on these and other populations before researchers and clinicians can state with confidence that DBT skills only is a first-line treatment for these treatment groups.

DBT Skills Only Conclusions

Another notable conclusion of this review is that the definition of "DBT Skills Only" lacks clarity and standardization across studies. In this review, skills-only studies range from eight to 28 weeks, where some studies used the complete model (which includes a therapist consultation team), some studies incorporated individualized treatment plans and/or diary cards into skills training, and still other research teams only utilized select DBT skills. The use of a "pared down" or adapted skills package for certain settings and populations, while potentially quite reasonable and indicated, is often delivered in these studies without any strong rationale provided. Due to the heterogeneity of the skills-only studies reviewed, it is difficult to develop a cogent statement about the clinical implication for DBT skills only—other than "some DBT skills work for some populations some of the time". The next steps for researchers are to provide more detail on DBT skills used, as well as sound rationale for deviations from the standard skills group content and structure. Several studies reviewed (see Harley et al., 2008; Hirvikoski et al., 2011; Neacsiu et al., 2014) provide excellent and thorough explications of the content of their DBT skills programmes, which enable researchers and clinicians to replicate the skills content in future programmes. Furthermore, researchers such as Courbasson et al. (2012) reported specific feedback from DBT participants; participants rated mindfulness, validation, and the therapeutic alliance as particularly helpful, in that these elements helped address their multiple problems simultaneously in a supportive therapeutic context. While this feedback is anecdotal, future researchers would benefit from collecting such information as it begins to suggest specific treatment mechanisms of action. Providing more detail on DBT skills used and clear rationale for treatment deviations will also enable consumers of the literature to meaningfully consider which treatment components (and specific DBT skills) are most effective with which populations.

Limitations and Strengths

Limitations of this review include its exclusive focus on RCTs and exclusion of effectiveness trials, quasi-experimental (controlled, non-randomized) trials, case studies, and unpublished literature. We recognize that excluding unpublished papers, known as "grey literature" can yield an overestimation of RCT efficacy (McAuley, Pham, Tugwell, & Moher, 2000). Researchers and clinicians would profit from a follow-up review that encompasses a wider scope of DBT studies and research designs. Finally, this review did not include RCTs currently underway (e.g. Linehan, Asarnow, and McCauley, forthcoming), which are investigating the efficacy for DBT with adolescents with suicidal and self-injurious behaviours. Lastly, use of a single-rater approach regarding the quality assurance scale prevents the calculation of inter-rater reliability scores. Further, the decision to modify the rating instrument used in this review presents a dialectical dilemma—while the addition of sub-criteria for the rating scales provided more specificity and consistency during the rating process, modifying a standardized instrument naturally compromises its validity. Regardless, one strength of this review was the systematic scoring of all RCT studies on an instrument designed to quantify quality assurance (the use of the RCT-PQRS; Kocsis et al., 2010) and using the ratings to inform our interpretation of efficacy of DBT for various populations and clinical problems. An additional strength is attempted email contact with each author to augment the published information on use of quality assurance methods such as supervision, training, and adherence methods.

Future Directions

Ultimately, there is a need for more extensive and feasible formal adherence ratings. While a greater proportion of studies are conducting adherence ratings as compared to the last DBT review (see Lynch et al., 2007), still as many as 60% of the published RCTs to date are not reporting specific adherence ratings derived from a standardized adherence instrument. Given that RCTs are considered the "gold standard" in the field of clinical science due to their use of randomization and comparison treatment, it is concerning that only roughly 50% of the studies reviewed used adherence monitoring of any kind. Furthermore, there appears to be variability in what the authors categorize as "adherent" across the studies; while some earlier researchers cite 3.8 as "adequate adherence" (Koons et al., 2001; Verheul et al., 2003) more recent studies cite 4.0 as the adherence cut-off score (Linehan et al., 2006; Mehlum et al., 2014; Pistorello et al., 2012). These findings are consistent with NREPP's observation that lack of clarity around adherence monitoring is one of DBT's general weaknesses in treatment outcome research (NREPP, 2006). We conjecture that time and monetary resources, as well as lack of access to and training on standardized adherence rating instruments, were obstacles to adherence monitoring, although such obstacles were not systematically assessed in this review. Obstacles to obtaining adherence ratings merit further investigation.

As mentioned previously, a minority of studies conducted self-assessed adherence or adherence assessed by DBT supervisor. While it is commendable that these researchers recognize the importance of adherence assessment for quality control purposes, it is unclear whether adherence collected in these ways yields reliable adherence results, particularly if these self-administered measures have not been validated against the standardized DBT adherence instrument, known as the DBT Expert Rating Scale (Linehan et al., 1996). Researchers should consider ways to increase access to adherence measurement without compromising adherence quality, perhaps by devising a validated self-assessment version of the standardized adherence instrument and/or creating sustainable training programmes to expand the base of qualified adherence coders. It is quite likely that community-based clinics with fewer resources would have even less access to quality-assurance measures such as adherence ratings, supervision, and tape review than RCTs, and therefore, devising time- and cost-effective quality control methods is of high priority. When adherence and fidelity are not assessed, researchers cannot be certain what treatment is being investigated, clinicians cannot be certain what treatment they are delivering, and clients cannot be certain what treatment they are receiving.

The need for systematic assessment of therapist competency. While adherence refers to the degree to which the treatment strategies were delivered at sufficient "dose and timing", clinician competence assesses the level of skill with which an intervention is delivered (Waltz, Addis, Koerner, & Jacobson, 1993). Yet despite the growing attention to the importance of adherence monitoring, little has been done to address and assess therapist *competency* in the context of DBT delivery; for example, a literature search of "Dialectical Behavior Therapy" and "competency" yields only six results. Koerner (2013) begins to address this underexplored area in suggesting six clear principles and corresponding skill domains in which a DBT clinician must gain competency, all of which are speculated to link to good clinical outcomes. She introduces the benefits of a "practice-based modular competency" approach, which supports the flexible application of areas of clinical competency that can be used within multiple treatment frameworks and manuals. Further empirical attention to the validation and dissemination of DBT competency checklists for clinicians and exploration of how said competencies relate to clinical outcomes is warranted.

The need for definitions and delivery of evidence-based training and supervision. Future attention to what constitutes "adequate" and evidence-based training and supervision is needed, as little is empirically known at this time about the link between certain DBT training models and therapist and client outcomes. For example, is video review-based supervision a necessary component for successful trainee and client outcomes, or is the relationship between video review and outcomes moderated by trainee experience? What training models are linked to clinician competence and client behaviour change over time? A quick literature search of "DBT Training" as of 2015 yields a mere eight peer-reviewed publications to date, 38% of which are theoretical in nature. Preliminary associations have been found between training dose and client outcomes; in one study, clients of clinicians with ten-day intensive training demonstrated greater reductions in suicidal and NSSI behaviour as compared to clients of clinicians who received a basic four-day training (Pasieczny & Connor, 2011).

There is also preliminary support for an association between DBT intensive training and use of DBT modes; in a nationwide study of 129 clinicians, those clinicians with intensive training incorporated skills groups, consultation team, and phone coaching more frequently into DBT treatment than those clinicians who had received two- to five-day workshops, although this study is limited by clinician self-report (DiGiorgio, Glass, & Arnkoff, 2010). While those in the field recognize the ten-day DBT intensive training and core clinical training (or equivalent) to be standard models for baseline training in DBT, more rigorous research is needed to compare those with this type of training to those with other non-intensive-equivalent DBT training on client outcomes and therapist competence before any further conclusions can be drawn about how much, and what type, of DBT training is necessary for clinician competence and client improvement. Further, we recognize that our ratings of clinician training for the purposes of this review likely are biased favourably towards more recent trials, since more recent trials have clearer parameters and more options as compared to training options in earlier studies.

The need for transparency and strategic decisions on treatment adaptations. This review included 13 DBT RCTs published in the last five years, roughly half of which tested DBT skills-only interventions. Such prolific development is promising and suggests wide applicability of the skills to treat a variety of clinical problems and populations. At the same time, it is important that authors are transparent in terms of the skills tested, treatment schedule, and the decision-making process that led to those choices. Otherwise, critically analysing the findings from this research area will be challenging, and questions regarding what skills work, for which clinical problems, under what type of conditions, will be very difficult to answer.

Conclusion

Overall, DBT efficacy studies have moved far beyond the site of treatment development, with results having been replicated across eight countries, 21 treatment sites, and 12 distinct patient populations. This expansion of RCT research investigating DBT with a wide variety of clinical problems and populations performed by many independent research sites speaks to the potential of DBT to effectively address clinical problems across diagnosis, levels of severity, and treatment settings. This research expansion is exciting and likely to lead to varied and important clinical implications for the efficacy of DBT. Moving forward, it is important for the research community to follow quality assurance procedures such that quality is not exchanged for quantity and findings can be interpreted with confidence. This will allow researchers to continue to strategically build upon a knowledge base of DBT to benefit clinicians in the pursuit of adequate training, and clients in the pursuit of compassionate, evidence-based care.

Key Messages for Clinicians

- Efficacy of Comprehensive DBT is substantiated for suicidal and self-injurious treatment populations, and comorbid BPD and substance use, and DBT generally evidenced superior treatment retention to control treatments.
- DBT-Skills only has well-established empirical evidence for efficacy with treatment resistant depression, anxiety, binge eating, and bulimia disorders.
- Quality assurance method strengths included standardized assessments, blind raters, and adequate randomization. Limitations included lack of power analyses, in-study reliability, and only 13% of trials conducted follow up assessment at least one year later.
- 35% of all DBT trials utilized formal adherence ratings, when reported scores ranged from 3.8–4.2, indicating generally adequate treatment adherence.
- 58% of studies reported some or all clinicians received intensive or intensive-equivalent DBT training, most prior to study start.
- More attention is needed towards increasing accessibility and prevalence of ongoing adherence monitoring, supervision, and baseline DBT training.

APPENDIX

PSYCHOTHERAPY QUALITY RATING SCALE-REVISED[a]

Description of subjects

Item 1. Diagnostic method and criteria for inclusion and exclusion

0 = poor description and inappropriate method/criteria

1 = full description or appropriate method/criteria

- *explanation of how a psychological construct (MR, psychosis, cognitive impairment) was not included or missing for 1 or more constructs*

2 = full description and appropriate method/criteria

- *if the inclusion criterion is not a diagnosis (e.g., trauma) a validated self report measure was employed*
- *used SCID or IPDE interview or an experienced clinician made a diagnosis based on the DSM or the ICD*

---

[a] Scale information provided in full. Information provided in italics are specific sub-criteria generated by authors of this review to ensure that each item is operationally defined.

Item 2. Documentation or demonstration of reliability of diagnostic methodology

0 = poor or no reliability documentation

1 = brief reliability documentation (documentation in the literature is sufficient, even if not explicitly cited)

- *measure has reliability and validity support from the literature but no in-study reliability data presented*

2 = full reliability documentation (documentation of within-study reliability necessary)

- *for interviews—kappas, ICCs, or % agreement is presented*
- *for self report—authors present cronbach alpha for the sample*

Item 3. Description of relevant comorbidities

0 = poor or no description of relevant comorbidities

1 = brief description of relevant comorbidities

- *relevant comorbidities listed but no specific %'s indicated*

2 = full description of relevant comorbidities

- *presents % of participants with affective disorders and substance use disorders (common comorbidities with BPD and other emotion regulation problems), unless disorder explicitly stated as an exclusionary criteria*

Item 4. Description of numbers of subjects screened, included, and excluded

0 = poor or no description of numbers screened, included, and excluded

- *e.g., information about only the included participants is given*

1 = brief description of numbers screened, included, and excluded

- *incomplete information regarding why people were excluded (e.g., no % excluded listed)*

2 = full description of numbers screened, included, and excluded

- *diagram or complete narrative description that clearly indicates how many were included and excluded at each stage of the study*

Definition and delivery of treatment

Item 5. Treatment(s) (including control/comparison groups) are sufficiently described or referenced to allow for replication

0 = poor or no treatment description or references

- *multiple criteria from below are missing*

1 = brief treatment description or references (also if full description of one group and poor description of another)

- *even if DBT condition is sufficiently described (as outlined below), may still receive a 1 if any element of other condition (e.g., TAU) is vaguely described or not cited such that another study could not replicate*

- *1 of the criteria below are missing*

2 = full treatment description or references (manual not required)

- *there is description of all modes*
- *there is mention that the strategies and philosophy common to DBT are used (clear citation is also sufficient)*
- *if the study is a skills training adaptation we have exact info about what skills were taught*
- *if any adaptation there is clear explanation and rationale for all modifications used*
- *if an active treatment lists a specific citation, and DBT condition is sufficiently detailed*

Item 6. Method to demonstrate that treatment being studied is treatment being delivered (only satisfied by supervision if transcripts or tapes are explicitly reviewed)

0 = poor or no adherence reporting

1 = brief adherence reporting with standardized measure or full adherence reporting with non-standardized measure (e.g., non-independent rater)

- *authors state self-assessed or supervisor assessed adherence conducted*

2 = full adherence reporting with standardized measure (must be quantitative and completed by an independent rater)

- *independent raters rated sessions for adherence using standardized instrument; scores included*

Item 7. Therapist training and level of experience in the treatment(s) under investigation

0 = poor description and underqualified therapists

1 = full description or well-qualified therapists

2 = full description and well-qualified

- *DBT therapists intensively trained and/or trained or supervised by expert and/or rated at adherence*

Item 8. Therapist supervision while treatment is being provided

0 = poor description and inadequate therapist supervision

1 = full description or adequate therapist supervision

2 = full description and adequate therapist supervision

- *expert supervision*
- *at least monthly*

- *full description (how often, how long)*
- *criteria above applies to both DBT and control treatment*

Item 9. Description of concurrent treatments (e.g., medication) allowed and administered during course of study

0 = poor or no description of concurrent treatments

1 = brief description of concurrent treatments

2 = full description of concurrent treatments

Outcome measures

Item 10. Validated outcome measure(s) (either established or newly standardized)

0 = poor or no validation of outcome measure(s)

1 = brief validation of outcome measure(s) (shown or cited)

- *incomplete information or at least one instrument doesn't have validation data*

2 = full validation of outcome measure(s) (shown or cited)

Item 11. Primary outcome measure(s) specified in advance (although does not need to be stated explicitly for a rating of 2)

0 = poor or no specification of primary outcome measure(s) in advance

1 = brief specification of primary outcome measure(s) in advance

- *unclear or vague identification of primary outcome measures hypotheses (e.g., will test between condition differences in psychopathology)*

2 = full specification of primary outcome measure(s) in advance

Item 12. Outcome assessment by raters blinded to treatment group and with established reliability

0 = poor or no blinding of raters to treatment group (e.g., rating by therapist, non-blind independent rater, or patient self-report) and reliability not reported

1 = blinding of independent raters to treatment group or established reliability

- *no mention of reliability and/or incomplete reliability info given for self reports within the sample, but do have blind raters*

2 = blinding of independent raters to treatment group and established reliability

- *study reliability reported for actual outcome measures (including self-report and interview-based outcome measures)*

Item 13. Discussion of safety and adverse events during study treatment(s)

0 = poor or no discussion of safety and adverse events

1 = brief discussion of safety and adverse events

2 = full discussion of safety and adverse events

Item 14.   Assessment of long-term post-termination outcome

0 = poor or no post-termination assessment of outcome

1 = medium-term assessment of post-termination outcome (2–12 months post-termination)

- *assessment f/up defined as 2–11 months upon termination to distinguish from "2" rating*

2 = long-term assessment of post-termination outcome (≥ 12 months post-termination)

Data analysis

Item 15.   Intent-to-treat method for data analysis involving primary outcome measure

0 = no description or no intent-to-treat analysis with primary outcome measure

1 = partial intent-to-treat analysis with primary outcome measure

- *all identified outcomes do not have ITT analyses or ITT definition changes*

2 = full intent-to-treat analysis with primary outcome measure

Item 16.   Description of drop-outs and withdrawals

0 = poor or no description of drop-outs and withdrawals

1 = brief description of drop-outs and withdrawals

2 = full description of drop-outs and withdrawals (must be explicitly stated and include reasons for drop-outs and withdrawals)

Item 17.   Appropriate statistical tests (eg, use of Bonferroni correction, longitudinal data analysis, adjustment only for a priori identified confounders)

0 = inappropriate statistics, extensive data dredging, or no information about appropriateness of statistics

1 = moderately appropriate, though unsophisticated, statistics and/or moderate data dredging

- *Bonferroni correction lacking or incomplete*

2 = fully appropriate statistics and minimal data dredging in primary findings

Item 18.   Adequate sample size

0 = inadequate justification and inadequate sample size

- *if no power analyses or power analyses on odd outcome*

1 = adequate justification or adequate sample size

- *if power analysis with poor methodology/doesn't match analytic method in rest of paper*

- *if the study is pilot/preliminary trial and no power analyses*

2 = adequate justification and adequate sample size

- *if power analysis using proper methodology (same as used in the outcome analyses)*

Item 19. Appropriate consideration of therapist and site effects

0 = therapist and site effects not discussed or considered

1 = therapist and site effects discussed or considered statistically

2 = therapist and site effects discussed and considered statistically

- *if analyses include specific individual therapist characteristics and site characteristics, and both characteristics are discussed at some point*

Treatment assignment

Item 20. A priori relevant hypotheses that justify comparison group(s)

0 = poor or no justification of comparison group(s)

1 = brief or incomplete justification of comparison group(s)

- *justification that too few studies exist for the current guidelines is not sufficient to explain choice of control condition (ex of rating 1)*

2 = full justification of comparison group(s)

Item 21. Comparison group(s) from same population and time frame as experimental group

0 = comparison group(s) from significantly different population and/or time frame

- *>2 significant differences and differences not covaried*

1 = comparison group(s) from moderately different population and/or time frame

- *≤ 2 significant differences and differences not covaried*

2 = comparison group(s) from same population and time frame

- *<2 significant differences and differences covaried*

Item 22. Randomized assignment to treatment groups

0 = poor (e.g., pseudo-randomization, sequential assignment) or no randomization

1 = adequate but poorly defined randomization procedure

2 = full and appropriate method of randomization performed after screening and baseline assessment

Overall quality of study

Item 23. Balance of allegiance to types of treatment by practitioners

0 = no information or poor balance of allegiance to treatments by study therapists (e.g., therapy in experimental and control groups both administered by therapists with strong allegiance to therapy being tested in the experimental group)

1 = some balance of allegiance to treatments by study therapists

2 = full balance of allegiance to treatments (e.g., therapies administered by therapists with allegiance to respective techniques)

- *if TAU therapists have roughly equivalent training/experience background in respective treatments then can rate a 2. The word "allegiance" does not have to be specifically referenced to receive a full rating*

Item 24. Conclusions of study justified by sample, measures, and data analysis, as presented (note: useful to look at conclusions as stated in study abstract)

0 = poor or no justification of conclusions from results as presented or insufficient information to evaluate (e.g., sample or treatment insufficiently documented, data analysis does not support conclusions, or numbers of withdrawals or drop-outs makes findings unsupportable)

1 = some conclusions of study justified or partial information presented to evaluate

2 = all conclusions of study justified and complete information presented to evaluate

Item 25. Omnibus rating: please provide an overall rating of the quality of the study, taking into account the adequacy of description, the quality of study design, data analysis, and justification of conclusions

The following elements were assessed for this rating:
- *active control (TAU) or rigorous control (active control + controlling for specific treatment elements (e.g., CV + 12s; CTBE));*
- *adequate analyses (Bonferroni and/or intent to treat analyses);*
- *adequate measurement (in-study reliability, blind raters, standardized instruments);*
- *1 year follow up; adequate justification of conclusions.*

7 (exceptionally good): rigorous control and data analysis, and f/up assessment at 1 year or longer

6 (very good): one of above criteria missing

5 (moderately good): 2+ criteria missing

4 (average): 3+ criteria missing

3 (moderately poor): 4+ criteria missing

2 (very poor)

1 (exceptionally poor)

References

Bedics, J., Atkins, D. C., Comtois, K. A., & Linehan, M. M. (2012). Treatment differences in the therapeutic relationship and introject during a 2-year randomized controlled trial of dialectical behavior therapy versus non-behavioral psychotherapy experts for borderline personality disorder. *Journal of Clinical and Consulting Psychology, 80*(1), 66–77.

Beidas, R. S., & Kendall, P. C. (2010). Training therapists in evidence-based practice: A critical review of studies from a systems-contextual perspective. *Clinical Psychology: Science and Practice, 17*(1), 1–30.

Bellg, A. J., Borrelli, B., Resnick, B., Hecht, J., Minicucci, D. S., Ory, M., . . . Czajkowski, S. (2004). Enhancing treatment fidelity in health behavior change studies: best practices and recommendations from the NIH Behavior Change Consortium. *Health Psychology, 23*(5), 443.

Bohus, M., Dyer, A. S., Priebe, K., Krüger, A., Kleindienst, N., Schmahl, C., . . . Steil, R. (2013). Dialectical behaviour therapy for post-traumatic stress disorder after childhood sexual abuse in patients with and without borderline personality disorder: A randomised controlled trial. *Psychotherapy and Psychosomatics, 82*(4), 221–233.

Bradley, R. G., & Follingstad, D. R. (2003). Group therapy for incarcerated women who experienced interpersonal violence: a pilot study. *Journal of Traumatic Stress, 16*(4), 337–340.

Carter, G. L., Willcox, C. H., Lewin, T. J., Conrad, A. M., & Bendit, N. (2010). Hunter DBT project: a randomized controlled trial of dialectical behaviour therapy in women with borderline personality disorder. *Australian & New Zealand Journal of Psychiatry, 44*, 162–173.

Chambless D. L., & Hollon, S. D. (1998). Defining empirically supported therapies. *Journal of Consulting and Clinical Psychology, 66*, 7–18.

Clarkin, J. F., Levy, K. N., Lenzenweger, M. F., & Kernberg, O. F. (2007). Evaluating three treatments for borderline personality disorder: a multiwave study. *American Journal of Psychiatry, 164*, 922–928.

Clarkin, J. F., Yeomans, F., & Kernberg, O. F. (1999). *Transference-focused psychodynamic therapy for borderline personality disorder patients.* Arlington, VA: American Psychiatric Publishing.

Cohen, J. A., Mannarino, A. P., & Deblinger, E. (2006). *Treating trauma and traumatic grief in children and adolescents.* New York: Guilford Press.

Courbasson, C., Nishikawa, Y., & Dixon, L. (2012). Outcome of dialectical behaviour therapy for concurrent eating and substance use disorders. *Clinical Psychology & Psychotherapy, 19*(5), 434–449.

Craighead, L. W. (2006), *The appetite awareness workbook: How to listen to your body and overcome bingeing, overeating, and obsession with food.* Oakland, CA: New Harbinger Publications.

Crowell, S. E., Beauchaine, T. P., & Linehan, M. M. (2009). A biosocial developmental model of borderline personality: Elaborating and extending Linehan's theory. *Psychological Bulletin, 135*(3), 495.

DBT: Comprehensive Training for Independent Practitioners™ (n.d.). Retrieved 13 December 2014, from http://behavioraltech.org/training/IndependentPractitioners.cfm

DiGiorgio, K. E., Glass, C. R., & Arnkoff, D. B. (2010). Therapists use of DBT: A survey study of clinical practice. *Cognitive and Behavioral Practice, 17*(2), 213–221.

Dixon-Gordon, K. L., Chapman, A. L., & Turner, B. J. (2013). A preliminary investigation of the specificity of effects of dialectical behavior therapy emotion regulation skills training. *Psychotherapy*: Invited article under review.

Feigenbaum, J. D., Fonagy, P., Pilling, S., Jones, A., Wildgoose, A., & Bebbington, P. E. (2012). A real-world study of the effectiveness of DBT in the UK National Health Service. *British Journal of Clinical Psychology, 51*(2), 121–141.

Feldman, G., Harley, R., Kerrigan, M., Jacobo, M., & Fava, M. (2009). Change in emotional processing during a dialectical behavior therapy-based skills group for major depressive disorder. *Behaviour Research and Therapy, 4*(4), 316–321.

Fleming, A. P., McMahon, R. J., Moran, L. R., Peterson, A. P., & Dreessen, A. (2015). Pilot randomized controlled trial of dialectical behavior therapy group skills training for ADHD among college students. *Journal of Attention Disorders, 19*(3), 260.

Goldstein, T. R., Fersch-Podrat, R. K., Rivera, M., Axelson, D. A., Merranko, J., Yu, H., ... Birmaher, B. (2015). Dialectical behavior therapy for adolescents with bipolar disorder: results from a pilot randomized trial. *Journal of Child and Adolescent Psychopharmacology, 25*(2), 140–149.

Harley, R., Sprich, S., Safren, S., Jacobo, M., & Fava, M. (2008). Adaptation of dialectical behavior therapy skills training group for treatment-resistant depression. *The Journal of Nervous and Mental disease, 196*(2), 136–143.

Harned, M. S., Chapman, A. L., Dexter-Mazza, E. T., Murray, A., Comtois, K. A., & Linehan, M. M. (2008). Treating co-occurring axis I disorders in recurrently suicidal women with borderline personality disorder. *Personality Disorders: Theory, Research, and Treatment, 1*, 35–45.

Henggeler, S. W., Melton, G. B., Brondino, M. J., Scherer, D. G., & Hanley, J. H. (1997). Multisystemic therapy with violent and chronic juvenile offenders and their families: the role of treatment fidelity in successful dissemination. *Journal of Consulting and Clinical Psychology, 65*(5), 821.

Henggeler, S. W., Schoenwald, S. K., Borduin, C. M., Rowland, M. D., & Cunningham, P. B. (1998). *Multisystemic treatment for antisocial behavior in children and adolescents.* New York: Guilford Press.

Hesslinger, B., Philipsen, A., & Richter, H. (2004). *Psychotherapie der ADHS im Erwachsenenalter: Ein Arbeitsbuch.* Göttingen: Hogrefe Verlag GmbH & Co. KG.

Hill, D. M., Craighead, L. W., & Safer, D. L. (2011). Appetite-focused dialectical behavior therapy for the treatment of binge eating with purging: a preliminary trial. *The International Journal of Eating Disorders, 44*(3), 249–261.

Hirvikoski, T., Waaler, E., Alfredsson, J., Pihlgren, C., Holmström, A., Johnson, A., ... Nordström, A. (2011). Reduced ADHD symptoms in adults with ADHD after structured skills training group: Results from a randomized controlled trial. *Behaviour Research and Therapy, 49*(3), 175–185.

Jüni, P., Altman, D. G., & Egger, M. (2001). Assessing the quality of controlled clinical trials. *British Medical Journal, 323*(7303), 42–46.

Kliem, S., Kröger, C., & Kosfelder, J. (2010). Dialectical behavior therapy for borderline personality disorder: A meta-analysis using mixed-effects modeling. *Journal of Consulting and Clinical Psychology, 78*(6), 936.

Kocsis, J. H., Gerber, A. J., Milrod, B., Roose, S. P., Barber, J., Thase, M. E., ... Leon, A. C. (2010). A new scale for assessing the quality of randomized clinical trials of psychotherapy. *Comprehensive Psychiatry, 51*(3), 319–324.

Koerner, K. (2013). What must you know and do to get good outcomes with DBT? *Behavior Therapy, 44*(4), 568–579.

Koons, C. R., Robins, C. J., Tweed, J. L., Lynch, T. R., Gonzalez, A. M., Morse, J. Q., ... Bastian, L. A. (2001). Efficacy of dialectical behavior therapy in women veterans with borderline personality disorder. *Behavior Therapy, 32*, 371–390.

Linehan, M. M. (1993a). *Cognitive-behavioral treatment of borderline personality disorder.* New York: Guilford Press.

Linehan, M. M. (1993b). *Skills training manual for treating borderline personality disorder.* New York: Guilford Press.

Linehan, M. M., Armstrong, H. E., Suarez, A., Allmon, D. & Heard, H.L. (1991). Cognitive-behavioral treatment of chronically parasuicidal borderline patients. *Archives of General Psychiatry, 48*, 1060–1064.

Linehan, M. M., Comtois, K. A., Murray, A. M., Brown, M. Z., Gallop, R. J., Heard, H. L., … Lindenboim, N. (2006). Two-year randomized controlled trial and follow-up of dialectical behavior therapy vs therapy by experts for suicidal behaviors and borderline personality disorder. *Archives of General Psychiatry, 63*, 757–766.

Linehan, M. M., Dimeff, L. A., Reynolds, S. K., Comtois, K. A., Welch, S. S., Heagerty, P., & Kivlahan, D. R. (2002). Dialectical behavior therapy versus comprehensive validation therapy plus 12-step for the treatment of opioid dependent women meeting criteria for borderline personality disorder. *Drug and Alcohol Dependence, 67*(1), 13–26.

Linehan, M. M., Heard, H. L., & Armstrong, H. E. (1993). Naturalistic follow-up of a behavioral treatment for chronically parasuicidal borderline patients. *Archives of General Psychiatry, 50*(12), 971–974.

Linehan, M. M., & Korslund, K. E. (2003). *Dialectical behavior therapy adherence manual.* Seattle, WA: University of Washington.

Linehan, M. M., Korslund, K. E., Harned, M. S., Gallop, R. J., Lungu, A., Neacsiu, A. D., … Murray-Gregory, A. (2015). Dialectical behavior therapy for high suicide risk in individuals with borderline personality disorder: A randomized clinical trial and component analysis. *JAMA Psychiatry, 72*(5), 475–482.

Linehan, M. M., Lockard, J. S., Wagner, A. W., & Tutek, D. (1996). *DBT expert rating scale.* Unpublished manuscript. Seattle, WA: University of Washington.

Linehan, M. M., & Schmidt, H., III., (1995). The dialectics of effective treatment of borderline personality disorder. In W. O'Donohue & L. Krasner (Eds.), *Theories in behavior therapy: Exploring behavior change* (pp. 553–584). Washington, DC: American Psychological Association.

Linehan, M. M., Schmidt, H., III., Dimeff, L. A., Craft, J. C., Kanter, J., & Comtois, K. A. (1999). Dialectical behavior therapy for patients with borderline personality disorder and drug-dependence. *American Journal of Addictions, 8*, 279–292.

Linehan, M. M., Tutek, D. A., Heard, H. L., & Armstrong, H. E. (1994). Interpersonal outcome of cognitive behavioral treatment for chronically suicidal borderline patients. *American Journal of Psychiatry, 151*(12), 1771–1775.

Lynch, T. R., Cheavens, J. S., Cukrowicz, K. C., Thorp, S. R., Bronner, L., & Beyer, J. (2007). Treatment of older adults with co-morbid personality and depression: a dialectical behavior therapy approach. *International Journal of Geriatric Psychiatry, 22*, 131–143.

Lynch, T. R., Morse, J. Q., Mendelson, T., & Robins, C. J. (2003). Dialectical behavior therapy for depressed older adults: A randomized pilot study. *American Journal of Geriatric Psychiatry, 11*, 33–45.

Lynch, T. R., Trost, W. T., Salsman, N., & Linehan, M. M. (2007). Dialectical behavior therapy for borderline personality disorder. *Annual Review of Clinical Psychology, 3*, 181–205.

McAuley, L., Pham, B., Tugwell, P., & Moher, D. (2000). Does the inclusion of grey literature influence estimates of intervention effectiveness reported in meta-analyses? *The Lancet, 356*(9237), 1228–1231.

McHugh, R. K., & Barlow, D. H. (Eds.) (2012). *Dissemination and implementation of evidence-based psychological interventions.* Oxford: Oxford University Press.

McHugo, G. J., Drake, R. E., Teague, G. B., & Xie, H. (1999). Fidelity to assertive community treatment and client outcomes in the New Hampshire dual disorders study. *Psychiatric Services, 50*(6), 818–824.

McMain, S. F., Links, P. S., Gnam, W. H., Guimond, T, Cardish, R. J., Korman, L., … Streiner, D. L. (2009). A randomized clinical trial of dialectical behavior therapy versus general psychiatric management for borderline personality disorder. *American Journal of Psychiatry*, *166*, 1365–1374.

Mehlum, L., Tørmoen, A. J., Ramberg, M., Haga, E., Diep, L. M., Laberg, S., & Grøholt, B. (2014). Dialectical behavior therapy for adolescents with repeated suicidal and self-harming behavior: a randomized trial. *Journal of the American Academy of Child and Adolescent Psychiatry*, *53*(10), 1082–1091.

Miller, W. R., Yahne, C. E., Moyers, T. B. Martinez, J., & Pirritano, M. (2004). A randomized trial of methods to help clinicians learn motivation interviewing. *Journal of Consulting and Clinical Psychology*, *72*, 1050–1062.

Moher, D., Pham, B., Jones, A., Cook, D. J., Jadad, A. R., Moher, M., & Klassen, T. P. (1998). Does quality of reports of randomised trials affect estimates of intervention efficacy reported in meta-analyses? *The Lancet*, *352*(9128), 609–613.

National Register for Evidence-based Programs and Practices (2006). Retrieved from nrepp. samsha.gov.

Neacsiu, A. D., Eberle, J. W., Kramer, R., Wiesmann, T., & Linehan, M. M. (2014). Dialectical behavior therapy skills for transdiagnostic emotion dysregulation: A pilot randomized controlled trial. *Behaviour Research and Therapy*, *59*, 40–51.

Neacsiu, A. D., Lungu, A. L., Harned, M., Rizvi, S. L., & Linehan, M. M. (2014). Impact of dialectical behavior therapy versus community treatment by experts on emotional experience, expression, and acceptance in borderline personality disorder. *Behavior Research and Therapy*, *53*, 47–54.

O'Connor, C., Small, S. A., & Cooney, S. M. (2007). Program fidelity and adaptation: Meeting local needs without compromising program effectiveness. *What works, Wisconsin–Research to Practice Series*, *4*, 1–5.

Öst, L. G. (2008). Efficacy of the third wave of behavioral therapies: A systematic review and meta-analysis. *Behaviour Research and Therapy*, *46*(3), 296–321.

Pasieczny, N., & Connor, J. (2011). The effectiveness of dialectical behaviour therapy in routine public mental health settings: An Australian controlled trial. *Behaviour Research and Therapy*, *49*(1), 4–10.

Pistorello, J., Fruzzetti, A. E., MacLane, C., Gallop, R., & Iverson, K. M. (2012). Dialectical behavior therapy (DBT) applied to college students: A randomized clinical trial. *Journal of Consulting and Clinical Psychology*, Advance online publication. doi: 10.1037/a0029096

PracticeGround | Learning Community Tracks (n.d.). Retrieved 13 December 2014, from http://www.practiceground.org/willow-wellbeing-which-path-is-right/

Priebe, S., Bhatti, N., Barnicot, K., Bremner, S., Gaglia, A., Katsakou, C., … Zinkler, M. (2012). Effectiveness and cost-effectiveness of dialectical behaviour therapy for self-harming patients with personality disorder: a pragmatic randomised controlled trial. *Psychotherapy and Psychosomatics*, *81*(6), 356–365.

Rockland, L. H. (1992). *Supportive therapy for borderline patients: A psychodynamic approach*. New York: Guilford Press.

SAMHSA's National Registry of Evidence-Based Programs and Practices (2006). *Dialectical behavior therapy*. Retrieved from http://legacy.nreppadmin.net/ViewIntervention.aspx?id=36

SAMHSA's Comparative Effectiveness Research Series (2012). *Dialectical behavior therapy: An informational resource*. Retrieved from http://www.nrepp.samhsa.gov/pdfs/DBT_Booklet_Final.pdf

Safer, D. L., & Joyce, E. E. (2011). Does rapid response to two group psychotherapies for binge eating disorder predict abstinence? *Behaviour Research and Therapy*, 49(5), 339–345.

Safer, D. L., Telch, C. F., & Agras, W. S. (2001). Dialectical behaviour therapy for bulimia nervosa. *American Journal of Psychiatry*, 58, 632–634.

Safer, D. L., Telch, C. F., & Chen, E. Y. (2009). *Dialectical behavior therapy for binge eating and bulimia*. New York: Guilford Press.

Safer, D., Robinson, A., & Jo, B. (2010). Outcome from a randomized controlled trial of group therapy for binge eating disorder: Comparing dialectical behavior therapy adapted for binge eating to an active comparison group therapy. *Behavior Therapy*, 41, 106–120.

Schoenwald, S. K., Garland, A. F., Chapman, J. E., Frazier, S. L., Sheidow, A. J., & Southam-Gerow, M. A. (2011). Toward the effective and efficient measurement of implementation fidelity. *Administration and Policy in Mental Health and Mental Health Services Research*, 38(1), 32–43.

Sholomskas, D. E., Syracuse-Siewert, G., Rounsaville, B. J., Ball, S. A., Nuro, K. F., & Carroll, K. M. (2005). We don't train in vain: a dissemination trial of three strategies of training clinicians in cognitive-behavioral therapy. *Journal of Consulting and Clinical Psychology*, 73(1), 106.

Soler, J., Pascual, J. C., Tiana, T., Cebria, A., Barrachina, J., Campins, M. J., ... Perez, V. (2009). Dialectical behaviour therapy skills training compared to standard group therapy in borderline personality disorder: A 3-month randomised controlled clinical trial. *Behaviour Research and Therapy*, 47, 353–358.

Stoffers, J. M., Vollm, B. A., Rucker, G., Timmer, A., Huband, N., & Lieb, K. (2012). Psychological therapies for people with borderline personality disorder. *Cochrane Database Systems Review*, 8: CD005652. doi: 10.1002/14651858.CD005652.pub2

Telch, C. F., Agras, W. S., & Linehan, M. M. (2000). Group dialectical behavior therapy for binge-eating disorder: A preliminary, uncontrolled trial. *Behavior Therapy*, 31, 569–582.

Telch, C. F., Agras, W. S., & Linehan, M. M. (2001). Dialectical Behavior Therapy for binge eating disorder. *Journal of Consulting and Clinical Psychology*, 69, 1061–1065.

Test, M. A. (1992). Training in community living. In R. P. Liberman (Ed.), *Handbook of psychiatric rehabilitation*. New York: Macmillan.

Test, M. A., & Stein, L. I. (1976). Practical guidelines for the community treatment of markedly impaired patients. *Community Mental Health Journal*, 12, 72–82.

Turner, R. M. (2000). Naturalistic evaluation of dialectical behavior therapy-oriented treatment for borderline personality disorder. *Cognitive and Behavioral Practice*, 7(4), 413–419.

Van den Bosch, L., Verheul, R, Schippers, G. M., & van den Brink, W. (2002). Dialectical behavior therapy of borderline patients with and without substance use problems: implementation and long-term effects. *Addictive Behaviors*, 2, 911–923.

Verheul, R., van den Bosch, L. M., Koeter, M. W., de Ridder, M. A, Stijnen, T., & van den Brink, W. (2003). Dialectical behaviour therapy for women with borderline personality disorder: 12-month, randomised clinical trial in The Netherlands. *British Journal of Psychiatry*, 182, 135–140.

Van Dijk, S., Jeffrey, J., & Katz, M. R. (2012). A randomized, controlled, pilot study of dialectical behavior therapy skills in a psychoeducational group for individuals with bipolar disorder. *Journal of Affective Disorders*, 145(3), 386–393.

Waltz, J., Addis, M. E, Koerner, K., & Jacobson, N. S. (1993). Testing the integrity of a psychotherapy protocol: Assessment of adherence and competence. *Journal of Consulting and Clinical Psychology*, 61, 620–630.

Wiser, S., & Telch, C. F. (1999). Dialectical behavior therapy for binge-eating disorder. *Journal of Clinical Psychology*, 55, 755–768.

CHAPTER 21

DIALECTICAL BEHAVIOUR THERAPY IN ROUTINE CLINICAL SETTINGS

CARLA J. WALTON AND
KATHERINE ANNE COMTOIS

EVIDENCE-BASED psychological treatments are usually developed and evaluated under ideal conditions in controlled settings. This allows researchers to demonstrate that the changes that occur are due to the effects of the therapy, and not to chance or other factors like the passage of time (Chambless & Hollon, 1998). These studies, called efficacy studies, are the focus of the chapter by Miga et al. (this volume). Those studies generally evaluate "standard DBT," i.e., 12 months of therapy including weekly individual therapy, weekly group skills training, access to phone coaching outside of sessions, and a consultation group attended by all DBT therapists (see Schmidt and Russo, this volume for more information). However, evidence-based therapies are developed and evaluated with the ultimate goal of broad use for persons presenting for help in routine clinical settings. The only way to determine if the results of efficacy studies generalize to applied clinical settings (and how well they generalize) is to test the therapy in these applied settings (Borkovec & Castonguay, 1998).

The conditions in routine clinical settings usually differ from those that occur in tightly controlled efficacy studies in a number of ways. In efficacy studies, there are typically restrictions on the inclusion-exclusion criteria, specially selected therapists, close supervision of therapists by experts, and rigorous monitoring of treatment adherence (Borkovec & Castonguay, 1998). Evaluating whether these treatments work without these restrictions provides vital evidence about the real-world benefit of new treatments. This chapter focuses on these so-called effectiveness studies that examine how treatments hold up when delivered to usual clinical populations, by routine therapists, in real world settings (Chambless & Hollon, 1998). In particular, it examines effectiveness studies of DBT in routine clinical settings where the population is either wholly or primarily comprised of those with Borderline Personality Disorder (BPD). This review includes studies that delivered standard DBT, as well as studies that have modified the duration and/or other aspects of treatment.

It is necessary to include a number of components in effectiveness trials to adequately test whether the treatments are feasible in routine clinical settings and whether they have measurable positive effects. Effectiveness research typically includes clinical populations with comorbid psychopathology and varying length of illness. Generally, experts do not closely supervise the clinicians in these studies, nor are their sessions monitored for how closely they adhere to the treatment protocol (Nathan, Stuart, & Dolan, 2000).

In order to identify relevant studies two online databases were searched: Medline and PsycInfo, using the search terms Dialectical Behaviour Therapy (both US and UK spellings), DBT, and were restricted to English language publications. Additional studies were identified in reference sections of the identified papers. Studies kept were those where the therapy was delivered in standard care. Any identified studies conducted in University settings, where the therapists were trained specifically for the purpose of the research trial or where therapists were coded for adherence and given feedback throughout the research, were not included for this chapter, as they were not considered to be representative of what occurs in routine clinical settings. Those studies are discussed in Miga et al. (this volume).

The identified effectiveness studies were either carried out in public sector community mental health services or in specialist personality disorder/DBT/substance use services within the public sector, and a small number were both RCTs and community-based (Feigenbaum et al., 2012; Pasieczny & Connor, 2011; Priebe et al., 2012).

CHARACTERISTICS OF ROUTINE CARE STUDIES

Table 21.1 shows details of the seven published 12-month studies that investigated standard DBT. The information indicates there was marked variability in the sample sizes of the studies, ranging from 27 to 80 participants.

Table 21.2 presents information regarding a further eight published studies that investigated standard DBT for six or fewer months' duration, where there was even greater variability in the sample sizes, ranging from 9 to 90 participants.

The profile of the samples was fairly similar across studies, including a formal diagnosis of BPD and age of participants between 18–65 years. Suicidal or non-suicidal self-injury (NSSI) was not an inclusion criterion for all studies, which made comparison across studies difficult in terms of suicidal outcomes. Further, they showed marked variability in outcome measures used across the studies, which further limited comparison. Exclusion criteria were fairly consistent across studies and were few in number; the most common being mental retardation and/or substance dependence. Some studies had tighter exclusion criteria, e.g., Carter, Willcox, Lewin, Conrad, & Bendit (2010), while others were more open as to whom they accepted, e.g., Comtois, Elwood, Holdcraft, Smith, & Simpson (2007). Hence, in a sense the profile of participants included in these samples was fairly homogenous in terms of age and diagnostic criteria, but differed in terms of their severity.

Not all studies (either effectiveness or efficacy) have reported on consistent outcomes, and the duration of the information collected prior to the delivery of the intervention was highly variable; therefore, we decided to calculate Cohen's D Effect sizes to provide a more standardized comparison, and Table 21.1 shows the results. Effect sizes are most straightforwardly interpreted as one of three categories: small (0.2), moderate (0.5), and large (0.8).

Interestingly, nearly all teams had a portion or all of their staff complete DBT standard training—a ten-day intensive training course (Landes & Linehan, 2012)—before or during the study. It is hard to know whether this is truly representative of the level of training completed by most therapists in routine clinical settings, or whether it is consistent with the level of teams who are willing to evaluate their outcomes and write them up for publication. Pasieczny and Connor (2011) discussed the outcomes of therapists who had completed intensive training compared with those who did not and reported that those therapists who completed intensive training had superior outcomes. Thus far, little research exists on patient outcomes depending on the level of therapist DBT training, and is an area that requires further work.

There was also marked variability in the follow-up consultation that therapists received after training, from weekly with a DBT expert, to monthly with a DBT expert, to ad hoc with a DBT expert, to no consultation with DBT experts at all. Four studies attempted to measure therapist adherence to the treatment (Hjalmarsson, Kaver, Perseius, Cederberg, & Ghaderi, 2008; Pasieczny & Connor, 2011; Priebe et al., 2012; Stiglmayr et al., 2014) and feedback was given to the therapists. Measuring therapist adherence involves watching recordings of sessions and assessing how closely the treatment delivered adheres to the treatment manual. As such, it measures whether the intended treatment was actually delivered. Measuring therapist adherence and providing feedback to the therapists is not standard in routine clinical settings, and unfortunately, it is not possible to determine whether measuring therapist adherence improved the therapy that was delivered, or its participants' outcomes.

SUICIDAL AND NON-SUICIDAL SELF-INJURY

In four studies (Carter et al., 2010; Feigenbaum et al., 2012; Pasieczny & Connor, 2011; Priebe et al., 2012) that compared DBT with a control group (either Treatment as Usual (TAU) or Waiting List + TAU), suicidality and NSSI decreased in all of the studies for both groups. However, Pasieczny and Connor (2011) and Priebe et al. (2012) were the only studies to find a significant difference between those receiving DBT and the control group. Both Tables 21.1 and 21.2 in this chapter show the *within*-treatment effect sizes for both DBT and the control group and the significance level as was reported in the published studies regarding the statistical difference between DBT and the control group.

Table 21.1 DBT for borderline personality disorder (BPD): Effectiveness studies of duration 12 months and two benchmarking studies

Authors	Setting and Country	Sample and Design	Mean age, gender	Inclusion criteria	Exclusion criteria
Comtois et al. (2007)	Community Mental Health USA	n = 38, Pre-Post.	34, 96% female.	Extensive suicide attempts or crisis service use.	Mental retardation, substance dependence without concurrent treatment.
Feigenbaum et al. (2012)	Specialist service for PDs in National Health Service United Kingdom	n = 41, RCT of DBT vs TAU.	35, 73% female.	Axis II: Cluster B.	Forensic history + current risk, Primary dx substance dependence, severe cognitive impairment, Axis I: Bipolar, Schizophrenia.
Hjalmarsson et al. (2008)	Psychiatric health care service Sweden	n = 27, Pre-Post.	20 (63% 18 or over), 100% female.	BPD, Ages >15, Self-harm.	Axis I: Psychosis, severe eating disorder, drug addiction.

Training received	Supervision/ consultation	Assessment points	DBT Outcomes in effect sizes (for studies with a control group, effect sizes are in parentheses)	Drop-out at post
All clinicians completed ten-day intensive training.	First author provided weekly individual supervision for at least six months, then, supervised by other experienced clinicians.	0, 12 (post) months.	Suicidal and Non-Suicidal Self-Injury (THI): 0.13. Psychiatric Hospital Days (THI): 0.55**.	DBT = 24%.
Two days' training in UK from a DBT trainer, followed by ten-day DBT intensive training in US.	One day of expert consultation every 12 months throughout study; 2.5 hours of weekly DBT consultation and skills development meetings.	0, 6, 12 (post) months.	Suicidal Self-Injury (SASII): 0.32 (control = 0.86). Non-Suicidal Self-Injury (SASII): 0.40 (control = 1.0) Psychiatric Hospital Days (THI & medical notes): -0.2 (control = -0.23). General Psychiatric Symptoms (CORE-OM): 0.36 (control = 0.38). Depression (BDI-II): 0.31 (control = 0.54).	DBT = 56%. TAU = 6%.
110 hours of theory of DBT; 51 hours of seminars and workshops.	Three hours/week group supervision and individual supervision (frequency not specified). Therapy sessions were videotaped and treatment discussed based on DBT adherence scale.	0, 6, 12 (post) months.	Suicidal and Non-Suicidal Self-Injury (BPD-TOA & diary cards): 0.44 * General Psychiatric Symptoms (SCL-90-R): 1**. General Functioning (GAF): 2.24***. Depression (KABOSS-S): 0.73**.	DBT = 19%.

(continued)

Table 21.1 Continued

Authors	Setting and Country	Sample and Design	Mean age, gender	Inclusion criteria	Exclusion criteria
Priebe et al. (2012) & Barnicot et al. (2014)[1]	National Health Service United Kingdom	N = 80, Pragmatic RCT of DBT vs TAU.	32, 88% female	Axis II dx, Age >16; Five or more days self-harm in past 12 months.	Severe learning difficulties, inability to read or write English.
Stiglmayr et al. (2014)	Routine mental health care Germany	N = 70, Pre-Post.	30, 84% female.	BPD, Ages >16.	Schizophrenia, bipolar I, acute suicidality, substance dependence in last six months, BMI lower than 18, IQ lower than 80, Axis II: ASPD.
Benchmarking studies					
Linehan et al. (2006)	University clinic USA	N = 101, RCT of DBT vs Therapy by Experts (TBE).	29, 100% female.	BPD, 18–45; Two suicide attempts and/or NSSI in past five years, at least one suicide attempt or NSSI in past eight weeks.	Lifetime diagnosis of schizophrenia, schizoaffective, bipolar, or psychotic disorder; seizure disorder requiring medication; mandate to treatment; need for primary treatment for another debilitating condition.

Training received	Supervision/ consultation	Assessment points	DBT Outcomes in effect sizes (for studies with a control group, effect sizes are in parentheses)	Drop-out at post
Not specified.	Not specified. Only 10% of individual sessions assessed for adherence. Feedback given to therapists.		Non-Suicidal Self-Injury (interview): Means and SDs not provided. Participants in DBT condition showed significantly greater reduction in self-harm over time. For every two months in DBT, the risk of self-harm decreased relative to TAU by an additional 9%. General Psychiatric Symptoms (BPRS): 0.36 (control = 0.18). Quality of Life (MANSA): 0.5 (control = 0.22).	DBT = 52%. TAU = not reported.
Attended at least 64 hours of DBT training at certified DBT institute.	Weekly consultation team and 55% had "regular DBT supervision." Adherence measured using Adherence Coding Scale.	0, >5 sessions, 4, 12 (post), 24 (FU), 48 (FU) months.	Non-Suicidal Self-Injury (LPC): 0.33[**2] Psychiatric Hospital Days (THI): 0.61[***] General Psychiatric Symptoms (BSI-GSI): 0.60[*] Depression (BDI): 0.99[*] Depression (HAM): 0.55[*]	DBT = 33%.
DBT seminar of 45 hours followed by supervised practice. Therapists were hired once six of eight consecutive training case sessions were rated as adherent to DBT.	Weekly consultation meeting. Adherence was assessed during the study.	0, 4, 8, 12, 16 (FU), 20 (FU), 24 (FU).	Suicidal and Non-Suicidal Self-Injury (SASII): 0.43 (TBE = 0.29)[*]. Depression (HAM-D): 1.05 (TBE = 0.64).	DBT = 19%. TBE = 43%.

(continued)

Table 21.1 Continued

Authors	Setting and Country	Sample and Design	Mean age, gender	Inclusion criteria	Exclusion criteria
McMain et al. (2009 & 2012)	Public health (teaching hospital) Canada	N = 180, RCT of DBT and GPM.	30, 86% female	BPD, two episodes of suicidal or NSSI in past five years and one in three months prior to enrolment.	Psychotic disorder, Bipolar 1 disorder, delirium, dementia, or mental retardation; Substance dependence in past 30 days; Medical condition that precluded psychiatric medications or required hospitalization within the next year; living outside a 40 mile radius of Toronto; plans to leave the Province in the next two years.

* p < .05;

** p < .01;

*** p < .001.

Effect sizes for all outcomes reported in this Table (for both pre-post studies and studies with a comparison group) are for within treatment, not between treatment. The significance level reported in this Table is that which was reported in the original paper. For the pre-post studies, the significance level refers to significant change over time; whereas for the studies where there was a comparison group, the significance levels shown are for time by group interaction.

Effect sizes are most straightforwardly interpreted as one of three categories: small (0.2), moderate (0.5), and large (0.8). Note that effect sizes are not ideal for non-normally distributed data, although they are acceptable and were used in this chapter in order to have a standardized number with which to compare outcomes across studies. Effect sizes were calculated by calculating the difference between the Means at pre- and post-treatment and dividing by the SD at pre-treatment.

Note: Age is >17 unless otherwise specified. Outcome measures: THI = Treatment History Interview; SASII = Suicide Attempt Self-Injury Interview; CORE-OM = Clinical outcomes in routine evaluation–outcome measurement; BDI-II = Beck Depression Inventory II; BPD-TOA = BPD Treatment Outcome Assessment; SCL-90-R = Symptom Checklist 90 Revised; GAF = Global Assessment of Functioning; KABOSS-S = Karolinska Affective and Borderline Symptom Scale–Self-Assessment; CSRI = Client Service Receipt Inventory; BPRS = Brief Psychiatric Rating Scale; MANSA = Manchester Short Assessment of Quality of Life; LPC = Lifetime Parasuicide Count; BSI-GSI = Brief Symptom Inventory–Global Severity Index; BDI = Beck Depression Inventory I; HAM = Hamilton-Depression Scale; EQ-5D = Euroqol Quality of Life Measure

[1] NB: Barnicot, Savill, Bhatti, & Priebe (2014) reported follow-up data and effects on hospitalization in a subsequent paper of the same study.

[2] Effect size shown in the Table for NSSI is that which was reported in the published study (as Means and SDs were not reported in the study for NSSI and hence, it could not be manually calculated to be consistent with all other effect sizes shown in the Table). All other effect sizes shown for this study in the Table were manually calculated as the Means and SDs were provided.

Training received	Supervision/ consultation	Assessment points	DBT Outcomes in effect sizes (for studies with a control group, effect sizes are in parentheses)	Drop-out at post
DBT intensive training and/or other training workshops.	Weekly individual supervision plus approximately monthly expert consultation. Adherence coding conducted and feedback provided to therapists.	0, 4, 8, 12, 18 (FU), 24 (FU), 30 (FU), 36 (FU).	Suicidal and Non-Suicidal Self-Injury (SASII): 0.50 (GPM = 0.24). Psychiatric Hospital Days (THI): 0.29 (GPM = 0.26). General Psychiatric Symptoms (SCL-90R): 0.47 (GPM = 0.49). Depression (BDI): 1.2 (GPM = 1.0). Quality of Life (EQ-5D): 0.29 (GPM = 0.21). Benefits were maintained at two-year follow-up.	DBT = 39%. GPM = 38%.

Table 21.2 DBT for borderline personality disorder (BPD): Effectiveness studies of duration of five or six months[1]

Authors	Setting and Country	Sample and Design	Mean age, gender	Inclusion criteria	Exclusion Criteria
Axelrod et al. (2011)	Substance use clinic USA	27, Pre-Post	38, 100% female	BPD & substance dependence.	Actively psychotic, actively suicidal, do not speak English.
Ben-Porath et al. (2004)	Community Mental Health USA	26, Pre-Post	35, 96% female	BPD & comorbid severe Axis I mental illness.	Nil reported.
Blennerhassett et al. (2009)	Community Mental Health Ireland	9, Pre-Post	29, 100% female	BPD.	Organic brain disorder, substance dependence, significant physical illness.
Brassington (2006)	Community Mental Health New Zealand	10, Pre-Post	34, 100% female	BPD.	Nil reported.

Training received	Supervision/ consultation	Assessment points	DBT outcomes in effect sizes (for studies with a control group, effect sizes are in parentheses)	Drop-out at post
"Train-the-trainer" model.	A DBT trainer attended the consultation meetings and supervised the clinicians for treatment adherence.	0, 10, 20 (post) weeks	Depression (BDI): 1.08***. Difficulties in emotion regulation (DERS): 1.26***. Substance use: 39.1% had weekly substance use in 30 days prior to the start of treatment. 8.6% had weekly substance use in 30 days prior to the end of treatment**.	44%
Two-day workshop & six-month-long study group. Five of the eight therapists attended a one-week training by Marsha Linehan.	Consultation team (as per the model). Staff that left replaced by individuals with little to no experience in DBT.	0, 6 (post) months	Suicidal and Non-Suicidal Self-Injury (from diary cards): 0.13 (NB: Only seven were self-harming at start of treatment). General Functioning (SCL-90-R) = 0.57*.	12%
Reading group; Three of the seven therapists had completed DBT intensive prior to the study.	Consultation team (as per the model). Nil external consultation.	0, 3, 6 (post) 9 FU months	Suicidal and Non-Suicidal Self-Injury (diary card): 0.61 (NB: Only four self-harming at start of treatment). Psychiatric Hospital Days: M = 57.83 days in year prior to treatment. M = 3.83 days in year of treatment. (SDs & signif not provided). General Psychiatric Symptoms (SCL-90-R—GSI): 1.34**.	11%
Seven therapists attended ten days of DBT intensive. Other three "familiarized themselves with DBT theory and practice."	Weekly (internal) therapist consultation meeting.	0, 6 (post) months. Although clinically therapy continued until 12 months	Psychiatric Hospital Days (interview): M = 0.57 days per patient per month prior to treatment. M = 0.2 days per patient per month during six months of treatment (SDs and signif not provided). General Psychiatric Symptoms (SCL-90-R—GSI): 7.3***.	0%

(continued)

Table 21.2 Continued

Authors	Setting and Country	Sample and Design	Mean age, gender	Inclusion criteria	Exclusion Criteria
Carter et al. (2010)	Specialist service for BPD within public mental health Australia	73, RCT of DBT vs WL + TAU	25, 100% female	BPD three episodes of deliberate self-harm in past 12 months.	Disabling organic condition, schizophrenia, bipolar affective disorder, psychotic depression, florid ASPD or developmental disability.
Pasieczny & Connor (2011)[2]	Public Mental Health service Australia	90, DBT vs WL/ TAU, but not randomized; based on group availability	34, 93% female	BPD Ongoing suicidal/ NSSI; At least one acute hospitalization or 3 ED presentations in past six months.	Nil, however, assessment was deferred if patients were at imminent risk of suicide or acute psychosis.
Prendergast & McCausland (2007)	Public mental health and women's health service Australia	16, Pre-Post	36, 100% female	BPD	Current psychotic episode, substance dependence.

Training received	Supervision/consultation	Assessment points	DBT outcomes in effect sizes (for studies with a control group, effect sizes are in parentheses)	Drop-out at post
Self-directed reading; Four team members completed DBT intensive during study.	Therapist participation in weekly supervision groups. "Several episodes of supplementary training" by Kelly Koerner and Kate Comtois (DBT Consultants).	0, 3, 6 (months). Although clinically, therapy continued until 12 months.	Suicidal and Non-Suicidal Self-Injury (Parasuicide History Interview): 0.58 (control = 0.22) Quality of Life (WHOQOL-BREF): Physical—0.91 (control = 0.07)* Psychological—1.85 (control = 0.78)** Social—1.28 (control = 0.56) Environmental—0.83 (control = 0.22)*.	DBT = 47%. TAU = 11%. (NB: People in this WL + TAU group were waiting to commence DBT).
All therapists received four days of basic DBT training from Australian DBT trainers; Four of the 18 therapists attended a ten-day DBT intensive training.	Peer supervision in weekly consultation group. Nil external consultation. Developed own adherence scale using Linehan's (1993) book.	0, 6 (post) months. Although clinically, therapy continued until 12 months and some 12-month data is reported.	Suicidal Self-Injury (Interview + medical records): 1.08 (control = -0.03)** Non-Suicidal Self-Injury (Interview + medical records): 0.55 (control = 0.03)**. Psychiatric Hospital Days (medical records): 0.60 (control = -0.14) **. General Psychiatric Symptoms (BSI-GSI): 0.74 (control = -0.004)*. Depression (BDI-II): 1.3 (control = 0.36)**.	DBT = 7%. TAU = 13%.
"All therapists had undergone intensive training in DBT."	In first year, weekly supervision for 1.5 hours. In second year, fortnightly supervision for two hours.	0, 6 (post) months.	Suicidal and Non-Suicidal Self-Injury (interview): 0.03 Psychiatric Hospital Days (medical records): 0.43*. General Functioning (GAF): 0.99*. Depression (BDI): 0.92*.	31%

(continued)

Table 21.2 Continued

Authors	Setting and Country	Sample and Design	Mean age, gender	Inclusion criteria	Exclusion Criteria
Williams et al. (2010)	Public mental health Australia	31,[3] Pre-Post	36, 86% female	BPD; residing within catchment area.	Current, severe and uncontrolled psychotic illness; Severe substance abuse; Significant aggressive or antisocial traits.

* p < .05;

** p < .01;

*** p < .001.

Outcome measures: WHOQOL-BREF = World Health Organization (WHO)—Quality of Life Brief Version; BSI = Brief Symptom Inventory; BASIS-32 (Behaviour and Symptom Identification Scale).

1 N.B. Exceptions were Axelrod and Williams study, which was 20 weeks.

2 NB: The self-report measures were not introduced until after 45 patients had been recruited; hence, the outcomes reported based on self-report measures are for n=45.

3 In the study by Williams, Hartstone, & Denson (2010) all 140 participants received group skills training, although only 31 of those received concurrent individual DBT, with the remaining 109 participants receiving individual TAU. Only the data from the 31 participants receiving both individual and group DBT was included in this review.

Training received	Supervision/consultation	Assessment points	DBT outcomes in effect sizes (for studies with a control group, effect sizes are in parentheses)	Drop-out at post
	"Regular consultation meetings were held for facilitator support and development"— further details not provided.	0, 20 (post).	Psychiatric Hospital Days (medical records): 0.11 Depression (BDI-II): 0.53*. Quality of Life (BASIS-32) = 1.04**.	32%

Pre-Post studies of DBT outcomes in routine clinical settings have been conducted in a number of community mental health settings. The clientele and structure of mental health settings vary across the world, which makes it hard to compare between settings. Most of the studies reviewed in this chapter focused on total reductions in behaviour rather than changes in frequency and severity. In the studies that looked at Pre-Post scores for those that had completed DBT, Stiglmayr et al. (2014) found a significant reduction in median scores. The majority of the participants (88%) were engaging in suicidal behaviour and NSSI prior to the treatment in Hjalmarsson et al.'s (2008) study, which dropped to 50% of the participants after 12 months of treatment. In the Blennerhassett, Bamford, Whelan, Jamieson, and O'Raghaillaigh (2009) study, only four of the nine participants had a history of self-harm and for all four the self-harm significantly reduced. The Brassington and Krawitz (2006) study reported that, of the seven participants with a history of self-harm, four of them showed clinically significant reductions in self-harm. In Ben-Porath, Peterson, and Smee (2004), only 30% of the sample reported a history of self-harm in the six months preceding the study and the reduction in their self-harming behaviour across the six months was not significant. Participants in Prendergast and McCausland's (2007) study did not change markedly in terms of presence or absence of the behaviour, although the authors note that 45% of the sample had a significant reduction in the severity of self-harming incidents, such that all of the self-harming behaviour occurring at post-treatment met their criteria of "no danger," e.g., scratching. Of note is that a number of these studies measured NSSI and suicidal behaviour by self-report on diary card. It is not clear how reliable this is as a source of data as participants may under report, over report, or accurately report.

TREATMENT DROP-OUT

There was a large range in drop-out rates from therapy between the different effectiveness studies, ranging from 0% of 10 participants (Brassington & Krawitz, 2006) to 56% of 41 participants (Feigenbaum et al., 2012). In the original DBT text (Linehan, 1993), the definition of drop-out is missing four consecutive appointments of either individual therapy or skills training, and most effectiveness studies have adopted this same definition. The way that a study defines drop-out will naturally have an impact on the rate of drop-out. For example, Priebe et al. (2012) defined drop-out as missing four consecutive sessions of either individual therapy, skills training, or any combination of the two and showed one of the highest rates of drop-out. Similarly, Williams, Hartstone, and Denson (2010) defined completion as attendance of at least 70% of sessions, not missing more than two consecutive sessions, and attendance at the final group session, and also found high drop-out rates.

There was no consistent picture across the drop-out rates for the identified studies except that the two studies from the UK reported higher drop-out rates (Feigenbaum et al., 2012; Priebe et al., 2012). A number of authors have identified the higher drop-out rates in studies of DBT in the UK compared with those in other countries (Gaglia, Essletzbichler, Barnicot, Bhatti, & Priebe, 2013; Priebe et al., 2012) and have speculated that the difference may be that reasonable alternate management or treatment options are available in the UK. Gaglia et al. (2013) looked at predictors of drop-out in a sample of 102 who began DBT in the UK National Health Service and found that a history of care coordination was a significant predictor of drop-out. They explained that care co-ordination "is arguably more oriented towards helping patients manage rather than treat or change the mental health symptoms and can provide the experience of compre-hensive and always available care" (p. 270).

Priebe et al. (2012) speculated that participants may be more likely to stay in treat-ment in places where there are fewer other available treatment options, e.g., in the US, in contrast to places that provide free healthcare, and where there might be greater treat-ment options, such as the UK and Australia. Two of the Australian studies had drop-out rates of 7% and 47%. Interestingly, therapists from the team of the Carter et al. (2010) study—the 47% drop-out rate—provided the initial training for the therapists in the Pasieczny and Connor (2011) study, which had the 7% drop-out rate. At the time of the Pasieczny and Connor (2011) study, there was a lack of any alternative treatment options in the community, which may have led to greater buy-in and retention by the patients (N. Pasieczny, personal communication, October 7, 2016).

Overall, it is hard to interpret the variability in drop-out rates, given that the studies are from a range of different contexts with slightly different inclusion and exclusion criteria. Regardless, the results of the effectiveness studies show that a substantial por-tion of people drop out of DBT treatment in routine clinical settings and while there has been some work in understanding this, the reasons for it are largely unclear. Many of these studies only had data for those that completed treatment, not those who dropped out. Hence, there is no information if those who dropped out showed similar improvement to those that stayed in therapy, or whether they had a poorer outcome. Comtois et al. (2007) included outcomes for both those who did and did not drop out of treatment, and many who had dropped out showed comparable outcomes to completers. Stiglmayr et al. (2014) explored the difference in outcomes depending on how frequently therapists attended consultation team meetings and found that fewer patients dropped out of treatment when their therapists attended consultation team meetings more regularly. More research is needed to explore reasons for drop-out and ways to decrease drop-out, as well as how to determine when drop-out reflects im-provement, and when it might be an indication of a subgroup for whom 12 months of DBT is too long.

QUALITY OF LIFE OUTCOMES

Among the four studies (Carter et al., 2010; Feigenbaum et al., 2012; Pasieczny & Connor, 2011; Priebe et al., 2012) that compared DBT with a control group (either TAU or Waiting List + TAU), the secondary outcomes that were measured varied, with some overlaps and some distinct constructs assessed. On the secondary outcomes measured, three of the studies (Carter et al., 2010; Feigenbaum et al., 2012; Priebe et al., 2012) found largely no significant difference in DBT when compared with the control group, with some minor exceptions. Carter et al. (2010) found a significant difference in favour of DBT for reduction in bed days and quality of life. Priebe et al. (2012) showed that those in DBT had significantly fewer days in hospital by the end of 12 months. However, in addition to showing a reduction in self-harming behaviour, Pasieczny and Connor (2011) found significant results on all secondary outcomes. It is not clear why they found this while the other studies did not. As discussed, one possibility is that the TAU in their setting was less satisfactory than in the other studies.

Of the Pre-Post studies, a number of studies showed a reduction in unemployment (Ben-Porath et al., 2004; Pasieczny & Connor, 2011) following treatment, even with only six months of treatment. On measures of general psychiatric symptoms as measured by the SCL-90-R, Ben-Porath et al. (2004) showed a significant reduction on seven of the 12 subscales and Brassington and Krawitz (2006) on ten of the 12 subscales.

The focus of the Axelrod, Perepletchikova, Holtzman, and Sinha (2011) study was slightly different given that the sample targeted was women with BPD and substance dependence. They found a significant reduction on substance use, depression, and difficulties with emotion regulation.

Benchmarking Effects between Routine Care and Randomized Controlled Trials

Given the importance of knowing how well DBT works in real-world settings compared with those in tightly controlled research settings, similarly to Comtois et al. (2007) we looked at the range of outcomes for the effectiveness studies described in this chapter and compared them against two randomized controlled trials (RCT) discussed by Miga et al. (this volume). Both of those studies are of high quality, with one by the treatment developer (Linehan et al., 2006) and one by an independent researcher (McMain, Guimond, Streiner, Cardish, & Links, 2012; McMain et al., 2009).

The variability in outcomes found in the studies set in routine clinical settings is also present in more well-controlled settings. Hence, we chose two studies that are representative of the overall findings of the efficacy RCTs. Both had reasonable sample sizes to identify a main effect of treatment. In both studies, therapists were trained and identified as being able to deliver DBT to a level of adherence prior to the trial. There are a number of RCTs conducted by the treatment developer Marsha Linehan, and the selected study of DBT compared with treatment by experts was chosen as a large-scale study with the greatest sample size of all of her studies. Shelley McMain and colleagues conducted a trial in a routine clinical setting but with a rigour associated with an efficacy study (2009). In addition to having a large sample size, the study is unique in that among the investigators there were those with allegiance to DBT and those with allegiance to the other treatment. Table 21.1 shows, as would be expected of efficacy studies, that the list of exclusion criteria are longer for both the Linehan and McMain studies than it is for the effective studies.

For NSSI and suicidal behaviour, effect sizes ranged from small to large in the effectiveness studies compared to moderate in the efficacy trials. These results were variable according to the specific behaviours assessed. For example, Comtois et al. (2007) reported only medically treated self-inflicted injuries; if all self-inflicted injuries including those that did not require medical treatment were reported, the effect size may have been greater. The studies of six months' duration or less had equal or greater effect sizes for reducing self-harming behaviour than the 12-month studies, which is consistent with life-threatening behaviour being the highest priority problem targeted early in DBT. Studies have consistently shown a reduction in those behaviours within the initial few months of treatment (Linehan et al., 2006). Some of the studies of six months' duration went on to deliver 12 months of treatment, but only evaluated the first six months. As such, the impact on patients between knowing treatment involved a full 12 months, compared with a clear termination at six months, is unclear.

In terms of impact of treatment on hospitalization, among the studies of treatments lasting 12 months, effect sizes varied from a negative small effect, i.e., an increase in hospital rate (Feigenbaum et al., 2012), to a moderate positive effect size. This compares favourably with the efficacy studies of moderate positive effect sizes. Differences may be to do with the availability of hospital as an option as patients' behaviour decreases in severity or the extent to which a particular programme emphasizes patients' decreasing reliance on the mental health system.

Across the effectiveness studies, what is most striking is the lack of consistency of outcomes across studies. The pattern of results is more consistent within studies than between studies, such that some studies found very few significant findings across their outcomes while others found a range of significant outcomes. There are a number of possible interpretations; while the inclusion criteria are fairly homogenous, there may be a different profile of patients in terms of their severity and comorbidities between services. Alternately, it may be that different aspects of the treatment are emphasized in different settings. Regardless, the overall picture is that treatment with DBT leads to improvement in terms of reducing NSSI and suicidal behaviour, days admitted to psychiatric hospital, depression, general psychiatric symptoms, and quality of life. There was not a clear pattern of outcomes between those studies with smaller samples versus larger samples.

The level of improvement in these domains varied between studies, however, and possible reasons for this variation are worth considering. In the studies that incorporated a control or comparative condition, the alternate condition also showed improvement, but none of the studies have large enough sample sizes to detect whether DBT was superior or equal to the control or comparative condition. It is possible that the delivery of DBT in the effectiveness trials is inferior to the quality in the RCTs, and further effort is required to improve the quality of DBT in routine clinical settings. Furthermore, perhaps some studies accepted more psychiatrically disabled persons into their treatments; e.g., Comtois et al. (2007) and Priebe et al. (2012) had very few exclusion criteria.

There is also a lack of agreement regarding definitions of who has responded well to treatment (Rizvi, 2011). The DBT model aims to achieve behavioural control as its Stage 1 target (Linehan, 1993), but there is a lack of clarity regarding whether behavioural control refers to complete cessation of suicidal and self-harming behaviour and, if so, for what period of time. In the outcomes measured across both efficacy and effectiveness studies, less emphasis has been placed on the importance of an increase in functioning or quality of life.

Naturally there are a number of limitations with these studies—without a control group, it is not possible to attribute the gains to the specific DBT intervention in some studies, and small samples limit generalizability. These limitations notwithstanding, the comparability of outcomes between routine care studies as benchmarked against clinical trials provides strong support for the feasibility and potential effectiveness of DBT and offers ideas about where studies beyond standard DBT should investigate further.

The effectiveness studies reported have been conducted in a number of Western countries (the UK, Ireland, Sweden, Germany, the US, New Zealand, and Australia). DBT has now been implemented across a number of different cultures (Landes & Linehan, 2012), although the extent to which it is generalizable across different cultures remains to be established.

ADAPTATIONS OF DBT IN ROUTINE CARE

DBT in routine care is often an adaptation of standard DBT as used in clinical trials. Minor adaptations were found among these studies. For example, Ben-Porath et al. (2004) reduced the length of the weekly skills training to 90 minutes due to concerns regarding individuals with diagnosis of BPD and comorbid severe mental illness being able to attend to and comprehend the material presented in the group therapy component. For similar reasons, Comtois et al. (2007) offered the usual 2.5 hours skills training group into two 90-minute groups at different times during the week.

Another fairly consistent adaptation among the studies reported relates to the times when phone coaching is provided; most studies described individual therapists being available during office hours only. Outside of office hours, patients had to contact someone else, such as a local hospital extended hours service or a crisis line. Research studies have not examined the impact that this adaptation from the original model has on outcomes, or the relative effect of the amount or type of phone coaching vs. whether it is provided within or outside standard work hours. Given that the DBT treatment manual instructs that phone coaching be available outside work hours, it is interesting that so many of the studies reported in this chapter did not incorporate it, nor explained why they did not do so. Landes et al. (2017) explored barriers to implementation of DBT in the American Veterans Health Administration. The study concluded that even where there is willingness among clinicians to provide between session coaching, the barriers such as policies and funding remain. Chalker et al. (2015) found more frequent phone contacts (regardless of the calls being during or outside of the work day) were associated with a decrease in drop-out and psychological symptoms, and an increase in client and therapist satisfaction in DBT. However, there is no research currently in the DBT literature on the impact of phone coaching hours. Outside of DBT, Nadort et al. (2009) in a study of Schema Therapy which randomized patients to receive phone support from their individual therapist after hours or not, found that access out-of-hours made no difference to outcomes. Gunderson (1996) has suggested around the clock availability may help reduce drop-out rates and hence, the lack of phone support by the individual therapist may be one of the contributing factors to the higher drop-out rates in the effectiveness studies.

There have been a number of considerable adaptations of standard DBT. As a whole package, DBT is very labour intensive and, while overall it has been shown to be cost effective (Krawitz & Miga this volume), many teams have found it hard to justify to administrators the amount of resources required. Andion and colleagues (2012) are one such group that identified limited resources as an issue to implementing DBT as a standard package. They sought to identify whether DBT delivered individually, i.e., without the skills group (to 37 patients) would be as effective as standard DBT (delivered to 14 patients), and found significant improvements across both DBT delivered individually and standard DBT and no significant difference between the two modes of delivery. It is not clear which mode (if either) the therapists preferred or the toll on the therapists of carrying individual patients without a skills training group, but regardless, such a study deserves to be replicated with a larger sample.

Turner (2000) compared DBT-informed intervention in a community mental health setting compared with a client-centred therapy (CCT) treatment protocol with two modifications to the DBT intervention: psychodynamic techniques were incorporated with DBT case conceptualization, and skills were taught during individual therapy instead of in a group environment. Frequency of deliberate self-harm was measured by an independent assessor on "Target Behaviour Ratings" along with anger, impulsive behaviour, and emotional instability on a 0–8 scale (where 0 is no symptoms and 8 is severe symptoms). Those in the DBT condition did significantly better in terms of reducing suicide and self-harm behaviour, impulsivity, anger, and depression while also improving in terms of their global mental health functioning. A number of these domains were significant at 12 months, but not at six months. The DBT applied was also modified from that in other studies (incorporating psychodynamic techniques and being taught individually rather than in a group), precluding us from determining if the treatment effect is of DBT or the added psychodynamic and individual application component. However, as in efficacy studies of DBT, hospitalization days significantly decreased for those in the DBT condition, and, in this study, increased for those in the CCT condition.

Blackford and Love (2011) evaluated the effectiveness of DBT in a community mental health setting utilizing DBT skills training group alone for six months for 18 patients. They found a significant reduction in depression scores across the six months and also noted a positive correlation with attendance and outcome, such that higher levels of attendance were associated with greater reduction in symptoms and improvement in functioning.

In the Williams et al. (2010) study, 31 participants received individual DBT concurrently to skills training and 109 received TAU concurrently to skills training. Participants who received individual DBT had a lower drop-out rate than those that received TAU. In the community, it is fairly common for people to attend a DBT skills training group while receiving TAU for the individual therapy. Hence, the outcomes from the Williams et al. (2010) study prompt the need for further studies identifying how the different modes work together. This was not a randomized trial and hence, the conclusions that can be made are limited. However, the pattern of results is similar to those found in Linehan et al.'s (2015) RCT comparing standard DBT with DBT skills training + case management, where there was a higher drop-out rate in the group that received DBT skills training + case management than there was for those receiving standard DBT.

Routine Use of DBT Adapted
for Graduates of Standard DBT

The following studies have developed an intervention to put in place beyond completion of standard DBT.

Comtois, Kerbrat, Atkins, Harned, and Elwood (2010) developed a treatment— DBT Accepting the Challenges of Employment and Self-Sufficiency (formerly DBT Accepting the Challenges of Exiting the System: DBT-ACES)— designed to follow a year of standard DBT for those who are psychiatrically disabled by BPD or a related psychiatric condition. The treatment is one year with standard DBT modes of therapy that focuses on DBT orientated goal-setting and problem-solving strategies paired with exposure and contingency management to assist clients to find and keep competitive employment and attend college or technical programmes to achieve a living wage career and financial self-sufficiency. Pre-Post evaluation of DBT-ACES found significant improvement in participants' odds of competitive employment and school matriculation, working at least 20 hours per week, and subjective quality of life. Gains were largely maintained after completion of DBT-ACES treatment.

Lopez and Chessick (2013) reported on a pilot study of a DBT graduate group that included 11 group members (five male and six female) ranging in age from 29 to 57 years who had completed DBT skills training. A meeting with group members about their needs and expectations helped to develop the curriculum for the graduate group and included a specific focus on helping group members to implement the skills into day-to-day problem solving. The group met weekly for 90 minutes over nine months. This group appeared to have a similar focus to DBT-ACES as group members identified a personal target to work towards such as "furthering education, finding a job, and making a new friend" (p. 146). The group members led the skills review, and the clients chose the order of the skills. Results showed significant improvement in depression scores with a large effect size as measured by the Patient Health Questionnaire (PHQ-9), as well as all reaching attainment of their target goal. There was a significant change in employment status across the nine months, with many returning to work, and eight of the 11 group members transitioned out of therapy.

TRAINING AND ADHERENCE IN ROUTINE USE OF DBT

One of the differences between efficacy trials and effectiveness trials that look at a treatment as applied in a routine clinical setting is the level of training of therapists and supervision. Pasieczny and Connor (2011) provided an important contribution with their study, which, in addition to looking at patient outcomes from participation in DBT, also set out to compare the clinical outcomes between patients treated by therapists who had attended a ten-day DBT intensive training with the clinical outcomes of patients receiving treatment from a basically trained therapist. They found that after six months of DBT, patients assigned to intensively trained therapists had significantly greater reductions in terms of suicide attempts and NSSI, while there were no significant differences in terms of hospital use or any of the self-report measures.

In the studies described in this chapter, there is a large amount of variability in the amount of therapist training and supervision. The minimal amount of training and supervision required for therapists to reach a level of adherence or for optimal outcomes has yet to be established. Hawkins and Sinha (1998) found that a broad range of health professionals were able to acquire a decent grounding in the theory of DBT and that knowledge acquisition improved by reading the treatment manual and attending the DBT consultation meeting. The results reported in this chapter would suggest that teams with a majority of members trained in DBT with ten days of intensive training and expert consultation/regular supervision can produce comparable results to efficacy studies on self-harm and hospitalization, but with greater drop-out rates and more variability on other outcomes.

Only four of the studies reported using some form of adherence coding to establish fidelity to the model, and two of those were adherence instruments developed by the authors of the studies. The majority of the effectiveness studies did not include a measure of fidelity or adherence, and therefore, it is unclear to what extent DBT, as it was developed, was delivered. As such, while the authors intended to measure the impact of DBT on their participant groups, there is not much information about the DBT provided. Adherence data is usually collected in RCTs where the range of adherence is most likely both higher and narrower than in routine clinical practice. It is likely that, in the settings of the studies reported in this chapter, teams that are willing to do research on top of their clinical work are people that are fairly invested (and confident) in what they're doing. No studies exist that look at whether there is a relationship between low adherence and outcome in DBT. Ben-Porath et al. (2004) write that, while adherence monitoring is important, it may not be feasible in real-world settings, and further suggest the importance of having a strong, committed and knowledgeable Team Leader to provide a foundation for fidelity.

BARRIERS TO THE ROUTINE USE OF DBT

There are a number of barriers to implementing standard DBT in routine clinical settings. Studies reported here identified the challenge of high staff turnover, limited funds, and lack of adherence to the treatment programme. Readers interested in further detail are referred to Comtois and Landes (this volume).

The majority of the studies reported studied DBT over a five- to six-month period, rather than the standard 12-month duration that is outlined in the majority of the RCTs. Most of these studies had small sample sizes. Some of these papers described the rationale for this being service constraints to deliver the full 12 months; some of the authors were emailed to enquire about the reason for choosing six months and responded similarly. Given that what is frequently occurring in routine clinical settings is to deliver five to six months of treatment, future studies are required to investigate more fully the results of a condensed version of the therapy compared with standard DBT of 12 months.

Ben-Porath et al. (2004) discuss the importance of staff selection in establishing a DBT programme and make the point that individuals working with a BPD population need to have "higher than normal threshold for ambiguity, stress and uncertainty" (p. 428), or, in other words, strong emotion regulation and distress tolerance skills themselves. They also discuss the importance of therapists being able to respect their own limits without personalizing challenging interactions between themselves and the client. They highlight the importance of selecting "volunteers" to be therapists in DBT programmes rather than drafting them. In Ben-Porath et al.'s (2004) study in a Community Mental Health setting, three of the eight clinicians involved in the study left the agency during the six-month study period. They cite evidence that the average annual rate of staff turnover was approximately 40% in a community-based facility (Riediger & Baine, 1987).

In many of the studies reported, therapists only had a small caseload. For example, in the Brassington study, each therapist only took on one to two patients each so as not to get overloaded. It is not clear how representative this is of routine clinical settings. Interestingly, this was the only study with 0% drop-out. The number of patients on a clinician's caseload may potentially have big implications for both the quality of care they can deliver and potential burnout. Large DBT caseloads could lead to burnout but small caseloads lead to limited practice and make sustaining a consultation team relatively more expensive to the clinic. Small teams also run the risk that they have too little critical mass to be available for referrals and to cover for each others' absences.

Qualitative Studies of Routine Use of DBT

Thus far this chapter has outlined the quantitative data on the effectiveness of DBT in routine clinical settings. It now discusses the qualitative research describing the experience of participants receiving DBT in routine clinical settings, specifically, Cunningham, Wolbert, and Lillie (2004), Hodgetts, Wright, and Gough (2007), McSherry, O'Connor, Hevey, and Gibbons (2012), and Perseius, Ojehagen, Ekdahl, Asberg, and Samuelsson (2003).

McSherry et al. (2012) held interviews and focus groups for eight participants who were currently attending the community mental health service about their experience of an adapted DBT programme. Hodgetts et al. (2007) interviewed five participants about their experience of DBT; three of these had completed 12 months of DBT, one was currently doing DBT, and another had prematurely completed the programme. Cunningham et al. (2004) interviewed 14 participants who were currently participating in DBT (involvement in the programme ranged from six months to three years, with a median time of 15 months). Perseius et al. (2003) interviewed ten patients who had been in DBT for 12 months or longer and four therapists. Each of the three studies used interpretative analyses to identify the main themes from the interviews. A number of themes emerged that focused on the impact of DBT on patients' lives generally, as well as on relationships, ability to regulate their emotions, level of suffering, and level of hope. Additional themes included their experience of the different modes of treatment, the challenges of DBT, and perceptions of psychiatric care before entering DBT.

A common response across the four studies was that participants considered DBT to be "life saving" or "life changing" and that it was reassuring to know that there were other people like them. The relationship with their therapist was considered to be respectful and validating, but challenging. Two of the studies found that the telephone skills coaching was difficult for individuals to initiate, but helpful, and that skills group was difficult, but important for learning as well as gaining support from others with similar issues (Cunningham et al., 2004; Perseius et al., 2003). Cunningham and colleagues described the DBT skills that participants found most useful and reported that some individuals did not use particular skills as they found them too difficult to understand. Both McSherry et al. (2012) and Cunningham et al. (2004) also described the particular effects of the treatment on clients' daily lives as improved relationships, ability to control emotions, decrease in self-harm, enjoying life more, and increased levels of hope. Although some participants of the Cunningham et al. (2004) study described a decrease in suffering, most described that their suffering remained the same, but that it no longer controlled them. Participants in the McSherry et al. (2012) study expressed frustration with the highly structured nature of the therapy and not being able to talk more freely in the group environment. Hodgetts and co-authors additionally identified the reasons for participating in DBT and grouped them as either "internal" (role of past behaviours and motivation to change) or "external" reasons (therapy choice limited and other's belief of DBT's helpfulness). Participants in the Hodgetts et al. study also found the structure of DBT novel and helpful and that DBT "provided a form of identity" (p. 175). The participants in the Perseius et al. (2003) study highlighted the difference between how they were treated in psychiatric care prior to DBT, and then in DBT. They described encountering respect, understanding, and support in DBT in contrast to "disrespectful and condemning attitudes" (p. 223) they had received previously in psychiatric care.

Brassington and Krawitz (2006) also conducted qualitative interviews with their ten participants following completion of six months of treatment in addition to the quantitative data collected, and reported on the common themes that emerged in those interviews. These included the practical utility of the treatment, learning alternate skillful ways to respond for their identified target problems, achieving long-term goals, developing a sense of responsibility for their own recovery, and hope and happiness.

Conclusions

On the whole, DBT appears to be maintaining many of its outcomes when evaluated in routine care instead of in the academic research environment. As found in data about most behavioural health and medical treatments, many outcomes are smaller and there is more variability in findings between effectiveness studies than observed in randomized trials. Pre-Post and quasi-experimental designs require more cautious evaluation than randomized trials, but the generalizability of these studies is compelling. This review of DBT in routine care has examined adaptations of DBT to adapt to routine care as well as asking innovative questions such as the impact of hours of phone coaching availability and consultation team attendance by therapists. These adaptations and questions reflect the needs of real-world DBT clinicians and clients, and suggest high impact DBT research yet to be conducted.

KEY MESSAGES FOR CLINICIANS

- Overall, in routine clinical settings, treatment with DBT leads to improvement in terms of decreasing suicidal and non-suicidal self-injury (NSSI), days admitted to psychiatric hospitals, depression, and general psychiatric symptoms.
- In the settings reported in this chapter, most of the clinicians had attended ten-day intensive DBT training, either before or during the study.
- There is large variability in routine clinical settings regarding the amount of follow-up consultation received after initial training.
- Drop-out rates for treatment are higher when DBT is delivered in routine clinical settings, as compared to research settings. More research is needed to explore reasons for drop-out and ways to decrease drop-out.
- Many routine clinical settings include phone coaching only during office hours. It is unclear what impact, if any, this modification from the standard protocol has on outcomes.

REFERENCES

Andion, O., Ferrer, M., Matali, J., Gancedo, B., Calvo, N., Barral, C., … Casas, M. (2012). Effectiveness of combined individual and group dialectical behavior therapy compared to only individual dialectical behavior therapy: A preliminary study. *Psychotherapy (Chic)*, 49(2), 241–250.

Axelrod, S. R., Perepletchikova, F., Holtzman, K., & Sinha, R. (2011). Emotion regulation and substance use frequency in women with substance dependence and borderline personality disorder receiving dialectical behavior therapy. *The American Journal of Drug and Alcohol Abuse*, 37(1), 37–42. doi: 10.3109/00952990.2010.535582

Barnicot, K., Savill, M., Bhatti, N., & Priebe, S. (2014). A pragmatic randomised controlled trial of dialectical behaviour therapy: Effects on hospitalisation and post-treatment follow-up. *Psychotherapy and Psychosomatics*, 83(3), 192–193.

Ben-Porath, D. D., Peterson, G. A., & Smee, J. (2004). Treatment of individuals with Borderline Personality Disorder using Dialectical Behavior Therapy in a community mental health setting: Clinical application and a preliminary investigation. *Cognitive and Behavioral Practice*, 11(4), 424–434. doi: 10.1016/S1077-7229%2804%2980059-2

Blackford, J. U., & Love, R. (2011). Dialectical behavior therapy group skills training in a community mental health setting: A pilot study. *International Journal of Group Psychotherapy*, 61(4), 645–657. doi: 10.1521/ijgp.2011.61.4.645

Blennerhassett, R., Bamford, L., Whelan, A., Jamieson, S., & O'Raghaillaigh, J. W. (2009). Dialectical Behaviour Therapy in an Irish community mental health setting. *Irish Journal of Psychological Medicine*, 26(2), 59–63.

Borkovec, T. D., & Castonguay, L. G. (1998). What is the scientific meaning of empirically supported therapy? *Journal of Consulting and Clinical Psychology*, 66(1), 136–142.

Brassington, J., & Krawitz, R. (2006). Australasian dialectical behaviour therapy pilot outcome study: Effectiveness, utility and feasibility. *Australasian Psychiatry, 14*(3), 313–319. doi: 10.1111/j.1440-1665.2006.02285.x

Carter, G. L., Willcox, C. H., Lewin, T. J., Conrad, A. M., & Bendit, N. (2010). Hunter DBT project: Randomized controlled trial of dialectical behaviour therapy in women with borderline personality disorder. *Australian & New Zealand Journal of Psychiatry, 44*(2), 162–173. doi:10.3109/00048670903393621

Chalker, S. A., Carmel, A., Atkins, D. C., Landes, S. J., Kerbrat, A. H., & Comtois, K. A. (2015). Examining challenging behaviors of clients with borderline personality disorder. *Behaviour Research and Therapy, 75*, 11–19.

Chambless, D. L., & Hollon, S. D. (1998). Defining empirically supported therapies. *Journal of Consulting and Clinical Psychology, 66*(1), 7–18.

Comtois, K. A., Elwood, L., Holdcraft, L. C., Smith, W. R., & Simpson, T. L. (2007). Effectiveness of dialectical behavior therapy in a community mental health center. *Cognitive and Behavioral Practice, 14*(4), 406–414. doi:10.1016/j.cbpra.2006.04.023

Comtois, K. A., Kerbrat, A. H., Atkins, D. C., Harned, M. S., & Elwood, L. (2010). Recovery from disability for individuals with borderline personality disorder: A feasibility trial of DBT-ACES. *Psychiatric Services, 61*(11), 1106–1111.

Cunningham, K., Wolbert, R., & Lillie, B. (2004). It's about me solving my problems: Clients' assessments of dialectical behavior therapy. *Cognitive and Behavioral Practice, 11*, 248–256.

Feigenbaum, J. D., Fonagy, P., Pilling, S., Jones, A., Wildgoose, A., & Bebbington, P. E. (2012). A real-world study of the effectiveness of DBT in the UK National Health Service. *British Journal of Clinical Psychology, 51*(2), 121–141. doi: 10.1111/j.2044-8260.2011.02017.x

Gaglia, A., Essletzbichler, J., Barnicot, K., Bhatti, N., & Priebe, S. (2013). Dropping out of dialectical behaviour therapy in the NHS: The role of care coordination. *The Psychiatrist, 37*(8), 267–271.

Gunderson, J. G. (1996). Borderline patient's intolerance of aloneness: Insecure attachments and therapist availability. *American Journal of Psychiatry, 153*(6), 752–758.

Hawkins, K. A., & Sinha, R. (1998). Can line clinicians master the conceptual complexities of dialectical behavior therapy? An evaluation of a State Department of Mental Health training program. *Journal of Psychiatric Research, 32*(6), 379–384. doi: 10.1016/S0022-3956%2898%2900030-2

Hjalmarsson, E., Kaver, A., Perseius, K.-I., Cederberg, K., & Ghaderi, A. (2008). Dialectical behaviour therapy for borderline personality disorder among adolescents and young adults: Pilot study, extending the research findings in new settings and cultures. *Clinical Psychologist, 12*(1), 18–29. doi: 10.1080/13284200802069035

Hodgetts, A., Wright, J., & Gough, A. (2007). Clients with borderline personality disorder: Exploring their experience of dialectical behaviour therapy. *Counselling & Psychotherapy Research, 7*(3), 172–177.

Landes, S. J., & Linehan, M. M. (2012). Dissemination and implementation of dialectical behavior therapy: An intensive training model. In D. H. Barlow & R. K. McHugh (Eds.), *Disemination and implementation of evidence-based psychological interventions* (pp. 187–208). New York, NY: Oxford University Press.

Landes, S. J., Rodriguez, A. L., Smith, B. N., Matthieu, M. M., Trent, L. R., Kemp, J., & Thompson, C. (2017). Barriers, facilitators and benefits of implementation of Dialectical

Behaviour Therapy in routine care: Results from a national program evaluation survey in the Veterans Health Administration. *Translational Behavioral Medicine, 7*, 1–13.

Linehan, M. M. (1993). *Cognitive-behavioral treatment of borderline personality disorder.* New York, NY: Guilford Press.

Linehan, M. M., Comtois, K. A., Murray, A., Brown, M. Z., Gallop, R. J., Heard, H. L., . . . Lindenboim, N. (2006). Two-year randomized controlled trial and follow-up of dialectical behavior therapy vs therapy by experts for suicidal behaviors and borderline personality disorder. *Archives of General Psychiatry, 63*, 757–766.

Linehan, M. M., Korslund, K. E., Harned, M. S., Gallop, R. J., Lungu, A., Neacsiu, A. D., . . . Murray-Gregory, A. M. (2015). Dialectical behavior therapy for high suicide risk in individuals with borderline personality disorder: A randomized clinical trial and component analysis. *JAMA Psychiatry, 72*(5), 475–482. doi: 10.1001/jamapsychiatry.2014.3039

Lopez, A., & Chessick, C. A. (2013). DBT graduate group pilot study: A model to generalize skills to create a "life worth living." *Social Work in Mental Health, 11*(2), 141–153.

McMain, S. F., Guimond, T., Streiner, D. L., Cardish, R. J., & Links, P. S. (2012). Dialectical behavior therapy compared with general psychiatric management for borderline personality disorder: Clinical outcomes and functioning over a 2-year follow-up. *The American Journal of Psychiatry, 169*(6), 650–661.

McMain, S. F., Links, P. S., Gnam, W. H., Guimond, T., Cardish, R. J., Korman, L., & Streiner, D. L. (2009). A randomized trial of dialectical behavior therapy versus general psychiatric management for borderline personality disorder. *The American Journal of Psychiatry, 166*(12), 1365–1374. doi: 10.1176/appi.ajp.2009.09010039

McSherry, P., O'Connor, C., Hevey, D., & Gibbons, P. (2012). Service user experience of adapted dialectical behaviour therapy in a community adult mental health setting. *Journal of Mental Health, 21*(6), 539–547.

Nadort, M., Arntz, A., Smit, J. H., Giesen-Bloo, J., Eikelenboom, M., Shiphoven, P., . . . Van Dyck, R. (2009). Implementation of outpatient schema therapy for borderline personality disorder with versus without crisis support by the therapist outside office hours: A randomized trial. *Behaviour Research Therapy, 47*, 961–973.

Nathan, P. E., Stuart, S. P., & Dolan, S. (2000). Research on psychotherapy efficacy and effectiveness: Between Scylla and Charybdis? *Psychological Bulletin, 126*(6), 964–981.

Pasieczny, N., & Connor, J. (2011). The effectiveness of dialectical behaviour therapy in routine public mental health settings: An Australian controlled trial. *Behaviour Research and Therapy, 49*(1), 4–10. doi: 10.1016/j.brat.2010.09.006

Perseius, K.-I., Ojehagen, A., Ekdahl, S., Asberg, M., & Samuelsson, M. (2003). Treatment of suicidal and deliberate self-harming patients with borderline personality disorder using dialectical behavioral therapy: The patients' and the therapists' perceptions. *Archives of Psychiatric Nursing, 17*(5), 218–227.

Prendergast, N., & McCausland, J. (2007). Dialectic behaviour therapy: A 12-month collaborative program in a local community setting. *Behaviour Change, 24*(1), 25–35.

Priebe, S., Bhatti, N., Barnicot, K., Bremner, S., Gaglia, A., Katsakou, C., . . . Zinkler, M. (2012). Effectiveness and cost-effectiveness of dialectical behaviour therapy for self-harming patients with personality disorder: A pragmatic randomised controlled trial. *Psychotherapy and Psychosomatics, 81*(6), 356–365.

Riediger, E., & Baine, D. (1987). Turnover of staff in residential facilities for people with mental handicaps in Alberta. *Canadian Journal of Rehabilitation, 1*, 29–36.

Rizvi, S. L. (2011). Treatment failure in dialectical behavior therapy. *Cognitive and Behavioral Practice*, *18*(3), 403–412. doi: 10.1016/j.cbpra.2010.05.003

Stiglmayr, C., Stecher-Mohr, J., Wagner, T., Meibner, J., Spretz, D., Steffens, C., ... Barbette, R. (2014). Effectiveness of dialectic behavioral therapy in routine outpatient care: The Berlin Borderline Study. *Borderline Personality Disorder and Emotional Dysregulation*, *1*(10). doi: 10.1186/2051-6673-1-20

Turner, R. M. (2000). Naturalistic evaluation of dialectical behavior therapy-oriented treatment for borderline personality disorder. *Cognitive and Behavioral Practice*, *7*(4), 413–419. doi: 10.1016/S1077-7229%2800%2980052-8

Williams, S. E., Hartstone, M. D., & Denson, L. A. (2010). Dialectical behavioural therapy and borderline personality disorder: Effects on service utilisation and self-reported symptoms. *Behaviour Change*, *27*(4), 251–264.

CHAPTER 22

COST-EFFECTIVENESS OF DIALECTICAL BEHAVIOUR THERAPY FOR BORDERLINE PERSONALITY DISORDER

ROY KRAWITZ AND ERIN M. MIGA

SERVICE PROVISION CHALLENGES OF BORDERLINE PERSONALITY DISORDER

A 35,000-person, US epidemiological study showed a lifetime prevalence of borderline personality disorder (BPD) between 2.7% (Tomko, Trull, Wood, & Sher, 2014) and 5.9% (Grant et al., 2008), depending on criteria used. People with BPD represent 20% of psychiatric inpatients, and 10% of community psychiatric patients (Swartz, Blazer, George, & Winfield, 1990). Research has found that individuals with BPD had more extensive histories of outpatient, inpatient, and pharmacological treatment than people with major depressive disorder and more extensive treatment histories than those with other personality disorders (Bender et al., 2001). As a complex and severe disorder, BPD individuals make up 42% (Comtois & Carmel, 2016) to 50% (Ferrero, Piero, Zirilli, Lanteri, & Fassino, 2008, as cited in Amianto et al., 2011)) of the highest mental health service utilizers, making BPD among the most expensive of psychiatric disorders. Upon post-mortem psychological autopsy, 33% of suicides met criteria for BPD (Runeson, Beskow, & Waern, 1996). The lifetime suicide rate among those with BPD is approximately 10% (50 times that of general population), and similar to that of schizophrenia and bipolar affective disorder. Across all mental disorders, this is the highest suicide rate for women and second highest for men (Qin, 2011).

This chapter proceeds with an overview of dialectical behaviour therapy (DBT), including efficacy and effectiveness research. It presents research on the financial cost-effectiveness of DBT for people with BPD (core reason for this chapter) particularly research on reduction in acute mental health hospital days as a common major contributing measure of financial cost effectiveness. It ends with brief financial data on four different BPD treatments, relevance of DBT adherence to financial cost effectiveness, and chapter conclusions.

Overview of Dialectical Behaviour Therapy

Standard comprehensive DBT includes four treatment modes organized across stages of treatment with identified hierarchical treatment targets. The treatment modes are individual therapy; group skills training; as-needed skills-based telephone coaching for the client; and clinician consultation team meeting. DBT stage 1 treatment primarily addresses severe behavioural dyscontrol such as suicidal and self-harming behaviour; stage 2 addresses severe emotional suffering with actions (suicide and self-harm, and sometimes other actions associated with severe Axis 1 conditions such as substance use) under control; stage 3 addresses basic problems in living and less severe Axis 1 disorders; and stage 4 addresses a sense of incompleteness or emptiness. (Linehan, 1993a). The overwhelming majority of DBT research has been on stage 1 DBT, usually of a one-year duration. It is important to note that, based on clinical experience, some clients will require a treatment longer than what has existed in research contexts. A hierarchy of priorities guides stage 1 treatment targets, without which treatment could be chaotic and likely ineffective. This hierarchy is decreasing life-threatening behaviour (including homicide, suicide, and other self-harm actions and thoughts), followed by "therapy interfering behaviour" (TIB) (any behaviour of client or therapist that interferes with treatment—for example client non-attendance, therapist lateness, or inattentiveness), followed by increasing "quality of life (QoL) behaviours" (for example, addressing depression, anxiety, joblessness) and increasing skills (Linehan, 1993a).

Outcomes of Dialectical Behaviour Therapy for BPD

DBT is a mindfulness-based cognitive-behavioural therapy for treating people with complex, challenging, hard-to-treat multi-diagnostic conditions, of which BPD has been the exemplar. Thirteen randomized controlled trials (some of these in "real-world" settings) exist to date that support DBT's efficacy and effectiveness in treating people with BPD; and numerous other randomized controlled trials have been conducted for other disorders (for more details on DBT's treatment efficacy, see Miga,

Neacsiu, Lungu, Heard, & Dimeff, this volume). DBT has been shown to be effective in non-academic "real world" settings as well (see Walton & Comtois, this volume). For example, DBT has effectively treated individuals with BPD in otherwise routine public mental health funded services, as evidenced by an RCT in England (Priebe et al., 2012), a non-randomized controlled trial in Australia (Pasieczny & Connor, 2011), and in pre-post studies (see Table 22.3 for those studies with data on hospital days used) throughout Europe and the US (American Psychiatric Association, 1998) (awarded an American Psychiatric Association Gold Award); Ireland (Blennerhassett, Bamford, Whelan, Jamieson, & O'Raghaillaigh, 2009) and New Zealand (Brassington & Krawitz, 2006).

Meta-analyses of DBT

DBT is the only treatment for BPD to date with a sufficient number of outcome studies to conduct a meta-analysis. One meta-analysis of DBT efficacy for BPD found a moderate effect size of .62 for suicidal and self-injurious behaviour, while DBT was only marginally more effective than TAU at treatment retention (Ost, 2008). Kliem, Kroger, and Kosfelder (2010) found effect sizes ranging from 0.37–0.51 depending on variables used, which are small to medium effects (Cohen, 1992). Similar to Ost, Kliem and colleagues found a moderate effect size for DBT in treating suicidal and self-injurious behaviour when pooling both RCT and non-RCTs. Furthermore, other meta-analyses have also found that DBT for BPD leads to a decrease in suicidal ideation and self-harm (Binks et al., 2006); and efficacy in stabilizing and controlling self-destructive behaviour (Panos, Jackson, Hasan, & Panos, 2014).

While several studies have found moderate effects for DBT's treatment of BPD-related behaviours, it is worth noting that effect sizes were reduced to small and non-significant when comparing DBT to BPD-specific evidence-based treatments (Clarkin, Levy, Lenzenweger, & Kernberg, 2007; McMain et al., 2009). No significant differences were found between DBT and alternative BPD-specific evidence-based treatments on drop-out rate in the aforementioned trials.

Most recently, Stoffers et al. (2012) found that DBT had the best meta-analytic evidence for its efficacy across all treatments for people with BPD. More specifically, this meta-analytic review compared DBT to TAU, finding medium- to large-effect sizes for DBT in reducing anger (-.83), self injurious behaviour (-.54) and improving general mental health outcomes (.65), while again, no differences were found in treatment retention. Sneed, Fertuck, Kanellopoulos, and Culang-Reinlieb (2012) write that because DBT has been shown to be efficacious by three independent groups, that it is the only treatment that meets criteria for a well-established treatment for BPD. As the body of empirical evidence supporting DBT has grown, so have its endorsements by professional organizations (see Table 22.1).

Table 22.1   DBT treatment efficacy research for BPD—professional organizational validation

Author	Outcomes & Comments	Quotes
National Institute for Health and Clinical Excellence (2009)	UK government NICE guidelines provide the only specific, favourable naming of a specialist treatment (i.e., DBT).	"For women with BPD, for whom reducing recurrent self-harm is a priority, consider a comprehensive DBT programme."
Australian Psychological Society (2010) (174-page review)	Names DBT for BPD meeting the highest rating of evidence possible (Level I), with schema-focused therapy and transference-focused therapy as moderate (Level II) evidence.	"... with insufficient evidence to indicate that any of the remaining interventions were effective."
Substance Abuse and Mental Health Administration (2011)	DBT named as the only therapy (apart from psycho-educational multi-family groups) listed as an evidence-based practice for BPD in report to US Congress.	"DBT has a large empirical base compared with other treatments and is largely considered one of the best, if not *the* best, treatments for BPD."
American Psychological Association Division 12 (2012)	Considers DBT to be the only current treatment for BPD that has Level I (highest level) strong evidence for its use, with mentalization-based therapy and schema-focused therapy having "modest" evidence and transference-focused therapy "controversial" evidence.	
Stoffers et al. (2012)	Stoffers et al., reporting on Cochrane Database of Systematic Reviews Plain Language Summary, cautiously name DBT as helpful.	"... best meta-analytic evidence for its efficacy" across all treatments for BPD.

BPD: Borderline Personality Disorder
DBT: Dialectical Behaviour Therapy

Cost-effectiveness in Treating People with BPD

Brazier et al. (2006) analysed data from six trials (four trials of DBT vs TAU or client-centred therapy [CCT]; one trial comparing manual-assisted CBT [MCBT] to an alternative treatment; and one trial comparing mentalization-based therapy [MBT] to an alternative treatment). Separate economic analyses were conducted for each trial, given the complexity of care models for those with BPD and obstacles to pooling data and conducting more formal decision modelling analyses. Cost-effectiveness was defined as quality-adjusted life year (QALY—quality plus quantity economic measure of disease burden where one QALY is equal to one year of life in perfect health) gained and cost per self-injury event (financial cost incurred to prevent one episode of self-injury) avoided.

Results suggested potential dominance of DBT as compared to comparison treatments: three out of four DBT trials revealed that DBT was more cost-effective (ranging from 53–85% probability), with one trial that dealt with a less suicidal population (Koons et al., 2001) revealing TAU as more cost-effective than DBT. Brazier's (2006) systematic review reported that the Linehan and Heard (1999a) economic report, where DBT treatment resulted in US$9,000 fewer health costs than TAU, was "a good-quality study that scored highly on the *BMJ* checklist for economic evaluations". Finally, MBT favored TAU in cost-effectiveness (45% probability) and results comparing MCBT to TAU were equivocal and difficult to interpret with any degree of certainty, partially due to methodological problems. Furthermore, the 2014 systematic review by Brettschneider, Riedel-Heller, & Köning regarding the economics of treating BPD concludes that the economic evidence is limited; that it is possible that some treatments are cost-effective with some preliminary support for the cost-effectiveness of DBT.

Cost-effectiveness studies in treating people with BPD are few in number and highly varied in their design and variables measured, so conclusions need to be considered with caution (Brazier et al., 2006; Brettschneider et al., 2014). Problems include using incompatible outcome variables; the difficulty of comparing studies across jurisdictions, states, or countries with different health care structures and costs; and the fact that studies published in different years are not necessarily comparable, even when compounding inflation is taken into account. Currency differences, which have fluctuated, and will continue to fluctuate, mean that inter-country cost comparisons are not necessarily entirely reliable. Yet despite these current limitations, funders and administrators still have to make decisions on the best current information available.

Cost-Savings of DBT: Reductions in Hospital Days

While Brazier et al. (2006) considered cost-effectiveness via two commonly researched variables, self-injury events avoided and quality-adjusted life years, mental health cost savings are also commonly measured through a reduction in inpatient psychiatric hospitalization. For example, Brettschneider et al. (2014), in their review of 15 trials, indicated that the greatest proportion of studies (67%) utilized inpatient care as one metric of cost-effectiveness. Psychiatric inpatient care also appears to be the cost variable that has been most often recorded in published BPD efficacy and effectiveness studies. Therefore, this section focuses on hospital days as a proxy of cost-effectiveness (see Table 22.2 and Table 22.3). DBT is committed to treating clients whenever possible in the community so that clients learn coping skills (including regulating urges for life-threatening behaviour) in the real world setting in which they live. This has translated to reports of substantial reductions in hospital days used (see Table 22.2 and Table 22.3). Descriptive data on RCTs (Table 22.2) comparing within-subject acute mental health hospital days in the year pre-DBT with year of DBT or year post-DBT is not available. However, seven studies are available where objective or extrapolated data on pre-post and controlled trials (Table 22.3) compare one year pre-DBT with either one year of DBT or one year post-DBT. These seven studies all report a reduction in hospital days used (range: 4.44–54.0) with a mean of 17.58.

For financial context, Pasieczny and Connor (2011) reported a mean total cost of a day in a psychiatric hospital day as A$953 in 2011 and Amner (2012) reported £288. Taking inflation (say 3%) and 2012 currency rates (as of October 31, 2012) into account, this translates in October 31, 2016 figures into a daily hospital cost of US $1,138 (Pasieczny & Connor, 2011) and US$521 (Amner, 2012). The mean reduction of 17.58 days reported results in a mean financial saving of between US$9,086 (using Amner's [2012] reported daily hospital costs of US$521) and US$19,847/client (using Pasieczny & Connor's [2011] reported daily hospital costs of US$1,138). These savings are somewhat larger than the reported costs (see Table 22.5) of providing DBT in the respective studies by both Amner, and Pasieczny & Connor.

Long-term Cost-Savings of DBT

It is reasonable to expect cost savings to increase over the years following treatment as positive client outcomes mean that health cost savings remain, while costs of providing treatment often decrease or stop. Most of the studies reported only direct psychiatric costs (see Table 22.4), meaning that other health costs, costs of other services (e.g., police, justice, ambulance, social services, housing), and lost income productivity would further enhance the cost-effectiveness analysis. More research is needed on the long-term cost savings of DBT as compared to other treatments.

Costs of Four Different Treatments

Evaluating cost-effectiveness requires not only cost-savings data, but data on the costs of the delivery of the new treatment. Table 22.5 reports the costs of treatment for funders who might want to know comparative costs across these four different treatments; however, it is the opinion of the authors that these results are confounding. For reasons

Table 22.2 Psychiatric inpatient days (or days in prison) reported on in DBT randomized controlled trials (adherence rated unless stated)

Author	Outcomes & Comments
Linehan et al. (1991, 1993b)	12-month DBT programme used 30.4 hospital days/client fewer than TAU; reductions in hospital days were maintained and improved upon at one-year follow-up.
Linehan et al. (1999b)	BPD and drug dependence: DBT outperformed TAU clinically. No statistical difference between DBT and TAU in hospital days used during the 12-month treatment and four-month follow-up.
Koons et al. (2001)	After six months of DBT, reduction from 30% to 10% of people admitted to a mental health hospital in the three–six month period of treatment compared to the three months pre-treatment (TAU 20% to 10%). Hospital days not reported.
Linehan et al. (2002)	DBT outperformed the comparator treatment (12 step+comprehensive validation) of people with BPD and opioid dependence. Mean number of nights in prison was 7.7 for the DBT clients and 18.8 for comparison clients.
Linehan et al. (2006)	DBT outperformed treatment by experts on most measures. In the year of treatment, statistically fewer DBT clients than treatment by experts' clients were admitted to a psychiatric hospital (19.6% vs 48.9%; $p < .007$) or admitted to a psychiatric hospital for suicide ideation (9.8% vs 35.6%; $p < .004$). There were essentially no differences in admission percentages in the 12 months post treatment. Pre-post comparisons of hospital days in each treatment arm not reported.
McMain et al. (2009)	DBT and "general psychiatric management" equally effective across most measures, including hospital days used. DBT arm: reduction in hospital days/client in the last four months of a 12-month treatment, compared to the four months pre-treatment (10.52 days to 3.73 days).
Carter et al. (2010)	Six-month DBT vs TAU: DBT resulted in a non-significant but greater reduction in hospitalizations vs. TAU (0.61 vs. 0.91 psychiatric admissions/client in six-month treatment; 0.5 vs.1.4 general hospital admissions in six-month treatment). Hospital days not reported (not adherence rated).
Feigenbaum et al. (2012)	12 months DBT vs TAU: No between- or within-group changes in hospitalization noted (not adherence rated).
Barnicot et al. (2014)	5% of DBT and 27.5% of TAU clients hospitalized during one year of treatment using a mean of 4.0 hospital days in DBT vs 8.4 days in TAU.
Mehlum et al. (2014)	DBT-A > EUC with 50% fewer hospitalizations (one person vs two people) and emergency department visits (two people vs five people); however, numbers too small for statistical significance; days in hospital not recorded.
Linehan et al. (2015)	Standard DBT including DBT skills group vs individual DBT+activities group (no DBT skills group): no difference in psychiatric hospitalization rates in year of treatment; decrease in psychiatric hospitalization rates in year after treatment (3% vs 13%; $p = .03$).

Two DBT RCTs not included as no data on hospitalization reported (Clarkin et al., 2007; Verhuel et al., 2003).

BPD: Borderline Personality Disorder

DBT: Dialectical Behaviour Therapy

DBT-A: Dialectical Behaviour Therapy for Adolescents

EUC: Enhanced Usual Care

RCT: Randomized Controlled Trial

TAU: Treatment as Usual

Table 22.3   Psychiatric inpatient days (and other cost–savings data when relevant) in pre-, post-, or non-randomized controlled DBT studies (not adherence rated); in otherwise routine state or publicly funded mental health services (unless otherwise stated).

Author	Outcomes & Comments
The American Psychiatric Association (1998)	Public and private insurance-funded service. Reductions in hospital days (2–3/client) comparing the 12 months pre-treatment with the 12 months of DBT treatment; and 76 % reduction in partial hospitalization days; 56 % reduction in crisis beds; and 80% reduction in ER contacts.
Turner (2000)	RCTs included in this table as DBT was adapted; "DBT oriented therapy" had fewer days in hospital in previous six months after six months (2.67 vs 10.75) and 12 months (.75 vs 13) treatment compared to client-centred therapy.
Rathus & Miller (2002)	Not routine mental health service, non-randomized controlled trial; shortened 12 week adolescent adapted DBT vs TAU; in the 12 weeks of treatment fewer clients admitted to hospital (0% vs 13%; p = .04).
Perseius et al. (2004)	Not routine mental health service: Mean days in hospital/client essentially unchanged comparing the 12 months pre-DBT with the 12 months of DBT (89.57 to 86.80); however, 50% reduction in hospital days comparing the 12 months pre-DBT with the 12 month period comprising the last six months of DBT and the six months post-one year DBT (89.57 to 44.12).
Batcheler (2005)	Pre-post DBT study: reduction in hospital days (25.04 to 4 to 1.09 days) comparing the 12 months pre-treatment, the 12 months of DBT treatment, and 12 months post-DBT treatment.
Brassington and Krawitz (2006)	Reduction in hospital days (3.42 to 1.2 days) comparing the six months pre-treatment with the six months of DBT treatment.
Comtois et al. (2007)	Reduction in median hospital days (17 to 0; p < .001) comparing the 12 months pre-treatment, with the 12 months of DBT treatment.
Comtois et al. (2010)	Reduction in mean number of inpatient admissions (5.23 to 0.67) comparing the year before DBT with the year of DBT.
Pasieczny and Connor (2011)	Six-month DBT vs waitlist TAU: DBT had significantly fewer hospital days (2.23 vs 13.6; p < .01) (local adherence rather than Linehan adherence rating used).
Prendergast and McCausland (2007)	Reduction in hospital days used (6.09 to 1.73 days) comparing the six months pre-treatment with the six months of DBT treatment.
Blennerhassett et al. (2009)	Six months DBT: Mean hospital days reduced from 57.83 to 3.83, comparing the one year pre-DBT with the one year post-DBT.
Williams et al. (2010)	Twenty-week DBT skills group+either individual DBT or individual TAU: "significant decrease in number of inpatient days during group therapy for group completers (2.79 to 0.57 days)", accounted mostly for by "high service utilisers" greater reductions (16.18 to 1.36 days) that were sustained over the six months follow-up (17.56 to 3.33 days; p = .06).
Meyers et al. (2014)	USA study of war veterans with symptoms of BPD treated with 46 weeks of DBT. Comparing one year before DBT vs one year after DBT revealed a 50% reduction in number of clients hospitalized and of those with a hospitalization, reduced average length of stay in hospital (5.2 to 1.6; p = .01).

DBT: Dialectical Behaviour Therapy

RCT: Randomized Controlled Trial

TAU: Treatment as Usual

outlined earlier of variability and paucity of studies, different jurisdictions costs, different country costs, currency differences, and time of reporting, the authors believe that decision-makers should be cautious in how interpretation of results might influence decision-making. In addition, the data in Table 22.5 for mentalization-based therapy are for partial hospitalization. A subsequent randomized controlled trial of outpatient mentalization-based therapy (Bateman & Fonagy, 2009) presumably involved lower costs, but these have not yet been reported.

DBT Adherence

Several of the randomized trials demonstrating the efficacy of DBT to date have been conducted with clinicians meeting a required standard of proficiency in DBT practice—important for client, clinician, organizational, and financial outcomes (see Walton & Comtois, this volume). However, the Substance Abuse and Mental Health Administration (2011) reported to the US Congress widespread concern about clinicians offering non-adherent DBT, and achieving poorer outcomes than that attained in the efficacy research. DBT adherence is therefore an important variable in financial cost-effectiveness decision-making by funders, managers, and clinicians, although the extent to which DBT adherence plays a clear role in clinical outcomes remains an empirical question worthy of further study. DBT standards for "real-world" contexts (outside research units) have been developed since 2014 with formal DBT therapist certification and DBT programme accreditation pathways in place to independently assess therapist and programme proficiencies and adherence to the DBT model. Such efforts have made great progress towards addressing concerns about the delivery of non-adherent DBT, although ongoing efforts and attention to this dilemma is needed.

Much of the extensive "gold standard" research of DBT's efficacy in working with complex, highly suicidal people is based on adherent DBT; so, if clinicians and organizations want to provide the treatment with reference to the evidence base, DBT adherence is required. In their 2007 study, Koerner, Dimeff, and Swenson suggest that "adapting (rather than adopting) DBT can heighten risk and legal liability", and that practising adherent DBT, "is likely to be more credible than trying to justify an untested modification of DBT".

CONCLUSIONS

Future focus on a range of different efficacious and effective BPD treatments is needed so as to be able to best match each unique client and treatment modality and to have another treatment to offer those clients when a previous treatment has been unsuccessful. Additionally, more head-to-head cost-effectiveness studies across a range of different

Table 22.4 Financial cost-effectiveness of DBT: reports to date.

Author	Outcomes & Comments
The American Psychiatric Association (1998)	USA community service study: "Total" treatment costs decreased by US $26,000/patient (US $46,000 to US $20,000) in the year of DBT, compared to the year pre-treatment; despite outpatient costs increasing by US$6,600 (US$3,500 to US$10,100) with hospital costs decreasing by US$26,500 (US$32,400 to US$5,900).
Linehan and Heard (1999a)	Linehan and Heard (1999a) report on the Linehan et al. (1991) study that DBT treatment resulted in US$9,000 less health costs than TAU.
Perseius et al. (2004)	Swedish community treatment study showed US$17,000 less costs (320,000SEK vs 210SEK; 1SEK = 0.1494 US$) comparing year pre-DBT vs year of DBT (6–18 month period of DBT). Comparing the month before DBT treatment with the 18th month of DBT treatment demonstrated cost savings of US$6,000/patient (US$8,000 vs US$2,000; 1SEK = 0.1494 US$).
Aos et al., Washington State Institute for Public Policy (2004)	A Washington State juvenile offender institution DBT programme achieved a US$38.05 financial benefit for every dollar spent on the DBT programme, and a benefits minus costs of US$31,243/client after costs of DBT subtracted.
Prendergast and McCausland (2007)	Australian public psychiatric service study: Reduced hospitalization rates resulted in a pre-post treatment cost reduction of A$4,501/client over 6 months of DBT.
Pasieczny and Connor (2011)	Australian public psychiatric service study: Decreased total treatment costs of A$5,927/patient over 6 month DBT vs. TAU (A$12,196 vs. A$18,123).
Amner (2012)	Welsh public psychiatric service DBT study: Reduction in all healthcare costs of £1,741 during the 1 year follow-up, compared with the 12 months pre-treatment; 20% reduction in inpatient costs.
Priebe et al. (2012)	"Real world" UK national health service study, total costs were higher in DBT (£5685) vs TAU (£3754) for every two months of treatment. DBT outperformed TAU with a 9% reduction in self-harm compared to TAU for every two months of treatment. This 9% reduction therefore costs £322 more than TAU; put differently, it costs £36 to achieve a 1% reduction in self-harm.
Wagner et al. (2014)	German study, using 2010 pricings: societal cost-of-illness was €28,026 in the one year pre-treatment, reducing to €18,758 during the one year of outpatient DBT (including DBT treatment costs); and reducing further to €14,750 in the year post-DBT treatment. Cost savings were mainly due to decreased inpatient costs. This data needs to be interpreted very cautiously as 20% of the sample were treated in an inpatient DBT programme in the year prior to the outpatient DBT, which would have affected pre-outpatient DBT costs and may have improved the clinical outcomes, including subsequent rate of hospitalizations.

Brown et al. (2013)	Pre–post study with people with intellectual disability and "challenging behaviours" (physical aggression 88%, stealing 65%, self-injury 48%, fire setting 23%) showed a 76% reduction of serious behaviours, incarceration, and hospitalization resulting in a 74% reduction of costs (reduced costs of US$491,340/client/year).
Wunsch et al. (2014)	Financial projected cost–benefit analysis estimated that for each dollar invested in DBT treatment, 1.52 dollars would be gained within one year; 55% of these savings from direct costs and 45% from indirect costs (e.g. work attendance, social benefits).
Meyers et al. (2014)	USA study of war veterans with symptoms of BPD treated with 46 weeks of DBT. Cost of DBT was US$8,443/client, essentially the same as the pre–DBT outpatient mental health treatment costs. Comparing one year before DBT vs one year after DBT, revealed a 28% (US$5,967) reduction in overall health costs/client (US$21,183 to US$15,216); US$3,670 reduction of outpatient mental healthcare costs/client (US$8,889 to US$5,219); For the 41 clients in the study the reduction in overall health care costs for the one year post treatment was a total of US$244,647

(Financial amounts reported as in cited publications and not updated for inflation.)

BPD: Borderline Personality Disorder

DBT: Dialectical Behaviour Therapy

ER: Emergency Room

SEK: Swedish krona

TAU: Treatment as Usual

Table 22.5   BPD costs across four treatment models

Author	Program	Country	Cost (US$)
Bateman and Fonagy (2003)	MBT—partial hospitalization	UK	22,680
Van Asselt et al. (2008)	TFP	Netherlands	5,938
Van Asselt et al. (2008)	SFT	Netherlands	7,139
Pasieczny and Connor (2011)	DBT	Australia	16,221
Amner (2012)	DBT	Wales	8,490

(Studies ranged from six months to three years, so costs are extrapolated to 12 months of treatment, expressed in US$ on basis of currency conversions as of October 31, 2012, and compounded inflation adjusted to 2016 US$ amounts on the assumption of inflation of 3%/year).

DBT: Dialectical Behaviour Therapy

MBT: Mentalization-based Therapy

SFT: Schema-focused Therapy

TFP: Transference-focused Therapy

client groups are needed, as well as more prospective cost-effectiveness studies with methodological strength built into such studies.

This article does not assume that DBT is necessarily more cost-effective than other evidence-based treatments for BPD; rather, that it has the most published data available on cost effectiveness. It might be worth, by proxy, in considering the hypothesis that other evidence-based BPD treatments might have similar cost-effectiveness. We strongly encourage such research to be conducted in order to better inform treatment for consumers.

Data on cost-effectiveness is variable and somewhat limited, hence the dominance of descriptive data in this paper. However, funders need to make decisions based on existing data, including when this is short of ideal. At the current time, DBT offers an evidence-based option for treating people with BPD that is likely to meet the objectives of funders, economists, accountants, administrators, providers, and consumers.

ACKNOWLEDGEMENTS

We thank Tony DuBose, Chief Training Executive at Behavioral Tech, and Alexis Karlson, MSSW, Director of Business Operations, Linehan Institute, who along with Erin Miga, from the original unabridged manuscript by Roy Krawitz, wrote an abridged version. The original manuscript and the abridged version were then synthesized for this chapter. We also thank André Ivanoff, PhD, Columbia University/Linehan Institute, who worked on an earlier version of this synthesized chapter. Roy Krawitz receives remuneration for delivering four days of DBT training on average per year in a private capacity.

KEY MESSAGES FOR CLINICIANS

- DBT is the treatment for BPD that offers Level 1 (highest level) evidence of efficacy and effectiveness and is the only treatment with sufficient data for meta-analyses.

- Cost-effectiveness studies in treating people with BPD are few in number and highly varied in their design and variables measured, so conclusions need to be considered with caution; more prospective methodologically robust studies are needed.

- Data on cost-savings from reduced hospital days remains largely descriptive although DBT has the most objective data, to date.

- Despite these current limitations, funders and administrators must make decisions on the best current information available.

- Current information of means of reduced mental hospital days suggest that providing DBT is in most situations likely to be financially cost-effective by virtue of hospital cost savings alone.

- In addition, it is reasonable to expect cost savings to increase over the years following treatment as positive client outcomes translate into both increased health cost savings and decreased costs of providing treatment.

- More systematic assessment of health costs, costs of other services (police, justice, ambulance, social services, housing), and lost income productivity would further enhance future cost-effectiveness analyses.

- DBT offers an evidence-based option for treating people with BPD that is likely to meet the financial objectives of funders, economists, accountants, administrators, providers, and consumers.

References

American Psychiatric Association (1998). Gold award: integrating dialectical behavior therapy into a community mental health program. *Psychiatric Services, 49*, 1138–1340.

American Psychological Association Division 12, Society of Clinical Psychology (2012), *Website on Research-Supported Psychological treatments*. Retrieved November 2, 2012 from http://www.div12.org/PsychologicalTreatments/disorders/bpd_main.php

Amianto, F. A., Ferrero, A., Piero, A., Cairo, E., Rocca, G., Simonelli, B., … Fassino S. (2011). Supervised team management, with or without structured psychotherapy, in heavy users of a mental health service with borderline personality disorder: a two-year follow-up preliminary randomized study. *BioMed Central 11*, 18.

Amner, K. (2012). The effect of DBT provision in reducing the cost of adults displaying the symptoms of BPD. *British Journal of Psychotherapy, 28*, 336–352.

Aos, S., Lieb, R., Mayfield, J., Miller, M., & Pennucci, A. (2004). *Benefits and costs of prevention and early intervention programs for youth*. Seattle: Washington State Institute for Public Policy.

Australian Psychological Society (2010). *Evidence-based psychological interventions in the treatment of mental disorders: a literature review.* Retrieved November 2, 2012 from http://www.psychology.org.au/Assets/Files/Evidence-Based-Psychological-Interventions.pdf

Barnicot, K., Savill, M., Bhatti, N., & Priebe, S. (2014). A pragmatic randomized controlled trial of dialectical behavior therapy: effects on hospitalization and post-treatment follow-up. *Psychotherapy and Psychosomatics, 83,* 192–193.

Batcheler, M. (2005). Dialectical behaviour therapy in New Zealand. *New Zealand Clinical Psychologist,* July, 11–16.

Bateman, A., & Fonagy, P. (2003). Health service utilization costs for borderline personality disorder patients treated with psychoanalytically orientated partial hospitalization versus general psychiatric care. *American Journal of Psychiatry, 160,* 169–171.

Bateman, A., & Fonagy, P. (2009). Randomized controlled trial of outpatient mentalization-based treatment versus structured clinical management for borderline personality disorder. *American Journal of Psychiatry, 166,* 1–10.

Bender, S., Dolan, R. T., Skodol, A. E., Sanislow, C. A., Dyck, I. R., McGlashan, T. H., ... Gunderson, J. G. (2001). Treatment utilization by patients with borderline personality disorder. *American Journal of Psychiatry 158,* 295–302.

Binks, C. A., Fenton, M., McCarthy, L., Lee, T., Adams, C. E., & Duggan, C. (2006). Psychological therapies for people with borderline personality disorder. *The Cochrane Database of Systematic Reviews, 1*(CD005652). doi: 10.1002/14651858.CD005652

Blennerhassett, R., Bamford, L., Whelan, A., Jamieson, S., & O'Raghaillaigh, J. W. (2009). Dialectical behaviour therapy in an Irish community mental health setting. *Journal of Psychological Medicine, 26,* 59–63.

Brassington, J., & Krawitz, R. (2006). Australasian dialectical behaviour therapy pilot outcome study: effectiveness, utility and feasibility. *Australasian Psychiatry, 14,* 313–319.

Brazier, J., Tumur, I., Holmes, M., Ferriter, M., Parry, G., Dent-Brown, K., & Paisley S. (2006). Psychological therapies including dialectical behavior therapy for borderline personality disorder: a systematic review and preliminary economic evaluation. *Health Technology Assessment, 10,* 1–138.

Brettschneider, C., Riedel-Heller, S., & Köning, H. (2014). A systematic review of economic evaluations of treatments for borderline personality disorder. *PLoS ONE, 9*(9), e107748. doi:10.1371/journal.pone.0107748

Brown, J. F., Brown, M. Z., & Dibasio, P. (2013). Treating individuals with intellectual disabilities and challenging behaviors with adapted dialectical behavior therapy. *Journal of Mental Health Research in Intellectual Disabilities, 6,* 280–303.

Carter, G. L., Willcox, C. H., Lewin, T. J., Conrad, A. M., & Bendit, N. (2010). Hunter DBT project: randomly controlled trial of dialectical behavior therapy in women with borderline personality disorder. *Australian & New Zealand Journal of Psychiatry, 44,* 162–173.

Clarkin, J. F., Levy, K. N., Lenzenweger, M. F., & Kernberg, O. F. (2007). Evaluating three treatments for borderline personality disorder: a multiwave study. *American Journal of Psychiatry, 164,* 922–928.

Cohen, J. (1992). A Power Primer. *Psychological Bulletin, 112,* 155–159.

Comtois, K. A., Elwood, L., Holdcraft, L. C., Smith, W. R., & Simpson, T. L. (2007). Effectiveness of DBT in a community mental health center. *Cognitive and Behavioral Practice, 14,* 406–414.

Comtois, K. A., Kerbrat, A. H., Atkins, D. C., Harned, M. S., & Elwood, L. (2010). Recovery from disability for individuals with borderline personality disorder: a feasibility trial of DBT-ACES. *Psychiatric Services, 61,* 1106–1111.

Comtois, K. A., & Carmel, A. (2016). Borderline personality disorder and high utilization of inpatient psychiatric hospitalization: concordance between research and clinical diagnosis. *Journal of Behavioral Health Services and Research, 43,* 272–280.

Feigenbaum, J. D., Fonagy, P., Pilling, S., Jones, A., Wildgoose, A., & Bebbington, P. E. (2012). A real-world study of the effectiveness of DBT in the UK National Health Service. *British Journal of Clinical Psychology, 51,* 121–141.

Ferrero, A., Piero, A., Zirilli, F., Lanteri, A., & Fassino, S. (2008). Clinical and sociodemographic features associated with high and prolonged utilization of resources by outpatients of a community psychiatric service. *Epidemiology and Psychiatric Sciences, 17,* 82–87.

Grant, B. F., Chou, S. P., Goldstein, R. B., Huang, B., Stinson, F. S., Saha, T. D., ... Ruan W. J. (2008). Prevalence, correlates, disability, and comorbidity of DSM-IV borderline personality disorder: results from the Wave 2 National Epidemiologic Survey on Alcohol and Related Conditions. *Journal of Clinical Psychiatry, 69,* 533–545.

Kliem, S., Kroger, C., and Kosfelder, J. (2010). Dialectical behavior therapy for borderline personality disorder: a meta-analysis using mixed-effects modeling. *Journal of Consulting and Clinical Psychology, 78,* 936–951.

Koerner, K., Dimeff, L. A., & Swenson, C. R. (2007). Adopt or adapt?: Fidelity matters. In L. A. Dimeff & K. Koerner (Eds.), *Dialectical behavior therapy in clinical practice: applications across disorders and settings* (pp. 19–36). New York: Guilford Press.

Koons, C. R., Robins, C. J., Tweed, J. L., Lynch, T. R., Gonzalez, A. M., Morse, J. Q., ... Bastian, L. A. (2001). Efficacy of dialectical behaviour therapy in women veterans with borderline personality disorder. *Behavior Therapy, 32,* 371–390.

Linehan, M. M., Armstrong, H., Suarez, L., & Allmon, D. (1991). Cognitive-behavioral treatment of chronically parasuicidal borderline patients. *Archives of General Psychiatry, 48,* 1060–1064.

Linehan, M. M. (1993a). *Cognitive behavioral treatment of borderline personality disorder.* New York: Guilford Press.

Linehan, M. M., Heard, H. L., & Armstrong, H. E. (1993b). Naturalistic follow-up of a behavioral treatment for chronically parasuicidal borderline patients. *Archives of General Psychiatry, 50,* 971–974.

Linehan, M. M., & Heard, H. L. (1999a). Borderline personality disorder: costs course and treatment outcomes. In N. Miller & K. Magruder (Eds.), *The cost effectiveness of psychotherapy: a guide for practitioners* (pp. 291–305). New York: Oxford University Press.

Linehan, M. M., Schmidt, H., Dimeff, L. A., Kanter, J., & Comtois, K. A. (1999b). Dialectical behavior therapy for patients with borderline personality disorder and drug dependence. *American Journal on Addiction, 8,* 279–292.

Linehan, M. M., Dimeff, L., Reynolds, S. K., Comtois, K. A., Welch S. S., Heagerty, P., & Kivlehan, D. (2002). Dialectical behavior therapy versus comprehensive validation therapy plus 12-step for the treatment of opioid dependent women meeting criteria for borderline personality disorder. *Drug and Alcohol Dependence, 67,* 13–26.

Linehan, M. M., Comtois, K. A., Murray, A. M., Brown, M. Z., Gallop, R. J., Heard, H. L., ... Lindenboim, N. (2006). Two-year randomized controlled trial and follow-up of dialectical behavior therapy vs therapy by experts for suicidal behaviours and borderline personality disorder. *Archives of General Psychiatry, 63,* 7573–7766.

Linehan, M. M., Korslund, K. E., Harned, M. S., Gallop, R. J., Lungu, A., Neasciu, A. D., ... Murray-Gregory, M. (2015). Dialectical behavior therapy for high suicide risk individuals with borderline personality disorder: a randomized controlled trial and component analysis. *JAMA Psychiatry, 72,* 475–482.

McMain, S. F., Links, P. S., Gnam, W. H., Guimond, T., Cardish, R. J., Korman, L., & Streiner, D. L. (2009). A randomized trial of dialectical behavior therapy versus general psychiatric management for borderline personality disorder. *American Journal of Psychiatry*, *166*, 1365–1374.

Mehlum, L., Tørmoen, A. J., Ramberg, M., Haga, E., Diep, L. M., Laberg, S., ... Grøholt, B. (2014). Dialectical behavior therapy for adolescents with repeated suicidal and self-harming behavior: a randomized controlled trial. *Journal of the American Academy of Child and Adolescent Psychiatry*, *53*, 1082–1091.

Meyers, L. L., Landes, S. J., & Thuras, P. (2014). Veteran's service utilization and associated costs following participation in dialectical behavior therapy: a preliminary investigation. *Military Medicine*, *179*, 1368–1373.

National Institute for Health and Clinical Excellence (2009). *Borderline personality disorder: treatment and management*. London: National Institute for Health and Clinical Excellence.

Ost, L. (2008). Efficacy of the third wave of behavioral therapies: a systematic review and meta-analysis. *Behaviour Research and Therapy*, *46*, 296–301.

Panos, P. T., Jackson, J. W., Hasan, O., & Panos, A. (2014). Meta-analysis and systematic review assessing the efficacy of dialectical behavior therapy (DBT). *Research on Social Work Practice*, *24*, 213–223.

Pasieczny, N., & Connor, J. (2011). The effectiveness of dialectical behavior therapy in routine public mental health settings: an Australian controlled trial. *Behavior Research and Therapy*, *49*, 4–10.

Perseius, K., Samuelsson, M., Andersson, E., Berndtsson, T., Gotmatk, H., Henriksson, F., ... Asberg, M. (2004). Does dialectical behavioural therapy reduce treatment costs for patients with borderline personality disorder? A pilot study. *Vard I Norden*, *72*, 27–30.

Prendergast, N., & McCausland, J. (2007). Dialectic behaviour therapy: a 12-month collaborative program in a local community setting. *Behaviour Change* *24*, 25–35.

Priebe, S., Bhatti, N., Barnicot, K., Bremner, S., Gaglia, A., Katsakou, C., ... Zinkler, M. (2012). Effectiveness and cost-effectiveness of dialectical behavior therapy for self-harming patients with personality disorder: a pragmatic randomized controlled trial. *Psychotherapy and Psychosomatics*, *81*, 356–365.

Qin, P. (2011). The impact of psychiatric illness on suicide: differences by diagnosis of disorders and by sex and age of subjects. *Journal of Psychiatric Research*, *45*, 1445–1452.

Rathus, J. H., & Miller, A. L. (2002). Dialectical behavior therapy adapted for suicidal adolescents. *Suicide and Life-Threatening Behavior*, *32*, 146–157.

Runeson, B. S., Beskow, J., & Waern, M. (1996). The suicidal process in suicides among young people. *Acta Psychiatrica Scandinavica*, *93*, 35–42.

Substance Abuse and Mental Health Administration (2011). *Report to Congress on borderline personality disorder*. Retrieved November 2, 2012 from http://store.samhsa.gov/shin/content/SMA11-4644/SMA11-4644.pdf

Sneed, J. R., Fertuck, E. A., Kanellopoulos, D., & Culang-Reinlieb, M. E. (2012). Borderline personality disorder. In P. Sturmey & M. Hersen (Eds.), *Handbook of evidence-based practice in clinical psychology* (Vol. 2, pp. 507–529). Hoboken: Wiley.

Stoffers, J. M., Völlm, B. A., Rücker, G., Timmer, A., Huband, N., & Lieb, K. (2012). Psychological therapies for people with borderline personality disorder. *Cochrane Database of Systematic Reviews*, doi: 10.1002/14651858.CD005652.pub2

Swartz, M., Blazer, D., George, L., & Winfield, I. (1990). Estimating the prevalence of borderline personality disorder in the community. *Journal of Personality Disorders*, *4*, 257–272.

Tomko, R. L., Trull, T. J., Wood, P. K., & Sher, K. J. (2014). Characteristics of borderline personality disorder in a community sample: comorbidity, treatment utilization, and general functioning. *Journal of Personality Disorders*, *28*, 734–750.

Turner, R. (2000). Naturalistic evaluation of dialectical behavior therapy-oriented treatment for borderline personality disorder. *Cognitive and Behavioural Practice*, *7*, 413–419.

Van Asselt, A. D., Dirksen, C. D., Arntz, A., Giesen-Bloo, J. H., Van Dyck, R., Spinhoven, P., … Severens, J. L. (2008). Out-patient psychotherapy for borderline personality disorder: cost-effectiveness of schema-focused therapy v. transference-focused psychotherapy. *British Journal of Psychiatry*, *192*, 450–457.

Verhuel, R., Van den Bosch, L. M. C., Koeter, M. W. J., Ridder, M. A. J., Stijnen, T., & van den Brink, W. (2003). Dialectical behavior therapy for women with borderline personality disorder. *British Journal of Psychiatry*, *182*, 135–140.

Wagner, T., Fydrich, T., Stiglmayr, C., Marschall, P., Salize, H-J., Renneberg, B., … Roepke, S. (2014). Societal cost-of-illness in patients with borderline personality disorder one year before, during and after dialectical behavior therapy in routine outpatient care. *Behaviour Research and Therapy*, *61*, 12–22.

Williams, S. E., Hartstone, M. D., & Denson, L. A. (2010). Dialectical behavioural therapy and borderline personality disorder: effects on service utilization and self-reported symptoms. *Behaviour Change*, *27*, 251–264.

Wunsch, E., Kliem, S., & Kroger, C. (2014). Population-based cost-offset estimation for the treatment of borderline personality disorder: projected costs in a currently running ideal health system. *Behaviour Research and Therapy*, *60*, 1–7.

CHAPTER 23

MECHANISMS OF CHANGE IN DIALECTICAL BEHAVIOUR THERAPY

TALI BORITZ, RICHARD J. ZEIFMAN, AND
SHELLEY F. MCMAIN

INTRODUCTION

DIALECTICAL Behaviour Therapy (DBT) is a structured therapy that was initially designed for the treatment of chronically suicidal individuals with borderline personality disorder (BPD) (Linehan, 1993). DBT is a comprehensive treatment that blends cognitive-behavioural approaches with acceptance-based practices embodied by Zen Buddhism (Linehan, 1993). At the core of treatment is dialectical philosophy, which stresses the value of searching for and finding syntheses between natural tensions in order to bring about change. In DBT, the fundamental dialectic involves striking a balance between change and acceptance; clients are encouraged, on the one hand, to acknowledge and accept emotional experience and, on the other, to use skills to decrease intense emotions and change problematic responses (for an overview of DBT, see Linehan, 1993; McMain, Korman, & Dimeff, 2001). There is strong evidence supporting the use of DBT in BPD (for review, see Stoffers et al., 2012, and Miga et al., this volume), and with suicidal adults and adolescents (e.g., Mehlum et al., 2014). Despite its demonstrated efficacy, little is known about what accounts for positive clinical outcomes in DBT.

There is growing interest in understanding specific change processes and mechanisms of change in DBT. This focus is consistent with growing research and discussions on processes and mechanisms of change in the field of psychotherapy research, which aim to explain *how* and *why* an intervention leads to change. Research on the processes and mechanisms of change is important for several reasons. When we understand how a treatment operates or which elements of a treatment drive its effects we are, (1) better able to optimize the active ingredients of the treatments we are offering; (2) in a better position to adapt treatments to real-world settings; and, (3) more able to personalize treatments to fit the needs of specific clients, through client-therapist or client-treatment matching (Kazdin, 2007).

The question of how DBT produces effects can be studied from a number of approaches. Change process research entails observing, identifying, and describing the specific therapist-level and client-level processes that lead to change in symptoms (Greenberg, 1986). This research can be conducted through the intensive study of significant therapy events, the microanalysis of client and therapist in-session behaviours, or through quantitative statistical designs. Correlational studies allow us to determine associations between process variables and outcomes, but have little predictive ability, and do not allow us to draw conclusions about causation. Mediation analyses are the most common approach and are used to study causal relationships between processes and outcome in psychotherapy (Nock, 2007). Mediation analyses determine the relationship between interventions, outcomes, and intermediate variables, by testing whether the relationship between the intervention and outcome is significant after variance on the intermediate variable is parsed out.

While the identification of statically significant mediators is frequently used to support the search for mechanisms of change, mediators are not in and of themselves mechanisms of change (Kazdin, 2007; Kraemer, Wilson, Fairburn, & Agras, 2002; Nock, 2007). A mediator is a construct that demonstrates a statistical relationship between an intervention and an outcome; it suggests a critical process about *why* a change occurs but not *how* the change comes about (Kazdin, 2009). To determine how change in therapy comes about we need a testable theory about the intervening steps between a mediator and outcome, and how these steps unfold (i.e., mechanisms of change).

Mechanisms of change describe the pathways between mediators and outcome; the processes through which mediators lead to change, the reason why change occurred, or how change came about (Kazdin, 2007, 2009). Psychotherapy researchers frequently use the terms mediators and mechanisms interchangeably, which has contributed to some confusion in the literature. However, as the field evolves, there are new calls to study mediators and mechanisms with increased rigor. Kazdin (2007, 2009) and Nock (2007) propose that the term "statistical mediator" be used to indicate when requirements for statistical mediation have been satisfied (i.e., whether a proposed mechanism can statistically explain the relationship between an independent and dependent variable). They further propose that the term "mechanism of change" be reserved for instances where additional criteria are met (see Box 23.1 for summary of these criteria).

Consider the following example to illustrate mediators and mechanisms underlying the phenomenon of developing an "ice cream headache." How and why does eating ice cream (intervention) cause a headache (outcome)? As it turns outs, an important mediator is the chilling of the palate or pharynx. If the palate of the mouth does not become cold, an ice cream headache will not occur: it mediates the relationship between eating something cold and experiencing a headache. However, this explanation does not tell us how or why a chilled palate leads to a headache (i.e., the mechanisms of change). To

Box 23.1 Requirements for demonstrating mechanisms of change

Data from Kazdin, A. E. (2009), Understanding how and why psychotherapy leads to change. *Psychotherapy Research*, *19*(4–5), 418-28. http://dx.doi.org/10.1080/10503300802448899

Strong association: Demonstration of a strong association between the therapeutic intervention (A) and the hypothesized mediator of change (B) and an association between the proposed mediator (B) and therapeutic change (C).

Specificity: Demonstration of the specificity of the association among the intervention, proposed mediator, and outcome (i.e., change in the intervention is uniquely related to change in the proposed mechanism, and change in the proposed mechanism is uniquely related to change in treatment outcome).

Consistency: Replication of an observed result across studies, samples, and conditions. However, inconsistency in findings may suggest the operation of a moderator rather than serve as evidence that the mechanism does not exist.

Experimental manipulation: Direct experimental manipulation of the proposed mediator to show the impact on outcome (C).

Temporal Relation: Demonstrating a timeline or ordering of the proposed mediator and outcome (i.e., the mediator changes before the outcome). This requires simultaneous and repeated assessment of the proposed mechanisms and outcome throughout the course of treatment.

Gradient: Amount of change in the intervention is directly related to the amount of change in the proposed mechanism, which consequently influences the degree of client change. Greater activation of the proposed mechanism that corresponds with greater change in outcome supports the operation of a change mechanism or mediator.

Plausibility or coherence: A plausible, coherent, and reasonable process that explains precisely what the construct does and how it works to lead to the outcome. The steps along the way (from construct to change) can be tested directly.

understand this, we need to know the steps or processes that lead to our outcome of interest. We would need to first formulate a testable theory about the intervening steps between our mediator and outcome (i.e., additional possible mediators). For example, ice cream headaches are purported to occur through the following steps: eating ice cream leads to decreased palate temperature, which then leads to increased constriction and swelling of blood vessels, followed by increased activation of pain receptors in the facial area and the head, resulting in the ice cream headache (Robb-Nicholson, 2009). We could then test this hypothesis by measuring each of these potential mediators and our outcome of interest at multiple time points, to ensure that these mechanisms occur following the intervention (eating an ice cream) and before the outcome (headache). Finally, we may decide to conduct an experiment wherein we manipulate our proposed mechanisms to determine whether the relationship holds if we omit or alter one of these purported mechanisms.

In order to begin conceptualizing potential mechanisms of change in DBT, we first consider how DBT conceptualizes the aetiology and maintenance of dysfunction. Next, we theorize how active ingredients in DBT treatment produce client change and we propose four key mechanisms of change that have emerged from DBT studies. Finally, we review the research evidence to support these putative mechanisms of change.

DBT's Biosocial Theory: The Core Problem of Emotion Dysregulation

DBT conceptualizes pervasive emotion dysregulation as the core dysfunction underlying BPD and other clinical disorders (e.g., substance abuse, eating disorders). Emotion dysregulation is defined as the "inability, even when one's best efforts are applied, to change or regulate emotional cues, experiences, actions, verbal responses and/or nonverbal expressions under normative conditions" (Linehan, Bohus, & Lynch, 2007, p. 584). In its extreme form, such as in the case of BPD, emotion dysregulation is pervasive, occurring with frequency and intensity across many contexts (e.g., work, school, relationships). Pervasive emotion dysregulation disrupts all aspects of an individual's emotional response system: physiological, cognitive, behavioural, and interpersonal (Lynch, Chapman, Rosenthal, Kuo, & Linehan, 2006). From a DBT perspective, dysfunction across multiple domains of functioning is an inevitable consequence of dysregulated emotions, or maladaptive attempts to cope with intense and distressing emotion. For example, emotion dysregulation leads to an increased risk for engaging in aggressive, impulsive, and risk-taking behaviours to alleviate emotional distress (Harned, Banawan, & Lynch, 2006).

DBT's biosocial theory posits that dysregulation of the emotion system is the product of a transaction between an individual's biological predisposition towards emotional vulnerability and an invalidating developmental environment (Linehan, 1993). Individuals who are emotionally vulnerable experience high sensitivity to emotion (i.e., quick reactions to emotion cues even at a low threshold), high reactivity (i.e., the intense experience and expression of emotions), and slow return to baseline (i.e., emotional arousal is long lasting). When biological emotional vulnerability is combined with an invalidating developmental environment, individuals learn to regulate emotion through maladaptive strategies.

An invalidating environment is one that trivializes, ignores, dismisses, or punishes the expression of emotion. The invalidating environment communicates to the child that their understandings of their experience and description of their internal experiences are fundamentally wrong, and due to unacceptable and socially undesirable character traits. Invalidating childhood environments contribute to the development of emotion dysregulation as they fail to teach the child how to understand, label, modulate, and tolerate emotional distress, or how to solve the problems contributing to these emotional reactions (Linehan, 1993; McMain et al., 2001). Extreme behaviours, such as self-harm and substance abuse, are understood as attempts to regulate emotion, or as the result of failed attempts to regulate emotion. Over time, these behaviours become reinforced as escape behaviours from aversive emotional states.

How and Why DBT Leads to Change

In DBT, all treatment strategies directly or indirectly aim to decrease emotion dysregulation and enhance emotion regulation. Treatment strategies in DBT are dialectically balanced between accepting the client as they are within a context of trying to teach them how to change (i.e., use more effective coping strategies). A dialectical pattern of therapist interaction that balances therapist affirmation (validation) and control (change) has been shown to predict reductions of non-suicidal self-injury (NSSI) (Bedics, Atkins, Comtois, & Linehan, 2012b). Treatment strategies target all aspects of the emotion regulation system: cognition, phenomenological experience, expressive-motor behaviour, and action tendencies.

The effectiveness of DBT treatment strategies depends upon the presence of a positive therapeutic relationship. Research on the therapeutic alliance in DBT has demonstrated that client-rated alliance between therapist and client is a consistent predictor of outcome (Bedics, Atkins, Harned, & Linehan, 2015; Hirsh, Quilty, Bagby, & McMain, 2012; Turner, 2000). A strong therapy relationship is the means for engaging clients in treatment and increasing motivation and willingness to change dysfunctional behaviours (Linehan, 1993). DBT therapists are encouraged to engage in a warm, reciprocal, and collaborative manner. This manner of engaging with clients promotes trust in the relationship, which in turn allows the client to be open to emotional experiencing and expression, and new learning experiences. Indeed, in DBT the therapeutic relationship is "the vehicle through which the therapist can effect the therapy; it *is* also the therapy." (Linehan, 1993, p. 514). While we are not able to address research on the therapeutic relationship in depth in this chapter, clinicians may wish to review the following studies addressing the therapeutic relationship in DBT: Boritz, Barnhart, Eubanks, & McMain, in press; Barnicot, Gonzalez, McCabe, & Priebe, 2016; Bedics et al., 2015; Bedics et al., 2012a; Bedics et al., 2012b; Shearin & Linehan, 1992.

Acceptance Strategies

Acceptance strategies refer to therapist behaviours that attempt to create a non-judgmental therapeutic environment that enables clients to explore, experience, and express emotionally difficult material. Therapists use reflection, empathy, and validation to communicate to the client that their responses make sense and are understandable within their current context or given their learning history. Validation helps to reduce in-session emotional arousal and enhance opportunities for new learning. However, when therapists validate clients they also model how to symbolize experiences in words and validate their own emotional responses.

Change Strategies

Change strategies produce and maintain positive client change by helping clients generate, evaluate, and implement alternative solutions to problematic situations, behaviours, or emotional responses. DBT's main change strategies include problem assessment (e.g. chain analysis) and solution analysis, skills training, and exposure protocols. These strategies help clients contextualize their thoughts, feelings, and behaviours, which facilitates emotional awareness and decreases emotional arousal. Exposure to primary adaptive emotional information in the context of problem solving helps decrease emotional avoidance and increases the client's ability to tolerate distressing emotion. Finally, identifying solutions/practising alternative behaviours leads to the development of new coping skills.

Dialectical Strategies

Therapists use dialectical strategies to help navigate and resolve tension and impasses in treatment through balancing or synthesizing dialectics occurring in the session (Linehan, 1993). The therapist actively models dialectical thinking by helping the client consider different perspectives, and identifying potential syntheses between extreme positions. Dialectical strategies such as irreverent communication can help shift a client's attention from ruminative or rigid thought, emotional, or behavioural patterns, and in turn, help to decrease in-session dysregulation. Dialectical strategies also teach clients to learn to engage with themselves and others more dialectically.

Structural Strategies

Structural strategies are used to create a therapeutic atmosphere that is transparent, predictable, and safe. These strategies are the organizing framework that makes the expectations of treatment explicit (e.g., roles; duration of treatment; frequency, length, and structure of sessions; fees; between-session contact). When clients know what to expect from their therapist and the treatment, emotional arousal associated with uncertainty, ambiguity, and the threat of abandonment are decreased, thereby allowing the client to engage more openly in the treatment without becoming overwhelmed. Thus, the treatment structure serves a regulatory function, containing intense client affect while allowing for its exploration under controlled conditions.

PUTATIVE MECHANISMS OF CHANGE IN DBT

Possible mechanisms of change in DBT were first proposed by Lynch et al. (2006). In their article, the authors identified specific interventions in DBT (e.g., mindfulness, opposite action, and chain analyses) and suggested theoretical mechanisms they believed may lead to the intervention's impact on outcome (e.g., enhanced attentional control). Empirical research on mechanisms of change remains an emerging area of study in DBT. To broaden our thinking on mechanisms of change in the facilitation of emotions regulation, we consider four mechanisms of change that have been the focus of scientific efforts in DBT research to date. We propose that within the context of a strong therapeutic relationship, specific DBT strategies (structural, acceptance, change, and dialectical strategies) exert their effects on outcomes (e.g., decreases in personality disorder symptoms, general distress, behavioural dyscontrol) by enhancing emotion regulation through the following mechanisms: (1) increased awareness and acceptance of emotion, (2) increased attentional control, (3) increased ability to modulate emotion, and (4) increased use of adaptive coping skills.

Empirical Evidence Supporting Specific Change Mechanisms

The current evidence base for proposed mechanisms is limited and focuses mainly on the relationship between change processes and outcome. Most DBT studies to date have employed correlational designs to investigate associations between change processes and outcome, often in the context of secondary analyses of controlled treatment trials. A smaller set of studies have employed statistical tests of mediation to investigate causal relationships between the change processes and outcome. No studies have yet employed experimental designs with random assignment to conditions and careful manipulation of the proposed causal agent to demonstrate a causal relation. This type of research is essential for showing that manipulation changes the proposed mechanism, which then changes the proposed outcome (Nock, 2007). Here we review the evidence for each of the putative mechanisms of change.

Increased Awareness and Acceptance of Emotion.

Awareness of emotions consists of paying attention to one's current internal experiences, while acceptance of emotions consists of being present and open to experiencing affective responses, even in situations where they are distressing (Campbell-Sills, Barlow, Brown, & Hofmann, 2006). Acceptance of emotion is the opposite of emotional suppression, which is associated with higher levels of negative mood, as well as lower levels of positive mood, social adjustment, and well-being (Gross & John, 2003; Moore, Zoellner, & Mollenholt, 2008). It is hypothesized that many individuals with pervasive emotion dysregulation engage in problematic behaviours as a method of avoiding aversive psychological experiences (Hayes, Wilson, Gifford, Follette, & Strosahl, 1996).

Whereas emotion suppression is an attempt to avoid experiencing affective responses in the present, awareness and acceptance allow individuals to change their relationship with their emotions (Gross & Thompson, 2007) and their long-term affective responses (Williams, 2010). Similarly, research suggests that individuals with negative attitudes toward distressing emotions are likely to engage in ruminative processes that escalate negative emotions (Teasdale, Segal, & Williams, 1995), while awareness and acceptance of one's emotions help to thwart engagement in ruminative processes (Singer & Dobson, 2009). Thus, it is proposed that increasing individuals' awareness and acceptance of their emotions is a mechanism of change through which DBT results in improved therapeutic outcomes.

Though much research remains to be done to fully test this purported mechanism, one study, conducted by Berking and colleagues (2009), explored the association between experiential avoidance and depression. The study drew 81 female BPD outpatients from a randomized controlled trial comparing one year of DBT with treatment by community experts (TBE). It was found that experiential avoidance, measured using the Acceptance and Action Questionnaire (AAQ; Hayes, Strosahl, Wilson, & Bissett, 2004), was associated with symptoms of depression before, during, and after treatment. Furthermore, higher levels of experiential avoidance were predictive of less subsequent changes in depression. Importantly, the study also found that, over time, decreases in experiential avoidance were associated with decreases in symptoms of depression.

While the evidence base for this particular mechanism is limited, the research suggests that reductions in experiential avoidance contribute to outcomes in DBT. Further studies should continue to explore this relationship. Additionally, it will be important to determine whether changes in experiential avoidance contribute to outcomes of DBT other than depression.

Increased Attentional Control

Attentional control refers to the ability to control the focus of attention rather than the object of attention (i.e., observing emotional experience without trying to change it). Improved attentional control involves being able to turn attention away from emotionally evocative stimuli and shift focus between different aspects of one's experience (e.g., emotions, cognitions, physical sensations).

Mindfulness skills are used in DBT to promote attentional control and enhance emotion regulation. In particular, improved attentional control helps clients disengage from emotional stimuli, which reduces their tendency to experience negative affect (Ellenbogen, Schwartman, Steward, & Walker, 2002) and increases their ability to modulate attention processes in emotional contexts (Teasdale et al., 1995). Mindfulness skills also involve teaching clients to non-judgmentally observe and bring one's full attention to current experience. This can act as an informal exposure to negative emotion, which over time helps to increase distress tolerance and extinguish maladaptive avoidance responses (e.g., rumination) (Linehan, 1993).

Several studies have demonstrated a relationship between mindfulness practice and outcomes in DBT. For instance, Soler and colleagues (2012) completed a non-randomized controlled trial where 59 individuals with diagnoses of BPD participated in either DBT-Mindfulness training plus general psychiatric management (DBT-M+GPM) or GPM alone. DBT-M consisted of eight group psychotherapy sessions of 120 minutes, which focused on teaching mindfulness skills and assignments to practise these skills throughout the week. They found that more time spent (e.g. number of minutes per week) engaged in formal mindfulness practice was associated with improvements in several symptom outcomes, including depression, general psychopathology, and confusion. Similarly, number of minutes of mindfulness practice per week was associated with improvements in non-reactivity to inner experience, a mindfulness subscale.

Feliu-Soler and colleagues (2014) conducted a study that utilized the same design and included 35 individuals with BPD. They found that greater time spent engaged in formal mindfulness practice was strongly associated with improvements in depressive symptoms and lower self-reported, but not biologically indexed, emotional reactivity. It is noteworthy that in this study, the association between mindfulness practice and general psychopathology did not reach significance.

Furthermore, Perroud and colleagues (2012) conducted a non-randomized study that included 52 individuals with BPD who participated in four weeks of Intensive-DBT (McQuillan et al., 2005; Perroud, Uher, Dieben, Nicastro, & Huguelet, 2010) followed by ten months of standard DBT. After accounting for changes in symptoms of depression and pessimism, there was a significant increase in mindfulness-accepting without judgment over time, which was most pronounced during standard DBT. Furthermore, after adjusting for baseline borderline personality scores, increases in acceptance without judgment were associated with decreased BPD symptoms. However, it should be noted, that this association was no longer significant after correcting for multiple statistical tests.

Overall, these studies indicate that increased attentional control (through the uptake of mindfulness) is associated with positive outcomes in DBT. Increased mindfulness appears to be particularly helpful for decreasing emotional reactivity.

Increased Ability to Modulate Emotion

Emotion modulation refers to the ability to influence physiological, experiential, or behavioural responses directly (Gross & Thompson, 2007). Emotion modulation deficits can be impacted by heightened negative emotional reactivity and intensity and deficits in the ability to turn negative affect on or off. Indeed, there is evidence that individuals with BPD show greater activation of the insula (Schulze et al., 2011) and less reduction in amygdala activity compared to healthy controls (Goodman et al., 2014; Koenigsberg et al., 2009). There is also evidence of dysfunction in the hypothalamic pituitary adrenal axis in BPD; this is the part of the brain that activates the sympathetic nervous system and is responsible for triggering neuro-hormonal changes (Zimmerman & Choi-Kain, 2009).

The study of emotion modulation has mostly centred on neurobiological activity. A number of recent studies have examined the role of neural correlates of change in DBT. Our search identified four neuroimaging studies in DBT that employed correlational designs to explore brain activity associated with emotion reactivity and negative affect modulation including areas in the limbic system and prefrontal cortex. All of these studies involved an investigation of neural correlates of treatment response in BPD samples.

Goodman et al. (2014) explored the effect of DBT for the treatment of BPD on amygdala hyperactivity using functional magnetic resonance imaging (fMRI). In this non-randomized controlled trial, 11 individuals with BPD receiving standard DBT were compared to healthy controls on fMRI assessed pre- and post-12 months. Emotion regulation was assessed via self-report using the Difficulties in Emotion Regulation Scale (DERS; Gratz & Roemer, 2004). DBT participants showed significant improvements on the DERS between pre- and post-treatment, whereas the healthy control group showed no change over time. Furthermore, the DBT group showed decreased amygdala activation during processing of emotionally adverse stimuli, and these changes were associated with improved emotion regulation on the DERS.

Another non-randomized controlled study by Schmitt and colleagues (2016) utilized fMRI to study neural correlates of treatment response in a sample of 32 females with BPD who were treated in a 12-week DBT inpatient programme. The DBT group was compared to 24 healthy controls and 16 BPD controls. Participants were assessed before and after 12 weeks of inpatient DBT. Between pre- and post-treatment, in response to a reappraisal task, the DBT group showed decreased activity in brain regions associated with hyperarousal (e.g. amygdala, insular and anterior cingulate cortex) and increased connectivity in the medial and superior frontal gyrus and the superior temporal gyrus. Reduced activity in the anterior insula was associated with improvements in affective dysregulation and symptom severity. Increased dorsal anterior cingulate cortex activity was also associated with improvements in BPD symptoms and depression scores while viewing negative pictures. The results of the study indicate that DBT is associated with the down-regulation of limbic hyperactivation and the enhancement of brain regions associated with cognitive control (e.g. prefrontal network).

A third non-randomized controlled study (Winter et al., 2016) also employed fMRI to examine performance on a distraction task. Thirty-one BPD individuals enrolled in a 12-week DBT programme were compared to 15 BPD individuals who were receiving treatment as usual and 22 healthy controls. Neuroimaging was conducted before and after participation in a 12-week DBT residential programme. The findings showed the

DBT participants had decreased activity during a distraction task in the right inferior parietal lobe/supramarginal gyrus, a brain region associated with emotion regulation. These decreases in activity were correlated with decreases in BPD symptom severity. Furthermore, treatment responders in the DBT group showed decreased activity in the anterior cingulate.

Furthermore, in a small neuroimaging study, Schnell and Herpertz (2007) conducted fMRI scans with six individuals with BPD who were enrolled in a 12-week DBT in-patient programme. The DBT participants were compared to six healthy controls. The main finding was that, compared to the healthy controls, the DBT participants showed decreased activation in regions of the brain involved in affect modulation, including the anterior cingulate cortex, posterior cingulate, and the insula. A favourable response in DBT was associated with decreased activity in the left amygdala and bilateral hippocampus.

Finally, an exploratory study recruited 129 individuals that met DSM-IV criteria for BPD and had a recent history of suicidal or non-suicidal self-injurious (NSSI) behaviours (McMain et al., 2013). Participants were referred from a trial that included either standard DBT or general psychiatric management. Self-reported affect balance, which is a measure of symmetry between positive and negative affect, was measured using the Derogatis Affects Balance Scale (DABS; Derogatis, 1975). Results indicated that, over time, participants reported significantly improved affect balance. Moreover, even after accounting for the effect of working alliance, improvements in affect balance were significantly associated with decreased psychiatric symptom distress and interpersonal problems. The results of this study suggest that one of the mechanisms through which DBT, and alternative treatments of BPD, may effectively reduce symptom distress and interpersonal problems is through greater symmetry of positive and negative affect.

Overall, these studies indicate that DBT appears to have a role in changing regions of brain functioning and psychological processes that are involved in affect reactivity and the ability to modulate negative affect. Since participants in these studies received comprehensive forms of DBT, it is unknown which modes of treatment or specific strategies are linked to the observed effects on neuro-functioning. Future studies are needed to parse out which treatment strategies contribute to change in the neuro-functioning of patients.

Increased Use of Adaptive Coping Skills

The DBT model suggests that emotion dysregulation and associated dysfunctional behaviours result, in part, from deficient coping skills (Linehan, 1993). BPD has been found to be associated with deficits in four coping skills, in particular, a) mindfulness skills (Wupperman, Neumann, Whitman, & Axelrod, 2009), b) emotion regulation skills (Carpenter & Trull, 2013), c) interpersonal relationship skills (Kremers, Spinhoven, Van der Does, & Van Dyck, 2006), and d) distress tolerance skills (Gratz, Rosenthal, Tull, Lejuez, & Gunderson, 2006). The model, therefore, suggests that deficits in these coping skills result in individuals engaging in maladaptive responses to temporarily alleviate their emotional distress. For example, research suggests that suicidal behaviours function as a maladaptive strategy for coping with distress (Brown, Comtois, & Linehan, 2002; Bryan, Rudd, & Wertenberger, 2013). These maladaptive coping strategies, in turn, become reinforced, due to their temporary alleviation of distress (Linehan, 1993). Furthermore, use of maladaptive coping strategies, such as rumination, may intensify negative emotions and thereby lead to engaging in dysfunctional behaviours as a means of coping with emotional distress (Selby, Anestis, & Joiner, 2008).

In contrast to maladaptive coping strategies, the adaptive coping skills taught and reinforced within DBT allow individuals to shape and respond to their environment and experiences in an effective manner (Linehan, 1993). It is thought that increased use of adaptive coping skills results in improved emotion regulation (Neacsiu, Bohus, & Linehan, 2013). Thus, by alleviating emotional and interpersonal distress, adaptive coping skills thereby reduce reliance on maladaptive coping strategies and result in decreases in symptomology and dysfunctional behaviours.

A few studies have examined coping skills in DBT. A non-randomized pre/post study of 70 individuals diagnosed with BPD who were enrolled in 12 months of DBT found that increased coping skills were associated with decreased self-harm behaviours (Barnicot et al., 2016). Skills use was measured using a self-report questionnaire, which asked participants how many days they had used mindfulness, interpersonal effectiveness, emotion regulation, and distress tolerance skills. The practice of skills was associated with decreased self-harm behaviours, and importantly, this association was independent of common treatment processes, such as treatment credibility, self-efficacy, and therapeutic alliance.

Another study included 108 women with BPD, 63 of whom were recurrently suicidal and 45 who had comorbid drug dependence (Neacsiu, Rizvi, & Linehan, 2010). Participants were drawn from three randomized control trials (RCT) where they were randomly assigned to either DBT (n=52) or one of three non-BPD specific control treatments. Results of the study indicated that increased use of DBT skills—as measured by the Dialectical Behavior Therapy Ways of Coping Checklist (DBT-WCCL; Neacsiu, Rizvi, Vitaliano, Lynch, & Linehan, 2010)—mediated decreases in suicide attempts, NSSI behaviours, and depressive symptoms, as well as increases in control of anger, over time. Additionally, in a randomized controlled trial (Neacsiu, Eberle, Kramer, Wiesmann, & Linehan, 2014), 44 individuals with high levels of emotion dysregulation and concurrent depressive or anxiety disorder were randomly assigned to either activities-based support group (ASG) or dialectical behaviour therapy skills training (DBT-ST). This study found that DBT-ST was superior to ASG in increasing skills use (also measured by the DBT-WCCL) and reducing emotion dysregulation and anxiety severity. Moreover, increased skills use mediated the relationship between study condition and the decreases in both emotion dysregulation and anxiety severity.

Finally, in a non-randomized study that included 27 outpatients with features of BPD, 17 of whom met criteria for a diagnosis of BPD, enrolled in 12 months of standard DBT treatment (Stepp, Epler, Jahng, & Trull, 2008), the number of skills used weekly (collected from diary card data) was associated with a reduction in the total number of borderline symptoms. Skills use was also associated with borderline symptom subscales including affective instability, identity disturbance, and negative relationships, measured over time. Although total skills use was not significantly associated with frequency of NSSI, greater use of mindfulness skills was marginally associated with decreases in NSSI.

Overall, these studies suggest that DBT operates through the uptake of coping skills. Limitations of this research include the potential for biased reporting of skills use and the possibility that patient improvement may be explained by high patient motivation, rather than an increase in coping behaviours assessed by client performance in the real world. Future research should further clarify which aspects of DBT contribute toward increased use of skills and which individual skills contribute to specific outcomes associated with DBT.

LIMITATIONS OF CURRENT MECHANISMS RESEARCH

The research presented in this chapter provides preliminary support for the proposed mechanisms of change in DBT. As with the larger psychotherapy literature, most of the studies that have been conducted on processes and mechanisms of change in DBT include correlational studies on the processes of change or mediator analyses used as a proxy for mechanisms of change. While these studies serve an important step in determining mechanisms of change in DBT, they do not satisfy all the criteria set forth by Kazdin (2007, 2009) and Nock (2007). This is partly due to the fact that most of the change process research in DBT has been conducted as secondary analyses of data from RCTs: the original studies were not designed to test specific mediators of outcome. As a result, the timing and frequency of measurement of mediator and outcome variables are not necessarily optimal for mechanisms research.

An additional limitation of the current research is the variability across studies in the operationalization and measurements of the change processes of interest. Indeed, the broadness of constructs like mindfulness or coping skills makes the interpretation of study findings challenging. For example, the construct of coping skills covers many different DBT skills; it is difficult to determine whether there are specific DBT skills driving symptom improvement. In regard to measurement, a range of tools can be used to assess change processes (e.g. ecological momentary assessment and in-session client verbalizations). However, the most common method used was self-report questionnaires. Since self-report does not necessarily correspond to actual behaviour, we are limited in our ability to draw conclusions about objective behavioural change.

TREATMENT IMPLICATIONS
AND FUTURE DIRECTIONS

In spite of the limitations of the available evidence base, the research provides some important directions for DBT treatment and future DBT research. Future studies on mechanisms of change in DBT must ensure that they are clear in their purpose and process. Research studies aimed at elucidating mechanisms of change should follow established research guidelines (e.g., Kazdin, 2009; Nock, 2007). DBT research studies should be designed to test multiple mediators with theory-driven hypotheses about how they lead to specific outcomes. Experimental study designs with random assignment to conditions and manipulation of the proposed causal agent can be used to demonstrate impact on outcome (Nock, 2007).

Once mechanisms of change are established, clinicians should be encouraged to integrate this research into their clinical practice. For example, if skills use is determined to be a mechanism of change in DBT, clinicians should ensure that this is a focus in their sessions. Additionally, understanding mechanisms of change allows clinicians to individualize treatments based on the characteristics of their clients. For example, if a patient with BPD is highly depressed, research suggests that it may be wise to work on improving their awareness and acceptance of emotion.

Current research supports increased emotional awareness and acceptance, attentional control, emotional modulation, and use of adaptive coping skills as change processes associated with positive outcomes in DBT. While more research is needed in each of these domains, therapist interventions focused on enhancing each of these processes are likely to yield beneficial effects.

KEY POINTS FOR CLINICIANS

- When reviewing literature on mediators and mechanisms of change, determine whether the researchers have established "statistically significant mediators" or met additional criteria necessary to be considered a mechanism of change.
- The effectiveness of DBT treatment strategies depends upon a strong therapeutic relationship. When DBT therapists adopt a dialectical stance that balances acceptance and change, clients are more open to emotional experiencing and expression, and new learning experiences.
- Increased emotional awareness and acceptance, attentional control, emotional modulation, and use of adaptive coping skills are change processes associated with positive outcomes in DBT. Therapist interventions focused on enhancing each of these processes are likely to yield beneficial effects.

REFERENCES

Barnicot, K., Gonzalez, R., McCabe, R., & Priebe, S. (2016). Skills use and common treatment processes in dialectical behaviour therapy for borderline personality disorder. *Journal of Behavior Therapy and Experimental Psychiatry*, *52*, 147–156.

Bedics, J. D., Atkins, D. C., Harned, M. S., & Linehan, M. M. (2015). The therapeutic alliance as a predictor of outcome in dialectical behavior therapy versus non-behavioral psychotherapy experts for borderline personality disorder. *Psychotherapy*, *52*, 67–77.

Bedics, J. D., Atkins, D. C., Comtois, K. A., & Linehan, M. M. (2012a). Weekly ratings of the therapeutic relationship and introject during the course of dialectical behavior therapy for the treatment of borderline personality disorder. *Psychotherapy: Theory, Research, Practice, Training*, *49*, 231–240.

Bedics, J. D., Atkins, D. C., Comtois, K. A., & Linehan, M. M. (2012b). Treatment differences in the therapeutic relationship and introject during a 2-year randomized controlled trial of dialectical behavior therapy versus nonbehavioral psychotherapy experts for borderline personality disorder. *Journal of Consulting and Clinical Psychology*, *80*, 66–77.

Boritz, T., Barnhart, R., Eubanks, C., & McMain, S. (in press). Alliance rupture and resolution in dialectical behavior therapy for borderline personality disorder. *Journal of Personality Disorders*.

Berking, M., Neacsiu, A., Comtois, K. A., & Linehan, M. M. (2009). The impact of experiential avoidance on the reduction of depression in treatment for borderline personality disorder. *Behaviour Research and Therapy*, *47*, 663–670.

Brown, M. Z., Comtois, K. A., & Linehan, M. M. (2002). Reasons for suicide attempts and nonsuicidal self-injury in women with borderline personality disorder. *Journal of Abnormal Psychology*, *111*, 198–202.

Bryan, C. J., Rudd, M. D., & Wertenberger, E. (2013). Reasons for suicide attempts in a clinical sample of active duty soldiers. *Journal of Affective Disorders*, *144*, 148–152.

Campbell-Sills, L., Barlow, D. H., Brown, T. A., & Hofmann, S. G. (2006). Effects of suppression and acceptance on emotional responses of individuals with anxiety and mood disorders. *Behaviour Research and Therapy*, *44*, 1251–1263.

Carpenter, R. W., & Trull, T. J. (2013). Components of emotion dysregulation in borderline personality disorder: A review. *Current Psychiatry Reports*, *15*, 335.

Derogatis, L. R. (1975). *Affects Balance Scale*. Baltimore, MD: Clinical Psychometrics Research Unit.

Ellenbogen, M. A., Schwartzman, A. E., Stewart, J., & Walker, C. D. (2002). Stress and selective attention: The interplay of mood, cortisol levels, and emotional information processing. *Psychophysiology*, *39*, 723–732.

Feliu-Soler, A., Pascual, J. C., Borràs, X., Portella, M. J., Martín-Blanco, A., Armario, A., ... Soler, J. (2014). Effects of dialectical behaviour therapy-mindfulness training on emotional reactivity in borderline personality disorder: Preliminary results. *Clinical Psychology and Psychotherapy*, *21*, 363–370.

Goodman, M., Carpenter, D., Tang, C. Y., Goldstein, K. E., Avedon, J., Fernandez, N., ... Hazlett, E. A. (2014). Dialectical behavior therapy alters emotion regulation and amygdala activity in patients with borderline personality disorder. *Journal of Psychiatric Research*, *57*, 108–116.

Gratz, K. L., & Roemer, L. (2004). Multidimensional assessment of emotion regulation and dysregulation: Development, factor structure, and initial validation of the difficulties in emotion regulation scale. *Journal of Psychopathology and Behavioral Assessment*, *26*, 41–54.

Gratz, K. L., Rosenthal, M. Z., Tull, M. T., Lejuez, C. W., & Gunderson, J. G. (2006). An experimental investigation of emotion dysregulation in borderline personality disorder. *Journal of Abnormal Psychology*, 115, 850.

Greenberg, L. S. (1986). Change process research. *Journal of Consulting and Clinical Psychology*, 54, 4–9.

Gross, J. J., & John, O. P. (2003). Individual differences in two emotion regulation processes: Implications for affect, relationships, and well-being. *Journal of Personality and Social Psychology*, 85, 348–362.

Gross, J. J., & Thompson, R. A. (2007). Emotion regulation: Conceptual foundations. In J. J. Gross (Ed.), *Handbook of emotion regulation* (pp. 3–24). New York: Guilford Press.

Harned, M. S., Banawan, S. F., & Lynch, T. R. (2006). Dialectical behavior therapy: An emotion-focused treatment for borderline personality disorder. *Journal of Contemporary Psychotherapy*, 36, 67–75.

Hayes, S. C., Strosahl, K., Wilson, K. G., & Bissett, R. T. (2004). Measuring experiential avoidance: A preliminary test of a working model. *The Psychological Record*, 54, 553–578.

Hayes, S. C., Wilson, K. G., Gifford, E. V., Follette, V. M., & Strosahl, K. (1996). Experiential avoidance and behavioral disorders: A functional dimensional approach to diagnosis and treatment. *Journal of Consulting and Clinical Psychology*, 64, 1152–1168.

Hirsh, J. B., Quilty, L. C., Bagby, R. M., & McMain, S. F. (2012). The relationship between agreeableness and the development of the working alliance in patients with borderline personality disorder. *Journal of Personality Disorders*, 26, 616–627.

Kazdin, A. E. (2007). Mediators and mechanisms of change in psychotherapy research. *Annual Review of Clinical Psychology*, 3, 1–27.

Kazdin, A. E. (2009). Understanding how and why psychotherapy leads to change. *Psychotherapy Research*, 19, 418–428.

Koenigsberg, H. W., Siever, L. J., Lee, H., Pizzarello, S., New, A. S., Goodman, M., ... Prohovnik, I. (2009). Neural correlates of emotion processing in borderline personality disorder. *Psychiatry Research: Neuroimaging*, 172, 192–199.

Kraemer, H. C., Wilson, G. T., Fairburn, C. G., & Agras, W. S. (2002). Mediators and moderators of treatment effects in randomized clinical trials. *Archives of General Psychiatry*, 59, 877–883.

Kremers, I. P., Spinhoven, P., Van der Does, A. J. W., & Van Dyck, R. (2006). Social problem solving, autobiographical memory and future specificity in outpatients with borderline personality disorder. *Clinical Psychology and Psychotherapy*, 13, 131–137.

Linehan, M. (1993). *Cognitive-behavioral treatment of borderline personality disorder*. New York: Guilford Press.

Linehan, M., Bohus, M., & Lynch, T. (2007). Handbook of emotion regulation. In J. Gross (Ed.), *Dialectical behavior therapy for pervasive emotion dysregulation: Theoretical and practical underpinnings* (pp. 581–605). New York: Guilford Press.

Lynch, T. R., Chapman, A. L., Rosenthal, M. Z., Kuo, J. R., & Linehan, M. M. (2006). Mechanisms of change in dialectical behavior therapy: Theoretical and empirical observations. *Journal of Clinical Psychology*, 62, 459–480.

McMain, S., Korman, L. M., & Dimeff, L. (2001). Dialectical behavior therapy and the treatment of emotion dysregulation. *Journal of Clinical Psychology*, 57, 183–196.

McMain, S., Links, P. S., Guimond, T., Wnuk, S., Eynan, R., Bergmans, Y., & Warwar, S. (2013). An exploratory study of the relationship between changes in emotion and cognitive processes and treatment outcome in borderline personality disorder. *Psychotherapy Research*, 23, 658–673.

McQuillan, A., Nicastro, R., Guenot, F., Girard, M., Lissner, C., & Ferrero, F. (2005). Intensive dialectical behavior therapy for outpatients with borderline personality disorder who are in crisis. *Psychiatric Services*, *56*, 193–197.

Mehlum, L., Tørmoen, A. J., Ramberg, M., Haga, E., Diep, L. M., Laberg, S., ... Grøholt, B. (2014). Dialectical behavior therapy for adolescents with repeated suicidal and self-harming behavior: A randomized trial. *Journal of the American Academy of Child and Adolescent Psychiatry*, *53*, 1082–1091.

Moore, S. A., Zoellner, L. A., & Mollenholt, N. (2008). Are expressive suppression and cognitive reappraisal associated with stress-related symptoms? *Behaviour Research and Therapy*, *46*, 993–1000.

Neacsiu, A. D., Bohus, M., & Linehan, M. M. (2013). Dialectical behavior therapy skills: An intervention for emotion dysregulation. In J. J. Gross (Ed.), *Handbook of emotion regulation, Vol. 2* (pp. 491–508). New York: Guilford Press.

Neacsiu, A. D., Eberle, J. W., Kramer, R., Wiesmann, T., & Linehan, M. M. (2014). Dialectical behavior therapy skills for transdiagnostic emotion dysregulation: A pilot randomized controlled trial. *Behaviour Research and Therapy*, *59*, 40–51.

Neacsiu, A. D., Rizvi, S. L., & Linehan, M. M. (2010). Dialectical behavior therapy skills use as a mediator and outcome of treatment for borderline personality disorder. *Behaviour Research and Therapy*, *48*, 832–839.

Neacsiu, A. D., Rizvi, S. L., Vitaliano, P. P., Lynch, T. R., & Linehan, M. M. (2010). The dialectical behavior therapy ways of coping checklist: Development and psychometric properties. *Journal of Clinical Psychology*, *66*, 563–582.

Nock, M. K. (2007). Conceptual and design essentials for evaluating mechanisms of change. *Alcoholism: Clinical and Experimental Research*, *31*, 4S–12S.

Perroud, N., Nicastro, R., Jermann, F., & Huguelet, P. (2012). Mindfulness skills in borderline personality disorder patients during dialectical behavior therapy: Preliminary results. *International Journal of Psychiatry in Clinical Practice*, *16*, 189–196.

Perroud, N., Uher, R., Dieben, K., Nicastro, R., & Huguelet, P. (2010). Predictors of response and drop-out during intensive dialectical behavior therapy. *Journal of Personality Disorders*, *24*, 634–650.

Robb-Nicholson, C. (2009). By the way, doctor. What exactly happens when I eat something cold and get an ice-cream headache? Is it harmful in any way? *Harvard Women's Health Watch*, *16*(12), 8.

Schmitt, R., Winter, D., Niedtfeld, I., Herpertz, S. C., & Schmahl, C. (2016). Effects of psychotherapy on neuronal correlates of reappraisal in female patients with borderline personality disorder. *Biological Psychiatry: Cognitive Neuroscience and Neuroimaging*, *1*, 548–557.

Schnell, K., & Herpertz, S. C. (2007). Effects of dialectic-behavioral-therapy on the neural correlates of affective hyperarousal in borderline personality disorder. *Journal of Psychiatric Research*, *41*, 837–847.

Schulze, L., Domes, G., Krüger, A., Berger, C., Fleischer, M., Prehn, K., ... Herpertz, S. C. (2011). Neuronal correlates of cognitive reappraisal in borderline patients with affective instability. *Biological Psychiatry*, *69*, 564–573.

Selby, E. A., Anestis, M. D., & Joiner, T. E. (2008). Understanding the relationship between emotional and behavioral dysregulation: Emotional cascades. *Behaviour Research and Therapy*, *46*, 593–611.

Shearin, E. N., & Linehan, M. M. (1992). Patient-therapist ratings and relationship to progress in dialectical behavior therapy for borderline personality disorder. *Behavior Therapy*, *23*, 730–741.

Singer, A. R., & Dobson, K. S. (2009). The effect of the cognitive style of acceptance on negative mood in a recovered depressed sample. *Depression and Anxiety*, 26, 471–479.

Soler, J., Valdepérez, A., Feliu-Soler, A., Pascual, J. C., Portella, M. J., Martín-Blanco, A., Pérez, V. (2012). Effects of the dialectical behavioral therapy-mindfulness module on attention in patients with borderline personality disorder. *Behaviour Research and Therapy*, 50, 150–157.

Stepp, S. D., Epler, A. J., Jahng, S., & Trull, T. J. (2008). The effect of dialectical behavior therapy skills use on borderline personality disorder features. *Journal of Personality Disorders*, 22, 549–563.

Stoffers, J. M., Völlm, B. A., Rücker, G., Timmer, A., Huband, N., & Lieb, K. (2012). Psychological therapies for people with borderline personality disorder. *Cochrane Database of Systematic Reviews*, 2012(8). doi:10.1002/14651858. CD005652.pub2

Teasdale, J. D., Segal, Z., & Williams, J. M. G. (1995). How does cognitive therapy prevent depressive relapse and why should attentional control (mindfulness) training help? *Behaviour Research and Therapy*, 33, 25–39.

Turner, R. M. (2000). Naturalistic evaluation of dialectical behavior therapy-oriented treatment for borderline personality disorder. *Cognitive and Behavioral Practice*, 7, 413–419.

Williams, J. M. G. (2010). Mindfulness and psychological process. *Emotion*, 10, 1–7.

Winter, D., Niedtfeld, I., Schmitt, R., Bohus, M., Schmahl, C., & Herpertz, S. C. (2016). Neural correlates of distraction in borderline personality disorder before and after dialectical behavior therapy. *European Archives of Psychiatry and Clinical Neuroscience*, 267, 1–12.

Wupperman, P., Neumann, C. S., Whitman, J. B., & Axelrod, S. R. (2009). The role of mindfulness in borderline personality disorder features. *The Journal of Nervous and Mental Disease*, 197, 766–771.

Zimmerman, D. J., & Choi-Kain, L. W. (2009). The hypothalamic-pituitary-adrenal axis in borderline personality disorder: A review. *Harvard Review of Psychiatry*, 17, 167–183.

···

DBT

A Client Perspective

···

LOUISE BRINTON CLARKE

Introduction

My idea of therapy had always been that of "talking about the past"; I'll talk about my past and I'll be "fixed." My only barrier would be managing to talk about those past experiences. My interpretation was that if I could discuss my past, then clearly, it would lead to healing and my life would be wonderful. However, DBT did not fit this preconception. Instead, it focused primarily on the present and how those past experiences affected my current state, and how my reactions to that state affected other people. Changing my mindset was a struggle; not only was it difficult to complete tasks like chain analysis, but being completely honest about why I was engaging in certain behaviours was even more challenging. Because it was, and is, difficult, I came to recognize that something important was occurring, and that I needed to fully accept it.

My past has been difficult and complex. From a young age, I was subject to neglect, abuse, and abandonment. I spent the majority of my childhood, up to the age of 18, in the care system, which is likely to have been the precursor to my attachment issues. Experiencing sexual, physical, and emotional abuse resulted in my having severe trust issues, a lack of interpersonal skills, and high levels of distress. I was also severely lacking in skills to help me verbalize these problems, as well as the inability to recognize them as problems. I used substance misuse, self-harming behaviour, and support-seeking behaviours in order to gain the validation I craved.

This chapter describes my personal experience of DBT. It covers my experience of the borderline personality disorder diagnosis, and my conviction that a deep understanding of this label is crucial for any practitioner working with this client group. It then describes my journey through DBT, and where my life is currently. I hope that my discussion of my experiences aids practitioners in delivering DBT, as well as demonstrates that many of the more destructive symptoms of BPD can be managed effectively.

MY EXPERIENCE OF BPD DIAGNOSIS

My journey with my BPD diagnosis has been long and convoluted. The term "BPD" was originally mentioned when I was just 15 years of age, and with hindsight, I think the application of this diagnostic label was premature and unhelpful. I had recently disclosed, at 14, that I had been sexually abused over a long period of time, and the disclosure required that I leave a long-term foster care placement to live in a children's home. Prior to the disclosure, I was quiet and reserved, excelled in school, and generally had no [external] problems. I had lived a life controlled to the extreme. I had no friends, I was bullied in school, and I had no typical teenage social life. I was accustomed to having to ask permission for things like using the bathroom, and I lived in constant fear for my safety. Upon entering the children's home and given the freedom I so desperately craved, I was unable to regulate myself. It is no surprise that I became uncontrollable. This change in circumstances and my behaviour was a move from one extreme to the other—I went from no freedom to total freedom. I began engaging in self-harm and substance misuse, and placing myself in dangerous situations.

At the time, the Child and Adolescent Mental Health Services team I was seeing were talking about the diagnoses of Post-Traumatic Stress Disorder (PTSD) or BPD. Not only was my understanding of these terms very limited, but at no point were they ever explained to me. I believed BPD meant "almost" a personality disorder. As time went on and my understanding of the diagnosis increased through self-education, I came to resent the diagnosis (I was officially diagnosed at the age of 18). I learned about, and experienced, the stigma attached to BPD, and it felt extremely invalidating. Simply being viewed as difficult, attention seeking, and manipulative left me feeling even more victimized, and angry. I felt as though I had survived my experiences, and rather than receiving support, I felt instead blamed for being who I was. I argued with professionals that I had merely reacted normally to abnormal circumstances. It was only when a psychologist pointed out that it was this very reaction that was the problem did I begin my recovery. Prior to this, practitioners had avoided challenging me, and I see now this was for several reasons. I could be argumentative, and I often elicited pity. Most therapists, however, refused both to acknowledge my difficult start in life and to treat me, believing I had no chance of recovery. Both then and now, knowing that there is a therapy devised for people like me is validation in itself.

Currently, I am conflicted about the BPD diagnosis. I struggle to accept both that I did fit the label, but also that I have *been* labelled. I believe there was a time where I fully accepted the diagnosis, but my current perspective suggests otherwise. At one time I met all of the diagnostic criteria, and both then and now I recognize the difficulties I have caused myself and others. In other words, externally, I have been a textbook case of BPD. At present, I do not meet the criteria for the diagnosis; however, as far as general mental health services are concerned, it remains. I am deemed currently to have a disordered personality because I responded to my circumstances then with the only tools at my disposal. Over the years, in using the more helpful tools that I found in DBT, I have flourished; on paper, however, this is not the case. According to current practice, I will retain the diagnosis of BPD for the rest of my life unless the wider mental health system changes its methods of diagnosis. In order to maintain my recovery, and to move forward with my life, I must accept that this is the current set of circumstances in UK mental health services. I am still angry and hurt that this label, which bears a stigma, has been given to me, but I recognize and allow myself to feel those emotions without resorting to old behaviours. There is an irony in that I choose to use DBT skills to accept the diagnosis that I so resent. I am not seeking to place blame, as I did previously, although I often wonder where responsibility begins and ends. However, I feel I am assuming complete responsibility for myself, as well as constantly working towards acceptance.

I have found myself stereotyped by many different professionals; because of the diagnosis, some professionals assumed I *must* be feeling/behaving a certain way. I have learned to tolerate this attitude much more effectively than previously, although I still become annoyed. However, I now own my anger, my frustration, and my sadness; I do not say "you made me angry," but rather, "I feel angry." This gives me back my control. I understand that I cannot change *how* others respond, but I can *influence* their response. I can also change my perception of responses. "It is not my fault, but it is my responsibility" is something I remind myself of daily. There is another irony. I am working incredibly hard on accepting myself, my past, and my experiences, but often I find that professionals do not accept that recovery from trauma is possible. Professionals must believe in the reality of recovery to inspire those people who have to do the hard work of change.

BEGINNING IN DBT

When I started DBT, I was in constant crisis. I had managed to function crisis-free for some time, primarily due to previous group therapy in a therapeutic community (TC). However, I had relapsed and was again self-harming. The TC had enabled me to recognize that thoughts and feelings are not facts, but it had not given me the skills I needed to continue my recovery. When I was referred for DBT, I had allowed myself to indulge in old thinking patterns: attempting to convince those around me that I was mentally ill, and that I [secretly] wanted to be in hospital. In truth, I simply did not want the responsibility of life. Although my self-harming was life-threatening, I did not wish to die (although I know many in similar circumstances do). When asked directly about my motivations, I would not deny suicide attempts—I would allow people to assume that I wanted to die. To me, my open acknowledgement that I did not want to die would have meant that I was not worthy of help or support. Although I experienced depression and anxiety, I was constantly making things worse for myself. My reactions to my mental and emotional states simply prolonged my problems and took the focus off the underlying issues. Although I experienced distress regarding my past experiences, I was unable to seek help for this distress; the therapeutic focus was on keeping me physically safe. This pattern of behaviour began at the age of 14; I entered DBT when I was 31.

The TC had also had an undesired effect. While the TC taught me to take responsibility for myself and my behaviours, even when I was behaving destructively, I also assumed responsibility for everyone else's feelings. My self-worth and self-esteem were still non-existent, and I still struggled massively with expressing my wishes, and I continued to allow others to take advantage of me. What I needed were methods and skills that were clear cut—a set of specific rules that I could follow—but I did not recognize this because I had completed group therapy; I should be "cured." Everything I experienced in my relapse, I proclaimed, was "fake"; I was "putting it on," I "wasn't distressed" and "I didn't deserve help." Although I was often not entirely honest about my motivations for self-harm, I was genuinely distressed. I craved validation from others, without knowing how to validate myself. I called myself an "attention-seeker," and was seemingly quite happy and comfortable to call myself that. My negative self-image had not altered at all, and was once again contributing to my behaviours.

Upon entering DBT, I felt motivated to engage. I had had a difficult start with my individual therapist, but this had been resolved thanks to her ability to quickly recognize where my difficulty was. I was feeling defensive and misunderstood; my therapist was not afraid to challenge me and she set very clear limits immediately. She outlined that we were a partnership, whereas I was used to being "boss." It became clear that I would not be dictating the sessions; there would be no "game" playing without consequences and if I wanted to remain in the therapy, I would have to adhere to the rules. Initially, this did not sit well with me; in one of our very first sessions, I walked out. My therapist wrote to me, and it was done in such a manner that it broke any tension immediately—it was quite a personal letter, and contained a pressed flower. She had given me this flower in the session I walked out of; I had looked at the flower and thought it was ridiculous. Hindsight tells me I was actually embarrassed and did not manage the exposure effectively. Pressing the flower and posting it to me made me laugh, and I respected my therapist for her daring and the risk she had taken.

Despite being motivated when starting DBT, I was not sure what I was motivated to do. I knew it was a therapy, and that it was a therapy originally devised for those with a diagnosis of BPD. As with all therapy, the patient needs to be motivated to engage. I had had some pre-DBT sessions, which I believe looked at my motivation. These sessions also laid out some rules and expectations of me for when I joined the group.

With hindsight I think it would have been helpful for my therapist to be even more explicit that attending DBT required me to put aside working on my trauma to engage in the programme. As programme participants, we are asked to accept the trauma we have experienced and also perhaps accept that we may *always* live a life in which there is a level of emotional pain. To acknowledge this is extremely difficult and painful. In dealing with patients who have often experienced multiple, life-changing, traumatic events requires practitioners who can be open and direct about the programme, recognize that they are being trusted with the emotions of highly vulnerable individuals, and the challenges patients are likely to face in completing the programme.

REFLECTIONS ON THE DBT SKILLS CLASS

Initially, I found DBT quite rigid—one size doesn't fit all— and I spent quite a long time battling this perceived rigidity. I struggled to verbalize my frustration effectively, and instead became angry, ultimately fulfilling the beliefs I believed others held about me. I began to believe the messages about myself that I had heard from others—that I was untreatable, "damaged beyond repair," "broken," manipulative, attention seeking, and even dangerous. Hindsight tells me this was one of the reasons DBT was appropriate for me. Not only did I require time, patience, and validation to help recover from my difficult start in life, but I also needed to begin recovery from the attitudes I had met from my teenage years to my adult life.

During the course of my time in group I came to appreciate that I was somewhat correct in my initial thought that "one size doesn't fit all," but my viewpoint was very one-sided. If one skill did not work for me, then there were others to which I could turn. I initially saw DBT as a whole, or single, thing; soon I began to see DBT as something made up of many different parts and elements, some glaringly obvious, some much more subtle; I still hold this view today. How I interpret and use one skill will be interpreted and viewed entirely differently by another, and this is the beauty of attending a group. However, I feel as though I came to this conclusion alone. Perhaps because of my experience in a TC, I was able to tolerate certain attitudes and situations in order to gain what I could from group; this was a massively important part of the therapy for me. I witnessed others, however, who were unable to understand that simply attending group, and experiencing and resolving conflict in a different way is actually part of the therapeutic experience. This reminds me of my original thought—"if I talk about my past, I'll be cured." Therapy is so much more than that.

I feel as though the skills programme of DBT makes up about 50% of the therapy; the other 50% is the group experience and the relationship with the individual practitioner. I was constantly mindful of this, primarily because I had experienced group therapy previously. However, this concept feels difficult to relay to other individuals attending group and it was not something that was highlighted very often. I often heard, "I don't do groups, I'm too anxious." This would suggest the exact reason why someone should attend group, but it is difficult to both relay and to understand this if you are the one living with the anxiety. For me, learning different social cues and recognizing my thought patterns and emotions when with others has been a massively important part of my learning. I began to see that this was true for others, even if they did not recognize this themselves.

The DBT Skills Group Rule on Discussing Self-Harm: Pros and Cons

Because I had already had group therapy experience, I had already begun to learn to speak openly about why I self-harmed. This has been one of the most important aspects of my recovery. When not being honest about my reasons, I was incredibly lonely and feeling the need to maintain the pretence simply added to my pre-existing anxiety. I wanted to be viewed as mentally ill, as well as being the "best" at self-harm. I was prepared to go great lengths in order to get the validation I so desperately craved. Because DBT has a focus on validation and recognition that group members may have been raised in an invalidating environment, this was immediately helpful. It gave me permission to openly address the function of my behaviours in the group; being able to do this also helped others to come forward and acknowledge that they may be support-seeking, or enjoy the "drama" of certain behaviours. It is extremely relieving and liberating to be able to talk about these controversial topics in an environment where those who listen do so without judgment; many also have had the same experiences. Many of those who listened to me suddenly said, "I'm the same." I can remember the relief, but also fear, on their faces. During my entire time in group, I was the group member who would address this difficult topic. It may be that the facilitators did not need to address it as I already had, but I believe it is useful for individuals to know they can talk about this.

I also believe that clients should not specify the type of self-damaging behaviours they have engaged in, and that this omission of type is one of the most important factors of DBT group. I fully understand and appreciate the reasons behind this. There was something enjoyable talking about what I might have done to myself, and it can become competitive; occasionally, I would glorify my behaviours. Additionally, in the past I have "taken ideas" from others' stories, and others have taken ideas from mine. Based on my experiences, I believe it would be useful to have a session on this very topic. It is a crucial part of learning about ourselves and it could also be useful for practitioners to witness responses to this type of talk. It opens up conversation—why do we like talking about it? What are we getting from it? That part of the therapy has been essential for me and my recovery; if I was unable to look at these things, I do not believe I would be where I am now.

Skills Class Content

Once learned, the skills seem relatively simply; initially, however, they seem complex, alien, and difficult to grasp. Skills Trainers need to clearly communicate the purpose of particular skills, as well as how to use the skills. An individual with lower intelligence may struggle with understanding some of the more challenging skills unless they are explained in a clear and simple way. My experience is that most people have difficulty grasping the skill of "radical acceptance"; I have struggled with the notion of acceptance for years as it feels as though it is something that cannot be explained, but only experienced. I have learned and accepted that some things can only be experienced and not explained, but the simple idea of "acceptance" was quite frustrating. With this in mind, it is important to consider that there may be people who do not have the ability to understand what we may view as clear-cut. Practitioners need not only to have the ability to deliver the programme, but also to teach the programme in a way that is suitable for the individual receiving the therapy. I had a therapist who delivered therapy in a way I understood it, and I am grateful for it.

Learning how to manage my initial responses via the interpersonal effectiveness module has changed my life. Previously, my initial responses would lead to other, external responses, which in turn would further negatively affect my interpersonal effectiveness. The DEAR MAN skill is the one that has had the most benefit. It has allowed me to break down what I need to convey without becoming argumentative, frustrated, or simply shutting down; for me, this skill is invaluable. I have also started learning how to validate my own thoughts and feelings using DEAR MAN. Initially, when the skills did not appear to be successful, I would lose hope; after a while, I learned patience, gave myself time to remember the DEAR MAN skill, and went through each step. It can still feel frustrating, however, when my efforts to use skills don't result in others responding effectively; nonetheless, as I have completed so many rounds of DBT, I have learned how the skills work together. The frustration levels fall when I accept that I have done all I can using distress tolerance, mindfulness, and emotion regulation. When, despite my best efforts, a relationship continues to be fraught with problems, I can use the skill of ending relationships—where acceptance comes around again!

Initially, my least favourite module was the mindfulness module. What I have learned, however, is that this was because I had a preconceived, judgmental attitude towards mindfulness. I believed mindfulness was simply "getting to know your raisin". I typically felt embarrassed and extremely self-conscious during mindfulness exercises, but going through them has been extremely useful for me; if I can survive the gut-wrenching, cringe-worthy three minutes of throwing sounds to another person, I can survive most things! Being able to sit with those feelings was direct evidence that difficult feelings can be managed. Although I feel as though I now have a clear understanding of these types of exercises, it was not always so, as demonstrated powerfully when my therapist gave me the flower. I also appreciate how exercises like these are exposure for the practitioner; it takes courage to do them in a group of highly emotional individuals. I typically attempt to engage in some type of mindfulness on a daily basis; this can be eating mindfully, being aware of the present moment, or being mindfully mindless! I am now able to recognize how the modules and skills work together and complement each other. Initially, they were all separate and distinct entities; now, each time I repeat a module, I take away something new and view it through a new lens.

MY EXPERIENCE OF INDIVIDUAL THERAPY

Previously, I had managed to acknowledge that the majority of my self-harming behaviours were done in order to seek support, hence my labelling myself as "attention-seeker." But it was easier to acknowledge this when some time had passed after these self-damaging events. Talking about it as it was happening, or even very recently afterwards in my individual therapy, was incredibly difficult. I would still deny any attempt at support seeking and say it was something else. It would have been useful for me had my therapist challenged me more. I understand that, for many practitioners, challenging their clients is a difficult task. As a client, I have been extremely confrontational at times, often seeing things in a somewhat skewed manner, misinterpreting situations, and wanting to be "in charge" of the situation, which made challenging me difficult.

This misinterpretation of situations—including body language, what is being said, and even trying to "mind read"—has been, and sometimes still is, a huge problem for me. Making assumptions drove many of my problem behaviours—self-harming, substance misuse, and not taking responsibility for my feelings. The problem with the latter, in particular, was that I never really knew what I wanted others to do, nor did I realize that I did not know what I wanted. People typically gave up on me, or apologized (usually in an attempt to appease me, or because I had, unintentionally, manipulated their words to make them believe they were in the wrong). Both of these outcomes fulfilled my original beliefs that "everyone hates me" and/or "I was right." I needed whoever was working with me to not get drawn in to my demands, to challenge my behaviour in a non-judgmental manner, and to remain focused on the moment. I also needed that individual to explain to me what was happening and why they were doing what they were doing. I do not feel as though I have fully experienced this; I have drawn my own conclusions as to why my therapists were doing particular things. I do not know if I am correct, but these reflections have helped me better challenge myself.

I found doing chain analyses frustrating. I often could not grasp what the precipitating event was, or what it "should" be. A feeling would have been triggered by an external event, yet I often could not name such events. This often led to lengthy discussions and my looking for something that perhaps was not there. Hindsight tells me that whatever situation may have occurred does not matter when considering the bigger picture; I can feel angry, for example, but what needs to be managed is the anger. What may have been more helpful would have been to simply focus on the feeling and work on my reaction to that feeling. Despite not experiencing this during my own therapy, I am able to recognize that this will be helpful for me as I move forward.

In my experience, when someone has a BPD diagnosis, their experience of other mental disorders, such as depression and anxiety, is often disregarded. For me, depression and anxiety have been almost debilitating. Without old behaviours to distract from these states, I experience depression and anxiety fully. I lose energy and hope, and I stop caring. I become paranoid and nihilistic. I no longer make things worse, but the state itself is distressing enough. Because I have previously engaged in support-seeking behaviours, the depressive states I experience are often ignored. The anxiety I experience leaves me in a constant state of hypervigilance. What I am attempting to accept—while simultaneously remembering that acceptance cannot be forced—is that my depression and anxiety may never go away. I still feel invalidated by some practitioners regarding the depression and anxiety; I can practise my skills at every given opportunity, yet still feel depressed and anxious. This is painful and exhausting. My experience leads me to believe that practitioners should always bear in mind that each client is not just a label, or a group of labels. It is possible for an individual to be grappling with more than one mental health issue, just as an individual can have two broken bones at the same time. Sometimes, the same bone may be broken in different parts of the body, meaning the same treatment will work for each; however, different bones may be broken, meaning different treatments are needed. This is the same for the brain and mind.

During my time in DBT, I had two individual therapists. It was unfortunate that the first one had to leave because of illness. However, during my two years in group (one year as a client, one year as a graduate facilitator), I witnessed a stream of practitioners come and go. I understood it was because the practitioners were not being granted time to deliver DBT. The practitioners were either mental health nurses or mental health social workers. The group was supposed to be multi-disciplinary, consisting of psychologists and mental health workers. By the time the group finished, there were three psychologists running the group, and through its demise, the group became a statistic. I understand that many programmes end without support from the organization to keep them going (Comtois & Landes, this volume). This was true for the group I attended.

MY EXPERIENCE AS A GRADUATE FACILITATOR

I completed two rounds of DBT modules as a client, following which my DBT programme offered me the opportunity to stay on as a graduate facilitator. This was a novel role developed by my team and meant that I was able to complete a further two rounds of the modules. At the time, I did not understand that it was a privilege to continue attending group; I viewed my place as helping others to become more accepting of themselves. Although I believe I did this with some members, the opportunity of further self-education was greatly appreciated. While I learned a lot for myself and was able to encourage and support others, the role of a DBT graduate facilitator was completely new to me. It felt unclear and I often felt isolated; I had no access to a therapist, nor was I a part of the Consultation Team. I was the only graduate facilitator at the time; I did not belong as a group member, nor was I a member of staff. Even more confusingly, some of the psychologists believed I should be paid for my time. My experience as a graduate facilitator has convinced me that such a role has potential in group; having someone in the group who understands from personal experience what it is like to begin and struggle with the treatment may benefit those who are new to group. However, such roles require a clear purpose and structure with an opportunity to receive support and feedback from the team about issues that arise in the role.

AFTER DBT

I have lived a life of trauma; trauma inflicted by others and trauma inflicted by myself. I have repeated patterns and tried to convince others and myself I am mentally ill. I have done the latter because of the former. I have learned that only I can ultimately determine my future. I have required support to do this, and may require further support in the future.

When I started DBT, I was nearing the end of completing a degree in psychology. I did complete it, with a 2:1. I have also completed a post-graduate diploma in counselling. I completely and voluntarily came off state benefits over a year ago and am working full time. I work as a mentor in a university, supporting students with mental ill health, learning disabilities, and/or autism spectrum disorders. I also work in a residential drug and alcohol rehabilitation unit. I married my partner of seven years in 2016 and I recently passed my driving test, which has been a huge achievement for me. Previously, I was unsafe to drive. I was substance dependent and engaged in too many risky, impulsive behaviours.

DBT has prepared me for life without trauma and drama. It has enabled me to get up every day, engage in routine, contribute positively to society, and assume responsibility for myself, my actions, and the effect I may have on others. What DBT has not done is resolve the trauma I experienced. Although I think more in wise mind, I often feel as though my feelings are the same; I'm simply not making things worse. I find myself being highly effective in most areas of my life. I am able to communicate as needed, and express my needs and wishes effectively. I still struggle, however, to express how I am feeling.

KEY MESSAGES FOR CLINICIANS

- The label of borderline personality disorder can be more damaging than helpful.
- Non-DBT services that continue to label clients as having BPD when they no longer meet the criteria for the disorder are unhelpful—once a broken leg is healed, it is no longer a broken leg. Clinicians need to emphasize this point to their clients, as well as to the systems in which they work.
- DBT should be delivered by confident, competent, and courageous practitioners who are not afraid to both challenge and set limits for their clients.
- The rationale behind some of the skills (e.g., exposure via mindfulness) require repeated explanation; clients may have difficulty in understanding the purpose of learning the skills.
- Consistency is key; DBT needs practitioners who are prepared to engage for at least two cycles of the skills programme. They must also be willing to work consistently as an individual therapist with their clients.
- DBT works, if the correct elements are in place—motivation from the client, a certain level of understanding from the client, and the appropriate, skilled practitioner are all needed for success in DBT.

I can recognize a negative emotion as I am experiencing it, but I am often unable to name the emotion. Reflecting upon this, I am attempting to utilize acceptance—I accept that perhaps I will always sometimes struggle with the trauma I experienced, and that I simply cannot name some of my emotions. I have some hope that this may change, but I wonder if it matters. Accepting what is in the moment is what enables me to live my life.

I have been fortunate enough to receive some individual therapy around a year after I left the DBT programme. This therapy is due to end before its time, which feels difficult, but I am able to address this in an effective manner. I feel as though ongoing therapy and support through this post-DBT time would help. I often feel as though I need a sounding board—someone who will listen, understand, validate, and not judge my internal experiences; sometimes, I need to be emotionally held by someone who is stronger than me. I am accepting that this is not the case for me right now, and I will continue to try and improve myself and my situation to the best of my ability, given the skills I have. Typically, I am content.

CONCLUSION

Would I recommend DBT? Definitely. I'm not sure anyone can be prepared for the painful realizations that may arise from completing the therapy; in my opinion, this is both a blessing and a curse. I'm living my life much more effectively, but I still struggle. I contribute to society and to myself, but I am in a place right now that feels difficult. After I completed DBT, I did not receive any trauma therapy, which I believe would have been beneficial to me. I understand the constraints of the NHS—its waiting lists, lack of staff. I understand that if I am not presenting as a risk, then I may not receive a service. What I no longer do is place myself at risk in order to receive that service. January 2018 marks two years since I have engaged in any self-harming behaviours. This time last year was the first time I experienced a depressive episode without resorting to previous behaviours. More recently, I have been formally discharged—through planning and collaboration—from the community mental health team. This is the first time in my life that I have been completely independent of any type of service. The evidence, for me, speaks for itself—DBT works.

ADAPTING THE TREATMENT FOR NEW CLINICAL POPULATIONS

CHAPTER 25

DBT WITH ADOLESCENTS

JILL H. RATHUS, ALEC L. MILLER, AND
LAUREN BONAVITACOLA

INTRODUCTION

MARSHA Linehan's Dialectical Behavior Therapy (DBT; Linehan, 1993a, b) has revolutionized cognitive behavioural therapy. Her biosocial model of disorder and balance of change and acceptance strategies for treating complex problems of emotional and behavioural dysregulation have brought compassionate treatment to clients previously regarded as too challenging to help. The dialectical world view underlying the treatment considers reality as consisting of bipolar opposites, and the core dialectic in DBT is the balance of clients working to accept things as they are while simultaneously working to change them, and the assumption that those contradictory goals can co-exist. Linehan originally developed her treatment for suicidal and self-injurious clients diagnosed with borderline personality disorder (BPD); since then, DBT has become a more transdiagnostic treatment. Linehan designed a comprehensive treatment package designed to handle multi-problem clients who often experienced numerous past treatment failures (Linehan, 1993a, b).

In the 1990s, we began applying DBT to suicidal multi-problem adolescents and families in an inner-city outpatient clinic. At the time, no comprehensive evidence-based treatments for suicidal adolescents existed, and the treatments researched for depression and related disorders excluded data on suicidal youth. We began our work by seeking training and applying the original Linehan (1993a, b) text and skills training manual as the best available comprehensive treatment for individuals with suicidal behaviours, multiple disorders, and complex presentations. This chapter describes DBT as we adapted it for adolescents.

Adapting Adult DBT for an Adolescent Population

Recognizing that adolescents had different developmental needs, and that many youths and parents had difficulty comprehending material on the skills handouts, we nevertheless piloted the adult manual as written with cohorts of adolescent patients and their caregivers in order to gain clinical information before modifying. Adolescent developmental literature, direct participant feedback, and clinical observations informed our initial alterations (Miller, Rathus, Linehan, Wetzler, & Leigh, 1997; Rathus & Miller, 2002), and we continued to make minor modifications based on developmental and family contextual needs and our research, as reflected in our volumes, *Dialectical Behavior Therapy with Suicidal Adolescents* (Miller, Rathus, & Linehan, 2007), and *DBT Skills Manual for Adolescents* (Rathus & Miller, 2015). We modified only where we believed changes were needed while maintaining the essential elements of DBT, including its dialectical underpinnings; biosocial theory of disorder; treatment functions; assumptions about patients and therapists; primary treatment targets and targeting procedures; change and acceptance procedures; treatment strategies (i.e., core, dialectical, stylistic, commitment, case management); and skills.

Adolescents differ from adult clients with regard to developmental level, and context: they overwhelmingly attend school and reside with their families. Thus, we identified adolescent quality-of-life (QoL) treatment targets (e.g., school- and peer-related problems) and adolescent-family secondary treatment targets; considered parent-teen confidentiality issues; increased use of environmental intervention, primarily by including parents in treatment through as-needed family and parenting sessions as well as including parents in skills training (data suggests a treatment focus on parents positively impacts outcomes for suicidal youth; see, e.g., Pineda & Dadds, 2013); and added a family-based skills module, "Walking the Middle Path," as well as several adolescent-focused skills. In addition, we modified the language and appearance of the skills materials to enhance accessibility for adolescents, and provided skills teaching examples and practice exercises tailored to teens and family members (Rathus & Miller, 2015).

How DBT Conceptualizes the Emotionally Dysregulated Adolescent

DBT treats youth presenting with multiple, serious problems that may include suicidal behaviours, non-suicidal self-injury (NSSI), disordered eating, alcohol and drug use, risky sexual behaviours, and other harmful behaviours. Youth may also have less severe problems, such as: light social drinking; first signs of non-suicidal and non-severe self-harm behaviour; anger dyscontrol; school avoidance; impulsive on-line behaviours; impaired self-awareness of emotions, goals, and values; and frequent relationship break-ups. DBT views these problems as consequences of emotional dysregulation or as attempts to re-regulate intense emotions.

DBT conceptualizes problematic adolescent behaviours as influenced primarily by: 1) a lack of important attentional, emotional, interpersonal, self-regulation, and distress tolerance capabilities; and 2) contextual and individual factors that inhibit use of capabilities teens may already have, and reinforce ineffective behaviours.

DBT addresses these factors through five treatment functions: (1) improving motivation, (2) increasing capabilities, (3) increasing generalization, (4) structuring the environment to motivate and reinforce adaptive behaviours, and (5) providing support for therapists. In DBT for adolescents, we added to the second function—increasing capabilities—in balanced thinking and interacting for individuals and their families ("Walking the Middle Path" module) as shown in Table 25.1.

To fulfil these functions, Linehan (1993a) developed four treatment modes: individual therapy, group skills training, between-session telephone coaching, and therapist consultation team. Comprehensive adolescent outpatient DBT conducts skills training with adolescents and parents together in a multi-family skills group, providing phone coaching for both adolescents and parents, and offering family and parenting sessions as needed (Miller et al., 2007). (See Table 25.2.)

Core elements of DBT also include: a biosocial theory of emotion dysregulation, an overall dialectical stance; a hierarchical prioritizing of behavioural treatment targets; and sets of acceptance, change, communication, commitment, structural, and dialectical strategies. The following sections discuss the application of these elements and our adapted treatment modes with adolescents. The chapter concludes with a case example, a summary of the outcome literature on DBT with adolescents, and future directions of DBT with youth.

DBT's Biosocial Theory

Linehan (1993a) theorized that chronic problems of emotional dysregulation stem from a biological vulnerability to emotional dysregulation transacting with an invalidating environment—hence the term "biosocial" theory.

Biological vulnerability. Emotional vulnerability is high sensitivity to emotion-triggering stimuli, high reactivity (i.e., intense emotional responses), and slow return to baseline emotional state. Added to this vulnerability is difficulty modulating emotional reactions; the person experiencing strong emotions lacks capacities to re-direct attention and behaviour in non-mood-dependent ways.

The neurobiology of BPD biological vulnerability in adolescents. In adults, amgydala hyperactivity in individuals with BPD has been widely demonstrated through fMRI

Table 25.1   Characteristics of dysregulation and corresponding DBT skills modules

Some characteristics of dysregulation	DBT skills modules
Emotion dysregulation	
Emotional vulnerability; emotional reactivity; emotional lability; angry outbursts; steady negative emotional states such as depression, anger, shame, anxiety, and guilt; deficits in positive emotions, and difficulty in modulating emotions.	Emotion Regulation
Interpersonal dysregulation	
Unstable relationships, interpersonal conflicts, chronic family disturbance, social isolation, efforts to avoid abandonment, and difficulties getting needs met in relationships, and keeping self-respect in relationships.	Interpersonal Effectiveness
Behavioural dysregulation	
Impulsive behaviours such as cutting classes, blurting out in class, spending money, risky sexual behaviour, risky online behaviours, binging and/or purging, drug and alcohol abuse, aggressive behaviours, suicidal and NSSI behaviour.	Distress Tolerance
Cognitive dysregulation & family conflict	
Non-dialectical thinking and acting (i.e., extreme, polarized, or black-or-white), poor perspective taking and conflict resolution, invalidation of self and other, difficulty effectively influencing own and other's behaviours (i.e., obtaining desired changes).	Walking the Middle Path
Self dysregulation	
Lacking awareness of emotions, thoughts, action urges; poor attentional control; unable to reduce one's suffering while also having difficulty accessing pleasure; identity confusion, sense of emptiness, and dissociation.	Core Mindfulness

Adapted from Alec L. Miller, Jill H. Rathus, & Marsha M. Linehan, *Dialectical Behavior Therapy with Suicidal Adolescents*, p. 36, Table 2.1 © Guilford Press, 2007, with permission.

Table 25.2   Modes in comprehensive outpatient DBT with multi–problem adolescents

- Multi-family skills training group
- Individual DBT therapy
- Telephone coaching for teens *and* family members
- Family sessions (as needed)
- Parenting sessions (as needed)
- Therapist consultation team meeting
- Possible ancillary treatments
    - Pharmacotherapy
    - Therapeutic/residential schools

Reprinted from Jill H. Rathus & Alec L. Miller, *DBT® Skills Manual for Adolescents*, p. 6, Table 1.2 © Guilford Press, 2015, with permission.

studies compared to healthy controls (Goodman et al., 2014; Hazlett et al., 2012; Koenigsberg et al., 2014; Krause-Utz et al., 2014), but to date, no fMRI studies have been conducted on amgydala activity in adolescents with BPD (Ensink, Biberdzic, Normandin, & Clarkin, 2015). Amgydala activity is notable due to its key role in emotion processing and fear and stress responses. Other neurobiological studies have been conducted with adolescents with BPD assessing volumetric abnormalities in the anterior cingulate cortex (ACC) and anterior cingulate gyrus (ACG), which are structures that are functionally connected to the amgydala. Some evidence suggests a decrease in volume in the left ACC in adolescents with BPD (Whittle et al., 2009) and decreased ACG volume in adolescents with BPD (Goodman et al., 2011). These results provide preliminary evidence that neurobiological vulnerabilities may exist in the development of BPD.

The invalidating environment. The invalidating environment consists of the tendency of people in the emotionally sensitive person's environment to pervasively dismiss, negate, punish, or respond erratically to the person's expression of emotions. These others are often parents/family members, and their invalidation may be well-meaning ("come on; it's not such a big deal! You'll get over it!"). For teens, the invalidating environment can also include peers, teachers, other school personnel, and health professionals. Moreover, teens may experience bullying, social exclusion, or social media provocations that elicit trauma reactions or a chronic sense of being different (e.g., an LGBTQ adolescent experiencing the hetero-normative culture as highly invalidating). In an invalidating environment, one's emotional experiences are not received as valid responses, and are instead trivialized, ignored, or attributed to unacceptable characteristics such as over-reactivity, inability to see things realistically, lack of motivation, attention-seeking, or being dramatic. At times, however, individuals in the environment may reinforce escalating communications of distress, such as by providing attention and soothing, or removing demands after a suicidal communication, inadvertently intermittently reinforcing escalated emotional displays. Invalidating environments emphasize controlling emotional expressiveness ("Why are you freaking out over this? Toughen up!"), oversimplify ease of solving problems ("Just pull yourself together and do better next time!") and are generally intolerant of displays of negative affect ("You're ruining this for everybody!"). Coaching in emotion regulation is lacking and maladaptive learning takes place (i.e., emotions are "bad," "I shouldn't feel what I feel; my reactions are wrong so I cannot trust them," "I can only be taken seriously if I *really* let them know how upset I am.").

Emotional vulnerability transacts with an invalidating environment such that both sides co-create each other over time (see Crowell et al., this volume). A person with extreme emotional vulnerability may develop dysregulation in a family with "normal" levels of invalidation, and may even inadvertently elicit invalidation (e.g., the well-meaning parent who doesn't understand why only this one, sensitive child cries and shuts down at dinner each night and finally snaps, "Enough! Go to your room!"). Or, a highly invalidating environment might transact with a lower level of emotional vulnerability to yield persistent emotional dysregulation (e.g., the coach throughout high school who screams, criticizes rest breaks as weakness, shames emotional displays, and tells the injured player to ignore the pain and "get back in the game.").

This emotional-environmental transaction results in lack of capacities to regulate arousal, tolerate distress, or trust internal emotional responses (Linehan, 1993a). This mistrust of one's own states often results in confusion about identity, goals, and values. The invalidating environment's response to emotional expression, while intermittently reinforcing its escalation, results in vacillation between emotion suppression and extreme emotional displays. Behaviours such as skipping school, drug use, running away, and self-injury may function to regulate affect and can be reinforced through sometimes eliciting support from an environment that generally dismisses expressions of emotional pain.

In DBT for adolescents, we teach the biosocial theory to teens and their parents (see Rathus & Miller, 2015). Teaching the model non-judgmentally, we ask family members which parts of the model apply to them, and elicit a discussion. We normalize the transaction and explain that the good news is that DBT addresses both parts of the model by teaching emotion regulation and validation skills.

DBT TREATMENT STAGES AND PRIMARY TREATMENT TARGETS

DBT conceptualizes treatment in stages that correspond to the client's problem severity, and each has its own treatment priorities or targets (Table 25.3). Pre-treatment typically lasts several sessions and involves assessing the client by meeting with parents and the adolescent, orientating them to DBT, and securing commitment from both parents and the teen. Pre-treatment commitment also involves obtaining consent for treatment from parents and assent from the teen (unless the teen is 18 or over, when only teen consent is needed). In cases in which a parent is reluctant to give consent, we recommend assessing treatment barriers or parent concerns and then validate, problem solve, or provide psychoeducation as needed, and use DBT commitment strategies. In addition, practitioners should become familiar with state laws as to how young a client can be to consent to their own treatment independently of their parent(s).

Clients in Stage One are severely dysregulated with impulsive and often high-risk behaviours, including self-harm or suicidal behaviours. The main task in Stage One is to help clients attain basic capacities and establish safety and behavioural control: the vast majority of outcome data pertains to this stage. For Stage One adolescents, we ask for a six-month commitment. For some this suffices and for some, follow-up care will entail either a graduate group or possibly another six months of Stage One treatment (see Miller et al., 2007).

In Stage One, clients participate in individual and skills training sessions and each mode has different treatment priorities (Table 25.3). The client completes daily self-monitoring through diary cards, which help set the session agenda. When problem behaviours are noted on the diary card, the individual therapist conducts behavioural chain and solution analyses. This process identifies places in the behavioural sequence

Table 25.3 Standard DBT stages and their hierarchies of primary treatment targets

Pretreatment stage: Orientation and commitment to treatment, agreement on goals
Targets: Inform adolescent about, and orientating adolescent to, DBT.
Inform adolescent's family about, and orientating family to, DBT.
Secure adolescent's commitment to treatment.
Secure adolescent's family's commitment to treatment.
Secure therapist's commitment to treatment.

Stage one: Attaining basic capacities, increasing safety, reducing behavioural dyscontrol
Hierarchy of primary targets in individual DBT therapy:
1. Decrease life-threatening behaviours.
2. Decrease therapy-interfering behaviours.
3. Decrease QoL-interfering behaviours.
4. Increase behavioural skills.

Hierarchy of primary targets in DBT skills training:
1. Decrease behaviours likely to destroy therapy.
2. Increase skill acquisition, strengthening, and generalization.
    a. Core Mindfulness Skills.
    b. Interpersonal Effectiveness.
    c. Emotion Regulation.
    d. Distress Tolerance.
    e. Walking the Middle Path.
3. Decrease therapy-interfering behaviours.

Stage two: Increasing non-anguished emotional experiencing; reducing traumatic stress
Primary target in individual DBT:
1. Decrease avoidance of emotional experience and post-traumatic stress.

Stage three: Increasing self-respect and achieving individual goals, addressing normal problems in living
Primary targets in individual DBT:
1. Increase respect for self.
2. Achieve individual goals.

Stage four:
Primary targets in individual DBT:
1. Resolve a sense of incompleteness.
2. Find freedom and joy.

Adapted from Alec L. Miller, Jill H. Rathus, and Marsha M. Linehan, *Dialectical Behavior Therapy with Suicidal Adolescents*, p. 45, Table 3.1 and p. 47, Table 3.2 © Guilford Press, 2007 and Marsha M. Linehan, *Cognitive-Behavioral Treatment of Borderline Personality Disorder*, p167, Table 6.1 © Guilford Press, 1993, with permission.

where DBT problem solving strategies such as skills training, exposure, cognitive modification, and contingency management can be applied.

In order to organize the session, individual therapy hierarchically prioritizes the following treatment targets from highest to lowest: decreasing life-threatening behaviours (which often includes self-injury), decreasing therapy-interfering behaviours

(TIBs), decreasing severe QoL-interfering behaviours, and increasing behavioural skills. QoL-interfering targets common with teens include such behaviours as school avoidance, disordered eating, social media-related risk behaviours, substance use, and peer conflict.

Stage Two involves either emotionally processing past trauma and grief (Linehan, 1993a), or a more intensive family-focused intervention, and often a graduate group to strengthen skills application (Miller et al., 2007).

DBT TREATMENT STRATEGIES IN INDIVIDUAL THERAPY

DBT uses specific treatment strategies to address treatment targets: 1) dialectical strategies, 2) validation strategies, 3) problem-solving strategies, 4) stylistic (communication) strategies, and 5) case management strategies. Dialectical strategies primarily concern how the therapist structures interactions, works toward synthesis of extreme positions, and constantly balances acceptance with change. Validation strategies focus on acceptance and include warm, reciprocal communication, explicitly conveying that the client's emotions make sense. Problem-solving strategies focus on traditional behavioural therapy strategies, including skills training, exposure, and cognitive modification, as well as techniques based on behavioural principles of positive and negative reinforcement, shaping, extinction, and punishment.

Stylistic communication strategies include balancing reciprocal communication with irreverence—a blunt, direct, often unorthodox or unexpected way of framing things to get the patient's attention and help them to see things differently. Irreverence with teens is essential as they tend to be suspect of "sugar-coating" and sensitive to hints of insincerity, over-soothing, or patronizing.

DBT case management balances consultation-to-the-patient with consultation-to-the-environment. Consultation-to-the-patient strategies teach adolescents how to be their own advocates with their environment, e.g., parents, teachers, coaches, or therapists. At the other end of the dialectic lie environmental intervention strategies, wherein therapists contact care providers, parents, or school personnel on behalf of the teen; therapists consult with the environment when the outcome is crucial and when the patient does not have the power or skill set to effect change (Linehan, 1993a). Since youth have less power with adult authority figures and often require more support, adolescent DBT includes more environmental intervention than adult DBT. However, whenever possible, direct communication from adolescents to others in their environment is coached and encouraged toward development of greater self-efficacy and mastery.

Often, individual therapists collaborate with others in the teen's environment, including family members as well as other mental health providers, such as a psychopharmacologist or school psychologist. Therapists may need to orient school personnel to DBT telephone coaching, and problem solve the use of this mode at school, i.e., identifying an office the teen can use and planning what to do if the therapist does not answer right away.

DBT also uses a set of orientating and commitment strategies. Orientating includes validating caregiver's concerns and emotions (such as shame, anxiety, and hopelessness) and providing the rationale for multi-family skills group. DBT commitment strategies, such as considering the pros and cons of entering treatment versus keeping things as they are, and playing the devil's advocate by challenging entering clients' commitment (e.g., "why would you want to be in such a demanding treatment?") to prompt the client to argue on behalf of engaging in comprehensive DBT, are used with both teens and parents. We informally add another commitment strategy with adolescents who say, "I don't have any problems; they made me come here!" We affectionately refer to this as the "How can we help you get your parents off your back?" strategy, since seeking more trust, freedom, and privacy will often motivate reluctant teens. Commitment strategies are used not only in pretreatment, but also throughout treatment as the therapist pulls for new behaviours and pushes for change.

Multi-family Skills Groups for Adolescents and Families

We recommend a multi-family group format when possible when conducting skills training with adolescents. Including caregivers increases understanding and skillful interactions in the teens' home environment, and including multiple families helps maintain the didactic agenda, as opposed to drifting into a single family's problem of the week. Having several families offers a support network; provides coping models, motivation, and hope; and expands group members' skills repertoires. For example, homework review exposes each member to many examples of a skill's use. A multiple family format allows for behavioural rehearsal across families, such as a teen practising a skill with another teen's parent, or a parent gently providing input to another parent's teen. With such interactions, clients' emotions tend to remain better regulated, and thus new learning is enhanced, while gradually working toward the exposure of interactions with one's own family members. Additionally, members often benefit from mastery when explaining a concept to a newer member, and report feeling validated when hearing that other families share similar struggles. Finally, at the graduation ceremony, teens and parents offer their parting constructive feedback and encouragement to one another, which powerfully affects the graduates *and* remaining group members. Most graduating members report dramatic improvement in relationships with participating family members; this feedback demonstrates to remaining members how life can be improved, models the need for perseverance, and inspires them to remain hopeful.

DBT Skills Taught

DBT skills for adolescents span five modules (Table 25.4): Mindfulness, Emotion Regulation, Interpersonal Effectiveness, Distress Tolerance, and a module we designed for teens and families, called Walking the Middle Path (WMP; Miller et al., 2007; Rathus & Miller, 2000; Rathus & Miller, 2015). Completing the modules typically takes 24 weeks. Group members are taught all the strategies and practise them all in weekly homework assignments.

Adaptations to Skills

In adolescent DBT, we retained virtually all of Linehan's skills (1993b, 2015). Changes included a) slightly reducing the amount of content, b) limiting the amount of text and simplifying language on handouts, c) adjusting teaching exercises and examples on handouts and in the teaching notes as to be developmentally relevant, d) adding graphics to make handouts more accessible, and e), adding the WMP module to target teen/family issues such as polarizing conflict, behavioural extremes, invalidation, and ineffective behaviour change strategies.

We added the teaching of dialectics directly to teens and families in the WMP module as we saw an opportunity to reframe family conflict. Dialectical truth, and thus change, emerges by considering elements of truth on both sides of an argument (the "thesis" and "antithesis"). This process results in a "synthesis," and rather than working to prove the merits of one side, a dialectical stance acknowledges the tension between sides, and through this consideration, new solutions emerge. Replacing "either/or" with a "both/and" perspective reminds clients that ideas that seem at odds with each other can both be true (e.g., "this is really hard, and we've got to keep working at it;" "I want to stay out late with friends, and you're concerned about my safety and want me home early."). Adolescents often become polarized with their family members regarding problems and potential solutions; thus, skills from WMP and family sessions help work toward synthesis.

Linehan (1993a) observed that individuals with pervasive emotion dysregulation tend to alternate between behavioural extremes that either under-regulate or over-regulate emotion, and noted these patterns as dialectical dilemmas for the client; the patterns themselves are targeted in treatment. We observed additional extreme, vacillating behaviour patterns with teens and caregivers and thus identified three teen-family dialectical dilemmas (Rathus & Miller, 2000):

- Excessive leniency versus authoritarian control.
- Normalizing pathological behaviours versus pathologizing normative behaviours.
- Forcing autonomy versus fostering dependence.

Walking the Middle Path addresses these dilemmas; parents, therapists, and adolescents can all vacillate between being quite loose or quite strict, making light of problem behaviours or making much of normative or typical teen behaviour, and pushing for independence too soon or fostering dependence. For each pattern, we developed

Table 25.4   Overview of DBT skills by module

Core mindfulness skills:
"Wise Mind" (States of Mind)
"What Skills" (Observe, Describe, Participate)
"How Skills" (Don't Judge, Stay Focused, Do What Works)

Distress tolerance skills:
Crisis Survival Skills:
Distract with Wise Mind ACCEPTS
    (Activities, Contributing, Comparisons, Emotions, Pushing away, Thoughts, Sensations)
Self-Soothe with six senses
    (vision, hearing, touch, smell, taste, movement)
IMPROVE the moment
    (Imagery, Meaning, Prayer, Relaxing, One thing in the moment, Vacation, Encouragement)
Pros and Cons

TIPP skills (Temperature, Intense exercise, Paced breathing, Progressive relaxation):
Reality Acceptance Skills
Half-Smile
Radical Acceptance
Turning the Mind
Willingness

Module—Walking the Middle Path:
Dialectics
Dialectical Thinking and Acting
Dialectical Dilemmas
Validation
Validation of Others

Self-validation:
Behaviour Change
    Positive reinforcement
    Negative reinforcement
    Shaping
    Extinction
    Punishment

Emotion regulation skills:
Understanding Emotions:
    Observing and Describing Emotions
    What Emotions Do for You
Reducing Emotional Vulnerability:
    ABC PLEASE:
Accumulate positives long and short term
Parent-Teen Shared Pleasant Activities
Adolescent Wise Mind Values and Priorities
Build mastery
Cope Ahead

PLEASE (treat PhysicaL illness, balance Eating, avoid mood–Altering drugs; balance Sleep, get Exercise):
Changing Unwanted Emotions:
    Check the Facts
    Problem Solving

(continued)

Table 25.4 Continued

Opposite action (to the current emotion)
Reduce emotional suffering
The Wave Skill: Mindfulness of current emotion

Interpersonal effectiveness skills:
Goals and priorities

Maintaining relationships and reducing conflict—GIVE:
(be Gentle, act Interested, Validate, use an Easy manner)
Getting what you want or saying no: DEAR MAN
    (Describe, Express, Assert, Reinforce, be Mindful, Appear confident, Negotiate)
    Keeping your self-respect: FAST
    (be Fair, no Apologies, Stick to your values, be Truthful)

Wise Mind self-statements to combat worry thoughts:
Factors to Consider in Asking or Saying No
Optional: Reducing conflict and negative emotion: THINK
    (Think from the other's perspective, Have empathy, other Interpretations, Notice the other, be Kind)

Adapted from Alec L. Miller, Jill H. Rathus, & Marsha M. Linehan, *Dialectical Behavior Therapy with Suicidal Adolescents*, p. 74, Table 4.2 © Guilford Press, 2007, with permission.

Table 25.5 Adolescent Dialectical Dilemmas with Corresponding Secondary Treatment Targets

Dilemma	Targets
Excessive leniency versus authoritarian control.	Increasing authoritative discipline; decreasing excessive leniency. Increasing adolescent self-determination; decreasing authoritarian control.
Normalizing pathological behaviours versus pathologizing normative behaviours.	Increasing recognition of normative behaviours; decreasing pathologizing of normative behaviours. Increasing identification of pathological behaviours; decreasing normalization of pathological behaviours.
Forcing autonomy versus fostering dependence.	Increasing individuation; decreasing excessive dependence. Increasing effective reliance on others; decreasing excessive autonomy.

Adapted from Alec L. Miller, Jill H. Rathus, & Marsha M. Linehan, *Dialectical Behavior Therapy with Suicidal Adolescents*, p. 98, Table 5.2 © Guilford Press, 2007, with permission.

secondary treatment targets: one to decrease the maladaptive behaviour, the other to increase a more adaptive response. Table 25.5 lists the dialectical dilemmas for adolescents and parents, and corresponding secondary treatment targets. These are explicated in WMP in order to allow families to identify patterns and problem solve to reach "middle path" solutions; individual therapists highlight such patterns when observed and address them in family sessions.

Walking the Middle Path teaches: a) dialectics and adolescent-family dialectical dilemmas to reduce extreme thinking/behaviours while enhancing perspective-taking skills, b) validation skills, and c) behaviour change principles—strategies for obtaining changes in one's own or others' behaviours (along with parenting strategies). To determine impact of the WMP module, we evaluated its treatment acceptability in families receiving DBT (Rathus, Campbell, Miller, & Smith, 2015). Adolescents and parents found the module acceptable (overall mean score of 4.23 out of 5 on the Treatment Acceptability Scale), and reported that it was helpful, interesting, and relevant. Additionally, three of the five most highly rated skills in perceived helpfulness for both adolescents and their caregivers across the full DBT skills curriculum were WMP skills, with validation the most highly rated skill across both adolescents and caregivers.

Additional Skills for Adolescents and Family Members

Adolescent DBT skills include the majority of Linehan's original (1993b) skills, those from our WMP module, and several additional skills. These additional skills, included in the adolescent DBT manual (Rathus & Miller, 2015), are either adapted from Linehan's revised skills manual (Linehan, 2015) or developed specifically for teens and families.

Adolescent additions adapted from Linehan's revised manual include: the TIPP skills for rapid decrease in emotional arousal in Distress Tolerance; and Cope Ahead, Check the Facts, Problem Solving, and Wise Mind Values and Priorities, which are all Emotion Regulation skills. To date, with the exception of Cope Ahead, these skills have not been included in adolescent research trials.

Several additions are original to our teen adaptation (Rathus & Miller, 2015). Parent-Teen Shared Pleasant Activities extends the Emotion Regulation skill of Accumulating Positives in the short term to address the deficit in positive interactions that we have noted within many families seeking DBT. This skill thus aims to add ways to increase positive emotions while improving parent-teen relationships. We also include two supplemental handouts to the Emotion Regulation PLEASE skill for managing eating (Food and your Mood) and sleep (Best Ways to get Rest). In Interpersonal Effectiveness, we added the optional THINK skill. We developed this skill based on Crick and Dodge's (1994) social information processing model after noticing that teens and families often assumed the worst about other's intentions, which increased negative emotions and ineffective interactions, and needed more help with perspective taking. THINK skills have not yet been included in clinical trials.

Telephone Contact with Family Members

Teens are encouraged to call their individual DBT therapists for inter-session telephone coaching of skills before engaging in problem behaviours. We observed that family members could benefit from telephone coaching as well. While adolescents called their individual therapist, parents did not have an individual therapist to call, and phoning their teen's therapist posed problems involving privacy and trust. We thus offer parents the opportunity to call skills group leaders or their parenting therapist (see parent training section later in this chapter) for as-needed phone coaching for skills generalization (as opposed to other purposes, such as repairing the relationship). In cases where one of the skills group leaders is the primary therapist for their child, parents may call the other leader. If the primary therapist is also the sole skills trainer, and there is no separate therapist available for parents, allowing parents to call the adolescent's therapist puts the teen's trust at risk. In these types of situations, the parent and adolescent would need to agree to clear guidelines on what can be discussed in the therapist-parent skills coaching call, and the parent and therapist should routinely disclose to the teen any calls made. Alternatively, coaching for parents may need to be restricted to only skills group or family sessions. Even if the parent's phone coach is someone other than the adolescent's primary therapist, we encourage parents to disclose when a phone contact has been made so the adolescent remains confident that the treatment team is not operating in a deceptive manner.

Managing confidentiality is an important part of the adolescent DBT skills process. Outside of coaching calls, our guidelines for parent calls to the teen's primary therapist include that the parent may share information with the therapist (of which the teen will be informed), but that the therapist will not share confidential information with the parent. Parents are urged to copy their teen into any email that goes to the therapist and notify their teen when leaving a voicemail message so the teen is kept abreast of parent-therapist correspondence. Therapists typically protect teen privacy by keeping any of the teen's ongoing low-level risk behaviours or thoughts confidential; therapists inform teens and parents that to disclose such information would violate trust and impede therapy. However, for any concerning escalation or new behaviour/urge, or any event that portends imminent risk, therapists will inform parents, often with the teen present and participating in the disclosure after therapist coaching and support (see the Suicidal Crises section in this chapter).

Family Therapy and Parent Sessions

In adolescent DBT, family therapy sessions are offered as needed. Reasons to schedule a family session include when a problematic interaction with a family member plays a significant role in an adolescent's target behaviour as revealed in a chain analysis, a crisis erupts within the family, a teen's treatment would be enhanced by orienting parents to a set of skills or treatment targets, contingencies at home reinforce maladaptive behaviour or punish adaptive behaviour, or parents are needed to participate in a crisis plan. Skills often emphasized in family sessions include Interpersonal Effectiveness and WMP skills, particularly increasing validation and identifying dialectical dilemmas that may be contributing to problem behaviours. The use of family behavioural analyses, or collaboratively assessing the chain of antecedent and consequent events surrounding a teen's target behaviour from multiple perspectives, can further understanding of both maladaptive and adaptive familial interactions. Family sessions also provide in vivo opportunities for adolescents and caregivers to apply skills to help with their generalization. Lastly, it may be critical to use such a session to help clarify parents' roles during suicidal crises (e.g., close monitoring, removing pills or sharps), while not inadvertently reinforcing maladaptive behaviours or escalated emotions. Parents may themselves become emotionally dysregulated during crises and it is important to emphasize the importance of validation, adhering to the crisis plan, and perhaps utilizing their own telephone coach to help with tolerating their own distress during these moments. If resources allow, additional parenting sessions are recommended when parents need additional support beyond what can be addressed during more crisis-oriented telephone coaching calls.

Over the years many parents have told us they need more individualized practice with the strategies introduced in WMP—dialectics, validation, and behaviour change strategies. Many report erratic, reactive, and ineffective parenting toward their dysregulated teens, as well as experiences of emotional dysregulation and despair themselves while trying to manage their teens. We thus offer optional, separate parenting sessions with a team therapist other than the adolescent's primary therapist. This therapist works with a teen's parent(s) to implement effective parenting strategies, while including other DBT skills as needed (e.g., mindfulness, distress tolerance). We typically offer parenting sessions as a short-term modality; many receive substantial help in six to 12 parent-focused sessions, and during this time, the parent-training therapist provides parent phone coaching. Research is needed to investigate the incremental value of parenting sessions in adolescent DBT.

Consultation team

An essential component of DBT with adolescents, as in DBT for adults, is the weekly therapist consultation meeting. This functions to improve therapists' motivation to engage in the challenging task of working with multi-problem adolescents and their families, as well as enhance their capabilities to do so. Consultation team aims to reduce therapist burnout by providing "therapy to the therapists" while working to ensure fidelity to the treatment model. The structure of the consultation team when working with adolescents is identical to how it is structured for adult DBT teams; however, therapist consultation topics may differ due to the unique challenges that therapists can face when working with adolescents and their families, such as erring on one side of the dialectic with a teen-parent struggle, addressing caregiver therapy-interfering behaviour, knowing when to step in and consult on behalf of the teen, and being mindful of confidentiality parameters.

Managing Suicidal Behaviours with Adolescents

Clinicians working with emotionally dysregulated, multi-problem patients assess and treat suicidal behaviours. Even patients initially presenting without suicidal behaviour may become suicidal as circumstances change. Thus, it remains critical to assess for suicidal risk factors at intake, recognize signs and risk factors during treatment, assess and treat when suicidal behaviour emerges, and handle a suicidal crisis competently. We recommend as starting points reading Linehan's original text (1993a), which includes suicidal behaviour protocols, becoming familiar with comprehensive structured assessments, such as the Linehan Suicide Risk Assessment and Management Protocol (LRAMP, Linehan, Comtois, & Ward-Ciesielski, 2012), and considering intensive training in DBT.

When working with adolescents, suicide crisis management takes on an extra complication—managing confidentiality and involving family members in a crisis plan. Clinicians working with teens often struggle with maintaining much information as private to maintain trust of the teen, while determining when a behaviour, urge, or thought becomes important and risky enough to break confidentiality. Clear situations requiring sharing information with a caregiver would include an imminent suicide plan or suicidal intent, while less clear ones include behaviours such as escalating substance use and risky sexual behaviours in a minor, or even escalating self-injury with no suicide plan. We recommend consultation with one's team, and considerations of risk, ethics, and liability. When a decision is made that it is in the patient's best interest to inform the parents, we recommend consultation to the patient, a collaborative approach, and coping ahead with the adolescent. Once informed, parents can play a crucial role in crisis plans, including removing dangerous objects such as pills and sharps, and monitoring the teen closely.

A Case Example of Adolescent DBT

A was a 16-year-old white female diagnosed with major depression, substance abuse, and BPD who presented with suicidal threats, suicidal ideation, self-injury with cutting on her arms, and intermittent school refusal since eighth grade. Her parents were divorced and her father had been out of touch for years. Her mother complained of A's rages (screaming, hitting, throwing phone and other objects), impulsive behaviours (e.g., sneaking out at night and taking the car without a licence), constant care-taking of friends who make risky decisions, erratic school performance with skipping class or coming late. A's mother reported no longer being able to control her, because of A's lying, such as by visiting her drug dealer when saying she's seeing a female friend; staying out past curfew, while not answering her mother's calls/texts; and an overall minimization of her problem behaviours. After several past treatment failures—"talk therapy" that did not help, her mother brought her to DBT following an arrest for shoplifting.

A reported marijuana and alcohol use three to five times per week, to decrease her emotions, and risky sexual behaviour including unprotected sex and sexting, to keep her boyfriend interested and reduce feelings of emptiness. She described a sense of feeling "different," intensely emotional and sensitive, with sleep problems, sad mood and daily bouts of crying. She described her boyfriend as controlling and verbally abusive, and stated she wanted to leave but would get panicky when apart from him and felt terrified of change. She admitted to lying to her mother to avoid "unfair and over-the-top punishments." She reported feeling depressed and worthless. She wanted to attend college but could not imagine living away or managing college-level work.

In DBT, A would forget her diary card and at times withhold the extent of impulsive behaviours from her therapist for "fear of being sent to residential treatment."

Regarding transactional development of her problems, her mother had trouble understanding her intense emotions and extreme jealous rage reactions when siblings were born; her mother would punish, send her to her room, yell, and tell her she had no reason to be upset, leading to A's feeling further excluded and alone. She would thus cry, scream, or break things, and her mother, seeing how upset she was, would at times comfort her or spend special one-on-one time with her.

A's mother generally responded to A's behaviours by either shutting down and "just letting her go" because of feeling overwhelmed, or over-punishing A, taking away privileges, grounding her, and taking her phone. Her mother reported "overindulging her" at times, trying to soothe her and make her happy when highly distressed.

A was able to generate reasons for living and long-term goals, including living for her mother, younger siblings, her dogs, and her friends, and goals of finishing high school, completing college, having a career working with animals or children. Her immediate treatment goals were to feel better, make better decisions, improve relationships, reduce drinking and drug use, and be less sensitive and depressed.

A's problems could be organized into the following primary treatment targets:

Decrease life-threatening behaviours:

Decrease suicidal ideation/communication, and non-suicidal self-injury

Decrease therapy-interfering behaviours:

Increase completion of diary card
Increase self-disclosure of target behaviours

Decrease severe QoL-interfering behaviours:

Increase school attendance and improve academic performance
Increase self-respect with regard to her boyfriend
Decrease intense anger and explosive behaviour
Decrease depression and hopelessness
Decrease marijuana and alcohol use
Decrease impulsive sexual behaviours

Decrease anxiety

Improve sleep hygiene

Increase behavioural skills:

Increase skills in Mindfulness, Emotion Regulation, Distress Tolerance, Interpersonal Effectiveness, Walking the Middle Path.

Chain analyses of A's suicidal ideation and communication revealed they were respondent to her boyfriend's verbally abusive comments, which left her feeling worthless, hopeless about ever feeling happy, and thus wanting to die; her ideation was negatively reinforced by relief of having a plan to "escape it all." Her suicidal communication was negatively reinforced by the boyfriend's cessation of hurtful comments and positively reinforced by his comforting her, and thus also negatively reinforced by reducing the intensity of her emotional pain.

Solution analyses included: wise mind planning to leave her boyfriend since she recognized this as a harmful and destructive relationship and that this escape plan had fewer negative side effects than suicide (cognitive modification), and also replacing suicidal communication with FAST skills for self-respect, letting her boyfriend know she would no longer tolerate such denigrating comments (skills training). These solutions gave her a sense of control and hope.

Chain analysis of a self-cutting incident (3 horizontal cuts with a razor on her upper left arm) revealed key antecedents were mother's punishment for lying about where she was by grounding her and taking away her phone for the weekend, leading to frantically fearing her boyfriend's reaction, feeling disconnected from friends and world, and leading to rage, despair, and feeling alone; cutting was negatively reinforced by reducing pain.

Solutions included A asking her mother to secure razors in a locked cabinet; practicing mindfulness to her current emotions to observe and describe their fluctuations without rapidly escaping from them (exposure); and distress tolerance skills such as TIPP skills (intense exercise), Distracting with Activities (drawing and watching movies) and creating other Emotions with music and funny TV shows. The therapist also scheduled a family session to address A's behaviours and communication with her mother, and her mother's tendency to use excessive consequences while often not positively reinforcing A's effective behaviours including attending school on time, coming home on time, and doing schoolwork (contingency management).

A central dialectical dilemma addressed in family sessions was "authoritarian control versus excessive leniency." The secondary treatment target was to increase authoritative parenting and apply clear, consistent rules while monitoring friends and whereabouts, while also applying more measured consequences, and allowing A to earn more freedom with effective behaviours. A's mother sought additional parenting sessions with the multi-family skills group leader to learn how she could be more proactive and less crisis-oriented and reactive.

Outcomes after six months of DBT included a cessation of cutting and suicidal communication, decreased suicidal ideation ratings on diary card from 4s and 5s to 1s and 2s, consistent completion of diary card and honest communication with therapist, breaking up with abusive boyfriend and working on self-respect skills and honest communication in her relationships, reduced marijuana and alcohol use, and significantly reduced impulsive behaviours. Depression and anxiety decreased; school attendance and grades increased. She attained an after-school job in a pet grooming business which better structured her time and increased her sense of mastery and working toward valued goals. She still struggled with emotional sensitivity and promiscuity and wanted to continue to work on these. After several parenting and family sessions, her mother had begun to shape positive behaviours, help extinguish anger explosions, and apply more moderate wise-minded consequences that "fit the crime," such as making curfew one hour earlier the night after A returned home one hour late. A and her mother were communicating better, A felt supported, and they were able to shop and take walks together, beginning to find ways to enjoy each other's company. A agreed to join the adolescent graduate group to maintain her gains by strengthening and generalizing her new DBT skills and by obtaining peer validation and reinforcement.

OUTCOME RESEARCH ON DBT-A PROGRAMMES

To date, two reviews and one meta-analysis exist that examine the outcomes of DBT for adolescents in various treatment settings (Cook & Gorraiz, 2016; Groves, Backer, van den Bosch, & Miller, 2011; MacPherson, Cheavens, & Fristad, 2013). The most recent review (MacPherson et al., 2013) lists 18 open and quasi-experimental trials of DBT with adolescents, and since this review was published several other non-randomized trials were published (e.g., Chu, Rizvi, Zendegui, & Bonavitacola, 2014; Fisher & Peterson, 2015). Also completed are several randomized controlled trials (RCTs) of DBT with adolescents.

Quasi-experimental studies on DBT with adolescents indicated that the treatment was promising in reducing numerous target behaviours found among suicidal multi-problem youth (Fleischhaker et al., 2011; Katz, Gunasekara, Cox, & Miller, 2004; Rathus & Miller, 2002). These studies demonstrated feasibility and promising outcomes. Numerous open trials of DBT indicate promising applications for adolescents with: 1) Multiple-diagnoses with suicidal and NSSI behaviours (Courtney & Flament, 2015; Fleischhaker et al., 2006; James, Taylor, Winmill, & Alfoadari, 2008; Sunseri, 2004; Woodberry & Popenoe, 2008); 2) BPD (Goldstein, Axelson, Birmaher, & Brent, 2007); 3) externalizing disorders in forensic settings (Trupin, Steward, Beach, & Boesky, 2002), and outpatient settings (Marco, Garcia-Palacios, & Botella, 2013; Nelson-Gray et al., 2006); 4) eating disorders, including bulimia, binge eating, and anorexia nervosa (Fisher & Peterson, 2015; Safer, Lock, & Couturier, 2007; Salbach-Andrae et al., 2009; Salbach-Andrae, Bohnekamp, Pfeiffer, Lehmkuhl, & Miller, 2008); and 5) school refusal (Chu et al., 2014).

Other open trials highlight application of DBT to settings beyond traditional outpatient, short-term inpatient, and forensic settings. These include applying DBT to adolescents in residential treatment (Sunseri, 2004), long-term inpatient care (McDonell et al., 2010), school settings (Mason, Catucci, Lusk, & Johnson, 2009; Perepletchikova et al., 2011; Sally, Jackson, Carney, Kevelson, & Miller, 2002), and in a children's hospital who are non-compliant with treatment for chronic medical conditions (Hashim, Vadnais, & Miller, 2013).

Mehlum and colleagues conducted a large RCT in Oslo, Norway, comparing 16 weeks of outpatient DBT (with our adolescent materials translated to Norwegian) to Enhanced Usual Care (EUC) for suicidal and self-harming adolescents (Mehlum et al., 2014). EUC consisted of any non-DBT therapy coupled with suicide risk assessment protocol training. DBT consisted of weekly individual therapy and multi-family skills training group, telephone coaching for adolescents, as-needed family sessions, and weekly therapist consultation team meetings.

The sample consisted of 77 adolescents with recent and repetitive self-harm and at least three borderline features. Treatment retention was generally good in both treatment conditions and use of emergency services was low. DBT was superior to EUC in reducing self-harm, suicidal ideation, depression, and BPD symptoms. Effect sizes were large for treatment outcomes in patients who received DBT, whereas effect sizes were small for outcomes in patients receiving EUC. One-year follow up data (Mehlum et al., 2016) demonstrated a continued significant between-groups difference of self-harm episodes, with DBT faring better than EUC. Both groups continued to show reductions in depression, hopelessness, and borderline symptoms, with no significant differences at one-year follow up. There was a trend approaching significance that those in the DBT group utilized outpatient therapy less than their EUC counterparts over the follow-up year, and long-term follow up research is underway.

Goldstein and colleagues (Goldstein et al., 2015) conducted a small RCT comparing DBT (n=14) to TAU (n=6) for suicidal adolescents diagnosed with bipolar disorder. Goldstein and colleagues used our adolescent skills manual and added psycho-education regarding bipolar disorder. DBT was delivered alternating one individual therapy session and one family skills training session; each was received every other week for 12 months. Subjects receiving DBT had significantly greater reductions in depression and trends toward significantly greater reductions in suicidal ideation and emotion dysregulation. The DBT group was more severe at baseline and the study was not adequately powered to expect significance. Therefore, the trends toward significance were noteworthy.

McCauley and colleagues (2016, October) have completed a large multi-site RCT (Collaborative Adolescent Research on Emotions and Suicide; CARES) comparing comprehensive DBT to Supportive Therapy for recent and repeated suicidal behaviour in adolescents with at least three BPD features. The DBT intervention spanned six months and employed a multi-family group format with telephone coaching for teens and parents. Preliminary results indicate a sharp decline in suicide attempts over the course of treatment and a significantly lower rate of suicide attempts at the end of the six-month treatment in the DBT condition compared to the control group. Investigators also found significantly reduced self-harm and suicidal ideation among adolescents receiving DBT compared to the control condition.

Other nascent adaptions of DBT-A have taken into account cultural differences of various racial and ethnic groups to enhance the treatment. These include suicidal Latinas (German et al., 2015) and substance using Native Americans/Alaska Natives (Beckstead, Lambert, DuBose, & Linehan, 2015).

Results reported from a range of studies indicate that adolescent DBT appears to reduce suicidal behaviour, NSSI, depression, and BPD features, as well as have strong treatment feasibility, acceptability, and treatment retention rates (Cook & Gorraiz, 2016; Cooney et al., 2012; Goldstein et al., 2007; Goldstein et al., 2015; Groves et al., 2011; McCauley et al., 2016; Mehlum et al., 2014; Rathus & Miller, 2002). Our adaptation of DBT for adolescents was designed as a comprehensive treatment package. Since then, however, clinicians and researchers have applied DBT to a broader range of adolescents, many of whom have never been suicidal (cf., Groves et al., 2011). Mental health practitioners can, therefore, apply DBT with adolescents across diagnoses and behavioural problems who struggle to control their emotions and behaviours. As adolescents fall along a continuum from typical, relatively asymptomatic, to severely emotionally and behaviourally dysregulated teens who may require a restrictive setting (i.e, inpatient or residential treatment), we believe DBT elements, ranging from skills training only to the comprehensive treatment, can be beneficial to all these populations, applied within a primary, secondary, and tertiary prevention framework.

FUTURE DIRECTIONS: CHILDREN, SCHOOLS, AND PREVENTION

DBT has recently been adapted for pre-adolescent children with emotion dysregulation, often diagnosed with disruptive mood dysregulation disorder (Perepletchikova et al., 2011; Perepletchikova et al., 2017; Perepletchikova et al., this volume). Perepletchikova and colleagues further modified handouts, simplified behavioural chain analyses, and added a large parent training component.

DBT has also been recently disseminated into elementary, middle, and high school settings as primary, secondary, and tertiary prevention programmes (Mason et al., 2009; Mazza, Dexter-Mazza, Miller, Rathus, & Murphy, 2016; Sally et al., 2002).

Implementation of DBT in the schools as secondary and tertiary prevention has shown very preliminary evidence of reducing a number of adverse outcomes, including the number of disciplinary referrals at school (Catucci, 2011), anxiety, social stress, anger, and depression, as well as increasing school attendance and GPA (e.g., Hanson, 2012). The application of DBT skills only as a universal, primary prevention programme to enhance social-emotional learning in school settings (Skills Training for Emotional Problem Solving for Adolescents [STEPS-A; Mazza et al., 2016]; Mazza & Dexter-Mazza, this volume) has also begun and will need evaluation. In lesson-plan form and classroom-length segments, the STEPS-A curriculum guides teachers on how to in-struct middle- and high-school students on the DBT-A skills in a general education classroom setting.

In the vein of intervening earlier and more broadly, an important direction concerns the early detection and prevention of BPD. The Global Alliance for Prevention and Early Intervention (GAP) for BPD (Chanen, Sharp, Hoffman, & The Global Alliance for Prevention and Early Intervention for Borderline Personality Disorder, 2017), has developed a set of evidence-based clinical, research, and social policy strategies and recommendations. These include early identification and diagnosis, training mental health providers in evidence-based interventions for BPD in youth, targeting preven-tion efforts within indicated/subthreshold BPD cases, reducing BPD stigma in the healthcare system, and creating skills and education programmes for families with a child with BPD.

Conclusion

We are excited that data support the adaptation of DBT-A for self-harming adolescents with BPD features and that emerging data support its use with other populations and settings. We hope this description of our adaptation of DBT for teens and families will help clinicians and researchers as they work toward improving the lives of adolescents who suffer and struggle with emotional and behavioural dysregulation. We further hope that with ongoing efforts to make DBT and its set of skills accessible to youth earlier in their lives, ideally before they exhibit multiple diagnoses, self-injury, and other harmful behaviours, we can prevent chronic struggles with emotion dysregulation and its ac-companying suffering for large numbers of adolescents.

Acknowledgement

Parts of this chapter are adapted, with permission, from Alec L. Miller, Jill H. Rathus, and Marsha M. Linehan, *Dialectical Behavior Therapy with Suicidal Adolescents*, Guilford Press, New York: NY, USA © Guilford Press, 2007, and Jill H. Rathus and Alec L. Miller, *DBT® Skills Manual for Adolescents*, Guilford Press, New York: NY, USA © Guilford Press, 2015.

KEY MESSAGES FOR CLINICIANS

- Dialectical Behaviour Therapy has been adapted and has been shown to be effective for multi-problem, complex adolescents with and without risk for suicide and/or non-suicidal self-injury.

- DBT-A includes all of the same modes of standard, adult DBT—individual therapy, group skills training (offered in the teen adaptation in a multi-family skills training group format), telephone consultation, and therapist consultation team.

- Parental support and involvement is a critical component of DBT-A, which is facilitated through additional modes of family sessions, parenting sessions, and parent phone coaching.

- There are particular challenges to working with multi-problem youth and their families, such as managing confidentiality, suicidal risk, rapport, and establishing/maintaining commitment to the treatment.

- Research, including the completion of two randomized controlled trials, now supports the adaptation of DBT for adolescents. Future directions include applying DBT with younger children and in school settings.

REFERENCES

Beckstead, D. J., Lambert, M. J., DuBose, A. P., & Linehan, M. M. (2015). Dialectical behavior therapy with American Indian/Alaska Native adolescents diagnosed with substance use disorders: Combining an evidence based treatment with cultural, traditional, and spiritual beliefs. *Addictive Behaviors*, *51*, 81–87.

Catucci, D. (2011). Dialectical behavior therapy with multi-problem adolescents in school setting. *New York School Psychologist Newsletter*, pp. 12–14. Retrieved from http://nysap.org/newsletters/news2011fall.pdf

Chanen, A., Sharp, C., Hoffman, P., & the Global Alliance for Prevention and Early Intervention for Borderline Personality Disorder (2017). Prevention and early intervention for borderline personality disorder: A novel public health priority. *World Psychiatry*, *16*(2), 215–216.

Chu, B. C., Rizvi, S. L., Zendegui, E. A., & Bonavitacola, L. (2014). Dialectical behavior therapy for school refusal: Treatment development and incorporation of web-based coaching. *Cognitive and Behavioral Practice*, *22*, 317–330.

Cook, N. E., & Gorraiz, M. (2016). Dialectical behavior therapy for nonsuicidal self-injury and depression among adolescents: Preliminary meta-analytic evidence. *Child and Adolescent Mental Health*, *21*(2), 81–89.

Cooney, E., Davis, K., Thompson, P., Wharewera-Mika, J., Stewart, J., & Miller, A. L. (2012). Feasibility of comparing dialectical behavior therapy with treatment as usual for suicidal & self-injuring adolescents: Follow-up data from a small randomized controlled trial. In A. L. Miller (Chair), *Is DBT effective with multi-problem adolescents? Show me the data! An international presentation of three randomized trials evaluating DBT with adolescents*. Symposium presented at the annual meeting of the Association of Behavioral and Cognitive Therapies. 15–18 November 2012, National Harbor, MD.

Courtney, D. B., & Flament, M. F. (2015). Adapted dialectical behavior therapy for adolescents with self-injurious thoughts and behaviors. *The Journal of Nervous and Mental Disease*, 203(7), 537–544.

Crick, N. R., & Dodge, K. A. (1994). A review and reformulation of social information-processing mechanisms in children's social adjustment. *Psychological Bulletin*, 115, 74–101.

Ensink, K., Biberdzic, M., Normandin, L., & Clarkin, J. (2015). A developmental psychopathology and neurobiological model of borderline personality disorder in adolescence. *Journal of Infant, Child, and Adolescent Psychotherapy*, 14(1), 46–69.

Fisher, S., & Peterson, C. (2015). Dialectical behavior therapy for adolescent binge eating, purging, suicidal behavior, and non-suicidal self-injury: A pilot study. *Psychotherapy*, 52(1), 78–92.

Fleischhaker, C., Böhme, R., Sixt, B., Brück, C., Schneider, C., & Schulz, E. (2011). Dialectical behavioral therapy for adolescents (DBT-A): A clinical trial for patients with suicidal and self-injurious behavior and borderline symptoms with a one-year follow-up. *Child and Adolescent Psychiatry and Mental Health*, 5, 3: doi: 10.1186/1753-2000-5-3

Fleischhaker, C., Munz, M., Böhme, R., Sixt, B., & Schulz, E. (2006). Dialectical Behaviour Therapy for adolescents (DBT-A)—a pilot study on the therapy of suicidal, parasuicidal, and self-injurious behaviour in female patients with a borderline disorder. *Zeitschrift für Kinder- und Jugendpsychiatrie und Psychotherapie*, 34(1), 15–25.

German, M., Smith, H. L., Rivera-Morales, C., Gonzalez, G., Haliczer, L. A., Haaz, C., & Miller, A. L. (2015). Dialectical behavior therapy for suicidal latina adolescents: Supplemental dialectical corollaries and treatment targets. *American Journal of Psychotherapy*, 69(2), 179–197.

Goldstein, T. R., Axelson, D. A., Birmaher, B., & Brent, D. A. (2007). Dialectical behavior therapy for adolescents with bipolar disorder: A 1-year open trial. *Journal of the American Academy of Child and Adolescent Psychiatry*, 46, 820–830.

Goldstein, T. R., Fersch-Podrat, R. K., Rivera, M., Axelson, D. A., Merranko, J., Yu, H., Brent, D. A., & Birmaher, B. (2015). Dialectical behavior therapy for adolescents with bipolar disorder: Results from a pilot randomized trial. *Journal of Child and Adolescent Psychopharmacology*, 25(2), 140–149.

Goodman, M., Carpenter, D., Tang, C. Y., Goldstein, K. E., Avedon, J., Fernandez, N., . . . Hazlett, E. A. (2014). Dialectical behavior therapy alters emotion regulation and amygdala activity in patients with borderline personality disorder. *Journal of Psychiatric Research*, 57, 108–116.

Goodman, M., Hazlett, E. A., Avedon, J. B., Siever, D. R., Chu, K. W., & New, A. S. (2011). Anterior cingulate volume reduction in adolescents with borderline personality disorder and co-morbid major depression. *Journal of Psychiatric Research*, 45(6), 803–807.

Groves, S. S., Backer, H. S., van den Bosch, L. M. C., & Miller, A. L. (2011). Dialectical behavior therapy with adolescents: A review. *Child and Adolescent Mental Health*, 17, 65–75.

Hanson, J. B. (2012). *Dialectical behavior therapy in the public schools*. Retrieved from PowerPoint presentation (PPT, 9.8MB).

Hashim, R., Vadnais, M., & Miller, A. L. (2013). Improving adherence in adolescent chronic kidney disease: A DBT feasibility trial. *Clinical Practice in Pediatric Psychology*, 1(4), 369–379.

Hazlett, E. A., Zhang, J., New, A. S., Zelmanova, Y., Goldstein, K. E., Haznedar, M. M., . . . Chu, K. W. (2012). Potentiated amygdala response to repeated emotional pictures in borderline personality disorder. *Biological Psychiatry*, 72(6), 448–456.

James, A., Taylor, A, Winmill, L., & Alfoadari, K. (2008). A preliminary community study of dialectic behavioural therapy (DBT) with adolescent females demonstrating persistent, deliberate self-harm (DSH). *Child and Adolescent Mental Health*, 13, 148–152.

Katz, L. Y., Gunasekara, S., Cox, B. J., & Miller, A. L. (2004). Feasibility of dialectical behavior therapy for parasuicidal adolescent inpatients. *Journal of the American Academy of Child and Adolescent Psychiatry, 43*, 276–282.

Koenigsberg, H. W., Denny, B. T., Fan, J., Liu, X., Guerreri, S., Mayson, S. J., . . . Siever, L. J. (2014). The neural correlates of anomalous habituation to negative emotional pictures in borderline and avoidant personality disorder patients. *The American Journal of Psychiatry, 171*(1), 82–90.

Krause-Utz, A., Elzinga, B. M., Oei, N. Y., Paret, C., Niedtfeld, I., Spinhoven, P., . . . Schmahl, C. (2014). Amygdala and dorsal anterior cingulate connectivity during an emotional working memory task in borderline personality disorder patients with interpersonal trauma history. *Frontiers in Human Neuroscience, 8*, 848.

Linehan, M. M. (1993a). *Cognitive-behavioral treatment of borderline personality disorder.* New York, NY: Guilford Press.

Linehan, M. M. (1993b). *Skills training manual for treating borderline personality disorder.* New York, NY: Guilford Press.

Linehan, M. M. (2015). *DBT skills training manual*, 2nd Edition. New York, NY: Guilford Press.

Linehan, M. M., Comtois, K. A., & Ward-Ciesielski, E. F. (2012). Assessing and managing risk with suicidal individuals. *Cognitive and Behavioral Practice, 19*(2), 218–232.

MacPherson, H. A., Cheavens, J. S., & Fristad, M. A. (2013). Dialectical behavior therapy for adolescents: Theory, treatment adaptations, and empirical outcomes. *Clinical Child and Family Psychology Review, 16*(1), 59–80.

Marco, J. H., Garcia-Palacios, A., & Botella, C. (2013). Dialectical behavioural therapy for oppositional defiant disorder in adolescents: A case series. *Psicothema, 25*(2), 158–163.

Mason, P., Catucci, D., Lusk, V., & Johnson, M. (2009). *An initial program evaluation of modified dialectical behavioral therapy skills training in a school setting.* Poster presentation at the International Society for the Improvement and Teaching of Dialectical Behavior Therapy conference. New York, NY.

Mazza, J. J., Dexter-Mazza, E. T., Miller, A. L., Rathus, J. H., & Murphy, H. E. (2016). *DBT skills in schools: The skills training for emotional problem solving for adolescents (DBT STEPS-A) curriculum.* New York, NY: Guilford Press.

McCauley, E., Berk, M. S., Asarnow, J. R., Korslund, K., Adrian, M., Avina, C., . . . Linehan, M. M. (2016). Collaborative adolescent research on emotions and suicide (CARES): A randomized controlled trial of DBT with highly suicidal adolescents. In M. S. Berk and M. Adrian (Chairs), *New outcome data on treatments for suicidal adolescents.* Symposium conducted at the meeting of the 50th Annual Convention of the Association for Behavioral and Cognitive Therapies (ABCT). 27–30, October 2016, New York, NY.

McDonell, M. G., Tarantino, J., Dubose, A. P., Matestic, P., Steinmetz, K., Galbereath, H., & McClellan, J. M. (2010). A pilot evaluation of dialectical behavioural therapy in adolescent long-term inpatient care. *Child and Adolescent Mental Health, 15*, 193–196.

Mehlum, L., Ramberg, M., Tormoen, A., Haga, E., Diep, L. M., Stanley, B. H., . . . Groholt, B. (2016). Dialectical behavior therapy compared with enhanced usual care for adolescents with repeated suicidal and self-harming behavior: Outcomes over a one-year follow-up. *Journal of the American Academy of Child and Adolescent Psychiatry, 55*(4), 295–300.

Mehlum, L., Tormoen, A., Ramberg, M., Haga, E., Diep, L. M., Laberg, S., . . . Groholt, B. (2014). Dialectical behavior therapy for adolescents with recent and repeated self-harming behavior—first randomized controlled trial. *Journal of the American Academy of Child and Adolescent Psychiatry, 53*, 1082–1091.

Miller, A. L., Rathus, J. H., & Linehan, M. M. (2007). *Dialectical behavior therapy with suicidal adolescents.* New York, NY: Guilford Press.

Miller, A. L., Rathus, J. H., Linehan, M. M., Wetzler, S., & Leigh, E. (1997). Dialectical behavior therapy adapted for suicidal adolescents. *Journal of Practical Psychiatry and Behavioral Health, 3*, 78–86.

Nelson-Gray, R. O., Keane, S. P., Hurst, R. M., Mitchell, J. T., Warburton, J. B, Chok, J. T., & Cobb, A. R. (2006). A modified DBT skills training program for oppositional defiant adolescents: Promising preliminary findings. *Behaviour Research and Therapy, 44*, 1811–1820.

Perepletchikova, F., Axelrod, S. R., Kaufman, J., Rounsaville, B. J., Douglas-Palumberi, H., & Miller, A. L. (2011). Adapting dialectical behaviour therapy for children: Towards a new research agenda for paediatric suicidal and non-suicidal self-injurious behaviours. *Child and Adolescent Mental Health, 16*(2), 116–121.

Perepletchikova, F., Nathanson, D., Axelrod, S. R., Merrill, C., Walker, A., Grossman, M., ... Walkup, J. (2017). Randomized clinical trial of dialectical behavior therapy for preadolescent children with disruptive mood dysregulation disorder: Feasibility and outcomes. *Journal of the American Academy of Child and Adolescent Psychiatry, 56*(10), 832–840.

Pineda, J., & Dadds, M. R. (2013). Family treatment and suicidal youth. *Journal of the American Academy of Child and Adolescent Psychiatry, 52*(8), 851–862.

Rathus, J. H., & Miller, A. L. (2000). DBT for adolescents: Dialectical dilemmas and secondary treatment targets. *Cognitive and Behavioral Practice, 7*, 425–434.

Rathus, J. H., & Miller, A. L. (2002). Dialectical behavior therapy adapted for suicidal adolescents. *Suicide and Life-Threatening Behaviors, 32*(2), 146–157.

Rathus, J. H., & Miller, A. L. (2015). *DBT skills manual for adolescents.* New York, NY: Guilford Press.

Rathus, J., Campbell, B., Miller, A., & Smith, H. (2015). Treatment acceptability study of walking the middle path, a new DBT skills module for adolescents and their families. *American Journal of Psychotherapy, 69*(2), 163–178.

Safer, D. L., Lock, J., & Couturier, J. L. (2007). Dialectical behavior therapy modified for adolescent binge eating disorder: A case report. *Cognitive and Behavioral Practice, 14*, 157–167.

Sally, M., Jackson, L., Carney, J., Kevelson, J., & Miller, A. L. (2002). *Implementing DBT skills training groups in an underperforming high school.* Poster presented at the International Society for the Improvement and Teaching of Dialectical Behavior Therapy Conference. Reno, NV.

Salbach-Andrae, H., Bohnekamp, I., Bierbaum, T., Schneider, N., Thurn, C., Stiglmayr, ... Lehmkuhl, U. (2009). Dialectical behavioral therapy (DBT) and cognitive behavioral therapy (CBT) for adolescents with anorexia and bulimia nervosa in comparison. *Childhood and Development, 3*, 180–190.

Salbach-Andrae, H., Bohnekamp, I., Pfeiffer, E., Lehmkuhl, U., & Miller, A. L. (2008). Dialectical behavior therapy of anorexia and bulimia nervosa among adolescents: A case series. *Cognitive and Behavioral Practice, 15*, 415–425.

Sunseri, P. A. (2004). Preliminary outcomes on the use of dialectical behavior therapy to reduce hospitalization among adolescents in residential care. *Residential Treatment for Children & Youth, 21*, 59–76.

Trupin, E. W., Stewart, D. G., Beach, B., & Boesky, L. (2002). Effectiveness of a dialectical behavior therapy program for incarcerated female juvenile offenders. *Child and Adolescent Mental Health, 7*, 121–127.

Whittle, S., Chanen, A. M., Fornito, A., McGorry, P. D., Pantelis, C., & Yücel, M. (2009). Anterior cingulate volume in adolescents with first-presentation borderline personality disorder. *Psychiatry Research, 172*(2), 155–160.

Woodberry, K. A., & Popenoe, E. A. (2008). Implementing dialectical behavior therapy with adolescents and their families in a community outpatient clinic. *Cognitive and Behavioral Practice, 15*(3), 277–286.

CHAPTER 26

....

DBT FOR EATING DISORDERS

An Overview

....

KELLY A. C. BHATNAGAR,
CAITLIN MARTIN-WAGAR,
AND LUCENE WISNIEWSKI

AN OVERVIEW OF EATING DISORDERS

EATING disorders (ED) such as anorexia nervosa (AN), bulimia nervosa (BN), and binge-eating disorder (BED) are serious conditions characterized by a persistent disturbance of eating behaviours that results in the altered consumption or absorption of food (American Psychiatric Association [APA], 2013). Maladaptive eating disorder behaviours may include extreme attempts to limit food intake and/or other weight management behaviours such as self-induced vomiting, excessive/compulsive exercise, and laxative or diuretic abuse. Eating disorder behaviours can be life-threatening and have dire medical consequences. For example, excessive dietary restriction causes cardiac abnormalities, endocrine and metabolic irregularities, renal complications, decreased bone density, abdominal bloating, delayed gastric emptying, and dry and thin skin (Pomeroy, Mitchell, Roerig, & Crow, 2002). Recurrent compensatory behaviours such as self-induced vomiting and laxative abuse can lead to oesophageal tears, sodium and potassium deficiencies, cardiac hypotension, and permanent erosion of dental enamel (Kaplan & Noble, 2007; Pomeroy et al., 2002). The combined medical and psychosocial impairments lead to substantially higher morbidity and mortality rates when compared to the general population and to other psychiatric conditions (Arcelus, Mitchell, Wales, & Nelson, 2011; Fichter & Quadflieg, 2016; Klump, Bulik, Kaye, Treasure, & Tyson, 2009). These statistics make identification of efficacious treatment models for ED vastly important.

TRADITIONAL EATING DISORDER
TREATMENT MODELS

Cognitive-behavioural therapy (CBT) and interpersonal psychotherapy (IPT) have the strongest evidence-base for the treatment of adult BN and BED (Hay, 2013; Wilson, Grilo, & Vitousek, 2007). Therefore, CBT and IPT are recommended as first-line treatments for those illnesses (National Institute for Health and Care Excellence [NICE], 2004). CBT challenges distorted thoughts and maladaptive behaviours that maintain ED symptoms, while IPT addresses interpersonal difficulties that maintain ED symptoms (Kass, Kolko, & Wilfley, 2013). CBT is also the most commonly tested treatment for adult AN, although research has yet to identify an approach that demonstrates its superiority over others for AN (Kass et al., 2013).

For adolescents, results of a comprehensive review highlighted the efficacy of family-based interventions for the treatment of ED (Downs & Blow, 2013). Family-Based Treatment (FBT) or the "Maudsley Model" (Lock, le Grange, Agras, & Dare, 2001; Lock & le Grange, 2012) is considered particularly efficacious in treating adolescents with AN and BN. Studies have reported approximately two-thirds of adolescent patients to be recovered at the end of FBT with 75%–90% maintaining full weight restoration at five-year follow-up (Downs & Blow, 2013; Eisler et al., 1997).

Despite the empirical support for CBT, IPT, and FBT, there continues to be a substantial number of individuals that do not fully recover using these approaches, especially adults with AN (Anderson & Maloney, 2001; Ball & Mitchell, 2004; Carter et al., 2011; Lundgren, Danoff-Burg, & Anderson, 2004; McIntosh et al., 2005). Additionally, a 2010 study by Lock and colleagues found as many as 50% of adolescent patients do not achieve *full* ED remission using FBT alone, and consequently, require alternative or supplementary treatment (Lock et al., 2010). These data, along with clinical experiences, have prompted clinicians and researchers alike to look to other empirically validated treatments for guidance managing patients with EDs (e.g. Fairburn, Cooper, & Shafran, 2003; Wonderlich, Mitchell, Peterson, & Crow, 2001). If research can identify predictors of treatment response, then novel or adapted approaches can be developed in the hope of ameliorating outcome. Although still early in the scientific study process, certain variables have been found to be related to successful or poorer outcomes in standard models of ED treatment. Adults with multidiagnostic, complex clinical pictures (e.g. dual diagnosis of Borderline Personality Disorder (BPD), Substance Abuse (SA)/Dependency, recurrent suicidality or self-harm behaviours, and/or deficits in emotion regulation abilities) may not benefit as greatly from CBT (e.g., Chen, Matthews, Allen, Kuo, & Linehan, 2008; Johnson, Tobin, & Enright, 1989; Wilfley et al., 2000). For youth, there are data to suggest patients with moderate to severe ED symptoms, slow rate of weight gain, comorbid psychiatric disorders, parent history of psychiatric illness, greater emotion dysregulation (e.g. suicidal/self-injurious behaviours, anger management problems), and/or personality disorder features (e.g. emerging BPD traits) may not do as well in FBT and are considered "difficult to treat" using FBT alone (Doyle, le Grange, Leob, Doyle, & Crosby, 2010; Le Grange, Crosby, & Lock, 2008). Families scoring high in expressed criticism and expressed emotion may also decrease the effectiveness of the FBT model (Eisler, Simic, Russell, & Dare, 2007; Treasure et al., 2008).

WHY DIALECTICAL BEHAVIOUR THERAPY FOR THE TREATMENT OF EATING DISORDERS?

The rationale for applying Dialectical Behaviour Therapy (DBT; Linehan, 1993) to the treatment of ED has been described comprehensively in the literature (Bankoff, Karpel, Forbes, & Pantalone, 2012; Ben-Porath, Wisniewski, & Warren, 2009; Lenz, Taylor, Fleming, & Sherman, 2014; McCabe, LaVia, & Marcus, 2004; Ritschel, Lim, & Steward, 2015; Wiser & Telch, 1999; Wisniewski, Bhatnagar, & Warren, 2013; Wisniewski & Kelly, 2003; Wisniewski, Safer, & Chen, 2007). While the etiology of ED is complex and not yet entirely understood, there is evidence that affect and emotion regulation deficits have a role transdiagnostically in the development and maintenance of the illnesses (Harrison, Sullivan, Tchanturia, & Treasure, 2009; Haynos & Fruzzetti, 2011; Svaldi, Griepenstroh, Tuschen-Caffier, & Ehring, 2012). It has been suggested that eating pathology (e.g. dietary restraint and restriction, self-induced vomiting, binge-eating, etc.) may function as a mechanism to cope with emotion sensitivity and vulnerability (Fairburn, 2008; Telch, Agras, & Linehan, 2000). DBT is proposed as a logical, alternative choice to traditional models, therefore, because it is based on an affect regulation model of treating symptoms (Telch et al., 2000).

In addition to its focus on affect regulation, other components of DBT may make it a viable option for ED treatment. The unique blend of behavioural principles, dialectical philosophy, and Zen influence may be useful in helping ED patients who struggle with motivation and commitment to treatment. AN, in particular, differs from other mental illnesses (such as depression and anxiety) in that patients often hold a considerable degree of ambivalence regarding symptom reduction/elimination and recovery as a whole (Williams & Reid, 2010). Treatment of such "ego syntonic" symptoms requires use of motivational strategies that delicately balance the need to change while simultaneously accepting a patient's present state and condition. DBT acknowledges the presence of dialectics and holds a firm stance on the necessity of both change-based and acceptance-based therapeutic strategies to bring about symptom relief (Linehan, 1993). Acceptance-based strategies may be particularly useful in ED treatment because patients are challenged to accept their current progress (including history of relapses), fluctuating weight and shape, and other difficult-to-change aspects of treatment. The focus on acceptance is also helpful for clinicians and family members in that it offers a framework for meeting a patient where he/she is and allows for a more flexible time course for which lasting change can be expected to occur (Wisniewski et al., 2013).

The DBT model may also be useful in addressing premature termination rates that are unfortunately common in ED treatment population. Drop-out rates in traditional treatment models range from 20.2 to 70% (e.g., Swan-Kremeier, Mitchell, Twardowski, Lancaster, & Crosby, 2005; Wallier et al., 2009). DBT has specific strategies to target treatment drop-out that might help ameliorate this problem. A small number of studies have indeed reported fewer drop-outs than typically seen in ED treatment, although this has been primarily observed to date in the BN and BED populations (Hill, Craighead, & Safer, 2011; Safer, Telch, & Agras, 2001b; Safer, Robinson, & Jo, 2010; Telch et al., 2000). While the number of studies examining DBT drop-out with AN is more limited, there are at least two studies to date that have promising preliminary results. One case series found a premature drop-out rate of 13.3% and another study focusing on Radically Open-DBT (RO-DBT) found a drop-out rate of 27.7% (Chen et al., 2015; Lynch et al., 2013). More research is needed to better understand DBT's impact on treatment compliance and completion, particularly for AN.

Other aspects of the DBT model, such as therapist and patient case-management strategies, also make DBT a feasible treatment option. ED patients and their symptoms (particularly those that can be a risk to life) have been noted to evoke strong emotions in their treatment providers (Warren, Schafer, Crowley, & Olivardia, 2012). Similar to symptoms related to BPD, ED symptoms are often conceptualized as conniving, dishonest, and superficial by mental health providers, family, and friends (Golan, Yaroslavski, & Stein, 2009). Such negative attributions can create significant challenges in the client's life and treatment, particularly if these beliefs are held by the therapist. DBT's solution is to emphasize the importance of maintaining a "non-judgmental stance" (Linehan, 1993) by posing that all behaviours, including those that appear dangerous and unhealthy, should be viewed without judgment. Therapists may be challenged to understand how any behaviour might be useful to the patient, and DBT reminds clinicians that the behaviour is likely indicative of a reinforced response that falls within a patient's current skill repertoire. Reframing a behaviour as "effective" or "ineffective" allows a patient to explore alternative behaviours for more adaptive environmental responses throughout the therapeutic process. Therapists treating ED patients can greatly benefit from the "therapy for the therapists" that a DBT consultation team meeting offers in order to receive support in managing strong feelings towards patients and upholding fidelity to DBT principles and interventions, even when treatment appears slow and frustrating for all. The authors believe this support to be fundamental to the successful treatment of chronic ED.

Case-management strategies encourage patients to deal with his/her own problems in the environments in which they occur, with the appropriate help and support of the therapist. Patient case-management strategies such as aiding (but not directly managing oneself) a patient in the management of an often-extensive health provider network (i.e. medical team, psychiatric team, nutrition team, hospitalizations, etc.) may help develop an ED patient's sense of mastery, control, and self-efficacy. This DBT strategy of consultation-to-the-patient promotes a therapeutic partnership that encourages patients to learn new behaviours that result in the achievement of developmental and interpersonal goals; this likely reinforces the collegial nature of the therapeutic alliance. A strong alliance can assist with a client's commitment to the therapist, and ultimately, to treatment in general.

Finally, it is important to consider the high frequency in which ED co-occur with other mental health issues, such as BPD and SA (Holderness, Brooks-Gunn, & Warren, 1994; Linehan et al., 2006). This is particularly important because rates of comorbid BPD and ED range from 3% of AN patients, to 21% of BN patients, making it likely for those that treat ED frequently to encounter these patients (Cassin & von Ranson, 2005). It is difficult to successfully treat eating pathology without addressing the symptoms of other diagnoses that may interfere with treatment or exacerbate ED symptoms. Also, both BPD and ED symptoms can be highly life-threatening, making priority in addressing harmful behaviours complicated. DBT for EDs provides a structure to address the co-occurring maladaptive behaviours (e.g., purging, self-harm, suicide attempts) that individuals with EDs often experience, which may make DBT especially useful for individuals with complex diagnostic presentations (Chen et al., 2008; Federici & Wisniewski, 2013; Harned et al., 2008; Kröger et al., 2010; Palmer et al., 2003).

THE DBT FOR ED TREATMENT MODEL

DBT was first adapted for use with ED patients meeting criteria for a primary diagnosis of BN or BED (Wiser & Telch, 1999). This DBT for ED adaptation consists of providing six months of DBT skills training either in a group format for BED patients (Telch et al., 2000; Wiser & Telch, 1999) or individually for BN (Safer et al., 2001b). As part of this treatment model, all skills except the Interpersonal Effectiveness skills are taught and the adaptation does not include the provision of individual DBT therapy or telephone skills coaching. This adaptation, which has accumulating evidence supporting its effectiveness, has been developed into an easy-to-use and widely available clinician's manual (Safer, Telch, & Chen, 2009) for use with primary, uncomplicated ED patients. However, DBT has a reputation for providing an evidenced-based model for patients considered "difficult to treat". There are likely clinicians who are interested in using DBT with ED patients who have more complex and comorbid presentations. While the literature on this is evolving, the authors have recommended elsewhere that complex and comorbid individuals be treated with comprehensive and standard DBT, as opposed to the adapted version of DBT (Wisniewski et al., 2007). The next section presents eligibility criteria for the use of DBT with ED patients and guidance to clinicians for deciding when to use the full DBT model versus the adapted version.

Eligibility Criteria

When determining course of treatment for individuals with ED, it is important to consider both the level of medical compromise and the state of nutritional insufficiency. Psychological interventions such as DBT may have limited effectiveness if a patient's physical health and cognitive processes are ill-functioning due to extreme starvation or other ED-related symptoms. The APA published guidelines can assist with decision-making surrounding the appropriateness of various treatment settings and levels of care during times of medical compromise (American Psychiatric Association, 2006). It is recommended that these guidelines be consulted prior to initiating DBT (or any other outpatient psychological treatment approach) with ED patients.

Given the success of CBT and FBT respectively for adult and adolescent ED patients, the authors view DBT as a treatment that can be offered if those treatments are not successful. Complex or comorbid patients can be identified as eligible for comprehensive DBT if a course of CBT, IPT, or FBT has not resulted in adequate symptom reduction. Additionally, if the patient describes ED symptoms being used for emotion regulation, engages in self harm, experiences chronic suicidality, or has a history of engaging in behaviours that interfere with treatment, DBT can be a viable treatment option (Federici & Wisniewski, 2013; Federici, Wisniewski, & Ben-Porath, 2013). The authors recommend that therapists consult the literature to guide the determination of whether or not a patient has responded to first-line ED treatment models. Table 26.1 shows specific admissions criteria developed and being tested at the authors' clinic to determine whether or not a patient may be an ideal candidate for DBT for ED.

Table 26.1 Dialectical behaviour therapy for eating disorders eligibility criteria

	Eligibility Criteria
(A)	Meets diagnostic criteria for eating disorders and is medically stable for outpatient treatment.
(B)	Presents with an established and documented history of emotion regulation difficulties, supported by a clinically significant Difficulties in Emotion Regulation Scale (DERS; Gratz & Roemer, 2004).
(C)	Exhibits two or more symptoms that DBT has evidence in managing (e.g. recurrent self-harm, suicidality, impulsivity with the potential for danger, substance abuse/dependence, pattern of affective instability, disturbance in interpersonal relationships).
For Patients Already Participating in Standard Treatment (CBT or FBT)	
(D)	Presents with comorbid diagnoses that are complicating standard ED treatment.
(E)	There is evidence that the patient is not being fully helped by standard CBT or FBT alone, as evidenced by slow treatment response or inability to meet treatment goals.
(F)	There is evidence of Therapy-Interfering Behaviours that make it difficult to follow the manualized CBT or FBT agenda and contribute to ineffectiveness of the standard models.

Orientation and Commitment
to Treatment: Target Hierarchy
Adaptations to Reflect ED Symptoms

Once it has been determined that a particular patient may benefit from standard, comprehensive DBT, the commitment process in DBT for complex, comorbid ED is not unlike the commitment for DBT in general. However, a clinician will need to understand how ED behaviours are evaluated in the hierarchy of treatment targets and adapt the target hierarchy accordingly for each ED patient.

It is typical that during orientation and commitment sessions, patients are advised of the treatment targets and how they will be addressed both in and across sessions (Linehan, 1993). In addition to the Life-Threatening Behaviours (Target I), such as self-harm and suicidal behaviour, that are traditionally addressed in standard DBT, each of these occur with some frequency in the ED client (Paul, Schroeter, Dahme, & Nutzinger, 2002; Stein, Lilenfeld, Wildman, & Marcus, 2004) and therefore, clinicians and patients alike need to understand that ED behaviours can also be lethal. During periods of medical instability, ED behaviours may be considered life-threatening (Wisniewski et al., 2007), as imminent risk of death is increased during these periods (see e.g., Sachs, Harnke, Mehler, & Krantz, 2016). Furthermore, if an individual meets criteria for medical conditions such as bradycardia, arrhythmia, or electrolyte abnormalities, then any ED behaviour would be considered life-threatening. Examples of behaviours that would be considered life-threatening include engaging in self-induced vomiting while hypokalaemic, exercising or restricting while bradycardic, and excessive drinking of water when hyponatraemic.

In addition to the general Therapy-Interfering Behaviours (TIB; Target II) of failure to complete diary cards or being late for a session, patients with ED may engage in TIB that are unique and directly related to their illness. For example, when a patient exhibits non-attentive behaviours such as being unable to focus in session or to remember what was discussed between sessions, the non-attentive behaviour is considered a TIB. The therapist may hypothesize, given the relationship between food deprivation and cognitive functioning (Keys, Brozek, & Henscheo, 1950), that restriction is a significant link on the chain leading to the non-attention. Another TIB related specifically to EDs includes non-collaborative behaviours such as drinking water before being weighed to give the illusion of weight gain (i.e. "water-loading").

ED behaviours that occur outside of periods of medical instability or that do not interfere with treatment, are considered Quality-Of-Life-Interfering-Behaviours (Target III). It may not always be clear where an ED symptom lies on the treatment hierarchy. Some behaviours will straddle the border between two categories and the therapist must carefully consider where such behaviours will be targeted. Consultation with the treatment team as well as a collaborative conversation with the patient is often necessary to determine where more complicated behaviours fall on the treatment hierarchy.

TREATMENT COMPONENTS

Individual Therapy & Diary Cards

The role of the individual therapist (IT) in DBT for ED is no different to their role in standard DBT. The IT must review diary cards, conduct behaviour chain analyses, work to set the session agenda collaboratively, and support the patient staying in treatment and generalizing skills. The authors recommend that the diary card for ED patients receiving DBT should monitor food and beverage consumption, as well as the time of day and location where the food or beverage was consumed. Some typical urges and behaviours to monitor on the diary card include restriction, binge-eating, vomiting, laxative, diuretic or diet pill use, and over-exercise. Having this information on the diary card will aid the patient and therapist in understanding how food- and exercise-related issues might trigger behaviours and how they might make an individual vulnerable to emotions, as in the PLEASE Master skills. PLEASE Master is a DBT technique used to reduce emotional vulnerability. This includes treating *p*hysical i*l*lness, balanced *e*ating, avoid mood *a*ltering drugs, balanced *s*leep, get *e*xercise, and achieve *mastery* (Linehan, 2015). Figure 26.1 provides an example of how the diary card has been adapted for ED treatment.

Although the *role* of the therapist is not different, the knowledge base of the DBT therapist that works with ED patients should ideally be skilled in ED-related issues and treatments. In working with complex and comorbid ED patients and using DBT, the authors have found it to be important to enhance standard DBT with some specific strategies for directly addressing ED behaviours. There is a robust treatment literature employing CBT strategies in the treatment of disordered eating (e.g., Fairburn, 2008). The authors have recommended some additions to the DBT model from CBT model that directly address ED issues (e.g., incorporating ED behaviours in the target hierarchy; weight, food and medical monitoring; food exposures and meal planning). In conclusion, the DBT therapist working with an ED patient needs to have a solid knowledge base of nutrition, exercise physiology, and traditional ED-treatment approaches.

Skills Training

In comprehensive DBT for EDs skills training, all four skills modules are taught without editing or alteration from how they are written in the published manuals (Linehan, 1993, 2015; Rathus & Miller, 2015). There are, however, some special considerations for clinicians working with ED patients. First, due to the medical issues related to ED behaviours, some DBT skills may not be physically safe. For example, given the impact that changes in temperature have on the heart, ED patients, especially those with a history of bradycardia, should not use the TIP skills (i.e., distress tolerance skills that encourage

DIARY CARD

The Emily Program

Name: _____ Date: _____

Mark (*) if you engaged in behaviour.
Rate (0–5) if you had an urge but did not engage in the behaviour.

Food Intake – Include approximate quantity and description of food
Hunger Scale – Graph hunger level from start to end of meal

TIME OF DAY	MEALS (PLAN / ACTUAL)	Food Intake / Hunger Scale	Location	Fluid Intake (cups/ozs.)	Binge	Purge	Restrict	Exercise	Lax/diuretics	Suicidal Ideation	Self-Harm	Alcohol/drug	Body Diss.
	BREAKFAST — Protein, Vegetable, Grain, Lipid N., Fruit, Dairy	empty 2 3 4 neutral 6 7 8 9 stuffed											
	SNACK	empty 2 3 4 neutral 6 7 8 9 stuffed											
	LUNCH — Protein, Vegetable, Grain, Lipid N., Fruit, Dairy	empty 2 3 4 neutral 6 7 8 9 stuffed											
	SNACK	empty 2 3 4 neutral 6 7 8 9 stuffed											
	DINNER — Protein, Vegetable, Grain, Lipid N., Fruit, Dairy	empty 2 3 4 neutral 6 7 8 9 stuffed											
	SNACK	empty 2 3 4 neutral 6 7 8 9 stuffed											
	VITAMINS	yes no											
	PROTOCOLS	Bradycardia Tachycardia Orthostasis N/A											

Emotions Today — Rating (0–5):
- Pain/Misery _____
- Anxiety/Fear _____
- Sadness _____
- Shame _____
- Anger _____
- Joy _____
- Urge to quit tx/recovery _____
- Lying/Withholding _____

Meds I am prescribed: — Took today?
- _____ Y N U
- _____ Y N U
- _____ Y N U
- _____ Y N U

Obstacles to med use:
- ☐ Forgot
- ☐ Not helpful
- ☐ Don't need it anymore
- ☐ Fear of side effects
- ☐ Ran out of rx
- ☐ Other: _____

FIGURE 26.1 Example of a diary card used in adult eating disorder treatment.

clients to engage in temperature change, intense exercise, and progressive relaxation) unless cleared by a medical professional (Linehan, 2015). This may also be true for exercise in the PLEASE skills. Second, given the nature of ED, there are some skills considered over-used or used to the exclusion of others, such as patients who self-soothe with taste or who exclusively use exercise to change body chemistry (TIP skill). A clinician may use a dialectical and non-judgmental framework when discussing these issues with patients. It can be helpful to acknowledge with patients that they may have been using these skills regularly to regulate emotion and that it is the therapist's job to teach them quite a few more skills with which to manage that do not reinforce the ED. Using the strategies of irreverence, a clinician faced with patients who had engaged in binge eating after becoming emotionally dysregulated might state "you already have mastered using taste to self-soothe! We want to help you develop a range of skills to manage emotions".

With respect to mindfulness skills and EDs, the authors are often asked about the use of mindful eating in DBT for eating disorders. In order to effectively answer this question, one of the authors conducted a study evaluating the impact of Mindfulness versus Distraction during a snack with AN and BN patients in a day treatment programme (Marek, Ben-Porath, Federici, & Wisniewski, 2013). The study found that using mindfulness decreased negative affect after meals for normal controls only and that negative affect actually *increased* after the mindfulness intervention compared to the distraction intervention for the ED group. Other research has shown that post-meal use of distracting activities (e.g., playing a computer game) leads to decreases in negative affect and intrusive thoughts and increases in positive affect in hospitalized, underweight ED patients (Griffiths, Hawkes, Gilbert, & Serpell, 2016). Taken together, these data suggest that distraction may be an effective skill to use for restricting and purging patients experiencing a high level of behavioural dyscontrol (e.g., when individuals are meeting criteria for hospitalization or day treatment). However, for individuals with BED, disconnection from internal cues and over-focus on external, hedonic cues can encourage mindless overeating and binge-eating. For BED patients, mindful eating approaches have been found to be helpful in decreasing binge and overeating episodes and for increasing internal awareness (Allen & Craighead, 1999; Kristeller, Wolever, & Sheets, 2014). Further, one study showed that improvements in eating disorder symptomology were related to the degree to which individuals practiced mindfulness (Kristeller et al., 2014). Additional research is needed to determine if mindful eating may be taught to individuals with AN or BN later in recovery, or with patients whose illness is mild to moderate.

Telephone Skills Coaching (TSC)

With ED patients, the TSC protocol for non-suicidal self-injurious (NSSI) and suicidal behaviour shares the same elements (e.g. 24-hour rule) as Linehan's original guidelines. As in standard DBT's telephone coaching, ED patients are instructed to call if they need help managing urges for suicidal or NSSI behaviours. However, there are some modifications recommended when working with an ED population (Wisniewski & Ben-Porath, 2005). First, ED patients are instructed to call for coaching prior to engaging in any eating disorder behaviours (e.g., restricting, binging, purging). This adaptation was adopted due to the high morbidity and mortality associated with ED behaviours. A second and related modification of standard TSC was an adjustment to DBT's 24-hour rule that accounted for eating behaviour. Because eating disordered patients are likely to be exposed to food repeatedly over the course of a day, the *Next Meal/ Snack Rule* was implemented. The *Next Meal/Snack Rule* states that if a patient engages in an ED behaviour, she is not permitted to call her therapist for TSC until the next scheduled meal or snack. However, if the patient has engaged in an ED behaviour and elects to call at the next scheduled meal or snack to receive coaching, the previous ED behaviour(s) is not addressed on the call and must wait until the next scheduled therapy appointment to do so. This adaptation was developed because a 24-hour waiting period for a behaviour that must occur at a minimum of three times per day might have the unintended consequence of preventing an individual from ever being able to call for coaching or get back on track. Additionally, because ED patients can exhibit avoidant ED behaviours, patients often report that calling for "accountability" is helpful. When calling for accountability, the patient schedules a coaching call with her therapist before eating a particular meal (Limbrunner, Ben-Porath, & Wisniewski, 2011).

Consultation Team

There are no specific adaptations for the DBT consultation team when working with ED patients. It will be important that all members of the team have expertise in the treatment of EDs. If members of a team do not have ED expertise, the consultation team could be the place to work on increasing competency via web trainings or expert consultation. For a list of topics suggested for a DBT therapist to learn in order to increase competence when treating EDs, see Wisniewski et al., 2007.

Child and Adolescent Adaptations and Considerations

In 2007, Miller and colleagues published a DBT treatment manual designed specifically for adolescents. The adolescent DBT treatment model closely resembles the adult model in that it shares the same theoretical framework, targeting structure, treatment modes, and strategies (Klein & Miller, 2011); however, seven key adaptations were proposed to make DBT more developmentally suitable for youth and their families (Chapter 25, this volume; Miller, Rathus, & Linehan, 2007). In summary, the adaptations include: 1) family members attend skills training groups and are offered telephone skills coaching by the multi-family skills group leader; 2) family therapy sessions are held on an as-needed basis to address familial conflict and crises that arise; 3) dialectical dilemmas specific to adolescents and families are introduced and are considered secondary be-havioural targets; 4) treatment length was decreased from 12 months to six months; 5) a second phase of treatment, a 16-week optional graduate group, is offered to youth who continue to experience symptom-related challenges after the first phase of treatment; 6) the number of skills taught within each module decreased and a fifth adolescent-inspired skills module, "Walking the Middle Path", was added; and 7) group handouts were modified to be more appealing and use language understandable to most ado-lescents (please see Miller et al., 2007 for a detailed description and rationale for the changes).

When working with youth with EDs, most of the adaptations proposed by Miller et al. (2007) apply strikingly well. For example, not only can family participation in skills training be helpful with enhancing an adolescent's potential for skills generalization and reinforcement outside of the treatment (Miller et al., 2007), but if an adolescent's cognitive functioning is impaired due to the effects of malnutrition, as is commonly seen in AN (Chui et al., 2008), it can be helpful to have an adult with a "healthy brain" present to help re-teach and interpret information that is not being completely under-stood. The modified handouts and condensed worksheets can also be helpful when assisting a patient with cognitive difficulties secondary to starvation. Furthermore, additional intervention in the form of a DBT graduate group may improve long-term successful outcomes for an illness where relapse is common (Berkman, Lohr, & Bulik, 2007). Symptom interruption and health/weight restoration in a severely ill adoles-cent can sometimes take much longer than six months to occur. An option for peer-led, ongoing support after the first treatment phase can help the recovering adolescent to improve motivation, improve effective behaviour, and promote skills generalization (MacPherson, Cheavens, & Fristad, 2013), which could theoretically serve as a pro-tective factor against a relapse.

Despite the fact that most of the adaptations do have relevance to adolescent ED treatment as well, the authors do suggest one significant variation specific to ED treat-ment. As opposed to offering family therapy "as needed", as suggested in the original model, it is proposed that family therapy in the form of FBT be offered regularly and *in conjunction with* standard DBT to create a blended FBT/DBT ED treatment model for youth. A blended model is recommended for two reasons. First, there is a signifi-cant amount of research data to support the effectiveness of the FBT treatment model (Downs & Blow, 2013) and because of this, it has emerged as the "gold standard" treat-ment for youth with ED. The level of empirical support FBT has obtained suggests adding to (as opposed to replacing) the model may make more sense. Second, parent/caregiver accountability and support are considered well-established key factors in suc-cessful ED treatment for children and adolescents (Le Grange, Lock, Loeb, & Nicholls, 2010). FBT empowers parents to take charge of eating and weight management behav-iours until an ill adolescent becomes less behaviourally and psychologically involved with the ED and can make healthy decisions on his/her own. This is accomplished in therapy by staying "laser-focused" on ED symptoms until they are in remission and/or the child is weight restored (Lock & le Grange, 2012). Maintaining a "laser-focus" on ED symptoms can be quite difficult to do, particularly when adolescents present with other life-threatening or safety-compromising behaviours (e.g. NSSI, suicidality, etc.). When working with children and adolescents with EDs, however, there is a narrow window of opportunity (i.e. approximately three years) to intervene so that symptoms do not progress into a more chronic and even more difficult-to-treat form of illness (Eisler et al., 1997; Russell, Szmukler, Dare, & Eisler, 1987), so an ideal treatment approach would be one that continues to rapidly and aggressively target ED symptoms and other dangerous comorbidities simultaneously. In the proposed blended FBT/DBT blended treatment model, each adolescent would be assigned a specially trained DBT individual therapist (one well-versed in FBT principles) to target life-threatening, therapy- and quality-of-life-interfering symptoms along with a specially trained FBT family therapist (one well-versed in DBT principles) who will remain hyper-focused on empowering parents to manage ED symptoms. For a detailed theoretical overview of the FBT/DBT treatment model, please see Bhatnagar & Wisniewski, 2015.

DATA SUPPORTING DBT FOR EATING DISORDERS

Since the first DBT with EDs study in 2000, additional modifications and various types of trials have been published, such as single case presentations, case series, uncontrolled trials, and randomized clinical trials. DBT treatment has been examined within AN, BN, BED, and multidiagnostic populations. Early results have found overall support for low drop-out rates, reduced therapist burnout, and reduced ED pathology and general symptomology. A primary goal of studies examining DBT with ED is to determine whether DBT is effective in reducing ED behaviours and conducive to reaching remission. To the authors' knowledge, there have been no randomized trials of DBT compared directly to another evidence-based ED treatment to date. However, evidence has been accumulating from case studies and wait-list control/treatment as usual (TAU) trials that DBT can be effective in facilitating the reduction of BED symptoms (Masson, von Ranson, Wallace, & Safer, 2013; Safer et al., 2010; Telch et al., 2000; Telch, Agras, & Linehan, 2001) and BN symptoms (Hill et al., 2011; Safer, Telch, & Agras, 2001a; Safer et al., 2001b). While research on DBT with AN patients is scarce, preliminary findings have found increases in BMI and reductions in ED psychopathology (Chen et al., 2015; Lynch et al., 2013). Some studies have examined DBT with a mixed sample of patients with AN, BN, or an eating disorder not otherwise specified (EDNOS) to increase knowledge of how DBT functions transdiagnostically. Transdiagnostic and multidiagnostic studies have also found significant support for the utility of DBT as an ED treatment (Chen et al., 2008; Courbasson, Nishikawa, & Dixon, 2012; Federici & Wisniewski, 2013;

Kröger et al., 2010; Lenz et al., 2014; Palmer et al., 2003). These findings are especially important because comorbity is very high among those who have ED (Hudson, Hiripi, Pope, & Kessler, 2007).

Follow-up study results provide additional support for DBT as a viable ED treatment option. ED behaviour abstinence rates and eating pathology reductions are observed at three and six months post-treatment, although at somewhat reduced levels in some studies (Chen et al., 2008; Safer et al., 2010; Telch et al., 2001). For individuals who needed to gain weight as part of their treatment, BMI increases were also reasonably retained, although more studies are needed to more thoroughly examine how DBT impacts BMI (Chen et al., 2015). Interestingly, while DBT may help achieve symptom improvements more quickly than active comparison group therapy (ACGT), long-term remission rates are comparable to ACGTs (e.g., Safer et al., 2010). Due to the complexity of some ED presentations, extended versions of DBT or follow-up skills groups may be helpful in furthering skills generalization and ED symptom reductions (Chen et al., 2008; Hill et al., 2011). Continued booster sessions may also support sustained rates of ED symptom reductions in the long term.

While reducing ED symptoms and behaviours is vital for the treatment of an ED, other factors may also impact the success of ED treatment. For instance, it is important to prevent the premature treatment termination that is common for individuals with EDs (Swan-Kremeier et al., 2005; Wallier et al., 2009). A crucial strength of DBT for EDs is the low rate of premature drop-out, which has been found to range from 0% to 28% (Chen et al., 2008; Chen et al., 2015; Courbasson et al., 2012; Federici & Wisniewski, 2013; Hill et al., 2011; Lynch et al., 2013; Palmer et al., 2003; Safer et al., 2001b; Safer et al., 2010; Telch et al., 2000) or similar to rates found in control groups (Masson et al., 2013; Telch et al., 2001). These low rates of premature drop-out may be because DBT targets TIB that obstruct patients from receiving their full dose of treatment. While many of these studies have very few participants, early results are promising. Finally, in line with traditional DBT goals, DBT with EDs has also been found to improve emotion regulation (Courbasson et al., 2012; Hill et al., 2011; Telch et al., 2000).

ADOLESCENT DATA

Over the last decade, DBT has been examined in adolescent ED populations as well. While only a handful of studies have looked at adapting DBT to adolescents with EDs, early results suggest DBT can aid in the reduction of eating disorder symptoms, depression symptoms, and general psychopathology (Johnston, O'Gara, Koman, Baker, & Anderson, 2015; Safer, Couturier, & Lock, 2007; Salbach, Klinkowski, Pfeiffer, Lehmkuhl, & Korte, 2007; Salbach-Andrae, Bohnekamp, Pfeiffer, Lehmkuhl, & Miller, 2008). Increases in BMI for AN patients have also been found in DBT-ED treatment (Salbach et al., 2007; Johnston et al., 2015). Further research examining DBT in adolescent ED populations, especially those with complicated presentations, comorbidity, and/or treatment-resistant EDs, is needed.

Taken together, the results thus far are promising and exciting, but more is needed to solidify DBT as an evidence-based treatment, particularly for AN. Direct comparisons of DBT to other, more heavily researched standard treatments are needed to inform clinical interventions. It may also be helpful in understanding which types of patients benefit best from established treatments, such as CBT and IPT, and which may need DBT to reach recovery.

CONCLUSIONS AND FUTURE DIRECTIONS

Given that ED can be resistant to traditional treatments, and that ED symptoms can be life-threatening, as well as severely impact the lives of both patients and their families, understanding additional viable treatment options is essential. This is especially true for when other evidence-based treatments have not been successful for an individual with an ED or who exhibits complex comorbidity. As this chapter shows, adapting traditional DBT to the needs of EDs is achievable and useful. The research evaluating the use of comprehensive DBT with ED patients is small but growing (e.g., Ben-Porath et al., 2009; Chen et al., 2008; Chen et al., 2015; Federici & Wisniewski, 2013; Groves, Backer, van den Bosch, & Miller, 2011; Kröger et al., 2010; Palmer et al., 2003), with the research consistently finding a reduction in ED behaviours and/or ED cognitions. However, DBT has not been examined at the same level and with the same rigour as other established ED treatments. More research is needed to aid in the understanding of DBT for the treatment of EDs.

There are numerous areas in which future research might focus. First, it is important that research directly compare DBT to standard, well-established ED treatments in RCTs. Larger sample sizes and increased control within future studies may be helpful in providing additional support (or contradiction) to the use of DBT with ED patients. Studies comparing adapted versions of DBT to the more comprehensive, original version of DBT may also be helpful in guiding clinicians in their treatment decision-making process. While DBT was originally adapted for use with BED and BN patients, much less is known about the effectiveness of DBT for patients with AN, thus, leaving an important gap in the literature.

Finally, DBT has been studied primarily in white women, making knowledge on how effective DBT is with men and minority populations difficult to discern. Prevalence rates of ED indicate men and minority populations experience a substantial number of ED symptoms, although much less is known about the factors that influence treatment seeking, barriers to recovery, and unique needs. For example, specific barriers present with low socio-economic status individuals, such as lack of insurance or the reduced ability to take time away from work due to limited financial resources, may impact DBT for ED treatment because the course of treatment is lengthy and intensive. Understanding more about the barriers present within various populations can help find ways for all individuals diagnosed with ED to access and maintain treatment. Hopefully, through the information provided in this chapter, clinicians can feel better equipped to use DBT with relevant ED patients and researchers can find additional areas of inquiry.

KEY POINTS FOR CLINICIANS

- Because eating pathology can function as a strategy to cope with emotion sensitivity and vulnerability, dialectical behaviour therapy (DBT) can fill a needed gap for individuals who have not responded to standard treatment approaches.
- The following characteristics in individuals with eating disorders (ED) may indicate the utility of a DBT approach:
  a. Failed treatment attempts with evidence-based treatment approaches.
  b. Affect or emotion regulation deficits.
  c. Multidiagnostic, complex clinical presentations, especially:
     i. Recurrent suicidality or self-harm behaviours
     ii. Borderline Personality Disorder or Substance Use Disorders.
  d. Slow rate of weight gain (for adolescents who need to gain weight as part of their treatment recommendations).
- The "non-judgmental stance" in DBT can be a powerful tool for clinicians to help reduce their burnout and prevent judgments related to behaviours that are often considered as dangerous, shallow, or deceitful. Participating in "therapy for the therapists" in DBT consultation teams is vital in order to receive support from other DBT clinicians and to uphold treatment fidelity.
- ED behaviours can fit into the target hierarchy by assessing the level of threat the behaviour poses. The ED behaviours may move targets over time depending on medical instability and implications of the behaviour.
- While the standard DBT protocol utilizes a 24-hour rule for phone coaching, for ED behaviours, this rule should be adapted to the "Next Meal/Snack Rule" due to the frequency of exposure to food and expected meals/snacks in one 24-hour period.

REFERENCES

Allen, H., & Craighead, L. (1999). Appetite monitoring in the treatment of binge eating disorder. *Behavior Therapy*, 30(2), 253–272.

American Psychiatric Association. (2006). *Practice guideline for the treatment of patients with eating disorders*, 3rd Edition. Arlington, VA: American Psychiatric Publications.

American Psychiatric Association. (2013). *Diagnostic and statistical manual of mental disorders*, 5th Edition. Arlington, VA: American Psychiatric Publishing.

Anderson, D. A., & Maloney, K. C. (2001). The efficacy of cognitive-behavioral therapy on the core symptoms of bulimia nervosa. *Clinical Psychology Review*, 21(7), 971–988.

Arcelus, J., Mitchell, A. J., Wales, J., & Nielsen, S. (2011). Mortality rates in patients with anorexia nervosa and other eating disorders: a meta-analysis of 36 studies. *Archives of General Psychiatry*, 68(7), 724–731.

Ball, J., & Mitchell, P. (2004). A randomized controlled study of cognitive behavior therapy and behavioral family therapy for anorexia nervosa patients. *Eating Disorders*, 12(4), 303–314.

Bankoff, S. M., Karpel, M. G., Forbes, H. E., & Pantalone, D. W. (2012). A systematic review of dialectical behavior therapy for the treatment of eating disorders. *Eating Disorders*, 20(3), 196–215.

Ben-Porath, D. D., Wisniewski, L., & Warren, M. (2009). Differential treatment response for eating disordered patients with and without a comorbid borderline personality diagnosis using a dialectical behavior therapy (DBT)-informed approach. *Eating Disorders*, 17(3), 225–241.

Berkman, N. D., Lohr, K. N., & Bulik, C. M. (2007). Outcomes of eating disorders: A systematic review of the literature. *International Journal of Eating Disorders*, 40(4), 293–309.

Bhatnagar, K., & Wisniewski, L. (2015). Integrating dialectical behavior therapy with family therapy for adolescents with affect dysregulation. In K. L. Loab, D. Le Grange, & J. Lock (Eds.), *Family therapy for adolescent eating and weight disorders* (pp. 305–327). New York: Taylor & Francis.

Carter, F. A., Jordan, J., McIntosh, V. V., Luty, S. E., McKenzie, J. M., Frampton, C.,...Joyce, P. R. (2011). The long-term efficacy of three psychotherapies for anorexia nervosa: A randomized, controlled trial. *International Journal of Eating Disorders*, 44(7), 647–654.

Cassin, S. E., & von Ranson, K. M. (2005). Personality and eating disorders: A decade in review. *Clinical Psychology Review*, 25(7), 895–916.

Chen, E. Y., Matthews, L., Allen, C., Kuo, J. R., & Linehan, M. M. (2008). Dialectical behavior therapy for clients with binge-eating disorder or bulimia nervosa and borderline personality disorder. *International Journal of Eating Disorders*, 41(6), 505–512.

Chen, E. Y., Segal, K., Weissman, J., Zeffiro, T. A., Gallop, R., Linehan, M. M.,...Lynch, T. R. (2015). Adapting dialectical behavior therapy for outpatient adult anorexia nervosa—A pilot study. *International Journal of Eating Disorders*, 48(1), 123–132.

Chui, H. T., Christensen, B. K., Zipursky, R. B., Richards, B. A., Hanratty, M. K., Kabani, N. J.,...Katzman, D. K. (2008). Cognitive function and brain structure in females with a history of adolescent-onset anorexia nervosa. *Pediatrics*, 122(2), e426–e437.

Courbasson, C., Nishikawa, Y., & Dixon, L. (2012). Outcome of dialectical behaviour therapy for concurrent eating and substance use disorders. *Clinical Psychology & Psychotherapy*, 19(5), 434–449.

Downs, K. J., & Blow, A. J. (2013). A substantive and methodological review of family-based treatment for eating disorders: The last 25 years of research. *Journal of Family Therapy*, 35(S1), 3–28.

Doyle, P., Le Grange, D., Loeb, K., Doyle, A. C., & Crosby, R. (2010). Early response to family-based treatment for adolescent anorexia nervosa. *International Journal of Eating Disorders*, 43(7), 659–662.

Eisler, I., Dare, C., Russell, G. F. M., Szmukler, G. I., Le Grange, D., & Dodge, E. (1997). Family and individual therapy in anorexia nervosa: A five-year follow-up. *Archives of General Psychiatry*, 54(11), 1025–1030.

Eisler, I., Simic, M., Russell, G. F. M., & Dare, C. (2007). A randomised controlled treatment trial of two forms of family therapy in adolescent anorexia nervosa: A five-year follow-up. *Journal of Child Psychology and Psychiatry*, 48(6), 552–560.

Fairburn, C. G. (2008). *Cognitive behavior therapy and eating disorders*. New York: Guilford Press.

Fairburn, C. G., Cooper, Z., & Shafran, R. (2003). Cognitive behaviour therapy for eating disorders: A "transdiagnostic" theory and treatment. *Behaviour Research and Therapy*, 41(5), 509–528.

Federici, A., & Wisniewski, L. (2013). An intensive DBT program for patients with multidiagnostic eating disorder presentations: A case series analysis. *International Journal of Eating Disorders, 46*(4), 322–331.

Federici, A., Wisniewski, L., & Ben-Porath, D. (2013). Description of an intensive dialectical behavior therapy program for multidiagnostic clients with eating disorders. *Journal of Counseling & Development, 90*(3), 330–338.

Fichter, M. M., & Quadflieg, N. (2016). Mortality in eating disorders—results of a large prospective clinical longitudinal study. *International Journal of Eating Disorders, 49*(4), 391–401.

Golan, M., Yaroslavski, A., & Stein, D. (2009). Managing eating disorders: Countertransference processes in the therapeutic milieu. *International Journal of Child and Adolescent Health, 2*(2), 213–227.

Gratz, K. L., & Roemer, L. (2004). Multidimensional assessment of emotion regulation and dysregulation: Development, factor structure, and initial validation of the difficulties in emotion regulation scale. *Journal of Psychopathology and Behavioral Assessment, 26*(1), 41–54.

Griffiths, E., Hawkes, N., Gilbert, S., & Serpell, L. (2016). Improving the post-meal experience of hospitalised patients with eating disorders using visuospatial, verbal and somatic activities. *Journal of Eating Disorders, 4*(9), 1–5.

Groves, S., Backer, H. S., van den Bosch, W., & Miller, A. (2011). Dialectical behaviour therapy with adolescents. *Child and Adolescent Mental Health, 17*(2), 65–75.

Harned, M. S., Chapman, A. L., Dexter-Mazza, E. T., Murray, A., Comtois, K. A., & Linehan, M. M. (2008). Treating co-occurring Axis I disorders in recurrently suicidal women with borderline personality disorder: A 2-year randomized trial of dialectical behavior therapy versus community treatment by experts. *Journal of Consulting and Clinical Psychology, 76*(6), 1068–1075.

Harrison, A., Sullivan, S., Tchanturia, K., & Treasure, J. (2009). Emotion recognition and regulation in anorexia nervosa. *Clinical Psychology & Psychotherapy, 16*(4), 348–356.

Hay, P. (2013). A systematic review of evidence for psychological treatments in eating disorders: 2005–2012. *International Journal of Eating Disorders, 46*(5), 462–469.

Haynos, A. F., & Fruzzetti, A. E. (2011). Anorexia nervosa as a disorder of emotion dysregulation: Evidence and treatment implications. *Clinical Psychology: Science and Practice, 18*(3), 183–202.

Hill, D. M., Craighead, L. W., & Safer, D. L. (2011). Appetite-focused dialectical behavior therapy for the treatment of binge eating with purging: A preliminary trial. *International Journal of Eating Disorders, 44*(3), 249–261.

Holderness, C. C., Brooks-Gunn, J., & Warren, M. P. (1994). Co-morbidity of eating disorders and substance abuse review of the literature. *International Journal of Eating Disorders, 16*(1), 1–34.

Hudson, J. I., Hiripi, E., Pope, H. G., & Kessler, R. C. (2007). The prevalence and correlates of eating disorders in the National Comorbidity Survey Replication. *Biological Psychiatry, 61*(3), 348–358.

Johnson, C., Tobin, D., & Enright, A. (1989). Prevalence and clinical characteristics of borderline patients in an eating-disordered population. *Journal of Clinical Psychiatry, 50*(1), 9–15.

Johnston, J. A., O'Gara, J. S., Koman, S. L., Baker, C. W., & Anderson, D. A. (2015). A pilot study of Maudsley family therapy with group dialectical behavior therapy skills training in an intensive outpatient program for adolescent eating disorders. *Journal of Clinical Psychology, 71*(6), 527–543.

Kaplan, A. S., & Noble, S. (2007). Medical complications of eating disorders. In S. Wonderlich, J. E. Mitchell, M. de Zwaan, & H. Steiger (Eds.), *Annual review of eating disorders* (Part 1, pp. 101–111). Oxford: Radcliffe.

Kass, A. E., Kolko, R. P., & Wilfley, D. E. (2013). Psychological treatments for eating disorders. *Current Opinions in Psychiatry*, 26(6), 549–555.

Keys, A., Brozek, J., & Henscheo, A. (1950). *The biology of human starvation.* Minneapolis: University of Minnesota Press.

Klein, D. A., & Miller, A. L. (2011). Dialectical behavior therapy for suicidal adolescents with bordeline personality disorder. *Child and Adolescent Psychiatric Clinics of North America*, 20(2), 205–216.

Klump, K. L., Bulik, C. M., Kaye, W. H., Treasure, J., & Tyson, E. (2009). Academy for eating disorders position paper: Eating disorders are serious mental illnesses. *International Journal of Eating Disorders*, 42(2), 97–103.

Kristeller, J., Wolever, R. Q., & Sheets, V. (2014). Mindfulness-based eating awareness training (MB-EAT) for binge eating: A randomized clinical trial. *Mindfulness*, 5(3), 282–297.

Kröger, C., Schweiger, U., Sipos, V., Kliem, S., Arnold, R., Schunert, T., & Reinecker, H. (2010). Dialectical behaviour therapy and an added cognitive behavioural treatment module for eating disorders in women with borderline personality disorder and anorexia nervosa or bulimia nervosa who failed to respond to previous treatments. An open trial with a 15-month follow-up. *Journal of Behavior Therapy and Experimental Psychiatry*, 41(4), 381–388.

Le Grange, D., Crosby, R. D., & Lock, J. (2008). Predictors and moderators of outcome in family-based treatment for adolescent bulimia nervosa. *Journal of the American Academy of Child and Adolescent Psychiatry*, 47(4), 464–470.

Le Grange, D., Lock, J., Loeb, K., and Nicholls, D. (2010). Academy for Eating Disorders position paper: The role of the family in eating disorders. *International Journal of Eating Disorders*, 43(1), 1–5.

Lenz, A. S., Taylor, R., Fleming, M., & Serman, N. (2014). Effectiveness of dialectical behavior therapy for treating eating disorders. *Journal of Counseling & Development*, 92(1), 26–35.

Limbrunner, H. M., Ben-Porath, D. D., & Wisniewski, L. (2011). DBT telephone skills coaching with eating disordered clients: Who calls, for what reasons, and for how long? *Cognitive and Behavioral Practice*, 18(2), 186–195.

Linehan, M. M., Comtois, K. A., Murray, A. M., Brown, M. Z., Gallop, R. J., Heard, H. L., … Lindenboim, N. (2006). Two-year randomized controlled trial and follow-up of dialectical behavior therapy vs therapy by experts for suicidal behaviors and borderline personality disorder. *Archives of General Psychiatry*, 63(7), 757–766.

Linehan, M. M. (1993). *Cognitive-behavioral treatment of borderline personality disorder.* New York: Guilford Press.

Linehan, M. M. (2015). *DBT skills training manual*, 2nd edition. New York: Guilford Press.

Lock, J., & Le Grange, D. (2012). *Treatment manual for anorexia nervosa: A family-based approach*, 2nd Edition. New York: Guilford Press.

Lock, J., Le Grange, D., Agras, W. S., & Dare, C. (2001). *Treatment manual for anorexia nervosa: A family-based approach.* New York: Guilford Press.

Lock, J., Le Grange, D., Agras, W. S., Moye, A., Bryson, S. W., & Jo, B. (2010). Randomized clinical trial comparing family-based treatment with adolescent-focused individual therapy for adolescents with anorexia nervosa. *Archives of General Psychiatry*, 67(10), 1025–1032.

Lundgren, J. D., Danoff-Burg, S., and Anderson, D. A. (2004). Cognitive-behavioral therapy for bulimia nervosa: An empirical analysis of clinical significance. *International Journal of Eating Disorders, 35*(3), 262–274.

Lynch, T. R., Gray, K. L., Hempel, R. J., Titley, M., Chen, E. Y., & O'Mahen, H. A. (2013). Radically open-dialectical behavior therapy for adult anorexia nervosa: feasibility and outcomes from an inpatient program. *BMC Psychiatry, 13,* 293–309.

MacPherson, H. A., Cheavens, J. S., & Fristad, M. A. (2013). Dialectical behavior therapy for adolescents: Theory, treatment adaptations, and empirical outcomes. *Clinical Child and Family Psychology Review, 16*(1), 59–80.

Marek, R. J., Ben-Porath, D. D., Federici, A., Wisniewski, L., & Warren, M. (2013). Targeting premeal anxiety in eating disordered clients and normal controls: A preliminary investigation into the use of mindful eating vs. distraction during food exposure. *International Journal of Eating Disorders, 46*(6), 582–585.

Masson, P. C., von Ranson, K. M., Wallace, L. M., & Safer, D. L. (2013). A randomized wait-list controlled pilot study of dialectical behaviour therapy guided self-help for binge eating disorder. *Behaviour Research and Therapy, 51*(11), 723–728.

McCabe, E., LaVia, M., & Marcus, M. (2004). The use of dialectical behavior therapy in the treatment of eating disorders. In J. K. Thompson (Ed.), *Handbook of eating disorders and obesity* (pp. 232–244). Hoboken, NJ: John Wiley and Sons.

McIntosh, V. V., Jordan, J., Carter, F. A., Luty, S. E., McKenzie, J. M., Bulik, C. M., … Joyce, P. R. (2005). Three psychotherapies for anorexia nervosa: A randomized, controlled trial. *American Journal of Psychiatry, 162*(4), 741–747.

Miller, A. L., Rathus, J. H., & Linehan, M. M. (2007). *Dialectical behavior therapy with suicidal adolescents.* New York: Guilford Press.

National Institute for Clinical Excellence. (2004). *Core interventions in the treatment and management of anorexia nervosa, bulimia nervosa, and binge eating disorder* (National Clinical Practice Guideline CG9). Retrieved from www.nice.org.uk/nicemedia/pdf/CG9FullGuideline.pdf

Palmer, R. L., Birchall, H., Damani, S., Gatward, N., McGrain, L., & Parker, L. (2003). A dialectical behavior therapy program for people with an eating disorder and borderline personality disorder—description and outcome. *International Journal of Eating Disorders, 33*(3), 281–286.

Paul, T., Schroeter, K., Dahme, B., & Nutzinger, D. O. (2002). Self-injurious behavior in women with eating disorders. *American Journal of Psychiatry, 159*(3), 408–411.

Pomeroy, C., Mitchell, J. E., Roerig, J., & Crow, S. (2002). *Medical complications of psychiatric illness.* Washington, DC: American Psychiatric Press.

Rathus, J. H., & Miller, A. L. (2015). *DBT® Skills Manual for Adolescents.* New York: Guilford Press.

Ritschel, L. A., Lim, N. E., & Stewart, L. M. (2015). Transdiagnostic applications of DBT for adolescents and adults. *Americal Journal of Psychotherapy, 69*(2), 111–128.

Russell, G. F., Szmukler, G. I., Dare, C., & Eisler, I. (1987). An evaluation of family therapy in anorexia nervosa and bulimia nervosa. *Archives of General Psychiatry, 44*(12), 1047–1056.

Sachs, K. V., Harnke, B., Mehler, P. S., & Krantz, M. J. (2016). Cardiovascular complications of anorexia nervosa: A systematic review. *International Journal of Eating Disorders, 49,* 238–248.

Safer, D. L., Couturier, J. L., & Lock, J. (2007). Dialectical behavior therapy modified for adolescent binge eating disorder: A case report. *Cognitive and Behavioral Practice, 14*(2), 157–167.

Safer, D. L., Robinson, A. H., & Jo, B. (2010). Outcome from a randomized controlled trial of group therapy for binge eating disorder: comparing dialectical behavior therapy adapted for binge eating to an active comparison group therapy. *Behavior Therapy, 41*(1), 106–120.

Safer, D. L., Telch, C. F., & Agras, W. S. (2001a). Dialectical behavior therapy adapted for bulimia: A case report. *International Journal of Eating Disorders, 30*(1), 101–106.

Safer, D. L., Telch, C. F., & Agras, W. S. (2001b). Dialectical behavior therapy for bulimia nervosa. *American Journal of Psychiatry, 158*(4), 632–634.

Safer, D. L., Telch, C. F., & Chen, E. Y. (2009). *Dialectical behavior therapy for binge eating and bulimia.* New York: Guilford Press.

Salbach, H., Klinkowski, N., Pfeiffer, E., Lehmkuhl, U., & Korte, A. (2007). Dialectical behavior therapy for adolescents with anorexia and bulimia nervosa (DBT-AN/BN): A pilot study. *der Kinderpsychologie und Kinderpsychiatrie, 56,* 91–108.

Salbach-Andrae, H., Bohnekamp, I., Pfeiffer, E., Lehmkuhl, U., & Miller, A. L. (2008). Dialectical behavior therapy of anorexia and bulimia nervosa among adolescents: A case series. *Cognitive and Behavioral Practice, 15*(4), 415–425.

Stein, D., Lilenfeld, L. R., Wildman, P. C., & Marcus, M. D. (2004). Attempted suicide and self-injury in patients diagnosed with eating disorders. *Comprehensive Psychiatry, 45,* 447–451.

Svaldi, J., Griepenstroh, J., Tuschen-Caffier, B., & Ehring, T. (2012). Emotion regulation deficits in eating disorders: A marker of eating pathology or general psychopathology? *Psychiatry Research, 197*(1), 103–111.

Swan-Kremeier, L. A., Mitchell, J. E., Twardowski, T., Lancaster, K., & Crosby, R. D. (2005). Travel distance and attrition in outpatient eating disorders treatment. *International Journal of Eating Disorders, 38*(4), 367–370.

Telch, C. F., Agras, W. S., & Linehan, M. M. (2000). Group dialectical behavior therapy for binge-eating disorder: A preliminary, uncontrolled trial. *Behavior Therapy, 31*(3), 569–582.

Telch, C. F., Agras, W. S., & Linehan, M. M. (2001). Dialectical behavior therapy for binge eating disorder. *Journal of Consulting and Clinical Psychology, 69*(6), 1061.

Treasure, J., Sepulveda, A. R., MacDonald, P., Whitaker, W., Lopez, C., Zabala, M., … Todd, G. (2008). The assessment of the family of people with eating disorders. *European Eating Disorders Review, 16*(4), 247–255.

Wallier, J., Vibert, S., Berthoz, S., Huas, C., Hubert, T., & Godart, N. (2009). Dropout from in-patient treatment for anorexia nervosa: critical review of the literature. *International Journal of Eating Disorders, 42*(7), 636–647.

Warren, C. S., Schafer, K. J., Crowley, M., & Olivardia, R. (2012). A qualitative analysis of job burnout in eating disorder treatment providers. *Eating Disorders: The Journal of Treatment & Prevention, 20*(3), 175–195.

Wilfley, D. E., Friedman, M. A., Dounchis, J. Z., Stein, R. I., Welch, R. R., & Ball, S. A. (2000). Comorbid psychopathology in binge eating disorder: Relation to eating disorder severity at baseline and following treatment. *Journal of Consulting and Clinical Psychology, 68,* 641–649.

Williams, S., & Reid, M. (2010). Understanding the experience of ambivalence in anorexia nervosa: The maintainer's perspective. *Psychology & Health, 25*(5), 551–567.

Wilson, G. T., Grilo, C. M., & Vitousek, K. M. (2007). Psychological treatment of eating disorders. *American Psychologist, 62,* 199–216.

Wiser, S., & Telch, C. F. (1999). Dialectical behavior therapy for binge-eating disorder. *Journal of Clinical Psychology, 55*(6), 755–768.

Wisniewski, L., & Ben-Porath, D. D. (2005). Telephone skill-coaching with eating-disordered clients: clinical guidelines using a DBT framework. *European Eating Disorders Review, 13*(5), 344–350.

Wisniewski, L., Bhatnagar, K., & Warren, M. (2013). Using dialectical behavior therapy for the treatment of eating disorders: A model for DBT enhanced CBT. In I. Dancyger & V. Fornari (Eds.), *Evidence-based treatments for eating disorders: Children, adolescents and adults* (pp. 275–290). New York: Nova Science Publishers.

Wisniewski, L., & Kelly, E. (2003). The application of dialectical behavior therapy to the treatment of eating disorders. *Cognitive and Behavioral Practice, 10*(2), 131–138.

Wisniewski, L., Safer, D., and Chen, E. (2007). Dialectical Behavior Therapy and Eating Disorders. In L. Dimeff & K. Koerner (Eds.), *Dialectical behavior therapy in clinical practice* (pp. 174–221). New York: Guilford Press.

Wonderlich, S. A., Mitchell, J. E., Peterson, C. B., and Crow, S. (2001). Integrative cognitive therapy for bulimic behavior. In R. Striegel-Moore & L. Smolak (Eds.), *Eating disorders: Innovative directions in research and practice* (pp. 173–195). Washington, DC: American Psychological Association.

CHAPTER 27

DIALECTICAL BEHAVIOUR THERAPY FOR SUBSTANCE USE DISORDERS

SETH R. AXELROD

INTRODUCTION

IMMEDIATELY after establishing the initial empirical support for Dialectical Behavior Therapy (DBT) for chronically suicidal and self-injurious individuals with Borderline Personality Disorder (BPD, see Linehean, Armstrong, Allmon, & Heard, 1991), Marsha Linehan set out to adapt DBT for an even higher-risk population for suicide and accidental death by overdose: those with co-occurring BPD and Substance Use Disorders (SUDs; Linehan et al., 1999), and specifically those with opioid dependence (Linehan et al., 2002). The co-occurrence of these disorders is quite common and includes more than half of those diagnosed with BPD, and more than a quarter of those diagnosed with SUDs (Trull, Sher, Minks-Brown, Durbin, & Burr, 2000). Linehan's approach to developing the DBT-SUD adaptation involved maintaining all aspects of standard model outpatient DBT (i.e., principles, strategies, and the treatment modalities), while introducing additional components that reflected established best practice (e.g., toxicology screening); had a high-level of empirical support (i.e., replacement medication for opioid users); synthesized formulations and interventions from leading SUD interventional models (i.e., abstinence-focused and harm-reduction models of recovery); addressed clinically observed skills deficits related to addiction (i.e., "DBCA" skills, described below); and addressed specific challenges with treatment engagement and retention (i.e., attachment strategies). In addition to providing an overview of these modifications, this chapter reviews the DBT biosocial model as it applies to the development of SUD, DBT-SUD clinical formulation, empirical support, and clinical recommendations for managing some of the common clinical implementation challenges of working with BPD and SUD from a DBT framework, such as case management, responding to lying, coordinating with standard SUD interventions, and problems of contagion.

Biosocial Model of BPD + SUD

All aspects of Marsha Linehan's biosocial model for understanding the aetiology and maintenance of chronic emotion dysregulation as stemming from the transacting forces of an emotionally vulnerable biological temperament and an emotionally invalidating social system (see chapters by Niedtfeld & Bohus and Grove & Crowell, this volume; Linehan, 1993) fully generalize to those individuals with co-occurring BPD and SUD. Certain aspects of this model, and particularly the addition of an impulsive biological vulnerability that extended and further elaborated the model by Crowell, Beauchaine, and Linehan (2009), is particularly relevant to co-occurring BPD and SUD. This extended model is highly comparable to a similar aetiological model proposed by Trull and colleagues (2000) that also adds a reciprocal relationship of BPD and SUD maintaining each other. The role of impulsivity as a predictor of both substance use and BPD features has been supported in multivariate models (Johnson, Ashe, & Wilson, 2016). Importantly, impulsivity is a multidimensional construct in which certain aspects may be more relevant than others in the development of BPD and SUDs and their potential interaction (Bornovalova, Lejuez, Daughters, Rosenthal, & Lynch, 2005). For example, Hahn and colleagues (2016) found negative urgency and low perseverance to be most predictive of BPD features and subsequent alcohol problems, perhaps indicating difficulty tolerating negative emotions, while pleasure-seeking forms of impulsivity including positive urgency, sensation seeking, and low premeditation (as well as negative urgency) were found to predict antisocial personality disorder features and subsequent alcohol problems.

Individuals who go on to develop SUDs (with or without BPD) are also likely to have additional biological vulnerabilities demonstrated by structural and functional features of the dopamine neurotransmitter system (Anokhina, Veretinskaya, Vasil'eva, & Ovchinnikov, 2000), differences in inhibitory control and reward neurocircuitry (Heitzeg, Cope, Martz, & Hardee, 2015), and a genetic heritability of SUDs between 30% and 80% (Agrawal & Lynskey, 2006; Verhulst, Neale, & Kendler, 2015). Such individuals may also be more likely to be sensitive to and/or experience invalidating messages within family environments that are either over-protective and unsupportive, or poorly defined and combative (Rhodes et al., 2003); that are marked by substance misuse, high stress, and excessive leniency (Milaniak, Watson, & Jaffee, 2015); and/or that communicate unrealistic expectations for individual control or responsibility (e.g., the "Just say no" and DARE campaigns of the 1980s; Rosenbaum, 2007).

As with Linehan's original formulation, the transaction between biology and environment is bi-directional, and within any specific case might originate with relatively greater biological vulnerability (e.g., very low inhibitory control) or more severe environmental invalidation (e.g., intensely controlling); however, once the pattern begins a positive feedback loop may ensue with each part making the other stronger over time. Ultimately, the individual becomes caught in an internalized dilemma between an under-regulated "Addict Mind" that is completely governed by thoughts, feelings, and sensations motivating use, and an over-regulated "Clean Mind" that is categorically opposed to further use and oversimplifies the ease of achieving abstinence to the point of even dismissing the possibility of further use. The original DBT biosocial model can be very useful for countering judgment and BPD stigma by grounding the clinician in a phenomenologically compassionate formulation of emotionally dysregulated and potentially aversive behaviour. Similarly, a biosocial formulation of addictions can help clinicians foster a compassionate perspective on individuals who struggle with addictions, and help counter the stigmatized impressions that mental health professionals may hold toward addiction (e.g., Van Boekel, Brouwers, Van Weeghel, & Garretsen, 2013). Whereas the overarching pathology of BPD identified within standard model DBT is understood to involve chronic emotional dysregulation produced from vacillating between under- and over-controlled efforts to emotionally regulate, DBT-SUD similarly understands the chronic inability to control substance use as a failure to synthesize Addict Mind and Clean Mind into a "Clear Mind" that is grounded in and fully accepting of both the ongoing vulnerability to be pulled toward using, as well as the necessity of avoiding use due to its aversive consequences. When individuals learn to access and follow their Clear Mind, they proceed towards recovery as a continuing and effortful process that avoids giving up on self-controls or trusting simplified solutions, and instead faces recovery head on as a process of vigilant, non-judgmental openness about vulnerability and willingness to take practical steps towards a non-using lifestyle.

TREATMENT STRUCTURE

Functions

As a comprehensive DBT treatment, DBT-SUD fulfils the five functions of standard outpatient DBT, including: 1) enhancing client capabilities, 2) enhancing client motivation, 3) generalizing to the environment, 4) structuring the environment, and 5) enhancing clinician capabilities and motivation. Each function has added emphasis to address the challenges of co-occurring BPD and SUD.

Enhancing Client Capabilities

The Distress Tolerance module of DBT-SUD provides clients with added skills for self-management and crisis survival reorganized into the mnemonic "DCBA" in Linehan's revised skills manual (Linehan, 2015). *Dialectical Abstinence* frames the SUD recovery process for clinicians and clients as a synthesis of the two leading, yet contradictory, models of addiction recovery and treatment, namely, abstinence approaches such as 12-step, and harm-reduction approaches such as relapse prevention. DBT-SUD strives to bring together the strengths and benefits of the abstinence approach (i.e., achieving longer episodes without use) and harm-reduction approaches (i.e., more rapid return to abstinence after lapses), while avoiding the primary weakness of each approach (i.e., use spiralling into full relapses and greater difficulty achieving abstinence, respectively). This synthesis is enacted in DBT-SUD with an expectation of total commitment for successful abstinence on one hand, and on the other, complete acceptance that substance use may occur as an expected part of the recovery process, and that relapse can be a learning experience. Like an Olympic athlete, the client fully commits to training with the intention of getting the gold, all the while knowing inplicitly that they may fail to get the gold at any given competition; any shortcomings will be analysed in order to increase the chances of getting the gold next time. A non-judgmental approach is used to mitigate any experience of shame of failure from plummeting into hopelessness and resignation (i.e., the abstinence violation effect, Marlatt, 1985).

Additional DCBA skills for enhancing capabilities include *Clear Mind* (mentioned previously) and *Community Reinforcement* (i.e., developing lifestyle contingencies that reward abstinence, such as a work schedule that is inconsistent with a using lifestyle and developing relationships with non-users); *Burning Bridges* to use (e.g., erasing contacts of dealers; ending relationships centred on use) and *Building Bridges* to replace sight and smell drug cues in one's environments with new sights and smells to become cues to recovery; *Alternate Rebellion* by practising options to functionally validate the desire to shock, break the rules, or push back on expectations in ways that are non-destructive and values-consistent (e.g., dying hair a bright colour or wearing unusual makeup) and *Adaptive Denial* by deliberately telling oneself falsehoods that ease the distress of moving forward towards abstinence (e.g., "I only have to get through today" or "that drug dealer is part of a sting operation"). Importantly, all of these skills are also perfectly suitable for targeting non-substance-related "addictions" including common DBT targets such as self-injury or binge eating, as well as more mundane ineffective habits like shopping or checking email (Linehan, 2015).

Enhancing Client Motivation

Individuals who struggle with SUDs often have strong ambivalence around stopping their use and often minimize or hide their use from those invested in helping them. For this reason and consistent with SUD treatment best practice, DBT-SUD incorporates random toxicology screenings to help manage issues of inaccurate reporting. DBT's hierarchical treatment plan structure of targeting treatment-interfering-behaviour directly and ahead of quality-of-life-interfering targets including SUD guide the clinician to treating inaccurate communication as an expected treatment obstacle and to maintain a non-judgmental orientation. A relevant DBT formulation for clients' inaccurate communication involves understanding them as struggling with a shame-ridden dialectical dilemma that leads them to vacillate between *apparent competence,* or inaccurately presenting as doing better than they actually are (including falsely projecting the ability to maintain abstinence), and *active-passivity,* or effortful withdrawal from participating in coping or collaborating in the help that they need (see further discussion and suggested clinical interventions for this dilemma later in this chapter).

A final common problem area that occurs frequently in the BPD with SUD target population is referred to as *butterfly attachment*, or the tendency to flit in and out of treatment with little desire to form bonds with clinicians or clinical agencies (unlike many individuals with BPD and no SUD, that tend to seek such attachments), and that results in problems with treatment attendance and treatment retention, which DBT-SUD refers to as *falling out of therapy.* To address these issues, DBT-SUD utilizes a variety of *attachment strategies* and contingency management (e.g., rewarding attendance with shorter sessions if that appears to be reinforcing). Some examples of attachment strategies include orienting individuals to the problem of butterfly attachment (e.g., "Have you found that you are often very excited about new commitments, but then lose interest fairly suddenly and quit?"); scheduling regular phone check-ins during the early phase of treatment; developing preemptive *getting found* plans, such as getting members of the client's support network to commit to helping find and convince clients to return to treatment if contacted by the clinician; social networking meetings to introduce supports to the clinicians; and reaching out to clients in their natural environments to break cycles of avoidance if they miss sessions.

Generalizing to the Environment

As with standard DBT, DBT-SUD includes diary cards, skills homework assignments, and telephone skills coaching to help generalize new skills acquired in therapy into the clients' natural environments. Consistent with the DBT assumption that clients "must learn behaviours in all relevant contexts" and following the principles of state-dependent learning, DBT-SUD includes an expectation for clients to continue practising their skills even when using substances to ensure that skills generalize to that specific relevant context when they might be at highest risk (Linehan & Dimeff, 1997).

Structuring the Environment

Because individuals with co-occurring BPD and SUD often struggle with significant life chaos such as homelessness, unemployment, and legal issues, DBT-SUD places greater emphasis on delivering case management strategies. There is particular attention given to assisting clients with restructuring their environments to reduce contact with substance use cues and options, and to introduce reinforcement of abstinence (see the section Path to Clear Mind). The added focus on case management in DBT-SUD may include the addition of a case manager as a resource for the individual therapists and/or the clients (Linehan & Dimeff, 1997).

DBT-SUD teams also structure the therapy environment to prevent substance use contagion among the clients by requiring clients to observe rules such as not engaging in secret relationships with other group members, including any sharing of drugs or alcohol. To help ensure a functional skills group environment, clients are directed to avoid appearing to be under the influence of substances during groups as to not trigger others to have cravings, even if they have actually been using.

Enhancing Clinician Capabilities and Motivation

Working with BPD with SUD *butterfly attached* clients who show patterns of missing sessions, falling out of therapy, coming late to sessions, wanting to leave early, and difficulty calling for help can be quite demoralizing for a clinician, and can feel similar to an experience of being rejected repeatedly by someone you are trying to be friends with. Consultation team members, therefore, vigilantly support each other through these trials and tribulations by soothing each other's wounds, celebrating the smallest of discernible indications of progress, and reinforcing each other for going above and beyond in their efforts to engage and re-engage their clients.

Targets

DBT-SUD involves a modified hierarchy of targets that places substance use, specifically, abstinence from the drug of choice, as the top quality-of-life-interfering behaviour. This means that the direct focus on treating SUD falls below the higher priorities of addressing life-threatening behaviours (i.e., suicide, non-suicidal self-injury, and homicide), as well as the next priority of addressing treatment-interfering behaviours (e.g., non-attendance, inaccurate reporting, etc.). As with standard DBT, additional quality-of-life interfering behaviours beyond SUD (e.g., homelessness, behaviours resulting from out-of-control anger, and other clinical problems) are then prioritized based on clinical considerations including the client's preferences, followed by a final target priority of enhancing capabilities (e.g., addressing skills deficits with DBT skills and learning self-management).

Precise targeting of SUD on the treatment hierarchy can become quite complicated when substance use is determined to be life-threatening or treatment-interfering. The general guideline for keeping the treatment hierarchy organized is to maintain a sharp focus on whether the substance use is done with suicidal intent (e.g., intentional overdose, using in order to get the confidence to overdose, or clear ambivalence about potential death by overdose even without clear suicidal intent); the use is done with an intention of bodily harm (e.g., drinking with liver disease in order to hurt the liver further); or if there is medical evidence that any further use creates imminent risk of death (e.g., using cocaine with a severe heart condition), all of which would be consistent with placing that particular topography of substance use on the top tier of the hierarchy, or life-threatening behaviour. Alternatively, if the substance use is non-life-threatening but limits the client's ability to participate in or benefit from treatment (e.g., non-attendance or inability to take in new learning due to intoxication, or further use during legal probation that risks treatment termination due to incarceration), then it would be targeted on the second tier of the hierarchy, or treatment-interfering behaviour. In such cases, it is important to keep in mind that not all use is necessarily targeted the same, so the exact topography of use identified as life threatening or treatment interfering might still be prioritized above any other use, even within the same substance (e.g., drinking as part of a suicide attempt, drinking leading to being too hungover to attend treatment, and drinking that is non-suicidal and that does not directly impact treatment).

Balancing Prioritizing and Blending of Targets

A final indication for targeting substances as life-threatening or treatment-interfering behaviour is when substance use shows up within chains (i.e., behavioural chain analysis) leading to these other higher targets (e.g., drinking leading to shame leading to non-suicidal self-injury). A way to maintain a fairly consistent focus on treating SUD throughout treatment is to attend to a synthesis of *prioritizing* primary targets on the hierarchy (i.e., targeting anything life threatening first), with *blending* of targets on the hierarchy by vigilantly targeting SUD-related vulnerability factors and controlling variables (links) on chains leading to non-SUD primary targets.

Path to Clear Mind

The SUD quality-of-life-interfering target is further subdivided and prioritized in the DBT-SUD treatment hierarchy as a *Path to Clear Mind* (McMain, Sayrs, Dimeff, & Linehan, 2007) that addresses substance use relevant sub-targets in the following order: 1) eliminating active substance use (e.g., soliciting commitment to abstinence and conducting chain analyses and solution analyses on instances of use towards the goal of abstinence); 2) decreasing the physical and emotional discomforts associated with withdrawal and/or that motivate use (e.g., opioid replacement medication; non-opioid pain management); 3) decreasing urges, cravings, and temptations to use (e.g., by employing Distress Tolerance Crisis Survival skills); 4) decreasing the options to use drugs by Burning Bridges to available pathways to use (see Enhancing Client Capabilities), 5) decreasing contact with cues for use, including "apparently irrelevant behaviours," or behaviours that may be superficially safe, but that actually create heightened risk of use (e.g., adopting alternative routes to avoid liquor stores; avoiding music that one knows to be associated with use); and 6) increasing Community Reinforcement of Clear Mind behaviours (see Enhancing Client Capabilities).

STRATEGIC MODIFICATIONS

Case Management Strategies

Standard Model Outpatient DBT includes a dialectical balance of change-focused *Consultation to the Client* strategies that involve helping the client better advocate and influence the various people and systems in their lives, with acceptance-focused *Environmental Intervention* strategies in which the therapist directly communicates with such people and systems to effect needed change. While the former is focused on increasing the client's active coping, problem solving, and assertiveness, the latter accepts the client's limitations in effectiveness and the greater probability of the therapist in effecting change in certain circumstances, particularly in those in which the client clearly does not have the necessary skills and the situation is extremely important and must be acted upon quickly. Standard DBT defaults strongly to the Consultation to the Client position, and places great effort into maximizing the client's direct involvement in those situations in which Environmental Intervention is necessary (e.g., having the client participate in meetings even when the therapist intends to speak on their behalf). While this same dialectic with preference toward Consultation to the Client is applied in DBT-SUD, there tend to be frequent indications for Environmental Intervention that must be accommodated related to substance use and/or common legal involvements. The most basic of these relates to the well-established challenge of individuals with SUDs hiding and/or lying about their use, and the resultant clinical best practice of performing biological drug and alcohol testing such as urine toxicology and breathalyser tests. The therapist places more trust into the drug/alcohol test results (their consultation with the environment) than in the client's report (consultation with the client). As it turns out, there is some indication that the self-reports of individuals receiving DBT-SUD might be more accurate than those receiving alternative treatment (Linehan et al., 2002); however, it is still standard practice in DBT-SUD to obtain regular toxicology screenings to confirm self-report.

The challenges related to unreliable SUD self-reporting also effect the decision-making within the clients' social, work, treatment, and/or legal systems, and again, the stakeholders within each of these domains may require drug/alcohol use monitoring and/or direct communication with the therapists to confirm issues of use and treatment participation. While adult clients may technically have autonomy around their choice of the therapist releasing information to these systems, frequently such systems will leverage power that will control clients' choice requiring them to release the desired information. For example, if a therapist were to indicate that a client had not consented to release information to child protective services, a probation officer, or organizations responsible for clearing individuals wanting to return to work (e.g., recovering medical professionals), such organizations would simply direct the client to provide the therapist with the necessary release. DBT-SUD therapists quickly learn to orient clients to such contingencies, as well as providing assurance that the therapist will inform the client about the information that they provide and will advocate for the client to continue to participate in treatment even in the face of lapses, as clinically indicated.

Responding Strategically to Lying

Individuals struggling with SUDs often become very adept at bending or hiding the truth to support their continued use and avoid consequences. Fortunately, in her identification of common behavioural patterns complicating the work of individuals with BPD, Marsha Linehan identified one pattern characterized by inaccurate communication that lends itself well for formulating and addressing such behaviour. Specifically, Linehan identified that some individuals struggle with an unresolved dialectical dilemma that goes from extremes of an *Actively-Passive* coping style, in which they vigorously refuse or withdraw from needed problem solving efforts—possibly until others step in when they hit rock bottom—to an opposite extreme of presenting a façade of *Apparent Competence* for managing their problems without assistance. The underlying struggle of this dilemma involves these individuals feeling completely overwhelmed and doubting their capacity to face problems independently, while simultaneously feeling utterly hopeless about the possibility of getting others to respond with the help they perceive themselves as needing. As a result, they exhibit marked ambivalence towards actively working on problems and severe deficits in their assertiveness characterized by non-response and inaccuracy. Without a notion that accurate, assertive communication could be well received and effective for getting the help needed, the possibility of the individual acting assertively is not considered or even conceived to be an option. They instead develop habitual and reflexive extreme Active-Passivity and Apparent Competence behaviours, such as quitting efforts to stop using and denying problems with use in the first place.

Formulating patterns of lying by individuals with SUDs within the Active-Passivity/ Apparent Competence framework can help to inform validating and problem-solving interventions, as well as significantly mitigate therapist burnout due to frustration or hopelessness. Key to this formulation is replacing any judgmental or moralistic responses to lying with the phenomenological and benign interpretation that these behaviours are completely understandable when individuals doing the best they can (first patient assumption of DBT; Linehan, 1993, p. 106) have learned that others will be unavailable, uninterested, uncaring, and/or punitive in the face of neediness or failings. As such, clients have learned to avoid making efforts on problem solving in order to prevent the shame of failure, and to prevent others from witnessing their problems and needs in order to protect themselves from disappointment or harsh punishment. It is crucial for therapists to seek consultation as needed to re-establish this formulation in the face of feeling hurt, angry, or confused by such behaviour.

This perspective of lying as an understandable behaviour developed from the expectations and habits of past learning history (classified as Level-4 Validation; Linehan, 1997) can inform specific validating responses. For example, when evidence of lying emerges, the therapist might say, "Listen, you've had years of being punished for not getting your use under control, so it totally makes sense that you've learned to hide it." Equally important is carefully assessing and acknowledging any legitimate concerns about aversive consequences of honesty in therapy (Level-5 Validation), such as situations in which providing accurate information could negatively affect legal decisions due to the therapist being required to share information about lapses with probation officers, disability determinations, child protective services, divorce proceedings, etc. Commitment to being "on their side" is balanced with openness about the limitations of confidentiality and the inherent dilemma the client faces in telling the truth.

Importantly, these formulations also lend themselves to making compassionate responses to suspected lying in the absence of concrete evidence or divulgence (classified as a Level-3 Validation, or mind-reading; Linehan, 1997; Fruzzetti & Ruork, this volume), a particularly useful strategy for working with Active-Passivity/Apparent Competence presentations. Here the therapist might say something like, "You know, while part of me hopes that what you're saying about staying clean is true, a lot of people who struggle with substance use learn to hide it because they've always been punished or blamed for it, so, I want to make clear that if at some point I learn that you were using and didn't feel like you could say so, I'll totally understand and it won't change my interest in wanting to help you with this." It is essential for the therapist to attend to all sources of information that might help them catch inaccuracies, including the gut feeling that something is "off" with the client's account (the source of which might later be behaviourally operationalized). An advantage of DBT-style mindreading over a more confrontational approach is that the therapist minimizes conflict by sharing their understanding as a hypothesis, without insisting that their hunch must be correct. At the same time, the therapist can openly assert an acceptance to not knowing the truth in these situations, rather than communicating agreement with the client's initial report or joining in rejecting the therapist's hypothesis and potentially colluding with inaccuracy. When reviewing the client's account for potential inaccuracy either during sessions or in reviewing them after the fact, therapists are encouraged to be vigilant for client explanations that are superficially plausible and may, in fact, be true, but that are nonetheless non-causal and do not seem to fully account for the behaviours under question.

With this level of acceptance of potential inaccuracy communicated by the therapist—and without even being asked to confirm what is or isn't true—many clients who struggle with honest reporting often respond by revealing themselves with more accurate communication, if not immediately, over time. It is actually preferable to avoid directly asking clients if they are telling the truth or to confirm that a validating statement about their lying is correct. As with outright accusations of lying, such actions tend to bring up reactance and lead such clients further away from revealing themselves. Whether the client reveals themselves or not, as needed, the therapist must also orient the client to how inaccuracy prevents therapy effectiveness. To the extent that the therapist should label the possibility of therapy being terminated due to this limitation, it is essential to assure the client that such withdrawal of support is done reluctantly and despite the therapist's continued desire to help, and that such a consequence is ultimately under the client's control if they push away the therapist and the treatment. The therapist should carefully balance validating the client's difficulty with openness and honesty, with their ownership of the consequences for the behaviour—including that they are distancing themselves from the support that individuals with this dialectical struggle tend to be desperate for—and counteracting any perceived experience of judgment and rejection by the therapist.

As soon as the therapist sees evidence of their validation "landing" with the client, including some acknowledgement of the inaccuracy, they actively proceed towards establishing commitment and collaboration on targeting this problem behaviour, including establishing shared non-judgmental language for the behaviour (e.g., "hiding," "withholding," "glossing over," etc.), careful monitoring of lies by omission or commission on the diary card, chain analysis of incidents, and attending to inaccurate communication as an expected secondary target on other primary target chains.

Implementation Challenges

Challenges involved with implementing DBT-SUD include synthesizing standard SUD interventions into a DBT framework and managing common complications of treating individuals with SUD. Several SUD treatment interventions that have some dialectical tension with DBT include opioid replacement medications (the DBT commitment to incorporate empirically supported interventions vs. the DBT preference for "skills over pills" active coping self-management); toxicology screenings (DBT prefers to work with the subjective self-report vs. accepting the reality of difficulties with lying); and, at least in the United States, working alongside a 12-step treatment philosophy that is a major source of support for many SUD treatment-seeking individuals and dominates many institutions that work with SUDs including residential rehabilitation facilities and legal systems.

Replacement Medications

DBT-SUD recommends using replacement medications for treating withdrawal symptoms and for facilitating abstinence from illicit medications. Opioid agonist medications such as methadone and buprenorphine are encouraged in DBT-SUD, given their "overwhelming" support for treating opioid addiction (Linehan et al., 2002; NIH Consensus Conference, 1998). Research has continued to accumulate supporting the efficacy of opioid agonist treatments with outcomes such as reduced crime-related costs (Krebs et al., 2016), improved quality of life (Nosyk et al., 2015), reduced rates of opioid overdose (Schwartz et al., 2013), and long-term survival, treatment retention, and reduced psychiatric symptoms (Soyka, Strehle, Rehm, Bühringer, & Wittchen, 2017). Stimulant agonist treatment was also incorporated in the first DBT-SUD trial (Linehan et al., 1999); however, the efficacy of stimulant agonists is still being determined (Stoops & Rush, 2012) and has not been included in other DBT-SUD studies to date. General guidelines for integrating psychopharmacology into DBT that apply to agonist treatments include: that medications be adjunctive to the primary DBT intervention; that medications be selected to treat specific symptoms without undue side effects that might interfere with psychosocial therapy (e.g., that significantly limit attention or concentration beyond a titration period); and that efforts be made to keep prescribing parsimonious and limit polypharmacy (Dimeff, McDavid, & Linehan, 1999).

The logistics of opioid replacement prescribing often involve challenges beyond standard psychopharmacology due to clinician attitudes, controlling legislation, and public policies which may be complicated by misconceptions about efficacy, stigma about addiction, and/or moral concerns about providing drugs with abuse potential. For example, clinicians with less exposure to opioid replacement treatment tend to be less open to incorporating them (Rieckmann, Daley, Fuller, Thomas, & McCarty, 2007). In the United States, federal regulations limit methadone prescribing and access to opioid treatment centres, which are predominantly located in urban areas, and regulations limit the buprenorphine prescribing only to physicians who have completed an approved course or are board certified in addiction medicine or addiction psychiatry. Such limitations contribute to the wide gaps between the availability of opioid replacement treatment and the prevalence of those needing such services (Jones, Campopiano, Baldwin, & McCance-Katz, 2015). While there are some trends in the United States toward increasing opioid agonist treatment availability including an increased number of states incorporating public insurance (Medicaid) policies covering agonist treatment (Burns et al., 2016) and an increase in the maximum number of buprenorphine patients physicians may carry at a time (from 30 to 100; Stein et al., 2015); there have also been new barriers introduced, such as added co-pay and pre-authorization insurance requirements (Burns et al., 2016). A variety of access barriers have been identified in the regulations of Eastern European countries, including consistently stigmatizing language (Vranken et al., 2017), while greater variability has been observed in the regulations controlling opioid agonist treatments in Western European countries (Brandt, Unger, Moser, Fischer, & Jagsch, 2016).

Finally, while opioid replacement therapies have very well established empirical support, significant questions remain for how to best maximize their effectiveness, such as the choice of prescribing methadone vs. buprenorphine, and how to accommodate individuals with comorbid psychiatric disorders or who abuse multiple substances (Alho et al., 2014). Some of the lingering questions identified by Alho and colleagues (2014) on these prescribing practices are reflected in the different methodologies of past DBT-SUD, such as the relative effectiveness of tapering patients off replacement medications (e.g., Linehan et al., 1999), using antagonist opioid medications such as naltrexone (e.g., Axelrod et al., 2011), or continuing patients on maintenance agonist medication (e.g., Linehan et al., 2002).

Ancillary 12-Step Participation

Because Marsha Linehan originally under-appreciated the active treatment components of 12-step support groups, she included 12-step as part of a non-active control condition for a DBT-SUD randomized controlled trial (Linehan et al., 2002). However, when she obtained findings showing DBT-SUD and the control condition had fairly equivalent positive results, she became impressed with the large overlap between many aspects of DBT and 12-step to the point of calling them "twin daughters of distant mothers." For example, DBT's central dialectic of acceptance and change is captured by the 12-step serenity prayer, and 12-step interventions involve skills building to manage urges and problematic thinking, as well as a strong focus on restructuring individuals' environments. On the other hand, there are some points of divergence between the two approaches. Specifically, 12-step programmes view addiction as a disease and require individuals in recovery to accept themselves as flawed, while DBT's behaviourism and Zen philosophy attempts to help individuals see their problems as completely understandable learned behaviours given their histories and skills deficits, and to honour themselves as perfect as they are while also mastering more effective behaviours. Ultimately, it is useful for DBT providers to become knowledgeable of 12-step language in order to help translate and support clients' 12-step work, and to adopt a dialectical philosophy looking to accept the kernels of truth and wisdom within any contradictory positions and support clients' agency in determining their Wise Mind resolutions. In practice, these treatment approaches can be successfully integrated (e.g., Beckstead, Lambert, DuBose, & Linehan, 2015).

Medications with Abuse Potential

There are several other clinical issues that may require thought in the implementation of DBT-SUD, particularly for clinicians that are less experienced working with SUD populations. For example, policies and procedures are helpful for responding to those clients prescribed medications with abuse potential such as those treated for acute or chronic pain who may be prescribed opioids, or more recently in the United States, cannabis. While programmatic restrictions might be applied to limit such prescribing, exceptional cases are likely to emerge offering new dialectics to consider (e.g., a patient prescribed a benzodiazepine controlling a seizure condition).

Case Management

Struggles with untenable living situations are also more common in DBT-SUD, including living with a substance-using partner, in drug-infested neighbourhoods, in homeless shelters or "sober" houses in which there is widespread substance use, or outright homelessness. While it may be possible, using commitment and attachment strategies, to engage many individuals in a productive outpatient DBT-SUD despite such challenges, clinicians should be open to acknowledging failure if it becomes apparent that the best DBT-SUD efforts were unable to effect change under such circumstances with given clients. In such situations, clinicians should carefully apply the DBT vacation protocol (Linehan, 1993, pp. 310–312) and stop treatment until the apparent environmental obstacles to treatment have been resolved, such as obtaining stable housing. If this is enacted, referrals to alternative treatments should be offered, such as a residential drug-rehabilitation programme.

Substance Use Contagion

Challenges related to the potential contagion of problem behaviours among clients are avoided in standard DBT with established guidelines (Linehan, 2015). It is necessary to ensure that DBT-SUD clients are specifically orientated that the standard guideline prohibiting "secret relationships" includes any sharing or selling of medications or substances. Such behaviour can quickly become therapy destroying; therefore, policies and procedures should be considered, such as a pre-defined programme suspension/vacation for individuals involved with giving or receiving substances or with using substances together.

RESEARCH EVIDENCE

Randomized Controlled Trials for BPD with SUD

With six randomized controlled trials (RCTs) supporting it, DBT is a recognized leading treatment for co-occurring BPD and SUD (Lee, Cameron, & Jenner, 2015; Substance Abuse and Mental Health Services Administration, 2014). RCTs have supported DBT-SUD for reducing substance use relative to treatment as usual (TAU; Linehan et al., 1999) and for reducing use in a way that was comparable to somewhat stronger when compared with manualized SUD treatments (Linehan et al., 2002; Linehan, Lynch, Harned, Korslund, & Rosenthal, 2009) or non-manualized dual-diagnosis treatment (McMain et al., 2004). Although most of these studies were limited to treating women, one included men and women (Linehan et al., 2009). Two additional RCTs found standard DBT (without SUD modifications) to outperform TAU and treatment by experts in the substance use outcomes for outpatients with BPD with and without co-occurring SUDs (Harned et al., 2008; van den Bosch, Verheul, Schippers, & van den Brink, 2002). Remarkably, Harned and colleagues (2008) found that 87.5% of those with substance dependence who received standard DBT achieved full remission for at least four weeks, as compared to only 33.3% of those who received comparison treatment by non-behavioural experts. On the other hand, several of these studies had mixed results for their substance use outcomes. For example, two of the studies found reductions in alcohol use, but not in use of other substances (McMain et al., 2004; van den Bosch et al., 2002; van den Bosch, Koeter, Stijnen, Verheul, & van den Brink, 2005), and one multi-site study targeting opioid dependence found DBT-SUD to outperform the comparison manualized treatment for cocaine use (as well as HIV-related risk behaviours), but not to outperform the comparison treatment for opioid use (both improved; Linehan et al., 2009). DBT-SUD has also had mixed results for treatment retention, with RCTs showing higher retention than TAU (Linehan et al., 1999), but equivalent (Linehan et al., 2009) or even lower retention than some comparison manualized treatments (Linehan et al., 2002).

Dialectical Behaviour Therapy for SUD without BPD

While DBT-SUD could be an effective intervention for SUD without BPD, it might not be advantageous in comparison to other empirically supported SUD treatments that tend to be more straightforward and less resource intensive to implement (Dimeff & Linehan, 2008). Also, the focus on chronic emotional dysregulation as the underlying pathology driving the substance use in DBT-SUD, supported as its mechanism of change (Axelrod, Perepletchikova, Holtzman, & Sinha, 2011), might not be broadly applicable to individuals with SUD in the absence of BPD. On the other hand, DBT-SUD could be justified for individuals with SUD and other co-occurring disorders marked by emotional dysregulation, such as eating disorders. One RCT applied to co-occurring SUD and eating disorders found DBT-SUD to have significantly better treatment retention (to the point that the control condition recruitment was stopped), and was supported by significant reductions in both eating disorder symptoms and drug use, but not alcohol use (Courbasson, Nishikawa, & Dixon, 2012).

DBT-SUD might also prove beneficial for targeting substance use within other hard-to-treat and under-served populations. Nyamathi and colleagues (2017) conducted a multisite RCT of a brief DBT-SUD case management (DBT-CM) intervention for recently incarcerated homeless women with substance use histories. DBT-CM was composed of six group sessions emphasizing the DCBA skills and six individual sessions that included diary card review and chain analysis of substance use targets. In comparison to a Health Promotion control treatment, women who received DBT-CM were more likely to initiate abstinence from drugs and alcohol during the intervention period and they were more likely to be abstinent of drugs and alcohol at six-month follow-up. DBT-SUD has also been applied to primary SUD in a large treatment-outcome study with an under-served group that faces a variety of treatment challenges, Native American/Alaskan Native adolescents (Beckstead et al., 2015). Although this study had no comparison group, 96% of the adolescents had either recovered or improved substance use status.

Culture and Diversity in DBT-SUD Research

While most of the earlier investigations supporting DBT for SUD involved Causian women in the United States or Europe (e.g., Harned et al., 2008; Linehan et al., 1999; Linehan et al., 2002; van den Bosch et al., 2002), some more recent investigations have extended its support to new groups including men in the United States (Linehan et al., 2009); men and women in Egypt (Abdelkarim, Molokhia, Rady, & Ivanoff, 2017); men in Iran (Azizi, Borjali, & Golzari, 2010); forensically-involved and homeless African American and Latina women (Nyamathi et al., 2017); and Native American/Alaskan Native adolescent boys and girls (Beckstead et al., 2015). This last study is noteworthy for its cultural adaptation of DBT-SUD that included the involvement of a medicine man/spiritual counsellor who led the adolescents in traditional Native practices and related these practices to their DBT mindfulness instruction. Taken together these studies show that DBT-SUD has potential efficacy for benefting a wide variety of individuals and groups.

Conclusion

DBT-SUD is a well-developed, research-supported extension of the original DBT model that includes skills, strategies, and formulations to address problems of addiction and related complications such as treatment engagement. Furthermore, the dialectical framework of DBT-SUD can flexibly incorporate best addiction treatment practices such as drug replacement therapies and toxicology screenings, and common addictions supports such as 12-step participation. Specific guidance is provided to help clinicians understand and address lying behaviour in a DBT-consistent way. Clinicians already providing DBT for individuals with BPD will undoubtedly encounter SUD presentations, and would therefore benefit from integrating the DBT-SUD modifications into their repertoire, if not developing DBT-SUD programmes within their practice settings. Moreover, as indicated in her revised DBT skills manual (2015), Marsha Linehan recommends applying the DBT-SUD skill package for mastering any non-substance use ineffective habits or "addictions" (e.g., internet use, shopping, etc.), making them relevant for all DBT target populations.

KEY MESSAGES FOR CLINICIANS

- Co-occurring Borderline Personality Disorder (BPD) and Substance Use Disorders (SUD) are associated with higher risk behaviours and with greater treatment engagement challenges than either independently.

- DBT adapted for SUDs includes all aspects of the standard model of DBT for BPD with added formulations, strategies, and skills for addressing problems of addiction.

- DBT-SUD includes attachment strategies to help prevent individuals with BPD and SUDs from "falling out of treatment."

- DBT-SUD addresses the challenges involved with structuring clients' living environments and the treatment environment with a re-balancing of the Consultation to the Client and Intervening in the Environment DBT case management strategies.

- A modified primary target treatment hierarchy helps provide an integrated treatment of BPD and SUD related problem behaviours.

- The Active Passivity vs. Apparent Competency dialectical dilemma formulation and related secondary targets of passive coping and inaccurate communication are particularly useful for maintaining phenomenological empathy and responding strategically to lying, a common challenge in SUD presentations.

- Implementation challenges of DBT-SUD involve synthesizing standard DBT principles and strategies with SUD treatment best practices such as opioid replacement medications, and addressing common complications of individuals struggling with SUDs such as severe life chaos and the potential for SUD contagion among clients.

- Several RCTs provide at least modest to moderate support of DBT with and without SUD modifications for co-occurring BPD and SUD. Preliminary evidence extends DBT-SUD effectiveness to new populations including co-occurring SUD and eating disorders and primary substance use disorders, and to diverse ethnic, linguistic, and geographic settings.

REFERENCES

Abdelkarim, A., Molokhia, T., Rady, A., & Ivanoff, A. (2017). DBT for co-morbid borderline personality disorder and substance use disorder without drug replacement in Egyptian outpatient settings: A non-randomized trial. *European Psychiatry, 41*, S260–S261.

Agrawal, A., & Lynskey, M. T. (2006). The genetic epidemiology of cannabis use, abuse and dependence. *Addiction, 101*(6), 801–812.

Alho, H., Fischer, G., Torrens, M., Maremmani, I., Ali, R., & Clark, N. (2014). Guidelines in the treatment of opiate addiction: a review and recommendation. *Heroin Addiction and Related Clinical Problems, 16*(4), 33–39.

Anokhina, I. P., Veretinskaya, A. G., Vasil'eva, G. N., & Ovchinnikov, I. V. (2000). Homogeneity of the biological mechanisms of individual predispositions to the abuse of various psychoactive substances. *Human Physiology, 26*(6), 715–721.

Axelrod, S. R., Perepletchikova, F., Holtzman, K., & Sinha, R. (2011). Emotion regulation and substance use frequency in women with substance dependence and borderline personality disorder receiving dialectical behavior therapy. *American Journal of Drug and Alcohol Abuse, 37*(1), 37–42.

Azizi, A., Borjali, A., & Golzari, M. (2010). The effectiveness of emotion regulation training and cognitive therapy on the emotional and addictional problems of substance abusers. *Iranian Journal of Psychiatry, 5*(2), 60.

Beckstead, D. J., Lambert, M. J., DuBose, A. P., & Linehan, M. (2015). Dialectical behavior therapy with American Indian/Alaska Native adolescents diagnosed with substance use disorders: Combining an evidence based treatment with cultural, traditional, and spiritual beliefs. *Addictive Behaviors, 51*, 84–87.

Bornovalova, M. A., Lejuez, C. W., Daughters, S. B., Rosenthal, M. Z., & Lynch, T. R. (2005). Impulsivity as a common process across borderline personality and substance use disorders. *Clinical Psychology Review, 25*(6), 790–812.

Brandt, L., Unger, A., Moser, L., Fischer, G., & Jagsch, R. (2016). Opioid maintenance treatment—a call for a joint European quality care approach. *European Addiction Research, 22*(1), 36–51.

Burns, R. M., Pacula, R. L., Bauhoff, S., Gordon, A. J., Hendrikson, H., Leslie, D. L., & Stein, B. D. (2016). Policies related to opioid agonist therapy for opioid use disorders: the evolution of state policies from 2004 to 2013. *Substance Abuse, 37*(1), 63–69.

Courbasson, C., Nishikawa, Y., & Dixon, L. (2012). Outcome of dialectical behavior therapy for concurrent eating and substance use disorders. *Clinical Psychology & Psychotherapy, 19*(5), 434–449.

Crowell, S. E., Beauchaine, T. P., & Linehan, M. M. (2009). A biosocial developmental model of borderline personality: Elaborating and extending Linehan's theory. *Psychological Bulletin*, *135*(3), 495.

Dimeff, L. A., & Linehan, M. M. (2008). Dialectical behavior therapy for substance abusers. *Addiction Science & Clinical Practice*, *4*(2), 39–47.

Dimeff, L. A., McDavid, J., & Linehan, M. M. (1999). Pharmacotherapy for borderline personality disorder: a review of the literature and recommendations for treatment. *Journal of Clinical Psychology in Medical Settings*, *6*(1), 113–138.

Hahn, A. M., Simons, R. M., & Hahn, C. K. (2016). Five factors of impulsivity: Unique pathways to borderline and antisocial personality features and subsequent alcohol problems. *Personality and Individual Differences*, *99*, 313–319.

Harned, M. S., Chapman, A. L., Dexter-Mazza, E. T., Murray, A., Comtois, K. A., & Linehan, M. M. (2008). Treating co-occurring Axis I disorders in recurrently suicidal women with borderline personality disorder: A 2-year randomized trial of dialectical behavior therapy versus community treatment by experts. *Journal of Consulting and Clinical Psychology*, *76*(6), 1068.

Heitzeg, M. M., Cope, L. M., Martz, M. E., & Hardee, J. E. (2015). Neuroimaging risk markers for substance abuse: recent findings on inhibitory control and reward system functioning. *Current Addiction Reports*, *2*(2), 91–103.

Johnson, B. N., Ashe, M. L., & Wilson, S. J. (2016). Self-control capacity as a predictor of borderline personality disorder features, problematic drinking, and their co-occurrence. *Journal of Personality Disorders*, *31*(3), 1–17.

Jones, C. M., Campopiano, M., Baldwin, G., & McCance-Katz, E. (2015). National and state treatment need and capacity for opioid agonist medication-assisted treatment. *American Journal of Public Health*, *105*(8), e55–e63.

Krebs, E., Urada, D., Evans, E., Huang, D., Hser, Y. I., & Nosyk, B. (2016). The costs of crime during and after publicly-funded treatment for opioid use disorders: a population-level study for the state of California. *Addiction*, *112*(5), 838–851.

Lee, N. K., Cameron, J., & Jenner, L. (2015). A systematic review of interventions for co-occurring substance use and borderline personality disorders. *Drug and Alcohol Review*, *34*(6), 663–672.

Linehan, M. M. (1993). *Cognitive behavioral therapy of borderline personality disorder* (Vol. 51). New York, NY: Guilford Press.

Linehan, M. M. (1997). Validation and psychotherapy. In A. C. Bohart & L. S. Greenberg (Eds.), *Empathy reconsidered: New directions in psychotherapy* (pp. 353–392). Arlington, VA: APA Publishing.

Linehan, M. M., Armstrong, H. E., Allmon, D., & Heard, H. L. (1991). Cognitive-behavioral treatment of chronically parasuicidal borderline patients. *Archives of General Psychiatry*, *48*(12), 1060–1064.

Linehan, M. M., & Dimeff, L. A. (1997). *Dialectical behavior therapy for substance abuse treatment manual*. University of Washington, Seattle, WA.

Linehan, M. M. (2015). *DBT® skills training manual*, 2nd Edition. New York, NY: Guilford Press.

Linehan, M. M., Schmidt, H., Dimeff, L. A., Craft, J. C., Kanter, J., & Comtois, K. A. (1999). Dialectical behavior therapy for patients with borderline personality disorder and drug-dependence. *The American Journal on Addictions*, *8*(4), 279–292.

Linehan, M. M., Dimeff, L. A., Reynolds, S. K., Comtois, K. A., Welch, S. S., Heagerty, P., & Kivlahan, D. R. (2002). Dialectical behavior therapy versus comprehensive validation therapy plus 12-step for the treatment of opioid dependent women meeting criteria for borderline personality disorder. *Drug and Alcohol Dependence, 67*(1), 13–26.

Linehan, M. M., Lynch, T. R., Harned, M. S., Korslund, K. E., & Rosenthal, Z. M. (November, 2009). Preliminary outcomes of a randomized controlled trial of DBT vs. drug counseling for opiate-dependent BPD men and women. Presented at the 43rd Annual Convention of the Association for Behavior and Cognitive Therapies, New York, NY.

Marlatt, G. A. (1985). Cognitive assessment and intervention procedures for relapse prevention. In G. A. Marlatt & J. R. Gordon (Eds.), *Relapse prevention: Maintenance strategies in treatment of addictive behaviors* (pp. 201–279). New York, NY: Guilford Press.

McMain, S., Korman, L., Blak, T., Dimeff, L., Collis, R., & Beadnell, B. (2004). Dialectical behavior therapy for substance users with borderline personality disorder: A randomized controlled trial in Canada [Presentation]. In *New Orleans: Association for the Advancement of Behavior Therapy Annual Meeting.*

McMain, S., Sayrs, J. H., Dimeff, L. A., & Linehan, M. M. (2007). Dialectical behavior therapy for individuals with borderline personality disorder and substance dependence. In L. Dimeff & K. Koerner (Eds.), *Dialectical behavior therapy in clinical practice* (pp. 145–173). New York, NY: Guilford Press.

Milaniak, I., Watson, B., & Jaffee, S. R. (2015). Gene-environment interplay and substance use: A review of recent findings. *Current Addiction Reports, 2*(4), 364–371.

Nyamathi, A. M., Shin, S. S., Smeltzer, J., Salem, B. E., Yadav, K., Ekstrand, M. L., . . . Faucette, M. (2017). Achieving drug and alcohol abstinence among recently incarcerated homeless women: A randomized controlled trial comparing dialectical behavioral therapy-case management with a health promotion program. *Nursing Research, 66*(6), 432–441.

NIH Consensus Conference 1998. Effective medical treatment of opiate addiction. *Journal of the American Medical Association, 280*, 1936–1943.

Nosyk, B., Bray, J. W., Wittenberg, E., Aden, B., Eggman, A. A., Weiss, R. D., . . . Schackman, B. R. (2015). Short term health-related quality of life improvement during opioid agonist treatment. *Drug and Alcohol Dependence, 157*, 121–128.

Rhodes, T., Lilly, R., Fernández, C., Giorgino, E., Kemmesis, U. E., Ossebaard, H. C., . . . Spannow, K. E. (2003). Risk factors associated with drug use: the importance of "risk environment". *Drugs: Education, Prevention and Policy, 10*(4), 303–329.

Rieckmann, T., Daley, M., Fuller, B. E., Thomas, C. P., & McCarty, D. (2007). Client and counselor attitudes toward the use of medications for treatment of opioid dependence. *Journal of Substance Abuse Treatment, 32*(2), 207–215.

Rosenbaum, D. P. (2007). Just say no to DARE. *Criminology & Public Policy, 6*(4), 815–824.

Schwartz, R. P., Gryczynski, J., O'Grady, K. E., Sharfstein, J. M., Warren, G., Olsen, Y., . . . Jaffe, J. H. (2013). Opioid agonist treatments and heroin overdose deaths in Baltimore, Maryland, 1995–2009. *American Journal of Public Health, 103*(5), 917–922.

Soyka, M., Strehle, J., Rehm, J., Bühringer, G., & Wittchen, H. U. (2017). Six-year outcome of opioid maintenance treatment in heroin-dependent patients: Results from a naturalistic study in a nationally representative sample. *European Addiction Research, 23*(2), 97–105.

Stein, B. D., Pacula, R. L., Gordon, A. J., Burns, R. M., Leslie, D. L., Sorbero, M. J., . . . Dick, A. W. (2015). Where is buprenorphine dispensed to treat opioid use disorders? The role of private offices, opioid treatment programs, and substance abuse treatment facilities in urban and rural counties. *Milbank Quarterly, 93*(3), 561–583.

Stoops, W. W., & Rush, C. R. (2012). Agonist replacement for stimulant dependence: a review of clinical research. *Current Pharmaceutical Design, 19*(40), 7026–7035.

Substance Abuse and Mental Health Services Administration. (2014). An introduction to co-occurring borderline personality disorder and substance use disorders. *In Brief, 8*(3), 1–8.

Trull, T. J., Sher, K. J., Minks-Brown, C., Durbin, J., & Burr, R. (2000). Borderline personality disorder and substance use disorders: a review and integration. *Clinical Psychology Review, 20*(2), 235e253.

Van Boekel, L. C., Brouwers, E. P., Van Weeghel, J., & Garretsen, H. F. (2013). Stigma among health professionals towards patients with substance use disorders and its consequences for healthcare delivery: systematic review. *Drug and Alcohol Dependence, 131*(1), 23–35.

van den Bosch, L. M., Verheul, R., Schippers, G. M., & van den Brink, W. (2002). Dialectical behavior therapy of borderline patients with and without substance use problems: Implementation and long-term effects. *Addictive Behaviors, 27*(6), 911–923.

van den Bosch, L. M., Koeter, M. W., Stijnen, T., Verheul, R., & van den Brink, W. (2005). Sustained efficacy of dialectical behaviour therapy for borderline personality disorder. *Behaviour Research and Therapy, 43*(9), 1231–1241.

Verhulst, B., Neale, M. C., & Kendler, K. S. (2015). The heritability of alcohol use disorders: a meta-analysis of twin and adoption studies. *Psychological Medicine, 45*(05), 1061–1072.

Vranken, M. J., Mantel-Teeuwisse, A. K., Jünger, S., Radbruch, L., Scholten, W., Lisman, J. A., … Schutjens, M. H. D. (2017). Barriers to access to opioid medicines for patients with opioid dependence: a review of legislation and regulations in eleven central and eastern European countries. *Addiction, 112*(6), 1069–1076.

CHAPTER 28

DBT IN FORENSIC SETTINGS

ANDRÉ IVANOFF AND PHILLIP L. MAROTTA

Soon after DBT expanded from standard outpatient settings into psychiatric inpatient units, DBT for incarcerated or mandated individuals became a popular application. As early as 1995, Rampton and Broadmoor Secure Forensic Hospitals in the UK and Echo Glen Children's Center of the Washington State Juvenile Rehabilitation Administration sought training and began implementing DBT. The compassionate stance of DBT, along with the fact that DBT was originally designed to treat individuals possessing many of the problems common among justice-involved populations, fuelled this popularity. Although many programmes focused on the most difficult-to-treat mentally disordered individuals, applications introduced into general correctional programming offer pioneering examples of DBT applied to "non-clinical" populations and treatment targets.

This chapter focuses on DBT carried out in "forensic" settings, including residential settings such as detention centres, jails, and prisons, as well as forensic hospitals and outpatient settings where individuals participate in legally mandated interventions, either as a part of their judicial judgment or to avoid incarceration. The goal may be restoring mental health or reducing aggressive behaviour and recidivism. In short, if you've come in the front door as a result of legal action, your treatment is forensic. Finer distinctions are made as needed when describing individual studies.

First, the chapter reviews why DBT is a desirable treatment for individuals in forensic settings. To some providers, DBT's use is logical because it treats learning deficits with skills and offers a compassionate view of severe behavioural disorder. Additionally, however, this chapter also discusses theoretical, nosological, and practical bases for this extension, including compatibility with risk-need-responsivity principles from the criminal justice literature and forensic-specific treatment targets. An international review of applications describes populations treated, DBT elements, and their dosage/titration, along with identified adaptations, design, and outcomes. Next is a brief chronology of the DBT–forensic landscape that lays bare the challenges and obstacles and the modifications and adaptations used to address them. Our plan is to provide both data and practical information to programme administrators, evaluators, clinicians, and line staff using DBT principles and practices in forensic settings.

THE APPEAL OF DBT AS A FORENSIC INTERVENTION

Ashleigh L., 21, had been in jail three times since she was 15, the first two incarcerations related to minor drug trafficking charges and the most recent to a robbery charge. She sustained back injuries in a gang-related fight at 16 and started using opioids at 17. Inside jail, she reports daily headaches and is irritable, sometimes picking fights and frequently infracting, receiving additional charges related to violence. She was sent to the Intensive Treatment Unit (ITU) where the correctional counsellors and clinicians conduct daily DBT skills groups across all four modules, use DBT language, and encourage the women to create posters and signage describing skills and their use. Individuals meet with clinicians weekly. Correctional officers were offered training in DBT skills and wear belt rings of skills cards to assist in coaching the women through difficult or crisis moments on the unit. Although they are quick to denounce playing a "clinical" role, some describe the programme as making their jobs a bit easier.

DBT holds broad appeal as programming in forensic settings for several reasons. First, clients in these settings frequently suffer from emotion regulation problems that are often related to the activities that prompted legal action. Second, these settings and the events of daily life while living in these settings can create crises of their own; further emotional dysregulation is common in highly restrictive settings. Third, and not to be understated, suicidal and other crisis/egregious behaviours consume costly resources. Current methods limited to managing, rather than treating, these behaviours prevent the use of newer behavioural technologies that actually reduce crisis and its costs. Finally, in working with individuals who reside in correctional and forensic settings, it is evident that they lack fundamental life skills needed to function in the free world. Self-management, the ability to problem-solve and self-correct, is often lacking. Identifiable transactions between individual vulnerabilities and environmental obstacles propel individual lives towards incarceration (cf. Dodge & Pettit, 2003). Once inside the system, the cycle can become self-perpetuating and increasingly difficult to escape. DBT offers hope to both clinicians and their service recipients in recognizing these pathways, and in identifying teachable skills with the potential to improve functioning now and into the future (California Department of Corrections and Rehabilitation, 2005; Leschied, 2011).

THE RATIONALE FOR DBT IN FORENSIC SETTINGS

There are multiple rationales provided for the use of DBT in forensic settings. They include:

1) the comorbidity of borderline personality disorder (BPD) and antisocial personality disorder (ASPD);

2) the applicability of the biosocial theory to characteristics of forensically involved individuals;

3) that DBT addresses the top dynamic risk factors associated with criminal behaviour and fits within a risk-need-responsivity framework; and

4) the risk-need-responsivity model forms the basis for evidence-based assessment and practice in corrections, and onto which DBT clearly maps.

A discussion of each rationale is to follow.

Comorbidity of BPD and ASPD

In forensic mental health settings, the comorbidity between BPD and ASPD supports the use of DBT as an appropriate intervention for this population. Although DBT focuses more on behaviour than on diagnostic criteria (and indeed, DBT only became identified with BPD at the insistence of early funders), its wide acceptance as a treatment for BPD encourages examination of multiple comorbidities associated with BPD—in this case, ASPD. The costs of both disorders represent major public health problems for both justice and healthcare systems. ASPD is historically cited as affecting up to 50% of those incarcerated (Teplin, 1994).

Overlap of diagnostic symptoms and clinical presentation include emotional lability, elevated rates of depression and suicide, trait impulsivity, and higher rates of childhood abuse/neglect (Paris, 1997). There is variable, but documented, comorbidity in general population (Grant et al., 2008) and clinical samples (Howard, Huband, Duggan, & Mannion, 2008; Tadić et al., 2009) and in forensic population samples (Grant et al., 2008). A review examining the comorbidity between BPD and ASPD found that the comorbidity of BPD and ASPD is enhanced in the general population relative to expected levels. Unfortunately, it was not possible to identify which symptoms were most prevalent, or whether anger and impulsivity (the shared symptoms) alone were responsible for the comorbidity (Ivanoff & Heyes, 2010). Clinicians in forensic settings describe generally high correspondence between presentations of BPD and ASPD.

Beauchaine and colleagues (2009) propose a common model of antisocial and borderline personality development that takes into account biological and environment influences, placing special emphasis on genes that are implicated in the expression of impulsivity, aggression, anxiety, or depression. The advantage of studies like that of Beauchaine and colleagues (2009) that identify transactional pathways to BPD and ASPD is the development of interventions that target the causal processes directly.

Significantly, for this chapter, personality disorders are frequently omitted from discussions on the interactions between mental disorders and crime. Reasons for this include the fact that personality disorders are controversial, rarely considered in the cases of criminal responsibility, e.g., ASPD, and difficult to distinguish from general predispositions toward criminal behaviour (Peterson, Skeem, Kennealy, Bray, & Zvonkovic, 2014). Including discussion of personality disorders varies widely between countries, however, with personality disorders given consideration in mental capacity cases in the UK, Germany, Belgium, and the Netherlands, but never in the US or Sweden. Psychotic symptoms, clearer and less controversial, do not encounter these differences.

Ashleigh was diagnosed with conduct disorder at age 14½ and as suffering from bi-polar disorder at 17. Although not formally diagnosed, she shares several common and distinct characteristics of BPD and ASPD (NB: since diagnosing ASPD inside a correctional facility is often regarded as invalid, no efforts were made to clarify diagnosis). Her clinical picture was complicated given her ongoing medical problems and substance dependence. Although she denies wanting to die, she has several reported instances of hopeless "I don't care" drug use, most recently after being physically abused and abandoned on the street by her boyfriend. In jail, she presents behaviourally as similar to the majority of the women: wary, tough talking, with tired eyes and omnipresent hopelessness. She emotionally dysregulates easily, often later saying, "I don't know why that happened."

Extension of Biosocial Theory to Antisocial Behaviour

Linehan (1993a) used a biosocial theory to model the underlying mechanisms that lead to the development of BPD. She proposed that BPD is the product of extensive transactional influences between biological emotional vulnerabilities, deficits in emotion regulation, and environmental invalidation (Linehan, 1993a). Emotional vulnerabilities include emotional sensitivity, emotional intensity, and prolonged return to emotional baseline, while the deficits in emotion regulation are primarily characterized as an under-regulation of emotions. When such emotional vulnerabilities and deficits are coupled with external invalidation of the individual's private experience, dysfunctional consequences often follow. As a result, these individuals may not develop the ability to trust their own private experience, label emotions correctly, or modulate emotional reactions. This, in turn, can lead to further invalidation from the environment in response to the individual's reaction, perpetuating a cycle that reinforces dysfunctional behaviour.

The biosocial theory was not only developed as a method of understanding the developmental psychopathology of BPD, but it also served as a framework for the development of therapeutic strategies (Crowell, Beauchaine, & Linehan, 2009). These strategies serve as the basis for DBT and are key components in the treatments of a variety of different clinical populations, including those in forensic settings.

Those applying DBT with forensic clients (Kletzka, Lachat, Echols, & Witterholt, 2014; Marotta, Ivanoff, Terrell, Perez, & Nathanson, 2012; McCann, Ball, & Ivanoff, 2000; McCann, Ivanoff, Schmidt, & Beach, 2007; Rosenfeld et al., 2007; Sampl, Wakai, & Trestman, 2010; Shelton, Kesten, Zang, & Trestman, 2011; Shelton, Sampl, Kesten, Zang, & Trestman, 2009; Trupin, Stewart, Beach, & Boesky, 2002) extend the biosocial theory Linehan uses, hypothesizing that individuals who engage in antisocial behaviour may fall into two general subtypes: (i) emotionally sensitive, and (ii) emotionally insensitive. The first subtype generally corresponds to the original biosocial model (Linehan, 1993a), in which emotionally sensitive individuals are characterized by an elevated baseline of negative affectivity, decreased ability to tolerate intense emotions, intense emotional reactions, and prolonged return to baseline once emotional arousal is experienced. In contrast, the emotional vulnerability factor for the second subtype is an over-regulated emotional insensitivity, corresponding with characteristics such as attenuated physiological arousal (Eysenck, 1977), hypo-responsivity to stress and anxiety (Lykken, 1995), reduced behavioural inhibition (Frick, 1998), deficits in processing emotional stimuli (Hare, 2003), and sensation-seeking behaviours as a means of regulating emotions (Quay, 1977). This type of emotional insensitivity represents an over-regulation of emotions (Galietta & Rosenfeld, 2012; McCann et al., 2000; McCann et al., 2007).

The application of the biosocial theory to individuals with emotionally insensitive vulnerabilities presents a number of parallels to the trajectory of their emotionally sensitive counterparts, but with a few distinctive differences. McCann and colleagues (2007) describe how the transactional relationship between emotional vulnerabilities, emotional insensitivity, in this case, and prolonged exposure to an invalidating environment may contribute to the emergence of antisocial behaviours and disorders such as ASPD. Unlike the emotionally sensitive subtype, which appears more heavily influenced by invalidating environmental factors that range in type and severity, there is evidence suggesting that the emotionally insensitive subtype may be heavily impacted by coercive caregiving methods during childhood (Frick, 2012; Frick & Morris, 2004). Emotionally insensitive individuals may present unique challenges to caregivers as a result of their emotional vulnerabilities. In an attempt to control or deter frequent disruptive behaviour, caregivers may employ insensitive, harsh, or coercive parenting strategies, often being inconsistent and relying heavily on punishment. Emotionally insensitive individuals may respond to these methods by escalating their oppositional behaviour, influencing the caregiver to intensify the coercive strategies. This cycle serves as reinforcement for both the caregiver and child and increases the likelihood that antisocial behaviours will develop (Frick, 2012; Frick & Morris, 2004).

Ashleigh was the middle of three children, born to married parents. Her father was a civil engineer; her mother did not work outside the home but was very involved in community volunteer work. Ashleigh, who was small in stature, had several medical problems as a child, including double hernia surgery, frequent urinary infections, and severe food allergies, which resulted in her missing a fair amount of school in her early years. An undiagnosed learning disability impeded her progress in school, and when her family moved when she was 12, Ashleigh began skipping school. Ashleigh's mother used excessively harsh physical discipline such as slapping her across the face for food infractions; Ashleigh to this day blames herself for this. During high school, Ashleigh began hanging out with youth three to four years older than she, drinking, smoking, and taking various "pills" (collected from parents' medicine cabinets) on a regular basis, and ignoring her parents' demands that she attend school. Following an incident when she ran away from home to avoid punishment for these activities, and a later highly dysregulated episode, her parents had her involuntarily committed to a psychiatric unit. Ashleigh ran away from the hospital, beginning an extended period of drug use/dealing and living with older, drug-involved men. As an unfortunate bystander at a gang fight, she was drawn into the fight. She was left with severely damaged cervical discs which began her addiction to pain medications.

Risk, Need, and Responsivity Model

Reducing recidivism is the ultimate goal in forensic intervention. While individuals who find themselves incarcerated may have many needs that would benefit from treatment, not all of these needs link directly to the risk of re-offence or recidivism (Polaschek, 2012; Taxman, 2006). Overall, there is a consensus that untreated serious mental disorders do not meaningfully predict recidivism: there is little evidence that mental health-focused programmes alone will reduce recidivism (Skeem, Winter, Kennealy, Louden, & Tatar, 2014).

The Risk, Need & Responsivity model (RNR) developed by Canadian researchers Andrews and Bonta (2006) is considered the most influential model that exists for assessment and treatment of offenders (Blanchette & Brown, 2006; Ward et al., 2007); some of the best risk-assessment tools used on offenders are based on the RNR model (Andrews et al., 2011). According to the RNR model, rehabilitation efforts must be applied differentially based on offender risk level, the risk factors for crime most relevant to the individual, and individual differences in responsiveness to rehabilitation (Dowden & Andrews, 1999). The recommendations RNR makes for treatment provide an exceptionally strong argument for using DBT in forensic programming and what follows expands on the RNR model.

Risk factors for crime, also referred to as *criminogenic needs*, are factors that motivate and sustain antisocial behaviour and criminal activity (Andrews & Bonta, 2006, 2015). Static needs such as race, family history, and number of previous convictions are unchangeable. Dynamic needs are those that *are* amenable to intervention such as antisocial peer affiliation and antisocial thinking (Andrews et al., 2006, 2011). Criminogenic needs are better predictors of recidivism over time than are symptoms of mental disorder (Peterson et al., 2014; Prins, Skeem, Mauro, & Link, 2015; Skeem et al., 2014). Substantial evidence exists that criminogenic needs largely account for the relationship between serious mental disorder and crime.

The *Risk* principle (Andrews & Bonta, 2006) posits that recidivism will decrease if the level of treatment services provided is proportional to the offender's risk to re-offend. This principle has two parts to it: i) the intensity of treatment, and ii) the individual's risk to re-offend. The *Need* principle (Andrews & Bonta, 2006) requires that the focus of correctional treatment is *criminogenic needs*. Criminogenic needs are dynamic risk factors directly linked to criminal behaviour. While static risk factors can only increase, criminogenic needs can increase and decrease and are the major

Table 28.1 Dynamic risk factors and DBT skills

Risk/Need Factor	Indicators	Intervention Goals	DBT Skills
Antisocial personality	Impulsive, risk taking, seeking, aggressive, irritable	Increase self-management skills, anger management	Mindfulness, Distress Tolerance, Emotion Regulation
Procriminal attitudes	Rationalizations for crime, negative attitudes towards the law	Counter rationalizations with prosocial attitudes; build prosocial identity	Mindfulness, Emotion Regulation
Social supports for crime	Criminal friends, no prosocial contacts	Replace friends and associates with prosocial friends and associates	Interpersonal Effectiveness
Substance abuse	Abuse of alcohol and/or drugs	Reduce substance abuse, enhance alternatives to substance use	Emotion Regulation, SUD
Family/marital relationships	Inadequate parental monitor and discipline, poor family relationships	Parenting skills, improve caring and warmth	Interpersonal Effectiveness, Mindfulness
School/vocational	Poor performance, low satisfactions	Improve work/study skills, facilitate prosocial relationships at school and work	Interpersonal Effectiveness, Mindfulness
Prosocial recreational activities	No involvement in prosocial recreational/leisure activities	Increase participation in prosocial recreational activities, teach prosocial hobbies/sports	Interpersonal Effectiveness

Reproduced from D.A. Andrews, James Bonta, and J. Stephen Wormith, The Risk–Need–Responsivity (RNR) Model. Does Adding the Good Lives Model Contribute to Effective Crime Prevention? *Criminal Justice and Behavior*, 38(7), p. 6, Table 1, doi: 10.1177/0093854811406356, Copyright © 2011, © SAGE Publications. Reprinted by Permission of SAGE Publications, Inc.

predictors of criminal behaviour (Andrews & Bonta, 2006; Andrews et al., 2006, 2011). Table 28.1 presents a cursory overview of the seven dynamic major risk/criminogenic need factors and their target behaviours, illustrating the DBT skills that address these targets.

Responsivity refers to the fact that social learning, i.e., skills-based, CBT interventions, are the most effective way to teach individuals new behaviours across behavioural domains. Effective social learning strategies operate according to two foundational CBT principles: i) the establishment of a collaborative and respectful relationship with the client, and ii) the use of social learning and problem-solving methods to teach new behaviour, i.e., didactic strategies, modelling, behaviour rehearsal, reinforcement (Andrews & Bonta, 2006). Specific responsivity calls for the consideration of personal strengths and biosocial factors in designing treatment interventions. Treatment can be tailored to these factors, as they have the potential to facilitate or hinder treatment. Andrews & Bonta (2006) demonstrate the close alignment between DBT and RNR principles (text in square brackets, added):

> The essence of this principle is that treatment can be enhanced if the treatment intervention pays attention to personal factors *[DBT places critical importance on idiographic assessment, e.g., behavioral analysis]* that can facilitate learning. Most have heard the pedagogical advice that one must vary teaching methods to suit visual learners and auditory learners. Offender treatment programs involve teaching offenders new behaviors and cognitions *[DBT skills training]*; maximizing this learning experience requires attention not only to whether the offender is a visual learner or an auditory learner but a whole range of personal-cognitive-social factors *[further DBT idiographic assessment]*. Treatment providers may need to first deal with an individual's debilitating anxiety or mental disorder in order to free the individual to attend and participate fully *[DBT skills: general mindfulness and mindfulness to current emotion]* in a program targeting criminogenic needs. If the offender has limited verbal skills and a concrete thinking style then the program must ensure that abstract concepts are kept to a minimum and there is more behavioral practice *[DBT skills rehearsal]* than talking. Increasing motivation and reducing barriers to attending treatment *[one of the five functions of comprehensive DBT; cf. Linehan, Cochran, & Keher, 2001]* must be well thought-out. This may be particularly important for women offenders (e.g., provide child care so the mother can attend treatment) and for Aboriginal offenders (e.g., include elders and spiritual ceremonies along with structured cognitive behavioral treatment).

Cognitive-behavioural programmes that target changeable dynamic risk factors, i.e., antisocial peer affiliation, antisocial cognitions, and antisocial personality traits, are able to reduce recidivism by up to 55% (Landenberger & Lipsey, 2005; McGuire et al., 2008; Wheeler & Covell, 2014). These programmes have recently proliferated (Howells, 2010). Specifically, programmes that are *intensive, structured, skills-based, and that focus on emotion regulation and interpersonal skills*, all *essential DBT treatment components*, have been most widely implemented as they have been found, consistently, to reduce recidivism among forensic populations (Landenberger & Lipsey, 2005; Lipsey, Chapman, & Landenberger, 2001).

DBT is compatible with risk-need-responsivity treatment principles and structure. First, it addresses specific treatment targets in hierarchical order. Life-threatening behaviours to self or others are first. Behaviours that are proximally related, e.g., self-harm, suicide urges or verbalizations or, in most forensic settings, violence toward others, are included in this category (McCann et al., 2000; Trupin et al., 2002). Treatment-interfering behaviours of residents, staff, and quality-of-life-interfering behaviours follow in the hierarchy. DBT also requires documentation of progress, integrating feedback, and accountability. Finally, data have now demonstrated that DBT is a cost-effective method of treating these high-risk and extreme behaviours (Amner, 2012; Botanov, 2015; Meyers, Landes, & Thuras, 2014; Priebe et al., 2012). Explicitly identifying treatment targets can increase accurate problem definition for staff and administration, improving ease of communication across disciplines and staff functions, and allowing quicker progress from assessment to intervention.

As an example, see the following target hierarchy for Ashleigh. The majority of forensic settings broaden hierarchies by adding additional foci regarded as essential in these settings. Escape or absconding as treatment-interfering behaviours and operating "stings" in the milieu as treatment-destroying behaviour are two examples (McCann et al., 2000; Trupin et al., 2002).

Ashleigh's Target Hierarchy

I. *Life-threatening behaviours*
   a. *Suicidal ideation*
   b. *Violent and aggressive behaviour toward others*
II. *Treatment-interfering behaviours*
   a. *Infracting such that cannot leave cell to attend groups*
   b. *Angry irritable outbursts at others in group or in milieu*
   c. *Angry irritable outbursts at clinician*
III. *Quality-of-life-interfering behaviours*
   a. *Drug use*

CLINICAL EFFECTIVENESS OF DBT IN FORENSIC SETTINGS

DBT's compatibility with RNR frameworks and the similarity in presentation between clients with severe emotion regulation disorders and those within forensic systems led to interest in its adoption in forensic systems. But does it work? Does it accomplish the goals or move individuals closer to the goals set by RNR and those of individual mental health? A burgeoning body of empirical literature supports cognitive-behavioural interventions for addressing a constellation of clinical and criminological factors among individuals who are in forensic secure and supervised community settings. DBT contains general cognitive behaviour therapy principles and practices designed to treat high-risk life-threatening self-harm and externalizing behaviours as well as therapy-interfering behaviours by staff and inmates.

The first survey of DBT in forensic settings identified 14 programmes in the United States, Canada, and the United Kingdom (Ivanoff, 1998). Forensic mental health hospitals were the most common settings with the remainder in the criminal justice system. All of the UK sites and the majority of those in the US and Canada were working to implement comprehensive DBT at that time. All but one site in the US/Canada reported ongoing empirical evaluation and the UK sites were part of an organized collaborative evaluation programme (personal communication with Shapiro, D., July 1998, Leeds, UK). Berzins and Trestman (2004), in designing a large US federally funded correctional trial of DBT, reviewed implementations by interviewing clinicians in seven correctional/forensic settings in North America. Three of these programme descriptions are published, while the other four were limited to personal communication. Four programmes (Ashlock, 2003; Giles, 2003; McDonough, 2003; Trupin et al., 2002) were in prison system psychiatric units, including one with juvenile females (Trupin et al., 2002), one was in an inpatient forensic hospital (McCann et al., 2000), and the other was outpatient treatment with sex offenders (Gordon & Hover, 1998). Four programmes offered individual psychotherapy and skills groups (Ashlock, 2003; Giles, 2003; McDonough, 2003), while three offered only DBT skills and other groups of widely varying duration and session length (Gordon & Hover, 1998; McCann et al., 2000; Trupin et al., 2002). Consultation team was mentioned at only one site (McCann et al., 2000).

Looking at these efforts through a current implementation science lens (Landes & Comtois, this volume), it can be that their early adoption may have developmentally disadvantaged them in some respects. Many of these programmes had one individual as primary champion who was responsible for motivating both staff and administrators. Almost all of these champions were also new to DBT, learning alongside other staff. Issues such as modifying skills examples to make them more salient to men with antisocial characteristics became larger obstacles for clinicians and staff who were both newly trained and less experienced with DBT.

Current Review of DBT: Overview and Method

This section reviews extant literature to aid those weighing the merits of implementing DBT in forensic settings to treat a number of problematic behaviours. This chapter synthesizes findings from evaluation studies to provide an overview of the use and effectiveness of DBT in forensic settings with a particular emphasis on programme implementation, adaptations to meet the needs of forensic settings, and changes on behavioural, cognitive, affective, and criminological outcomes (i.e., rearrests, recidivism).

Clinicians considering implementing DBT in forensic settings must weigh several important factors. Specifically, we identified the following clinical characteristics in forensic studies: i) setting; ii) sample characteristics (inclusion criteria, demographics, and diagnosis); iii) design; iv) DBT treatment modes (individual sessions, skills groups, coaching, consultation team); v) treatment delivery characteristics (duration of treatment, frequency and length of sessions, supervision); vi) supervision and fidelity efforts; vii) forensic adaptations or modifications (including treatment targets); viii) outcomes; and ix) reported implementation factors. At the time of writing this chapter in 2017, we identified 18 articles in peer-reviewed journals on 15 treatment evaluation studies examining the implementation of DBT in forensic settings. During our search, we also identified several dissertations and reports in the grey literature. For the purposes of this chapter, we only synthesized information reported in published peer-reviewed evaluation studies of forensic DBT. Table 28.2 provides a summary of the studies discussed here.

Setting, Study Design, and Sample Characteristics

We classified the studies by setting into three categories: i) prison, ii) forensic secure hospital, and iii) forensic outpatient. The milieux of these categories vary considerably internationally and clinicians must pay careful attention to the type of setting that will house their forensic DBT intervention. The review of the literature identified ten articles reporting on seven evaluation studies in prisons (Asmand, Mami, & Valizadeh, 2015; Banks, Kuhn, & Blackford, 2010; Bradley & Follingstad, 2003; Eccleston & Sorbello, 2002; Nee & Farman, 2005, 2007, 2008; Sampl et al., 2010; Shelton et al., 2009; Shelton et al., 2011; Trupin et al., 2002). A total of six articles report evaluations of separate studies of inpatient DBT in forensic hospitals (Evershed et al., 2003; Gee & Reed, 2013; Long, Fulton, Dolley, & Hollin, 2010; Low, Jones, Duggan, Power, & MacLeod, 2001; Sakdalan, Shaw, & Collier, 2010; Sakdalan et al., 2012). Two articles reported studies in outpatient forensic clinics (Rosenfeld et al., 2007; Van den Bosch, Hysaj, & Jacobs, 2012).

In addition to setting, clinicians considering implementing forensic DBT interventions must scrutinize the quality of empirical evaluation studies. At the time of this writing (late in 2017), there are no published randomized controlled trials examining the effectiveness of DBT interventions in forensic settings. However, DBT received positive support in pilot studies of interventions in forensic facilities using quasi-experimental, Pre-Post study designs. Our review found 6/15 studies (eight articles) with treatment comparison groups: Rational Emotive Therapy (Asmand et al., 2015), DBT for non-mental health individuals (Banks et al., 2010), case management (Sampl et al., 2010; Shelton et al., 2009, 2011), treatment as usual (Evershed et al., 2003) and no-treatment control groups (Bradley & Follingstad, 2003; Trupin et al., 2002). Most studies had only a single treatment group with no comparison (Eccleston & Sorbello, 2002; Gee & Reed, 2013; Long et al., 2010; Low et al., 2001; Nee & Farman, 2005, 2007, 2008; Rosenfeld et al., 2007; Sakdalan et al., 2010, 2012;

Table 28.2 Studies reviewed

Authors	Study Characteristics, Setting, Design, Inclusion, Sample	Tx Characteristics: Duration (D) 1:1 Sessions (IS) Skills Groups (SG) Skills Modules (SM)	Consult Team (CT) Supervision/Training (S/T) Fidelity (F) Coaching (C)	Implementation Facilitators or Barriers	Significant Behavioural (B), Cognitive (C), & Affective (A) Outcomes
Asmand, P., Mami, S., & Valizadeh, R. (2015).	prison, Iran, pre–post DBT-TG[1], TCG[2], no follow-up, n=64, men, Dx[13]: APD.[3]	D: 16 sessions. SG: one hr twice/wk.			C: reduced irrational beliefs (e.g., need to conform, high expectations of self, tending to blame, reaction to failure, emotional irresponsibility, anxiety and stress); avoidance of exposition of pitfalls, dependence, helplessness to change others, and perfectionism.
Banks, B, Kuhn, T., & Blackford, J. U. (2010).	prison, US[4], pre–post DBT-TG[1], TCG[2], no follow-up, n=12, adolescent females.	D: 12 sessions IS: weekly check-in SG: 1.5 hr once/wk, two wks SM: M[5] ER[6] IE[7] DT.[8]	CT: weekly S/T: group facilitators received no formal training, on-site supervision by counsellor with formal DBT training.	no extra cost to facility; collaboration with security officers; did not impose staffing demands; administered by nurse practitioner interns; reported no logistical problems related to running groups (e.g., resources, space, security).	C: reduced overall problems. A: reduced depression and internalizing problems and increased satisfaction

Study	Setting/sample	Design	Training/fidelity	Modifications	Outcomes
Bradley, R. G., & Follingstad, D. R. (2003).	prison, US[4], pre-post DBT-TG[1], CG[9], no follow up, n=49, women, trauma history.	D: 18 sessions IS: none SM: M[5] ER[6] IE[7] DT.[8] Other: education on interpersonal victimization and affect regulation, writing assignments.	S/T: one leader from each group completed 40-hour DBT training programme.	incorporated issues common to women in prison (e.g., anger).	A: reduced depression, anxious arousal, and intrusive experiences.
Eccleston, L., & Sorbello, L (2002).	prison, Australia, pre-post DBT-TG[1], no CG[9], no follow up, n=29, women, history of suicide or self-harm, Dx[13]: BPD.[10]	D: 20 sessions IS: "as needed" SG: 2hr 2/wk SM: M[5] ER[6] IE[7] DT.[8]	F: facilitator therapy notes.	incorporated poetry reading, role-play, analogies, games and quizzes; changed order of modules (1. mindfulness, 2. distress management, 3. emotion regulation, and 4. interpersonal effectiveness); reported high staff engagement, were motivated to participate in intervention.	A: reduced depression, anxiety, and stress.
Evershed, S., Tennant, A., Boomer, D., Rees, A., Barkham, M., & Watson, A. (2003).	forensic hospital, UK,[15] pre-post DBT-TG[1] + six-month follow up, n=17, TAU[12], no follow up, n=17, Dx[13]: BPD[10] and other PD.[11]	D: 18 months (treatment group) 12 months (comparison group). IS: 1x/wk SG: 1x/wk SM: M[5] ER[6] IE[7] DT.[8]	CT: weekly consultation group operated according to DBT principles. S/T: some clinicians attended two-week DBT training course, skills coaches attended two-day introductory DBT course, weekly supervision to review and practise DBT skills and formulate case conceptualization. F: DBT summary sheets used following each session and compared to skills manual.	incorporated violent behaviours into curriculum (e.g. ideation, urges, emotions); skills coaches available on treatment wards; changed self-soothing tools to incorporate items relevant to high-security environments and gender-specific examples; made material more relevant to offending population; quizzes.	B: reduced serious violent behaviours. C: reduced hostility. A: reduced hostility and anger.

(continued)

Table 28.2 Continued

Authors	Study Characteristics, Setting, Design, Inclusion, Sample	Tx Characteristics: Duration (D) 1:1 Sessions (IS) Skills Groups (SG) Skills Modules (SM)	Consult Team (CT) Supervision/ Training (S/T) Fidelity (F) Coaching (©)	Implementation Facilitators or Barriers	Significant Behavioural (B), Cognitive (C), & Affective (A) Outcomes
Gee, J., & Reed, S. (2013).	prison UK,[15] pre-post DBT-TG[1], no CG[9], no follow-up, n=62.	D: 24 weeks IS: 50 min once/wk SG: 1.5hr twice/wk SM: M[5] ER[6] IE[7] DT.[8]	CT: two hr/wk		B: recidivism: reduced adjudication during and after intervention; overall positive reports of impact of programme on positive life changes; reduced self-harm behaviours; all improved overall health. C: reduced suicidal ideation; improved perceptions of lives, mental health, and relationships with family and friends.
Long, C. G., Fulton, B., Dolley, O., & Hollin, C. R. (2010).	prison, UK[15], pre-post DBT-TG[1], no CG[9], no follow-up, n=44, women, index offences, violent crimes, arson, and assault, Dx[13]: PD,[14]	D: 17 sessions IS: weekly, practise skills, relapse prevention SG: 1.5hr once/wk SM: M[5] ER[6] IE[7] DT.[8]			B: reduced physical aggression against self and others, and total number of risk behaviours. C: reduced anxiety, depression, suicidality, guilt, hostility; increased coping skills, recognized changes in mood, and distress tolerance.

	schizophrenia, schizoaffective, and bipolar depressive disorders.		
Low, G., Jones, D., Duggan, C., Power, M., & MacLeod, A. (2001).	forensic hospital, UK[15], pre–post DBT–TG[1], six-month follow up, no CG[9] n=10, women, self harm, Dx[13]: BPD.[10]	D: 52 sessions: IS: once/wk SG: once/wk SM: M[5] ER[6] IE[7] DT.[8]	B: reduction in self-harm post-treatment. C: reduction in depression during treatment not at follow-up; reduction in dissociation post-treatment and at follow-up; increase in survival and coping beliefs post treatment and follow-up; reduction in suicidal ideation post treatment; reduction in impulsiveness during treatment.
Nee, C., & Farman, S. (2005). Nee, C., & Farman, S. (2007). Nee, C., & Farman, S. (2008).	prison, UK[15], case study, pre–post, six-month follow up, no CG[9], n=3, women, suicide, parasuicide history, Dx[13]: BPD.[10]	D: 52 sessions IS: one hr once/ wk, diary cards, behavioural chain analyses SG: two hr/wk SM: M[5] ER[6] IE[7] DT.[8]	B: decreased BPD symptoms, anger, suicidal ideation, and suicidal behaviour; increased locus of control, coping skills.

(continued)

Table 28.2 Continued

Authors	Study Characteristics, Setting, Design, Inclusion, Sample	Tx Characteristics: Duration (D) 1:1 Sessions (IS) Skills Groups (SG) Skills Modules (SM)	Consult Team (CT) Supervision/Training (S/T) Fidelity (F) Coaching (©)	Implementation Facilitators or Barriers	Significant Behavioural (B), Cognitive (C), & Affective (A) Outcomes
Rosenfeld, B., Galietta, M., Ivanoff, A., Garcia-Mansilla, A., Martinez, R., Fava, J., ... & Green, D. (2007).	outpatient forensic, US[4], pre-post DBT–TG[1], 12.2 months mean follow up, no CG[9], n=29, men, Dx[13] : psychosis, mood disorders, substance abuse disorders, Axis 2: personality disorders with primarily cluster B traits.	D: 24 sessions IS: 45min once/wk SG: one hr once/wk SM: M[5] ER[7] IE[7] DT.[8]	CT: ongoing supervision provided by DBT clinician S/T: treatment delivered by DBT trainers or trained graduate students, weekly reminder calls to participants.		B: lower recidivism rates than published data on stalking; greater acknowledgement of anger.
Sakdalan, J. A., Shaw, J., & Collier, V. (2010).	forensic hospital, New Zealand, multiple case study, pre-post DBT-TG[1], no CG[9], n=6, men and women, Dx: ID.[16]	D: 13 sessions IS: 1.5hr once/wk SG: one hr once/wk SM: M.[5]	CT: DBT group supervision S/T: training of vocational and residential staff in DBT principles, structured milieu to support DBT principles.	focus on quality and therapy-interfering behaviours instead of self-harm; adapted behavioural targets to match needs of participants; milieu emphasized DBT principles.	C: participants scored high on DBT intervention learning comprehension; high satisfaction in course; decrease in criminogenic factors.

Sakdalan, J. A., & Collier, V. (2012).	forensic hospital, New Zealand, multiple case study, pre-post DBT-TG[1], no CG[9], n=3, men, Dx[13]: ID[16], prior sex offenses.	D: Seven months IS: one hr once/wk SG: two hr/wk SM: M[5] ER[6] IE[7] DT.[8] Other: manualized sex offender treatment		B: reduction in sexually abusive behaviours, physical aggression, verbal aggression; increase in frustration tolerance. C: sexual knowledge and empathy.
Shelton, D., Sampl, S., Kesten, K. L., Zhang, W., & Trestman, R. L (2009).; Shelton, D., Kesten, K., Zhang, W., & Trestman, R. L (2011).; Sampl, S., Wakai, S., & Trestman, R. L (2010).	prison, US[4], pre-post, DBT-TG[1], CM-CG[17], 12-month follow-up, n=124.	D: 24 sessions IS: 30 min once/wk SG: weekly.	lengthy clearance process for study delayed start; participant removal for security reasons, unanticipated release or transfer, staff turnover.	B: post-DBT intervention; lower physical aggression and fewer disciplinary tickets. C: improved anger management; increased ways of coping (e.g., seeking social support, accepting responsibility, planful problem-solving, escape avoidance).
Trupin, E. W., Stewart, D. G., Beach, B., & Boesky, L. (2002).	juvenile detention, pre-post, DBT-TG[1], CG[17], n=90.	D: ten months SG: 60–90min once-twice/wk SM: M[5] ER[6] IE[7] DT.[8] Other: self-management.	CT: one to two hr/wk S/T: staff members received DBT intensive training (80 hours on mental health unit, 16 hours on general population unit). adapted behavioural targets to meet needs of forensic setting including primarily in domains of: 1. "unit-destructive behaviours" (violence, oppositional defiance, victimization), and 2. quality-of-life-interfering behaviours (high-risk sexual behaviours, mental health problems, offence-related behaviours).	B: reduced behavioural problems (e.g., aggression, parasuicide); increased access to rehabilitative services within institution.

(continued)

Table 28.2 Continued

Authors	Study Characteristics, Setting, Design, Inclusion, Sample	Tx Characteristics: Duration (D) 1:1 Sessions (IS) Skills Groups (SG) Skills Modules (SM)	Consult Team (CT) Supervision/Training (S/T) Fidelity (F) Coaching (©)	Implementation Facilitators or Barriers	Significant Behavioural (B), Cognitive (C), & Affective (A) Outcomes
Van den Bosch, L. M. C., Hvsaj, M., & Jacobs, P. (2012).	forensic outpatient, Netherlands, pre-post, DBT-TG[1] CG[9], n=29, men and women, Dx[13]: BPD.[10]	D: 52 weeks IS: one hr/wk SG: 2–2.5 hours SM: M, DT, ER, IE.	S/T: DBT supervision provided by member of international DBT training group in Seattle focused on application of DBT and occurred after skills training groups, case consultation occurred weekly for one hr; 17 individual therapists and six trainers received ten-day intensive DBT course. F: adherence coder provided scoring to video-taped therapy sessions selected at random, reviewed session notes, adherence score 3.5 for forensic setting.	compared forensic outpatient to non-forensic patients found that implementation of standard DBT was feasible in a forensic outpatient setting.	feasibility study, no outcomes reported.

[1] Dialectical Behavioural Therapy—Treatment Group; [2] Treatment Comparison Group; [3] Antisocial Personality Disorder; [4] United States; [5] Mindfulness; [6] Emotional Regulation; [7] Interpersonal Effectiveness; [8] Distress Tolerance; [9] Comparison Group; [10] Borderline Personality Disorder; [11] Personality Disorder; [12] Treatment as Usual; [13] Diagnosis; [14] Personality Disorder; [15] United Kingdom; [16] Intellectual Disability; [17] Case Management-Comparison Group

Van den Bosch et al., 2012). Only 5/15 studies (eight articles) included any follow-up period, ranging from six months (Evershed et al., 2003; Low et al., 2001; Nee 2005, 2007, 2008), to a year or more (Rosenfeld et al., 2007; Shelton et al., 2009, Shelton et al., 2011). Sample sizes of the 15 studies ranged from the smallest sample of three (Sakdalan & Collier, 2010) to the study with the largest sample of 124 (Shelton, 2010, Shelton et al., 2009, 2011).

Determining who in the forensic population may benefit most from DBT is an important concern for clinicians in forensic settings. This includes clinical diagnoses (i.e., borderline personality disorder), behavioural targets (i.e., suicide attempts, self-harm, violent behaviour, substance abuse), and comorbid psychiatric conditions that show improvement as a result of receiving DBT interventions, e.g., BPD and PTSD (Harned, Korslund, Foa, & Linehan, 2012; Harned, Korslund, & Linehan, 2014).

DBT shows promise for widely diverse forensic populations based on demographic, clinical, and criminological factors. Several studies recruited participants with histories of self-harm and suicide (Eccleston & Sorbello, 2002; Nee & Farman, 2005, 2007, 2008). Samples included diagnosed BPD (Evershed et al., 2003; Low et al., 2001; Nee & Farman, 2005, 2007, 2008; Van den Bosch et al., 2012), ASPD (Asmand et al., 2015), and other personality disorders (Evershed et al., 2003). A wide range of other psychiatric issues, including psychosis, schizophrenia, schizoaffective disorder, mood disorders (bipolar, depression), were also reported (Bradley & Follingstad, 2003; Long et al., 2010, Rosenfeld et al., 2007). One study recruited a population of women with histories of traumatic experiences and trauma symptoms (Bradley & Follingstad, 2003). In addition to clinical characteristics, studies recruited participants with histories of violent, sex, and other major criminal offences (Sakdalan & Collier, 2012; Shelton et al., 2009, 2011; Sampl et al., 2010). Two studies by the same investigators examined DBT for a small population of individuals in forensic settings with intellectual disability (Sakdalan et al., 2010, 2012).

Although the majority of studies were conducted with adults, three studies (five articles) evaluated the utility of DBT with adolescents in forensic settings (Banks et al., 2010; Sampl et al., 2010; Shelton et al., 2009, 2011; Trupin et al., 2002). Across all 15 studies, five included only men (Asmand et al., 2015; Eccleston & Sorbello, 2002; Evershed et al., 2003; Rosenfeld et al., 2007; Sakdalan et al., 2010), while seven (nine articles), included women or girls exclusively (Banks et al., 2010; Bradley & Follingstad, 2003; Gee & Reed, 2013; Long et al., 2010; Low et al., 2001; Nee & Farman, 2005, 2007, 2008; Trupin et al., 2002) and three (five articles) treated both men and women (Sakdalan et al., 2010; Sampl et al., 2010; Shelton et al., 2009, 2011; Van den Bosch et al., 2012). The UK (Evershed et al., 2003; Gee & Reed, 2013; Long et al., 2010; Low et al., 2001; Nee & Farman, 2005, 2007, 2008) and US each contributed five studies (seven articles); it is notable that US samples included African-American, Hispanic, Asian, Native-American, and White participants (Banks et al., 2010; Bradley & Follingstad, 2003; Rosenfeld et al., 2007; Sampl et al., 2010; Shelton et al., 2009, 2011; Trupin et al., 2002). Of the remaining studies, two were conducted in New Zealand (Sakdalan et al., 2010, 2012), one each was conducted in

Iran (Asmand et al., 2015), Australia (Eccleston & Sorbello, 2002), and the Netherlands (Van den Bosch et al., 2012).

DBT Treatment Modes and Delivery Characteristics

Treatment delivery characteristics, including the length and structure of treatment sessions, depended upon many factors including the clinical needs of the service recipients and the available resources in the treatment setting (prison, forensic hospital, and forensic outpatient). Eleven of the 15 studies included both regular individual sessions and skills groups, three conducted skills-only and one reported individual sessions "as needed." Six studies reported some version of consultation team. Individual (1:1) sessions lasted from 30 minutes (Sampl et al., 2010; Shelton et al., 2009, 2011) to 90 minutes in length (Sakdalan et al., 2010). All of the studies implemented weekly skills groups lasting between 60 (Trupin et al., 2002) and 180 minutes (Van den Bosch et al., 2012) and most covered all four DBT skills modules. There were "extra" elements reported that could be classified as coaching or milieu support, including orientation (Gee & Reed, 2013; Long et al., 2010), weekly "check-in" about DBT skills application (Banks et al., 2010), review of diary cards (Gee & Reed, 2013; Nee & Farman, 2005, 2007, 2008), behavioural chain analyses (Nee & Farman, 2005, 2007, 2008), and milieu skills reinforcement (Banks et al., 2010; Sakdalan et al., 2012). Treatment length ranged from three (Banks et al., 2010) to 18 months (Bradley & Follingstad, 2003) and sessions were held once or twice per week. Consultation teams met for one hour (Van den Bosch et al., 2012) to two hours weekly (Gee & Reed, 2013; Trupin et al., 2002) and conducted according to DBT principles and practices (Banks et al., 2010; Evershed et al., 2003).

Training, Supervision, and Fidelity

Only a small portion of studies reported the training received by individual therapists and skills group leaders. Training varied widely, from a 40-hour basic training (Bradley & Follingstad, 2003), to a ten-day intensive (Evershed et al., 2003; Trupin et al., 2002; Van den Bosch et al., 2012), to a two-day introductory course (Evershed et al., 2003) and "on-site training" (Sakdalan et al., 2010). Behavioural Tech trainers and graduate students delivered one intervention (Rosenfeld et al., 2007). In most of the evaluation studies, staff members received the DBT training and co-led groups with untrained facilitators.

Five studies reported on-site DBT supervision provided in group format by a DBT clinician (Banks et al., 2010; Evershed et al., 2003; Rosenfeld et al., 2007; Sakdalan et al., 2010; Van den Bosch et al., 2012). Supervision also included reviewing and practising DBT skills as well as formulating DBT-orientated case conceptualizations (Evershed et al., 2003). In the only study reporting adherence, Van den Bosch and colleagues (2012) randomly selected session videos and coded for adherence, reporting a mean adherence score of 3.5/5, which does not constitute adherent DBT.

Clinical and Criminological Outcomes

Reported changes on behavioural and cognitive factors provide promising results for implementing DBT forensic interventions. Behavioural changes reported in the evaluation studies include significant reductions in self-harm/parasuicide (Gee & Reed, 2013; Long et al., 2010; Low et al., 2001; Trupin et al., 2002), other suicidal behaviours (Nee & Farman, 2005, 2007, 2008), violent behaviour (Evershed et al., 2003), aggressive outbursts (Gee & Reed, 2013; Sakdalan et al., 2012; Sampl et al., 2010; Shelton et al., 2009, 2011; Trupin et al., 2002), sexual aggression (Sakdalan et al., 2012), disciplinary infraction tickets (Gee & Reed, 2013; Sampl et al., 2010; Shelton et al., 2009, 2011), and criminal recidivism (Gee & Reed, 2013; Rosenfeld et al., 2007) and other risk behaviours (Long et al., 2010).

Although behavioural outcomes are the strongest indicators of treatment success, some studies suggest DBT may improve several cognitive factors closely related to poor psychological health and high-risk behaviours. Forensic DBT reduced suicidal ideation (Gee & Reed, 2013), dissociation (Low et al., 2001), cognitive symptoms of BPD (Low et al., 2001), irrational beliefs, e.g., need to conform, high expectations of self, tending to blame, reaction to failure (Asmand et al., 2015), and impulsivity (Low et al., 2001). DBT also increased empathy (Sakdalan & Collier, 2012) and positive perceptions of lives and attitudes toward family and friends (Gee & Reed, 2013). Several studies using inventories of coping skills found significantly increased ways of coping with distressing thoughts or unpleasant feelings including anger (Nee & Farman, 2005, 2007, 2008; Sampl et al., 2010; Shelton et al., 2009, 2011). Teaching individuals in forensic settings DBT skills may enable those with behavioural problems to more effectively deal with challenges presented by the constraints of the immediate physical and social environment. In addition to cognitive and behavioural outcomes, a number of affective outcomes improved following DBT, including reductions in anxiety, (Asmand et al., 2015; Bradley & Follingstad, 2003; Eccleston & Sorbello, 2002), depression (Banks et al., 2010; Bradley & Follingstad, 2003; Eccleston & Sorbello, 2002; Low et al., 2001), and anger (Evershed et al., 2003; Nee & Farman, 2005, 2007, 2008; Rosenfeld et al., 2007; Sampl et al., 2010; Shelton et al., 2009, 2011).

Adaptations and Modifications

Adaptations and modifications include differences from standard DBT (Linehan, 1993a, b). As described elsewhere, these generally include: i) inpatient or residential setting, including a DBT milieu, ii) service delivery (frequency and length of sessions) (cf. Linehan, 2015a), and iii) selection of treatment modes. More unique to forensic settings is the addition of targets prevalent among forensic populations, including violence and aggressive behaviours toward others (ideation, emotions, urges), high-risk sexual behaviours, and offence-related behaviours as well as trauma and anger (Bradley & Follingstad, 2003; Evershed et al., 2003; Trupin et al., 2002). Examples, activities, and skills practice were modified for relevance to the restricted setting (Evershed et al., 2003; Sakdalan, Shaw, & Collier, 2010; Trupin et al., 2002). Eccleston & Sorbello (2002) used poetry reading, role-play, analogies, games, and quizzes to facilitate skill acquisition. Taken together, the adaptations to meet the needs of the clinical population and the constraints imposed by secure environments were critical to the delivery of DBT forensic interventions reported in the evaluation studies.

Implementation Facilitators and Barriers

A small number of studies provided details on setting characteristics that either facilitated implementation or created barriers challenging DBT implementation in forensic settings. Barriers to implementation noted in articles by Shelton and colleagues (2009, 2011) and Sampl and colleagues (2010) included the lengthy clearance process to implement studies, unanticipated facility lockdowns, staff turnover, removal of participants for security reasons, and unanticipated participant release or transfer from the facility.

Banks and colleagues (2010) reported that high engagement and motivation among staff were major factors facilitating implementation. This was despite the highly stringent conditions imposed on implementation: i) no extra cost to the facility, ii) no increased staffing demands, and iii) no logistical burden to facility as a result of running groups.

CHALLENGES TO IMPLEMENTING DBT IN FORENSIC SETTINGS

Despite DBT's appeal and applicability and the significant efforts to implement the model in forensic settings, the challenges remain daunting for many. These challenges are, in the broadest view, tensions between treatment/programming and security/safety. They may be regarded as simultaneously philosophical, structural, and logistical (Berzins & Trestman, 2004; Chapman & Ivanoff, 2017; Ivanoff, 1998; McCann, Ball, & Ivanoff, 2000). Figure 28.1 provides a visual of these overlapping challenges.

The primary philosophical tension in these settings is between security and treatment or security and rehabilitative programming. The goal of security is safety and efficiency in managing the system. The goal of clinical care is the improvement of

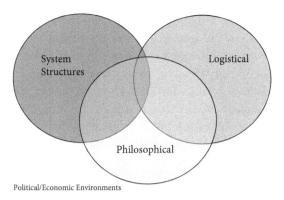

FIGURE 28.1 Challenges to implementing DBT in forensic settings.

individual functioning. The goals of programming frequently include both addressing factors linked to recidivism and the management of behaviour within the institution. The result is a constant need to weigh and balance these priorities. Unfortunately, in prison settings, security always trumps mental health needs. In forensic hospitals, the first mandate is treatment, although security and public safety cannot be ignored. From political pressure, usually of a conservative nature, to efforts by unions to protect workers' rights, these influences shape the feasibility of implementation, and the dose and structure of treatment. Particularly in correctional facilities, the challenges to sustaining a DBT programme have not benefited from the lessons of recent implementation science.

The Axis II DBT programme was implemented at the US Medical Center for Federal Prisoners in Springfield, Missouri in 2002. Designed for inmates identified as highly dysregulated and responsible for the most behavioural disruptions throughout the US, the programme was comprehensive and milieu-based, training correctional officers as well as mental health staff. Two difficult years into its implementation, an episode of "This American Life", a popular public radio show, reported on this innovative programme for that system's most severely disordered inmates (Glass, 2004). Custody staff interviewed used words like "coddling" and suggested patients were being given things they "didn't deserve" as part of contingency management, focusing on the frequent severe crisis and egregious behaviours prevalent in this population. Despite its careful design from the beginning, this ongoing backlash from custody staff angered by inmate patients participating in an "undeserved" contingency management programme in the institution, forced the programme to severely tighten standards for programme admission and instigate frequent expulsions. Unfortunately, the behaviours resulting in expulsion were often the exact behaviours inmate patients were originally included in the programme to address, i.e., patients were expelled from the programme for demonstrating that they should be in the programme! The resulting high number of expulsions (cf. Berzins & Trestman, 2004, personal communication with Ashlock, G., 2003; personal communication with Terrell, D., 2010) contributed to that programme's demise.

In another federal facility, a decade later, a systematic feasibility study examined the use of DBT mindfulness groups and a "crisis prevention" skills programme based on inmate needs assessment. Designed to address needs of identified vulnerable detainees in a large urban facility (Ivanoff, 2012), the programme took a year to set up and obtain various clearances to commence. Despite encouraging pilot data, a year later the Warden's retirement and the consequent change in facility administration decided the programme was inconsistent with security needs and ended it abruptly. The CMHIP programme in Pueblo (McCann et al., 2002) and the Washington State Juvenile Rehabilitation Administration programme (Schmidt & Salisbury, 2009; Trupin et al., 2002), internationally popular exemplars that spawned numerous other programmes over the years, have also succumbed to leadership changes that limited or eliminated implementation of DBT programme components.

Structural challenges concern both the environment and the systems. Incurring criminal charges in a forensic hospital system may or may not result in transfer to a prison. In addition, carrying a designation as "in need of mental health services" does not ensure that adequate treatment is provided. Prisons trying to establish a therapeutic milieu run into conventions that insist "treatment" occurs only with a clinician present or in an area, e.g., the treatment "mall," designated for "mental health." In residential settings, if custodial staff cannot provide milieu coaching because of union rules, frequent staff changes, or too few staff, the skills taught in group cannot be generalized to the living environment. There are numerous examples of systems so low on resources that DBT implementation is simply not possible. In some cases, staff or clinicians providing DBT skills training or individual psychotherapy are so thinly distributed the dose is ineffective. Illustrations from current programmes include:

1) One skills trainer to conduct a group of 15–20 patients;
2) Skills groups run only once weekly for 45 minutes;
3) No coaching or follow-through on subsequent skills use; and
4) Individual sessions on an "as-needed" or twice-monthly basis.

Unfortunately, in many situations, it is common to hear the DBT model itself is viewed as the problem and labelled as ineffective or inappropriate for the population.

Logistical issues concern details, from large to small, about how the intervention will be provided. Day, time, location, staffing, escorts, materials, and voluntary participation are only a few of the many items on the logistics checklist. While holding skills groups sitting in the middle of eight secure treatment modules, i.e., cages, or with participants each shackled to the wall may appall some clinicians and lack clinical warmth, individuals with behaviours requiring these restrictions also deserve (and should not be deprived of) treatment.

The John T. Montford Psychiatric Center in Lubbock, Texas, began a DBT skills programme after an extended period of high-frequency violence and self-harm. Here, as in many other secure, intensive behaviour management or segregated housing units, even arranging where and how to hold a skills group was a challenge (Berzins & Trestman, 2004). A lack of readily available skills training manuals for the group leaders and for the participants is common when group venues are physically distant from offices or copying machines. While carrying out skills groups in residential settings on the actual living units theoretically bodes well for incorporating skills into daily unit use, the realities of ongoing noise and frequent interruptions create significant distraction for impulsive, hypervigilant residents (personal communication with Novak, M., May, 2017, NY).

CONCLUSIONS AND FUTURE DIRECTIONS

This review suggests DBT holds considerable promise to address the most salient behavioural health problems prevalent in forensic populations. DBT skills, taught with minor modifications for language and context, address emotion dysregulation and criminogenic dynamic risk factors. While most programmes aspire to implement comprehensive DBT, the limited availability of out-of-session coaching and confusion about the distinctive differences between case consultation and DBT consultation team create challenges. Absence of thorough basic and specialized training and ongoing supervision or expert consultation are also common. Methodologically, research in these settings suffers from weak designs, high variability in measurement type and quality, lack of follow-up, and absence of fidelity or adherence monitoring.

Clinically and administratively, decisions about the pace and rate of implementation are frequently determined by political and social mandates. Beginning small, i.e., with a single pilot unit, and doing less to do better and "get the bugs out" are virtues in the field of implementation science. Many systems are under pressure to roll out system-wide from the beginning, risking unevenness and jeopardizing fidelity. The trajectory of effort presented here demonstrates the willingness and perseverance of numerous dedicated clinicians and other service providers. Notably absent from this review are the many dissertations, grey sources, and conference presentations describing and evaluating DBT programmes in forensic settings that never see peer-reviewed publication. Lacking academic supports, public agency staff frequently have no resources to support such writing. Lessons learned from their efforts should also be gathered and used to problem-solve challenges and augment the outcomes in this review. There are many lessons from implementation science, particularly DBT implementations, which can also inform future work in this area. As we arrive at two decades of DBT use in forensic settings, we still have far to go. Communication, systematic assessment, and common problem-solving of our challenges may help reduce compassion fatigue and improve sustainability of both individual providers and programmes.

KEY MESSAGES FOR CLINICIANS

- DBT is adopted in forensic settings as a treatment model for characteristics of Borderline Personality Disorder and other emotion regulation disorders.
- DBT is also adopted in forensic settings as general behavioural programming to address risk factors of criminal recidivism.
- Examples and language used throughout DBT standard manuals need to be modified to match a forensic population and setting conditions: this does not constitute treatment "adaptation."
- Modifications to standard DBT (Linehan, 1993a, b) in forensic settings most commonly include skills-only interventions, shortening group session length, incorporating targets related to dynamic criminogenic risk factors, and adding coping skills related to stressors in the institution.
- Variation across studies and lack of methodological rigor call for more research to reach conclusions regarding the effectiveness of implementing DBT in forensic settings.

AUTHOR NOTE

We dedicate this chapter to Hans Toch and Dudley J. (Duke) Terrell, Jr.

REFERENCES

Amner, K. (2012). The effect of DBT provision in reducing the cost of adults displaying the symptoms of BPD. *British Journal of Psychotherapy*, *28*, 336–352.

Andrews, D. A., & Bonta, J. (2006). *The psychology of criminal conduct*, 4th Edition. New York, NY: Routledge.

Andrews, D. A., Bonta, J, & Wormith, J. S. (2011). The risk-need-responsivity (RNR) model: Does adding the good lives model contribute to effective crime prevention? *Criminal Justice and Behavior*, *38*(7), 735–755.

Ashlock, G. (2003). Personal communication.

Asmand, P., Mami. S., & Valizadeh, R. (2015). The effectiveness of dialectical behavior therapy and rational emotive behavior therapy in irrational believes treatment among young male prisoners who have antisocial personality disorder in Ilam Prison. *International Journal of Health System and Disaster Management*, *3*(2), 68–73.

Banks, B., Kuhn, T., & Blackford, J. U. (2010). Modifying dialectical behavior therapy for incarcerated female youth: A pilot study. *Journal of Juvenile Justice*, *4*(1), 1.

Berzins, L. G., & Trestman, R. L. (2004). The development and implementation of dialectical behavior therapy in forensic settings. *International Journal of Forensic Mental Health*, *3*, 93–103.

Beauchaine, T. P., Klein, D. N., Crowell, S. E., Derbidge, C., & Gatzke-Kopp, L. (2009). Multi-finality in the development of personality disorders: A biology, sex, environment interaction model of antisocial and borderline traits. *Development and Psychopathology, 21*, 735–770.

Blanchette, K., & Brown, S. L. (2006). *The assessment and treatment of women offenders: An integrative perspective.* Chichester, England: John Wiley & Sons.

Botanov, Y. (2015). *Cost-offset of dialectical behavior therapy: A white paper.* Seattle, WA: Linehan Institute.

Bradley, R. G., & Follingstad, D. R. (2003). Group therapy for incarcerated women who experienced interpersonal violence: A pilot study. *Journal of Traumatic Stress, 16*(4), 337–340.

California Department of Corrections and Rehabilitation (2005). *Status Report on Juvenile Justice Reform.* Retrieved from: http://www.cdcr.ca.gov/Divisions_Boards/DJJ/Status_Report_JJ.html

Chapman, A., & Ivanoff, A. (in press, 2017). Forensic issues in borderline personality disorder. In B. Stanley & A. New (Eds.), *Borderline personality disorder.* New York, NY: Oxford University Press.

Crowell, S. E., Beauchaine, T. P., & Linehan, M. M. (2009). A biosocial developmental model of borderline personality: Elaborating and extending Linehan's theory. *Psychological Bulletin, 135*(3), 495–510.

Dowden, C., & Andrews, D. A. (1999). What works in young offender treatment: A meta-analysis. *Forum on Corrections Research, 11*(2), 21–24.

Dodge, K. A., & Pettit, G. S. (2003). A biopsychosocial model of the development of chronic conduct problems in adolescents. *Developmental Psychology, 39*(2), 349–371.

Eccleston, L., & Sorbello, L. (2002). The RUSH program—real understanding of self-help: A suicide and self-harm prevention initiative within a prison setting. *Australian Psychologist, 37*(3), 237–244.

Evershed, S., Tennant, A., Boomer, D., Rees, A., Barkham, M., & Watson, A. (2003). Practice-based outcomes of dialectical behaviour therapy (DBT) targeting anger and violence, with male forensic patients: A pragmatic and non-contemporaneous comparison. *Criminal Behaviour and Mental Health, 13*(3), 198–213.

Eysenck, H. J. (1977). Personality and factor analysis: A reply to Guilford. *Psychological Bulletin, 84*(3), 405–411.

Frick, P. J. (1998). *Conduct disorders and severe antisocial behavior.* New York, NY: Plenum.

Frick, P. J. (2012). Developmental pathways to conduct disorder: Implications for future directions in research, assessment, and treatment. *Journal of Clinical Child and Adolescent Psychology, 41*, 378–389.

Frick, P. J., & Morris, A. S. (2004). Developmental pathways to conduct problems. *Journal of Clinical Child and Adolescent Psychology, 33*, 54–68.

Galietta, M., & Rosenfeld, B. (2012). Adapting dialectical behavior therapy (DBT) for the treatment of psychopathy. *The International Journal of Forensic Mental Health, 11*(4), 325–335.

Gee, J., & Reed, S. (2013). The host programme: A pilot evaluation of modified dialectical behaviour therapy with female offenders diagnosed with borderline personality disorder.*European Journal of Psychotherapy & Counselling, 15*(3), 233–252

Giles, C. (2003). Personal communication.

Glass, I. (2004, May 7). Special treatment [Episode 264]. *This American Life* [Audio podcast]. Retrieved from http://www.thisamericanlife.org/radio-archives/

Grant, B. F., Chou, S., Goldstein, R. B., Huang, B., Stinson, F. S., Saha, T. D., & Ruan, W. (2008). Prevalence, correlates, disability, and comorbidity of DSM-IV borderline personality disorder: Results from the Wave 2 National Epidemiologic Survey on Alcohol and Related Conditions. *Journal of Clinical Psychiatry, 69*(4), 533–545.

Hare, R. D. (2003). *Manual for the revised psychopathy checklist*, 2nd Edition. Toronto, ON: Multi-Health Systems.

Harned, M. S., Korslund, K. E., Foa, E. B., & Linehan, M. M. (2012). Treating PTSD in suicidal and self-injuring women with borderline personality disorder: Development and preliminary evaluation of a dialectical behavior therapy prolonged exposure protocol. *Behavior Research and Therapy*, 50(6), 381–386.

Harned, M. S., Korslund, K. E., & Linehan, M. M. (2014). A pilot randomized controlled trial of dialectical behavior therapy with and without the dialectical behavior therapy prolonged exposure protocol for suicidal and self-injuring women with borderline personality disorder and PTSD. *Behavior Research and Therapy*, 55, 7–17.

Howard, R. C., Huband, N., Duggan, C., & Mannion, A. (2008). Exploring the link between personality disorder and criminality in a community sample. *Journal of Personality Disorders*, 22(6), 589–603.

Howells, K. (2010). The "third wave" of cognitive-behavioural therapy and forensic practice. *Criminal Behaviour and Mental Health*, 20(4), 251–256.

Ivanoff, A. (1998). *Survey of criminal justice and forensic dialectical behaviour therapy in the U.S. and U.K.* Seattle, WA: Linehan Training Group.

Ivanoff, A. (2012, May). *Using brief DBT skills training to avoid crisis in federal confinement.* Invited address at the Yale NEA-BPD conference, New Haven, CT.

Ivanoff, A., & Heyes, M. (2010, July). *Comorbidity between borderline and antisocial personality disorders: Salient but not unique.* Invited presentation at the 1st International Conference on Borderline Personality Disorder, Berlin, Germany.

Kletzka, N., Lachat, C., Echols, S., & Witterholt, S. (2014, November). *Structuring dialectical behavior therapy treatment in a forensic inpatient setting: Patient progress and staff perceptions.* 19th Annual ISITBT DBT Conference. Philadelphia, PA.

Landenberger, N. A., & Lipsey, M. W. (2005.) The positive effects of cognitive–behavioral programs for offenders: A meta-analysis of factors associated with effective treatment. *Journal of Experimental Criminology*, 1(4), 451–476.

Leschied A. (2011). *The treatment of incarcerated mentally disordered women offenders: A synthesis of current research (Corrections research: User report)*. Ottawa, ON: Public Safety Canada. Retrieved from http://publications.gc.ca/collections/collection_2011/sp-ps/PS3-1-2011-3-eng.pdf

Linehan, M. M. (1993a). *Cognitive-behavioral treatment of borderline personality disorder.* New York, NY: Guilford Press.

Linehan, M. M. (1993b). *Skills training manual for treating borderline personality disorder.* New York, NY: Guilford Press.

Linehan, M. M. (2015a). *DBT skills training manual*, 2nd Edition. New York, NY: Guilford Press.

Linehan, M. M. (2015b). *DBT skills training handouts and worksheets*, 2nd Edition. New York, NY: Guilford Press.

Linehan, M. M., Cochran, B., Kehrer, C. A. (2001). Borderline personality disorder. In D. H. Barlow (Ed.), *Clinical handbook of psychological disorders*, 3rd Edition. (pp. 470–522). New York: Guilford Press.

Lipsey, M. W., Chapman, G. L., & Landenberger, N. A. (2001). Cognitive-behavioral programs for offenders. *The Annals of the American Academy of Political and Social Science*, 578(1), 144–157.

Long, C. G., Fulton, B., Dolley, O., & Hollin, C. R. (2010). Dealing with feelings: The effectiveness of cognitive behavioural group treatment for women in secure settings. *Behavioural and Cognitive Psychotherapy*, 39(2), 243–247.

Low, G., Jones, D., Duggan, C., Power, M., & MacLeod, A. (2001). The treatment of deliberate self-harm in borderline personality disorder using dialectical behaviour therapy: A pilot study in a high security hospital. *Behavioural and Cognitive Psychotherapy*, 29(1), 85–92.

Lykken, D. T. (1995). *The antisocial personalities*. Hillsdale, NJ: Lawrence Erlbaum Associates.

Marotta, P., Ivanoff, A., Terrell, D., Perez, G., & Nathanson, D. (2012, April). *Brief* dialectical behavior therapy skills training to treat distress among federal detainees: Pilot feasibility & outcomes. Paper presented at 12th Annual International Association for Forensic Mental Health Treatment Conference, Miami, FL.

McCann, R. A., Ball, E. M., & Ivanoff, A. (2000). DBT with an inpatient forensic population: the CMHIP model. *Cognitive and Behavioral Practice*, 7, 447–456.

McCann, R.A., Ivanoff, A., Schmidt, H., & Beach, B. (2007). Implementing dialectical behavior therapy in residential forensic settings with adults and juveniles. In L. A. Dimeff & K. Koerner (Eds.), *Dialectical behavior therapy in clinical practice: Applications across disorders and settings* (pp. 112–144). New York, NY: Guilford Press.

McDonough, D. (2003). Personal communication.

McDonough, D., Taylor, K., & Blanchette, K. (2003). Correctional adaptation of dialectical behaviour therapy (DBT) for federally sentenced women. In *Forum on Corrections Research*, 14, 36–39. Conference Proceedings, Ottawa, ON: Correctional Service of Canada. Retrieved from http://www.csc-scc.gc.ca/research/rl 45-eng.shtml

McGuire, J., Bilby, C. L., Hatcher, R., Hollin, C., Hounsome, J., & Palmer, E. (2008). Evaluation of structured cognitive-behavioural treatment programmes in reducing criminal recidivism. *Journal of Experimental Criminology*, 4(1), 21–40.

Meyers, L. L, Landes, S. J., & Thuras, P. (2014). Veterans' service utilization & associated costs following participation in dialectical behavior therapy: A preliminary investigation. *Military Medicine*, 179, 1368–1373. doi:10.7205/MILMED-D-14-00248

Nee, C., & Farman, S. (2005). Female prisoners with borderline personality disorder: Some promising treatment developments. *Criminal Behaviour and Mental Health*, 15(1), 2–16.

Nee, C., & Farman, S. (2007). Dialectical behaviour therapy as a treatment for borderline personality disorder in prisons: Three illustrative case studies. *The Journal of Forensic Psychiatry & Psychology*, 18(2), 160–180.

Nee, C., & Farman, S. (2008). Treatment of borderline personality disorder in prisons: Findings from the two dialectical behaviour therapy pilots in the UK. In J. Hagen & E. Jensen (Eds.), *Personality disorders: New research* (pp. 107–121). New York, NY: Nova Science Publishers.

Paris, J. C. (1997). Childhood trauma as an etiological factor in the personality disorders. *Journal of Personality Disorders*, 11, 34–49.

Peterson, J. K., Skeem, J., Kennealy, P., Bray, B., & Zvonkovic, A. (2014). How often and how consistently do symptoms directly precede criminal behavior among offenders with mental illness? *Law and Human Behavior*, 38(5), 439–449.

Polaschek, D. L. L. (2012). An appraisal of the Risk-Need-Responsivity (RNR) model of offender rehabilitation and its application in correctional treatment. *Legal and Criminological Psychology*, 17(1), 1–17.

Priebe, S., Bhatti, N., Barnicot, K., Bremner, S., Gaglia, A., Katsakou, C., & Zinkler, M. (2012). Effectiveness and cost-effectiveness of dialectical behaviour therapy for self-harming patients with personality disorder: A pragmatic randomized controlled trial. *Psychotherapy and Psychosomatics*, 81(6), 356–365.

Prins, S. J., Skeem, J. L., Mauro, C., & Link, B. G. (2015). Criminogenic factors, psychotic symptoms, and incident arrests among people with serious mental illnesses under intensive outpatient treatment. *Law and Human Behavior, 39*(2), 177–188.

Quay, H. C. (1977). The three faces of evaluation. *Criminal Justice and Behavior, 4*, 341–354.

Rosenfeld, B., Galietta, M., Ivanoff, A., Garcia-Mansilla, A., Munoz, R., Fava, J., … Green, D. (2007). Dialectical behavior therapy for the treatment of stalking offenders. *Journal of International Forensic Mental Health, 6*(2), 95–103.

Sakdalan J.A & Collier, V. (2012), Piloting an Evidence-Based Group Treatment Programme for High Risk Sex Offenders with Intellectual Disability in the New Zealand Setting. *New Zealand Journal of Psychology, 41*(3), 5–11.

Sakdalan, J. A., Shaw, J., & Collier, V. (2010). Staying in the here-and-now: A pilot study on the use of dialectical behaviour therapy group skills training for forensic clients with intellectual disability. *Journal of Intellectual Disability Research, 54*(6), 568–572.

Sampl, S., Wakai, S., & Trestman, R. L. (2010). Implementation and evaluation of DBT-CM in correctional settings: Implications for translating evidence-based practices from community to corrections. *Journal of Behavioral Analysis of Offender and Victim Treatment and Prevention, 2*(2), 114–123.

Schmidt, H. III, & Salisbury, R. E. III. (Spring, 2009). Fitting treatment to context: Washington state's integrated treatment model for youth involved in the juvenile justice system. *Report on Emotional and Behavioral Disorders in Youth.*

Shelton, D., Sampl, S., Kesten, K. L., Zang, W., & Trestman, R. L. (2009). Treatment of impulsive aggression in correctional settings. *Correctional Mental Health Care, 27*(5), 787–800.

Shelton, D., Kesten, K. L., Zang, W., & Trestman, R. L. (2011). Impact of a Dialectic Behavior Therapy—Corrections Modified (DBT-CM) upon behaviorally challenged incarcerated male adolescents. *Journal of Child and Adolescent Psychiatric Nursing, 24*(2), 105–113.

Skeem, J. L., Winter, E., Kennealy, P. J., Louden, J. E., & Tatar, J. R. II (2014). Offenders with mental illness have criminogenic needs, too: Toward recidivism reduction. *Law and Human Behavior, 38*(3), 212–224.

Tadić, A., Wagner, S., Hoch, J., Başkaya, O., von Cube, R., Skaletz, C., Lieb, K., & Dahmen, N. (2009). Gender differences in axis I and axis II comorbidity in patients with borderline personality disorder. *Psychopathology, 42*, 257–263.

Taxman, F. S. (2006). Risk, need, and responsivity (RNR): It all depends. *Crime & Delinquency, 52*(1), 28–51.

Teplin, L. A. (1994). Psychiatric and substance abuse disorders among male urban jail detainees. *American Journal of Public Health, 8*, 290–293.

Terrell, D. J. (2010). Personal communication.

Trupin, E. W., Stewart, D. G., Beach, B., & Boesky, L. (2002). Effectiveness of a dialectical behavior therapy program for incarcerated female juvenile offenders. *Child and Adolescent Mental Health, 7*, 121–127.

Van den Bosch, L. M. C., Hysaj, M., & Jacobs, P. (2012). DBT in an outpatient forensic setting. *International Journal of Law and Psychiatry, 35*(4), 311–316.

Ward, T., Mesler, J., & Yates, P. (2007). Reconstructing the risk-need-responsivity model: A theoretical elaboration and evaluation. *Aggression and Violent Behavior, 12*, 08–228.

Wheeler, J., & Covell, C. (2014) Recidivism risk reduction therapy (3RT): Cognitive behavioral approaches to treating sexual offense behavior. In R. C. Tafrate & D. Mitchell (Eds.), *Forensic CBT: A handbook for clinical practice* (pp. 302–326). New York: Wiley-Blackwell.

CHAPTER 29

DELIVERING DBT IN AN INPATIENT SETTING

EMILY FOX

Introduction

Of those people diagnosed with borderline personality disorder (BPD), as many as 72% across their lifetime may find themselves treated on an inpatient unit (Lieb, Zanarini, Schmahl, Linehan, & Bohus, 2004). Some will be admitted as voluntary patients, and others will be detained under mental health legislation. Some will be in and out of hospital quickly, once an acute suicidal crisis has passed, while others may be detained in units for months or years; the decision as to where each patient ends up may appear arbitrary.

In some jurisdictions, inpatient treatment is not advised. In the United Kingdom (UK), the National Institute for Health and Care Excellence (NICE) recommends that inpatient admissions for patients with BPD should be avoided unless there is the need for "management of crisis involving significant risk to self or others" or "detention under the Mental Health Act (for any reason)" (NICE Clinical Guidance, 2009, p. 338). This injunction to keep BPD patients out of hospital if at all possible is based on sound behavioural principles, as there is a risk of contagion of self-harming behaviours (Swenson, Witterholt, & Bohus, 2007), and patients incarcerated in artificial environments (e.g., single-sex, restricted access, carefully controlled) find it difficult to practise skills for the real world that they will encounter when they leave. Thus, ensuring there is a comprehensive psychological programme that focuses on learning skills to build a life outside hospital seems vital.

In the UK, patients with apparently similar behaviours can be placed in medium-secure and low-secure units, locked rehabilitation settings, or Psychiatric Intensive Care Units (PICUs). These decisions are influenced by a variety of factors, including funding arrangements, bed availability, geographical proximity to the patient's home, access to specific treatments, and whether patients are being referred from Court, prisons, or national or local commissioning teams. Of those hospitalized with BPD, 75% will be female (Gunderson, 2011) and men with BPD are more likely to be incarcerated under the criminal justice system than admitted to hospital (Sansome & Sansome, 2011). To complicate matters further, each of these different environments will have a different recommended length of stay. Some researched programmes range from days (Silk et al., 1994; Simpson et al., 1998), others weeks (Booth, Keogh, Doyle, & Owens, 2012; Kroger et al., 2006), and yet others months (Barley et al., 1993; Fox, Krawczyk, Staniford, & Dickens, 2015). Some patients are admitted to hospital expressly for the purpose of engaging in the DBT programme as an alternative to community-based treatment (Roepke et al., 2011; van den Bosch, Sinnaeve, Hakkaart-van Roijen, & van Furth, 2014), while others are admitted to a long-stay hospital that has a DBT treatment unit as one of the available options (Fox et al., 2015). Even some short-stay psychiatric units describe using some aspects of DBT treatment (Simpson et al., 1998; Springer, Lohr, Buchtel, & Silk, 1996).

There is no doubt that the structured design of DBT fits well within the confines of controlled environments. Treatment hierarchies have face validity in targeting the specific behaviours that have led to the patient's hospitalization, while also focusing on discharge from the day of admission. As the evidence base grows, DBT has increasingly been used as the treatment of choice in inpatient settings for patients with behavioural dyscontrol. Reviews conducted by Swenson et al. (2007) and Bloom, Woodward, Susmarus, & Pantalone (2012) clearly outline how variations to standard outpatient DBT have been adapted for hospital-based programmes. This chapter reviews the data for inpatient DBT and looks at differences between short-stay and longer-term programmes. In particular it explores how the functions and modes of treatment can be provided in diverse settings. It then assesses factors influencing the patient's journey through treatment, those enhancing the likelihood of good clinical outcomes, and those contributing to patient drop out.

PUBLISHED RESEARCH ON DBT INPATIENT UNITS

Attempts by each research group to modify and apply DBT to their unique inpatient psychiatric unit make it very difficult to either compare programmes with each other or to identify the factors which lead to better clinical outcomes. As of October 2016, no consistent DBT programme protocol exists for use in inpatient settings (see Table 29.1 for recent articles published), and teams continue to decide, depending on their environment and the patients being treated, the modes in which the standard DBT functions (Linehan, 1993) are delivered. Bloom and colleague's (2012) review of 11 inpatient-based studies noted the diversity of programmes on offer, suggesting the testing of different programme structures in a step-wise manner is required to get some sense of what is most effective. This has not yet been achieved as clinicians continue to adapt DBT for the unique inpatient setting where they work. The next two sections discuss some key points from studies both in the review and subsequent to it with relation to short- and longer-term programme development.

This current review and that of Bloom et al. (2012) demonstrate that DBT programmes in inpatient settings roughly fall into two types. In the short-term programmes, the main aim is to restore the patient to the community as quickly as possible. These acute admissions are often unplanned, as a result of a crisis, and the function of any intervention is to resolve the immediate problem and, if possible, give the patient enough skills to prevent a recurrence. In the longer-term programmes, the patient is more likely to have been referred for specialist treatment that cannot be delivered in the community, either because the patient's behaviour is considered too risky, or the therapy is not available locally in an outpatient format.

Shorter-Term Inpatient DBT Programmes

For the purposes of this chapter we have arbitrarily defined short-term inpatient DBT programmes as those that admit patients for fewer than six weeks, although there is a paucity of research in this area. Having a short admission often means increasing the number of sessions during the week. Silk and colleagues (1994) devised a programme for BPD patients with an average length of stay of only ten to 17 days. They provided shortened modules of Emotion Regulation (five sessions) and Interpersonal Effectiveness (four sessions). While they included only one formal session on Distress Tolerance, patients were encouraged throughout the entire programme to focus on new methods and options for tolerating distress. Only anecdotal evidence was provided for the treatment's effectiveness, which was reportedly well-received by patients, staff, and commissioners.

Booth et al. (2012) developed a DBT Skills Training programme of eight core DBT skills taught over a two-week period, which then repeated over three cycles. These groups were delivered four days a week and were designed for patients admitted with repeated self-injurious behaviours and suicidal ideation, regardless of the diagnosis. The results indicated a significant reduction in self-injurious behaviours and an increase in patients' distress tolerance levels that were maintained at three-month follow-up. There was also a reduction in inpatient days at one-year and two-year follow-up.

Simpson and colleagues (1998) developed a partial hospital programme, with a minimum of five days inpatient treatment that included on each day a one-to-one session with their DBT therapist, a mindfulness practice, and a taught DBT skill. Patients were also provided with an overview of the DBT skills training modules and an orientation to the biosocial theory. The unit milieu had clearly defined behavioural principles, meetings during the day that reinforced DBT skills, and medications managed in individual DBT sessions. Those patients that graduated from this inpatient treatment were then eligible for a six-month outpatient DBT programme. After running for two years this format provided promising (but still anecdotal) evidence that DBT can be effectively modified to a partial hospital setting and with a more diverse psychiatric population.

Table 29.1 Literature review (June 2011 to present) for adult inpatient DBT programmes

Study	Enhancing capabilities	Improving motivation	Ensuring generalization	Structuring environment	Motivating and supporting staff
Booth et al. (2012) Group only—four days a week over six weeks. For patients with repeated self-injurious behaviours/ suicidal ideation regardless of diagnosis.	Eight core DBT skills taught—one cycle = two weeks. Three cycles to complete the course.				
Fox et al. (2015) Patients in treatment for minimum of one year with the average length of stay is two years.	Two hours of DBT skills group a week.	One-to-one weekly sessions.	Skills coaching—face-to-face and telephone from DBT therapist.	Operational policy—Risk management—Incentive programme—staff training—OT programme.	Two hours a week for therapists.
Kroger et al. (2013) 12-week admission Also, twice weekly movement therapy and art therapy (each at 100 minutes).	Weekly group psycho-education (50 minutes). DBT Skills training (Twice 100 minutes per week). Weekly Mindfulness (Once per week at 60 minutes).	One-to-one weekly for 50 minutes.		Practice groups Weekly "Patient Parliament". Every six weeks a trialogue meeting with patients and relatives/friends. Staff trained to have "basic knowledge of DBT ... discussed patients on a daily basis ... twice yearly in a half-day workshop"	Three times per week team leaders available for "supervisory and structural matters".

Kroger et al. (2014) 12-week admission. Also, active physical therapy (once weekly for 90 minutes); Occupational Therapy (90 minutes).	Psychoeducative basic group (once a week for 50 minutes). DBT Skills Training (twice a week for 90 minutes). Mindfulness training (15 minutes once a week and five to ten minutes at the start of each one-to-one or group session).	One-to-one weekly for 50 minutes. "Team and team leader met once a week with the patient to address patient's needs, modify techniques, and determine how to overcome obstacles".	Skills practice group arranged by the patients. Staff having a "basic knowledge of DBT". Team discussed patients on a daily basis.	Once a week Consultation Meeting for 60 minutes. Team was supervised once a week by "state-registered supervisor for behaviour therapy and a certified DBT therapist".
Van den Bosch et al. (2014). Outlines programme from previous pilot (van den Bosch et al., 2013). No outcomes. Accommodation for nine patients. Partial hospitalization—5 days and no staff in evenings. Two hours drama therapy, psycho-education about sexuality, substance abuse and medication, teaching on getting help but using validation and behavioural analysis skills.	Skills Training and Homework (2.5 hours per week) but separated during week. Daily mindfulness classes.	Weekly one-to-one sessions for 45 minutes.	Housekeeping meeting. Psycho-educational sessions in evening giving information on BPD and DBT, followed by a training programme (six sessions for two hours) in which patients, together with family and friends, can get help in applying the skills.	One-hour weekly consultation for trainers and therapists. Staff also receive supervision twice-weekly (orientation not mentioned).

While it is difficult to generalize findings, the common denominator in these short-term DBT programmes is the delivery of concentrated DBT skills groups training. Ensuring that the newly acquired DBT skills are learned, rehearsed, and practised in as short a period as possible is their core feature. Teaching a smaller number of skills, and selecting those that will assist in crisis resolution rather than each entire module, is pragmatic given the time constraints (Linehan, 2015). In addition, training the milieu staff to reinforce and build on DBT skills makes the best of every skills strengthening opportunity. It is in these extra hours available for on-ward coaching, if used correctly, that inpatient programmes have potential to garner additional benefits over a community intervention of a similar duration.

For acute admissions there is a danger of being over-ambitious in the treatment objectives. This type of programme can only realistically achieve a goal of the patient being discharged with a few enhanced skills (Silk et al., 1994). It is a common mistake to believe that on discharge the intervention is finished, when in reality these are the opening moves in a game of chess. The structure of these shorter-term DBT programmes should focus on specific skills likely to assist in future crises and prevent further hospitalization.

Longer-Term Inpatient DBT Programmes

These are arbitrarily defined as more than 12 weeks in duration. Much of the evidence base for these inpatient DBT programmes comes from Bohus, Haaf, Stiglmayr, et al. (2000) and Bohus, Haaf, Simms, et al. (2004) where patients were referred from a wide geographical area. Patients were admitted to 12-week comprehensive DBT programmes then discharged back to home areas to continue with long-term outpatient therapy (Bohus et al., 2000). All programmes that were reviewed (see Table 29.1) refer to the delivery of the five functions of a DBT programme, apart from Kroger et al. (2006) and Roepke et al. (2011) who do not describe the generalization function. Each study demonstrated a reduction in psychopathology. However, only Fox et al. (2015) reported a reduction in self-injurious behaviours. Kroger et al. (2006) decided not to use parasuicidal behaviour as an outcome, as self-ratings are often "conservatively" estimated and the individual's baseline scores differ in frequency (van den Bosch, Sinnaeve, & Nijs, 2013). One pilot study showed a reduction in interpersonal problems but parasuicidal behaviours were not significantly reduced (van den Bosch et al., 2014). All studies emphasize that milieu staff must have the knowledge of DBT skills to coach patients in crisis and have the support and training to work with this challenging patient group.

Predictors of Outcome in Inpatient DBT Services

There is limited research looking at factors that predict improvement, termination, or drop-out from inpatient DBT programmes. Bohus and colleagues reported that "approximately 50% of the treated patients failed to show clinically significant improvement". The authors reported that "no measure of psychopathology at admission or any sociodemographic participant variable predicted response" (Bohus et al., 2004, p. 497). When looking at effectiveness, response, and drop-out of DBT for BPD, Kroger, Harbeck, Armbrust, and Kliem (2013) found that the predictive variables were the presence of substance use disorders and a younger age at pre-treatment. Kroger, Roepke, and Kliem (2014) went on to find that more than nine suicide attempts, antisocial personality disorders, and more than 86 weeks in psychiatric hospital were significant risk factors of treatment drop-out. In their earlier study they reported reasons for *expulsion* from a DBT inpatient setting included:

- Treatment-disturbing behaviours (17%).
- Substance/alcohol abuse or possession of illicit substances (14.8%).
- Offences, threats, and use of violence (4%).
- Suicide attempts (3.4%).
- Not gaining pre-arranged weight (2.3).
- Starting a sexual relationship with another inpatient (1.7%).

These reasons contrast with those given by those patients who dropped out of therapy, which include a lack of motivation (13.1%), getting into arguments with others (10.8%), no willingness to tolerate emotional distress (10.2%), critical life events (9.1%), feeling stable but discharged against medical advice (7.4%), unknown reasons (4%), substance dependence (2.8), or death by overdose (0.6%).

IMPLEMENTING AN INPATIENT PROGRAMME

Having established whether an environment is delivering acute care or a longer-term intervention, the next question is how the DBT programme delivers the five functions of treatment (Schmidt & Russo, this volume). Decisions on how the programme will look will depend on such things as average length of stay, whether patients can return as outpatients to complete treatment, whether patients are detained under mental health legislation or liable to be transferred at short notice, the safety of others, risk of absconding, the average attention span of the patient group, competing demands (like school attendance for adolescents), and staff shift patterns.

Structuring the Environment

Sadly, in inpatient settings the very behaviours identified as the highest target in a DBT programme (e.g., life-threatening self-injury) are often reinforced by the system responses (Swenson, Sanderson, Dulit, & Linehan, 2001). Therefore, of the five functions of treatment, "Structuring the Environment" needs to be prioritized. The DBT programme itself becomes a structural component of the milieu, although how much structure it provides will vary. Prospective patients do well to establish what exactly is on offer, as, based on the review of studies reported here, all of the following have at some stage been described as DBT:

- Comprehensive DBT including staff consultation meeting, individual therapy, group skills training, telephone coaching, psycho-education for staff and patients, and contingency management in the milieu.
- Skills groups only.
- Individual sessions and groups, but without in-vivo coaching.
- Individual sessions and groups where coaching is outsourced to a community DBT team.
- Patients receiving individual sessions from one therapist, and one-to-one skills coaching from another. Often considered where patients are considered a risk to others.

Further, it would be a mistake for commissioners to think that because ward staff are trained to deliver DBT, and because the patient is being cared for on that ward, that when the patient is admitted they will immediately commence their DBT treatment. This is not always the case and it is possible for a patient to be admitted to a unit where, despite staff attending intensive DBT training, there are no DBT skills groups, no individual therapy, nor consultation meetings. If referring a patient for an inpatient DBT programme it is essential to establish which functions of the DBT programme are being delivered.

When building a programme the first task is to establish an implementation team of key personnel responsible for ensuring that the DBT programme is set up correctly with adequate resources. The project team should contain at least one person with managerial status sufficient to recruit organizational support, book rooms, allocate staff time, and, if necessary, halt the implementation process rather than deliver an under-resourced treatment. The implementation team should begin by researching whether there is a *clinical* justification for the choice of DBT, rather than a financial or system-serving one. Delivering a partial programme because there is no funding for a comprehensive one is akin to saving money by giving patients their medication only on alternate days.

Structuring the Environment to Manage Risk

Whether the treatment is short- or longer-term, an overriding feature of inpatient care is the need to structure the milieu to manage the risky behaviours that necessitated admission. When accepting responsibility for highly suicidal patients it would be understandable if the team decided to manage this risk by having a member of staff constantly with the patient. Placing the patient in rip-proof clothing in a sterile environment might also alleviate the fear of litigation or public humiliation should a patient die in a hospital spe-cifically designated for his or her protection. If staff prevent self-harming behaviours, they are further rewarded by not having to fill in forms to officially record an untoward event. Clinicians may keep patients on enhanced observations (one-to-one, two-to-one, or even three-to-one) for excessive periods, rather than risk having to face an investiga-tion if the patient were to die by suicide. Encouraging the team to hold their nerve and not just contain but *treat* patients, requires exactly the structure and understanding of behavioural principles that is given in DBT.

Within inpatient settings there is often a tension between ensuring safety and decreasing adverse events, which is all too frequently achieved by overly restrictive practices while simultaneously allowing patients the freedom to manage their own be-haviour independently using skills. Having clear protocols around managing risk while minimizing restrictions is often the solution to this dialectic. DBT provides a structure that demands patients stop engaging in the behaviours that have resulted in them being hospitalized, while recognizing that these behaviours have been their solutions to life's problems. Contingencies are created that link risk-reduction to patient privileges, while understanding that one person's privilege (such as weekend leave) is another's dread. Transparency for the patient and staff allows patients to work safely towards achievable goals and ensures that there is objectivity in decision-making around risk. The proce-dural and environmental structure of the unit could be usefully viewed as initially 100% structured and containing, with a move towards environmental leniency as the risk di-minishes (see Box 29.1).

While formal policies for responding to risk give some clear direction to the patient and staff about which consequence to apply, there needs to be a response that not only applies the contingency, but also helps the patient to understand how they reached the point at which the freedom was removed or the restriction enforced. A compassionate approach to helping patients attain a "life worth living" takes them step-by-step through what went awry, and how they might behave differently if the same provocation was encountered again.

The unit staff have a responsibility to manage incidents of suicidal and self-harm be-haviours and violence towards others in a manner which protects the individual con-cerned as well as others. In managing such behaviours the initial focus is always on the prevention of further incidents and DBT explicitly encourages the individual to seek out the assistance of DBT therapists or others for more adaptive resolution of crises instead of engaging in harmful behaviours. Linehan (1993) refers to this as an "egregious behav-iour protocol." Box 29.2 provides an example of one that may be used in an inpatient programme:

Staff Training

Frontline staff dealing with day-to-day crises on the unit who have most contact with patients require training in the approach, yet often the amount of training required is

Box 29.1   Decreasing harm versus minimizing restrictions

- Dialectical synthesis is the desired attainment in any DBT treatment programme.
- Everything in the treatment is designed to move the patient away from rigid, dichotomous, extreme behaviours towards flexible, adaptive behaviours that reflect a synthesis of contradictions.
- A synthesis of reducing risky behaviours versus increasing freedoms is to provide a structure under which as the patient reduces their harmful actions they are allowed more control and less supervision within the unit. The following is an example of how this would work in practice.

Examples of restrictions	Examples of freedoms
Highly supervised in the toilet or bathroom.	Hourly observations instead of five or 15 minutes.
Confined to shared areas in the daytime.	Access to toilet/bedroom area.
No access to bedroom unsupervised.	Supervised access to the grounds.
Continuous observations.	Unescorted access to the grounds.
Fifteen-minute observations.	Escorted trips away from the unit.
Five-minute observations.	Unsupervised trips out of the hospital.
	Overnight stays in the community.

Transparency: Each risk level should be articulated in the unit's Operational Policy, with clear guidelines on timescales and behavioural requirements for the patient to move up or down the levels of restrictions. Patients are involved in discussions about their own care, honouring the DBT principle of "consultation to the patient."

Contingency management: Factors controlling behaviour vary with each individual patient. While most patients want to work toward getting out of hospital, they also have good reason to fear being away from the security and support offered within it. Hitting a member of staff may result in a restrictive practice (such as being under continuous observation) which, rather than being disliked by the patient, is valued. This may result in the behaviour increasing rather than decreasing when the contingency of continuous observation is applied. Risk management practices need to be dialectical in their application and focus on effectiveness, rather than rules.

underestimated. Unit managers may be reluctant to allow all staff delivering DBT the time to attend consultation team, and yet this is an essential part of the treatment for people delivering any aspect of DBT. On a unit where all patients are attending DBT skills group, this time can be used to offer consultation to milieu staff to ensure contingency management and that DBT principles are being adhered to with a degree of accuracy and consistency.

Box 29.2   Egregious behaviour protocol

After an incident of suicidal or self-harm behaviour, appropriate medical attention will be provided either on the Unit or, if necessary, at the local General Hospital. Subsequently, a senior member of the nursing staff will decide on the appropriate form of management to ensure the safety of the individual concerned. At all times, it is useful to respond to such behaviours in a "matter of fact" manner, as over-concern can inadvertently increase the likelihood of future recurrences. Interest, warmth, and support should always be evident when the patient is engaging in skillful behaviour, rather than when engaging in egregious behaviours.

In the management of aggression, the initial focus is always on the prevention of such incidents. This may involve the minimization of potential triggers in the environment, or the appropriate intervention at an early stage to prevent a situation escalating to one of aggression. The procedures used to manage incidents of aggressive behaviour are the "least restrictive" possible.

At the earliest opportunity, the patient is required to work on completing a Behavioural Chain and Solution Analysis (BCA) of the target behaviour (e.g., self-injurious behaviour or aggression) which is then presented to and shaped by her DBT therapist at their next meeting. The patient can be offered a BCA template by staff following an egregious behaviour. The spirit of conducting BCA is one of genuine enquiry and learning, as chain analysis is also a part of regular DBT sessions and we do not want patients to associate BCA with being blamed or subjected to punitive measures.

For 24 hours after an incident, the patient does not have access to the individual therapist for coaching or repair, as a natural contingency of failing to ask for help *before* the incident occurred. This is to reinforce the message that if help is requested ahead of time, something can be done, whereas *after* the event, coaching is redundant. However, the therapist should not ignore the patient if they see them in passing on the unit and, as in standard DBT, if there is a scheduled DBT session this should still go ahead.

Following any incident of an egregious behaviour which has impacted adversely on the members of the Ward community, the patient will share at the Community Meeting the Solution Analysis and Plan for Repair parts of the Behavioural Chain Analysis.

All incidents of egregious behaviours are monitored and discussed with patients and the multi-disciplinary team (MDT) at their next MDT care meeting (e.g., ward round).

The type and depth of staff training delivered depends upon the admission criteria for the unit. Staff on the unit might be divided by their functional role with patients as follows:

1. Clinicians delivering individual DBT therapy.
2. Clinical/ward staff running skills training groups.
3. Clinical/ward staff co-leading skills training groups.
4. Clinical/ward staff offering DBT skills coaching to patients on the unit.
5. Support staff offering day-to-day patient care on the unit, but not participating in therapy.
6. Ancillary service staff (cooks, cleaners, gardeners, porters, etc.).

> ## Box 29.3   Possible training programmes for staff
>
> - Understanding personality disorders.
> - Orientation to DBT with focus on biosocial theory, diagnosis re-organized, and how this links to the skills modules being taught.
> - Contingency management.
> - Overview of DBT skills modules.
> - DBT assumptions about patients, staff and teams (Swenson et al., 2007, pp. 82–84).
>
> Roles of staff on the unit to ensure roles are clear with particular attention being paid to the role of the care co-ordinator and individual DBT therapist.

Assessment of training needs is always required, based on the clinical outcomes in the unit. Poor outcomes might relate to specific difficulties experienced by a particular patient group, and up-scaling the level of training can equip staff to deal with these more challenging problems. While all milieu staff can benefit from the training programme described in Box 29.3, staff who are delivering different functions of the DBT programme will need to attend relevant additional training specific to their role on the programme. Staff who are delivering DBT skills groups (the Enhancing Skills function) will need to trained to be familiar with the skills, handouts, and worksheets as well as the specific roles of the facilitator and co-facilitator. Staff who are coaching patients (the Skills Generalization function) will need training in both DBT skills and how to elicit a commitment to use skills when in a crisis. Professionals who are conducting individual DBT therapy (the Improving Motivation function) should be trained to Intensive Level and receive external supervision.

In short, concentrated programmes, where patients are moving quickly in and out of the unit, it becomes more important to maximise their learning opportunities in DBT. There is an argument, therefore, that the more people trained to prompt skillful means, the more coaching opportunities there will be (Bohus et al., 2004; Kroger et al., 2013; van den Bosch et al., 2014). In rare cases organizations have trained even ancillary personnel in basic behavioural principles—to avoid reinforcing unskilled behaviour. Maintaining an active training programme will assist in increasing staff's knowledge and empathy towards the patients' challenging behaviours.

Enhancing Patients' Capabilities

Programmes may consider limiting, extending, or dividing the time spent on teaching each skill according to the learning ability of the patients, and the average length of stay on the ward. Some units provide drop-in sessions for patients to get help with homework practice, or additional mindfulness groups for patients and staff, and some deliver more frequent DBT Skills Groups across the week rather than teaching the modules sequentially (e.g., for four days of the week a different module is taught). Frontline care providers may be trained to prompt patients in skills use on the unit, which can both enhance capabilities and also improve generalization. Access to information from posters, leaflets, and worksheets strategically placed on walls, surfaces, and the inside of the toilet doors can assist skills acquisition. Patients may be encouraged to practise the skill of the day, and be rewarded for skills use through tokens, a points system, raffle tickets, or stickers. Other interventions available on site may add to the skills enhancement process—for example, attending an anxiety management group or a 12-step addiction programme is entirely compatible with DBT. Attending family therapy, unless based on DBT principles (see Fruzzetti, this volume) or psychodynamic therapy alongside DBT, however, is not recommended.

If tempted to customize the materials, therapists are encouraged to make a proper assessment. It is not uncommon for inpatient therapists to decide their patients will be unable to understand DBT materials which have already been used extensively with all abilities. Changes do not automatically deliver better or, indeed, equal results. There are advantages to utilising the standard handouts (Linehan, 2015) as these will be used in other environments in which patients may subsequently find themselves: using the same handouts may provide much needed continuity. If patients cannot understand the materials it is advisable to review other research before creating bespoke handouts.

Improving Patient Motivation

Weekly individual therapy may be delivered in exactly the same way as in standard outpatient DBT, if the length of stay allows. Ideally, in longer-term programmes the individual DBT therapist will be allocated prior to admission and pre-treatment work will commence as soon as possible. In very short programmes, it might be useful to consider which individual will motivate the patient to achieve their goals in the shortest time frame, or consider meeting with patients in small groups to target behaviours (Swenson et al., 2007). Ensuring that discussions around self-harm are not held at these meetings could be resolved with strong ground rules, while chain analyses can still be reviewed and more skillful behaviours rehearsed (Springer et al., 1996).

Ideally the patient will meet for one hour per week with her primary therapist to review the diary card, select a target behaviour, conduct a chain and solution analysis, and rehearse alternative skillful means. The therapist will troubleshoot the solutions, and gain a commitment to practise more effective skills. Inpatient therapists are encouraged to use the word "psychotherapy" for these individual sessions, to distinguish them from the universal "one-to-one" time that will involve unstructured conversation with a named nurse or other professional. The routine of a set time and place for individual DBT sessions is also helpful to avoid the professional fitting the session in around other ward tasks. The increased availability of patients in an inpatient setting means that individual therapy can be delayed or rescheduled with more ease than for an outpatient session, but this can reduce the discipline that both parties bring to this very important work. On the other hand, if a patient remains in bed instead of coming to therapy on more than one occasion, the regular slot can be moved to a time at which she will definitely be up and about. If the new time conflicts with another activity, so be it. It is a natural consequence of failing to attend the earlier appointments. Inpatient staff need to convey the message that this is a life-saving treatment that neither they nor the patient can afford to miss and, therefore, they should do their best to supply cover for one another during therapists' absence.

Ensuring Generalization

Inpatient DBT staff must regularly remind patients that the skills they are learning relate directly to the problems they face outside hospital (e.g., managing strong emotions, dealing with angry people, and managing stress). The patient is encouraged to call for assistance when trying to implement a skill outside of skills training group. Initially, these coaching sessions may be offered as face-to-face meetings by staff trained to coach DBT skills on the unit and then expanded as the patient is allowed out on leave to telephone calls. In-vivo coaching can be accessed by paging or telephoning the individual therapist, asking staff trained specifically to deliver DBT skills coaching, or via a nominated "coach of the day."

All methods by which milieu staff coach skills will help in generalization, but it must be remembered that using the skills on the unit is not generalizing to the real world. What *is* possible in the milieu is the chance for some staff members to replicate real-world responses (for example, getting angry when a patient breaks the rules), while a DBT coach helps the patient handle the scenario skillfully. This is why it is important that not everyone prompts skills use with the patient, as this would present an unrealistic expectation of life outside hospital. Graded exposure to actual triggers and challenging situations must be achieved while the patient still has access to coaching from the ward. Trips out, initially escorted and then without support, are essential.

Enhancing Therapist Motivation

In a DBT milieu, staff attendance at a consultation meeting should become integral to life on the unit. This can sometimes be a challenge given different shift patterns. The fact that staff may meet for other clinical and managerial meetings on the unit can result in consultation meetings being de-prioritized in the belief that DBT queries can be discussed elsewhere. However, a DBT consultation meeting is unique to the therapy—it is a "team of therapists" (Koerner, 2012) treating the inpatients and working together to achieve the mutual goals, with adherence to DBT principles. In some establishments there will be two consultation meetings each week, one for late shift workers, and the other on early shift. In others, all therapists are scheduled on the daytime rota to fit in with skills group and consultation team. Keeping a register of attendance and asking all to sign a commitment to attend and adhere to the DBT principles can help when individuals drift.

Issues of authority and seniority can sometimes be exaggerated in environments where power over decisions is a desirable commodity, so teams should maintain a dialectical approach. In inpatient settings, DBT therapists can be psychologists, psychiatrists, occupational therapists, social workers, and nurses, but hierarchies that exist outside the meeting (e.g., psychiatrists often being the clinical lead on the unit) are not relevant in Consultation Team. Again, including an equal-status agreement in the commitment that is signed by all can help if this tension arises. Consultation Team provides "therapy for the therapist" (Koerner, 2012) and allows for fallibility, so it is important that the blame-culture endemic to secure environments should not infiltrate this meeting. Therapists need to feel able to admit to mistakes and problem solve them without fear.

Phases of DBT Treatment in Inpatient Settings

Although the phases of treatment in an inpatient setting will be the same for all patients requiring hospitalization, they will vary in length depending upon the unit's criteria for admission (e.g. psychiatric Intensive Care Unit—PICU, locked rehab, specialist inpatient treatment, secure units) and the needs of the patient being admitted. Swenson et al. (2007) describe a three-phased approach when delivering DBT in an inpatient setting:

- Getting in (Phase 1—pre-treatment).
- Getting in control (Phase 2).
- Getting out (Phase 3).

The metaphor of an inpatient unit being like a swimming pool can help patients and staff understand these phases. Phase 1 involves getting patients to commit to getting into the water. Phase 2 involves getting patients from the baby pool (small, warm, few people, a helper alongside) to the deep end (teenagers splashing and jumping in, inflatables to negotiate). Phase 3 involves planning and moving from the controlled waters in the swimming pool to open-water swimming.

Phase 1: Getting In (Pre-Treatment)

The earlier the patient can be orientated to DBT the better—ideally at a pre-admission assessment. Increasingly, patients have had some experience of DBT prior to admission and it is important to clarify what has been offered previously. All too often, therapists find out that the patient who reports that they have already "done DBT" have only been taught some of the DBT skills (perhaps Distress Tolerance) and, because this was unsuccessful, the patient feels despondent. Here, the therapist can orientate the patient to the programme currently on offer by providing information booklets, discussing the obligations of both therapist and patient, and offering to talk to family members where desired. Maintaining a mindful stance, the therapist reminds all parties that the patient has never done *this* programme before.

A danger for inpatient services is losing focus on the patient's "life worth living" outside of the establishment, particularly so for long-stay admissions. Patients can quickly feel "at home" as inpatients, but it is a home where the "rent" must be paid in continued pathology—when the patient stops producing risky and harmful behaviours they are considered for eviction. For this reason, therapists must ensure that from the patient's first day on the unit, they keep alive the possibility of a better place for the patient to ultimately reside, and an improved lifestyle beyond the unit. The patient's life-goals have to be fleshed out in detail: where they will be living (geographically and what type of placement), how they will be filling their time (e.g., attending college to complete an animal care course, working part time in an office, etc.), what hobbies they will be engaging in (e.g., horse riding, cinema, Zumba, attending church, etc.) and who they will be socializing with (e.g., friends, family, partner). Ensuring that patients and therapists have in their minds a clear picture of these life goals is crucial when someone is newly admitted as it keeps the focus, throughout treatment, on exiting the unit. The "life worth living" option must be preferable to the inpatient one as, without this incentive, patients will deteriorate whenever discharge is mooted, whether intentionally or just through pure fear. It cannot be left until the later stages of therapy when the patient has already made an emotional investment in staying put.

Commitment is sought to work on the behaviours that led to hospitalization and those required for discharge, which is formulated as a goal of treatment. This focus requires the unit to be behaviourally specific about both the reasons for admission and the criteria for discharge, and to move away from the sometimes vague notion of patients being discharged "when they are ready." It also means that whatever the remit of the unit (e.g., treating eating disorders, alcohol consumption, self-harming, aggressive behaviour, etc.), the treatment will aim to decrease the undesired behaviours and increase those that are considered essential for onward progress, be that discharge back to their home or to step-down care.

Building a Target Hierarchy

In Phase 1, as in outpatient DBT, a target hierarchy is drawn up. It is important to consider the behaviours that have resulted in treatment not being offered in the community. Life-threatening behaviours (in terms of both harm to self and others) are often obvious, but the therapist must also attend to behaviours that are restricted by the inpatient environment. For example, if the patient was admitted for setting fires, just being in a controlled setting can inhibit the behaviour. In this case the therapist will add "urges to set fires" to the hierarchy. The patient may report that these urges occur in a variety of situations—classically conditioned (she sees some cardboard and it triggers an association with fire-setting) or operant (she has an argument with another patient and has an urge to set a fire "to teach her a lesson"). These urges become the subject of a chain and solution analysis in individual therapy.

Therapy-interfering behaviours, as in outpatient DBT, will include all behaviours that result in the patient being out of the DBT treatment programme. Additionally, in an inpatient setting, any behaviours that result in the patient being discharged from the unit and, therefore, out of the DBT programme, can also be included in the target hierarchy (e.g., breaking the unit rules/expectations leading to discharge from the unit, bringing substances/alcohol onto the unit).

Therapists often struggle to identify quality-of-life interfering behaviours once the patient has stopped the main problematic actions that prompted her admission. It is helpful to ask what the factors are currently that maintain the patient's inpatient status. This may be the presence of "flaggable offences" (Christine Dunkley, personal communication, 29 October 2015) which are any behaviours by the patient that if a mental health review were called would prevent them being considered for discharge. Milieu staff often say, "Well, she's not harming herself any more but we're not confident that she can be discharged." This needs to be operationalized; what behaviours are either present or absent that lead to the staff's concern? Also, therapists need to consider the "seriousness" test, i.e., if the patient did the same thing in the community, would it be a reason to admit her into hospital? If not, then it should not be cited as the sole reason to keep her in hospital.

In some cases, the criteria for discharge from hospital are based on maintaining a harm-free status for a period of time, in which case, this should be clearly articulated to the patient, i.e., how long is long enough for the staff to consider discharge? The expression, "when we are confident in your ability to cope" is an opportunity to name what those confidence-provoking behavioural markers will be, e.g., "when you have had no self-harm for three months despite utilizing unescorted leave for six weeks".

Not every problem and diagnosis the patient has needs to be treated during the current admission. For some patients, treating social anxiety, trauma, or substance misuse is needed to ensure that they stay out of hospital. Others can be discharged once the life-threatening behaviours are under control, with comorbid mental health problems being treated by the receiving community team. A sample target hierarchy is given in Box 29.4.

Building the target hierarchy offers the patient a comprehensive view of what will be worked on during therapy, and then they are asked to formally opt in or out. Once commitment to the DBT programme has been made (either a literal or metaphorical handshake or signing of an agreement), this is celebrated on the unit with comment and praise being given at the next Community Meeting. Some units have a DBT Notice Board which is used to welcome patients once they have joined the DBT programme.

Of course, the patient must also be allowed to choose non-engagement, no matter how much the team or therapist believe DBT will help. However, patients may be nudged slightly towards the DBT option if the opt-out plan is less appealing. It will not

Box 29.4   Case example of target hierarchy

Life-threatening behaviours—Self-directed

- Tying ligatures around neck.
- Taking lethal overdoses of prescribed and over-the-counter medication.
- Jumping from heights (bridges/buildings).
- Cutting arteries/blood letting.
- Headbanging walls.
- Cutting forearms/legs.
- Burning hands/arms/legs.
- Urges to engage in the above behaviours.

Life-threatening behaviours—Violence towards others

- Fire-setting.
- Hitting others.
- Urges to engage in the above behaviours.

Therapy-interfering behaviours

- Not attending DBT groups or individual sessions.
- Not completing diary cards.
- Lying face down on the floor during therapy sessions.
- Breaking unit rules that will result in discharge/transfer from the unit.

Quality-of-life interfering behaviours/behaviours maintaining inpatient status

- Making pointed sexual remarks to staff.
- Illicit substance and/or alcohol misuse.
- Not attending scheduled careers sessions.
- Binge eating and purging.
- Urges to engage in the above behaviours.

enhance the patient's motivation to attend DBT if the alternative is art classes, one-to-one time, or trips off-site. Whereas recommending the patient has "quiet time" while she waits for others to finish in skills group and that she completes a chain and solution analysis on the factors that led to her missing the session might make it more likely that she will reconsider entering the programme. What is not recommended is offering "DBT through the back door", i.e., teaching skills and strategies without the patient ever making a commitment to follow through. Specific DBT input should be reserved for those who opt in, although the unit may leave the door open for the patient to reconsider at a later date.

Phase 2—Getting In Control

In Phase 2, the target is reducing life-threatening behaviours and behaviours that compromise treatment in an outpatient setting. The treatment plan emphasizes the acquisition and practice of DBT skills in the environment, spreading from the unit to wider opportunities to practise use of skills. Staff are looking for the maximum number of practice opportunities for the patient. Lee and Harris (2010) have described an effective occupational therapy treatment pathway that provides opportunities, as risk diminishes, to engage in both activities of daily living, hobbies, and vocational pursuits. Further, Comtois, Kerbrat, Atkins, Harned, and Elwood (2010) have discussed the importance of patients exiting systems and engaging in meaningful vocational activity that would be relevant when considering the needs of patients as they are being discharged from inpatient care.

As in standard outpatient DBT, diary cards are reviewed with the primary therapist and the highest target on the hierarchy addressed by completing a chain and solution analysis. As patients live together, and are attended by a cohort of staff, there is scope for more in-vivo coaching than in outpatient settings. This includes peer-to-peer support, making repairs to the community, and demonstrating skillful negotiation during ward meetings. The behaviours agreed during Phase 1 are worked on and, as the patient becomes more in control of their life-threatening behaviours, the therapist moves down the target hierarchy.

Despite the milieu being a vital component of the phase "getting in control", it is equally important to avoid creating a "DBT bubble". This is where everyone uses the same DBT language that is not transferrable to life outside hospital (e.g. "Have you attended to your PLEASE skills?"), someone is always available to offer skills coaching when needed, and skills use is consistently rewarded. Many inpatient therapists ask the question: "What do we do when other staff members don't know DBT and reinforce unskilled behaviour, or suggest non-DBT solutions?" The answer is, "Be grateful, for in the community your patient may encounter people who demand they desist from DBT, ridicule their skills, and encourage illegal or harmful actions." Teach the patient to be her own advocate in the face of opposing forces. It is always a dialectical dilemma—too little reinforcement of skills will lead to lack of learning, while too much will create unrealistic expectations.

Once therapy is under way, the most common difficulty for inpatient settings is that staff members are pulled away from therapy to manage the day-to-day running of the ward. Staff rotas in hospitals are a constant source of frustration. Therapists are encouraged to remind the establishment that the treatment of life-threatening self-harm is as high in priority as the provision of chemotherapy for cancer. It is in the mid-phase of treatment that both patients and staff members can become complacent—paradoxically, the patient is more available to the therapist than a community patient would be, but this can result in less therapy as both parties assume DBT will happen by osmosis simply because the patient is in the unit. Regular, reliable therapy slots are important for effective treatment.

During this phase, the patient may access in-vivo coaching to help with skills implementation. Ideally this will be someone who knows the patient and therefore what skills are in her response hierarchy. However, some units nominate a "coach of the day" or staff specifically trained to deliver DBT skills coaching who will attend any of the patients who request help with DBT as an alternative to self-harm.

A dialectical dilemma sometimes arises when addressing trauma-focused work with both patients and community teams preferring for this work to be addressed while in hospital, so that risk can be more readily managed. However, an inpatient is often not able to address some of the "in vivo" exposure work that would typically be addressed while they are many miles away from home. Protocols for simultaneous PTSD work are now available (Harned, Korslund, Foa, & Linehan, 2012) and can be utilized if appropriate training and supervision is available.

Phase 3—Getting Out

In the final phase of inpatient treatment, the focus moves to getting out and staying out of hospital. Having a clear idea of the discharge setting allows the patient and therapist to design management plans that reduce the risk of relapse and increase the likelihood of staying in the community. Content of individual therapy moves subtly to include coping ahead with high risk situations that are likely to occur on discharge.

During this phase of therapy, it is not unusual for staff attitudes to polarize between those who think the patient needs to do more work, and those championing immediate discharge. A synthesis is achieved by replicating some of the structure provided by treatment with routines more appropriate to a life outside the unit. Vocational, educational, and leisure activities must be set up prior to discharge. Patients who have been free of self-injurious behaviours need to be tested in the presence of the triggers they will encounter outside, e.g., peers who might encourage drinking/drug taking, family arguments, or specific cues that elicit traumatic memories. They often find it hard to believe that this will be an issue on discharge, yet the failure to generalize skills from the security of the inpatient setting to the real world is a known hazard on discharge. There is really no substitution for incrementally more challenging trips into the environment where the patient needs to use skills, eventually "scaffolding out" the support of the unit staff. A robust risk management plan is constructed in collaboration with the patient to reduce the likelihood of readmission.

Graduate groups are sometimes provided for DBT completers, where problems implementing skillful behaviour outside the hospital can be debated and solved. Peers take responsibility for the group discussion and for generating solutions, thereby reducing reliance on staff input. Successful graduates can be invited back to the unit to inspire newly admitted patients, providing hope in the possibility of a "life worth living." Some units have a graduation ceremony or party for the patient on discharge where the community celebrates their achievement, and remaining patients can look forward to marking their own progress the same way.

Dialectical Dilemmas

While milieu interventions can be hugely effective, the inpatient environment offers many opportunities for tensions to arise. When problems occur they most likely involve a dialectical imbalance, and frequently mirror those cited by Rathus and Miller (2000) in their DBT adaptation for adolescents. Members of staff often act *in loco parentis* and may get into the type of arguments that parents have with their adolescent children. Messy patient bedrooms become battle grounds while more pathological behaviours (e.g., scratching arms with a broken pen) are minimized. Staff hold opposing views and argue that their position is right; having an understanding of the adolescent dialectic tensions in these situations will help both sides find the synthesis. In each of the adolescent dilemmas that follow, we describe how this relates to the inpatient setting.

Pathologizing Normative Behaviours vs Normalizing Pathological Behaviours

Here, the staff may overemphasize behaviours that outside the unit might be considered little more than an unhealthy lifestyle choice (e.g., not washing daily, not filling their time with meaningful activity, eating "junk" food over a healthy option). At the same time, they may minimize risky behaviours (e.g., staff in hospital expecting to get hit and not involving the police, or allowing patients to stay in bed all day despite mood significantly deteriorating).

Fostering Dependence vs Forcing Autonomy

A member of staff could tidy patients' bedrooms, express groundless fears about their ability to move on, or act as go-between when there are disputes. Crucial to this dilemma is that patients may feel that this is the first place they feel safe and understood by their treating team. At the same time, patients are sometimes perceived as "wilful", "not trying," or "quite happy where they are," when they actually lack skill to do better and need additional help. Patients can be told to "use your DBT skills" by staff members who have not themselves conceptualized what skill would be helpful or how it could be implemented. Instead, they expect the patient to know or they are quickly given increased home leave without adequate preparation and consolidation of skills.

Excessive Leniency vs Authoritarian Control

Members of the care team can get in the habit of removing demands from patients when they are highly aroused or display hostile or uncooperative behaviours, such that normal courtesy and consideration for others is not expected. They may allow lateness, swearing, spitting, and disregard for property in order to not provoke the patient further. At the same time, patients are sometimes ignored while they are quiet almost to the point of inducing loneliness, yet at the first sign of misbehaviour they may receive excessive social contact. Risky behaviour may result in increasing the level of observation such that it is impossible for the patient to develop self-regulatory skills.

Inpatients can be blamed for deliberately or otherwise acting in ways which cause disagreements and ruptures among their treating teams. In such instances, the behavioural approach of DBT would lead to careful assessment of behaviours and contingencies, rather than relying on concepts (which may come from other models, e.g., "splitting") or jumping to conclusion. Maybe the patient is simply going about her day, responding differently to a variety of people as anyone might. Some staff members will be more agreeable to her and she to them, and some decisions in the unit will be more acceptable than others. At times, the patient may ask for something from one person and then, if refused, ask another with whom she thinks she may have more chance of success. This might be termed skillful pursuit of a goal. It is the staff team that responds to this behaviour by taking polarized positions and holding them rigidly. Once professionals are willing to engage with each other in a dialectical manner and search for what makes sense in each position, there are opportunities to build a synthesis in how to approach the situation (Ritter and Platt, 2016; Swenson et al., 2007). For example, one patient wanted the staff to move the time of skills group so she could do an unrelated class off the unit. The team polarized into those saying she was being skillful in asking, and those observing that she frequently got other people to change their schedules to make sure she was not inconvenienced, describing this as "active passivity." Once the team acknowledged a little truth in both sides they decided to ask the patient to do the legwork for the change, assessing when everyone was free, and making sure this coincided with the group room availability. This rewarded her skillful request, without reinforcing any active passivity.

Conclusions

The structure and clarity of DBT lend themselves to implementation in inpatient settings. While it is possible to adopt many of the principles of a standard DBT outpatient service (e.g., patient assumptions, functions of a comprehensive DBT programme, the 4-miss rule, the 24-hour rule, etc.), the restrictions around length of stay, focus on risk reduction, and security issues mean that adjustments are necessary. The huge variation in types of setting means that, despite numerous studies, there is no recognized standardized approach to delivering DBT in these contexts. The research thus far shows some promise for inpatient DBT, provided the goals and programme structures are clear, staff are well trained, and there is a consistent focus on helping the patient achieve the necessary skills to live outside the inpatient setting.

Key Messages for Clinicians

- Decide on whether what is being offered is a crisis resolution programme, where there is a need for a brief admission focused on quick discharge, or a specialist treatment unit. This might depend more on the actual length of stay versus the desired one. The length of stay for patients will inform treatment targets in individual therapy and also the breadth of DBT skills taught in the Skills Training Groups.

- In terms of treatment targets, focus on those behaviours that got the patient into inpatient treatment and keep them there—watch for "mission creep" and having to treat every last problem that actually could be managed in the community once the risk has abated.

- The evidence for short-term DBT programmes indicates teaching a concentrated version of DBT skills (fewer skills taught more frequently) with a focus on crisis resolution.

- The evidence for longer-term DBT programmes emphasizes the importance of structuring the environment with a strong emphasis on behavioural principles and discharge.

- Maximize the opportunities to strengthen and generalize the use of skillful behaviour.

- Pay attention to Rathus and Miller's (2000) dialectical dilemmas for treating suicidal adolescents and their families, and how they manifest themselves in inpatient settings.

References

Barley, W. D., Buie, S. E., Peterson, E. W., Hollingsworth, A. S., Griva, M., Hickerson, S. C., ... Bailey, B. J. (1993). Development of an inpatient cognitive-behavioral treatment program for borderline personality disorder. *Journal of Personality Disorders, 7*(3), 232–240.

Bloom, J. M., Woodward, E. N., Susmaras, T., & Pantalone, D. W. (2012). Use of dialectical behavior therapy in inpatient treatment of borderline personality disorder: A systematic review. *Psychiatric Services, 63*(9), 881–888.

Bohus, M., Haaf, B., Stiglmayr, C., Pohl, U., Bohme, R., & Linehan, M. M. (2000). Evaluation of inpatient dialectical behavioural therapy for borderline personality disorder. *Behaviour Research and Therapy, 38,* 875–887.

Bohus, M., Haaf, B., Simms, T., Limberger, M. F., Schmahl, C., Unckel, C., ... Linehan, M. M. (2004). Effectiveness of inpatient dialectical behavioural therapy for borderline personality disorder: a controlled trial. *Behaviour Research and Therapy, 42,* 487–499.

Booth, R., Keogh, K., Doyle, J., & Owens, T. (2012). Living through distress: A skills training group for reducing deliberate self-harm. *Behavioural and Cognitive Psychotherapy, 42,* 156–165.

Comtois, K. A., Kerbrat, A. H., Atkins, D. C., Harned, M. S., & Elwood, L. (2010). Recovery from disability for individuals with borderline personality disorder: A feasibility trial of DBT-ACES. *Psychiatric Services*, 61(11), 1106–1111.

Fox, E., Krawczyk, K., Staniford, J., & Dickens, G. L. (2015). A service evaluation of a 1-year dialectical behaviour therapy programme for women with borderline personality disorder in a low secure unit. *Behavioural and Cognitive Psychotherapy*, 43, 676–691.

Gunderson, J. G. (2011). Borderline personality disorder. *New England Journal of Medicine*, 364, 2037–2042.

Harned, M. S., Korslund, K. K., Foa, E. B., & Linehan, M. M. (2012). Treating PTSD in suicidal and self-injuring women with borderline personality disorder: Development and preliminary evaluation of a dialectical behavior therapy prolonged exposure protocol. *Behaviour Research and Therapy*, 50(6), 381–386.

Koerner, K. (2012). *Doing dialectical behavior therapy: A practical guide*. New York, NY: Guilford Press.

Kroger, C., Schweiger, U., Sipos, V., Arnold, R., Kahl, K. G., Schunert, T., ... Reinecker, H. (2006). Effectiveness of dialectical behaviour therapy for borderline personality disorder in an inpatient setting. *Behaviour Research and Therapy*, 44, 1211–1217.

Kroger, C., Harbeck, S., Armbrust, M., & Kliem, S. (2013). Effectiveness, response, and dropout of dialectical behavior therapy for borderline personality disorder in an inpatient setting. *Behaviour Research and Therapy*, 51, 411–416.

Kroger, C., Roepke, S., & Kliem, S. (2014). Reasons for premature termination of dialectical behavior therapy for inpatients with borderline personality disorder. *Behaviour Research and Therapy*, 60, 46–52.

Lee, S., & Harris, M. (2010). The development of an effective occupational therapy assessment and treatment pathway for women with a diagnosis of borderline personality disorder in an inpatient setting: implementing the Model of Human Occupation. *British Journal of Occupational Therapy*, 73(11), 559–563.

Lieb, K., Zanarini, M. C., Schmahl, C., Linehan, M. M., & Bohus, M. (2004). Borderline personality disorder. *The Lancet*, 364, 453–461.

Linehan, M. M. (1993). *Cognitive-behavioral treatment of borderline personality disorder*. New York, NY: Guilford Press.

Linehan, M. M. (2015). *DBT skills training manual*. New York, NY: Guilford Press.

National Collaborating Centre for Mental Health (2009). *Borderline personality disorder: Treatment and management*. (National Clinical Practice Guideline Number 78). London: The British Psychological Society and The Royal College of Psychiatrists.

Rathus, J. H., & Miller, A. L. (2000). DBT for adolescents: Dialectical dilemmas and secondary treatment targets. *Cognitive Behavioral Practice*, 7(4), 425–434.

Ritter, S., & Platt, L. M. (2016). What's new in treating inpatients with personality disorders?: Dialectical behaviour therapy and old-fashioned, good communication. *Journal of Psychosocial Nursing and Mental Health Services*, 54(1), 38–45.

Roepke, S., Schroder-Abe, M., Schutz, A., Jacob, G., Dams, A., Vater, A., ... Lammers, C. H. (2011). Dialectic behavioural therapy has an impact on self-concept clarity and facets of self-esteem in women with borderline personality disorder. *Clinical Psychology and Psychotherapy*, 18, 148–158.

Sansome, R. A., & Sansome, L. A. (2011). Gender patterns in borderline personality disorder. *Innovations in Clinical Neuroscience*, 8(5), 18–20.

Silk, K. R., Eisner, W., Allport, C., DeMars, K., Miller, C., Justice, R. W., & Lewis, M. (1994). Focused time-limited inpatient treatment of Borderline Personality Disorder. *Journal of Personality Disorders, 8*(4), 268–278.

Simpson, E. B., Pistorello, J., Begin, A., Costello, E., Levinson, J., Mulberry, S., . . . Stevens, M. (1998). Use of dialectical behaviour therapy in a partial hospital program for women with borderline personality disorder. *Psychiatric Services, 49,* 669–673.

Springer, T., Lohr, N. E., Buchtel, H. A., & Silk, K. R. (1996). A preliminary report of short-term cognitive-behavioral group therapy for inpatients with personality disorders. *Journal of Psychotherapy Practice and Research, 5,* 57–71.

Swenson, C. R., Sanderson, C., Dulit, R. A., & Linehan, M. M. (2001). The application of dialectical behavior therapy for patients with borderline personality disorder on inpatient units. *Psychiatric Quarterly, 72*(4), 307–324.

Swenson, C. R., Witterholt, S., & Bohus, M. (2007). Dialectical behavior therapy on inpatient units. In L. Dimeff & K. Koerner (Eds.), *Dialectical behavior therapy in clinical practice; applications across disorders and settings* (pp. 69–111). New York, NY: Guilford Press.

van den Bosch L. M. C., Sinnaeve R., & Nijs, M. G. (2013). In Dutch. Kortdurende klinische dialectische gedragstherapie voor de borderline persoonlijkheidsstoornis: ontwerp van programma en resultaten pilotstudie. *Tijdschrift voor Psychiatrie, 55,* 165–175.

van den Bosch, L. M. C., Sinnaeve, R., Hakkaart-van Roijen, L., & van Furth, E. F. (2014). Efficacy and cost-effectiveness of an experimental short-term inpatient dialectical behavior therapy (DBT) program: study protocol for a randomized controlled trial. *Trials, 15,* doi: 10.1186/1745-6215-15-152

DIALECTICAL BEHAVIOUR THERAPY IN COLLEGE COUNSELLING CENTRES

AMANDA A. ULIASZEK, CARLA D. CHUGANI, AND GREGORY E. WILLIAMS

COLLEGE COUNSELLING CENTRES: AN OVERVIEW

COLLEGE counselling centres (CCCs) are often the first line of defence in the identification and treatment of a variety of mental disorders in emerging adult populations. CCCs vary across universities in terms of their staff, size, policies, and expertise; however, there are some commonalities found across the majority of sites: 1) CCCs are located on campus to increase access for students; 2) tuition payments typically cover CCCs services and do not incur an additional cost for registered students; 3) a majority of CCCs have session limits or promote the centre as a short-term counselling service. Below we review the primary mental health concerns of college students, based on large scale surveys, and the common challenges currently faced by many CCCs.

University Student Mental Health

The climate of mental health is changing in colleges and universities. Where severe psychopathology would have precluded many from attending college in the past, improvements in the treatment and diagnosis of adolescents, reduced stigma related to mental health difficulties, and legal emphasis on early identification of challenges and the development of individualized education plans to address these associated with the Individuals with Disabilities Education Act (IDEA) has enabled many more students to attend college. In fact, in a survey of 275 CCC directors representing over 3 million North American students, 94% report a steady increase in the number of students arriving on campus with severe psychological problems (Gallagher, 2014). With research estimating that as many as 25% of college students report treatment for or diagnosis of a psychiatric condition in the previous year (ACHA, 2016), it is not surprising CCCs are treating more students each year.

While mental health concerns vary across student populations, large-scale international surveys consistently report significant impairment regarding instances of anxiety, depression, and suicidality on college campuses. An international study of 380 CCCs reported that anxiety continues to be a primary mental health concern across campuses (Reetz, Barr, & Krylowicz, 2013). Several studies in the United States and Canada also found that a majority of students reported overwhelming anxiety or feeling overwhelmed by all they have to do, and a quarter of students report that anxiety negatively affected their academic performance (ACHA, 2016; NCHA, 2013). Mental health concerns about anxiety are followed closely by high rates of depression, hopelessness, and sadness, with 37–39% of students reporting levels of depression high enough to affect daily functioning (ACHA, 2016; NCHA, 2013; Reetz et al., 2013). Finally, suicidality continues to be a major concern across campuses, with estimates of students experiencing suicidal ideation as high as 18% (Reetz et al., 2013), and up to 10% seriously considering suicide in the previous year (ACHA, 2016; NCHA, 2013).

Approximately 10% of college students will seek treatment from their CCC this year (ACHA, 2016; Gallagher, 2014); this 10% represents hundreds of thousands of students who are in need of help, support, and psychological intervention. The increasing rates of psychopathology in college students present a campus-wide challenge that is especially acute for those working in the CCC. Regarding types of psychopathology, CCC directors report an increase in all types of severe psychopathology, with a majority noting an increase in anxiety disorders, crises requiring immediate response, and clinical depression (Gallagher, 2014). The idea that CCCs primarily deal with mild anxiety and sadness is no longer accurate. Currently, 52% of students would be categorized as having severe psychological problems, with 8% so severe that they cannot remain in school (Gallagher, 2014).

Changes and Challenges in CCCs

Changes in the CCC context are necessary to combat the increase in prevalence and complexity of college student mental health concerns. CCCs now must treat a larger number of students with more severe symptomatology, and to adequately address these concerns, changes are necessary at clinician, CCC policy, and university policy levels. Over the previous decade, many CCCs have attempted to meet these new challenges with a number of strategies, including increasing the amount of time dedicated to training and a focus on making appropriate referrals and dealing with difficult cases (Gallagher, 2014). At the university level, a majority of schools report staff serving on interdisciplinary committees to identify troubled students. This increase in training and preventive measures are important first steps. However, only 26% of surveyed CCCs listed increasing counselling staff as a measure to address these problems and only 14% increased training for staff in time-limited therapy. Even fewer cited offering skills training for students (Gallagher, 2014). Further, Gallagher (2014) reported that referrals to external practitioners applied to only 9% of clients, demonstrating that the CCC still remains the primary mode for treatment delivery for many students.

To summarize, universities must acknowledge and respond to the high rates of students displaying increasingly complex and severe psychopathology. While CCCs have taken a number of steps to address these problems, limited access to resources adversely affects efficacy, and the majority of CCCs must operate with fewer personnel and less training in evidence-based, time-limited therapies than needed, given student demand. In fact, those employed by CCCs cite their most time-consuming issues to be administrative issues related to students with severe psychopathology; balancing their varying demands for services; and the growing demand for services without an appropriate increase in resources (Gallagher, 2014).

DBT in CCCs: An *Almost* Perfect Fit

DBT is a cognitive-behavioural treatment with strong foundations in behavioural principles, Zen Buddhism, and dialectical theory. In DBT, clients are conceptualized through a biosocial framework, which focuses on the interaction between an invalidating environment and inherent emotional vulnerabilities (Linehan, 1993). The comprehensive DBT protocol includes weekly individual therapy sessions, skills group, team consultation, and as-needed telephone coaching, and typically requires a one-year commitment. There is consistent evidence supporting DBT as a gold standard psychological intervention for a range of disorders (Robins & Chapman, 2004). While DBT began as a treatment for borderline personality disorder (BPD), suicidality, and self-harm (Linehan, Tutek, Heard, & Armstrong, 1994; Linehan et al., 2006), several randomized controlled trials support its efficacy in the treatment of substance use (Linehan et al., 2002), severe and comorbid depression (Lynch et al. 2007), and eating disorders (Telch, Agras, & Linehan, 2001). Recent research also has supported DBT as an efficacious treatment for adolescents with emotion dysregulation and suicidality (James, Taylor, Winmill, & Alfoadari, 2008; Uliaszek, Rashid, Williams, & Gulamani, 2016; Uliaszek, Wilson, Mayberry, Cox, & Maslar, 2014; Woodberry & Popenoe, 2008). Presently, DBT is characterized as a treatment for severe emotion dysregulation (Linehan, 2015), a transdiagnostic construct underlying the cognitive, behavioural, and interpersonal dysregulation that is characteristic of many types of psychopathology (Fairholme, Boisseau, Ellard, Ehrenreich, & Barlow, 2010).

Unfortunately, CCCs face two primary difficulties: 1) increasing prevalence, complexity, and severity of student psychopathology, and 2) limited resources to increase training in evidence-based therapies or number of staff. We assert that DBT may be uniquely suited to help address a portion of these problems within the CCC. First, as a transdiagnostic treatment, DBT can help treat an array of presenting problems—an important feature for CCCs charged with serving *all* students who seek services. This includes those presenting the most severe concerns, as DBT has consistently resulted in reduced suicidality and self-harm (e.g., Kliem, Kroger, & Kosfelder, 2010; Panos, Jackson, Hasan, & Panos, 2014). The breadth of relevant treatment targets and large body of research support for DBT can address the problems of the increasing severity of college student psychopathology and dearth of evidence-based practice offered.

Second, because DBT is a modular treatment (both in terms of individual vs. group components and the skills modules themselves), modifications are available to address the specific needs of the CCC and the student population (see Strategic Modifications for the CCC Practice Setting). This not only increases its utility, but it makes it possible to reduce training demands by only training staff in one DBT modality—typically DBT skills group. Third, because there are limited resources to increase staff to address the growing number of students needing counselling, DBT skills group as a standalone or adjunct treatment allows simultaneous treatment of several students using an evidence-based, time-limited approach. In fact, research has already accumulated supporting this strategy (Valentine, Bankoff, Poulin, Reidler, & Pantalone, 2015). Below, we review the empirical evidence for DBT in CCCs, as well as a number of clinical strategies that may aid in the implementation of DBT in this setting.

Research Evidence

As recognition of the demands placed on CCCs has increased in recent years, so too has the research examining DBT in this context (see Table 30.1 for a summary of research evidence). A survey of CCC directors regarding non-suicidal self-injury (NSSI) revealed that, as of 2009, DBT (43% of respondents) trailed only cognitive behaviour therapy (67%) in frequency of treatment approach for this behaviour (Whitlock, Eells, Cummings, & Purington, 2009). The survey revealed that estimates of prevalence rates of NSSI among college students were between 12–17%, highlighting a clear need for efficacious interventions. Despite the reported frequency of DBT use to this point, no published research at the time had empirically tested DBT in a CCC setting.

Pistorello, Fruzzetti, MacLane, Gallop, and Iverson (2012) were the first group to conduct a randomized trial of DBT in a CCC, comparing a comprehensive DBT programme to an "optimized" treatment-as-usual (TAU) condition. The latter condition was modelled after a study by Linehan et al. (2006), who also mandated that expert clinicians led their control group. The sample included 63 treatment-seeking college students who reported suicidal ideation and had at least one prior act of NSSI or suicidal behaviour. All participants also met at least three criteria for BPD, and did not require inpatient care or show evidence of psychotic symptoms. Four modifications to the DBT programme from the manualized standard (1-year) treatment included: 1) condensation of the distress

Table 30.1 Summary of studies examining dialectical behaviour therapy in college counselling centres

Study	Sample Size	Sample Description	DBT Treatment Description	Control or Comparison Group	Main Findings
Pistorello, Fruzzetti, MacLane, Gallop, & Iverson (2012)	63	Ages 18–25 ($M = 21$), 81% female, suicidal at baseline, >1 lifetime self-injury or suicide attempt, ≥3 BPD symptoms	7–12 months of comprehensive DBT	TAU	DBT group reported greater decreases in suicidal behaviour and BPD symptom severity, and greater improvements in social adjustment
Engle, Gadischkie, Roy, & Nunziato (2013)	30–42 per semester	Diagnosis of BPD	At least one semester of comprehensive DBT	Time–limited psychodynamic treatment (8–10 sessions)	DBT group had fewer psychiatric hospitalizations and fewer mental health or medical leaves
Chugani, Ghali, & Brunner (2013)	19	Mean age = 21, 95% female, diagnoses of cluster B personality disorder or traits, >1.5 SD above the mean on GEDM	11-week DBT skills training group	TAU	DBT group showed a greater decrease in emotion regulation difficulties, and greater improvements in adaptive coping skills use
Meaney-Tavares & Hasking (2013)	17	Ages 18–28 ($M = 22.5$), 76.5% female, diagnosis of BPD	8 modified DBT skills group sessions	None	Participants showed significant reductions in depression and BPD (but not anxiety) symptoms; participants reported significant improvements in adaptive coping skills use

(continued)

Table 30.1 Continued

Study	Sample Size	Sample Description	DBT Treatment Description	Control or Comparison Group	Main Findings
Panepinto, Uschold, Olandese, & Linn (2015)	110	Ages 18–48 (M = 25.5), 77% female, identified behavioural deficits and/or self-damaging impulsive behaviours	Modified comprehensive DBT (i.e., biweekly individual session and consultation team meetings, 6–13 weeks of skills group)	None	Participants reported significant reductions in psychopathological symptom severity and life problems
Uliaszek, Rashid, Williams, & Gulamani (2016)	54	Ages 18–46 (M = 22), 78% female, inclusion based on CCC clinician recommendation	Semester-long DBT skills group (11–12 sessions)	Positive Psychotherapy	Both groups led to symptom improvement; DBT group had better retention and larger effect sizes with regard to decreases in emotion regulation difficulties and increases in mindfulness and life satisfaction

Note. BPD = borderline personality disorder; GEDM = General Emotion Dysregulation Measure; CCC = college counselling centre; DBT = dialectical behaviour therapy; TAU = treatment as usual.

tolerance skills module to make room for a dialectics mini-module, 2) modification of the drop-out rules to accommodate breaks in the university schedule, 3) the skills group was 1.5 hours per week, and 4) the skills modules followed the timeline of the university schedules, such that one module was taught per academic semester. While both groups presented elevated drop-out rates (35% for DBT and 47% for TAU), the DBT group reported greater decreases in suicidal behaviour, greater reductions in BPD symptom severity, and greater improvement in social adjustment relative to the control group.

Engle, Gadischkie, Roy, and Nunziato (2013) also noted positive outcomes following the implementation of a comprehensive DBT programme in a CCC setting, in this case, for students who met criteria for BPD. It compared those who took part in the programme with those with BPD who elected not to participate in DBT, and instead completed eight to ten sessions of psychodynamic treatment (referred to as TAU). Results showed that, of the individuals who took part in DBT, none required hospitalization for psychiatric or substance use reasons, while 13 TAU treatment receivers did require hospitalization for these reasons over the same time frame. Similarly, one student in the DBT treatment programme took a mental health or medical leave as compared to 13 leaves for those taking part in TAU.

More recently, Panepinto, Uschold, Olandese, and Linn (2015) evaluated the efficacy of a modified comprehensive DBT treatment among 110 students at a CCC, although no comparison group was included. Modifications to the standardized treatment included holding both individual sessions and consultation team meetings on a biweekly basis, and offering an abbreviated skills group to match semester timelines (i.e., 6-13 weekly 90-minute sessions). The study accepted students based on CCC counsellors having identified them as having behavioural skills deficits or coping strategy deficits at initial assessment. Students could also participate if they endorsed one of several possible self-damaging impulsive behaviours, including suicidal or non-suicidal self-injury, substance abuse, eating disorder behaviours, risky sexual behaviours, or excessive gambling or shopping. Analyses indicated that the treatment contributed to improvements in a number of areas, including reductions in global psychopathological symptom severity and self-reported life problems.

While these findings hold promise, challenges and barriers remain with regard to implementation of comprehensive DBT programmes, including difficulties with implementation, and cost and time required (see Implementation Challenges). Modified DBT programmes may also offer similar benefits to high-need students at a fraction of the time and cost. Chugani and Landes (2016) surveyed CCC employees regarding trends and barriers to implementing DBT programmes in CCC settings, and suggested that CCCs may wish to offer a DBT skills training group while partnering with community providers who may be able to offer additional services, including crisis management. In this spirit, studies have begun to examine the potential efficacy of short-term DBT-based skills groups, independent of other DBT components (i.e., individual DBT treatment, consultation team, and telephone coaching).

Meaney-Tavares and Hasking (2013) examined an eight-session DBT-based skills group for students who had received a BPD diagnosis and who were all individually seeing a community provider. Seventeen participants completed pre- and post-treatment measures, including self-reported depression and anxiety symptoms, coping skills, and BPD diagnostic criteria. Participants showed significant reductions with regard to depression and BPD, but not anxiety symptoms, although anxiety symptoms may have been inflated at post-treatment due to its timing (i.e., just prior to upcoming exams). Additionally, there were noted improvements in coping skills regarding increased problem solving and reduced self-blame. While the absence of a comparison group limited the conclusions reached, the study highlighted the potential of a skills group-only DBT intervention.

Adding to these findings, Chugani, Ghali, and Brunner (2013) compared an 11-week DBT skills group to TAU for 19 individuals with DSM-IV Cluster B disorders (i.e., antisocial personality disorder, borderline personality disorder, histrionic personality disorder, or narcissistic personality disorder) or traits who also endorsed high levels of emotion dysregulation. The group consisted of weekly 90-minute sessions; telephone coaching and individual DBT sessions were optional, and staff did participate in a consultation team. TAU was typically comprised of weekly individual therapy sessions. Results showed that those in the DBT group showed marginally greater reductions with regard to emotion regulation difficulties compared to the TAU group. Unlike TAU subjects, however, the DBT group also showed significant increases in use of adaptive coping strategies and significant decreases in maladaptive coping strategies.

Most recently, Uliaszek et al. (2016) compared a semester-long (i.e., 11-12 weeks) DBT skills group to another active treatment, positive psychotherapy (PPT). The study randomized 54 university students who sought treatment through the CCC to either treatment condition. There were no specific diagnostic criteria necessary for inclusion, as the study design assessed efficacy across a range of psychopathology. Results indicated that both treatment approaches led to symptom improvement, including significant reductions in depression, anxiety, and BPD symptoms, though there were also some notable differences. One such difference involved the drop-out rates; the DBT-based intervention maintained significantly higher retention (85%) relative to PPT (56%). In addition, larger effect sizes presented for the DBT group with regard to decreases in emotion regulation difficulties and increases in mindfulness and life satisfaction.

Modified DBT treatments have also shown efficacy among college students outside of CCCs, and CCCs could conceivably adapt such interventions as needed. For example, Rizvi and Steffel (2014) offered two brief (eight-week) forms of DBT skills training for college students, though not within a CCC setting. Results indicated that both an emotion regulation group and an emotion regulation/mindfulness group led to similar improvements in emotion regulation and skills use, and decreases in depression, anxiety, and stress symptoms. In addition, Fleming, McMahon, Moran, Peterson, and Dreessen (2015) offered a DBT skills group for college students with ADHD. They found that those in the DBT group showed greater treatment response with regard to ADHD symptoms and quality-of-life improvements relative to a control group who received self-guided handouts for skills training. Taken together, findings to date show promise for the efficacy of brief, DBT-based skills groups designed to accommodate students' schedules while also minimizing the monetary and time demands of the CCC treatment providers.

Strategic Modifications for the CCC Practice Setting

Potential Changes to the Treatment Structure

Given that the CCC mission is to serve and support the mental wellness of diverse body of students, it does not come as a surprise that a specialized treatment model such as DBT may not initially fit well into the traditional CCC practice structure. As mentioned above, the multi-modal nature of DBT, as well as its focus on the transdiagnostic symptom of emotion dysregulation, may make it suitable for adaptation. Adapting DBT for CCCs requires that one consider the limits of their specific centre, the resources available, and the population to be served, and proceed by making strategic modifications to the original DBT model. It is important to make only the minimal modifications truly required, while still adhering to the overarching principles and practices of DBT. The next subsection discusses the various modifications to DBT specific to CCCs that have available research evidence, as well as those modifications based on clinical experience.

Challenges to Implementing Standard DBT

Standard DBT involves individual therapy, skills group, phone coaching, and team consultation with a one-year commitment. While recommended, it is likely that many CCCs cannot offer this level of intensity. This is both due to policy and/or clinician limitations, as well as a mismatch between the student's needs and the standard DBT protocol. Three primary areas that may limit the implementation of standard DBT are session limits, opportunity for consultation team, and limitations around contact with students outside of sessions and/or business hours.

Since most CCCs do observe general session limits that are much less than the one-year commitment desired in standard DBT, one possibility is to create CCC policies specific for the DBT programme so that it can operate under different parameters from the rest of the CCC; programme pilots have achieved some success. For example, one large university in the US has assembled a group of clinicians within their centre whose sole focus is to treat severely distressed students. This group of clinicians is responsible for offering DBT services to the subsection of students who need a higher level of care. In this way, the CCC maintains its normal scope of operations, while the DBT programme operates inside of it with more expansive services. Because students with the most severe psychopathology take up the most time in administrative issues and crisis management (Gallagher, 2014), providing expanded services to these students may actually reduce their impact on the CCC as a whole.

The regular meeting of a consultation team may pose a challenge in the CCC setting. Among CCCs who currently have a DBT programme, 68% report that difficulty meeting or sporadic attendance at consultation team was a barrier to implementation (Chugani & Landes, 2016), with productivity demands or large caseloads potentially to blame. Emphasizing the importance of consultation team and elevating its priority within the CCC may address the problem. Even CCCs that offer only DBT skills groups are likely to encounter challenging situations that could benefit from consultation team.

Finally, contact with students outside of session or business hours is something not only impacted by CCC policies, but clinician limits. In many CCCs, students have no access (i.e., cell phone numbers) to immediate contact with their clinician outside of regular business hours. Clinicians may also be reticent to offer coaching outside of scheduled sessions, as it is not typical in the CCC setting and may not be offered to non-DBT students. The availability of phone coaching depends on the scope of the DBT programme, the target population intended for treatment, and the desired outcomes. For example, if a CCC wishes to offer DBT skills training to any student wishing to learn healthy coping skills, phone coaching may be unnecessary. However, if the intent of the DBT programme is to provide a higher level of care for students presenting with serious mental health issues and/or chronic suicidal and self-injuring behaviours, it is likely that this population of students will have difficulties implementing and generalizing skills learned during the group without coaching. In this case, a reliable crisis hotline may be a viable alternative to manage student crises outside of the CCC hours.

Modifications to Modes

In addition to making decisions about which of the primary DBT modes to offer, CCCs may wish to modify the modes themselves in order to help the treatment fit more realistically into the CCC practice setting. The most researched and popular modification is to shorten DBT skills groups from the standard six-month cycle to a more manageable six- to 12-week programme (e.g., Uliaszek et al., 2016). Reducing the length required to deliver a group has several advantages for CCCs. First, it can be helpful to offer skills training in a format that allows a student to complete the treatment experience during a single semester due to changes in availability across semesters. Second, research supports DBT skills training as sufficient to achieve positive clinical outcomes with emotionally dysregulated students (see Rizvi & Steffel, 2014; Uliaszek et al., 2016). Third, it requires less training of clinicians to implement a brief skills training protocol than standard DBT. Fourth, it may be easier to elicit commitment from students to participate in a more time-limited treatment. Taken together, the implementation of a brief DBT skills group is a treatment from which any CCC could benefit and may be a good place to test the waters if DBT is new to a CCC.

While it may not be possible for some CCCs to offer standard DBT telephone coaching, there may be a way to provide opportunities for students to receive coaching within the CCC's operational limits. Possible modifications include offering phone coaching during business hours only, having DBT team members take turns as the "on call" clinician for receiving after hours coaching calls, or utilization of an after-hours crisis hotline. Another way to offer coaching is through the use of smart phone applications designed to assist in practising DBT skills. While many DBT apps correspond to daily diary cards, some (e.g., DBT Skills Coach; Rizvi, Dimeff, Skutch, Carroll, & Linehan, 2011) allow users to customize a set of emergency skills, provide a glossary of skills, and can send email updates directly to the clinician.

Modifications to Length and Intensity

Another set of considerations relates to the length and intensity of the treatment offered. A guiding principle in deciding when and where to modify should be to focus on the goals of the programme. In other words, *what is the need that you are trying to fill by implementing the DBT or DBT-informed programme?* If you aim to treat suicidal and self-injuring students, we suggest adherence to the original model whenever possible. Offering only DBT skills group might be most appropriate if the goals of the CCC are to offer an adjunct to individual therapy for students with personality disorders (Chugani, Ghali, & Brunner, 2013; Meaney-Tavares & Hasking, 2013), severe emotion dysregulation (Rizvi & Steffel, 2014; Uliaszek et al., 2016), or for students in need of developing coping skills (Panepinto et al., 2015). Offering only the skills group may work particularly well if there is also a consultation team where all individual therapists can review DBT skills. An additional consideration is which skills to offer when the duration of DBT skills group is significantly shortened to accommodate the CCC setting (see Modifications to Modes). One option is to distil all the DBT skills into a shorter protocol, specifically one that fits within the confines of a single semester (see Uliaszek et al., 2016). Students might then elect to repeat the group in a following semester in order to fully solidify skill usage; this is similar to what we see as standard practice where clients typically complete two rotations of all skills over the course of one year. A second option is to offer multiple DBT skills groups simultaneously, with each group focusing on a different set of skills. For example, one group might focus on distress tolerance skills and mindfulness, where another focuses on interpersonal effectiveness and mindfulness. Thus, a student could elect to attend any or all groups that seem particularly germane to their treatment needs.

Another possible approach to varying the length and intensity of DBT within a CCC is the stepped care approach (e.g., Pistorello et al., 2012). CCCs wishing to implement this type of model might consider what levels of care they are able to offer and what levels best address the presenting problems. On the lowest level (e.g., mental wellness), the CCC could offer drop-in workshops on a selection of DBT skills. The second level might be a brief skills group appropriate for a range of students. The third level could be brief DBT group as an adjunct to individual therapy, and the fourth level would be standard DBT services. The advantage of this approach is that the investment of resources for training and implementation benefits a much broader group of the campus population.

Finally, the "4-miss rule," which states that clients who miss four consecutive appointments must terminate treatment, and may only negotiate a new therapy contract after the current contract has expired, may not be appropriate for the abbreviated treatment length offered in the CCC. Thus, CCCs may wish to consider modifying this rule to be a "3-miss rule" or consider establishing some reasonable exceptions to the 4-miss rule. Alternatively, many CCCs do not allow the implementation of this policy as students may be "guaranteed" treatment through the CCC due to funding through fees/tuition paid by students.

Considerations Related to Biosocial Theory

Originally, the biosocial theory was presented as an aetiological model of BPD (Linehan, 1993); however, it is now regarded as a theory of emotion dysregulation (Linehan, 2015). Most students that present for treatment at a CCC citing emotional (e.g., depression, anxiety) and/or behavioural (e.g., substance abuse, self-harm) difficulties relate to the idea and tenets of emotion dysregulation as central to their experience. Thus, we see no need to modify this theory for the CCC setting. In fact, framing students' concerns within the biosocial theory can be both validating for the student and provide a starting point for naming treatment targets within a historical context.

We believe that understanding the tenets of biosocial theory is important for nearly every treatment-seeking student. Being able to recognize invalidating environments and the associated consequences can help clinicians and students make sense of and validate ineffective behaviour. Here we emphasize the importance of the *perception* of invalidation; nearly everyone has experienced their environment as invalidating at some point and this can be an important source of clinical information regarding current emotional and behavioural patterns.

The biological piece of biosocial theory also continues to be useful for helping students understand their difficulties. Students may present with a variety of biological vulnerabilities that make them more prone to experiencing emotional or psychological difficulties. It can be helpful to work with students to acknowledge and accept these vulnerabilities. Clinicians may find it helpful to use the metaphor of the dandelion and the orchid to explain biological vulnerabilities in a non-judgmental manner (Ellis & Boyce, 2008). Dandelions pop up anywhere and can thrive even when neglected, while the quality and specificity of the nurturing behaviour relates directly to the flourishing of the orchid. There is nothing wrong with the orchid—it simply has different biological requirements.

Implementation Challenges

Best Practices and Guidelines

In writing about best practices for implementation of DBT in CCCs, we believe it is important to note that the research in this field is quite nascent and data to inform a list of CCC-specific best practices are limited. This subsection provides suggestions for consideration based upon our experience in implementing these programmes as well as our experiences in assisting others in their implementation efforts. Primarily, we recommend that CCCs interested in implementing DBT conduct an assessment to determine the feasibility of implementation. This can be a daunting task for those unfamiliar with DBT and it may be helpful to seek expert consultation to support this process. We recommend that this type of assessment include consideration of (at a minimum) the following questions:

1. What group(s) of students are we seeking to treat with DBT?
2. What components of DBT can we realistically and feasibly implement?
3. Will these components be sufficient to treat the targeted students?
4. How well do these components fit within our CCC structure, standard mode of service provision, and/or scope of practice?
5. What resources are available to support DBT programme development and implementation?
6. What resources are needed to support DBT programme development and implementation?
7. If resources available and needed are not aligned, how do we propose to address this discrepancy?

A more detailed discussion of CCC-specific areas for consideration in programme development and implementation can be located in Chugani (2017).

Second, we recommend that CCC clinicians receive support from administrators in seeking formal DBT training. This includes time and expenses related to the training event, as well as release time or reduced productivity demands to provide for time and energy to read, study, and master the materials. It has been our experience that when clinicians have no protected time during work hours to complete the necessary learning tasks associated with DBT, it can foster resentment and diminished interest and commitment to the DBT programme. As mentioned, the level and intensity of training obtained can be adjusted to match the level and intensity of the desired programme. We also encourage the use of ongoing, expert consultation during the programme development and implementation phase to ensure that adaptations remain true to DBT practices and principles.

While it is advisable to implement empirically evaluated adaptations, it is still recommended to conduct an outcome evaluation of any new programme. Outcome evaluation is particularly important given the resource investment often required to implement a DBT programme. Outcome evaluations not only provide information regarding the comparison of expectations to performance, but can also point to specific areas in need of change. These evaluations need not take the structure of a formal research project—as this often requires a significant amount of investment in both time and cost—but instead can be as simple as collecting pre- and post-assessments on a few measures of interest, along with elicited feedback from participating clinicians, students, and policy makers.

Challenges and Solutions in Implementation

The challenges CCCs face in implementing DBT programmes will naturally vary depending on several factors. At the same time, there are some challenges that CCCs may be more likely to encounter. These issues include (1) misfit between CCC structure or scope of practice and DBT treatment practices, (2) low support from university administration, (3) misfit between DBT theory and clinician's beliefs about treatment or pre-existing theoretical orientations, (4) difficulties obtaining commitment from students to participate in new treatment modalities, and (5) challenges arising from students in treatment together who know one another from classes or elsewhere on campus.

Misfit between CCC structure/scope and DBT practices is a serious issue that many types of clinical practices face in implementing DBT. Although the type of fit issue will vary between centres, we believe that successful implementation of DBT is achievable with flexibility on both the part of the CCC and the DBT model. Flexibility, willingness to engage in continued problem solving, and support from the CCC director and university administration can be very helpful in figuring out how to manage fit issues. This is not to say that DBT cannot be successfully implemented in CCCs where no structural flexibility is permissible. It will simply be more easily accomplished with flexibility on the part of the clinicians responsible for implementing the programme as well as from the directors and administrators who oversee the programme and centre operations.

A related issue is that of low support from university administration. Low administrative support can take a variety of forms including failure to provide funds for training, lack of flexibility to make adjustments in CCC structure/scope to accommodate DBT, not allowing staff time for weekly team consultation, or not providing staff involved with the programme with protected learning time. One suggestion is to use data to make a direct argument to the administration regarding the need for a DBT programme. In one case (see Chugani, 2017), we implemented a small scale DBT programme and evaluated the clinical outcomes of this programme (Chugani, Ghali, & Brunner, 2013). We then used the outcome data to support our request for funds to have interested staff participate in a DBT Intensive Training. Another potential solution may be to use CCC statistics already available to demonstrate the need on your campus. For example, CCCs with electronic charting programmes may be able to pull data showing the numbers of crisis walk-in appointments, thus justifying efforts to invest in a DBT programme. Whether you aim to increase areas such as emotion regulation and coping skills or to decrease suicide attempts or waitlist times, outcome evaluation of a trial DBT programme can be very useful in convincing administrators of the value of the programme for the campus community.

Misfit between DBT theory and clinician theoretical orientations can arise when clinicians bring a variety of expertise, experiences, and expectations to a new DBT team. Those clinicians who have had previous training in structured and/or behaviourally oriented therapies may have less difficulty adopting DBT theory than those trained in approaches that are less congruent with DBT practices and principles. Team members who initially commit to participating in the DBT programme initiatives may find that they are less committed as they learn more about DBT or other requirements.

There are multiple ways to remedy this issue. First, prospective team members must learn about DBT to make educated decisions if they wish to participate. Second, there should be no requirement for staff to participate in DBT programmes. While it can be challenging to invest resources in training only to discover that a staff member no longer wishes to participate, we have observed instances in which a single individual who was not interested in practising DBT led to significant dysfunction among the DBT team as a group. A final option is to hire a trained DBT therapist to lead programme implementation. This could be a full-time staff position dedicated to developing and leading the DBT programme or a clinician working in the local community who is interested in having a part-time position working with the CCC. In cases where only a single staff member is interested in DBT, that individual may be able to offer DBT services within the CCC by participating in a local or virtual consultation team.

A fourth implementation challenge relates to generating student interest and willingness to participate in the DBT programme. One challenge we have observed is that some CCCs do not have a "group culture." That is, the CCC has historically not offered many groups; thus, there is not an expectation among the student body that this activity is part of the CCC experience. It may take time for students to warm up to group therapy as a treatment option and the use of DBT orientation and commitment strategies (see Linehan, 1993) at intake sessions can be helpful in readying students for that type of intervention.

A related implementation challenge is the fact that students who are participating in DBT skills group may know each other prior to beginning group and/or are likely to see each other outside of group on campus. This can be particularly challenging due to concerns about the maintenance of confidentiality, as well as stigma associated with treatment-seeking behaviour. Group leaders should talk with students directly about the particular issues that may arise and plan ahead for how to manage them. Such issues may include seeing group members around campus, connecting with group members through social media, living in the same residence hall, or participating in the same classes or extracurricular activities. The goal is open discussion and problem-solving before any issues arise. Students may benefit from problem-solving tasks and role-playing how to handle such situations.

Problems with dual roles exist when close friends are in group together. Students may be friends prior to group entry, while in other cases students may meet in the group and develop close friendships during the course of treatment. While friendships among group members can be problematic, we have not found a way to prevent them from occurring and note that they often exist as strong instances of support and empathy in a student's life. This is a dialectic; close friendships among group members may both cause myriad challenges and contribute to the life worth living.

Concluding Remarks

As demonstrated by national and international survey research, it is quite clear that the mental health of college and university students is changing on campuses around the world. Students are arriving on campus with a greater diversity and severity of psychological issues than ever before. The CCC is often the first line of defence against treating both chronic conditions and acute periods of mental illness. While CCCs formerly provided supportive therapy for mildly anxious or sad students, they are quickly becoming places where crisis management and evidence-based, time-limited, and cost-effective therapy is a necessity. DBT is particularly suited to address many of these concerns; its efficacy at treating emotion dysregulation, a symptom of many disorders, and severe psychological behaviours (i.e., suicidality and self-harm) make it an appropriate treatment choice for many students. In addition, its varied modes of delivery provide tailor-made methods that address the specific needs of the students and the CCC itself.

To date, research on DBT in the CCCs has consistently supported its efficacy in reducing suicidality, life problems, and psychopathology in college students. However, several studies have been marred by small sample size and a lack of control group. In addition, few studies have examined standard DBT or actual implementations of DBT in the real-world setting. This research is promising, particularly for the DBT skills group as a standalone or adjunct treatment, but much more is needed to fully understand the place for DBT within the CCC.

There are several ways to strategically alter DBT in order to address common policy issues within the CCC. This includes instituting DBT-specific policies that will allow the DBT clinic within the CCC to extend session limits and to provide protected time for consultation team and training. Amendments to typical phone coaching and the

"4-miss rule" may offer further adjustments that still preserve the integrity of the DBT model. We also suggest offering brief DBT skills group in the CCC setting as this addresses several environmental constraints and has consistent research support. Finally, while there may be several challenges in implementation of a DBT programme, careful planning and the utilization of data can address many of these concerns for students, staff, and administrators. This highlights the importance of a thorough assessment of needs and available resources before implementing a programme, followed by outcome evaluation during and post-implementation. The collection of clinical outcome data as well as clinician and centre driven data (e.g., addressing acceptability, feasibility, and sustainability) supports CCCs in achieving an effective and sustainable intervention that is well suited to their specific environments, but also provides critically important knowledge to others seeking information to inform new programme development.

KEY MESSAGES FOR CLINICIANS

- The complexity and severity of mental illness are increasing across college campuses; this includes increasing rates of anxiety, depression, and suicidality.
- Of the surveyed CCC directors, 94% report a steady increase in the number of students arriving on campus with severe psychological problems (Gallagher, 2014).
- Research on DBT in the CCC shows promising results regarding reductions in suicidality, life problems, and psychopathology and increases of adaptive coping skills. More research is needed examining implementation, standard DBT protocol, and utilizing more controlled designs.
- Designing a DBT programme within your CCC operating under different policies and parameters than the CCC as a whole may be a way to implement standard DBT without violating policies regarding session limits and contact outside of business hours.
- Implementing brief DBT skills group is an evidence-based, time-limited treatment for a wide range of students that requires a lesser degree of training than standard DBT.
- The biosocial theory in its current form as a theory of emotion dysregulation is relevant and appropriate for explaining many common symptoms found in college students.
- Before implementing DBT, a thorough assessment of the needs and goals of the CCC and student body is necessary.
- After implementing a new DBT programme, the CCC should conduct a thorough outcome evaluation to assess progress toward goals.

- Challenges to implementation include (1) misfit between CCC structure or scope of practice and DBT treatment practices, (2) low support from university administration, (3) misfit between DBT theory and clinician's beliefs about treatment or pre-existing theoretical orientations, (4) difficulties obtaining commitment from students to participate in new treatment modalities, and (5) challenges arising from students in treatment together who know one another from classes or elsewhere on campus.

References

American College Health Association (2016). *American College Health Association—National College Health Assessment II: Reference Group Executive Summary Fall 2015.* Hanover, MD: American College Health Association.

Chugani, C. D. (2017). Adapting dialectical behavior therapy for college counseling centers. *Journal of College Counseling, 20*(1), 67–80.

Chugani, C. D., Ghali, M. N., & Brunner, J. (2013). Effectiveness of short term dialectical behavior therapy skills training in college students with Cluster B personality disorders. *Journal of College Student Psychotherapy, 27*(4), 323–336.

Chugani, C. D., & Landes, S. J. (2016). Dialectical behavior therapy in college counseling centers: Current trends and barriers to implementation. *Journal of College Student Psychotherapy, 30*(3), 176–186.

Ellis, B. J., & Boyce, W. T. (2008). Biological sensitivity to context. *Current Directions in Psychological Science, 17*(3), 183–187.

Engle, E., Gadischkie, S., Roy, N., & Nunziato, D. (2013). Dialectical behavior therapy for a college population: Applications at Sarah Lawrence College and beyond. *Journal of College Student Psychotherapy, 27*(1), 11–30.

Fairholme, C. P., Boisseau, C. L., Ellard, K. K., Ehrenreich, J. T., & Barlow, D. H. (2010). Emotions, emotion regulation, and psychological treatment. In A. M. Kring & D. Sloane (Eds.), *Emotion regulation and psychopathology: A transdiagnostic approach to etiology and treatment* (pp. 283–309). London: Guilford.

Fleming, A. P., McMahon, R. J., Moran, L. R., Peterson, A. P., & Dreessen, A. (2015). Pilot randomized controlled trial of dialectical behavior therapy group skills training for ADHD among college students. *Journal of Attention Disorders, 19*(3), 260–271.

Gallagher, R. P. (2014). *National survey of college counseling centers 2014.* Alexandria, VA: International Association of Counseling Services, Inc.

James, A. C., Taylor, A., Winmill, L., & Alfoadari, K. (2008). A preliminary community study of dialectical behaviour therapy (DBT) with adolescent females demonstrating persistent, deliberate self-harm (DSH). *Child and Adolescent Mental Health, 13*, 148–152.

Kliem, S., Kroger, C., & Kosfelder, J. (2010). Dialectical behavior therapy for borderline personality disorder: a meta-analysis using mixed-effects modeling. *Journal of Consulting and Clinical Psychology, 78*, 936–951.

Linehan, M. M. (1993). *Cognitive behavioral treatment of borderline personality disorder.* New York, NY: Guilford Press.

Linehan, M. M. (2015). *DBT skills training manual*, 2nd Edition. New York, NY: Guilford Press.

Linehan, M. M., Tutek, D., Heard, H. L., & Armstrong, H. E. (1994). Interpersonal outcome of cognitive-behavioral treatment for chronically suicidal borderline patients. *American Journal of Psychiatry, 51*, 1771–1776.

Linehan, M. M., Comtois, K. A., Murray, A. M., Brown, M. Z., Gallop, R. J., . . . Lindenboim, N. (2006). Two-year randomized controlled trial and follow-up of dialectical behavior therapy vs therapy by experts for suicidal behaviors and borderline personality disorder. *Archives of General Psychiatry, 63*, 757–766.

Linehan, M. M., Dimeff, L. A., Reynolds, S. K., Comtois, K. A., Welch, S. S., . . . Kivlahan, D. R. (2002). Dialectical behavior therapy versus comprehensive validation therapy plus 12-step for the treatment of opioid dependent women meeting criteria for borderline personality disorder. *Drug and Alcohol Dependence, 67*, 13–26.

Lynch, T. R., Cheavens, J. S., Cukrowicz, K. C., Thorp, S. R., Bronner, L., & Beyer, J. (2007). Treatment of older adults with co-morbid personality disorder and depression: A dialectical behavior therapy approach. *International Journal of Geriatric Psychiatry, 22*, 131–143.

Meaney-Tavares, R., & Hasking, P. (2013). Coping and regulating emotions: A pilot study of a modified dialectical behavior therapy group delivered in a college counseling service. *Journal of American College Health, 61*(5), 303–309.

National College Health Assessment (2013). *Canadian Reference Group Executive Summary, Spring 2013.* Hanover, MD: American College Health Association.

Panepinto, A. R., Uschold, C. C., Olandese, M., & Linn, B. K. (2015). Beyond borderline personality disorder: Dialectical behavior therapy in a college counseling center. *Journal of College Student Psychotherapy, 29*, 211–226.

Panos, P. T., Jackson, J. W., Hasan, O., & Panos, A. (2014). Meta-analysis and systematic review assessing the efficacy of dialectical behavior therapy (DBT). *Research on Social Work Practice, 24*, 213–223.

Pistorello, J., Fruzzetti, A. E., Maclane, C., Gallop, R., & Iverson, K. M. (2012). Dialectical behavior therapy (DBT) applied to college students: A randomized clinical trial. *Journal of Consulting and Clinical Psychology, 80*(6), 982–994.

Reetz, D. R., Barr, V., & Krylowicz, B. (2013). *The Association for University and College Counseling Center Directors Annual Survey.* Indianapolis, IN: Association for University and College Counseling Center Directors.

Rizvi, S. L., & Steffel, L. M. (2014). A pilot study of 2 brief forms of dialectical behavior therapy skills training for emotion dysregulation in college students. *Journal of American College Health, 62*, 434–439.

Rizvi, S. L., Dimeff, L. A., Skutch, J., Carroll, D., & Linehan, M. M. (2011). A pilot study of the DBT coach: an interactive mobile phone application for individuals with borderline personality disorder and substance use disorder. *Behavior Therapy, 42*, 589–600.

Robins, C. J., & Chapman, A. L. (2004). Dialectical behavior therapy: Current status, recent developments, and future directions. *Journal of Personality Disorders, 18*, 73–89.

Telch, C. F., Agras, W. S., & Linehan, M. M. (2001). Dialectical behavior therapy for binge eating disorder. *Journal of Consulting and Clinical Psychology, 69*, 1061–1065.

Uliaszek, A. A., Rashid, T., Williams, G. E., & Gulamani, R. (2016). Group therapy for university students: A randomized control trial of dialectical behavior therapy and positive psychotherapy. *Behavior Research and Therapy, 77*, 78–85.

Uliaszek, A. A., Wilson, S., Mayberry, M., Cox, K., & Maslar, M. (2014). Treatment effectiveness of dialectical behavior group therapy in a treatment-seeking adolescent population: Effects on teens and their caregivers. *The Family Journal, 22*, 206–215.

Valentine, S. E., Bankoff, S. M., Poulin, R. M., Reidler, E. B., & Pantalone, D. W. (2015). The use of dialectical behavior therapy skills training as stand-alone treatment: a systematic review of the treatment outcome literature. *Journal of Clinical Psychology*, 71, 1–20.

Whitlock, J., Eells, G., Cummings, N., & Purington, A. (2009). Nonsuicidal self-injury in college populations: Mental health provider assessment of prevalence and need. *Journal of College Student Psychotherapy*, 23(3), 172–183.

Woodberry, K. A., & Popenoe, E. J. (2008). Implementing dialectical behavior therapy with adolescents and their families in a community outpatient clinic. *Cognitive and Behavioral Practice*, 15, 277–286.

CHAPTER 31

DIALECTICAL BEHAVIOUR THERAPY FOR PRE-ADOLESCENT CHILDREN

FRANCHESKA PEREPLETCHIKOVA

THEORETICAL MODEL

Biosocial Theory

BIOSOCIAL Theory (Linehan, 1993) suggests that individuals with emotional dysregulation are usually born sensitive or vulnerable to their emotions, and are unable to effectively modulate their emotional experiences. They display high emotional arousal, high reactivity, and a slow return to baseline. Parents often describe these children as "going from a 0 to a 100 in a split second." Additionally, events that trigger these extreme emotional reactions are not always due to the external environment, and instead may involve just a thought, memory, or stressor so minute it is indiscernible to observers. Children with emotional dysregulation problems often describe their emotional experiences as "tsunamis" that are quite overwhelming, painful, and almost impossible to control.

The environment may not be ready to effectively manage the challenges such children present and "good-enough parenting" may not be sufficient to meet these children's needs. Winnicott's (1973) concept of "good enough parenting" focused on the parental ability to survive a child's anger at the world and their shock of the loss of the omnipotence, as well as to help the child accept reality and relate to it in more realistic terms (Bingham & Sidorkin, 2004; Phillips & Taylor, 2009). With emotionally dysregulated children, surviving the child's frustration with reality frequently becomes an almost insurmountable challenge for both child and parent. This inborn sensitivity significantly exacerbates the child's frustration, as well as feelings of parental hopelessness and defeat because they do not understand the reasons for, nor have methods to deal with, their child's reactivity.

This poor fit between a child's needs and the parental ability to satisfy them may create an invalidating environment over time. It is reasonable to expect that "good enough parenting" will include some level of direct criticism, punishment, and dismissal of a child's feelings, thoughts, and behaviours as invalid. What makes an environment invalidating is the pervasive nature of such events. The invalidating environment indiscriminately rejects private experiences and behaviours as invalid (e.g., "Why are you angry? There is nothing to be angry about!"), oversimplifies the ease of solutions (e.g., "Just snap out of it," "Why can't you be like your brother?"), and intermittently reinforces escalated emotional displays (e.g., child learns that s/he can receive the coveted care and support primarily when she threatens suicide to communicate suffering, while lower levels of such expression are invalidated).

An invalidating environment fails to teach a child how to 1) label private experiences; 2) trust experiences as valid responses to events; 3) accurately express emotions; 4) communicate pain effectively; 5) use self-management to solve problems; and 6) effectively regulate emotions. Instead, an invalidating environment teaches a child how to 1) respond with high negative arousal to failure; 2) form unrealistic goals and expectations; 3) rely on the external environment for cues on how to respond; 4) actively self-invalidate; and 5) oscillate between emotional inhibition and extreme responses.

Transactional Model

Thomas and Chess (1985) have extensively discussed the notion of the "poorness of fit" between an environment and a child as a critical factor in the aetiology of psychopathology. They have also highlighted the pattern of reciprocal influence in the child-environment system. Indeed, the characteristics of a child and an environment are not static, but rather change through reciprocal interaction or transaction where components continuously adapt to each other. Such mutual influence may lead to an exacerbation of a child's emotional dysregulation, as well as the development of an invalidating environment. When a child's needs cannot be adequately met by the environment, the child becomes destabilized. As the increasingly destabilized child continues to stretch an environment's ability to respond adequately, further invalidation ensues, and over time this transaction may lead to the development of a psychopathology.

Research indicates that impulsivity and chronic irritability of the kind exhibited in children with emotional dysregulation are associated with a range of impairments. Problematic relationships with parents, siblings, peers, and teachers, persistent difficulties in multiple settings, and negative feedback may lead to the development of negative self-concept in affected children, impede their emotional, social, and cognitive development, and increase chances of psychopathology in adolescence and adulthood (e.g., personality disorders, substance abuse, mood disorders, and suicidality)

(Althoff, Verhulst, Retlew, Hudziak, & Van der Ende, 2010; Okado & Bierman, 2015; Pickles et al., 2009).

DBT-C Hierarchy of Treatment Targets

DBT-C aims to stop the harmful transaction between a child and an environment, and replace it with an adaptive pattern of responding. The main goal is to reduce the risk of psychopathology in the future, while intervening to ameliorate presenting problems. Intervention and prevention are primarily achieved via 1) teaching parents how to create a validating and change-ready environment; 2) empowering parents to become coaches for their children to promote adaptive responding during treatment and after therapy is completed; and 3) teaching children and their parents effective coping and problem-solving skills.

In order to incorporate these goals, the hierarchy of treatment targets was greatly extended for DBT-C as compared to DBT for adults and adolescents. While the original DBT hierarchy includes four main categories (i.e., life-threatening behaviours, therapy-interfering behaviours, quality-of-life interfering behaviours, and skills training), DBT-C includes three main categories, which are subdivided into ten subcategories (see Table 31.1). The DBT-C treatment target hierarchy is the same for outpatient, residential, and inpatient settings. In inpatient and residential settings, milieu and nursing staff share a caregiving role with parents, and in many ways, these assume more caregiving responsibility as children spend more time with the staff than with their parents. Thus, the parent-related treatment targets discussed below apply to all caregivers in contact with a child.

Table 31.1   DBT-C hierarchy of the treatment targets

I. Decrease risk of psychopathology in the future	1. Life-threatening behaviours of a child
	2. Therapy-destroying behaviours of a child
	3. Therapy-interfering behaviours of parents
	4. Parental emotion regulation
	5. Effective parenting techniques
II. Target parent-child relationship	6. Improve parent-child relationship
III. Target child's presenting problems	7. Risky, unsafe, and aggressive behaviours
	8. Quality-of-life-interfering problems
	9. Skills training
	10. Therapy-interfering behaviours of a child

I. Decreasing the Risk of Psychopathology in Adolescence and Adulthood

1. *Life-Threatening Behaviours of a Child*

The primary focus of treatment is to keep a child alive and well. If a child is at risk of suicide-related behaviours, this target is treated as a priority. The target includes 1) suicidal acts; 2) non-suicidal self-injury (NSSI); 3) suicidal communications and ideations; 4) suicide-related expectations and beliefs; and 5) suicide-related affect. Pre-adolescent children with emotional dysregulation are at an increased risk of suicidal behaviours and ideations and NSSI (Holtman et al., 2011; Tamás et al., 2007). In a study with children with Disruptive Mood Dysregulation disorder (DMDD), where emotion regulation is seen as a core dysfunction, more than 50% of children reported suicidality and/or NSSI (Perepletchikova, Nathanson, et al., 2017).

2. *Therapy-destroying behaviours of a child*

Most of the problematic behaviours a child can exhibit during a treatment session (e.g., verbal aggression, threats, cursing, screaming, running around) are addressed with planned ignoring (i.e., removing attention from undesirable behaviours and immediately attending to any positive responses). Additionally, these behaviours are treated as informative (i.e., they help the therapist observe parent-child interactions in the real time) and target-relevant (i.e., they allow the therapist to model and coach effective responding methods to parents and a child).

However, there are behaviours that cannot be ignored. Therapy-destroying behaviours are subdivided into those that occur during a session and those that occur outside a session. Therapy-destroying behaviours that occur in sessions include physical aggression to a therapist and/or parent(s), severe destructive behaviours (e.g., trashing therapist's office, throwing objects), and running out of a treatment room (unless a child stays right outside the therapist's office, when this behaviour can be safely ignored). These behaviours are dangerous for a child, other people, and property, and have to be immediately suppressed. If a behaviour can be addressed in any other way instead of immediate suppression (e.g., ignoring, removing opportunities for behaviour to occur), then this behaviour is treated as therapy-interfering, and not as therapy-destroying.

When therapy-destroying behaviours occur in session, parents (not the therapist) can put a child into a time out, but only if this technique was already covered with parents in prior sessions and practised at home. Or, the therapist can end the session with the child while continuing the session with parent(s) if possible. It is important to keep in mind that ending a session can reinforce maladaptive behaviours, especially if the child does not want to continue with a session. This issue is easier to prevent than to resolve. Prevention efforts may include focusing on developing a strong therapist-child relationship, promoting the child's motivation for change, creating a validating environment, and reinforcing treatment engagement (e.g., praise, tangible rewards). If a dangerous behaviour still occurs, safety is prioritized.

Out-of-session therapy-destroying behaviours include dangerous levels of aggression to parents, siblings, peers, and other people, as well as severe property destruction. These behaviours become therapy-destroying when the level of escalation precludes application of therapeutic techniques due to safety concerns. Aggressive and property-destroying behaviours can become especially detrimental to conducting effective treatment when temper outbursts and other undesirable behaviours are put on an extinction schedule. Extinction bursts, which occur when a response is no longer reinforced, may escalate to a degree where it is no longer safe to continue to ignore a behaviour. Thus, there is an increased risk that extinction will be terminated and an escalation of an aggressive behaviour will be reinforced by attention, removing an unwanted demand, giving in to a request, granting a coveted privilege, etc. For example, a child starts to scream because her parents refused to grant her request. The parents implement planned ignoring, which is followed by an anticipated extinction burst. However, for this child, escalation is likely to quickly reach dangerous levels and may involve running out of the house into traffic, attempting to choke a sibling, flipping furniture, breaking windows, etc. At this point parents are likely to attempt to pacify a child, or call the police, or resort to a hospitalization. All of these outcomes are highly counterproductive. They reinforce escalated behaviours, and subsequent attempts to follow an extinction protocol will become increasingly futile. Thus, it is important to conduct a very thorough assessment of a child's level of severity before accepting a family into a treatment to determine if the child's needs can be addressed on an outpatient level of care. Further, a psychiatric intervention can be considered to ameliorate reactivity with a psychotropic medication at the beginning stages of treatment, with a plan to start titrating medications down as soon as possible. In the randomized clinical trial of DBT-C for children with DMDD, all improvements were achieved without additional psychopharmacological interventions (Perepletchikova, Nathanson, et al., 2017). Although more research is needed, the results of this study suggest that psychosocial treatment alone without additional medication management may be sufficient, in most cases, for treatment in outpatient settings. However, when there is a choice between placing a child in a residential setting or continuing to address problematic behaviours in an outpatient setting with an addition of a psychotropic medication, it is advised to attempt the latter first. With all things being equal, implementation of the most benign treatment possible is important for any therapeutic approach.

3. *Therapy-interfering behaviours of parents and therapists*

DBT-C views parental adaptive patterns of responding as key to achieving lasting changes in a child's emotional and behavioural regulation. Thus, DBT-C focuses on teaching parents how to create a validating and change-ready environment for their child in order to address presenting problems and to reduce risk of psychopathology in the future. Parents are trained to become coaches for their children, and to continue the intervention after a treatment ends. Significant and lasting treatment gains cannot be achieved without parental commitment to treatment, engagement in therapy, and willingness to follow the agreed-upon plan. Thus, treatment cannot successfully continue if parents frequently miss sessions, fail to bring a child to treatment, keep re-scheduling appointments, refuse to take part in therapy, fail to follow therapist's recommendations, and continue to use prolonged or harsh punishments or other ineffective parenting techniques to force a child's compliance.

Therapists also can engage in therapy-interfering behaviours. DBT for adults and adolescents highlights a whole range of such behaviours, including a failure to be dialectical (e.g., imbalance of reciprocal versus irreverent communication) and engaging in behaviours that are disrespectful to clients (e.g., coming in late, missing appointments, appearing dishevelled). All of these issues apply to DBT-C therapists as well. However, a behaviour that may be specifically problematic for a DBT-C therapist is an inability to tolerate intense emotional displays. A therapist's difficulties with tolerating children's temper outbursts and other behavioural escalations may lead to attempts to pacify a child in a moment and, thus, a reinforcement of dysfunctional behaviours, as well as modelling of ineffective problem resolution to parents.

4. *Parental emotion regulation*

In order for parents to model effective coping and problem solving, ignore maladaptive responses, validate a child's suffering, reinforce desirable behaviours, among other techniques, parents have to be in control of their own emotional reactivity. That is one of the reasons why, in DBT-C, parents not only learn everything that their child is learning (e.g., skills and didactics on emotions), but they must also participate in the parent training component. A DBT-C therapist continues to stress throughout the treatment that while the child's emotion regulation is the main target, the main focus in achieving this goal is parental behaviour, and the therapist also closely monitors parental emotion regulation and the use of DBT-C skills. At times, this may include advising parents to seek treatment for their own psychopathology, as well as marriage counselling.

5. *Effective parenting techniques*

Frequently by the time parents decided to enter treatment with their child, the disruption in the child-environment system has reached a significant level, and parents are greatly stressed. Screaming and yelling at a child, as well as excessive, prolonged, and/or physical punishment are quite common. It is imperative to ensure parental willingness to employ effective parenting techniques, to rely primarily on validation, reinforcement, ignoring, and natural consequence, and to use punishment only sparingly and strategically. The use of effective parenting techniques is paramount to decrease invalidation, start healing the parent-child relationship, and reduce parental modelling of dysfunctional behaviours.

Parental behaviours can help ameliorate the child's emotional dysregulation or can exacerbate it through the process of the transaction discussed earlier. In DBT-C, whether an incident was effectively resolved is evaluated primarily by the environmental response. For example, if a parent responded to a stressful event in an effective way (e.g., stayed calm, modelled use of skills, validated or ignored as needed) while a child had a two-hour temper outburst, the situation is considered to have been effectively resolved. In this case, the environment was no longer transacting with a child in a dysfunctional way. If applied consistently, parental adaptive responding over time may result in the creation of a validating environment, and the resulting transaction may help ameliorate the child's emotional and behavioural dysregulation. Conversely, in a situation when a child responded effectively to a stressor (e.g., used coping skills, walked away to prevent escalation) while parental responses were dysfunctional (e.g., used inappropriate punishment, resorted to screaming or threatening), the incident was not effectively resolved. Without environmental support, the observed child's adaptive behaviours are likely to remain isolated and sporadic incidents. DBT-C indeed upholds that a child's behaviour is *irrelevant* until the environment is able to consistently and effectively promote progress. Consequently, parental responses are treated as a higher priority than the child's behaviours throughout the duration of treatment. Table 31.2 presents the list of topics of the parent training component.

II. Improving the Parent-Child Relationship

6. *Improve Parent-Child Relationship*

DBT-C Behaviour Change Model maintains that in order for any behaviour change to occur, three factors have to be present: 1) awareness of an action urge before an action occurs; 2) willingness not to follow an action urge if it is not justified by a situation, and instead respond in an adaptive way; and 3) a capability to engage in an effective behaviour.[1] A positive parent-child relationship is required for a child to accomplish each of these tasks successfully.

In order to decrease reactive responding and enhance adaptive functioning, an individual has to be aware of an action urge before it becomes an action. An action urge is a directive from our emotions on how to react to a situation. Although emotions are our main motivators to initiate and sustain behaviours needed to achieve specific goals, they are, so to speak, blind to whether their directives are justified by a situation. To regulate our emotions means to be in control of a decision on whether or not to follow an action urge, given the environmental demands. In other words, an emotion provides the fuel and direction but cannot be in the driver's seat. For example, an action urge of fear to run away from a lion is justified on the open plains of the Serengeti, but not justified when a lion is in a cage in a zoo.

The *awareness* of action urges can be gradually enhanced by practising mindfulness. Mindfulness means being fully present in the moment, purposefully, and in a non-judgmental way. Mindfulness is a complicated concept. Adults frequently take a considerable amount of time to fully appreciate its meaning and function and to start practising

---

[1] The DBT-C Behaviour Change Model discusses factors that have to be present to change one's *own* behaviour. A behaviour can be changed without a person's awareness through shaping and reinforcement.

Table 31.2   Parent-training curriculum

Pre-treatment phase

Biosocial theory, transactional model, and goal	Discussion of the biosocial theory, transactional model, and the DBT-C hierarchy of treatment targets.
Orientation and commitment	Discussion of the treatment model and how it will address specified goals. Commitment is elicited and required from parents to start treatment.

Didactics on emotions and problem solving

Didactics on emotions	Discussion of the following topics: definition of emotions, function of emotions, myths about emotions, emotions vs mood, feeling/thought/behaviour triangle, levels of emotional intensity, Emotions Wave, Behaviour Change Model, Emotion Regulation Model, radical acceptance, and STOP skill.
Problem solving	Discussion of the following topics: four responses to any problem, pros and cons, cognitive restructuring and five steps of problem solving.

DBT-C skills

Skills training	Mindfulness, distress tolerance, emotion regulation, and interpersonal effectiveness.

Parent training

Creating a change-ready environment	Discussion of the following topics: definition of a behaviour, three steps to behaviour change, main factors that maintain undesirable behaviours, definition of a problem, five cardinal rules of parenting, and importance of a positive parent-child relationship.
Creating a validating environment	Discussion of the following topics: definition of validation, function of validation, levels of validation, what validation is not, invalidating behaviours, and troubleshooting validation.
Introduction to behaviour change techniques	Discussion of the following topics: definitions of reinforcement, punishment, extinction, and shaping, and how to give effective prompts.
Reinforcement	Discussion of the following topics: function of reinforcement, types of reinforcers, factors that enhance the effectiveness of reinforcement, and using a point chart to reinforce skills use and other adaptive behaviours.
Punishment	Discussion of the following topics: function of punishment, punishment vs retaliation, punishment vs natural consequences, side effects of punishment, punishment traps for caregivers, myths about punishment, factors that enhance effectiveness of punishment, when and how to use each punishment technique (reprimands, time out, chores, and taking away privileges).
A-VCR model of responding	Putting it all together by using an A-VCR model: **A**ttend/**A**ssess, **V**alidate, **C**oach skills use, **R**einforce.
Introduction to dialectics	Discussion of the guiding principles of dialectics (there is not absolute nor relative truth, opposite things can both be true, change is the only constant, and change is transactional), how these principles apply to parenting, and ways to practise dialectics.

Table 31.2 Continued

Dialectical dilemmas	Discussion of dialectical dilemmas of parenting: permissive vs restrictive parenting, overprotective vs neglectful parenting, overindulging vs depriving parenting, and pathologizing normative behaviours vs normalizing pathological behaviours.
Walking the middle path	Discussion on how to walk the middle path by balancing the opposites and looking for a synthesis, balancing extremes of parenting styles, searching for what is valid, and using behavioural principles and effective parenting strategies.

mindfulness consistently. Therefore, to expect pre-adolescent children to practise mindfulness without support and encouragement from their families is unrealistic. However, even if mindfulness practice becomes a daily routine for parents, a child's interest and motivation to join in largely depend on the relationship they have with their parents. For children, mindfulness practice usually involves mindful participation in games and other activities with family members. If a parent-child relationship is severely strained, a child is more likely to avoid parents and resist joint activities (Kerns, Tomich, Aspelmeier, & Contreras, 2000). The above discussed issues in a strained parent-child relationship, of course, apply to any skills practice (not just mindfulness) and any parental modelling. Mindfulness practice is a special, albeit very important, case as mindfulness is a core DBT skill on which the use of all other skills depends.

Awareness of an emotional reaction and a corresponding action urge are required, but not sufficient, for a desired response to occur. An individual has to be willing not to follow an action urge if it is not justified by the demands of a situation. This is difficult, especially for children with severe emotional sensitivity. The difficulty comes from a need to somehow harness the willingness to go against our main motivators—our emotions. Willingness is not the same as acceptance, but it is a first step leading to it. Willingness is *acting as if* one has already accepted and is ready for a change. It is starting to walk towards change and away from a wilful stance; it is exhaling fighting and inhaling acceptance.

There are four main sources of willingness—intrinsic motivation, extrinsic motivation, reciprocity, and satisfying functions of the behaviour (Ryan & Deci, 2000). Intrinsic motivation occurs when the activity itself is rewarding, satisfies our basic needs (e.g., food, shelter, companionship) and enhances a sense of pride, self-esteem, self-determination, interest to learn, and the ability to gain self-mastery and achieve goals. Extrinsic motivation occurs when an activity is rewarded by incentives not inherent in the task, such as external attention, accolades, praise and recognition from others, as well as material rewards, money, or tokens (e.g., stickers, points). The younger the child, the higher the tendency to be motivated by extrinsic, rather than intrinsic, rewards (Hayamizu, 1997). Extrinsic rewards that are contingent and tied to performance levels can over time establish interest in activities that lack initial interest, as well as enhance effort and persistence, increase perception of self-determination and reliance on intrinsic motivation to continue to achieve desired outcomes (Cameron, Banko, & Pierce, 2001). Thus, without a strong extrinsic motivational system, any improvements in children's behaviour may be isolated and sporadic.

Reciprocity is the middle ground between internal and external motivation. It is a transaction in which parents and the child share a mutual goal to act in ways to meet each other's expectations, satisfy interests, and benefit the relationship. To build reciprocity, parents need to focus on doing what their child finds enjoyable (playing a video game) and not what they think may be better for the child (e.g., reading a book). Reciprocity enhances both internal and external motivation and helps build a positive parent-child relationship.

Furthermore, parents need to help their child understand the function of his/her maladaptive behaviour and aid in addressing this function in adaptive ways. No amount of skills training and reinforcement will produce a consistent behaviour if a function is not satisfied. For example, if a child's aggression towards a sibling leads to coveted parental attention and physical contact (even if this means being restrained to prevent injury to self and others), showering this child with rewards for using skills may only produce isolated and sporadic instances of the prosocial behaviour, if the desired attention and contact are not obtained. Understanding and addressing functions are imperative to eliciting and sustaining motivation.

Consistent progress can be achieved when an environment is supportive, reinforcing, and validating. A positive parent-child relationship serves four main functions: 1) modelling a relationship built on acceptance, trust, reinforcement, shared interests, and mutual respect; 2) increasing a child's desire to spend time with parents, which provides parents with more opportunities to model and prompt skills use, and to offer validation and reinforcement; 3) increasing a child's motivation to do desired behaviours to please parents, make parents proud, and earn rewards; and 4) building pathways in the child's brain associated with adaptive functioning. A relationship where parents are punishing, critical, judgmental, and invalidating not only dysregulates a child and models ineffective patterns of relating, but may also lead to the child avoiding, distrusting, and retaliating against the parents (Morris et al., 2002; Strand, 2000). Avoidance and distrust can significantly decrease the frequency and quality of reinforcement. If a child avoids parents, this may greatly limit the amount of time they spend together, and, thus, the number of opportunities a parent may have to model, prompt, and reinforce the child's effective responding. The quality of reinforcement may also be negatively affected, as children of abusive parents are shown to be less receptive to reinforcement (Strand, 2000). Retaliation against parents is also quite common when the parent-child relationship is severely strained. One function of a child's negative behaviour may be an attempt to inflict upon the parent the same feelings of "misery" that the child feels by being pervasively invalidated. When this function predominates, it is unlikely that reinforcement and skills training will produce a desired behaviour change. This is because the main goal of reinforcement and skills training is to increase the frequency of positive and prosocial behaviours, which contradicts the goal of inflicting misery.

Additionally, retaliation (e.g., screaming, yelling, and inflicting pain) can be modelled by parents as a way to respond to problems. Unfortunately, retaliation is frequently confused with punishment. The function of punishment is to suppress an undesirable behaviour in a moment. Punishment, as a behaviour modification technique, should be applied consistently and strategically (e.g., in DBT-C it is only used to suppress unsafe behaviours, such as physical aggression). The function of retaliation, on the other hand, is to inflict suffering in a response to an aversive event. Retaliation is used inconsistently and indiscriminately because it is a mood-dependent response. While punishment targets a suppression of another person's dysfunctional behaviour, retaliation targets a decrease of one's own aversive emotional state. A parent-child relationship where mutual retaliation is frequent will continue to exacerbate the pattern of invalidation and, thus, decrease the child's willingness to engage in adaptive behaviours.

Awareness and willingness are only instrumental when an individual has a behavioural capability to act in an effective way. Behavioural *capability* is achieved via learning and practising adaptive skills. Learning is initiated during treatment sessions. However, most of the work on the application of the techniques occurs outside of the office. Parents are entrusted with eliciting further discussions of the concepts, practising techniques, and, most importantly, demonstrating the use of skills via modelling. Skills can be practised with children in four main ways, such as: 1) during an actual problematic situation; 2) while processing a problematic response after an outburst has occurred and rehearsing alternative solutions; 3) during the practice of skills in hypothetical problematic situations via role-plays; and 4) while coping ahead of problematic situations that are likely to happen in a near future and deciding on how to respond. All four situations necessitate parental participation. The first scenario requires parental attention to prompt, refine, and reinforce adaptive responding, while the last three are primarily elicited by parents.

In DBT-C, parental modelling of skills use is seen as one of the most important ingredients of change. A child's adaptive responding cannot be expected if the environment is consistently reacting in dysfunctional ways, and is not promoting the child's learning by demonstrating skillful behaviours. Developmental psychologists have always maintained that children learn by imitating adults (Bandura & Kupers, 1964). The importance of modelling for behaviour acquisition has been championed by Albert Bandura and his famous Bobo doll experiment (Bandura, Ross, & Ross, 1961). Bandura's social learning theory postulated that behaviours are learned through the environment by observing, encoding, and imitating modelled responses (1977). More recent research actually indicates that children will imitate everything that adults demonstrate, including actions that are obviously irrelevant (something other primates do not do) (Horner & Whiten, 2005; Nielsen, 2006). It appears that children assume that all actions demonstrated by adults have a purpose (even if unknown), have been tested and presumed rational, and are attempts to transmit knowledge (Gergely & Csibra, 2005; Gergely, Egyed, & Kiraly, 2007). Indeed, our motivation to do things like those around us may be a universal human activity and may be the way that human culture is transmitted (Nielsen & Tomaselli, 2010).

III. Targeting the Child's Presenting Problems

7. Risky or Unsafe Behaviours

Emotional dysregulation is often associated with aggression toward other people (Okado & Bierman, 2015; Roy et al., 2013). Aggressive behaviours can be high risk and can sometimes result in injury or destruction of property. Yet, they are lower on the hierarchy than parental behaviours because addressing them without first targeting changes in the environment is not likely to produce lasting results. Aggression towards others can be divided into four main categories: 1) physical aggression (e.g., kicking, punching, throwing objects with an intent to hit a person, scratching, spitting, pulling hair); 2) verbal aggression (e.g., screaming, yelling, threatening; duration is for longer than one minute); 3) destructive behaviours (e.g., breaking objects, ripping paper, throwing objects without an intent to hit a person); and 4) talking back (e.g., swearing, "smart alec" comments, name calling; duration is one minute or less).

The risky or unsafe behaviours category includes any behaviours that threaten the safety of other people or property, and thus, cannot be ignored. These usually include physical aggression and destructive behaviours. These behaviours are not dangerous enough to be included into the therapy-destroying category, as they are mild to moderate in severity and are not likely to cause significant damage to the child, other people or property, or severely disrupt a treatment process.

DBT-C teaches parents to rely almost exclusively on modelling, acceptance, validation, reinforcement, ignoring, and natural consequences. Punishment techniques (i.e., reprimands, time out, assignment of chores, and removal of privileges as a back-up strategy) are used primarily to suppress behaviours that cannot be ignored because they are a safety risk (e.g., a child is throwing objects at her sibling). Punishment procedures are always supported by the reinforcement of desired alternative responses and shaping programmes (i.e., reinforcement of the successive approximation of a response in order to produce a final desired behaviour). Parents are made explicitly aware that, even in circumstances when a behaviour has to be suppressed, short-term gains are achieved at the expense of long-term outcomes, as punishment is associated with a slew of detrimental side effects (e.g., emotional escalation, modelling force as a conflict resolution strategy, reinforcement of unwanted behaviours by attention, straining the parent-child relationship, and consequent avoidance of parents) (Strand, 2000). Although DBT-C supports zero tolerance of physical aggression and destructive behaviours and teaches parents punishment techniques, the emphasis is on the reinforcement, shaping, and learning skills. Thus, it is easy to appreciate why parental behaviours are given a priority even over the child's physical aggression, as effective punishment, reinforcement, and skills practice will not occur without first addressing parental capabilities.

8. Quality-of-life-interfering problems

The quality-of-life-interfering problems include child and environmental issues that interfere with a child's functioning. These may include a child's behaviours (e.g., verbal aggression, severe interpersonal problems) and comorbid psychiatric disorders, as well as insufficient environmental supports (e.g., school services) (see Table 31.3). Although physical aggression can also be viewed as a quality-of-life-interfering behaviour, it is separated into its own category to ensure that it is treated as a higher priority, and is therefore targeted before other quality-of-life (QoL) issues are addressed. For example, it is advisable to implement a shaping programme to reduce verbal aggression only after physical aggression is eliminated. Implementation of multiple reinforcement and shaping programmes is undesirable and counterproductive, as a child may have too many venues to earn rewards. Goals that are higher on the target hierarchy are usually more difficult to attain. If a child receives a sufficient number of points and rewards for behaviours that are lower on a target hierarchy (e.g., completing chores, doing homework), it may decrease a child's motivation to work on higher-level targets (cutting, physical aggression).

Issues that do not qualify as interfering with QoL are usually not extensively addressed during therapy and are instead left for parents to continue to resolve once treatment is completed. However, therapists have to be prepared that parents may have strong opinions on what is a priority and will expect therapists to address most of their preferred targets (e.g., academic achievements, attending extracurricular activities) during the treatment. Additionally, parents may have difficulty agreeing with a need to change their own behaviours and may especially find it problematic to accept a notion that their behaviours take precedence over their child's behaviours. Therefore, parents' orientation to the biosocial theory, transactional model, and a treatment target hierarchy and commitment to the model are prerequisites to initiating treatment, while a child's commitment is not required. Given that it is not always possible to address all of the concerns parents have regarding their child's functioning during the treatment, it is always helpful

---

Table 31.3 Pre-adolescent children quality-of-life-interfering behaviours

1. Comorbid Axis I disorders (e.g., ADHD, anxiety, depression)
2. Neurophysiological problems (e.g., sensory processing disorder)
3. Verbal aggression (e.g., screaming, yelling, threatening for longer than one min.)
4. Talking back (e.g., cursing, smart-aleck comments, dismissive or disrespectful responses for ≤ one min.)
5. Issues with delayed gratification and impulse control behaviours (e.g., stealing, lying, cheating)
6. Severe interpersonal difficulties with siblings, peers, teachers, family members (other than primary caregivers)
7. Parent/family issues (e.g., child's response to parental divorce)
8. School problems (e.g., school refusal, detentions, suspensions, difficulties with homework)
9. Need for further services (e.g., special services at school, occupational therapy)
10. Problems with maintaining physical health (e.g., refusing to take prescribed medication, refusing to go to medical appointments)

for parents to understand that they will be taught techniques that can be used to develop any child behaviours that are desired, but that are not yet fully established at treatment completion.

9. *Skills Training*

As discussed above, in order for a change to occur, an individual has to have behavioural capabilities. DBT-C requires the skills training curriculum to be completed by children as well as their parents. At least one parent has to attend treatment sessions consistently to learn the material, with a goal of communicating this learning to other caregivers (e.g., the other parent, grandparents, babysitters). DBT-C incorporates almost all of the adult DBT skills into the curriculum, with some exceptions that may not be developmentally appropriate for pre-adolescent children (e.g., finding meaning, sticking to values, no apologies; see Table 31.4). In DBT-C, "skills" is a general term that encompasses all of the didactic material taught during individual therapy (see Table 31.5) and skills training (see Table 31.6). Topics are taught in the sequence presented, and further discussion about treatment structure is discussed in Section III.

10. *Therapy-Interfering Behaviours of the Child*

DBT-C is quite tolerant of child behaviour that may interfere with conducting a session. This stems from its ability to rely almost exclusively on parental learning, when necessary, which significantly relieves the pressure of ensuring the child's full engagement during a session. In DBT-C, problematic behaviours (verbal aggression, threats, cursing, screaming, using threatening body language, devaluing treatment as a waste of time, running around, and other distracting behaviours) are just ignored with a plan to help a child re-regulate and re-focus attention when appropriate. If such behaviours occur consistently, they are targeted by a shaping programme.

Furthermore, problematic behaviours that occur during sessions, such as temper outbursts, can be very informative and target relevant, as they allow a therapist to: 1) observe parent-child interactions; 2) model to parents how to respond to problematic situations; 3) coach parental responses in the moment; and 4) model effective conflict resolution, problem solving, and skills use to parents and a child. Ignoring of problem behaviours in session also helps with extinction generalization (e.g., swearing is not attended to at home and in therapy).

If DBT-C is conducted in a residential setting or inpatient unit, skills training is usually delivered in groups and parents are not present. However, ignoring the above-described behaviours is still practised to the fullest extent possible. For other participants, a temper outburst of a group peer (unless a behaviour is aggressive or dangerous) is viewed as an opportunity to practise ignoring, distress tolerance, and other skills.

Attempts to correct therapy-interfering behaviours as they are occurring during a session via discussions, behaviour analysis, suppression of behaviours via punishment (except if dangerous) etc., can reinforce these behaviours with attention, interfere with addressing higher level targets (e.g., teaching skills to parents), lead to escalation, strain the therapist-child relationship, and decrease a child's willingness to attend further

Table 31.4 DBT for adults skills vs DBT for children skills

DBT adult skills	DBT-C skills	DBT-C individual	Parent training	Not covered
Mindfulness				
Three states of mind	Three states of mind			
What skills	What skills			
How skills	How skills			
Interpersonal effectiveness				
Factors reducing Interpersonal Effectiveness	What gets in the way of being effective			
Myths	Worry thoughts			
Cheerleading	Cheerleading			
DEAR	DEAR			
MAN, GIVE, FAST	FRIEND			(no) Apologies Stick to values
Walking the middle path			Walking the middle path	
Dialectics			Dialectics	
Validation			Validation	
Behaviour change skills			Behaviour change skills	
Distress tolerance				
STOP		STOP		
Wise mind ACCEPTS	DISTRACT	Self-reinforcement		Comparisons
IMPROVE the moment		Self-validation		Meaning
TIP skills				Prayer

(continued)

Table 31.4 Continued

DBT adult skills	DBT-C skills	DBT-C individual	Parent training	Not covered
Self-soothe	Self-soothe			
Pros and cons	Pros and cons			
Radical acceptance	Letting it go			
Willingness/wilfulness	Willingness/wilfulness			
Emotion regulation				
Understanding emotions		What am I feeling?		
		Feeling thermometer		
		Feeling/thought/behaviour triangle		
Myths about emotions		Myths about emotions		
Model for describing emotions		Emotion Wave		
What good are emotions?		Why emotions are important?		
Letting go of emotional suffering	Surfing Your Emotions			
Check the facts		Check the facts		
Problem solving		Problem solving		
Opposite action	Opposite action			
PLEASE	PLEASE			
ABC	LAUGH			

Table 31.5 Individual counselling curriculum

Pre-treatment phase

Biosocial model and treatment goals	Discussion of emotional sensitivity, invalidating environment, and resulting problems. Long-term and short-term goals are discussed and an "Eiffel Tower" of the child's own treatment target hierarchy is created.
Orientation and commitment	Discussion of the treatment model and how it will address specified goals. Commitment is elicited (only if therapist is confident that a child is willing and likely to commit.

Didactics on emotions

What am I feeling?	Discussion of emotions, corresponding sensations and action urges, changes in face and body.
Feelings/thought/ behaviour triangle	Discussion of how feelings, thoughts, and behaviours are different, how emotions can be turned into mood, and how emotions have different levels of intensity (as a "Feeling Thermometer").
Why are emotions important?	Discussion of the functions of emotions and myths about emotions.
Emotion Wave	Emotion Wave is seen as going through six stages: event, thought, feeling, action urge, action, and after effect.
Food for emotions	Discussion of three sources of food for emotions: doing what emotion wants, thinking what emotions wants, and maintaining tension in the body that emotion brings.
Behaviour change model	Three main factors that are needed to change your own behaviour: awareness, willingness and capability.
Wilfulness and willingness	Being willing to accept reality as it is as opposed to being wilful in refusing to do what works.
Letting it go	Techniques for accepting events that cannot be changed with mind and body.
STOP skill	Avoiding impulsive reactions using STOP skills: *S*top and do not move a muscle, *T*ake a step back and breathe, *O*bserve what is going on inside and outside of you to collect information, *P*roceed mindfully by considering goals.

Individual therapy following stage 1 targets

Four responses to any problem	Solve a problem, change the way you feel, tolerate and accept, stay miserable.
Short-term and long-term pros and cons	To select an effective solution to a problem, consider pros and cons of each response, and note which consequences are short term and long term.
Check the facts	Cognitive restructuring by catching ineffective cognitions, challenging, and changing them.
Problem solving	Five steps to problem solving: describe the situation, consider the "Eiffel Tower of Goals," brainstorm all possible solutions, choose one that fits bets, act on your choice, and note results to consider next time.

Table 31.6   DBT–C skills training curriculum

Mindfulness

Introduction	Meaning, importance, and goals of mindfulness skills.
What is mindfulness?	Paying attention to paying attention on purpose, in this one moment, and non-judgmentally.
Three states of mind	"Emotion mind" is when thoughts and behaviours are controlled mostly by emotions and it is hard to think straight. "Reasonable mind" is when thoughts and behaviours are controlled by logic and rules and emotions are not considered. "Wise mind" is when we take into account information from our feelings and thoughts and add intuition when making decisions. Steps to connect to Wise mind are discussed.
What skills	Observing, describing, and participating with awareness.
How skills	Don't judge, stay focused, and do what works.
Review	Review and discussion of the learned mindfulness skills.

Distress tolerance

Introduction	Meaning and goals of distress tolerance skills.
DISTRACT	Controlling emotional and behavioural responses in distress using DISTRACT skills: *D*o something else, *I*magine pleasant events, *S*top thinking about it, *T*hink about something else, *R*emind yourself that feelings change, *A*sk others for help, *C*ontribute, *T*ake a break, and *T*ense and Relax.
TIP	When at a breaking point, use TIP skills: *T*ense and Relax, *I*ntense sensation, *P*aced Breathing.
Self-soothe	Tolerating distress by using the five senses: vision, hearing, taste, smell, and touch.
Review	Review and discussion of the learned distress tolerance skills.

Emotion regulation

Introduction	Meaning and goals of emotion regulation.
Surfing your emotion	Decreasing the intensity of emotional arousal by attending to sensations the emotion produces in the body without distracting or ruminating.
Opposite action	Changing emotion by acting opposite to the action urge.
PLEASE skills	Reducing emotional vulnerability with PLEASE skills: attend to *P*hysica*L* health, *E*at healthy, *A*void drugs/alcohol, *S*leep well, and *E*xercise.
LAUGH skills	Increasing positive emotions with LAUGH skills: *L*et go of worries, *A*pply yourself, *U*se coping skills ahead of time, set *G*oals, and *H*ave fun.
Review	Review and discussion of the learned emotion regulation skills.

Interpersonal effectiveness

Introduction	Meaning and goals of interpersonal effectiveness.
Worry thoughts & cheerleading	Goals of interpersonal effectiveness, what gets in the way of being effective and cheerleading statements.
Goals	Two kinds of interpersonal goals, "getting what you want" and "getting along."

Table 31.6 Continued

DEAR skills	How to "get what you want" using DEAR skills: **D**escribe the situation, **E**xpress feelings and thoughts, **A**sk for what you want, **R**eward or motivate the person for doing what you want.
FRIEND skills	How to "get along" by using the FRIEND skill: (be) **F**air, **R**espect the other person, (act) **I**nterested, **E**asy manner, **N**egotiate and (be) **D**irect.
Review	Review and discussion of the learned interpersonal effectiveness skills.

sessions. For example, in a situation when a child will only attend therapy if allowed to play on his iPhone during a session, instead of wrestling over electronic devices, this behaviour is ignored, and engagement is prompted and reinforced, while a therapist is teaching skills to parents. Similarly, if a child is very hyperactive and keeps moving and exploring objects in a room, focusing on having him sit quietly in one place will not be productive. In such situations, a therapist continues to teach and ask the child questions to assess attention and comprehension, as well as to engage the child in task-relevant activities.

A child's therapy-interfering behaviours are addressed primarily via 1) developing a strong therapist-child relationship; 2) reinforcing desired behaviours in the moment and shaping adaptive responding over time; 3) ignoring problematic behaviours (except if dangerous); 4) relying on natural consequences (i.e., a child does not get a participation reward); 5) conducting a chain and solution analysis of a behaviour in subsequent sessions; and 6) if child is not engaging, teaching the material to parents with the goal for them to communicate this material to a child at home via modelling, discussions, and prompting, reinforcing, and practising skills use.

OVERVIEW OF ADAPTATIONS

DBT-C adaptations to therapeutic strategies, skills training, and individual treatment, as well as the parent-training component have been discussed elsewhere (Perepletchikova et al., 2011; Perepletchikova & Goodman, 2014). Therefore, they will only be briefly reviewed in this section. DBT-C retains all principles, therapeutic strategies, didactic information, and skills modules of DBT for adults (Linehan, 1993, 2015). However, significant deviations from the original DBT permeate the entire DBT-C model, starting with how the presenting problem is discussed with children and their families. In working with this population, clinicians have to ensure that the term "sensitive" does not continue to be associated with a child being touchy, defensive, uptight, paranoid, or neurotic. To aid this goal, the term "supersenser" may be used as a better descriptor.

This word was derived from terms describing people with heightened sensitivity to sensory perceptions. Indeed, there are those who have an increased number of taste buds and experience the sense of taste with far greater intensity than an average person; these people are referred to as supertasters (Hayes & Keast, 2011). There are also supersmellers who have an increased olfactory acuity that causes them to have a lower threshold for odour, or hyperosmia (Hummel, Landis, & Huttenbrink, 2011). Having "super" abilities may present with some advantages as it allows such people to appreciate the nuances of tastes and smells to a greater extent; however, the intensity of their experiences can be overwhelming. Similarly, those who have a lower threshold for emotional arousal and experience it with greater intensity and duration than an average person may be referred to as supersensers. Just like the others with "super" abilities, supersensers can be easily overpowered by their reactions; however, their abilities may have some advantages. Research and clinical practice indicate that these people are not only sensitive to their own emotions, but also may be more attuned to other people's emotional states and may be very empathic (see, e.g., Spinrad & Stifter, 2006; Zahn-Waxler, Robinson, & Emde, 1992). Perhaps people who are reactive themselves have an enhanced understanding and concern about another person's distress. Explaining the notions of emotional sensitivity from a perspective of supersensers' special abilities and challenges rather than a vulnerability can achieve multiple functions. It may help avoid the risk of invalidation, provide a dialectical view of the presenting issue, and in many cases, give children and their parents a sense of relief and even contentment. Furthermore, a child's interest and willingness to learn techniques can be greatly enhanced when s/he understand that emotional sensitivity is a special ability that needs to be better controlled, rather than a problem to be corrected.

DBT-C maintains emotion dysregulation as its main target. In DBT-C concepts are simplified to promote better comprehension, given the developmental level of the target population. For example, DBT-C Emotion Change Model discusses emotion regulation as "not feeding" an unwanted emotion. Children are taught that emotions have three main sources of food: 1) doing what an emotion is saying to do (i.e., following an action urge); 2) thinking what an emotion is saying to think (e.g., rumination about a triggering event); and 3) maintaining tension in the body that is associated with emotional arousal. So, if an action urge is not justified by a situational demand, in order for an emotion to subside or change, all three sources of "food" have to be interrupted. Emotion regulation skills, such as "Surfing Your Emotion" and "Opposite Action," can change an emotional experience because they include techniques that interrupt all three sources of "food" for an emotion. For example, "Surfing Your Emotion" skill 1) interrupts action by performing a skill instead of a dysfunctional behaviour, 2) interrupts rumination by re-orienting attention from thoughts to sensations in the body that are associated with an emotion (e.g., "butterflies in the stomach" for fear), and 3) releases tension by doing half smile and willing hands. Most of the distress tolerance skills, on the other hand, are designed to tolerate a situation without making it worse and not to change an emotional experience, as they usually interrupt just one or two of the "food" sources (e.g., "Do Something Else" skill interrupts dysfunctional actions, and the "Tense and Release" skill interrupts a dysfunctional action and releases tension). Figure 31.1 presents the Emotion Change Model within the context of the Behaviour Change Model.

DBT-C aims to improve emotion regulation through intervening into each step of the Emotion Wave paradigm that is taught to participants (Figure 31.2): Step 0) vulnerabilities or events that increase chances of a dysfunctional response occurring, targeted through mindfulness and problem-solving; Step 1) an event, which can be internal (e.g., thought, memory, another feeling) or external (e.g., being called names, not getting a coveted item) is targeted through teaching effective problem-solving and conducting exposure; Step 2) a thought or interpretation of an event is targeted through mindfulness and cognitive restructuring; Step 3) physical feeling or sensations in the body is targeted through mindfulness; Step 4) an action urge or a directive from an emotion on how to respond to an event (e.g., pushing or kicking for anger) is targeted through mindfulness; Step 5) an action, whether or not to follow an action urge, is targeted through skills training and teaching effective problem-solving; and Step 6) the after-effects or consequences of an action (e.g., being rewarded or punished, other thoughts or emotions) are targeted through implementing and teaching contingency management procedures.

DBT-C favours practices, experiential exercises, role-plays, and games to didactic presentations and lengthy intellectual discussions. Active learning (through experiencing or practising a technique) is preferred to passive learning (through reading and discussing) for several reasons: 1) to help engage and sustain children's attention; 2) to promote understanding of the discussed skills; and 3) to allow the therapist to directly observe the use of a technique and provide immediate feedback to further refine skills use. *Experiential exercises* help participants experience aspects of the presented skills and may greatly aid in the understanding of techniques. For example, asking a child to

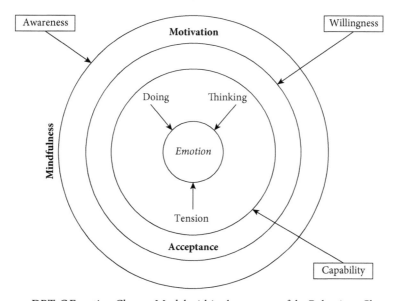

FIGURE 31.1 DBT-C Emotion Change Model within the context of the Behaviour Change Model.

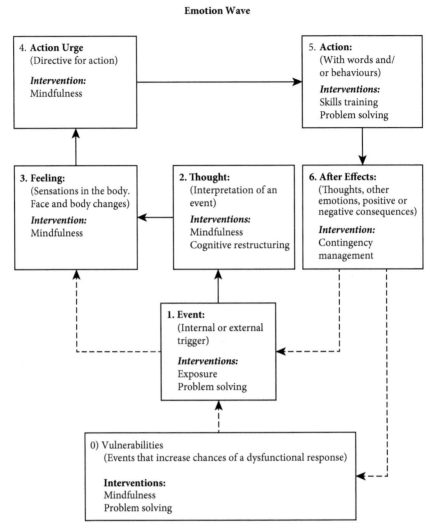

Emotion Wave

FIGURE 31.2 Emotions Wave and targets for intervention.

balance a peacock feather on a tip of her finger will require a mindful participation in order to keep the feather from falling, thus eliciting an experience of mindfulness. *In-session practice* is also used to enhance understanding of techniques, as well as to help refine skills use. Practices follow the presentation of didactic materials and include the therapist's modelling of a skill, eliciting the child's performance of a skill, and providing corrective feedback. *Role plays* give a child an opportunity to practise skills in a playful way and to apply techniques to real-life situations.

During individual sessions, therapists address specific concerns, review Diary Cards, perform behavioural analyses, exposure, and cognitive restructuring, provide contingency management, and help the child apply learned skills to everyday problems. During the first several individual sessions of DBT-C, the child and caregivers receive didactic instructions on emotions. The child also learns problem-solving and cognitive restructuring techniques. Information taught during skills training is simplified and condensed from DBT for adults. For example, "Wise Mind ACCEPTS," "IMPROVE the moment" and "TIP" skills were combined into one skill: "DISTRACT" (see Table 31.5). DBT-C skills training is also augmented by multimedia and games. Multimedia presentations utilize video clips with cartoon characters performing skills effectively or ineffectively, which helps engage children in a discussion of techniques. Several games also have been developed for DBT-C. The "Skills Master" card game was created to assist with review of the learned skills at the end of each skill module. The "Three-Headed Dragon" game was developed to assist with chain and solution analysis. Additionally, a parent-training component has been added to the model, with some strategies adapted from Kazdin (2005). Parents are required to learn everything their child is learning (i.e., didactics on emotions and DBT-C skills), and participate in the parent training (i.e., validation, creation of change-ready environment, behaviour modification techniques, and dialectics of parenting).

Therapy structure largely depends on organizational demands and family needs. For example, on an outpatient basis, all treatment components are provided individually to family units. Children and their parents are seen once weekly for 90 minute sessions (30 min for individual child therapy, 20 min for individual parent component, and 40 min for skills training with a child and a parent together). A substantial difference in the developmental levels between seven-year-old and twelve-year-old children can make it quite a challenge to conduct effective skills training in a group format on an outpatient level of care. In residential care facilities, on the other hand, children and parents participate in separate skills trainings. Also, children are typically housed by age which allows a natural opportunity to conduct group skills training by units.

DBT highlights function over form. DBT-C does not prescribe a specific form for implementing treatment components, but rather emphasizes adherence to DBT principles and strategies, which enhances the flexibility of implementation. For example, didactics on emotions and DBT-C skills are usually taught to children together with their parents. However, separate training can be conducted when a parent-child relationship is so strained that a child becomes extremely reactive in his parents' presence, and where that reactivity interferes with learning. Separate trainings continue to be conducted until the relationship sufficiently improves to allow joint sessions.

EMPIRICAL SUPPORT

Two randomized clinical trials were recently completed on DBT for pre-adolescent children (seven to 12 years of age). The outpatient setting trial targeted children with DMDD (Perepletchikova et al., 2017). More than half of these children reported suicidality and/or non-suicidal self-injury (NSSI), with Attention Deficit Hyperactivity Disorder (ADHD) and Anxiety Disorders being the most prevalent comorbid conditions. Results of this trial indicated that DBT-C was acceptable to children and their parents and was significantly more effective in decreasing DMDD symptoms than Treatment As Usual (TAU). DBT-C had a significantly higher rate of attendance, treatment acceptability, and satisfaction, and a significantly lower drop-out rate as compared to TAU. Further, 90% of children in DBT-C responded to the intervention as compared to 45.5% in TAU, despite three times as many subjects in TAU as in DBT-C receiving additional psychopharmacological treatment. Differences between groups were shown for both mood symptoms and behaviour outbursts. Observed changes were also clinically significant and maintained at three-month follow-up.

The residential care trial was completed with male children with a range of psychiatric conditions, with ADHD, Disruptive Behaviour Disorders, and Anxiety Disorders being most prevalent (Perepletchikova, Klee et al., manuscript in preparation). Most children had three or more comorbid disorders, and reported suicidality and/or NSSI. The mean IQ for participants was 88.9. The results of this trial indicated no significant differences in the attendance and drop-out rates between groups, which was expected given the nature of the residential setting programme. However, significant differences were observed on the main measures of outcome—the *Child Behaviour Checklist* (CBCL) and the milieu staff report. Children in the DBT-C condition as compared to TAU had significantly greater reduction in scores on both the CBCL Internalizing and Externalizing scales. Results were maintained at follow-up, and observed changes were clinically significant.

Significant differences between groups were reported on the CBCL only by the milieu staff, and not by teachers or parents. One of the factors that may have contributed to the disparity in the results was the degree to which these caregivers received DBT-C training. Teachers were not trained in DBT-C, and the same teachers were in contact with both groups of children. Parents unfortunately attended only a fraction of parent training groups in both conditions and, thus, also did not receive sufficient training. DBT-C milieu staff, on the other hand, received intensive training in the DBT-C strategies, coping skills, didactics on emotions, and the parent-training component, and were supervised weekly on the application of the techniques. As noted, the goal of caregiver training is to help create a validating and change-ready environment with the expectation that this will facilitate children's progress. Indeed, results of both studies indicated significant and rapid symptom reduction for children receiving DBT-C within the trained environment. More research is needed to further examine the caregivers' role in treatment and to evaluate the efficacy of DBT for children; however, the obtained results are promising and provide preliminary support for the model.

CONCLUSION

DBT for pre-adolescent children retained the theoretical model, principles, and therapeutic strategies of standard DBT. DBT-C incorporates almost all of the adult DBT skills and didactics into the curriculum; however, the presentation and packaging of the information are considerably different to accommodate for the developmental and cognitive levels of pre-adolescent children. One of the major departures from the original model is the treatment target hierarchy, which has been greatly expanded to incorporate DBT-C's emphasis on the parental role in attaining the child's treatment goals. DBT-C views parental adaptive patterns of responding as key to achieving lasting changes in a child's emotional and behavioural regulation.

KEY MESSAGES FOR PRACTITIONERS

- DBT-C retains the theoretical model, principles, and therapeutic strategies of standard DBT.

- DBT-C incorporates almost all of the adult DBT skills and didactics into the curriculum, but modified to the developmental and cognitive level of pre-adolescent children.

- DBT-C includes a parent-training component.

- A major departure from standard DBT is the treatment target hierarchy, which emphasizes increasing adaptive patterns of parental responding as central to improving the child's emotional and behavioural regulation.

REFERENCES

Althoff, R. R., Verhulst, F. C., Retlew, D. C., Hudziak, J. J., & Van der Ende, J. (2010). Adult outcomes of childhood dysregulation: A 14-year follow-up study. *Journal of the American Academy of Child and Adolescent Psychiatry, 49*, 1105–1116.

Bandura, A. (1977). *Social learning theory*. Englewood Cliffs, NJ: Prentice Hall.

Bandura, A, & Kupers, C. J. (1964). Transmission of patterns of self-reinforcement through modeling. *Journal of Abnormal and Social Psychology, 69*, 1–9.

Bandura, A., Ross, D., & Ross, S. A. (1961). Transmission of aggression through imitation of aggressive models. *Journal of Abnormal and Social Psychology, 63*, 575–582.

Bingham, C. W., & Sidorkin, A. M. (2004). *No education without relation*. New York: Peter Lang Publishing.

Cameron, J., Banko, K. M., & Pierce, D. (2001). Pervasive negative effects of rewards on intrinsic motivation: The myth continues. *The Behavior Analysis, 24*, 1–44.

Gergely, G., & Csibra, G. (2005). The social construction of the cultural mind: Imitative learning as a mechanism of human pedagogy. *Interaction Studies, 6*, 463–481.

Gergely, G., Egyed, K., & Kiraly, I. (2007). On pedagogy. *Developmental Science, 10*, 139–146.

Hayamizu, T. (1997). Between intrinsic and extrinsic motivation: Examination of reasons for academic study based on the theory of internalization. *Japanese Psychological Research, 39*, 98–108.

Hummel, T., Landis, B. N., & Huttenbrink, K. B. (2011). Smell and taste disorders. *GMS Current Points in Otorhinolaryngology, 10*, 1–15.

Hayes, J. E., & Keast, R. S. J. (2011). Two decades of supertasting: where do we stand? *Physiology & Behaviors 104*, 1072–1074.

Holtman, M., Buchmann, A. F., Esser, G., Schmidt, M. H., Banaschewski, T., & Laucht, M. (2011). The Child Behavior Checklist—Dysregulation Profile predicts substance use, suicidality, and functional impartment: a longitudinal analysis. *Journal of Child Psychology and Psychiatry, 52*, 139–147.

Horner, V., & Whiten, A. (2005). Causal knowledge and imitation/emulation switching in chimpanzees (Pan troglodytes) and children (Homo sapiens). *Animal Cognition, 8*, 164–181.

Kazdin, A. E. (2005). *Parent management training: Treatment of oppositional, aggressive and antisocial behavior in children and adolescents.* New York, NY: Oxford University Press.

Kerns, K. A., Tomich, P. L., Aspelmeier, J. E., & Contreras, J. M. (2000). Attachment-based assessment of parent-child relationships in middle childhood. *Developmental Psychology, 36*, 614–626.

Linehan, M. M. (1993). *Cognitive-behavioral treatment of borderline personality disorder.* New York, NY: Guilford Press.

Linehan, M. M. (2015). *DBT skills training manual.* New York, NY: Guilford Press.

Morris, A. S., Silk, J. S., Steinberg, L., Sessa, F. M., Avenevoli, S., & Essex, M. J. (2002). Temperamental vulnerability and negative parenting as interacting predictors of child adjustment. *Journal of Marriage and Family, 64*, 461–471.

Nielsen, M. (2006). Copying actions and copying outcomes: Social learning through the second year. *Developmental Psychology, 42*, 555–565.

Nielsen, M., & Tomaselli, K. (2010). Overimitation in Kalahari Bushman children and the origin of human cultural cognition. *Psychological Science, 21*, 729–736.

Okado, Y., & Bierman, K. L. (2015). Differential risk for late adolescent conduct problems and mood dysregulation among children with early externalizing behavior problems. *Journal of Abnormal Child Psychology, 43*, 735–747.

Perepletchikova, F., Axelrod, S. R., Kaufman, J., Rounsaville, B. J., Douglas-Palumberi, H., & Miller, A. L. (2011). Adapting Dialectical Behavior Therapy for children: Towards a new research agenda for pediatric suicidal and non-suicidal self-injurious behaviors. *Child and Adolescent Mental Health, 16*, 116–121.

Perepletchikova, F., & Goodman, G. (2014). Two approaches to treating pre-adolescent children with severe emotional and behavioral problems: Dialectical Behavior Therapy adapted for children and Mentalization-Based Child Therapy. *Journal of Psychotherapy Integration, 24*, 298–312.

Perepletchikova, F., Klee, S., Davidowitz, J., Nathanson, D., Merrill, C., Axelrod, S., . . . Walkup, J. (2017). Dialectical Behavior Therapy with pre-adolescent children in residential care: Feasibility and primary outcomes.

Perepletchikova, F., Nathanson, D., Axelrod, S., Merrill, C., Grossman, M., Rebeta, J., . . . Walkup, J. (manuscript in preparation). Dialectical Behavior Therapy for pre-adolescent children with Disruptive Mood Dysregultion Disorder: Feasibility and primary outcomes. *Journal of the American Academy of Child and Adolescent Psychiatry, 56*, 832–840.

Phillips, A. & Taylor, B. (2009). *On Kindness.* London: Hamish Hamilton.

Pickles, A., Aglan, A., Collishaw, S., Messer, J., Rutter, M., & Maughan, B. (2009). Predictors of suicidality across the life span: the Isle of Wight study. *Psychological Medicine, 26*, 1–14.

Roy, A. K., Klein, R. G., Angelosante, A., Bar-Heim, Y., Leibenluft, E., Hulvershorn, L., . . . Spindel, C. (2013). Clinical features of young children referred for impairing temper outbursts. *Journal of Child and Adolescent Psychopharmacology, 23*, 588–596.

Ryan, R. M., & Deci, E. L. (2000). Intrinsic and extrinsic motivations: Classic Definitions and new directions. *Contemporary Educational Psychology*, *25*, 54–67.

Spinrad, T. L., & Stifter, C. A. (2006). Toddlers' empathy-related responding to distress: Predictions from negative emotionality and maternal behavior in infancy. *Infancy*, *10*, 97–121.

Strand, P. S. (2000). A modern behavioral respective on child conduct disorder: Integrating behavioral momentum and matching theory. *Clinical Psychology Review*, *20*, 593–615.

Tamás, Z., Kovacs, M., Gentzler, A. L., Tepper, P., Gádoros, J., Kiss, E., . . . Vetró, A. (2007). The relationship of temperament and emotion self-regulation with suicidal behavior in a clinical sample of depressed children in Hungary. *Journal of Abnormal Child Psychology*, *35*, 640–652.

Thomas, A., & Chess, S. (1985). The behavioral study of temperament. In J. Strelau, F. H. Farley, & A. Gale (Eds.), *The biological bases of personality and behavior: Vol. 1. Theories, measurements techniques and development* (pp. 213–235). Washington, DC: Hemisphere.

Winnicott, D. W. (1973). *The Child, the Family, and the Outside World*. Harmondsworth: Penguin Books.

Zahn-Waxler, C., Robinson, J. L., & Emde, R. N. (1992). The development of empathy in twins. *Developmental Psychology*, *28*, 1038–1047.

CHAPTER 32

DBT SKILLS IN SCHOOLS

Implementation of the DBT STEPS—A Social Emotional Curriculum

JAMES J. MAZZA AND
ELIZABETH T. DEXTER-MAZZA

RATIONALE AND DEVELOPMENT FOR DBT STEPS-A

THE history of developing the DBT Skills in Schools: Skills Training for Emotional Problem Solving for Adolescents (DBT STEPS-A) curriculum began in 2005 and 2006 with numerous conversations among leading experts in the field of suicidology regarding designing a preventive intervention programme to reduce the rate of adolescent non-suicidal self-injury (NSSI) and suicidal thinking and behaviour (STB). The rationale for designing such a programme was to build an upstream approach versus the common approach of "waiting to fail" where adolescents need to engage in the symptomatic behaviour before being identified for mental health services (Cook, 2015; Cook, Burns, Browning-Wright, & Gresham, 2010). As preliminary conversations centered around NSSI and STB, the areas of expertise for the authors, the preliminary design of DBT STEPS-A focused on trying to utilize the evidence-based treatment programme of Dialectical Behaviour Therapy (DBT) (Linehan, 1993, 2015a, b; Miller, Rathus, & Linehan, 2007). However, the multi-component structure of standard DBT did not lend itself well to school-based settings and/or school personnel for a preventive approach. Thus, we focused on a single component, the DBT Skills, as a place where we could adapt the treatment content into structured lesson plans that comprised a universal social emotional learning (SEL) curriculum.

Once we had identified DBT Skills as the foundation, we initially focused the curriculum for high-risk adolescents, i.e., those who have engaged in NSSI and STB, or those considered to be at Tier III service provision (requiring more specialist input) within a multitiered systems of support (MTSS)(Stoiber, 2014; Stoiber & Gettinger, 2016). As the curriculum began to develop, it became increasingly clear that adolescents who were experiencing emotional distress in areas of peer relationships, intimacy and dating, family relationships, substance use, bullying, and academic pressures could also benefit from learning DBT Skills, since they too could be at-risk for engaging in NSSI and STB. Given that most adolescents will experience emotional stress in one or more of these areas, we changed our lens from Tier III to Tier I (universal), which became the focus. The development of the curriculum at the universal level also provided a broader expansion of the DBT Skills to all students, thus lending itself to a classroom structure and format. The universal approach also provided a proactive design to stem the flow of students becoming at-risk by providing them with skills for current and possible future situations that may cause emotional distress.

The DBT STEPS-A curriculum represents ten years of ongoing development and a process of revising the lessons and handouts to make them more teacher and student friendly, respectively, while also accounting for implementation in a school-based setting. Given the varying mental needs of student within schools, we also provided supplemental strategies for working with students at the Tier II and Tier III levels, with DBT STEPS-A as the foundation of the service delivery model. These strategies are discussed in detail in *DBT Skills in Schools: Skills Training for Emotional Problem Solving for Adolescents* (Mazza, Dexter-Mazza, Miller, Rathus, & Murphy, 2016). This chapter discusses the school-based application of DBT STEPS-A as well as the implementation strategies, curriculum structure, potential barriers, preliminary findings, and future directions.

RATES OF SUICIDE AND SELF-HARM CONTINUE TO RISE

Suicide is the second leading cause of death among youth ages 10–19 years-old in the United States (Centers for Disease Control and Prevention, 2017). Unfortunately, these rates over the past five years have been slowly increasing despite greater awareness of the issue of youth suicide. The frequency rate of NSSI among community adolescents is equally high, if not higher, with between 14% to 39% engaging in some form of NSSI in the past 12 months (Lloyd-Richardson, Perrine, Dierker, & Kelley, 2007; Muehlenkamp, Hoff, Licht, Azue, & Hasenzahl, 2009). Leading experts in the field of suicidology have suggested that tertiary approaches, such as psychotherapy, which may be effective are limited in their reach and availability, and proposed the need to find novel approaches that expand the utilization of evidence-based programmes (Miller & Mazza, 2017). Because emotional dysregulation is a core component of both NSSI and STB, as well as a symptom in borderline personality disorder, PTSD, substance use, and eating disorders, focusing on emotional regulation interventions and skills seemed like a worthy area to target for broad based dissemination (Mehlum et al., 2014; Muehlenkamp et al., 2009; Nelson-Gray et al., 2006).

The Role of Schools

With the high number of youth experiencing mental health difficulties and the barriers of trying to access mental health care, schools have become "de facto" mental health providers (Cook et al., 2010). In fact, schools appear to be the logical setting to provide services given most youth attend schools. Recent research findings provide substantial support for utilizing schools in this role of mental health provider. The estimated number of high-school students who are experiencing mental health difficulties/disorders that warrant mental health services is estimated as between 20 to 25% (Kilgus, Reinke, & Jimerson, 2015). Unfortunately, research shows that when schools refer these cases to outside agencies, more than 80% of these students do not receive the referred mental health services due to accessibility and implementation barriers, such as burdensome geography, lack of availability (months-long waiting lists), and financial hardship (National Institute of Mental Health, 2015). This stands in stark contrast to the 20% of students referred for services within school-based settings—for this group, over 95% successfully received mental health services (Kilgus et al., 2015). This finding, coupled with the increased rates of adolescent suicide and NSSI (CDC, 2017), suggests that evidence-based interventions delivered in community/outpatient settings need to be accessible, adapted, and delivered within school-based settings in order to make a substantial difference in the mental health needs of adolescents.

Schools offer numerous advantages over community agencies' outpatient settings for delivering mental health services to adolescents. First, school-based settings have a captive audience, meaning that, as students are already coming to the setting for the delivery of academic instruction, providing complementary mental health services would be a natural fit. Second, schools are places where adolescents experience some significant stressors, although schools can also provide positive support and assistance to students who are struggling, and offer them a real-life setting to practise their mental health strategies under close monitoring of school staff. Third, the school-based setting is not parent-dependent, meaning adolescents do not need to rely on their parents to transport them to community agencies or outpatient settings to receive services. Although parents are an important part of a therapeutic process, their inconsistencies can often lead to lack of adolescent involvement. Wagner (1997) reported that parents' life stressors can often be obstacles in helping their children get the mental health services they need. Finally, school-based settings offer an opportunity to deliver mental health strategies in classroom settings (i.e., 15–30 students), thus providing a cost-effective means with a broader reach than individual models of service delivery. The primary disadvantage of using schools for delivering mental health services is access to mental health professionals and/or therapists to provide the service. Most schools do not have the financial resources to employ dedicated school-based mental health professionals, which unfortunately may end up costing schools more money in the long-run when students with high intensive needs are placed in restrictive settings such as residential treatment, where often school districts need to pay the cost.

STANDARD DBT TO DBT STEPS-A

There is strong empirical support showing the effectiveness of implementing standard DBT with highly emotionally dysregulated adults (Harned et al., 2008) and adolescents who engage in NSSI and STB (Mehlum et al., 2014; Nelson-Gray et al., 2006), as well as other mental health disorders (i.e., substance abuse, PTSD) (Mehlum et al., 2014; Muehlenkamp et al., 2009; Nelson-Gray et al., 2006). However, the structure of standard DBT does not generalize easily to school-based settings, given the intensive resource demands needed for standard components of phone coaching 24/7, 90–120 minute skills training groups, and trained personnel to provide individual therapy 45–50 minutes per week per student. Therefore, the dilemma was how to adapt a programme as effective as standard DBT that would translate well into school-based settings for a larger number of students.

Research on adaptations of standard DBT applied in school-based settings have shown promising results among high-risk adolescents in high school, showing a reduction in NSSI and STB, levels of depression and anxiety, and disciplinary issues while also improving GPAs, school attendance, and subjective well-being (Mazza & Hanson, 2015; Miller, Mazza, Dexter-Mazza, Steinberg, & Courtney-Seidler, 2014). In addition, one study examining the effectiveness of the skills component only among 32 adolescents showed that DBT skills alone improved adolescent levels of depression, NSSI, and STB; this suggests that DBT skills alone is an effective treatment (Nelson-Gray et al., 2006). Using this information and examining the skills component of standard DBT, it seemed feasible to adapt the skills training materials and convert them to teacher lesson plans that would provide instruction for skill acquisition and practice. Prior to the development of DBT STEPS-A, we consulted with Marsha Linehan (treatment developer of DBT), and Alec Miller and Jill Rathus (developers of standard DBT for outpatient adolescents) regarding the feasibility and design in adapting the DBT Skills for universal dissemination. With their support and guidance, we began developing the DBT STEPS-A curriculum.

CURRICULUM STRUCTURE OF DBT STEPS-A

The curriculum structure of DBT STEPS-A is consistent throughout each lesson. The structured format of the 30 lessons are similar to provide consistency and predictability to students and instructors in teaching the lessons. In addition, the consistent structure allows for efficiency in planning as well as providing substitute teachers with an established format. Each lesson begins with a mindfulness exercise/activity that is approximately five minutes. The lesson provides instructions for the different mindfulness exercises/activities. Homework review is the second lesson component, which typically comprises student dyads reviewing the skills practice of one another, and offering praise for skill use practice and/or coaching/suggestions to overcome barriers in skill use practice. The peer-to-peer review was designed to take advantage of the fact that adolescents often disclose information to other adolescents before talking to adults regarding issues of mental health. The allocated time for home review is ten minutes. Teaching the new skill/s is the third part of the lesson, which usually has 25–30 minutes allocated to it. This part of the lesson focuses on helping the students understand what the new skill is, examples of what it might look like, and different environments where it might be practised. The lesson summary and homework assignment occurs at the end of every lesson and takes three to five minutes to complete. During each lesson, students are given homework assignments that focus on the practice of the skill just taught. Homework assignments are due the next time the class meets.

The curriculum comprises four modules: mindfulness, distress tolerance, emotion regulation, and interpersonal effectiveness; the same four modules found in standard DBT. The recommended module sequence for DBT STEPS-A is as follows. Orientation and mindfulness need to be first in the sequence of instruction to provide students with an understanding of what the curriculum is about, establish classroom guidelines, and develop skills to increase awareness. Following mindfulness, the next module is distress tolerance, followed by emotion regulation and interpersonal effectiveness. However, there is flexibility in the ordering of modules following mindfulness, and schools may opt to implement interpersonal effectiveness or emotion regulation before distress tolerance. The rationale for sequencing distress tolerance after the initial mindfulness lessons was to provide students who are currently experiencing high levels of emotional distress with skills to resist the strong urges that are often accompanied by emotional dysregulation. However, instructors have the flexibility to interchange sequence of the other three modules, as long as each module is covered.

Tests

Because the curriculum is designed to be taught as a class, we created three knowledge tests that can be used for grading purposes that correspond to the modules of distress tolerance, emotion regulation, and interpersonal effectiveness. The knowledge test of the fourth module, mindfulness, is dispersed throughout the other three tests, underscoring its importance and relationship to the other three modules. The knowledge tests are one component of the recommended grading structure, with class participation and diary card completion being the other two.

Short-Term vs Long-Term Goals of the DBT STEPS-A Curriculum

It is important to keep in mind that the development of DBT STEPS-A was designed with both short- and long-term goals in mind. The short-term goals are: 1) to provide students with a structured format to learn DBT skills in a non-judgmental environment; 2) to teach students skills that apply to their own personal situation/environment; and 3) to provide ongoing support and coaching during skills development. Thus, the short-term goals focus on skill acquisition and teaching skills. The long-term goals are: 1) to practise skills so they become automatic; 2) to polish and refine skill use so they become more effective across different environments; and 3) to create a school environment that supports students using the DBT skills. In comparison to the short-term goals, the long-term goals focus on skills practice and generalization; the short- and long-term goals are complementary and extend beyond the classroom and/or school-based setting, and provide students with lifelong social emotional skills.

Implementing DBT STEPS-A within Multitiered Systems of Support (MTSS)

The DBT STEPS-A curriculum was developed to be implemented primarily at the universal level, meaning by all students in school-based settings. Yet all students do not learn at the same level or at the same time, and some students need additional services. Thus, specific strategies were developed for students in Tier II and Tier III that align with the DBT STEPS-A curriculum. With different educational and social emotional needs of their students, many school have adopted the multitiered systems of support (MTSS) structure, which has been effective in addressing the varying needs of students within a school environment. While developing DBT STEPS-A, utilizing the MTSS framework allowed us to address and provide strategies for students who may have more emotion regulation needs than at the universal level. A discussion of the different strategies to use with students in the Tier II and/or Tier III levels follows. It is important to keep in mind that even though students may be identified for needing Tier II and/or Tier III services, all students receive DBT STEPS-A as the foundation which supplements the other strategies.

Supplemental Tier II Strategies

The supplemental support strategies in working with Tier II students are designed to bolster the effectiveness and impact of the DBT STEPS-A curriculum. Tier II students, by definition, need some additional mild to moderate support. The recommended Tier II supplemental support strategies for DBT STEPS-A include, but are not limited to, the following:

1. The size of the class should be smaller, such as 10–15 students, compared to the universal size of 15–30 students. This strategy provides students with more opportunities to practise skills and receive feedback and mentoring on their skills practice. In addition, smaller class sizes will increase the participation of students during the teaching of the lessons and opportunities to ask questions.
2. Adjusting the DBT STEPS-A curriculum to fit the needs of the particular students. For example, slower learners may benefit from two cycles through the curriculum, rather than the one recommended for Tier I students. A second cycle through the curriculum gives students additional opportunities to learn all the skills, and provides additional practice. The two-cycle strategy is sometimes used in the DBT skills groups for outpatient adolescents (Rathus & Miller, 2015). A second alternative to this strategy is to split the content of one lesson over two days (class periods), allowing more time to grasp the information and receive coaching during class time opportunities.
3. Offering individual coaching by the instructor on an as needed basis to students who are experiencing emotionally stressful situations due to current circumstance or near-term future events. This strategy is dependent on the availability of the instructor, and is to be utilized during school hours. During these individual sessions, coaching should consist of assisting Tier II students in identifying what skills are required in any given situation, as well as providing opportunities for the students to role-play using their skills in learning what to say or do. Telephone coaching of skill use is one component of standard DBT for outpatient adolescents (Miller et al., 2007) on an as-needed basis. For this strategy to work effectively, instructors need to orient each student about when coaching is available and under what circumstances the student may ask for coaching.

Supplemental Tier III Strategies

The supplemental strategies for Tier III students include all those strategies discussed for Tier II students (smaller class size, an instructor with extensive training in adolescent mental health issues, a two-cycle rotation through the curriculum, and individual coaching as needed), plus some additional strategies. By definition within an MTSS structure, students identified as Tier III need intensive services that are provided by school personnel in different classroom-structured settings. These supplemental strategies include, but are not limited to:

1. Designating individual coaching/mentorship time for each student. The time allocation would be dependent on the instructor's availability, but somewhere

between 15–45 minutes would be sufficient. Unlike Tier II students, who can ask for coaching/mentoring as the situation requires, this strategy provides Tier III students with a predictable time that they can talk about ongoing distressing issues and/or practise individual skills for upcoming situations and receive coaching. This strategy also helps the instructor stay up to date on the individual issues, and assist at the individual level in applying the warranted skills. It is important to note that this individual coaching is not considered psychotherapy or a replacement for individual psychotherapy if it is warranted.

2. Bringing in parents and facilitating a group discussion with parents and their Tier III child who is taking the DBT STEPS-A class/curriculum. This group would meet once or twice per month during the evening to provide exposure regarding the DBT STEPS-A curriculum. Having the students there is optional, but should be encouraged. The rationale behind this strategy is threefold. First, it would help parents understand the skills and rationale behind the skills that are currently taught in curriculum. Second, it can teach parents how to support their children during difficult times, and increase support in the home environment for both students and parents. Finally, parents would have an opportunity to support one another in the challenges of having a child who needs intensive-level services. This strategy aligns with standard adolescent DBT where multi-family parent-child groups have been used successfully as part of treatment strategy among outpatient adolescents receiving DBT (Mehlum et al., 2014; Miller et al., 2007). For details on how to facilitate these parent groups, see Rathus & Miller (2015).

3. The instructor teaching the curriculum to Tier III students should have at least a moderate level of formal mental health training. Given the fact that students at this tier are going to have, or be at more risk for, mental health issues, including possible NSSI and STB, having an instructor who has received formal training in working with these high-risk students is warranted.

4. Provide additional support to the DBT STEPS-A instructor/s by developing a within-school consultation team. This team would consist of other school personnel who are supporting the implementation of the DBT STEPS-A curriculum, such as the school psychologist, school social worker, counsellors, and administrative staff that support services to Tier III students. The consultation meeting times would occur weekly or bimonthly to discuss student progress or difficulty, the skills and strategies particular students are learning, to receive support from peers who are also working with challenging students, and provide a mechanism for sharing information about what worked well and what didn't. The consultation team meeting times, once established, need to be protected by the school administration, as they are often scheduled over. Similar to some of the other supplemental strategies, implementing team consultation is a formal component of standard DBT shown to keep treatment on track, to provide an opportunity to get collegial supervision and support, and to reduce burnout. The team consultation meetings can take place before or after school,

if schedules are too hectic to find a common time during the day. The meetings can last between 45 to 90 minutes, depending on the needs of the team (Sayrs & Linehan, in press; this volume).

PROGRESS MONITORING

One of the core components of MTSS is using a data-based decision-making process to identify students who may need more intensive services (universal screening) as well as an ongoing progress monitoring system to evaluate the effectiveness of the intervention/services that are being delivered. As DBT STEPS-A was designed for implementation at the universal level, a universal screening tool was not formally integrated into the curriculum. Schools implementing the programme could consider adding this in to evaluate the effectiveness of their implementation. DBT STEPS-A does formally monitor progress through a self-report diary card, which is similar to the diary card used in standard DBT, except personal goals and self-harming behaviour are not monitored on the DBT STEPS-A tool. The diary card for DBT STEPS-A consists of only the skills that are taught in the curriculum, the daily use of the skill (yes or no), and the effectiveness of the skill when implemented (0 to 7 categorical scale). The instructor uses the diary card to monitor the skill use of each student and to determine which skills appear to be effective and/or which skills need more practice/coaching.

Figure 32.1 provides a graphic representation of the implementation of DBT STEPS-A and the supplemental strategies within a MTSS structure.

DBT STEPS-A IMPLEMENTATION ISSUES

Due to the content and focus of the DBT STEPS-A curriculum, there are several unique implementation issues that need to be addressed before implementing the curriculum in a classroom setting. These issues are often best addressed by a team of school personnel who support the dissemination of mental health services in school-based settings, such as school psychologists, school social workers, counsellors, and administrators. The implementation issues and the strategies to address the issues are often setting specific.

The first implementation issue is the type of class format in which DBT STEPS-A is taught, open versus closed; there are advantages and disadvantages to both. In an open-type format, students are allowed to join the class upon entering the school system or changing classes. The advantage of this format is that students are more likely to adhere to established group/classroom rules. In addition, students entering the school-based setting midyear do not need to wait until the next academic year to take the class. The

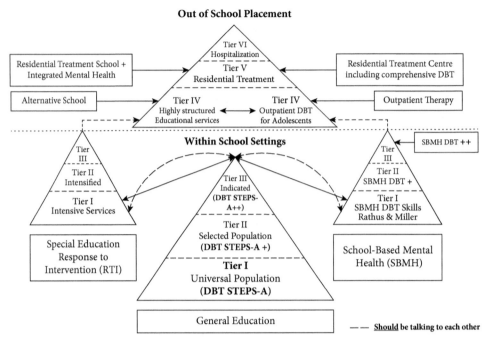

FIGURE 32.1 DBT Skills and Therapy Continuum using a Multitiered Systems of Support (MTSS).

disadvantage of open-type formats is that a new student may disrupt the group cohesion that has been established and may undermine the trust students have developed with each other. A second disadvantage is that late-entry students may have missed a significant portion of the curriculum and bringing that student up to date can be burdensome on the instructor.

The closed-type format is defined as a group where, once the class is established and has met for an allotted amount of time (i.e., two to four weeks), no other students can join the group/class, and that any student who drops out of the group/class is not replaced. The advantages of closed-type format are that it provides early establishment of group/class norms, fosters greater participation and self-disclosure due to established trust, and helps in instruction planning knowing which students will be in the group/class. The primary disadvantage of a closed-type format is that students cannot be added to the group/class after an allotted time has passed.

The second implementation issue pertains to the academic curriculum schedule of the school in deciding if the class that is implementing the curriculum is required, or if it is an elective. If offered as an elective, addressing issues of how students are identified for the class and what enrollment requirements entail will be important. If the class is mandatory for all students, the issues of who can take the class and under what circumstance become less important.

CURRENT DEVELOPMENT AND RESEARCH
WITH DBT STEPS-A

DBT STEPS-A is fairly new to the field of DBT, with the curriculum being available publicly in May of 2016, and represents one of the first formal expansions of DBT skills beyond clinical settings. The novel approach of implementing DBT skills in school-based settings at universal level has piqued the interests of mental health professionals and school-based personnel as a viable means for stemming the flow of adolescents who may engage in future NSSI and STB. In examining the school settings that were early implementers of DBT STEPS-A and collected data, the preliminary findings are encouraging, but more formal research needs to be conducted. We now discuss briefly the data from two separate school-based settings.

The first setting is an alternative middle school in Washington State where NSSI and STB had been identified as being problematic over the past five years. DBT STEPS-A was initially taught in the eighth grade classroom (13–14 years-old) after the teacher completed the formal DBT STEPS-A training. Given the school was an alternative setting, the teacher decided to be methodical and deliberate regarding the initial implementation of the curriculum. After asking for permission to slow down the implementation speed from the curriculum developers, only mindfulness and distress tolerance skills were taught in the first year, followed by three of the modules, mindfulness, distress tolerance, and interpersonal effectiveness in the second. The results showed that the vast majority of young adolescents believed that the skills taught in DBT STEPS-A can/are useful to them and/or their peers. The results are provided in Table 32.1.

The second school-based setting is in Cork, Ireland. There were nine schools that participated in a research study which aimed to evaluate the effectiveness of DBT STEPS-A in an Irish universal schools-based population. The study compares data from eight schools where the intervention was delivered with a control group at two sites. The results discussed here are preliminary data from the overall study; results which focus on reporting of descriptive statistics for a cohort of students at pre- and post-intervention. A total of 479 students, aged 15 and 16 years old, participated in the study. There were 385 participants in the intervention group and 94 in the control group. Results showed similar scores across groups on broadband and narrowband measures at pre-intervention. Participants scores were classified as high if they scored in the "at risk" or "clinically significant" categories for clinical scales in the Behavioral Assessment System for Children—Second Edition (BASC-2; broadband measure). There was a significant reduction in the percentage of participants who reported high scores on the Emotion Symptom Index from pre- to post-intervention (37.8% versus 26.6%, $p < .001$). Similarly, the percentage of participants who scored low on self-esteem significantly decreased in the intervention group from pre- to post-intervention (32.9% versus 25.6%, $p < .01$). On examination of the narrowband measure of the DBT Ways of Coping Checklist

Table 32.1   Results from Washington State Middle School

2014

Question (n = 64)	Yes	No	Sometimes	?
Will you use DBT STEPS-A?	51(80%)	11(17%)	1(1.5%)	1(1.5%)
Do you think this programme can help others?	57(89%)	4(6.0%)	2(3.0%)	1(1.5%)

2015

Question (n = 72)	Yes	No	Sometimes
Do you think the DBT STEPS-A programme can help you and others?	69(96%)	3(4%)	0(0%)

Cross-Sectional Data

Self Report Cutting Behaviour	Winter 2011-2014 (avg. = 500)	Winter 2014-2015 (n = 497)	Winter 2015-2016 (n = 485)
Number of students who have cut in the past year	10–12/years	3	0

(DBT-WCCL; narrowband measure), a measure directly aligned with the DBT STEPS-A curriculum, participants in the intervention group showed significant improvement overall as well as for male and females separately. As promising as these findings appear, the overall results should be interpreted with caution until the final analyses have been completed.

FUTURE DIRECTIONS

With DBT STEPS-A being a fairly new curriculum, there are many avenues to explore regarding its implementation, student and teacher acceptability, and proximal/distal student outcomes. Large-scale systematic trials that examine different student populations and utilize a comparison control group also need to be conducted. Of particular interest are those students who struggle with emotion dysregulation and social skills difficulties, such as students identified with Emotion and Behaviour Disorder (EBD), or those on the autism spectrum.

Future directions for DBT STEPS-A also include finding ways to broaden its reach and increase its utilization in educational settings. One such approach is having the curriculum translated into other languages. In addition, we are encouraging teachers and instructors to adapt some of the language and examples used in the curriculum to make it more tangible for their student populations. Again, research examining these adapted versions would be also a future endeavour.

Finally, the ideas of trying to reduce adolescents' NSSI and STB in school-based settings, which was the impetus for developing this curriculum, will still need exploration. This long-term goal will likely take five to ten years of wide-spread implementation in order to determine if DBT STEPS-A has an impact on emotional dysregulation behaviours, specifically NSSI and STB. While hoping to reduce NSSI and STB among adolescents, the implementation of DBT STEPS-A may have beneficial side effects in reducing emotional distress, reducing school disciplinary issues, and increasing adolescents' decision-making abilities and relationship skills.

Guidelines in Implementing DBT STEPS-A

1. Gain familiarity and training with the curriculum before teaching it.
2. Formally incorporate DBT STEPS-A into the academic curriculum as part of a universal application to all students in a particular grade and/or class.
3. Obtain administrative support for the implementation of the curriculum.
4. Develop a school-based support team (i.e., school-based mental health professional) to provide direct and indirect support to the instructors of the curriculum as well as to the students who are receiving it.
5. Adapt the language and examples to align with the student population.
6. Use the diary card as a progress monitoring tool.

SUMMARY

DBT STEPS-A is a universal SEL curriculum designed to be taught by general education teachers (i.e., health, wellness) in school-based settings for adolescents. The curriculum focuses on teaching emotion regulation, decision-making, and relationship skills, and was developed as a novel upstream approach to help reduce emotionally dysregulated behaviours within a MTSS framework. Developed from comprehensive DBT, DBT STEPS-A provides a structured approach that goes beyond the clinical setting and offers DBT skills to all adolescents. Given the uniqueness of this curriculum, implementation strategies and guidelines were provided. It is our hope that through this chapter, others will see the potential benefits of implementing DBT STEPS-A and reduce the likelihood of adolescents engaging in emotionally dysregulated behaviours.

KEY POINTS FOR CLINICIANS

- DBT Skills in schools offers a unique upstream approach to provide adolescent emotion regulation skills.
- DBT STEPS-A is designed at the universal level and to be delivered by general education teachers.
- DBT STEPS-A is part of a continuum of DBT services that can be provided in school-based settings, is developed for school-based adolescents, and is adapted from Marsha Linehan's DBT.

REFERENCES

Centers for Disease Control and Prevention, National Center for Injury Prevention and Control (2017). *Leading causes of death reports, 1981–2015*. Retrieved from http://webappa.cdc.gov/sasweb/ncipc/leadcause.html.

Cook, C. R. (2015, Spring). *Universal screening and selective mental health services within a multi-tiered system of support: Building capacity to implement the first two tiers*. Paper presented as part of the Washington State Association of School Psychologists Lecture Series.

Cook, C. R., Burns, M., Browning-Wright, D., & Gresham, F. M. (2010). *Transforming school psychology in the RTI era: A guide for administrators and school psychologists*. Palm Beach Gardens, FL: LRP.

Harned, M. S., Chapman, A. L., Dexter-Mazza, E. T., Murray, A., Comtois, K. A., & Linehan, M. M. (2008). Treating co-occurring Axis I disorders in recurrently suicidal women with borderline personality disorder: a 2-year randomized trial of dialectical behavior therapy versus community treatment by experts. *Journal of Consulting and Clinical Psychology, 76*, 1068–1075.

Kilgus, S. P., Reinke, W. R., & Jimerson, S. R. (2015). Understanding mental health intervention and assessment within a multi-tiered framework: Contemporary science, practice and policy. *School Psychology Quarterly, 30*, 159–165.

Linehan, M. M. (1993). *Skills training manual for treating borderline personality disorder*. New York: Guilford Press.

Linehan, M. M. (2015a). *DBT® skills training manual*, 2nd Edition. New York: Guilford Press.

Linehan, M. M. (2015b). *DBT® skills training handouts and worksheets*, 2nd Edition. New York: Guilford Press.

Lloyd-Richardson, E. E., Perrine, N., Dierker, L., & Kelley, M. L. (2007). Characteristics and functions of non-suicidal self-injury in a community sample of adolescents. *Psychological Medicine, 37*, 1183–1192.

Mazza, J. J., Dexter-Mazza, E. T., Miller, A. L., Rathus, J. L., & Murphy, H. E. (2016). *DBT Skills in the Schools: The Skills Training for Emotional Problem Solving for Adolescents (DBT STEPS-A) Curriculum*. New York: Guilford Press.

Mazza, J. J., & Hanson, J. B. (2015, February). *Implementing DBT emotion regulation skills for Tier II-III students*. Invited workshop presented at the national conference of the National Association of School Psychologists. Orlando, FL.

Mehlum, L., Tormoen, A. J., Ramberg, M., Haga, E., Diep, L. M., Laberg, S., … Groholt, B. (2014). Dialectical behavior therapy for adolescents with repeated suicidal and self-harming behavior: A randomized trial. *Journal of the American Academy of Child and Adolescent Psychiatry, 53*, 1082–1091.

Miller, A. L., Mazza, J. J., Dexter-Mazza, E. T., Steinberg, S., & Courtney-Seidler, E. (2014, November). *DBT in schools: The do's and don'ts.* Paper presented at the annual conference of the International Society for the Improvement and Teaching of Dialectical Behavior Therapy. Philadelphia, PA.

Miller, A. L., Rathus, J. H., & Linehan, M. M. (2007). *Dialectical behavior therapy with suicidal adolescents.* New York: Guilford Press.

Miller, D. N., & Mazza, J. J. (2017). Evidence-based interventions for suicidal behavior in children and adolescents. In L. A. Theodore (Ed.), *Handbook of evidence-based interventions for children and adolescents* (pp. 55–66). New York, NY: Springer.

Muehlenkamp, J. J., Hoff, E. R., Licht, J. G., Azue, J. A., & Hasenzahl, S. J. (2009). Rates of non-suicidal self-injury: a cross-sectional analysis of exposure. *Current Psychology, 27*, 234–241.

National Institute of Mental Health. (2015). *Strategic Plan for Research.* NIH publication number 15-6368.

Nelson-Gray, R. O., Keane, S. P., Hurst, R. M., Mitchell, J. T., Warburton, J. B., Chok, J. T., & Cobb, A. R. (2006). A modified DBT skills training program for oppositional defiant adolescents: Promising preliminary findings. *Behaviour Research and Therapy, 44*(12), 1811–1820.

Rathus, J. H., & Miller, A. L. (2015). *DBT® skills manual for adolescents.* New York: Guilford Press.

Sayrs, J. H. R., & Linehan, M. M. (in press). *Developing therapeutic treatment teams: The DBT model.* New York. Guilford Press.

Stoiber, K. C. (2014). A comprehensive framework for multitiered systems of support in school psychology. In A. Thomas & P. Harrison (Eds.), *Best practices in school psychology: Data-based and collaborative decision making* (pp. 41–70). Bethesda, MD: National Association of School Psychologists.

Stoiber, K. C., & Gettinger, M. (2016). Multi-tiered systems of support and evidence-based practices. In S. R. Jimerson, M. K. Burns, & A. M. VanDerHeyden (Eds.), *Handbook of response to intervention* (pp. 121–141). New York: Springer.

Wagner, B. M. (1997). Family risk factors for child and adolescent suicidal behavior. *Psychological Bulletin, 121*, 246–298.

CHAPTER 33

....

DIALECTICAL BEHAVIOURAL THERAPY SKILLS FOR EMPLOYMENT

....

JANET D. FEIGENBAUM

INTRODUCTION

....

Mental Health and Employment

THE complex relationship between mental health and employment is transactional and unique to each individual (Milner, Page, & Lamontagne, 2014). Many models of recovery from mental health difficulties suggest that employment is important for providing individuals with "meaningful occupied time" in line with their values (Leamy, Bird, Le Boutillier, Williams, & Slade, 2011). The structure and demands of employment provide the opportunity for behavioural activation (Mazzucchelli, Kane, & Rees, 2009), social interaction, and positive feedback. Employment may also provide distraction from the ruminative cognitive processes common across mental health disorders (Smith & Alloy, 2009). Conversely, employment may lead to an increase or onset of mental health disorders due to the stressors in the workplace (Kelloway & Barling, 1991). Additionally employment not in line with the individual's values, talents, or interests may lead to mental health difficulties (Warr, 1994). Thus, the decision to commence (or return) to employment for individuals with mental health difficulties requires an individualized formulation with an emphasis on the dialectical tension between the benefits of employment and the stressors of the workplace.

From a cognitive perspective, individuals with mental health difficulties commonly hold negative core beliefs about their competence in the workplace; thus, each failure at interview to be appointed to a position, or loss of employment, provides further support for their beliefs and increases the levels of anxiety when seeking employment and within employment. This repeated activation of beliefs about competence will likely lead to increased symptoms of depression and anxiety, resulting in reduced motivation to engage with the employment process. Thus, equipping an individual with skills to identify and manage problematic cognitions and their related emotions is important in the process of obtaining or returning to employment (Overland, Grasdal, Løvvik, Lie, & Reme, 2014).

According to the Layard report (2012) for the United Kingdom, "mental illness reduces GDP by 4.1% or £52 billion a year." In February 2013, 2.51 million people in Britain claimed incapacity benefit (now Employment Support Allowance). Of those on incapacity benefit, 38% have a mental disorder (Layard, 2006), and of these at least 10% will have a PD (Sansone & Sansone, 2010). In addition, long-term unemployment is associated with an increased risk of substance abuse, which has implications for health and criminal justice systems (Levitas et al., 2007), leading to further NHS and societal economic impact. Furthermore, unemployment is associated with social exclusion factors that have an impact upon families, such as divorce (Blekesaune, 2008) and poor education attainment and behaviour in children (Murali & Oyebode, 2004); these may lead to an increased likelihood of mental illness and unemployment in the next generation.

Personality Disorder and Employment

There are ten personality disorders identified in the *Diagnostic and Statistical Manual for Mental Disorders* (DSM-5; APA, 2013). Personality Disorder (PD) affects approximately 5% of the UK adult population (Coid, Yang, Tyrer, Roberts, & Ullrich, 2006). While symptom presentation is different for each PD, most share common difficulties including, emotional instability (excessive or constricted), behavioural regulation problems (impulsive or restricted), identity disturbance, and difficulties with relationships. Employment settings create significant challenges across these domains, requiring individuals with PD to demonstrate both self-awareness and self-control across all domains of personal functioning.

Vocational functioning in those with PD is more compromised than social functioning (McMahon & Enders, 2009; Zanarini, Frankenburg, Reich, & Fitzmaurice) and does not improve in direct association with change in mental health symptoms, thus suggesting that vocation may need to be targeted directly. A review by Sansone and Sansone (2012) found that nearly half of all individuals with PD were unemployed in longitudinal follow-up (both after treatment and in non-treatment seekers). Furthermore, PD was associated with a greater number of jobs since age 18, less overall time in employment, a greater likelihood of "cash in hand" employment, and a greater likelihood of being fired (Sansone, Leung, & Wiederman, 2012). PD is also associated with "losing a job on purpose" (Sansone & Wiederman, 2013). Across the spectrum of personality disorders, those with a cluster A (paranoid/schizotypal) personality disorder are more likely to be unemployed, to work in less cognitively challenging jobs, or to be employed in jobs with less social contact (McGurk et al., 2013). PD is also associated with early retirement (Korkeila et al., 2011).

Vocational rehabilitation programmes have identified factors related to seeking employment. Rogers and colleagues (2001) found that "contemplation" was a key factor using the Change Assessment Scale. Mee and Sumsion (2001) found three factors—generating motivation, building competence, and developing self identity—were key in readiness for employment. Ward and Riddle (2003) divided the challenges between employability dimensions and support for dealing with challenges. A number of mediating factors reduce the likelihood of an individual with PD in obtaining employment. These include impulsivity (Sio, Chanen, Killackey, & Gleeson 2011), degree of neuroticism and disagreeableness (Michon et al., 2008), level of social dysfunction (Newton-Howes, Tyrer, & Weaver, 2008), and symptom severity (Rymaszewska et al., 2007; Sansone & Sansone, 2010). Thus, any intervention aimed at improving employment in those with a PD will need to address these factors.

Dialectical Behavioural Therapy

Based on a biosocial model of the transaction between emotional vulnerability and invalidating environments, Dialectical Behavioural Therapy (DBT; Linehan, 1993) was developed initially for the treatment of suicidal and impulsive individuals with a diagnosis of Borderline Personality Disorder (BPD). The treatment provides a theoretical framework and associated clinical techniques to address problems across several domains of dysfunction, with specific emphasis on emotional regulation, distress tolerance, interpersonal effectiveness, mindfulness, dialectical thinking, problem solving, and self-validation. DBT is the evidence-based recommended treatment for BPD across most western cultures including the United Kingdom (UK; the National Institute for Clinical Excellence, 2009), United States (US; American Psychological Association, 2001) and Australia (Australian Department of Health, 2012). Furthermore, the evidence supports the effectiveness of DBT for the wider range of personality disorders (Lynch & Cheavens, 2008), comorbid substance misuse (Dimeff & Linehan, 2008), and other disorders characterized by emotional dysregulation and impulsivity (Feigenbaum, 2007).

ADAPTATIONS OF DBT FOR EMPLOYMENT

DBT-W

Evidence has been emerging from the US for adaptations of DBT with a dual focus on mental health and employment. Koons and colleagues (2006) developed an adaptation for individuals with mental health disorders who were engaged in a vocational rehabilitation programme (DBT-W) in the US. The primary inclusion criteria was "very significantly disabled" in ability to attain employment. Participants were excluded if they had a suicide attempt in the past six months or were self-harming, based on the target hierarchy of DBT in which parasuicidal behaviour takes precedence over quality of life (QoL) targets. Of those in the study, 83% had a diagnosis of a PD, and the majority had significant comorbidity including major depressive disorder, substance abuse, psychotic disorders, and anxiety disorders. Eight participants (66.7%) completed the intervention and four dropped out. Koons and colleagues (2006) demonstrated a significant improvement in mental well-being and a small increase in hours worked.

The DBT-W programme ran weekly for six months, and was comprised of skills training of two hours weekly, and a 90-minute per week diary card and chain and solution analysis review. In addition the facilitators met weekly for DBT consultation. The programme delivered on all functions of fully programmatic DBT.

While the outcomes were positive for the small number of individuals (n = 8) who received DBT-W, the DBT-W intervention has not been evaluated outside of the vocational rehabilitation setting in which the clients were receiving a number of additional supports for return to employment. In addition, the intervention involved the deployment of four facilitators due to the challenges of the population which may be beyond the staffing limitations of many services, thus increasing costs.

DBT-W is based on the standard skills outlined in the original Linehan (1993b) skills manual. Figure 33.1 shows the individual formulations based on Koon et al.'s (2006) path to working mind.

Decrease Behaviours Likely to Prevent Getting a Job

Initially the therapist and client will consider the range of current behaviours which prevent the individual from obtaining and retaining employment. As high-risk behaviours

Decrease behaviours likely to prevent getting a job.

↓

Acquire mindfulness, interpersonal effectiveness, emotion regulation, and distress tolerance skills.

↓

Increase use of skills to get ready to work.

↓

Decrease behaviours likely to interfere with keeping a job.

↓

Increase use of skills on the job.

↓

Working mind.

FIGURE 33.1 The pathway to working mind.

Reprinted from *Cognitive and Behavioral Practice*, 13 (2), Cedar R. Koons, Alexander L. Chapman, Bette B. Betts, Beth O'Rourke, Nesha Morse, and Clive J. Robins, Dialectical Behavior Therapy Adapted for the Vocational Rehabilitation of Significantly Disabled Mentally Ill Adults, pp. 146–56, https://doi.org/10.1016/j.cbpra.2005.04.003 Copyright © 2006 Association for Behavioral and Cognitive Therapies. Published by Elsevier Ltd.

take precedence over QoL in the DBT programme individuals with high-risk behaviours are excluded from DBT for employment adaptations and standard DBT is recommended until the risk behaviours have ceased (Linehan, 1993a). After risk, the most common behaviours likely to prevent getting a job involve substance misuse or abuse. Many individuals partake of alcohol and/or recreational substances prior to the working day, but excessive use leads to physical consequences the next day (e.g., a hangover) or the substances may still be present in the body at the time of needing to be in the workplace. Therefore, the therapist and individual will need to address the timing, frequency, and amount of substance use. Other examples of behaviours likely to prevent getting a job would include criminal behaviour, poor compliance with medical recommendations for physical disorders, behaviours associated with severe eating disorders, and lack of activity associated with moderate to severe depression or significant anxiety.

Acquire Mindfulness, Interpersonal Effectiveness, Emotional Regulation, and Distress Tolerance Skills

The four main sets of skills delivered in standard DBT are needed to engage successfully with the processes of preparing for and obtaining employment. The acquisition of these four sets of skills may take some time in a standard DBT programme, or may be acquired in adaptations of DBT for employment. At this stage of the pathway the individual will be acquiring and practising the skills within their daily life. As employment requires interactions with others in the workplace it is important for the individual to engage in regular social interactions to strengthen and generalize their use of skills. Therefore, individuals at this stage are expected to engage with community-based activies such as hobbies, volunteer work, or religious activities to increase opportunities to practise the skills in social settings where emotions and relationship difficulties may be present.

Increase Use of Skills to Get Ready to Work

The next step on the pathway involves generalization of the DBT skills to the process of applying for and obtaining employment. Individuals with PD frequently lack the skills for self-management (i.e., keeping a diary of appointments, waking to an alarm clock, regular eating, and exercise routines). In addition they may require the skills to self-motivate to undertake tasks. The relevant skills may include strengthening pros and cons and wise mind decision making to facilitate self management.

Decrease Behaviours Likely to Interfere with Keeping a Job

Once employment has been obtained, the individual will require the full range of skills to manage the emotional and interpersonal stressors common in employment. Thus, the focus of this step in the path to regular and sustained employment is the generalization of the DBT skills in the workplace. Frequently the integration of a number of skills will be required to function successfully in employment. At this stage the individual may need to strengthen their distress tolerance skills, as it is common for an individual to be required to continue in their work tasks while experiencing strong emotions. The common dialectical tension in these situations is the balance between using distress tolerance skills (for example, distraction or self-soothe) to manage the action urges associated with intense emotions without engaging in problematic behaviours versus the impact of the distress tolerance skills on the ability of the individual to continue to perform their role at work. For example, it may not be possible for a cashier at the supermarket to repeatedly ask for a break to change temperature or self-soothe, or for a phone sales person or receptionist to use distraction while taking continuous calls.

The most common behaviours that interfere with keeping a job include regular absences from work, leaving work part way through a shift, arriving late for work (which may be related to using substances the night before or due to poor sleep which is common in mental health disorders), and engaging in excessive displays of emotion in the work place (particularly behaviours associated with anger).

Additionally, the individual will need to develop a balanced mind position on the dialectical tension between being overly or insufficiently assertive in the work place. The ablity to use wise mind to recognize the appropriate time to be appropriately assertive with colleagues and managers, and when to acknowledge, with radical acceptance, the power and position of those in authority.

Increase Use of Skills on the Job

While the full range of DBT skills is needed to be successful in employment, leading to both job retention and hopefully promotion, of primary importance is the use of effective mindfulness to ensure focus of attention, remaining in the moment, being effective, and maintaining a non-judgmental stance in relation to colleagues, managers, and customers/consumers. Throughout this step in the pathway to working mind, the emphasis is on the ongoing strengthening and generalization of the skills as the demands and challenges of the workplace continually change.

Working Mind

The destination of the pathway to employment is to remain in working mind. Linehan (1993) initially outlined the primary dialectical tension for individuals with a personality disorder as the tension between emotional mind and rational (reasonable) mind. In this dialectic, emotional mind triggers a number of urges, cognitions, physiological sensations, and behaviours in response to the primary, or mixture, of emotions. Emotional mind considers the short-term consequences and seeks to reduce or eliminate painful emotions or prolong positive emotions. For example, frustration or anger may lead to the desire to shout or be physically violent, or love may lead to the urge to remain with the object of desire rather then go to work. On the other end of the dialectic, rational mind considers the long-term consequences of the actions. A wise mind decision is achieved when both the short-term needs of emotional mind and the long-term consequences identified by rational mind are addressed in a synthesis.

In another adaptation of DBT, Comtois and colleagues (2006, 2007, 2010) have sought to assist individuals who have been engaged with mental health services to leave the system and engage in recovery-based activities, including employment. The DBT Accepting the Challenges of Employability and Self-Sufficiency (ACES; formerly known as Accepting the Challenges of Exiting the System) (DBT-ACES) programme was designed for individuals after they have completed stage one of DBT (Linehan, 1993a). DBT-ACES is a year-long programme in which the individual attends both weekly individual and ongoing group based skills training. During this "second year" there is an emphasis on "self sufficiency" with additional training in goal setting, problem solving, trouble shooting, dialectical thinking, and use of reinforcement (to change behaviour in self and others).

DBT-ACES

DBT-ACES (Comtois et al., 2010), originally conceived as a follow-up for committed completers of one year of DBT, adapts standard DBT in several ways. The first adaptation is the development of a target hierarchy based on recovery goals which include: 1) choosing a career path to employment that provides a living wage, 2) being capable of financially supporting oneself and family without state benefits or family support, 3) having "back up" employment to support oneself, and 4) engaging in employment-appropriate behaviour (attendance, appropriate dress and manner, task completion, following directions). DBT-ACES places an emphasis on interpersonal recovery goals such as: 1) being "easy to get on with" even with difficult people or when stressed, 2) regulating emotions in challenging interpersonal situations, 3) awareness of personal limits of self and others, and 4) able to receive praise, promotions, and wage raises. In addition to the aforementioned employment-based goals, DBT-ACES promotes social recovery goals (which will have a bearing on employment goals) such as: 1) having friends with similar values, 2) having casual friendships (e.g., people to have lunch or coffee with), 3) at least one close social support person, 4) belonging to at least one group who would notice if you were not around, 5) being a member of an organized recreational activity, 6) disengaging from destructive family relationships or friendships, and 7) engaging in a supportive romantic relationship if desired. The final set of recovery goals relate to self-sufficiency and include: 1) generating savings in the event of unemployment, 2) managing time, and 3) managing one's own psychiatric and physical symptoms. DBT-ACES emphasizes the need to manage emotions effectively in all employment, familial, and social situations.

The second adaptation in DBT-ACES is an emphasis on ambition, progress, and effectiveness. The skills curriculum includes skills addressed in the Walking the Middle Path module of the new skills manual (Linehan, 2015) and areas such as perfectionism, time management, and anger management. The final area of adaptation is the emphasis on contingency management with a requirement that participants in the programme engage in increasing hours of social or employment activity, and an emphasis on the self-regulation of contingencies. Individuals in the DBT-ACES programme continue to receive all standard modes of DBT, but the expectation is that the individual therapist and skills training facilitators will "keep the bar high" and expect ongoing improvement in the behaviours associated with the recovery hierarchy.

The feasibility study of DBT-ACES (Comtois et al., 2010; n = 30; 24 completers and six drop-outs) demonstrated a significant increase in employment (odds ratio: 3.34) following treatment completion and again at one year follow-up. In addition there was an increase in subjective QoL and a reduction in inpatient admissions. At one year follow-up from the DBT-ACES programme, 36% of participants were no longer engaged with mental health services. DBT-ACES has been further evaluated outside the US (in Germany) and found to be effective. While the DBT-ACES programme is clinically- and cost-effective, it remains costly for some services as the individuals continue in fully programmatic DBT for a second year. Thus, there continues to be the need to evaluate whether shorter adaptations or adaptations with fewer modes may be effective. In addition, there is a potential need for adaptations that are available for individuals with PD who may not previously have been engaged in standard DBT.

DBT-Skills for Employment (DBT-SE): A Brief DBT Adaptation

A growing evidence base is emerging for the delivery of DBT skills in a group-only format (Valentine, Bankoff, Poulin, Reidler, & Pantalone, 2015). The current evidence suggests that for those individuals who are of low risk to self or others and have limited comorbidity with other mental health disorders, DBT skills training alone may be effective if combined with regular risk assessment and management processes. With the constant pressure on health services to deliver timely and cost-effective interventions, group treatments are becoming more prevalent and desirable to commissioners of services. With this in mind, DBT-SE was developed as a brief group-based intervention.

Functions and Modes of DBT

Koerner, Dimeff, and Swenson (2007) provide a useful summary of the important factors to consider when developing an adaptation of DBT. The main emphasis is on the five important functions of standard programmatic DBT and the modes most commonly used to deliver each of these functions (Linehan, 1993). The DBT-SE adaptation delivers on all five functions of standard DBT.

1) *Enhancing capabilities*: the DBT-SE skills are taught in a group-based setting with 45 minutes of teaching with associated handouts, worksheets for recording between-session practice, and examples of completed worksheets to support comprehension.

2) *Improving motivation*: clinical progress is strengthened and factors that inhibit progress are identified in the weekly chain and solution analyses section of the intervention.

3) *Ensuring generalization*: telephone coaching during working hours is provided to all participants from the facilitator or co-facilitator. In addition, the DBT-SE manual provides a handout on the importance of consistent rehearsal of skills in a range of contexts.

4) *Enhancing therapist skill and motivation*: all DBT-SE facilitators and co-facilitators are expected to attend weekly DBT-SE consult (as described in Linehan (1993a)).

5) *Structuring the environment*: a handbook for employers is provided to all participants to give to their employers/managers upon obtaining employment if they feel this would be helpful. The handbook provides information for employers on "reasonable adaptations" in the workplace for individuals with PD, based on the DBT-SE skills and principles of reinforcement. The pros and cons of disclosing mental health difficulties to managers is discussed in the pre-group meeting when the handbook is provided to participants.

The DBT-SE adaptation is based upon the format piloted by Koons and colleagues (2006). The programme is a sixteen-week curriculum delivered in a group format for three hours once a week. The feedback from staff and clients in the initial piloting and feasibility study of DBT-SE suggests that clients are very willing and able to attend and participate for the full three hours. As is highlighted to them in the initial meeting, most employment requires attendance and participation for more than three hours a day.

The group facilitator and co-facilitator provide the same roles as described in standard DBT, with the facilitator responsible for the teaching of the material and the co-facilitator responsible for the learning environment. Both facilitators may change roles at any moment in the session.

The initial piloting and feasibility study of DBT-SE (Feigenbaum et al., in preparation) enrolled twelve clients in each of four groups. The main entry criteria were a diagnosis of a personality disorder (not BPD-specific), no suicide attempt in the past three months, no self-harm in the past month, and eligible and interested in obtaining or returning (from long-term sick leave) to employment. The feasibility study began with 41 participants (18 males, 19 females, one transgender), and 13 dropped out before completing the full 16 weeks, indicating a 69% retention rate. Of the participants, 25% attended all 16 sessions. The mean score on the Standardised Assessment of Personality Disorder—Abbreviated Scale (SAPAS; Moran et al., 2003) cut-off was 5.5 7 + 1.44 (cut-off on the SAPAS for probable PD = 3) indicating considerable issues related to personality disorder. Of this number, 26 (63%) had been unemployed for longer than one year (Mean 115.05 months; SD 124.44 Range 15–540 months). During the 16-week intervention, ten participants obtained employment (25%) and an additional six participants (14%) attended an interview. One commenced volunteer work and one began an employment-related training course. In the one-month follow-up period, a further five individuals obtained employment. The average number of hours of "employment-seeking activity" ranged from 5.96 + 10.96 hours by week two to 8.87 + 13.58 by week 16. In addition, measures of well-being indicated a decrease in symptoms of depression, substance misuse, and anger and improvements in interpersonal effectiveness and social adjustment.

Structure of DBT-SE Sessions

The structure of the sessions is detailed in Table 33.1 It should be noted that based on feedback from clients in the piloting and feasibility studies, the term "between-session practice" is used rather than "homework" to emphasize the importance of ongoing rehearsal of skills.

Based on the experience of the developers of the DBT-SE adaptation, it was identified that many of the clients who are interested and ready for DBT-SE (at the "increase use of skills to get ready for work" step in the path to working mind) have experience of many of the distress tolerance skills. Therefore it was decided to incorporate the teaching of a distress tolerance skill modified for the workplace at the end of each session. This has the additional effect of acting as a wind-down exercise to finish the session. The distress tolerance skills were taken directly from the Linehan DBT skills manual (2014), using examples and suggestions specific to the workplace (see Box 33.1 for an example of the minor modification to the TIPP skill for the workplace).

The DBT-SE Curriculum

Table 33.2 shows details of the curriculum for the DBT-SE programme . All participants are given a ring binder in the first session that contains the full set of handouts and worksheets for recording the details of their between-session practice. They are provided with a sample completed worksheet for each skill to show how to complete the worksheet. The curriculum includes the four modules of standard DBT, a brief introduction to cognitive restructuring, and skills for self-management, which includes practical issues and

Table 33.1   DBT–SE session plan

15 minutes	Mindfulness practice and feedback
45 minutes	Review of weekly between-session practice
45 minutes	Teaching topic and between-session practice setting
15 minutes	Coffee/tea break
50 minutes	Review of chain and solution analyses
10 minutes	Distress tolerance skill

Box 33.1 TIPP in the workplace

Distress Tolerance at Work

TIPP

TEMPERATURE

Change your temperature—if hot cool down/if cold warm up
Hot coffee/tea
Extra jumper
Heater—lean on the radiator
Hot meal

Cold drink with ice
Lean on a cold wall
Face against a cold window
Open the windows
Fan
Cold cloth on neck or face
Ice cubes on the wrists
Air conditioner
Clear out the refrigerator in staff kitchen
Intense Exercise (engage your body without your mind)

- Star jumps
- Lunchtime run
- Run up the stairs at work
- Use heavy books to weight lift (safely)

Paired Progressive Muscular Relaxation

- Tighten and relax each muscle group while saying a specific word (e.g., relax)

Desk chair yoga
www.huffingtonpost.com/meredith-nordhem/office-yoga-poses_b_5604195.html
www.verywell.com/yoga-stretches-at-your-desk-3567200
Facial massage (self)
Shoulder massage (self)
Paced Breathing

- Breathe in slowly, pause, breathe out slowly for longer than on the in breath
- Pay attention to your breath mindfully

Reproduced from Marsha M. Linehan, *DBT® Skills Training Handouts and Worksheets Second Edition*, Distress Tolerance Handout 4, p. 376. Copyright © 2015, Guilford Press. Adapted with permission of Guilford Press.

Table 33.2   DBT–SE curriculum

Week 1	**Introductions**
	Orientation to DBT-SE
	Pathway to Employment
	Dialectical Thinking
	How to conduct a chain analysis
	Distress Tolerance
	TIPP (Temperature)
Week 2	**Mindfulness 1: What Skills**
	Observe, Describe, Participate
	Distress Tolerance
	TIPP (Intensive) Exercise
	Paced Breathing
Week 3	**Mindfulness 2: How Skills**
	(Non-Judgmental, One Mindful, Effective)
	Distress Tolerance
	TIPP (Paired Muscular Relaxation)
Week 4	**Mindfulness 3: Wise Mind/Balanced Mind/Employee Mind**
	STOPP
	Distress Tolerance
	ACCEPTS (Activities)
Week 5	**Emotional Regulation 1:**
	Model of Emotions
	Functions of Emotions
	Mindfulness of Emotions
	Distress Tolerance
	ACCEPTS (Contributing)
Week 6	**Emotional Regulation 2:**
	Check the Facts
	Opposite Action
	Distress Tolerance
	ACCEPTS (Comparisons)
Week 7	**Emotional Regulation 3:**
	Problem Solving
	Distress Tolerance
	ACCEPTS (Emotions)

Table 33.2 Continued

Week 8	**Emotional Regulation 4:** ABC PLEASE at work and home **Distress Tolerance** ACCEPTS (Pushing Away)
Week 9	**Emotional Regulation 5:** Cope Ahead Avoid Avoiding **Distress Tolerance** ACCEPTS (Thoughts)
Week 10	**Interpersonal Effectiveness 1:** The art of small talk The art of sharing—personal limits **Distress Tolerance** ACCEPTS (Sensations)
Week 11	**Interpersonal Effectiveness 2:** Changing Behaviour with Reinforcement/Contingencies **Distress Tolerance** IMPROVE (Imagery/Meaning)
Week 12	**Interpersonal Effectiveness 3:** Values at work IE What Skill—DEAR **Distress Tolerance** IMPROVE (Prayer (serenity)/Relaxing)
Week 13	**Interpersonal Effectiveness 4:** IE How Skill—MAN GIVE FAST **Distress Tolerance** IMPROVE (One thing in the moment/Vacation)
Week 14	**Interpersonal Effectiveness 5:** IE Intensity and Effectiveness **Distress Tolerance** IMPROVE (Encouragement)
Week 15	**Managing your mind** Noticing and challenging unhelpful thinking patterns **Distress Tolerance** Self-soothe

(continued)

Table 33.2 Continued	
Week 16	Managing a work routine
	Putting it all together
	How to carry on practising
	Where to get support in using the skills
	Finding motivation

issues of self-motivation to develop and utilize skills (both during the treatment and in employment).

Pre-DBT-SE Session

One of the challenges of providing DBT-SE is the absence of the individual therapy mode where motivation to practise skills for strengthening and generalization is traditionally undertaken. Therefore DBT-SE facilitators must identify how to provide the function of motivation to practise (see Box 33.2, which provides an example of a motivational handout highlighting the importance of practice to achieve success in a new skill).

Another aspect to consider when working to increase motivation is the importance of values in the workplace (see Box 33.3) both with respect to selecting the type of employment to consider and the important issue of satisfaction in the workplace. Differences in values can be a source of considerable emotional dysregulation and as such are returned to in more detail again in the interpersonal effectiveness teaching. The early identification of how employment may fit with values was highlighted by most participants as important in facilitating attendance and skills practice.

DBT-SE and Working Mind

In the original 2006 model developed by Koons and colleagues, the final step of the pathway to employment is working mind. This has been further elaborated in the DBT-SE model (Figure 33.2) as the dialectic between "perfect employee mind" ("I must never make a mistake at work", "I must always please my managers") and "unemployed mind" ("I am not able to work", "It is too hard", "No one will employ me", "My manager is looking for ways to fire me"). Perfect employee mind leads to anxiety-driven behaviours including extended working hours, not taking breaks, vigilance behaviours, and worry. Unemployed mind leads to hopeless and helpless cognitions with the associated decrease in behaviour and most commonly the emotions of sadness, guilt, and shame. Social

---

Box 33.2 Motivation to practise skills handout

PPPrepared

(in DBT-SE and at work)

Why?
Peace of mind
     Positive Relationships
         Practical Ability

How?
Procure: learn by reading, watching, asking
Practice: over and over again
Patience: learning takes time and mistakes

Image source: Stones on the Beach: iStock.com/pixonaut

---

isolation and an absence of employment-seeking behaviour tend to follow from un-employed mind. The synthesis of these two dialectical poles is wise "effective" employee mind in which one strives to do the best in one's employment at any given time, but ac-knowledges that everyone has times when they are not able to achieve what is expected or hoped for in the workplace. Clients struggling with the synthesis of this dialectic are reminded of the DBT principle "you are doing the best you can, and you can always do better." Radical acceptance of one's performance in this moment in time is emphasized.

Chain and Solution Analysis in DBT-SE

In the pilot of DBT-W, Koons and colleagues (2006) deployed employment advisors to meet individually with each client in the group to review their chain and solution analysis of the week and prepare what to share in the wider group setting. This was fea-sible in an intensive vocational rehabilitation setting, but not considered pragmatic for many services. Thus, DBT-SE has incorporated weekly chain analysis reviews within the three-hour session.

Using the handouts from Linehan (2015), all clients in the group are taught in the first session how to conduct their own chain analysis of a target (problem) behaviour that interferes with their ability to seek, return to, or retain employment. They are informed that each week two individuals will be selected to share their chain anal-ysis with the group and receive assistance from the group on identifying solutions to break key links in the chain. Two individuals are selected in a pseudorandom fashion by the facilitator, ensuring that everyone in the group is called upon to share their chain analysis at least twice in the sixteen weeks. A missing links analysis (Linehan, 2015) is conducted by the facilitator if an individual has not produced a chain analysis

Box 33.3 Values in the workplace

Values (Priorities) at work

What is a value?
Principles or standards of behaviour; one's personal judgment of what is important in life.

How do I know something is a value for me?
Is this something you feel is important to you or is it something that you think other people want from you?

Knowing and acknowledging our values helps us both to identify the type of employment in which we will feel content/satisfied and also helps to shape our behaviour in the workplace.

Remember—values are personal and others may not share our same values.

Common values at work:

1. Relationships—getting on with my co-workers and managers.
2. Being part of a group—working together with others to create/provide.
3. Being powerful and influencing others.
4. Having a sense of achievement (even without recognition).
5. Getting credit for my achievements from others.
6. Being productive.
7. Behaving respectfully to others (and self).
8. Being generous (time, knowledge).
9. Being self-directed.
10. Security.
11. Self-development.
12. Interest.
13. Being wealthy.
14. Being healthy.
15. Time for my friends and family.
16. Time for my personal pursuits (hobbies, interests).

when called upon. Asking the whole group to participate in the generation of solutions for key links in the chain provides the impetus for brainstorming ideas, problem solving, identification of barriers, and active participation, rather than passive listening (Nierenberg, 1998).

The transcript in Box 33.4 demonstrates a chain analysis being conducted in the second week of a DBT-SE programme. Undertaking a chain analysis in a group setting

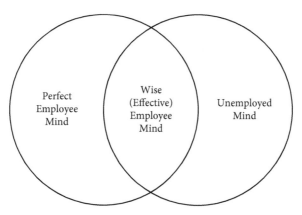

FIGURE 32.2 Wise (effective) employee mind.

can be a potentially embarrassing or anxiety-provoking situation for participants. Thus, additional validation is used to reinforce their willingness to engage with the process. As the participants in a DBT-SE intervention are currently unemployed or on long-term sick leave, many of their problematic behaviours will initially be related to non-employment situations. The facilitator looks for opportunities to link the problem behaviour under discussion to employment experiences. Following the identification of the key links in the chain analysis, the whole group participates in the generation of potential solutions for each link.

Following this particular chain analysis the group identifies a number of solutions including: distraction for the worry thoughts, cooling down when hot (get out of bed and open the window), muscular relaxation for the tense muscles, regular eating of "easy to eat food" (PLEASE skill), arranging for a friend to go to the appointment with them, playing games on the phone so that the client will not notice if anyone is staring, and writing down pros and cons of going to the appointment in order to remember the long-term consequences earlier. To emphasize the links to employment and assist with generalization, the facilitators highlight the importance of ringing one's employer as early as possible if one is not going to be able to come to work, the relevance of managing sleep for performance in the workplace, and how catastrophizing may be a problem in the workplace.

DBT-SE Diary Card

The diary card for DBT-SE (Table 33.3) has been developed to provide both a place for the participant to review and consider their skills rehearsal each week, but also to assist with considering the different tasks in moving towards employment (or returning to employment from long-term illness leave). The diary card functions both as a prompt for rehearsal and as an outcome measure for the facilitators and participants to review progress. The diary card does not provide space to monitor risk behaviours which may

Box 33.4   Example of eliciting a chain analysis

Facilitator: What did you do that you wish you hadn't done?

Client: Cancelling an appointment

Facilitator: ... you know a lot of people do that, they cancel an appointment or they cancel with the job centre or they cancel with the benefit office or they cancel with the GP or they don't go to an interview. [validation; linking to employment tasks] So let's work backwards just before you made the call? [orienting to the time frame of links in the chain] How did you cancel it?

Client: By phone.

Facilitator: Just before you picked up the phone, what did you feel in your body? [physical sensations link]

Client: Anxious

Facilitator: Anxious is the emotion. But what were you experiencing in your body? [emotion link; physical sensations]

Client: Shaking

Facilitator: So you were shaking. What were you doing with your body? [behavioural link]

Client: Lying in bed

Facilitator: Tell me about your breathing. [physiology link]

Client: Heavy breathing, no fast breathing

Facilitator: Fast breathing. Okay, what was your temperature? [physiology link]

Client: I was hot

Facilitator: What were your thoughts? [cognitive link]

Client: Catastrophizing

Facilitator: So the way you were thinking was catastrophizing, what were your specific thoughts? Give me some catastrophic thoughts. [clarification of difference between cognitive distortions and cognitions]

Client: I'll collapse, I'll be sick, because I'm agoraphobic and I don't like going outside.

Facilitator: How about people will stare at me? [validation; hypothesis testing]

Client: Yep

Facilitator: Notice everyone that I'm right up against her behaviour, I haven't asked her what the prompting event was, we'll get to that in a moment. [orientation to key links in the chain] First let's look at the consequences. How did your body feel after you cancelled the appointment?

Client: Relief.

Facilitator: So you felt relaxed? [contingency clarification; negative reinforcement]

Client: Yeah.

Facilitator: Relaxed body, what happened to the heavy breathing and the hot temperature? [physical links]

Client: Calmed down.

Facilitator: You felt calm. What happened to the catastrophic thoughts?

Client: They went away.

Facilitator: So the thoughts went away. What happened then to anxiety?

Client: It lowered.

Facilitator: It makes sense why you cancelled the appointment as it made you feel better in the moment. [validation] So what are the long term consequences, was this an important appointment?

> **Box 33.4 Continued**
>
> Client: Yep. Now I have guilt.
> Facilitator: So in the longer term you've got guilt, are there other long term consequences like is your health going to deteriorate or are you going to lose benefits as a result?
> Client: I'll have to make another appointment.
> Facilitator: Now one final question: When did you find out about the appointment?
> Client: About a week before.
> Facilitator: Did you cancel it last minute?
> Client: Yes.
> Facilitator: So, you had a whole week to cancel but you waited until minutes before you had to leave the house?
> Client: About an hour before.
> Facilitator: What shifted in the hour before you called to cancel? [identification of prompting event]
> Client: I was being sick and stuff, because my anxiety gets that bad.
> Facilitator: So the prompting event was being sick. Were there any other vulnerability factors?
> Client: Vulnerability factors?
> Facilitator: Other things happening that made you more anxious or left you feeling unable to attend the appointment?
> Client: I hadn't slept during the night and hadn't eaten since the day before.

re-emerge during the course of the sixteen-week intervention. It is recommended that facilitators identify a risk-monitoring protocol and process suitable to their setting. The diary card is collected by the co-facilitator at the start of each session and reviewed by both facilitators (half each) briefly during the first break. Very brief feedback, usually in the form of encouragement, to rehearse less-frequently rehearsed skills or praise for engagement in skills practice and/or steps to employment is given at the start of the teaching session.

Mindfulness and DBT-SE

Mindfulness in the workplace is an essential set of skills for productivity and healthy relationships with colleagues. Based on the practice of mindfulness defined by Linehan (1993b) and elaborated by Dunkley and Stanton (2013), clients are provided with both the What and How mindfulness skills from standard DBT, and information on the three "As" of mindfulness: Attention, Awareness, and Attitude of Acceptance (see Box 33.5).

Each session begins with a mindfulness practice designed to support the use of mindfulness in the workplace. For example, in one mindfulness exercise designed to assist with focusing attention while working in a noisy or shared plan office, clients select either a proofreading task or a budget task and are asked to focus attention

Table 33.3 Diary card for weekly employment activity

Diary card for weekly employment activity	ID Number:			Date			How often during the week did you fill out this diary?			□ I filled it out today □ 2-3 times □ 1-2 times □ 4-5 times □ 6-7 times		
Employment seeking activity	MON			TUE			WED			THUR		
	FRI			SAT			SUN					
Visited Job Centre												
Looked for jobs in newspaper												
Online job searching												
Worked on CV												
Attended training/course												
Working through a job application form												
Job related phone calls												
Job related visits												
Doing research about jobs												
Studying for formal recognised qualification e.g. University degree, NVQ, A-Levels												
Volunteering												

Employment Support Service																				
Interview preparation, a: route planning																				
Interview preparation, b: gathering outfit																				
Interview preparation, c: mock interview																				
Job Interview																				
Other:																				
Other:																				
How many hours of paid employment have you completed? e.g. 7.5 hrs																				

KEY

✔ : Tick if you participated in this activity

🕐 : Enter time taken to complete activity e.g. 30m, 1.5hrs

✖ : Enter whether you used skills:

0: Not thought about using skills/did not use them

1: Thought about using skills, but did not want to use them

2: Thought about using skills, did not use them but wanted to

3: Consciously tried to use skills, but could not use them

4: Consciously tried to use skills, could do them but they did not help

5: Consciously tried to use skills, could do them and they helped

6: Did not consciously try to use skills, used them but they did not help

7: Did not consciously try to use skills, used them, they helped

(continued)

Table 33.3 Continued

	MON	TUE	WED	THUR	FRI	SAT	SUN	Wise Mind/Balanced Mind/Employee Mind	
Mindful-ness	MON	TUE	WED	THUR	FRI	SAT	SUN		Listen to both emotional and rational mind, make sure both get heard
	MON	TUE	WED	THUR	FRI	SAT	SUN	What skills: Observe	Just notice
	MON	TUE	WED	THUR	FRI	SAT	SUN	What skills: Describe	Put into words, just the facts
	MON	TUE	WED	THUR	FRI	SAT	SUN	What skills: Participate	Enter into the experience
	MON	TUE	WED	THUR	FRI	SAT	SUN	How skills: Non-Judgmental	State the facts only
	MON	TUE	WED	THUR	FRI	SAT	SUN	How skills: One mindfully	Present moment
	MON	TUE	WED	THUR	FRI	SAT	SUN	How skills: Effective	Focus on what works
	MON	TUE	WED	THUR	FRI	SAT	SUN	The art of small talk	Objectives, relationship, self respect
	MON	TUE	WED	THUR	FRI	SAT	SUN	The art of sharing: limits	How not to say too much (or too little)
	MON	TUE	WED	THUR	FRI	SAT	SUN	Changing behaviour – rein-forcement	Increasing a behaviour with reward or relief
Interpersonal	MON	TUE	WED	THUR	FRI	SAT	SUN	What skills: DEAR	Describe, Express, Assert, Reinforce
	MON	TUE	WED	THUR	FRI	SAT	SUN	How skills: MAN	Broken record, ignore attacks; Mindfully, Appear confident, Negotiate
Effective-ness	MON	TUE	WED	THUR	FRI	SAT	SUN	How skills: GIVE	Gentle, Interested, Validate, Easy Manner
	MON	TUE	WED	THUR	FRI	SAT	SUN	How skills: FAST	Fair, no Apologies, Stick to values, Truthful
	MON	TUE	WED	THUR	FRI	SAT	SUN	Intensity and effectiveness,	Focus on what works; neither too loud nor to softly
	MON	TUE	WED	THUR	FRI	SAT	SUN	Models of emotions, func-tions of emotions	Noticing and understanding the value of your emotions

Category	MON	TUE	WED	THUR	FRI	SAT	SUN	Skill	Description
Emotional Regulation	MON	TUE	WED	THUR	FRI	SAT	SUN	Mindfulness of emotion	Observing emotions whilst letting go of emotional suffering
	MON	TUE	WED	THUR	FRI	SAT	SUN	Avoid avoiding	Experience your emotions fully
	MON	TUE	WED	THUR	FRI	SAT	SUN	Check the facts	Mindfully and dialectically look at what IS
	MON	TUE	WED	THUR	FRI	SAT	SUN	Opposite action	Use action opposite to the emotions
	MON	TUE	WED	THUR	FRI	SAT	SUN	Problem solving	Identify the problem from the situation. Think of the skills to solve it.
	MON	TUE	WED	THUR	FRI	SAT	SUN	PLEASE at work and home	Physical Illness, Eating, Avoid Drugs, Sleep, Exercise
	MON	TUE	WED	THUR	FRI	SAT	SUN	Cope ahead	Prepare for the worst, do your emotional preparation
	MON	TUE	WED	THUR	FRI	SAT	SUN	Dialectical Thinking	Looking for other perspectives/ possibilities
Distress Tolerance	MON	TUE	WED	THUR	FRI	SAT	SUN	TIP	Temperature, ice or heat/Intense exercise/Prog muscle relaxation
	MON	TUE	WED	THUR	FRI	SAT	SUN	Paced breathing	Breath out more than in, drop into the pause
	MON	TUE	WED	THUR	FRI	SAT	SUN	Distract (ACCEPTS)	Activities, Contributing, Comparisons, Opposite emotions, Pushing Away, Other thoughts, Intense Sensations
	MON	TUE	WED	THUR	FRI	SAT	SUN	IMPROVE the moment	Imagery, Meaning, Prayer, Relaxing, One thing, Vacation, Encouragement
	MON	TUE	WED	THUR	FRI	SAT	SUN	Self Soothe	Nurture yourself using your five senses
	MON	TUE	WED	THUR	FRI	SAT	SUN	FAIL WELL	Find kernel of truth, accept fallibility, identify opportunity, learn, wise, effective, live in the moment, let it go
Managing the challenges	MON	TUE	WED	THUR	FRI	SAT	SUN	DEALING with POWER	Dialectical, Effective, Acknowledge Authority, Respectful, Interested, non-judgemental, genuine, proceed mindfully, offer opinions, activate willingness, engage wise mind, represent self well
	MON	TUE	WED	THUR	FRI	SAT	SUN	COFFEE BREAK	Chat, open listening, find commonalities, form ideas, engage in conversation, end with an entrance, boundaries, realistic expectations, effective, accept differences, know your values
	MON	TUE	WED	THUR	FRI	SAT	SUN	APPRAISAL	Accept, prepare, proceed mindfully, row, allow, interested, stick to values, accumulate positives, learn (make lemonade)
	MON	TUE	WED	THUR	FRI	SAT	SUN	INTERRUPTIONS	
	MON	TUE	WED	THUR	FRI	SAT	SUN	STOPP	Step Back, take breath, observe, perspective, practice

Box 33.5 The three "As" of mindfulness

Attention
  One thing at a time
  In the moment
  Inside or outside of self

Awareness
  Observing sensations
  Observing thoughts
  Observing urges
  Observing tone of voice
  Observing posture
  Observing facts

Spotlight of attention

Attitude of Acceptance
  It is as it should be
  It is only as it is in this moment
  This is where I am now

Spotlight of Attention: Shutterstock.com

on their selected task while the facilitator and co-facilitator speak loudly on their telephones.

Box 33.6 provides an example of setting up and receiving feedback on a mindfulness task, where the facilitator has linked the cognitions and action urges described by the client to experiences in the workplace. The mindfulness task has become a metaphor of a common experience at work.

Judgmental thoughts frequently lead to an increase in emotional experience and often interfere with effective interpersonal functioning. In an effort to assist clients with identifying judgments, Box 33.7 provides an example of the vignette which is read out to the clients to listen to mindfully (participate). In the feedback, clients are asked if they noticed any judgments about anyone in the vignette.

When deciding upon mindfulness practices for each week, it is suggested that the facilitator consider mindfulness practices that could usefully and easily be undertaken in the workplace, for example, mindful tea/coffee making, mindfulness of eating, mindful handwashing, and mindful desk chair yoga. Of importance is making the link with clients of the value in remaining mindful at work for performance, and the subsequent retention and promotion at work.

Box 33.6   Example of a mindfulness participate task and metaphor

---

Facilitator: Now we're going to do our mindfulness practice. I'm going to give you a task—this is a participate. Throw yourself in, to do this one mindfully. Notice judgments, notice any urges to give up, notice any wilful thoughts, just notice what's going on and keep turning your mind back to "this is what I'm doing". You may not notice any emotion come up, but if you do notice any emotion arise just see if you can mindfully notice it and go back to doing the task.

Client: So what about judgments, what do you mean by that?

Facilitator: So if you have any thoughts like "she shouldn't make us do this, this isn't fair, it isn't right, I don't like this, this isn't the way it should be". For this mindfulness participate task, I am going to give you a handful of jigsaw puzzle pieces from a single puzzle and they may or may not fit but your task is to mindfully try to put your pieces together.

[All members of the group commence mindfully working with their jigsaw pieces, and half way through the task the facilitator says . . .]

Facilitator: If your mind has wandered from the task, just gently bring it back.

[Group members continue working with puzzle pieces . . .]

Facilitator: That was five minutes of puzzle putting together. So, what was your experience of trying to be mindful?

Client: The last song they played on the radio kept going round in my head.

Facilitator: Oh right! And did that distract you?

Client: Yeah, a little bit.

Facilitator: I'm wondering if, when the song was going through your mind, you had any thoughts like "I can't do this, the pieces don't go together", or was there an urge to give up?

Client: Yeah, a little bit thinking "oh this is a little bit pointless, I've only got two pieces that fit together."

Facilitator: Do you think that these types of thoughts ever come up at work? Do you think in a work setting that you're ever given a task that you have the thought "this is a bit pointless, can't see the bigger picture, the pieces don't fit together".

[turning to whole group] Can anyone give some ideas what we can do when judgments arise?

Client 2:   Let them go like helium balloons.

Client 3:   Accept that we often don't have the whole picture or all the information we would like.

Client 4:   Just keep moving your mind back to the task.

Emotional Regulation and DBT-SE

The emotional regulation skills taught in DBT-SE are taken directly from the Linehan (2015) DBT skills manual. As with the mindfulness skills, the teaching, metaphors, and examples are designed to highlight the importance and relevance of the emotional regulation skills in the workplace. Box 33.8 shows an example of scenarios identified to assist clients with practising the skill of Cope Ahead in the workplace.

Box 33.7   Mindfulness Vignette—Judgments

Vignette: Issues about the Work Roster

You are employed in a job where you are given rostered shifts each week. You have told your manager that you can only work morning shifts as you have childcare issues. The manager gives you a roster in which you only have one shift and it finishes at 4pm on Thursday. You mention to your colleague at work in the tea room that you only have one shift and you will need to pay for childcare which will mean you actually only get half your pay that day. Your colleague, who does not have children, looks a bit embarrassed and looks away. You ask them what is up and they say "I was given five shifts all in the morning for next week". You ask if you can swap your shift for one of theirs, and they say "no". When you try to speak to your manager she says she is busy at the moment and will think about the shifts next week, then rushes off.

What judgments are you having about the manager?
What judgments are you having about your colleague?
What judgments are you having about yourself?

As homework: restate the above judgments as facts and consequences.

Three emotions which are prevalent in the workplace are: irritation, frustration, and disappointment. Additional handouts elaborating on these three emotions are provided in the DBT-SE manual. An example of one of these is the frustration handout shown in Box 33.9.

Interpersonal Effectiveness and DBT-SE

The Interpersonal Effectiveness skills in DBT-SE are taken directly from the Linehan (2015) DBT skills manual and the Rathus and Miller (2014) manual for adolescents. The emphasis and examples provided to the clients are again relevant and important to the workplace.

An area potentially challenging for those with mental health difficulties, and in particular those with a PD, are to know what to share or not share in the workplace. As a result of difficult experiences in childhood (i.e., abuse, bullying, neglect) and the cognitive and behavioural consequences of emotional dysregulation, individuals with a PD will frequently either overdisclose or underdisclose information, or oscillate between the two extremes. Either end of the dialectic may lead to ostracism in the workplace. Many individuals with a PD additionally have difficulties with understanding appropriate levels of intimacy in some situations (Chelune, Sultan, & Williams, 1980; Hill et al., 2008). Hence, time is spent in DBT-SE on the discussion of personal limits (Box 33.10).

Integrating across DBT skills

While learning each of the specific DBT skills is important for individuals seeking employment, there are specific work-based experiences which require an integration

Box 33.8   COPE AHEAD scenarios

COPE AHEAD with Difficult Situations

Scenarios for practising COPE AHEAD include:

1. Being made redundant.
2. Being accused at work of stealing.
3. Not being invited to a staff party after work.
4. Getting to work late.
5. Not meeting a deadline.
6. Not knowing how to do a task at work.
7. Going to work the day after the staff Christmas party where you drank too much alcohol.
8. Denting your manager's car in the staff car park.
9. Being criticized by a colleague repeatedly.
10. Dropping/ruining an expensive product at work.

My examples of difficult situations I am catastrophizing (excessive worry) about:

   a)

   b)

   c)

and extension of the DBT skills. For DBT-SE a set of integrating skills have been developed for: COFFEE BREAK (managing self disclosure and building relationships at work), FAIL WELL (see Box 33.11), DEALING with POWER (see Box 33.12), APPRAISALS (managing the challenges of evaluation in the workplace), and INTERRUPTIONS.

Individuals with mental health difficulties, including PD, frequently have a number of problematic core beliefs of incompetence that, when activated, contribute to painful and problematic emotions which escalate rapidly and result in dysfunctional behaviours such as lashing out at colleagues or escaping by leaving work abruptly. Failure in the workplace (and in education) is a common experience as targets are changed, productivity is increased, and demands are made. Thus, learning to "fail well" is an important achievement.

Box 33.9 Frustration

Frustration

Frustration FITS THE FACTS of a situation whenever:

A. You are unable to reach a desired goal or target (e.g., your boss has set targets which you find difficult to reach).

B. You are putting in a lot of effort yet not getting a positive result (e.g., you have applied for several jobs but have not received any interviews).

C. Your efforts do not match the desired outcome (e.g., you work overtime but do not receive extra pay or get any time off).

D. You are unable to change something (e.g., your colleagues prefer doing tasks in a way that you don't agree with).

E. Provide another example: _____

Follow these suggestions when frustration is **NOT JUSTIFIED** by the facts or is **NOT EFFECTIVE.**

Opposite Actions for Frustration

Do the opposite of your frustrated action urges. For example:

1. **Take a time out**
    - Step away from the task you are trying to complete or the person you are interacting with.

2. **Breathe in and out deeply and slowly.**

3. **Take a brief mental vacation for no more than 3–5 minutes (e.g., imagine yourself on a beach, in the woods, or go for a short walk).**

4. **Briefly watch or read something that makes you laugh (no more than 3–5 minutes).**

All-the-Way Opposite Actions for Frustration

1. **Get curious about the other person's point of view.**
    - Ask questions (e.g., what may I need to change in order to improve my chances of getting an interview? Why do my colleagues like doing things in a particular way?).

2. **Change your body posture.**
    - Relax your chest and stomach muscles.
    - Relax facial muscles; half smile.

3. **Change your body chemistry.**
    - For example, go to the bathroom and splash cold water on your face.

Box 33.10 Limits

What is a limit in a relationship?

Limits are what set the space between where you end and the other person begins.

What types of limits should I think about?

- Personal information
- Physical contact
- Contact information (address, phone, email)
- Willingness to actions
- Spiritual/religious
- Health/mental health

How do I know whether my limits have been crossed?

- Physical tension
- Worry about being "hurt" or "used"
- Warnings from friends/family
- Not wanting to be around someone

THINK BEFORE YOU SPEAK!

Head silhouette: Michael Brown © 123RF.com

The principle behind the integrating skills is to link the tasks in the skill to the DBT skills learned. As can be seen in FAIL WELL (Box 33.11), the main skills are the full range of mindfulness skills. Accepting fallibility requires an attitude of acceptance, or radical acceptance (distress tolerance skill) and a letting go of judgments (about the self and about the colleague or manager who highlighted the "failure").

Another relevant issue for individuals in the workplace is dealing with power. For those who have been abused or bullied in childhood, or who have suffered consistent

---

Box 33.11   FAIL WELL

FAIL (what) WELL (how)

What
Find the kernel of truth [Check the facts]
Accept fallibility [Radical acceptance]
Identify the opportunity [make lemonade out of lemons]
Learn

How
Wise [Mindfulness: Wise mind]
Effective [Mindfulness: being effective in relation to values and goals]
Live in the moment [Mindfulness: in the moment]
Let it go [Mindfulness: in the moment, effective]

---

invalidation and control from others in their home life, acknowledging and managing the reality of the role and rights of managers can be challenging. DEALING with POWER (Box 33.12) requires the integration of dialectical thinking, mindfulness, interpersonal effectiveness, and willingness.

Phone Coaching in DBT-SE

In programmatic DBT the function of generalization is provided through phone coaching. In the employment setting, if an individual is having difficulties with a task they will seek advice and support from their colleagues or managers. However, this

---

Box 33.12   DEALING with POWER

DEALING with POWER (Managers)
Dialectical [take multiple perspectives]
Effective [mindfulness]
Acknowledge authority [radical acceptance; Mindfulness: Effective]
RespectfuL [Interpersonal Effectiveness]
Interested [Interpersonal Effectiveness: GIVE]
Non-judgmental [Mindfulness]
Genuine [Interpersonal Effectiveness: GIVE]

WITH

Proceed mindfully [Mindfulness: Effective, Wise mind]
Offer opinions
Activate Willingness [Distress tolerance]
Engage wise mind [Mindfulness]
Represent self well [Interpersonal Effectiveness: FAST]

support would not typically be available outside of work hours. Therefore, the decision was taken to provide telephone coaching of the DBT-SE skills during "working hours" to provide a more realistic and natural experience of seeking support from others. As many mental health and employment services are not funded to provide for out-of-hours phone coaching, this was identified as a more financially viable and realistic option for services considering offering DBT-SE.

Clients in DBT-SE are given the option of leaving a voice message, texting, or sending an email to the facilitators, who agree to respond within the same or next working day to the request for skills coaching.

Conclusion

Vocational functioning is a key aspect of recovery from mental health illness. Many of the challenges in obtaining and retaining employment for individuals with mental health issues arise from difficulties with managing emotions, tolerating distress, managing cognitions, and being effective in interpersonal relationships. DBT is an evidence-based approach to assisting individuals with these key areas of functioning. This chapter has outlined three adaptations of DBT for employment (DBT-W, DBT-ACES, and DBT-SE). All three programmes have shown success in feasibility studies with high retention in treatment and good return to employment rates. All three adaptations are grounded in the principles and practice of DBT, and focus on the integration of skills for use in employment settings.

ACKNOWLEDGEMENTS

The development and evaluation of DBT-SE is funded by the National Institute for Health Research (Programme Grants for Applied Research, RP-PG-1212-20011). The views expressed in this chapter are those of the author(s) and not necessarily those of the NHS, the National Institute for Health Research, or the Department of Health, UK.

KEY POINTS FOR CLINICIANS

- Vocational activity is an important goal for recovery from mental ill health.
- Adaptations of DBT focusing on employment have shown positive results.
- DBT for employment can be delivered as a group-based treatment, thus improving cost-effectiveness.
- All three adaptations of DBT for employment provide all five functions of standard DBT.
- The adaptations of DBT for employment have been developed as stage 2 treatments, provided to those individuals who are no longer engaging in high-risk behaviours.

REFERENCES

American Psychiatric Association. (2013). *Diagnostic and statistical manual of mental disorders (DSM-5®)*, 5th Edition. American Psychiatric Publishing.

American Psychiatric Association Practice Guidelines. (2001). Practice guideline for the treatment of patients with borderline personality disorder. *American Journal of Psychiatry, 158*(10 Suppl), 1–52.

Blekesaune, M. (2008). *Unemployment and partnership dissolution.* ISER Working Paper No. 2008-21. Colchester: Institute for Social & Economic Research.

Chelune, G. J., Sultan, F. E., & Williams, C. L. (1980). Loneliness, self-disclosure, and interpersonal effectiveness. *Journal of Counseling Psychology, 27*(5), 462.

Coid, J., Yang, M., Tyrer, P., Roberts, A., & Ullrich, S. (2006). Prevalence and correlates of personality disorder in Great Britain. *The British Journal of Psychiatry, 188*(5), 423–431.

Comtois, K. A., Huus, K., Hoiness, M., Marsden, J., Mullen, C., Elwood, L., et al. (2006), Dialectical behaviour therapy: Accepting the Challenges of Exiting the System (ACES) manual. (unpublished manuscript).

Comtois, K. A., Kerbrat, A. H., Atkins, D., Harned, M., & Elwood, L. (2010). Recovery from disability for individuals with borderline personality disorder: a feasibility trial of DBT-ACES. *Psychiatric Services, 61*(11), 1106–1111.

Comtois, K. A., Koons, C. R., Kim, S. A., Manning, S. A., Bellows, E., & Dimeff, L. A. (2007). Implementing standard dialectical behavior therapy in an outpatient setting. In L. A. Dimeff & K. Koerner (Eds.), *Dialectical behavior therapy in clinical practice: applications across disorders and settings* (pp. 37–68). New York: Guilford Press.

Dimeff, L. A., & Linehan, M. M. (2008). Dialectical behavior therapy for substance abusers. *Addiction Science & Clinical Practice, 4*(2), 39.

Dunkley, C., & Stanton, M. (2013). *Teaching clients to use mindfulness skills: A practical guide.* New York: Routledge.

Feigenbaum, J. (2007). Dialectical behaviour therapy: An increasing evidence base. *Journal of Mental Health, 16*(1), 51–68.

Feigenbaum, J., Swales, M., Fonagy, P., Stansfeld, S., Morris, S., Hoare, Z., … Cattrell, A., (in preparation). Dialectical Behavioural Therapy Skills for Employment (DBT-SE): a Feasibility Study.

Hill, J., Pilkonis, P., Morse, J., Feske, U., Reynolds, S., Hope, H., & Broyden, N. (2008). Social domain dysfunction and disorganization in borderline personality disorder. *Psychological Medicine, 38*(1), 135–146.

Kelloway, E. K., & Barling, J. (1991). Job characteristics, role stress and mental health. *Journal of Occupational and Organizational Psychology, 64*(4), 291–304.

Koons, C. R., Chapman, A. L., Betts, B. B., O'Rourke, B., Morse, N., & Robins, C. J. (2006). Dialectical behavior therapy adapted for the vocational rehabilitation of significantly disabled mentally ill adults. *Cognitive and Behavioral Practice, 13*(2), 146–156.

Korkeila, J., Oksanen, T., Virtanen, M., Salo, P., Nabi, H., Pentti, J., … Kivimäki, M. (2011). Early retirement from work among employees with a diagnosis of personality disorder compared to anxiety and depressive disorders. *European Psychiatry, 26*(1), 18–22.

Layard, R. (2006). Health policy: The case for psychological treatment centres. *British Medical Journal, 332*(7548), 1030.

Layard, R; The Centre for Economic Performance Mental Health Policy Group (2012). *How mental illness loses out in the NHS.* London: The London School of Economics and Political Science.

Leamy, M., Bird, V., Le Boutillier, C., Williams, J., & Slade, M. (2011). Conceptual framework for personal recovery in mental health: systematic review and narrative synthesis. *The British Journal of Psychiatry, 199*(6), 445–452.

Levitas, R., Pantazis, C., Fahmy, E., Gordon, D., Lloyd, E., & Patsios, D. (2007). *The multidimensional analysis of social exclusion: A Research Report for the Social Exclusion Task Force.* Bristol: University of Bristol.

London Mental Health and Employment Partnership. (2012). *Work, Mental Health, and Welfare: the case for co-ordinated action to achieve shared benefit.* London: National Health Service.

Linehan, M. (1993a). *Cognitive-behavioral treatment of borderline personality disorder.* New York: Guilford Press.

Linehan, M. M. (1993b). *Skills training manual for treating borderline personality disorder.* New York: Guilford Press.

Linehan, M. M. (2015). *DBT® skills training manual.* New York: Guilford Press.

Lynch, T. R., & Cheavens, J. S. (2008). Dialectical behavior therapy for comorbid personality disorders. *Journal of Clinical Psychology, 64*(2), 154–167.

Mazzucchelli, T., Kane, R., & Rees, C. (2009). Behavioral activation treatments for depression in adults: a meta-analysis and review. *Clinical Psychology: Science and Practice, 16*(4), 383–411.

McGurk, S. R., Mueser, K. T., Mischel, R., Adams, R., Harvey, P. D., McClure, M. M., . . . Siever, L. J. (2013). Vocational functioning in schizotypal and paranoid personality disorders. *Psychiatry Research, 210*(2), 498–504.

McMahon, R. C., & Enders, C. (2009). Personality disorder factors predict recovery of employment functioning among treated cocaine abusers. *American Journal of Drug and Alcohol Abuse, 35*(3), 138–144.

Mee, J., & Sumsion, T. (2001). Mental health clients confirm the motivating power of occupation. *British Journal of Occupational Therapy, 64*(3), 121–128.

Michon, H. W. C., Ten Have, M., Kroon, H., Van Weeghel, J., De Graaf, R., & Schene, A. H. (2008). Mental disorders and personality traits as determinants of impaired work functioning. *Psychological Medicine, 38*(11), 1627.

Milner, A., Page, A., & Lamontagne, A. D. (2014). Cause and effect in studies on unemployment, mental health and suicide: a meta-analytic and conceptual review. *Psychological Medicine, 44*(5), 909–917.

Moran, P., Leese, M., Lee, T., Walters, P., Thornicroft, G., & Mann, A. (2003). Standardised Assessment of Personality–Abbreviated Scale (SAPAS): preliminary validation of a brief screen for personality disorder. *British Journal of Psychiatry, 183*(3), 228–232.

Murali, V., & Oyebode, F. (2004). Poverty, social inequality and mental health. *Advances in Psychiatric Treatment, 10*, 216–224.

National Institute for Health and Clinical Excellence, (2009). *Borderline personality disorder: treatment and management (National Clinical Practice Guideline Number 78).* Leicester: British Psychological Society/London: Royal College of Psychiatrists. Available at: https://www.nice.org.uk/guidance/cg78/evidence/cg78-borderline-personality-disorder-bpd-full-guideline3

Newton-Howes, G., Tyrer, P., & Weaver, T. (2008). Social functioning of patients with personality disorder in secondary care. *Psychiatric Services, 59*(9), 1033–1037.

Nierenberg, D. W. (1998). The challenge of "teaching" large groups of learners: Strategies to increase active participation and learning. *The International Journal of Psychiatry in Medicine, 28*(1), 115–122.

Overland, S., Grasdal, A., Løvvik, C., Lie, S. A., & Reme, S. E. (2014). EPA-1090–The effectiveness of a work-focused cognitive behavioural therapy and individual job support on return to work for common mental disorders: randomized controlled multicenter trial. *European Psychiatry, 29,* 1.

Rathus, J. H., & Miller, A. L. (2014). *DBT® skills manual for adolescents.* New York: Guilford Press.

Rogers, E. S., Martin, R., Anthony, W., Massaro, J., Danley, K., Crean, T., & Penk, W. (2001). Assessing readiness for change among persons with severe mental illness. *Community Mental Health Journal, 37*(2), 97–112.

Rymaszewska, J., Jarosz-Nowak, J., Kiejna, A., Kallert, T., Schützwohl, M., Priebe, S., . . . Raboch, J. (2007). Social disability in different mental disorders. *European Psychiatry, 22*(3), 160–166.

Sansone, R. A., Leung, J. S., & Wiederman, M. W. (2012). Employment histories among patients with borderline personality disorder symptomatology. *Journal of Vocational Rehabilitation, 37*(2), 131–137.

Sansone, R. A., & Sansone, L. A. (2010). Personality dysfunction and employment dysfunction: double, double, toil and trouble. *Psychiatry (Edgmont), 7*(3), 12.

Sansone, R. A., & Sansone, L. A. (2012). Employment in borderline personality disorder. *Innovations in Clinical Neuroscience, 9*(9), 25.

Sansone, R. A., & Wiederman, M. W. (2013). Losing a job on purpose: relationships with borderline personality symptomatology. *Early Intervention in Psychiatry, 7*(2), 210–212.

Sio, I. T., Chanen, A. M., Killackey, E. J., & Gleeson, J. (2011). The relationship between impulsivity and vocational outcome in outpatient youth with borderline personality features. *Early Intervention in Psychiatry, 5*(3), 249–253.

Smith, J. M., & Alloy, L. B. (2009). A roadmap to rumination: A review of the definition, assessment, and conceptualization of this multifaceted construct. *Clinical Psychology Review, 29*(2), 116–128.

Valentine, S. E., Bankoff, S. M., Poulin, R. M., Reidler, E. B., & Pantalone, D. W. (2015). The use of dialectical behavior therapy skills training as stand-alone treatment: A systematic review of the treatment outcome literature. *Journal of Clinical Psychology, 71*(1), 1–20.

Ward, V.G., & Riddle, D. I. (2003). *Measuring Employment Readiness.* NATCON Papers, Les Actes du CONAT (Canada).

Warr, P. (1994). A conceptual framework for the study of work and mental health. *Work & Stress, 8*(2), 84–97.

Zanarini, M. C., Frankenburg, F. R., Reich, D. B., & Fitzmaurice, G. (2010). The 10-year course of psychosocial functioning among patients with borderline personality disorder and axis II comparison subjects. *Acta Psychiatrica Scandinavica, 122*(2), 103–109.

CHAPTER 34

....

IMPROVING ACCESSIBILITY TO DIALECTICAL BEHAVIOUR THERAPY FOR INDIVIDUALS WITH COGNITIVE CHALLENGES

....

JULIE F. BROWN

INTRODUCTION

....

THE development of Dialectical Behaviour Therapy (DBT) expanded treatment options for individuals with borderline personality disorder (BPD), who, prior to Linehan's work (1993a, 1993b), were largely perceived as untreatable. DBT is a comprehensive model that includes a foundational theory, principles, and strategies to support people with BPD to improve core regulation capacities. There is a new group of perceived "untreatables," individuals with intellectual disabilities (ID) who experience various types of dysregulation. Again, DBT is a potential solution, but because of this population's intensified needs, delivery mechanisms need adjusting and additional scaffolding is necessary to improve accessibility to DBT. This chapter addresses specific strategies to help the DBT practitioner treat people with ID and emotion regulation challenges.

The goal is to make accommodations *and* remain adherent to DBT. This is best achieved by examining the functions of the DBT treatment mechanisms, keeping essential concepts, and adjusting delivery systems to improve access, while not disturbing core curative elements. This process—evaluating and altering of the delivery methods—must focus on the treatment needs and available resources of the individual. To strengthen the evidence-base of this adaptation, it is necessary to rely on research in alternate fields of study (e.g., ID, emotion regulation, and cognitive load theory) to understand barriers and solutions. This chapter reviews one approach to delivering DBT to patients with ID. While limited direct evidence is available, the chapter draws on principles of DBT and relevant findings from the field of ID.

Biosocial Theory and
the Beginning of DBT

Biosocial theory, which is the theoretical underpinning of DBT, posits that there are transactional relationships between vulnerable individuals and invalidating environments that intermittently reinforce emotionally dysregulated responses. Individuals diagnosed with ID experience deficits in cognitive and executive processing which increase vulnerability and hinder adaptive functioning. Broad spectrums of aetiologies exist within the diagnosis of ID, as well as diverse constellations of strengths and weaknesses related to individual functioning capacities that create heterogeneity within this group. Generally speaking, deficits impact the individual's abilities to manage cognitive load demands in complex situations and impede the execution of adaptive chains of goal-directed behaviour.

In addition to cognitive difficulties, the literature highlights multiple factors that can increase the vulnerability of individuals with ID. For example, a diagnosis of co-occurring mental illnesses in this group is more likely than in that of its non-disabled counterparts (Hove & Havik, 2008; Weiss, 2012). These individuals also experience higher rates of victimization (e.g., neglect, physical, sexual, and witnessing violence; Beadle-Brown, Mansell, Cambridge, Milne, & Whelton, 2010; Mevissen, Lievegoed, Seubert, & Jongh, 2011; Sullivan & Knutson, 2000). Sullivan and Knutson (2000) found that youth with ID were 30% more likely to experience abuse. Although this is alarming, researchers predict that the prevalence rates are even higher because of the widespread underreporting of victimization (McCormack, Kavanagh, Caffrey, & Power, 2005; Bedard, Burke, & Ludwig, 1998). A concerning double-bind exists; despite heightened risks, this population experiences fewer treatment options specifically designed to accommodate the impact of the ID (Emerson & Hatton, 2014).

Transactional Social Relationships

The biosocial theory contends that negative transactions between vulnerable individuals and invalidating environments create and maintain patterns of dysregulation. These patterns can happen within families, support environments, and potentially within the DBT treatment relationship. Therefore, it is vital to be aware of how various micro- and macro-biosocial factors may transact to ensure effective management of the DBT therapeutic relationship.

Vulnerable Environments

Individuals with ID have intensified needs which potentially creates increased pressures for the families/systems supporting them. Norona and Baker (2014) studied 225 families and examined transactional parenting behaviours and emotion regulation capacities of both ID and non-disabled youths across three time points. These authors found that children with ID were significantly more dysregulated at all time points when compared to non-disabled age-mates. Additionally, the mothers of the children with ID demonstrated fewer "scaffolding behaviors" at ages three and five (Norona & Baker, 2014, p. 3209). The authors found that a lack of effective parental scaffolding behaviours contributed to the emotion regulation skills deficits of the children. Because of the increased demands implicit in supporting a person with ID and co-occurring mental health issues, it may be useful to reframe the elements of the biosocial theory for individuals with ID as a transactional relationship between a vulnerable person and a vulnerable environment. This reframe will aid the DBT practitioner in understanding and validating the experiences of people within the support system to facilitate change.

Power Imbalances

Individuals with ID experience higher levels of social stigmatization (Ali et al., 2013; Ditchman et al., 2013). Jahoda et al. (2009) highlight how receptive and expressive language problems impact power distributions in the relationships between individuals with ID and their therapists. The authors assert that bi-directional transactional communication dissonances can complicate the assessment and treatment processes for both participants and care providers. Beyond therapy settings, power imbalances commonly occur within relationships between individuals with ID and other people in social contexts (Coons & Watson, 2013; Irvine, 2010; Jahoda et al., 2009). On an institutional level, these imbalances may hinder transactions that include processes associated with autonomy and self-determination (Petner-Arrey & Copeland, 2014).

Transactions: The Problem and the Fix

It is vital that DBT therapists and skills trainers understand personal and social contexts that are relevant for this population. Linehan describes how "individual functioning and environmental conditions are mutually and continuously interactive, reciprocal, and interdependent" (1993a, p. 39). Within these types of transactional relationships, the entities are continually adapting and bi-directionally influencing each other. Factors associated with stigma and power differential processes emerge continually within therapy sessions, skills training groups, and interactions with support providers. These events create learning opportunities or the continuation of recursive problematic patterns. Fortuitously, DBT contains a myriad of practices designed to create and maintain egalitarian relationships between the client and the therapist.

DIALECTICAL DILEMMAS

Emotional Vulnerability Versus Self-invalidation

There is emerging literature related to the psychological functioning of individuals with ID, yet serious knowledge gaps remain. Although there are numerous barriers related to diagnostic precision (e.g., heterogeneity of this population, communication issues, lack of provider awareness, etc.), there is general consensus that individuals with ID appear to experience heightened emotional vulnerabilities. This means that a formal diagnosis of BPD in individuals with ID is rare, yet many may experience similar processes that underlie BPD. The combination of (a) reinforced patterns of emotional escalation in transactional relationships with invalidating/vulnerable environments and (b) inadequate learning experiences related to building effective emotion regulation skills contribute to patterns of emotional, cognitive, and behavioural dysregulation.

The conceptualization of emotional vulnerability in DBT (e.g., high sensitivity, slow return to emotional baseline, impact on cognitive processing capacities, and problematic behaviour functioning as a desperate attempt to regulate escalating emotions) are key for DBT therapists (and collaterals such as staff and family members) to understand. Oversimplifying the ease of coping and misattributing behaviours as manipulative fosters conflict and, ultimately, self-invalidation by the individual. The combination of acceptance strategies (that support the individual in the moment, as it is) and change strategies (that support the individual to be effective while in the moment) helps the individual develop a stronger sense of self- awareness, self-acceptance, self-value, and self-trust (e.g., self-validation).

Active Passivity Versus Apparent Competency

Several factors contribute to the individual with ID presenting with behaviours labelled as active passivity. For example, it can be difficult for support providers to accurately assess the specific support needs and shape interventions to build increasing capacities; teams often oscillate between over-doing and under-doing. Simultaneously, individuals experience skills deficits that affect their abilities to effectively manage intra- and interpersonal environments; individuals frequently oscillate between over-doing and under-doing. Additionally, the lack of foundational skills to complete complex tasks such as problem solving can promote resignation and derailment, often misattributed to passivity, while the root issue is a lack of adequate requisite problem solving and self-regulation competencies that are components of complex skills chains. In addition to skills deficits, individuals with ID tend to have low self-efficacy that can reduce engagement.

Competency is a complex construct in relation to people with ID. For example, the level of emotional and cognitive dysregulation may impact behavioural competency in the moment. Environments that provide ample scaffolding and supports specifically tailored to the needs of the individual are likely to witness the individual demonstrating increased competency. Additionally, how the therapist conceptualizes competency impacts the evaluation of capacities. If the therapist defines competency as quantitative and academic abilities, they will view the client as more incompetent. If the therapist acknowledges areas of strength (e.g., creativity, compassion, spirituality, wisdom, humour, and intuition), they will assess the client as more competent.

Unrelenting Crisis Versus Inhibited Grieving

Individuals with ID often experience heightened risks and recursive challenges that block change. Cognitive processing deficits coupled with higher rates of mental illness, victimization, medical problems, and stigmatization affect the individual. Additionally, factors such as congregate living situations, staff supervision, vocational supports, and state involvement associated with their lives add stress. Psychiatric and psychological treatment options are often limited. Unfortunately, despite best intentions, supports can augment difficulties, rather than mitigate them. Often their lives are rich in crisis and light on resources to support adaptive emotional processing. Justified overwhelming stress and insufficient skills to correct the myriad of systemic factors that perpetuate negative transactions may initially appear as unrelenting crisis and inhibited grieving.

The DBT therapist has to see the individual, the world that surrounds the client, and the human potential that exists to address dialectical dilemmas. Building "a life worth living" requires that the individual actively self- and system manage to bridge these gaps. Building emotion regulation and social effectiveness skills that support these processes are essential to facilitate synthesis.

OVERVIEW OF TREATMENT STRATEGIES

DBT Therapist Preparation Assumptions

In addition to the basic DBT assumptions highlighted by Linehan (1993a, pp. 106–108), the DBT practitioner treating this population should consider engaging in behaviours that promote self-, social, and academic awareness of factors associated with ID. For example, DBT therapists require mindfulness of stereotypes related to developmental delays. Perceiving people with ID as "simple" and/or equating developmental status of adults to school-age children (e.g., mental age of five) blocks the treatment providers' visions about strengths and the complexity of human development.

Alternatively, Greenspan discusses the "individual developmental time-table" (Greenspan & Lourie, 1981, p. 729), related to the psychological development of individuals with ID. Greenspan explains that the individual can "catch up" and "such learning, however, may have a different developmental sequence and final configuration" (p. 726).

If the DBT therapist characterizes the adult with ID as a non-disabled child, it may create power imbalances, oversimplify developmental processes, and invalidate the person being an adult human. No amount of DBT craft related to strategies will offset this type of foundational inequity.

Behavioural Targets in Treatment

Dialectical Thinking

One of the goals of DBT therapy is to help the individual cultivate dialectical thinking capacities; these perspectives in turn increase activation of dialectical or balanced life-style behaviours. Dialectical thinking involves having the capacity to appraise thesis and antithesis forces (e.g., [thesis] I dislike my staff when they tell me what to do *and* [antithesis] I like it when my staff pays attention to me). A dialectical synthesis would involve reconciling the polarities through a reappraisal process (e.g., re-thinking the situation) in a way that integrates both perspectives. An example of dialectical thinking in this case would be: Even though it bugs me [appraisal], I know my staff are helping me reach my goals [reappraisal/synthesis].

Assessing Dialectical Thinking

DBT therapists need to understand the transactional elements of assessing dialectical thinking. Individuals with ID often engage in concrete or black and white cognitive processing. Executive functioning deficits impact the person's capacities to sequence/organize and ultimately communicate complex perceptions in a way that others can understand fully. Both (a) the individual's level of arousal and (b) the receptivity-status of the other person impact the individual's ability to communicate multifaceted concepts to someone. Support providers with biases/narrow interpretations of capacity, lack of experience with dysregulation, or who fail to establish effective bi-directional communication that supports non-judgmental exploration create barriers to effective communication. Just because the individual struggles to effectively communicate the nuances and "grey" areas within complex situations does not mean that they do not understand it on various levels.

Using the word "and" to link the thesis and anti-thesis can be a useful tool to promote dialectical thinking capacities. This joining creates an opportunity for dialectical synthesis and reappraisal. It is a simple word that is accessible to even non-readers; writing it on a note card and using it as a visual cue can facilitate exploration of dialectical perspectives.

Primary Behavioural Targets

The DBT therapist is thoughtful about the targeting process. Assessing the difference between life-threatening, therapy-interfering, and quality of life issues is an important process in DBT. All of the standard DBT targeting strategies are relevant when treating individuals with ID. The role of staff support may reduce the level of apparent danger-ousness of a behaviour, yet this layer of containment should not influence the decision about whether an action is life threatening or not.

Therapy-interfering Behaviours

Therapy-interfering behaviour (TIB) management follows standard DBT practice. Carefully examining the function of the TIB to (a) understand the reason behind the action and to (b) explore any transactional factors associated with the therapist's be-haviour results in more effective intervention. Communication deficits and power imbalances may reduce the individual's capacities to address problems in the therapy relationship directly or in a pro-active way.

Quality of Life

Often the individual has a primary goal of increasing independence, self-determination, and/or autonomy. For example, if the individual currently lives in a group home where he has 24-hour per day supervision, perhaps lower levels of supervision, supported living, or independent living are long-term goals. The highest threats to this increased freedom (behaviours that may result in incarceration or homelessness, e.g., child mo-lestation, fire-setting, and non-homicidal aggression) would become the focus of quality-of-life targets. Behaviours that negatively impact the individual's independent functioning (e.g., rule infractions that result in privilege losses and increases in re-strictive procedures) are often the next priority.

In addition to the salient residential factors, the DBT therapist supports the indi-vidual to define and reach short- and long-term goals related to personal functioning (e.g., mind, body, and spirit), social connections, vocational opportunities, and family relationships. These changes hinge on the individual enhancing adaptive intra-personal and interpersonal coping skills. The myriad of challenges (e.g., cognitive, trauma, co-occurring mental illness, challenging behaviours, polypharmacy, and stigmatization) create multi-factorial transactional patterns that complicate the change process. Skill deficits, low self-efficacy, and incalcitrant complex environmental factors can negatively affect follow-through and execution of adaptive behaviours.

Increasing Behavioural Skills

Because of pervasive skills deficits, increasing behaviour skills is integrated into all target levels. Designed for individuals who have academic capacities (e.g., reading and writing), the standard DBT skills curriculum features complex language and acronyms that increase cognitive load demands, and hinder encoding, recognition, and recall. In addition, the standard model assumes intact executive functioning; individuals are able to learn the material in four modules and synthesize discrepant information into elabor-ated chains of adaptive behaviour while experiencing moderate or strong emotions. The standard model anticipates a degree of impairment in learning consequent to clients' difficulties with emotion regulation, and teaches every skill twice within a 12-month treatment programme to address these difficulties. However, this modification alone is insufficient to address the challenges faced by clients with an ID. Deficits in executive functioning, attentional control, and memory hinder an individual with ID's capacities to know (a) which skills (or elements of skills) to use, (b) how many skills to use, (3) the sequence of skills to use, and (4) the timing of skills use, even at low levels of emotion. Because of the barriers to learning essential DBT skills and the inability to execute multiple skills together in adaptive chains (replacing maladaptive patterns across the spam of dysregulated emotions), accommodations are required.

The Skills System, presented in *Emotion Regulation Skills System for the Cognitively Challenged Client: A DBT°-Informed Approach* (Brown, 2016), is an adapted skills curriculum specifically designed for use in treating individuals diagnosed with moderate or mild ID. The term DBT-SS reflects an adapted model for vulnerable learners that integrates DBT individual therapy and the Skills System curriculum for skills training.

Structuring DBT-SS Treatment: Who Can Participate?

Individuals who have (a) moderate or mild severity ID, (b) basic verbal communication skills, and (c) emotional, cognitive, behavioural, self, and relationship dysregulation are candidates for DBT-SS treatment. Individuals referred for therapy often have multiple mental health diagnoses, take several psychotropic medications, and demonstrate challenging behaviours (CBs). Because there are few adequate solutions for the individual, he or she may be a multiple-system user that may include numerous psychiatric hospitalizations, ER visits, residential placements, and involvement with the criminal justice system. CBs are often the reason for referral.

Remaining adherent to DBT is essential. For example, the modes of treatment used with this population include individual therapy, group skills training, consultation team involvement, and phone skills coaching. Although there are trends towards skills-only DBT treatment, individual DBT therapy is the foundation of the treatment for individuals with ID. Individual therapy offers comprehensive supports and essential scaffolding to sustain the skills building process.

THE FIVE FUNCTIONS OF DBT

This section highlights factors within DBT-SS that support fulfillment of the five functions of DBT, i.e., enhancing client capacities, improving motivation to change, generalizing skills into the environment, structuring the environment, and enhancing therapist capabilities. The information focuses on (a) additional interventions that address the unique needs of this population, (b) prerequisites for the function to be addressed, and (c) specific conditions that commonly impact individuals with ID related to the DBT function.

Enhancing Client Capabilities

Learning new skills lies at the heart of standard DBT. For clients with an ID the standard curriculum requires modification to enable increased access to the treatment. Brown (2016) extracted the core functions and altered the delivery system of the skills to improve accessibility to DBT, and the Skills System is a tool used to enhance the individual's capacities in multiple ways. The design of the skills model, as well as strategies that integrate the concepts into DBT treatment, bridge gaps for vulnerable learners.

Skills System Design

The Skills System has nine core DBT-based skills and three System Tools that help the individual cognitively assemble and execute adaptive chains of behaviour throughout each day. The three base skills lead the individual to engage in mindfulness (Skill 1. Clear Picture), goal-directed thinking/cognitive restructuring (Skill 2. On-Track Thinking), and behavioural activation (Skill 3. On-Track Action) in each situation. Linking these skills together helps individuals to (a) be present, (b) create effective plans (even at high levels of emotion, and (c) demonstrate goal-directed behaviours. The other six skills (Safety Plan, New-Me Activities, Problem Solving, Expressing Myself, Getting It Right, and Relationship Care) supplement the base skills to manage diverse situations.

The Skills System is designed to fit all learning abilities. For example, each of the nine skills have sub-skills that provide elaborated skill options for individuals that have advanced capacities. Conversely, individuals with greater impairment may use single skills or partial skills chains. DBT therapists who use the Skills System should be competent in the model to be able to maximize benefits in teachable moments with individuals with complex learning profiles.

Skills System Skills Training

It is important to consider an individual's functioning capacities (e.g., academic and communication abilities) when designing a skills training programme. For example, due to the high cognitive load demands of instruction and the need to adjust teaching to optimize comprehension, group sessions are limited to one hour. Similarly, adherence to the Skills System concepts is imperative, yet the delivery methods of the concepts must be tailored to fit the individual's situation. Individuals with ID often live in complex support environments, and the skills training format realistically needs to fit within the support context to promote sustainability.

Although Brown's (2016) manual provides a detailed 12-week group curriculum of 60-minute groups (multiple 12-week cycles are recommended), it is only one option. Therapists may need to consider individual one-to-one skills instruction; often there are too few clients with ID to form a group in a geographical area. If an individual is unable to learn information, because of high levels of behavioural dysregulation in groups, 1:1 training may be necessary as a preliminary step. While it is preferable to separate one-to-one instruction from DBT individual therapy, setting up a second appointment during the week for skills training, or dividing the session into two discrete sections, are options.

Skills System Pilot Data

Brown, Brown, and DiBiasio (2013) reported outcome data of a pilot study of DBT-SS, which reported statistically significant reductions in behavioural outcomes for 30 individuals with co-occurring ID and mental illness with histories of challenging behaviours. Currently, the Skills System is the only manualized adapted-DBT™ skills curriculum for this population.

Improving Motivation to Change

The primary task of the therapist is to collaborate with the individual with ID to create a strong therapeutic relationship that can sustain the movement and flow of DBT strategies across the connection. For example, tactics to increase awareness and motivation include oscillating between validation and change strategies, commitment strategies, didactic instruction, and dialectical strategies. Behavioural strategies can reinforce adaptive patterns of behaviours, as well as provide contingencies for less-effective ones to increase motivation. There may be a tendency to over-rely on behavioural strategies with individuals with ID, especially if there are communication challenges that appear to hinder the use of strategies that foster intrinsic motivation.

There are two related factors that are essential elements that help create an environment within which a therapeutic relationship can develop and sustain motivation. The first is bi-directional communication. Establishing reciprocal communication is a prerequisite for developing a functional therapeutic relationship. Second, the DBT therapist needs to be continually aware of and actively manage cognitive load demands of all interactions and interventions, so the individual can remain present in the dialogue. Understanding how the individual's ID may impact these processes will optimize progress toward this DBT function.

Communication and Cognitive Load

Many factors can impact communication patterns within transactional client-therapist relationships. For example, in a study of non-disabled individuals, Hansen, Kutzner, and Wanke (2013) reported that, in low-demand situations, people tend to have increased capacity for "abstract, top-down processing" (p. 1155), while in more stressful situations, concrete thinking helps to adjust for the increased cognitive load. This natural shift in high-stress situations, coupled with other cognitive deficits (e.g. executive functioning) may increase concrete processing for the client. Therefore, the therapist may notice that at low levels of arousal the client may be able to process and communicate abstract concepts more effectively than when experiencing stress.

Sweller (1988, 2010) highlights several factors related to the design of teaching interventions that increase and/or decrease cognitive load demands for the learner. Processing is impeded by interventions that increase extraneous cognitive load, for example, complex language and concepts. Similarly, unlinked or divergent information that lacks association connecting essential elements causes extraneous cognitive load that strains processing abilities. Information that is similar, difficult to differentiate, and/or lacks transitions also increases extraneous cognitive load. Likewise, high levels of emotional content can contribute to cognitive overload. Continually evaluating cognitive load demands during interactions will aid the DBT therapist to accurately assess behaviour and adjust strategies.

Cognitive overload can impact bi-directional communication patterns (Sweller, 2010; Brown, 2016). For example, when the individual experiences high cognitive load demands, his or her ability to organize and sequence his narrative may reduce. In this state, the individual may be more likely to shift to an associated topic without transition. When experiencing stress, the individual may use fragmented/partial sentences or concrete terms to express abstract or complex concepts. Similarly, the individual may be more likely to shift between polarities, because expressing synthesis-oriented points may be more difficult during cognitive over-load. When overwhelmed in this way, the individual may demonstrate idiosyncratic communication styles such as mono-syllabic answers, disclosures that appear to be random, and/or perseveration.

As a result, the therapist may also experience increased cognitive load demands. It may be difficult for the therapist to fully understand what the individual is saying. During this type of transaction communication breakdowns and relationship ruptures are more likely. Therapists will benefit from taking time to explore (in a non-judgmental way) what is being communicated. If the therapist is able to establish reciprocal communication in these situations, important therapeutic work can happen. Misattribution of cognitive load as a lack of insight, resistance, and/or wilfulness can hinder the development of and even destroy the therapeutic relationship.

Reciprocal communication breakdowns should prompt the therapist to notice (a) what potentially clinically-relevant material discussed is increasing demands and (b) whether the client-therapist communication pattern itself is contributing to cognitive and communication challenges. The therapist must continually self-monitor related to communication behaviours, making adjustment such as simplifying language, using visual aids, and/or breaking complex concepts into component parts (Brown, 2016). The therapist may want to ask clarifying questions to ensure reciprocal understanding of points. Creating positive versus negative transactions requires the DBT therapist to persist to bridge communication gaps when discussing relevant topics, rather than shifting the focus of the conversation.

Quick Step Assessment

Brown (2016) introduced the Quick Step Assessment strategy, based on Sweller's (1988, 2010) Cognitive Load Theory, which is intended to help therapists design effective interventions:

- Step 1 prompts therapists to be mindful of the cognitive load demands of an intervention prior to implementation. Factors such as complexity, simultaneous processing, emotional content, divergent topics, and rapid transitions without orientation create extraneous cognitive load, potentially causing cognitive over-load for the client.

- Step 2 asks the therapist to monitor the individual's responses to the intervention, watching for direct and indirect signs of emotional and/or cognitive processing difficulties. Cognitive over-load may manifest as confusion, disorganization, avoidance, resistance, and/or wilfulness.
- Step 3 helps the therapist adjust the intervention to reduce cognitive load demands. Simplifying the language, using a metaphor that is easily understandable, and breaking down complex concepts into component parts (e.g. task analysis) can reduce cognitive load demands.

When the individual appears resistant, the therapist needs to use the Quick Step Assessment immediately to explore the therapist contribution to the strained transaction.

Generalizing into the Natural Environment

There is general consensus in the disabilities field that individuals with ID have difficulty generalizing skills into natural contexts. A multi-level approach is necessary to ensure the individual has adequate supports in place to build competency in executing adaptive patterns of behaviour. For example, the design of the Skills System, the enhanced teaching strategies outlined in the text, and individual therapy techniques create in-session learning experiences that are the foundation for generalization. Extending supports beyond the therapy office offers scaffolding that facilitates competency in real-life situations. Phone skills coaching as well as training support providers to be in-vivo skills coaches can enhance generalization of Skills System concepts. The skills coach needs to (a) learn skills and sub-skills and (b) be able to apply the DBT-based Skills System coaching techniques.

Structuring the Environment

Standard case management strategies (e.g., environmental interventions, consultation-to-the-patient, and consultation-to-the-therapist) are all *vital* aspects of DBT and DBT-SS. Consultation-to-the-patient strategies guide the DBT-SS therapist to function as a consultant to the client, rather than to the support system. The tendency might be for the therapist to destabilize the client and over-engage with members of the support team, undermining the power and responsibility of the client. The DBT-SS therapist orients and discusses these consultation-to-the-patient strategies with the individual on an ongoing basis.

The consultation-to-therapist strategies, as applied in the consultation team, provide the DBT therapist with support to maintain intra- and interpersonal balance within the therapeutic relationship. The consultation team is mindful of judgment, biases, frustrations, ethical dilemmas, confidentiality, environmental interventions, and managing the consultation-to-the-patient strategies. Practicing dialectical perspectives in consultation team increases the likelihood those attitudes will generalize into the therapist's DBT practice.

These consultation team practices are of special value when clients may also be in receipt of other interventions in their wider environment, and the DBT therapist must balance consultation to the patient with environmental intervention. For example, an individual's support plan often includes Applied Behaviour Analysis (ABA) interventions. Baseline data and a functional analysis generally delineates four functions of behaviour escape/avoidance, attention seeking, seeking access for materials, and sensory stimulation. This process yields behavioural treatment plans that include (a) positive reinforcement (e.g., incentive programmes), and (b) contingencies (e.g., restricted access to the community), both of which are designed to increase adaptive behaviours.

Although behavioural strategies are an important ingredient of DBT, the process of understanding and explaining the functions involves a more comprehensive, interactive, transactional, ongoing data collection approach that informs the implementation of behavioural strategies. Through a DBT lens, the functions of behaviours are not divided into four categories; it could be considered invalidating to over-simplify the complex/dynamic processes involved in motivation. Additionally, replacement behaviours in ABA plans do not tend to integrate instruction of comprehensive skills sets designed to enhance intrinsic emotion regulation capacities. Therefore, pairing ABA behavioural strategies and Skills System concepts can create a valuable synthesis.

Interacting with the Individual's Support Team

Whenever possible it is optimal to prompt the individual to engage with his or her psychologist (behavioural treatment plan developer) to improve the plans. For example, encouraging the client to advocate for the team to pair ABA-based incentives with the Skills System concepts (e.g., incentives for effective Safety Planning or engaging in New-Me Activities). The DBT-SS therapist may encourage the individual to self-advocate to change behavioural plans and ultimately terminate them as capacities improve.

Enhancing Therapist Capabilities

Successful therapists depend both on a sound knowledge base, as well as adequate funding, when treating their clients. Intensive training in DBT for therapists is crucial, and advanced training and supervision by a DBT expert is recommended. Optimally, the consultant should have experience in treating individuals with ID. Staying abreast of current disabilities field literature can increase DBT therapists' understanding of the myriad of relevant processes that impact this heterogeneous population.

Additionally, funding can be challenging. Payments for each element of comprehensive DBT services (over a year or more) may require the therapist to explore available resources through the State, provider agencies, and/or insurance companies. The Brown,

Brown, and DiBiasio (2013) Skills System pilot data article contains an analysis of the State's cost savings; sharing the article with funders may be helpful.

Beginning DBT-SS Treatment

Intake Process

The individual's family, agency staff, or a state social worker are likely to initiate the referral for DBT therapy. Orienting the care providers to DBT to ensure adequate resource allocation to support the multi-modal treatment process will be a good investment of time. It is also important to make consistent transportation arrangements at the outset. Determining the team members' commitment to learning the DBT Skills and functioning as in-vivo skills coaches are important. Additionally, the team should acknowledge that the client will need to have access to phone skills coaching with the therapist in between sessions.

The person making the referral may initially not have all of this information. The DBT therapist may need to have multiple conversations with different team members prior to the first session with the client. Although the team discusses preliminary arrangements, without contact with the client, it is impossible to accurately assess whether a bridge between the client and therapist will form.

Receiving a comprehensive packet of referral information from collateral contacts prior to the first session can be useful. The DBT therapist will want information from the individual, yet gaining clarity about historical information may be an evolving process. Asking the team for any past evaluations and summaries can supply the therapist with frames of reference that can structure the history gathering process with the individual.

Optimally, the client contacts the therapist directly (with staff assistance if necessary) to arrange a first session. It may be easier to speak with the staff, but it is important for the therapist to begin immediately investing in the relationship with the individual. This approach hopefully signals to the individual that the DBT relationship is radically different from other helping relationships previously experienced.

Initial Sessions and Understanding Autonomy

During the first session, the DBT therapist tries to establish communication and a rapport with the individual. If possible, the therapist talks to the individual without the staff in the room. This demonstrates that DBT therapy is a 1:1 relationship between equal people, it assumes capacity.

Completing an informed consent document is one of the preliminary activities the therapist and individual do. The DBT therapist needs to orient the individual about the therapy process, so that the client can make a self-determined, autonomous decision about being in the session and what the guidelines are. Posing clarifying questions and asking the individual to re-explain concepts to the therapist creates an opportunity for the therapist to ensure comprehension and rectify misunderstood points.

There may be intra-personal and environmental factors associated with individuals with ID acting autonomously. For example, Petner-Arrey and Copeland (2014) highlighted that there are "significant challenges within the support service system that often prevent promotion of autonomy for people with ID" (p. 42). The barriers included, consumers and staff having competing interests or mandates, staff asserting their agenda rather than including the individuals' priorities, disagreement between the consumer and staff about safety being a primary focus of support, and institutional goals outweighing individual goals.

The therapist must be aware of engaging in similar patterns, assess whether the individual may be deferring to authority or offering superficial compliance to placate the therapist. The DBT therapist will want to have ample discussions related to goal setting and commitment. Asking multiple clarifying questions and DBT commitment strategies can help determine the client's level of commitment to engaging in therapy or attempting to satisfy others.

Assessing Whether DBT Fits the Dyad

As in standard DBT, the dyad of therapist and client discuss the client's challenges, goals, and commitment. Regarding the exploration of historical information, executive functioning and memory deficits may impede the person's ability to sequence and organized synthesized timelines. In addition to cognitive processing difficulties, the individual is likely to have experienced challenges and/or trauma associated with a myriad of social systems from family relationships, education systems, community settings, vocational placements, and congregate living arrangements that may produce emotions during the assessment process. During interactions, the therapist can use the Quick Step Assessment to evaluate the individual's level of dysregulation and adjust interview strategies. It is the evolving process, rather than external time frames, that determines the pace of therapy.

If the individual demonstrates CBs on a regular basis, it may make sense to discuss a safety plan prior to delving into challenging topics. Initially, the client may opt to speak to the staff member, call a support person, or take a brief walk with staff. Being familiar with the client's support plan helps the DBT therapist generate solutions that fit within the individual's guidelines. Once the therapist and client have a therapeutic relationship, in-session activities such as paced breathing or a card sort (dividing a standard deck of playing cards first by colour and then by suit) help decrease arousal and allow the client to remain engaged in the session.

Therapy Agreements

The DBT therapist will orient the individual to the concept of therapy agreements. Developing written therapy agreements (client and therapist) may be helpful, provided that they use simple language and/or images to address elements included in standard

DBT agreements. For example, the statement "I agree to be in DBT therapy for one year," followed by a check box labelled "yes" or "no" creates a tangible reference to the client and therapist committing to the therapy process. Be sure the client clearly understands how long a year is. A thorough discussion of all related topics needs to happen prior to writing, reviewing, and signing therapy agreements so that genuine commitment exists.

Ending Sessions

Prior to ending a session, the DBT therapist communicates with the individual about his level of emotion, regulation status, and strategies the individual will use to manage stress between sessions. Reviewing basic concepts related to the Safety Planning and New-Me Activities can be helpful. If there is a staff or family member present, the therapist may consider consulting with the individual about checking in with the support person prior to leaving the office. This conversation can be an in-vivo practice session where the client communicates about his or her status and advocates about regulation and co-regulation activities (involving collateral supports) that may facilitate his or her effective self-management between sessions.

BASIC TREATMENT STRATEGIES

Dialectical Strategies

Understanding vulnerability factors, transactional communication patterns, and managing cognitive load (e.g., Quick Step Assessment) help the DBT-SS therapist use standard DBT strategies, such as dialectical strategies, effectively with the ID population. Standard dialectical strategies are key with this client group, as long as the DBT therapist is mindful of the individual's cognitive load status during the intervention. Although speed and flow are crucial, rapid shifts without ample explanation or transition can induce cognitive overload. Similarly, the individual must understand any metaphors used. When overloaded, the individual is unlikely to discuss the confusion; conversely, some form of conflict, avoidance, and/or superficial compliance may happen. The therapist may misattribute the controlling variable of this TIB as wilfulness, rather than cognitive overload, potentially creating a negative transaction. When the client comprehends all of the points in the discussion, he or she may be more likely to remain cognitively regulated and benefit from the DBT "dancing" experience (Linehan, 1993a, p. 203).

Validation Strategies

As in standard DBT, validation strategies are vital with this client group. The major difference is in the enhanced responsibilities of the therapist to provide functional validation related to (a) establishing effective bi-directional communication and (b) making adjustments to interventions to improve accessibility for the individual with ID. Similarly, the therapist must understand the complex environmental factors that the individual has dealt with throughout their lifetime in order to provide salient verbal validation.

Stepping back and attempting to live within the individual's context can augment awareness and increase the relevance of validation. For example, an adult with ID may receive 24-hour supervision. Individual monitoring and behaviour-related feedback are available to the client 24/7, every year. Supervision and instructions for the client may come from a therapist far younger than themselves, which might be demoralizing. The staff may not have adequate training about how to interact in a way that fosters respect and self-determination. The staff may be from a culture that has different norms related to disabilities. The staff may speak English only as a second language, which may impact communication transactions. Programmes may be chronically mismanaged or under-funded; under-staffing may reduce opportunities for community access and choice. Unfortunately, individuals with ID often experience highly complex problems within the care system framework, and may have limited resources to address them.

The DBT therapist needs to empathize with the individual related to these issues, rather than treat the client with ID as different from herself. The therapist must be mindful not to recreate similar problematic transactions. Additionally, these types of environmental factors can exacerbate target behaviours and therapists should acknowledge any possible antecedents during the behaviour chain analysis processes. Solution analysis must include tactics to alter systemic problems and accept factors that are temporarily unchangeable.

Problem Solving

Problem solving is a dynamic, multiple-step process. Individuals with ID often experience difficulties with problem solving because (a) the support systems are complex, (b) power imbalances and biases impact transactions, and (c) the ID impacts the individual's execution of problem-solving strategies. The Skills System provides a structured framework that teaches the steps of problem solving, as well as the requisite emotion regulation tactics that support those processes.

Behaviour Analysis and Solution Analysis Strategies

Diary cards function to help the therapist "obtain information on a daily basis about relevant behavior" (Linehan, 1993a, p. 184). The goal is to be able to efficiently address target behaviours through the spectrum of DBT strategies (e.g., validation, behaviour chain analysis, solution analysis). The individual's academic abilities impact the design of the diary card (Figure 34.1); non-readers will need simple text and visual

Dates:_____   **MARY's Diary Card**

	Targets I am Working On			Stressful Event	Label & Rate	Skills I Used
Mon.	Self Harm: Urges: Yes No Action: Yes No	Run Away: Urges: Yes No Action: Yes No	Pacing: Urges: Yes No Action: Yes No	HOME WORK What start it?	Feeling: 0-1-2-3-4-5	
Tues.	Self Harm: Urges: Yes No Action: Yes No	Run Away: Urges: Yes No Action: Yes No	Pacing: Urges: Yes No Action: Yes No	HOME WORK What start it?	Feeling: 0-1-2-3-4-5	
Wed.	Self Harm: Urges: Yes No Action: Yes No	Run Away: Urges: Yes No Action: Yes No	Pacing: Urges: Yes No Action: Yes No	HOME WORK What start it?	Feeling: 0-1-2-3-4-5	
Thur.	Self Harm: Urges: Yes No Action: Yes No	Run Away: Urges: Yes No Action: Yes No	Pacing: Urges: Yes No Action: Yes No	HOME WORK What start it?	Feeling: 0-1-2-3-4-5	
Fri.	Self Harm: Urges: Yes No Action: Yes No	Run Away: Urges: Yes No Action: Yes No	Pacing: Urges: Yes No Action: Yes No	HOME WORK What start it?	Feeling: 0-1-2-3-4-5	
Sat.	Self Harm: Urges: Yes No Action: Yes No	Run Away: Urges: Yes No Action: Yes No	Pacing: Urges: Yes No Action: Yes No	HOME WORK What start it?	Feeling: 0-1-2-3-4-5	
Sun.	Self Harm: Urges: Yes No Action: Yes No	Run Away: Urges: Yes No Action: Yes No	Pacing: Urges: Yes No Action: Yes No	HOME WORK What start it?	Feeling: 0-1-2-3-4-5	

FIGURE 34.1 Example of an adapted diary card.

representations (e.g. cue pictures, circling images, and check boxes) to document the frequency and intensity of emotions, urges, and actions. Creating individualized modified diary cards in session with the client to target specific behaviours currently addressed in treatment can be helpful. Adjusting the diary card form until it functions effectively is often necessary.

In addition to a modified diary card, if the client receives staff supervision, creating a daily communication sheet that support staff complete during day and evening activities may also help. The communication sheet should highlight targets, activities, and skills use. The client may want to work collaboratively with collaterals to complete the communication sheet each day. Reviewing the diary card and communication sheet in the beginning of session together can facilitate targeting and the behaviour chain analysis process. Greater amounts of information results in less time spent to gain clarity of time frames (i.e., sequencing can be challenging due to executive functioning difficulties in those with ID).

The client and therapist should discuss possible power imbalances that may occur related to collaterals completing communication sheets. On the positive side, reading the staff reports may aid evaluation and intervention with staff behaviours that contribute to problematic transactions. If the client cannot read and write, seeing people write notes about them may understandably elicit strong emotions. Overall, the benefits may outweigh the difficulties in Stage 1 of treatment, when there are complex targets that require behaviour chain analysis, solution analysis, and practising adaptive alternative behaviours.

As in standard DBT, conducting behaviour chain analyses are primary strategies. The DBT therapist helps the client define the problem behaviour, conducts a chain analysis, and generates hypotheses. In DBT-SS, the six parts of Skill 1: Clear Picture (e.g., notice the breath, notice surroundings, do a body check, label and rate feelings, notice thoughts, and notice urges) explore the micro-transitions of behaviour that comprise the chain links. The DBT-SS therapist helps the client get a Clear Picture of the antecedents, the problem, and the consequences. Additionally, Skill 2: On-Track Thinking (e.g., Stop and Check It [thumbs up for on-track urges and thumbs down for off-track urges], Turn It, Cheerleading, and Make a Skills Plan) are integrated into this investigation. Finding the discriminating stimulus or point when the client gave thumbs up, instead of thumbs down, to off-track urges is important. The behaviour chain analysis includes Skill 3: On-Track Action as the dyad discusses whether actions were, upon reflection, on-track or off-track to the individual's goals.

Using the Skills System framework to understand problem behaviour chains lays the foundation for developing a solution analysis plan. Often the individual goes off-track when he engages in Calm Only skills (i.e., Skill 6: Problem Solving, Skill 7: Expressing Myself, Skill 8: Getting It Right, and/or Skill 9: Relationship Care) at too high a level of emotion, reducing effectiveness. The dyad produces an improved skills chain that takes into account the situation and any forces that may undermine the success of the chain. Ideally, each chain contains mindfulness processes (Clear Picture), reappraisal and planning (On-Track Thinking), and behavioural activation (On-Track Action) of adaptive responses (e.g. Safety Plan, New-Me Activity, Problem Solving, Expressing Myself, Getting It Right, and Relationship Care).

When conducting a behaviour chain and solution analysis, the therapist uses the Quick Step Assessment and other tactics to accommodate cognitive challenges. Memory deficits, executive functioning impairment, and communication difficulties can affect the process of assembling synthesized time lines. Visual aids representing elements of the chain can help the dyad put the puzzle together. Accomplishing an effective assessment of the situation combined with an adequate solution analysis with an opportunity for practice of the adaptive skills requires effective time management and is frequently a challenge.

The following case example exemplifies how various strategies can be integrated during a behaviour chain analysis (Box 34.1). The client, Mary, a 33-year-old woman, has been diagnosed with PTSD, BPD, and Mild ID. She reads and writes at approximately a second-grade level. Mary has a history of self-harm that includes cutting, swallowing objects/toxic chemicals, tying cords around her neck, head banging, and darting into traffic. She lives in a community residence with three other women and receives 24-hour supervision and attends a vocational day programme. She has been in DBT-SS treatment for 10 months. This dialogue begins after Mary entered the therapy office,

Box 34.1 Case example (treatment strategies in bold)

Dialogue	Therapist Thoughts and Strategies
Therapist: (Reading the diary card) Mary, I see that you circled that you had urges to self-harm on Wednesday and that you did self-harm on Thursday. Is that right?	**Diary card review:** I need to make sure I know about all of the level 1 targets. I need to have a clear sense of Mary's week related to her targets so I can use all DBT strategies effectively.
Mary: Yes.	
Therapist: You and I spoke on Wednesday afternoon, right?	**Reinforcing adaptive behaviour:** I positively reinforce her calling for skills coaching on Wednesday.
Mary: Yeah, after I got home from work.	
Therapist: Calling was an On-Track Action. We talked about your urges to swallow a battery. We talked on the speaker phone with Kate (staff) about you doing a written safety plan together.	**Secondary target:** Not calling on Thursday is a therapy-interfering behaviour that will get addressed at some point.
Mary: We did it.	
Therapist: So, Thursday. You and I didn't talk.	**Assessing vulnerability factors:** Justin seems to be a stressor.
Mary: No, had a problem at the day programme. I was mad at Justin (boyfriend).	**Assessing primary target:** Mary has executive functioning deficits; I need to triangulate data from multiple sources to pinpoint target.
	Validation strategies: I validated the feeling and reinforced skill use.
Therapist: Were there any other targets this week?	**Assess transactional patterns:** The staff sheets can help me find missing information and diagnose transactional patterns that trigger Mary.
Mary: No.	
Therapist: How about you and I read through the staff communication sheets. Are you OK with doing that?	**Selection of primary target:** I reinforced adaptive behaviour and pivoted to non-judgmentally highlighting of TIB. We need to stay focused on the self-harm primary target chain analysis.
Mary: I hate it when they write about me, it gets me upset.	**Behaviour Chain Analysis:** I define the problem behaviour. I want to partner with her so I get informed consent about moving ahead.
Therapist: I can understand that, ... Good Clear Picture of your feeling, though that sounds like the "anger" emotion. Ok if we look through the sheets?	**Reinforcing dialectical functioning:** I highlight that she is feeling uncomfortable and facing the moment as it is; the "good news" comment addresses dialectics in a concrete way.
Mary: Yes, I guess so. Staff piss me off. They don't listen to me.	**Defining beginning, middle, and end of the chain:** I use the Feeling Rating Scale (0–5) to map the chaining process. I confirm the rating to be sure she is not under- or over-rating (at a level 3 she can talk and listen and be on-track).
Therapist: Ok, I see here that you talked to staff on Wednesday. Kate said you did a good job on the Safety Plan. I see you went to the ER on Thurday night.	
Mary: I swallowed a AA battery from the TV remote.	

Therapist: I don't see any other incidents in the staff sheets. Did you have any other self-harming behaviours this week?

Mary: No, I know I should've called you. I was just really upset.

Therapist: We can talk about that in a few minutes. We have to do our behaviour chain about your self-harm on Thursday so we can see what happened. You good with that?

Mary: I hate talking about this because it makes me upset all over again.

Therapist: I get that. The good news is, you are a skills master when you do On-Track Actions like this. We can both know what happened and then we can talk about what we can do differently next time. What level are you at now?

Mary: About a 3.

Therpist: So, you are saying that you can talk and listen and still be on-track right now?

Mary: Yeah, but I might go to a 4.

Therapist: True. It isn't easy doing our behaviour chains. If you go to a level 4 what should we do?

Mary: Maybe take a break. Do some breathing.

Therapist: Last week you did really well when we practised the seated mountain pose.

Mary: That was pretty good. I'll try that.

Therapist: Ok, so Thursday. What happened?

Mary: I was really mad at Justin. He was sitting with Carol at lunch— you remember his ex at day programme. I started looking around for stuff.

Therapist: Stuff?

Cope Ahead: Mary has difficulty with transitions. I want her to know what to do at a 4 (strong emotion with off-track action urges), before she gets there, so that she can shift gears and be effective at all levels of emotions.

Searching for the discriminating stimulus: I need to find the second she shifted from on-track to off-track. When did she shift from a 4 to a 5 emotion (overwhelming emotion: harming self, other, or property)?

Quick Step Assessment: Mary has difficulty with sequencing. I chunk the time frames, so we are oriented.

Assessing antecedents: I want to see if she was stressed in the morning before lunch. I want to map her escalation pattern.

Continually assess accuracy: I have to be sure the rating is accurate in relation to her behaviour versus self-reported affect.

Didactic strategy: I positively reinforced her adjusting the rating and highlighted how we can (dialectically) feel terrible and still be on-track.

Reciprocal strategy: I get consent for the shift to another activity.

Quick Step Assessment: The worksheet will offer structure to abstract concepts/time frames; it also teaches the skill Clear Picture.

Mindful awareness: I want to start with what Mary already is aware (rating the emotion) of to increase self-efficacy. Then we expand to the other parts of Clear Picture.

Pinpointing the discriminating stimulus: She said the urge, great! I think she is still at a 4 at this point. I positively reinforce her having a Clear Picture and wanted to separe the urge and action.

Antecedent: Mary was cognitively dysregulated ("spaced out"). Pacing is on her diary card as an antecedent behaviour. We have talked before about her doing a Talking Safety Plan in that situation. She shifted from a 4 to a 5 at this point.

(continued)

Box 34.1 Continued

Dialogue	Therapist Thoughts and Strategies
Mary: Stuff I could swallow. Therapist: When did you swallow the battery? Mary: I'm not sure. Therapist: Was it before or after lunch? Mary: It was right after lunch. Therapist: How were you doing before lunch? Mary: I was cleaning the offices. Then I went to the day programme. Therapist: Tell me about when you got there. Mary: Not good! I saw him sitting with HER. Therapist: Tell me about that moment when you saw them? Mary: I was at a 5. Therapist: You hurt yourself right then? Mary: No, it was after that. I guess I was a 4. But it felt like a 5. Therapist: True, good observation. A level 4 can feel super intense, the difference is that at a 5 we are hurting ourselves, others, or property. (Mary nods). How about we go through the Clear Picture handout so we understand a little more about what was happening. Mary: OK, that's fine. Therapist: So you were at a 4 … what emotion were you feeling? Mary: Pissed off. Therapist: What's next on the sheet? Mary: My breath. I think I was breathing really fast. Therapist: Excellent (Therapist points to the next picture). How about your surroundings in that moment? Mary: I was coming in the door and *they* were at the table by the window. Therapist: Good job, how about this one? Mary: Body check. My heart was pounding. I wanted to run. Therapist: Good Clear Picture of your urge. Did you run? Mary: No, I started pacing.	**Solution analysis:** I positively reinforce her engaging in the behaviour analysis. I orient her to our need to look at two situations (with the visual aid of my fingers) that need solution analysis. I ask for consent before moving ahead.

Therapist: What was happening when you were pacing?

Mary: I was spaced out. I start staring at stuff.

Therapist: Did you say anything to staff? Or did they say anything to you?

Mary: No. They weren't paying attention. I walked by the clicker and grabbed it. I took the battery out and ate it.

Therapist: I know it isn't easy to go back over this and you did a good job. I feel like I understand what happened. Thank you. Now, how about we go back over two important times and think about what skills could help you in that moment. (counting on my fingers) First, is when you walked into the day programme and saw them. And then second, when you get spaced out and start pacing. We have to know what to do at both of these times. Does that make sense?

Mary: OK.

greetings were exchanged, and the therapist has started reviewing the documentation (diary card and staff communication sheets).

Insight Strategies

Although insight is not a mechanism of change in DBT, the ability to understand patterns of one's own behaviour is a useful skill. It is a myth that individuals with ID lack the capacity for insight and self-awareness. To support the standard DBT insight strategies, the DBT-SS therapist integrates the Skills System language to scaffold complicated constructs creating a common language that the dyad can build upon. Using the Quick Step Assessment helps the therapist adjust communication so that there are seamless transitions across complex ideas, rather than gaps that derail the individual's ability to fully understand abstract concepts.

Commitment Strategies

Commitment strategies are used in their standard forms, as low self-efficacy, academic failures, traumatic experiences, and foundational skill deficits can reduce the individual's enthusiasm for engaging in novel activities. Taking sufficient time to explore commitment and non-commitment alternatives using multiple commitment strategies can help individuals make informed choices. The DBT therapist should assess the client's level of commitment, or whether he is verbalizing commitment that reflects merely superficial compliance. Additionally, revisiting commitment is necessary; validating the changeable nature of commitment can foster the shift from polarization to synthesis processes during treatment.

Change Procedures

As in standard DBT evaluating whether the individual with ID has requisite behaviour in his behaviour repertoire is a first step. The Skills System builds basic emotion regulation, distress tolerance, interpersonal effectiveness, and mindfulness capacities. Salient points to evaluate should include an examination of what reinforces problem behaviours.

The in-session use of contingencies is similar to standard DBT. The DBT-SS therapist orients the individual to contingency management, uses reinforcement, highlights natural consequences, and implements extinction to shape behaviours. Similar to standard DBT, aversive contingencies warrant thoughtful consideration. Communication breakdowns can confuse situations, and any misunderstandings need clearing up before using an aversive contingency due to the deleterious potential impact to the therapeutic relationship. As with standard DBT, DBT-SS includes informal exposure practices; the

Skills System offers strategies to help the individual experience uncomfortable emotions in session and to assemble effective responses. Limited data exists relating to formal exposure techniques with this population.

Observing Limits Procedures

Communication challenges may enhance the need to explain limits thoroughly and confirm comprehension of the parameters. Memory deficits may impede recognition and recall. Verbal cues and visual aids may remind the individual about the issue and prompt more adaptive responses.

Suicide Crisis Protocol

Communication and cognitive processing challenges may impact the delivery of the standard DBT special treatment strategies, but not the functions. Higher cognitive load may happen when an individual is in crisis, which can impede communication patterns. Ensuring clear communication is a foundational step to managing crisis and suicidal behaviours. Creating written safety plans (using language and/or visual aids as needed) for use during high-risk times can help the individual manage behaviours.

The therapist may need to orient the client and communicate with the team directly when the client verbalizes intent to self-injure or harm others. The therapist should ensure that the agency has adequate procedures in place to manage high-risk situations as well as a framework to evaluate when the individual requires emergency services. Additionally, the therapist may need to foster inter-team communication (e.g., nurse, primary care doctor, and/or psychiatrist) related to managing acute behaviours to ensure the safety of the individual.

SUMMARY

Many individuals diagnosed with ID experience emotional, cognitive, and behavioural dysregulation. Standard DBT includes comprehensive treatment elements essential to addressing these problems, yet accommodation is necessary to improve accessibility to DBT for individuals with cognitive impairment and co-occurring mental health issues. This chapter highlights transactional and vulnerability factors that commonly impact both the intra- and interpersonal patterns of behaviour. The material also offers practitioners strategies to facilitate adjusting standard individual therapy techniques in terms of cognitive load demands, while maintaining adherence to DBT. Additionally, it shows an adapted DBT-informed skills curriculum (Skills System) specifically designed for this population, as well as information relative to how to integrate the skills framework.

Key Points for Clinicians

- Accommodations to DBT for individuals with ID need to remain adherent to the model; the delivery mechanisms are altered, rather than core processes.

- It is essential for the DBT therapist to have heightened self-awareness regarding perceptions and communication patterns to foster positive transactional patterns in the client.

- The DBT therapist treating individuals with ID must understand how to manage factors associated with cognitive load in order to design and adjust treatment interventions.

- The therapist needs to understand, be empathetic about, and manage the complex environmental factors that impact the lives of individuals with ID.

- The complex and detailed skills curricula that form part of standard DBT require some adaptation for clients with ID. The Skills System is one such adaptation that provides the client with an accessible emotion regulation skills framework that promotes self-regulation and co-regulation processes to enhance the generalization of skills into the individual's natural environment.

References

Ali, A., Scior, K., Ratti, V., Strydom, A., King, M., & Hassiotis, A. (2013). Discrimination and other barriers to accessing health care: Perspectives of patients with mild and moderate intellectual disability and their carers. *PLOS One, 8*(8), 1–13.

Beadle-Brown, J., Mansell, J., Cambridge, P., Milne, A., & Whelton, B. (2010). Adult protection of people with intellectual disabilities: Incidence, nature and responses. *Journal of Applied Research in Intellectual Disabilities, 23*(6), 573–584.

Bedard, C., Burke, L, & Ludwig, S. (1998). Dealing with sexual abuse of adults with a developmental disability who also have impaired communication: Supportive procedures for detection. *The Canadian Journal of Human Sexuality, 79*(1), 79–92.

Brown, J. (2016). *The emotion regulation skills system for the cognitively challenged client: A DBT approach*. New York: The Guilford Press.

Brown, J. F., Brown, M. Z., & Dibiasio, P. (2013). Treating individuals with intellectual disabilities and challenging behaviors with adapted dialectical behavior therapy. *Journal of Mental Health Research in Intellectual Disabilities, 6*(4), 280–303.

Coons, K. D., & Watson, S. L. (2013). Conducting research with individuals who have intellectual disabilities: Ethical and practical implications for qualitative research. *Journal on Developmental Disability, 19*(2), 14–25.

Ditchman, N., Kosyluk, K., Werner, S., Jones, N., Elg, B., & Corrigan, P. W. (2013). Stigma and intellectual disability: Potential application of mental illness research. *Rehabilitation Psychology, 58*(2), 206–216.

Emerson, E., & Hatton, C. (2014). *Health inequities and people with intellectual disabilities*. Cambridge University Press: Cambridge, UK.

Greenspan, S. I., & Lourie, R. S. (1981). Developmental structuralist approach to the classification of adaptive and pathological personality organizations: Application to infancy and early childhood. *American Journal of Psychiatry*, *138*(6), 725–735.

Hansen, J., Kutzner, F., & Wanke, M. (2013). Money and thinking: Reminders of money trigger abstract construal and shape consumer judgments. *Journal of Consumer Research*, *39*, 1154–1156.

Hove, O., & Havik, O. E. (2008). Mental disorders and problem behavior in a community sample of adults with intellectual disability: Three-Month Prevalence and Comorbidity. *Journal of Mental Health Research in Intellectual Disabilities*, *1*(4), 223–237.

Irvine, A. (2010). Conducting qualitative research with individuals with developmental disabilities: Methodological and ethical considerations. *Developmental Disabilities Bulletin*, *38*(1–2), 21–34.

Jahoda, A., Selkirk, M., Trower, P., Pert, C., Kroese, B. S., Dagnan, D. & Burford, B. (2009). The balance of power in therapeutic interactions with individuals who have intellectual disabilities. *British Journal of Clinical Psychology*, *48*, 63–77.

Linehan, M. M. (1993a). *Cognitive behavioral treatment for borderline personality disorder.* New York: Guilford Press.

Linehan, M. M. (1993b). *Skills training manual for treating borderline personality disorder.* New York: Guilford Press.

McCormack, B., Kavanagh, D., Caffrey, S., & Power, A. (2005). Investigating sexual abuse: Findings of a 15-year longitudinal study. *Journal of Applied Research in Intellectual Disabilities*, *18*, 217–227.

Mevissen, L., Lievegoed, R., Seubert, A., & Jongh, A. D. (2011). Do persons with intellectual disability and limited verbal capacities respond to trauma treatment? *Journal of Intellectual & Developmental Disability*, *36*(4), 278–283.

Norona, A. N,. & Baker, B. L. (2014). The transactional relationship between parenting and emotion regulation in children with or without developmental delays. *Research in Developmental Disabilities*, *35*, 3209–3216.

Petner-Arrey, J., & Copeland, S. R. (2014). "You have to care." Perceptions of promoting autonomy in support setting for adults with intellectual disabilities. *British Journal of Learning Disabilities*, *43*, 38–48.

Sullivan, P. M., & Knutson, J. F. (2000). Maltreatment and disabilities: A population-based epidemiological study. *Child Abuse & Neglect*, *24*(10), 1257–1273.

Sweller, J. (1988). Cognitive load during problem solving: Effects on learning. *Cognitive Science*, *12*, 257–285.

Sweller, J. (2010). Element interactivity and intrinsic, extraneous, and germane cognitive load. *Educational Psychology Review*, *22*(2), 123–138.

Weiss, J. A. (2012). Mental health care for Canadians with developmental disabilities. *Canadian Psychology*, *53*(1), 67–69.

CHAPTER 35

....

INTEGRATING POST-TRAUMATIC STRESS DISORDER TREATMENT INTO DIALECTICAL BEHAVIOUR THERAPY

Clinical Application and Implementation of the DBT Prolonged Exposure Protocol

....

MELANIE S. HARNED AND SARA C. SCHMIDT

DIALECTICAL Behaviour Therapy (DBT; Linehan, 1993) is intended to be a comprehensive treatment capable of flexibly targeting the full range of problems that manifest in multi-diagnostic clients. Research supports DBT's efficacy in treating a wide variety of problem behaviours, mental health disorders, and psychosocial impairment. Historically, however, DBT has been less effective in targeting post-traumatic stress disorder (PTSD), a common and often debilitating disorder among individuals receiving DBT. This chapter describes the rationale for and structure of the DBT Prolonged Exposure (DBT PE) protocol that has been developed to be integrated into DBT to facilitate routine and direct targeting of PTSD. In addition, it reviews the evidence base for this integrated treatment approach and discusses challenges that may arise during implementation of the DBT PE protocol in routine practice settings.

BACKGROUND

....

Linehan's (1993) biosocial model posits that borderline personality disorder (BPD) and pervasive emotion dysregulation develop due to a transaction between biologically based emotional vulnerability and an invalidating social environment. Accordingly, many individuals receiving DBT report a history of various types of severe invalidation, which can include sexual and physical violence and other forms of trauma, and these experiences are often associated with significant post-traumatic stress symptoms. Among individuals with BPD receiving DBT, the rate of PTSD ranges from 36–50% in research settings (Linehan et al., 1999; Linehan et al., 2006; McMain et al., 2009) and 57–83% in routine practice settings (Barnicot & Priebe, 2013; Barnicot, 2016). In addition, PTSD is associated with greater impairment among individuals with BPD, including more frequent suicidal and self-injurious behaviour, greater depression, poorer physical health, and more impaired global functioning (e.g., Bolton, Mueser, & Rosenberg, 2006; Harned, Rizvi, & Linehan, 2010; Rüsch et al., 2007).

Although PTSD is one of the most common and impairing disorders among individuals receiving DBT, it is the disorder least likely to remit during treatment (Harned et al., 2008) with rates of diagnostic remission ranging from 12–35% (Barnicot, 2016; Harned, Korslund, & Linehan, 2014; Harned et al., 2008). Moreover, individuals entering treatment with PTSD, particularly severe PTSD, exhibit poorer outcomes during DBT, including more frequent self-harm, lower likelihood of eliminating acute suicide risk and suicidal and self-injurious behaviour, and higher dissociation (Barnicot, 2016; Barnicot & Priebe, 2013; Harned et al., 2010). These poorer outcomes are likely due to the fact that PTSD maintains or exacerbates other problems; for example, individuals with BPD and PTSD report a greater likelihood of engaging in self-harm in response to flashbacks, nightmares, and thoughts about sexual abuse and rape than those with BPD alone (Harned, Rizvi, & Linehan, 2010). Taken together, these findings indicate the importance of developing more effective methods of treating PTSD during DBT both to improve PTSD outcomes and to more effectively address other functionally related problems.

The Treatment Model

DBT utilizes a stage model of treatment with each stage addressing different and progressively more functional treatment goals (Linehan, 1999). Stage 1 focuses on achieving control over life-threatening and other severe behaviours, Stage 2 aims to reduce "quiet desperation" by treating PTSD and increasing the ability to experience emotions effectively, Stage 3 addresses non-disabling problems in living, and Stage 4 focuses on achieving the capacity for sustained joy. The integrated DBT and DBT PE protocol treatment adheres to DBT's stage model of treatment, which is also consistent with expert consensus treatment guidelines for complex PTSD (Cloitre et al., 2012). Specifically, the treatment begins by using DBT to stabilize problems that are likely to make trauma-focused treatment unsafe or ineffective (Stage 1). Once sufficient stability has been achieved, the DBT PE protocol is integrated into ongoing DBT to directly target PTSD (Stage 2). The final stage of treatment focuses on addressing any problems in living that remain after PTSD has been treated (Stage 3). The primary targets and treatment strategies of each stage of the treatment are described in the next section.

Pre-Treatment: Orientation and Commitment

Prior to starting Stage 1, clients complete a pre-treatment phase that is focused on identifying treatment goals, orientating to DBT and the DBT PE protocol, and obtaining commitments to stay alive and engage in treatment. During this initial pre-treatment phase, therapists complete all of the standard DBT pre-treatment tasks while also weaving in discussion of PTSD and its treatment. For example, clients are asked whether they wish to make reducing PTSD a treatment goal and are orientated to the general rationale and procedures of the DBT PE protocol as a means of treating PTSD. During this discussion, it is often helpful to provide clients with psychoeducation about PTSD and common reactions to trauma. Orientation to the biosocial model typically includes discussion of how trauma and severe invalidation impact the development of BPD and/or emotion regulation problems. In addition, when orientating clients to the DBT target hierarchy, PTSD is described as a quality-of-life (QoL)-interfering behaviour that cannot be addressed until life-threatening and therapy-interfering behaviours (TIB) are sufficiently controlled. Clients are also orientated to the requirement that they must achieve at least two months of abstinence from all forms of suicidal and non-suicidal self-injury (NSSI) before they can begin PTSD treatment. Clarification of this contingency during pre-treatment often has the effect of increasing client motivation to achieve control over these life-threatening behaviours quickly in order to receive a treatment they view as critical to their recovery. Whereas clients are required to commit to engaging in DBT (at least for some period of time) before progressing to Stage 1, they do not have to commit to engaging in the DBT PE protocol. Although many clients are clearly committed to receiving DBT PE from the beginning of treatment, for others this is a decision that is made during Stage 1.

Stage 1:   Reducing Behavioural Dyscontrol and Increasing Behavioural Skills

In the first stage of treatment, standard DBT is delivered without adaptation according to Linehan's manuals (1993, 2015a, b). The overarching goal of Stage 1 is to prepare clients to safely and effectively engage in subsequent PTSD treatment by reducing behavioural dyscontrol and increasing behavioural skills. Treatment includes weekly individual therapy, weekly group skills training, between-session phone coaching, and weekly therapist consultation team. Standard DBT strategies and protocols are used to target behaviours that are a higher-priority than PTSD due to their life-threatening nature (e.g., acute suicide risk, suicidal and non-suicidal self-injury) or because they are likely to interfere with later PTSD treatment (e.g., severe dissociation, uncontrolled substance use, frequent refusal to engage in treatment tasks). In many cases, these higher-priority behaviours function as a way to cope with PTSD symptoms and painful trauma-related emotions and cognitions. In such cases, a present-focused approach is used in which clients are taught behavioural skills to more effectively cope with PTSD, with the goal of reducing its impact on current functioning. For example, crisis survival skills can be used to help clients cope with intense intrusive symptoms (e.g., flashbacks), mindfulness skills are taught to increase awareness of the present moment and reduce dissociation, emotion regulation skills help clients learn to reduce the intensity of painful trauma-related emotions, and reality acceptance skills can be used to help clients accept their PTSD and the suffering it causes until it can be treated. In sum, Stage 1 DBT can be viewed as helping clients to effectively manage their PTSD using a combination of change- and acceptance-focused skills without directly targeting the underlying disorder.

Importantly, trauma processing (i.e., in-depth discussion of the details of past trauma) is proscribed in Stage 1 due to concerns about high-risk clients' ability to safely manage the intense emotions elicited by this work (Linehan, 1993). Instead, Stage 1 treatment focuses on helping clients acquire the skills necessary to effectively engage in subsequent trauma-focused treatment. Given that the DBT PE protocol is an exposure-based treatment, particular emphasis is placed on increasing clients' capacity to experience intense emotions without avoiding or suppressing by using skills such as mindfulness of current emotion, radical acceptance, and willingness. As treatment progresses, clients are encouraged to apply these skills specifically in the context of low- to moderate-intensity exposure-like tasks; for example, using the skill of opposite action to approach feared situations that are not actually dangerous (e.g., going to a crowded store, riding in an elevator) and then using mindfulness of current emotion while in the feared situation to allow the experience of uncomfortable emotions and physical sensations. These types of exposure-like tasks are often assigned towards the end of Stage 1 as behavioural tests to evaluate clients' readiness to move on to Stage 2 PTSD treatment.

As Stage 1 progresses and clients express interest in receiving the DBT PE protocol, therapists orientate clients to the specific criteria for determining readiness to begin the treatment, including: (1) not at imminent risk of suicide, (2) no suicidal or non-suicidal self-injury for at least two months, (3) ability to control urges to engage in suicidal and non-suicidal self-injury when in the presence of cues for those behaviours, (4) no serious therapy-interfering behaviour, (5) PTSD is the client's highest-priority goal, and (6) ability and willingness to experience intense emotions without escaping. For each of these readiness criteria, therapists work with clients to collaboratively define specific behaviours that must change and select a target start date for the DBT PE protocol. Thus, the treatment is delivered in an idiographic and principle-driven manner, with clients achieving readiness for Stage 2 at different times, depending on their progress toward their individual readiness goals.

For clients who are ambivalent about or not interested in receiving the DBT PE protocol, therapists actively work during Stage 1 to increase client motivation to engage in the treatment if/when treating PTSD is believed to be necessary for the client to achieve their "life worth living" goals (Linehan, 1993). A variety of motivational strategies can be used, such as assessing and addressing the client's concerns about the DBT PE protocol, linking the ability to achieve other goals the client views as important to the need to treat PTSD, and highlighting the problems caused by untreated PTSD. Ultimately, however, the decision to engage in the DBT PE protocol is completely under the control of the client, and some clients may choose not to progress to Stage 2 PTSD treatment.

Stage 2: Targeting PTSD via the DBT PE Protocol

The DBT PE protocol is based on Prolonged Exposure (PE) therapy (Foa, Hembree, & Rothbaum, 2007), a highly effective evidence-based treatment (EBT) for PTSD. Approximately 60–78% of adults and adolescents receiving PE achieve diagnostic remission from PTSD (e.g., Foa et al., 1999; Foa, McLean, Capaldi, & Rosenfield, 2013) and 93% show a reliable improvement in PTSD severity (Jayawickreme et al., 2014). The DBT PE protocol utilizes all core strategies from PE, including in vivo exposure to feared, but objectively safe, situations and imaginal exposure to trauma memories, followed by processing. Adaptations to PE were made when necessary to more effectively address the characteristics of severe, multi-problem clients and to improve compatibility with DBT principles and strategies.

Importantly, while PE is a structured protocol that is delivered in a pre-determined session-by-session format, DBT is a principle-driven treatment that requires therapists to flexibly select from a wide variety of potential treatment strategies in any given moment. The integrated DBT+DBT PE treatment combines these approaches in that therapists deliver the DBT PE protocol while adhering to standard DBT principles. Broadly, this means that therapists use DBT strategies as needed to increase clients' willingness and ability to effectively complete DBT PE protocol procedures. For example, therapists rely on DBT strategies to target problems that may occur during DBT PE sessions, such as urges to engage in life-threatening behaviours, dissociation, and unwillingness to complete treatment tasks. In addition, principle-based guidelines are used to aid therapists in making clinical decisions about when to stop the protocol due to the occurrence of higher-priority behaviours, when to resume the protocol after stopping, and when to end the treatment. Finally, therapists use the principles underlying both treatments to tailor the DBT PE protocol to most effectively address the specific needs of individual clients.

The DBT PE protocol is integrated into DBT individual therapy sessions, and clients continue to receive all modes of DBT treatment, including skills training and phone coaching. During implementation of DBT PE, clients either receive one combined individual therapy session per week (90 minutes of the DBT PE protocol and 30 minutes of DBT), or two separate individual therapy sessions per week (one 60-minute DBT session and one 90-minute DBT PE session), depending on logistical considerations and the number of other, non-PTSD treatment targets. As with standard PE, the DBT PE protocol includes three treatment phases: pre-exposure, exposure, and termination/consolidation.

Pre-exposure sessions. During Session 1, clients first receive an overview of the treatment, including the rationale for exposure, and complete a trauma history interview. The trauma history interview is used to collaboratively determine which traumatic memory or memories to target during DBT PE, and to establish the client's preferred order of targeting for the top three most distressing memories. Next, the therapist obtains commitment from the client to (1) not engage in any suicidal or self-injurious behaviours during DBT PE; (2) actively participate in DBT PE; and (3) control any other problematic behaviours that might interfere with exposure (e.g., dissociation, substance use). The therapist also works with the client to develop a Post-Exposure Skills Plan that includes skills from DBT, which can be used to manage distress following both in and out of session exposure tasks.

In Session 2, the therapist reviews a dialectical framework for understanding common reactions to trauma, provides the client with the rationale for in vivo exposure, introduces the Subjective Units of Distress (SUDs) scale, and collaborates with the client in constructing the in vivo exposure hierarchy. While the in vivo hierarchy includes tasks that are standard in PE (e.g., situations the client perceives as dangerous or that are reminders of the trauma, or activities in which the client has lost interest), it is modified in DBT PE to also include situations that elicit unjustified shame (e.g., saying "no" to a request, disclosing trauma to a friend). The session concludes with assigning clients to complete their first in vivo exposure as homework, which typically involves two moderately distressing (SUDs = 40–60) tasks from the hierarchy that are each expected to be repeated multiple times before the next session.

Finally, DBT PE includes an optional pre-exposure session that may be conducted with the client and one or more support people (e.g., a partner, friend, or parent(s)) at any point in the pre-exposure phase of treatment. The goal of this session is to orientate the relevant support people to the treatment and enlist their help and support throughout the process. If a client does not wish to include friends or family members in their treatment, this session may be skipped.

Exposure sessions. In Session 3, the assigned in vivo exposure homework is reviewed and any difficulties completing the tasks are addressed. A detailed rationale for imaginal exposure is provided and clients then complete their first imaginal exposure followed by processing of the emotions and thoughts that arose during the exposure experience. Imaginal exposure follows the same procedures as in standard PE, including repeatedly recounting the trauma memory out loud in the present tense in as much detail as possible while monitoring the clients' SUDs ratings. However, in DBT PE, additional monitoring is completed before and after all exposure tasks to obtain ratings of pre-, peak, and post-exposure urges to commit suicide, self-injure, quit therapy, and use substances, as well as levels of state dissociation. Additionally, clients provide pre- and post-exposure ratings for several specific emotions (sadness, anger, shame, guilt, disgust, fear, and joy), and rate the degree to which they radically accept that the trauma happened. Finally, clients provide pre- and post-exposure ratings of the likelihood and severity of feared outcomes, as well as whether or not the feared outcome occurred. These ratings are used to guide the focus of processing after imaginal exposure by providing therapists with important information about which unjustified emotions and problematic beliefs were activated and may require targeting. The imaginal exposure is recorded for clients to listen to as homework (ideally daily) and in vivo exposure tasks are also assigned.

During each subsequent exposure session, the same general session structure is followed. The session first begins with a brief review of the DBT diary card in order to ensure that no higher order target behaviours (e.g., self-injury) have occurred (and that would merit the need to stop the DBT PE protocol). Next, in vivo and imaginal exposure homework is reviewed and the agenda is presented. Then, the therapist conducts and processes the imaginal exposure and assigns in vivo and imaginal homework. During in vivo and imaginal exposure, DBT strategies are used to target emotional under- and over-engagement as needed. For example, DBT crisis survival skills can be used to decrease the intensity of emotions during exposure, whereas DBT mindfulness and reality acceptance skills can be used to up-regulate emotions during exposure. Additionally, DBT therapist strategies (e.g., validation, self-disclosure, challenging cognitions, dialectics, irreverence) are used during processing of imaginal exposure to flexibly address the problematic beliefs underlying unjustified trauma-related emotions and facilitate corrective learning.

As the treatment progresses, clients approach increasingly more difficult tasks on their in vivo exposure hierarchy, always being sure to target the most feared situation by the end of treatment. As habituation (reduction in distress) begins to occur during imaginal exposure, clients progress to addressing hotspots, which are the most difficult moments within a larger trauma memory. In addition, once one trauma memory is sufficiently addressed (e.g., peak SUDs are low), additional trauma memories are targeted via imaginal exposure as needed. Typically, clients target 2–3 trauma memories via imaginal exposure in order to reach diagnostic remission of PTSD. Of note, there is no pre-determined number of exposure sessions. Instead, the duration of the DBT PE protocol is determined collaboratively by therapist and client through ongoing assessment of the client's PTSD symptoms and treatment goals.

Final session. When a client determines she has made sufficient progress and is ready to end targeted PTSD treatment, the therapist moves into the final session of the DBT PE protocol. As in standard PE, this session includes a brief imaginal exposure, a review of progress, and a discussion of relapse prevention strategies. Additionally, the DBT PE protocol includes a structured set of relapse prevention handouts and worksheets that are reviewed in the final session and include creating a plan for continued, self-directed practice of exposure, discussing skills for adopting an "exposure lifestyle", preparing for future high-risk situations, and discussing strategies for managing potential future relapses of PTSD symptoms.

Stage 3: DBT after the DBT PE Protocol

Upon completion of the DBT PE Protocol, clients return to standard DBT to address remaining targets. These often include increasing self-respect and self-validation, improving psychosocial functioning (e.g., relationships and connections to others, school, and employment), addressing non-disabling problems in living (e.g., uncomplicated major depression, marital problems), dealing with residual sadness/grieving from Stage 2, and achieving ordinary happiness.

CURRENT RESEARCH EVIDENCE

The DBT PE treatment approach involves the integration of two EBTs that are considered "gold standards" for the problems they are designed to treat. Extensive research already supports the use of DBT for the treatment of suicidal and self-injurious behaviour, particularly among individuals with BPD (Kliem, Kröger, & Kosfelder, 2010; Stoffers et al., 2012) and the use of PE for the treatment of PTSD (Powers, Halpern, Ferenschak, Gillihan, & Foa, 2010). Thus, research on the integrated DBT+DBT PE treatment has focused on confirming the feasibility, acceptability, safety, and effectiveness of combining these two EBTs.

Efficacy Studies

To date, DBT+DBT PE has been evaluated as a one-year treatment in our research clinic in an open trial (n=13; Harned, Korslund, Foa, & Linehan, 2012) and a randomized controlled trial (RCT) that compared DBT with and without the DBT PE protocol (n=26, Harned et al., 2014). Both studies involved samples of women (ages 18–60) with PTSD, recent (past 2–3 months) suicidal self-injury or serious NSSI, BPD, and an average of five additional diagnoses. Participants in these studies reported experiencing an average of 11–14 types of trauma beginning before the age of six, and childhood sexual abuse was the most common index trauma (50–62%).

Acceptability and feasibility. At intake, 74% of clients reported a preference for DBT+DBT–PE compared to DBT alone (26%) or PE alone (0%), and this was predicted by more severe PTSD re-experiencing symptoms and a childhood index trauma (Harned, Tkachuck, & Youngberg, 2013). Across both the open trial and RCT, 60% of clients started the DBT PE protocol, which occurred after an average of 20 weeks of DBT; of these, 73% completed the protocol in an average of 13 sessions (range = 6–19). The primary barrier to initiating the DBT PE protocol was premature drop-out during Stage 1 of DBT. The treatment was highly acceptable to clients and therapists in terms of positive treatment expectancies and satisfaction.

Safety. In both studies, urges to commit suicide and self-injure were low both before and after exposure tasks (M's = 0.3–0.6 out of 5) and these urges rarely increased immediately after completing an exposure task (6–11% of tasks). During the DBT PE protocol, 20–25% of clients engaged in suicidal and/or self-injurious behaviour. Over the entire treatment year, few clients in the open trial attempted suicide (9%) or engaged in NSSI (27%). In the RCT, clients who completed the DBT PE protocol were 2.4 times less likely to attempt suicide (17% vs. 40%) and 1.5 times less likely to self-injure (67% vs. 100%) than those completing DBT alone. These findings suggest that adding the DBT PE protocol to DBT is likely to decrease, rather than increase, the risk of suicidal and self-injurious behaviours.

Effectiveness. In the open trial, 71% of clients who completed the DBT PE protocol achieved diagnostic remission from PTSD at post-treatment, and 57% remained in remission three months after treatment ended. In the RCT, clients who completed the DBT PE protocol were twice as likely as those in DBT to achieve diagnostic remission from PTSD at post-treatment (80% vs. 40%); these remission rates decreased to 60% and 0%, respectively, at 3-month follow-up. In both studies, clients in DBT+DBT PE showed large pre- to post-treatment improvements in dissociation, depression, anxiety, guilt, shame, and social and global functioning and, in the RCT, these improvements were larger in DBT+DBT PE than in DBT alone. Of particular note, in the RCT, 80% of DBT+DBT PE completers both reliably improved and reached a normative level of functioning in terms of global symptom severity, compared to 0% of completers in DBT.

Mechanisms and Processes of Change

Using data from the above efficacy trials, several studies have begun to evaluate factors that account for improvements during DBT+DBT PE as well as the typical course of change during treatment. Analyses of treatment mechanisms indicate that diagnostic remission of PTSD is predicted by greater between-session habituation in global distress, sadness, and anger from the first to last imaginal exposure trial (Harned, Ruork, Liu, & Tkachuck, 2015). Improvement in PTSD severity is, in turn, associated with subsequent improvements in suicidal ideation, dissociation, depression, global severity, social adjustment, and health-related QoL (Harned, Wilks, Schmidt, & Coyle, 2016). Analyses of the course of change across the three stages of DBT+DBT PE indicate that PTSD severity significantly improves in Stages 2 and 3, whereas BPD severity and state dissociation significantly improve in Stage 3 (Harned, Gallop, & Valenstein-Mash, in press). Taken together, these findings indicate that: (1) PTSD is unlikely to significantly improve until it is directly targeted via the DBT PE protocol, (2) reduction in the intensity of trauma-related emotions across imaginal exposure trials is critical to achieving remission from PTSD, and (3) improvements in comorbid problems are likely to occur after, and as a result of, successful treatment of PTSD.

Effectiveness Studies

To date, one study has been completed that evaluated the DBT PE treatment approach in a routine practice setting. Using an open trial design, a combined DBT and PE treatment was evaluated as a 12-week intensive outpatient programme in a Veterans

Administration medical centre (Meyers et al., 2017). Participants were 33 veterans with PTSD (51% male) with a prior incomplete attempt at standard PE or Cognitive Processing Therapy, where the factors interfering with completion were due to BPD symptoms (e.g., suicidality, self-harm, dissociation, extreme emotions). A majority of veterans completed the treatment (67%) and none dropped out during PE. Among the treatment completers, nearly all achieved a reliable improvement in PTSD (91%), large pre- to post-treatment effect sizes were found for decreases in PTSD and dysfunctional coping, and a moderate effect size was found for decreases in suicidal ideation. Three additional effectiveness studies are currently underway with adolescents and adults in residential, partial hospital, intensive outpatient, and outpatient routine care settings.

IMPLEMENTATION CHALLENGES

To date, an estimated 1,700 therapists in four countries have received training in the DBT PE protocol that has ranged from one-day introductory workshops to four-day intensive trainings. Therapists attending these workshops are typically already trained in and delivering DBT and are seeking to add the DBT PE protocol to the services they provide. Trainees have subsequently implemented the DBT PE protocol with adolescents and adults in a wide variety of treatment settings. Based on our experience of providing training and consultation, as well as preliminary findings of several ongoing implementation studies, a number of common difficulties have emerged. The following section describes these implementation challenges and suggests potential solutions.

Lack of Foundational Training in Exposure

The DBT PE protocol is an exposure-based treatment and therefore requires therapists to have a solid working knowledge of the basic principles and procedures of exposure. However, few therapists have received prior training in exposure therapy and many are unfamiliar with how exposure is used to treat PTSD. For example, a survey of US psychologists found that only 27–28% had received training in imaginal or in vivo exposure for PTSD (Becker, Zeyfert, & Anderson, 2004). Although most therapists report that the basic procedures of the DBT PE protocol are relatively straightforward to learn and implement, many find it more difficult to determine what to do when these procedures are not working as expected (e.g., habituation is not occurring after multiple sessions of imaginal exposure) and/or they must make important clinical decisions (e.g., when to progress to hotspots or move to a new trauma memory during imaginal exposure).

The ability to effectively assess and address problems that may arise during the DBT PE protocol, as well as to determine an effective duration and course of treatment, requires knowledge of the principles underlying exposure therapy. For therapists without prior training in exposure, it is recommended that they acquire this knowledge in more depth in preparation for attending training. This can include reading books (e.g., Abramowitz, Deacon, & Whiteside, 2010) or taking online courses (e.g., http://behavioraltech.org/ol/details_exp.cfm) that teach the general principles and procedures of exposure therapy, and/or reviewing educational resources specific to standard Prolonged Exposure therapy for PTSD (e.g., Foa et al., 2007; Foa, Chrestman, & Gilboa-Schechtman, 2008; http://pe.musc.edu). Having this foundational knowledge of exposure therapy and its application to PTSD appears to help therapists learn the DBT PE protocol more readily and implement it in a principle-driven manner to overcome clinical obstacles and make effective clinical decisions.

Concerns about Exposure Therapy for PTSD

Common clinical lore suggests that exposure therapy is insensitive, contraindicated for many clients, potentially damaging, and perhaps even unethical (Olatunji, Deacon, & Abramowitz, 2009). Although these concerns are not supported by research (e.g., Foa, Zoellner, Feeny, Hembree, & Alvarez-Conrad, 2002; Jayawickreme et al., 2014; Olatunji et al., 2009), many therapists remain hesitant or unwilling to use exposure therapy. Concerns about exposure typically stem from the fact that these treatments require therapists to deliberately elicit intense and uncomfortable emotions by having clients confront the stimuli they are avoiding in order for new learning to occur. This emotion-induction approach stands in contrast to standard therapy approaches in which therapists are encouraged to help clients quickly reduce the intensity of painful emotions when they occur. Moreover, given the high risk for suicide and general severity of clients treated in DBT, many therapists are understandably anxious about whether the use of trauma-focused exposure may cause clients to get worse, including in potentially life-threatening ways.

Several strategies appear helpful in decreasing therapist concerns about using the DBT PE protocol to treat PTSD. First, providing research data that supports the safety of the DBT PE protocol (discussed previously) is often critical to reducing therapist concerns about the potential for client worsening. Similarly, it is often helpful to share this data with clients and their families, colleagues, ancillary treatment staff, and agency administrators who may also express these concerns. Second, given that most therapists have no, or minimal, prior experience with exposure, it is often helpful for therapists to engage in "exposure to exposure" to reduce their own anxiety about the treatment. To that end, DBT PE workshops utilize extensive videos of actual therapy sessions, including many of clients engaging in imaginal exposure, so that therapists can see what it actually looks like and how clients typically respond. Similarly, when possible, it can be very helpful for therapists to observe exposure sessions conducted by colleagues on their team. Third, we recommend therapists gain personal experience in the use of exposure by completing exposure tasks to address their own fears. Personal use of exposure not only helps therapists to gain better understanding of how the procedure works and feels, but can also serve as excellent modelling when working to increase client willingness to engage in the treatment. Finally, therapists are encouraged to obtain support and consultation from their DBT consultation team to help address concerns they may have about using the DBT PE protocol with specific clients.

PTSD Screening and Referral Procedures

Although trauma is highly prevalent among individuals receiving mental health services, PTSD symptoms often go unrecognized. In a multi-site study of community mental health centres, only 2% of the sample had received a PTSD diagnosis even though 42% were found to meet diagnostic criteria for PTSD (Mueser et al., 1998). This discrepancy reflects the lack of routine assessment of trauma history and PTSD in many service settings (e.g., Chessen, Comtois, & Landes, 2011; Frueh et al., 2002). Accordingly, many therapists receiving training in the DBT PE protocol report that PTSD is not routinely assessed among clients entering their DBT programmes. Routine PTSD screening is essential to the successful implementation of the DBT PE protocol in order to identify clients in need of the treatment. Ideally, this screening should occur at intake so that discussion of PTSD and its treatment can be initiated during the pre-treatment phase of DBT. We recommend the self-report PTSD Checklist (Weathers et al., 2013) for routine screening as it assesses both trauma exposure and DSM-5 PTSD diagnostic criteria, has strong psychometric properties, can be administered quickly (5–10 minutes), and is freely available. In addition, in DBT programmes where only some therapists are trained to deliver the DBT PE protocol, it is critical to establish procedures to ensure that clients screening positive for PTSD are referred to DBT PE trained therapists.

Difficulties with Client Engagement

Therapists trained to deliver trauma-focused EBTs report that client unwillingness to engage in these treatments (e.g., due to perceived intolerability, or not wanting to talk about traumatic experiences) is a significant barrier to implementation (e.g., Hamblen et al., 2015; Lu, Plagge, Marsiglio, & Dobscha, 2016; Osei-Bonsu et al., in press). Similarly, many clients who have received trauma-focused EBTs report originally being ambivalent and delaying initiation of these treatments due to fear of symptom worsening, beliefs that avoidance of trauma-related cues is helpful, scepticism about the treatment rationale, and lack of knowledge about the treatments (Hundt et al., 2015). Although our research has indicated that approximately 75% of clients with PTSD entering DBT programmes prefer to receive DBT with the DBT PE protocol over DBT alone (Harned et al., 2013), it is not unusual for clients to be at least somewhat ambivalent about actually initiating the treatment.

As described, much of the work to provide psychoeducation about the DBT PE protocol and increase client motivation and willingness to engage in the treatment falls to the individual therapist. In addition, it is imperative that individual therapists convey confidence in the treatment and the client's ability to do it (eventually, if not now); hesitant therapists are likely to create hesitant clients. However, even when individual therapists convey confidence in the treatment to their clients, problems may occur when other members of the treatment team (e.g., skills trainers, pharmacotherapists) do not. From a programme perspective, it it therefore important to structure the larger treatment environment to provide a unified and confident message that encourages clients to engage in the DBT PE protocol when they are ready. This will also help to shape a pro-DBT PE attitude among clients in the programme more generally. In addition, allowing clients who have completed the DBT PE protocol to serve as role models for clients who are considering the treatment can be very helpful in increasing client engagement. This may occur informally through client interactions in DBT skills groups or other shared treatment settings, or can be structured to occur more formally via peer support models or client testimonials.

Logistical Issues

As described, in research settings the DBT PE protocol has been delivered via either two individual sessions per week (one 90-minute DBT PE session and one 60-minute DBT session) or one two-hour individual session per week (90 minutes of DBT PE and 30 minutes of DBT). Both session formats are longer and/or more frequent than is typical in DBT (usually 60 minutes/week). This more intensive treatment format may pose challenges for both clients and therapists due to logistical barriers (e.g., schedule conflicts, work demands) and financial considerations (e.g., extra cost of additional treatment, reimbursement limitations). One potential solution is to shorten the length of the DBT PE sessions (or portions of sessions) from 90 to 60 minutes, which is supported by research indicating that both session lengths yield comparable outcomes (van Minnen & Foa, 2006). However, therapists must still contend with how to provide clients with some amount of DBT individual therapy concurrently with DBT PE. Therapists utilizing the DBT PE protocol in routine practice settings report that the most commonly used session formats are either a single 90-minute session per week (60 minutes of DBT PE and 30 minutes of DBT) or two 60-minute sessions per week (one DBT PE and one DBT). Thus, it is important for therapists and programmes to consider in advance how to accommodate these longer or more frequent therapy sessions during the portion of the treatment (approximately 10–15 weeks) in which the DBT PE protocol is delivered. Another notable logistical issue to consider is how to audio-record therapy sessions so that clients can listen to the in-session imaginal exposure as homework. Most often, clients are expected to provide and manage their own recording devices (e.g., smartphones, digital recorders), although in some cases programmes may need to provide equipment to clients who are unable to access such devices.

Access to Supervision and Consultation

A significant barrier to the dissemination of EBTs in general, including DBT+DBT PE, is the limited availability of expert supervision or consultation for therapists after training. These types of ongoing support are often critical to increase adoption of and competence in newly learned treatments. Indeed, research generally indicates that training alone is unlikely to substantially change therapist behaviour or impact client outcomes without the addition of ongoing support (Beidas & Kendall, 2010; Herschell, Kolko, Baumann, & Davis, 2010), including for PE specifically (Karlin et al., 2010). However, as with other EBTs, there is a shortage of experts in DBT PE to provide consultation and these services are both costly and time-intensive for therapists. Accordingly, research is ongoing to develop and evaluate feasible and scalable methods of providing ongoing support in the DBT PE protocol after workshop training, including group consultation via telephone or virtual conferencing platforms, advanced case-consultation based workshops, and train-the-supervisor models.

SUMMARY AND CONCLUSIONS

The integrated DBT and DBT PE protocol treatment offers a promising approach for DBT therapists to more directly and effectively treat PTSD. Although historically there has been concern that trauma-focused treatments may be contraindicated for the high-risk, severe, and multi-problem clients typically treated in DBT, research now supports the feasibility, acceptability, safety, and effectiveness of integrating this type of treatment into DBT using a stage-based approach. Moreover, successfully treating PTSD is likely to improve other serious problems that are maintained or exacerbated by untreated PTSD. Thus, it is not only possible, but imperative to provide effective PTSD treatment to DBT clients suffering from this debilitating disorder, and the DBT PE protocol offers a structured method for doing so.

ACKNOWLEDGEMENTS

This work was supported by grants R34MH082143 and R34MH106598 from the National Institute of Mental Health to the first author. Dr. Harned is a trainer and consultant for Behavioral Tech, LLC. Dr. Schmidt is a consultant for Behavioral Tech, LLC.

KEY POINTS FOR CLINICIANS

- DBT+DBT PE is delivered in three stages, with Stage 1 using DBT to achieve behavioural control, Stage 2 targeting PTSD via the DBT PE protocol, and Stage 3 using DBT to address any problems that remain after PTSD is treated.

- During the pre-treatment phase of DBT, therapists begin orienting clients to the DBT PE protocol and establishing effective contingencies regarding achieving behavioural control in order to receive PTSD treatment.

- Stage 1 DBT is delivered without adaptation with the goal of helping clients to achieve the stability and skills necessary to safely and effectively engage in subsequent PTSD treatment.

- Clients must meet specified, principle-driven readiness criteria to begin the DBT PE protocol in Stage 2, including a requirement of abstinence from all forms of suicidal self-injury and NSSI for at least two months.

- The DBT PE protocol is an adapted version of Prolonged Exposure (PE) therapy that uses the core procedures of in vivo exposure to feared but objectively safe situations and imaginal exposure and processing of trauma memories.

- The DBT PE protocol includes three treatment phases: pre-exposure (2–3 sessions), exposure (flexible number of sessions), and termination/consolidation (1 session).

- On average, the DBT PE protocol is started after 20 weeks of DBT and lasts 13 sessions.

- Research supports the feasibility, acceptability, safety, and effectiveness of integrating the DBT PE protocol into DBT for suicidal and self-injuring clients with BPD, PTSD, and multiple additional diagnoses.

- Successful implementation of the DBT PE protocol in routine practice settings requires attention to several common client-, therapist-, and programme-level barriers.

REFERENCES

Abramowitz, J. S., Deacon, B. J., & Whiteside, S. P. H. (2010). *Exposure therapy for anxiety: Principles and practice*. New York: Guilford Press.

Barnicot, K. (2016). Personality disorder and post-traumatic stress disorder: Implications for the psychological treatment of deliberate self-harm. Presentation at the 23rd British Isles Research Workshop on Suicide and Self-Harm (Oxford, UK).

Barnicot, K., & Priebe, S. (2013). Post-traumatic stress disorder and the outcome of dialectical behaviour therapy for borderline personality disorder. *Personality and Mental Health*, 7, 181–190.

Becker, C. B., Zayfert, C., & Anderson, E. (2004). A survey of psychologists' attitudes towards and utilization of exposure therapy for PTSD. *Behaviour Research and Therapy*, 42, 277–292.

Beidas, R. S., & Kendall, P. C. (2010). Training therapists in evidence-based practice: A critical review of studies from a systems-contextual perspective. *Clinical Psychology Review*, 17, 1–30.

Bolton, E. E., Mueser, K. T., & Rosenberg, S. D. (2006). Symptom correlates of posttraumatic stress disorder in clients with borderline personality disorder. *Comprehensive Psychiatry*, 47, 357–361.

Chessen, C. E., Comtois, K. A., & Landes, S. J. (2011). Untreated posttraumatic stress among persons with severe mental illness despite marked trauma and symptomatology. *Psychiatric Services*, 62, 1201–1206.

Cloitre, M., Courtois, C. A., Ford, J. D., Green, B. L., Alexander, P., Briere, J., ... van der Hart, O. (2012). *The ISTSS Expert Consensus Treatment Guidelines for Complex PTSD in Adults.* Retrieved from https://www.istss.org/ISTSS_Main/media/Documents/ISTSS-Expert-Concesnsus-Guidelines-for-Complex-PTSD-Updated-060315.pdf

Foa, E. B., Chrestman, K., & Gilboa-Schechtman, E. (2008). *Prolonged exposure therapy for adolescents with PTSD: Emotional processing of traumatic experiences.* New York: Oxford University Press.

Foa, E. B., Dancu, C. V., Hembree, E. A., Jaycox, L. H., Meadows, E. A., & Street, G. P. (1999). A comparison of exposure therapy, stress inoculation training, and their combination for reducing posttraumatic stress disorder in female assault victims. *Journal of Consulting and Clinical Psychology*, 67(2), 194–200.

Foa, E. B., Hembree, E., & Rothbaum, B. O. (2007). *Prolonged exposure therapy for PTSD: Emotional processing of traumatic experiences.* New York: Oxford University Press.

Foa, E. B., McLean, C. P., Capaldi, S., & Rosenfield, D. (2013). Prolonged exposure vs supportive counseling for sexual abuse-related PTSD in adolescent girls: A randomized clinical trial. *JAMA: The Journal of the American Medical Association*, 310(24), 2650–2657.

Foa, E. B., Zoellner, L. A., Feeny, N. C., Hembree, E. A., & Alvarez-Conrad, J. (2002). Does imaginal exposure exacerbate PTSD symptoms? *Journal of Consulting and Clinical Psychology*, 70, 1022–1028.

Frueh, B. C., Cousins, V. C., Hiers, T. G., Cavenaugh, S. D., Cusack, K. J., & Santos, A. B. (2002). The need for trauma assessment and related clinical services in a state-funded mental health system. *Community Mental Health Journal*, 38, 351–356.

Hamblen, J. L., Bernardy, N. C., Sherrieb, K., Norris, F. H., Cook, J. M., Louis, C. A., & Schnurr, P. P. (2015). VA PTSD clinic director perspectives: How perceptions of readiness influence delivery of evidence-based PTSD treatment. *Professional Psychology: Research and Practice*, 46, 90–96.

Harned, M. S., Chapman, A. L., Dexter-Mazza, E. T., Murray, A., Comtois, K. A., & Linehan, M. M. (2008). Treating co-occurring Axis I disorders in chronically suicidal women with borderline personality disorder: A 2-year randomized trial of Dialectical Behavior Therapy versus Community Treatment by Experts. *Journal of Consulting and Clinical Psychology*, 76(6), 1068–1075.

Harned, M. S., Gallop, R. J., & Valenstein-Mash, H. R. (in press). What changes when? The course of improvement during a stage-based treatment for suicidal and self-injuring women with borderline personality disorder and PTSD. *Psychotherapy Research*.

Harned, M. S., Jackson, S. C., Comtois, K. A., & Linehan, M. M. (2010). Dialectical Behavior Therapy as a precursor to PTSD treatment for suicidal and/or self-injuring women with borderline personality disorder. *Journal of Traumatic Stress*, 23, 421–429.

Harned, M. S., Korslund, K. E., Foa, E. B., & Linehan, M. M. (2012). Treating PTSD in suicidal and self-injuring women with borderline personality disorder: Development and preliminary evaluation of a Dialectical Behavior Therapy Prolonged Exposure protocol. *Behaviour Research and Therapy*, *50*, 381–386.

Harned, M. S., Korslund, K. E., & Linehan, M. M. (2014). A pilot randomized controlled trial of Dialectical Behavior Therapy with and without the Dialectical Behavior Therapy Prolonged Exposure protocol for suicidal and self-injuring women with borderline personality disorder and PTSD. *Behaviour Research and Therapy*, *55*, 7–17.

Harned, M. S., Rizvi, S. L., & Linehan, M. M. (2010). The impact of co-occurring post-traumatic stress disorder on suicidal women with borderline personality disorder. *American Journal of Psychiatry*, *167*, 1210–1217.

Harned, M. S., Ruork, A. K., Liu, J., & Tkachuck, M. A. (2015). Emotional activation and habituation during imaginal exposure for PTSD among women with borderline personality disorder. *Journal of Traumatic Stress*, *28*, 253–257.

Harned, M. S., Tkachuck, M. A., & Youngberg, K. A. (2013). Treatment preference among suicidal and self-injuring women with borderline personality disorder and PTSD. *Journal of Clinical Psychology*, *69*, 749–761.

Harned, M. S., Wilks, C., Schmidt, S. C., & Coyle, T. (2016). The impact of PTSD severity on treatment outcomes in DBT with and without the DBT Prolonged Exposure protocol. In C. Wilks (Chair), *The how and the why: Mechanisms and change processes of Dialectical Behavior Therapy*. Symposium presented at the 50th Annual Convention of the Association for Behavioral and Cognitive Therapies (New York, NY).

Herschell, A. D., Kolko, D. J., Baumann, B. L., & Davis, A. C. (2010). The role of therapist training in the implementation of psychosocial treatments: A review and critique with recommendations. *Clinical Psychology Review*, *30*, 448–466.

Hundt, N. E., Mott, J. M., Miles, S. R., Arney, J., Cully, J. A., & Stanley, M. A. (2015). Veterans' perspectives on initiating evidence-based psychotherapy for posttraumatic stress disorder. *Psychological Trauma: Theory, Research, Practice, and Policy*, *7*, 539–546.

Jayawickreme, N., Cahill, S. P., Riggs, D. S., Rauch, S. A. M., Resick, P. A., Rothbaum, B. O., & Foa, E. B. (2014). Primum non nocere (first do no harm): Symptom worsening and improvement in female assault victims after Prolonged Exposure for PTSD. *Depression and Anxiety 31*, 412–419.

Karlin, B. E., Ruzek, J. I., Chard, K. M., Eftekhari, A., Monson, C. M., Hembree, E. A., … Foa, E. B. (2010). Dissemination of evidence-based psychological treatments for posttraumatic stress disorder in the Veterans Health Administration. *Journal of Traumatic Stress*, *23*, 663–673.

Kliem, S., Kröger, C., & Kosfelder, J. (2010). Dialectical behavior therapy for borderline personality disorder: a meta-analysis using mixed-effects modeling. *Journal of Consulting and Clinical Psychology*, *78*(6), 936.

Linehan, M. M. (1993). *Cognitive-Behavioral Treatment of Borderline Personality Disorder*. New York: Guilford Press.

Linehan, M. M. (1999). Development, evaluation, and dissemination of effective psychosocial treatments: Levels of disorder, stages of care, and stages of treatment research. In M. G. Glantz & C. R. Hartel (Eds.), *Drug abuse: Origins and interventions* (pp. 367–394). Washington, DC: American Psychological Association.

Linehan, M. M. (2015a). *DBT® skills training manual,* 2nd Edition. New York: Guilford Press.

Linehan, M. M. (2015b). *DBT® skills training handouts and worksheets,* 2nd Edition. New York: Guilford Press.

Linehan, M. M., Comtois, K. A., Murray, A. M., Brown, M. Z., Gallop, R. J., Heard, H. L., … Lindenboim, N. (2006). Two-year randomized controlled trial and follow-up of dialectical behavior therapy vs. therapy by experts for suicidal behaviors and borderline personality disorder. *Archives of General Psychiatry, 63*, 757–766.

Linehan, M. M., Schmidt, H., Dimeff, L. A., Craft, J. C., Kanter, J., & Comtois, K. A. (1999). Dialectical behavior therapy for patients with borderline personality disorder and drug dependence. *American Journal on Addictions, 8*, 279–292.

Lu, M. W., Plagge, J. M., Marsiglio, M. C., & Dobscha, S. K. (2016). Clinician documentation on receipt of trauma-focused evidence-based psychotherapies in a VA PTSD clinic. *Journal of Behavioral Health Services & Research, 43*, 71–87.

McMain, S. F., Links, P. S., Gnam, W. H., Guimond, T., Cardish, R. J., Korman, L., & Streiner, D. L. (2009). A randomized trial of dialectical behavior therapy versus general psychiatric management for borderline personality disorder. *American Journal of Psychiatry, 166*, 1365–1375.

Meyers, L., Voller, E. K., McCallum, E. B., Thuras, P., Shallcross, S., Velasquez, T., & Meis, L. (2017). Treating veterans with PTSD and borderline personality symptoms in a 12-week intensive outpatient setting: Findings from a pilot program. *Journal of Traumatic Stress, 30*, 178–181.

Mueser, K., Goodman, L. A., Trumbetta, S. L., Rosenberg, S. D., Osher, F. C., Vidaver, R., … Foy, E. W. (1998). Trauma and posttraumatic stress disorder in severe mental illness. *Journal of Consulting and Clinical Psychology, 66*, 493–499.

Olatunji, B. O., Deacon, B. J., & Abramowitz, J. (2009). The cruelest cure? Ethical issues in the implementation of exposure-based treatments. *Cognitive and Behavioral Practice, 16*, 172–180.

Osei-Bonsu, P. E., Bolton, R. E., Stirman, S. W., Eisen, S. V., Herz, L., & Pellowe, M. E. (in press). Mental health providers' decision-making around the implementation of evidence-based treatment for PTSD. *Journal of Behavioral Health Services & Research.*

Powers, M. B., Halpern, J. M., Ferenschak, M. P., Gillihan, S. J., & Foa, E. B. (2010). A meta-analytic review of prolonged exposure for posttraumatic stress disorder. *Clinical Psychology Review, 30*, 635–641.

Rüsch, N., Corrigan, P. W., Bohus, M., Kuhler, T., Jacob, G. A., & Lieb, K. (2007). The impact of posttraumatic stress disorder on dysfunctional implicit and explicit emotions among women with borderline personality disorder. *Journal of Nervous and Mental Disease, 195*, 537–539.

Stoffers, J. M., Völlm, B. A., Rücker, G., Timmer, A., Huband, N., & Lieb, K. (2012). Psychological therapies for people with borderline personality disorder. *Cochrane Database of Systematic Reviews, 8*, doi: 10.1002/14651858.CD005652.pub2

van Minnen, A., & Foa, E. B. (2006). The effect of imaginal exposure length on outcome of treatment for PTSD. *Journal of Traumatic Stress, 19*, 427–438.

Weathers, F. W., Litz, B. T., Keane, T. M., Palmieri, P. A., Marx, B. P., & Schnurr, P. P. (2013). *The PTSD Checklist for DSM-5 (PCL-5)*. Scale available from the National Center for PTSD. Retrieved from www.ptsd.va.gov

CHAPTER 36

DBT – PTSD

A Treatment Programme for Complex PTSD After Childhood Abuse

MARTIN BOHUS AND KATHLEN PRIEBE

PSYCHOLOGICAL CONSEQUENCES OF CHILDHOOD ABUSE

IDENTIFYING the specific psychological consequences of sexual and/or physical abuse in childhood presents several difficulties, not least because sexual and physical abuse frequently occur together, often alongside other critical factors such as emotional abuse, neglect, or violence between parents. Notwithstanding these challenges, the data from prospective cohort studies and epidemiological studies fairly consistently establish that sexual abuse is associated with a multitude of psychological problems in adulthood and is a nonspecific risk factor for psychopathology in general (Gilbert et al., 2009; Maniglio, 2009). In a New Zealand cohort study, 13% of mental disorders could be traced back to sexual abuse (Fergusson, Boden, & Horwood, 2008). In an Australian cohort study, individuals with a history of sexual abuse compared to those without were approximately 2.5 times more likely to exhibit an Axis I disorder (18.4% vs. 7.0%) and five times more likely to exhibit a personality disorder (3.6% vs. 0.7%) (Cutajar et al., 2010). In a number of studies, the incidence in people with a history of childhood sexual abuse was increased for post-traumatic stress disorders (PTSD), depression, sleep disorders, substance-related disorders, and borderline personality disorders (BPD) (Chen et al., 2010; Cutajar et al., 2010; Maniglio, 2010). In addition to psychiatric diagnoses, those with a history of childhood sexual abuse have increased risks for further psychological and psycho-social problems, for example, dissociative symptoms, interpersonal difficulties, self-esteem problems, self-harming behaviour, and suicidal tendencies (Chen et al., 2010; Paolucci, Genuis, & Violato, 2001; Yates, Carlson, & Egeland, 2008). On the other hand, about 56% of individuals with BPD meet criteria for co-occuring PTSD, mostly after childhood sexual abuse (Yen et al., 2002; Zanarini et al., 1998; Zlotnick, Franklin, & Zimmerman, 2002). There is ample evidence that these patients show exaggerated psychopathology and are more likely to experience chronic problems (Cackowski, Neubauer, & Kleindienst, 2016; Harned, Rizvi, & Linehan, 2010).

Symptoms of Post-traumatic Stress Disorder After Childhood Abuse

Post-traumatic stress disorder (PTSD) is characterized by the re-experiencing of the traumatic event(s) accompanied by symptoms of increased arousal and by avoidance of stimuli associated with the trauma. The DSM-IV conceptualized PTSD mainly as a fear condition and required the experience of fear, helplessness, and horror during the traumatic event. However, for those with PTSD after sexual abuse, the traumatic experience and the memories are often associated with emotions of disgust and a sense of being dirty, as well as shame and guilt, alongside the feelings of fear and helplessness (Görg et al., 2017). Unlike traumatization in the context of uncommon experiences (such as traumatization by natural disaster, war experiences, or accidents), sexual abuse is often associated with everyday stimuli, so that affected persons encounter triggers for memories everywhere. Thus, the experience of human proximity, intimacy, and sexuality—a source of joy and happiness for healthy people—is a typical trigger for distressing memories. Accordingly, the avoidance behaviour relates to precisely these everyday things such as partnership, intimacy, and sexuality, as well as physical care and medical visits (mainly gynaecologists, cardiologists, and dentists). From a behavioural perspective, multiple dysfunctional behaviours (e.g., non-suicidal self harm (NSSI), suicide ideations, aggressive outbursts, high-risk behaviour, drug and alcohol intake) can be conceptualized as escape strategies from distressing intrusions or severe dissociative states.

Patients with PTSD related to childhood sexual abuse often exhibit addional problems such as emotion dysregulation, dissociative symptoms, and interpersonal difficulties. Many of them have negative self-concepts, characterized by persistent thoughts of being inferior, worthless, and unlovable. This rejection often also pertains to their own body, which they perceive as dirty and disgusting. They find it hard to trust other people or feel close to others. Against the backdrop of the belief that they are not worthwhile and do not deserve a loving relationship, sufferers may often remain in dysfunctional relationships and experience violence again.

This complex picture of PTSD has been described under the terms Disorders of Extreme Stress Not Otherwise Specified (DESNOS) and Complex PTSD (cPTSD). Both the DSM-5 (APA, 2013) and the upcoming ICD-11 modified the diagnostic criteria of PTSD to accommodate these more complex presentations. The DSM-5 added symptoms to the PTSD diagnosis that have frequently been viewed as symptoms of cPTSD, such as distorted beliefs about self and others, and reckless behaviour, and introduced a dissociative subtype of PTSD. The ICD-11 proposes a distinct cPTSD diagnosis that comprises the three core symptoms of PTSD along with enduring disturbances in the domains of affect, self, and interpersonal relationships (Maercker et al., 2013).

Data for the Treatment of Post-traumatic Stress Disorder After Childhood Abuse

Numerous meta-analyses have demonstrated the effectiveness of trauma-focused psychotherapies (Bisson, Roberts, Andrew, Cooper, & Lewis, 2013; Bradley, Greene, Russ, Dutra, & Westen, 2005; Watts et al., 2013). The meta-analysis by Watts and colleagues (2013) included 112 randomized controlled trials and reported a mean effect size of 1.1 for the post-traumatic symptoms, i.e., very effective. There were no significant differences between treatments focusing on exposure and treatments focusing on cognitive processing and EMDR (Eye Movement Desensitization and Reprocessing). Exposure-based procedures include the repeated exposure to the distressing memories in imagination, and to feared and avoided triggers. Cognitive procedures mainly focus on identifying, challenging, and modifying unhelpful trauma-related cognitions, e.g., "I am to blame for the abuse," "Closeness means danger." In EMDR, patients are asked to observe their emerging thoughts, feelings, and body reactions during "bilateral physical stimulation" (usually horizontal eye movements) without judgment. The results obtained in the meta-analyses with PTSD-remission rates of about 50–60% indicate that these treatments work well for many patients with PTSD. Prolonged Exposure (Foa, Hembree, & Rothbaum, 2007), Cognitive Processing Therapy (Resick, Monson, & Chard, 2016) and EMDR (Shapiro, 2018) are all well-studied treatment programmes demonstrating good outcomes. Despite these promising results, there is room for improvement. Regardless of which treatment programme is used, approximately 20% of patients terminate the treatment prematurely (Imel, Laska, Jakupcak, & Simpson, 2013). While remission rates of 50–60% are good, 40–50% of patients continue to suffer from PTSD after psychotherapeutic treatment.

In addition, it is unclear to what extent the results of these meta-analyses apply to the treatment of cPTSD, since many studies have excluded patients with symptoms like suicidal ideation, self-harming behaviour, or substance abuse (Bradley et al., 2005). In a meta-analysis of treatment studies on the psychotherapy of PTSD after sexual or physical abuse in childhood, typically associated with more complex presentations, Ehring and colleagues (2014) report an effect size of 0.72 for post-traumatic symptoms. Dorrepaal and colleagues (2014) conclude, in their review on the treatment of PTSD following sexual and physical abuse in childhood, that the studies with patients with cPTSD show lower PTSD remission rates, higher post-treatment symptoms scores, and lower rates of clinically significant improvement. In addition, it is still largely unclear whether the additional symptom domains of cPTSD—that is, problems in the areas of the regulation of emotions, self-esteem, and interpersonal relationships—improve with classic trauma-focused treatments.

The absence of sufficient data on the psychotherapy of cPTSD has prompted the International Society for Traumatic Stress Studies (ISTSS) to conduct an expert survey on cPTSD (Cloitre et al., 2011). The majority of experts recommended a phase-oriented, multimodal treatment. Training in the regulation of emotions and exposure to the traumatic memory were rated as the most effective interventions. In line with this, several working groups developed treatment programmes that combine emotion regulation skills and trauma-focused interventiones. Cloitre and colleages (2002, 2010) have investigated such a two-phase treatment consisting of eight sessions of emotion regulation training and subsequent eight-session exposure in two randomized-controlled trials. In the first study, however, there were a number of exclusion criteria, for example, BPD and dissociative disorders, and thus probably excluding most patients with cPTSD. With Dialectical Behavioural Therapy plus Prolonged Exposure (DBT + PE, Harned, Korslund, Foa, & Linehan, 2012; Harned, Korslund, & Linehan, 2014) and Dialectical Behavioural Therapy for post-traumatic stress disorder (DBT-PTSD, Bohus et al., 2013; Steil, Dyer, Priebe, Kleindienst, & Bohus, 2011), there are now two treatment programmes combining DBT and trauma-focused interventions. In DBT + PE, patients receive trauma-focused exposure sessions in addition to standard DBT as soon as they have stopped self-harming behaviour for at least two months. In a US pre-post study in 13 patients, there was a significant improvement in post-traumatic symptoms with an effect size of 1.4 (Harned et al., 2012). In a randomized controlled trial (Harned et al., 2014), although there were significant effects on the post-traumatic symptoms, only eight patients (less than half) of the 17 patients included received the trauma-specific treatment.

In contrast to the previously highly linearly organized treatment programmes, DBT-PTSD is based on a modular organization. This takes into account that a large number of symptom presentations can be present in cPTSD, which are likely to require specific interventions. In addition, the modular organization allows a more dynamic response to the highly fluctuating symptoms and the many everyday problems. In the first pre-post study, which was conducted under residential conditions with 29 females with PTSD related to childhood sexual abuse, there was an effect size of 1.22 and no drop-outs from treatment (Steil, Dyer, Priebe, Kleindienst, & Bohus, 2011). In a randomized controlled trial including 74 female patients, also under residential conditions, DBT-PTSD resulted in significantly greater reductions in post-traumatic symptoms at discharge and three months post-discharge compared to treatment-as-usual (TAU). The intent to treat between group effect size for the post-traumatic symptoms was 1.35. Only 5% of the patients (two out of 36) discontinued the treatment prematurely. Individual analysis did not reveal any symptom worsening in any subject treated with DBT-PTSD. About 50% of the patients in this study met DSM-IV criteria for BPD. Patients with ongoing self-harm and severe dissociative features and suicidal thoughts were not excluded. The last life-threatening suicide attempt had to have been more than eight weeks past. Post-hoc analyses revealed that neither the severity of BPD symptomatology nor the number of episodes of self-harm at the beginning of the treatment influenced the outcome of the therapy. No increase in suicidal thoughts or urges for self-harm occurred during the exposure phases (Krüger et al., 2014). Long-term analysis of the data showed highly significant decreases in admission rates and persistence of recovery one year after discharge (Priebe et al., 2017).

Based on these highly promising data on safety, feasibility, acceptability, and efficacy under residential conditions, the treatment programme was subsequently tailored for outpatient conditions. Outpatient DBT-PTSD comprises up to 45 sessions of individual therapy. For practical reasons we abstained from a skills group. A pilot study showed excellent feasibility under outpatient conditions (Steil et al., 2018). Within the scope of a multi-centre therapy study supported by the German Federal Ministry of Education and Research (RELEASE project), we conducted a randomized controlled trial to investigate feasibility, acceptance, and effectiveness of DBT-PTSD under outpatient conditions; 206 female patients suffering from cPTSD after childhood sexual or physical abuse were randomized to either one year of DBT-PTSD or one year of Cognitive Processing Therapy (CPT) as designed and supervised by the treatment developer, P. Resick. Data will be published in 2019. However, thus far (2018), we have found no indications of high drop-out rates or serious incidents such as suicide attempts in DBT-PTSD—otherwise, we would not have published this chapter! Even without the final analysis of the outpatient study, currently available data converge to suggest that DBT-PTSD has strong empirical evidence for acceptability and effectiveness in the treatment of cPTSD after childhood abuse.

STRUCTURE AND PRINCIPLES OF DBT-PTSD

DBT-PTSD was specifically developed for patients with complex PTSD with and without co-occurring BPD. The **overriding aim** of DBT-PTSD is to help the clients to live a meaningful life in accordance with their own values. Figure 36.1 provides an overview of the sources of DBT-PTSD. In addition to trauma-specific cognitive and skills-based exposure-based techniques, DBT-PTSD comprises a variety of interventions of the so-called "third wave" of behavioural therapy with elements of DBT (Linehan, 1993a, b), Compassion Focused Therapy (CFT; Gilbert, 2010) and Acceptance and Commitment Therapy (ACT; Hayes, 2016). Patients affected by sexual and physical abuse in childhood often cannot completely revise their cognitive-affective schemata developed early in life. Often patients have to learn to deal with these problematic schemas and take goal-orientated action in spite of their fears and their disturbing thoughts. According to DBT's dialectical principles, changing emotional and cognitive processing is balanced by a strong focus on acceptance, metacognitive awareness (observing), and self-compassion. These aspects play a central role in ameliorating the more persistent symptom areas of cPTSD—i.e., components of self-worth.

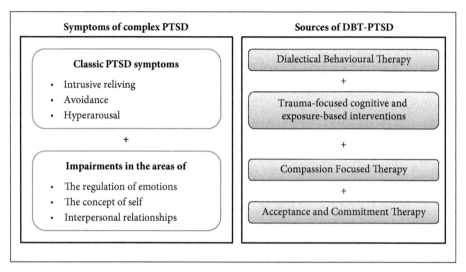

FIGURE 36.1 Sources of DBT-PTSD.

In addition to the treatment framework, the principles, and the therapeutic approach of DBT, DBT-PTSD uses many DBT interventions to improve the regulation of emotions. The identification and description of emotions and thoughts using mindfulness creates an inner distance (in the sense of *"I am not my emotion but I have an emotion."*). The attitude of ACT that it is more helpful in the case of some thoughts and feelings (so-called "bodyguards"), not to fight them but to accept them as old and once useful thoughts, has proved useful particularly in the case of basic assumptions (in the sense of *"I have learned familiar thoughts, and I can decide whether I should act in accordance with these thoughts."*). In addition, ACT provides many helpful interventions for recognizing and implementing personal values and thus for improving the quality of life. The strengthening of compassion towards oneself and towards others in accordance with CFT has proved to be particularly helpful for treating issues in the areas of self-worth and interpersonal relations.

DBT-PTSD Basic Assumptions

1. The overarching goal is to empower the clients to live a life according to their values (life worth living).
2. Currently, trauma-related symptoms, cognitions, emotions, and behaviour hinder clients in achieving their goals (or even to define their individual values and goals).
3. Thus, the treatment primarily focuses on reduction of trauma-related symptoms, cognitions, emotions, and behaviour.
4. Most trauma-related symptoms are maintained by either escape or avoidance of trauma-related primary emotions.

5. The key components of negative self-esteem have been developed as maladaptive coping strategies to survive feelings of unescapable threat, powerlessness, irritation, helplessness, and loss of belonging.

6. The key components of DBT-PTSD are skills-assisted exposure; development of compassion for self and others; radical acceptance of the past; and developing a life worth living (in this order).

7. DBT-PTSD is a highly intensive treatment provided by highly trained experts.

8. DBT-PTSD is a treatment in a team.

DBT-PTSD Treatment Phases

DBT-PTSD is divided into a pre-treatment phase and seven consecutive thematic treatment phases (Figure 36.2), which extend over a period of 12 weeks in a residential setting and comprise up to 45 therapy sessions in an outpatient setting. Each treatment phase includes mandatory and optional treatment modules. The latter allow tailoring the treatment to the many different symptom constellations that present in cPTSD. While one patient in the third therapy phase is focused, for example, primarily on the reduction of dissociative symptoms, the treatment of the feelings of guilt can be the focus of another patient. In addition to the chronologically organized treatment process, DBT-PTSD is also oriented to the dynamic treatment hierarchy as defined by standard DBT. Whenever present, therefore, life-threatening or crisis-generating or therapy-interfering behaviours take precedence.

Pre-Treatment. Prior to treatment, diagnosis of PTSD and co-occurring psychiatric disorders is required. We recommend the Structured Clinical Interview for DSM-5 (SCID-5; First, Williams, Karg, & Spitzer, 2015) and the Clinician-Administered PTSD Scale (CAPS; Weathers et al., 2013). We further require an overview of any current crisis-generating behaviour, including ongoing self-harm behaviour, suicide attempts, high-risk behaviour, aggressive outbursts, etc. We recommend the Severe Behavioural Dyscontrol Interview (SBD; Bohus, 2011) for this purpose. In case of a life-threatening suicide attempt within the last six weeks, we apply a short version of individual DBT in order to figure out the main reasons for this suicide attempt and clarify whether the related problems are still of relevance, can be solved, or can be coped with using specific individualized skills. Ongoing NSSI, parasuicidal behaviour, suicidal ideation, or severe dissociative states are no reason to exclude patients from this treatment. As a next step, we educate the client about the form and function of the treatment and work on a non-suicidal contract. The latter includes a promise, mostly in the form of a written contract, not to committ suicide during the therapy phase and—under residential conditions—for six months after discharge from the unit. In return, clients are offered telephone consultation to assist with managing suicidal crises according to the standard DBT suicide crisis protocol.

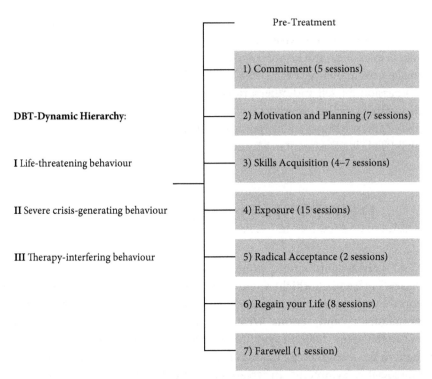

FIGURE 35.2 Modular DBT-PTSD with dynamic treatment hierarchy

Commitment phase. During this phase, we conduct a short biographical and medical history, explore the individual's PTSD presentation, and orientate our clients to the treatment and try to understand the experience and potential problems with previous psychosocial treatments. Clients are informed about the basic concept of mindfulness exercises and encouraged to practise mindfulness daily for at least ten minutes, based on MP3 file mindfulness instructions, read by their therapist.

Motivation and planning. This second phase begins with a short overview of the circumstances of the major traumatic events: "What happened to you? At which age did it happen? Who was involved? Who was informed? Did you have any emotional support? When and why did it end? And how did the perpetrator(s) frighten and intimidate you not to report to anybody?" The focus in this early phase is not to elicit strong emotional responses, but rather to encourage the clients in speaking openly about previously taboo subjects with their therapists. A longer focus on motivational issues follows helping the clients to clarify their personal values and to formulate specific, measurable, attainable, relevant, and time-bound (SMART) treatment goals. The central question is: "How would you create your life if you were not hindered by PTSD symptoms?" In order to avoid problems in the therapeutic relationship based on replicating patterns in previous significant relationships, we briefly assess the characteristics of significant others like the mother, father, or siblings of the client. One further important topic is the development of an individualized trauma-model including explanations of the form and function of trauma-networks (i.e., relative fixed associations of trauma-related thoughts, emotions, and somatic experiences), initiating cues, maladaptive mechanisms of avoidance and escape, including behavioural (e.g., self-harm), emotional (e.g., guilt, dissociation), and cognitive strategies.

Skills Acquisition. Due to lack of a group, in DBT-PTSD skills are taught by the individual therapist. We selected a small number of essential skills: anti-dissociation skills (e.g., balance board, ammonia, ice-packs), distress tolerance skills, emotion regulation of guilt, shame, anger, and disgust.

Skills-assisted Exposure. As a first step, the index-trauma (the currently most distressing and shameful memory) is selected. Next, the patient's concerns and apprehensions regarding the exposure are thoroughly discussed and addressed. Central to the fourth treatment phase is in-sensu exposure to the most distressing memory. In order to keep stress within a tolerable range and to prevent dissociative symptoms, exposure is based on the principle of skills-assisted exposure. Through the use of skills, a balance between the activation of trauma-associated feelings and present relevance is established. This phase typically lasts for about five to seven sessions per index trauma. After remission, we can process a second or third traumatic memory.

Radical Acceptance. Linehan's (1993 a, b) radical acceptance requires acceptance of the facts of the past, the sequelae of past events, and the current emotional response to both of these. Accordingly, we added a phase of intensively working on radical acceptance at the end of the exposure phase.

Regain your Life. Most of our patients experience dramatic changes within a relatively short time frame. This often revolutionizes the client's perspective on his/her entire life: Partnership, sexuality, friendships, supportive systems, occupational conditions—almost every aspect has to be questioned and re-arranged. Making these behavioural changes requires time and support.

Farewell. After such an intensive and life-changing therapy saying farewell is not easy and so we provide a structured approach to this process.

DBT-PTSD INTERVENTIONS

DBT-PTSD in general follows the principles and rules of standard DBT and adds in a set of trauma-specific interventions such as exposure to the index-trauma. Some additional non-trauma-specific interventions like "compassion for self and others" or "follow your values" are in line with the DBT-principles as outlined by Linehan (1993a, b); however, we elaborated on these concepts to enhance their relevance for this specific patient group.

In general, the DBT-PTSD manual is designed as a comprehensive and detailed textbook for therapists, including a set of handouts and worksheets for the patients. The entire focus is on trauma, avoidance of trauma-related emotions, and related cues, as well as trauma-related sequelae on self-esteem and self-concepts, including maladaptive guilt, shame, disgust, self-contempt, and suspiciousness.

The key element of the programme is skills-assisted exposure. Therapists should thoroughfully prepare these sessions by selecting the appropriate index-trauma(s) (the currently most distressing and shameful event(s)). Furthermore, they should be familiar with the key primary emotions (emotions that were experienced during the trauma), mostly disgust, and other relevant cognitions and sensations, such as power-lessness, threat, or sexual arousal. Emotions like guilt, shame, and self-contempt are seen as secondary emotions and mostly function as escapes from primary emotions. Therapists should actively guide their patients to experience and tolerate the primary emotions. We do not apply classic prolonged exposure (PE) as proposed by Foa and colleagues (2007), since most patients meeting criteria for cPTSD are highly prone to dissociative features under stress conditions, and the level of activated dissociative features negatively correlates with treatment-outcome (Kleindienst et al., 2016). The neural mechanisms underlying dissociative features are not completely understood. There is ample evidence, however, that during dissociation the functions of amygdala and hippocampus are blunted (Krause-Utz et al., 2017; Winter et al., 2015), and there-fore emotional learning is attenuated if not completely inhibited (Ebner-Priemer et al., 2009). Therapeutic in-sensu or in-vivo activation of traumatic memories induces stress, stress induces dissociative features, and dissociative features inhibit emotional learning. To facilitate emotional learning during stressful in-sensu exposure, therapists apply anti-dissociative skills. Any kind of strong sensory input can be used as anti-dissociative skills: loud noise, pain (ammonia), cold temperature (ice-cubes), eye-movement, as well as proprio-sensoric stimuli such as balancing boards, or even juggling. Most patients are rather creative and quickly learn to find their own techniques to also inhibit dissociative symptoms when listening to the audiotaped exposure-sessions at home.

In most cases, five to seven exposure sessions should be sufficient to reduce the fre-quency and the distress of index-related intrusions and nightmares. Secondary trauma related emotions like guilt, shame, and self-contempt or self-hatred need more specific interventions. We use a combination of psychoeducation, meta-cognitive training and compassion-based interventions to address these issues. The results for this approach are quite convincing: the three-month residential programme resulted in a strong de-crease of guilt, shame, and disgust. By the end of the intervention 82% of the patients had achieved a level of trauma-related guilt (shame 67%; disgust 51%) that resembled the level of a healthy control group (Görg et al., 2017; Görg et al., in prep).

The standard DBT manual provides no specific interventions for changing habits or creating a life worth living. Chain—or behavioural analyses—are helpful tools to understand and modify maladaptive behaviour such as self-harm, suicidal thoughts, or aggressive outbursts. However, when it comes to modifying your patient's sexual sensi-tivity, to encourage seeking a nicer partner, or applying for a better job—chain analyses are of little help. We found a useful and practical solution in a recently developed ACT tool—the Matrix (Polk, Schoendorff, Webster, & Olaz, 2016). The Matrix is a simple-to-use format developed initially for groups, but subsequently utilized with individuals. Based on an original idea by Kevin Polk, the Matrix discriminates between direct ex-periencing with the senses and indirect experiencing in the mind encouraging clients to sort behaviour into two categories, broadly described as "Towards" whom or what is important to us, and "Away" from what we want to avoid feeling or thinking. Therapists orientate clients to the difference between five-sense experiencing and observable behaviour—which is the immediate experience we have of the world outside, and inner experiencing—which is the world of the mind and emotions. Using a diagrammatic format, the Matrix helps clients rapidly develop clarity about these differences and move toward valued living, also known as psychological flexibility.

The focus of the Matrix is more on dragging out new behaviour than on analysing hindering cognitions and emotions. DBT skills can be used as both mental reminders and motivators as well as functional behaviours.

Summary

With DBT-PTSD, a treatment programme is available that is specifically tailored for the needs of patients with complex PTSD and/or borderline patients with co-occuring PTSD. The treatment has proved to be effective and safe under residential and outpatient treatment conditions. Training in DBT-PTSD requires four days, plus one supervised case for therapists who are already experienced in standard DBT.

Key Points for Clinicians

- DBT-PTSD is a safe and highly effective multicomponent treatment programme for complex PTSD.
- Thus far, there is no evidence that ongoing self-harm is a safety risk or negative predictor for treatment outcome.
- Borderline patients with co-occurring PTSD should search for a trauma-focused treatment.
- In most cases, there is no need for patients with complex PTSD or PTSD and BPD to complete standard DBT ahead of a specifically designed treatment programme for treating trauma.

References

American Psychiatric Association (2013). Diagnostic and statistical manual of mental disorders (DSM-5®). Washington, DC: American Psychiatric Pub.

Bisson, J. I., Roberts, N. P. Andrew, M., Cooper, R., & Lewis, C. (2013). Psychological therapies for chronic post-traumatic stress disorder (PTSD) in adults. *Cochrane Database of Systematic Reviews*. doi: 10.1002/14651858.CD003388.pub4

Bohus. M. (2011). Checkliste zu schweren Störunegn der Verhaltenskontrolle (SBDI). In G. Meinlschmidt, S. Schneider, & J. Margraf (Eds.), *Lehrbuch der Verhaltenstherapie: Band 4: Materialien für Psychotherapie*. Berlin: Springer Verlag.

Bohus, M., Dyer, A., Priebe, K., Krüger, A., Kleindienst, N., Schmahl, C. ... Steil, R. (2013). Dialectical behaviour therapy for post-traumatic stress disorder after childhood sexual abuse in patients with and without borderline personality disorder: a randomised controlled trial. *Psychotherapy and Psychosomatics, 82*, 221–233.

Bradley, R., Greene, J., Russ, E., Dutra, L., & Westen, D. (2005). A multidimensional meta-analysis of psychotherapy for PTSD. *American Journal of Psychiatry, 162*, 214–227.

Cackowski, S., Neubauer, T., & Kleindienst, N. (2016). The impact of posttraumatic stress disorder on the symptomatology of borderline personality disorder. *Borderline Personality Disorder and Emotion Dysregulation, 3*, 7.

Chen, L. P., Murad, M. H., Paras, M. L., Colbenson, K. M., Sattler, A. L., Goranson, E. N. ... Zirakzadeh, A. (2010). Sexual abuse and lifetime diagnosis of psychiatric disorders: systematic review and meta-analysis. *Mayo Clinic Proceedings, 85*, 618–629.

Cloitre, M., Koenen, K. C., Cohen, L. R., & Han, H. (2002). Skills training in affective and interpersonal regulation followed by exposure: A phase-based treatment for PTSD related to childhood abuse. *Journal of Consulting and Clinical Psychology, 70*, 1067–1074.

Cloitre, M., Stovall-McClough, K. C., Nooner, K., Zorbas, P., Cherry, S., Jackson, C. L. ... Petkova, E. (2010). Treatment for PTSD related to childhood abuse: A randomized controlled trial. *American Journal of Psychiatry, 167*, 915–924.

Cloitre, M., Courtois, C. A., Charuvastra, A., Carapezza, R., Stolbach, B. C., & Green, B. L. (2011). Treatment of complex PTSD: Results of the ISTSS expert clinician survey on best practices. *Journal of Traumatic Stress, 24*, 615–627.

Cutajar, M. C., Mullen, P. E., Ogloff, J. R., Thomas, S. D., Wells, D. L., & Spataro, J. (2010). Psychopathology in a large cohort of sexually abused children followed up to 43 years. *Child Abuse & Neglect, 34*, 813–822.

Dorrepaal, E., Thomaes, K., Hoogendoorn, A. W., Veltman, D. J., Draijer, N., & van Balkom, A. J. (2014). Evidence-based treatment for adult women with child abuse-related complex PTSD: A quantitative review. *European Journal of Psychotraumatology, 5*, https://doi.org/10.3402/ejpt.v5.23613

Ebner-Priemer, U. W., Mauchnik, J., Kleindienst, N., Schmahl, C., Peper, M., Rosenthal, Z., ... Bohus, M. (2009). Emotional learning during dissociative states in borderline personality disorder. *Journal of Psychiatry and Neuroscience, 34*, 214–222.

Ehring, T., Welboren, R., Morina, N., Wicherts, J. M., Freitag, J., & Emmelkamp, P. M. (2014). Meta-analysis of psychological treatments for posttraumatic stress disorder in adult survivors of childhood abuse. *Clinical Psychology Review, 34*, 645–657.

Fergusson, D. M., Boden, J. M., & Horwood, L. J. (2008). Exposure to childhood sexual and physical abuse and adjustment in early adulthood. *Child Abuse & Neglect, 32*, 607–619.

First, M. B., Williams, J. B. W., Karg, R. S., & Spitzer, R. L. (2015). *Structured clinical interview for DSM-5 disorders, clinician version* (SCID-5-CV). Arlington, VA: American Psychiatric Association.

Foa, E. B., Hembree, E. A., & Rothbaum, B. O. (2007). *Prolonged exposure therapy for PTSD: Emotional processing of traumatic experiences*. Oxford: Oxford University Press.

Gilbert, P. (2010). *Compassion focused therapy*. New York: Routledge.

Gilbert, R., Widom, C. S., Browne, K., Fergusson, D., Webb, E., & Janson, S. (2009). Burden and consequences of child maltreatment in high-income countries. *The Lancet, 373,* 68–81.

Görg, N., Priebe, K., Böhnke, J. R., Steil, R., Dyer, A. S., & Kleindienst, N. (2017). Trauma-related emotions and radical acceptance in dialectical behavior therapy for posttraumatic stress disorder after childhood sexual abuse. *Borderline Personality Disorder and Emotion Dysregulation, 4,* 15.

Görg et al. in prep. *Changes in trauma-related emotions following treatment with Dialectical Behavior Therapy for Posttraumatic Stress Disorder after childhood abuse.*

Harned, M., Rizvi, S., & Linehan, M. (2010). Impact of co-occurring posttraumatic stress disorder on suicidal women with borderline personality disorder. *American Journal of Psychiatry, 67,* 1210–1217.

Harned, M. S., Korslund, K. E., Foa, E. B., & Linehan, M. M. (2012). Treating PTSD in suicidal and self-injuring women with borderline personality disorder: Development and preliminary evaluation of a dialectical behavior therapy prolonged exposure protocol. *Behaviour Research and Therapy, 50,* 381–386.

Harned, M. S., Korslund, K. E., & Linehan, M. M. (2014). A pilot randomized controlled trial of dialectical behavior therapy with and without the dialectical behavior therapy prolonged exposure protocol for suicidal and self-injuring women with borderline personality disorder and PTSD. *Behaviour Research and Therapy, 55,* 7–17.

Hayes S. (2016). *Acceptance and commitment therapy: The process and practice of mindful change.* New York: Guilford Press.

Imel, Z. E., Laska, K., Jakupcak, M., & Simpson, T. L. (2013). Meta-analysis of dropout in treatments for posttraumatic stress disorder. *Journal of Consulting and Clinical Psychology, 81,* 394–404.

Kleindienst, N., Priebe, K., Görg, N., Dyer, A., Steil, R., Lyssenko, L., … Bohus, M. (2016). State dissociation moderates response in women receiving dialectical behavior therapy for posttraumatic stress disorder with or without borderline personality disorder. *European Journal of Psychotraumatology, 7.* https://doi.org/10.3402/ejpt.v7.30375

Krause-Utz, A., Winter, D., Schriner, F., Chiu, C. D., Lis, S., Spinhoven, P. … Elzinga, B. (2017). Reduced amygdala reactivity and impaired working memory during dissociation in borderline personality disorder. *European Archhives of Psychiatry and Clinical Neuroscience,* 1–15. https://doi.org/10.1007/s00406-017-0806-x

Krüger, A., Kleindienst, N., Priebe, K., Dyer, A., Steil, R., Schmahl, C., & Bohus, M. (2014). Non-suicidal self-injury during an exposure-based treatment in patients with posttraumatic stress disorder and borderline features. *Behavior Research and Therapy, 61,* 136–141.

Linehan, M. M. (1993a). *Cognitive behavioral treatment of borderline personality disorder.* New York: Guilford Press.

Linehan, M. M. (1993b). *Skills training manual for borderline personality disorder.* New York: Guilford Press.

Maercker, A., Brewin, C. R., Bryant, R. A., Cloitre, M. Reed, G. M., van Ommeren, M. … Rousseau, C. (2013). Proposals for mental disorders specifically associated with stress in the International Classification of Diseases-11. *The Lancet, 381,* 1683–1685.

Maniglio, R. (2009). The impact of child sexual abuse on health: a systematic review of reviews. *Clinical Psychology Review, 29,* 647–657.

Maniglio, R. (2010). Child sexual abuse in the etiology of depression: a systematic review of reviews. *Depression and Anxiety, 27,* 631–642.

Paolucci, E. O., Genuis, M. L., & Violato, C. (2001). A meta-analysis of the published research on the effects of child sexual abuse. *The Journal of Psychology, 135*, 17–36.

Polk, K. L., Schoendorff, B., Webster, M., & Olaz, F. O. (2016). *The essential guide to the ACT Matrix: A step-by-step approach to using the ACT Matrix model in clinical practice*. Oakland, CA: New Harbinger Publications.

Priebe, K., Roth, M., Krüger, A., Glöckner-Fink, K., Dyer, A., Steil, R. … Bohus, M. (2017). [Costs of Mental Health Care in Patients with Posttraumatic Stress Disorder Related to Sexual Abuse One Year Before and After Inpatient DBT-PTSD]. *Psychiatrische Praxis, 44*, 75–84.

Resick, P. A., Monson, C. M., & Chard, K. M. (2016). *Cognitive processing therapy for PTSD*. New York: Guilford Press.

Shapiro, F. (2018). *Eye movement desensitization and reprocessing (EMDR) therapy, second edition: Basic principles, protocols, and procedures*. New York: Guilford Press.

Steil, R., Dyer, A., Priebe, K., Kleindienst, N., & Bohus, M. (2011). Dialectical behavior therapy for posttraumatic stress disorder related to childhood sexual abuse: a pilot study of an intensive residential treatment program. *Journal of Traumatic Stress, 24*, 102–106.

Steil, R., Dittmann, C., Müller-Engelmann, M., Dyer, A., Maasch, A. M., & Priebe, K. (2018). Dialectical behaviour therapy for posttraumatic stress disorder related to childhood sexual abuse: a pilot study in an outpatient treatment setting. *European Journal of Psychotraumatology, 9*(1), 1423832.

Watts, B. V., Schnurr, P. P., Mayo, L., Young-Xu, Y., Weeks, W. B., & Friedman, M. J. (2013). Meta-analysis of the efficacy of treatments for posttraumatic stress disorder. *The Journal of Clinical Psychiatry, 74*, 541–550.

Weathers, F. W., Blake, D. D., Schnurr, P. P., Kaloupek, D. G., Marx, B. P., & Keane, T. M. (2013). The clinician-administered PTSD scale for DSM-5 (CAPS-5). Interview available from the National Center for PTSD at www.ptsd.va.gov

Winter, D., Krause-Utz, A., Lis, S., Chiu, C. D., Lanius, R. A., Schriner, F. … Schmahl, C. (2015). Dissociation in borderline personality disorder: Disturbed cognitive and emotional inhibition and its neural correlates. *Psychiatry Research, 15*, 339–351.

Yates, T. M., Carlson, E. A., & Egeland, B. (2008). A prospective study of child maltreatment and self-injurious behavior in a community sample. *Development and Psychopathology, 20*, 651–671.

Yen, S., Shea, M. T., Battle, C. L., Johnson, D. M., Zlotnick, C., Dolan-Sewell, R. … McGlashan, T. H. (2002). Traumatic exposure and posttraumatic stress disorder in borderline, schizotypal, avoidant, and obsessive-compulsive personality disorders: findings from the Collaborative Longitudinal Personality Disorders Study. *Journal of Nervous and Mental Disease, 190*, 510–518.

Zanarini, M. C., Frankenburg, F. R., Dubo, E. D., Sickel, A. E., Trikha, A., Levin, A., & Reynolds, V. (1998). Axis I comorbidity of borderline personality disorder. *American Journal of Psychiatry, 155*, 1733–1739.

Zlotnick, C., Franklin, C. L., & Zimmerman, M. (2002). Is comorbidity of post-traumatic stress disorder and borderline personality disorder related to greater pathology and impairment? *American Journal of Psychiatry, 159*, 1940–1943.

SECTION VII

IMPLEMENTATION OF DBT

CHAPTER 37

IMPLEMENTING DBT

An Implementation Science Perspective

KATHERINE ANNE COMTOIS AND SARA J. LANDES

INTRODUCTION

This chapter reflects the combination of our experience. Dr. Comtois has led a DBT programme in Seattle for 20 years, has been a research therapist in DBT, and has developed a version of DBT focused on helping psychiatrically disabled clients with BPD return to work. In addition to her experience implementing DBT in her own programme, she conducts DBT trainings internationally with a focus on implementation, consults across a wide range of systems on the implementation of DBT, and is the founder and past president of the Society for Implementation Research Collaboration (SIRC). Dr. Landes is a DBT therapist and trainer as well as an implementation scientist who conducts research on the implementation of DBT in large systems and an officer of SIRC as well as other dissemination and implementation organizations. This chapter includes an introduction to implementation science from a DBT perspective and a review of implementation research on DBT. Given that implementation research is still in its early days, we have also embedded observations and conclusions from our experience of implementing DBT and from our consulting with others implementing DBT. Finally, we note that future implementation research needs to answer some key questions.

DEFINING IMPLEMENTATION SCIENCE AND QUESTIONS IT CAN ANSWER

As described elsewhere in this volume, DBT is an effective psychotherapy that has been adapted for a variety of disorders and treatment settings. Many of these adaptations have themselves been evaluated for effectiveness such that there is a wide published literature on the efficacy and effectiveness of DBT (see Chapters 20 and 21, this volume).

However, there are a great deal fewer evaluations of the *implementation* of DBT. It is important to immediately make a distinction between studying whether DBT works when implemented with a new disorder or in a new setting versus studying DBT implementation itself. The former is an *effectiveness* study of DBT where the outcomes are changes in a new subgroup of DBT clients. The latter is an *implementation* study of *how* DBT is used and the outcome is changes in clinicians, the setting, or the system, but *not* the clients. Of course, there are effectiveness-implementation hybrid studies that seek to achieve both outcomes (Curran, Bauer, Mittman, Pyne, & Stetler, 2012).

To put it another way, DBT does not magically arrive in a new setting—rather, the use of explicit and implicit strategies gets it there. The most obvious, and certainly necessary, strategy is training—in DBT language, enhancing the capabilities and motivation of the clinicians to do DBT. Thus, a DBT training course is an implementation strategy. Consultation to or supervision of clinicians is another implementation strategy. Then there are less-obvious implementation strategies, including changes to programme structure, changes to clinician schedules, changes to medical record templates, changes in supervision expectations or job descriptions, changes to billing codes, changes to intake or exit procedures, changes to suicide risk management protocols, etc. Then there are implementation strategies, such as implementation consultation (i.e., external facilitation) to help clinics choose, plan, and use such implementation strategies (Kirchner et al., 2014; Ritchie, Dollar, Kearney, & Kirchner, 2014). All of these activities are part of the implementation of DBT and, to date, we have little empirical data on how to do them effectively, which are more successful than others, or how to order them to achieve an effective and sustained DBT programme. And so DBT programmes—even those focused on data—are generally attending to client outcomes, but not implementation outcomes.

Implementation science is the study of strategies to promote the integration of research findings and evidence into healthcare policy and practice. Again, the outcome is whether research is integrated into policy and practice—not whether clients improve. Implementation science studies different strategies, such as training, consultation, systemic changes, incentives, etc., to determine which bring about successful integration. But how do we measure successful integration of research into practice if we are not looking at client success? In 2011, Proctor and colleagues (2011) organized and codified implementation outcomes. As shown in Figure 37.1 from their seminal paper, implementation outcomes precede service outcomes—such as the safety, effectiveness, and equity of the intervention—because, of course, the intervention needs to be in place before evaluating its service outcomes. The client outcomes of satisfaction, symptoms, and function are the final link in the chain. While client outcomes are the ultimate goal, the figure illustrates how difficult and noisy it is to evaluate implementation strategies by using client outcomes when such outcomes are dependent on a whole host of service outcomes as well. There is also the risk that if DBT was ineffective for clients in a new setting, it will be impossible to determine whether this was a DBT failure (it didn't work) or an implementation failure (DBT was deployed incorrectly) (Proctor et al., 2011).

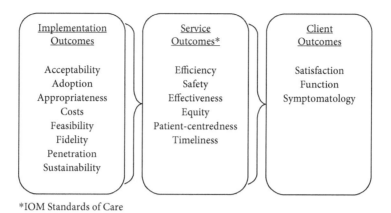

*IOM Standards of Care

FIGURE 37.1 Types of outcomes in implementation research.

Reproduced from Enola Proctor, Hiie Silmere, Ramesh Raghavan, Peter Hovmand, Greg Aarons, Alicia Bunger, Richard Griffey, and Melissa Hensley, Outcomes for Implementation Research: Conceptual Distinctions, Measurement Challenges, and Research Agenda, *Administration and Policy in Mental Health, 38*(2), pp. 65–76, Figure 2, doi: 10.1007/s10488-010-0319-7 © The Author(s) 2010. This work is licensed under the Creative Commons Attribution Noncommercial 2.0 License (CC BY-NC 2.0). It is attributed to the authors Enola Proctor, Hiie Silmere, Ramesh Raghavan, Peter Hovmand, Greg Aarons, Alicia Bunger, Richard Griffey, and Melissa Hensley.

Thus, to successfully evaluate implementation, it is helpful to focus on the eight implementation outcomes—acceptability, appropriateness, adoption, feasibility, fidelity, penetration, cost, and sustainability—accepted as standards when evaluating implementation of a variety of evidence-based practices (EBPs). These outcomes have been assessed empirically with contingency management (Hartzler, Jackson, Jones, Beadnell, & Caslyn, 2014), multisystemic therapy (MST; Schoenwald, Henggeler, Brondino, & Rowland, 2000), and prolonged exposure (PE) and cognitive processing therapy (CPT; Karlin et al., 2010), and other EBPs, but DBT research and community providers have not yet considered them. This chapter examines each implementation outcome in terms of DBT, including both empirical implementation research as well as our own observations from implementation practice.

Acceptability and Appropriateness

The first two outcomes—acceptability and appropriateness—are measures of how key stakeholders within a clinic or health system (e.g., clients, providers, clinic managers, facility leadership) view DBT. Acceptability reflects whether DBT is generally viewed as a good idea—i.e., are stakeholders agreeable or satisfied with the DBT approach including its functions, modes, outcomes, principles, interventions, and demands on clients and the clinical setting. Appropriateness is the perceived fit of DBT to this particular clinic or system—i.e., is it relevant, compatible, suitable, and useful.

Empirical studies generally show that DBT is considered acceptable, but that it is not always appropriate for particular settings. Herschell and colleagues (2009) interviewed leaders of ten community mental health agencies across four counties in the US who were embarking on an implementation of DBT who reported high acceptability; describing DBT as "reasonable", "worthwhile", "practical", "ideal", "humane", "common sense", and a "complement to established services". Swales, Taylor, and Hibbs (2012) interviewed leaders and clinicians from NHS mental health organizations across the UK who had implemented DBT. They described benefits of DBT as both improved client outcomes and benefits to the clinicians in improving their own skills and experience of support at work. Hazelton, Rossiter, and Milner (2006) interviewed leaders and clinicians across a county in Australia before and after a countywide DBT training. Prior to training, clinicians had negative attitudes toward clients with borderline personality disorder (BPD) and pessimistic attitudes toward their treatment. After initial trainings in DBT, clinicians reported increased confidence in treatment and that DBT provided structure and logic for treatment and benefits to the clinicians' personal lives.

Landes and colleagues (2017) surveyed leads of DBT programmes across the Veterans Health Administration (VHA) in the US and found high acceptability for DBT who saw a wide range of benefits for clients, for providers, and for the clinic/system. The client benefits endorsed by the majority of programme leads were increased hope, improvement in clients' symptoms or functioning, reduced number of psychiatric hospitalizations, reduced use of emergency services, and longer-term treatment options. The benefits for clinicians reported by the majority of programmes were increased self-efficacy, increased compassion (for themselves, co-workers, and veterans), increased sense of challenge and accomplishment at work, increased job satisfaction, increased support and connection with co-workers, decreased burnout, and improved therapy skills. A majority of programmes also identified four system benefits: ability to offer EBP for clients with self-injury and suicidality, ability to offer an additional opportunity for trainees, community of providers/team approach for therapy, and better efficiency/productivity for EBPs for Post-traumatic Stress Disorder (PTSD). While about half the programmes identified a non-behavioural orientation as a barrier, they reported this was a barrier they had already overcome or were working on, and none described it as a barrier they could not overcome. Other theoretical or philosophy barriers to DBT (such as difficulty adopting DBT assumptions or team agreements, buying into the biosocial theory, dialectical orientation, etc.) were not a barrier, or only a small barrier, for the majority of programmes and were almost never described as a barrier that could not be overcome.

These studies, however, also heard leaders and clinicians expressing concern about the appropriateness of DBT to their specific setting. Herschell and colleagues (2009) found concerns that DBT done to fidelity did not fit with the community mental health payment structure and that clinicians taking calls at home did not fit their agency structure. There were also concerns that DBT was too time- and cost-intensive. Swales and colleagues (2012) also found that struggles with resources and administrative support were the primary reasons that DBT programmes in the UK had closed, rather than due to concerns about DBT per se. Hazelton and colleagues (2006), however, found more administrative support during the initial implementation of DBT that matched clinical support and positive attitude change. Landes et al. (2017) found the primary barriers that DBT programmes in the VHA were still working on or could not overcome in-cluded difficulty implementing telephone coaching outside of business hours due to VHA rules. Chugani and Landes (2016) surveyed college counselling centres across the US to determine barriers to DBT and found that more than half thought that DBT was beyond their scope or only relevant to a minority of students, and that over 60% found that it did not fit with their structure primarily due to after-hours calls and non-behavioural orientation of counselling centre clinicians.

Based on our experience implementing DBT, worse appropriateness outcomes are due to an underestimation of DBT's flexibility, lack of a core DBT mode (e.g., individual therapy) in that setting, or perception that DBT would be too expensive. As seen in Hazelton et al. (2006), initial or introductory trainings and clinician testimonials have often been found to improve acceptability and appropriateness. Trainings that facilitate discussion or answering questions or consultation are often more important for appro-priateness as the stakeholders work through the potential fit of DBT with their setting. When acceptability and appropriateness outcomes are assessed, this information can be used by DBT intermediaries (i.e., trainers, consultants, facilitators) or clinic leadership early on to shape the implementation process or as factors to consider as to why DBT was not implemented.

For successful DBT implementation, DBT training and consultation methods need to succeed in demonstrating that DBT is a strong treatment in general and that it is ap-propriate to that particular site. Trainings vary tremendously in their ability to do this depending on the content and process of training. Given perspectives that DBT is ac-ceptable and effective, but too costly, too big, or otherwise not appropriate for their system, some academic presentations do not provide enough contextual information or examples of DBT in practice to demonstrate its flexibility. It is critical for trainers to have experience with a range of solutions to the typical appropriateness concerns so that clinicians, agencies, or systems don't implement DBT in a rigid way that conforms to the manual, but clashes with the clinical structure. A key example is out of session coaching, often described as 24/7, and thus considered a non-starter for community settings. The result of this emphasis on coaching outside of work hours is that clinicians and teams reject out of session coaching (or DBT) entirely, rather than considering how to use coaching during work hours. Our practical experience is focusing on generalization of skills outside of sessions through coaching during work hours first (if this is a setting limitation) achieves a key DBT function. Without this being seen as a make-or-break issue, more DBT clinicians and programmes eventually start to want coaching options outside of work hours because they see the utility and figure out options to do it.

Adoption

Adoption—or the intention or initial decision to employ an EBP—has been a particu-larly strong outcome for DBT. DBT has been adopted not only by counties and vet-erans' services in many countries (Carmel, Rose, & Fruzzetti, 2014; Hazelton et al.,

2006; Herschell et al., 2009; Herschell, Lindhiem, Kogan, Celedonia, & Stein, 2014; Landes et al., 2017), but it has also been adopted by national government health systems or mental health organizations like the Government of Ireland (2006), the National Institute of Health and Care Excellence (NICE, 2009), the US Substance Abuse and Mental Health Services Administration (SAMHSA, 2013) and by the VHA as an appropriate treatment for suicidality or BPD (Department of Veterans Affairs/Department of Defense, 2013).

Adoption is ideally based on key stakeholders' determination that DBT is both acceptable and appropriate. But in the real world, adoption sometimes comes without either, such as when a county or state puts out a request for applications to come to a DBT training contingent on adopting DBT at the agency. The agency leadership applies for the training, and clinicians and supervisors are tasked to start a DBT programme, sometimes knowing very little about what that entails. Anecdotally, those who have provided training in such circumstances have seen it fail as one might predict, but have also seen it succeed where acceptability and appropriateness were developed through the process of training and adoption (Ditty, Landes, Doyle, & Beidas, 2015; Hazelton et al., 2006; Herschell et al., 2009, 2014; Landes et al., 2017). No research evidence has evaluated this question.

This is a good place to note the value of "trialability" in implementation. Trialability, as articulated by Rogers (2010), is the ability to try a new intervention and, if it isn't working, to remove it; additionally, it is associated with increased willingness to adopt innovations. This form of adoption is seen in DBT implementation through the use of pilot programmes where DBT is tried with a small group of clients over the course of the training period and may be implemented more widely based on the results. Thus, a DBT pilot programme is an implementation strategy that can be evaluated with these implementation outcomes as results.

Feasibility and Fidelity

Once a system adopts DBT, then the next implementation outcome evaluated is either feasibility or fidelity. Feasibility is the extent to which DBT can be successfully used in a given setting or system. It is the reality side of appropriateness—rather than perceived fit, feasibility is the actual fit or suitability of DBT for practical use in that setting, and is generally measured by stakeholder surveys or administrative data. Fidelity is the extent to which DBT is adherent or delivered as intended. Often there is a dialectical tension between feasibility and fidelity in a complex and multi-modal treatment such as DBT; unpaid or unusual aspects of DBT such as out-of-session contact and consultation teams buck up against the clinicians' schedule or agency's structure. This does not usually occur for EBPs that involve changing the content of treatment but not the modes of treatment (e.g., changing individual therapy from standard care to cognitive behavioural therapy, or one medication for another).

Multiple survey studies show evidence of DBT feasibility with at least minimal fidelity in community settings. Ditty and colleagues (2015) found that DBT programmes endorsed 70% of the DBT elements established by the treatment developer and colleagues. Herschell and colleagues (2014) in their evaluation of DBT across four counties found DBT providers moved from using some to most of the DBT components over the two-year training period. An evaluation of community mental health clinicians across one state (Hawkins & Sinha, 1998) found that there was high post-training content knowledge of DBT. Landes and colleagues (2017) found DBT programmes were implemented in the VHA despite any formalized VHA training or endorsement and the majority of programmes were established with only low- or medium-intensity training such as reading the treatment manuals or attending one- or two-day workshops (Landes et al., 2016). Likewise, Chugani and colleagues (2017) found that only a quarter of the DBT programmes established in college counselling centres had received formal training.

Significant barriers comparable to those that led to lower appropriateness were also associated with lower feasibility. Carmel and colleagues (2014) found significant barriers in implementing DBT in a US community mental health system. Almost half (47%) of key informants reported that staffing issues and turnover were significant barriers, as were a lack of administrative support (42%) and insufficient time to conduct DBT (42%). Landes et al. (2017) found that only 42% of DBT programmes implemented in the VHA employed all four DBT treatment modes. Difficult barriers to overcome in the VHA included insufficient numbers and/or availability of therapists to do DBT, lack of resources for training, difficulty meeting or sporadic consultation team attendance, and clients' difficulty with new treatment methods or resistance to change. Of note, the three most-frequently endorsed "most difficult" barriers were all related to the logistics of implementing phone coaching outside of business hours. This did not reflect clinician resistance to coaching per se, as clinician willingness to take calls or extend limits when needed was not a barrier for one-third, and only 12% of DBT programmes could not overcome this barrier. Half the programmes did not find coaching during business hours to be a barrier at all, and only 6% of DBT programmes could not overcome barriers to coaching during business hours.

In a DBT context, adherence is divided into programme adherence and therapist adherence. Programme adherence to DBT has been measured using the Program Elements of Treatment Questionnaire (PETQ; Schmidt, Ivanoff, Korslund, & Linehan, 2008; Ditty et al., 2015) and the more detailed Landes Implementation of DBT Scale (Landes et al., 2016). These measures assess the presence or absence of key DBT elements. Therapist adherence is measured by the DBT Global Rating Scale (Linehan & Korslund, 2003). However, the Global Rating Scale requires trained and reliable coders and is therefore of limited availability. DBT certification processes, which are another measure of fidelity, are underway in the US and UK; again this is not yet widely used and is expensive, so few clinicians have yet to pursue it. DBT programme certification has only recently been launched. Thus, for practical purposes, therapist fidelity is evaluated using the tables provided in the DBT manual (Linehan, 1993). These tables list DBT and anti-DBT therapist behaviours upon which the Global Rating Scale is based and DBT programme fidelity is measured according to the number of DBT elements in place. Most studies of DBT fidelity developed their own measures based on these sources.

DBT fidelity appears to be associated with more training. Hawkins and Sinha (1998) found that greater DBT knowledge was associated with more reading about DBT as well as more expert and peer consultation. Frederick and Comtois (2006) found that more extensive DBT training in residency predicted more use of DBT overall and greater use of DBT strategies by psychiatrists after graduation. Ditty and colleagues (2015) found that supervision was a predictor of programme fidelity, as was team cohesion and positive organizational climate. In their survey of DBT therapists, DiGiorio and colleagues (2010) found that while ≤ 50% of therapists trained in DBT reported the use of key DBT strategies such as chain analysis, problem solving, or validation, greater use of these strategies was found for those participating in ten-day vs. two-day trainings. They also found greater adherence by those therapists who had a behavioural orientation prior to DBT training.

Feasibility and fidelity are often in conflict during DBT programme adoption and implementation. DBT is a complex intervention that includes a large number of sessions, need for two group leaders, weekly consultation team, access to therapists between sessions, and a long list of DBT skills and therapy strategies to master to the point where they can be mixed and matched. When the focus is on new therapists learning and implementing the treatment to fidelity, a programme can develop which is infeasible in the long term, such as each therapist having only one or two clients plus receiving supervision and attending a consultation team. However, if trainees are able to work through the pilot or "implementation phase" and then have their client load increased and supervision decreased, then feasibility is achievable. By contrast, programmes that focus their initial use of DBT on feasibility sacrifice either programme fidelity by only implementing parts of DBT, or therapist fidelity by starting with a large number of clients and providing little time for supervision and consultation team. Again, hopefully over time, clinicians build skill and achieve fidelity. Currently, however, there is no real solution to this dilemma and little data on how to organize DBT implementation to maximize both feasibility and fidelity.

Reach or Penetration

Reach is also known as the penetration or integration of DBT into the setting. It is measured in two ways: the number of clients receiving DBT divided by the number of clients appropriate for or eligible to receive DBT, or alternatively, the number of providers delivering DBT divided by the number of providers trained and expected to provide it. Administrative data or caseload audit determine reach, which is generally the primary goal of implementation. Studies of DBT implementation almost never assess reach. The exception is Landes and colleagues (2017) who attempted to determine the reach of DBT in the VHA. They measured the percentage of each clinic's population receiving DBT and found they ranged from 1% to 75%, with a mode of 1%, and an average of 15%.

Penetration is often a downfall for DBT implementation. Many providers do not want to provide DBT to very many clients at once and there is a natural limit for most clinicians on how many chronically suicidal clients and/or clients with BPD whom they can see simultaneously without becoming burned out. Often this number is nowhere near the prevalence of clients with chronic suicidality and BPD in the setting. Some providers do not turn out to be a good fit with the DBT model, or with the personalities or behaviour of DBT clients, and do not continue. On the up side, DBT is often very effective with more severe levels of disorder, so some programmes are able to reach a greater percentage of more extreme cases in their setting than the percentage of eligible or appropriate clients overall (Comtois, Elwood, Holdcraft, Smith, & Simpson, 2007).

Reach or penetration should also be highlighted as the downfall of trialability and pilot programmes in DBT implementation, as described previously. A pilot programme is purposefully small for training or trialability reasons. But it can also become an implicit norm in the setting so that the number of DBT clients seen in the pilot phase becomes the number that can or should be seen. For example, Swales et al. (2012) found that, relatively speaking, programmes had a lot of staff, but only small amounts of time devoted to the programme, and therefore only saw a small number of patients. This leads to a low penetration rate and/or DBT missing its target population.

Cost

The incremental cost or cost of implementation is a combination of the cost of the intervention itself, the cost of the strategies used to implement it (e.g., training, consultation, lost productivity), and the costs of the setting. The complexity of DBT leads to high costs of both DBT itself and both the DBT training and implementation strategies. The meaning of these costs, however, depends on the cost-effectiveness perspective, because there are often substantial savings in inpatient and medical care for clients in DBT. From the perspective of a stakeholder contending with all costs (e.g., county, state, or federal government, or a commercial insurance company), DBT varies from manageable costs to a net savings. However, from the perspective of the outpatient provider—especially in a capitated system—there are considerable costs to an intensive multi-session treatment, and no savings beyond care being more predictable with fewer crisis outreach expenses. So the cost-effectiveness of DBT varies from high (cost-offset) to little or none; depending on which costs and revenue are included (Meyers, Landes, & Thuras, 2014; Priebe et al., 2012; Wagner et al., 2014).

Two studies of the cost of DBT found costs from one year comparable to standard care the year prior to DBT (Meyers et al., 2014; Priebe et al., 2012). Meyer and colleagues found a US$6000 decrease in client costs in the year following DBT compared to the year prior to DBT. Savings in inpatient and community nursing expenses fuelled a GB£36,000 saving for DBT (Amner, 2012). A review of economic evaluations of DBT showed reduction in costs when compared to the prior treatment year, reduction in costs when compared to treatment-as-usual, decreases in long-term service utilization in high service-utilizing individuals, potential financial benefits to the treatment institution depending on perspective, and a potential decrease in societal costs (see Krawitz and Miga, this volume).

Sustainability

Sustainability is the extent to which DBT is maintained or institutionalized within the setting's ongoing, stable operations. This can be considered in three stages: (1) moving from a pilot to a permanent DBT programme, (2) becoming embedded in institutional procedures such as documentation, budget, supervisory responsibilities, intake practices, job descriptions, etc., and (3) "niche saturation," or the extent to which DBT is integrated into all subsystems of an organization. Case audits, checklists, semi-structured interviews, or questionnaires can all help assess sustainability.

Swales and colleagues (2012) conducted a review of 105 programmes started in the UK from 1994 to 2007 and found most (63%) were still functioning and the rest had "died". DBT programme "deaths" related primarily to lack of organizational support (68%), staff turnover (63%), and insufficient time for DBT (56%). Examining the time of "death" of DBT programmes showed two important turning points that programmes should attend to. The first time is in the year following completion of training. Most core training in DBT occurs over a period of time through ongoing classes, or a Part 1/ Part 2 format to allow time to practise and report back. Thus, the first risk period is after the completion of Part 2, and that contingency for doing DBT disappears. The second risk period found by Swales and colleagues was five years after beginning. In the UK NHS, given natural turnover patterns, this is when a significant percentage of DBT programme staff will have left or been promoted out of the programme. This speaks to the importance of a mechanism to bring on new staff trained sufficiently to keep the programme steady (Carmel et al., 2014; Herschell et al., 2009; Swales et al., 2012). Herschell and colleagues (2014) also found turnover to be a significant problem in US community health, where 45% of clinicians participating in a training across four counties were lost to turnover by the end of the two-year DBT training process.

When considering a plan for turnover, there are two main strategies—provide ongoing training from outside the programme, and train internal trainers (aka "train the trainer"). Dr. Comtois has considerable experience in both mechanisms and it is important to consider which will be more effective and efficient. "Train the trainer" models have intuitive appeal—if staff train within the system, there is no longer need to pay a training company or academic trainer to support the DBT programme(s). In DBT, "train the trainer" models generally have the DBT trainers and the system or agencies' leaders identify clinicians in the core training who show particular aptitude for DBT and/or leadership skills. These "trainers in training" receive additional clinical consultation or training in DBT, as well as how to train others in DBT. Across several large training initiatives, it is clear these individuals exist and can be trained in this way. Additionally, internal trainers have the advantage of local perspective on the barriers and facilitators for DBT. However, it is important to consider the "day job" of the internal trainer before choosing an external training vs. internal training model. Frequently, that person already has a clinical job. Thus, when it is time for them to train others, their supervisor—while initially supportive of the plan—may baulk at patient session cancellations and clinic disruptions that their staff member's off-site training engagements or consultations will entail. This problem tends to increase over time; in one state-wide system in the US, Dr. Comtois trained 13 "train the trainers," of whom, after two years, only three were still training others themselves, and considerably less frequently than planned. Thus, it is important that a "train the trainer" model provides release time for the trainers, carefully considers the impact of any absence, and provides compensation to the trainer's clinic. This compensation allows the clinic to hire staff to backfill what is lost to training time. An alternative is to create a trainer position within a system and to hire a successful graduate of the DBT training programme into that position. This has been tried successfully in several US states, but it means losing a strong clinician from the DBT provider pool, and it is only affordable for larger care systems. It is also apparent that there are considerable costs to training a clinician as an internal trainer, as well as risks of the trainer leaving the agency or system. The alternative is to hire a training company or academic trainer who provides training on an annual or other regular basis. Dr. Comtois has provided annual DBT training at her university for twenty years. While the training began primarily for residents and interns in the psychiatry department, it has expanded to become the annual training vehicle for DBT staff across the multiple hospitals and associated outpatient clinics of the medical school. DBT training companies have developed five-day training sessions with the goal of giving staff new to DBT sufficient training in DBT so that their consultation team can integrate them and provide the rest of the training. For independent clinics and smaller systems, this will be far more cost-effective than training internal trainers. Even for large care systems, the costs of bringing in trainers or sending even a fair number of staff to a single training once a year are lower, and the efficiency higher than training and maintaining an internal trainer.

Conclusion

Taken together, implementation outcomes (acceptability, appropriateness, adoption, feasibility, fidelity, reach, cost, and sustainability) are the "implementation targets" for DBT. In a clinical DBT hierarchy, quality of life is core to the development of a "life worth living," but it is hard to achieve if life-threatening and therapy-interfering behaviours are not targeted first. Client outcomes are the core goal of DBT implementation. To achieve this, it is critical to assure that the implementation outcomes are achieved. If DBT can't be made acceptable, appropriate, feasible, and cost-effective, it will not be implemented. DBT must be adopted with reasonable fidelity and reach sufficient proportion of clients and be sustained over time. Thus, both the DBT programme and the larger system have to keep these targets in mind, from the planning stage, through the implementation process, and beyond.

And like DBT clinically, what is targeted is what changes. DBT therapists prioritize therapy-interfering behaviour over quality-of-life targets because working on quality of life when the therapy is not working is neither more effective nor more efficient; bluntly, it probably just won't work. Instead, we target therapy-interfering behaviour, and resolve it, and then quality-of-life targets become the focus, and are resolved faster and more fully. Similarly, client outcomes are the goal of the DBT implementation. But targeting client outcomes without prioritizing implementation outcomes will not provide a faster solution. A programme will not achieve outcomes when it is not fully implemented, or is not really working. Instead, by targeting implementation outcomes first, the resulting resolve and focus can move to achieving client outcomes in a faster and sustained way.

KEY MESSAGES FOR CLINICIANS

- When considering DBT trainings to enhance implementation, trainings that facilitate discussion or answering of questions or consultation are important as stakeholders work through determining how DBT will fit in their setting.
- Trainers must have experience with a range of solutions to typical appropriateness concerns so clinicians, agencies, or systems do not implement DBT in a rigid way that fits the manual, but not their clinical structure.
- A DBT pilot programme is an implementation strategy that can be evaluated to determine whether it should be implemented more widely.
- Once a pilot project is determined to be successful, expanding the programme to improve reach to appropriate clients is a vital next step.
- Those considering implementing DBT could use the data presented within this chapter about barriers to inform an implementation plan (e.g., knowing that staff turnover is an issue, plan for how to address it using the suggestions provided).
- DBT fidelity appears to be associated with more training.

REFERENCES

Amner, K. (2012). The effect of DBT provision in reducing the cost of adults displaying the symptoms of BPD. *British Journal of Psychotherapy, 28*, 336–352.

Carmel, A., Rose, M. L., & Fruzzetti, A. E. (2014). Barriers and solutions to implementing dialectical behavior therapy in a public behavioral health system. *Administration and Policy in Mental Health and Mental Health Services Research, 41*, 608–614.

Chugani, C. D., Mitchell, M. E., Botanov, Y., & Linehan, M. M. (2017). Development and initial evaluation of the psychometric properties of the Dialectical Behavior Therapy Barriers to Implementation Scale (BTI-S). *Journal of Clinical Psychology*, online first version. doi:10.1002/jclp.22478

Chugani, C., & Landes, S. J. (2016). Dialectical behavior therapy in college counseling centers: Current trends and barriers to implementation. *Journal of College Student Psychotherapy, 30*, 176–186. doi:10.1080/87568225.2016.1177429

Comtois, K. A., Elwood, L., Holdcraft, L. C., Smith, W. R., & Simpson, T. L. (2007). Effectiveness of dialectical behavior therapy in a community mental health center. *Cognitive and Behavioral Practice, 14*, 406–414. https://doi.org/10.1016/j.cbpra.2006.04.023

Curran, G. M., Bauer, M., Mittman, B., Pyne, J. M., & Stetler, C. (2012). Effectiveness-implementation hybrid designs. *Medical Care, 50*, 217–226. doi:10.1097/MLR.obo 13e3182408812

Department of Veterans Affairs/Department of Defense. (2013). The clinical practice guideline for the assessment and management of patients at risk for suicide [Internet]. Available from: http://www.healthquality.va.gov/suicideRisk.asp

DiGiorgio, K. E., Glass, C. R., & Arnkoff, D. B. (2010). Therapists' use of DBT: A survey study of clinical practice. *Cognitive and Behavioral Practice, 17*, 213–221. https://doi.org/10.1016/j.cbpra.2009.06.003

Ditty, M. S., Landes, S. J., Doyle, A., & Beidas, R. S. (2015). It takes a village: A mixed method analysis of inner setting variables and dialectical behavior therapy implementation. *Administration and Policy in Mental Health and Mental Health Services Research, 42*, 672–681. doi:10.1007/s10488-014-0602-0

Frederick, J. T., & Comtois, K. A. (2006). Practice of dialectical behavior therapy after psychiatry residency. *Academic Psychiatry, 30*, 63–68.

Government of Ireland. (2006). Vision for change [Internet]. Available from: https://www.hse.ie/eng/services/Publications/Mentalhealth/VisionforChange.html

Hartzler, B., Jackson, T. R., Jones, B. E., Beadnell, B., & Caslyn, D. A. (2014). Disseminating contingency management: Impacts of staff training and implementation at an opiate treatment program. *Journal of Substance Abuse Treatment, 46*, 429–438. http://dx.doi.org/10.1016/j.jsat.2013.12.007

Hawkins, K. A., & Sinha, R. (1998). Can line clinicians master the conceptual complexities of dialectical behavior therapy? An evaluation of a State Department of Mental Health training program. *Journal of Psychiatric Research, 32*, 379–384. https://doi.org/10.1016/S0022-3956(98)00030-2

Hazelton, M., Rossiter, R., & Milner, J. (2006). Managing the "unmanageable": Training staff in the use of dialectical behaviour therapy for borderline personality disorder. *Contemporary Nurse, 1*, 120–130. doi:http://dx.doi.org/10.5172/conu.2006.21.1.120

Herschell, A. D., Lindhiem, O. J., Kogan, J. N., Celedonia, K. L., & Stein, B. D. (2014). Evaluation of an implementation initiative for embedding Dialectical Behavior Therapy in community settings. *Evaluation and Program Planning, 43*, 55–63. https://doi.org/10.1016/j.evalprogplan.2013.10.007

Herschell, A., Kogan, J. N., Celedonia, K. L., Gavin, J. G., & Stein, B. D. (2009). Understanding community mental health administrators' perspectives on dialectical behavior therapy implementation. *Psychiatric Services, 60*, 989–992.

Karlin, B. E., Ruzek, J. I., Chard, K. M., Eftekhari, A., Monson, C. M., Hembree, E. A., Resick, P. A., & Foa, E. B. (2010). Dissemination of evidence-based psychological treatments for posttraumatic stress disorder in the Veterans Health Administration. *Journal of Traumatic Stress, 23*, 663–673. doi:10.1002/jts.20588

Kirchner, J. E., Ritchie, M. J., Pitcock, J. A., Parker, L. E., Curran, G. M., & Fortney, J. C. (2014). Outcomes of a partnered facilitation strategy to implement primary care-mental health. *Journal of General Internal Medicine, 29*, 904–912.

Landes, S. J., Matthieu, M. M., Smith, B. N., Trent, L. R., Rodriguez, A. L., Kemp, J., & Thompson, C. (2016). Dialectical behavior therapy training and desired resources for implementation: Results from a national program evaluation in the Veterans Health Administration. *Military Medicine, 181*, 747–752. doi: http://dx.doi.org/10.7205/MILMED-D-15-00267

Landes, S. J., Rodriguez, A. L., Smith, B. N., Matthieu, M. M., Trent, L. R., Kemp, J., & Thompson, C. (2017). Barriers, facilitators, and benefits of implementation of dialectical behavior therapy in routine care: Results from a national program evaluation survey in the Veterans Health Administration. *Translational Behavioral Medicine*, online first version. doi: 10.1007/s13142-017-0465-5

Linehan, M. (1993). *Cognitive-behavioral treatment of borderline personality disorder*. New York, NY: Guilford Press.

Linehan, M., & Korslund, K. (2003). *Dialectical behavior therapy adherence manual*. University of Washington. Unpublished manuscript.

Meyers, L. L., Landes, S. J., & Thuras, P. (2014). Veterans' service utilization & associated costs following participation in dialectical behavior therapy: A preliminary investigation. *Military Medicine*, *179*, 1368–1373. doi:10.7205/MILMED-D-14-00248

National Institute of Health and Care Excellence. (2009). Clinical guidelines on borderline personality disorder: Recognition and management [Internet]. Available from: https://www.nice.org.uk/guidance/cg78

Priebe, S., Bhatti, N., Barnicot, K., Bremner, S., Gaglia, A., Katsakou, C., ... Zinkler, M. (2012). Effectiveness and cost-effectiveness of dialectical behaviour therapy for self-harming patients with personality disorder: A pragmatic randomised controlled trial. *Psychotherapy and Psychosomatics*, *81*, 356–365.

Proctor, E., Silmere, H., Raghavan, R., Hovmand, P., Aarons, G., Bunger, A., Griffey, R., & Hensley, M. (2011). Outcomes for implementation research: Conceptual distinctions, measurement challenges, and research agenda. *Administration and Policy in Mental Health and Mental Health Services Research*, *38*, 65–76.

Ritchie, M. J., Dollar, K., Kearney, L. K., & Kirchner, J. E. (2014). Responding to needs of clinical operations partners: Transferring implementation facilitation knowledge and skills. *Psychiatric Services*, *65*, 141–143. doi:10.1176/appi.ps.201300468

Rogers, E. M. (2010). *Diffusion of innovations*, 4th Edition. New York, NY: The Free Press.

SAMHSA. (2013). National Registry of Evidence-Based Programs and Practices [Internet]. Available from: http://www.nrepp.samhsa.gov/

Schmidt, H., Ivanoff, A., Korslund, K., & Linehan, M. M. (2008). *Program Elements of Treatment Questionnaire*. Seattle, WA: Behavioral Research & Therapy Clinics.

Schoenwald, S. K., Henggeler, S. W., Brondino, M. J., & Rowland, M. D. (2000). Multisystemic therapy: Monitoring treatment fidelity. *Family Process*, *39*, 83–103. doi:10.1111/j.1545-5300.2000.39109.x

Swales, M. A., Taylor, B., & Hibbs, R. A. (2012). Implementing Dialectical Behaviour Therapy: Programme survival in routine healthcare settings. *Journal of Mental Health*, *21*, 548–555.

Wagner, T., Fydrich, T., Stiglmayr, C., Marschall, P., Salize, H. J., Renneberg, B., ... Roepke, S. (2014). Societal cost-of-illness in patients with borderline personality disorder one year before, during and after dialectical behavior therapy in routine outpatient care. *Behaviour Research and Therapy*, *61*, 12–22. https://doi.org/10.1016/j.brat.2014.07.004

....

CHAPTER 38

THE DIALECTICAL DILEMMAS OF IMPLEMENTATION

....

HELEN BEST AND JIM LYNG

THE CHALLENGES OF IMPLEMENTING DBT

....

Over the last 30 years, as described across this volume, DBT has been applied to several clinical populations and age groups and has been widely implemented across all levels of care. As with any evidence-based treatment, success in translating DBT into real-world settings is far from assured (Swales, Taylor, & Hibbs, 2012; Comtois & Landes, this volume). A common misconception is that implementation of a treatment is a passive process simply synonymous with the provision of appropriate training to providers (Fairburn & Wilson, 2013). Where training clinicians and teams is relatively formulaic, despite taking time, commitment and effort, implementation is far more difficult to accomplish and is a deliberate, focused, planned, and iterative endeavour. It requires behaviour change across every level of an organization, engagement with all stakeholders, and careful evaluation of the system's needs, fit, and readiness. Well-defined objectives, reinforcement for all components of the implementation (i.e., system, programme, team, clinician), leadership participation, stable funding, policy flexibility, outcome evaluation, and clinical oversight are among the critical factors in the long-term success of implementing a psychological therapy programme (Karlin & Cross, 2014; Smith et al., 2017). Some implementation activities may be established or resolved in a single meeting, others may take years.

Comprehensive DBT is a multifunctional (i.e., it addresses client capability, motivation, and generalization, while also structuring the environment, and treating therapist motivation), multi-modal (i.e., comprises skills group, individual therapy,

This chapter was influenced by a discussion between HB and DBT trainer colleague Annie McCall, which helped HB map several dialectical dilemmas encountered in implementing DBT.

phone consultation, and team consultation), and is a lengthy treatment for severe and life-threatening disorders (Manning, 2007; Rizvi, Steffel, & Carson-Wong, 2013). This combination of characteristics contributes to unique challenges and threats to success-fully implementing and sustaining a DBT programme (Swales, 2010a). One of us (HB) has consulted on more than fifty implementation projects in the United States, Canada, New Zealand, and Norway, which have ranged from tiny, courageous, single-location projects, to vast, ambitious, State- or Province-wide projects. The other (JL) is a DBT Trainer and has co-ordinated a five-year, cross-border, multi-site Northern Irish and Irish "practice-based research network" (Barkham, 2014) committed to implementing and sustaining DBT for borderline personality disorder (BPD) in community services. This chapter is an effort to share some of our perspectives on several signature di-lemmas posed by the implementation of DBT and how dialectics can assist with these dilemmas.

Dialectics as a World view and a Method of Persuasion

DBT is a recursive treatment, meaning that providers utilize treatment strategies for themselves, as well as teaching and employing such strategies with their clients (Swales, 2010b). Running through the veins of DBT is a commitment to dialectics as both a world view and a method of persuasion (Swales & Heard, 2017). From a dia-lectical position, polarization and disagreement are considered as natural and inev-itable, and all the more so when working with intense emotional dysregulation and suicidality which can lead to entrenched and narrow perspectives (Chapman, 2006; Lynch, Chapman, Rosenthal, Kuo, & Linehan, 2006). Dialectics, as described by Linehan (1993, 2015), provide a coherent philosophy and framework for approaching tensions associated with competing, yet valid, perspetives. Dialectical thinking pro-motes flexibility and runs counter to rigidity (Swenson, 2016). Our experience across time, settings, systems, and countries has informed us that the improvisational rhythms of dialectics can assist clinicians and services foster movement and reso-lution in the face of conflict and disagreement. As teams work to implement DBT, it is normal to run into sources of tension which block movement (Swales, 2010a). When a team recognizes these dialectical dilemmas as junctures where more than one position may have validity, progress becomes possible. This involves letting go of the concepts of right and wrong, finding an "and" instead of an "or," and building a synthesis from different positions that honours each grain of truth while considering what has been left out (Koerner, 2012, 2013).

Dialectical strategies in DBT include highlighting tensions, allowing natural change, employing metaphors and stories, extending, activating wise-mind, entering the paradox, and making lemonade out of lemons (see Linehan, 1993, for a full discussion of

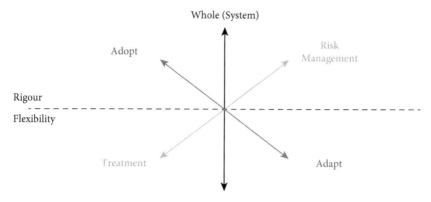

FIGURE 38.1. Dialectical dilemmas of implementation.

dialectics). Such dialectical strategies can help with finding bridge-building commonalities, e.g., recognizing that services, staff, and clients are all just people trying to make the best of their lives or pursue their values at any given moment. Dialectical strategies also facilitate a synthesis in the face of opposite views, e.g., taking a stance which acknowledges the wisdom in each position, no matter how fierce the disagreement or dispute, and eschewing simplistic, rigid, or blaming viewpoints. Furthermore, dialectical strategies draw attention to the ubiquity of change, e.g., remembering that no matter how much an impasse appears to lack a resolution, this too will pass, since change will inevitably happen around the impasse, if not within it, thus changing the context. For the remainder of this chapter we identify and explore three dialetical dilemmas commonly encountered in implementing DBT (see Figure 38.1).

THE DIALECTICAL DILEMMAS OF IMPLEMENTATION

The Dilemma of Adopting or Adapting

A central dialectical dilemma surrounding the implementation of DBT is whether to "adopt or adapt" the treatment (Koerner, Dimeff, & Swenson, 2007). A tension often arises between implementing all modes of the comprehensive DBT model and the decision to employ only components of the full treatment, such as standalone group skills training (Valentine, Bankoff, Poulin, Reidler, & Pantalone, 2015). DBT was developed for chronically suicidal and self-harming women in a community-based university clinic (Linehan & Wilks, 2015). It follows that the dilemma of adopting or adapting is more frequently encountered in contexts which differ the most from this original setting, e.g., forensic, residential, and inpatient services. Yet, this dilemma is not exclusively the preserve of less-traditional settings for psychotherapy and can occur in community services for BPD, especially where resources are limited.

In our experience, such tensions emerge within treatment teams as well as between teams and management. Disagreement is especially prone in relation to treatment duration (e.g., weeks/months vs. one year), duties and role of providers (e.g., scope of responsibilities of the DBT therapist), frequency of modalities (e.g., daily or weekly), clinical and diagnostic appropriateness (e.g., whether to offer DBT to clients who do not meet criteria for BPD), problems related to generalizing skills (e.g., getting the use of skills off the hospital ward and into the client's regular life), difficulties with the allocation of necessary resources (e.g., two leaders for group skills training sessions), and problems around consultation meetings (e.g., allowing staff sufficient time to attend and ensuring staff commitment to attend). Resolving such tensions requires thoughtful, deliberate action informed by context and nuance, rather than simplistic, over-generalized strategies taken from the proverbial shelf. It is worth keeping in mind that the best of intentions often sit behind the worst decisions. Reaching a synthesis between the tensions surrounding adapting or adopting requires a clear understanding of the treatment, the system in which it is being delivered, and can be helped by a practical use of dialectics.

As a case example, HB recalls consulting on the introduction of DBT to an inpatient mental health facility for adolescents which was part of a large, centrally administered, but geographically separate, health system in North America. A non-negotiable three-week length of stay was rigidly enforced at the facility, dramatically shorter than the treatment duration usually offered in DBT. Several models of shortened inpatient DBT have been described elsewhere (for a review see Swenson, Witterhold, & Bohus, 2007, and Fox, this volume), but the major tension among stakeholders here was whether this should operate as a comprehensive inpatient DBT programme with all five modes (albeit over an unavoidably condensed time period of three weeks), or whether the programme would be better served as a DBT-informed, standalone skills training group. Local advocates on the side of comprehensive DBT pointed out that a comprehensive DBT programme, characterized by responsiveness and multiple points of support, had some chance of successfully meeting needs of "at-risk" youth in the community, whereas non-intensive interventions, such as the treatment-as-usual approach in use, were failing. The view on the side of adaptation, endorsed most strongly by clinical and administrative leadership, was that a standalone skills group was realistic and sustainable, given budgets and concerns about the complexity of clinical skills needed to deliver comprehensive DBT.

Dialectically informed solutions evolve from acknowledging and drawing out tensions and polarities, rather than suppressing or avoiding them (Linehan, 1993). This assists creativity and can lead to new understandings while promoting flexibility (Swales, 2009). Dialectics helped decision-making here by reminding all involved that no one position was singularly "right" or "wrong," and that complexity such as this was a natural phenomenon, rather than a problem to be resisted (Wan, 2012). At the same time, dialectics is not simply a compromise where, as in *Alice's Adventures in Wonderland*, all who run win prizes (Carroll, 1865). After much discussion, a synthesis was arrived at where the facility decided to introduce a brief, adapted version of DBT. Since lower intensity interventions were not working, it was agreed that the DBT programme would provide adaptations of several of the functions of standard DBT, all within a three-week window. The function of enhancing client capability would be the central focus of the programme, with daily group skills training. Enhancing client motivation would be delivered by case workers in short, informal, regular meetings, rather than structured, individual hour-long DBT therapy sessions. Generalization would be supported through ward staff on an as-needed basis, rather than phone coaching. Weekly DBT team consultation meetings would serve the function of supporting clinicians.

Dialectical assessment is an ongoing, rather than fixed, process, and as this skills-orientated DBT adaptation was rolled out, new dilemmas became apparent. It was clear that the complicated and urgent needs of clients (and their families) were still not being adequately met by this adapted intervention, which lacked the individual therapist mode of comprehensive DBT. A decision was reached to increase the time, staffing, and training available for DBT. This supported more one-to-one time with providers and patients, allowing for the use of a wider range of DBT strategies, such as targeting commitment and conducting behavioural chain and solution analysis. As the implementation widened in scope and penetration, existing non-DBT interventions, such as anger management and psychotherapy process groups, were scaled back and staff not willing to participate in DBT were transferred to other programmes or settings in the wider health system. Also, consistent with growing trends in the provision of DBT to adolescents, family members were also included in treatment as a means of structuring the environment (Rathus & Miller, 2015). Management provided support with staffing changes and amended policy in ways which supported the provision of DBT with greater fidelity. In making these changes within the seemingly insurmountable obstacle of the fixed three-week length of stay, clients and their families who accessed this programme received high doses of treatment within a brief window. Subsequent unpublished programme evaluations, an essential part of the implementation, have shown these changes were associated with improvements in clinical and functional outcomes for clients using the facility.

In another case example of the dilemma of adopting or adapting, JL was part of a DBT team faced with the problem of high drop-out rates among young adults engaged in an adult DBT programme for BPD. Some among the team drew attention to the established pattern of young adult premature termination from psychological therapies (Edlund et al., 2002; Reneses, Munoz, & Lopez-Ibor, 2009) and queried whether early drop-out was simply an inevitable feature of working with young adults. Others on the team, while unsure of the best way forward, were passionate in their determination to proactively work with this age group and highlighted the potential benefits of early intervention in arresting long term disability among young adults before disorders become entrenched and chronic (Chanen, Sharp, Hoffman, & the Global Alliance for Prevention and Early Intervention for BPD, 2017; McGorry, 2015; McGorry, Goldstone, Parker, Rickwood, & Hickie, 2014). The synthesis involved accepting the presence of problems in providing care to this cohort and at the same time recognizing that DBT remained a promising treatment for young adults given its demonstrated viability with adolescents (Mehlum et al., 2014). A decision was reached to introduce a young-adult only DBT programme for clients with BPD between 18 and 25 years, in parallel to the existing adult DBT programme. The associated increase in workload during the launch of the programme required some temporary stretching of personal limits from team members. In addition, management made some accommodations around resources and time available due to the demonstrated benefits of a local early intervention strategy for psychosis, with the hope these could be replicated for BPD.

Dialectical enquiry (e.g. arguing for opposite positions) helped the team decide that the young adult programme would adopt DBT with fidelity to the comprehensive model. This is consistent with the practice in DBT of only modifying treatment when necessary (Comtois & Landes, this volume). Initial outcomes from a pilot evaluation were encouraging (Lyng, Swales, & Hastings, 2015), which led to the mainstreaming of the young adult programme. Completion rates reversed among 18 to 25 year olds who attended the young adult DBT programme with almost three in four completing a full year of young adult DBT, a number that remained stable over the first four years of the programme. 70% of a total of 35 completers have since been fully discharged from statutory adult mental health services (Steve Doherty, personal communication, 1 March 2018). Interestingly, greater levels of clinically significant change have also been found among completers of the young adult DBT programme when compared with the same age group in a general (i.e., all ages 18+) adult DBT programme (Lyng, Swales, Hastings, Millar, & Duffy, under review), although these findings need cautious interpretation and replication in a well controlled study. At major decision points relating to implementation, each complex with competing valid views, dialectics served as a compass which orientated the team. Rather than pushing for rigid and narrow solutions (or giving up), dialectics allowed the team to remain open to competing possibilities and information, yet also proceed in a deliberate and flexible manner.

The Dilemma of Managing Risk or Providing Treatment

DBT is intended for clients with challenging, often high-risk behaviours (Wheelis, 2009). This can vary from clients in an outpatient setting to those serving multiple life sentences in a maximum-security prison (Miller, 2015). DBT will seek to address problems by assessing, coaching, and supporting the client to make changes using a range of solutions (Heard & Swales, 2016). Inevitably, the level and type of a client's risky behaviour (e.g., non-suicidal self-injury or assaultive behaviours) will intersect with standard policy in how that behaviour is managed in a given setting. Frequently, once a patient engages in the problematic behaviour which brought them to treatment in the first place (which is the very behaviour that needs to change), "risk management" and standard policy often mandates a response that presumes to create safety for the client, others, and the system. For example, in residential services patients are sometimes removed from usual settings and placed on enhanced observation or might be restrained. In community settings a client might be hospitalized or receive increased access to therapists. These responses, while well-meaning and understandable, often reinforce the problematic behaviour targeted in treatment, making it likely to recur (National Institute of Clinical Excellence, 2011), while blocking any opportunity to practise more skillful replacement behaviours. The resulting tensions between managing risk and providing opportunities for DBT to work are a common dialectical dilemma for DBT programmes.

HB remembers consulting to an adolescent service which had introduced a high-fidelity, comprehensive DBT programme for self-injury and suicidal behaviours. Administrative management were supportive of DBT, but showed reluctance in dropping the established policy of organized psychiatric admission for clients following any incidence of self-injury or a suicide attempt. A similar policy was also in place following suicidal communication and ideation. At the time, one particular client in DBT was engaged in repetitive, medically dangerous self-injury. This resulted in regular emergency room visits and frequent inpatient hospitalizations. The DBT team drew attention to the dialectical tensions between existing, well-intentioned risk management strategies and the provision of DBT. On the side of risk management, standard policy was designed with the aim of keeping clients safe, and as this client's self-injury had increased, the attending psychiatrist became more averse to anything other than immediate hospitalization. On the side of DBT, there were concerns about possible iatrogenic effects from repeated hospitalization, especially given evidence that this client's suicidal behaviours actually increased following each hospital discharge. The DBT team wished to inhibit repeated hospitalization in order to allow the DBT to work with the client on solving the problem of self-injury through self-management.

In taking a dialectical stance, it was recognized that both sides of this dilemma held potentially life-saving truths. Administrative leadership appreciated that standard policy appeared to be unintentionally escalating risky behaviour, yet also recognized myriad legal, ethical, professional, and moral consequences in the event of a tragic death of a young person due to self-injury while in their care. Clinical leadership understood that the DBT team was working on long-term behavioural control, where tolerating a degree of risk, or "positive risk taking," is often unavoidable in working effectively with chronic self-injury (Royal College of Psychiatrists, 2010; Swenson, 2016). A dialectical synthesis was reached with the assistance of executive leadership, including the medical director and legal advisors, who worked in tandem with the DBT treatment team. There was agreement to avoid automatically moving to hospitalization when the client conveyed suicidal urges or ideation or engaged in self-injury, and instead to carry out a clinical assessment of needs at that time. All stakeholders committed to work together to define when hospitalization made sense in terms of immediate risk management, which itself was moved from being a first-line response to the intervention of last resort. Where immediate medical intervention was not indicated, the client was instructed to take care of his own injuries (e.g., washing blood and applying band aids). Over time, this policy shift was associated with a reduction in the frequency of hospitalization. The view was ultimately shared by both the client and his therapists that this new policy, and the associated contingencies, provided him with greater incentives and opportunities to modify his behaviour and eventually make progress.

JL also recalls another situation with an implementation dilemma familiar to many teams and administrators, i.e., the tension between providing timely response for an at-risk population and providing resource-intensive, evidence-based care. The standard model of DBT places a greater-than-usual burden on resources due to the multiple modes of delivery (Comtois et al., 2007). Throughput of access to standard DBT can be slow due to this demand on resources, and questions have been posed about the practicality of delivering standard DBT on a large scale in the real world (Brodsky & Stanley, 2013; Swenson, Torrey, & Koerner, 2002). Several teams involved in JL's practice-based research network held long waiting lists of up to one year, largely due to resource deficits. Within a short space of time two teams each reported the suicide of a prospective client waiting to be assessed for treatment. In both instances, sustaining comprehensive DBT was threatened due to external and internal pressures and distress resulting from these tragedies.

Configuring a careful, considered, and non-impulsive response was greatly helped by adopting a dialectical stance where the validity of several competing positions was explicitly recognized. On the side of emphasizing risk management were those stakeholders who viewed the elimination of waiting lists as the top priority in the interest of immediate safety, regardless of compromises that might need to be made to treatment offered. On the side of waiting lists for comprehensive DBT were those stakeholders who drew attention to the history of negative experiences from so-called "revolving-door" crisis service utilization, typically characterized by superficial (but timely) crisis responses by providers. These stakeholders argued for the greater good of tolerating the short-term risks of waiting lists in order to be in a position to provide meaningful (albeit delayed) treatment, such as comprehensive DBT, which could help clients break free from the demoralizing and vicious cycle of repeated crises, as well as the long-term risk associated with recurrent problems.

Dialectics helped find a synthesis which acknowledged both the life-saving benefits of timely care and the advantages of resource-intensive, comprehensive treatment. A client-led, stepped-model of care was piloted by the DBT teams. Here, all clients were triaged from a chart review and a single assessment session after which clients themselves were given the option to choose between immediately available six-month standalone DBT group skills training (thus surrendering their place on the waiting list for comprehensive DBT), or electing to wait for the next available place on the comprehensive DBT programme, aware this would be months, or longer, away. Those clients judged most "at-risk" (i.e., those with medically dangerous self-harm and recent suicide attempts) were not offered standalone skills, and instead efforts were made to actively link such clients with community teams while waiting for comprehensive DBT. Consistent with the findings of Linehan et al. (2015), no difference was found between the measured clinical outcomes in the standalone skills and standard DBT treatment pathways at six months (Lyng et al., under review). Dialectics helped all concerned to hold their nerve and commitment to DBT, while recognizing the need for change and adaptation to an unfolding and demanding reality. It is also useful to note that in the spirit of dialectical thinking, other services in similar situations have reached entirely different solutions, such as Shelly McMain and her colleagues (McMain, Guimond, Barnhart, Habinski, & Streiner, 2017), who describe the use of standalone DBT skills as an effective waiting list intervention for clients who subsequently progress to being offered comprehensive DBT. Dialectics reminds us there is no one shoe for all sizes.

Meeting the Needs: The Whole System or the People in the System?

Systems like more systems. Tidy numbers, standardized operational policies, easily defined pay grades, shared IT applications, common compliance standards, and clearly demarcated hierarchies are among system specialities. Responding to individual needs, context, change, and messiness can be difficult for systems (Alter, 2013; Checkland, 1999). When implementing DBT in an organization there is frequently a tension between supporting the larger system and getting behind the needs of the people in the system, whether this involves the team as a whole, individual clinicians, clients, or caregivers and families. In our experience, commonly occurring pressure points between systems and people in DBT include scheduling and resource demands, financial supports, stabilizing staffing on units, the voluntary "opt-in" nature of the treatment, allocating time for staff to attend consultation meetings and training, obtaining permissions for video and audio recording of sessions, enabling clinicians to carry mobile phones to receive out-of-hours telephone coaching calls, and enacting policies to cover the management of such calls. Policies which dismantle or mutate the defining characteristics of DBT run the risk of disarming the treatment, potentially leaving nothing more than a costlier version of treatment-as-usual. New thinking is often needed within organizations, including the extension of existing limits, especially in relation to risk. On the other hand, people providing services need to be cognizant of the inherently limited systems in which they often operate. Sometimes resolution is swift. More often, a long arc of engagement is required for progress to unfold, typically involving new employee practices. Such tensions often lean on systems and people to tolerate uncomfortable and unfamiliar positions.

When considering systems, dialectical assessment draws attention to how organizations often have good reasons to behave as they do, i.e. how the behaviour of systems is valid. The emphasis on careful scrutiny and oversight which are characteristic of high functioning systems is frequently on the side of ensuring a focus on the best interest of those served by the system (Carayon & Wood, 2010). Organizations are also often tasked with addressing multifaceted ethical questions and devising ways of responding to complex matters relating to risk and safety. Effective organizational leadership must consistently keep the big picture in mind with respect for fiscal realities and constraints. It is not uncommon for organizational management to have accountability to higher-order paymasters or stakeholders, such as government bodies, macro-level funders, professional regulators, and the judiciary, not to mention citizens and the public (Tang, Eisenberg, & Meyer, 2004). On the other side, treatment providers seek to be facilitated when delivering treatment, in the manner that has been supported by research, without obstruction. It has been our experience that the most successful DBT implementations involve organizational leadership that is well orientated to DBT and contributes to clinical operations, e.g., through a programme steering committee that understands the objectives and strategies in routine interactions as well as crisis situations. At the same time, the capacity of a DBT programme to resolve an organizationally driven impasse is helped when front-line providers appreciate the challenges and operational objectives of leadership and know how decisions are reached. At the heart of this dialectical dilemma of meeting the needs of systems and people is moving from the familiar, rigid juxtaposition of "us vs. them" well documented by social psychologists as a recurring motif in human relations (Hamilton, Sherman, & Lickel, 1998; Tajfel, 1982), and instead turning to the connectedness of "we" by finding what both system and people have in common.

As a case example, HB recalls consulting on the implementation of DBT to a North American community mental health centre where initially the organization had clear, fixed policies restricting overtime and union-supported prohibitions on contact with clients outside regular work hours, and did not provide staff with mobile phones for work duties. The newly trained DBT team aspired to provide the full treatment model, including between-session telephone coaching. This led to an inevitable tension between the needs of the system and people. On carrying out careful dialectical assessment of the dilemma, the DBT team identified high levels of anxiety within the organization that telephone coaching calls would become frequent and lengthy. There was concern that these calls would overwhelm already strained staff resources and compromise staff resilience, as well as presenting problems with the allocation of clinical time for the purpose of billing third-party payers.

Adopting dialectics, once both system and people came to appreciate that they possessed the shared objective of providing high-quality, yet sustainable, mental health services, it was easier to find a synthesis that held true to all positions. The organization was eventually willing to organize direct billing for all coaching calls of up to 16 minutes duration, whereas calls that exceeded this would only receive compensatory time in lieu as remuneration and would be billed as case management time. Staff, in turn, agreed to take calls on secured personal devices and committed to working on very time-limited, focused telephone coaching. Such an approach to telephone coaching is entirely consistent with this mode of DBT, where phone coaching is intended to efficiently get the client to commit to a skillful solution and terminate the call once this generalization function has been achieved (Manning, 2009). With practice, the majority of the calls for this team were completed within the agreed time. The overall volume of coaching calls across the programme was managed within the observing-limits contingency of DBT, where DBT therapists directly target problems that get in the way of their motivation to deliver therapy as therapy-interfering behaviours (Foertsch, Manning, & Dimeff, 2003; Rizvi & Roman, this volume). Such behaviours could include receiving more calls from clients than the therapist was able to tolerate within her, or her organization's, limits.

Neither side compromised what was true and important, with both sides holding firmly to what mattered and finding a solution which attends to all positions.

Concluding Remarks On Implementing Dbt (And Ten Things To Avoid!)

DBT is complex and implementing DBT can be daunting. The good news is that there is no one way to be successful. There are ever-more resources to orient, guide, and support the installation of programmes and assist with supervising, monitoring, and evaluating existing programmes (of which this volume is a clear example!). Where failure occurs, it often takes place in the spaces between opposing goals, expectations, and mandates, or the ability to tolerate scary situations. Understanding the inevitable dialectical tensions that surround the implementation of DBT—rigour versus flexibility, adoption versus adaption, risk management versus treatment, the whole versus the part—may orientate teams and systems to expect these natural sources of tension. Different outcomes to such tensions are likely wherever and whenever they arise. A firm commitment to dialectically assess and respond to the truth in all sides may enhance the likely success of any efforts to install and sustain a DBT programme.

By way of concluding, we thought it might be useful to share a few morsels of specific advice on implementing DBT. These are intended for clinicians as well as for administrators, teams, and systems. From a dialectical perspective everything always depends on everything else, yet from the vantage points of our own experiences these are ten rules-of-thumb which we think will seldom lead a DBT implementation astray (and our own journeys in implementing DBT might have been easier if we had heeded some of these earlier!).

1. Implementation is an iterative process. Everything that sustains movement requires fuel and refuelling. Do not expect one cycle of DBT training to change the world.
2. Organizations, treatment teams, and their clients are best served when clinicians providing DBT do the treatment regularly and extensively. It is almost impossible to become an expert in a complex treatment with one to two clients every year. Do not expect clinicians to learn DBT as an "add on" to their existing full time case load or responsibilities.
3. In advance of any training, begin a wide-ranging consultative process, identify drivers, define goals, plan programmes, and only then determine who to send to training. Do not send a team of clinicans to training and expect them to return with the ability to manage implementation in your setting.
4. Assess contingencies operating in your settings—a team needs to know what will reward the system for tolerating more risk and the system needs to understand how clinicians will be rewarded for enduring commitment to more work with challenging clients.

5. Commit to gathering and monitoring data (e.g., client outcomes, clinical performance, system evaluation, etc.). It will help you defend your programme and know when you need to change course.

6. Do not mandate clinicians to training or clients to treatment.

7. Do not proceed without a firm commitment from leadership to participate and support implementation issues such as staffing, clinical supervision, and job descriptions. Some implementation issues may be easily addressed, but others can be hard to resolve once a programme has been started. At the same time, don't wait too long to move—not everything can be mapped in advance.

8. DBT is not a panacea. It is an effective treatment, for some clients with certain problems to varying degrees.

9. Expect failure, and be willing to learn from it.

10. DBT requires persistence and perseverance, and progress can be slow, but it can also transform services, teams, the lives of patients, and their therapists.

KEY MESSAGES FOR CLINICIANS

- Successful implementation of DBT involves multi-level change within organizations.
- As a complex activity, tensions are inevitable among stakeholders when implementing DBT. Dialectics offer a means of promoting flexibility and resolving the challenges of implementation.
- Three common dialectical dilemmas occur during implementation of DBT:
  1. Tension between adopting and adapting DBT.
  2. Tension between risk management and delivering the treatment as intended.
  3. Tension between meeting both the needs of the system and the needs of providers.

REFERENCES

Alter, S. (2013). Work system theory: Overview of core concepts, extensions, and challenges for the future. *Journal of the Association for Information Systems*, 14, 72–121.

Barkham, M. (2014). Practice-based research networks: Origins, overview, obstacles, and opportunities. *Counselling and Psychotherapy Research*, 14, 167–173

Brodsky, B. S., & Stanley, B. (2013). *The dialectical behavior therapy primer: How DBT can inform clinical practice*. Oxford, UK: Wiley-Blackwell.

Carayon, P., & Wood, K. E. (2010). Patient safety: The role of human factors and systems engineering. *Studies in Health Technology and Informatics*, 153, 23–46.

Carroll, L. (1865). *Alice's Adventures in Wonderland*. New York: Macmillan.

Chanen, A.M., Sharp, C., & Hoffman, P. (2017). Prevention in early intervention for borderline personality disorder: A novel public health priority. *World Psychiatry*, 16, 215–216.

Chapman, A. L. (2006). Dialectical behaviour therapy: Current indications and unique elements. *Psychiatry (Edgmont)*, *3*, 62–68.

Checkland, P. (1999). *Systems thinking, systems practice (Includes a 30-year retrospective)*. Chichester, UK: John Wiley & Sons.

Comtois, K. A., Koons, C. R., Kim, S. A., Manning, S. Y., Bellows, E., & Dimeff, L. A. (2007). Implementing standard dialectical behavior therapy in an outpatient setting. In L. A Dimeff & K. Koerner (Eds.), *Dialectical behavior therapy in clinical practice: Applications across disorders and settings* (pp. 37–68). New York: Guilford Press.

Doherty, S. (2018). Personal communication.

Edlund, M.J., Wang, P.S., Berglund, P.A., Katz, S.J., Lin, E., & Kessler, R.C. (2002). Dropping out of mental health treatment: Patterns and predictors among epidemiological survey respondents in the United States and Ontario. *American Journal of Psychiatry*, *159*, 845–851.

Fairburn, C. G., & Wilson, G. T. (2013). The dissemination and implementation of psychological treatments: Problems and solutions. *International Journal of Eating Disorders*, *46*, 516–521.

Foertsch, C., Manning, S. Y., & Dimeff, L. (2003). Difficult-to-treat patients: The approach from Dialectical Behaviour Therapy. In R. L. Leahy (Ed.), *Roadblocks in cognitive-behavioral therapy: Transforming challenges into opportunities for change* (pp. 255–273). New York: Guilford Press.

Hamilton, D. L., Sherman, S. J., & Lickel, B. (1998). Perceiving social groups: The importance of the entitativity continuum. In C. Sedikides, J. Shopler, & C. Insko (Eds.), *Intergroup cognition and intergroup behavior* (pp. 47–74). Mahwah, NJ: Lawrence Erlbaum.

Heard, H. L., & Swales, M. A. (2016). *Changing behavior in DBT: Problem solving in action*. New York: Guilford Press.

Karlin, B. E., & Cross, G. (2014). From the laboratory to the therapy room: National dissemination and implementation of evidence-based psychotherapies in the U.S. Department of Veterans Affairs Health Care System. *American Psychologist*, *69*, 19–33.

Koerner, K. (2012). *Doing dialectical behavior therapy*. New York: Guilford Press.

Koerner, K. (2013). What must you know and do to get good outcomes with DBT? *Behaviour Therapy*, *44*, 568–579.

Koerner, K., Dimeff, L. A., & Swenson, C. (2007). Adopt of adapt?: Fidelity matters. In L. A. Dimeff & K. Koerner (Eds.), *Dialectical behavior therapy in clinical practice: Applications across disorders and settings* (pp. 19–26). New York: Guilford Press.

Linehan, M. M. (1993). *Cognitive-behavioral treatment of borderline personality disorder*. New York: Guilford Press.

Linehan, M. M. (2015). *DBT skills training manual*, 2nd Edition. New York: Guilford Press.

Linehan, M. M., & Wilks, C. R. (2015). The course and evolution of dialectical behavior therapy. *American Journal of Psychotherapy*, *69*, 97–110.

Linehan, M. M., Korslund, K. E., Harned, M. E., Gallop, R. J., Lungu, A., Neacsiu, A. D., McDavid, J., . . . Murray-Gregory, A. M. (2015). Dialectical behaviour therapy for high suicide risk in individuals with borderline personality disorder: A randomised controlled trial and component analysis. *Journal of the American Medical Association Psychiatry*, *72*, 475–482.

Lynch, T. R., Chapman, A. L., Rosenthal, M. Z., Kuo, J. R., & Linehan, M. M. (2006). Mechanisms of change in dialectical behaviour therapy: Theoretical and empirical observations. *Journal of Clinical Psychology*, *62*, 459–480.

Lyng, J.L., Swales, M.A., & Hastings, R.P. (2015). Dialectical behaviour therapy for younger adults: Evaluation of 22 weeks of community delivered dialectical behaviour therapy for females 18–25 years. *Irish Journal of Psychological Medicine*, *32*, 299–306.

Lyng, J. L., Swales, M. A., Hastings, R. P., Millar, T., Booth, R., & Duffy, D. J. (under review). Outcomes for six months of standalone DBT group skills training compared to standard DBT for adults with Borderline Personality Disorder: A community-based study.

Lyng, J. L., Swales, M. A., Hastings, R. P., Millar, T., & Duffy, D. J. (under review). Outcomes for 18–25 year olds with borderline personality disorder in a young adult only DBT programme compared to a general adult DBT programme.

Manning, S. Y. (2007) Dialectical behaviour therapy (DBT). In C. Freeman & M. Cooper (Eds.), *Handbook of evidence-based psychotherapies: A guide for research and practice* (pp. 83–92). Chichester, UK: John Wiley & Sons.

Manning, S. Y. (2009). Common errors made by therapists providing telephone consultation in dialectical behaviour therapy. *Cognitive and Behavioural Practice, 18,* 178–185.

McGorry, P.D. (2015). Early intervention with psychosis: Obvious, effective, overdue. *The Journal of Nervous and Mental Disease, 203,* 310–318.

McGorry, P.D., Goldstone, S.D., Parker, A.G., Rickwood, D.J., & Hickie, I.B. (2014). Cultures of mental health care of young people: An Australian blueprint for reform. *Lancet Psychiatry, 1,* 559–568.

McMain, S. F., Guimond, T., Barnhart, R., Habinski, L., & Streiner, D. L. (2017). A randomised trial of brief dialectical behavior therapy skills training in suicidal patients suffering from borderline personality disorder. *Acta Psychiatrica Scandinavica, 135,* 138–148.

Mehlum, L., Tormoen, A.J., Ramberg, M., Haga, E., Diep, L.M., Laberg, S., . . . & Groholt, B. (2014). Dialectical behaviour therapy for adolescents with repeated suicidal and self-harming behaviours: A randomised trial. *Journal of the American Academy of Child and Adolescent Psychiatry, 53,* 1082–1091.

Miller, A. L. (2015). Introduction to a special issue Dialectical Behaviour Therapy: Evolution and adaptations in the 21st century. *American Journal of Psychotherapy, 69,* 91–95.

National Institute of Clinical Excellence. (2011). *Self-harm; Longer term management.* London: Department of Health.

Rathus, J. H., & Miller, A. L. (2015). *DBT skills manual for adolescents.* New York: Guilford Press.

Reneses, B., Munoz, E., & Lopez-Ibor, J.J. (2009). Factors predicting drop-out in community mental health centres. *World Psychiatry, 8,* 173–177.

Rizvi, S. L., Steffel, L. M., & Carson-Wong, A. (2013). An overview of dialectical behaviour therapy for professional psychologists. *Professional Psychology: Research and Practice, 44,* 73–80.

Royal College of Psychiatrists. (2010). *Self harm, suicide, and risk: Helping people who self harm.* London: Royal College of Psychiatrists.

Smith, T. L., Landes, S. J., Lester-Williams, K., Batdorf, W., Brown, G. K., Trockel, M., . . . Healy, T. E. (2017). Developing alternative training delivery methods to improve psychotherapy implementation in the U.S. Department of Veterans Affairs. *Training and Education in Professional Psychology, 11,* 266–275.

Swales, M.A. (2009). Dialectical behaviour therapy: Description, research and future directions. *International Journal of Behavioural Consultation and Therapy, 5,* 164–177.

Swales, M. A. (2010a). Implementing DBT: selecting, training, and supervising a team. *The Cognitive Behavioural Therapist, 3,* 71–79.

Swales, M. A. (2010b). Implementing dialectical behaviour therapy: Organisational pre-treatment. *The Cognitive Behavioural Therapist, 3,* 147–157.

Swales, M. A., & Heard, H. L. (2017). *Dialectical behaviour therapy: The CBT distinctive features series,* 2nd Edition. London: Routledge.

Swales, M. A., Taylor, B., & Hibbs, R. A. (2012). Implementing dialectical behaviour therapy: programme survival in routine healthcare settings. *Journal of Mental Health*, *21*, 548–555.

Swenson, C. R. (2016). *DBT principles in action: Acceptance, change, and dialectics.* New York: Guilford Press.

Swenson, C. R., Torrey, W. C., & Koerner, K. (2002). Implementing dialectical behaviour therapy. *Psychiatric Services*, *53*, 171–178.

Swenson, C. R., Witterhold, S., & Bohus, M. (2007). Dialectical behaviour therapy on inpatient units. In L. A. Dimeff & K. Koerner (Eds.), *Dialectical behavior therapy in clinical practice: Applications across disorders and settings* (pp. 69–111). New York: Guilford Press.

Tajfel, H. (1982). Social psychology of intergroup relations. *Annual Review of Psychology*, *33*, 1–39.

Tang, N., Eisenberg, J. M., & Meyer, G. S. (2004). The roles of government in improving health care quality and safety. *Joint Commission Journal on Quality and Safety*, *30*, 47–55.

Valentine, S. E., Bankoff, S. M., Poulin, R. M., Reidler, E. B., & Pantalone, D. W. (2015). The use of dialectical behaviour therapy skills training as a stand alone treatment: A systematic review of the treatment outcome literature. *Journal of Clinical Psychology*, *71*, 1–20.

Wheelis, J. (2009). Theory and practice of dialectical behavior therapy. In G. O. Gabbard (Ed.), *Textbook of psychotherapeutic treatments* (pp. 727–756). Arlington, VA: American Psychiatric Publishing, Inc.

Wan, P. Y. (2012). Dialectics, complexity, and the systemic approach: toward a critical reconciliation. *Philosophy of the Social Sciences*, *43*, 411–452.

CHAPTER 39

··

DBT IN PRIVATE PRACTICE

··

SARAH K. REYNOLDS AND COLLEEN M. LANG

INTRODUCTION AND OVERVIEW

DIALECTICAL behaviour therapy (DBT; Linehan, 1993) was originally developed for individuals with suicidal behaviour in the context of borderline personality disorder (BPD) and multiple clinical trials support its efficacy (Miga et al., this volume). The treatment has since been expanded for use with a wide range of disorders (e.g., eating disorders, substance use disorders, adolescents with suicidal behaviour) with a growing body of research support (Ritschel, Lim, & Stewart, 2015). As popularity and demand for DBT rises, clinicians are increasingly interested in adapting it for their private practice settings. But how to best approach the implementation process for a broad-based and comprehensive model such as DBT? When delivered in its standard form DBT includes multiple treatment modes delivered by a team of clinicians. How does a solo practitioner feasibly provide DBT to fidelity? The purpose of this chapter is to answer such questions by identifying common challenges and offering practical guidance based on our own experience as DBT solo practioners.

There are a variety of general pitfalls in operating a private practice, but the focus of the present chapter is on the ways that these difficulties impact the delivery of DBT and the dialectical tensions that can result. Unlike most outpatient DBT settings (e.g., university counselling centre, hospital outpatient clinic), a solo practitioner has total autonomy. There is no pre-existing structure or administrative oversight, nor are there fellow clinicians on site. As attractive as this autonomy may be, it also means that clinicians have sole responsibility to design the practice structure that best suits their personal and professional goals. This structure must address both financial *and* clinical service needs, leading to a variety of potential challenges that are best approached dialectically.

Accordingly, our aim is to offer dialectical solutions to aid DBT clinicians in balancing the needs of their business, their clients, and their own personal and professional limits. We discuss options for structuring a solo DBT practice and ways to navigate clinical interactions that honour profit-making goals alongside clinical service goals. Although this chapter is not intended to be a detailed "how-to" guide, we provide practical wisdom and concrete tips taken from our combined experience and hard-earned lessons as DBT therapists, teachers, supervisors, and/or consultants across various settings including schools, hospitals, community mental health centres, forensic facilities, and both solo and group private practice.

Several caveats are in order. First, we presume that readers have at least a basic understanding of the principles, strategies, and theoretical foundations of DBT. Second, our focus is on a DBT practice that strives for treatment fidelity. The flexible, principle-based framework of DBT allows for fidelity when making setting-specific modifications, as long as those modifications are done mindfully, systematically, and consistent with the treatment model (Koerner, Dimeff, & Swenson, 2007). While many solo practitioners may be interested in partial implementation of DBT (e.g., skills group-only) or treatments that are DBT-informed, we caution against this approach without extensive training and experience in delivery of standard DBT. Finally, we use the term private practice to refer to a solo practitioner who is operating under one tax identification number. Accordingly, the present focus is on commonly encountered problems that arise in solo settings. Readers should note, however, that much of the presented information has relevance for DBT practices with a group private practice model. Table 39.1 provides a comparison of solo and group practice models.

SETTING THE STAGE

Many details of the implementation process are best understood from the vantage point of two DBT conceptual underpinnings: the functions of treatment as distinguished from modes of service delivery, and the paradigm of dialectics as a framework for the treatment. The subsequent sections highlight how these concepts can frame decision-making at both the macro-level (e.g., programme structure) and the micro-level (e.g., interacting with a client seeking a fee reduction).

DBT as Functions of Treatment and Modes of Service Delivery

Linehan has articulated that a psychotherapy intended to be *comprehensive* should fulfil five functions: 1) enhance client motivation by addressing factors that interfere with progress (e.g., painful emotions); 2) enhance client capabilities; 3) ensure generalization of skillful responses to relevant environments of the client; 4) enhance motivation and skills of therapists to deliver adherent DBT; and 5) structure the overall treatment environment (where needed) such that it promotes clinical progress. In standard DBT these

Table 39.1 Comprehensive DBT models in private practice

Structure	Description	Benefits	Pitfalls to Avoid
Group practice comprised of clinicians with equal ownership of business.	The practice is one legal entity with one tax ID; business ownership and decision making is equally shared.	• Enables standard DBT to be delivered most easily by clinicians with equal investment legally and financially. • Can share costs of administrative support.	• Significant commitment that is hard to dissolve. • May be hard to reach consensus; polarization can occur and lead to ongoing "stuckness".
Group practice led by one (or more) business owner who employ staff clinicians.	The practice is one legal entity with one tax ID; business owner(s) makes decisions regarding practice structure and policies.	• Decision making is easier with one leader. • Standard DBT in one location. • Easier to start.	• Employer-employee relationship can introduce new set of dialectical tensions. • Business owners may become removed from direct clinical relationship and clinicians have greater risk for burnout if they cannot observe own limits. • High risk clients might be seen by clinicians who are less impacted by legal liability issues.
Multiple solo practitioners (sole proprietors) who work together in shared location.	Each clinician remains a separate business entity but joins for purpose of consultation team and sharing clients. Cost of space is shared.	• Enables clinical collaboration without requiring business collaboration. • Shared space provides clinical benefits of a programme.	• Clinical investment can be unequal due to differing degrees of financial/legal risk. • May be difficult to find another clinician who is a good match.
Multiple solo practitioners treating DBT clients in separate locations.	Includes solo practitioners who commute for consultation team. For skills: clients travel to outside group or one practitioner provides all modes.	• Enables flexibility and is easy to start. • Adaptable to settings where other DBT clinicians are sparse (e.g., rural settings). • Consistent with classic private practice model.	• Requires most adaptation and best done by well-trained DBT clinicians. • Team-based approach can break down without strong commitment. • Skills acquisition can be more challenging due to logistical challenges.

tasks are divided across the following modes of service delivery, respectively: individual therapy; skills group; between-session phone coaching as needed; therapist consultation team; various methods when needed (e.g., family sessions).

The distinction between functions and modes creates flexibility for those adopting DBT in settings where the standard modes are difficult. For example, in the context of a three-week partial hospital programme, individual therapy may have a less prominent role and the motivational enhancement function could be shared by the additional mode of a twice-weekly group focusing on participant goals. The mistake would be to simply drop the individual therapy mode or offer a very watered-down replacement without adding a component responsible for motivational enhancement. The essential point is to stay grounded in the functions of treatment, and ensure that each mode provided, regardless of the particulars, is matched with a corresponding function. A solo practice may not offer modes identical to standard DBT, but the practitioner must be able to articulate how each function is served by the modes offered, and be mindful of any functions that are not being addressed

Earning a Profit in a Helping Profession: Take a Dialectical Stance

Among DBT clinicians, private practitioners are in the unique position of being also business owners. Embracing a dialectical philosophy is a helpful way to manage the complex interplay between needs related to service versus those related to business. The skilled *clinician* values altruism and seeks to improve the lives of their clients; a skilled *business owner* values entrepreneurship, and prioritizes profit-making and keeping "customers" happy (i.e., therapy clients, colleagues, and potential referents). Not surprisingly, many clinicians struggle to fully inhabit the role of business manager. They identify as "helpers", but struggle as "entrepreneurs" who must make difficult business decisions. These internal tensions are often heightened for the DBT practitioner treating a multi-disordered population who may be suffering and yet unable to bear the financial burden of full-price weekly sessions, let alone the cost of skills group. Certainly, there can be a perceived conflict of interest in not only making treatment recommendations, but also profiting from these very recommendations. Oscillation between extremes of altruism on one pole versus profit-making on the other may occur without ever finding a synthesis.

Perhaps to a greater degree than for other treatments, DBT may select for practitioners who are particularly altruistic and can quickly become emotionally invested in clients. As a result, DBT clinicians may be prone to negative judgments of earning a profit for their professional skills, and can become self-invalidating about both wanting session payment and also for failing to address it with the client. When the emphasis is exclusively on altruism, essential tasks such as targeting a client's non-payment may feel in direct conflict with the values of a helping profession. Without mindfulness of such attitudes, DBT clinicians may not recognize the ways they may be inadvertently reinforcing problem behaviours on the part of the clients, and how the need for financial reimbursement may actually foster clinical work. Reimbursement for our services symbolizes and reinforces the value of what we are providing and validates the effort we put into work for our clients. Also, earning money can help providers maintain and improve clinical skills over time by paying for additional training, which, by extension, means an improved capacity to be helpful. Most importantly, the profit a practitioner earns is what determines his/her ability to stay open and continue to help others.

Financial pressures and money-related attitudes may influence clinical work in the other direction, as well. For example, excessive focus on building one's business can lead to accepting too many clients, particularly to offset the out-of-session tasks required for DBT clinicians. It is true that many of the tasks of comprehensive DBT do not generate income, and at a minimum, include weekly consultation team and as-needed-phone coaching. Financial pressures may also influence a clinician to opt out of these important modes of treatment. Further, effective treatment of Stage 1 clients with complex emotional difficulties may involve additional out-of-session case management tasks, such as collaborating with ancillary providers and/or family members. A clinician may struggle with a wise mind goal of providing effective treatment, and yet feel a sense of burnout since the extra time is not financially reimbursed. These feelings may intensify when juggling a busy practice and a personal life—creating a cycle of constant pressure and re-evaluation about whether an unreimbursed activity is sufficiently valuable (i.e., reinforcing) given opportunity-costs.

A related dialectical tension arises from the business emphasis on "pleasing the customer" which will sometimes be at odds with a structured treatment that pushes for behavioural change. Doing DBT will not always feel good for the client (i.e., customer), particularly in instances where strong contingencies are applied. Other "customers" may also feel vital to business interests including referral sources, ancillary non-DBT providers, and inidividuals other than the client (e.g., parents) who may be paying for the treatment (often the case with adolescents and many young adults). As a result, the clinician may feel pulled in multiple directions. Common examples include a client who continues to "vent" during an individual session despite a clinician's effort to set an agenda, or a family member who pushes for an alternate treatment plan than the one a clinician has agreed upon with the client. Professional integrity and expertise will (rightfully) influence a DBT clinician to remain aligned with the treatment principles. However, polarization with referents, family members or clients may run counter to business interests and can be anxiety provoking for clinicians. The task for clinicians is to move away from characteristic response patterns that are unhelpful or extreme, and instead to access wise mind and find a synthesis among various perspectives (whether held by different parties, within the clinician, or both). In the present example a clinician may need to start by noticing his/her fear-based catastrophic thoughts that "all my clients might out" and could instead foster the notion, that a "customer" who expresses dissatisfaction or disagreement with treatment need not mean a failing business.

The overarching recommendation is to stay rooted in a dialectical framework and continually return to the task of dialectical assessment. In addition, we highlight two ways to help clinicians find and maintain a balanced approach.

Conduct a self-assessment. Clinicians should learn to recognize where and how they are vulnerable to polarization along these business-service tensions (and any other dialectical dilemmas that are relevant for their practice). Doing so will require clinicians to set aside time for mindful self-assessment: evaluate where you become "stuck" and the behavioural examples of your own non-dialectical responses (emotions, thoughts, actions) along with common prompting events. Where possible use the consultation team (or a trusted colleague) to conduct and discuss your self-assessment and ultimately to help each other with solution analyses and coaching toward more dialectical responses.

Follow a financial plan to minimize anxiety-driven decisions. Developing greater skill and confidence in the business landscape will make your practice more successful and more satisfying, particularly for clinicians who are tilted heavily toward a "helper" identification. To that end, develop and follow an a priori business plan with financial benchmarks in order to earn the income you need and also to make effective and balanced decisions related to weekly caseload, session fees, and other payment-related policies. One straightforward approach to identifying financial benchmarks and the minimum number of weekly visits needed to reach them is the following: determine the net income needed from the practice in order to meet household/living expenses; add your projected business expenses (include self-employment taxes if applicable) to the net income figure; divide by the total number of weeks the practice will be open, excluding holidays and vacations (e.g., 48 weeks) in order to calculate the minimum weekly practice income. From here, it is easier to estimate weekly individual caseload by dividing the weekly income figure by your session fee. The results may suggest areas for adjustment; for example, if the weekly caseload feels excessive the clinician could consider raising session fees, reducing business expenses, or evaluate what other changes might help with balancing workload and financial needs.

Clinicians who shy away from business management tasks should be proactive about developing their business skills. Various forms of help can be considered, ranging from self-study utilizing books or online classes to hiring an accountant or a business coach. The general point is to "avoid avoiding" and prioritize your role as a business manager if that is an area of weakness.

GETTING STARTED: STRUCTURING YOUR DBT PRACTICE

Structuring your DBT practice requires many decisions. *Who will you treat using DBT? Will you practise DBT exclusively, or will it be a small part of your practice? Is your physical location conducive to running a skills group?* This section discusses important questions and issues to consider in the decision-making process.

Identify the Clients Served and How they Fit Your Overall Practice

Decisions about intended client population should involve several interrelated factors including the comprehensiveness of the programme, a clinician's background and training in DBT, and personal and financial needs. Clinicians who make a purposeful "wise-minded" decision about *who* they will treat (even if later they decide to shift focus), as well as who they are competent and equipped to treat, are less likely to become unduly influenced by financial reinforcers and treat clients that their programme structure cannot effectively support.

Many private practitioners elect to provide transdiagnostic applications of DBT; that is, focus on problem behaviours other than suicidal behaviour in the context of BPD (e.g., eating disorders, school refusal, etc.). In such cases clinicians should consider whether other evidence-based CBT protocols are sufficient or more appropriate. Either way, the needs of the client population will inform whether a therapist provides all modes of DBT; for example, a therapist may aim to treat individuals who might typically be in Stage 2 of DBT in which case skills group may not be indicated and/or phone coaching may be expected to be less frequent. On the other hand, many individuals who present to private practice have low-level and infrequent suicidal ideation/urges to self-injure, and instead struggle primarily with problems best conceptualized as quality-of-life (QoL) targets. As such private practice clinicians may need to increase their skill in targeting and prioritizing multiple QoL behaviours, making consultation team a particularly important treatment mode.

Ultimately, the identity of the client population directly impacts the overall number of DBT clients that can be effectively treated at once. While greater financial needs and/or desire to please the customer (and referral network) might predict seeing numerous clients, becoming overly driven by business-related concerns can reduce treatment quality and/or eventually result in clinician burnout. One dialectical solution can be to offer DBT to a subset of clients within a larger CBT practice. Doing so allows clinicians to meet financial benchmarks, meet the needs of a broader array of clients and referral sources, and reduces chances of clinician burnout. In our experience, full-time solo practitioners treat a subset of DBT clients (at varying stages of treatment) that comprises between 35–75% of their overall caseload (typically ranging from 20-30 clients). By comparison, clinicians who work in a private group practice alongside multiple therapists tend to treat a greater number of actively suicidal clients (Sayrs, personal communication, August 4, 2017; Greenberg, personal communication, July 24, 2017).

Many practitioners will need to regularly re-evaluate the foregoing decisions as shifts in personal, professional, or financial goals dictate. A prime example is clinicians who are in the early stages of their DBT training or new to private practice who are working toward a 12-month goal of a comprehensive DBT programme. Decisions about the number and severity of DBT clients should differ when the clinician is conducting only partially implemented DBT (e.g., providing individual sessions and meeting sporadically with an inexperienced consultation team) as compared to a later time point when all modes are being provided.

Personal limits of the clinician are another obvious consideration and inevitably change over time. Life events (e.g., health problems, unexpected financial burden, etc.) may influence decisions about overall caseload or preclude clinicians from taking on clients with high treatment needs for a period of time or indefinitely. One useful strategy for sole proprieters can be to have new clients (in Stage 1) enter treatment on a periodic basis, hence allowing for additional time and thoughtfulness at the front end of treatment while greater stability is being achieved. (e.g., four to eight weeks for a new client). Overall, embracing the dialectical principle that reality is in constant change can be quite "freeing" for clinicians who tend to avoid firm decision-making or who are slow to make changes to their practice. That is, one need not feel forever confined by one particular choice, as change is always possible and in fact unavoidable.

Screening Prospective Clients

Developing a way to screen potential DBT clients helps practitioners uphold their a priori decisions about the client population they will serve and their target DBT caseload. Screening is best done by setting aside time for a 15- to 30-minute telephone conversation that allows for preliminary assessment of the goodness of fit in two areas: logistical factors (e.g., fee, scheduling, etc.) and clinical factors (type/severity of presenting problems, your general treatment approach). Our general strategy is to schedule an intake evaluation only after deciding there is sufficient likelihood that we would accept the client into our practice (should that be the resulting recommendation based on the intake). Doing so reduces the risk of having the prospective client invest significant financial and emotional resources involved in a lengthy intake evaluation only to be disappointed by not being accepted into treatment. For example, if a client absolutely requires an evening appointment and you do not foresee having an evening opening for months, it does not make sense for the client to come in for an intake. Likewise, if the client is describing frequent suicidal behaviour and/or history of difficulties engaging in treatment and you are not conducting comprehensive DBT, use the information to find an appropriate, alternate referral for that client. Also, even if you are providing comprehensive DBT to clients with more severe symptoms, use the initial call to determine the potential stage of treatment and whether your current caseload and programme structure can accommodate effective treatment. Where appropriate, this phone screening can even serve as a helpful precursor to the DBT pre-treatment conversation that may take place during the intake evaluation. Preliminary use of orienting and commitment strategies can make prospective clients aware of what would likely be expected of them should they enter treatment with you (e.g., engage in a structured change-oriented treatment).

Because detailed phone screening is non-reimbursable and may not ultimately result in a new client, some clinicians prefer to move quickly through this stage or simply schedule an intake via email. However, we find that careful screening of prospective DBT clients is often more cost effective in the long run. Ultimately, taking on a client whose needs cannot be met is not only unfair to the client, but may also lead to higher costs to a clinician, both with respect to time (i.e., treatment planning, collateral contact, coaching) and emotional energy. Moreover, clinicians who tend to get polarized around extreme altruism or pleasing the customer find it easier to say "no" to a distressed client via this phone screening, but nearly impossible in the context of a lengthy in-person evaluation for which the client is paying.

Relatedly, clinicians sometimes struggle with matter-of-fact questioning during an initial phone screen. However, direct inquiry about recent suicidal behaviour and/or hospitalization (even if you expect these questions may be uncomfortable for the potential client), enable better clinical decision-making. In some instances, the most helpful outcome of the call may be to make an alternate referral. However, for some clinicians, the more desperate the potential client seems, the more difficult it can be to honour personal limits. And yet, it is far easier and more effective to be honest about these limits at the outset than to do so after engaging in additional contacts. Further, doing so is consistent with a DBT-style of interacting that avoids treating clients as overly fragile and instead presumes they are capable of handling uncomfortable truths. It can be a communication of honesty and respect to say to a client: "I don't want you to spend needless time and resources coming in for a consultation if it is not reasonable to expect we will work together."

Choosing a Location

Choosing a location requires consideration of many factors general to private practice, including cost and convenience for your intended client population. For DBT you must also consider whether your space can accommodate a skills group and perhaps a consultation team. In an ideal world, DBT clinicians have access to a room adjacent to their private office that includes a table/chairs and whiteboard. A second room for skills group has two potential benefits: it allows for an easy transition for the tightly booked clinician with individual sessions scheduled immediately before/after skills group; additionally, there is often more space to accommodate more people, including a co-leader when available. However, such an arrangement could be cost-prohibitive and clinicians should be mindful that building a skills group that is reliably revenue-generating can take time and energy.

For these reasons, many clinicians simply use their private office and make small adaptations to create a more classroom like setting. For example, choosing an office that will comfortably fit at least four group members. However, clinicians working with adolescents who want to conduct a multi-family skills group will likely need a second room. A middle path approach to allow more space with the least financial burden would be to access a room for select periods at low or no additional cost; a large professional building is often a good bet.

Another consideration is proximity to your team members. Other things being equal, closer is better. It improves convenience of weekly team meetings and is often easier to cross-refer to each other's skills groups. Consider sharing the cost of an office suite with one or more consultation team members, even while you continue to operate under separate tax IDs. This approach integrates the DBT practice needs with the business needs: solo clinicians can provide services that approximate a DBT "clinic" while still remaining financially independent and keeping costs low.

Establishing Financial Policies

Having clear financial policies with clients is the key to a smoothly running business and is also a way for you to structure the business side of your relationship with prospective clients. Simply making policy decisions in advance and committing them to paper can act as an antidote for those clinicians prone to polarized responding on the service side of the dialectic. To that end, decide how you intend to handle the many payment-related aspects of your practice and put it in writing to be added to a larger document outlining all practice policies (e.g., emergencies, confidentiality, etc.). Provide this policy statement to clients at the initial consultation. Although the specific financial details to include in the policy statement may vary depending on practitioner needs, we suggest the following information at a minimum: your fees for each type of service, acceptable forms of payment, the time at which payment is expected, policy on cancellations and missed sessions, any insurance agreements, and any details about handling payment provided by an outside individual (e.g., the client's parent). Having a written policy ensures that the clinician remains mindful of the business manager role, even when face-to-face with a distressed client during the first meeting. Similarly, use of a written document tends to make the money conversation less about the individuals involved and more about "the business."

Fee-setting

In order to meet yearly income goals, clinicians must ensure that their session fee is properly balanced with their intended weekly caseload. As such, decisions regarding the session fee should be guided mainly by your overall financial plan as described earlier in the chapter. An important factor here is that most private practitioners use a business model in which they bill only for direct contact with the client. Therefore, the therapy session is essentially the "product" being offered (Grodzki, 2000), and the amount of available product is limited by the number of hours in a week and the amount of clinical demand a clinician can and should tolerate. Unlike most other types of business which can drive up profits by selling an array of products or by using various other means to increase production (e.g., mass-produce at lower cost), a therapy business cannot offer an automated or assembly-line approach to a therapy session; there is no low-cost alternate therapist who can be used as a substitute for a session. As a result, profit is capped by the relatively high costs of a therapy business—both in terms of direct (e.g., office rent) and indirect expense (e.g., time spent in unbilled work including administrative tasks and marketing, professional trainings).

Therefore your session fee should be sufficiently high to offset the substantial amount of unreimbursed time spent running your business. Clinicians who struggle with this reality may put themselves at risk for income loss or clinical burnout resulting from an excessive caseload. Revisiting the self-assessment on the business-service dialectic and evaluating cognitive biases may be helpful. For example, there are reasons to think that paying more for a session can sharpen the focus and motivation of clients in the same way that it can for clinicians. Research suggests that payment for services can be associated with improved outcomes, and most clinicians can point to experiences of clients who are not themselves paying for treatment and appear uninvested. Indeed, it's important to periodically raise the fees for your clients which can have the effect of increasing the energy level they put into the work.

Affordability of Treatment

At the same time, providing affordable treatment options is important to many DBT private practitioners. In fact the intended DBT target client population and their associated financial resources should be considered when setting financial policies; for example, charging high session fees may simply not make sense if you're providing DBT for disabled veterans. Moreover, comprehensive DBT is more expensive for clients than the typical once-weekly outpatient therapy e.g., Comtois et al. (2007). Insurance companies are not likely to pay for both individual and group therapy and will definitely not cover missed ("no-show") sessions. This requires sensitivity on the part of the DBT clinician to the high costs of treatment. On the other hand, DBT also requires clinicians to spend more time doing non-reimbursable activities (i.e., consultation team, phone coaching, collateral contacts) than is typical for other treatments.

Various approaches can be taken to increase the affordability of comprehensive DBT while maintaining profits. Some clinicians providing comprehensive DBT elect to charge high individual session fees that reflect the non-reimbursed time incurred and then encourage clients to negotiate with their insurance company for a "bundled" weekly rate. This approach can be justified on the grounds that DBT therapists are expected to continue to treat, independent of whether clients attend the sessions (e.g., by problem solving how to get to sessions, managing crises, etc.). If a bundled rate is not available and the insurance company limits reimbursement to one weekly session, then it is best to seek reimbursement for the weekly session with the highest fee.

Similarly, DBT can be made more affordable by offering a "package rate" when clients are being treated by one provider who is their individual therapist and skills group leader. A straightforward approach by sole proprietor clinicians might be to maintain their typical individual session fee but offer their own clients a spot in the skills group at a significantly reduced fee, hence enabling clients to keep their weekly treatment costs low. Doing so can have the added benefit of countering possible client perceptions that a clinician's treatment recommendations are driven solely by financial motives.

Clinicians may also offer a different "menu" of service options, each associated with a different cost based on session length. For example, some clients may benefit from more frequent, but shorter sessions that are offered at lower cost (e.g., twice weekly for 30-minute sessions). Another option is to provide reduced fees for hard-to-fill time

---

Box 39.1 Clinical Vignette No. 1

Anna tends to be flexible in reducing her session fee. When prospective clients (with whom she is not yet in a relationship) request a reduced fee, she typically offers up to a 15-20% reduction. When existing clients request a fee reduction, Anna may link their request to relevant treatment targets. For example, for a client working to increase active problem-solving skills or independent coping (such as may be the case with a young adult client), Anna may make a fee reduction contingent upon the client's efforts at budgeting. Anna's decision-making can also be influenced by a client's engagement in treatment. In one instance, Anna agreed to reduce her fee for a long-standing client whose financial status changed for reasons largely beyond her control (i.e., her husband lost his high-paying job). Anna continued to feel motivated and fulfilled in her work as her client continued to work hard in treatment, use coaching effectively, and communicate skillfully with Anna.

---

slots, whereas "prime" evening slots require payment of full fee. When possible, employ a trainee who can treat the client at a reduced cost in exchange for your clinical supervision.

Offering a reduced fee is always an option, and some DBT clinicians can afford to budget for a certain number of sliding fee slots in their caseload. At the same time, clinicians need not reflexively reduce their fee upon request, particularly for a prospective client with whom you don't yet have a relationship. Instead of an unqualified "yes" to a fee reduction request, seek some understanding of the reasons for the request and be sure to explain the rationale for your fee. In instances when you have agreed to a reduced fee, consider doing so for a time-limited period and then re-assessing. As highlighted in the section below, fee reduction requests may be handled somewhat differently for existing clients with whom you already have a relationship. Vignette 1 illustrates approaches to fee reduction and how they may differ with existing clients (Box 39.1).

SETTING UP MODES OF TREATMENT

A significant challenge for clinicians implementing comprehensive DBT in private practice is determining how to implement modes of treatment that meet all of functions of DBT outlined. This section discusses each mode of standard DBT with an emphasis on mode-specific barriers for private practitioners and options for addressing them. Box 39.2 summarizes common implementation challenges and potential solutions.

Individual Therapy

In a private practice setting, DBT individual therapists are especially likely to wear multiple hats (e.g., individual therapist and skills group leader, clinician and business owner) and "drifting" out of balance is easy, especially given the potential isolation of private

Box 39.2   DBT implementation: Summary of common challenges and possible solutions for private practitioners

General challenges

Can only provide partially-implemented DBT

- Give informed consent to prospective clients via a written handout that outlines differences between standard DBT and your services.
- Clarify what behavioural changes they can reasonably expect from the treatment.
- Be mindful of how services are advertised. To avoid misunderstanding, use accurate language such as "DBT-informed" services.

Clients cannot afford additional weekly sessions (e.g., skills group) recommended by DBT clinician

- Assess and define client's financial problem to see what solutions exist (aside from opting out of the additional sessions). Take an active role in helping clients address financial difficulties that interfere with treatment.
- Consider providing a low-fee skills group, especially if comprised of your individual clients.
- Offer a bundled rate for clients who are seen more than once per week.
- Budget for a certain number of reduced-fee individual therapy slots or provide the option of working with supervisees who have lower fees.
- Offer to reduce individual session fee for hard-to-fill time slots or provide twice weekly briefer sessions at a lower cost.

Individual Therapy Challenges

Difficult to turn away clients "in need" and become overwhelmed with a high number of Stage 1 clients

- Be mindful of personal and professional limits. Use consultation team to role-play orienting prospective clients why treating them is not feasible.
- Conduct a dialectical assessment: is it truly in a client's longer-term interest for a clinician to treat if you cannot provide all that is needed? Evaluate pros/cons in short and longer term.
- Before scheduling an in-person intake, conduct a thorough telephone screening to be sure there is a reasonable probability client will be accepted into one's practice:
  - Allow for 15–30 minutes to assess logistical (fees/schedule/etc.) and clinical fit.
  - Be direct in asking about suicidal behaviour and hospitalization history.
  - Be honest about reasons you can't take them as clients and have other referrals ready.
- If feasible, have prospective clients enter treatment at two-month intervals to enable a period of stabilization for each new client before admitting a new one.

Difficulty with setting fees and collecting payment

- Avoid mood-dependent decisions by relying on yearly financial goals to estimate weekly caseload and fee.

(continued)

Box 39.2 Continued

- Be mindful of greater amount of unpaid time required as a DBT individual therapist. Consider whether to charge higher fees for individual DBT clients (i.e., one rate that includes phone coaching, consultation team, collateral contacts).
- During pre-treatment phase: orient clients to fees and payment/cancellation policies. Identify and problem-solve potential difficulties as TIBs.
- When providing orientation during pre-treatment, use a written policy statement that clearly outlines business and payment information for the practice.
- Be proactive in coaching clients with insurance reimbursement.

Consultation Team Challenges
Distance between team members interferes with attendance at consultation team

- Consider videoconferencing or telephone if absolutely necessary.
- Shorter weekly team meetings can be supplemented by a longer team meeting once every month or every two months, where team members can focus more intensively upon case conceptualization.
- Periodically rotate the location of consultation team so that everyone has an opportunity for convenience.
- Create a culture of openness among team members and facilitate discussions of barriers to team attendance and/or any frustrations with loss of income associated with commuting to and attending team. Avoid "elephants in the room".
- Maximize the utility and reinforcing aspects of team in ways such as:
  - Come prepared to the team when in need of consultation: identify consultation questions, prepare chain.
  - Choose members carefully and start small if needed; seek team members with whom you are comfortable giving/receiving direct feedback and who are a good match regarding DBT experience/skill level and commitment to fidelity.
  - Seek team members who are existing colleagues and with whom you would value a long-term professional relationship.
  - When adding new members, balance overall size of team with the length of your scheduled meeting. Most private practice teams requiring members to commute tend be 60–75 min with four to six members.

Consultation team members do not share the same clients

- Cultivate equal investment in all clients: Emphasize team principle that members should treat team members' clients as if their own client. Add this agreement to standard consultation team agreements.
- Remain mindful that consultation team is *clinician*-centred rather than client-centred, so sharing clients is not a requirement.
- Refer individual clients to skills groups run by team members.
- Provide coverage for each other's clients for brief or extended leaves (e.g., maternity leave).

Box 39.2 Continued

Skills Group Challenges

Leading a skills training group without a co-leader

- Address potential TIBs directly by orienting and seeking commitment prior to group entry.
- Make a plan for most time-efficient ways to manage clinical administrative tasks related to group. Possible strategies include:
  - Using a sign-in sheet for attendance.
  - Having individuals pay up front for a block of sessions or for the entire module.
  - Developing a simple system for giving homework assignments to individuals who did not attend group; if necessary, ask clients to simply complete the same assignment from prior week.

Getting a sufficient number of clients to launch a new skills group

- Can start with three clients although four is preferable.
- Select from your individual clients.
- Foster cross-referrals within your own DBT consultation.
- Offer a reduced fee.
- If applicable, allow shorter minimum time commitment for group entry (e.g., for one module).

practice. At the same time, individual therapy is arguably the DBT treatment mode in which clinicians can exercise the most direct control. Given the right ingredients and level of mindfulness, this mode has the capacity to best represent dialectical balance. Cultivating this balance requires clinicians to take responsibility for identifying and observing their own limits (personal, professional, and business-related) and helping clients to do the same through use of orienting and problem-solving strategies. This process begins during the pre-treatment phase, which is the clinician's opportunity to set the stage by getting client commitment to the treatment plan and by anticipating and problem-solving potential treatment-interfering behaviours (TIBs) of the client that may occur along the way.

The dual roles of business manager and clinician can complicate the pre-treatment conversation and clinicians may fail to thoroughly target potential TIBs. As a result, prospective clients can be too readily accepted into treatment without a clear understanding of or commitment to all elements of treatment or to the financial policies of the practice. At times, conceptualizing a client's primary problems is the easier part of the pre-treatment phase. What is more difficult is attention to an important guiding principle: *What is necessary to comfortably and effectively treat the client?* A clinician who becomes too focused on pleasing their "customer" becomes vulnerable to influence by the client at the cost of clarifying contingencies and/or observing personal limits. For example, a client may flatly state that she is unwilling to engage in a group. Reflexively agreeing to such client requests without appropriate assessment will likely lead to ongoing treatment imbalance in which the clinician is struggling to conduct effective treatment, eventually leading to drop-out and/or treatment failure.

At the same time, rigidity about "rules and requirements" is not consistent with the principle-driven nature of DBT, which takes a dialectical stance on a client's capacities in the current moment and what the clinician must help the client *learn* to do as part of treatment. While clinicians must assess a client's willingness to commit to conditions considered standard to DBT (i.e., skills group, diary card, consistent attendance), *as well as* additional contingencies needed to effectively treat (e.g., collateral treatment, commitment to exposure), the other side of the dialectic is that *the therapist* needs to help a client meet those contingencies rather than expect the client can do so at the outset. This leads to a second guiding principle of *how much help will the client need in getting "there" and can the therapist do that?*

For example, if ancillary treatment is a recommendation, part of the individual therapist's job is to coordinate all other aspects of treatment (both DBT and non-DBT). The individual therapist must also get client commitment to additional treatment modes and provide the necessary coaching to ensure client follow-through—a task which can be difficult early in treatment when clients may have greater impairment and fewer skills to engage with an outside provider. Use of commitment strategies and problem-solving in such instances is crucial so that clients know exactly what is expected (e.g., the need to follow through with setting up an appointment and attending regular appointments with another provider in a different location) and have the motivation and ability to fulfil treatment requirements.

Several pointers are particularly relevant to the pretreatment conversation in private practice DBT. As noted, coordinating adjunctive treatments, (e.g., couples work, substance abuse services) is often more time-intensive for a private practitioner who lacks an external structure of practitioners or a resource-rich environment such as a hospital. Clinicians should consider the impact of any additional coordination when deciding whether to accept a client into their practice and what to emphasize during the pre-treatment phase. (Having a ready network of providers who are ancillary and yet DBT-friendly can be very helpful for such moments.)

Second, clinicians should avoid becoming overly acceptance-oriented in the pre-treatment phase and instead adopt a dialectical approach in which they seek commitment while maintaining a non-attached stance (i.e., allow a client to choose an alternative provider). Be mindful of urges to work excessively for commitment or to reduce treatment requirements in order to maintain the "customer." At times, clinicians with high financial needs or customer-service orientation may fear a client's negative reaction and "fast-forward" through the pre-treatment and commitment phase or even compromise on the treatment plan. However, allowing a client's negative reaction and potential refusal to enter treatment is critical. The therapist must seek commitment while simultaneously practising radical acceptance that clients may ultimately choose to find a different treatment provider. Doing otherwise can lead to treatment drop-out or failure, which is not only demoralizing but can be damaging for your business in the longer term: premature drop-outs result in a practice with heavy client turnover, requiring a clinician to repeatedly do the more time-intensive work of the early treatment phase (e.g., conducting a detailed assessment) at the expense of fostering longer-term relationships that yield more successful outcomes.

Third, it helps to define a minimum length of treatment as a way to structure treatment and leverage contingencies. Every client, even if demonstrating a strong level of commitment, should be asked to agree to a defined treatment interval. For standard DBT, this might be for the six months it takes to cycle through all of the DBT skills modules. Importantly, reaching the interval does not require that treatment ends, but rather that the therapist and the client collaboratively evaluate progress, make changes as necessary, and re-commit to treatment goals for another defined interval of time. Following this practice keeps both clinicians and clients working hard in treatment and aware of any ongoing TIB that needs to be addressed. From a behavioural standpoint, it can also provide a way to reinforce the client (i.e., with continued treatment) for reaching treatment goals and for remaining an active participant in the therapeutic work. For the clinician, it provides a chance to comprehensively address treatment progress and goals and use commitment strategies in a planful, wise-mind manner.

In instances where the client is unwilling or unable to engage in a recommended treatment mode (for whatever reason), defining a briefer treatment interval without that mode may serve as a middle path solution to refusing to treat. Incumbent on the clinician is to clearly communicate the possible negative treatment outcomes of following the client's wishes (e.g., refusing to engage in family sessions, doing self-study of skills rather than attending a group) rather than the prescribed treatment plan, define the length of the interval such as two to three months in order to "see if this approach can work," collaboratively identify benchmarks for success, and obtain clear agreement from the client that treatment must end or change if benchmarks are not met. Use this approach judiciously, as the idea is not to be punitive, but to fully and experientially assess both sides of your dialectic (e.g., your recommendations for treatment versus the client's view of what services are needed.). It is not to be used in a situation where the client is seeking a fundamentally different approach or is at high suicide risk. Clinicians should proceed only with input from the consultation team.

The pre-treatment phase also calls for orientation and commitment to all business policies. Just as other significant TIBs should be assessed and anticipated, so should possible difficulties that a client may have with the amount of payment, the frequency of payment, or cancellation policies. As noted, this is the time to have a written policy statement to review with clients. Doing so early on makes it much easier to raise problems that emerge later in treatment. The challenge here is that clinicians are often more comfortable assessing a client's problems and forming a relationship than discussing financial policies. However, money management and reciprocity in relationships are often difficulties for our clients, and avoiding such discussions is a disservice to them.

Once treatment commences, problems such as non-payment, late cancellations, etc., are targeted as TIBs and require problem solving with the client. Many such behaviours

Box 39.3   Clinical Vignette No. 2

Paul's client, Michelle, had been struggling with fee payment for nearly a month. Problem assessment indicated that Michelle, who had chronically low mood and associated avoidance behaviours, had stopped submitting the paperwork to her insurance company after they had rejected a claim for unclear reasons. She had stopped receiving reimbursement and had not followed up with them, primarily due to feelings of anxiety and shame—both of which were targets in treatment. During the behavioural assessment, Paul was able to target Michelle's shame in session and coach her on contacting her insurance company. They also developed a short-term payment plan so that she could begin paying Paul in the meantime.

Box 39.4   Clinical Vignette No. 3

Angela sought consultation on her work with a client whose frequent coaching calls, difficulties ending calls, leaving session angrily, and responding to redirection, had become increasingly difficult to manage. When asked by her consultation team to examine her difficulties with targeting these TIBs, Angela cited as a significant source of her difficulty her empathy regarding the client's recently escalating stressors, which included losing her job, a need to move, and financial destabilization. Angela then revealed to the team that while the client's contact and session length had increased, the client had not paid her session fee in months, despite a fee reduction to accommodate recent financial instability. Angela was unaware of how polarized she had become towards the role of helper and pleasing the customer (as well as away from fidelity to the model), and the consultation team gently confronted her. Team members expressed concern that Angela was treating the client as overly fragile; they observed their own limits that Angela should first address the client's TIB of non-payment before moving to discussion of other targets; they also obtained Angela's commitment to address payment in the next session.

The familiarity and respect among consultation team members, as well as their non-judgmental awareness of the specific ways they each tended to become polarized, enabled the team to give this gentle yet direct clinical feedback. Team members reminded Angela that her polarization was *not* truly altruistic nor inherently "pleasing" to the client and most importantly, it was not clinically effective. Through team discussion, Angela found a synthesis in that she became aware that honouring her own limits (which included being paid for her time) was also in the best interest of her client, who benefited from the chance to practice honouring and radically accepting the needs of others in relationships.

reflect broader problems that occur in the client's life and may already be targets of treatment (see Boxes 39.3 and 39.4.) Some difficulties commonly occur with many clients and can be addressed in a preventative way, such as insurance-related difficulties. One colleague orients clients the task of managing one's insurance company to the Emotion Regulation "PLEASE" Skills; creatively termed "PLEASE-I."

An important general point here is that DBT clinicians should take an active role in helping their clients to problem solve financial challenges as they relate to treatment, and non-payment should be targeted quickly before the amount increases (which often leads to increasing client shame). When a lower fee is requested, view it as one potential solution to a financial problem, and engage the client in defining the problem before considering an array of possible solutions. Reducing the fee for an agreed upon interval before re-assessing is also an option. Keep in mind that our motivation, effectiveness, and vulnerability against burnout is a function of feeling that our work is valued and results in meaningful change for the client. Sometimes a client's willingness and capacity to work hard in treatment, regardless of the severity of their problems, drive our willingness to reduce fees.

Because of the therapist/client relationship, some clinicians feel guilty about addressing issues with non-payment, seeming to follow an either/or attitude that requesting payment negates the connection and caring that are part of the therapy relationship. While it's true that clients may have a negative reaction that seems to conflate money with callousness, therapists would do well to remember that clients are paying for your training and therapeutic skill, while your caring comes naturally.

Out-of-Session Coaching

Providing out-of-session coaching (*as needed*) meets the important treatment function of improving generalization of new skills. In private practice the structural constraints frequently placed on hospital or agency-based clinicians are absent (e.g., no phone calls after 5pm), allowing freedom to choose a method best suited to the DBT programme needs. Some commonly used options include use of one mobile phone for both work and personal tasks, a separate mobile phone with a Google voice number, and the option of using SMS messages. This level of autonomy can make phone coaching much easier. However, many practitioners have an aversion to the idea of phone coaching. Since this is an important aspect of treatment, clinicians may feel more willingness toward phone coaching when there is clear orientation with clients related to its use and and clinicans clarify their limits (e.g., cannot be expected to call back in less than three hours, are not as effective for calls received in the middle of the night). Clinicians who elect not to provide it should consider what other modes they can implement to address skills generalization.

Consultation Team

Questions often arise about whether consultation team is necessary for private practitioners doing DBT. Our answer is consistently yes: the consultation team is required (e.g., Koerner, 2012). Regardless of the population being treated, the absence of a team should be viewed as partial implementation. The consultation team serves as the backbone of a DBT programme. The relatively higher degree of isolation associated with private practice increases vulnerability to the dialectical tensions described in this chapter, as well as tensions common to general practice of DBT. For private practitioners working alone and without oversight, having a strong team is one way to guard against these dialectical imbalances. Nonetheless, the consultation team can be a significant time investment that is not financially reimbursed, and atittudes emphasizing the business management side of the dialectic may compel a clinician to dismiss or accept a "watered-down" version of this mode of treatment. For example, clinicians may schedule shorter (e.g., one hour or less) and/or less frequent team meetings (e.g., less than once weekly). While honouring the value of dialectical syntheses, adaptations to team can devalue its purpose. Frustrations that a clinician may feel about potential income loss should be channelled towards his/her individual efforts to make consultation team sufficiently valuable and also time-efficient. All members are urged to approach team in the manner they would approach any mode where clients are physically present, and take the responsibility of creating a team that is highly reinforcing and advances their DBT skills.

Adaptations made with this spirit allow for a strong team that is adherent to DBT principles. For example, when clinicians are unable to devote the recommended amount of time, shorter weekly team meetings can be supplemented by a longer team meeting once every month or every two months, where team members can focus more intensively upon case conceptualization. Clinicians can also increase productivity of briefer team meetings by more mindfully preparing case presentations, consultation questions, and chain analyses ahead of time. Be mindful that differences may exist among team members in their attitudes about the value of consultation team, perhaps resulting from differences in financial pressures or logistical constraints such as scheduling or the commute time to/from the location of team meeting. Discussion of such differences allows teams to develop dialectical solutions (see Box 39.2).

Finding a Team

Clinicians have to decide upon the size of their consultation teams and, relatedly, who they want as members of their teams. Given the need for team to be sufficiently reinforcing, decisions about who can provide valuable consult are paramount. It is important to feel confident about any potential team member's experience, adherence to the model, and, importantly, capacity for dialectical thinking and awareness of the dialectical tensions unique to private practice. Prioritize your expected level of comfort discussing and providing feedback about imbalances in these tensions with a proposed team member. To this end, we have found it helpful to choose team members with whom we were already familiar and had already worked and/or participated in a team. (See Box 39.2 for an example of consultation team members providing feedback.)

Size of Team

Each team member needs sufficient time to receive consultation, so the size of the team should be determined by how many clients are being treated by each team member, balanced with how much time is being devoted to team overall. At the same time, it is not effective for clinicians treating very few clients to be part of larger teams where other members are seeing disproportionately more clients. In our experience, when teams are comprised of team members who are each treating a roughly equivalent number of clients, and are capable of committing the same amount of time to team each week, they are more likely to share equal investment in team. Also, the number of team members on the team should determine the length of time devoted to team, also accounting for mindfulness, and other agenda items. On average, each clinician may need to discuss one to three of their clients per week for five to 20 minutes each, depending upon target. We provide this parameter to help mindfully balance the amount of time devoted to team, given other scheduling and financial constraints, with the inclusion or incorporation of members on team. As an example, our own team is comprised of four clinicians, and we meet for 75 minutes per week; accounting for other agenda items, this allows each of us an average of about 15 minutes each per week. Because we experience a degree of time pressure, we have adopted some of the strategies described here for managing time constraints. Incorporating a fifth team member would require each of us to devote an additional 15 minutes per team. This decision would require all team members to balance financial and scheduling needs for this additional time against the potential benefit of a fifth team member's consultation.

When Team Members Do Not Share the Same Clients

Clinicians working alone in private practice often have to create or join teams comprised of other clinicians working alone in private practice. Members on teams structured in this way often do not have direct experience with each other's clients. Without sharing clients and, more explicitly, working in one programme, clinicians can be vulnerable to unique dialectical tensions. For example, without the same amount of felt investment in each other's clients (and business), clinicians may be less inclined to push for behavioural change in their team members and more inclined to instead protect their relationships with each other, resulting in "walking on eggshells" around TIBs. On the other hand, when team members do not have frequent interactions as co-workers in a clinic, and particularly in cases where team members use videoconferencing, clinicians may be less inclined to "please" one another and become very change-oriented without sufficient validation.

Team members can also adopt attitudes too far on either of these poles with respect to the clients of other team members. The lack of direct experience with a client can make it either easier or more difficult to validate the client's behaviour; in consultation, a greater sense of objectivity about clients and the treating clinician's perceptions of clients can be both enhanced and undermined by the consultant knowing a client. Alternatively, direct experience with a client can increase investment and facilitate validation through stronger emotional connection, and may make it more apparent to the consultant when the treating therapist is being overly validating or overly change-oriented.

To maintain a dialectal stance with team members and their clients, it is imperative in private practice to adopt and regularly review the team consultation agreement that all clients are to be treated by team members as if they are their own clients. Fostering an equal investment in all clients can best be facilitated by choosing team members with whom the therapist already has pre-existing relationships, and with whom long-term professional relationships can be expected, and then referring to team members for skills groups and for other DBT-related services (e.g., parenting sessions) is the best approach. Other approaches include taking notes each week on client-therapist dyads discussed and providing clinical coverage for each other when the primary therapist is away, including for shorter periods and for more extended leaves, such as for maternity leave.

Skills Group

In standard comprehensive DBT, clients typically attend individual therapy and skills group within one location and group is conducted by two skills trainers. Meeting this standard as a private practitioner is often challenging and when adaptations are necessary, clinicians should ensure they are addressing the skills group *function*: enhancing overall capabilities by acquiring, strengthening, and generalizing skills.

First, including two skills trainers may be difficult due to lack of availability of another DBT clinician and because of financial constraints when fees must be split between two trainers. One dialectical solution is to add a co-leader who is a DBT trainee, whose compensation is largely the learning opportunity, which can keep costs low. When such an option is not possible, conducting a group alone might make the most financial and logistical sense, but clinicians should bear in mind that the absence of a co-leader usually means more administrative burden for the sole skills trainer (e.g., tracking attendance, collecting/tracking payments, contacts with clients who missed group).

Also, because it is more difficult for a single skills group leader to manage TIB, it is wise to keep the group small (e.g., approximately 5–7 members) and to screen carefully. Use of orienting and commitment strategies in a scheduled pre-treatment session before group entry is the best strategy to prevent, or at least minimize, group TIBs. Doing so is especially important if leading a group comprised primarily of one's individual clients since polarization is more likely when one clinician is doing all the treatment. With that said, many private practitioners have run skills groups single-handedly and for many clients it can be preferable to attending a different location for skills group. For individual clients enrolling in group, the pre-treatment work may simply be a portion of one or more individual sessions during which the clinician clearly communicates his/her dual role as skills trainer *and* individual therapist and articulates the differing goals/targets of each. Willingness of the clinician to be radically genuine, to acknowledge his/her own TIBs, and to have open non-judgmental discussions with clients in the context of individual sessions is essential for addressing ongoing problems that may arise (see Table 39.2 for a summary).

The other option for skills training group is for the therapist to refer individual clients to an outside group. However, a skills group in a separate location may involve significant problem-solving to ensure the client attends regularly. The ideal solution is for team members to either work within the same office location (even while maintaining separate business IDs) or to be conveniently located to each other, and for the therapist to refer individual clients to team members' skills groups, and vice versa. Cross-referrals of this nature enable the best consulting opportunities, reduce the chance of polarization with individual clients, and allow the therapist to have a regular referral flow for her own skills group.

Other challenges may arise when clients are reluctant to commit to a weekly skills group for an interval of six months (i.e., the length of time needed to cycle through all modules once). In fact, the standard format requires one year to enable clients to repeat the cycle and thereby greatly strengthen and generalize their skills. However, many individuals seeking treatment in a self-pay private practice have full time employment and may have entered treatment with the expectation of once-weekly individual therapy. Obtaining agreement to six months of twice-weekly sessions may be difficult, and it is important to balance the client's need for skills with recognition that full-time employment is functional, goal-directed behaviour that should be reinforced. Some skills trainers develop policies that allow clients a shorter minimum time commitment while adding attendance policies in order to maintain the stability of the group. An example might be to require attendance for at least an eight-week module, and if there are more than two consecutive absences a client loses his/her their place in group and is asked to sit out the next module before re-applying. In some instances, reducing the time commitment for entry can make it easier to get the minimum number of clients needed to start a new group (i.e., at least three, although four is preferable).

Clients can also learn the skills on an individual basis. Ideally, individual skills sessions are conducted at a separate time and with a separate team member if at all possible. Additional permutations are suggested in the second edition of the DBT skills manual, where Linehan (2014) outlines variations on the standard skills group format and detailed guidelines for helping a client meet the function of capability enhancement. We encourage readers to review this detailed set of guidelines.

DBT Skills Training Only

Many solo practitioners run skills groups which include clients who are not in individual DBT and either receive no individual treatment or are working with a non-DBT individual therapist. Indeed, there is emerging research supporting the use of DBT skills as a standalone treatment for certain client groups (Linehan, 2015). However, remaining grounded in the treatment philosophy and theoretical assumptions is crucial for effective teaching of the DBT skills. In many ways, what is "most DBT" about DBT is the unique way in which its practitioners are asked to view their clients and therapy. In short, running a DBT skills group to fidelity requires that skills trainers apply *all other treatment strategies* throughout the group.

On the one hand, doing this is a natural place to start and to learn more about how to conduct the treatment and teach the skills. On the other hand, clients (and clinicians) may misunderstand the treatment model and come to think that a skills group is equivalent to "DBT." False expectations about what group-only can do (in the absence of addressing the function of motivational enhancement) are perpetuated and clients may feel increased shame and reduced motivation.

Clinicians who offer a skills group-only option should develop inclusion/ex-clusion criteria and ensure that Stage 1 clients are enrolled in comprehensive DBT. Client screening should attend to the fact that it may be difficult to address TIB within the group. Most importantly, therapists must orient clients to the fact that the group is a partially implemented form of DBT, describe the limitations of the group, and communicate what participants can expect to gain. Provision of a handout detailing the differences between standard DBT and the group may also be helpful. Many of these guidelines can also be applied to other forms of partially implemented DBT.

Summary and Conclusions

Implementing comprehensive DBT in a solo private practice involves complex chal-lenges that require dialectical solutions. DBT clinicians may struggle to embrace the fi-nancial/business aspects of their work and find it inconsistent with strongly held values of altruism and compassion. A dialectical philosophy can bridge the gap between busi-ness and service by helping DBT clinicians recognize when they are polarized and move towards a synthesis of their dual roles as business manager and clinician. Some clin-icians may need to increase their skill and comfort with the business-related tasks such as financial planning and targeting client non-payment as a TIB.

This chapter highlighted the major decisions clinicians must make in setting up a DBT practice. In our experience, the structure that best enables solo practice clinicians to deliver comprehensive DBT to fidelity is to share one location in which clinicians can have their weekly team meeting, run skills groups, and see individual DBT clients who can be referred to each other's skills groups. The cost of space is shared, but the clinicians are able to retain their individual business identity as a sole proprietor. This model addresses the logistical challenges of clients who must travel to a second location for skills group or consultation team members who must travel for weekly consultation team meetings. The principle-based nature of DBT allows flexibility in addressing the five functions of a comprehensive treatment. Solo practice settings may not offer modes identical to standard DBT, but the practitioner must be able to articulate how each func-tion is fulfilled by the modes provided, and be mindful of functions not being addressed. What can feel daunting is that there is not one single "right way" for how to precisely address thorny implementation issues from a DBT perspective. Instead, a practitioner must choose from a variety of possibilities to combine DBT principles and use their DBT expertise in order to decide what best meets their setting needs.

Proficiency in standard DBT is, therefore, a necessity before making significant adap-tations; otherwise, the resulting treatment approach may include anti-DBT elements or reflect a partially implemented programme. Particularly troubling is when such ap-proaches are advertised as "DBT." Market forces in the private sector are one likely factor that leads solo practitioners to claim they are delivering an evidence-based treatment when they are not. Insufficient DBT training and experience may also lead to misrepresentation of services. Clinicians providing partially implemented DBT should use accurate descriptors, such as "DBT-informed," and detail how the services differ from standard comprehensive DBT. The recently launched process of DBT certification for programmes and for individual practitioners may also aid in this endeavour (interested readers are referred to http://www.dbt-lbc.org for more information).

Despite the implementation challenges described, running a private practice DBT programme has many potential benefits in the form of improved client outcomes, enhancing the market appeal of the therapist's private practice, and a broader array of clinical skills for the provider. We believe solo practitioners can provide DBT and run a profitable business in a way that is values-driven and personally satisfying. Our hope is that the presented information aids in that endeavour.

KEY MESSAGES FOR CLINICIANS

- The challenge for clinicians implementing comprehensive DBT in private practice is to determine how to implement modes of treatment that meet all of functions of DBT. The modes may differ from standard DBT, but the practitioner must be able to articulate how each function is served by the modes provided.

- Solo practitioners can best deliver standard comprehensive DBT by utilizing a shared location that enables cross-referrals between therapists' skills groups while maintaining separate business entities.

- The dual roles of business manager and individual therapist can be difficult to balance. Many DBT clinicians may have negative judgments of earning money from clients "in-need" and must seek dialectical solutions that honour business, service to clients, and personal limits.

- For private practice DBT, an essential topic in the pre-treatment phase is orientation to all business and payment-related policies. Potential problems such as non-payment, late cancellations/no-shows, etc., are conceptualized and targeted as TIBs.

- The consultation team is an essential component for any practitioner wishing to use DBT in their solo practice.

REFERENCES

Comtois, K., Koons, C., Kim, S., Manning, S. Y., Bellows, E., & Dimeff, L. (2007). Implementing standard dialectical behavior therapy in an outpatient setting. In L. Dimeff & K. Koerner (Eds.), *Dialectical behavior therapy in clinical practice: Applications across disorders and settings* (pp. 37–68). New York, NY: Guilford Press.

Grodzki, L. (2000). *Building your ideal private practice: A guide for therapists and other healing professionals.* New York, NY: W.W. Norton & Company.

Koerner, K. (2012). *Doing dialectical behavior therapy: A practical guide.* New York, NY: Guilford Press.

Koerner, K., Dimeff, L., & Swenson, C. (2007). Adopt or adapt: Fidelity matters. In L. Dimeff & K. Koerner (Eds.), *Dialectical behavior therapy in clinical practice: Applications across disorders and settings* (pp. 19–36). New York, NY: Guilford Press.

Linehan, M. M. (1993). *Cognitive-behavioral treatment of borderline personality disorder.* New York, NY: Guilford Press.

Linehan, M. M. (2014). *DBT skills training manual*, 2nd Edition. New York, NY: Guilford Press.

Ritschel, L., Lim, N., & Stewart, L. (2015). Transdiagnostic applications of DBT for adolescents and adults. *American Journal of Psychotherapy, 69*, 111–128.

CHAPTER 40

IMPLEMENTATION IN NATIONAL SYSTEMS

DBT in an Irish Context

DANIEL M. FLYNN, MARY KELLS, AND MARY JOYCE

BACKGROUND

ESTIMATES of the prevalence of borderline personality disorder (BPD) in the general population are between 0.7% and 1%, although some estimates are higher (Coid, Yang, Tyrer, Roberts, & Ullrich, 2006; Jackson & Burgess, 2000; Torgersen, Kringlen, & Cramer 2001). In the Republic of Ireland ('Ireland'), BPD is a feature of approximately 11%–20% of clinical presentations to outpatient clinics within mental health services (Government of Ireland, 2006). These estimates are similar to other countries, including the United Kingdom (UK, e.g., Keown, Holloway, & Kuipers, 2002) and the United States (US, Zimmerman, Rothschild, & Chelminski, 2005). BPD is recognized as one of the most distressing disorders for clients and their families, and the most difficult for clinicians to treat. An Irish government policy framework for mental health services, published by an Expert Group on Mental Health Policy, outlines that people with this disorder can present with histories of abusive relationships, repeated self-harm behaviour, and emotional instability (Government of Ireland, 2006). This policy document highlights the fact that, given the complexity of their presentations, individuals with BPD can present a huge challenge for mental health services.

DBT AS AN EVIDENCE-BASED TREATMENT

Dialectical Behaviour Therapy (DBT) was initially formulated as a treatment for BPD, which is typically characterized by patterns of emotional and behavioural dysregulation that often manifest in self-harm and suicidal behaviours. Standard DBT (Linehan 1993a,

b) is delivered by a team of multidisciplinary mental health professionals, and comprises individual therapy sessions for each patient, group skills training sessions, phone coaching, and consultation meetings for the clinicians on the DBT team. All treatment modalities are delivered on a weekly basis over the course of a 12-month programme. DBT is noted to be an intervention with a growing body of evidence that demonstrates its effectiveness in treating individuals diagnosed with BPD. To date, more than a dozen controlled trials (e.g., Linehan, Armstrong, Suarez, Allmon, & Heard, 1991; Verheul, van den Bosch, de Ridder, & van den Brink, 2003) have investigated the efficacy of DBT at multiple independent sites (Carmel, Rose, & Fruzzetti 2014; Rizvi, Steffel, & Carson-Wong 2013; Miga et al., this volume). The results of these trials have shown that DBT results in a reduction in suicidal behaviours, inpatient hospitalizations, depression, hopelessness, and suicidal ideation among other constructs relevant for individuals with BPD (Bohus et al., 2004). The American Psychiatric Association (2001) and more recently the NHS National Institute for Health and Clinical Excellence (NICE, 2009) recommend DBT as an evidence-based treatment option for patients with BPD and comorbid presentations.

Early Adoption of DBT in Ireland

Throughout the early 2000s, a number of DBT training events were held in Ireland based on clinicians' interest in DBT as an evidence-based model that would meet the needs of the clinical population attending their local community mental health services. As opportunities to attend these training events were localized, there was no mechanism in place for services or teams to apply for training in a coordinated manner at a national level. At this time, matching of the intervention to population need was not done in a considered way. Wider systemic issues and potential barriers to implementation and sustainability were not considered beyond local clinicians' interest and ability to influence their local mental health management structures. At this time, there was no clear national mandate to provide an evidence-based treatment like DBT in a publicly funded health system.

Change in Political Climate

By the mid-2000s, advancement in procedures for recording epidemiological information, along with progressions in health service policy, made the issue of self-harm and suicide in Ireland more explicit. Firstly, the 2001 launch of the National Self-Harm Registry Ireland facilitated increasing awareness of the very significant rates of self-harm following the publication of annual reports derived from data gathered at hospital emergency departments across Ireland. These data provided robust evidence for the already existing awareness of clinicians about the magnitude of self-harm in Ireland. The reports generated clinical and political consideration, as well as discussions on approaches to managing this growing problem in an Irish population.

Secondly, a sequence of fundamental events followed the 1993 decriminalization of suicide in Ireland. This change in legislation resulted in the Irish Census of Population recording death by suicide in the population for the first time. This recording facilitated a focus on suicide mortality rates, which highlighted high rates of death by suicide in Ireland. In response to these high rates, Reach Out: National Strategy for Action on Suicide Prevention (Health Service Executive, 2005) was launched by the Minister for Health and Children and provided the policy framework for suicide prevention activities in Ireland from 2005 until 2014 (Health Service Executive, 2005). It was recommended that a National Office for Suicide Prevention be established to drive this implementation strategy, and to work with statutory and community partners to tackle high rates of suicide and self-harm in Ireland (Health Service Executive, 2005).

Thirdly, in 2003 the then-Minister for State with responsibility for mental health established the Expert Group on Mental Health Policy to formulate a blueprint for providing world-class service to meet the mental health needs of the Irish society. In 2006, the group published a government policy framework for mental health services titled "*A Vision for Change—Report of the Expert Group on Mental Health Policy*" (Government of Ireland, 2006), which recommended DBT as an evidence-based treatment for individuals with BPD. This report advised that each catchment area (300,000 population) in the public health service in Ireland should develop an agreed policy on the management of service users with BPD and other comorbid presentations. In order to do so, the report outlined that a dedicated DBT team should be established in each catchment area, where each team member would be seconded from their existing sector community mental health team.

While a number of clinicians had implemented DBT based on local clinical need or interest in a piecemeal fashion, the advancements in recording epidemiological information, the formation of an expert group for mental health policy, and the publication of subsequent policy documents were all fundamental advances for supporting clinicians and services in considering the value of DBT as a part of their service.

LOCAL IMPLEMENTATION—A CONSIDERED APPROACH

While there was a growing interest in providing DBT in Ireland, challenges regarding securing of funding for training and awareness of how to establish DBT in community mental health services continued. International implementation research (e.g., Swales, Taylor, & Hibbs, 2012; Swenson, Torrey, & Koerner, 2002) highlights a number of factors that can pose as common barriers to DBT implementation. Lack of support from public mental health authorities and programme leaders, and absence of organizational support (including staff turnover, and funding for administration, training, and supervision) are common barriers to implementation. Indeed, these were all key factors that impacted on the sustainability and longer-term viability of some of the early teams that trained in DBT in Ireland in the early and mid-2000s.

Given that there was no clear mandate or funding stream for services to provide DBT, implementation continued to be driven by local service need and champions of the model seeking an effective way of responding to service users who were emotionally dysregulated and often presenting and re-presenting to hospital with self-harm and suicide attempts. In view of the then-growing incidence of self-harm repetition in the Cork region (Natioanl Suicide Research Foundation, 2007–2009), the lack of specialized services available for the treatment of these behaviours, and the recommendation by the *"A Vision for Change"* report that DBT be offered, members of the North Lee Adult Mental Health Service (based in a community outpatient setting) self-funded to attend DBT training in the UK in 2010. The local mental health management team recognized the concerns of clinicians regarding the challenges of effectively treating individuals with BPD. While supportive of the rationale for establishing a DBT team to meet the needs of this client group, the local management team did not have access to a funding stream to support such an initiative. Despite this, management did agree that staff would be released for secondment to DBT 1.5 days per week to implement this evidence-based treatment. The team, which consisted of multidisciplinary team members (representing Psychology, Nursing, Psychiatry, and Art Therapy from the Community Mental Health Team), completed Intensive Training™ Part I (see duBose, Botanov, & Ivanoff, this volume for description and discussion) in April 2010, began delivery of their local DBT programme in September 2010, and completed Intensive Training™ Part II in January 2011.

The Health Service Executive (HSE) is the national health provider in Ireland and has the responsibility of delivering all public health services in Ireland. The HSE Change Model (Health Service Executive, 2008) provided a model for implementing and driving this local service change. This model is based on experience of what works in practice and focuses on engaging people in the process of culture change. This model (see Figure 40.1) is comprised of four steps: initiation, planning, implementation, and mainstreaming. Openness to ongoing review and ongoing communication with broader stakeholders set the scene for reciprocal feedback between the DBT team and the broader environment, with data collection being key to evaluating the benefits of a service change initiative.

THE IMPORTANCE OF EVALUATION

Internationally, DBT was attracting much research interest. Up to 2010, however, there were no known research studies reporting on the effectiveness of standard DBT programmes (i.e,. a 12-month programme offering all treatment modalities) in Community Mental Health Settings in Ireland.[1] Thus, the North Lee DBT team identified the critical

---

[1] Although one study did publish positive findings on a DBT programme which was six months in duration (Blennerhassett, Bamford, Whelan, Jamieson, & O'Raghaillaigh, 2009).

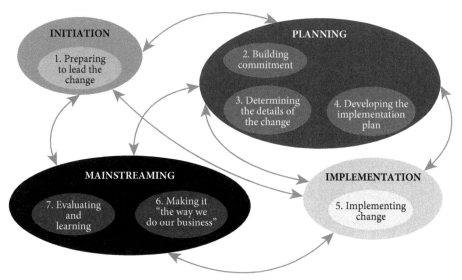

HSE Change Model

FIGURE 40.1 HSE Change Model—Model adapted from: Kolb, D. and Frohman, A., 1970; Huse, E., 1980; Neumann, J., 1989; Kotter, J. P., 1995; Ackerman Anderson, L. and Anderson, D., 2001; McAuliffe, E. and Van Vaerenbergh, C., 2006; and Project Management Institute, 2004.

Reproduced from The Organisation Development and Design Unit, The Health Service Executive, *Improving our Services: A users' guide to managing change in the health service executive*, Figure 3, p. 16 © The Health Service Executive, 2008.

importance of evaluating the effectiveness of their local DBT programme, which would provide evidence for, and understanding about, the outcomes for DBT in an Irish context. In order to do so, a detailed research protocol was developed which, based on international evidence, aimed to measure change in psychological constructs relevant for individuals with BPD using a battery of standardized measures. The significant reduction in outcome measures including borderline symptoms and suicidal ideation from pre- to post-intervention is presented in Figure 40.2. An increase in quality of life (psychological health) was also observed. These gains were maintained at six months following programme completion.

The evaluation also included an examination of health service utilization by recording information regarding Emergency Department (ED) visits and acute inpatient admissions for service users availing of the programme one year prior to, during, and six weeks after the intervention. This is shown in Table 40.1.

There was a significant reduction in the number of emergency department visits, inpatient admissions, and days spent in the acute psychiatric unit when comparing 12 months prior to, during, and 12 months following completion of the DBT programme as listed in Table 40.1 (Flynn & Kells, 2013).

Further to the positive outcome indicators of the DBT programme in the North Lee Adult Mental Health Service, the North Lee DBT team leader made a case to the local operations manager to expand DBT. The rationale for this expansion was to facilitate equity

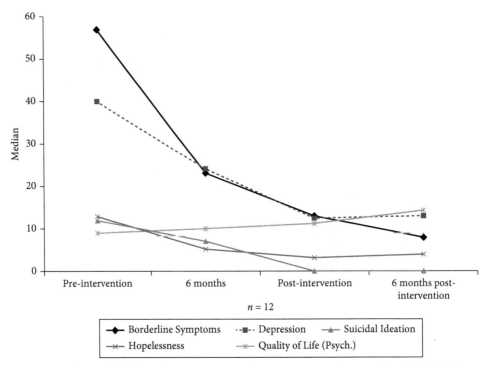

FIGURE 40.2 Results of outcome assessments for participants who completed the DBT programme in North Lee Adult Mental Health Service.

Table 40.1 Number of ED visits, acute inpatient admissions, days spent in acute psychiatric unit, and total cost for participants who completed the DBT programme in North Lee Adult Mental Health Service.

	12 months before DBT programme (n=12)	During DBT programme (n=12)	12 months after DBT programme (n=12)
No. of ED visits	49	6	7
No. of acute inpatient admissions	12	3	1
No. of bed days	207	45	1
Cost* (€)	144,900	31,500	700

* Costs were calculated conservatively based on typical bed stay in an acute inpatient facility in Cork, Ireland.

of access to this evidence-based treatment to the wider population of Cork county. This would represent an increase in population coverage (182,000 to 520,000) in the greater Cork region. A concurrent process involved the team leader approaching senior clinical psychology clinicians across the Cork County area to seek initial buy-in, build and strengthen clinician commitment, and mediate between direct service providers and system management. The National Office for Suicide Prevention (NOSP) agreed to fund this additional training (based on the positive outcomes of the preliminary pilot study analyses in North Lee) resulting in the three remaining adult mental health teams in the greater Cork region completing DBT training in 2012.

FROM LOCAL TO NATIONAL IMPLEMENTATION

By the late 2000s, the recommendations outlined in the "*A Vision for Change*" report were being considered in various catchment areas. Several community mental health teams across Ireland had independently requested funding from the NOSP to establish DBT programmes within their services. A natural consequence of this service-by-service approach, however, was the absence of a macro-level view of the overall needs of the BPD clinical population attending mental health services across Ireland. Coinciding with this, findings from the National Self-Harm Registry Ireland were consistently reporting high rates of self-harm and repetitive self-harm nationally. More specifically, significant increases in self-harm rates were reported between 2007–2011 (National Suicide Research Foundation, 2012). This significant and dramatic increase highlighted the growing urgency and need for a structured, stepped approach to implementation of DBT in Ireland.

Subsequent to the additional training in Cork in 2011–2012, discussions between the North Lee DBT team leader and the NOSP identified that funding requests were being submitted from individual teams for both DBT training and associated supports. While the role of the NOSP was to develop leadership and promote coordination with multiple statutory and community partners across Ireland on a broad range of suicide and self-harm prevention and intervention training programmes (Health Service Executive, 2005), it was beyond its remit to provide the extensive support required for implementation of a specialized treatment like DBT. The NOSP thus sought clinician support to lead and offer direction for a potential national coordinated implementation of DBT based on clinical and population need. In view of the effective implementation and evaluation of DBT in the North Lee Adult Mental Health Service, and the fact that the DBT team leader had gained experience and was successful in expanding DBT to a wider geographical area, the North Lee DBT team leader, with support from another clinical psychologist on the team, drafted a proposal for the NOSP requesting funding to train 16 DBT teams across Ireland over a two-year period and to evaluate this coordinated implementation. In doing so, an innovation champion (Rogers, 1995–cited Swales, 2010, p. 73) for implementation of DBT at a national level was proposed. The bid was successful and with the support of the NOSP, *The National DBT Project* was established in Ireland.

CONTEXT FOR NATIONAL IMPLEMENTATION IN A PUBLICLY FUNDED HEALTH SYSTEM

As earlier outlined, the HSE, Ireland's public health service, is a large organization staffed by over 100,000 people, and has the responsibility of delivering all public health services in Ireland (Health Service Executive, 2016). There are four core areas of health service for the Irish population: acute hospitals, social care and disability, mental health, and primary care. About 90% of mental health difficulties are addressed through the primary care system in Ireland (Government of Ireland, 2006). The remaining 10% (approximately) of individuals will require more specialist care, which is accessed through mental health services. This secondary-level care encompasses more specialist interventions delivered by mental health professionals such as psychiatrists, psychologists, or mental health nurses. Most of the activity of mental health services in Ireland is carried out in the community, which means that people with mental health difficulties are typically seen in outpatient settings, day hospitals, day centres, and at home (Government of Ireland, 2006).

The "*A Vision for Change*" report recommended that a dedicated DBT team should be established in each catchment area, where each team member is seconded from their existing sector community mental health team. Typically, this may involve multidisciplinary staff from multiple sector teams coming together in a geographical area and working together to provide specialized intervention for the population of that greater area (see Figure 40.3). This format facilitates each member of the DBT team to have dedicated time (1.5 days per week) to support the delivery of an adherent DBT programme ensuring all modalities of the treatment are delivered. In other jurisdictions (e.g., UK), other models of team structure exist where dedicated DBT services or personality disorder treatment service have been established. While there are advantages to having a specialist team for treating BPD, it requires additional funding as such teams operate in parallel to existing community mental health teams. Equally challenging is the recruitment of staff to work full time with a population that may be perceived as high risk, thus potentially leading to therapist burnout (Freestone et al., 2015). Given the recommendation of our national policy document, restraints in developing new services as a result of the economic climate in Ireland at this time, and in an attempt to maximize the likelihood of staff commitment to working with this population, the secondment model was adopted as most feasible for this national initiative.

FIGURE 40.3 DBT teams in context of the Public Health System (Health Service Executive).

Teams who had trained in DBT in Ireland prior to the *National DBT Project* were established in community-based second level care services (i.e., Adult Community Mental Health Teams or Child/Adolescent Mental Health Teams). Access to Community Mental Health teams is usually via General Practitioner (GP) referral or via the Liaison Psychiatry services attached to General Hospital Emergency Departments. Referrals are reviewed by the Community Mental Health Team; the processes by which referrals are considered varies by location, but would ordinarily involve review by a Consultant Psychiatrist (and in some areas, may include Multidisciplinary Team initial assessment, and/or triage by a Team Coordinator). Based on initial and ongoing assessment, the Community Mental Health Team will consider interventions such as DBT as part of an ongoing care plan to address the individual's clinical need (see Figure 40.4).

The structure of DBT teams in Ireland has followed the recommendations of the UK licensed training provider of Intensive Training™ (British Isles DBT Training) which specify that teams who want to train in DBT must have a minimum of four team members and a maximum of ten.[2] Each team must have either a clinical/forensic/counselling psychologist *or* a person with demonstrable graduate training in behaviour therapy. All teams must be genuine teams, i.e., teams that either already, or have explicit plans to, meet together to deliver a comprehensive DBT programme to a group of clients in a single setting, e.g., outpatient adult clients.

---

[2] In 2013, recommendations by BiDBT allowed up to a maximum of ten members per DBT team. This has since been revised and current training requirements allow a maximum of eight team members.

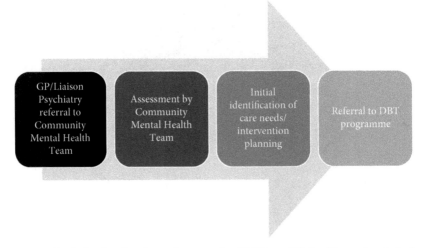

FIGURE 40.4   Typical referral pathway for accessing DBT in public health services in Ireland.

DEVELOPING A PROTOCOL FOR NATIONAL IMPLEMENTATION

Having showcased the potential of DBT in local systems, political and mental health system support was established to launch the *National DBT Project* with the financial support of the NOSP. Funding was initially granted for a two-year funded project that would train 16 new DBT teams with the aim of delivering DBT across adult and adolescent populations in Ireland. A comprehensive evaluation of this implementation would also be incorporated as part of the project. The coordination and management of this project would take place with the appointment of an assigned coordinator, administrator, and a research team who would support and carry out the evaluation of this national coordinated implementation of DBT. The project would be led by two clinicians who were DBT trained and who had experience of implementing DBT in a Community Mental Health Service in Ireland. The clinical leads were representative of innovation champions in this implementation initiative.

The coordinator monitored the implementation of DBT programmes by recently trained DBT teams, and led the multisite research evaluation of the overall project. The role of the administrator was to manage the budget for training and ongoing supervision for all teams, and provide financial assistance where possible for associated resources that were requested by teams. The administrator took responsibility for preparation of annual reports and budget submissions to the funding provider. Both the coordinator and administrator also acted as a point of contact for all teams who trained as part of the project and worked closely with the clinical leads to assist with providing direction and support to teams who faced implementation difficulties. Each newly trained DBT

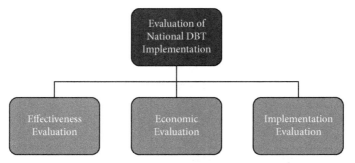

FIGURE 40.5 National DBT Project, Ireland: Overview of research evaluation.

team was also linked with a research officer from the coordinating team as points of contact for the purpose of the research evaluation. Thus, each member of the research team played a critical role in supporting the newly established teams.

To ensure a comprehensive evaluation of the *National DBT Project*, the research team consulted with mental health and research experts in the area. Such experts included DBT researchers, suicide and self-harm researchers, clinicians, and health economists. The research team were therefore responsible for designing the evaluation in line with research best practice, working with newly trained DBT teams to support and carry out the research evaluation at each of the multiple sites, and disseminating the findings of the research both nationally and internationally (Figure 40.5).

The established aims of the research evaluation for the *National DBT Project, Ireland* were to:

- Evaluate the effectiveness of DBT programmes in Community Mental Health Services in Ireland.
- Evaluate the coordinated implementation of DBT in a publicly funded health system.
- Complete an economic evaluation of DBT versus treatment as usual in Community Mental Health Services in Ireland.

CHALLENGES FOR NATIONAL IMPLEMENTATION

Despite having guidelines which assist in identifying best-practice care pathways, there can be multiple system barriers and challenges that impact on individuals' access to appropriate interventions. With this in mind, considering implementation science, and DBT implementation literature in particular, was central in steering this coordinated national initiative. While still an emerging discipline, implementation science offers frameworks to structure implementation whether it is at micro or macro level (e.g,.

Consolidated Framework for Implementation Research, Damschroder et al., 2009; PARIHS, Kitson, Harvey, & McCormack, 1998). For this national implementation, the Consolidated Framework for Implementation Research was identified as the most appropriate guiding framework. This framework facilitates revisiting, expanding, refining, and re-evaluating throughout the course of the implementation. This is discussed in more detail later in this section.

DBT Implementation Literature

From the outset, the project team reviewed literature regarding DBT implementation in health services to facilitate effective implementation at a national level. In particular, existing knowledge regarding barriers to, and facilitators for, DBT implementation was of particular relevance for this project. The team anticipated that this would avoid issues that have occurred previously when implementing an evidence-based treatment such as DBT. Work carried out by Swenson et al. (2002) identified the following barriers to implementation of DBT in community settings; lack of financial support by public mental health authorities; lack of prioritization of DBT as a treatment option by mental health programme leaders; and clinicians' prior therapeutic work (therapeutic beliefs, change in role). Swales et al. (2012) also identified funding difficulties and competing priorities as barriers for DBT implementation. In addition, they also noted the following barriers: insufficient protected time to deliver treatment; absence of management buy-in; staff turnover; and insufficient resources and absence of planning. With the outline in mind, the project team considered how best to overcome such barriers and how this knowledge could be used to best proceed with implementation at a national level.

Implementation Framework

The Consolidated Framework for Implementation Research (Damschroder et al., 2009) consists of five constructs, with essential criteria to be considered under each construct when planning for implementation. For this national implementation, the fifth construct—the process construct—held particular relevance for this coordinated effort. The four points listed under this construct proved to be of critical importance in this coordinated national implementation; planning, engaging, executing, and reflecting and evaluating. The consideration of each point for the national implementation of DBT is described in more detail here.

Planning refers to the degree to which a scheme or method of behaviour and tasks for implementing an intervention are developed in advance, and the quality of those schemes or methods. The planning phase for the *National DBT Project* involved, as an initial task, meeting with the NOSP to discuss funding opportunities for this national implementation initiative. When funding was secured (described earlier in more detail in "From Local to National Implementation"), the clinical leads needed to consider carefully and decide how best to structure and evaluate the overall project. In view of the fact that, to our knowledge, this was the first national coordinated implementation of DBT in a publicly funded health system, there was a natural opportunity to investigate the potential of this national initiative. Therefore, in addition to the provision of DBT training, a coordinating team was appointed to coordinate, administer, and evaluate this initiative. In the planning phase, a National Steering Group Committee was also established. This committee comprised mental health experts, mental health management representatives, DBT experts, research experts, and policy developers. A service user and a family representative were also invited to form part of the committee. The function of the group was to ensure robust governance of the investment made by the NOSP in the *National DBT Project*; to oversee how best to coordinate training in DBT and allied interventions in Ireland; to ensure continued high-quality research; and to ensure service users' meaningful involvement in DBT and allied interventions in Ireland.

The planning phase was an important time to consider previous implementation research in an attempt to avoid implementation barriers that may arise during the project. With this in mind, and as a natural consequence of this being the first coordinated effort to provide DBT training at a national level, the clinical leads decided on the application process for teams to apply for training. Based on the clinical leads' understanding of the research literature, their own experience of implementation, and following consultation with DBT training providers, an application form was developed which required, in addition to detail about the proposed DBT team, evidence of support from each area management team. This support was gathered in the form of the Executive Clinical Director or nominated Area Mental Health Management representative signing off on the application form to indicate their awareness of the application and training requirements. A two-year commitment, with each staff member committing to 1.5 days per week to deliver DBT to the service was required. All applications were collated by the coordinating team, minimum requirements for training were proposed (see Appendix I), and all applications were reviewed and considered by the Steering Group Committee, who had overall oversight and responsibility for prioritization of teams and allocation of training places.

In order to provide ongoing support for newly established teams, a budget for expert supervision for each team was also built into the overall funding proposal. To address the previously identified implementation barrier of staff turnover, additional training to facilitate the expansion of already established teams was also included in the budget for this national implementation.

Engaging involves attracting and involving appropriate individuals in the implementation and use of the intervention through a combined strategy of social marketing, education, role modelling, training, and other similar activities. The engaging phase for the *National DBT Project* involved informing and orientating appropriate individuals within the mental health framework to the implementation and use of the DBT intervention in their local mental health service. As previous research (Swales et al., 2012) highlighted the absence of management buy-in and insufficient protected time to deliver treatment as barriers to DBT implementation, an essential step in this national implementation involved engaging local and area management teams so that new DBT teams not only had the support of their service to complete training, but also received the recommended time to provide the treatment on a weekly basis. All management teams were required to participate in a meeting with the clinical leads and project coordinator, the purpose of which was to build commitment regarding the model of service and to clarify this fit with their service goals. This meeting involved providing information about DBT as a treatment option in community mental health services, and outlined the background, training requirements, commitment required from each team, and information about the research evaluation for the *National DBT Project*.

An orientation meeting also took place for teams who had received a place to train with the *National DBT Project*. The primary functions of this orientation meeting were to increase knowledge of the implementation requirements and to build team commitment. The information communicated at the orientation meeting was similar in content to that provided to management representatives in the meeting outlined earlier.

The project's clinical lead, who was championing DBT at a national level, recognized that, beyond gaining initial commitment from stakeholders, commitment strengthening within the broader system was also necessary. Six months after initial funding was secured, key stakeholders met to consolidate the proposal for a national implementation project. The meeting involved the DBT treatment developer, Professor Marsha Linehan, the then-Minister for State with responsibility for mental health in Ireland, the Director of a newly established Mental Health Division in the public health system, the Director of the NOSP, local managers, and DBT champions, including DBT therapists, service users, and family members who had benefited from participating in the DBT and allied family programmes in the greater Cork region. For the first time, clinicians, service users, the treatment developer, mental health service management, and political leadership had agreed to work collectively to support a systematic implementation of DBT.

Executing involves carrying out or accomplishing the implementation according to plan. When the tasks of the engagement phase were met, teams proceeded to attend Intensive Training Part I for the first of two weeks of required training to establish a new DBT team within a service. When teams completed Intensive Training Part I, the National DBT Project team made contact with each DBT team leader in the following weeks to encourage the implementation of a DBT programme in their service. All teams were encouraged to prepare for and implement a DBT programme before attending Intensive Training Part II, which typically takes place within eight months after attending Part I (Swales, 2010).

Reflecting and Evaluating refers to gathering quantitative and qualitative feedback about the progress and quality of implementation accompanied with regular personal and team debriefing about progress and experience. As newly trained DBT teams began preparations for the implementation of a DBT programme in their service, the research team planned for the extensive evaluation that was to be carried out of this coordinated implementation initiative. As depicted earlier in the section "Developing a Protocol for National Implementation", there were three established aims of the evaluation, including evaluating the effectiveness of the intervention, evaluating the coordinated

Table 40.2 Barriers and identified solutions relevant to a national implementation of DBT in Ireland

Previously identified barriers to implementation	Proposed solutions for coordinated implementation
Absence of management support and lack of organizational support	Treating the system at both local and national levels; educating service management and funding agents, building commitment of local champions and management teams.
Funding difficulties and lack of administrative support	Securing of national funding for training and supervision with the appointment of national coordinating team to support implementation.
Insufficient resources	Training contingent on local service management agreement to minimum team commitment for service provision and evaluation. Additional resources contingent on ongoing commitment.
Staff selection and turnover	Coordinated team selection based on population need (Steering Group Committee).
	Facility for training additional members to join existing teams based on need and productivity.

implementation of DBT, and conducting a comprehensive economic evaluation. Both qualitative and quantitative feedback would be obtained from various stakeholders (e.g., service users availing of the DBT programme, DBT therapists) to assess the quality of the implementation and inform future implementation of DBT in national health systems. This feedback would be regularly reviewed by both the Research Group and Steering Group Committee who were established to ensure governance of the *National DBT Project*.

In summary, implementation science and previous DBT implementation research highlighted the multiple challenges that needed to be overcome to maximize the likelihood of successful service improvement and sustainability of change. By proposing solutions to overcome relevant barriers highlighted by previous research, and using a framework to help guide this implementation, it was possible to pre-empt potential barriers for this national initiative and propose solutions for overcoming these likely barriers. Table 40.2 summarizes the key barriers relevant for this implementation initiative and the solutions that were proposed in this national coordinated effort.

IMPLEMENTATION OUTCOME

During the period from June 2013 to May 2015, multiple teams applied for DBT training; 16 teams were selected to complete Intensive Training as part of the *National*

DBT Project. The 16 teams consisted of nine adult treatment teams, and seven child/adolescent treatment teams. In total, 124 therapists were trained across the 16 teams. The first cohort of eight teams completed Intensive Training in July 2014, while the second cohort completed their training in May 2015. While staff turnover has resulted in attrition of some team members across the 16 teams, efforts have been made to replace DBT therapists through training, which facilitates the addition of new team members to established, existing teams. All 16 teams who trained as part of the *National DBT Project* are still functioning as DBT teams at 2.5 years (Cohort 1) and 1.7 years (Cohort 2) following training completion. While efforts have been made to manage the challenges that frequently result in teams typically disbanding at the second and fifth years (Swales et al., 2012), only time will tell if the systematic approach adopted for the coordinated national effort will lead to long-term viability and sustainability. Based on the evidence of team survival thus far, however, it would seem that coordinated efforts for implementation and sustainability are a worthwhile investment.

CONCLUSION

Successful implementation of changes in practice requires an innovation champion, and DBT is no exception (Rogers, 1995; Swales, 2010). In order to embed an evidence-based treatment such as DBT into a national system, the leader of such an initiative requires both knowledge of the organizational culture and expertise in the treatment model. This is similar to the role of the DBT champion within a team where the ability to persuade and influence in order to gain both system and political support is required. In our experience, this "champion" leader role is critical for a national initiative such as the current project.

Although the innovation champion may be ready for change, change is not possible unless the system itself is ready. Part of the success of a project such as this is attributable to the innovation champion recognizing that the system is ready to change and that commitment is possible from various stakeholders. Similar to treatment with a DBT client, unless there is motivation and willingness to change, it is very difficult to make progress and find success. High rates of self-harm and the recognition that suicide was a significant societal problem in Ireland led clinicians, service providers, politicians, and policy makers to seek effective ways of managing the problem. This was evidenced by the establishment of mental health expert groups, and policy documents to guide targeted approaches to address these issues. Both the political and health system were primed and ready to commit to considering an evidence-based approach in order to address this national problem. Having established commitment, part of the ongoing challenge is to manage commitment as it ebbs and flows, similarly to DBT treatment with clients. The role of the innovation champion in the project is to monitor and review commitment, provide research evidence where necessary, and continue to collaborate with stake-holders to highlight the benefit of continued efforts for sustainability. Ultimately, the innovation champion uses data to demonstrate to the system the benefit of its earlier commitment, and constantly seeks to encourage further commitment (investment in further training, advanced training, and supervision) to reaffirm and strengthen earlier commitments.

The project coordinating team provides a critical role as facilitators and sup-porters of successful implementation. By reflecting on the lived experiences of clinicians working within a public mental health system, in addition to the consid-eration of implementation science literature, the project coordinating team attempts to anticipate and understand potential barriers that can impact on successful im-plementation. In doing so, the project coordinating team provides a source of sup-port and knowledge base for implementation barriers encountered by DBT teams and therapists. The project coordinating team facilitates guidance to appropriate resources by directing teams to expert supervisors, local management or indeed bringing current issues to the Steering Group Committee who oversee the govern-ance of this project.

While the above outlined have contributed to the successful implementation of DBT at a national level in Ireland, there have been limitations with regard to the breadth of coverage of this initiative. While system level support was obtained for many teams across Ireland, at present, there is no documented national mandate from our public health service provider to maintain that an evidence-based treatment such as DBT be made available in all public health services. While there continues to be teams in parts of Ireland who are interested in receiving training and expanding their service provision, for some, there is still a lack of local management support which in effect prevents them from proceeding further in this endeavour. In other words, although training has been available at a national level, it does not mean that training oppor-tunities are available to all teams nationally which results in a lack of full population coverage. These frustrations are further highlighted by annual reports published by the National Self-Harm Registry Ireland where high rates of repetitive self-harm are reported in areas where management are not in a position to support a new initia-tive such as DBT. Unfortunately, such challenges are a reality of publicly funded sys-tems where limited budgets result in difficult choices being made as to what regional priorities might take precedence at a given point in time. Thus, the next challenge for this national implementation project is to highlight the benefits of the interven-tion, to garner support for a national mandate which outlines that DBT is not merely an "option" for local mental health service providers, but an expected part of core service delivery. Achieving this goal may require national funding for both training and supervision of staff, but also a considered workforce plan to ensure staff can be dedicated to providing the required services in key locations. The learning from this project thus far can be reviewed and applied in order to have the best chance at success in this undertaking.

KEY LEARNING AND RECOMMENDATIONS

In addition to the above outlined facilitators to implementation, there are some key events that, from our perspective, were inherent to successful implementation and sustainability of DBT at a national level. These include:

- Provision of additional training for established teams; from the outset, additional training to replenish teams who experienced staff turnover was built into our project plan. As staff turnover within any team is inevitable over time, having additional training available on an annual basis for teams helped to support teams in their implementation and sustainability. As with applications for Intensive Training™, all teams completed an application process to gain additional training places, having been established as a DBT team for at least one year and showing evidence of actively delivering the intervention.
- Including management representatives in the early stages of implementation was critical. Meetings with management prior to training events, and obtaining signature of support from management representatives, facilitated successful implementation for teams across Ireland. The difficulties and complexities of the management role must be highlighted however. Seeking managerial sign-off to release staff from their generic multi-disciplinary work to dedicate 1.5 days to DBT on a weekly basis without backfill for their time presents inherent challenges. While one can argue that in this manner, resources are simply used differently, this argument is less valid when a staff member's core work is not the provision of therapy. Thus, further problem solving for such issues requires constant consideration; neglecting to do so poses challenges for long-term sustainability.
- As funding for this initiative was provided by the public health provider, the coordinating project team attended review meetings with the funding providers on an annual basis. This facilitated not only a review of progress to date, but also the creation of a work plan and identification of goals for the upcoming year. Our team prepared detailed reports of implementation outcomes as well as research outcomes. In doing so, evidence was available for the stakeholders who supported DBT, which encouraged continued support for this initiative and investment in training.

Implementation and sustainability of an evidence based treatment such as DBT at a national level is an iterative process. As successive teams continue to be trained, the model for implementation at a national level in Ireland will continuously need to be refined to address new and unanticipated difficulties that arise in real world settings.

Key Messages for Clinicians

- Existing knowledge about DBT implementation for teams can be applied to implementation at a system-level.

- System change requires innovation champions who understand both the evidence-based treatment model as well as the political and societal climate within which it exists.

- Innovation champions cannot achieve change alone; change requires DBT champions and health service management working together to facilitate successful implementation.

- Research evaluation of all aspects of implementation is essential so as to understand, refine, and address potential implementation barriers.

APPENDIX I

National DBT Project

Criteria for the Selection of Teams for Training
- Evidence of need
  1. NSRF Registry Data 2013; 2012 (analysis of registry raw data)
  2. Therapist reports of need in their area (National DBT Project application)
  3. Availability of DBT intervention in area
- Evidence of team commitment
(National DBT Project application; phone calls; orientation meeting)
- Commitment from local management
(signatures; conference call)
- Evidence of evaluation/ research commitment
(National DBT Project application; phone calls; orientation meeting)
- Meeting BiDBT training requirements
(National DBT Project application; BiDBT application)
- Sample characteristics
  1. Effectiveness evidence (international evidence of effectiveness)
  2. National DBT Project research requirements

References

American Psychiatric Association. (2001). Practice guideline for the treatment of patients with borderline personality disorder. *American Journal of Psychiatry, 158,* 1–52.

Blennerhassett, R., Bamford, L., Whelan, A., Jamieson, S., & O'Raghaillaigh, J. W. (2009). Dialectical behaviour therapy in an Irish community mental health setting. *Irish Journal of Psychological Medicine, 26*(2), 59–63.

Bohus, M., Haaf, B., Simms, T., Limberger, M. F., Schmahl, C., Unckel, C., Lieb, K., & Linehan, M. M. (2004). Effectiveness of inpatient dialectical behaviour therapy for borderline personality disorder: a controlled trial. *Behaviour Research and Therapy*, 42(5), 487–499.

Carmel, A., Rose, M. L., & Fruzzetti, A. E. (2014). Barriers and solutions to implementing dialectical behaviour therapy in a public behavioural health system. *Administration and Policy in Mental Health and Mental Health Services Research*, 41(5), 608–614.

Coid, J., Yang, M., Tyrer, P., Roberts, A., & Ullrich, S. (2006). Prevalence and correlates of personality disorder in Great Britain. *British Journal of Psychiatry*, 188(4), 423–431.

Damschroder, L. J., Aron, D. C., Keith, R. E., Kirsh, S. R., Alexander, J. A., & Lowery, J. C. (2009). Fostering implementation of health services research findings into practice: a consolidated framework for advancing implementation science. *Implementation Science*, 4(50), doi:10.1186/1748-5908-4-50

Flynn, D., & Kells, M. (2013). *The Road to Endeavour: Development and Evaluation of a Programme for Those Presenting with Repeated Self-Harm and Chronic Suicidality*. Poster Presentation, Society for Dialectical Behaviour Therapy Conference, London, UK.

Freestone, M. C., Wilson, K., Jones, R., Mikton, C., Milsom, S., Sonigra, K., Taylor, C., & Campbell, C. (2015). The impact on staff of working with personality disordered offenders: a systematic review. *Plos One*, 10(8), doi:10.1371/journal.pone.0136378

Government of Ireland. (2006). *A Vision for Change: Report of the Expert Group on Mental Health Policy*. Dublin: Stationery Office.

Health Service Executive. (2005). *Reach out: national strategy for action on suicide prevention 2005-2014*. Health Service Executive.

Health Service Executive. (2008). *Improving our services: a user's guide to managing change in the health service executive*. Health Service Executive.

Health Service Executive (2016). 'Our structure'. Date accessed: 2 March 2017. http://www.hse.ie/eng/about/Who/

Jackson, H., & Burgess, P. (2000). Personality disorders in the community: a report from the Australian national survey of mental health and wellbeing. *Social Psychiatry and Psychiatric Epidemiology*, 35, 531–538.

Keown, P., Holloway, F., & Kuipers, E. (2002). The prevalence of personality disorders, psychotic disorders and affective disorders amongst the patients seen by a community mental health team in London. *Social Psychiatry and Psychiatric Epidemiology*, 37, 225–229.

Kitson, A., Harvey, G., & McCormack, B. (1998). Enabling the implementation of evidence based practice: a conceptual framework. *Quality in Health Care*, 7(3), 149–158.

Linehan, M. M. (1993a). *Cognitive behavioral therapy of borderline personality disorder*. New York: Guilford Press.

Linehan, M. M. (1993b.) *Skills training manual for treating borderline personality disorder*. New York: Guilford Press.

Linehan, M. M., Armstrong, H. E., Suarez, A., Allmon, D., & Heard, H. L. (1991). Cognitive-behavioural treatment of chronically parasuicidal borderline patients. *Archives of General Psychiatry*, 48, 1060–1064.

National Suicide Research Foundation. (2012). *National Registry of Deliberate Self Harm Annual Report 2011*. Cork: National Suicide Research Foundation.

National Institute for Health and Care Excellence (NICE). (2009). *Borderline Personality Disorder: Treatment and Management*. National Clinical Practice Guideline Number 78. London: Stanley L. Hunter (Printers) Ltd.

Rizvi, S. L., Steffel, L. M., & Carson-Wong, A. (2013). An overview of dialectical behavior therapy for professional psychologists. *Professional Psychology: Research and Practice*, *44*(2), 73–80.

Rogers, E. M. (1995). *Diffusion of innovations*, 4th Edition. New York: The Free Press.

Swales, M. A. (2010). Implementing DBT: selecting, training and supervising a team. *The Cognitive Behaviour Therapist*, *3*, 71–79.

Swales, M. A., Taylor, B., & Hibbs, R. A. (2012). Implementing dialectical behaviour therapy: programme survival in routine healthcare settings. *Journal of Mental Health*, *21*(6), 548–555.

Swenson, C. R., Torrey, W. C., & Koerner, K. (2002). Implementing dialectical behavior therapy. *Psychiatric Services*, *53*(2), 171–178.

Torgersen, S., Kringlen, E., & Cramer, V. (2001). The prevalence of personality disorders in a community sample. *Archives of General Psychiatry*, *58*(6), 590–596.

Verheul, R., van den Bosch, L. M. C., de Ridder, M. A. J., & van den Brink, W. (2003). Dialectical behaviour therapy for women with borderline personality disorder: 12-Month, randomized clinical trial in The Netherlands. *The British Journal of Psychiatry*, *185*, 135–140.

Zimmerman, M., Rothschild, L., & Chelminski, I. (2005). The prevalence of DSM-IV personality disorders in psychiatric outpatients. *American Journal of Psychiatry*, *162*(10), 1911–1918.

CHAPTER 41

INTERNATIONAL IMPLEMENTATION OF DIALECTICAL BEHAVIOUR THERAPY

The Challenge of Training Therapists Across Cultures

ANTHONY P. DUBOSE, YEVGENY BOTANOV, AND ANDRÉ IVANOFF

THE GLOBAL NEED FOR DIALECTICAL BEHAVIOUR THERAPY

THE global demand for dialectical behavior therapy (DBT) has increased since the publication of *Cognitive-Behavioral Treatment of Borderline Personality Disorder* in 1993 (Linehan, 1993a), in part, due to the following key factors: 1) high levels of mortality and morbidity due to suicide (World Health Organization [WHO], 2014); 2) the need for effective treatments for disorders of emotion regulation, including borderline personality disorder (BPD); 3) the ongoing exponential growth in DBT research conducted across the globe; and 4) an increased demand for evidence-based mental health treatment. While BPD was the focus of early studies on DBT due to high rates of suicide attempts and non-suicidal self-injury (NSSI; Zanarini, Frankenburg, Hennen, & Silk, 2003), the treatment is now viewed as an effective treatment for a range of populations and diagnoses, particularly for behaviours stemming from a skills deficit in emotion regulation (for review, see Harned & Botanov, 2016; MacPherson, Cheavens, & Fristad, 2013; Robins & Chapman, 2004). Consequently, DBT has been listed in the National Registry of Evidence Based Practices for the past ten years (United States Substance Abuse and Mental Health Services Administration, 2006) and has been disseminated globally due to its efficacy in treating challenging behavioural health problems. It is important to take note of challenges and modifications to implementing DBT as international interest continues to grow.

Suicide Rates

Suicide is a serious and widespread problem globally. WHO (2014) estimates that nearly one million people die by suicide annually and suicide is the third leading cause of death in the world for those aged 15–44 years. Moreover, figures provided by WHO may underestimate death by suicide in some parts of the world due to remarkable differences in the availability and quality of suicide mortality data across countries (e.g., Phillips, Li, & Zhang, 2002; Khan, 2005). Furthermore, it is estimated that about 10% of adolescents report self-harm, irrespective of suicidal ideation (Madge et al., 2008; Moran et al., 2012) making suicide and self-injury pervasive, widespread problems throughout the world and across age groups.

In the United States (US), suicide has reached its highest level since 1991 (13.4 deaths per 100,000 people), making it the tenth leading cause of death for all ages (Kochanek, Murphy, Xu, & Tejada-Vera, 2016). The rate of death by suicide has increased 28% from 1999 to 2014, leading to more than 51 billion USD in combined medical and work loss costs (Centers for Disease Control and Prevention, 2013). Unlike the other top ten leading causes of death in the US, only the suicide rate has increased over the past two decades and has shown no appreciable decline over the past 50 years.

Similar increases are found in the United Kingdom (UK), where the male suicide rate is the highest since 2001 (Office of National Statistics, 2015). Similarly, data for 28 European Union Member States (EU-28) indicates that on average, there were 11.7 deaths per 100,000 inhabitants in 2013 (Eurostat, 2017). However, the death rate from suicide varies greatly between countries. For example, Lithuania has the highest rate (36.1 deaths per 100 000), which is more than threefold higher than the EU-28 average. Likewise, in Latin America and the Caribbean the overall suicide rates have increased since 1990 for both sexes (Pan American Health Organization, 2014).

Suicide is pervasive throughout the lifespan and has become the second leading cause of death among 15–29-year-olds worldwide (WHO, 2014) and is increasing in children (Bridge et al., 2015) and middle-aged adults (Hempstead & Phillips, 2015). Due to the significant burden, suicide is among the top contributors to years lost to premature mortality and disability. Moreover, suicide research receives significantly less funding than other conditions with significantly lower mortality and disability rates (National Institutes of Health [NIH], 2016). This may, in part, explain why over 40% of individuals who attempt suicide do not receive mental health care, and half of those who do receive care report unmet treatment needs (Han, Compton, Gfroerer, & McKeon, 2014).

BPD Prevalence

DBT is conceptualized as a treatment for severe emotion dysregulation that often leads to suicidal behaviour (Linehan, 1993a). Within the DBT framework, severe emotion dysregulation encapsulates the clinical diagnosis of BPD. To better understand the prevalence of severe emotion dysregulation, BPD serves as a proxy representation. The incidence and prevalence of BPD has often been studied in numerous countries worldwide. Past estimates of prevalence have varied greatly from 0.4% in the US (Samuels, Nestadt, Romanoski, Folstein, & McHugh, 1994) to 5.4% in Sweden (Ekselius, Tillfors, Furmark, & Fredrikson, 2001). The *Diagnostic and Statistical Manual of Mental Disorders, Fifth Edition* (APA, 2013) identifies the prevalence as 1–2%. However, many studies are limited by small, unrepresentative samples, low response rates, or use of screening measures instead of diagnostic measures (for review, see Grant et al., 2008). In response to the lack of comprehensive and detailed information on BPD prevalence in the US, a recent epidemiological study conducted face-to-face interviews with nearly 35,000 people using a diagnostic interview measure. The lifetime prevalence of BPD in the US population was estimated at between 2.7–5.9% dependent on the operationalization of social or occupational dysfunction (Grant et al., 2008; Trull, Jahng, Tomko, Wood, & Sher, 2010). Grant and colleagues (2008) estimated a 5.9% prevalence rate, equally distributed among men (5.6%) and women (6.2%), when individuals endorsed at least five of the nine symptoms of BPD and at least a single symptom was associated with social or occupational dysfunction. In Trull and colleagues' (2010) reanalysis of the data, endorsement of significant distress was required to be associated with each BPD symptom, which reduced the prevalence to 2.7% and found a statistically significant difference in women (3.02%) compared to men (2.44%).

Severe Emotion Dysregulation Estimated Prevalence

Incorporating the literature on BPD prevalence to estimate the prevalence of individuals suffering from severe emotion dysregulation must be done carefully. Our conservative estimate, incorporating the aforementioned data, is that about 3% of the world's population will experience high levels of distress leading to functional impairment as a consequence of emotion dysregulation in their lifetime. The current global estimate of adults aged 15–65 is about 4.5 billion people (United Nations, 2015). Thus, the estimated global need—to help individuals experiencing high levels of distress from difficulties in emotion regulation sometime in their lifetime—is 135 million people. While there have been no clear ways to estimate the number of people who have received DBT, we are certain that the number falls far short of the many millions of people who need it.

Global DBT Research

From its inception, DBT has been a research-driven treatment emphasizing the need for a strong evidence base. At the time of this writing, at least 35 randomized controlled trials (RCTs) on DBT have been peer reviewed and published across ten countries (Linehan Institute, 2016). A PsycInfo search yielded an average of eight published and peer reviewed DBT publications per year from 1993 until 2000, 41 publications per year from 2001 to 2010, and 78 per year since 2011. The reliance on empirical findings may explain why the original DBT text (Linehan, 1993a) is considered the most influential modern book by mental health practitioners (Cook, Biyanova, & Coyne, 2009). Additionally, DBT is the most studied cognitive-behavioural treatment for suicidal behaviour (Tarrier, Taylor, & Gooding, 2008) and is superior to treatment as usual in reducing suicide attempts and NSSI (Stoffers et al., 2012). DBT also decreases suicide attempts by 50% when compared to treatment by non-behavioural experts (Linehan et al., 2006) and is superior at reducing hospitalization for suicide ideation, medical risk for suicide attempts and self-injury, treatment drop-out, psychiatric emergency room visits, and psychiatric hospitalizations. These findings indicate that DBT is uniquely effective in reducing suicidal behaviour beyond general therapeutic factors associated with expert psychotherapy (Linehan et al., 2006). With increasing interest in treating suicide, high BPD prevalence rates, and growing international research initiatives, the global demand for DBT implementation continues to grow.

DIFFUSION, DISSEMINATION, AND IMPLEMENTATION OF DBT: IMPACT TO DATE

Definitions

A discussion of global implementation of DBT is well-served by clarification of terms and identification of outcome variables in the field of dissemination and implementation (D&I) science. As an emerging field, key terms have only recently been accepted. Specifically, diffusion refers to the passive (i.e., untargeted, unplanned, uncontrolled) spread of new ideas, practices, or interventions (Lomas, 1993; Maclean, 1996). Conversely, dissemination is an active approach to spreading evidence-based interventions to the target audience via determined channels using planned strategies (Lomas, 1993; Maclean, 1996). Dissemination research is the systematic study of the processes and factors that lead to widespread adoption and use of an evidence-based treatment (Johnson, Green, Frankish, MacLean, & Stachenko, 1996; Sussman, Valente, Rohrbach, Skara, & Ann Pentz, 2006). Finally, implementation is the process by which a targeted setting puts into place or integrates an evidence-based intervention (NIH, 2010).

DBT Implementation Research in the US

The diffusion of DBT is exemplified by the prominence of the original text (Linehan, 1993a) among mental health practitioners (Cook et al., 2009). DBT research is just beginning to expand into D&I science. Since the standard outpatient DBT treatment model is more resource intensive than traditional outpatient treatment—requiring individual therapy, skills training, out-of-session coaching, and team consultation—implementation research is likely critical to more widespread adoption of DBT into the general community. That said, multiple models of implementation have been put forth in the field of D&I research with no consensus on adoption of specific models (Tabak, Khoong, Chambers & Brownson, 2012). DBT implementation has primarily been examined through the DBT Intensive Training™ (see DuBose, Botanov, Navarro-Haro, & Linehan, this volume), indicating high rates of initial implementation (Harned et al., 2016) and long-term sustainability (Swales, Taylor, & Hibbs, 2012). Several studies have found that DBT training and implementation efforts are successful in improving attitudes toward individuals with BPD and adherence to, confidence about, and knowledge of DBT (Hawkins & Sinha, 1998; Herschell, Lindheim, Kogan, Celedonia, & Stein, 2014). Finally, comparisons of different training methods find online training and in-person workshops superior to simply reading treatment manuals at increasing DBT knowledge (Dimeff, Woodcock, Harned, & Beadnell, 2011; Dimeff et al., 2009, 2015).

International Implementation Initiatives

Although DBT was originally developed in the US, interest in the treatment quickly crossed borders. International implementation of DBT primarily occurred through one of two mechanisms: 1) providers from other countries travelled to the US for training and then disseminated and implemented DBT in their own countries, or 2) US trainers travelled to countries where providers expressed interest in DBT implementation. Due to the many challenges and limitations related to these methods, some international providers have attempted other options such as reading manuals or online learning. To meet the global need, additional technology-based and remote learning alternatives are currently under development employing innovative synchronous and asynchronous teaching methods. Initially, international implementation efforts required healthcare providers from other countries to travel to the US for DBT Intensive Training™ that began in the mid-1990s. The first DBT programmes outside the US included the UK, Ireland, New Zealand, Canada, Germany, the Netherlands, and Scandinavian countries.

Due to increasing demand, it quickly became necessary to provide in-country training where there was interest. Training began being provided directly by organizations outside the US. The first of these to provide training in collaboration with the treatment developer and experts from the US was an organization in the UK and Ireland. Notably, these initial trainings were in English-speaking countries. Subsequently, regions with many English speakers (i.e., Scandinavia) received local training in English. Training also began in non-English speaking countries in the language of the country (i.e., Germany, the Netherlands). All of these developments occurred within a decade of the publication of the initial DBT text (Linehan, 1993a). While the non-English training efforts occurred with more independence from the treatment developer, the leaders of these initiatives collaborated closely with international DBT experts on research. In the mid-2000s, several mental health leaders in Latin America attended DBT trainings in the US. They repeated the transfer process, taking DBT to their home countries. Recently, the training company of the Linehan Institute, Behavioral Tech, has engaged in a systematic D&I effort based on advances in D&I science and the lessons learned from the early international implementation efforts. Some 20 years later, we see that the early international adopters who participated in these US-based trainings started a trend leading to DBT implementation in almost 30 countries across six continents. One recent example, the National DBT Project, is a government supported initiative across Ireland to train DBT therapists, already training over 100 therapists in its first two years (Flynn, Kells, Joyce & Suarez, 2014).

In addition to clinical implementation, early international adopters often study DBT as they apply it. RCTs have been conducted in Canada (McMain et al., 2009; Courbasson, Nishikawa, & Dixon, 2012: Van Dijk, Jeffrey, & Katz, 2013; Uliaszek, Rashid, Williams, & Gulamani, 2016), the Netherlands (Verheul et al., 2003), Australia (Carter, Willcox, Lewin, Conrad, & Bendit, 2010), Great Britain (Feigenbaum et al., 2012; Priebe et al., 2012), Germany (Bohus et al., 2013), Norway (Mehlum et al., 2014), Spain (Soler et al., 2009), Sweden (Hirvikoski et al., 2011), Denmark (Andreasson et al., 2016), and New Zealand (Cooney, Davis, Thompson, Wharewere-Mika, & Stewart, 2010). An additional RCT is currently being conducted in Taiwan (Clinical Trials, 2016). An uncontrolled clinical trial was also conducted in Egypt (Abdelkarim, Rizk, & Esmaiel, 2015; Abdelkarim, Rizk, Esmaiel, & Helal, 2016). These international trials and implementation efforts demonstrate that DBT, carried out with fidelity to the model, is effective when implemented in other countries and cultures.

What is Being Implemented

A complex treatment for complex problems. Since the publication of the initial DBT text (Linehan, 1993a) and its companion skills manual (Linehan, 1993b), DBT has been applied to many other clinical problems, most recently to well-being efforts. As such, an important consideration in determining the most effective implementation approach is a clear understanding of the setting, population, and problems being targeted. Wherever DBT is being implemented, we have found it important that treatment providers be trained in the standard model, regardless of the extended or adapted application of the treatment. For example, even in settings where service providers intend to use DBT skills alone as an intervention for problems in living or as an enhancement to well-being, it is not uncommon for a portion of individuals attending skills training to also have more severe dysfunctional behaviours. It is essential that providers know both how to recognize these behaviour patterns and to appropriately guide these individuals toward more intensive treatment. Additionally, *knowledge* of skills content alone is not considered sufficient for effective skills *teaching*. Based on our experience, we find it is important that skills trainers are also able to apply the dialectical strategies of balancing change and acceptance in teaching the skills, in addition to accurate knowledge of skills content (Linehan, 2015).

DBT implementation can be divided into two broad categories: 1) the required programmatic elements of the treatment, and 2) the provider behaviours that need to align with the strategies of the treatment. The programme elements align with five functions of comprehensive treatment outlined further on. In terms of provider behaviours, trainees must be taught the core strategies of the treatment and specific procedures that must be used to treat the targeted problem behaviours. In addition, trainees must demonstrate facility with special treatment strategies and specific treatment protocols that are incorporated as needed.

DBT is a principle-based treatment in contrast to the many CBT protocol-driven manualized treatment models. As such, DBT has the flexibility to respond to novel situations presented by patients receiving the treatment. This is a necessary characteristic of the treatment, given the complexity of the problems faced by the populations targeted during the development of DBT. However, this core element of the treatment presents challenges in training. Training focused on principles, rather than relying only on standardized protocol and specific techniques, requires a deeper understanding of the content.

Several challenges arise when comparing implementation of DBT to manualized treatments or protocols that have been used in international settings. For example, peer providers or lay therapists have been trained to implement time-limited interventions for specific behavioural problems, such as depression (Patel et al., 2017) or harmful drinking (Nadkarni et al., 2017), with individuals living in low- and middle-income communities. DBT, on the other hand, is a treatment with an evidence base strongest for helping individuals with complex and severe problems who experience significant difficulties in functioning and are often at high risk for self-injury and suicide. As such, the models that have been used for standardized protocol driven interventions are not applicable to implementations of DBT.

This dilemma is one of teaching techniques and specific strategies versus teaching the principles of treatment, and an important question related to this is "who to train?" The advantage of teaching straightforward linear techniques allows for quicker and simpler transfer of specific skills. It also requires less educational background and training in mental health. Conversely, focusing on the principles of the treatment allows the provider to more easily apply the treatment to novel situations, which is necessary when working with individuals displaying complex problems. The challenge arises from a need for a higher level of academic preparation and more extensive training in the treatment. Moreover, implementation of DBT in residential or milieu-based settings requires training not only for direct clinical providers, but also some training for ancillary staff (e.g., nurses, psychiatric aides, recreation therapists, custodial staff). We are aware of recent initiatives that teach DBT skills for well-being or life enhancements; however, this chapter focuses on efforts to train mental health professionals to treat those with the highest need for the treatment.

Programme elements of treatment. Comprehensive DBT programmes attend to the motivation and capabilities of patients, assure generalization of treatment gains to the natural environment, structure the environment of patients to support accomplishment of their goals, and attend to the motivation and capabilities of treatment providers. In standard outpatient DBT programmes these elements are outlined in five functions that are met through four modes of treatment: 1) individual therapy, 2) skills training,

3) out-of-session coaching (typically via phone calls), and 4) a consultation team for the DBT providers. Some of the strongest data on instructor-led training in DBT are related to the implementation of these exact DBT programme elements. In a study of 52 teams attending US-based trainings, 75% implemented all four modes of DBT within a year of completing DBT Intensive Training™ (Harned et al., 2016) and 86% implemented at least three modes. Prevalent practices within cultures, countries, or even dominant models of psychotherapy often need to be addressed in the course of implementation. For example, in some contexts, the idea that mental health providers work in teams is inconsistent with current clinical practice. DBT's focus using the consultation team as an egalitarian group to improve the skills of therapists requires understanding and respecting cultural norms while maintaining the integrity of the treatment. Interestingly, individuals who conducted the first DBT trainings in the US were faced with some of the same concerns.

Many experience the tasks related to becoming a DBT clinician as overwhelming. Prior to beginning any implementation effort or course of training, an assessment is necessary to determine the system barriers to implementing the model and the individual therapist responses to a rigorous training process. Particular attention is needed to the structure of mental health care provision. For example, in many cultures it is highly irregular to engage in treatment without the involvement of family members, regardless of the age of the patient. In addition to implications for the context in which therapy occurs (e.g., the family home, clinic, inpatient unit), this may result in different guidelines and legal requirements about age of consent for treatment, confidentiality, and privilege, as well as expectations for how to balance the DBT case management strategies of consultation to the patient and direct environmental intervention. These issues have direct bearing on structuring skills training classes, conducting out-of-session coaching, and structuring the environment. Again, if the implementation of the treatment is to be successful, these cultural norms, regional professional standards of practice, and differing legal regulations must be taken into consideration with a view as to how to move forward while maintaining the integrity of the treatment. In our experience, dialectical assessment and understanding of the context results in solutions to problems.

Changing provider behaviours. Based on the outcomes of online and remote, computer-assisted, or wholly computer-driven training (Dimeff et al., 2009, 2011, 2015), we are encouraged to develop training methods that will allow for wider dissemination without the challenges of groups travelling long distances to a central location for instructor-led training. In addition to travel and scheduling logistics, instructor-led training tends to be the most expensive form of training. We believe that development of online training methods, similar to university online learning opportunities in multiple languages, is an important endeavour in the long-term goal of providing DBT to the many individuals who need it. At the same time, the costs and expertise required to develop interactive online training can be prohibitive as well. We believe that online courses and instructor-led training serve different, but important, purposes. Instructor-led training often results in higher satisfaction and may be required to develop an initial leadership team and gain a foothold in a new region. To date, we can point to key individuals around the world (e.g., Argentina, larger Latin America, Norway, Egypt, Russia, Israel, northern Europe, and New Zealand) who first obtained training for themselves and their teams, implemented programmes, developed relationships with other DBT providers via in-person training, and became champions for DBT within their regions. Whatever the methods chosen for training, the goal is to train providers to effectively deliver DBT strategies, procedures, and protocols *as designed in the treatment development laboratories*. It is essential that providers are able to dialectically apply the principles of behaviour change balanced with validation strategies. This requires the ability to create treatment target hierarchies and incorporate protocols as necessary. The amount of time and training this takes depends on the academic and experiential backgrounds that trainees have. This is often influenced by prevalent training methods and theoretical orientations in various regions of the world. For example, some countries place more emphasis on training in behaviour therapy and learning theory; something that greatly facilitates learning DBT. Conversely, if the prevalent practice is non-behavioural, more work will be needed in the key principles of behaviour therapy that are at the heart of DBT.

International Implementation: Considerations

Assessing Requests for DBT Implementation

Embarking on a DBT implementation requires careful assessment and consideration of the setting and need. Given the coverage of DBT in both professional and popular media, and the spread of DBT by word-of-mouth, expectations of the implementation process often vary widely. While the most common request for implementation of DBT is for the treatment of emotion dysregulation and suicidal behaviours, examples of additional inquiries include the use of DBT:

- in inpatient/residential substance abuse and other addiction treatment facilities;
- in eating disorders programmes;
- with incarcerated youth and adults;
- on college campuses;
- with homeless youth;
- in schools;
- in primary care and health-care liaison services;
- as a wellness initiative in community centres;
- for justice-involved youth and adults in the community;
- skills for caregivers of individuals with chronic illness;
- skills for family members of individuals with emotion dysregulation;

- skills training with refugees;
- skills training as a wellness measure in retreat centres and resorts;
- training standards/models for graduate programmes in mental health.

Given how widely these requests vary, those leading the implementation should carefully consider the request being made and who is initiating the request. Implementing standard outpatient DBT in populations supported by empirical evidence is disparate from DBT implementation as a preventive intervention or for well-being. Moreover, it is important to assess the resources and authority of the programme or individuals requesting the implementation to carry out and sustain the required effort. Consideration should also incorporate the ability of the individual requesting DBT to develop collaborative relationships with others in the country who may also have an interest in DBT D&I. For example, we have found it is important that beginning implementations in new countries or regions involve collaboration with partners who possess credible relationships with leaders in the professional mental health community or have the skills to develop such relationships. The next section provides an outline of some key factors to consider and Table 41.1 shows a brief summary.

Major Considerations

There are a number of practical legal and business factors that must be taken into consideration when working across international boundaries. These generally have to do with

Table 41.1   Important factors to consider for international DBT implementation efforts

Factors	Examples
Technology	Video/audio software/hardware Internet bandwidth Secure file sharing software
Working in Foreign Country	Visas Taxes Contracts regarding scope of services and responsible parties Currency agreements Prevailing jurisdiction
Language and Translation	Translation of treatment materials Translation of training materials Models of translation of written materials Translation of verbal training instructions
Variable Treatment Systems	Licensure types and scope of practice Laws/regulations regarding treatment of individuals who are suicidal Health management systems

geographical, technological, financial, and legal considerations. One of the most expensive factors related to implementing DBT internationally is the cost of travel for expert trainers to be on site for extended periods of time, often many time zones from their home base. Given the importance of ongoing consultation to implementation success (e.g., Beidas, Edmunds, Marcus, & Kendall, 2012; Miller, Yahne, Moyers, Martinez, & Pirritano, 2004), scheduling consultations across multiple time zones can be difficult. This means often requiring the consultant to participate very early in the morning while trainees are at the end of their day. We should also note that this can work out very well in countries such as Egypt, Greece, and Russia, where clinical practice extends to as late as 11 p.m.

Technology. It is also important to identify manageable communications technologies that address the needs of the training (e.g., audio, video, screen sharing, discussion mechanisms, embedded video) and can be reliably operated. Our experience indicates that the most effective consultation involves live video feed, particularly to help address the audio problems that can be exacerbated when the parties involved speak different native languages. While technological advances, platform options, and bandwidth have increased significantly in the past decade, interruptions and intermittent poor audio and video quality are not uncommon. All parties need to be trained and in agreement about the communications technologies that will be used.

Secure transfer of training materials between participants and trainers must be addressed as well. We have found that clearly identified cloud services, and procedures for how to use the services, are critical to avoid confusion and version control related to training materials. Our experience indicates that shipping or carrying hardcopy materials over long distances is the least effective solution and should only be a last resort. An impediment to training is the availability of quality of textbooks and manuals. Resolution of this problem may involve creating relationships with regional book distributors.

Working in a Foreign Country

Training and implementation projects, like any endeavour that crosses political and/or governmental boundaries, require a novel set of skills and specialized business acumen. While there is frequent free movement around the globe for professional conferences, providing training, particularly when payment is involved, can become quite complicated. Notably, visas for working in a country are usually not the same as those for tourism or when travelling for academic conferences. International laws frequently govern how business is conducted, and may require consultation with an attorney. Taxation associated with permission to conduct business in a foreign country and currency transfer taxes can boost the costs of training, making it, at times, infeasible in low-resourced countries.

When engaging in a commercial enterprise outside one's home country, it is important to have clear agreements about the currency in which payment will be made and how funds will be transferred. It is also wise to anticipate fluctuations in exchange rates. Recently shifting economies in many developing nations can leave those on both sides who think project cost agreements were reached facing significantly different costs based on changes in exchange rates.

It is important to reference applicable legal jurisdiction that will govern the agreements between agencies and potential disputes. Sensitivity is advised because discussions of negative possibilities are, in some cultures, interpreted as lack of commitment to move forward. Conversely, in other countries it is assumed that extended deliberation occur before agreements are completed. Cultural norms and business practice/etiquette are easily researched and this knowledge can help prevent misunderstandings and strained relationships. Ultimately, however, even the very idea of a written contract may be regarded as offensive, while US norms consider this critical before any business movement is initiated. Paying particular attention to the language of written documents such that they are culturally sensitive is advised. For example, the legal advice that will be given most American entities working in foreign countries is pitched toward protecting the interests of the American entity. This can seem patronizing and overbearing to those from other cultures.

Language and Translation

Implementing DBT in a region where English is not the native language presents a distinct set of challenges. Most individuals involved in broader translational research efforts across scientific fields have noted the need for standards in technical language translation. Typically, translation of materials related to DBT occurs in 3 arenas: 1) translation of materials used by training providers; 2) translation of verbal presentations, treatment demonstrations, and consultations; and 3) translation of treatment materials for patient use. In our experience, the first wave of training conducted in international regions is conducted with trainees who possess the best facility with English. While this may solve some problems of translation during initial training, it does not solve the longer-term problem that most recipients of training do not speak English and will be providing the treatment in the native language. Furthermore, providers will need materials in their native language to work with their patients. When a region only has a few individuals who are trained, they may be prematurely placed in a role of presenting DBT and even doing the training themselves. However, these individuals often have limited training and experience to be viewed as experts (both by themselves and others).

International standards set for translation typically fall along two lines: 1) concurrence by multiple experts; and 2) back translation. For example, Behavioral Tech employs guidelines that combine concurrence and back translation of selected samples of training materials. Translation of treatment materials or texts are typically dictated by publishing companies that hold the copyrights and their distributors. Familiarity with the entities holding the translation and distribution rights to materials is recommended prior to contracting for an implementation in a non-English-speaking region. As translations commonly take about two years, it is worthwhile to initiate conversations with the applicable entities early to ensure materials will be accessible to trainees and those receiving the service. During simultaneous translation in training events, we have found that it is useful to provide translators with the glossary of terms used specifically in DBT. Doing so facilitates an agreement about how the translation will occur before the live presentation is completed. It helps immensely for trainers to spend time with translators before the event to discuss meanings and missing words to facilitate a smooth working relationship. For example, in Spanish there is no English equivalent for "targeting," and after discussion, it was determined that the word "objectivos" would be used, while being clear that the patients' "goals" would be translated as "metas." Additionally, we have observed that training is particularly successful when the translators have read the treatment manuals before the event.

Culture

It is important that DBT training incorporates expectations of cultural competence that can then be applied in direct service care. Cross-cultural applications of DBT require acknowledging differences in numerous domains, including: 1) language and communication styles; 2) cultural, traditional, and spiritual practices; 3) experiences of system-level discrimination; 4) level of community and family engagement; and 5) attitudes about mental health treatment. Cultural competence includes understanding and respecting values, attitudes, beliefs, and norms that differ across cultural groups. Additionally, the delivery of services must be tailored to meet patients' social, cultural, and linguistic needs. Implementation efforts must also consider cultural differences in planning, implementing, and evaluating interventions.

Behaviour therapy in general, and DBT specifically, is based on idiographic assessment and solution generation. Detailed assessment of each patient's relevant inner-, outer-, and system-level contexts is necessary. Effective solutions must address all relevant contexts contributing to current problems. When applying DBT in a new cultural context, practitioners and trainers assume that the core components of DBT are viable across cultural groups. DBT was designed to be an idiographic treatment and practitioners must be careful not to make assumptions about broad groups (e.g., "Latinos," "lesbians," "men," "adolescents"). The principle base of the treatment allows for individual tailoring, including use of culturally specific language and metaphors, culturally appropriate therapeutic strategies.

The extensive efficacy and effectiveness of international DBT trials and less rigorous, more formative studies suggest acceptable cultural adaptability. RCTs have found that DBT is effective when implemented in other cultures and results are similar to those found in studies conducted in the US (i.e., DBT has been effectively implemented and demonstrated positive clinical outcomes across six continents). Additionally, within US subcultures, trials have examined the efficacy of DBT for American Indian/Alaskan Native adolescents (Beckstead, Lambert, DuBose, & Linehan, 2015), adolescents (Rathus & Miller, 2002), older adults (Lynch, Morse, Mendelson, & Robins, 2003; Lynch et al., 2007) and trials that have included large samples of individuals identifying as Hispanic (Rathus & Miller, 2002), non-heterosexual (Pistorello, Fruzzetti, MacLane, Gallop, & Iverson, 2012), African American (Koons et al., 2001), and biracial (Pistorello et al., 2012) also demonstrated positive treatment outcomes.

Variability in Mental Health Treatment Systems

Numerous issues arise in implementation from the variability in health care systems across countries. First, this includes the governmental policies that shape mental health care and determine preferred methods of treatment. Countries differ in use of public funding for mental health services and commonly are limited to inpatient or residential care only, and outpatient psychotherapy is available only to those who can privately afford it. In other countries, psychiatry and mental health treatment is still biologically driven and psychosocial interventions hold no place in treatment planning. In still yet other countries, BPD is not yet recognized as a disorder worthy of treatment. In many parts of the world, physicians and psychiatrists determine what defines mental health care; psychologists work under psychiatrists, and in many countries, social work is not considered a clinical discipline. Moreover, some health care systems specify which providers are permitted to treat suicidal individuals. For example, only psychiatrists are allowed to treat people considered at highest risk in some countries. We have had experience training providers who were required to be supervised by psychiatrists to treat patients using DBT. However, those supervisors were not included in the training. In some countries, neither private nor public funds are available for mental health services. In those cases, implementation requires skillful networking and collaboration among those working in the for-profit private sector with those working for non-profit and governmental organizations if DBT is to have a successful regional D&I, rather than a haphazard diffusion.

In regions that have the aforementioned problems, we have found that collaborations will need to be established by trainees. There may be a need for public relations experts who can run media campaigns to increase awareness or collaborators who have access to government ministries and can testify to the need for broadening the scope of practice of those being trained. Furthermore, making the case that individuals at high risk for suicide can be treated on an outpatient basis—instead of inpatient or residential care—requires knowledge of the evidence base and an ability to articulate the case to administrators.

LONG-TERM VIABILITY, TASK-SHARING, AND AFFILIATION

From our experience, the early identification and presence of local leadership and future in-country trainers is extremely advantageous. Working with in-country hosts responsible for venue procurement, marketing, application and registration processes, and event administration can predict the success or failure of an implementation initiative. Multiple factors lead to successful implementation and sustainability of efforts in a region over time. Those competencies that must be built within the regional system include skills related to public relations, administration and operations, and training. We have found it to be instrumental to develop teams of mentors internal to the system early on in international projects. This involves inviting individuals who have been through the initial DBT Intensive Training™ in the country to guide subsequent trainees through the process. This serves the function of keeping new trainees engaged while providing opportunities for potential trainers to learn the tasks related to training while being observed by expert trainers.

The long-term success of an international project relies on the ability to develop an independent group within the country to spearhead projects in the long term. For example, the Linehan Institute identifies several levels of involvement possible for its international affiliates. These range from individuals who are DBT dissemination champions to specific organizations or business entities that operate independent training programs in affiliation with the Linehan Institute.

Behavioral Tech, the training company founded by Marsha Linehan, outlines a mentorship model for becoming a trainer. The first step of this process is becoming a competent DBT clinician who is able to conceptualize and articulate treatment plans for complex cases. The process of becoming a DBT trainer requires more dedicated time and study than is required to become a DBT clinician. In addition to being able to deliver the treatment at a high level of competence, the individual must also be able to articulate the complex concepts and strategies of the treatment with accuracy. Furthermore, potential trainers must be able to convey this knowledge in a way that their trainees learn to apply the treatment in an effective and practical manner. Trainers must also be able to adequately assess the needs and questions of trainees so that they provide pertinent and useful answers when consulting. Given the array of skills required for effective training, the Behavioral Tech trainer-in-training model is based on competencies that develop over time, rather than a time-based model. The development of these competencies is influenced by individual factors related to the system or country in which they work. These factors include:

a. The rate at which the individual learns.
b. Background and clinical experience:
    i. The experience and background of the individual as a student and clinician. For example, an individual well-trained in behaviour therapy in their university graduate programme will likely possess the necessary knowledge to become a trainer more quickly than someone who does not have this background.
    ii. The number and variety of patients seen by the individual, as well as number of hours spent providing DBT, will increase the speed of the training mentorship. For example, an individual who is providing DBT to between 25 and 30 high-acuity patients per week with emotion dysregulation and suicidal behaviours will likely gain the experience and skills to train more quickly than an individual with more limited experience. Since DBT requires incorporating other

evidence-based protocols as necessary, experience treating problems like depression and anxiety in the context of DBT is necessary for DBT trainers. Since trainees often treat a variety of patients, experience in the adaptations of DBT for such groups, like adolescents and substance-dependent individuals, is also helpful.

   iii. Work in a variety of settings, such as outpatient programmes as well as milieu-based programmes (e.g., inpatient units and residential treatment facilities) is also valuable experience that will allow trainers to understand and meet the needs of those they will train.

c. Availability of mentorship, particularly when potential trainers are distant from expert DBT trainers, is essential to guide trainees through the process of becoming a trainer. This often requires coordination of time with someone in a distant time zone and the willingness of the expert to donate time. Otherwise, the financial cost of this can be considerable.

d. Opportunities to demonstrate training in the essential domains of DBT:

   i. Traditionally, individuals became DBT trainers by presenting and training with an experienced senior trainer. When the potential trainer is geographically close to the trainees, this model can work quite well. However, great geographical distance between trainer and trainees can significantly delay the process. While the model has worked well in North America, in order to meet the global need for the treatment, alternate means are necessary for potential trainers to demonstrate their ability to train in the various domains of the treatment.

   ii. These domains include such areas as the theoretical foundations and scientific underpinnings of DBT, the core strategies of the treatment, suicide risk assessment and management, DBT skills, and the various special treatment strategies and protocols used within the treatment. This is an area that clearly demands development of technologies that can be used remotely to provide this experience and observation.

SUMMARY

The field of clinical treatment science has made grand leaps in the past 50 years as advances in our understanding of behavioural disorder and psychopathology have led to the development of many empirically supported psychological treatments. DBT is an evidence-based treatment for disorders of emotion regulation that enjoys global reach with successful implementations in almost 30 countries across six continents. Despite these advances, the D&I of DBT does not meet the needs of the estimated 135 million people who will need the treatment at some point in their lifetime. The value of DBT has become recognized around the world as the desire for effective treatments for suicidal behaviours and emotion regulation-based disorders spread from healthcare policy advisors to the general public.

The need for increased international DBT implementation is critical, but implementations must be carried out and sustained with high standards to ensure quality care. To date, training practitioners in DBT has primarily occurred in traditional settings, whether based in the US, through strategically located affiliated training organizations, or the efforts of clinical scientists in other countries. Future training endeavours will increasingly incorporate technology to increase DBT's reach. Additionally, factors such as culture, language, legal issues, large scale economic instability, treatment elements and settings, healthcare systems, and evidence-driven methods for implementation must be systematically and carefully examined as this work continues.

KEY POINTS FOR CLINICIANS

- The global demand for DBT stems from high levels of mortality and morbidity due to suicide, the need for effective treatments for disorders of emotion regulation, and an increased demand for evidence-based mental health treatments.
- Due to the resource-intensive framework of DBT, careful examination of past implementation efforts is necessary for continued success in the international implementation of DBT.
- DBT implementation includes the required programmatic elements of the treatment and the provider behaviours that need to align with the strategies of the treatment.
- For successful international DBT implementation, factors including technology, language/translation, variability in healthcare systems, and challenges of working in a foreign country must be considered.

REFERENCES

Abdelkarim, A., Rizk, D. N., & Esmaiel, M. (2015). Compliance to DBT skills training among a sample of Egyptian female patients with borderline personality disorder. *European Psychiatry, 30*, 857.

Abdelkarim, A., Rizk, D. N., Esmaiel, M., & Helal, H. (2016). Impact of dialectical behavior therapy on incidence of suicidal attempts and non-suicidal self injury among a sample of Egyptian borderline personality disorder patients. *European Psychiatry, 33*, S270.

American Psychiatric Association. (2013). *Diagnostic and Statistical Manual of Mental Disorders (DSM-5®)*. Arlington, VA: APA Publishing.

Andreasson, K., Krogh, J., Wenneberg, C., Jessen, H. K., Krakauer, K., Gluud, C., . . . Nordentoft, M. (2016). Effectiveness of dialectical behavior therapy versus collaborative assessment and management of suicidality treatment for reduction of self-harm in adults with borderline personality traits and disorder—a randomized observer-blinded clinical trial. *Depression and Anxiety, 33*(6), 520–530.

Beckstead, D. J., Lambert, M. J., DuBose, A. P., & Linehan, M. (2015). Dialectical behavior therapy with American Indian/Alaska Native adolescents diagnosed with substance use disorders: Combining an evidence based treatment with cultural, traditional, and spiritual beliefs. *Addictive Behaviors, 51*, 84–87.

Beidas, R. S., Edmunds, J. M., Marcus, S. C., & Kendall, P. C. (2012). Training and consultation to promote implementation of an empirically supported treatment: A randomized trial. *Psychiatric Services, 63*(7), 660–665.

Bohus, M., Dyer, A. S., Priebe, K., Krüger, A., Kleindienst, N., Schmahl, C., . . . Steil, R. (2013). Dialectical behaviour therapy for post-traumatic stress disorder after childhood sexual abuse in patients with and without borderline personality disorder: A randomised controlled trial. *Psychotherapy and Psychosomatics, 82*(4), 221–233.

Bridge, J. A., Asti, L., Horowitz, L. M., Greenhouse, J. B., Fontanella, C. A., Sheftall, A. H., . . . Campo, J. V. (2015). Suicide trends among elementary school-aged children in the United States from 1993 to 2012. *JAMA Pediatrics, 169*(7), 673–677.

Carter, G. L., Willcox, C. H., Lewin, T. J., Conrad, A. M., & Bendit, N. (2010). Hunter DBT project: randomized controlled trial of dialectical behaviour therapy in women with borderline personality disorder. *Australian & New Zealand Journal of Psychiatry, 44*(2), 162–173.

Centers for Disease Control and Prevention (CDC). Web-based Injury Statistics Query and Reporting System (WISQARS) [Online]. (2013) National Center for Injury Prevention and Control, CDC (producer). Available from https://www.cdc.gov/injury/wisqars/index.html

Cook, J. M., Biyanova, T., & Coyne, J. C. (2009). Influential psychotherapy figures, authors, and books: An Internet survey of over 2,000 psychotherapists. *Psychotherapy: Theory, Research, Practice, Training, 46*(1), 42.

Cooney, E. B., Davis, K. L., Thompson, P., Wharewera-Mika, J., & Stewart, J. (2010). *Feasibility of evaluating DBT for self-harming adolescents: A small randomised controlled trial.* Auckland: Te Pou o Te Whakaaro Nui.

Courbasson, C., Nishikawa, Y., & Dixon, L. (2012). Outcome of dialectical behaviour therapy for concurrent eating and substance use disorders. *Clinical Psychology & Psychotherapy, 19*(5), 434–449.

Clinical Trials [ClinicalTrials.gov] (2016). Efficacy of dialectical behavior therapy in patients with borderline personality disorder: a controlled trial in Taiwan [Online]. National Library of Medicine (producer). Available from: https://clinicaltrials.gov/ct2/show/NCT01952405?term=dialectical+behavior+therapy&cntry1=ES%3ATW&rank=1

Dimeff, L. A., Harned, M. S., Woodcock, E. A., Skutch, J. M., Koerner, K., & Linehan, M. M. (2015). Investigating bang for your training buck: a randomized controlled trial comparing three methods of training clinicians in two core strategies of dialectical behavior therapy. *Behavior Therapy, 46*(3), 283–295.

Dimeff, L. A., Koerner, K., Woodcock, E. A., Beadnell, B., Brown, M. Z., Skutch, J. M., . . . Harned, M. S. (2009). Which training method works best? A randomized controlled trial comparing three methods of training clinicians in dialectical behavior therapy skills. *Behaviour Research and Therapy, 47*(11), 921–930.

Dimeff, L. A., Woodcock, E. A., Harned, M. S., & Beadnell, B. (2011). Can dialectical behavior therapy be learned in highly structured learning environments? Results from a randomized controlled dissemination trial. *Behavior Therapy, 42*(2), 263–275.

Ekselius, L., Tillfors, M., Furmark, T., & Fredrikson, M. (2001). Personality disorders in the general population: DSM-IV and ICD-10 defined prevalence as related to sociodemographic profile. *Personality and Individual Differences, 30*(2), 311–320.

Eurostat, 2017. Mental health and related issues statistics. Retrieved from http://ec.europa.eu/eurostat/statistics-explained/index.php/Mental_health_and_related_issues_statistics

Feigenbaum, J. D., Fonagy, P., Pilling, S., Jones, A., Wildgoose, A., & Bebbington, P. E. (2012). A real-world study of the effectiveness of DBT in the UK National Health Service. *British Journal of Clinical Psychology, 51*(2), 121–141.

Flynn, D., Kells, M., Joyce, M., & Suarez, C. (2014, February). The National Dialectical Behaviour Therapy Implementation Project [Poster]. In Health and Social Care Professions Annual Research Conference. Health Service Executive (HSE).

Grant, B. F., Chou, S. P., Goldstein, R. B., Huang, B., Stinson, F. S., Saha, T. D., . . . Ruan, W. J. (2008). Prevalence, correlates, disability, and comorbidity of DSM-IV borderline personality disorder: results from the Wave 2 National Epidemiologic Survey on Alcohol and Related Conditions. *The Journal of Clinical Psychiatry, 69*(4), 533.

Han, B., Compton, W. M., Gfroerer, J., & McKeon, R. (2014). Mental health treatment patterns among adults with recent suicide attempts in the United States. *American Journal of Public Health, 104*(12), 2359–2368.

Harned, M. S., & Botanov, Y. (2016). Dialectical behavior therapy skills training is an effective intervention. *Psychiatric Times, 33* (3), 13–14.

Harned, M. S., Navarro-Haro, M. V., Korslund, K. E., Chen, T., DuBose, A. P., Ivanoff, A., & Linehan, M. M. (2016). Rates and predictors of implementation after Dialectical Behavior Therapy Intensive Training. Proceedings of the 3rd Biennial Conference of the Society for Implementation Research Collaboration (SIRC) 2015: advancing efficient methodologies through community partnerships and team science. *Implementation Science, 11*(Suppl 1): A57.

Hawkins, K. A., & Sinha, R. (1998). Can line clinicians master the conceptual complexities of dialectical behavior therapy? An evaluation of a State Department of Mental Health training program. *Journal of Psychiatric Research, 32*(6), 379–384.

Hempstead, K. A., & Phillips, J. A. (2015). Rising suicide among adults aged 40–64 years: the role of job and financial circumstances. *American Journal of Preventive Medicine, 48*(5), 491–500.

Herschell, A. D., Lindheim, O. D., Kogan, J. N., Celedonia, K. L., & Stein, B. D. (2014). Evaluation of an implementation initiative for embedding dialectical behavior therapy in community settings. *Evaluation and Program Planning, 43*, 55–63.

Hirvikoski, T., Waaler, E., Alfredsson, J., Pihlgren, C., Holmström, A., Johnson, A., . . . Nordström, A. L. (2011). Reduced ADHD symptoms in adults with ADHD after structured skills training group: results from a randomized controlled trial. *Behaviour Research and Therapy, 49*(3), 175–185.

Johnson, J. L., Green, L. W., Frankish, C. J., MacLean, D. R., & Stachenko, S. (1996). A dissemination research agenda to strengthen health promotion and disease prevention. *Canadian Journal of Public Health, 87*, S5.

Khan, M. M. (2005). Suicide prevention and developing countries. *Journal of the Royal Society of Medicine, 98*(10), 459–463.

Kochanek, K. D., Murphy, S. L., Xu, J. Q., & Tejada-Vera B. (2016) *Deaths: Final data for 2014. National Vital Statistics Reports*: Vol. 65, No 4. Hyattsville, MD: National Center for Health Statistics.

Koons, C. R., Robins, C. J., Tweed, J. L., Lynch, T. R., Gonzalez, A. M., Morse, J. Q., . . . Bastian, L. A. (2001). Efficacy of dialectical behavior therapy in women veterans with borderline personality disorder. *Behavior Therapy, 32*(2), 371–390.

Linehan Institute. (2016). *DBT Data to Date*. Behavioral Tech, LLC, available at http://www.linehaninstitute.org/research/data-to-date.php

Linehan, M. M. (1993a). *Cognitive-behavioral treatment of borderline personality disorder*. New York, NY: Guilford Press.

Linehan, M. M. (1993b). *Skills training manual for treating borderline personality disorder.* New York, NY: Guilford Press.

Linehan, M. M. (2015). *DBT® skills training manual.* New York, NY: Guilford Press.

Linehan, M. M., Comtois, K. A., Murray, A. M., Brown, M. Z., Gallop, R. J., Heard, H. L., . . . Lindenboim, N. (2006). Two-year randomized controlled trial and follow-up of dialectical behavior therapy vs therapy by experts for suicidal behaviors and borderline personality disorder. *Archives of General Psychiatry, 63*(7), 757–766.

Lomas, J. (1993). Diffusion, dissemination, and implementation: who should do what? *Annals of the New York Academy of Sciences, 703*(1), 226–237.

Lynch, T. R., Cheavens, J. S., Cukrowicz, K. C., Thorp, S. R., Bronner, L., & Beyer, J. (2007). Treatment of older adults with co-morbid personality disorder and depression: A dialectical behavior therapy approach. *International Journal of Geriatric Psychiatry, 22*(2), 131–143.

Lynch, T. R., Morse, J. Q., Mendelson, T., & Robins, C. J. (2003). Dialectical behavior therapy for depressed older adults: A randomized pilot study. *The American Journal of Geriatric Psychiatry, 11*(1), 33–45.

MacLean, D. R. (1996). Positioning dissemination in public health policy. *Canadian Journal of Public Health, 87,* S40.

MacPherson, H. A., Cheavens, J. S., & Fristad, M. A. (2013). Dialectical behavior therapy for adolescents: theory, treatment adaptations, and empirical outcomes. *Clinical Child and Family Psychology Review, 16*(1), 59–80.

Madge, N., Hewitt, A., Hawton, K., Wilde, E. J. D., Corcoran, P., Fekete, S., . . . Ystgaard, M. (2008). Deliberate self-harm within an international community sample of young people: comparative findings from the Child & Adolescent Self-harm in Europe (CASE) Study. *Journal of Child Psychology and Psychiatry, 49*(6), 667–677.

McMain, S. F., Links, P. S., Gnam, W. H., Guimond, T., Cardish, R. J., Korman, L., & Streiner, D. L. (2009). A randomized trial of dialectical behavior therapy versus general psychiatric management for borderline personality disorder. *American Journal of Psychiatry, 166*(12), 1365–1374.

Mehlum, L., Tørmoen, A. J., Ramberg, M., Haga, E., Diep, L. M., Laberg, S., . . . Grøholt, B. (2014). Dialectical behavior therapy for adolescents with repeated suicidal and self-harming behavior: a randomized trial. *Journal of the American Academy of Child and Adolescent Psychiatry, 53*(10), 1082–1091.

Moran, P., Coffey, C., Romaniuk, H., Olsson, C., Borschmann, R., Carlin, J. B., & Patton, G. C. (2012). The natural history of self-harm from adolescence to young adulthood: a population-based cohort study. *The Lancet, 379*(9812), 236–243.

Miller, W. R., Yahne, C. E., Moyers, T. B., Martinez, J., & Pirritano, M. (2004). A randomized trial of methods to help clinicians learn motivational interviewing. *Journal of Consulting and Clinical Psychology, 72*(6), 1050.

Nadkarni, A., Weobong, B., Weiss, H. A., McCambridge, J., Bhat, B., Katti, B., . . . Wilson, G. T. (2017). Counselling for Alcohol Problems (CAP), a lay counsellor-delivered brief psychological treatment for harmful drinking in men, in primary care in India: a randomised controlled trial. *The Lancet, 389*(10065), 186–195.

Office for National Statistics (2015). *Suicides in the UK: 2015 registrations.* London: Office for National Statistics. Available from: https://www.ons.gov.uk/peoplepopulationandcommunity/birthsdeathsandmarriages/deaths/bulletins/suicidesintheunitedkingdom/2015registrations

National Institutes of Health (2016). Estimates of Funding for Various Research, Condition, and Disease Categories. Retrieved from https://report.nih.gov/categorical_spending.aspx

National Institutes of Health. (2010). Dissemination and implementation research in health (R01). Retrieved from http://grants.nih.gov/grants/guide/pa-files/PAR-10-038.html/

Pan American Health Organization (2014). *Suicide Mortality in the Americas: Regional Report.* Washington, DC.

Patel, V., Weobong, B., Weiss, H. A., Anand, A., Bhat, B., Katti, B., . . . Vijayakumar, L. (2017). The Healthy Activity Program (HAP), a lay counsellor-delivered brief psychological treatment for severe depression, in primary care in India: a randomised controlled trial. *The Lancet, 389*(10065), 176–185.

Pistorello, J., Fruzzetti, A. E., MacLane, C., Gallop, R., & Iverson, K. M. (2012). Dialectical behavior therapy (DBT) applied to college students: a randomized clinical trial. *Journal of Consulting and Clinical Psychology, 80*(6), 982.

Phillips, M. R., Li, X., & Zhang, Y. (2002). Suicide rates in China, 1995–99. *The Lancet, 359*(9309), 835–840.

Priebe, S., Bhatti, N., Barnicot, K., Bremner, S., Gaglia, A., Katsakou, C., . . . Zinkler, M. (2012). Effectiveness and cost-effectiveness of dialectical behaviour therapy for self-harming patients with personality disorder: a pragmatic randomised controlled trial. *Psychotherapy and Psychosomatics, 81*(6), 356–365.

Rathus, J. H., & Miller, A. L. (2002). Dialectical behavior therapy adapted for suicidal adolescents. *Suicide and Life-Threatening Behavior, 32*(2), 146–157.

Robins, C. J., & Chapman, A. L. (2004). Dialectical behavior therapy: Current status, recent developments, and future directions. *Journal of Personality Disorders, 18*(1), 73–89.

Samuels, J. F., Nestadt, G., Romanoski, A. J., Folstein, M. F., & McHugh, P. R. (1994). DSM-III personality disorders in the community. *American Journal of Psychiatry, 151*(7), 1055–1062.

Soler, J., Pascual, J. C., Tiana, T., Cebrià, A., Barrachina, J., Campins, M. J., . . . Pérez, V. (2009). Dialectical behaviour therapy skills training compared to standard group therapy in borderline personality disorder: a 3-month randomised controlled clinical trial. *Behaviour Research and Therapy, 47*(5), 353–358.

Stoffers, J. M., Völlm, B. A., Rücker, G., Timmer, A., Huband, N., & Lieb, K. (2012). Psychological therapies for people with borderline personality disorder. *Cochrane Database of Systematic Reviews, 8*(CD005652). doi: 10.1002/14651858.CD005652.pub2

Substance Abuse and Mental Health Services Administration's National Registry of Evidence-based Programs and Practices. (2006). *Dialectical behavior therapy.* Retrieved from http://www.nrepp.samhsa.gov/ViewIntervention.aspx?id=36

Sussman, S., Valente, T. W., Rohrbach, L. A., Skara, S., & Ann Pentz, M. (2006). Translation in the health professions: converting science into action. *Evaluation & the Health Professions, 29*(1), 7–32.

Swales, M. A., Taylor, B., & Hibbs, R. A. (2012). Implementing dialectical behaviour therapy: Programme survival in routine healthcare settings. *Journal of Mental Health, 21*(6), 548–555.

Tabak, R. G., Khoong, E. C., Chambers, D. A., & Brownson, R. C. (2012). Bridging research and practice: models for dissemination and implementation research. *American Journal of Preventive Medicine, 43*(3), 337–350.

Tarrier, N., Taylor, K., & Gooding, P. (2008). Cognitive-behavioral interventions to reduce suicide behavior: a systematic review and meta-analysis. *Behavior Modification*, 32(1), 77–108.

Trull, T. J., Jahng, S., Tomko, R. L., Wood, P. K., & Sher, K. J. (2010). Revised NESARC personality disorder diagnoses: gender, prevalence, and comorbidity with substance dependence disorders. *Journal of Personality Disorders*, 24(4), 412–426.

Uliaszek, A. A., Rashid, T., Williams, G. E., & Gulamani, T. (2016). Group therapy for university students: A randomized control trial of dialectical behavior therapy and positive psychotherapy. *Behaviour Research and Therapy*, 77, 78–85.

United Nations, Department of Economic and Social Affairs, Population Division (2015). *World Population Prospects: The 2015 Revision, Key Findings and Advance Tables*. Working Paper No. ESA/P/WP.241.

Van Dijk, S., Jeffrey, J., & Katz, M. R. (2013). A randomized, controlled, pilot study of dialectical behavior therapy skills in a psychoeducational group for individuals with bipolar disorder. *Journal of Affective Disorders*, 145(3), 386–393.

Verheul, R., van den Bosch, L. M., Koeter, M. W., de Ridder, M. A., Stijnen, T., & van den Brink, W. (2003). Dialectical behaviour therapy for women with borderline personality disorder. *The British Journal of Psychiatry*, 182(2), 135–140.

World Health Organization. (2014). *Preventing suicide: A global imperative*. Geneva, Switzerland.

Zanarini, M. C., Frankenburg, F. R., Hennen, J., & Silk, K. R. (2003). The longitudinal course of borderline psychopathology: 6-year prospective follow-up of the phenomenology of borderline personality disorder. *American Journal of Psychiatry*, 160(2), 274–283.

....

CHAPTER 42

USING NOVEL TECHNOLOGY IN DIALECTICAL BEHAVIOUR THERAPY

....

ANITA LUNGU, CHELSEY R. WILKS, AND
MARSHA M. LINEHAN

INTRODUCTION

....

The Case for Computerized Psychotherapy: An Overview

IN 2013, the World Health Organization (WHO) reported in its Mental Health Action Plan 2013–2020 that "Health systems have not yet adequately responded to the burden of mental disorders; as a consequence, the gap between the need for treatment and its provision is large all over the world" (WHO, 2013). At the same time, up to 50% of patients with severe mental health disorders in high-income countries, and up to 85% in low- and middle-income countries, do not receive treatment. The report also notes that almost half the world's population lives in countries where there is an average of one psychiatrist to serve 200,000 people or more, and that other mental health care providers trained in the use of psychosocial interventions are even scarcer.

Over the last several decades, significant progress has been made in creating and evaluating efficacious psychological treatments for a wide range of mental disorders. A review of meta-analyses for Cognitive Behaviour Therapy (CBT) found large effect sizes for unipolar depression, generalized anxiety disorder, panic disorder with or without agoraphobia, social phobia, post-traumatic stress disorder, and childhood depressive and anxiety disorders (Butler, Chapman, Forman, & Beck, 2006). CBT effect sizes for bulimia nervosa and schizophrenia were in the large range. Effect sizes for DBT for Borderline Personality Disorder (BPD) were in the moderate range including for suicidal and self-harm behaviours (Kliem, Kroger, & Kosfelder, 2010). Face-to-face psychotherapy treatment effect sizes are generally in the medium range (Lambert &

Ogles, 2009; Luborsky et al., 1999; Smith & Glass, 1977). Indeed, regarding the effectiveness of traditional, face-to-face evidence based psychotherapy Wampold concludes "Simply stated, *psychotherapy is remarkably efficacious*" (Wampold, 2001, p. 71).

However, as the WHO reports emphasize, most people in need of mental health treatments are unable to access and benefit from them. Barriers to wide-scale dissemination of treatment include: a) low availability of adequately trained practitioners, b) the resource intensive process of effectiveness studies when transitioning an evidence-based treatment (EBT) to clinical practice, c) the high cost of face-to-face therapy, d) the logistics involved in getting people to face-to-face appointments, and e) the stigma about mental health that keeps people from treatment (Lyons, Hopley, & Horrocks, 2009; Turner, Beidel, Spaulding, & Brown, 1995).

Computerized treatments (CT) can address at least some of the barriers to large-scale dissemination of EBTs. Treatment delivered entirely through software does not require training, does not tire, remains at initial fidelity, can be easily replicated, and can be easily updated. CTs can also be made available to individuals in need regardless of geographic location (provided there is access to computers and potentially the Internet). Cost savings compared to face-to-face psychotherapy can be significant (National Institute for Health and Clinical Excellence, 2002; Newman, Consoli, & Taylor, 1997; Newman, Consoli, & Taylor, 1999; Stuhlmiller & Tolchard, 2009) There is also less stigma associated with CTs. People are more likely to tell a computer, rather than a human, about sensitive information, such as suicide risk or an attempted suicide (Classen & Larkin, 2005; Greist et al., 1973), which is particularly relevant for DBT. Changes in treatments can propagate more quickly to consumers via software updates. The effort for adapting the treatment to a different target population might be contained only to generating new examples.

Based on meta-analyses, including randomized controlled trials (RCTs) of CTs for clinical problems such as mood and anxiety disorders, insomnia, and general psychological problems (Andersson & Cuijpers, 2009; Andrews, Cuijpers, Craske, McEvoy, & Titov, 2010; Cheng & Dizon, 2012; Cuijpers et al., 2009; Reger & Gahm, 2009; Richards & Richardson, 2012; Spek et al., 2007), CTs can be effective in treating clinical problems, even to an extent comparable to the efficacy of face-to-face therapies. However, to the best of our knowledge no equivalence studies have as yet been reported. Large effect sizes have been obtained particularly when treating anxiety disorders (Andrews et al., 2010; Cuijpers et al., 2009; Reger & Gahm, 2009), and medium effect sizes for depression (Richards & Richardson, 2012), with an overall efficacy of CT approaching that of face-to-face therapies of a medium effect (Barak, Hen, & Boniel-Nissim, 2008). Similarly, concerns over CTs having significantly higher drop-out rates compared to face-to-face therapy have not materialized; one meta-analysis reported drop-out rates between 2% and 29%, which is comparable to face-to-face therapy (Cuijpers et al., 2009). While one meta-analysis did find higher drop-out rates (74%) for treatments unsupported by human contact (Richards & Richardson, 2012), significant data regarding lack of engagement and reduced satisfaction with treatment have not materialized.

The vast majority of interventions have been designed based on CBT and have addressed mostly mood and anxiety disorders. More complex clinical presentations routinely addressed in DBT, e.g., individuals meeting criteria for personality disorders, or multiple co-occurring diagnoses including substance use, are yet to be targeted by CT. Specifically, one meta-analysis found that over 90% of RCTs of CBT excluded individuals at risk for suicide, and 74% excluded individuals engaging in addictive behaviour (Wilks, Zieve, & Lessing, 2015).

Thus far, most research on CTs has been conducted outside of the United States (US). However, within the US, as a result of recent changes to the health system (the Affordable Care Act; see, e.g., Koh & Sebelius, 2010), there are now financial incentives and interest in treatment dissemination as well as in decreasing inefficiencies in mental health and substance abuse treatment. Start-up companies have emerged in partnership with academic researchers to build digital behavioural health interventions (Empower Interactive http://www.empower-interactive.com/; Lyra Health https://www.lyrahealth.com/; SilverCloud Health Ltd https://silvercloudhealth.com), although the focus, for now, is still on less complex clinical presentations (such as social anxiety or mild or moderate depression).

DIALECTICAL BEHAVIOUR THERAPY AND TECHNOLOGY

Marsha Linehan developed DBT in the 1980s with the goal of treating individuals at high risk for suicide and with complex diagnostic presentations in order to help them build "lives worth living". Since its beginning the treatment has evolved continuously in its mission of finding the most effective ways to address, alleviate, and (whenever possible) solve the complex clinical problems of individuals at high risk for suicide. In its trajectory, DBT incorporated acceptance and change, techniques woven together through dialectical philosophy and through a pioneering incorporation of eastern philosophy principles such as mindfulness meditation. Today, similar to other hallmark treatments, DBT is faced both with a tremendous challenge and a tremendous opportunity. Via its multiple interfaces and increasing affordability, technology represents for many individuals an avenue for connection to information, relationships, work, and potential change. By incorporating technology into its structure, the potency, appeal, and reach of DBT increase to further promote behavioural change for building "lives worth living" for as many individuals as possible.

DBT has already taken some steps to incorporate technology among its treatment tools. This chapter highlights the promising research on computerized psychotherapy interventions, and discusses the specific characteristics in DBT's foundation and evolution to date that make the use of novel technology a good conceptual fit. It also provides an overview of existing DBT tools that incorporate novel technology, underlines their potential and limitations, and proposes new directions for the field.

DBT is in an excellent position to emerge as a strong CT. There is evidence that it reduces symptoms associated with a wide range of mental health conditions from BPD to depression (Lynch, 2000; Lynch et al., 2007), Attention Deficit Hyperactivity Disorder (ADHD; Fleming, McMahon, Moran, Peterson, & Dreessen, 2014), bipolar disorder (Van Dijk, Jeffrey, & Katz, 2013), transdiagnostic mood and anxiety disorders (Neacsiu, Eberle, & Linehan, 2014), a broad spectrum of severity for mental disorders, from high-risk, complex clinical presentations (Linehan et al., 2015; Linehan, McDavid, Brown, Sayrs, & Gallop, 2008) to families and caregivers of individuals with clinical problems (e.g., Wilks et al., 2015), as well as age ranges from older adults, adolescents, and even children (Perepletchikova et al., 2010). Additionally, DBT has a scientific approach, a theoretical foundation, and several structural advantages that fit very well within a technological framework, which is explored in the next section.

New Technology and the Science of DBT

At the highest level, DBT has a scientific foundation, and Linehan's motivation from the beginning has been to address—and if at all possible to solve—the very difficult and complex clinical problems found in the lives of those at high risk for suicide. As such, DBT has never been focused on prescribing specific tools and proscribing others to reach clinical goals. Instead, research and clinical effort was expended to try different clinical tools and approaches, closely observe the impact on patients, incorporate the feedback to refine a more effective treatment, and then try again. This constant loop of trial, observation, and incorporation of feedback has continued throughout the life of the treatment; DBT has continuously evolved since its inception to incorporate new scientific findings and become more efficacious and effective in its clinical impact. The Behavioral Research and Therapy Clinics at the University of Washington, where Linehan conducted her research, incorporates a Treatment Development Clinic that engages graduate students, post-doctoral trainees, and other researchers in finding new ways to transform the treatment for the better (Lungu, Rodriguez-Gonzalez, & Linehan, 2012). The second edition of the DBT Skills training manual (Linehan, 2015a, b) incorporates, through many additional skills, new research on mechanisms of action in emotion regulation, substance abuse, and general behavioural change through skills such as Paired Muscle Relaxation (Smith & Smoll, 1990), Dialectical Abstinence (Dimeff & Linehan, 2008), and Walking the Middle Path (Miller, Rathus, & Linehan, 2006).

Via its ability to collect, analyse, and derive insight from large data pools, new technology can change the fibre of behavioural research. When large groups of patients can be gathered to quickly observe the impact of using a specific skill in a particular context, or when behavioural analyses can be integrated to identify behavioural patterns for thousands of chain analyses, treatment could become more precise in its targeting. Theoretically, it becomes possible to conduct analyses to derive moderators of treatment success or failure as well as mechanisms of change and map specific skills for specific problems or user characteristics. Mobile devices can passively (meaning without involving patient effort) generate data on where a user is spending time in a skills training app, generating feedback into feasibility and acceptability of treatment.

Fundamentally, DBT remains true to behavioural principles that see experience as paramount in knowing and interacting with reality. With the advent of technology and the willingness to incorporate it into the therapeutic process, patients' experience can become more visible to clinicians. The user experience as it is stored in mobile devices can tell clinicians about patients' acceptability and use of clinical materials and tools in a different way than a discussion during the therapy hour. Thus far, the treatment has evolved through a dialectical resolution of tensions between clinical experience, theory, and research. Technology can add a new dimension of data—that of the user experience—to be considered in defining the clinical content and process.

New Technology and DBT Theory

DBT was theoretically founded on three frameworks: dialectics, social behavioural theory, and Zen practice. The next few sections discuss these theoretical underpinnings and how they work using the new technology approach.

Dialectical Philosophy and its Connection to New Technology

Dialectics emerged in DBT as the framework that could hold together DBT's un-wavering focus on both acceptance and change; the full dialectical philosophy as it applies to DBT has been elaborated elsewhere (Linehan & Schmidt, 1995; Sayrs & Linehan, this volume). This segment discusses some major ideas that are connected with technology: dialectics as method of persuasion, and the dialectics of the relationship between an individual and their environment (i.e., the futility of trying to understand an individual in isolation from their environment).

Within the context of DBT, dialectics highlights the role of *the therapist as an agent of persuasion* and change (Basseches, 1984; Kaminstein, 1987). Fundamentally, in both individual and group settings, psychotherapy can be understood as a process of persuasion, of convincing the patient to change his/her world view and behaviours in order to attain specific goals. DBT also includes a consultation team for therapists, in which the goal is to perform therapy for the therapists, i.e., to persuade and support therapists in continuing to efficaciously treat their patients.

Traditionally in DBT (and other treatments), the individual and group therapist represented the only agent and conduit of persuasion via a direct dialogue with the patient; a similar process takes place in DBT consultation teams, where the "patient" is a DBT therapist and the "therapist" is the team. Technology has the capacity to augment or support the role of the therapist as an agent of persuasion. Integrating technology to augment therapist's power of persuasion can be done haphazardly (sometimes reinventing the wheel) or strategically (e.g., taking advantage of research conducted in relevant areas such as human-computer interaction).

The next section describes the framework of persuasive technology and how it can be used to strengthen the presence of new technology tools within DBT. Persuasive technology is not the only framework for integrating novel technology into DBT, although it provides an example of a framework that can strategically organize such an integration.

Augmenting the DBT Therapist's Role: Using Persuasive Technology

Persuasive technology has emerged as an area of research that investigates the use of technology designed to change attitudes or behaviours of users through persuasion and social influence, but not through deception or coercion (Fogg, 2003). Similarly, *persuasive systems* are defined as "computerized software or information systems designed to reinforce, change or shape attitudes or behaviors or both without using coercion or deception" (Oinas-Kukkonen & Harjumaa, 2008a). As discussed previously, persuasion plays a critical role in DBT in that the "job" of the therapist is often to convince/persuade a patient to try a different behaviour in order to meet therapy goals. The persuasive technology framework also fits well with DBT's value of transparency and lack of deceit in empowering patients to change their behaviour. Tools that fit within the umbrella of persuasive technology could be incorporated into DBT to increase the treatment's persuasion properties.

Fogg (2003) conceptualized the field of persuasive technology by organizing the strategies and mechanisms through which computers can persuade. He proposes three different functions that computers can fulfil as persuasive agents: *computers as tools* (persuading towards change by making tasks and activities easier through technology); *computers as media* (persuading through sensory media, such as simulations or virtual reality environments to provide interactive experiences to motivate and engage); and *computers as social actors* (persuading based on the property that individuals using an interactive technology often respond emotionally to the technology, becoming attached to it). DBT and cognitive behaviour therapy more generally have an impact on patients' lives to the extent that patients change their behaviours as a result of the therapeutic encounter. Enfolding the persuasive functions of computers into DBT can translate into incorporating tools that can make the homework assignments easier for patients. For example, using computers as tools could be seamlessly inserting homework activities into a patient's calendar or making suggestions of distraction activities based on someone's already installed and used apps on their mobile devices could make doing these activities easier for patients. Similarly, in the computers as media category, the opposite action, DBT skill and exposure therapy, more broadly could be augmented with simulations and virtual reality elements. Virtual reality (VR) has already been used successfully in studies as an avenue for prolonged exposure. The accelerated pace of innovation in this area is bringing the technology for virtual reality into patients' households. VR headsets (e.g., Oculus Rift) powered by desktops and even by smartphones (e.g., the Merge VR googles working with Android and iOS devices; see https://mergevr.com/), and an increasingly diversified range of applications make VR experiences possible as a homework assignment in regular DBT outpatient therapy, which fits within the persuasive function of computers as media.

Persuasive technology has also identified two different *types* of technology-assisted persuasion: *computer-mediated persuasion* (humans persuading others through use of technology like email, messaging, social networking, etc.) and *human-computer persuasion* (persuading through the use of computer technology alone; Harjumaa & Oinas-Kukkonen, 2007; Oinas-Kukkonen & Harjumaa, 2008b). DBT therapists are already using technologies like text messaging and email to communicate with their patients (especially adolescents), albeit mostly for coaching purposes. Sometimes patients (again, especially adolescents) use social media to connect outside of the DBT framework to offer each other additional support. These tools could be used in DBT more strategically to support treatment goals. For example, text messages and emails could be routinely sent to refresh content taught during DBT groups, reinforce the homework assigned, or deliver suggestions for daily mindfulness practice. Newsletters and additional skills teaching and practice content can strengthen skills training representing an example of human-computer persuasion.

Five years after Fogg published his book, Oinas-Kukkonen and Marjumaa (Oinas-Kukkonen, 2010; Oinas-Kukkonen & Harjumaa, 2008b) reorganized his taxonomy within the Systematic Framework for Designing and Evaluating Persuasive Systems around four different *functions* that a persuasive system could fulfil: *primary task support, dialogue support, system credibility support,* and *social support.* Table 42.1 shows examples of persuasive strategies from each of Oinas-Kukkonen's four categories in the Systematic Framework for Designing and Evaluating Persuasive Systems.

Later, the section iDBT for Emotion Regulation provides an example of a CT system for teaching DBT skills for emotion regulation trans-diagnostically that incorporates many of the persuasive technology strategies presented in Table 42.1.

Patient/Environment Interaction: Augmenting Therapist Understanding

Another principle integrated in DBT pertaining to dialectics as a world view is that of seeing the world as being systemic, complex, and interconnected, made of "parts" that together create a "whole." The parts are in constant interaction with one another, which makes the system change constantly. Change is seen as the only constant of the system—a characteristic to be fully accepted and embraced. A "part" of the system can only be understood when its relationship to the system, and vice-versa, is considered. This dialectical principle impacts DBT's clinical work in that patients cannot be understood in isolation from their environment, i.e., the therapist must conceptualize both the aetiology of disorder as well as its maintenance, and consequently how he/she treats the disorder.

Technology can be tremendously helpful as a lens through which the DBT therapist can assess and understand a patient's environment. Through their pervasive use of technology, patients leave an information trace of their behaviour within their devices, particularly mobile ones. Information related to someone's social and support network, changes in activity levels, even changes in voice tone while speaking on the phone or in places frequented (particularly useful when substance misuse is relevant) can become available to the therapist (NB: only with full consent from the patient) to add a new

Table 42.1 Persuasive technology strategies and definitions

Persuasion category	Persuasion strategy	Definition
1. Primary task support	1.1 Reduction	Reduction is persuading the user to perform a behaviour by reducing complex tasks to easier or simpler steps.
	1.2 Tunnelling	Tunnelling refers to persuading a user by guiding him/her through a series of pre-determined steps, such that once the user has entered the "tunnel" he/she is likely to follow along.
	1.3 Tailoring	A message tailored to a user's specific needs, interests, and goals is likely to be more persuasive if it decreases the effort involved when exposed to non-relevant information.
	1.4 Personalization	Personalization refers to offering the users capabilities to personalize the content and services offered to them to increase persuasion.
	1.5 Self-monitoring	A persuasive system with self-monitoring support helps the user keep track of performance or status in achieving goals.
	1.6 Simulation	Simulation as a strategy persuades by allowing the user to immediately observe the cause-effect relationships.
	1.7 Rehearsal	Persuading through rehearsal refers to increasing the likelihood that a certain behaviour will take place in the real world if it is rehearsed during an interaction with a system.
2. Supporting dialogue/ relationship with users	2.1 Praise	Conveying praise to a client through a variety of tools (images, words, comments, or symbols) can reinforce the preceding behaviour.
	2.2 Rewards	Rewards given for performing behaviours targeted to increase can lead to behaviour change in the desired direction.
	2.3 Reminders	A persuasive system that reminds users to perform specific target behaviours is increasing the likelihood that those behaviours will happen.
	2.4 Suggestion	The principle of suggestion is that "a computing technology will have greater persuasive power if it offers suggestions at opportune moments."
	2.5 Similarity	Similarity refers to the fact that people are persuaded more easily by systems that resemble themselves in some ways.
	2.6 Liking	A system that is designed to be likeable and appealing to users can have increased power of persuasion.
	2.7 Social role	Social role refers to the system adopting a familiar, established social role to increase its persuasiveness.
3. System credibility support	3.1 Trustworthiness	A system viewed as trustworthy, unbiased, fair, and without using coercion or manipulation will have a greater power of persuasion.
	3.2 Expertise	A system viewed as incorporating a high level of expertise (knowledge, experience, and competence) will be more persuasive.

Table 42.1 Continued

Persuasion category	Persuasion strategy	Definition
	3.3 Surface credibility	Surface credibility highlights that the first impression a system makes on a user has a high impact on credibility of that system.
	3.4 Real-world feel	Real-world feel refers to having a system that underlines the people or organizations behind it to increase persuasion.
	3.5 Authority	Content viewed by users as being generated from a source of authority (person or organization) enhances persuasion.
	3.6 Third-party endorsement	Third-party endorsement, especially from well-reputed systems increases credibility of a system.
	3.7 Verifiability	Verifiability refers to enhancing credibility of a system by making its information easily verifiable against external sources.
4. Social influence	4.1 Social learning	Social learning refers to persuading people to perform a specific behaviour by enabling them to observe someone else performing that behaviour.
	4.2 Social comparison	Social comparison increases persuasion by allowing users to compare their performance to that of other users.
	4.3 Normative influence	Normative influence refers to leveraging peer pressure to increase persuasion.
	4.4 Social facilitation	Social facilitation refers to increasing persuasion by allowing the user to discern that others are performing intended behaviours along with them.
	4.5 Cooperation	Cooperation offered through a system can increase user's motivation to perform target behaviours.
	4.6 Competition	Competition can increase motivation to engage in a particular behaviour, leveraging human's natural tendency to compete.
	4.7 Recognition	Recognition of performing a particular behaviour can motivate users to continue to engage in the behaviour.

dimension of assessment. Along those lines, while mobile technology has the capacity to track almost every movement of a patient, there are considerable ethical concerns as it relates to big data collection and monitoring. That being said, the ethical aspects of monitoring and managing patient health is outside the scope of this chapter; for a review of the ethics of big data and privacy, see Boyd and Crawford (2012).

Nonetheless, this augmented assessment of environmental factors can be valuable during the initial case conceptualization phase to inform treatment planning. It can also be leveraged continuously during treatment to better identify how treatment is reflected in changes in environmental patterns of behaviour. Tech companies have already started to research and develop behavioural analytic solutions that can passively (without asking for information from the user) collect and analyse behavioural data to link it to health metrics (e.g., Ginger; https://ginger.io/). Data from mobile devices continuously accumulates, which fits the dialectical principle of embracing change. Such flows of data can be analysed to better identify changes in behaviour that might increase a patient's risk for dangerous behaviours—an important target in DBT. DBT therapists could, theoretically, integrate such data analytic solutions to improve their understanding of the patient's interaction with their environment, which is a goal fully in line with DBT's dialectical philosophy.

Social Behavioural Theory and New Technology

Another core component of DBTs theory is Staat's social behavioural model of personality (Staats, 1975; Staats & Staats, 1963). According to this model of personality, human behaviour can be understood through the interaction between three behaviour response systems: the overt behavioural response system, the cognitive response system, and the physiological/affective response system.

Emotions, a fundamental construct and unit of analysis in DBT, are understood as full organism responses that include all three response systems. In order to understand particular emotions as well as to work on regulating them—a main goal in DBT—therapists need to understand the full context surrounding that emotion, namely, the affect, cognitions, and behaviours that occur as part of that emotion. Moreover, in line with the dialectical principle of interdependence, the three systems are seen as interacting with one another such that changing an element in one system can enact change in the other two. New technology can assist in this process in multiple ways. First, advances in technology have enabled increasingly precise emotion recognition and identification by analysing voice, language (Lee, Narayanan, & Pieraccini, 2002), facial expression, and walking (Cui, Li, & Zhu, 2016), or a combination of physiological parameters, wearable devices, human behaviours and activities, and facial micro-expressions (Sokolova et al., 2015). Second, automatic collection of emotion and behavioural data can identify patterns and relationships that can be used in treatment to suggest targets for behaviour change.

Behavioural analysis has long been a strong tool in DBT to inform treatment planning in the long term (such as within the case conceptualization phase of treatment), as well as at the micro-level of the individual session, or even for individual therapeutic interactions within a session. Chain analysis is a particular behavioural analysis tool in DBT that consists of a step-by-step assessment of all environmental variables of interest (see Landes, this volume). The therapist attempts to gather all information relevant to a particular chain of events that lead to a behaviour that is a therapy target (either to decrease, as is the case for self-harm, or increase, as is the case for use of DBT skills). Some patients are good observers and reporters of environmental variables of interest, while others are quite poor. Technology can assist therapists in behavioural analysis tasks by supplying the information of interest when building a behavioural chain analysis. Records saved within mobile or desktop devices regarding activities, locations, and behavioural markers (such as placing a phone call that was labelled as high in a particular emotion) can supplement an interview with the patient to help the therapist better understand the environment surrounding a target behaviour. Technology can also prompt patients to conduct a chain analysis on their own after detection of a strong emotion or at a predetermined time, and it can guide a patient through the steps needed to supply all information required. Technology can also help by saving a sequence of a behavioural chain in treatment to il-lustrate a record of change and progress (or lack thereof) for both the therapist and the patient. Once the relevant factors involved in a behavioural chain analysis are collected, the therapist can move with the patient to "resolve" the chain or to figure out what links in the chain should be changed such that the next time similar environmental variables take place, the end behaviour is no longer a target behaviour. Technology can assist in col-lecting information across multiple chains, identifying links with high impact across dif-ferent scenarios, and suggesting those for change; it can also automatically identify when several environmental variables line up similarly to a problematic chain and alert the pa-tient to that alignment, or suggest a skill to use to change the outcome.

Although technology cannot (at least now) "read minds" and capture the cognitive component of Staat's social behavioural model of personality, computerized thought re-cords can facilitate collection of cognitive information.

To summarize the link between Staat's social behavioural model of personality and technology: in DBT, all dysregulated behaviour (including both suicidal and non-suicidal behaviours, as well as cognitions and emotions) targeted for change in therapy can be influenced by enacting change in the behavioural and environmental compo-nents, which could be facilitated via technology.

Zen Practice and New Technology

Zen was introduced in DBT as a result of Linehan's search for a technology of acceptance to counterbalance behaviourism as a technology of change (see Wolbert, this volume). One of the challenges described by Linehan in teaching mindfulness to patients was their adamant refusal (sometimes) of a classical meditation practice. Mindfulness represents a core foun-dation for DBT, considering the treatment's focus on awareness of cognitions, emotions, and behaviours as a precursor of change in those domains. Mindfulness is often practised in individual DBT sessions to navigate the intense waves of emotion that can emerge in sessions, or routinely to start and sometimes end DBT group sessions. It is practised also as a beginning ritual in DBT teams, and all DBT therapists are encouraged to develop and sus-tain their own personal mindfulness practice. However, despite the vast majority of therap-ists' and many patients' acknowledgement of the importance of mindfulness, mindfulness practice remains quite difficult. As with other behaviours that don't generate an immediate reinforcer, mindfulness practice is difficult for therapists and their patients. Technology can help support a consistent mindfulness practice for DBT therapists and patients. Many mindfulness apps have been created that can suggest different mindfulness practices, prompt users to engage in mindful moments throughout the day, and guide users through lengthier practices. They can also give physiological feedback following the practice, although mindfulness practice itself does not have any immediate goals in terms of changing physiology. Such tools can be integrated into therapy to strengthen therapists' and patients' dedication to the practice and support them in incorporating mindfulness practice in their own environment outside of the therapists' office. At a high level, mindfulness practice is a behaviour that is usually difficult for patients and providers to engage in; technology can support behavioural change and, therefore, could support mindfulness.

DBT Structure and New Technology

DBT has several structural characteristics that make it a good match for computerization and for integration with new technology, particularly its modularity and use of algorithms.

DBT as a Modular Treatment

Modularity is a design strategy used across domains to handle complexity. Modularity appears in mathematics, computer science, architecture, industrial design, and nature as a divide-and-conquer strategy that helps break down complex problems into easier-to-solve sub-problems. Thus, individual modules can be created to accomplish a sub-goal such that the outcome of all modules can be reassembled as a complete solution of the original problem. In DBT, modularity was introduced for the same goal of managing clinical complexity (Linehan & Wilks, 2015). DBT patients often present with multiple, complex problems that cannot be effectively solved via a single therapeutic modality or tool. Therefore, DBT's inherent modularity allows for a logical integration of technological solutions when sub-problems are identified.

DBT is conceptually modular at multiple levels, and breaks down the functions of treatment to: (a) enhance the individual's capability by increasing skillful behaviour, (b) improve and maintain a client's motivation to change and engage in treatment, (c) ensure generalization of skillful behaviour to all relevant contexts, (d) enhance motivation of therapists for treatment delivery, and (e) assist patients in influencing or changing relevant environmental variables (see Figure 42.1).

DBT is also modular in using multiple treatment modes, each of which serves different therapeutic functions: (a) individual therapy, (b) group skills training, (c) out-of-session coaching, and (d) therapist consultation team (see Figure 42.2). Modularity of treatment modes and functions can be advantageous when using new technology in that different tools and technology can be used to fulfil the distinct functions. For example, individual therapy might take place in person with a therapist, while the group skills training might be done via teleconferencing or via a computerized skills training modality. Similarly, out-of-session coaching can be "out-sourced" to a call centre functioning via telephone, email, or text message, or to a combination of automatic computerized coaching and human therapist coaching for crisis calls. The DBT therapist consultation team can also be facilitated by technology to enable DBT team members that are located far apart geographically. Similarly, improving patients' motivation can

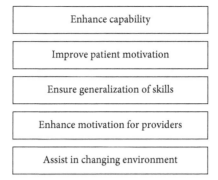

FIGURE 42.1 Modularity of Treatment Targets.

FIGURE 42.2 Modularity of treatment modes.

be conducted separately via an app that focuses on identifying and updating goals, and reminds patients of the purpose of therapy when motivation is low. The treatment function of helping patients influence or change their environment can be facilitated by technology if specific skills training modules are designed and offered for family members, caregivers, and even school personnel in the context of teenage patients going to school.

Modularity is also seen at a structural level for group skills content (see Figure 42.3) and flow—with all sessions having the same workflow (see Figure 42.4). The skills content follows the main dialectic in DBT between acceptance and change (with two of the four modules focused on acceptance and change skills each). Each module in turn is split into a sequence of individual skills, for example, the mindfulness module comprises seven individual skills (see Figure 42.3).

Skills sessions are also modular, and all follow a similar structure of starting with a mindfulness practice, followed by the homework review—with feedback and troubleshooting if homework was not entirely completed, and closing with teaching the new skills with practice and assignment of new homework.

At the level of treatment targets and flow, DBT is modular in that it permits other protocols to be seamlessly incorporated into DBT. Given the complexity of clinical presentations seen in DBT, it was not feasible to develop a treatment that would contain treatment protocols for all possible clinical problems. The solution was to allow DBT to incorporate evidence-based protocols to target specific clinical problems once

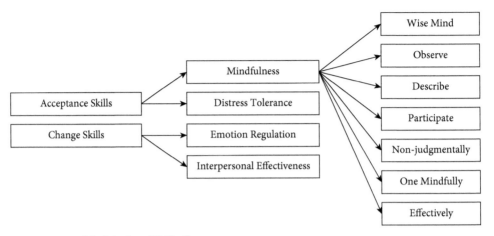

FIGURE 42.3 Modularity of Skills Content.

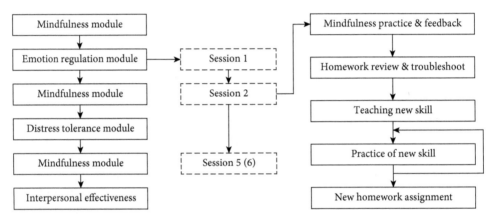

FIGURE 42.4 Modularity of skills structure.

such problems were clearly identified and assessed, and the timing was appropriate for targeting given DBT's overarching hierarchy of priorities. Specific protocols have been developed to describe how to safely transition ancillary treatments in and out of DBT. Such an example is the protocol developed for incorporating prolonged exposure treatment for patients meeting criteria for BPD and individuals at high risk for suicide (Bohus et al., 2013; Harned, Korslund, Foa, & Linehan, 2012; Harned & Linehan, 2008). Such a protocol defines the conditions needed to start the ancillary treatment, how to monitor successful progression, or when to discontinue the protocol when clinically indicated. This modularity can also translate, in the context of technology, to increased flexibility if the patient can undergo the ancillary treatment through a computerized tool.

DBT's Algorithmic Characteristic

Valid and precise behavioural assessment drives therapy progress in DBT at all stages of treatment. Fundamentally, no clinical problem can be addressed or solved before being correctly identified. DBT implementation has been refined over time and now incorporates multiple behavioural assessment tools that can be converted into an algorithm. An algorithm represents a description of a sequence of steps to be followed in problem-solving processes. Algorithms are often used in computer science, but they can be applied to provide logic and establish process in any field that requires problem solving.

Within clinical work, expert clinicians follow their own algorithms to uncover all pieces of information needed in order to understand the problem to be solved. In DBT, multiple such algorithms are relatively explicit and can be transformed into a more formal workflow that can be used in computerized psychotherapy. For example, DBT contains chain analysis (discussed earlier) to create a moment-by-moment understanding of relevant variables that lead to a behaviour that is a therapy target. Similarly, DBT contains missing links analyses, which represents a protocol of assessment via which a clinician can identify the needed but missing behaviour that resulted in expected behaviour not being accomplished (see Figure 42.5). The missing link analysis is typically used in DBT whenever the patient had homework assigned to him/her but returns to therapy without completing it (Linehan, 2015a, b). For example, the analysis begins by elucidating whether the patient was aware homework was assigned; if yes, whether he/she was willing to do it the moment it was assigned; if not, what he/she can do next time to increase the probability homework would be accomplished. The missing link analysis probes common reasons why people do not do a task expected of them (not hearing it, not being willing to do it, becoming hopeless about doing it, not knowing how to do it, postponing it, etc.). Once the reason the task was not done is identified, the next step is to propose different solutions to overcome the missing link such that the task is done next time. Such a succession of steps can easily be transformed into an algorithm to be conducted in a computerized way, with or without human clinician supervision.

Some of the skills taught in DBT involve a succession of steps and a logical progression through questions to see how to implement the skill. For example, the Opposite Action skill involves several branches in a decision tree. The patients need to first identify what emotion they are experiencing, whether they want to change that emotion or not, what is the action urge associated with that emotion, what is the opposite action to that urge, and a practical way to implement/engage in the opposite action to regulate the original emotion. This decision-making process can be translated into an algorithm through which a computerized tool can guide a user. Similar skills that involve several steps and decisions along the way for the skill to be applied correctly are Check the Facts (where patients are required to again identify their emotion, see what facts justify/ are in line with that emotion, then check if the facts in their own situation justify that emotion) and the DEAR MAN GIVE FAST interpersonal skills (where patients need to compose an assertive action towards another individual and decide on how strong that assertion should be based on a list of facts to check about the relationship and the situation).

The examples given here are not the only places where DBT follows an algorithmic path. Highlighting these skills provides some examples and may prompt others to identify ways in which behavioural assessment and skills training can be described in algorithmic formats more easily interpreted by computers and technology.

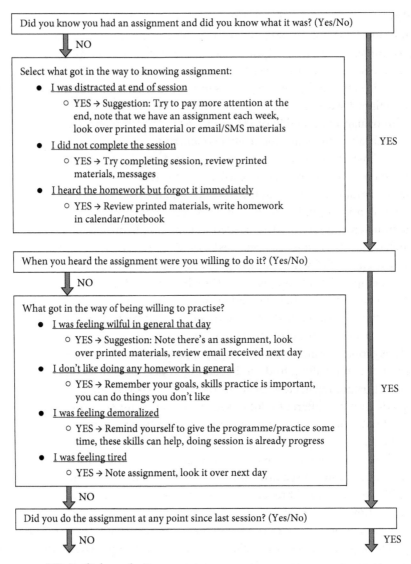

FIGURE 42.5 Missing links analysis.

EXISTING DBT TOOLS AND NEW TECHNOLOGY: AN OVERVIEW

The desire to use technology for the purpose of disseminating DBT to as many individuals in need as possible is not new. This section does not cover the technology-mediated tools developed for the purposes of training clinicians in DBT. Instead, it focuses on tools developed with direct-to-patient clinical work in mind.

Teaching DBT skills via DVDs

A series of DVDs were created in 2006/2007 in which Linehan teaches a subset of DBT skills directly via video (Linehan, 2000, 2002, 2003a, 2003b, 2003c, 2003d, 2003e). The DVDs are organized to include Linehan teaching the skills directly to the recording camera and to also incorporate, through video editing, additional schematics and animations to further elaborate specific points. The teaching material also includes suggestions for specific practices to incorporate the material taught into someone's life. Research has investigated the feasibility and efficacy of teaching patients the emotion regulation Opposite Action skill via video. Thirty patients meeting criteria for BPD who were naïve to DBT were randomly assigned using a within-subject design to watching a DBT skill via video or a control video (Waltz et al., 2009). Viewing the DBT skills video was associated with significant increase in knowledge of the skill and with increases in expectations of positive outcomes compared to watching the control video.

The DBT Coach

The DBT Coach is a software application developed for smartphones and is aimed at assisting patients in generalizing the DBT skills learned in therapy to their own environment outside of therapy. The DBT Coach starts by assessing the patient's rating of emotional intensity and urges to use drugs; the software then guides patients through identifying the emotion they want to change and assesses their willingness around wanting to change that emotion. An endorsement of willingness to change the emotion led to the DBT Coach guiding the patient through the steps of the DBT Opposite Action skill (including identifying the action urge associated with the emotion to be changed, finding the opposite to that urge, and encouraging the patient to take the action step that was opposite to the emotion urge). A feature called "follow-up DBT Coach" reassesses level of emotion and prior success with the skill and guides the patient through additional coaching. The DBT Coach was evaluated primarily for acceptability and feasibility in a quasi-experimental design in which 22 individuals were enrolled in a study to use the tool for ten to 14 days (Rizvi, Dimeff, Skutch, Carroll, & Linehan, 2011). Upon study completion, participants used the DBT Coach on a range of emotions (including sadness and fear) and gave good ratings of acceptability; participants also reported a decrease in depression and general distress. As a follow-up to this study, the DBT Coach was modified to include all four modules of the DBT skills training programme (Rizvi, Hughes, & Thomas, 2016). In this study, 16 participants enrolled in standard DBT evaluated the extended DBT Coach. Again, participants enrolled in the study endorsed high acceptability and usability of the app; however, with exception of reduction in non-suicidal self-injury (NSSI), usage of the app was not associated with any clinical variables.

DBT Apps on the Market

Simply typing in "DBT" in the app store produces 13 apps marketed to clients receiving DBT. These include apps related to tracking behaviour (e.g., Diary Card, DBT Diary Card and Skills Coach, A Simple and Free DBT Skills Coach, DBT Skills Diary, and DBT Diary). The costs of these apps range from free (A Simple and Free DBT Skills Coach) to US$4.99 (DBT Diary). Other apps provide skills training or coaching (e.g., DBT Interpersonal Relationship Tools, DBT Mindfulness Tools, DBT Distress Tolerance Tools, DBT Complete 4 Module Toolset, and Impulse DBT). The prices for these apps range from free (Impulse DBT) to US$22.99 (DBT complete 4 Module Toolset). These apps are specifically designed to prompt, coach, and teach clients how to use the skills. Finally, one free app (DBT Trivia and Quiz) is designed to strengthen skills acquisition through the use of quizzes. With the explosive market of tech-based intervention tools that can augment or supplant face-to-face psychotherapy, researchers have developed measures in which researchers and clinicians can formally evaluate apps (e.g., Mobile Application Rating Scale; Stoyanov et al., 2015). It is believed that, to date, none of these DBT apps have been formally evaluated with regard to usability, acceptability, and clinical efficacy.

iDBT for Emotion Regulation

This study focused on the pilot testing of a computerized, transdiagnostic DBT skills training programme to treat emotion dysregulation in individuals with mood and anxiety disorders. Women and men above a threshold on a measure of emotion dysregulation (DERS—Difficulties in Emotion Regulation; Gratz & Roemer, 2004) who met criteria for a mood and/or anxiety disorder who were not at imminent risk for suicide ($N = 34$) received an eight-week online DBT skills intervention plus two months of follow-up assessment. Contact with a clinician was limited to brief phone contact for suicide risk assessment and management; no other therapist time was involved. Over the duration of the study, the suicide risk management protocol was utilized only a few times, with no instances of additional intervention being necessary. The intervention also included daily reminders to practise mindfulness and assigned skills practice homework, and to log skills practised via an online diary card. The intervention was associated with significant reductions in emotion dysregulation, anxiety, depression, and general distress, as well as increases in mindfulness and skills practice (Lungu, 2015). A total of six individuals (17.6% of the intent-to-treat sample) dropped out of treatment, with drop-out being defined as not logging into the intervention for three weeks or more. Overall, the results indicate that this computerized format of DBT skills delivery is feasible to implement within an eight-week intervention, highly acceptable to patients, safe to administer, and shows promise as an effective computerized, trans-diagnostic intervention for emotion dysregulation across mood and anxiety disorders.

Development of iDBT for Emotion Regulation

This section considers the development of iDBT-ER in more detail to illustrate some of the principles in developing such an application. It also discusses how both principles from DBT and persuasive technology were used in its development.

iDBT-ER Treatment Structure

The structure of the iDBT-ER intervention was created keeping in mind the general structure of standard DBT skills training. It includes a welcome, orientation, and commitment video from the DBT creator going over the goal of skills training for emotion regulation, defining emotion regulation, asking about participant's goals, stressing the importance of practising the skills outside of the programme, and mentioning the strong research support for DBT skills training for emotion regulation. Briefly pointing to the development of the treatment at a renowned academic institution, the research support for the treatment, and delivering the skills training via video recordings with the treatment creator represent instances of persuasive technology system credibility support. Additionally, delivery of the iDBT-ER via video recordings with a therapist supports the social role strategy from persuasive technology.

A more detailed orientation to treatment logistics follows (including topics covered, number, duration, and frequency of sessions, homework assignment, and use of handouts and worksheets). All sessions, except the first, start with mindfulness practice and end with a different brief encouraging video message congratulating the participant for completing the session and encouraging practice. The last session concludes with congratulations on completing the programme and saying goodbye.

iDBT-ER Treatment Session Structure and Components

Figure 42.6 describes the session structure. Keeping the "session" structure for presenting the material also represents a tunnelling persuasive technology technique that sets the expectation that the entire section will be traversed as a unit. Each iDBT session beyond the first starts with an overview of the material to be covered, followed by a five- to seven-minute mindfulness practice, a review of the homework from the last session with feedback, troubleshooting barriers to practise if homework was not completed, teaching of new skills, in-session practice of the new skills to the extent possible, assignment of the new homework, and finally, troubleshooting what could prevent the assignment being completed for the following week. Both the initial mindfulness practice and practising the other skills taught in session represent rehearsal persuasive technology strategies.

Mindfulness practice. Each session starts with a longer mindfulness practice (approximately four to eight minutes; awareness of sounds, breath, sensation on skin, and thoughts); brief mindfulness practices of less than one minute are spread throughout the sessions to illustrate brief daily mindfulness practices.

Homework review and feedback. iDBT-ER checks completion of the following homework elements: a) the skills practice itself, b) writing down at least one practice, and c) completing the daily diary card at least three to four times during the week. Not doing the homework is followed by encouragement to practise the skill the following week and revisiting of rationale for practice. A positive response is followed by verbal praise and encouragement, which also represent rewards from a persuasive technology perspective.

iDBT-ER incorporates the "missing links analysis" that troubleshoots barriers to homework completion. For skills comprised of several steps, the homework review checks if components of the skill were done. Figure 42.6 illustrates the process for the check the facts skill. The algorithm guides the participant through the steps of the skills and, for the steps missed, suggests that the participant engage in that step right then. This is similar to the homework review process in a standard DBT group.

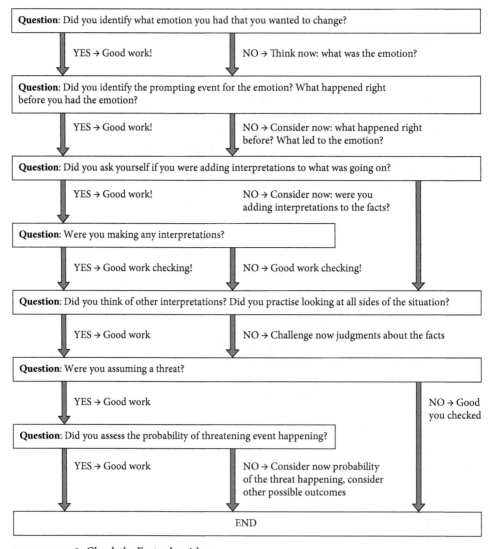

FIGURE 42.6 Check the Facts algorithm.

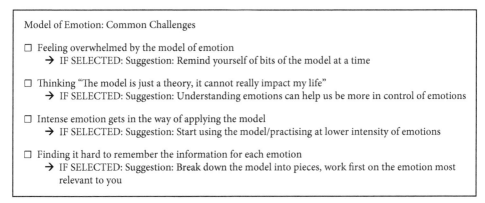

FIGURE 42.7 Common Challenges to the Model of Emotions.

Oftentimes participants encounter challenges in their skills practice, especially at the beginning of treatment. After homework review, iDBT-ER presents common challenges for that skill and asks the participants which were relevant for them and presents suggestions to overcome them (see Figure 42.7).

Teaching new skills. The new skills didactic content is presented via video segments between five and ten minutes in length which are interspersed with other engagement and practice activities grounded in DBT theory and clinical practice, as well as multimedia learning and information processing theories (called practice activities).

Self-Referencing practice activities. Research on memory and self-related processes argue that information about the self has superior elaborative and organizational properties in memory and is more frequently accessed (Kihlstrom et al., 1988; Klein & Loftus, 1988; Maki & Carlson, 1993; Markus, 1977). Indeed, information related to the self is better remembered than more general information (the Self-Referencing Effect—SRE; see Rogers, Kuiper, & Kirker, 1977; Symons & Johnson, 1997).

DBT skills training incorporates self-referencing by consistently asking participants to consider how the information presented is relevant to them. Such approaches are encouraged throughout the standard DBT skills training teaching notes. Self-referencing prompts were frequent in the video iDBT-ER skills training materials and were also incorporated into practice activities. Participants are prompted to consider their goals and areas in their lives in which they would be interested in applying specific skills. Figure 42.8 depicts a self-referencing practice asking participants to consider and select areas in their lives where they would like to be more mindful (e.g., be present more, become a better observer, become better at describing non-judgmentally, participating more).

Modelling and behavioural rehearsal practice activities. Modelling and behavioural rehearsal are behavioural change strategies extensively used in DBT during skills training (Naugle & Maher, 2003). Video and brief text- and narration-based vignettes of skills practice in different circumstances were incorporated as modelling practice activities. All the skills taught have activities supporting rehearsal. Figure 42.9 shows an in-session practice of the mindfulness describe skill where participants are instructed to

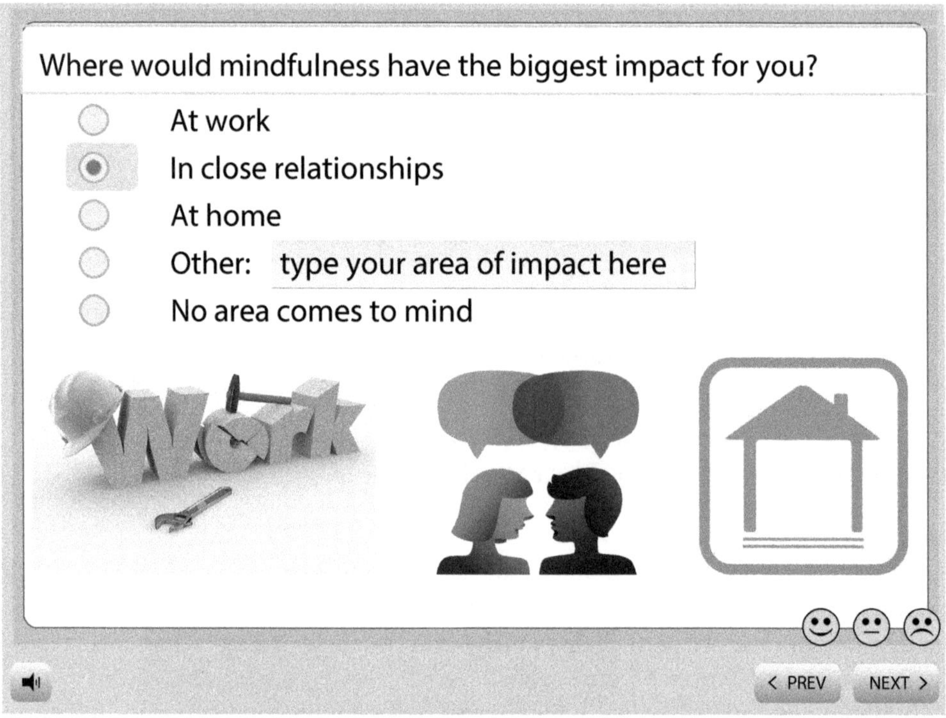

Where would mindfulness have the biggest impact for you?

- ○ At work
- ◉ In close relationships
- ○ At home
- ○ Other: type your area of impact here
- ○ No area comes to mind

< PREV   NEXT >

FIGURE 42.8 Where Would You Like to be More Mindful?

Source: Shutterstock.com

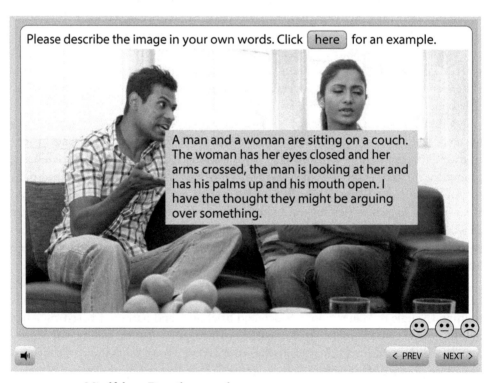

Please describe the image in your own words. Click [here] for an example.

A man and a woman are sitting on a couch. The woman has her eyes closed and her arms crossed, the man is looking at her and has his palms up and his mouth open. I have the thought they might be arguing over something.

< PREV   NEXT >

FIGURE 42.9 Mindfulness Describe example.

Source: Shutterstock.com

describe the image of a couple that appears to be arguing. Participants can compare their description with one provided.

Planning and scheduling practice activities. Participants are prompted throughout the intervention to consider changes they can make to their routines to increase generalization of specific skills (e.g., to practise the ICE water DBT skill, which needs some materials such as ice-packs or ice cubes in the freezer). Similarly, the programme asks the participant how their routine could change to incorporate practice of adding pleasant events in their lives.

Elaborative rehearsal practice activities. Elaborative rehearsal in which an individual actively thinks about the new content in a meaningful way (for example, by relating it to prior relevant information) increases learning more than maintenance rehearsal in which information is purely repeated (Goldstein, 2014). Interaction is a common feature of multimedia learning systems and supports a deeper level of content processing. Multiple activities in iDBT-ER promote elaborative rehearsal and interactivity. Figure 42.10 instructs to click to reveal how the same prompting event and different interpretations can lead to different emotions solidifying understanding of the theoretical model of emotion.

Homework assignment. The homework assignment reiterates several important aspects: a) the rationale of generalizing skillful behaviour to situations that will make a

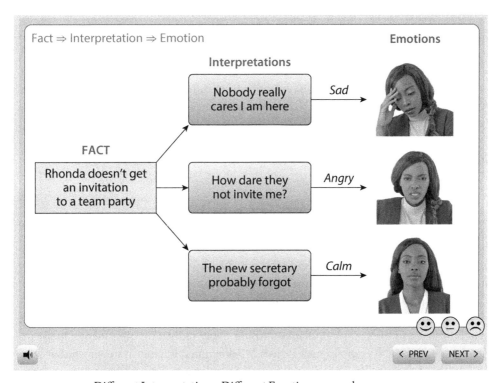

FIGURE 42.10   Different Interpretations, Different Emotions example.

Source: Shutterstock.com

difference in participants' lives; b) the specific homework assignment for that week; c) the emphasis on not being perfectionistic about the homework and having realistic expectations about the pace of learning new skills; d) anticipating potential urges to quit and practising not giving in to such urges; and e) suggestion to track skills practice using the daily diary card. iDBT-ER homework assignments include identifying barriers to homework completion as well as troubleshooting solutions. The participant selects solutions they are willing to try for the following week based on the barriers they anticipate.

In-between session skills practice prompts. Generalization of new skills is a critical aspect of DBT. If homework is only assigned at the end of a session with no reminder of it until the next session, the opportunity for generalization of skills practice is not fully maximized. Behavioural prompts are known to increase the frequency of engaging in a specific behaviour. Text messaging interventions have been found to be effective in the field of behavioural health (Cole-Lewis & Kershaw, 2010; Fogg & Adler, 2009). iDBT-ER includes daily messages delivered via text or email message encouraging participants to practise the skills assigned for homework and offering specific suggestions for practise. iDBT-ER also prompts participants to practise mindfulness daily, as mindfulness is such a core component of DBT and emotion regulation.

Daily diary card. At the end of the day, participants are sent an email or text message (based on their preference) that incorporates a link to an electronic survey type diary card that contains all the skills iDBT-ER covered until that point.

Technical Set-Up for iDBT-ER

Several information components are incorporated into each session. The videos teaching the DBT skills with the DBT treatment developer are professionally recorded, edited, and uploaded on the video streaming server vimeo.com (www.vimeo.com). The iDBT-ER lessons are assembled into the e-Learning course development software Articulate Storyline (www.articulate.com) and then hosted in the Articulate Online Learning Management System (LMS). Users login to access the iDBT-ER content through the Articulate Online LMS which, in turn, builds the content of the lesson by accessing Vimeo on demand to play the teaching videos.

iDBT for Suicidal and Heavy Episodic Drinkers

Building on work from Lungu (Lungu, 2015), iDBT-ER was modified to suit clients who engage in problematic drinking and who are suicidal. Because individuals at risk for suicide and who engage in addictive behaviour are often excluded from trials of online CBT (Wilks et al., 2017), and because Internet-delivered interventions are specifically designed to reduce barriers to dissemination, developing an Internet intervention for generalizable and high-risk populations would likely reduce the treatment gap for individuals engaging in complex and high-risk behaviours. Furthermore, given that DBT was designed specifically for individuals with complex and high-risk behavioural presentations, iDBT is particularly suitable for this population.

The biggest modification to iDBT-ER was the development and integration of skills designed for problematic alcohol use. While DBT has a set of skills for addictive behaviour (e.g., the Addiction skills; Linehan, 2015a, b), they were primarily developed for clients with opiate and methamphetamine addiction (Linehan et al., 1999; Linehan et al., 2002). Subsequently, the skills encouraged abstinence from their addictive behaviour, albeit using a dialectical approach. This heavy focus on abstinence is not inline with some of the evidence-based approaches for problematic alcohol use (e.g., Harm reduction, Marlatt, 1996). As a result, the skills of "Dialectical Drinking" and "Wise Mind Goals" were developed that teach 1) the abstinence violation effect, 2) motivational interviewing, and 3) goal setting (Wilks, Yin, Ang, Matsumiya, & Lungu, 2017). In goal setting, participants choose a goal that most likely fits their drinking behaviour and values; further, the other addiction skills were modified such that "abstinence" was changed to "your drinking goal."

The other major modification was to integrate a larger reliance on "human-in-the-loop," (see, e.g., Cranor, 2008). In other words, due to the high-risk nature of the participants, clinicians trained to work with suicidal and alcohol-using clients were dispatched to attend to acute suicidal crises and respond accordingly. Specifically, clinicians would be prompted to contact clients 1) during the first week of study participation, regardless of condition or suicide level, 2) whenever suicide risk increased from the previous week in terms of frequency or intensity, and 3) if urge to quit the treatment increased from the previous week. If clinicians were unable to reach the suicidal clients, a "caring email" was sent urging clients to use crisis services if they experienced urges to die. The calls and emails functioned as a safety check as well as a motivation enhancement.

FUTURE DIRECTIONS FOR RESEARCH

Advances in technology have opened up a new and exciting treatment frontier, where use of new technologies can potentially increase DBT treatment effectiveness. However, given the uniqueness of technology-delivered treatments, research is needed to identify the active ingredients of evidence-based treatment such that treatment delivery is maximally efficient without losing effectiveness, as well as adherent to DBT treatment guidelines. Along those lines, more research on the mechanisms of action in DBT is crucial in order to identify the active components of treatment and discover ways to incorporate those active ingredients through technology. In addition, technology can supplement, augment, and even supplant traditional face-to-face psychotherapy, and research is needed to determine how technology can best complement psychotherapy without sacrificing treatment effectiveness. Along those lines, technology is already being incorporated to assist researchers in collecting and analysing data. As developers build tools with an increased focus on increasing the ease of use, treatment providers may be more inclined to implement data collection and real-time evaluation to guide treatment in outpatient care. Finally, through the shared use of open-source data collection and collaboration, technology developers and users can come together to share and provide feedback with the shared goal of increasing access and effectiveness of therapy.

DBT as a treatment has continuously transformed to incorporate state-of-the-art science for behaviour change. Technology provides another platform upon which treatment efficacy can evolve and increase, treatment itself can be used by hard-to-reach populations, and treatment impact can improve for both the therapist and the client. It is critical that in incorporating technology DBT remains true to its core principles and values, such as putting the patient first, remaining grounded in science and the evidence base, and incorporating state-of-the-art research on behavioural change. At the same time, DBT can expand to incorporate findings from other disciplines and research areas, such as human-computer interaction, online learning, machine learning, and even advertising, entertainment, and video production. The goal of alleviating suffering and helping our patients build "lives worth living" remains the same, and technology can be another avenue for reaching that goal.

Key Points for Clinicians

- The demand for DBT is outpacing the supply of clinicians trained in delivering it effectively.
- DBT is compatible with the implementation of technology, including persuasive technology, modularity, and logical flow.
- There is growing research support for the use of technology to both augment and supplant DBT, including videos, mobile apps, and computerized interventions.
- There are several mobile apps on the market that can be downloaded and used in therapy, although there appears to be no research on these applications.

References

Andersson, G., & Cuijpers, P. (2009). Internet-based and other computerized psychological treatments for adult depression: A meta-analysis. *Cognitive Behavior Therapy*, 38(4), 196–205.

Andrews, G., Cuijpers, P., Craske, M. G., McEvoy, P., & Titov, N. (2010). Computer therapy for the anxiety and depressive disorders is effective, acceptable and practical health care: A meta-analysis. *PloS One*, 5(10). Retrieved from https://doi.org/10.1371/journal.pone.0013196

Barak, A., Hen, L., & Boniel-Nissim, N. (2008). A comprehensive review and a meta-analysis of the effectiveness of Internet-based psychotherapeutic interventions. *Journal of Technology in Human Services*, 26(2–4), 109–160.

Basseches, M. (1984). *Dialectical thinking and adult development*. Norwood, NJ: Ablex Publishing.

Bohus, M., Dyer, A. S., Priebe, K., Kruger, A., Kleindienst, N., Schmahl, C., & Steil, R. (2013). Dialectical behaviour therapy for post-traumatic stress disorder after childhood sexual abuse in patients with and without borderline personality disorder: a randomised controlled trial. *Psychotherapy and Psychosomatics, 82*(4), 221–233.

Boyd, D., & Crawford, K. (2012). Critical questions for big data: Provocations for a cultural, technological, and scholarly phenomenon. *Information, Communication & Society, 15*(5), 662–679.

Butler, A. C., Chapman, J. E., Forman, E. M., & Beck, A. T. (2006). The empirical status of cognitive-behavioural therapy: a review of meta-analyses. *Clinical Psychology Review, 26*(1), 17–31.

Cheng, S. K., & Dizon, J. (2012). Computerized cognitive behavioural therapy for insomnia: A systematic review and meta-analysis. *Psychotherapy and Psychosomatics, 81,* 206–216. doi: 10.1159/000335379

Classen, C., & Larkin, G. (2005). Occult suicidality in an emergency department. *British Journal of Psychiatry, 186,* 352–353.

Cole-Lewis, H., & Kershaw, T. (2010). Text messaging as a tool for behavior change in disease prevention and management. *Epidemiologic Reviews, 32*(1), 56–69.

Cranor, L. F. (2008). A framework for reasoning about the human in the loop. *UPSEC,* 8, 1–15.

Cui, L., Li, S., & Zhu, T. (2016, January). Emotion detection from natural walking. In International Conference on Human Centered Computing (pp. 23–33). Springer, Cham.

Cuijpers, P., Marks, I. M., Van Straten, A., Cavanagh, K., Gega, L., & Andersson, G. (2009). Computer-aided psychotherapy for anxiety disorders: A meta-analytic review. *Cognitive Behavior Therapy, 38*(2), 66–82.

Dimeff, L. A., & Linehan, M. M. (2008). Dialectical behavior therapy for substance abusers. *Addiction Science and Clinical Practice, 4*(2), 39–47.

Fleming, A. P., McMahon, R. J., Moran, L. R., Peterson, A. P., & Dreessen, A. (2014). Pilot randomized controlled trial of dialectical behavior therapy group skills training for ADHD among college students. *Journal of Attention Disorders, 19*(3), 260–271.

Fogg, B. J. (2003). *Persuasive technology using computers to change what we think and do,* Vol. 1. San Francisco: Morgan Kaufmann Publishers.

Fogg, B. J., & Adler, R. (2009). *Texting 4 health: A simple, powerful way to change lives.* Palo Alto, CA: Captology Media.

Goldstein, B. E. (2014). *Cognitive psychology: Connecting mind, research and everyday experience,* 4th Edition. Belmont, CA: Wadsworth Publishing.

Gratz, K. L., & Roemer, L. (2004). Multidimensional assessment of emotion regulation and dysregulation: Development, factor structure, and initial validation of the difficulties in emotion regulation scale. *Journal of Psychopathology and Behavioral Assessment, 26,* 41–54.

Greist, J. H., Laughren, T. P., Gustafson, D. H., Stauss, F. F., Rowse, G. L., & Chiles, J. A. (1973). A computer interview for suicide-risk prediction. *American Journal of Psychiatry, 130*(12), 1327–1332.

Harjumaa, M., & Oinas-Kukkonen, H. (2007). *Persuasion theories and IT design.* Berlin: Heidelberg.

Harned, M. S., Korslund, K. E., Foa, E. B., & Linehan, M. M. (2012). Treating PTSD in suicidal and self-injuring women with borderline personality disorder: development and preliminary evaluation of a dialectical behavior therapy prolonged exposure protocol. *Behaviour Research and Therapy, 50*(6), 381–386. PMCID: PMC3348973.

Harned, M. S., & Linehan, M. M. (2008). Integrating dialectical behavior therapy and prolonged exposure to treat co-occurring borderline personality disorder and PTSD: Two case studies. *Cognitive and Behavioral Practice, 15*(3), 263–276, http://dx.doi.org/210.1016/j.cbpra.2007.1008.1006

Kaminstein, D. S. (1987). Toward a dialectical metatheory for psychotherapy. *Journal of Contemporary Psychotherapy, 17*(2), 87–101.

Kihlstrom, J. F., Cantor, N., Albright, J. S., Chew, B. R., Klein, S. B., & Niedenthal, P. M. (1988). Information processing and the study of the self. In L. Berkowitz (Ed.), *Advances in experimental social psychology* (Vol. 21, pp. 145–180). New York: Academic Press.

Klein, S. B., & Loftus, J. (1988). The nature of self-referent encoding: The contribution of elaborative and organizational processes. *Journal of Personality and Social Psychology, 55*, 5–11.

Kliem, S., Kroger, C., & Kosfelder, J. (2010). Dialectical behavior therapy for borderline personality disorder: A meta-analysis using mixed-effects modeling. *Journal of Consulting and Clinical Psychology, 78*(6), 936–951.

Koh, H. K., & Sebelius, K. G. (2010). Promoting prevention through the Affordable Care Act. *New England Journal of Medicine, 363*(14), 1296–1299.

Lambert, M. J., & Ogles, B. M. (2009). Using clinical significance in psychotherapy outcome research: The need for a common procedure and validity data. *Psychotherapy Research, 19*(4–5), 493–501.

Lee, C. M., Narayanan, S. S., & Pieraccini, R. (2002). Combining acoustic and language information for emotion recognition. In Seventh International Conference on Spoken Language Processing.

Linehan, M. M. (2000). *Opposite action: Changing emotions you want to change.* Seattle: The Behavioral Technology Transfer Group.

Linehan, M. M. (2002). *From suffering to freedom through reality acceptance.* Seattle: Behavioral Tech, LLC.

Linehan, M. M. (2003a). *Crisis survival skills, part four: Skills for everyday mindfulness.* Seattle: Behavioral Tech, LLC.

Linehan, M. M. (2003b). *Crisis survival skills, part one: Distracting and self-soothing.* Seattle: Behavioral Tech, LLC.

Linehan, M. M. (2003c). *Crisis survival skills, part three: Practicing reality acceptance.* Seattle: Behavioral Tech, LLC.

Linehan, M. M. (2003d). *Crisis survival skills, part two: Improving the moment and pros & cons.* Seattle: Behavioral Tech, LLC.

Linehan, M. M. (2003e). *This one moment: Skills for everyday mindfulness.* Seattle: Behavioral Tech, LLC.

Linehan, M. (2015a). *DBT skills training handouts and worksheets,* 2nd Edition. New York: Guilford Press.

Linehan, M. (2015b). *DBT skills training manual,* 2nd Edition. New York: Guilford Press.

Linehan, M. M., Dimeff, L. A., Reynolds, S. K., Comtois, K. A., Welch, S. S., Heagerty, P., & Kivlahan, D. R. (2002). Dialectical behavior therapy versus comprehensive validation therapy plus 12-step for the treatment of opioid dependent women meeting criteria for borderline personality disorder. *Drug and Alcohol Dependence, 67*(1), 13–26.

Linehan, M., Korslund, K., Harned, M., Gallop, R., Lungu, A., Neacsiu, A. D., ... Murray-Gregory, A. (2015). Dialectical behavior therapy for high suicide risk in borderline personality disorder: a component analysis. *JAMA Psychiatry, 72*(5), 475–482.

Linehan, M. M., McDavid, J. D., Brown, M. Z., Sayrs, J. H. R., & Gallop, R. J. (2008). Olanzapine plus dialectical behavior therapy for women with high irritability who meet criteria for borderline personality disorder: A double-blind, placebo-controlled study. *Journal of Clinical Psychology, 69*, 999–1005.

Linehan, M. M., & Schmidt, H., III. (1995). The dialectics of effective treatment of border-line personality disorder. In W. O. O'Donohue & L. Krasner (Eds.), *Theories in behavior therapy: Exploring behavior change* (pp. 553–584). Washington DC: American Psychological Association (Reprinted from: IN FILE).

Linehan, M. M., Schmidt, H., Dimeff, L. A., Craft, J. C., Kanter, J., & Comtois, K. A. (1999). Dialectical behavior therapy for patients with borderline personality disorder and drug-dependence. *The American Journal on Addictions, 8*(4), 279–292.

Linehan, M.M., & Wilks, C.R. (2015). The course and evolution of dialectical behavior therapy. *American Journal of Psychotherapy, 69*(2), 97–110.

Luborsky, L., Diguer, L., Seligman, D. A., Rosenthal, R., Krause, E. D., Johnson, S., . . . & Schweizer, E. (1999). The researcher's own therapy allegiances: A "wild card" in comparisons of treatment efficacy. *Clinical Psychology: Science and Practice, 6*(1), 95–106.

Lungu, A. (2015). *Computerized trans-diagnostic dialectical behavior therapy skills training for emotion dysregulation* (Doctoral dissertation). University of Washington.

Lungu, A., Rodriguez-Gonzalez, M., & Linehan, M. M. (2012). Implementing a dialectical behavior therapy training program for graduate students. *The Behavior Therapist, 35*(1), 4–11.

Lynch, T. R. (2000). Treatment of elderly depression with personality disorder comorbidity using dialectical behavior therapy. *Cognitive and Behavioral Practice, 7*(4), 468–477.

Lynch, T. R., Cheavens, J. S., Cukrowicz, K. C., Thorp, S. R., Bronner, L., & Beyer, J. (2007). Treatment of older adults with co-morbid personality disorder and depression: a dialectical behavior therapy approach. *International Journal of Geriatric Psychiatry, 22*(2), 131–143.

Lyons, C., Hopley, P., & Horrocks, J. (2009). A decade of stigma and discrimination in mental health: plus ça change, plus c'est la même chose (the more things change, the more they stay the same). *Journal of Psychiatric and Mental Health Nursing, 16*(6), 501–507.

Maki, R. H., & Carlson, A. K. (1993). Knowledge of the self: Is it special? In T. K. Srull & R. S. Wyer (Eds.), *Advances in social cognition* (Vol. 5, pp. 101–110). New York: Lawrence Erlbaum.

Markus, H. R. (1977). Self-schemata and processing information about the self. *Journal of Personality and Social Psychology, 35*, 63–78.

Marlatt, G. A. (1996). Harm reduction: Come as you are. *Addictive Behaviors, 21*(6), 779–788.

Miller, A. L., Rathus, J. H., & Linehan, M. M. (2006). *Dialectical behavior therapy with suicidal adolescents*. New York: Guilford Press.

National Institute for Health and Care Excellence. (2002). *Guidance on the use of computerised cognitive behavioural therapy for anxiety and depression* (Vol. 51). London: NICE.

Naugle, A. E., & Maher, S. (2003). Modeling and behavioral rehearsal. In W. T. O'Donohue, J. E. Fisher, & S. C. Hayes (Eds.), *Cognitive behavior therapy: Applying empirically supported techniques in your practice* (pp. 238–246). Hoboken, NJ: John Wiley & Sons.

Neacsiu, A. D., Eberle, J. E., & Linehan, M. M. (2014). Dialectical behavior therapy skills for transdiagnostic emotion dysregulation: A pilot randomized controlled trial. *Behaviour Research and Therapy, 59*, 40–51.

Newman, M. G., Consoli, A., & Taylor, C. B. (1997). Computers in assessment and cognitive behavioral treatment of clinical disorders: Anxiety as a case in point. *Behavior Therapy, 28*(2), 211–235.

Newman, M. G., Consoli, A. J., & Taylor, C. B. (1999). A palmtop computer program for the treatment of generalized anxiety disorder. *Behavior Modification, 23*(4), 597–619.

Oinas-Kukkonen, H., & Harjumaa, M. (2008a). *A systematic framework for designing and evaluating persuasive systems*. Berlin: Heidelberg.

Oinas-Kukkonen, H., & Harjumaa, M. (2008b). *Towards deeper understanding of persuasion in software and information systems*. Proceedings of the First International Conference on Advances in Computer-Human Interaction (pp. 200–205). Piscataway, NJ: IEEE.

Perepletchikova, F., Axelrod, S. R., Kaufman, J., Rounsaville, B. J., Douglas-Palumberi, H., & Miller, A. L. (2010). Adapting dialectical behaviour therapy for children: Towards a new research agenda for paediatric suicidal and non-suicidal self-injurious behaviours. *Child and Adolescent Mental Health*, 16(2), 116–121.

Reger, M. A., & Gahm, G. A. (2009). A meta-analysis of the effects of Internet- and computer-based cognitive-behavioral treatments for anxiety. *Journal of Clinical Psychology*, 65(1), 53–75.

Richards, D., & Richardson, T. (2012). Computer-based psychological treatments for depression: A systematic review and meta-analysis. *Clinical Psychology Review*, 32, 329–342.

Rizvi, S., Dimeff, L., Skutch, J. M., Carroll, D., & Linehan, M. M. (2011). A pilot study of the DBT Coach: An interactive mobile phone application for individuals with borderline personality disorder and substance use disorder. *Behavior Therapy*, 42, 589–600.

Rizvi, S. L., Hughes, C. D., & Thomas, M. C. (2016). The DBT Coach mobile application as an adjunct to treatment for suicidal and self-injuring individuals with borderline personality disorder: A preliminary evaluation and challenges to client utilization. *Psychological Services*, 13(4), 380.

Rogers, T. B., Kuiper, N. A., & Kirker, W. S. (1977). Self-reference and the encoding of personal information. *Journal of Personality and Social Psychology*, 35, 677–688.

Smith, R. E., & Smoll, F. L. (1990). Sport performance anxiety. In H. Leitenberg (Ed.), *Handbook of social and evaluation anxiety* (pp. 417–454). Springer US.

Smith, M. L., & Glass, G. V. (1977). Meta-analysis of psychotherapy outcome studies. *American Psychologist*, 32(9), 752.

Sokolova, M. V., Fernández-Caballero, A., López, M. T., Martínez-Rodrigo, A., Zangróniz, R., & Pastor, J. M. (2015). A distributed architecture for multimodal emotion identification. In *Trends in Practical Applications of Agents, Multi-Agent Systems and Sustainability* (pp. 125–132). Springer, Cham.

Spek, V., Cuijpers, P., Nyklicek, I., Riper, H., Keyzer, J., & Pop, V. (2007). Internet-based cognitive behaviour therapy for symptoms of depression and anxiety: a meta-analysis. *Psychological Medicine*, 37(3), 319–328.

Staats, A. W. (1975). *Social behaviorism*. Homewood, IL: Dorsey Press.

Staats, A. W., & Staats, C. K. (1963). *Complex human behavior*. New York: Holt, Rinehart & Win.

Stoyanov, S. R., Hides, L., Kavanagh, D. J., Zelenko, O., Tjondronegoro, D., & Mani, M. (2015). Mobile app rating scale: a new tool for assessing the quality of health mobile apps. *JMIR mHealth and uHealth*, 3(1), e27.

Stuhlmiller, C., & Tolchard, B. (2009). Computer-assisted for depression & anxiety: increasing accessibility to evidence-based mental health treatment. *Journal of Psychosocial Nursing and Mental Health Services*, 47(7), 32–39.

Symons, C. S., & Johnson, B. T. (1997). The self-reference effect in memory: A meta-analysis. *Psychological Bulletin*, 121(3), 371–394.

Turner, S. M., Beidel, D. C., Spaulding, S. A., & Brown, J. M. (1995). The practice of behavior therapy: A national survey of cost and methods. *Behaviour Therapist*, 18, 1–4.

Van Dijk, S., Jeffrey, J., & Katz, M. R. (2013). A randomized, controlled, pilot study of dialectical behavior therapy skills in a psychoeducational group for individuals with bipolar disorder. *Journal of Affective Disorders*, 145(3), 386–393.

Waltz, J., Dimeff, L., Koerner, K., Linehan, M., Taylor, L., & Miller, C. (2009). Feasibility of using video to teach a dialectical behavior therapy skill to clients with borderline personality disorder. *Cognitive and Behavioral Practice*, 16(2), 214–222.

Wampold, B. E. (2001). *The great psychotherapy debate: Models, methods, and findings.* Mahwah, NJ: Lawrence Erlbaum Associates, Inc.

WHO. (2013). Mental health action plan 2013–2020.

Wilks, C., Yin, Q., Ang, S. Y., Matsumiya, B., Lungu, A., & Linehan, M. (2017). Internet-delivered dialectical behavioral therapy skills training for suicidal and heavy episodic drinkers: protocol and preliminary results of a randomized controlled trial. *JMIR Research Protocols*, 6(10).

Wilks, C. R., Zieve, G. G., & Lessing, H. K. (2015). Are trials of computerized therapy generalizable? A multidimensional meta-analysis. *Telemedicine and e-Health*, 22(5), 450–457.

SECTION VIII

TRAINING IN DBT

CHAPTER 43

EVIDENCE-BASED TRAINING

The Intensive Model of Training in Dialectical Behaviour Therapy

ANTHONY P. DUBOSE, YEVGENY BOTANOV, MARIA V. NAVARRO-HARO, AND MARSHA M. LINEHAN

BACKGROUND OF INTENSIVE TRAINING IN DIALECTICAL BEHAVIOUR THERAPY

Dialectical behaviour therapy (DBT) was developed through repeated attempts to apply the principles of behavioural science to treat individuals at high risk for suicide. After publication of the first randomized controlled trial on DBT (Linehan et al., 1991), and the original text outlining the treatment (Linehan, 1993), interest in DBT training increased rapidly. At the time, traditional psychotherapy training was conducted in university settings, psychotherapy training institutes, and medical residency programmes. However, it often requires many years of dissemination before traditional training institutions adopt a new treatment and begin training students in the intervention. Additionally, most psychotherapy training programmes do not provide both didactic and clinical supervision for evidence-based therapies (Weissman et al., 2006). Consequentially, traditional routes to psychotherapy training are too protractive in creating practitioners and researchers that are competent in doing DBT to meet the growing demand. Traditional training options also neglect practitioners who have completed academic training and are practising. To meet the rapidly growing demand for training without relying on traditional training institutions for a resource-intensive, evidence-based treatment, a new training method was needed. These factors led to the development of an intensive model of training in DBT.

The intensive model has its genesis in Marsha Linehan's research laboratory. As the treatment developer, she trained her graduate students using a model that integrated clinical training in DBT with their science training. Student courses were taught in a context of ongoing research on treatment development, provision of clinical services, and live review of clinical work. Quickly it became clear that this was insufficient to meet the needs outside of the academic setting. Moreover, there was often reticence to train students in graduate programmes to work with individuals with elevated risk for suicide due to concerns about liability, and the exposure of students to high-risk situations. To move the training beyond academic settings, Linehan began training clinicians in concert with her graduate students. When it was clear that this, in and of itself, would not meet the growing need to increase access to DBT, she then created a training company to meet the need, which also required developing a new training model.

DEVELOPMENT OF THE INTENSIVE TRAINING MODEL

The need to export the treatment into community settings, and the variability and structural differences across research and clinical settings, presented many obstacles to developing a training model. However, training of practitioners was central to increasing the dissemination, implementation, and sustainability of DBT. The development of an intensive, team-based, training model that focuses strongly on implementation of DBT programmes is, in part, responsible for much of the success of DBT dissemination (McHugh & Barlow, 2010).

An aspect of the DBT approach to treatment that differed from standard approaches of the time was the delivery of treatment in the context of a comprehensive programme. The comprehensive programme included numerous modes of treatment, not only individual therapy. DBT incorporated a team approach to treatment, a novel innovation for an evidence-based therapy. The team approach requires that a group of DBT trained practitioners – a DBT consultation team – establish a programmatic, team-based approach to treatment. DBT consultation teams are a core mode of treatment, which was incorporated into the training model. Groups of practitioners interested in DBT were required to form teams before implementing DBT. The team trains together, works jointly on implementation of DBT, maintains treatment fidelity within routine delivery, and ensures sustainability of a DBT programme. In effect, the community of clients is treated by a community of therapists. Therefore, all therapists who wish to pursue training must agree that, as members of the team, if there is a death by suicide for any client on the team, all therapists acknowledge that they have treated a client who has died by suicide. Furthermore, the DBT consultation team serves to monitor adherence, reduce burnout, and provide backup for clients. Regular meetings of the consultation team and systematic evaluation of treatment outcomes are considered essential to DBT and the training model (see Sayrs, this volume).

A single session or a few short workshops was prohibitive to training in DBT because the intensive model of training was replacing traditional apprenticeship training models, required teaching numerous programmatic elements and provider behaviours, and included multiple modes of treatment. Additional time was also needed for trainers to provide feedback and assist teams with implementation across varied treatment settings. Accordingly, the training model was constructed as two five-day workshops separated by a period for self-study and implementation wherein teams of practitioners are provided the necessary skills to implement a comprehensive DBT programme that includes four treatment modes. Intensive training focuses on providing therapists the skills necessary to conduct DBT and establish a sustainable programme.

DBT's principle-based focus of treatment, contrary to many other manualized cognitive behavioural therapies (CBTs), required further innovation. While DBT skills training is a core protocol-based mode of the treatment, and additional protocols are incorporated on an as-needed basis, the majority of the treatment is not manualized. Training in a principle-based treatment creates opportunities and challenges. While training in a strictly manualized treatment can be more straightforward, the complexities of the populations treated by DBT require a thorough knowledge of the principles of the treatment, and competence at applying the strategies informed by these principles. While learning such a treatment may not be as easily accomplished as training someone in a curriculum-driven manual, the principle-based approach prepares trainees to respond in novel situations that are inevitable when working with complex problems.

The Intensive Training Model

Elements

Foundationally, treatment providers must learn to 1) implement programmatic elements of the treatment and 2) engage in specific provider behaviours. DBT teams in training are encouraged to consider the five functions of comprehensive treatment in the development of their DBT programmes:

- Improving client motivation.
- Enhancing client capabilities.
- Generalizing treatment gains to the natural environment.
- Structuring the client's environment.
- Improving treatment providers' skills and motivation.

These functions map onto the four standard modes of treatment in outpatient DBT that include:

- Individual therapy—agenda-based: assist client in adopting new behaviours/ DBT skills
- Skills-training—protocol-based: learning, developing, and applying DBT skills
- Out-of-session coaching—generalization of skills
- Consultation team—team approach to treatment and assist treatment providers in providing adherent therapy

In addition to the programme elements of DBT, providers must be trained in a collection of strategies, procedures, and protocols, which dialectically balance change-orientated behaviour therapy with acceptance strategies. Crucially, implementing specific interventions of the treatment must be based on core dialectical treatment principles. Training reflects the delicate balance between procedures and principles, which is often more complicated than teaching a set of straight-forward protocols. The next section describes a training model that follows an implementation model of adoption, skills acquisition, implementation, practice improvement, and sustainability.

Training Structure

Developing an intensive model of training was an iterative process continued over numerous years. Dialectical Behavior Therapy Intensive Training™ is an example of the intensive model created by the treatment developer and provided by the Behavioral Research & Therapy Clinics at the University of Washington and Behavioral Tech, LLC and its International Affiliates. Intensive training is provided as a bipartite training consisting of two five-day workshops (Part 1 and Part 2) separated by a period for self-study and implementation. The typical interval between the two parts of training is six months. Training is team based with members seated together to facilitate discussion. Trainings typically consist of six to eight teams from different agencies or healthcare systems. Typically, teams range in size from three to eight members. A team is considered a group of mental health professionals who meets at least weekly to assist each other in applying DBT in their practice setting. Core structural elements are outlined here, and Table 43.1 provides a description of the training objectives.

Preparation. Prior to Part 1, participants are required to read the DBT texts authored by the treatment developer (Linehan, 1993, 2015) and discuss them within their teams. Alternatively, Behavioral Tech, LLC offers teams the option of preparation by joining Learning Communities, which occur six to 12 weeks before the start of Part 1. DBT-trained facilitators assist teams within the Learning Communities to review the DBT texts, discuss related DBT concepts, answer questions, and practise applying the treatment. These steps foster acceptability, adoption, and enhancement of knowledge before the first part of training.

Part 1. The initial five-day, in-person, instructor-led training encompasses the content of standard outpatient DBT. Table 43.2 provides a schedule for intensive training. The general structure of each day is as follows: Day 1 consists of an orientation to the training and focus on foundations of DBT (e.g., evidence for DBT, theoretical foundations, basic assumptions of treatment) and initial case conceptualization (biosocial model of emotion dysregulation). Experiential exercises, as well as team-based exercises, are conducted during each teaching section. Teams are often assigned homework over lunch periods and evenings. Day 2 continues with the functions and structure of DBT programmes. Case conceptualizations are further developed with focus on levels of disorder and targets of treatment. Day 2 ends with orientation and commitment to treatment. Day

Table 43.1   Training objectives for DBT intensive training

Part 1:
- Participate in a DBT Consultation Team.
- Demonstrate Consultation Team strategies used in DBT.
- List the modes, the functions, and the typical treatment agreements made in DBT.
- Implement the structure, goals, and stages of DBT.
- Teach the four DBT skills modules.
- Explain the biosocial model of severe emotion dysregulation, borderline personality disorder, and other disorders in all required treatment contexts.
- Create DBT treatment plans for clients using targeting procedures.
- Explain the dialectical nature of DBT and demonstrate how dialectics are used in DBT.
- Conduct cue exposure and response prevention.
- List the steps in problem solving.
- Conduct behavioural chain analyses and solution analyses.
- Implement the cognitive-behavioural strategies in DBT.
- Identify the levels of validation and the contexts in which they apply.
- Demonstrate the use of validation to balance change strategies.
- Demonstrate the different communication strategies of DBT.
- Implement the DBT case management, telephone coaching, and other generalization strategies of DBT.
- Apply suicide crisis protocols of DBT.
- Discuss the DBT research for different populations.

Part 2:
- Demonstrate comprehension and ability to apply important concepts in DBT.
- Demonstrate ability to appropriately apply DBT strategies.
- Demonstrate use of DBT commitment strategies.
- Identify in-session dysfunctional behaviours and use DBT strategies to treat them.
- Use DBT strategies to better manage skills training problems.
- Identify team problems and use DBT strategies to resolve them.
- Design DBT service programmes, appropriately implementing and modifying DBT protocols for different populations and settings.
- Formulate plans to evaluate programme/services.
- Discuss the take-home exam assigned in Part 1 to better understand important concepts in DBT.
- Discuss homework assignments involving the application of the treatment to better understand how to apply the treatment.
- Understand and apply the treatment after teams' presentations.
- Use techniques for strengthening and using the DBT consultation team.
- Practise the techniques of DBT by role playing, as coached by the instructors, and be better able to describe and apply treatment strategies.
- Teach DBT skills as detailed in the DBT skills training manual.
- View and discuss videotaped segments of DBT as modelled by expert therapists and be better able to describe and apply treatment strategies.
- Understand and apply the treatment after team case presentations.

Table 43.2   Typical schedule of in-person, instructor-led intensive training in DBT

8:30–9:00	Registration & Sign-In
9:00–12:30	Morning Session
12:30–1:30	Lunch
1:30–5:15	Afternoon Session
5:15–5:30 (Day 5 ends at 4:30pm)	Evaluations & Sign-out

Table 43.3   Key content domains taught in Part 1 of DBT intensive training

Day 1	Day 2	Day 3	Day 4	Day 5
Foundations of DBT • Behavioural Science • Acceptance Principles • Dialectical Principles DBT Case Formulation Structure of the Treatment • DBT Consultation Team	Functions of Comprehensive Treatment Levels of Disorder & Stages of Treatment Targets of Treatment Orientation & Commitment	DBT Problem Solving • Behavioural Analysis • CBT Procedures Validation Dialectical Strategies	Suicide Risk Assessment & Management Crisis Strategies Treatment of Suicidal Individuals	Stylistic Strategies Case Management Protocols & Special Treatment Strategies

3 concentrates on the core strategies of the treatment, behaviour therapy, and acceptance practices balanced by dialectical strategies. An emphasis on behaviour therapy constitutes a majority of the day's training and includes behavioural analysis, skills training, problem solving, cognitive modification, exposure procedures, and contingency management. Case conceptualization continues with a focus on assessment of skills and chain analyses of target behaviours. Specific exercises are also incorporated to integrate validation and dialectical strategies. Day 4 addresses the assessment, management, and treatment of suicidal behaviour in DBT. Recent trials on DBT (e.g., McMain et al., 2009) indicate that suicide risk assessment and management may be the critical component of the treatment that reduces suicidal behaviour. Teams learn how to incorporate suicidal behaviour and crisis management protocols within their programmes. Case conceptualization continues with a focus on treatment planning related to suicidal behaviours. Day 5 concentrates on stylistic strategies, case management, and special treatment strategies and protocols (e.g., when to conduct prolonged exposure, relationship strategies, ancillary treatments). Table 43.3 outlines the key content domains that are covered in each portion of training. Teams also have an opportunity to engage in planning related to the homework assignments that must be completed prior to Part 2.

Traditional didactic training is supported by discussion, various modelling methods (e.g., viewing recordings of authentic treatment sessions, demonstrations by trainers, and role play with trainees). The strategies and principles of the treatment are also incorporated within the training. For example, mindfulness is included at the start of each day and chain analyses are utilized to target behaviours that interfere with training, such as trainees arriving late. Teams also have opportunities to discuss strategic plans for their programmes and practise conducting DBT consultation team meetings. Team discussions focus on identifying steps for implementing DBT within their setting, defining inclusion and exclusion criteria, developing recruitment strategies for the target population, navigating and restructuring their setting if barriers to implementation exist, and developing strategies to increase the likelihood of implementing all four modes of DBT.

Self-Study and Implementation. The period between the in-person portions of training is designated for trainees to implement the programme, assess barriers, and continue studying DBT. During this period, homework tasks are assigned to facilitate clinical application and implementation of DBT. Trainees complete homework tasks individually (e.g., conduct a chain analysis, practise the DBT skills, read a book on DBT foundations) and on team (e.g., agree to consultation team agreements, define programme inclusion/exclusion criteria, identify barriers to implementation). Trainees must also complete a DBT knowledge exam prior to the second portion of in-person training. This period also provides opportunities to practise complex DBT strategies. A trainer will also initiate a mock suicide crisis call with at least one member of each team and, subsequently, the team must practise a call with each of its members. Additional consultations with a trainer may be included during this period (e.g., observation of the consultation team, review of client sessions).

Part 2. The final portion of training is a five-day in-person instructor-led training. Teams are required to provide a description of their progress in DBT implementation and a conceptualization of a clinical case. This part of the training focuses on assisting the teams to overcome barriers to implementation. Teams interact and learn from each other in a large group consultation format designed to identify successful strategies and methods for overcoming barriers. Trainers provide clinical consultation and a forum for live practice of the DBT strategies based on the presented case formulations. Constructive feedback is provided by trainers and other teams regarding programme structure and case treatment and conceptualization. Trainers structure consultation on cases and programme descriptions to ensure teams receive reinforcement for their work. Additional training on areas of weakness is provided didactically or through practice.

Methods

Didactics. In-person instructor-led training is used to conceptualize and discuss the application of treatment and the domains of knowledge necessary for implementation. An overview of these domains is outlined in Table 43.3.

Demonstration. Audio-visual recordings of authentic therapy sessions from the treatment development laboratory are incorporated to demonstrate treatment to trainees. These recordings have been coded as adherent to DBT and determined to effectively demonstrate a DBT principle, strategy, or skill for training. In addition, trainers maintain a flexibility to demonstrate any specific strategies or skills that arise in the course of training.

Rehearsal. Several methods are utilized to strengthen and generalize participants' skills. Demonstrations are replicated by participants in training events via role play. This allows for accuracy checks and strengthening of skills. In addition, participants are required to complete homework between the two in-person portions of training. Most of the homework requires rehearsal of interventions with team members and clients. For example, trainees are required to practise assessment and management of risk during a mock suicide crisis phone call while being observed by team members.

Implementation. Homework between the two instructor-led portions of training requires specific tasks to be accomplished to support programme development. These are described in a written document that is reviewed for Part 2 of the training and provides the basis for content covered in Part 2. In addition, the required programme description and case formulation provide the basis for consultation at Part 2. Homework also includes practising specific clinical skills, such as behavioural shaping, validation, teaching skills, communication strategies, and crisis calls.

Contingencies. Specific requirements, milestones, and incentives are built into the training to reinforce progress and provide disincentives for non-compliance with training requirements. These include homework score sheets that are required for receiving a Letter of Completion. In some cases, the homework score sheets are used as the basis for a prize that is awarded at Part 2. Participants complete a knowledge test that is scored as part of the training and the test score is included in the homework score sheet. There is also a requirement that teams remain intact for completion of the training.

Supplemental Training

Once DBT programmes with intensively trained teams were being implemented, a need arose for new team members to receive training. Dialectical Behavior Therapy Foundational Training™ was developed later for new members of existing, intensively-trained DBT teams. It provides the training necessary to conduct treatment within functioning DBT programmes. The content covered in foundational training is similar to that covered in the first portion of intensive training. The Dialectical Behavior Therapy Team Building Intensive Training Program™ was also developed to supplement the initial model of intensive training by bringing together solo practitioners and creating virtual teams. By design, the training team of practitioners becomes the DBT consultation team.

Caveats

Completion of intensive training in DBT is not equivalent to certification in DBT or an assessment of a trainee's ability to conduct DBT. Furthermore, the training does not provide certification to programmes. Training provides a thorough exposure to the principles and methods of DBT and allows for practice of important strategies; however, there are no assessments of each trainee's abilities or competencies. While intensive training programmes prepare practitioners for a certification process, the trainings alone do not constitute meeting a particular standard in the provision of DBT.

EVIDENCE FOR DBT INTENSIVE TRAINING

DBT Implementation

DBT is considered one of the most successful dissemination efforts pursued by treatment developers of evidence-based psychological treatments (McHugh & Barlow, 2010), although examination of the intensive training model is still in its infancy. The earliest extensive examination of DBT intensive training surveyed teams trained in the UK between 1994 and 2007 (Swales, Taylor, & Hibbs, 2012). Of the 105 intensively trained teams, nearly 63% were actively running DBT programmes in the two to 15 years since receiving training. DBT programmes were most at risk for failure in the second and fifth years after training. Early results indicated that large-scale training leads to effective implementation and sustainability of DBT, but more research was needed to improve long-term sustainability.

The core programme elements of DBT, modes of treatment, have often been chosen as the variable by which DBT implementation success is evaluated because each mode demonstrates an aspect of successful DBT implementation. As more modes of DBT are implemented, the greater the level of DBT adoption, and without a functioning programme, client outcomes cannot be delivered (Comtois & Landes, this volume). A recent prospective study (Harned et al., 2016) found that 75% of teams implemented all four modes of DBT five to 12 months after intensive training and nearly 87% of teams implemented at least three modes of DBT. Skills training (96.2%) and consultation team (92.3%) were the two modes of DBT most likely to be implemented. Ditty, Landes, Doyle, & Beidas (2015) found that at least one year after attending a DBT intensive training, a purposive sample of clinicians reported high rates of implementation of the four modes of DBT in their programmes. Rates of implementation were very high for individual therapy (96%), group skills training (99%), and consultation team (97%) while implementation of out-of-session phone coaching was moderately high (87%). Taken together, these findings indicate promising evidence for the effectiveness of DBT intensive training to implement the modes of treatment. However, further research is necessary to examine other aspects of treatment implementation.

The effectiveness of intensive training in DBT may be due to many potential factors. For instance, a model that bookends the training process with in-person trainings and includes an extended period of time between—typically six months—establishes protracted contact with trainers compared to traditional one-time workshop trainings. Additionally, a team-based training format may increase the likelihood of adoption and increase reach compared to standard workshops that focus on training individual clinicians. Receiving training as a team may help to reduce the impact of common organizational barriers to implementation of evidence-based therapies and improve clinician motivation. Finally, DBT trainers expressly target increasing clinician motivation throughout the trainings, including a focus on the use of contingency management strategies. Teams are reinforced for completing tasks and changing attitudes/behaviours. Similarly, the team with the highest rate of homework completion during the self-study and implementation phase may be publicly recognized for their achievement. Non-completion of assignments and other training-interfering behaviours are targeted with behavioural chain analyses, problem solving, and contingency management strategies. Finally, the expectation to present the outcomes to an audience may lead to more proactive, rather than passive, implementation actions by trainees.

Factors Influencing DBT Implementation

Different models of implementation (e.g., Beidas & Kendall, 2010) suggest multiple contextual factors are involved in subsequent therapist behaviour regarding treatment implementation after receiving training. Accordingly, it is important to also consider evidence evaluating therapist, organizational, and team factors that may influence successful DBT implementation after training. The role of theoretical orientation, therapist characteristics, attitudes toward evidence-based practices (EBPs), and confidence to deliver a treatment have been studied as factors that could influence DBT implementation. Previous research has indicated that therapists defining themselves within a cognitive-behavioural theoretical orientation have more positive attitudes toward EBPs and are more open to learning and applying EBPs (e.g., Aarons, 2004; Baer et al., 2009; Stewart, Chambless, & Baron, 2011). Although DBT falls under the umbrella of CBT, diverse theoretical orientations are endorsed by practitioners that attend DBT trainings. When examining over 300 intensively trained practitioners, openness to adopting an EBP was significantly lower in the participants that endorsed a theoretical orientation other than CBT/DBT. However, openness scores increased and negative views of EBPs decreased significantly for all participants who completed DBT intensive training, regardless of theoretical orientation (Botanov et al., 2016a). In addition to orientation and attitude, research indicates that therapists who report greater confidence in their ability to deliver a treatment are more likely to adopt the treatment after training (Shapiro, Prinz, & Sanders, 2012), a finding also observed for DBT (Herschell, Lindhiem, Kogan, Celedonia, & Stein, 2014).

Although less studied, another important therapist attribute to consider when implementing DBT is therapist burnout, which is defined as physical and psychological fatigue and exhaustion. Therapist burnout has been thought to be higher for practitioners working with high-risk and difficult-to-treat clients with BPD (Linehan, Cochran, Mar, Levensky, & Comtois, 2000). Two studies have found that receiving training in DBT decreased therapist burn-out and the experience of stress associated with providing treatment (Carmel, Fruzzetti, & Rose, 2014; Perseius, Kaver, Ekdahl, Åsberg, & Samuelsson, 2007), which may in turn facilitate successful DBT implementation. Additionally, when examining trainees attending intensive training in DBT, compared to the population norms for health service professionals, practitioners who did not endorse a CBT or DBT orientation demonstrated significantly higher personal and work burnout at the end of training (Botanov et al., 2016b). This may be potentially due to the added responsibilities of practising within a new theoretical orientation. Similarly, CBT/DBT practitioners scored significantly lower on client burnout at the end of training (Botanov et al., 2016b), which may indicate a reduction in stress when learning about new intervention strategies that correspond with an already adopted theoretical orientation. These findings indicate that theoretical orientation may be a significant factor to consider prior to initiation of intensive DBT training in relation to burnout.

With respect to team factors, Ditty and colleagues (2015) evaluated the relationship between inner setting variables that encompass structural, political, and cultural contexts and DBT implementation. Intensively trained DBT teams with better team cohesion, communication, and climate were associated with implementing a greater number of DBT elements. Furthermore, a prospective evaluation of nine DBT intensive trainings (Harned et al., 2016) found that the proportion of team members with a master's degree or higher, and greater prior DBT experience, predict implementation of more DBT modes. Additionally, a Dutch study (van den Bosch & Sinnaeve, 2015) of 25 intensively trained DBT teams found that sustainability of DBT programmes may be due to the commitment of both the consultation team and its managers. Feeling embedded in an organization as a whole, connection with other practitioners, and feeling supported may indicate that a well-functioning consultation team seems to be of crucial importance for DBT sustainability.

Organizational characteristics are also likely to influence implementation of DBT after training. Nonetheless, organizational factors remain under-discussed in the literature (McHugh & Barlow, 2010). Examining over 100 DBT teams intensively trained in the UK, the most commonly reported reason for programme "deat" was a lack of organizational support (68%), which included factors such as insufficient protected time to deliver DBT, absence of management buy-in, funding difficulties, and insufficient resources (Swales et al., 2012). In another study, organizational factors such as more training and programme needs led to fewer DBT elements implemented (Harned et al., 2016). Another important aspect to consider is penetration or the extent of clients treated after intensive training. Swales and colleagues (2012) found that active programmes (62.8%) reported an average of 15.8 clients per programme at any one time (range 2–60). Little other research has been done examining penetration of DBT after training.

Two studies examined barriers to DBT implementation in public health systems through qualitative interviews with clinicians (Carmel et al., 2014) and administrators

(Herschell, Kogan, Celedonia, Gavin, & Stein, 2009). Both studies found common organizational barriers, including lack of administrative support or investment in DBT, resource concerns, and lack of reduction in clinical responsibilities needed to deliver DBT. Another study (Chugani & Landes, 2016) examined barriers to DBT implementation for programmes in college counselling centers and concluded that productivity demands and lack of individual therapists, time for team consultation, and willingness to offer phone coaching were the most highly endorsed barriers to DBT implementation. These findings underscore common barriers that interfere with successful DBT implementation but further research is needed.

In addition to investigating DBT modes implemented, factors related to provider behaviours, such as adherence to the principles, strategies, and procedures of the treatment, may influence successful DBT implementation. Although more research is needed, knowledge of DBT is also strongly associated with completing intensive training across mental health disciplines (Hawkins & Sinha, 1998). It is important to develop instruments to measure in-session adherence in naturalistic settings. Currently, very few options are available to examine adherence to DBT by intensively trained practitioners.

Early examination of intensive DBT trainings and other DBT implementation efforts indicate that while immediate post-training implementation outcomes are strong, sustained implementation beyond the initial training effort requires additional organizational supports. Understanding the implementation process for DBT requires further refinement of valid and reliable measures. Recently, the psychometric properties of the DBT Barriers to Implementation Scale (BTI-S) were tested with data collected from intensive trainings (Chugani, Mitchell, Botanov, & Linehan, 2017). The findings indicate that the measure assesses four domains considered important for implementation of DBT reasonably well. However, the low reliability of the scores suggests that the BTI-S would be improved with further development. Refining measures to evaluate predictors of DBT implementation and elements implemented combined with more rigorous research designs including randomized controlled trials and follow-up after training, are needed. Adherence of provider behaviours, as well as reach, may be factors to explore in future research studies. Furthermore, the effect of client characteristics on successful DBT implementation may be another important variable to investigate.

CONCLUSIONS AND FUTURE DIRECTIONS

DBT is an evidence-based treatment for disorders of emotion regulation that has global reach with successful implementations in almost 30 countries across six continents. Adoption of DBT has been widespread and the demand from providers and mental health systems remains high. The intensive training model for DBT is, in part, the reason for the successful global dissemination. The model has, through an iterative process, evolved by consistent self-examination via empirical research over nearly 25 years. In these ways, the training model development has mirrored the development of DBT itself.

While significant gains have been made in the training of DBT providers, there are limitations. Trained DBT practitioners are reaching far fewer people than the total number of those who need the treatment. Our conservative estimate is that the global need—to help individuals experiencing high levels of distress from difficulties in emotion regulation during their lifetime—is 135 million people (for review, see DuBose, Botanov, & Ivanoff, this volume). While there have been no clear ways to estimate the number of people who have received DBT, we are certain that the number falls far short of the need. It may be that in-person instructor-led training will never be sufficient to reach the needed numbers, and new models of training must be developed and investigated. One area that needs serious consideration is remote training, specifically, the use of online media. Also, as treatment development studies further identify the therapeutic components of DBT, training models may become more parsimonious to address these specific critical components.

KEY MESSAGES FOR CLINICIANS

- Along with evidence-based psychological treatments, there is also a need for evidence-based training.
- An intensive model of training in DBT was developed to meet the growing demand that could not be met through traditional training methods.
- The model of DBT intensive training typically is provided as a bipartite training consisting of two five-day workshops separated by a period for self-study and implementation.
- Strategies and principles of the treatment are also incorporated within the training, such as mindfulness at the start of each training day and chain analyses targeting behaviours that interfere with training.
- Early evaluations of DBT intensive training have demonstrated successful initial implementation and adoption of DBT modes. However, further research is needed to examine long-term sustainability and treatment penetration.

REFERENCES

Aarons, G. A. (2004). Mental health provider attitudes toward adoption of evidence-based practice: The Evidence-Based Practice Attitude Scale (EBPAS). *Mental Health Services Research, 6*, 61–74.

Baer, J. S., Wells, E. A., Rosengren, D. B., Hartzler, B., Beadnell, B., & Dunn, C. (2009). Agency context and tailored training in technology transfer: A pilot evaluation of motivational interviewing training for community counselors. *Journal of Substance Abuse Treatment, 37*, 191–202.

Beidas, R. S., & Kendall, P. C. (2010). Training therapists in evidence-based practice: A critical review of studies from a systems-contextual perspective. *Clinical Psychology: Science and Practice, 17*, 1–30.

Botanov, Y., DuBose, A. P., Korslund, K. E., Ivanoff, A. M., Kikuta, B., & Linehan, M. M. (2016a). Implementing dialectical behavior therapy: The relationship between therapeutic orientation, burnout, and attitudes. Poster presented at The Dissemination and Implementation Science SIG of ABCT, New York, NY.

Botanov, Y., Kikuta, B., Chen, T., Navarro-Haro, M., DuBose, A. P., Korslund, K. E., & Linehan, M. M. (2016b). Attitudes toward evidence-based practices across therapeutic orientations. Proceedings of the 3rd Biennial Conference of the Society for Implementation Research Collaboration (SIRC) 2015: advancing efficient methodologies through community partnerships and team science. *Implementation Science, 11*(Suppl 1), A37.

Carmel, A., Fruzzetti, A. E., & Rose, M. L. (2014). Dialectical behavior therapy training to reduce clinical burnout in a public behavioral health system. *Community Mental Health Journal, 50*, 25–30.

Chugani, C. D., & Landes, S. J. (2016). Dialectical behavior therapy in college counseling centers: current trends and barriers to implementation. *Journal of College Student Psychotherapy, 30*(3), 176–186.

Chugani, C., Mitchell, M., Botanov, Y., & Linehan, M. M. (2017). Development and initial evaluation of the psychometric properties of the Dialectical Behavior Therapy Barriers to Implementation Scale (BTI-S). *Journal of Clinical Psychology, 73*(12), 1704–1716.

Ditty, M. S., Landes, S. J., Doyle, A., & Beidas, R. S. (2015). It takes a village: A mixed method analysis of inner setting variables and dialectical behavior therapy implementation. *Administration and Policy in Mental Health and Mental Health Services Research, 42*(6), 672–681.

Harned, M. S., Navarro-Haro, M. V., Korslund, K. E., Chen, T., DuBose, A. P., Ivanoff, A., & Linehan, M. M. (2016). Rates and predictors of implementation after Dialectical Behavior Therapy Intensive Training. Proceedings of the 3rd Biennial Conference of the Society for Implementation Research Collaboration (SIRC) 2015: advancing efficient methodologies through community partnerships and team science. *Implementation Science, 11*(Suppl 1), A57.

Hawkins, K. A. & Sinha, R. (1998). Can line clinicians master the conceptual complexities of dialectical behavior therapy? An evaluation of a State Department of Mental Health training program. *Journal of Psychiatric Research, 32*, 379–384.

Herschell, A. D., Kogan, J. N., Celedonia, K. L., Gavin, J. G., & Stein, B. D. (2009). Understanding community mental health administrators' perspectives on dialectical behavior therapy implementation. *Psychiatric Services, 60*(7), 989–992.

Herschell, A. D., Lindhiem, O. J., Kogan, J. N., Celedonia, K. L., & Stein, B. D. (2014). Evaluation of an implementation initiative for embedding Dialectical Behavior Therapy in community settings. *Evaluation and Program Planning, 43*(2), 55–63.

Linehan, M. M. (1993). *Cognitive-behavioral treatment of borderline personality disorder.* New York, NY: Guilford Press.

Linehan, M. M. (2015). *DBT® skills training manual*, 2nd Edition. New York, NY: Guilford Press.

Linehan, M. M., Cochran, B. N., Mar, C. M., Levensky, E. R., & Comtois, K. A. (2000). Therapeutic burnout among borderline personality disordered clients and their therapists: Development and evaluation of two adaptations of the Maslach Burnout Inventory. *Cognitive and Behavioral Practice, 7*(3), 329–337.

McHugh, R. K., & Barlow, D. H. (2010). The dissemination and implementation of evidence-based psychological treatments: a review of current efforts. *American Psychologist, 65*(2), 73.

McMain, S. F., Links, P. S., Gnam, W. H., Guimond, T., Cardish, R. J., Korman, L., & Streiner, D. L. (2009). A randomized trial of dialectical behavior therapy versus general psychiatric management for borderline personality disorder. *American Journal of Psychiatry*, *166*(12), 1365–1374.

Perseius, K. I., Kaver, A., Ekdahl, S., Åsberg, M., & Samuelsson, M. (2007). Stress and burnout in psychiatric professionals when starting to use dialectical behavioural therapy in the work with young self-harming women showing borderline personality symptoms. *Journal of Psychiatric & Mental Health Nursing*, *14*(7), 635–643.

Shapiro, C. J., Prinz, R. J., & Sanders, M. R. (2012). Facilitators and barriers to the implementation of an evidence-based parenting intervention to prevent child maltreatment: The Triple P-Positive Parenting Program. *Child Maltreatment*, *17*, 86–95.

Stewart, R. E., Chambless, D. L., & Baron, J. (2011). Theoretical and practical barriers to practitioners' willingness to seek training in empirically supported treatments. *Journal of Clinical Psychology*, *68*, 8–23.

Swales, M. A., Taylor, B., & Hibbs, R. A. (2012). Implementing dialectical behaviour therapy: Programme survival in routine healthcare settings. *Journal of Mental Health*, *21*(6), 548–555.

van den Bosch, L., & Sinnaeve, R. (2015). Dialectische gedragstherapie in Nederland: Implementatie en consolidatie. *Tijdschrift voor Psychiatrie*, *57*(10), 719–727.

Weissman, M. M., Verdeli, H., Gameroff, M. J., Bledsoe, S. E., Betts, K., Mufson, L., . . . Wickramaratne, P. (2006). National survey of psychotherapy training in psychiatry, psychology, and social work. *Archives of General Psychiatry*, *63*(8), 925–934.

CHAPTER 44

SHAPING THERAPISTS TOWARDS ADHERENCE
A How-to Guide

AMY GAGLIA

FIDELITY, ADHERENCE, COMPETENCE

Treatment fidelity, adherence, and competence are three essential constructs in the transfer of evidence-based psychotherapeutic interventions from controlled research conditions to community practice. Within the literature regarding the dissemination and implementation of evidence-based therapies, some authors refer to treatment fidelity (e.g., Dorsey, 2016) while others refer to treatment adherence (e.g., Perepletchikova & Kazdin, 2005) when describing the concept of whether a therapist actually provided the therapy as written about in the treatment manual. This latter use of the term adherence contrasts with the typical use of the term in medical treatment and in some psychological interventions, where adherence to treatment generally refers to the practice of the recipient of the intervention. For example, patient behaviour related to pill taking or engagement in prescribed therapeutic activities would typically be referred to as adherence and, in the treatment of Obsessive Compulsive Disorder, adherence to treatment might refer to the frequency and duration with which a client engaged in exposure and response prevention work in a given time period. Finally, competence relates to the practitioner skill level once they have already reached a minimum level of fidelity to a prescribed intervention.

Whilst therapists, patients, and commissioners can reasonably assume that an intervention provided in accordance with the evidence base will yield the same or similar results as those produced in the research establishing that evidence base, transferring treatments from research into practice settings is not so straightforward (Comtois & Landes, this volume). Using two terms, fidelity and adherence, to describe how closely a system follows a treatment manual in its delivery of an intervention could, in these circumstances, potentially be confusing. From a DBT perspective, however, the two terms can prove helpful in describing different aspects of implementation. First, with respect to fidelity, therapists and care systems choose to implement *specific* therapeutic interventions with *specific* populations based on the scientific validation of the efficacy of a treatment technology for use with a *specific* condition or set of behaviours. The extent to which the various components of a given model are implemented can be considered a measure of *fidelity* to the model. Delivering DBT with fidelity requires installation and execution of programme modalities according to the principles in the treatment manual. Based on research on DBT, a therapist with the intention to provide DBT with fidelity would establish a programme that provides manualized individual therapy and group skills training, between session generalization telephone contact, and therapist peer consultation meetings. From the perspective of fidelity to the model, these provisions also apply regardless of whether a therapist is implementing standard DBT or one of the evidence-based adaptions of DBT.

In DBT, therapist *adherence* refers to the accuracy with which the therapist delivers the strategies of the treatment as described in the manual. Therapists are often able to achieve fidelity, but may struggle to provide adherent DBT therapy, i.e., to engage in therapist behaviour that matches the manual. Later sections of this chapter will review common barriers to achieving adherence in DBT. While therapists may be able to provide therapy adherent to the manual, they may struggle to provide DBT at the highest level of competence. Fidelity and adherence are precursors to competence. Thus, how is adherence in DBT measured?

Early trials in DBT, like many clinical trials of other evidence-based practices conducted at that time, did not routinely assess whether therapists in the trial were delivering the treatment as specified. Scheel's (2000) review and critique of the research on DBT, as well as Koerner and Dimeff's direct response (2000), outline some of the issues with the earlier research on DBT. A lack of a measure of fidelity to the model is not specifically mentioned in these papers, although the implication is that the earlier positive results may be the result of a Type 1 error, which specifies that it is not possible to determine if the positive results of a study are attributable to the invention or to the presence of a contaminant, e.g., be receiving expert supervision in psychotherapy. As Resnick and Ziporkin (2012) suggest, a measure of treatment fidelity helps reduce Type 1 errors (although it does not guarantee that they have been eliminated) by establishing that the intervention was delivered in adherence with the manual. Thus, following some of the critiques of the early research on DBT and a general shift in the zeitgeist to favour fidelity measures to reduce Type 1 errors, a scale was developed and constructed to measure adherence in DBT.

Finalized in 2003, after many iterations, the University of Washington DBT Adherence Coding Scale (ACS: Linehan & Korslund, 2003) consists of 66 items distributed across 12 sub-scales that, with the exception of the subscale on validation, are addressed in Linehan's original (1993) manual; the subscale on validation was constructed from a later chapter (Linehan, 1997). The same scale measures adherence in individual sessions as well as group skills training classes. Behaviours of therapists providing adaptions of

DBT such as DBT-S or DBT for Adolescents can also be successfully measured using the DBT ACS. While the DBT ACS represents an important step in codifying adherent DBT practice and is intended for research purposes, it is not easily transferable to community practice because the tool is long and mastering reliability takes some time. As the scale is broad, technical, and focuses on observable behaviour, adherence to the model is not synonymous with competence in the model. A discussion of the finer details of the scale itself, including its sensitivity to quality, exceeds the scope of this chapter. However, the DBT-ACS captures the issues laid out by Perepletchikova and Kazdin (2005) regarding measuring therapist adherence to a manualized treatment: namely, the scale comprises the strategies in the textbook summarized in the boxes entitled "DBT therapist does" and "Anti-DBT" (Linehan, 1993) and the validation article (Linehan, 1997).

Adherence rating in DBT appraises a therapist's delivery of the intervention. The DBT ACS embodies a dialectical world view, perhaps most helpfully thought of here as an "it depends" world view. While the tool is anchored to the treatment manual, it is complex to administer because it frequently applies "if-then" rules. Of the 66 items, 16 are required in every session, i.e., the presence or absence of the majority of strategies is based on therapist reactions and responses to client behaviours in the moment. Some strategies, such as validation Level 5, are required in a DBT session, although many of the strategies are required only under certain conditions (described in the treatment manual). For example: two items on the coding scale ask for "commitment" and "troubleshooting." Neither of these items are required in every session. However, if commitment to treatment, to a new behaviour, or to a new intervention is required, then the therapist is required to "troubleshoot" with the client to identify what might get in the way of following through on that commitment. One potential risk arising from this construction of the adherence rating scale is that therapists may become overly focused on providing the "required" components of a DBT session, thereby limiting in-session flexibility, which may paradoxically diminish their effectiveness and competence with a given client in a given moment: adherent DBT is always about the moment.

The DBT-ACS manual specifies that adherence is not an objective quality of the therapist, but rather that the therapist may conduct an adherent session. In a dialectical manner, adherent sessions are a product of one moment in time between a particular dyad. Nevertheless, when the therapist produces multiple sessions that have been rated as adherent, the DBT community typically assumes that that given therapist possesses the skills to deliver adherent DBT; thus, if a reliably adherent therapist is not producing adherent sessions then there is an issue occurring in that moment in time with that specific dyad, which requires support of the consultation team or a supervisor.

DOES ADHERENCE IN DBT MATTER?

Randomized controlled trials (RCTs) are the gold standard of research with respect to psychological therapies, and are used to establish an evidence base for an intervention.

As such, in examining the issue of adherence, we examined the RCTs on DBT because RCTs are the studies most likely to include measures on adherence that establish that the intended intervention was actually delivered. DBT is the most studied intervention for the treatment of Borderline Personality Disorder (Stoffers, Völlm, Rücke, Huband, & Leib, 2012), with a total of twenty-one RCTs (see Miga et al., this volume; Andreasson et al., 2016; Bohus et al., 2013; Carter, Wilcox, Lewin, Conrad, & Bendit, 2010; Clarkin, Levy, Lenzenberg, & Kernberg, 2007; Courbasson, Nishikawa, & Dixon, 2012; Feigenbaum et al., 2012; Goldstein et al., 2015; Harned, Korslund, & Linehan, 2014; Koons et al., 2001; Linehan, 2002; Linehan, Armstrong, Suarez, Allmon, & Heard, 1991; Linehan, Tutek, Heard, & Armstrong, 1994; Linehan et al., 1999; Linehan et al., 2006; Linehan et al., 2015; Lynch et al., 2007; McMain et al., 2009; Mehlum et al., 2014; Pistorello, Fruzzetti, MacLane, Gallop, & Iverson, 2012; Priebe et al., 2012; Turner, 2000; van den bosch, Koeter, Stijnem, Verheul, & van den Brink 2002, 2005; Verheul et al., 2003). Adherence or fidelity to treatment is measured and mentioned in at least 16 of the studies, although when it is mentioned, it is generally to state that therapists have or have not been checked for their adherence to the treatment manual. Generally, model adherence is not a variable examined with respect to client outcome. The few instances in which therapist adherence to the model is correlated to client outcome are described next.

Linehan et al. (1999) published a RCT that compared DBT with treatment as usual (TAU) for women with a comorbid diagnosis of BPD and drug dependence. Patients in the DBT arm of the trial showed great reductions in drug use, as measured through structured interviews and urine analysis, while in treatment and in follow up than those receiving TAU. In addition, patients in the DBT arm stayed in treatment longer and showed greater gains in global and social adjustment at follow up than patients in the TAU arm of the study. From the perspective of adherence, a most interesting facet of this paper is that the authors measured adherence to the model using the DBT Expert Rating Scale (Linehan, Wagner, & Tutek, 1990), a precursor to the DBT ACS. Therapists in this study who were consistently more faithful to the model had client outcomes that were superior to therapists who were not consistently adherent to the model.

In contrast to the results related to therapist adherence and client outcomes, Koons et al.'s (2001) effectiveness study of DBT for women veterans also examined adherence to the model using the DBT Expert Rating Scale. Therapists providing DBT in the study were, on average, adherent to model. The sample size in the study was very small, with only ten in the treatment arm.

RCTs conducted after the empirical validation and publication of the DBT ACS (2003) that employed the scale demonstrated similar outcomes to the original Linehan et al. 1991 study (e.g., Harned et al., 2010; Linehan et al., 2006; Priebe et al., 2012; van den Bosch et al., 2005; Verheul et al., 2003) in terms of reductions in self-harming behaviour. Each of these studies benefited from the ability to answer the question: did research therapists actually provide DBT, irrespective of the study being an efficacy or effectiveness study and regardless of whether or not it employed intention to treat analysis? Verheul et al. (2003) and their follow-up study (van den Bosch et al., 2005) found that therapists whose average adherence rating was 3.8, just below adherence to DBT, were able to receive expected reductions in non-suicidal self-injurious behaviour while they did not achieve the same results in reduction in substance misuse as in other DBT research. Linehan et al. (2006), Harned et al. (2010), and Priebe et al. (2012) all reported that therapists were adherent to the model, but therapist adherence was not examined as a possible cause of change for clients. Thus, measures of adherence in RCTs generally only show whether therapists did DBT, but we are left to infer that doing DBT is necessary; additionally, the Verheul and van den Bosch studies each suggest that doing something close to DBT may also yield effective results.

If we broaden the question slightly and consider whether therapists' adherence to an evidenced-based treatment manual impacts client outcomes in other manualized treatments such as CBT, we are faced with mixed results, with some studies suggesting that therapist adherence to the evidence-based treatment positively impacts outcomes (e.g., Hogue et al., 2008) and others finding that strong adherence to a model hinders client progress in certain instances (Hauke et al., 2013; Huppert, Barlow, Gorman, Shear, & Woods, 2006). Boswell et al. (2013) suggest that the conflicting results regarding the importance of adherence to a model or not with respect to client outcomes has to do with the heterogeneous nature of patients and the importance of context specific interventions. Manualized treatments do not generally have attendance to the therapeutic relationship as part of the protocol, which turns out to be an extremely important factor as more recent research has demonstrated that therapist adherence to a model can shift from client to client (Boswell et al., 2013). Thus, with DBT's focus on the therapeutic relationship as an integral part of the treatment, it may be that, after further research into client outcomes and therapist adherence to the model, we will be able to definitively address the importance of adherence to the model.

TOWARDS ADHERENCE: STARTING WITH COMMITMENT

While data derived from RCTs thus far is ambiguous in terms of the relationship between adherence and clinical outcomes, endeavouring to deliver the treatment as designed is an important principle to follow until more is known about which aspects of the treatment are essential for good outcomes. Therapist commitment to strive for adherence to and competence in DBT represents the first step in this endeavour. Therapists commence with reading the texts (Linehan, 1993; Linehan, 2015a, b) and attending trainings that educate them about the different functions and modes of therapy as well as the treatment strategies. Swales (2010a) reviews the importance of commitment in the implementation literature and applies the principles of obtaining commitment to the organization seeking to implement DBT. Equally, commitment to learning and delivering the treatment adherently may require some work on the part of the therapist. Therapists working on research trials are hired with the explicit expectation that they will learn and apply a treatment adherently—but rarely is this a requirement for therapists in routine care settings. Some therapists embarking on learning DBT may find this insistence on delivering adherent therapy both surprising and onerous. Explicitly outlining this commitment to them and gaining their commitment to it is useful for DBT trainers and team leaders alike.

TRAINING, LEARNING THE DBT MODEL, SUPERVISION, AND CONSULTATION TEAM

The most common and standard route of training in DBT is "intensive training" described by Swales (2010b) and DuBose, Botanov, Navarro-Haro, & Linehan (this volume). Teams of at least four mental health professionals, including (in the UK at least) a psychologist trained to post-graduate level, attend ten days of training spread over six to eight months. The first week of training focuses on teaching the strategies. The team then goes away and practises what they have learned through providing the therapy, often establishing from scratch a functioning DBT provision, as well as through tailored homework assignments and an exam. They return for a second week of training and present their work, receive coaching and feedback designed to increase their adherence and competence to the model, as well as some additional didactic training. After intensive training, team members may seek additional training in DBT or arrange for supervision. Outcomes from Intensive Training are discussed in DuBose et al. (this volume).

DBT can be a "tricky" therapy in the sense that it brings together many different paradigms, and inevitably some aspects of the therapy will be more comfortable than others to a given therapist. Sometimes DBT therapists gravitate towards strategies that are most comfortable or familiar to them and furthermore, sometimes this behaviour can be rewarded! For example, because the scale encompasses all of DBT and is an off-shoot of CBT, it is possible that a CBT therapist might be able to have an adherent DBT session using primarily CBT strategies. Also, sometimes when learning DBT and observing the richness and inclusiveness of it, therapists may incorporate strategies that might not be in the model, for example, interpreting a client's behaviour in a psychodynamic manner.

Falling back on professional training and not "buying into" DBT as a discrete and unique treatment also hinders therapists' ability to adhere to the DBT model. Dorsey, Berliner, Lyon, Pullmann, & Murray (2014) write about therapists' decisions about whether to modify a CBT therapy or not, and the research suggests that therapists who are less experienced, have less confidence in the model, and are not trained in the model "voluntarily" (e.g., the motivation for doing so was related to career advancement, or as edicts from management) are more likely to modify the treatment to be closer to the paradigm with which they are more comfortable (Dorsey, 2016). Other research suggests that more highly trained and experienced therapists drift out of adherence in response to their perception of their client's needs or other issues related to the therapeutic interaction (Boswell et al., 2013).

Research on models for learning DBT suggests that there are a number of effective ways to acquire the model. Frederick and Comtois' 2006 study on DBT training for psychiatric residents found that the dose of training received impacts a therapist's practice. Dimeff, Woodcock, Harned, and Beadnell (2011) experimented with different teaching conditions to acquire DBT: one based on working with the manual only, one based on e-learning, and the third on doing nothing. Therapist knowledge of DBT was measured at various points. The control group that received no learning on DBT did not demonstrate any changes in DBT knowledge. After 15 weeks, e-learning, which was preferred by participants, out-performed learning from the manual for acquiring DBT knowledge. Dimeff, Harned, Woodcock, Skutch, Koerner, and Linehan (2015) tested three conditions for learning DBT: instructor led, e-learning, and reading the treatment manual. Instructor-led learning was rated highest in therapist satisfaction, self-efficacy, and motivation, whereas e-learning was the most effective method for increasing knowledge. Earlier research by Dimeff et al. (2009) suggested that certain strategies in DBT, such as validation strategies, are easily taught through e-learning, while more complex strategies, such as chain analysis, are more effectively taught with instructors.

The positive results related to e-learning match other work on the dissemination of evidenced-based manualized treatments. Sholomskas and Carroll (2006) demonstrated that computer-assisted learning versus studying the manual alone was more effective for therapists learning a skills-based intervention for alcohol use. Beidas and Kendall's (2010) review of existing literature on training of therapists in evidence-based psychotherapies concludes that training is very effective for teaching therapists new skills, but the degree to which these skills will be implemented depends on the system in which the therapist is working.

Finally, from a slightly different angle, Koerner (2013) recommends breaking DBT and other evidence-based therapies into component parts that are acquired by therapists, rather than using the current standard practice of attempting to have therapists acquire the entire manualized therapy at once. While acknowledging the lack of research on this, she suggests teaching therapists to conceptualize the treatment in terms of the biosocial theory, and ameliorating deficits in client functioning related to biological vulnerability and the invalidating environment. Koerner then suggests using problem-solving strategies that treat emotional dysregulation and to add validation and dialectics when needed. For therapist effectiveness, she suggests that consultation team treats the therapist and promotes mindfulness and reiterative practice of the treatment strategies, while finally teaching therapists how to structure the treatment environment.

In learning and improving one's ability to deliver a complex therapy such as DBT supervision is essential (Carmel, Vilatte, Rosenthal, Chalker, & Comtois, 2014; Milne and Westerman, 2001; Schoenwald, Mehta, Frazier, & Schenoff, 2013; Weissman et al., 2006). Swales (2010b) discusses the possibility that therapists in community practice without the same supervisory input may fail to achieve the same results as those obtained in DBT efficacy studies. Dorsey et al. (2013) similarly emphasizes that a component of successful community transfer of evidence-based practice must centre on creating similar supervision and training conditions as those that were provided in the research that established the evidence base to begin with.

Research and experimentation with different types of supervision provides guidance on useful methods to enhance learning of DBT strategies. A small study examined Bug in the Eye (BITE) technology, which provided directions to therapists during sessions with a supervisor suggesting strategies through a teleprompter behind the client's head as the session proceeded (Carmel et al., 2014). BITE recipients had more "book" knowledge as measured on a written exam than the control group that received supervision as usual. Rizvi (2016) presented a case study using BITE technology which suggested that therapist adherence as measured by the DBT ACS increased as a result of using the technology. One conclusion from this research is that recursive practice of strategy identification when paired with actual therapy sessions appears to be of high value in shaping therapist practice.

The type of activities engaged in through the supervisory process may influence the move towards fidelity or adherence to the model. Beidas, Cross, and Dorsey (2014) in their study of CBT examined the relationship between supervision and a clinician's fidelity to an evidence-based model. They discovered the most effective supervision condition requires supervisees to "show" their work through the use of tapes, as well as role play and checking on homework assignments, and not "tell" or describe their therapeutic engagement with a client. In order to demonstrate work, a therapist could bring in a video or audio recording of a segment of the session with a client, a process recording, or could be asked in the moment to role play the strategy with the supervisor.

DBT has ongoing supervision of the therapist built into using consultation team, which is described over two concise chapters in Swales and Heard (2017). Linehan (1993) describes the consultation team meeting as the forum in which therapists apply the therapy to themselves, and Koerner (2012) adds that consultation team members must come to the meeting prepared to discuss a situation with a client and then to analyse their own behaviour, hence "therapy for the therapist" (see Sayrs, this volume). The most common barrier to consultation team being the most effective form of supervision or shaping towards adherence is the DBT training structure. As a team training together, most of the consultation team members all have the same level of DBT skill and there will be no one with the skills and knowledge to correct drift from the model. Thus, input must come from an expert post training either to the team as a whole or to the team lead to prevent a team from developing anti-DBT practices, and to aid the team members in progressing their skill level.

Additionally, consultation teams develop cultures, and while there is no empirical evidence at present regarding the barriers to effective adherence to DBT on the consultation team, anecdotally from providing external consultation to teams, we know that consultation team members commonly experience, for example, unhelpful cognitions and aversive emotions about asserting themselves or "requiring" colleagues to demonstrate their work. Rizvi (2011) provides a useful discussion of treatment failure in DBT and the role of consultation team. Colleagues can be reluctant to benevolently demand behaviour from each other and will default to accepting a therapist's description.

Box 44.1   Clinical example of Consultation Team difficulty: Violation of consultation team agreement

Clinical example introduction

In a Consultation Team meeting of five members, the Team Leader Ann is presenting her client, Tracey, who, for the fourth week in a row, has self-harmed, after months of not doing so. Ann is very worried about the reoccurrence of this behaviour and has many thoughts about being an "awful" therapist. After the first episode of self-harm, Ann increased her contact with the client, and now after four weeks is having daily contact with the client, despite the fact that this violates the 24-hour rule. Ann reports that Tracey is "grateful" for the extra support, but everyone on the team notices that this "support" has not reduced the behaviour, while at the same time it appears that Ann is becoming more anxious, less effective, and appears increasingly more worn out. Ann has asked for consultation for the third time on "how to get Tracey to stop self-harming again." Various members of the team offer different skills that Ann might try to have Tracey use, and one member tries to discern the controlling variable for Tracey's behaviour. A number of team members have worry thoughts about Ann's behaviour with the client, and about Ann's ability to sustain her commitment to this client; some are experiencing low levels of annoyance that the same issue is coming up week after week, but no one addresses it. In fact, quite the opposite, as most people are speaking with sympathetic tones and offering Ann reassurance that she is a "good" therapist and that it will all work out well. In addition, one team member voices to Ann the thought that she is the team leader, so therefore she must be doing the "right" things.

What are some of the problems (and adherent corrections) here with the potentially common scenario?

In no particular order, the consultation team is not applying the principles of the therapy to Ann. A team adherent to the model would seek to perform a behavioural chain analysis (BCA) on Ann's interactions with Tracey around the issue of self-harm. Behavioural chain analysis would be followed by a solution analysis, and the solutions would include not only recommendations on what Ann might ask Tracey to do, but importantly also focus on changes Ann might make in her own behaviour, including potentially accepting that all therapists, including herself, are fallible. In doing the BCA, the team would be looking for the thoughts and changes in emotional experience that underpin or potentially reinforce Ann's behaviour with Tracey. There would be a number of different points that the team could help Ann to analyse. Ann could be encouraged to bring a recording to Consultation Team as well or to demonstrate her behaviour by interacting with a team member. She could also be asked to practise by role playing or putting into place one or more of the solutions generated. The team would also help Ann identify and troubleshoot anything that might get in the way of using the solutions when working with Tracey.

In terms of the Consultation Team itself, the person acting as the observer of the day would notice that Consultation Team agreements are potentially being violated. The observer, or if this is a separate role on this team, the person who is responsible in a given week will notice and alert the team to instances in which the therapists are treating each other as fragile, and not describing mindfully their own reactions and assessments of a

---

Box 44.1 Continued

---

colleague's behaviour. Firstly, Ann is violating the 24-hour rule. Ann also appears to be suffering a great deal, and no one is labelling this! Once someone names the "elephant in the room," it may be an opportunity to drop the agenda and do a mini-behavioural and solution analysis on how the "elephant" was allowed to roam, and to implement corrective solutions to remove the "elephant." Once this is done, the team moves back to the agenda item to remain dialectical and mindful that the moment has passed. However, if there is "merciless" elephant pursuit, this is observed as well. Additionally, the Consultation Team is treating Ann as fragile by soothing her. Here, soothing Ann is invalidating because at this moment in time thoughts about not being effective with Tracey are correct; however, the team may need to help Ann into expressing these thoughts non-judgmentally, rather than as "awful". Additionally, the statement that Ann is the team leader and must know what she is doing violates the fallibility agreement. Similarly, the dialectical agreement may be violated as well, as outwardly the team appears to be unanimously soothing to Ann, while offering solutions that are all based on Tracey changing in some way. The observer would notice these violations, highlight them for the team by ringing the bell, and describe what was observed. As a team moves towards greater competence in the model, it may enough for the observer to ring the bell as a signal for each member of the team to be mindful that an agreement has been violated and to cue proceeding more mindfully without describing the violation.

Individual supervision may be more likely to focus on therapist role play and showing their work, although it can be expensive to procure expert supervision. Swales (2010b) also addresses this issue and highlights the need to apply the strategies of the "therapy for the therapists," e.g., helping them mindfully describe practice, identify their own cognitions, emotions, action urges, and behaviours, engage in contingency management, exposure, cognitive modification or increased skills, etc., and accordingly increase "adherence" to the DBT model. Swales writes that "A vital strategy here, in the treatment of therapists just as much as for the client—is rehearsal, rehearsal, rehearsal" (2010b, p. 6). Box 44.1 offers a clinical example of violating the DBT Consultation Team Agreements, which is a common consultation team problem.

INDIVIDUAL THERAPIST ADHERENCE: COMMON OBSTACLES AND SOLUTIONS

While there are no systematic reviews or research into types of errors in acquiring the capacity to deliver adherent DBT, there have been only a small group of practitioners trained in the reliable measurement of DBT sessions using the DBT ACS. In clinical and research session reviews of therapists according to the DBT ACS, a body of knowledge has been acquired about common difficulties that therapists encounter in their journey into acquiring competency in the treatment. This section reviews problems that occur with session structure, session targeting, problem-solving, and dialectical balance.

Problems in Session Structure

Session structure shapes the content of the session. Thus, if the structure is awry, it is highly likely that the session will be ineffective. Required structural strategies include reviewing the diary card, reviewing homework or other changes since the last session, setting a session agenda based on the treatment hierarchy (i.e., life–destroying behaviours), followed by therapy-interfering behaviours (TIBs) and quality-of-life-interfering behaviours. The session ends with strategies that are designed to help a client "close up" from the session and convey that the therapeutic relationship continues after the interaction is over. A focus on emotion is also required as DBT is a treatment for problems of emotion dysregulation.

There are some structural strategies beyond those required that may apply in specific instances. For example, when a client comes to session in a high state of distress, the therapist is required to attend to this first before pursuing other agenda items and sometimes this requirement can create problematic patterns. For example, Sally comes into most sessions crying, hyperventilating, and complaining about how she will never be able to get home after becoming dysregulated by the bus ride to the clinic. Alexis, her therapist, spends the first 20 minutes of the session helping Sally regulate herself, and then has very little time, let alone energy, to review the diary card, which generally has at least one episode of self-harm on it, and conduct a behavioural chain and solution analysis with behavioural rehearsal. This pattern has been going on for two months. She needs the help of her consultation team to practise how she will address this TIB and find strategies to work through it. Options here might include focusing on mindfulness of the present moment and opposite action all the way to fear, which is an exercise Sally needs to practise in order to reduce her dysregulation prior to coming into the therapy room.

Targeting Problems

After pretreatment, the first few minutes of session involves the therapist asking for the diary card and reviewing it together with the client to pull out a problem to work on in the session. The problem or problems of the week are selected based on the treatment hierarchy. Sticking to the hierarchy can be problematic for therapists and clients who may believe that other issues are more pressing.

For example, a common targeting problem exists for Suzy, who came to session with a diary card indicating that she had self-harmed during the week. Suzy and her therapist Steve reviewed the diary card together, and Steve stated their top priority for the session was to behaviourally analyse the episode of self-harm. Suzy's reply was that this was not her real problem—she only self-harms when she binges and purges and that she believed they should be talking about her weight issues instead. Here, Steve is undecided about how to proceed; he believes that a therapist "should" be client centred, and he experiences the emotions of fear and shame when Suzy is irritated with him. He decides to proceed with Suzy's agenda, knowing that the DBT treatment hierarchy states that her life-threatening behaviour must be targeted ahead of quality-of-life-interfering behaviour, but he finds Suzy reluctant to discuss her self-harming and that she is much more collaborative when discussing her eating disorder. Steve decides to target Suzy's eating disorder, and in doing so experienced a reduction of his painful negative emotions. While the session contained many behaviours that are technically adherent to the model, at the same time, in true dialectical fashion, Steve failed to provide competent DBT because he did not address the life-threatening behaviour or the TIB. Steve would have been more effective had he stuck to the hierarchy and analysed the self-harming episode with guilt about purging as its prompting event. He could have used the client's willingness to work on eating disordered behaviour as a contingency to shape willingness to address self-harming, namely, by stating that he would like to look at that behaviour as well if there is time, assuring Suzy that once the self-harming is gone they will work on the eating disorder. Weaving in a light touch of irreverence about dead clients *never* having the opportunity to work on eating disorders—i.e., the first step in solving the eating disordered behaviour is being alive—may smooth the path to change. In addition, Steve may need the help of his consultation team to develop and implement skills to avoid mood-dependent action himself and to challenge some of his cognitions.

Problems also occur when therapists have not sufficiently learned the target hierarchy in their training. For example, it is not uncommon for a therapist to formulate a high-risk sexual behaviour as a life-threatening behaviour. Additionally, later on in treatment when a client is no longer engaging in life-threatening behaviours, therapists may fail to identify which quality-of-life-interfering issue is the most pressing. Commonly, novice therapists struggle to select a discrete quality of life-interfering problem and one instance of it to work on and may default to working on something global. For example, Anna and her client Margaret have decided to target high-risk sexual behaviour, namely, picking up random men in bars and engaging in unprotected sex with them. They spend the session talking generally about Margaret's sexual practice, when adherent and competent DBT recommends that one incident of the behaviour is targeted. As it is a quality-of-life-interfering behaviour and not severe enough to be leading to immediate crisis, the therapist has the choice of focusing in on the problem on a more macro level, namely, specifically identifying aspects of the problem—thoughts, emotions, actions, or to do a formal chain and solution analysis. From the perspective of competence in the model, chain analysis is recommended for at least several episodes of the behaviour to obtain a reasonable grasp of the controlling variables for the behaviour, but it is not required.

Issues in Executing Problem-Solving Strategies

Problem definition commonly presents as a difficulty with therapists either not getting enough specificity to help the client effectively solve their problem, or with therapists focusing too narrowly. Heard and Swales (2016) discuss the principles and practice of behavioural chain and solution analysis from targeting life-destroying behaviours to therapy-and quality-of-life-interfering behaviours. Chapman and Rosenthal (2016) provide useful assistance to readers who wish to enhance their knowledge and practice on targeting and addressing TIBs.

Behavioural chain analysis is not required for all issues; it is required for life-destroying behaviours and any therapy-interfering or quality-of-life-interfering behaviours likely to lead to imminent crisis, e.g., when a client is facing imminent homelessness. However, behavioural chain analysis can be very helpful in most instances and the expectation of doing one in every session seems anecdotally related to increased therapist competence in the model.

Related to the difficulties in structuring the session, it has been observed that therapists commonly struggle to identify a specific problem to work on when a client has given up self-harming. While a behavioural chain analysis may not be required in these instances, specific problem definition, namely, helping a client identify thoughts, emotions, and behaviours, is required. Therapists who are most adherent to the model also routinely ask questions about the fluctuating intensity of emotions and action urges. Finally, therapists can increase their adherence to the model by actually *analysing* chains with a client to elucidate the function of a behaviour as well as the controlling variables that strengthen the likelihood a behaviour will occur, i.e., does the behaviour occur to escape what has come before it, to obtain that which follows it, or is it some combination of both.

Chain analysis also helps with solution generation and is only complete when a solution analysis is done. The chain analysis ideally takes no longer than 20 minutes of the session. Once completed, the therapist and client generate different solutions to these links and therapists are then required to activate new behaviour from clients in session. The most common pitfall is that therapists "talk" with the client about new behaviour, rather than practising in session. In order to counteract this tendency to talk rather than act, it may be helpful for therapists to have in mind the sentence "if I have not seen them do the skillful behaviour in this situation, it is effective for me to assume the client does not know how to do it", which is an antidote to invalidation in the form of oversimplifying problem solving. And in the spirit of "if-then" rules, an individual therapist must be willing to teach the client a needed skill or procedure in the moment, including modelling it, providing corrective coaching feedback, and programming generalization to the client's wider environment through the use of contingency management if the client requires. Finally, possible approaches to problems are offered in a dialectical fashion. Thus, therapeutic dyads work on a balance of change-orientated solutions and acceptance-orientated solutions.

For example: Mark, the client, and Todd, the therapist, completed a chain analysis on Mark's behaviour of being late for session. The pair had worked out that the function of the behaviour was to reduce the intensity of shame that Mark experiences when thinking about presenting his diary card showing an episode of cocaine use. Mark notices that when he begins to prepare to leave home for session on one of the cocaine weeks, he starts to find more things to do around the house and becomes occupied with those tasks, thereby making himself up to 30 minutes late for the hour-long session. Todd and Mark generate some effective solutions and recognize that distress tolerance is ineffective here because engaging in distraction is causing Mark to be late in the first place. The pair discuss in depth how Mark could be mindful of the present moment, could notice the worry thoughts, could use cheerleading statements, could tolerate his shame, could act opposite to the shame in the moment when he was leaving. They seem to have covered all the bases, but next week the same pattern happened. When analysing what got in the way of using the skills they discussed, it transpired that Mark did not know how to use most of them. Todd did not teach Mark any of the skills or have him practise them in session with him in order to provide coaching and corrective feedback; he also did not troubleshoot issues that might stop Mark from using these skills.

A frequently occurring issue in the problem-solving segment of the session is that the therapist does not know which solutions to offer. Therapists, regardless of whether they are delivering the skills training segment of DBT or not, must also know all of the skills that are taught. However, the solutions used with clients are not confined to the DBT skills, but also include contingency management, cognitive modification, and exposure. Heard and Swales (2016) also cover problems in solution generation, evaluation, and implementation, and the problems that arise in considerable depth. An immediate tip for therapists struggling to know which solutions to offer is to ask themselves what they would do if they were in this situation. For example, for the majority of therapists, their first solution to the experience of an intensely painful emotion in the wake of a major falling out with a loved one is probably not to plan to kill oneself. The problem of relationship difficulties is ubiquitous to all humans, and therefore a therapist can genuinely state how they have handled it, i.e., offer solutions and practice related to experiencing pain, soothing oneself, being mindful of other connections, etc. A therapist can do this using the strategy of self-disclosure if appropriate—or can just briefly, silently, and mindfully check in with their own thoughts about the processes employed to manage similar situations and offer suggestions.

A final word on solution analysis: the most underused strategy is exposure. In a perusal of data from 1,200 coded sessions on file at the University of Washington, it emerged that less than 1% of those sessions used exposure, formal or informal

(Korslund, personal communication). Interestingly, this may relate to findings by Harned et al. (2013) who, in reviewing the effectiveness of DBT for treating Axis I disorders, found that, while DBT was effective in treating many domains including symptoms related to BPD, mood disorders, and substance-misuse, it was not as effective at treating anxiety disorders, despite anxiety disorders being the most common comorbid condition for people with BPD. We might expect that there was no great reduction in PTSD symptoms, as most therapists following the Linehan manual will defer exposure-based treatment of PTSD until Stage 2 of treatment. Yet DBT therapists also appear to avoid treating other anxiety disorders, perhaps because many standard treatments of anxiety disorder exclude people who are actively self-harming and or suicidal, making it difficult for people with comorbid BPD and anxiety disorders to access appropriate comprehensive treatment (Harned & Valenstein, 2013). Research suggests that if anxiety disorders remain untreated, remission from BPD is very unlikely (Harned & Valenstein, 2013). Therapists seem to shy away from this solution despite many client dysfunctional behaviours serving as attempts to avoid dreaded cues, either internal (e.g., related to emotions), or external (e.g., situations or activities). It has been noticed that therapists may become imbalanced by offering acceptance strategies such as distress tolerance or mindfulness skills, rather than opting for exposure, despite the fact that in the long run, exposure would be the most effective strategy and help a client build skills. To counteract this pervasive underuse, therapists can be encouraged to role play exposure procedures in consultation team, do additional reading around it, practise on themselves, and make it a goal to track how often they engage a client in exposure to ensure that they implement this strategy. Readers seeking to enhance their skills in the use of exposure may find Abramowitz, Deacon, and Whiteside (2013) or Barlow (2001) helpful.

Developing Dialectical Balance

An imbalance in strategies used in session is another obstacle that potentially causes therapists to veer from adhering to the manual. Sessions may become non-adherent when therapists overuse reciprocal strategies or, conversely, overuse irreverence, because while irreverence is not required in each session, speed, flow, and movement are. The imbalanced use of irreverence, reciprocal, or change versus validation strategies may also impact on effective use of the dialectical strategies. We recommend that therapists use/develop their mindfulness skills to be aware of which strategies they have used and to actively pursue a balance. Additionally, we recommend that therapists apply chain analysis to their own behaviour when observing and describing patterns of unevenness throughout the session. This analysis may reveal that the therapist has "rules" about how they are meant to behave with clients, and frequently these "rules" do not include the use of irreverence. They may find a matter-of-fact way of addressing behaviour aversive. Similarly, a therapist may be feeling anger and annoyance with a client and overuse irreverence, when it might be more effective to use contingency management strategies to observe and assert her own limits to the client. Consultation team can help therapists challenge their rules and practise new behaviours, both through role play regarding a client, but also in vivo when this behaviour emerges in consultation team meeting as well. See Box 44.1 about Consultation Team for an illustration of the way that therapist beliefs can impact both on therapy and Consultation Team behaviour.

DBT strategies are interrelated as they derive from the same principles. Thus, not adhering to session structure may impact on problem and solution analysis, or focusing too heavily on contingency management may be at the sacrifice of validation. Flexibility is the key as there are multiple roads to adherence and competence, but all roads will involve responsiveness and balancing change versus validation strategies.

GROUP SKILLS FACILITATOR ADHERENCE: COMMONLY OCCURRING OBSTACLES AND SOLUTIONS

As mentioned, in individual therapy as well as in skills class, DBT ACS is the research tool used to measure therapist adherence to the model. The emphasis in skills class is on the problem-solving strategies, particularly skills acquisition and strengthening strategies like teaching, coaching, providing feedback, and generalization of skills. However, there is still the expectation that structure is maintained, that life-destroying and therapy-destroying behaviours, as well as TIBs, are managed, that validation is provided, that dialectical balance is maintained, and so forth. When considering adherence to the model in skills class it may be helpful to know that the responses of the skills facilitator as well as the co-facilitator are taken as one, which may make achieving dialectical balance easier than if one person demonstrates all the strategies. As with the individual sessions, when the structure of the session is not maintained, often other aspects of DBT fall out of adherence (see Box 44.2).

CONCLUSION

Fidelity, adherence, and competence are important issues for effective dissemination of therapies from a laboratory setting to a community-based setting. In DBT, fidelity to the model centres on the implementation of all functions and modes of the therapy as well as the therapist putting into practice the strategies that are written in the treatment manual. We call this process adherence in DBT because of the assumption that DBT therapists engage in the same skills and strategies that they use

Box 44.2 Example of adherence issues in skills class

There is a group of eight people, plus Rachel the facilitator and Laura the co-facilitator. Rachel is teaching the group about Radical Acceptance and Laura is providing some coaching to Nancy, who returned from break in tears. Veronica is giving an example of turning the mind when Michelle calls out that this skill is rubbish and is teaching people to just take anything that anyone dishes out to them. A few other members of the group begin to echo Michelle's sentiment. Rachel feels flummoxed by the response she is receiving and stops teaching and starts engaging with the comments that are being made and while Laura has stopped coaching Nancy and is sitting still and not talking.

What problems can we identify here?

First, as Rachel's job is to teach the material, any distraction from this task means the structure of the session is then lost. Additionally, Laura's job is to attend to in-session behaviour and diffuse any interference in order for Rachel to teach. Thus, one possible solution is the use of aversive strategies, including extinguishing. As the session went off track, Laura could have stopped coaching Nancy in the moment and attended to Michelle immediately by moving next to her and asking her to stop and listen. Alternatively, Laura could have spoken over the group and asked everyone to take a moment to stop and breathe, and then have everyone practise the radical acceptance skill of willingness in the moment. In the next breath, Rachel would have gone back immediately to paying attention to Veronica's example or reinforcing with attention anyone else who is participating willingly, while she also ignores any disruptive behaviour. Here, contingency management strategies are needed to maintain the structure of the group and to focus on the primary target of the skills class, i.e., enhancing how group members attain their skills.

with their clients. It is complicated to measure adherence and competence in DBT because the dialectical philosophy that underpins the therapy precludes the use of tick box/yes or no forms. Strategies in DBT largely are applied using the principles of dialectics, i.e., an if/then approach (i.e., if client does "X," or "X" is the situation then do "Y" or a choice of different "Ys" in response). Therapists are responding to the moment in DBT and accept full well that the landscape will appear different in the next moment. Therapist strategies for increasing the likelihood of providing the therapy adherently comprise a commitment to and the practice of learning the therapy as thoroughly as possible, including beyond intensive-level training as well as making effective use of Consultation Team. Therapists may benefit from supervision in addition to participation in Consultation Team, as well as on-going training; however, the financial constraints of publicly funded agencies providing DBT may make this difficult. Finally, we have reflected on common mistakes that pull therapists out of adherence to the DBT model through some case examples and have offered some potential solutions.

KEY MESSAGES FOR CLINICIANS

- Translating evidence-based therapies from research settings to routine community settings requires that interventions provided, in both form and content, match those delivered as part of the research protocol in order to maintain outcomes.

- Treatment adherence and treatment fidelity: DBT uses "treatment adherence" to describe therapists' behaviours used when conducting the therapy, and "treatment fidelity" when discussing therapy modes offered in DBT programmes.

- DBT is a complex therapy to master given the abundance of treatment strategies, all of which are context specific. DBT is a principle-driven, not protocol-driven, therapy, although protocols do also exist within DBT.

- The DBT Adherence Coding Scale (DBT ACS), created for research purposes, establishes whether a therapist's therapy provision matches the behaviours set out in the treatment manual.

- The DBT ACS scale reflects the complexity of the treatment and requires the review of an entire therapy session and the subsequent coding of therapist strategies on 66 items, some of which embody complex "if-then" rules of therapy.

- Currently DBT does not have a scale that is briefer, easier to administer, or easier to deploy in community settings to measure therapist competence.

- Research on the acquisition of and the increase of competence in DBT suggests that more training and supervision leads to increased use of DBT strategies.

- Consultation team habits can shape the DBT practice of its team members.

REFERENCES

Abramowitz, J. S., Deacon, B. J., & Whiteside, S. P. (2013) *Exposure therapy for anxiety: Principles and practice*. New York, NY: Guilford Press.

Andreasson K, Krogh J., Wenneberg C., Jessen H. K., Krakauer K., Gluud C., Thomsen R. R., Randers L., & Nordentoft M. (2016). Effectiveness of dialectical behavior therapy versus collaborative assessment and management of suicidality treatment for reduction of self-harm in adults with borderline personality traits and disorder—a randomized observer-blinded clinical trial. *Depression and Anxiety, 33*(6), 520–530.

Barlow, D. (2001). *Clinical handbook of psychological disorders*. New York, NY: Guilford Press.

Beidas, R. S., Cross, W. F., & Dorsey, S. (2014). Show me don't tell me: Behavioral rehearsal as a training and fidelity tool. *Cognitive and Behavioral Practice, 21*(1), 1–11.

Beidas, R. S., & Kendall, P. C. (2010). Training therapists in evidence-based practice: a critical review of studies from a systems-contextual perspective. *Clincial Psychology, 17*(1), 1–30.

Bohus, M., Dyer, A., Priebe, K., Krüger, A., Kleindienst, N., Schmahl, C., ... Steil, R. (2013). Dialectical Behaviour Therapy for Post-traumatic Stress Disorder after childhood sexual abuse in patients with and without borderline personality disorder: a randomised controlled trial. *Psychotherapy and Psychosomatics, 82*(4), 221–233.

Boswell, J. F., Gallagher, M. W., Sauer-Zavala, S. E., Bullis, J., Gorman, J. M., Shear, M. K., ... Barlow, D. H. (2013). Patient characteristics, and varability in adherence and competence in cognitive-behavioral therapy for panic disorder. *Journal of Consulting and Clinical Psychology, 81* (3), 443–454.

Carmel, A., Villatte, J. L., Zachary Rosenthal, M., Chalker, S., & Comtois, K. A. (2014). Applying technological approaches to clinical supervision in dialectical behavior therapy: A randomized feasibility trial of the Bug-in-the-Eye (BITE) model. *Cognitive and Behavioral Practice, 23*(2), 221–229.

Carter, G. L., Wilcox, C. H., Lewin, T. J., Conrad, A. M., & Bendit, N. (2010). Hunter DBT project: Randomized controlled trial of dialectical behaviour therapy in women with borderline personality disorder. *Australian & New Zealand Journal of Psychiatry, 44*(2), 162–173.

Chapman, A. L., & Rosenthal, M. Z. (2016). *Managing therapy-interfering behavior strategies for dialectical behavior therapy.* Washington, DC: American Psychological Association.

Clarkin, J. F., Levy, K. N., Lenzenweger, M. F., & Kernberg, O. F., (2007). Evaluating three treatments for borderline personality disorder: A multiwave study. *American Journal of Psychiatry, 164*(6), 922–928.

Courbasson, C., Nishikawa, Y., & Dixon, L. (2012). Outcome of dialectical behaviour therapy for concurrent eating and substance use disorders *Clinical Psychology & Psychotherapy, 19*(5), 434–449.

Dimeff, L. A, Woodcock, E. A., Harned, M. S., & Beadnell, B. (2011). Can dialectical behavior therapy be learned in high structured learning environments? Results from a randomized controlled dissemination trial. *Behavior Therapy, 42*(2), 263–275.

Dimeff, L. A., Koerner, K., Beadnell, B., Woodcock, E. A., Brown, M. Z., Skutch, ... Harned, M. S. (2009). Which training method works best? A randomized controlled trial comparing three methods of training clinicians in dialectical behavioral skills. *Behaviour Research and Therapy, 47*, 921–930.

Dimeff, L. A., Harned, M. S., Woodcock, E. A., Skutch, J. M., Koerner, K., & Linehan, M. M. (2015). Investigating bang for your training buck: a randomized controlled trial comparing three methods of training clinicians in two core strategies of dialectical behavior therapy. *Behavior Therapy, 46*(3), 283–295.

Dorsey, S., Pullmann, M., Deblinger, E., Berliner, L., Kerns, S. E., Thompson, K., ... Garland, A. F. (2013). Improving practice in community-based settings: a randomized trial of supervision—study protocol. *Implementation Science, 8,* 89.

Dorsey, S., Berliner, L., Lyon, A. R., Pullmann, M., & Murray, L. K. (2014). A statewide common elements initiative for children's mental health. *Journal of Behavioral Health Services and Research, 43*(2), 246–261.

Dorsey, S. (2016). ESSPD Keynote Address: 4th International Congress on Borderline Personality Disorder and Allied Disorder, Vienna, Austria 8–10 September 2016.

Feigenbaum, J. D., Fonagy, P., Pilling, S., Jones, A., Wildgoose, A, & Bebbington, P. E. (2012). A real-world study of the effectiveness of DBT in the UK National Health Service. *British Journal of Clinical Psychology, 51*(2), 121–141.

Frederick, J. T., & Comtois, K. A. (2006). Practice of dialectical behavior therapy after psychiatry residency. *Academic Psychiatry, 30*(1), 63–68.

Goldstein, T. R., Fersch-Podrat, R. K., Rivera, M., Axelson, D. A., Merranko, J., Yu, H., ... Birmaher, B. (2015). Dialectical behavior therapy for adolescents with bipolar disorder: Results from a pilot randomized trial. *Journal of Child and Adolescent Psychopharmacology, 25*(2), 140–149.

Harned, M. S., Korslund, K. E., & Linehan, M. M. (2014). A pilot randomized controlled trial of Dialectical Behavior Therapy with and without the Dialectical Behavior Therapy Prolonged Exposure protocol for suicidal and self-injuring women with borderline personality disorder and PTSD. *Behaviour Research and Therapy*, 55, 7–17.

Harned, M. S., & Valenstein, H. R. (2013). Treatment of borderline personality disorder and co-occuring anxiety disorders. *F1000Prime Reports*, 5(15), doi: 10.12703/P5-15.

Harned, M. S, Jackson, S. C., Comtois, K. A., & Linehan, M. M. (2010). Dialectical behavior therapy as a precursor to PTSD treatment for suicidal and/or self injuring women with borderline personality disorder. *Journal of Traumatic Stress Aug*, 23(4), 421–429.

Heard, H. L., & Swales, M. A. (2016). *Changing behavior in DBT: Problem solving in action*. New York, NY: Guilford Press.

Hauke, C., Gloster, A., Gerlach, A., Hamm, A., Deckert, J., Fehm, L., … Wittchen, H. (2013). Therapist adherence to a treatment manual influences outcome and dropout rates: Results from a multicenter randomized clinical CBT trial for panic disorder with agoraphobia. *International Journal of Research Studies in Psychology*, 2(4), 3–16.

Hogue, A., Henderson, C. E., Dauber, S., Barajas, P. C., Fried, A., & Liddle, H. (2008). Treatment adherence, competence, and outcome in individual and family therapy for adolescent behavior problems. *Journal of Consulting and Clinical Psychology*, 76(4), 544–555.

Huppert, J. D., Barlow, D. H., Gorman, J. M., Shear, M. K., & Woods, S. W. (2006). The interaction of motivation and therapist adherence predicts outcome in cognitive behavioral therapy for panic disorder: preliminary findings. *Cognitive and Behavior Practice*, 13(3), 198–204.

Koerner, K., & Dimeff, L. A. (2000). Further data on dialectical behavior therapy. *Clinical Psychology: Science and Practice*, 7(1), 104–112.

Koerner, K. (2012). *Doing dialectical behavior therapy: A practical guide*. New York, NY: Guilford Press.

Koerner, K. (2013). What you must know and do to get good outcomes with DBT. *Behavior Therapy*, 44(4), 568–579.

Koons, C. R., Robins, C. J., Tweed, J. L., Lynch, T. R., Gonzalez, A. M., Morse, J. Q., … Bastian, L. A. (2001). Efficacy of dialectical behavior therapy in women veterans with borderline personality disorder. *Behavior Therapy*, 32(2), 371–390.

Linehan, M. M., Wagner, A. W., & Tutek, D. (1990). *DBT expert rating scale*. Seattle, WA: University of Washington Press.

Linehan, M. (1993). *Cognitive behavior therapy for the treatment of borderline personality disorder*. New York, NY: Guilford Press.

Linehan, M., Armstrong, H., Suarez, A., Allmon, D., & Heard, H. (1991). Cognitive-behavioral treatment of chronically parasuidical borderline patients. *Archives of General Psychiatry*, 48, 1060–1064.

Linehan, M. M., Heard, H. L., & Armstrong, H. E. (1993). Naturalistic follow-up of a behavioral treatment for chronically parasuicidal borderline patients. *Archives of General Psychiatry*, 50, 971–974.

Linehan, M. M., Tutek, D. A., Heard, H. L., & Armstrong, H. E. (1994). Interpersonal outcomes of cognitive behavioral treatment for chronically suicidal borderline patients. *American Journal of Psychiatry*, 151, 1771–1776.

Linehan, M. M. (1997). Validation and psychotherapy. In A. C. Bohart & L. Greenberg (Eds.), *Empathy Reconsidered: New directions in psychotherapy* (pp. 353–392). Washington, DC: American Psychological Association.

Linehan, M. M. & Korslund, K. E. (2003). Dialectical behavior therapy adherence coding scale™. Seattle, WA: University of Washington Press.

Linehan, M. M., Schmidt, H., Dimeff, L. A., Craft, J. C., Kanter J., & Comtois, K. A. (1999). Dialectical behaviour therapy for patients with borderline personality disorder and drug dependence. *American Journal on Addictions, 8*, 279–292.

Linehan, M. M, Dimeff, L. A., Reynolds, S. K., Comtois, K. A., Welch, S. S., Heagerty, P., & Kivlahan, D. R. (2002). Dialectical behavior therapy versus comprehensive validation therapy plus 12-step for the treatment of opioid dependent women meeting criteria for borderline personality disorder. *Drug and Alcohol Dependence, 67*(1), 13–26.

Linehan, M. M, Comtois, K. A., Murray, A. M., Brown, M. Z., Gallop, R. J., Heard, H. L., ... Lindenboim, N. (2006). Two-year randomized controlled trial and follow-up of dialectical behavior therapy vs treatment by experts for suicidal behaviors and borderline personality disorder. *Archives of General Psychiatry, 63*, 757–766.

Linehan, M. M., Korslund, K. E., Harned, M. S., Gallop, R. J., Lungu, A., Neacsiu, A. D., ... Murray-Gregory, A. M. (2015). Dialectical behavior therapy for high suicide risk in individuals with borderline personality disorder: a randomized clinical trial and component analysis. *JAMA Psychiatry, 72*(5), 475–482.

Linehan, M. M. (2015a). *DBT skills training manual*, 2nd Edition. New York: Guilford Press.

Linehan, M. M. (2015b). *DBT skills training handouts and worksheets*, 2nd Edition. New York: Guildford Press.

Lynch, T. R., Cheavens, J. S., Curkrowicz, K. C., Thorp, S. C., Brunner, L., & Beyer, J. (2007). Treatment of older adults with co-morbid personality disorder and depression: a dialectical behavior therapy approach. *International Journal of Geriatric Psychiatry, 22*(2), 131–143.

McMain, S. F., Links, P. S., Gnam, W. H., Guimond, T., Cardish, R. J., Korman, L., & Streiner, D. L. (2009). A randomized trial of dialectical behavior therapy versus general psychiatric management for borderline personality disorder. *American Journal of Psychiatry, 166*(12), 1365–1374.

Mehlum, L., Tormoen, A. J., Ramburg, M., Hagan, E., Diep, L. M., Lab erg, S., ... Groholt, B. (2014). Dialectical behavior therapy for adolescents with repeated suicidal and self-harming behavior: a randomized trial. *Journal of the American Academy of Child and Adolescent Psychiatry, 53*(10), 1082–1091.

Milne, D., & Westerman, C. (2001). Evidence-based clinical supervision: rationale and illustration. *Clinical Psychology & Psychotherapy, 8*(6), 444–457.

Perepletchikova, F., & Kazdin, A. (2005). Treatment integrity and therapeutic change: issues and research recommendations. *Clinical Psychology Science and Practice, 12*(4), 365–383.

Pistorello, J., Fruzzetti, A. E., MacLane, C., Gallop, R., & Iverson, K. M. (2012). Dialectical behavior therapy (DBT) applied to college students: A randomized clinical trial. *Journal of Consulting and Clinical Psychology, 80*(6), 982–994.

Priebe, S., Bhatti, N., Barn cot, K., Bremmer, S., Gaglia, A., Katsakou, C., ... Zinkler, M. (2012). Effectiveness and cost-effectiveness of dialectical behaviour therapy for self-harm patients with personality disorder: a pragmatic randomized controlled trial. *Psychotherapy and Psychosomatics, 81*, 356–365.

Resnick, B., & Ziporkin, S. (2012). Treatment fidelity in intervention research. https://nursing.jhu.edu/excellence/aging/center/gsa/2012/treatment-fidelity.pdf, accessed 27/6/2017

Rizvi, S. L. (2011). Treatment failure in dialectical behavior therapy. *Cognitive and Behavioral Practice, 18*(3), 403–412.

Rizvi, S. L., Yu, J., Geisser, S., & Finnegan, D. (2016). The use of "Bug-in-the-Eye" live supervision for training in dialectical behavior therapy: A case study. *Clinical Case Studies, 15*(3), 243–258.

Scheel, K. R. (2000). The empirical basis of dialectical behavior therapy: summary, critique, and implications. *Clinical Psychology: Science and Practice, 7*(1), 68–86.

Schoenwald, S. K., Mehta, T. G., Frazier, S. L., & Schernoff, E. S. (2013). Clinical supervision in effectiveness and implementation research. *Clinical Psychology: Science and Practice, 20*(1), 44–59.

Sholomskas, D. E., & Carroll, K. M. (2006) One small step for manuals: computer-assisted training in twelve-step facilitation. *Journal of Studies on Alcohol and Drugs, 67*(6), 939–945.

Stoffers, J., Völlm, B., Rücke, T. A., Huband, N., & Leib, K. (2012). Psychological therapies for people with borderline personality disorder. *Cochrane Database of Systematic Reviews.* doi: 10.1002/14651858.CD005652.pub2

Swales, M. A., & Heard, H. L. (2017). *Dialectical behaviour therapy: Distinctive features,* 2nd Edition. Abingdon, UK: Routledge.

Swales, M. A. (2010a). Implementing dialectical behaviour therapy: organizational pretreatment. *The Cognitive Behaviour Therapist, 3*(4), 145–157.

Swales, M. A. (2010b). Implementing dialectical behaviour therapy: organizational pretreatment. *The Cognitive Behaviour Therapist, 3*(2), 71–79.

Turner, R. (2000) Naturalistic evaluation of dialectical behaviour therapy-oriented treatment for borderline personality disorder. *Cognitive and Behavioral Practice, 7*(4), 413–419.

van den Bosch, L. M. C., Koeter M. W. J., Stijnem, T., Verheul, R., & van den Brink, W. (2002). Dialectical behavior therapy of borderline patients with and without substance problems: Implementation and long-term effects. *Addicitive Behaviors, 27,* 911–923.

van den Bosch, L. M. C., Koeter M. W. J., Stijnem, T., Verheul, R., & van den Brink, W. (2005) Sustained efficacy of dialectical behaviour therapy for Borderline Personality Disorder. *Behaviour Research Therapy, 43*(9), 1231–1241.

Verheul, R., van den Bosch, L. M. C., Koeter M. W. J., de Ridder, M. A., Stijnem, T., Verheul, R., & van den Brink, W. (2003). Dialectical behaviour therapy for women with borderline personality disorder: 12-month, randomized clinical trial in the Netherlands. *British Journal of Psychiatry, 182,* 135–140.

Weissman, M. M., Verdeli, H., Gameroff, M. J., Beldsoe, S. E., Betts, K., Mufson, L., ... Wickramaratne, P. (2006). National survey of psychotherapy training in psychiatry, psychology, and social work. *Archives of General Psychiatry, 63,* 925–934.

SECTION IX

IN CONCLUSION

....

CHAPTER 45

FUTURE DIRECTIONS FOR DIALECTICAL BEHAVIOUR THERAPY

Theory, Development, and Implementation

....

MICHAELA A. SWALES

INTRODUCTION

....

SINCE the first randomized controlled trial (RCT) of dialectical behaviour therapy (DBT) and its accompanying manuals were published (Linehan 1993a, b; Linehan, Armstrong, Suarez, Allmon, & Heard, 1991), the treatment landscape for clients with borderline personality disorder (BPD) has changed dramatically. DBT was at the start of that process and continues to contribute with further research, development, and investigation, as evidenced by the work represented in this volume. Considerable investment by researchers and clinicians into the development and successful investigation of other psychosocial treatments for BPD (e.g. mentalization-based therapy, transference focused therapy, and schema therapy) has also been a feature of the last two decades, although DBT remains the most widely practised of these new structured psychological therapies for BPD (Choi-Kain, Albert, & Gunderson, 2016; McHugh & Barlow, 2010). Among the successfully navigated challenges of the first 25 years was establishing that the treatment worked and was deliverable by those other than the treatment developer. This chapter asks what DBT has achieved in the last 25 years in terms of evidence in support of its biosocial theory, treatment outcomes, adaptations, and implementation, and looks ahead to future challenges in these areas and in the wider psychotherapy field.

Biosocial Theory

In constructing DBT, Linehan developed a truly integrative therapy, drawing on philosophies and theories in overt tension with each other and melding them into a seamless whole (Swales & Heard, 2017, Chapter 2; Swales, this volume). Blending western cognitive behavioural practices with eastern meditative traditions became part of what some have described as the *third wave* in CBT treatment development (Hayes, 2004), and arguably Linehan could be considered the first psychotherapy developer to have achieved a coherent synthesis of these contrasting theoretical traditions. At the time of writing her original treatment manual, Linehan drew together what was known about the origins and development of BPD and constructed a developmentally informed account of the aetiology of behavioural patterns associated with the diagnosis that was not only compassionate, but also that orientated the treatment towards a central focus on affect. The resulting biosocial theory not only articulates how clients' difficulties evolve and steers the structure of the treatment from a theoretical perspective, but it also directs therapists in treatment moment by moment. Placing emotion at the centre of the treatment validates clients' experiences of their essential vulnerabilities and also assists therapists in identifying and treating controlling variables for dysfunctional behaviour.

Since the early 1990s, significant advancements have been made in supporting Linehan's biosocial model, including understanding the neurological underpinnings of emotional dysregulation, impulsivity, and interpersonal disturbances (Niedtfeld & Bohus, this volume). What remains unknown is how unique these neurological differences are to clients with a BPD diagnosis or whether they might better be understood as consequences of early trauma conferring a transdiagnostic vulnerability. DBT as a behavioural treatment, however, is more interested in whether these identified neurological differences will open up new avenues for tailoring treatment or whether the neurological pathways identified will simply remain as alternative descriptions of the behavioural manifestations failing to result in treatment innovations or modification.

In terms of the environmental component of the model, while there is greater understanding about early invalidating environments, little is known about precisely how such environments confer risk and therefore what might be done to ameliorate it (Grove & Crowell, this volume). Also, while most research has focused on the invalidating family context, there are likely other contenders, for example, invalidation at the societal level, peer relationships in childhood and early adolescence, and the increasing influence of digital and social media, that are all potentially highly impactful sources of invalidation. For example, researchers and clinicians have recently utilized the DBT biosocial model to describe and integrate the particular forms of invalidation experienced by lesbian, gay, bisexual, and transgender youth, using the framework of the theory to conceptualize how their distress might be treated (Sloan, Berke, & Shipherd, 2017). Evaluation of these applications is just beginning (Beard, Kirakosian, Silverman, Winer, & Wadsworth, 2017).

The absence of prospective studies of the biosocial theory limits what can be said about causal pathways. Understanding more comprehensively the early transactions between invalidating environments and biological vulnerabilities in children and adolescents may pave the way for early interventions at the individual, familial, and school levels. Such an endeavour may reduce psychopathology more widely as well as addressing particular risk factors for the onset of behaviours that may evolve into behavioural patterns particularly identified with a diagnosis of BPD. The work of Dexter-Mazza and Mazza (this volume) is an example of this type of early intervention.

Linehan's focus on affect and its amelioration as central to effective outcomes has largely been supported by research into mediators and moderators of outcome. Current research supports emotional awareness and acceptance, attentional control, emotional modulation, and adaptive coping skills as mechanisms of change (Boritz, Zeifman, & McMain, this volume). Each of these mechanisms link to aspects of treatment, either relating to mindful experiencing of emotion or to behavioural change procedures to decrease emotional intensity. Unfortunately, mechanisms research is typically underpowered, leading to less certainty about which mechanisms are the most important and how different mechanisms relate to each other. Two challenges for the field stem from this research; first, conducting mechanisms studies that, both follow established guidelines for establishing mediators and moderators, and, have sufficient power to test multiple mediators based on theory-driven hypotheses. Funding such studies is expensive and complex and may be prohibitive, i.e., our understanding in this area may always remain less than perfect. Secondly, as knowledge about mechanisms improves, ensuring practitioners can access this research and use it clinically presents a challenge. Clinicians often do not have sufficient access to current research (the *research-practice gap*; McHugh & Barlow, 2012), nor is it always clear what the implications are of research findings in terms of how therapy should be conducted. Solving these problems to more precisely target change processes in routine clinical practice will likely require new methods of research, dissemination, and implementation.

TREATMENT OUTCOMES AND ADAPTATIONS

DBT has a strong record in both efficacy and effectiveness research (Miga et al.; Walton and Comtois; Krawitz and Miga; all this volume). The strength of the research findings has resulted in influential meta-analyses highlighting DBT's success with suicidal outcomes, in particular, (Stoffers-Winterling et al., 2012) and in recommendations by national bodies to implement DBT (National Collaborating Centre for Mental Health (NCCMH), 2009). Strong evidential support for using DBT for clients with suicidal behaviour in the context of BPD has been complemented by promising outcomes with other groups, specifically suicidal and self-harming adolescents, clients with eating disorders, and substance misuse. Adaptations with other populations and presenting problems have more limited evidence and for clinicians and researchers in those areas the forthcoming task is ensuring that further evidence for these adaptations accumulates.

DBT's flexible modular structure has aided the process of adopting and adapting the treatment for new client groups and new populations. There is still much we do not know about which modalities of treatment are actually required to obtain effective outcomes. Recent dismantling research by Linehan et al. (2015) challenged the established view that DBT individual therapy was necessarily required for effective outcomes, highlighting that a skills training emphasis combined with robust application of the DBT suicide protocol, as was included in the dismantling study, may be sufficient. Telephone consultation between sessions, a unique component of the model and one that frequently presents an implementation challenge, is notably understudied. How essential it is to obtaining clinical outcomes remains unknown. Others are examining what may be the effective length of the treatment (McMain, 2017a). Typically, DBT programmes have been one year long, yet little is known about whether this is the optimal length of treatment and whether or not treatment length may interact with severity in predicting clinical outcomes. Studying all the relevant variations in treatment to answer all relevant questions via the traditional method of the randomized clinical trial is unlikely. While some funding bodies have as part of their remit the investigation of these types of studies, as DBT becomes more accepted, obtaining funding to study further adaptations may be perceived as redundant. Research funding and practice frequently focuses on novelty and new innovation (Makel, Plucker, & Hegarty, 2012; Nosek, Spies, & Motyl, 2012) and establishing the finer-grained parameters of established interventions may prove of less interest. Innovative designs in the behavioural health field using the Multi-Phase Optimization Strategy (MOST) may prove helpful in identifying which components of a complex treatment such as DBT can be combined to maximize effect sizes (Collins, Murphy, Nair, & Strecher, 2005) Alternatively, big data methods to collect information from routine practice could be harnessed to systematically study clinical outcomes in naturally occurring variations in treatment delivery if the infrastructure to implement and utilize such structures was supported (Markowetz, Blaszkiewicz, Montag, Switala, & Schlaepfer, 2014). There is much enthusiasm for and anxiety concerning the possibilities of "big data" (Gray & Hyatt Thorpe, 2015). Whether it holds the promise some suggest for accessing more accurate outcomes to study individual variation and comparative treatment effectiveness only the next two decades will prove. Such investigations will certainly involve far more cross-service and cross-border collaboration than has heretofore been evident in the field of psychotherapy.

DBT as a modular, skills-based approach is a natural model for innovative methods of treatment delivery. New technological approaches may help in reaching new client groups by providing components of the treatment that may be difficult to deliver in some geographical locations, for example, online skills-training modules, and in incorporating what is known about mechanisms into new methods of delivering the treatment. Adaptations to synthesize the traditional psychotherapeutic delivery mechanisms of DBT with innovative technological approaches are in their infancy (Lungu et al., this volume). Establishing how technological innovation can most effectively complement or possibly replace traditional psychotherapeutic interventions is a field likely to evolve significantly in the next two decades.

DBT's major achievement over the last 25 years was demonstrating its efficacy and effectiveness in treating client groups with extreme difficulties in regulating emotion and behaviour. More recently, DBT has been augmented and restructured (Harned & Schmidt, this volume; Bohus & Priebe, this volume) to target a particularly hard-to-help client group, clients with diagnoses of both BPD and post-traumatic stress disorder (PTSD). Traditionally this group are excluded from treatment because of clinicians' concerns that their risk will escalate during conventional exposure-based treatments. The new adaptations based in DBT have now established safety and require further testing for efficacy and transferability into routine clinical settings.

DBT's effects on certain proximal outcomes, for example, suicide and self-harming behaviour, depression, substance misuse, eating disorders, are robust, yet despite positive treatment outcomes many clients remain functionally impaired in the medium to longer term. Dedicated research to understanding and scoping this problem would be a useful focus for the next decade. McMain and colleagues (2017b) have made a useful start on this problem by studying the treatment trajectories of clients who participated in their RCT of DBT compared to General Psychiatric Management (McMain et al., 2009). In the study there were three types of trajectory identified; those who made rapid progress and sustained it through follow-up; those who made slower progress but also sustained treatment gains; and those who made rapid progress but whose symptoms returned almost to baseline post-discharge. Clients with this latter trajectory tended to have higher baseline emergency department visits and depression and were more likely to be unemployed, the latter finding regarding employment status was replicated in Lyng (2017), who also found poorer outcomes for males with BPD in DBT. Studies such as these indicate that certain clinical presentations may require additional modifications to treatment. Understanding the factors that drive poor functional outcomes as well as which aspects of treatment may promote them deserves further more systematic study.

All of the groups for whom DBT has been tested share behavioural dysregulation stemming from emotional under-control as a common feature. More recently, attention has turned to clients with clinical presentations that may be characterized as over-controlled, where affect regulation is arguably so successful that it leads to extreme emotional inhibition which seriously impacts social communication leading to isolation, ostracism, and social disconnection (Lynch, 2018a, b; Lynch, Hempel, & Dunkley, 2015). Lynch's distinctive and pioneering work developed from the application of standard DBT to older clients with chronic depression, beginning more as an adaptation of the treatment (Lynch, Morse, Mendelson, & Robins, 2003; Lynch et al., 2007) but evolving into a distinctive treatment in its own right—Radically Open DBT (RO-DBT; Lynch, 2018a, b). RO-DBT shares many structural similarities with DBT: there is a targeted hierarchical approach to solving problems, with suicidal behaviours as top priority when they occur; the treatment addresses problematic behavioural patterns linked to the diagnosis rather than the diagnosis itself; there is a strong focus on learning new skills in a skills class environment; the treatment has a dialectical focus; and RO-DBT therapists conduct fine-grained analyses of target behaviours both in session and out of session to assist clients in making behavioural changes to improve their functioning and quality of life. Yet there are substantial differences. While the RO-DBT biosocial model is also transactional, it highlights different biological vulnerabilities, for example, insensitivity to reward as well as high sensitivity to threat, early learning environments that focus on perfectionism, avoiding making mistakes, and that prize emotional control. Rather than focusing on emotion regulation, the skills deployed in RO-DBT focus on increasing flexibility and openness, improving social signalling and social connectedness, activating the social-safety system, and increasing skills in accepting feedback. Early outcome research in treating anorexia has shown promise (Chen et al., 2014; Lynch et al., 2013), as has a group-based inpatient adaptation of the treatment (Keogh, Booth, Baird, & Davenport, 2016). Outcomes of a major RCT of RO-DBT for treatment-resistant depression in community settings are awaited with interest (Lynch et al., 2015). The testing and implementation of this evolved form of DBT will likely be a feature of the next decade.

IMPLEMENTATION

The last two decades have seen a blossoming of research in DBT and subsequent dissemination and implementation across the globe. In many senses, DBT has demonstrated a significant degree of implementation success; some have argued that the Intensive Training™ method training teams, rather than individuals, is responsible for this outcome (McHugh & Barlow, 2010). Numerous studies in a variety of settings indicate DBT's feasibility, acceptability, and adoptability (Comtois & Landes, this volume). Outcomes in clinical practice can reach the benchmark set in efficacy studies, although further work in understanding what levels of training and supervision are required to maintain these will be a useful focus for further investigation (Walton & Comtois, this volume). While not all DBT teams survive, 50% of teams trained will survive longer than five years, and this figure may improve with the availability of alternative training models to reseed teams (Swales, Taylor, & Hibbs, 2012).

Significant challenges remain, however. Perhaps the most significant of these is reach, and relatedly, scaleability. DuBose and colleagues in their chapter on global dissemination highlight how far short the number of trained practitioners and functioning programmes are for the size of the population that could realistically be helped by the treatment. Solving this problem requires methods to further enhance implementation outcomes from training as well as finding new and innovative methods to train and supervise practitioners that decrease the requirement for face-to-face time with an expert. Even in systems that have high-level sign up and investment in training and supervision, reach can be a challenge as highlighted by Flynn and colleagues in their chapter. DBT programmes often remain small and are not locally resourced to reach the maximal throughput of clients who may benefit (Comtois & Landes, this volume). Some of these challenges are typical of any healthcare intervention in practice. Encouraging systems to change how they conduct their business remains difficult, even when there is a clear financial case for doing so. The complexity of what needs to be implemented in a DBT programme, i.e., multiple modes of treatment with multiple therapy contacts per client per week, impacts scaleability. Making progress with this aspect of the challenge may be facilitated by current research into briefer less multi-modal methods of offering treatment. The most frequent modification seen and evaluated here is offering skills groups alone. Recent research indicates that such interventions are feasible and effective at least for some client groups in some contexts (Lyng, 2017; McMain, Guimond, Barnhart, Habinski, & Streiner, 2017c). Such modifications may facilitate delivery of the treatment in a wider range of public and private healthcare settings.

Partly in response to limited availability, many people and treatment programmes offer DBT with little or no training in DBT and advertise themselves as delivering DBT. Potential risks to clients are present in these circumstances as the safety or effectiveness of these unsupervised modified versions is unknown. In response to this there are now systems in a number of countries (e.g., Germany, US, UK) that provide a structure for verifying therapeutic capability in the treatment. These systems are time consuming and expensive to implement, creating a genuine tension between desires to disseminate and desires to maintain fidelity. Synthesizing this tension effectively is the challenge for the next 20 years in DBT research and practice.

CHALLENGES IN THE WIDER PSYCHOTHERAPY CONTEXT

Two particular changes in the wider context of psychological therapy will likely impact on DBT, its development, and its sustainability over the next two decades. Firstly, recently proposed changes to the systems of diagnostic classification may impact how research into therapy is funded. Secondly, the proliferation of new and effective therapeutic methods presents significant challenges for training and disseminating treatments.

In the last five years, both the DSM (the diagnostic classificatory systems for psychiatric diagnoses written by the American Psychiatric Association) and the ICD (the international classification of diseases written by the World Health Organization) both decided to revise their systems (American Psychiatric Association, 2013; Tyrer et al., 2011). Both classification systems actively considered changing the classification of personality disorder to a more dimensional rather than a categorical system that focused more on personality traits than on "disorder" diagnoses. DSM backed away at the eleventh hour from such a radical change publishing the suggested revisions as an appendix and leaving the DSM-5 criteria largely unchanged from DSM-IV. ICD-11 faced similar objections from the professional community, particularly over concerns that losing the category of BPD may prevent clients, long excluded from receiving treatment and only recently gaining access to effective interventions, from receiving treatment. Others were concerned that by abolishing the diagnosis, progress made across the last twenty years of research into the diagnosis would be lost. In the case of ICD-11, a recent set of compromise proposals have been presented that essentially make the category of personality disorder more dimensional and trait based while retaining the BPD diagnostic category as a transitional arrangement (WHO/ISSPD collaboration, 2017). In a parallel yet similar process, the National Institute of Mental Health in the US signalled a shift away from diagnosis driven research to research driven by the Research Domain Criteria (RDoC; Cuthbert, 2014) framework that also centres on dimensional psychological constructs relevant to human behaviour and mental disorders, potentially leading to a more transdiagnostic or common psychological processes approach to intervention research. For DBT, these changes in many ways are less challenging. While DBT has cooperated with the diagnostic zeitgeist in examining its efficacy in specific diagnostic groups, it began, and at heart still remains, a behavioural treatment that focuses on improving affect regulation and tolerance in clients for whom affect drives "out-of-control" behaviour. DBT has never been particularly attached to the diagnosis of BPD or indeed any diagnosis as representing a genuine entity, and indeed, Linehan herself has described DBT as a treatment for chronic suicidal behaviours that incorporated the use of the BPD label as part of the research grant application process (Linehan & Wilks, 2015; Swales, this volume). Diagnoses are simply labels that humans give to clusters of behaviours in an endeavour to explain and understand the world around them. In meeting with a client who has been labelled as having BPD, DBT therapists quickly move to define clients' difficulties in terms of behaviour, focusing on how to apply the principles of behavioural theory, wider cognitive behavioural practice, and skills to solve those problems. Clinically shifting away from categorical diagnosis to dimensional constructs that are more behaviourally defined and deleting BPD from the psychiatric lexicon is not much of a challenge for DBT. There may be greater challenges for researchers, however, in thinking about how to describe and assess for clinical trials and how to link what has been learned in a research era led by categorical diagnoses as we move towards more dimensional ways of conceptualizing clinical problems and processes.

In the last three decades, research into psychological treatments has flourished. There are now many evidence-based treatments and systems in place to summarize what is known about what works for whom in order to guide practitioners in their clinical practice. This is good news for clients—or at least it should be—although there is a problem. There is evidence that delivering an evidence-based treatment with fidelity leads to better outcomes (McHugh & Barlow, 2012), and yet it is just not possible for therapists to become proficient in multiple evidence-based therapies. Training and supervision to proficiency takes time, and in hard-pressed public services, ensuring staff are trained in any evidence-based therapy, never mind several, is a significant challenge. Concern about how realistic it is to implement, even the current list of known efficacious interventions has led some researchers to consider more actively the application of evidence-based principles of change (Marchette & Weisz, 2017).

In many senses DBT was ahead of this curve. It is a principle-based treatment that flexibly applies cognitive behavioural procedures to target behaviours and the controlling variables that drive them. DBT has a proven track record with disorders of under-control, and as such, has a demonstrated pedigree as a transdiagnostic treatment. Nevertheless, its complexity, emphasis on flexible application of principles rather than protocols and multi-modality which make it adaptable to a wider range of clinical presentations can be a hindrance in training and extensive implementation. The challenge of the next two decades is how to build on DBT's flexible transdiagnostic basis to realize its potential in reaching a greater number of clients suffering from difficulties in the experience and management of emotion.

CONCLUSION

This volume has brought together established and well-known researchers in the field of DBT who have contributed to its development in the last 25 years, and many of them wrote with more junior colleagues who will be responsible for taking DBT forward over the next quarter of a century. DBT has evolved from a little-known treatment, aspects of which garnered scepticism and suspicion, for example, the inclusion of dialectics and mindfulness, to a widely known and highly regarded evidence-based intervention for some of the most complex clinical problems presenting to services. Its success in delivering significant changes in highly distressing and costly outcomes, suicidal behaviours, and hospital admissions, has consistently persuaded hard-pressed systems to invest in this complex, intensive intervention. Clients desperate for solutions have dedicated hours in skills classes and individual therapy to changing their lives around.

The main challenge ahead, not just for DBT, but for all efficacious treatments is reach—how to ensure clients receive the latest evidence-based treatments and that these treatments are delivered by staff sufficiently trained and supervised to deliver efficacy-level outcomes in routine practice. Understanding more about mechanisms, both in treatment and in methods of training staff, to deliver consistently improved outcomes for clients should be the focus of future research. It could be argued that further research into new treatments is unnecessary—the challenge is effectively implementing those currently in use. Such an argument shifts the dialogue away from innovation in treatment development to systematic studies of implementation. For implementation issues and their study to become the central focus in psychotherapy research requires not only a change in emphasis, but also a paradigm shift. In such a changed environment, funding replicability in real-world settings will take precedence over funding novelty; study design and analysis will more likely occur in clinical practice settings and will utilize "big data" to answer more precise implementation questions. Only the next two decades will show whether the wider field changes in these new and promising ways, or whether it continually ploughs the current well-worn furrows. The DBT community has focused on implementation from the first; the sustained investigations of the last 25 years make DBT well placed to meet the challenges ahead.

KEY POINTS FOR CLINICIANS

- Since the publication of the first treatment trial in 1991 evidential support for using DBT for clients with suicidal behaviour in the context of BPD has been complemented by promising adaptations and outcomes in other populations.
- DBT's flexible modular structure has aided the process of adopting and adapting the treatment for new client groups and new populations.
- Building on DBT's flexible transdiagnostic basis to realize its potential to reach a greater number of clients suffering from difficulties in the experience and management of emotion should be a focus for the next two decades.
- Understanding more about effective mechanisms, both in treatment and for training staff, to deliver consistently improved outcomes for clients will aid the dissemination endeavour.
- Synthesizing the desire to disseminate the treatment and improving reach with ensuring fidelity to maintain clinical outcomes is a central issue for DBT now and into the future
- Despite DBT's success in delivering good clinical outcomes many clients remain functionally impaired in the medium to longer term. Dedicated research to understanding and scoping this problem would be a useful focus for the next decade.
- Funding research to examine which modes of treatment and which treatment lengths and intensities are most effective remains a priority. "Big data" collected in routine practice settings may assist with this task.
- DBT is well placed to adapt to forthcoming changes in diagnostic classification that utilize a dimensional trait based approach to describing difficulties.
- DBT as a principle-based treatment fits well with ideas of interventions that focus on evidence-based principles of change.

REFERENCES

American Psychiatric Association. (2013). *Diagnostic and statistical manual of mental disorders*, 5th Edition. Washington, DC: American Psychiatric Association.

Beard, C., Kirakosian, N., Silverman, A. L., Winer, J. P., & Wadsworth, L. P. (2017). Comparing treatment response between LGBQ and heterosexual individuals attending a CBT and DBT skills-based partial hospital. *Journal of Consulting and Clinical Psychology*, 83(12), 1171–1181.

Chen, E. Y., Segal, K., Weissman, J., Zeffiro, T. A., Gallop, R., Linehan, M. M., Bohus, M., & Lynch, T. R. (2014). Adapting dialectical behavior therapy for outpatient adult anorexia nervosa: A pilot study. *International Journal of Eating Disorders*. doi: 10.1002/eat.22360

Choi-Kain, L. W., Albert, E. B., & Gunderson, J. G. (2016). Evidence-based treatments for borderline personality disorder: Implementation, integration, and stepped care. *Harvard Review of Psychiatry*, 24(5), 342–356. doi: 10.1097/HRP.0000000000000113

Collins, L.M., Murphy, S.A., Nair, V.N., & Strecher, V.J. (2005). A strategy for optimizing and evaluating behavioral interventions. *Annals of Behavioral Medicine*, 30(1), 65–73.

Cuthbert, B. N. (2014). The RDoC framework: Facilitating transition from ICD/DSM to approaches that integrate neuroscience and psychopathology. *World Psychiatry*, 13(1), 28–35. PMCID: PMC2918011

Gray, E. A., & Hyatt Thorpe, J. (2015). Comparative effectiveness research and big data: balancing potential with legal and ethical considerations. *Journal of Comparative Effectiveness Research*, 4(1), 61–64.

Hayes, S. C. (2004). Acceptance and commitment therapy and the new behavior therapies: Mindfulness, acceptance and relationship. In S. C. Hayes, V. M. Follette & M. M. Linehan, *Mindfulness and acceptance: Expanding the cognitive-behavioural tradition.* New York: Guilford Press.

Keogh, K., Booth, R., Baird, K., & Davenport, J. (2016). A radically open DBT-informed group intervention for over-control: A controlled trial with 3-month follow-up. *Practice Innovations*, 1(2), 129–143.

Linehan, M. M. (1993a). *Cognitive-behavioral treatment of borderline personality disorder.* New York: Guilford Press.

Linehan, M. M. (1993b). *Skills trainng manual for treating borderline personality disorder.* New York: Guilford Press.

Linehan, M. M., Armstrong, H. E., Suarez, A., Allmon, D., & Heard, H. L. (1991). Cognitive behavioural treatment of chronically parasuicidal borderline patients. *Archives of General Psychiatry*, 48, 1060–1064.

Linehan, M. M., Korslund, K. E., Harned, M. S., Gallop, R. I., Lungu, A., Neacsiu A. D., McDavid, J., … Murray-Gregory, A. M. (2015). Dialectical behavior therapy for high suicide risk in individuals with borderline personality disorder: a randomized clinical trial and component analysis. *JAMA Psychiatry*, 72(5), 475–482.

Linehan, M. M., & Wilks, C. R. (2015). The course and evolution of dialectical behavior therapy. *American Journal of Psycholtherapy*, 69(2), 97–110.

Lynch, T. R. (2018a). *Radically open dialectical behaviour therapy: Theory and practice for treating disorders of overcontrol.* Oakland, CA: New Harbinger.

Lynch, T. R. (2018b). *The skills training manual for radically open dialectical behaviour therapy: A clinician's guide for treating disorders of overcontrol.* Oakland, CA: New Harbinger.

Lynch, T. R., Cheavens, J. S., Cukrowicz, K. C., Thorp, S. R., Bronner, L., & Beyer, J. (2007). Treatment of older adults with co-morbid personality disorder and depression: A dialectical behavior therapy approach. *International Journal of Geriatric Psychiatry*, 22(2), 131–143.

Lynch, T. R., Gray, K. L. H., Hempel, R. J., Titley, M., Chen, E. Y., & O'Mahen, H. A. (2013). Radically open-dialectical behavior therapy for adult anorexia nervosa: Feasibility and outcomes from an inpatient program. *BMC Psychiatry*, 13, 293.

Lynch, T. R., Hempel, R. J., & Dunkley, C. (2015). Radically open-dialectical behavior therapy for disorders of over-control: Signaling matters. *American Journal of Psychotherapy*, 69(2), 141–162.

Lynch T. R., Morse, J. Q., Mendelson, T., & Robins, C. J. (2003). Dialectical behavior therapy for depressed older adults: A randomized pilot study. *American Journal of Geriatric Psychiatry*, 11(1), 33–45.

Lynch, T. R., Whalley, B., Hempel, R. J., Byford, S., Clarke, P., Clarke, S., Kingdon, D., … Remington, B. (2015). Refractory depression: Mechanisms and evaluation of radically open dialectical behaviour therapy (RO-DBT) [REFRAMED]: Protocol for randomised trial. *BMJ Open*, 5, doi:10.1136/bmjopen-2015-008857

Lyng, J. (2017). Patient variables at baseline as predictors of outcomes of dialectical behaviour therapy for adults with a diagnosis of borderline personality disorder. Unpublished PhD thesis, Bangor University, chapter 5. http://ethos.bl.uk/OrderDetails.do?uin=uk.bl.ethos.731759

Makel, M. C., Plucker, J. A., & Hegarty, B. (2012). Replications in psychology research: How often do they really occur? *Perspectives on Psychological Science, 7*(6), 537–542.

Marchette, L. K., & Weisz, J. R. (2017). Practitioner review: Empirical evolution of youth psychotherapy toward transdiagnostic approaches. *Journal of Child Psychology and Psychiatry, 58*(9), 970–984. doi: 10.1111/jcpp.12747

Markowetz, A., Blaszkiewicz, K., Montag, C., Switala, C. L., & Schlaepfer, T. E. (2014). Psycho-Informatics: Big data shaping modern psychometrics. *Medical Hypotheses, 82,* 405–411.

McHugh, R. K., & Barlow, D. H. (2010). The dissemination and implementation of evidence-based psychological treatments: a review of current efforts. *American Psychologist, 65*(2), 73–84.

McHugh, R. K., & Barlow, D. H. (2012). The reach of evidence-based psychological interventions. In R. K. McHugh & D. H. Barlow (Eds.), *Dissemination and implementation of evidence-based psychological interventions* (pp. 3–15). New York: Oxford University Press.

McMain, S. F., Links, P. S., Gnam, W. H., Guimond, T., Cardish, R. J., Korman, L., & Streiner, D. L. (2009). A randomized trial of dialectical behavior therapy versus general psychiatric management for borderline personality disorder. *American Journal of Psychiatry. 166*(12), 1365–74.

McMain, S. (2017a). DBT for chronically self-harming individuals with BPD: Evaluating the clinical and cost-effectiveness of a six-month treatment (FASTER-DBT). Record retrieved from: https://clinicaltrials.gov/ct2/show/record/NCT02387736)

McMain, S. F., Fitzpatrick, S., Boritz, T., Barnhart, R., Links, P., & Streiner, D. L. (2017b). Outcome trajectories and prognostic factors for suicide and self-harm behaviors in patients with borderline personality disorder following one year of outpatient psychotherapy. *Journal of Personality Disorders, 14,* 1–16. doi: 10.1521/pedi_2017_31_309

McMain, S. F., Guimond, T., Barnhart, R., Habinski, L. & Streiner, D. L. (2017c) A randomized brief dialectical behavior therapy skills training in suicidal patients suffering from borderline disorder. *Acta Psychiatrica Scandinavica, 135,* 138–148.

National Collaborating Centre for Mental Health (NCCMH) (2009). *Borderline Personality Disorder: Treatment and Management.* Nice Clinical Guideline no. 78. Leicester: British Psychological Society.

Nosek, B.A., Spies, J.R., & Motyl, M. (2012). Scientific Utopial: II. Restructuring incentives and practices to promote truth over publishability. *Perspectives on Psychological Science, 7*(6), 615–631.

Sloan, C. A., Berke, D. S., & Shipherd, J. C. (2017). Utilizing a dialectical framework to inform conceptualization and treatment of clinical distress in transgender individuals. *Professional Psychology: Research and Practice, 48*(5), 301–309.

Stoffers-Winterling, J. M., Vollm, B. A., Rucker, G., Timmer, A., Huband, N., & Lieb, K. (2012). *Psychological therapies for people with borderline personality disorder.* Cochrane Database of Systematic Reviews. DOI: 10.1002/14651858.CD005652.pub2

Swales, M. A., & Heard, H. L. (2017). *Dialectical behaviour therapy: Distinctive features series,* 2nd Edition. London: Routledge.

Swales, M., Taylor, B., & Hibbs, R. A. B. (2012). Implementing dialectical behaviour therapy: Programme survival in routine healthcare settings. *Journal of Mental Health, 21*(6), 548–555.

Tyrer, P., Crawford, M., Mulder, R., Blashfield, R., Farnam, A., Fossati, A., Kim Y., . . . Reed, G. M. (2011). The rationale for the reclassification of personality disorder in the 11th revision of the International Classification of Disesases (ICD-11). *Personality and Mental Health, 5,* 246–259.

WHO/ISSPD collaboration on classification of Personality Disorders for ICD-11. Presentation delivered at the ISSPD conference in Heidelberg, 2017.

Index